1953	1954	1955	1956	1957	1958	1959	1960	1961	1962	1963	1964	1965	1966	1967
232.6	239.8	257.9	270.6	285.3	294.6	318.1	332.4	343.5	364.4	384.2	412.5	444.6	481.6	509.3
54.9	54.1	69.7	72.7	71.1	63.6	78.8	78.7	77.9	87.9	93.4	101.7	118.0	130.4	128.0
82.8	76.0	75.3	79.7	87.3	95.4	99.0	99.8	107.0	116.8	122.3	128.3	136.3	155.9	175.6
−0.8	0.4	0.4	2.3	3.9	0.4	−1.7	2.4	3.4	2.4	3.3	5.5	3.9	1.9	1.4
369.5	370.3	403.3	425.2	447.7	453.9	494.2	513.4	531.8	571.6	603.1	648.0	702.7	769.8	814.3
30.9	32.5	34.4	38.1	41.1	42.8	44.6	46.3	47.7	49.3	51.3	53.9	57.3	62.1	67.4
338.6	337.8	368.9	387.1	406.6	411.4	449.6	467.1	484.1	522.3	551.8	594.1	645.4	707.7	746.9
2.1	2.2	2.6	3.0	3.4	2.9	2.8	3.2	3.6	4.3	4.5	5.0	5.4	5.2	5.5
34.1	33.7	35.2	33.8	37.1	39.0	42.3	44.6	47.2	52.1	54.8	60.0	63.9	69.2	72.5
306.6	306.3	336.3	356.3	372.8	375.0	410.1	425.7	440.5	474.5	501.5	539.1	586.9	643.7	679.9
9.6	10.6	12.0	13.5	15.5	15.9	18.8	21.9	22.9	25.4	28.5	30.1	31.6	40.6	45.5
20.3	17.6	22.0	22.0	21.4	19.0	23.6	22.7	22.8	24.0	26.2	28.0	30.9	33.7	32.7
8.6	9.9	14.8	12.6	12.4	10.0	15.9	14.5	14.3	14.2	22.6	26.1	31.9	34.0	31.2
22.4	24.8	26.7	29.0	32.8	37.0	39.4	42.6	46.0	42.5	52.2	55.8	60.4	66.3	76.0
290.5	293.0	314.2	337.2	356.3	367.1	391.2	409.2	426.5	453.4	476.4	510.7	552.9	601.7	646.5
35.5	32.5	35.4	39.7	42.4	42.2	44.5	48.7	50.3	54.8	58.0	56.0	61.9	71.0	77.9
255.1	260.5	278.8	297.5	313.9	324.9	346.7	360.5	376.2	398.7	418.4	454.7	491.0	530.7	568.6
1,702.8	1,679.1	1,773.1	1,808.6	1,837.5	1,824.7	1,931.3	1,973.2	2,025.6	2,129.8	2,218.0	2,343.3	2,473.5	2,622.3	2,690.3
4.1	−1.4	5.6	2.0	1.6	−0.7	5.8	2.2	2.7	5.1	4.1	5.6	5.6	6.0	2.6
6,557.3	6,550.9	6,811.1	7,016.0	7,061.3	7,065.9	7,256.0	7,264.0	7,382.0	7,583.0	7,718.0	8,140.0	8,508.0	8,822.0	9,114.0

1953	1954	1955	1956	1957	1958	1959	1960	1961	1962	1963	1964	1965	1966	1967
26.7	26.9	26.8	27.2	28.1	28.9	29.1	29.6	29.9	30.2	30.6	31.0	31.5	32.4	33.4
0.8	0.7	−0.4	1.5	3.3	2.8	0.7	1.7	1.0	1.0	1.3	1.3	1.6	2.9	3.1
31.6	29.9	33.7	35.1	35.6	33.3	37.3	38.1	38.4	41.6	44.0	47.0	51.7	56.3	57.5
128.3	130.3	134.5	136.0	136.8	138.4	140.0	140.7	145.2	147.9	153.4	160.4	167.9	172.1	183.3
3.17	3.05	3.16	3.77	4.20	3.83	4.48	4.82	4.50	4.50	4.50	4.50	4.54	5.63	5.61
160.2	163.0	165.9	168.9	172.0	174.9	177.8	180.7	183.7	186.5	189.2	191.9	194.3	196.6	198.7
63.0	62.3	65.0	66.6	66.9	67.6	68.4	69.6	70.5	70.6	71.8	73.1	74.5	75.8	77.3
1.8	3.5	2.9	2.8	2.9	4.6	3.7	3.9	4.7	3.9	4.1	3.8	3.4	2.9	3.0
2.9	5.5	4.4	4.1	4.3	6.8	5.5	5.5	6.7	5.5	5.7	5.2	4.5	3.8	3.8
55.8	56.7	58.4	59.2	60.7	62.5	64.6	65.6	68.1	70.4	73.3	76.5	78.6	81.0	83.0
3.6	1.6	3.0	1.3	2.6	3.0	3.3	1.6	3.7	3.5	4.1	4.3	2.7	3.0	2.5
−1.3	0.2	0.4	2.7	4.8	0.8	−1.3	2.8	3.8	3.4	4.4	6.8	5.4	3.0	2.6
266.0	270.8	274.4	272.7	272.3	279.7	287.5	290.5	292.6	302.9	310.3	316.1	322.3	328.5	340.4

(Continued on back cover)

ECONOMICS

ECONOMICS
Principles, Problems, and Policies

TWELFTH EDITION

Campbell R. McConnell
Professor of Economics, Emeritus
University of Nebraska—Lincoln

Stanley L. Brue
Professor of Economics
Pacific Lutheran University

McGraw-Hill, Inc.
New York   St. Louis   San Francisco   Auckland
Bogotá   Caracas   Lisbon   London   Madrid
Mexico   Milan   Montreal   New Delhi   Paris
San Juan   Singapore   Sydney   Tokyo   Toronto

1 2 3 4 5 6 7 8 9 0   VNH VNH   9 0 9 8 7 6 5 4 3 2

ISBN 0-07-045559-7

This book was set in Century Oldstyle by York Graphic Services, Inc.
The editors were Scott D. Stratford, Michael R. Elia, and Edwin Hanson;
the designer was Joseph A. Piliero;
the production supervisor was Annette Mayeski.
The photo editor was Safra Nimrod;
the photo researcher was Debra Hershkowitz.
New drawings were done by Vantage Art.
Graphic illustrations in selected chapters were created by Cathy Hull.
Von Hoffmann Press, Inc., was printer and binder.

Photo Credits

10: Jan Staller/The Image Works   32: AP/Wide World   63: Mike Maples/Woodfin Camp & Associates   84: Montes De Oca/FPG International   167: AP/Wide World   192: John Zoiner/International Stock Photo   238: Tom McHugh/Photo Researchers   278: AP/Wide World   300: Spencer Grant/Stock, Boston   346: Spencer Grant/Photo Researchers   362: Monty Bancroft/Photo Researchers   380: Ken Straiton/The Stock Market   398: Larry Mulvehill/Science Source/Photo Researchers   402: Ormand Gigli/The Stock Market   409: William Curtsinger/Photo Researchers   434: John Madere/The Stock Market   460: Blaine Harrington III/The Stock Market   482: Jonathon Blair/Woodfin Camp & Associates   494: Debra P. Hershkowitz   514: Joel Gordon   530: FPG International   548: John Clark/The Stock Market   563: Bob Pizaro/Comstock   576: Hulton/Bettmann Newsphotos   596: Comstock   599: Wally McNamee/Woodfin Camp & Associates   634: Jon Feingersh/The Stock Market   616: Bettmann Newsphotos   650: Joel Gordon   669: Will & Demi McIntyre   692: Tim Davis/Photo Researchers   697: Michael A. Keller/The Stock Market   716: R. Michael Stuckey/Comstock   762: Mike Yamashita/Woodfin Camp & Associates   778: Andy Hernandez/SIPA Press

Library of Congress Cataloging-in-Publication Data

McConnell, Campbell R.
   Economics: principles, problems, and policies / Campbell R. McConnell, Stanley L. Brue.—12th ed.
      p.   cm.
   Includes index.
   ISBN 0-07-045559-7
   1. Economics.   I. Brue, Stanley L., (date).   II. Title.
HB171.5.M47   1993
330—dc20   92-6638

ABOUT THE AUTHORS

Campbell R. McConnell earned his Ph.D. from the University of Iowa after receiving degrees from Cornell College and the University of Illinois. He taught at the University of Nebraska–Lincoln from 1953 until his retirement in 1990. He is also coauthor of *Contemporary Labor Economics,* 3d ed. (McGraw-Hill) and has edited readers for the principles and labor economics courses. He is a recipient of both the University of Nebraska Distinguished Teaching Award and the James A. Lake Academic Freedom Award, and is past-president of the Midwest Economics Association. His primary areas of interest are labor economics and economic education. He has an extensive collection of jazz recordings and enjoys reading jazz history.

Stanley L. Brue did his undergraduate work at Augustana College (S.D.) and received his Ph.D. from the University of Nebraska—Lincoln. He teaches at Pacific Lutheran University, where he has been honored as a recipient of the Burlington Northern Faculty Achievement Award for classroom excellence and professional accomplishment. He is national President-elect and member of the International Executive Board of Omicron Delta Epsilon International Honor Society in Economics. Professor Brue is coauthor of *Economic Scenes: Theory in Today's World,* 5th ed. (Prentice-Hall); *The Evolution of Economic Thought,* 4th ed. (Harcourt Brace Jovanovich); and *Contemporary Labor Economics,* 3d ed. (McGraw-Hill). For relaxation, he enjoys boating on Puget Sound and skiing trips with his family.

To Mem
and to Terri and Craig

CONTENTS IN BRIEF

CONTENTS

 Note: All chapter sections with substantial global content are indicated in light blue ink.

PREFACE

The publication of the twelfth edition of *Economics* (and its accompanying editions of *Macroeconomics* and *Microeconomics*) follows the most successful edition of this book to date. Naturally, we are pleased that *Economics* continues to be the best selling economics text in the United States. Moreover, we are pleasantly surprised that the Russian translation of *Economics* will soon be the leading economics text in the former Soviet Union; Politizdat Press has taken orders for nearly 500,000 copies. This fact dramatizes how remarkable these times are for teaching and learning economics! The message of our day is clear: People who comprehend economic principles will have a great advantage functioning in, and making sense of, the emerging world. We express our sincere thanks to each of you using *Economics* for granting us a modest role in your efforts to teach or learn this globally important subject.

THE REVISION

The twelfth edition of *Economics* has been thoroughly revised, polished, and updated. Many of the changes have been motivated by the comments of 36 reviewers and another 13 participants in focus groups. We are especially grateful to these scholars and acknowledge them by name at the end of this preface.

We strive only for an overview of the changes in the twelfth edition here; chapter-by-chapter details are provided in the *Instructor's Resource Manual* accompanying this book.

Consolidation of Introductory Chapters

Responding to reviewer suggestions, we have reduced the number of introductory chapters from eight to six, allowing for a quicker start into the macroeconomics or microeconomics. The previous edition's Chapters 5 and 7 are consolidated into new Chapter 5 and old

Chapters 6 and 8 are combined into new Chapter 6. Parts of the material on taxation in old Chapter 8 are now found in new Chapter 32, which treats public choice and tax analysis. We have resisted the temptation to compress the introductory material even further, believing that most students inadequately understand the characteristics of capitalism (Chapter 3), the functioning of the market system (Chapter 5), and the extensive role of government in the modern economy (Chapter 6). A strong introduction helps students understand and apply macroeconomic and microeconomic theory. We believe we have provided such an introduction, but now in a more expeditious form.

New Topics and Analysis

Much attention has been given to applying economics to the major issues of our day. Also, this edition contains new formal economic analyses. Examples of new discussions and analyses include:

- **The switch to GDP (gross domestic product) accounting.** This edition fully incorporates the United States' recent switch from GNP to GDP accounting. In particular, Chapter 7 has been carefully revised to present the new accounting. Also, in the macro theory chapters we have designated real output as GDP, rather than NNP, and have substituted gross investment, I_g, for net investment, I_n, throughout the discussion and diagrams.
- **Soviet economy in transition.** A completely rewritten chapter (Chapter 40) presents an up-to-date, thorough analysis of the present crisis and reform efforts in the former Soviet Union.
- **Economics and the environment.** Chapter 31 is a new chapter on government and market failure. This chapter extends Chapter 6's discussion of externalities by examining the Coase theorem, liability rules and lawsuits, markets for externality rights, and society's optimal amount of externality abatement. A case study of pollution examines the dimensions, causes, and

solutions of this problem. Special attention is given to the Superfund law, the Clean Air Act of 1990, and solid waste disposal and recycling.

• **The crisis in American financial institutions.** A major section in Chapter 13 examines bank and thrift failures, including the role of deposit insurance.

• **Economics of information.** A lengthy new section of Chapter 31 looks at market failure associated with inadequate information by buyers about sellers and by sellers about buyers. Topics such as adverse selection and moral hazard are included here. Also, Chapter 25's discussion of advertising is completely rewritten to highlight advertising's informational role. The idea of imperfect information in decision making is introduced *early* in the book; Chapter 1's Last Word uses the economic perspective to analyze how customers decide which fast-food line to enter.

• **Strategic behavior.** Game theory—specifically the prisoner's dilemma model—is presented in the discussion of oligopoly (Chapter 26). Also, Chapter 37 contains a discussion of strategic international trade policy.

• **Public choice and tax analysis.** A full chapter (Chapter 32) is devoted to public choice and tax analysis. Also, we have placed much more emphasis on public choice theory in our explanation of the persistence of agricultural subsidies in Chapter 34, a chapter which has been extensively revised and updated.

• **Absorption of segments of monetarism and rational expectations theory into the mainstream macroeconomics.** Although we continue to contrast the various macroeconomic theories, a new section of Chapter 16 emphasizes that mainstream macroeconomics has absorbed important aspects of monetarism and rational expectations theory.

• **Principal–agent problem and pay-for-performance.** A new section of the chapter on wage determination (Chapter 28) explains the principal–agent problem and discusses pay-for-performance plans (piece rates, commissions and royalties, bonuses and profit sharing), seniority pay, and efficiency wages.

• **Economic growth in Japan.** Chapter 2 now applies production possibilities analysis to relative growth rates in Japan and the United States and stresses the higher saving and investment rates in Japan. Also, Chapter 19 on economic growth now concludes with a Last Word on the Japanese growth miracle.

• **Causes of the productivity slowdown.** Chapter 19 on economic growth contains a completely re-written section on the causes of the American productivity slowdown.

• **The economics of an aging American population.** Chapter 30 on general equilibrium traces the myriad implications of an aging American population.

• **Early introduction of comparative advantage theory.** In an optional new section in Chapter 3, we use production possibilities tables to illustrate comparative advantage. By combining this new material with Chapter 4's optional discussion of exchange rates, instructors can effectively introduce international economics early in the course.

• **Other new discussions.** There are numerous other new discussions in the twelfth edition, a few examples being: the Ricardian equivalence theorem; the Federal funds market; the social security surplus and the public debt; the Budget Consolidation and Budget Enforcement Acts of 1990; cross and income elasticities; rent controls; the absence of a monopoly supply curve; the Herfindahl index; growing inequality in the distribution of income; consolidation in the airline industry; immigration reform; world trade and farm policy; the Farm Act of 1990; the economic impact of import quotas; the proposed North American free-trade zone; Uruguay Round negotiations; and the purchasing power parity theory of exchange rates.

New "Last Words"

Reviewers indicate that they appreciate the "Last Word" minireadings and their placement toward the conclusion of each chapter. These selections serve several purposes: Some provide current or historical real-world applications of economic concepts; others reveal human-interest aspects of economic problems; and still others present economic concepts or issues in a global context. Eighteen Last Words are new and others have been extensively revised and updated.

We have selected Last Word topics that are both highly relevant to the chapter's discussion *and* interesting to the reader. New topics are fast-food lines viewed from the economic perspective (Chapter 1); the impact of Operation Desert Storm on Iraqi production possibilities (Chapter 2); the increasing use of barter (Chapter 3); the effect of supply interdiction on the price of marijuana (Chapter 4); the mystery of the $196 billion of paper money unaccounted for by the Federal Reserve (Chapter 13); the bank panics of 1930–1933 (Chapter 14); the Fed as a series of metaphors (Chapter 15); international comparisons of public debt among industrial nations (Chapter 18); the Japanese growth miracle

(Chapter 19); the market for health care (Chapter 20); monopoly in the national parks (Chapter 24); product differentiation and nonprice competition in the market for economics textbooks (Chapter 25); the market for "lemons" (Chapter 31); the special interest effect as reflected in the Tax Reform Act of 1986 (Chapter 32); causes of greater income inequality (Chapter 35); possible discrimination in professional basketball (Chapter 36); the difficulties of "buying American" when many product components are imported (Chapter 38); and an obituary of the Soviet Union (Chapter 40).

Pedagogical Improvements

The principles course has become increasingly demanding for students. Globalization of economies, developments in economic theory, and modern economic problems have added new, sometimes complex material to the course. Concise and understandable explanations are more important than ever before. Accordingly, we have directed much effort toward improving the pedagogy of *Economics*. We have "gone back to the basics," attempting to bolster what we believe to be this book's comparative advantages: its readability and accessibility. Examples of our pedagogical changes include:

• **"Quick Reviews" within each chapter.** Two or three new reviews within the body of each chapter allow the student to pause and ponder key points. We believe these "Quick Reviews" will also help students as they study for examinations.

• **"Key Graphs."** Students often have a difficult time distinguishing which of the hundreds of graphs in economics are of fundamental importance. To direct students' attention to the essential graphs, we have designated 22 figures as "Key Graphs." These graphs are specially designed and labeled to make them easily identifiable. Figures 2-1 and 4-5 are representative. A complete listing of the Key Graphs can be found in the Brief Table of Contents on page x.

• **Motivational introductions.** In many chapters new introductions are added to stimulate reader interest in the chapter's contents. These introductions relate to students' everyday experiences and observations. The opening material for Chapters 2, 6, 21, 29, and 37 is illustrative.

• **Full-color layout.** The full range of colors in the designer's palette makes for a more interesting text and is used functionally to clarify many graphs and diagrams.

• **Functional use of color photos.** Unobtrusive chapter-opening photos are employed as "teasers" for the content of the Last Words, where larger photos are found. The front and back photos visually unite the beginning and ends of the chapters and are designed to spark reader interest in the Last Words.

• **Shorter paragraphs.** In keeping with trends in popular and academic publishing, we have shortened scores of long paragraphs.

• **Tighter sentences.** The two authors and a talented McGraw-Hill editor scrutinized every sentence in this edition for unnecessary verbiage. Collectively, we were able to tighten hundreds of sentences without altering the overall style of writing. In economizing on words, we were careful *not* to reduce the thoroughness of our explanations. Where needed, the "extra sentence of explanation" remains a distinguishing characteristic of *Economics*.

• **Numbered lists and added subheads.** We have substituted numbered and labeled lists for verbal strings of "First," "Second," and "Third." The idea here is to break material into smaller parcels to help students more readily retain the content. Similarly, we have employed subheads more liberally so the organizational structure of each chapter and topic will be clearer.

• **Footnote deletion.** We have significantly reduced the number of footnotes. Several lengthy explanatory footnotes have been deleted; a number of shorter footnotes have been integrated into the text. Footnotes suggesting additional reading have been judiciously pruned.

• **Added labeling in graphs.** Taking great care to avoid clutter, in a number of cases we have added labeling in figures to help guide the reader through the analysis. These labels are set in strong type so they are highly readable both within the book and on transparencies.

• **New diagrams.** Some of the added diagrams depict new graphical analyses such as aggregate demand–aggregate supply analysis of growth (Figure 19-3), the economics of recycling (Figure 31-4), and a comparison of the effects of tariffs and quotas (Figure 37-3). Other new diagrams should help students visualize the interrelations of the concepts involved. Examples of these diagrams are Figures 8-4, 10-5, 11-4, 11-5, 32-1, and 33-1.

• **Clarified explanations of difficult subject matter.** We have continued to look for ways to explain difficult material more clearly. Even minor improvements in language or labeling of graphs can often help students better understand the material. Improvements of this sort have been made in numerous places throughout the text. Good examples are our revised discussions of efficiency (Chapter 2), the ratchet effect (Chapter 9), demand-pull and cost-push inflation in the long run (Chapter 17), the relationship between the demand curve and total revenue (Chapter 24), the efficiency effects of oligopoly (Chapter 26), and efficiency losses of taxes (Chapter 32).

New and Enhanced Ancillaries

The ancillaries in the twelfth edition package are discussed later in this Preface, but four new items are noteworthy.

• **Test Bank III.** New to the *Economics* package is a test bank allowing an alternative testing approach to the predominantly multiple-choice questions in Test Banks I and II. Written by Professors William Walstad and Joyce Gleason, Test Bank III contains questions that emphasize "constructive response" concepts. Students are more actively involved in creating answers to these questions, which provide a valuable alternative to conventional test questions.

• **Augmented Test Bank I.** We have added approximately 1200 questions to Test Bank I.

• **New macro simulation software.** *Macroeconomics: A Lab Course,* a new macro simulation program, greatly advances the art of economics software. This program is highly interactive and visually spectacular. Also, the successful *Concept Master* software introduced with the eleventh edition has been completely updated. Both these software programs are directly tied to the contents of *Economics*.

• **Enhanced video materials.** The power of videodisks is harnassed in this edition to provide enhanced classroom presentation of visual material. Also, there are new videotape materials that have been carefully designed for effective classroom use.

We trust that the outcome of this detailed revision effort is a text and package that are clearly superior to their predecessors.

FUNDAMENTAL GOALS

Although the twelfth edition bears little resemblance to the first, the basic purpose remains the same—to introduce the beginning economics student to those principles essential to an understanding of the fundamental economic problems and the policy alternatives available for dealing with these problems. We hope that the ability to reason accurately and objectively about economic matters and the development of a lasting interest in economics will be two valuable by-products of this basic objective. Our intention remains to present the principles and problems of economics in a straightforward, logical fashion. To this end, we continue to put great stress on clarity of presentation and on logical organization.

PRODUCT DIFFERENTIATION

This text embraces a number of features which perhaps distinguish it from other books in the field.

• **Comprehensive explanations at an appropriate level.** We have attempted to craft a comprehensive, analytical text that is challenging to better students, yet accessible—with appropriate hard work—to average students. We think the thoroughness and accessibility of *Economics* enables the instructor to select topics for special classroom emphasis with confidence that students can independently read and comprehend other assigned material in the book.

• **Comprehensive definition of economics.** The principles course sometimes fails to provide students with a comprehensive and meaningful definition of economics. To avoid this shortcoming, all of Chapter 2 is devoted to a careful statement and development of the economizing problem and an exploration of its implications. This foundation should help put the many particular subject areas of economics in proper perspective.

• **Early integration of international economics.** Comparative advantage is discussed in detail in Chapter 3, exchange rates are explained as an application of supply and demand in Chapter 4, and the international trade sector of the American economy is highlighted in Chapter 5. This strong introduction to international economics permits "globalization" of later discussions of macroeconomics and microeconomics, where appropriate. The Table of Contents highlights sections in all chapters with substantial global content.

• **Early treatment of government.** For better or worse, government is an integral component of modern capitalism. Its economic role, therefore, should not be treated piecemeal or as an afterthought. This text introduces the economic functions of government early and accords them systematic treatment in Chapter 6. Chapter 31 examines government and market failure in further detail and Chapter 32 looks at salient facets of public choice theory and public finance. Both the macroeconomics and the microeconomics sections of the text have problem- and policy-oriented chapters in which government's role is explored.

• **Emphasis on economic growth.** This volume continues to put considerable emphasis on economic growth. Chapter 2 uses the production possibilities curve to lay bare the basic ingredients of growth. Chapter 19 discusses the rate and causes of American growth, in addition to some of the controversies surrounding growth. Chapter 39 focuses on the less developed countries and the growth obstacles that confront them. A segment of Chapter 40 concerns the stalling of growth in the former Soviet Union. Also, the chapters on price theory stress the implications that the various market structures have for technological progress.

• **Resurgence of the market system.** Economies the world over are making the difficult transition from planning to markets. Our emphasis on general equilibrium analysis and the market *system* is thus even more relevant in the 12th edition than in earlier editions. A major portion of Chapter 5 is devoted to the interrelationships within the market system, and Chapter 30 explicitly outlines the nature and significance of general equilibrium analysis.

• **Emphasis on the theory of the firm.** We have purposely given much attention to microeconomics in general and to the theory of the firm in particular, for two reasons: First, the concepts of microeconomics are difficult for most beginning students. Short expositions usually compound these difficulties by raising more questions than they answer. Second, we have coupled analysis of the various market structures with a discussion of the impact of each market arrangement on price, output levels, resource allocation, and the rate of technological advance.

• **Chapters on economic issues.** As most students see it, Part 4 on macroeconomic issues and Part 6 on micro-oriented problems are where the action is. We have sought to guide the action along logical lines through the application of appropriate analytical tools. Our bias in these parts is in favor of inclusiveness; each instructor can effectively counter this bias by omitting those chapters felt to be less relevant for a particular group of students.

ORGANIZATION AND CONTENT

We believe that the basic prerequisite of an understandable economics text is the logical arrangement and clear exposition of subject matter. This book has been organized so that the exposition of each particular topic and concept is directly related to the level of difficulty which in our experience the average student is likely to encounter. For this reason microeconomics and macro employment theory are given comprehensive and careful treatments. Simplicity here is correlated with comprehensiveness, not brevity.

Furthermore, our experience suggests that in the treatment of each basic topic—aggregate demand and aggregate supply, money and banking, theory of the firm, and international economics—it is desirable to couple analysis with policy. A three-step development of basic analytical tools is employed: (1) verbal descriptions and illustrations; (2) numerical examples; and (3) graphical presentation based on these numerical illustrations.

The material in this book is organized into seven basic parts. They are: Part 1: An Introduction to Economics and the Economy; Part 2: National Income, Employment, and Fiscal Policy; Part 3: Money, Banking, and Monetary Policy; Part 4: Problems and Controversies in Macroeconomics; Part 5: Microeconomics of Product and Resource Markets; Part 6: Government and Current Economic Problems; and Part 7: International Economics and the World Economy. The Table of Contents lists the specific chapters in each part and details the contents within each chapter.

ORGANIZATIONAL ALTERNATIVES

Although economics instructors generally agree as to the basic content of a principles of economics course, there are differences of opinion on what particular arrangement of material is best. The structure of this book provides considerable organizational flexibility. Users of prior editions tell us they accomplished substantial rearrangements of chapters with little sacrifice of continuity.

Although we have chosen to move from macro- to microeconomics, the introductory material of Part 1 can be followed immediately by the micro analysis of Part 5. Similarly, in our judgment money and banking can best be taught after, rather than before, aggregate expenditure analysis. Those who disagree will encounter no special problems by preceding Chapter 7 with appropriate parts of Chapters 13, 14, and 15.

Furthermore, some instructors will prefer to intersperse the microeconomics of Part 5 with the problems chapters of Part 6. This is easily accomplished. Chapter 34 on the farm problem may follow Chapter 23 on pure competition; Chapter 33 on antitrust and regulation may follow Chapters 24 to 26 on imperfect competition. Chapter 36 on labor market issues may either precede or follow Chapter 28 on wages, and Chapter 35 on income inequality may follow Chapters 28 and 29 on the distributive shares of national income.

Those who teach the typical two-semester course and who feel comfortable with the book's organization will find that, by putting the first four parts in the first semester and Parts 5 through 7 in the second, the material is divided both logically in terms of content and satisfactorily in terms of quantity and level of difficulty between the two semesters. For those instructors who choose to emphasize international economics, Parts 1, 2, 3, and 7 may be treated the first semester and Parts 4, 5, and 6 the second.

For a course based on three quarters of work we would suggest Chapters 1 through 12 for the first quarter, 13 through 30 for the second, and 31 through 40 for the third.

Finally, those interested in the one-semester course will be able to discern several possible groups of chapters that will be appropriate to such a course. Tentative outlines for three one-semester courses, emphasizing macroeconomics, microeconomics, or a survey of micro and macro theory, follow this preface on page xxxi. Also included are several one-quarter course options.

STUDENT FRIENDLY: STUDY AIDS

As in its previous eleven editions, *Economics* is highly student oriented.

1 Students who are comfortable with graphical analysis and a few related quantitative concepts are in an advantageous position to understand principles of economics. To help students in this regard, an appendix to Chapter 1 carefully reviews graphing, line slopes, and linear equations.

2 The introductory paragraphs of each chapter state objectives, present an organizational overview of the chapter, and relate the chapter to what has been covered before and what will follow.

3 Because a significant portion of any introductory course is devoted to terminology, terms are given special emphasis. In particular, each important term is in **boldface type** where it first appears in each chapter. We have tried to make all definitions clear and succinct. At the end of each chapter all new terms are listed in the "Terms and Concepts" section. Finally, at the end of the book a comprehensive glossary of almost 1000 terms is found. This glossary also is contained in the *Study Guide.*

4 As we noted earlier, each chapter contains two or three "Quick Reviews" at appropriate places in the chapter to reinforce key points for students and help them study for examinations.

5 Figures worthy of intensive study are given special design treatment and designated as "Key Graphs."

6 The legends accompanying all diagrams are written so they are self-contained analyses of the relevant concepts shown. This is a strategic means of reinforcing student comprehension.

7 Much thought has gone into the end-of-chapter questions. Though purposely intermixed, the questions are of three general types. Some are designed to highlight the main points of each chapter. Others are "open-end" discussion, debate, or thought questions. Wherever pertinent, numerical problems which require the student to derive and manipulate key concepts and relationships are employed. Numerical problems are stressed in those chapters which deal with analytical material. Some optional "advanced analysis" questions accompany certain theory chapters. These problems usually involve the stating and manipulation of certain basic concepts in equation form.

8 Many of the end-of-chapter questions deal with subject matter that is reinforced by the excellent computerized tutorial, *Concept Master II,* that accompanies the text. A floppy disk symbol 💾 appears in conjunction with questions whose underlying content correlates to a lesson in the tutorial program.

9 In addition to its considerable esthetic merit, the full color format of the twelfth edition stresses the use of color so students will more quickly and easily perceive the ideas expressed in each diagram and chart.

INSTRUCTOR FRIENDLY: THE SUPPLEMENTS

The twelfth edition is accompanied by supplements that we feel equal or surpass competing texts in terms of both quantity and quality.

Study Guide

Professor William Walstad has prepared the twelfth edition of the *Study Guide* that many students find to be an indispensable aid. It contains for each chapter an introductory statement, a checklist of behavioral objectives, an outline, a list of important terms, fill-in questions, problems and projects, objective questions, and discussion questions. The glossary found at the end of *Economics* also appears in the *Study Guide.*

In the twelfth edition, Professor Walstad has added text page references for every question (true-false, multiple-choice, and discussion); has extensively revised the chapter learning objectives to add more detail; and has added discussion sections to the chapter outlines. He has also increased the number of multiple-choice questions for each chapter, and has increased the number of problems and projects for further study.

The *Guide* comprises, in our opinion, a superb "portable tutor" for the principles student. Separate *Study Guides* have been prepared to correspond with the individual macro and micro paperback editions of the text.

Economic Concepts

Economic Concepts provides carefully designed programmed materials for all the key analytical areas of the principles course. Revised by Professor W. H. Pope for use with the twelfth edition of *Economics,* it can be used as an effective supplement with any mainstream text.

Instructor's Resource Manual

Professor Joyce Gleason of Nebraska Wesleyan University has revised and updated the *Instructor's Resource Manual.* It comprises chapter summaries, listings of "what's new" in each chapter, teaching tips and suggestions, learning objectives, chapter outlines, data and visual aid sources with suggestions for classroom use, and questions and problems. Answers to all the text's end-of-chapter questions are also found in the *Manual.*

The new edition of the *Manual* includes a full, chapter-by-chapter overview of all changes in the revision. Also, the chapter outlines have been consolidated into a separate section of the *Manual,* so they can more readily be used as a resource in classroom lectures. We think instructors will find this *Manual* useful and time-saving.

Available again in this edition is a computerized version of the *Manual,* suitable for use with IBM-PC computers, IBM-PC compatibles, and MacIntosh computers. The version for IBM-PCs and compatibles is available in both 5¼-inch and 3½-inch formats. Users of *Economics* can print out portions of the *Manual's* contents, complete with their own additions or alterations, for use as student handouts or in whatever ways they might wish. This capability includes printing out answers to all end-of-chapter questions.

As with the *Study Guide,* separate editions of the *Instructor's Resource Manual* have been prepared to correspond with the individual macro and micro paperback editions of the text. Users of one or both of these volumes will find that the material in the accompanying *Manual* correlates with the chapter sequencing in the text.

Three Test Banks

The new edition of *Economics* is supplemented by two test banks of objective, predominantly multiple-choice, questions and a new test bank of short-answer and essay questions.

Test Bank I now comprises some 4800 questions, all written by the text authors; approximately 3600 are carried over from the previous edition and over 1200 have been prepared by the authors for the new edition.

Test Bank II, revised by Professor Walstad, contains approximately 3100 questions. For all test items in these two test banks, the nature of each question is identified (e.g., G, graphical; C, conceptual, etc.) as are the pages in the text containing the material which is the basis for each question. Also, each chapter in *Test Banks I* and *II* has an outline or table of contents which groups questions by topics.

New to this edition, *Test Bank III* will emphasize "constructive response" testing to evaluate student understanding in a manner different from conventional multiple-choice and true-false questions. Prepared by Professors Walstad and Gleason, this unique resource emphasizes short-answer and essay questions designed to enhance critical thinking skills.

Adopters of the text will be able to use this sizable number of questions, organized into three test banks of equal quality, with maximum flexibility. The fact that the text authors and *Study Guide* authors have prepared all the test items will assure the fullest possible correlation with the content of the text.

As with the *Study Guide* and *Instructor's Resource Manual,* separate versions of the test banks have been prepared to correspond with the individual macro and micro editions of the text.

Additional Supplements

Computerized testing *Test Banks I, II,* and, *III* are available in computerized versions, as well as print. Computerized test generation will be available for IBM-PCs and compatibles, and for MacIntosh computers. All of these systems include the capability to produce high-quality graphs from the test banks.

These systems will also feature the ability to generate multiple tests, with versions "scrambled" to be distinctive, and will have other useful features. They will meet the various needs of the widest spectrum of computer users.

Color transparencies Over 200 new full-color transparencies for overhead projectors have been prepared especially for the twelfth edition. These encompass all the figures which appear in *Economics* and are available on request to adopters. As with the *Study Guide, Instructor's Resource Manual,* and *Test Banks,* the transparencies are also available in versions corresponding to *Macroeconomics* and *Microeconomics.*

Student software For users of IBM-PCs and compatibles, a student software package, *Concept Master II,* has been prepared by Professor William Gunther, of the University of Alabama, and Irene Gunther. The previous version of this software was widely praised by its users, and it has been improved to provide even more flexibility. It provides the most extensive and varied computer-assisted study material of any software package available.

Over twenty graphics-based tutorial programs provide an opportunity for students to study key topics in the book in an interactive fashion. The tutorial programs are linked to the text. Selected end-of-chapter questions that relate to the content of one of the tutorial programs are highlighted by a floppy disk symbol 💾. The questions themselves are not necessarily contained within the tutorial program, but the tutorial does contain material that relates directly to the concepts underlying the highlighted questions.

In addition to the tutorial programs, students can quiz themselves with a self-testing program accompanying each test chapter. The package also features eight simulation games, divided between macroeconomics and microeconomics. Some of the simulations

are elementary, and others are more complex. Wherever possible, they include a global perspective. Also included in the package are a list of key terms, a pop-up calculator for computations, and a section that uses the "Key Graphs" in the text to direct students to the appropriate tutorial lesson.

Professor Norris Peterson of Pacific Lutheran University, working with the talented staff of Intellipro, Inc., has created a new software package, *Macroeconomics: A Lab Course,* to be used in macroeconomics courses. It builds the basic macroeconomic framework in sequential, "building block" laboratory simulations that allow students to grasp the fundamental concepts of macroeconomics in a dynamic and creative manner.

For users of MacIntosh computers, there is an exciting tutorial program, *VizEcon.* Developed by Professor William A. Phillips of the University of Southern Maine, this innovative package uses Apple's HYPER-CARD programming environment to produce an extremely interactive learning experience. Dynamic shifts of curves, screen animation, sound effects, and simple-to-use command keys are features of this program. Its development was underwritten by grant funds and consultation from Apple Computer, Inc.

Videodisks New to this edition are videodisks designed to harness this exciting new technology for classroom presentation. These videodisks offer an array of graphical illustrations of key economic concepts to further student understanding.

Videos New videotape materials have been assembled for this edition to illustrate fundamental concepts and economic issues in a manner that will be equally effective in classroom settings or media resource centers. Among these materials is the new "MacNeil/ Lehrer Quarterly Report on Economics", a new series of excerpts from the acclaimed PBS news program, "The MacNeil/Lehrer Newshour". Your local McGraw-Hill representative can provide details on all new video ancillaries for the text.

DEBTS

The publication of this twelfth edition will extend the life of *Economics* well into its fourth decade. The acceptance of *Economics,* which was generous from the outset, has expanded with each edition. This gracious reception has no doubt been fostered by the many teachers and students who have been kind enough to provide their suggestions and criticisms.

Our colleagues at the University of Nebraska–Lincoln and Pacific Lutheran University have generously shared knowledge of their specialties with us and have provided encouragement. We are especially indebted to Professors Harish Gupta, Jerry Petr, David Rosenbaum, Merlin Erickson, and Norris Peterson, who have been most helpful in offsetting our comparative ignorance in their areas of specialty.

As indicated, the twelfth edition has benefited from a number of perceptive reviews. In both quantity and quality, they provided the richest possible source of suggestions for this revision. These contributors are listed at the end of this Preface.

Professors Thomas P. Barbiero and W. H. Pope of Ryerson Polytechnical Institute in their role as coauthors of the Canadian edition of *Economics* have provided innumerable suggestions for improvement. Thanks also go to Professor Mark Lovewell who coded the new *Test Bank* items by type of questions and identified the corresponding text page number for all the items.

We are greatly indebted to the many professionals at McGraw-Hill—and in particular Phil Galea, Annette Mayeski, and Karen Jackson—for their expertise in the production and distribution of the book. Joe Piliero has given the book its unique design. Safra Nimrod and Debra Hershkowitz found suitable photos for the Last Word readings, and Cathy Hull provided the creative illustrations for several of them. Margaret Hanson's imaginative editing has been invaluable. Our greatest debts are to Scott Stratford, Edwin Hanson, and Mike Elia for their conscientious supervision of this revision. Their patience and many positive contributions are gratefully acknowledged.

Given this much assistance, we see no compelling reason why the authors should assume full responsibility for errors of omission or commission. But we bow to tradition.

Campbell R. McConnell
Stanley L. Brue

ACKNOWLEDGMENTS

We thank the following instructors for their written reviews and other comments, which greatly helped shape this edition:

Thomas P. Barbiero, *Ryerson Polytechnic Institute*
Arleigh T. Bell, *Loyola College*
Michael S. Blair, *Tarrant County Junior College*
Joseph P. Cairo, *La Salle University*
Robert Campbell, *Indiana University–Bloomington*
Gordon Crocker, *Community College of Allegheny County*
Paul G. Farnham, *Georgia State University*
Walter F. Gall, Jr., *Northeastern Junior College*
John A. Gould, *Garrett Community College*
Paul W. Grimes, *Mississippi State University*
Richard C. Harmstone, *Pennsylvania State University*
Gail A. Hawks, *Miami-Dade Community College*
R. Bradley Hoppes, *Southwest Missouri State University*
Matthew Hyle, *Winona State University*
Patrick Joyce, *Michigan Technological University*
James C. Koch, *St. Edwards University*
Fredric Kolb, *University of Wisconsin–Eau Claire*
Patrick Litzinger, *Robert Morris College*
Mark Lovewell, *Ryerson Polytechnic Institute*
George F. Muscat, *Camden County Community College*
Asghar Nazemzadeh, *University of Houston–Downtown*
Margaret O'Donnell, *University of Southwest Louisiana*
Ronald W. Olive, *New Hampshire College*
Diana Petersdorf, *University of Wisconsin–Stout*
David Priddy, *Piedmont Community College*
John J. Rapczak, *Community College of Rhode Island*
Theresa Riley, *Youngstown State University*
Peter Rupert, *SUNY–Buffalo*
Doris Sheets, *Southwest Missouri State University*
Steven P. Skinner, *Western Connecticut State University*
Robert Stuart, *Rutgers University*
Percy O. Vera, *Sinclair Community College*
Howard J. Wall, *West Virginia University*
Paul R. Watro, *Jefferson Community College*
Peter J. Watry, Jr., *Southwestern College*
Dieter Zschock, *SUNY–Stony Brook*

In addition, we thank the following instructors for participating in focus group sessions, which served as very useful complements to the reviewing process:

Barbara Brogan, *Northern Virginia Community College*
Robert F. Brooker, *Gannon University*
Christopher B. Colburn, *Old Dominion University*
Jacob Deutch, *University of Maryland–Baltimore County*
James Halteman, *Wheaton College*
Charles Jewell, *Charles County Community College*
George Kosicki, *College of the Holy Cross*
Patrick Litzinger, *Robert Morris College*
Craig MacPhee, *University of Nebraska–Lincoln*
Norris A. Peterson, *Pacific Lutheran University*
Donald Schilling, *University of Missouri–Columbia*
Robert Tansky, *St. Clair Community College*
Irvin Weintraub, *Towson State University*

SUGGESTED ONE-SEMESTER AND ONE-QUARTER COURSE OUTLINES
(Core chapters are indicated by "c"; optional chapters by "o")

Chapter	One-semester course			One-quarter course	
	Macro emphasis	Micro emphasis	Macro-micro survey	Macro emphasis	Micro emphasis
1	c	c	c	c	c
2	c	c	c	c	c
3	c	c	c	c	c
4	c	c	c	c	c
5	c	c		c	c
6	c	c		c	c
7	c		c	c	
8	c		c	c	
9	c		c	c	
10	c		c	c	
11	c		c	c	
12	c		c	c	
13	c		c	c	
14	c		c	c	
15	c		c	c	
16	c		c	o	
17	c		o	o	
18	c		o		
19	c		o		
20		c	c		c
21		o			
22		c	c		c
23		c	c		c
24		c	c		c
25		c	o		c
26		c	o		c
27		c			c
28		c			c
29		c			c
30		o			o
31		o			
32		o			
33		o[1]			
34		o[2]			
35		o[3]			
36		o[4]			
37	o	o			
38	o	o			
39	o				
40	o				

[1] If used, Chapter 33 may follow Chapter 26.
[2] If used, Chapter 34 may follow Chapter 23.
[3] If used, Chapter 35 may follow Chapter 28 or 29.
[4] If used, Chapter 36 may follow Chapter 28.

ECONOMICS

PART 1

An Introduction to Economics and the Economy

CHAPTER 1

The Nature and Method of Economics

Human beings, unfortunate creatures, are plagued with wants. We want, among other things, love, social recognition, and the material necessities and comforts of life. Our striving to improve our material well-being, to "make a living," is the concern of economics. Specifically, economics is the study of our behavior in producing, distributing, and consuming material goods and services in a world of scarce resources.

But we need a more sophisticated definition of economics. We are, indeed, characterized by both biologically and socially determined wants. We seek food, clothing, shelter, and many goods and services associated with a comfortable or affluent standard of living. We are also blessed with aptitudes and surrounded by quantities of property resources—both natural and manufactured. We use available human and property resources—labor and managerial talents, tools and machinery, land and mineral deposits—to produce goods and services which satisfy these material wants. This is done through the organizational mechanism we call the *economic system.*

Quantitative considerations, however, rule out an ideal solution. The blunt fact is that the total of all our material wants is beyond the productive capacity of all available resources. Hence, absolute material abundance is not a possible outcome. This unyielding fact is the basis for our definition of economics: Economics *is concerned with the efficient use or management of limited productive resources to achieve maximum satisfaction of human material wants.* Though it may not be self-evident, all the headline-grabbing issues of the day—inflation, unemployment, the collapse of communism, government and international trade deficits, free-trade agreements among nations, poverty and inequality, pollution, and government regulation of business—are rooted in the issue of using limited resources efficiently.

In this first chapter, however, we will not plunge into problems and issues. Our immediate concern is with some basic preliminary questions: (1) Of what importance or consequence is the study of economics? (2) How should we study economics—what are the proper procedures? What is the character of the method-ology of economics? (3) What specific problems, limitations, and pitfalls might we encounter in studying economics?

THE AGE OF THE ECONOMIST

Is economics a discipline of consequence? Is the study of economics worth your time and effort? Half a century ago John Maynard Keynes (1883–1946)—clearly the most influential economist of this century—offered a telling response:

> The ideas of economists and political philosophers, both when they are right and when they are wrong, are more powerful than is commonly understood. Indeed the world is ruled by little else. Practical men, who believe themselves to be quite exempt from any intellectual influences, are usually the slaves of some defunct economist.

Most of the ideologies of the modern world which compete for our minds have been shaped by the great economists of the past—Adam Smith, David Ricardo, John Stuart Mill, Karl Marx, and John Maynard Keynes.[1] And it is currently commonplace for world leaders to receive and invoke the advice and policy prescriptions of economists.

For example: The President of the United States benefits from the ongoing counsel of his Council of Economic Advisers. The broad spectrum of economic issues facing political leaders is suggested by the con-tents of the annual *Economic Report of the President.* Areas covered include unemployment and inflation, economic growth and productivity, taxation and public expenditures, poverty and income maintenance, the balance of payments and the international monetary system, labor-management relations, pollution, dis-crimination, immigration, and competition and anti-trust, among others.

Economics for Citizenship

A basic understanding of economics is essential if we are to be well-informed citizens. Most of the specific

problems of the day have important economic aspects, and as voters we can influence the decisions of our political leaders in coping with these problems. What are the causes and consequences of the "twin deficits"—the Federal budget deficit and the international trade deficit—that are constantly reported by the news media? What of the depressing stories of homeless street people? Is it desirable that corporate raiders be allowed to achieve hostile takeovers of corporations? Why is inflation undesirable? What can be done to re-duce unemployment? Are existing welfare programs effective and justifiable? Should we continue to subsi-dize farmers? Do we need further reform of our tax system? Does America need to "reindustrialize" to re-assert its dominant position in world trade and finance? Has the deregulation of the airlines, trucking, and banking industries been a boon or a bane to society? Since responses to such questions are determined largely by our elected officials, intelligence at the polls requires that we have a basic working knowledge of economics. Needless to say, a sound grasp of econom-ics is more than helpful to politicians themselves!

Personal Applications

Economics is also a vital discipline for more mundane, immediate reasons. It is of practical value in business. An understanding of the overall operation of the eco-nomic system enables the business executive to better formulate policies. The executive who understands the causes and consequences of inflation can make more intelligent business decisions during inflationary peri-ods than otherwise. Indeed, more and more econo-mists are appearing on the payrolls of large corpora-tions. Their job is to gather and interpret economic information on which rational business decisions can be made. Economics also gives the individual as a con-sumer and worker insights on how to make wiser buy-ing and employment decisions. What should one buy and how much? How can one "hedge" against the re-duction in the dollar's purchasing power which accom-panies inflation? Which occupations pay well; which are most immune to unemployment? Similarly, some-one who understands the relationship between budget and trade deficits, on the one hand, and security (stock

---

[1] Any of the following three volumes—Robert Heilbroner, *The Worldly Philosophers,* 6th ed. (New York: Simon and Schuster, Inc., 1986); Daniel R. Fusfeld, *The Age of the Economist,* 6th ed. (Chicago: Scott, Foresman and Company, 1990); or E. Ray Canterbery, *The Making of Economics,* 3d ed. (Belmont, Calif.: Wadsworth Publish-ing Company, 1987)—will provide the reader with a fascinating in-troduction to the historical development of economic ideas.

and bond) values, on the other, can make more enlightened personal investment decisions.

In spite of its practical benefits, however, you must be forewarned that economics is mainly an academic, not a vocational, subject. Unlike accounting, advertising, corporation finance, and marketing, economics is not primarily a how-to-make-money area of study. A knowledge of economics will help you run a business or manage personal finances, but this is not its primary objective. In economics, problems are usually examined from the *social,* rather than the *personal,* point of view. The production, exchange, and consumption of goods and services are discussed from the viewpoint of society as a whole, rather than from the standpoint of one's own bankbook.

METHODOLOGY

What do economists do? What are their goals? What procedures do they employ? The title of this volume—*Economics: Principles, Problems, and Policies*—contains a thumbnail answer to the first two questions. Economists formulate economic *principles* which are useful in the establishment of *policies* designed to solve economic *problems.* The procedures employed by the economist are summarized in Figure 1-1. The economist ascertains and gathers facts relevant to a specific economic problem. This task is sometimes called **descriptive** or **empirical economics** (box 1). The economist also states economic principles, that is, generalizes about the way individuals and institutions actually behave. Deriving principles is called **economic theory** or "economic analysis" (box 2).

As we see in Figure 1-1, economists are as likely to move from theory to facts in studying economic behavior as they are to move from facts to theory. Stated more formally, economists use both deductive and inductive methods. **Induction** distills or creates principles from facts. Here an accumulation of facts is arranged systematically and analyzed to permit the derivation of a generalization or principle. Induction moves from facts to theory, from the particular to the general. The inductive method is suggested by the left upward arrow from box 1 to box 2 in the figure.

Similarly, economists can begin with theory and proceed to the verification or rejection of this theory by an appeal to the facts. This is **deduction** or the hypothetical method. Economists may draw upon casual observation, insight, logic, or intuition to frame a tentative, untested principle called an **hypothesis.** For ex-

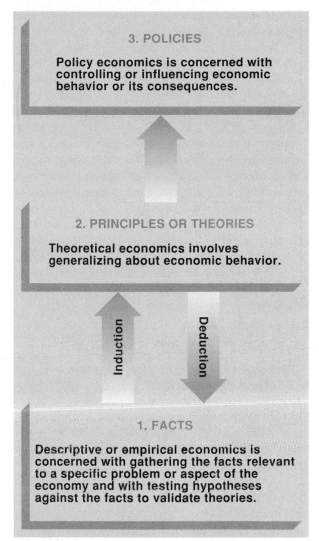

FIGURE 1-1   The relationship between facts, principles, and policies in economics

In analyzing problems or aspects of the economy, economists may use the inductive method whereby they gather, systematically arrange, and generalize on facts. Alternatively, the deductive method entails the development of hypotheses which are then tested against facts. Generalizations derived from either method of inquiry are useful not only in explaining economic behavior, but also as a basis for formulating economic policies.

ample, they may conjecture, on the basis of "armchair logic," that it is rational for consumers to buy more of a product when its price is low than when its price is high. The validity of this hypothesis must then be tested by the systematic and repeated examination of relevant facts. The deductive method goes from the general to the particular, from theory to facts. This method is implicit in the right downward arrow from box 2 to box 1 in Figure 1-1.

Deduction and induction are complementary, rather than opposing, techniques of investigation. Hypotheses formulated by deduction provide guidelines for the economist in gathering and systematizing empirical data. Conversely, some understanding of factual evidence—of the "real world"—is prerequisite to formulation of meaningful hypotheses.

Finally, the general knowledge of economic behavior which economic principles provides can then be used in formulating policies, that is, remedies or solutions, for correcting or avoiding the problem under scrutiny. This final aspect of the field is sometimes called "applied economics" or **policy economics** (box 3).

Continuing to use Figure 1-1 as a reference, we now examine the economist's methodology in more detail.

Descriptive Economics

All sciences are empirical; they are based on facts, that is, on observable and verifiable behavior of certain data or subject matter. In the physical sciences the factual data are inorganic. As a social science, economics examines the behavior of individuals and institutions engaged in the production, exchange, and consumption of goods and services.

Fact-gathering can be an infinitely complex task. Because the world of reality is cluttered with innumerable interrelated facts, the economist must use discretion in gathering them. One must distinguish economic from noneconomic facts and then determine which economic facts are relevant and which irrelevant for the problem under consideration. But even when this sorting process is complete, the relevant economic facts may appear diverse and unrelated.

Economic Theory

The task of economic theory or analysis is to systematically arrange, interpret, and generalize upon facts. Principles and theories—the end result of economic analysis—bring order and meaning to facts by tying them together, putting them in correct relationship to one another, and generalizing upon them. "Theories without facts may be barren, but facts without theories are meaningless."[2]

[2]Kenneth E. Boulding, *Economic Analysis: Microeconomics,* 4th ed. (New York: Harper & Row, Publishers, Incorporated, 1966), p. 5.

Principles and theories are meaningful statements drawn from facts, but facts, in turn, serve as a constant check on the validity of principles already established. Facts—how individuals and institutions actually behave in producing, exchanging, and consuming goods and services—may change with time. This makes it essential that economists continually check existing principles and theories against the changing economic environment.

Terminology   Economists talk about "laws," "principles," "theories," and "models." These terms all mean essentially the same thing: generalizations, or statements of regularity, concerning the economic behavior of individuals and institutions. The term "economic law" is a bit misleading because it implies a high degree of exactness, universal application, and even moral rightness. So, to a lesser degree, does the term **principle.** And some people incorrectly associate the term "theory" with ivory-tower dreams, divorced from the facts and realities of the world. The term "model" has much to commend it. A model is a simplified picture of reality, an abstract generalization of how relevant data actually behave. In this book these four terms will be used synonymously. The choice of terms in labeling any particular generalization will be governed by custom or convenience. Thus, the relationship between the price of a product and the quantity consumers purchase will be called the "law" of demand, rather than the theory or principle of demand, because this is the customary designation.

Several other points regarding the character and derivation of economic principles are in order.

Generalizations   Economic principles are **generalizations** and, as the term implies, characterized by somewhat imprecise quantitative statement. Economic facts are usually diverse; some individuals and institutions act one way and some another way. Economic principles are therefore frequently stated in terms of averages or statistical probabilities. For example, when economists say that the average household earned an income of about $35,000 in 1990, they are generalizing. It is recognized that some households earned much more and a good many others much less. Yet this generalization, properly handled and interpreted, can be very meaningful and useful.

Similarly, economic generalizations are often stated in terms of probabilities. A researcher may tell us there is a 95 percent probability that every $1.00 reduction in personal income taxes will result in a $.92 increase in consumer spending.

"Other Things Equal" Assumption Like other scientists, economists use the ***ceteris paribus*** or **other things being equal assumption** to construct their generalizations. That is, they assume all other variables except those under immediate consideration are held constant. This technique simplifies the reasoning process by isolating the relationship under consideration. For example, in considering the relationship between the price of Pepsi and the amount purchased, it helps to assume that, of all the factors which might influence the amount of Pepsi purchased (for example, the price of Pepsi, the prices of other goods such as Coke, consumer incomes and tastes), only the price of Pepsi varies. The economist can then focus on the "price of Pepsi–purchases of Pepsi" relationship without reasoning being blurred or confused by intrusion of other variables.

In the natural sciences controlled experiments usually can be performed where "all other things" are in fact held constant or virtually so. Thus, scientists can test the assumed relationship between two variables with great precision. But economics is not a laboratory science. The economist's process of empirical verification is based on "real-world" data generated by the actual operation of the economy. In this rather bewildering environment "other things" *do* change. Despite the development of complex statistical techniques designed to hold other things equal, such controls are less than perfect. As a result, economic principles are less certain and less precise in application than those of laboratory sciences.

Abstractions Economic principles, or theories, are necessarily abstractions. They do not mirror the full complexity of reality. The very process of sorting out noneconomic and irrelevant facts in the fact-gathering process involves abstracting from reality. Unfortunately, the abstractness of economic theory prompts the uninformed to identify theory as impractical and unrealistic. This is nonsense! Economic theories are practical simply because they are abstractions. The level of reality is too complex and bewildering to be very meaningful. Economists theorize to give meaning to a maze of facts which would otherwise be confusing and useless, and to put facts into a more usable, practical form. Thus, to generalize is to abstract or purposely simplify; generalization for this purpose is practical, and therefore so is abstraction.

An economic theory is a model—a simplified picture or map—of some segment of the economy. This model helps us understand reality better *because* it avoids the confusing details of reality. Theories—*good*

theories—are grounded on facts and therefore are realistic. Theories which do not fit the facts are simply not good theories.

Macro and Micro There are two different levels of analysis at which the economist may derive laws concerning economic behavior. The level of **macroeconomics** deals either with the economy as a whole or with the basic subdivisions or aggregates—such as the government, household, and business sectors—which make up the economy. An aggregate is a collection of specific economic units which are treated *as if* they were one unit. Thus, we might find it convenient to lump together the over eighteen million businesses in our economy and treat them as if they were one huge unit. In dealing with aggregates, macroeconomics is concerned with obtaining an overview, or general outline, of the structure of the economy and the relationships among the major aggregates which constitute the economy. No attention is given to specific units making up the various aggregates. Macroeconomics speaks of such magnitudes as *total* output, *total* level of employment, *total* income, *aggregate* expenditures, the *general* level of prices, and so forth, in analyzing various economic problems. In short, macroeconomics examines the forest, not the trees. It gives us a bird's-eye view of the economy.

On the other hand, **microeconomics** deals with *specific* economic units and a *detailed* consideration of these individual units. At this level of analysis, the economist figuratively puts an economic unit, or very small segment of the economy, under the microscope to observe details of its operation. Here we talk in terms of an individual industry, firm, or household, and concentrate upon such magnitudes as the output or price of a specific product, the number of workers employed by a single firm, the revenue or income of a particular firm or household, or the expenditures of a given firm or family. In microeconomics we examine the trees, not the forest. Microeconomics is useful in achieving a worm's-eye view of some very specific component of our economic system.

The macro–micro distinction does not mean that the subject matter of economics is so highly compartmentalized that each topic can be readily labeled as "macro" or "micro"; many topics and subdivisions of economics are rooted in both. Indeed, there has been a convergence of macro- and microeconomics in important areas in recent years. While the problem of unemployment was treated primarily as a macroeconomic topic some twenty or twenty-five years ago ("unemployment depends on *aggregate* spending"), economists now recognize that decisions made by *individual* workers in searching for jobs and the manner in which specific product and labor markets function are also critical in determining the unemployment rate.

Graphical Expression   Many of the economic models or principles presented in this book will be expressed graphically. The most important of these models are labeled "Key Graphs." You are strongly urged to read the appendix to this chapter to review graphing and other relevant quantitative relationships.

QUICK REVIEW 1-1

◆   *Economics is concerned with the efficient management of scarce resources.*

◆   *Induction involves observing regularities in factual data and drawing generalizations from them; deduction entails the creation of hypotheses which are then tested with factual data.*

◆   *Economic theories ("laws," "principles," or "models") are generalizations, based on facts, concerning the economic behavior of individuals and institutions.*

◆   *Macroeconomics deals with the economy as a whole; microeconomics focuses on specific units which comprise the economy.*

Policy Economics: Positive and Normative

As we move from the fact and principles levels (boxes 1 and 2) of Figure 1-1 to the policy level (box 3) we make a critical leap from positive to normative economics.

Positive economics deals with facts (once removed at the level of theory) and avoids value judgments. Positive economics attempts to set forth scientific statements about economic behavior. **Normative economics,** in contrast, involves someone's value judgments about what the economy should be like or what particular policy action should be recommended based on a given economic generalization or relationship.

Positive economics concerns *what is,* while normative economics embodies subjective feelings about *what ought to be.* Positive economics deals with what the economy is actually like; normative economics examines whether certain conditions or aspects of the economy are desirable or not.

Consider this example: Positive statement: "Unemployment is 7 percent of the labor force." Normative statement: "Unemployment ought to be reduced." Second positive statement: "Other things being the same, if tuition is increased, enrollment at Gigantic State University will fall." Normative statement: "Tuition should be lowered at GSU so that more students can obtain an education." Whenever words such as "ought" or "should" appear in a sentence, there is a strong chance you are dealing with a normative statement.

Most of the apparent disagreement among economists involves normative, value-based policy questions. To be sure, various economists present and support different theories or models of the economy and its component parts. But by far most economic controversy reflects differing opinions or value judgments as to what our society should be like. For example, there is greater agreement about the actual distribution of income in our society than how income should be distributed. The point we reemphasize is that value judgments or normative statements come into play at the level of policy economics.

As noted earlier, successful policy economics draws heavily on economic principles. For example, one almost universally accepted economic principle indicates that, within certain limits, there is a direct relationship between total spending and the level of employment in the economy. "If total spending increases, the volume of employment will rise. Conversely, if total spending decreases, the volume of employment will fall." This principle can be invaluable to government in determining its economic policies. If government economists note that available statistics indicate an actual slackening of total expenditures, the principle will permit them to predict the undesirable consequence of unemployment. Aware of this anticipated result, public officials can set in motion government policies designed to bolster total spending and head off or reduce expected unemployment. In short, we must be able to predict in order to effectively control. Economic principles help make prediction possible and are the basis for sound economic policy.

Economic Goals   A number of **economic goals** or value judgments are widely, though not universally, accepted in our own society and in many others. These goals may be briefly listed as follows:

1 Economic Growth   The production of more and better goods and services, or, more simply stated, a higher standard of living, is desired.

2 Full Employment Suitable jobs should be available for all willing and able to work.

3 Economic Efficiency We want maximum benefits at minimum cost from the limited productive resources available.

4 Price Level Stability Sizable upswings or downswings in the general price level, that is, inflation and deflation, should be avoided.

5 Economic Freedom Business executives, workers, and consumers should enjoy a high degree of freedom in their economic activities.

6 An Equitable Distribution of Income No group of citizens should face stark poverty while others enjoy extreme luxury.

7 Economic Security Provision should be made for those who are chronically ill, disabled, handicapped, laid off, aged, or otherwise unable to earn minimal levels of income.

8 Balance of Trade We seek a reasonable balance in our international trade and financial transactions.

This list of widely accepted goals[3] is the basis for several significant points.

1 Interpretation Note that this or any other statement of basic economic goals inevitably involves problems of interpretation. What are "sizable" changes in the price level? What is a "high degree" of economic freedom? What is an "equitable" distribution of income? Although most of us might accept the above goals as generally stated, we might also disagree substantially on their specific meanings and hence the types of policies needed to attain these goals. Although goals 1 to 4 and 8 are subject to reasonably accurate measurements, the inability to quantify goals 5 to 7 undoubtedly contributes to controversy over their precise meaning.

2 Complementary Certain of these goals are complementary in that when one goal is achieved, some other goal or goals will also be realized. For example, the achieving of full employment (goal 2) means elimi-

nation of unemployment, a basic cause of low incomes (goal 6) and economic insecurity (goal 7). Furthermore, the sociopolitical tensions which may accompany a highly unequal distribution of income (goal 6) are tempered somewhat when most incomes rise absolutely as a result of economic growth (goal 1).

3 Conflicting Some goals may be conflicting or mutually exclusive. For example, goals 1 and 6 may be in conflict. Some economists point out that efforts to achieve greater equality in the distribution of income may weaken incentives to work, invest, innovate, and take business risks, all of which promote rapid economic growth. They argue that government tends to equalize the distribution of income by taxing high-income people heavily and transferring those tax revenues to low-income people. The incentives of a high-income individual will be diminished because taxation reduces one's income rewards. Similarly, a low-income person will be less motivated to work and engage in other productive activities when government stands ready to subsidize that individual.

International example: Before recent events in the Soviet Union, central planning virtually eliminated unemployment with the result that this source of worker insecurity almost disappeared. However, with little fear of losing one's job, Soviet workers were quite cavalier regarding work effort and therefore productivity and efficiency in the Soviet Union were quite low. Here we have a conflict between goal 7, economic security, and goal 1, the growth of worker productivity.

4 Priorities When basic goals do conflict, society is forced to develop a system of priorities for the objectives it seeks. If full employment and price stability are to some extent mutually exclusive, that is, if full employment is accompanied by some inflation *and* price stability entails some unemployment, society must decide upon the relative importance of these two goals. There is clearly ample room for disagreement here.

Formulating Economic Policy The creation of specific policies designed to achieve the broad economic goals of our society is no simple matter. A brief examination of the basic steps in policy formulation is in order.

1 Stating Goals The first step is to make a clear statement of goals. If we say that we want "full employment," do we mean that everyone between, say, 16 and 65 years of age should have a job? Or do we mean that

[3]There are other goals which might be added. For example, improving the physical environment is a widely held goal.

everyone who wants to work should have a job? Should we allow for some "normal" unemployment caused by workers' voluntarily changing jobs?

2 Policy Options Next, we must state and recognize the possible effects of alternative policies designed to achieve the goal. This requires a clear-cut understanding of the economic impact, benefits, costs, and political feasibility of alternative programs. Thus, for example, economists currently debate the relative merits and demerits of fiscal policy (which involves changing government spending and taxes) and monetary policy (which entails altering the supply of money) as alternative means of achieving and maintaining full employment.

3 Evaluation We are obligated to both ourselves and future generations to review our experiences with chosen policies and evaluate their effectiveness; it is only through this type of evaluation that we can hope to improve policy applications. Did a given change in taxes or the supply of money alter the level of employment to the extent originally predicted? Did deregulation of a particular industry (for example, the airlines) yield the predicted beneficial results? If not, why not?

QUICK REVIEW 1-2

♦ *Positive economics deals with factual statements ("what is"), while normative economics concerns value judgments ("what ought to be").*

♦ *Some of society's economic goals are complementary while others are conflicting.*

PITFALLS TO OBJECTIVE THINKING

Our discussion of the economist's procedure has, up to this point, skirted some specific problems and pitfalls which frequently hinder our thinking objectively about economic problems. Consider the following impediments to valid economic reasoning.

Bias

In contrast to a neophyte physicist or chemist, the budding economist ordinarily brings into economics a bundle of biases and preconceptions about the field. For example, one might be suspicious of business profits or feel that deficit spending is invariably evil. Needless to

say, biases may cloud our thinking and interfere with objective analysis. The beginning economics student must be willing to shed biases and preconceptions which are simply not warranted by facts.

Loaded Terminology

The economic terminology to which we are exposed in newspapers and popular magazines is sometimes emotionally loaded. The writer—or more frequently the particular interest group he or she represents—may have a cause to further or an ax to grind, and terms will be slanted to solicit the support of the reader. A governmental flood-control project in the Great Plains region may be called "creeping socialism" by its opponents and "intelligent democratic planning" by its proponents. We must be prepared to discount such terminology to objectively understand important economic issues.

Definitions

No scientist is obligated to use popularized or immediately understandable definitions of his or her terms. The economist may find it convenient and essential to define terms in such a way that they are clearly at odds with the definitions held by most people in everyday speech. So long as the economist is explicit and consistent in these definitions, he or she is on safe ground. For example, the term "investment" to the average citizen is associated with the buying of bonds and stocks in the securities market. How often have we heard someone talk of "investing" in General Motors stock or government bonds? But to the economist, "investment" means the purchase of real capital assets such as machinery and equipment, or the construction of a new factory building, not the purely financial transaction of swapping cash or part of a bank balance for a neatly engraved piece of paper.

Fallacy of Composition

Another pitfall in economic thinking is assuming that "what is true for the individual or part of a group is necessarily also true for the group or whole." This is a logical **fallacy of composition;** it is *not* correct. The validity of a particular generalization for an individual or part does *not* necessarily ensure its accuracy for the group or whole.

A noneconomic example may help: You are watching a football game and the home team executes an outstanding play. In the excitement, you leap to your feet to get a better view. Generalization: "If you, *an individual*, stand, then your view of the game is improved." But does this also hold true for the group—for everyone watching the game? Certainly not! If everyone stands to watch the play, everyone—including you—will probably have the same or even a worse view than when seated.

Consider two examples from economics: A wage increase for Smith is desirable because, given constant product prices, it increases Smith's purchasing power and standard of living. But if everyone realizes a wage increase, product prices may rise, that is, inflation might occur. Therefore, Smith's standard of living may be unchanged as higher prices offset her larger salary.

Second illustration: An *individual* farmer fortunate enough to reap a bumper crop is likely to realize a sharp gain in income. But this generalization does not apply to farmers as a *group*. For the individual farmer, crop prices will not be influenced (reduced) by this bumper crop, because each farmer produces a negligible fraction of the total farm output. But to farmers as a group, prices vary inversely with total output.[4] Thus, as *all* farmers realize bumper crops, the total output of farm products rises, thereby depressing crop prices. If price declines are relatively greater than the increased output, farm incomes will *fall*.

Recalling our earlier distinction between macroeconomics and microeconomics, the fallacy of composition reminds us that *generalizations which are valid at one of these levels of analysis may or may not be valid at the other.*

Cause and Effect: Post Hoc Fallacy

Still another hazard in economic thinking is to assume that simply because one event precedes another, the first is necessarily the cause of the second. This kind of faulty reasoning is known as the **post hoc, ergo propter hoc,** or **after this, therefore because of this, fallacy.**

A classic example clearly indicates the fallacy inherent in such reasoning. Suppose that early each spring the medicine man of a tribe performs his ritual by cavorting around the village in a green costume. A week or so later the trees and grass turn green. Can we safely conclude that event A, the medicine man's gyrations, has caused event B, the landscape's turning

green? Obviously not. The rooster crows before dawn, but this doesn't mean the rooster is responsible for the sunrise!

It is especially important in analyzing various sets of empirical data *not* to confuse **correlation** with **causation.** *Correlation* is a technical term which indicates that two sets of data are associated in some systematic and dependable way. For example, we may find that when X increases, Y also increases. But this does not necessarily mean that X is the cause of Y. The relationship could be purely coincidental or determined by some other factor, Z, not included in the analysis.

Example: Economists have found a positive correlation between education and income. In general, people with more education earn higher incomes than do people with less education. Common sense prompts us to label education as the cause and higher incomes as the effect; more education suggest a more productive worker and such workers receive larger monetary rewards.

But, on second thought, might not causation run the other way? That is, do people with higher incomes buy more education, just as they buy more automobiles and steaks? Or is the relationship explainable in terms of still other factors? Are education and income positively correlated because the bundle of characteristics—ability, motivation, personal habits—required to succeed in education are the same characteristics required to be a productive and highly paid worker? Upon reflection, seemingly simple cause-effect relationships—"more education means more income"—may prove to be suspect or perhaps flatly incorrect.

In short, cause-and-effect relationships are typically not self-evident in economics; the economist must look carefully before concluding that event A caused event B. The fact that A preceded B is not sufficient to warrant any such conclusion.

THE ECONOMIC PERSPECTIVE

The methodology used by economists is common to all the natural and social sciences. Similarly, all scholars try to avoid the reasoning errors just discussed. Hence, economists do *not* think in a special way. But they *do* think about things from a special perspective. Economists have developed a keen alertness to certain aspects of everyday conduct and situations. Specifically, they look for *rationality* or *purposefulness* in human actions and economic institutions. This purposefulness

---

[4]This assumes there are no government programs which fix farm prices.

LAST WORD

FAST-FOOD LINES: AN ECONOMIC PERSPECTIVE

How might the economic perspective help us understand the behavior of fast-food consumers?

When you enter a fast-food restaurant, which line do you select? What do you do when you are in a long line in the restaurant and a new station opens? Have you ever gone to a fast-food restaurant, only to see long lines, and then leave? Have you ever had someone in front of you in a fast-food line place an order which takes a long time to fill?

The economic perspective is useful in analyzing the behavior of fast-food customers. These customers are at the restaurant because they expect the benefit or satisfaction from the food they buy to match or exceed its cost. When customers enter the restaurant they scurry to the *shortest* line, believing that the shortest line will reduce their time cost of obtaining their food. They are acting purposefully; time is limited and most people would prefer using it in some way other than standing in line.

All lines in the fast-food establishment normally are of roughly equal lengths. If one line is temporarily shorter than other lines, some people will move toward that line. These movers apparently view the time saving associated with the shorter line to exceed the cost of moving from their present line. Line changing normally results in an equilibrium line length. No further movement of customers between lines will occur once all lines are of equal length.

Fast-food customers face another cost-benefit decision when a clerk opens a new station at the counter. Should customers move to the new station or stay put? Those who do shift to the new line decide that the benefit of the time savings from the move exceeds the extra cost of physically moving. In so deciding, customers must also consider just how quickly they can get to the new station compared to others who may be contemplating the same move. (Those who hesitate in this situation are lost!)

Customers at the fast-food establishment select lines without having perfect information. For example, they do not first survey those in the lines to determine what they are ordering before deciding on which line to enter. There are two reasons for this. First, most customers would tell them "It is none of your business,"

and therefore no information would be forthcoming. Second, even if they could obtain the information, the amount of time necessary to get it (cost) would most likely exceed any time saving associated with finding the best line (benefit). Because information is costly to obtain, fast-food patrons select lines on the basis of imperfect information. Thus, not all decisions turn out to be as expected. For example, some people may enter a line in which the person in front of them is ordering hamburgers and fries for the forty people in the Greyhound bus parked out back! Nevertheless, at the time the customer made the decision, he or she thought that it was optimal.

Imperfect information also explains why some people who arrive at a fast-food restaurant and observe long lines decide to leave. These people conclude that the total cost (monetary plus time costs) of obtaining the fast food is too large relative to the benefit. They would not have come to the restaurant in the first place had they known the lines were so long. But, getting that information by, say, employing an advance scout with a cellular phone would cost more than the perceived benefit.

Finally, customers must decide what to order when they arrive at the counter. In making these choices they again compare costs and benefits in attempting to obtain the greatest personal well-being.

Economists believe that what is true for the behavior of customers at fast-food restaurants is true for economic behavior in general. Faced with an array of choices, consumers, workers, and businesses rationally compare costs and benefits in making decisions.

implies that people, individually and collectively, make choices by comparing costs and benefits. It therefore might be said that the **economic perspective** is a *cost-benefit perspective*.

Because people make economic choices from a wide array of alternatives, all choices entail sacrifices or costs. To buy a new VCR may mean not being able to afford a new personal computer. Taking a course in economics may preclude taking a course in accounting, political science, or computer science. A decision by government to provide improved health care for the elderly may mean deteriorating health care for children in poverty. Alas, costs are everywhere! Naturally, people are most aware of personal monetary costs—expenses incurred when paying tuition, buying hamburgers, hiring babysitters, renting apartments, or attending concerts. But in Chapter 2 we will see that costs occur in *all* situations in which incomes or resources are scarce relative to wants.

Economic actions of workers, producers, and consumers, of course, also produce personal economic benefits. Workers receive wages, producers garner profits, and consumers obtain satisfaction. People *compare* these benefits with costs in deciding how to spend their time, which products to buy, whether or not to work, or which goods to produce and sell. If the added benefits associated with a given course of action exceed the added costs, then it is rational to take that action. But if added costs are greater than added benefits, that action is not rational and should not be undertaken. Furthermore, when costs or benefits *change,* people *alter* their behavior accordingly.

Economists look carefully at costs and benefits to understand the everyday activities of people and institutions in the economy. This economic perspective will become increasingly evident as you advance through this book. The accompanying Last Word provides an everyday application of the economic perspective.

QUICK REVIEW 1-3

✦ *Beware of logical errors such as the fallacy of composition and the post hoc fallacy when engaging in economic reasoning.*

✦ *The economic perspective is a cost-benefit perspective; it helps us analyze the everyday behavior of individuals and institutions.*

CHAPTER SUMMARY

1 Economics deals with the efficient use of scarce resources in the production of goods and services to satisfy material wants.

2 Economics is studied for several reasons: **a** It provides valuable knowledge about our social environment and behavior; **b** it equips a democratic citizenry to render fundamental decisions intelligently; **c** although not chiefly a vocational discipline, economics may provide the business executive or consumer with valuable information.

3 The tasks of descriptive or empirical economics are **a** gathering those economic facts relevant to a particular problem or specific segment of the economy, and **b** testing hypotheses against facts to validate theories.

4 Generalizations stated by economists are called "principles," "theories," "laws," or "models." The derivation of these principles is the task of economic theory.

5 Induction distills theories from facts; deduction states a hypothesis and then gathers facts to determine whether the hypothesis is valid.

6 Some economic principles deal with macroeconomics (the economy as a whole or major aggregates), while others pertain to microeconomics (specific economic units or institutions).

7 Economic principles are particularly valuable as predictive devices; they are the bases for the formulation of economic policy designed to solve problems and control undesirable events.

8 Positive statements deal with facts ("what is"), while normative statements encompass value judgments ("what ought to be").

9 Economic growth, full employment, economic efficiency, price level stability, economic freedom, equity in the distribution of income, economic security, and reasonable balance in our international trade and finance are all widely accepted economic goals in our society. Some of these goals are complementary; others are mutually exclusive.

10 In studying economics the beginner may encounter numerous pitfalls. Some of the more important are **a** biases and preconceptions, **b** terminological difficulties, **c** the fallacy of composition, and **d** the difficulty of establishing clear cause-effect relationships.

11 The economic perspective envisions individuals and institutions making rational decisions based on costs and benefits.

TERMS AND CONCEPTS

| economics | economic theory | hypothesis | *ceteris paribus* or |
| descriptive or empirical economics | induction and deduction | principles or generalizations | "other things being equal" assumption |

policy economics
macroeconomics and
    microeconomics
economic goals

positive and normative
    economics
correlation and
    causation

post hoc, ergo propter
    hoc or "after this,
    therefore because of
    this" fallacy

fallacy of composition
economic perspective

QUESTIONS AND STUDY SUGGESTIONS

1 Explain in detail the interrelationships between economic facts, theory, and policy. Critically evaluate: "The trouble with economics is that it is not practical. It has too much to say about theory and not enough to say about facts."

2 Analyze and explain the following quotation.[5]

Facts are seldom simple and usually complicated; theoretical analysis is needed to unravel the complications and interpret the facts before we can understand them . . . the opposition of facts and theory is a false one; the true relationship is complementary. We cannot in practice consider a fact without relating it to other facts, and the relation is a theory. Facts by themselves are dumb; before they will tell us anything we have to arrange them, and the arrangement is a theory. Theory is simply the unavoidable arrangement and interpretation of facts, which gives us generalizations on which we can argue and act, in the place of a mass of disjointed particulars.

3 Of what significance is the fact that economics is not a laboratory science? What problems may be involved in deriving and applying economic principles?

4 Explain each of the following statements:

    a "Like all scientific laws, economic laws are established in order to make successful prediction of the outcome of human actions."[6]

    b "Abstraction . . . is the inevitable price of generality . . . indeed abstraction and generality are virtually synonyms."[7]

    c "Numbers serve to discipline rhetoric."[8]

5 Indicate whether each of the following statements pertains to microeconomics or macroeconomics:

    a The unemployment rate in the United States was 6.8 percent in August of 1991.

    b The Alpo dogfood plant in Bowser, Iowa, laid off 15 workers last month.

    c An unexpected freeze in central Florida reduced the citrus crop and caused the price of oranges to rise.

    d Our national output, adjusted for inflation, grew by about 1 percent in 1990.

    e Last week Manhattan Chemical Bank lowered its interest rate on business loans by one-half of 1 percentage point.

    f The consumer price index rose by more than 6 percent in 1990.

6 Identify each of the following as either a positive or a normative statement:

    a The high temperature today was 89 degrees.

    b It was too hot today.

    c The general price level rose by 4.4 percent last year.

    d Inflation eroded living standards last year and should be reduced by government policies.

7 To what extent would you accept the eight economic goals stated and described in this chapter? What priorities would you assign to them? It has been said that we seek simply four goals: progress, stability, justice, and freedom. Is this list of goals compatible with that given in the chapter?

8 Analyze each of the following specific goals in terms of the eight general goals stated on pages 6 and 7, and note points of conflict and compatibility: **a** the lessening of environmental pollution; **b** increasing leisure; and **c** protection of American producers from foreign competition. Indicate which of these specific goals you favor and justify your position.

9 Explain and give an illustration of **a** the fallacy of composition, and **b** the "after this, therefore because of this" fallacy. Why are cause-and-effect relationships difficult to isolate in the social sciences?

10 "Economists should never be popular; men who afflict the comfortable serve equally those who comfort the afflicted and one cannot suppose that American capitalism would long prosper without the critics its leaders find such a profound source of annoyance."[9] Interpret and evaluate.

11 Use the economic perspective to explain why someone who normally is a light eater at a standard restaurant may become somewhat of a glutton at a buffet-style restaurant which charges a single price for all you can eat.

---

[5]Henry Clay, *Economics for the General Reader* (New York: The Macmillan Company, 1925), pp. 10–11.

[6]Oskar Lange, "The Scope and Method of Economics," *Review of Economic Studies,* vol. 13, 1945–1946, p. 20.

[7]George J. Stigler, *The Theory of Price* (New York: The Macmillan Company, 1947), p. 10.

[8]Victor R. Fuchs, *How We Live* (Cambridge, Mass.: Harvard University Press, 1983), p. 5.

[9]John Kenneth Galbraith, *American Capitalism,* rev. ed. (Boston: Houghton Mifflin Company, 1956), p. 49.

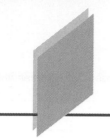
Graphs and Their Meaning

If you glance quickly through this text, you will find graphs. Some will appear to be relatively simple, while others seem more formidable. Contrary to student folklore, graphs are *not* designed by economists to confuse students! On the contrary, graphs are employed to help students visualize and understand important economic relationships. Economists express their theories or models with graphs. The physicist and chemist sometimes illustrate their theories by building Tinker-Toy arrangements of multicolored wooden balls representing protons, neutrons, and so forth, held in proper relation to one another by wires or sticks. Economists often use graphs to illustrate their models, and by understanding these "pictures" students can more readily comprehend what economists are saying.

Most of our principles or models will explain the relationship between just two sets of economic facts; therefore, two-dimensional graphs are a convenient way of visualizing and manipulating these relationships.

Constructing a Graph

A graph is a visual representation of the relationship between two variables. Table 1 is a hypothetical illustration showing the relationship between income and con-

sumption. Without ever having studied economics, one would expect intuitively that high-income people would consume more than low-income people. Thus we are not surprised to find in Table 1 that consumption increases as income increases.

How can the information in Table 1 be expressed graphically? Glance at the graph shown in Figure 1. Now look back at the information in Table 1 and we will explain how to represent that information in a meaningful way by constructing the graph you just examined.

What we want to show visually, or graphically, is how consumption changes as income changes. Since income is the determining factor, we represent it on the horizontal axis of the graph, as is customary. And, because consumption depends on income, we represent it on the vertical axis of the graph, as is also customary. Actually, what we are doing is representing the inde-

TABLE 1 The relationship between income and consumption

Income (per week)	Consumption (per week)	Point
$ 0	$ 50	a
100	100	b
200	150	c
300	200	d
400	250	e

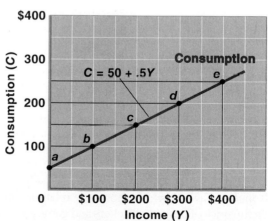

FIGURE 1 Graphing the direct relationship between consumption and income

Two sets of data which are positively or directly related, such as consumption and income, graph as an upsloping line. In this case the vertical intercept is 50 and the slope of the line is $+\frac{1}{2}$.

pendent variable on the horizontal axis and the dependent variable on the vertical axis.

Now we must arrange the vertical and horizontal scales of the graph to reflect the range of values of consumption and income, as well as mark the steps in convenient graphic increments. As you can see, the ranges in the graph cover the ranges of values in Table 1. Similarly, as so happens in this example, the increments on both scales are $100 for approximately each half-inch.

Next, we must locate for each consumption value and the income value that it depends upon a single point which reflects the same information graphically. Our five income–consumption combinations are plotted by drawing perpendiculars from the appropriate points on the **vertical** and **horizontal axes.** For example, in plotting point *c*—the $200 income–$150 consumption point—perpendiculars must be drawn up from the horizontal (income) axis at $200 and across from the vertical (consumption) axis at $150. These perpendiculars intersect at point *c,* which locates this particular income–consumption combination. You should verify that the other income–consumption combinations shown in Table 1 are properly located in Figure 1. By assuming that the same general relationship between income and consumption prevails at all other points between the five points graphed, a line or curve can be drawn to connect these points.

Using Figure 1 as a benchmark, we can now make several additional important comments.

Direct and Inverse Relationships

Our upsloping line depicts a direct relationship between income and consumption. By a positive or **direct relationship** we mean that the two variables—in this case consumption and income—change in the *same* direction. An increase in consumption is associated with an increase in income; conversely, a decrease in consumption accompanies a decrease in income. When two sets of data are positively or directly related, they will always graph as an *upsloping* line as in Figure 1.

In contrast, two sets of data may be inversely related. Consider Table 2, which shows the relationship between the price of basketball tickets and game attendance at Gigantic State University. We observe a negative or **inverse relationship** between ticket prices and attendance; these two variables change in *opposite* directions. When ticket prices decrease, attendance increases. Conversely, when ticket prices increase, atten-

TABLE 2 The relationship between ticket prices and attendance

Ticket price	Attendance (thousands)	Point
$25	0	a
20	4	b
15	8	c
10	12	d
5	16	e
0	20	f

dance decreases. In Figure 2 the six data points of Table 2 are plotted following the same procedure outlined above. Observe that an inverse relationship will always graph as a *downsloping* line.

Dependent and Independent Variables

Although the task is sometimes formidable, economists seek to determine which variable is "cause" and which "effect." Or, more formally, we want to ascertain the independent and the dependent variable. By definition, the **dependent variable** is the "effect" or out-

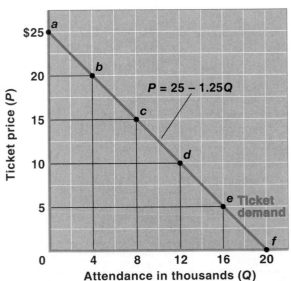

FIGURE 2 Graphing the inverse relationship between ticket prices and game attendance

Two sets of data which are negatively or inversely related, such as ticket price and the attendance at basketball games, graph as a downsloping line. The slope of this line is −1¼.

come; it is the variable which changes because of a change in another (independent) variable.

Similarly, the **independent variable** is the "cause"; it is the variable which causes the change in the dependent variable. As noted earlier in our income–consumption example, generally, income is the independent variable and consumption the dependent variable. Income causes consumption to be what it is rather than the other way around. Similarly, ticket prices determine attendance at GSU basketball games; attendance does not determine ticket prices. Ticket price is the independent variable and the quantity purchased is the dependent variable.

You may recall from your high school courses that mathematicians always put the independent variable (cause) on the horizontal axis and the dependent variable (effect) on the vertical axis. Economists are less tidy; their graphing of independent and dependent variables is more arbitrary. Thus, their conventional graphing of the income–consumption relationship is consistent with mathematical presentation. But economists put price and cost data on the vertical axis. Hence, the economist's graphing of GSU's ticket price–attendance data conflicts with normal mathematical procedure.

Other Variables Held Constant

Our simple two-variable graphs ignore many other factors which might affect the amount of consumption which occurs at each income level or the number of people who attend GSU basketball games at each possible ticket price. When economists plot the relationship between any two variables, they invoke the *ceteris paribus* or "other things being equal" assumption discussed previously. Thus, in Figure 1 all other factors (that is, all factors other than income) which might affect the amount of consumption are presumed to be constant or unchanged. Similarly, in Figure 2 all factors other than ticket price which might influence attendance at GSU basketball games are assumed constant. In reality, we know that "other things" often change, and when they do, the specific relationships presented in our two tables and graphs will change. Specifically, we would expect the lines we have plotted to shift to new locations.

For example, what might happen to the income–consumption relationship if a stock market "crash" such at that of October 1987 occurred? The expected impact of this dramatic fall in the value of stocks would be to make people feel less wealthy and therefore less willing to consume at each income level. In short, we

would anticipate a downward shift of the consumption line in Figure 1. You should plot a new consumption line, assuming that consumption is, say, $20 less at each income level. Note that the relationship remains direct, but the line has merely shifted to reflect less consumer spending at each level of income.

Similarly, factors other than ticket prices might affect GSU game attendance. If the government abandoned its program of student loans, GSU enrollment and hence attendance at games might be less at each ticket price. You should redraw Figure 2, assuming that 2000 fewer students attend GSU games at each ticket price. Question 2 at the end of this appendix introduces other variables which might cause the relationship shown in Figure 2 to shift to another position.

Slope of a Line

Lines can be described in terms of their slopes. The **slope of a straight line** between any two points is defined as the ratio of the vertical change (the rise or fall) to the horizontal change (the run) involved in moving between those points. In moving from point b to point c in Figure 1 the rise or vertical change (the change in consumption) is +$50 and the run or horizontal change (the change in income) is +$100. Therefore:

$$\text{Slope} = \frac{\text{vertical change}}{\text{horizontal change}} = \frac{+50}{+100} = +\frac{1}{2}$$

Note that our slope of $\frac{1}{2}$ is positive because consumption and income change in the same direction, that is, consumption and income are directly or positively related.

This slope of $+\frac{1}{2}$ tells us that there will be a $1 increase in consumption for every $2 increase in income. Similarly, it indicates that for every $2 decrease in income there will be a $1 decrease in consumption.

For our ticket price–attendance data the relationship is negative or inverse with the result that the slope of Figure 2's line is negative. In particular, the vertical change or fall is 5 and the horizontal change or run is 4. Therefore:

$$\text{Slope} = \frac{\text{vertical change}}{\text{horizontal change}} = \frac{-5}{+4} = -1\frac{1}{4}$$

This slope of $-5/+4$ or $-1\frac{1}{4}$ means that lowering the price of a ticket by $5 will increase attendance by 4000 people. Or, alternatively stated, it implies that a $1 price reduction will increase attendance by 800 persons.

In addition to its slope, the only other information needed in locating a line is the vertical intercept. By definition, the **vertical intercept** is the point at which the line meets the vertical axis. For Figure 1 the intercept is $50. This means that, if current income was somehow zero, consumers would still spend $50. How might they manage to consume when they have no current income? Answer: By borrowing or by selling off some of their assets. Similarly, the vertical intercept in Figure 2 shows us that at a $25 ticket price GSU's basketball team would be playing in an empty auditorium.

Given the intercept and the slope, our consumption line can be succinctly described in equation form. In general, a linear equation is written as $y = a + bx$, where y is the dependent variable, a is the vertical intercept, b is the slope of the line, and x is the independent variable. For our income–consumption example, if C represents consumption (the dependent variable) and Y represents income (the independent variable), we can write $C = a + bY$. By substituting the values of the intercept and the slope for our specific data, we have $C = 50 + .5Y$. This equation allows us to determine consumption at *any* level of income. At the $300 income level (point d in Figure 1), our equation predicts that consumption will be $200 [=$50 + (.5 × $300)]. You should confirm that at the $250 income level consumption will be $175.

When economists reverse mathematical convention by putting the independent variable on the vertical axis and the dependent variable on the horizontal axis, the standard linear equation solves for the independent, rather than the dependent, variable. We noted earlier that this case is relevant for our GSU ticket price–attendance data. If P represents the ticket price and Q represents attendance, our relevant equation is $P = 25 - 1.25Q$, where the vertical intercept is 25 and the negative slope is $-1\frac{1}{4}$ or -1.25. But knowing the value for P lets us solve for Q, which is actually our dependent variable. For example, if $P = 15$, then the values in our equation become: $15 = 25 - 1.25(Q)$, or $1.25Q = 10$, or $Q = 8$. You should check this answer against Figure 2 and also use this equation to predict GSU ticket sales when price is $7.50.

Slope of a Nonlinear Curve

We now move from the simple world of linear relationships (straight lines) to the slightly more complex world of nonlinear relationships (curves). By definition, the slope of a straight line is constant throughout. In contrast, the slope of a curve changes as we move from one point to another on the curve. For example, consider the upsloping curve *AA* in Figure 3a. Although its slope is positive throughout, it diminishes or flattens as we move northeast along the curve. Given

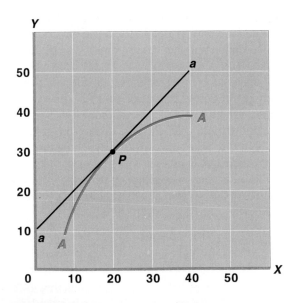 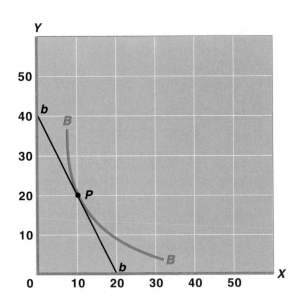

FIGURE 3 Determining the slopes of curves

The slope of a nonlinear curve changes as one moves from point to point on the curve. The slope at any point can be determined by drawing a straight line tangent to that point and calculating the slope of that straight line.

that the slope is constantly changing, we can only measure the slope at some particular point on the curve.

We begin by drawing a straight line which is tangent to the curve at that point where we want to measure its slope. By definition, a line is **tangent** at that point where it touches, but does not intersect, the curve. Thus, line *aa* is tangent to curve *AA* at point *P* in Figure 3a. Having done this, we can measure the slope of *AA* at point *P* by measuring the slope of the straight tangent line *aa*. Specifically, in Figure 3a, when the vertical change (rise) in *aa* is +10, the horizontal

change (run) is also +10. Thus, the slope of the tangent *aa* line is 10/10 or +1 and therefore the slope of *AA* at *P* is also +1.

Now consider the downsloping curve *BB* in Figure 3b. In this case the slope of *BB* is negative and it diminishes as we move southeast along the curve. What is the slope at point *P*? Again, we draw line *bb* which is tangent to curve *BB* at *P*. Here, when the vertical change (fall) in *bb* is −10, the horizontal change is only +5. Thus, the slope of *BB* at point *P* is −10/+5 or −2. Question 6 at the end of this appendix is relevant.

APPENDIX SUMMARY

1 Graphs are a convenient and revealing means of presenting economic relationships or principles.

2 Two variables are positively or directly related when their values change in the same direction. Two variables which are directly related will plot as an upsloping line on a graph.

3 Two variables are negatively or inversely related when their values change in opposite directions. Two variables which are inversely related will graph as a downsloping line.

4 The value of the dependent variable ("effect") is determined by the value of the independent variable ("cause").

5 When "other factors" which might affect a two-variable

relationship are allowed to change, the plotted relationship will likely shift to a new location.

6 The slope of a straight line is the ratio of the vertical change to the horizontal change in moving between any two points. The slope of an upsloping line is positive, while that of a downsloping line is negative.

7 The vertical (or horizontal) intercept and the slope of a line establish its location and are used in expressing the relationship between two variables as an equation.

8 The slope of a curve at any point is determined by calculating the slope of a straight line drawn tangent to that point.

APPENDIX TERMS AND CONCEPTS

vertical and horizontal axes	**dependent and independent**	**vertical intercept**	**direct and inverse relationships**
slope of a straight line	**variables**	**tangent**	

APPENDIX QUESTIONS AND STUDY SUGGESTIONS

🖫 *1 Briefly explain the use of graphs as a means of presenting economic principles. What is an inverse relationship? How does it graph? What is a direct relationship? How does it graph? Graph and explain the relationships one would expect to find between **a** the number of inches of rainfall per month and the sale of umbrellas, **b** the amount of tuition and the

level of enrollment at a university, and **c** the size of a university's athletic scholarships and the number of games won by its football team.

In each case cite and explain how considerations other than those specifically mentioned might upset the expected relationship. Is your second generalization consistent with the fact that, historically, enrollments and tuition have both increased? If not, explain any difference.

🖫 2 Indicate how each of the following might affect the data shown in Table 2 and Figure 2 of this appendix:

   a GSU's athletic director schedules higher-quality opponents.

   b GSU's Fighting Aardvarks experience three losing seasons.

   c GSU contracts to have all its home games televised.

*Note to the reader: A floppy disk symbol 🖫 precedes each of the questions in this appendix. This icon is used throughout the text to indicate that a particular question relates to the content of one of the tutorial programs in the student software which accompanies this book. Please refer to the Preface for more detail about this software.

3 The following table contains data on the relationship between saving and income. Rearrange these data as required and graph the data on the accompanying grid. What is the slope of the line? The vertical intercept? Interpret the meaning of both the slope and the intercept. Write the equation which represents this line. What would you predict saving to be at the $12,500 level of income?

Income (per year)	Saving (per year)
$15,000	$1,000
0	−500
10,000	500
5,000	0
20,000	1,500

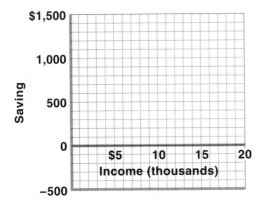

4 Construct a table from the data shown on the accompanying graph. Which is the dependent and which the independent variable? Summarize the data in equation form.

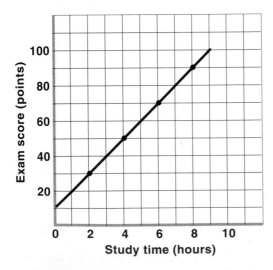

5 Suppose that when the interest rate which must be paid to borrow funds is 16 percent, businesses find it unprofita-

ble to invest in machinery and equipment. However, when the interest rate is 14 percent, $5 billion worth of investment is profitable. At 12 percent, a total of $10 billion of investment is profitable. Similarly, total investment increases by $5 billion for each successive 2 percentage point decline in the interest rate. Indicate the relevant relationship between the interest rate and investment verbally, tabularly, graphically, and as an equation. Put the interest rate on the vertical axis and investment on the horizontal axis. In your equation use the form $i = a - bI$, where i is the interest rate, a is the vertical intercept, b is the slope of the line, and I is the level of investment. Comment on advantages and disadvantages of verbal, tabular, graphical, and equation forms of presentation.

6 The accompanying diagram shows curve *XX* and three tangents at points *A, B,* and *C.* Calculate the slope of the curve at these three points.

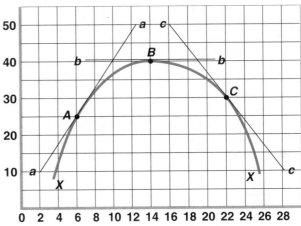

7 In the accompanying diagram, is the slope of curve *AA'* positive or negative? Does the slope increase or decrease as we move from *A* to *A'*? Answer the same two questions for curve *BB'*.

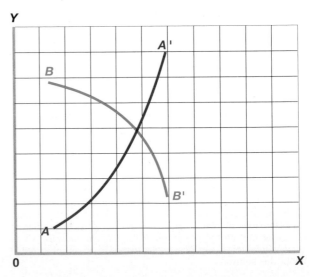

CHAPTER 2

The Economizing Problem

You make decisions every day which capture the essence of economics. Suppose you have $20 and are deciding how to spend it. Should you buy a new pair of blue jeans? A couple of compact discs? A ticket for a rock concert? Similarly, what to do with the time between three and six o'clock on, say, a Thursday afternoon? Should you work extra hours on your part-time job? Do research on a term project? Prepare for an economics quiz? Watch TV? Take a nap? Money and time are both scarce and making decisions in the context of scarcity implies costs. If you choose the jeans, the cost is the forgone CDs or concert. If you nap or watch TV, the cost might be a low grade on your quiz. Scarcity, choices, and costs—these are the building blocks of the present chapter.

This chapter introduces and explores certain fundamental considerations which constitute the foundation of economic science. Basically, we expand on the definition of economics introduced in Chapter 1 and explore the essence of the economizing problem. To this end, we will illustrate, extend, and modify our definition of economics by using so-called production possibilities tables and curves. Finally, we will survey briefly different ways in which institutionally and ideologically diverse economies "solve" or respond to the economizing problem.

THE FOUNDATION OF ECONOMICS

Two fundamental facts which constitute the **economizing problem** provide a foundation for the field of economics. We must carefully state and fully understand these two facts, because everything that follows in our study of economics depends directly or indirectly upon them.

1 *Society's material wants, that is, the material wants of its citizens and institutions, are virtually unlimited or insatiable.*
2 *Economic resources—the means of producing goods and services—are limited or scarce.*

Unlimited Wants

In the first statement, precisely what is meant by "material wants"? We mean, first, the desires of consumers to obtain and use various *goods* and *services* which provide **utility,** the economist's term for pleasure or satisfaction.[1] An amazingly wide range of products fills the bill in this respect: houses, automobiles, toothpaste, compact-disc players, pizzas, sweaters, and the like. In short, innumerable products which we sometimes classify as *necessities* (food, shelter, clothing) and *luxuries* (perfumes, yachts, mink coats) all can satisfy human wants. Needless to say, what is a luxury to Smith may be a necessity to Jones, and what is a commonplace necessity today may have been a luxury a few years ago.

But services satisfy our wants as much as tangible products. A repair job on our car, the removal of our appendix, a haircut, and legal advice have in common with goods the fact that they satisfy human wants. On reflection, we realize that we indeed buy many goods, for example, automobiles and washing machines, for the services they render. The differences between goods and services are often less than they seem to be at first.

Material wants also include those which businesses and units of government seek to satisfy. Businesses want factory buildings, machinery, trucks, warehouses, communications systems, and other things that help them realize their production goals. Government, reflecting the collective wants of its citizenry or goals of its own, seeks highways, schools, hospitals, and military hardware.

As a group, these material wants are, for practical purposes, *insatiable,* or *unlimited,* meaning that material wants for goods and services cannot be completely satisfied. Our wants for a *particular* good or service can be satisfied; that is, over a short period of time we can get enough toothpaste or beer. Certainly one appendicitis operation is par for the course. But goods *in general* are another story. Here we do not, and presumably cannot, get enough. A simple experiment will help verify this point: Suppose we are asked to list those goods and services we want but do not now possess. If we ponder our unfilled material wants, chances are our list will be impressive.

Furthermore, over a period of time, wants multiply so that, as we fill some of the wants on the list, we add new ones. Material wants, like rabbits, have a high reproduction rate. The rapid introduction of new products whets our appetites, and extensive advertising

tries to persuade us that we need items we might not otherwise consider buying. Not long ago, the desire for personal computers, light beer, video recorders, fax machines, and compact discs was nonexistent. Furthermore, we often cannot stop with simple satisfaction: The acquisition of an Escort or Geo has been known to whet the appetite for a Porsche or Mercedes.

At any given time the individuals and institutions which constitute society have innumerable unfulfilled material wants. Some—food, clothing, shelter—have biological roots. But some are also influenced by the conventions and customs of society: The specific kinds of food, clothing, and shelter we seek are frequently determined by the general social and cultural environment in which we live. Over time, wants change and multiply, fueled by development of new products and extensive advertising and sales promotion.

Again, let us stress that the overall objective of all economic activity is the attempt to satisfy these diverse material wants.

Scarce Resources

In considering the second fundamental fact, *economic resources are limited or scarce,* what do we mean by "economic resources"? In general, we mean all natural, human, and manufactured resources that go into the production of goods and services. This covers a lot of ground: factory and farm buildings and all equipment, tools, and machinery used to produce manufactured goods and agricultural products; a variety of transportation and communication facilities; innumerable types of labor; and land and mineral resources of all kinds. Economists broadly classify such resources as either (1) *property* resources—land or raw materials and capital; or (2) *human* resources—labor and entrepreneurial ability.

Resource Categories   Let's examine these various resource categories.

Land   By **land** the economist means much more than do most people. Land is all natural resources—all "gifts of nature"—usable in the productive process. Such resources as arable land, forests, mineral and oil deposits, and water resources come under this classification.

Capital   **Capital,** or investment goods, is all manufactured aids to production, that is, all tools, machinery,

---

[1] This definition leaves a variety of wants—recognition, status, love, and so forth—for the other social sciences to worry about.

equipment, and factory, storage, transportation, and distribution facilities used in producing goods and services and getting them to the ultimate consumer. The process of producing and purchasing capital goods is known as **investment.**

Two other points are pertinent. First, *capital goods* ("tools") differ from *consumer goods* in that the latter satisfy wants directly, whereas the former do so indirectly by facilitating production of consumable goods. Second, the term "capital" as here defined does *not* refer to money. True, business executives and economists often talk of "money capital," meaning money available to purchase machinery, equipment, and other productive facilities. But money, as such, produces nothing; hence, it is not considered an economic resource. *Real capital*—tools, machinery, and other productive equipment—is an economic resource; *money* or *financial capital* is not.

Labor Labor is a broad term the economist uses for all the physical and mental talents of men and women which are available and usable in producing goods and services. (This excludes a special set of human talents—entrepreneurial ability—which, because of their special significance in a capitalistic economy, we will consider separately.) Thus the services of a logger, retail clerk, machinist, teacher, professional football player, and nuclear physicist all fall under the general heading of labor.

Entrepreneurial Ability Finally, there is the special human resource which we label **entrepreneurial ability,** or, more simply, *enterprise.* We can assign four related functions to the entrepreneur.
1 The entrepreneur takes the initiative in combining the resources of land, capital, and labor to produce a good or service. Both a sparkplug and a catalyst, the entrepreneur is at once the driving force behind production and the agent who combines the other resources in what is hoped will be a profitable venture.
2 The entrepreneur makes basic business-policy decisions, that is, those nonroutine decisions which set the course of a business enterprise.
3 The entrepreneur is an innovator—the one who attempts to introduce on a commercial basis new products, new productive techniques, or even new forms of business organization.
4 The entrepreneur is a risk bearer. This is apparent from a close examination of the other three entrepreneurial functions. The entrepreneur in a capitalistic

system has no guarantee of profit. The reward for his or her time, efforts, and abilities may be attractive profits *or* losses and eventual bankruptcy. In short, the entrepreneur risks not only time, effort, and business reputation, but his or her invested funds and those of associates or stockholders.

Resource Payments We will see shortly how these resources are provided to business institutions in exchange for money income. The income received from supplying property resources—raw materials and capital equipment—is called *rental* and *interest income,* respectively. The income accruing to those who supply labor is called *wages* and includes salaries and various wage and salary supplements in the form of bonuses, commissions, royalties, and so forth. Entrepreneurial income is called *profits,* which, of course, may be a negative figure—that is, losses.

These four broad categories of economic resources, or *factors of production* or *inputs* as they are often called, leave room for debate when it comes to classifying specific resources. For example, suppose you receive a dividend on some newly issued Exxon stock which you own. Is this an interest return for the capital equipment the company bought with the money you provided in buying Exxon stock? Or is this return a profit which compensates you for the risks involved in purchasing corporate stock? What about the earnings of a one-person general store where the owner is both entrepreneur and labor force? Are the owner's earnings considered wages or profit income? The answer to both queries is "some of each." The point is that while we might quibble about classifying a given flow of income as wages, rent, interest, or profits, all income can be fitted under one of these general headings.

Relative Scarcity Economic resources, or factors of production, have one fundamental characteristic in common: *They are scarce or limited in supply.* Our "spaceship earth" contains only limited amounts of resources to use in producing goods and services. Quantities of arable land, mineral deposits, capital equipment, and labor (time) are all limited; that is, they are available only in finite amounts. Because of the scarcity of productive resources and the constraint this scarcity puts on productive activity, output will necessarily be limited. Society will *not* be able to produce and consume all the goods and services it might want. Thus, in the United States—one of the most affluent nations—output per person was limited to $22,419 in 1991. In the poorest nations annual output per person is as low as $200 or $300!

ECONOMICS AND EFFICIENCY

We have arrived once again at the basic definition of economics first stated at the beginning of Chapter 1. *Economics is the social science concerned with the problem of using or administering scarce resources (the means of producing) to attain the greatest or maximum fulfillment of society's unlimited wants (the goal of producing).* Economics is concerned with "doing the best with what we have." If our wants are virtually unlimited and our resources scarce, we cannot satisfy all of society's material wants. The next best thing is to achieve the greatest possible satisfaction of these wants.

Full Employment and Full Production

Economics is a science of efficiency—efficiency in the use of scarce resources. Society wants to use its limited resources efficiently; that is, it wants to get the maximum amount of useful goods and services produced with its available resources. To achieve this it must realize both full employment and full production.

Full Employment By **full employment** we mean that all available resources should be employed. No workers should be involuntarily out of work; the economy should provide employment for all who are willing and able to work. Nor should capital equipment or arable land sit idle. Note we say all *available* resources should be employed. Each society has certain customs and practices which determine what particular resources are available for employment. For example, legislation and custom provide that children and the very aged should not be employed. Similarly, it is desirable for productivity to allow farmland to lie fallow periodically.

Full Production But the employment of all available resources is insufficient to achieve efficiency. Full production must also be realized. By **full production** we mean that all employed resources should be used to make the most valued contributions to the domestic output. If we fail to realize full production, economists say that our resources are *underemployed.*

Full production implies that two kinds of efficiency—allocative and productive efficiency—are achieved.

Allocative efficiency means that resources are devoted to goods most wanted by society; for example, compact discs and cassettes, rather than 45 rpm or long-play records. Society wants resources apportioned to word processors, not mechanical typewriters, and to xerox, not mimeograph, machines. Nor do we want Iowa's farmland planted to cotton and Alabama's to corn when the opposite assignment would provide the nation with substantially more of both products from the same amount of land.

Productive efficiency means that the least costly production techniques are used to produce wanted goods and services. Efficiency requires that Tauruses and Grand Ams be produced with computerized and roboticized assembly techniques rather than with the primitive assembly lines of the 1920s. Nor do we want our farmers harvesting wheat with scythes or picking corn by hand when elaborate harvesting equipment will do the job at a much lower cost per bushel.

In summary, allocative efficiency means that resources are apportioned among firms and industries to obtain the particular mix of products society wants the most. Productive efficiency means that each good or service in this optimal product mix is produced in the least costly fashion. Full production means producing the "right" goods (allocative efficiency) in the "right" way (productive efficiency).

QUICK REVIEW 2-1

◆   *Human material wants are virtually unlimited.*

◆   *Economic resources—land, capital, labor, and entrepreneurial ability—are scarce or limited.*

◆   *Economics is concerned with the efficient management of these scarce resources to achieve the maximum fulfillment of our material wants.*

◆   *Economic efficiency entails full employment and full production.*

Production Possibilities Table

The nature of the economizing problem can be clarified by the use of a production possibilities table. This device reveals the core of the economizing problem: *Because resources are scarce, a full-employment, full-production economy cannot have an unlimited output of goods and services. As a result, choices must be made on which goods and services to produce and which to forgo.*

Assumptions Several specific assumptions will set the stage for our illustration.

1 Efficiency The economy is operating at full employment and achieving full production.

2 Fixed Resources The available supplies of the factors of production are fixed in both quantity and quality. But, of course, they can be shifted or reallocated, within limits, among different uses; for example, a relatively unskilled laborer can work on a farm, at a fast-food restaurant, or in a gas station.

3 Fixed Technology The state of the technological arts is constant; that is, technology does not change during the course of our analysis. The second and third assumptions are another way of saying that we are looking at our economy at a specific point in time, or over a very short period of time. Over a relatively long period it would be unrealistic to rule out technological advances and the possibility that resource supplies might vary.

4 Two Products To simplify our illustration further, suppose our economy is producing just two products—industrial robots and pizza—instead of the innumerable goods and services actually produced. Pizza is symbolic of **consumer goods,** those goods which directly satisfy our wants; industrial robots are symbolic of **capital goods,** those goods which satisfy our wants *indirectly* by permitting more efficient production of consumer goods.

Necessity of Choice It is evident from our assumptions that a choice must be made among alternatives. Available resources are limited. Consequently, the total amounts of robots and pizza that our economy can produce are limited. *Limited resources mean a limited output.* Since resources are limited in supply and fully employed, any increase in the production of robots will mean shifting resources away from the production of pizza. And the reverse holds true: If we step up the production of pizza, needed resources must come at the expense of robot production. *Society cannot have its cake and eat it, too.* Facetiously put, there's no such thing as a "free lunch." This is the essence of the economizing problem.

Let's generalize by noting in Table 2-1 alternative combinations of robots and pizza which our economy might choose. Though the data in this and the following **production possibilities tables** are hypothetical, the points illustrated have tremendous practical significance. At alternative A, our economy would be devoting all its resources to the production of robots (capital

TABLE 2-1 Production possibilities of pizza and robots with full employment, 1993 *(hypothetical data)*

Type of product	Production alternatives				
	A	B	C	D	E
Pizza (in hundred thousands)	0	1	2	3	4
Robots (in thousands)	10	9	7	4	0

goods). At alternative E, all available resources would go to pizza production (consumer goods). Both these alternatives are clearly unrealistic extremes; any economy typically strikes a balance in dividing its total output between capital and consumer goods. As we move from alternative A to E, we step up the production of consumer goods (pizza), by shifting resources away from capital goods (robot) production.

Remembering that consumer goods directly satisfy our wants, any movement toward alternative E looks tempting. In making this move, society increases the current satisfaction of its wants; but there is a cost involved. This shift of resources catches up with society over time as its stock of capital goods dwindles—or at least ceases to expand at the current rate—with the result that the potential for greater future production is impaired. In short, in moving from alternative A toward E, society chooses "more now" at the expense of "much more later."

In moving from E toward A, society chooses to forgo current consumption. This sacrifice of current consumption frees resources which can now be used to increase production of capital goods. By building up its stock of capital in this way, society can anticipate greater production and, therefore, greater consumption in the future.

At any point in time, a full-employment, full-production economy must sacrifice some of product X to obtain more of product Y. The basic fact that economic resources are scarce prohibits such an economy from having more of both X and Y.

Production Possibilities Curve

To ensure our understanding of the production possibilities table, let's view these data graphically. We employ a simple two-dimensional graph, arbitrarily putting the output of robots (capital goods) on the vertical

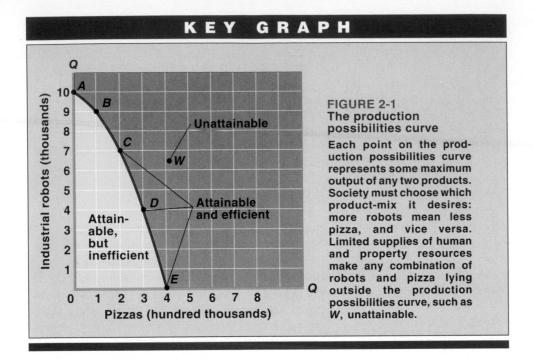

KEY GRAPH

FIGURE 2-1
The production
possibilities curve

Each point on the prod-
uction possibilities curve
represents some maximum
output of any two products.
Society must choose which
product-mix it desires:
more robots mean less
pizza, and vice versa.
Limited supplies of human
and property resources
make any combination of
robots and pizza lying
outside the production
possibilities curve, such as
W, unattainable.

axis and the output of pizza (consumer goods) on the horizontal axis, as in Figure 2-1 (Key Graph). Following the plotting procedure discussed in the appendix to Chapter 1, we can locate the "production possibilities" curve, as shown in Figure 2-1.

Each point on the production possibilities curve represents some maximum output of the two products. Thus the curve is, in effect, a frontier. To realize the various combinations of pizza and robots which fall on the production possibilities curve, society must achieve full employment and full production. All combinations of pizza and robots *on* the curve represent maximum quantities attainable only as the result of the most efficient use of all available resources. Points lying *inside* the curve are also attainable, but are not as desirable as points on the curve. These points imply a failure to achieve full employment and full production. Points lying *outside* the production possibilities curve, like point W, would be superior to any point on the curve; but such points are unattainable, given the current supplies of resources and technology. The production barrier of limited resources prohibits production of any combination of capital and consumer goods lying outside the production possibilities curve.

Optimal Product-Mix

If all outputs on the production possibilities curve reflect full employment and full production, which combination will society prefer? Consider, for example, points C and D in Figure 2-1. Which output-mix is superior or "best"? This is a nonscientific or normative matter; it reflects the values of society as expressed by its control group—the dictatorship, the party, the electorate, the citizenry, the individual institutions, or some combination thereof. What the economist can say is this: If a society's production possibilities are as in Table 2-1 *and* if that society seeks the product-mix indicated by, say, alternative C, it is *not* using its resources efficiently if it realizes a total output composed only of 6 units of robots and 1 unit of pizza. And the economist can also say that the society cannot hope to achieve a domestic output of 8 units of robots and 3 units of pizza with its available resources. These are quantitative, objective, positive statements. But, although the economist may have opinions as an individual, as a social scientist he or she cannot say that combination C is "better" or "worse" than combination D. This is a qualitative or normative matter.

Law of Increasing Opportunity Costs

We have stressed that resources are scarce relative to the virtually unlimited wants which these resources can be used to satisfy. As a result, choices among alternatives must be made. Specifically, more of X (pizza) means less of Y (robots). *The amount of other products which must be forgone or sacrificed to obtain some amount of any given product is called the opportunity cost of that good.* In our case the amount of Y (robots) which must be forgone or given up to get another unit of X (pizza) is the *opportunity cost,* or simply the *cost,* of that unit of X.

In moving from possibility A to B in Table 2-1, we find that the cost of 1 unit of pizza is 1 unit of robots. But, as we now pursue the concept of cost through the additional production possibilities—B to C, C to D, and so forth—an important economic principle is revealed. In shifting from alternative A to alternative E, the sacrifice or cost of robots involved in getting each additional unit of pizza *increases.* In moving from A to B, just 1 unit of robots is sacrificed for 1 more unit of pizza; but going from B to C sacrifices 2 units of robots for 1 more unit of pizza; then 3 of robots for 1 of pizza; and finally 4 for 1. Conversely, you should confirm that in moving from E to A the cost of an additional robot is $\frac{1}{4}$, $\frac{1}{3}$, $\frac{1}{2}$, and 1 unit of pizza respectively for each of the four shifts.

Note that this discussion of opportunity cost is couched in terms of an *added* or *marginal* unit of a good rather than *total,* or cumulative, opportunity cost. For example, the opportunity cost of the third unit of pizza in Table 2-1 is 3 units of robots ($=7-4$). But the total opportunity cost of 3 units of pizza is 6 units of robots ($=10-4$ or $1+2+3$).

Concavity Graphically, the **law of increasing opportunity costs** is reflected in the shape of the production possibilities curve. Specifically, the curve is *concave* or bowed out from the origin. As verified by the white lines in Figure 2-1, when the economy moves from *A* toward *E,* it must give up successively larger amounts of robots (1, 2, 3, 4) as shown on the vertical axis to acquire equal increments of pizza (1, 1, 1, 1) as shown on the horizontal axis. This means that the slope of the production possibilities curve becomes steeper as we move from *A* to *E* and such a curve, by definition, is concave as viewed from the origin.

Rationale What is the economic rationale for the law of increasing opportunity costs? *Why* does the sac-

rifice of robots increase as we get more pizza? The answer is rather complex, but, simply stated, it amounts to this: *Economic resources are not completely adaptable to alternative uses.* As we step up pizza production, resources which are less and less adaptable to this use must be induced, or "pushed," into this line of production. If we start at *A* and move to *B,* we can first pick resources whose productivity of pizza is greatest in relation to their productivity of robots. But as we move from *B* to *C,* *C* to *D,* and so on, resources highly productive of pizza become increasingly scarce. To get more pizza, resources whose productivity in robots is great in relation to their productivity in pizza will be needed. It will take more and more of such resources—and hence a greater sacrifice of robots—to achieve a given increase of 1 unit in the production of pizza. This lack of perfect flexibility, or interchangeability, on the part of resources and the resulting increase in the sacrifice of one good that must be made in acquiring of more and more units of another good is the rationale for the law of increasing opportunity costs. In this case, these costs are stated as sacrifices of goods and not in terms of dollars and cents.

QUICK REVIEW 2-2

The production possibilities curve illustrates four basic concepts:

♦ **The scarcity of resources is implicit in that all combinations of output lying outside the production possibilities curve are unattainable.**

♦ **Choice is reflected in the need for society to select among the various attainable combinations of goods lying on the curve.**

♦ **The downward slope of the curve implies the notion of opportunity cost.**

♦ **The concavity of the curve reveals increasing opportunity costs.**

UNEMPLOYMENT, GROWTH, AND THE FUTURE

It is important to understand what happens when the first three assumptions underlying the production possibilities curve are released.

Unemployment and Underemployment

The first assumption was that our economy is characterized by full employment and full production. How would our analysis and conclusions be altered if idle resources were available (unemployment) or if employed resources were used inefficiently (underemployment)? With full employment and full production, our five alternatives represent a series of maximum outputs; they illustrate combinations of robots and pizzas which might be produced when the economy is operating at full capacity. With *un*employment or *under*employment, the economy would produce less than each alternative shown in Table 2-1.

Graphically, a situation of unemployment or underemployment can be illustrated by a point *inside* the original production possibilities curve, which has been reproduced in Figure 2-2. Point *U* is such a point. Here the economy is falling short of the various maximum combinations of pizza and robots reflected by all the points *on* the production possibilities curve. The arrows in Figure 2-2 indicate three of the possible paths back to full employment and full production. A move toward full employment and full production will entail a greater output of one or both products.

A Growing Economy

When we drop the remaining assumptions that the quantity and quality of resources and technology are fixed, the production possibilities curve will shift position; that is, the potential total output of the economy will change.

Expanding Resource Supplies Let's now abandon the simplifying assumption that our total supplies of land, labor, capital, and entrepreneurial ability are fixed in both quantity and quality. Common sense tells us that over time a nation's growing population will bring about increases in supplies of labor and entrepreneurial ability.[2] Also, labor quality usually improves over time. For example, the percentage of the labor force with a high school education rose from 30 percent in 1960 to 40 percent in 1989. Historically, our stock of capital has increased at a significant, though unsteady, rate. And although we are depleting some of our energy and mineral resources, new sources are being discovered. The drainage of swamps and the development of irrigation programs add to our supply of arable land.

Assuming continuous full employment and full production, the net result of these increased supplies of the factors of production will be the ability to produce more of both robots and pizza. Thus, in the year 2013, the production possibilities of Table 2-1 for 1993 may be obsolete, having given way to those shown in Table 2-2. Observe that the greater abundance of resources results in a greater potential output of one or both products at each alternative; economic growth, in the sense of an expanded potential output, has occurred.

But note that such a favorable shift in the production possibilities curve does not guarantee that the economy will actually operate at a point on that new curve. The economy might fail to realize fully its new potentialities. Some 125 million jobs will give us full employment now, but ten or twenty years from now our labor force, because of a growing population, will be larger, and 125 million jobs will not be sufficient for

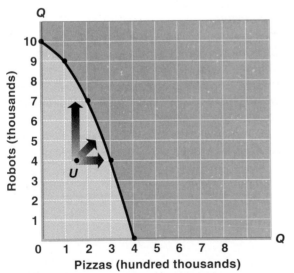

FIGURE 2-2 Unemployment and the production possibilities curve
Any point inside the production possibilities curve, such as *U*, indicates unemployment or underemployment. By moving toward full employment and full production, the economy can produce more of either or both of the two products, as the arrows indicate.

---

[2]This does not mean that population growth as such is always desirable. In Chapter 39 we will discover that overpopulation can be a constant drag on the living standards of many less developed countries. In advanced countries overpopulation can have adverse effects on the environment and the quality of life.

TABLE 2-2 Production possibilities of pizza and robots with full employment, 2013 (*hypothetical data*)

Type of product	Production alternatives				
	A'	B'	C'	D'	E'
Pizza (in hundred thousands)	0	2	4	6	8
Robots (in thousands)	14	12	9	5	0

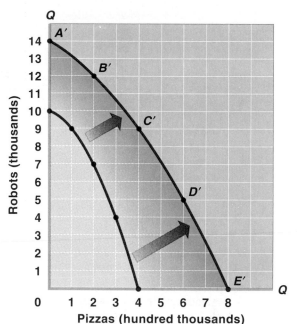

FIGURE 2-3 Economic growth and the production possibilities curve

The expanding resource supplies, improved resource quality, and technological advances which characterize a growing economy move the production possibilities curve outward and to the right. This permits the economy to enjoy larger quantities of both types of goods.

full employment. In short, the production possibilities curve may shift, but the economy may fail to produce at a point on that new curve.

Technological Advance   Our other simplifying assumption is a constant or unchanging technology. We know that technology has progressed remarkably over a long period. An advancing technology entails new and better goods *and* improved ways of producing these goods. For now, let's think of technological advance as comprising merely improvements in capital facilities—more efficient machinery and equipment. Such technological advance alters our earlier discussion of the economizing problem by improving productive efficiency, thus allowing society to produce more goods with fixed resources. As with increases in resource supplies, technological advance permits the production of more robots *and* more pizza.

When the supplies of resources increase or an improvement in technology occurs, the production possibilities curve of Figure 2-2 shifts outward and to the right, as illustrated by the *A'B'C'D'E'* curve in Figure 2-3. **Economic growth**—*the ability to produce a larger total output—is reflected in a rightward shift of the production possibilities curve; it is the result of increases in resource supplies, improvements in resource quality, and technological progress.* The consequence of growth is that our full-employment economy can enjoy a greater output of *both* robots and pizza. While a static, no-growth economy must sacrifice some of X to get more Y, a dynamic, growing economy can have larger quantities of both X and Y.

Economic growth does *not* typically mean proportionate increases in a nation's capacity to produce various products. Note in Figure 2-3 that, while the economy can produce twice as much pizza, the increase in robot production is only 40 percent. On Figure 2-3 you should pencil in two new production possibilities curves: one to show the situation where a better tech-

nique for producing robots has been developed, the technology for producing pizza being unchanged, and the other to illustrate an improved technology for pizza, the technology for producing robots being constant.

Present Choices and Future Possibilities   An economy's current choice of position on its production possibilities curve is a basic determinant of the future location of that curve. Let's designate the two axes of the production possibilities curve as "goods for the future" and "goods for the present," as in Figures 2-4a and b. "Goods for the future" are such things as capital goods, research and education, and preventive medicine, which increase the quantity and quality of property resources, enlarge the stock of technological information, and improve the quality of human resources. As we have already seen, "goods for the future" are the ingredients of economic growth. "Goods for the present" are pure consumer goods such as foodstuffs, clothing, "boom boxes," and automobiles.

Now suppose there are two economies, Alphania and Betania, which are identical in every respect ex-

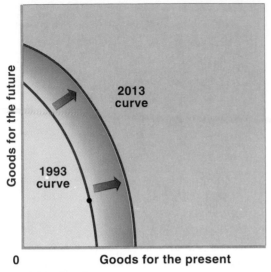

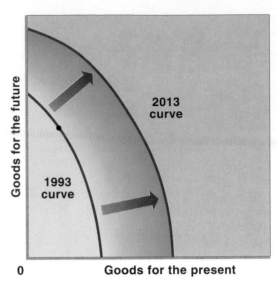

(a) Alphania   (b) Betania

FIGURE 2-4   **An economy's present choice of position on its production possibilities curve helps determine the curve's future location**

A current choice favoring "present goods," as rendered by Alphania in (a), will cause a modest rightward shift of the curve. A current choice favoring "future goods," as rendered by Betania in (b), will result in a greater rightward shift of the curve.

cept that Alphania's current (1993) choice of position on its production possibilities curve strongly favors "present goods" as opposed to "future goods." The dot in Figure 2-4a indicates this choice. Betania, on the other hand, makes a current (1993) choice which stresses large amounts of "future goods" and lesser amounts of "present goods" (Figure 2-4b).

Now, all other things being the same, we can expect the future (2013) production possibilities curve of Betania to be farther to the right than that of Alphania. That is, by currently choosing an output more conducive to technological advance and to increases in the quantity and quality of property and human resources, Betania will tend to achieve greater economic growth than Alphania, whose current choice of output places less emphasis on those goods and services which cause the production possibilities curve to shift rightward. In terms of capital goods, Betania is choosing to make larger current additions to its "national factory"—that is, to invest more of its current output—than Alphania. The payoff or benefit from this choice is more rapid growth—greater future productive capacity—for Betania. The opportunity cost is fewer consumer goods in the present.

QUICK REVIEW 2-3

♦ *Unemployment and underemployment (the inefficient use of employed resources) cause the economy to operate at a point inside its production possibilities curve.*

♦ *Expanding resource supplies, improvements in resource quality, and technological progress cause economic growth, that is, an outward shift of the production possibilities curve.*

♦ *An economy's present choice of output—particularly of capital and consumer goods—helps determine the future location of its production possibilities curve.*

Real-World Applications

There are many possible applications of the production possibilities curve.

1 Microeconomic Budgeting   While our discussion is in macroeconomic terms—that is, in terms of the output of the entire economy—the concepts of scarcity, choice, and opportunity cost also apply at the microeconomic level. You should reread the first paragraph of this chapter at this point.

2 Going to War   In beginning to produce war goods for World War II (1939–1945), the United States found itself with considerable unemployment. Our economy was able to produce an almost unbelievably large quantity of war goods and at the same time increase the output of consumer goods (Figure 2-2). The Soviet Union, on the other hand, entered World War II at almost capacity production; that is, the Soviet economy was operating close to full employment. Its military preparations entailed considerable shifting of resources from production of civilian goods with a drop in the standard of living.

Curiously, the United States' position during the Vietnam War was similar to that of the Soviet Union during World War II. Our economy was at full employment in the mid-1960s and the Johnson administration accelerated military spending for Vietnam while simultaneously increasing expenditures on domestic "war on poverty" programs. This attempt to achieve simultaneously more pizza and more robots—or, more accurately, more guns and more butter—in a full-employment economy was doomed to failure. The attempt to spend beyond our capacity to produce—to realize a point like W in Figure 2-1—contributed significantly to the double-digit inflation of the 1970s.

3 Discrimination   Discrimination based on race, gender, age, or ethnic background impedes the efficient allocation or employment of human resources, keeping the economy operating at some point inside its production possibilities curve. Discrimination prevents blacks, women, and others from obtaining jobs in which society can use efficiently their skills and talents. Elimination of discrimination would help move the economy from some point inside the production possibilities curve toward a point on the curve.

4 Productivity Slowdown   Since the mid-1960s the United States has experienced a rather alarming decline in the rate of growth of labor productivity; that is, the growth of output per worker-hour has diminished. Some economists feel a major cause of this decline is that the rate of increase in the mechanization of labor has slowed because of insufficient investment. One proposed remedy is to increase investment as compared to consumption. That is, a D to C type of shift in Figure 2-1 is recommended. Special tax incentives to

make business investment more profitable are an appropriate policy to facilitate this shift. The expectation is that the restoration of a more rapid rate of productivity growth will accelerate the growth of the economy (that is, the rightward shift of the production possibilities curve) through time.

5 Growth: Japan versus United States   The growth impact of a nation's decision on how much of its domestic output will be devoted to investment and how much to consumption is illustrated vividly in comparing Japan and the United States. Recently, Japan has been investing over 25 percent of its domestic output in productive machinery and equipment compared to only about 10 percent for the United States. The consequences are in accord with our earlier discussion. Over the 1960–1990 period Japan's domestic output expanded at about 6.4 percent per year compared to only 3.2 percent for the United States. In other words, Japan's production possibilities curve shifted outward more rapidly than the United States' curve. This is reflected in living standards. In 1980 the per capita output of Japan was $16,711 as compared to $17,643 for the United States. By 1989 these figures had changed to $22,884 and $21,404 respectively.

6 International Trade Aspects   The message of the production possibilities curve is that a nation cannot live beyond its means or production potential. When the possibility of international trade is taken into account, this statement must be modified in two ways.

Trade and Growth   We will discover in later chapters that a nation can circumvent the output constraint imposed by its domestic production possibilities curve through international specialization and trade. International specialization and trade have the same impact as having more and better resources or discovering improved production techniques. Both have the effect of increasing the quantities of both capital and consumer goods available to society. International specialization and trade are the equivalent of economic growth.

Trade Deficits   Within the context of international trade, a nation can achieve a combination of goods outside its domestic production possibilities curve (such as point W in Figure 2-1) by incurring a *trade deficit*. A nation may buy and receive an amount of imported goods from other nations which exceeds the amount of goods it exports. The United States has been doing just that recently. In 1990 the United States had a trade deficit of approximately $108 billion. In other words, we imported $108 billion more worth of goods than we exported. The net result was that in 1990 the United States enjoyed some $108 billion of output over what it produced domestically.

This looks like a very favorable state of affairs. Unfortunately, there is a catch. To finance its deficit—to pay for its excess of imports over exports—the United States must go into debt to its international trading partners *or* it must give up ownership of some of its assets to those other nations. Analogy: How can you live beyond your current income? Answer: Borrow from your parents, the sellers of goods, or a financial institution. Or, alternatively, sell some of your real assets (your car or stereo) or financial assets (stocks or bonds) which you own. This is what the United States has been doing.

A major consequence of our large and persistent trade deficits is that foreign nationals hold larger portions of American private and public debt and own larger amounts of our business corporations, agricultural land, and real estate. To pay our debts and repurchase those assets we must in the future live well *within* our means. We must settle for some combination of goods within our production possibilities curve so that we can export more than we import—that is, incur a *trade surplus*—to pay off our world debts and reacquire ownership of those assets. On the other hand, to the extent that some of our imports are capital goods, our future production possibilities curve will be farther rightward than it might otherwise be.

7 Famine in Africa Modern industrial societies take economic growth—more-or-less continuous rightward shifts of the production possibilities curve—for granted. But, as the recent catastrophic famine in Ethiopia, Chad, the Sudan, and other African nations indicates, in some circumstances the production possibilities curve may shift leftward. In addition to drought, an important cause of the African famine is ecological degradation or, more simply, poor land-use practices. Land has been deforested, overfarmed, and overgrazed, causing the production possibilities of these highly agriculturally oriented countries to diminish. In fact the per capita national outputs of most of these nations declined in the 1980s.

8 Operation Desert Storm This chapter's Last Word chronicles how the Gulf War devastated Iraq's property

and human resources and had the effect of shifting its production possibilities curve inward.

THE "ISMS"

A society can use many different institutional arrangements and coordinating mechanisms to respond to the economizing problem. Historically, the industrially advanced economies of the world have differed essentially on two grounds: (1) the ownership of the means of production, and (2) the method by which economic activity is coordinated and directed. Let's briefly examine the main characteristics of two "polar" types of economic systems.

Pure Capitalism

Pure, or **laissez faire, capitalism** is characterized by the private ownership of resources and the use of a system of markets and prices to coordinate and direct economic activity. In such a system each participant is motivated by his or her own self-interests; each economic unit seeks to maximize its income through individual decision making. The market system functions as a mechanism through which individual decisions and preferences are communicated and coordinated. The fact that goods and services are produced and resources are supplied under competitive conditions means there are many independently acting buyers and sellers of each product and resource. As a result, economic power is widely dispersed. Advocates of pure capitalism argue that such an economy is conducive to efficiency in the use of resources, output and employment stability, and rapid economic growth. Hence, there is little or no need for government planning, control, or intervention. Indeed, the term *laissez faire* roughly translates as "let it be," that is, keep government from interfering with the economy, because such interference will disturb the efficiency with which the market system functions. Government's role is therefore limited to protecting private property and establishing an appropriate legal framework in which free markets function.

The Command Economy

The polar alternative to pure capitalism is the **command economy** or **communism,** characterized by public ownership of virtually all property resources and the rendering of economic decisions through central economic planning. All major decisions concerning the level of resource use, the composition and distribution of output, and the organization of production are determined by a central planning board. Business firms are governmentally owned and produce according to state directives. Production targets are determined by the planning board for each enterprise and the plan specifies the amounts of resources to be allocated to each enterprise so that it might realize its production goals. The division of output between capital and consumer goods is centrally decided and capital goods are allocated among industries in terms of the central planning board's long-term priorities.

Mixed Systems

Real-world economies are arrayed between the extremes of pure capitalism and the command economy. The United States economy leans toward pure capitalism, but with important differences. Government plays an active role in our economy in promoting economic stability and growth, in providing certain goods and services which would be underproduced or not produced at all by the market system, and in modifying the distribution of income. In contrast to the wide dispersion of economic power among many small units which characterizes pure capitalism, American capitalism has spawned powerful economic organizations in the form of large corporations and strong labor unions. The ability of these power blocs to manipulate and distort the functioning of the market system to their advantage is a further reason for governmental involvement in the economy. While the former Soviet Union historically approximated the command economy, it relied to some extent upon market-determined prices and had some vestiges of private ownership. Recent reforms in the former Soviet Union, China, and most of the eastern European nations are designed to move these command economies toward more capitalistic, market-oriented systems.

But note that private ownership and reliance on the market system do not always go together, nor do public ownership and central planning. For example, the *fascism* of Hitler's Nazi Germany has been dubbed **authoritarian capitalism** because the economy was subject to a high degree of governmental control and direction, but property was privately owned. In contrast, the Yugoslavian economy was **market socialism,** characterized by public ownership of resources

coupled with increasing reliance on free markets to organize and coordinate economic activity. The Swedish economy is also a hybrid system. Although over 90 percent of business activity is in private hands, government is deeply involved in achieving economic stability and in redistributing income. Similarly, the capitalistic Japanese economy entails a great deal of planning and "coordination" between government and the business sector. Table 2-3 summarizes the various ways economic systems can be categorized based on the two criteria we are using. Keep in mind that the real-world examples in this framework are only rough approximations.

The Traditional Economy

Table 2-3 is couched in terms of industrially advanced or at least semideveloped economies. Many less developed countries have **traditional** or **customary economies.** Production methods, exchange, and distribution of income are all sanctioned by custom. Heredity and caste circumscribe economic roles of individuals and socioeconomic immobility is pronounced. Technological change and innovation may be closely constrained because they clash with tradition and threaten the social fabric. Economic activity is often secondary to religious and cultural values and society's desire to perpetuate the status quo. In deciding to pursue economic development, traditional economies must face the question as to which model in Table 2-3 will result in growth and simultaneously be the most compatible with other economic and noneconomic goals valued by that society.

The point is that there is no unique or universally accepted way to respond to the economizing problem. Various societies, having different cultural and historical backgrounds, different mores and customs, and

TABLE 2-3 **Comparative economic systems**

		Coordinating mechanism	
Ownership of resources		Market system	Central planning
	Private	United States	Nazi Germany
	Public	Yugoslavia	Soviet Union

LAST WORD

OPERATION DESERT STORM AND IRAQ'S PRODUCTION POSSIBILITIES

War can seriously diminish a nation's production possibilities.

The quick and decisive military victory of the United States and its allies in Operation Desert Storm has had a devastating economic impact on Iraq. Forty-three days of intensive Allied bombing inflicted great physical damage to Iraq's productive facilities and infrastructure. Civilian factories, roads, bridges, railroads, power plants, water purification plants, and communication facilities were all severely impaired. Commerce and communications have been greatly disrupted. Furthermore, despite Iraq's greatly diminished productive potential, the United Nations has ordered it to pay up to 30 percent of its future oil revenues as war reparations to Kuwait and others harmed by the war. This means that a significant portion of Iraq's future domestic output will be unavailable for its consumers or to rebuild its productive facilities.

Devastation to Iraq's human resources was also severe. One estimate suggests that as many as 100,000 to 120,000 Iraqi troops plus 5,000 to 20,000 civilians were killed in the war. Another 20,000 lost their lives in the postwar rebellion against Saddam Hussein. Finally, an estimated 15,000 to 30,000 Kurds and other displaced people have died in camps and on the road. A Harvard medical team has predicted that 170,000 Iraqi children will die because of delayed effects of the Persian Gulf war. In particular,

typhoid, cholera, diarrhea, malnutrition and other health problems will cause the death rate of children under age 5 to be two or three times higher than before the war. Without electric power water treatment plants are silent; sewage cannot be pumped or treated. Backed-up pipes now drain into rivers and canals from which people have no choice but to bathe and drink. Further, there is no power to run irrigation pumps and little gasoline is available for harvesting machines. Food harvests are in doubt and refrigeration is no longer available to store existing food supplies.

In short, Iraq invaded Kuwait to bring Kuwait's oil resources under its control and by so doing increase Iraq's production possibilities. Instead, Iraq's physical and human resources—and hence its production possibilities—have been seriously diminished by Operation Desert Storm.

contrasting ideological frameworks—not to mention resources which differ both quantitatively and qualitatively—use different institutions in dealing with the reality of relative scarcity. The former Soviet Union, the United States, and Great Britain, for example, are all—in terms of their accepted goals, ideology, technolo-

gies, resources, and culture—attempting to achieve efficiency in the use of their respective resources. The best method for responding to the unlimited wants–scarce resources dilemma in one economy may be inappropriate for another economic system.

CHAPTER SUMMARY

1 Economics centers on two basic facts: first, human material wants are virtually unlimited; second, economic resources are scarce.

2 Economic resources may be classified as property resources—raw materials and capital—or as human resources—labor and entrepreneurial ability.

3 Economics is concerned with the problem of administering scarce resources in the production of goods and services to fulfill the material wants of society. Both full employment and full production of available resources are essential if this administration is to be efficient.

4 At any time a full-employment, full-production economy

must sacrifice the output of some types of goods and services to achieve increased production of others. Because resources are not equally productive in all possible uses, shifting resources from one use to another gives rise to the law of increasing opportunity costs; that is, the production of additional units of product X entails the sacrifice of increasing amounts of product Y.

5 Over time, technological advance and increases in the quantity and quality of human and property resources permit the economy to produce more of all goods and services.

Society's choice as to the composition of current output is a determinant of the future location of the production possibilities curve.

6 The various economic systems of the world differ in their ideologies and also in their responses to the economizing problem. Critical differences center on **a** private versus public ownership of resources, and **b** the use of the market system versus central planning as a coordinating mechanism.

TERMS AND CONCEPTS

economizing problem	full production	law of increasing	authoritarian
utility	allocative efficiency	opportunity costs	capitalism
land, capital, labor,	productive efficiency	economic growth	market socialism
and entrepreneurial	consumer goods	pure or laissez faire	traditional or
ability	capital goods	capitalism	customary
investment	production possibilities	command economy or	economies
full employment	table (curve)	communism	

QUESTIONS AND STUDY SUGGESTIONS

1 "Economics is the study of the principles governing the allocation of scarce means among competing ends when the objective of the allocation is to maximize the attainment of the ends."[3] Explain. Why is the problem of unemployment a part of the subject matter of economics?

2 Critically analyze: "Wants aren't insatiable. I can prove it. I get all the coffee I want to drink every morning at breakfast." Explain: "Goods and services are scarce because resources are scarce." Analyze: "It is the nature of all economic problems that absolute solutions are denied us."

3 What are economic resources? What are the major functions of the entrepreneur? "Economics is . . . neither capitalist nor socialist: it applies to every society. Economics would disappear only in a world so rich that no wants were unfulfilled for lack of resources. Such a world is not imminent and may be impossible, for time is always limited."[4] Carefully evaluate and explain these statements. Do you agree that time is an economic resource?

4 Distinguish between allocative efficiency and productive efficiency. Give an illustration of **a** achieving allocative, but not productive, efficiency; and **b** achieving productive, but not allocative, efficiency.

5 Comment on the following statement from a newspaper article: "Our junior high school serves a splendid hot meal for $1 without costing the taxpayers anything, thanks in part to a government subsidy."

6 The following is a production possibilities table for war goods and civilian goods:

Type of production	Production alternatives				
	A	B	C	D	E
Automobiles (in millions)	0	2	4	6	8
Guided missiles (in thousands)	30	27	21	12	0

a Show these production possibilities data graphically. What do the points on the curve indicate? How does the curve reflect the law of increasing opportunity costs? Explain. If the economy is currently at point *C*, what is the cost of 1 million more automobiles in terms of guided missiles? Of 1000 more guided missiles in terms of automobiles?

b Label point *G* inside the curve. What does it indicate? Label point *H* outside the curve. What does this point indicate? What must occur before the economy can attain the level of production indicated by point *H*?

c Upon what specific assumptions is the production possibilities curve based? What happens when each of these assumptions is released?

d Suppose improvement occurs in the technology of producing guided missiles but not in the production of

---

[3]George J. Stigler, *The Theory of Price* (New York: The Macmillan Company, 1947), p. 12.

[4]Joseph P. McKenna, *Intermediate Economic Theory* (New York: Holt, Rinehart and Winston, Inc., 1958), p. 2.

automobiles. Draw the new production possibilities curve. Now assume that a technological advance occurs in producing automobiles but not in producing guided missiles. Draw the new production possibilities curve. Finally, draw a production possibilities curve which reflects technological improvement in the production of both products.

7 What is the opportunity cost of attending college?

8 Suppose you arrive at a store expecting to pay $100 for an item, but learn that a store two miles away is charging $50 for it. Would you drive there and buy it? How does your decision benefit you? What is the opportunity cost of your decision? Now suppose that you arrive at a store expecting to pay $6000 for an item, but learn that it costs $5950 at the other store. Do you make the same decision as before? Perhaps surprisingly, you should! Explain why.

9 "The present choice of position on the production possibilities curve is a major factor in economic growth." Explain.

10 Contrast the means by which pure capitalism, market socialism, and a command economy attempt to cope with economic scarcity.

11 Explain how an international trade deficit may permit an economy to acquire a combination of goods in excess of its domestic production potential. Explain why nations try to avoid having trade deficits.

Pure Capitalism and the Circular Flow

Fact: In the past few years the media have inundated us with stories of how the centrally planned economies are trying to alter their systems in the direction of capitalism. Question: Precisely what are the features and institutions of capitalism which these nations are trying to emulate?

Fact: You have virtually nothing whatsoever to do with the production of the vast majority of goods and services you consume. Question: Why is it that production is so specialized in modern economies?

Fact: Nearly every day you exchange paper dollars—whose intrinsic value is virtually nil—for a wide variety of products of considerable value. Question: Why do such seemingly irrational monetary transactions occur?

The foregoing questions are just some addressed in the pages that follow. Our initial task is to describe the capitalist ideology and to explain how pure, or laissez faire, capitalism would function.

Strictly speaking, pure capitalism has never existed and probably never will. Why, then, do we bother to consider the operation of such an economy? Because it provides us with a useful first approximation of how the economies of the United States and many other industrially advanced nations function. And approximations or models, when properly handled, can be very useful. In other words, pure capitalism constitutes a simplified model which we will then modify and adjust in later chapters to correspond more closely to the reality of these modern economies.

In explaining the operation of pure capitalism, we will discuss: (1) the institutional framework and basic assumptions which make up the capitalist ideology; (2) certain institutions and practices common to all modern economies; (3) capitalism and the circular flow of income; (4) how product and resource prices are determined; and (5) the market system and the allocating of economic resources. The first three topics are explored in the present chapter; the latter two will be discussed in Chapters 4 and 5.

35

CAPITALIST IDEOLOGY

Unfortunately, there is no neat, universally accepted definition of capitalism. We therefore must examine in some detail the basic tenets of pure capitalism to clearly understand what it entails. In short, the framework of capitalism embraces the following institutions and assumptions: (1) private property, (2) freedom of enterprise and choice, (3) self-interest as the dominant motive, (4) competition, (5) reliance on the price or market system, and (6) a limited role for government.

Private Property

Under a capitalistic system, property resources are owned by private individuals and private institutions rather than by government. **Private property,** coupled with the freedom to negotiate binding legal contracts, permits private persons or businesses to obtain, control, employ, and dispose of property resources as they see fit. The institution of private property is sustained over time by the *right to bequeath,* that is, by the right of a property owner to designate the recipient of this property at the time of death.

Needless to say, there are broad legal limits to this right of private ownership. For example, the use of one's resources for the production of illicit drugs is prohibited. Nor is public ownership nonexistent. Even in pure capitalism, public ownership of certain "natural monopolies" may be essential to the achievement of efficiency in the use of resources.

Freedom of Enterprise and Choice

Closely related to private ownership of property is freedom of enterprise and choice. Capitalism charges its component economic units with the responsibility of making certain choices, which are registered and made effective through the free markets of the economy.

Freedom of enterprise means that under pure capitalism, private business enterprises are free to obtain economic resources, to organize these resources in the production of a good or service of the firm's own choosing, and to sell it in the markets of their choice. No artificial obstacles or restrictions imposed by government or other producers block an entrepreneur's choice to enter or leave a particular industry.

Freedom of choice means that owners of property resources and money capital can employ or dispose of these resources as they see fit. It also means

that laborers are free to enter any lines of work for which they are qualified. Finally, it means that consumers are at liberty, within the limits of their money incomes, to buy that collection of goods and services they feel is most appropriate in satisfying their wants.

Freedom of *consumer* choice may well be the most profound of these freedoms. The consumer is in a particularly strategic position in a capitalistic economy; in a sense, the consumer is sovereign. The range of free choices for suppliers of human and property resources is circumscribed by the choices of consumers. The consumer ultimately decides what the capitalistic economy should produce, and resource suppliers must make their free choices within these constraints. Resource suppliers and businesses are not really "free" to produce goods and services consumers do not desire.

Again, broad legal limitations prevail in the expression of all these free choices.

Role of Self-Interest

The primary driving force of capitalism is the promotion of one's **self-interest;** each economic unit attempts to do what is best for itself. Hence, entrepreneurs aim to maximize their firm's profits or, as the case might be, minimize losses. And, other things being equal, owners of property resources attempt to achieve the highest price obtainable from the rent or sale of these resources. Given the amount and irksomeness of the effort involved, those who supply human resources will also try to obtain the highest possible incomes from their employment. Consumers, in purchasing a given product, will seek to obtain it at the lowest price. Consumers also apportion their expenditures to maximize their utility or satisfaction. In short, capitalism presumes self-interest as the fundamental *modus operandi* for the various economic units as they express their free choices. The motive of self-interest gives direction and consistency to what might otherwise be an extremely chaotic economy.

Note that pursuit of economic self-interest should not be confused with selfishness. The stockholder who receives corporate dividends may contribute a portion to the United Way or leave bequests to grandchildren. Similarly, a local church official may compare price and quality among various brands in buying new pews for the church.

Competition

Freedom of choice exercised in terms of promoting one's own monetary returns is the basis for **competi-**

tion, or economic rivalry, as a fundamental feature of capitalism. Competition, as economists see it, entails:

1 The presence of large numbers of independently acting buyers and sellers operating in the market for any particular product or resource.

2 The freedom of buyers and sellers to enter or leave particular markets.

Large Numbers The essence of competition is the widespread diffusion of economic power within the two major aggregates—businesses and households—which comprise the economy. When many buyers and sellers are present in a particular market, no one buyer or seller will be able to demand or offer a quantity of the product sufficiently large to noticeably influence its price. Let's examine this statement in terms of the selling or supply side of the product market.

We know that when a product becomes unusually scarce, its price will rise. An unseasonable frost in Florida may seriously curtail the output of citrus crops and sharply increase the price of oranges. Similarly, *if* a single producer, or a small group of producers acting together, can somehow control or restrict the total supply of a product, then price can be raised to the seller's advantage. By controlling supply, the producer can "rig the market" on his or her own behalf. Now the essence of competition is that there are so many independently acting sellers that each, *because he or she is contributing an almost negligible fraction of the total supply,* has virtually no influence over the supply or, therefore, over product price.

For example, suppose there are 10,000 farmers, each of whom is supplying 100 bushels of corn in the Kansas City grain market when the price of corn is $4 per bushel. Could a single farmer who feels dissatisfied with the existing price cause an artificial scarcity of corn and thereby boost the price above $4? The answer clearly is "No." Farmer Jones, by restricting output from 100 to 75 bushels, exerts virtually no effect on the total supply of corn. In fact, the total amount supplied is reduced only from 1,000,000 to 999,975 bushels. This obviously is not much of a shortage! Supply is virtually unchanged, and, therefore, the $4 price persists. In brief, competition means that each seller is providing a drop in the bucket of total supply. Individual sellers can make no noticeable dent in total supply; hence, a seller cannot *as an individual producer* manipulate product price. This is what is meant when it is said that an individual competitive seller is "at the mercy of the market." The same rationale applies to the demand side of the market. Buyers are plentiful and act inde-pendently. Thus single buyers cannot manipulate the market to their advantage.

The widespread diffusion of economic power underlying competition controls the use and limits the potential abuse of that power. Economic rivalry prevents economic units from wreaking havoc on one another as they attempt to further their self-interests. Competition imposes limits on expressions of self-interest by buyers and sellers. Competition is a basic regulatory force in capitalism.

Entry and Exit Competition also assumes that it is simple for producers to enter or leave a particular industry; there are no artificial legal or institutional obstacles to prohibit expansion or contraction of specific industries. This aspect of competition is prerequisite to the flexibility which is essential if an economy is to remain efficient over time. Freedom of entry is necessary for the economy to adjust appropriately to changes in consumer tastes, technology, or resource supplies. (This is further explored in Chapter 5.)

Markets and Prices

The basic coordinating mechanism of a capitalist economy is the market or price system. *Capitalism is a market economy.* Decisions rendered by buyers and sellers of products and resources are made effective through a system of markets. Indeed, by definition, a **market** is simply a mechanism or arrangement which brings buyers or "demanders" and sellers or "suppliers" of a good or service into contact with one another. A McDonald's, a gas station, a grocery supermarket, a Sotheby's art auction, the New York Stock Exchange, and worldwide foreign exchange markets are but a few illustrations. The preferences of sellers and buyers are registered on the supply and demand sides of various markets, and the outcome of these choices is a system of product and resource prices. These prices are guideposts on which resource owners, entrepreneurs, and consumers make and revise their free choices in furthering their self-interests.

Just as competition is the controlling mechanism, so a system of markets and prices is a basic organizing force. The market system is an elaborate communication system through which innumerable individual free choices are recorded, summarized, and balanced against one another. Those who obey the dictates of the market system are rewarded; those who ignore them are penalized by the system. Through this communication system, society decides what the economy should produce, how production can be efficiently organized, and how the fruits of productive endeavor are distributed among the individual economic units which make up capitalism.

Not only is the market system the mechanism through which society decides how it allocates its resources and distributes the resulting output, but it is through the market system that these decisions are carried out.

Economic systems based on the ideologies of socialism and communism also depend on market systems, but not to the same degree or in the same way as pure capitalism. Socialistic and communistic societies use markets and prices primarily to implement decisions made wholly or in part by a central planning authority. In capitalism, the market system functions both as a device for registering innumerable choices of free individuals and businesses *and* as a mechanism for carrying out these decisions.

In Chapters 4 and 5 we will analyze the mechanics and operation of the market system.

Limited Government

A competitive capitalist economy promotes a high degree of efficiency in the use or allocation of its resources. There is allegedly little real need for governmental intervention in the operation of such an economy beyond its role of imposing broad legal limits on the exercise of individual choices and the use of private property. The concept of pure capitalism as a self-regulating and self-adjusting economy precludes any significant economic role for government. However, as we will find in Chapter 6, a number of limitations and potentially undesirable outcomes associated with capitalism and the market system have resulted in an active economic role for government.

QUICK REVIEW 3-1

◢ *Pure capitalism rests on the private ownership of property and freedom of enterprise and choice.*

◢ *Economic entities—businesses, resource suppliers, and consumers—seek to further their own self-interests.*

◢ *The coordinating mechanism of capitalism is a competitive system of prices or markets.*

◢ *The efficient functioning of the market system under capitalism allegedly precludes significant government intervention.*

OTHER CHARACTERISTICS

Private property, freedom of enterprise and choice, self-interest as a motivating force, competition, and reliance on a market system are all institutions and assumptions more or less exclusively associated with pure capitalism. In addition, there are certain institutions and practices which are characteristic of all modern economies: (1) the use of advanced technology and large amounts of capital goods, (2) specialization, and (3) the use of money. Specialization and an advanced technology are prerequisites to efficient employment of any economy's resources. The use of money is a mechanism which allows society more easily to practice and reap the benefits of specialization and advanced productive techniques.

Extensive Use of Capital Goods

All modern economies—whether they approximate the capitalist, socialist, or communist ideology—are based on advanced technology and the extensive use of capital goods. Under pure capitalism it is competition, coupled with freedom of choice and the desire to further one's self-interest, which provides the means for achieving technological advance. The capitalistic framework is felt to be highly effective in harnessing incentives to develop new products and improved techniques of production, because monetary rewards accrue directly to the innovator. Pure capitalism therefore presupposes extensive use and relatively rapid development of complex capital goods: tools, machinery, large-scale factories, and facilities for storage, transportation, and marketing.

Why are the existence of an advanced technology and the extensive use of capital goods important? Because the most direct method of producing a product is usually the least efficient.[1] Even Robinson Crusoe avoided the inefficiencies of direct production in favor of **roundabout production.** It would be ridiculous for a farmer—even a backyard farmer—to go at production with bare hands. It pays huge dividends in terms of more efficient production and, therefore, a more abundant output, to fashion tools of production, that is, capital equipment, to aid in the productive process. There is a better way of getting water out of a well than to dive in after it!

---

[1]Remember that consumer goods satisfy wants directly, while capital goods do so indirectly through the more efficient future production of consumer goods.

But there is a catch involved. Recall our discussion of the production possibilities curve and the basic nature of the economizing problem. With full employment and full production, resources must be diverted from the production of consumer goods to be used in the production of capital goods. We must currently tighten our belts as consumers to free resources for the production of capital goods which will increase productive efficiency and give us a greater output of consumer goods in the future.

Specialization and Efficiency

The extent to which society relies on **specialization** is astounding. The vast majority of consumers produce virtually none of the goods and services they consume and, conversely, consume little or nothing of what they produce. The hammer-shop laborer who spends a lifetime stamping out parts for jet engines may never "consume" an airplane trip. The assembly-line worker who devotes 8 hours a day to installing windows in Corsicas may own a Honda. Few households seriously consider any extensive production of their own food, shelter, and clothing. Many farmers sell their milk to the local dairy and then buy margarine at the Podunk general store. Society learned long ago that self-sufficiency breeds inefficiency. The jack-of-all-trades may be a very colorful individual, but is certainly not efficient.

Division of Labor

In what specific ways might human specialization—the **division of labor**—enhance productive efficiency?
1   Specialization permits individuals to take advantage of existing differences in their abilities and skills. If caveman A is strong, swift, and accurate with a spear, and caveman B is weak and slow, but patient, this distribution of talents can be most efficiently used by making A a hunter and B a fisherman.
2   Even if the abilities of A and B are identical, specialization may be advantageous. By devoting all one's time to a single task, the doer is more likely to develop the appropriate skills and to discover improved techniques than when apportioning time among a number of diverse tasks. One learns to be a good hunter by hunting!
3   Finally, specialization—devoting all one's time to, say, a single task—avoids the loss of time involved in shifting from one job to another.
    For all these reasons the division of labor results in greater productive efficiency in the use of human resources.

Geographic Specialization

Specialization also is desirable on a regional and international basis. Oranges could be grown in Nebraska, but because of the unsuitability of the land, rainfall, and temperature, the costs involved would be exceedingly high. Florida could achieve some success in the production of wheat, but for similar reasons such production would be relatively costly. As a result, Nebraskans produce those products—wheat in particular—for which their resources are best adapted, and Floridians do the same, producing oranges and other citrus fruits. In so doing, both produce surpluses of their specialties. Then, very sensibly, Nebraskans and Floridians swap some of their surpluses. Specialization permits each area to turn out those goods which its resources can most efficiently produce. In this way both Nebraska and Florida can enjoy a larger amount of both wheat and oranges than would otherwise be the case.
    Similarly, on an international basis the United States specializes in such items as commercial aircraft and computers which it sells abroad in exchange for video recorders from Japan, bananas from Honduras, shoes from Italy, and woven baskets from Thailand. In short, human and geographical specialization are both essential in achieving efficiency in the use of resources.

Specialization and Comparative Advantage[2]

These simple illustrations clearly show that specialization is economically desirable because it results in more efficient production. Indeed, the point is almost self-explanatory. But, because the concept of specialization is so vital to understanding the production and exchange processes of modern economies, let's tackle a more exacting illustration of the gains which accrue from specialization.

Comparative Costs   Let's pursue our Nebraska–Florida example of specialization at a more advanced level, relying on an already familiar concept—the production possibilities table—as a basic analytical device. Suppose production possibilities data for the Nebraska and Florida economies are as in Tables 3-1 and 3-2, respectively.
    These production possibilities tables are "different" from those of Chapter 2 in that we here assume

---

[2]This section may be skipped by instructors who wish to defer detailed treatment of comparative advantage to Part 7 on the world economy.

TERMS AND CONCEPTS

private property	competition	specialization and	bartering
freedom of enterprise	market	division of labor	resource and product
freedom of choice	roundabout production	terms of trade	markets
self-interest	comparative advantage	medium of exchange	circular flow model

QUESTIONS AND STUDY SUGGESTIONS

1 "Capitalism may be characterized as an automatic self-regulating system motivated by the self-interest of individuals and regulated by competition."[5] Explain and evaluate.

2 Explain how the market system is a means of communicating and implementing decisions concerning allocation of the economy's resources.

3 What advantages result from "roundabout" production? What problem is involved in increasing a full-employment, full-production economy's stock of capital goods? Illustrate this problem in terms of the production possibilities curve. Does an economy with unemployed resources face the same problem?

4 What are the advantages of specialization in the use of human and material resources? The disadvantages? Explain: "Exchange is the necessary consequence of specialization."

5 Answer question 7 at the end of Chapter 37.

6 What problems does barter entail? Indicate the economic significance of money as a medium of exchange. "Money is the only commodity that is good for nothing but to be gotten rid of. It will not feed you, clothe you, shelter you, or amuse you unless you spend or invest it. It imparts value only in parting."[6] Explain this statement.

7 Describe the operation of pure capitalism as portrayed by the circular flow model. Locate resource and product markets and emphasize the fact of scarcity throughout your discussion. Specify the limitations of the circular flow model.

---

[5]Howard R. Bowen, *Toward Social Economy* (New York: Holt, Rinehart and Winston, Inc., 1948), p. 249.

[6]Federal Reserve Bank of Philadelphia, "Creeping Inflation," *Business Review,* August 1957, p. 3.

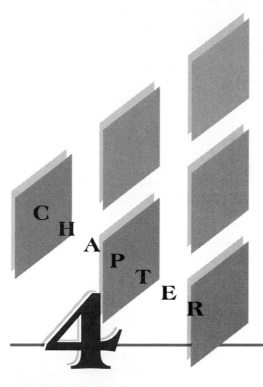

C H A P T E R

4

Understanding Individual Markets: Demand and Supply

Teach a parrot to say, "Demand and supply," and you have an economist! There is a strong element of truth in this quip. The simple tools of demand and supply can take us far in understanding not only specific economic issues, but also the operation of the entire economic system.

In this chapter we will examine the nature of markets and how prices and outputs are determined. Our circular flow model in Chapter 3 identified the participants in both product and resource markets. But we assumed there that product and resource prices were "given"; no attempt was made to explain how prices are "set" or determined. We now build on the circular flow model by discussing the concept of a market more fully.

MARKETS DEFINED

A **market** is *an institution or mechanism which brings together buyers ("demanders") and sellers ("suppliers") of particular goods and services.* Markets exist in many forms. The corner gas station, the fast-food outlet, the local music store, a farmer's roadside stand—all are familiar markets. The New York Stock Exchange and the Chicago Board of Trade are highly organized markets where buyers and sellers of stocks and bonds and farm commodities, respectively, from all over the world are brought into contact with one another. Similarly, auctioneers bring together potential buyers and sellers of art, livestock, used farm equipment, and sometimes real estate. The all-American quarterback and his agent bargain with the owner of an NFL team. A graduating finance major interviews with Citicorp or Chase Manhattan at the university placement office. All these situ-

ations which link potential buyers with potential sellers constitute markets. As our examples imply, some markets are local while others are national or international in scope. Some are highly personal, involving face-to-face contact between demander and supplier; others are impersonal in that buyer and seller never see or know one another.

This chapter concerns the functioning of *purely competitive markets.* Such markets presume large numbers of independently acting buyers and sellers interested in exchanging a standardized product. These markets are not the music store or corner gas station where products have price tags, but competitive markets such as a central grain exchange, a stock market, or a market for foreign currencies where the equilibrium price is "discovered" by the interacting decisions of buyers and sellers. Similarly, we see how prices are established in resource markets by demand decisions of competing businesses and supply decisions of competing households (Figure 3-2). We shall concentrate on the *product market,* then later in the chapter examine the *resource market.* Our goal is to explain the mechanics of prices.

DEMAND

Demand is *a schedule which shows the various amounts of a product consumers are willing and able to purchase at each price in a series of possible prices during a specified period of time.*[1] Demand portrays a series of alternative possibilities which can be set down in tabular form. It shows the quantities of a product which will be demanded at various possible prices, *all other things being equal.*

We usually view demand from the vantage point of price; that is, we read demand as showing the amounts consumers will buy at various possible prices. It is equally correct and sometimes more useful to view demand from the reference point of quantity. Instead of asking what quantities can be sold at various prices, we ask what prices can be gotten from consumers for various quantities of a good. Table 4-1 is a hypothetical **demand schedule** for a single consumer purchasing bushels of corn.

This tabular portrayal of demand reflects the relationship between the price of corn and the quantity the consumer would be willing and able to purchase at each of these prices. Note that we say willing and *able,* because willingness alone is not effective in the market. I may be willing to buy a Porsche, but if this willingness is not backed by the necessary dollars, it will not be effective and, therefore, not reflected in the market. In Table 4-1, if the price of corn were $5 per bushel, our consumer would be willing and able to buy 10 bushels per week; if it were $4, the consumer would be willing and able to buy 20 bushels per week; and so forth.

The demand schedule does not tell us which of the five possible prices will actually exist in the corn market. This depends on demand *and supply.* Demand is simply a tabular statement of a buyer's plans, or intentions, with respect to the purchase of a product.

To be meaningful the quantities demanded at each price must relate to a specific period—a day, a week, a month. To say "a consumer will buy 10 bushels of corn at $5 per bushel" is meaningless. To say "a consumer

---

TABLE 4-1 **An individual buyer's demand for corn (hypothetical data)**

Price per bushel	Quantity demanded per week
$5	10
4	20
3	35
2	55
1	80

will buy 10 bushels of corn *per week* at $5 per bushel" is clear and meaningful. Without a specific time period we would not know whether demand for a product was large or small.

Law of Demand

A fundamental characteristic of demand is this: All else being constant, as price falls, the quantity demanded rises. Or, other things being equal, as price increases, the corresponding quantity demanded falls. In short, there is a negative or *inverse* relationship between price and quantity demanded. Economists call this inverse relationship the **law of demand.**

The "other things being constant" assumption is critical here. Many factors other than the price of the product under consideration affect the amount purchased. For example, the quantity of Nikes purchased will depend not only on the price of Nikes, but also on the prices of such substitute shoes as Reeboks, Adidas, and L.A. Gear. The law of demand in this case says that fewer pairs of Nikes will be purchased if the price of Nikes rises *and the prices of Reeboks, Adidas, and L.A. Gear all remain constant.* In short, if the *relative price* of Nikes increases, fewer Nikes will be bought. If the prices of Nikes and all other competing shoes increase by some amount—say $5—consumers might buy more, less, or the same amount of Nikes.

On what foundation does the law of demand rest? There are several levels of analysis on which to argue the case.

1 Common sense and simple observation are consistent with the law of demand. People ordinarily *do* buy more of a given product at a low price than they do at a high price. Price is an obstacle which deters consumers from buying. The higher this obstacle, the less of a product they will buy; the lower the price obstacle, the more they will buy. A high price discourages consumers from buying, and a low price encourages them to buy. The fact that businesses have "sales" is concrete

---

[1] In adjusting this definition to the resource market, substitute the word "resources" for "product" and "businesses" for "consumers."

evidence of their belief in the law of demand. "Bargain days" are based on the law of demand. Businesses reduce their inventories by lowering prices, not by raising them.

2   In any given time period each buyer of a product will derive less satisfaction or benefit or utility from each successive unit of a product. The second "Big Mac" will yield less satisfaction to the consumer than the first; and the third still less added benefit or utility than the second. Because consumption is subject to **diminishing marginal utility**—consuming successive units of a particular product yields less and less extra satisfaction—consumers will only buy additional units if price is reduced.

3   The law of demand also can be explained in terms of income and substitution effects. The **income effect** indicates that, at a lower price, you can afford more of the good without giving up other goods. In other words, a decline in the price of a product will increase the purchasing power of your money income, enabling you to buy more of the product than before. A higher price will have the opposite effect.

The **substitution effect** suggests that, at a lower price, you have the incentive to substitute the cheaper good for similar goods which are now relatively more expensive. Consumers tend to substitute cheap products for dear products.

For example, a decline in the price of beef will increase the purchasing power of consumer incomes, enabling them to buy more beef (the income effect). At a lower price, beef is relatively more attractive and is substituted for pork, mutton, chicken, and fish (the substitution effect). The income and substitution effects combine to make consumers able and willing to buy more of a product at a low price than at a high price.

The Demand Curve

This inverse relationship between product price and quantity demanded can be represented on a simple graph wherein, by convention, we measure quantity demanded on the horizontal axis and price on the vertical axis. We locate on the graph those five price–quantity possibilities shown in Table 4-1 by drawing perpendiculars from the appropriate points on the two axes. Thus, in plotting the "$5-price–10-quantity-demanded" possibility, we draw a perpendicular from the horizontal (quantity) axis at 10 to meet a perpendicular drawn from the vertical (price) axis at $5. If this is done for all five possibilities, the result is a series of points as shown in Figure 4-1. Each point represents a specific price and the corresponding quantity the consumer will purchase at that price.

Now, assuming the same inverse relationship between price and quantity demanded at all points between the ones graphed, we can generalize on the inverse relationship between price and quantity demanded by drawing a curve to represent *all* price–quantity-demanded possibilities within the limits shown on the graph. The resulting curve is called a **demand curve,** labeled *DD* in Figure 4-1. It slopes

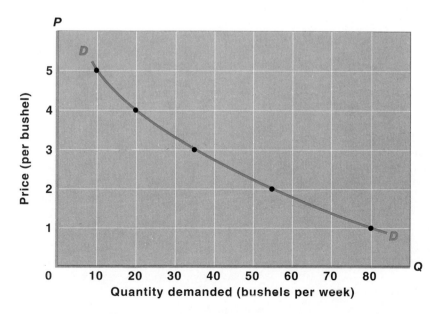

FIGURE 4-1   An individual buyer's demand curve for corn

An individual's demand schedule graphs as a downsloping curve such as *DD*, because price and quantity demanded are inversely related. Specifically, the law of demand generalizes that consumers will buy more of a product as its price declines.

downward and to the right because the relationship it portrays between price and quantity demanded is negative or inverse. The law of demand—people buy more at a low price than at a high price—is reflected in the downward slope of the demand curve.

What is the advantage of graphing our demand schedule? After all, Table 4-1 and Figure 4-1 contain exactly the same data and reflect the same relationship between price and quantity demanded. The advantage of graphing is that we can represent clearly a given relationship—in this case the law of demand—more simply than if we relied on verbal and tabular presentation. A single curve on a graph, if understood, is simpler to state *and manipulate* than tables and lengthy verbal descriptions. Graphs are invaluable tools in economic analysis. They permit clear expression and handling of sometimes complex relationships.

Individual and Market Demand

Until now we have assumed just one consumer. Competition assumes many buyers are in the market. The transition from an *individual* to a *market* demand schedule can be accomplished easily by summing the quantities demanded by each consumer at the various possible prices. If there were just three buyers in the market, as is shown in Table 4-2, it would be easy to determine the total quantities demanded at each price. Figure 4-2 shows the same summing procedure graphically, using only the $3 price to illustrate the adding-up process. Note that we are simply summing the three individual demand curves *horizontally* to derive the total demand curve.

TABLE 4-2 Market demand for corn, three buyers (hypothetical data)

Price per bushel	Quantity demanded			Total quantity demanded per week
	First buyer	Second buyer	Third buyer	
$5	10 +	12 +	8	= 30
4	20 +	23 +	17	= 60
3	35 +	39 +	26	= 100
2	55 +	60 +	39	= 154
1	80 +	87 +	54	= 221

Competition, of course, entails many more than three buyers of a product. So—to avoid a lengthy addition process—suppose there are 200 buyers of corn in the market, each of whom chooses to buy the same amount at each of the various prices as our original consumer does. Thus, we can determine total or market demand by multiplying the quantity-demanded data of Table 4-1 by 200, as in Table 4-3. Curve D_1 in Figure 4-3 indicates this market demand curve for the 200 buyers.

Determinants of Demand

An economist constructing a demand curve such as D_1 in Figure 4-3 assumes that price is the most important influence on the amount of any product purchased. But the economist knows that other factors can and do affect purchases. Thus, in locating a given demand curve such as D_1, it must also be assumed that "other things are equal"; that is, certain *determinants* of the amount demanded are assumed to be constant. When any of

FIGURE 4-2 The market demand curve is the sum of the individual demand curves

Graphically the market demand curve (*D* total) is found by summing horizontally the individual demand curves (*D₁*, *D₂*, and *D₃*) of all consumers in the market.

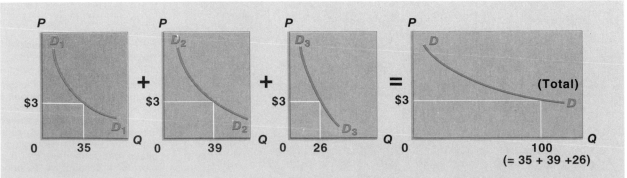

TABLE 4-3 Market demand for corn, 200 buyers (hypothetical data)

(1) Price per bushel	(2) Quantity demanded per week, single buyer		(3) Number of buyers in the market		(4) Total quantity demanded per week
$5	10	×	200	=	2,000
4	20	×	200	=	4,000
3	35	×	200	=	7,000
2	55	×	200	=	11,000
1	80	×	200	=	16,000

these determinants do change, the location of the demand curve will shift to the right or left of D_1. For this reason determinants of demand are referred to as *demand shifters*.

The basic determinants of market demand are: (1) the tastes or preferences of consumers, (2) the number of consumers in the market, (3) the money incomes of consumers, (4) prices of related goods, and (5) consumer expectations about future prices and incomes.

Changes in Demand

A change in one or more of the determinants of demand will change the demand schedule data in Table 4-3 and therefore the location of the demand curve in Figure 4-3. A change in the demand schedule data, or, graphically, a shift in the location of the demand curve, is called a *change in demand*.

If consumers become willing and able to buy more of this particular good at each possible price than is reflected in column 4 of Table 4-3, the result will be an *increase in demand*. In Figure 4-3, this increase in demand is reflected in a shift of the demand curve to the *right*, from D_1 to D_2. Conversely, a *decrease in demand* occurs when, because of a change in one or more of the determinants, consumers buy less of the product at each possible price than indicated in column 4 of Table 4-3. Graphically, a decrease in demand is shown as a shift of the demand curve to the *left*, for example, from D_1 to D_3 in Figure 4-3.

Let's now examine how changes in each determinant affects demand.

1 Tastes A change in consumer tastes or preferences favorable to a product—possibly prompted by

FIGURE 4-3 Changes in the demand for corn

A change in one or more of the determinants of demand—consumer tastes, the number of buyers in the market, money incomes, the prices of other goods, or consumer expectations—will cause a change in demand. An increase in demand shifts the demand curve to the right, as from D_1 to D_2. A decrease in demand shifts the demand curve to the left, as from D_1 to D_3. A change in the quantity demanded is caused by a change in the price of the product, and is shown by a movement from one point to another—as from *a* to *b*—on a fixed demand curve.

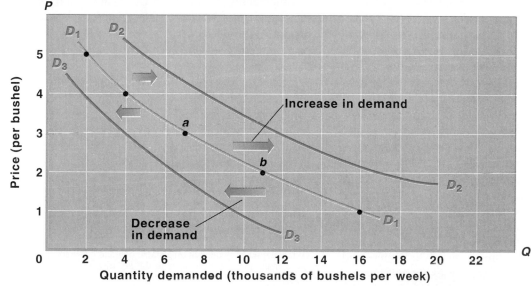

advertising or fashion changes—will mean that more will be demanded at each price; that is, demand will increase. An unfavorable change in consumer preferences will cause demand to decrease, shifting the curve to the left. Technological change in the form of a new product may prompt a revision of consumer tastes. For example, the introduction of compact discs has decreased the demand for long-playing records. Demand for oat bran has increased greatly because of health studies linking it to lower cholesterol levels.

2 Number of Buyers An increase in the number of consumers in a market will increase demand. Fewer consumers will be reflected by a decrease in demand. For example, dramatic improvements in communications have made financial markets international in scope, increasing demand for stocks, bonds, and other financial instruments. And the "baby boom" after World War II increased demand for diapers, baby lotion, and services of obstetricians. When the "baby boom" generation reached their twenties in the 1970s, the demand for housing increased dramatically. Conversely, the aging of the baby boomers in the 1980s and 1990s has been an important factor in the recent "slump" in housing demand. Also, increasing life expectancy has increased demands for medical care, retirement communities, and nursing homes. Note, too, that American trade negotiators are trying to reduce foreign trade barriers to American farm products to increase demands for those products.

3 Income The impact of changes in money income on demand is more complex. For most commodities, a rise in income will cause an increase in demand. Consumers typically buy more steaks, sunscreen, and stereos as their incomes increase. Conversely, the demand for such products will decline in response to a fall in incomes. Commodities whose demand varies *directly* with money income are called **superior,** or **normal, goods.**

Although most products are normal goods, there are a few exceptions. As incomes increase beyond some point, the amounts of bread or lard or cabbages purchased at each price may diminish because higher incomes allow consumers to buy more high-protein foods, such as dairy products and meat. Rising incomes may also decrease demands for used clothing and third-hand automobiles. Similarly, rising incomes may cause demands for hamburger and margarine to decline as wealthier consumers switch to T-bones and butter. Goods whose demand varies *inversely* with a change in money income are called **inferior goods.**

4 Prices of Related Goods Whether a given change in the price of a related good will increase or decrease the demand for a product will depend on whether the related good is a substitute for it or a complement to it. A substitute is a good which can be used in place of another good. A complement is a good used in conjunction with another good.

Substitutes For example, butter and margarine are **substitute goods.** When the price of butter rises, consumers will buy less butter, and this will increase the demand for margarine.[2] Conversely, as the price of butter falls, consumers will buy more butter, causing the demand for margarine to decrease. *When two products are substitutes, the price of one good and the demand for the other are directly related.* So it is with Millers and Budweiser, sugar and Nutrasweet, Toyotas and Hondas, and Coke and Pepsi.

Complements Other pairs of products are **complementary goods;** they "go together" in that they are jointly demanded. If the price of gasoline falls and, as a result, you drive your car more, this extra driving will increase your demand for motor oil. Conversely, an increase in the price of gasoline will diminish the demand for motor oil.[3] Thus gas and oil are jointly demanded; they are complements. So it is with ham and eggs, tuition and textbooks, VCRs and video cassettes, golf clubs and golf balls, cameras and rolls of film. *When two commodities are complements, the price of one good and the demand for the other are inversely related.*

Many pairs of goods, of course, are not related at all—they are *independent* goods. For such pairs of commodities as, for example, butter and golf balls, potatoes and automobiles, bananas and wristwatches, a change in the price of one would have little or no impact on the demand for the other.

5 Expectations Consumer expectations about future product prices, product availability, and future income can shift demand. Consumer expectations of higher future prices may prompt them to buy now to "beat" anticipated price rises; similarly, the expectation of rising incomes may induce consumers to be freer in

---

[2]Note that the consumer is moving up a stable demand curve for butter. But the demand curve for margarine shifts to the right (increases). Given the supply of margarine, this rightward shift in demand means more margarine will be purchased and that its price will also rise.

[3]While the buyer is moving up a stable demand curve for gasoline, the demand for motor oil shifts to the left (decreases). Given the supply of motor oil, this decline in the demand for motor oil will reduce both the amount purchased and its price.

current spending. Conversely, expectations of falling prices and income will decrease current demand for products. First example: If freezing weather destroys much of Florida's citrus crop, consumers may reason that forthcoming shortages of frozen orange juice will escalate its price. They may stock up on orange juice by purchasing extraordinarily large quantities now. Second example: Several years ago Johnny Carson jokingly predicted a toilet paper shortage. Many of his TV fans took this seriously and within a few days toilet paper was not to be found on the shelves of many supermarkets. Third example: A first-round NFL draft choice might splurge for a new Mercedes in anticipation of a lucrative professional football contract. Final example: Additional Federal excise taxes imposed on beer, wine, and distilled liquor on January 1, 1991, sharply increased demand in December of 1990 as consumers "bought early" to beat anticipated price increases.

In summary, an *increase* in demand—the decision by consumers to buy larger quantities of a product at each possible price—can be caused by:

1 A favorable change in consumer tastes
2 An increase in the number of buyers
3 Rising incomes if the product is a normal good
4 Falling incomes if the product is an inferior good
5 An increase in the price of a substitute good
6 A decrease in the price of a complementary good
7 Consumer expectations of higher future prices and incomes

Be sure you can "reverse" these generalizations to explain a *decrease* in demand. Table 4-4 provides additional illustrations to reinforce your understanding of the determinants of demand.

Changes in Quantity Demanded

A "change in demand" must not be confused with a "change in quantity demanded." A **change in demand** is a shift in the entire demand curve either to the right (an increase in demand) or to the left (a decrease in demand). The consumer's state of mind concerning purchases of this product has been altered. The cause: a change in one or more of the determinants of demand. The term "demand" refers to a schedule or curve; therefore, a "change in demand" means that the entire schedule has changed and that graphically the curve has shifted its position.

In contrast, a **change in the quantity demanded** designates the movement from one point to another point—from one price-quantity combination to an-

---

TABLE 4-4 Determinants of demand: factors that shift the demand curve

1 **Change in buyer tastes** Example: Physical fitness increases in popularity, increasing the demand for jogging shoes and bicycles

2 **Change in number of buyers** Examples: Japanese reduce import quotas on American telecommunications equipment, thereby increasing the demand for such equipment; a decline in the birthrate reduces the demand for education

3 **Change in income** Examples: An increase in incomes increases the demand for such normal goods as butter, lobster, and filet mignon, while reducing the demand for such inferior goods as cabbage, turnips, retreaded tires, and used clothing

4 **Change in the prices of related goods** Examples: A reduction in air fares reduces the demand for bus transportation (substitute goods); a decline in the price of compact disc players increases the demand for compact discs (complementary goods)

5 **Change in expectations** Example: Inclement weather in South America causes the expectation of higher future coffee prices, thereby increasing the current demand for coffee

---

other—on a fixed demand curve. The cause of a change in quantity demanded is a change in the price of the product under consideration. In Table 4-3 a decline in the price from $5 to $4 will increase the quantity of corn demanded from 2000 to 4000 bushels.

The distinction between a change in demand and a change in the quantity demanded can be seen in Figure 4-3. The shift of the demand curve D_1 to either D_2 or D_3 is a "change in demand." But the movement from point a to point b on curve D_1 is a "change in the quantity demanded."

You should decide whether a change in demand or a change in quantity demanded is involved in each of the following illustrations:

1 Consumer incomes rise, with the result that more jewelry is purchased.
2 A barber raises the price of haircuts and experiences a decline in volume of business.
3 The price of Toyotas goes up, and, as a consequence, the sales of Chevrolets increase.

QUICK REVIEW 4-1

♪ *A market is any arrangement which facilitates purchase and sale of goods, services, or resources.*

♪ *The law of demand indicates that, other things being constant, the quantity of a good purchased will vary inversely with its price.*

♦ The demand curve will shift because of changes in **a** consumer tastes, **b** the number of buyers in the market, **c** incomes, **d** the prices of substitute or complementary goods, and **e** expectations.

♦ A "change in quantity demanded" refers to a movement from one point to another on a stable demand curve; a "change in demand" designates a shift in the entire demand curve.

SUPPLY

Supply *is a schedule which shows the amounts of a product a producer is willing and able to produce and make available for sale at each price in a series of possible prices during a specified period.*[4] This **supply schedule** portrays a series of alternative possibilities, such as shown in Table 4-5, for a single producer of corn. Supply tells us the quantities of a product which will be supplied at various prices, all other factors held constant.

Our definition of supply indicates that supply is usually viewed from the vantage point of price. That is, we read supply as showing the amounts producers will offer at various prices. It is equally correct and more useful in some instances to view supply from the reference point of quantity. Instead of asking what quantities will be offered at various prices, we can ask what prices will be required to induce producers to offer various quantities of a good.

Law of Supply

Table 4-5 shows a positive or *direct* relationship between price and quantity supplied. As price rises, the corresponding quantity supplied rises; as price falls, the quantity supplied also falls. This particular relationship is called the **law of supply.** Producers will produce and offer for sale more of their product at a high price than at a low price. This again is basically a commonsense matter.

Price is a deterrent from the consumer's standpoint. The obstacle of a high price means that the consumer, being on the paying end of this price, will buy a relatively small amount of the product; the lower the price obstacle, the more the consumer will buy. The supplier is on the receiving end of the product's price.

[4]In talking of the resource market, our definition of supply reads: a schedule which shows the various amounts of a resource which its owners are willing to supply in the market at each possible price in a series of prices during a specified time.

TABLE 4-5 An individual producer's supply of corn (hypothetical data)

Price per bushel	Quantity supplied per week
$5	60
4	50
3	35
2	20
1	5

To a supplier, price is revenue per unit and therefore an inducement or incentive to produce and sell a product. Given production costs, a higher product price means greater profits for the supplier and thus an incentive to increase the quantity supplied.

Consider a farmer who can shift resources within limits among alternative products. As price moves up in Table 4-5, the farmer will find it profitable to take land out of wheat, oats, and soybean production and put it into corn. Furthermore, higher corn prices will make it possible for the farmer to cover the costs associated with more intensive cultivation and the use of larger quantities of fertilizers and pesticides. All these efforts result in more output of corn.

Now consider a manufacturing concern. Beyond some point manufacturers usually encounter increasing production costs per added unit of output. Therefore, a higher product price is necessary to cover these rising costs. Costs rise because certain productive resources—in particular, the firm's plant and machinery—cannot be expanded quickly. As the firm increases the amounts of more readily variable resources such as labor, materials, and component parts, the fixed plant will at some point become crowded or congested. Productive efficiency will decline and the cost of successive units of output will increase. Producers must receive a higher price to produce these more costly units. Price and quantity supplied are directly related.

The Supply Curve

As with demand, it is convenient to represent graphically the concept of supply. Our axes in Figure 4-4 are the same as those in Figure 4-3, except for the change of "quantity demanded" to "quantity supplied" on the horizontal axis. The graphing procedure is the same, but the quantity data and relationship involved are different. The market supply data graphed in Figure 4-4 as S_1 are shown in Table 4-6, which assumes there are 200 suppliers in the market having the same supply

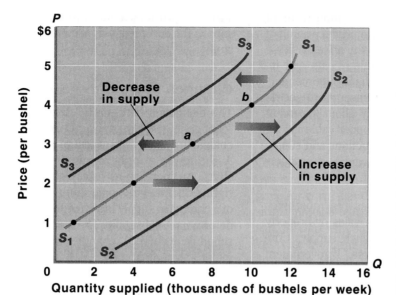

FIGURE 4-4   Changes in the supply of corn

A change in one or more of the determinants of supply—resource prices, productive techniques, the prices of other goods, taxes and subsidies, price expectations, or the number of sellers in the market—will cause a change in supply. An increase in supply shifts the supply curve to the right, as from S_1 to S_2. A decrease in supply is shown graphically as a shift of the curve to the left, as from S_1 to S_3. A change in the quantity supplied is caused by a change in the price of the product and is shown by a movement from one point to another—as from *a* to *b*—on a fixed supply curve.

schedules as the producer previously portrayed in Table 4-5.

Determinants of Supply

In constructing a supply curve, the economist assumes that price is the most significant influence on the quantity supplied of any product. But, as with the demand curve, the supply curve is anchored on the "other things are equal" assumption. The supply curve is drawn assuming that certain determinants of the amount supplied are given and do not change. If any of these determinants of supply do change, the supply curve will shift.

The basic determinants of supply are (1) resource prices, (2) the technique of production, (3) taxes and

TABLE 4-6   Market supply of corn, 200 producers (hypothetical data)

(1) Price per bushel	(2) Quantity supplied per week, single producer		(3) Number of sellers in the market		(4) Total quantity supplied per week
$5	60	×	200	=	12,000
4	50	×	200	=	10,000
3	35	×	200	=	7,000
2	20	×	200	=	4,000
1	5	×	200	=	1,000

subsidies, (4) prices of other goods, (5) price expectations, and (6) the number of sellers in the market. A change in any one or more of these determinants or *supply shifters* will cause the supply curve for a product to shift either to the right or the left. A shift to the *right*, from S_1 to S_2 in Figure 4-4, designates an *increase in supply:* Producers are now supplying larger quantities of the product at each possible price. A shift to the *left*, S_1 to S_3 in Figure 4-4, indicates a *decrease in supply:* Suppliers are offering less at each price.

Changes in Supply

Let's consider how changes in each of these determinants affect supply.

1 Resource Prices   As indicated in our explanation of the law of supply, the relationship between production costs and supply is an intimate one. A firm's supply curve is based on production costs; a firm must receive higher prices for additional units of output because those extra units cost more to produce. It follows that a decrease in resource prices will lower production costs and increase supply, that is, shift the supply curve to the right. If prices of seed and fertilizer decrease, we can expect the supply of corn to increase. Conversely, an increase in resource prices will raise production costs and reduce supply, that is, shift the supply curve to the left. Increases in the prices of iron ore and coke will increase the cost of producing steel and reduce its supply.

Observe in column 4 that at this price, quantity demanded is in excess of quantity supplied by 15,000 units. This relatively low price discourages farmers from devoting their resources to corn production and encourages consumers to attempt to buy more than is available. The result is a 15,000-bushel **shortage** of, or *excess demand* for, corn. This price of $1 cannot persist as the market price. Competition among buyers will bid up the price to something greater than $1. At a price of $1, many consumers who are willing and able to buy at this price will be left out in the cold. Many potential consumers will express a willingness to pay a price above $1 to ensure getting some of the available corn.

Suppose this competitive bidding up of price by buyers boosts the price of corn to $2. This higher price has reduced, but not eliminated, the shortage of corn. For $2, farmers are willing to devote more resources to corn production, and some buyers who were willing to pay $1 for a bushel of corn will choose not to buy at $2. But a shortage of 7000 bushels still exists at $2. We can conclude that competitive bidding among buyers will push market price above $2.

Equilibrium

By trial and error we have eliminated every price but $3. At a price of $3, *and only at this price,* the quantity which farmers are willing to produce and supply in the market is identical with the amount consumers are willing and able to buy. As a result, there is neither a shortage nor a surplus of corn at this price. A surplus causes price to decline and a shortage causes price to rise.

With neither a shortage nor a surplus at $3, there is no reason for the actual price of corn to move away from this price. The economist calls this price the *market-clearing* or **equilibrium price,** equilibrium meaning "in balance" or "at rest." At $3, quantity supplied and quantity demanded are in balance; that is, **equilibrium quantity** is 7000 bushels. Hence $3 is the only stable price of corn under the supply and demand conditions shown in Table 4-8. Or, stated differently, the price of corn will be established where the supply decisions of producers and the demand decisions of buyers are mutually consistent. Such decisions are consistent with one another only at a price of $3. At any higher price, suppliers want to sell more than consumers want to buy and a surplus will result; at any lower price, consumers want to buy more than producers are willing to offer for sale, as shown by the consequent

shortage. Discrepancies between supply and demand intentions of sellers and buyers will prompt price changes which will bring these two sets of plans into accord with one another.

A graphical analysis of supply and demand should yield the same conclusions. Figure 4-5 (Key Graph) puts the market supply and market demand curves for corn on the same graph, the horizontal axis now measuring both quantity demanded and quantity supplied. At any price above the equilibrium price of $3, quantity supplied will exceed quantity demanded. This surplus will cause a competitive bidding down of price by sellers eager to rid themselves of their surplus. The falling price will cause less corn to be offered and will simultaneously encourage consumers to buy more.

Any price below the equilibrium price will entail a shortage; quantity demanded will exceed quantity supplied. Competitive bidding by buyers will push the price up toward the equilibrium level. And this rising price will simultaneously cause producers to increase the quantity supplied and ration buyers out of the market, thereby eliminating the shortage. *Graphically, the intersection of the supply curve and the demand curve for the product will indicate the equilibrium point.* In this case equilibrium price and quantity are $3 per bushel and 7000 bushels.

Rationing Function of Prices

The ability of the competitive forces of supply and demand to establish a price where selling and buying decisions are synchronized or coordinated is called the **rationing function of prices.** In this case, the equilibrium price of $3 clears the market, leaving no burdensome surplus for sellers and no inconvenient shortage for potential buyers. The composite of freely made individual buying and selling decisions sets this price which clears the market. In effect, the market mechanism of supply and demand says that any buyer willing and able to pay $3 for a bushel of corn will be able to acquire one; those who are not, will not. Similarly, any seller willing and able to produce bushels of corn and offer them for sale at $3 will be able to do so; those who are not, will not.

Changes in Supply and Demand

We know that demand might change because of fluctuations in consumer tastes or incomes, changes in consumer expectations, or variations in the prices of related goods. Supply might vary in response to changes

KEY GRAPH

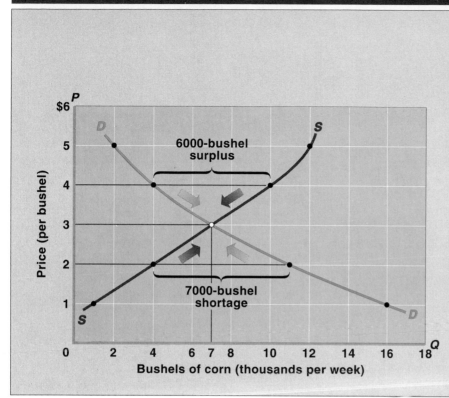

FIGURE 4-5

The equilibrium price and quantity for corn as determined by market demand and supply

The intersection of the down-sloping demand curve *D* and the upsloping supply curve *S* indicates the equilibrium price and quantity, $3 and 7000 bushels in this instance. The shortages of corn which would exist at below-equilibrium prices, for example, 7000 bushels at $2, drive price up, and in so doing, increase the quantity supplied and reduce the quantity demanded until equilibrium is achieved. The surpluses which above-equilibrium prices would entail, for example, 6000 bushels at $4, push price down and thereby increase the quantity demanded and reduce the quantity supplied until equilibrium is achieved.

in technology, resource prices, or taxes. Our analysis would be incomplete if we did not consider the effect of changes in supply and demand on equilibrium price.

Changing Demand First, we analyze the effects of a change in demand, assuming supply is constant. Suppose demand increases, as shown in Figure 4-6a. What is the effect on price? Since the new intersection of the supply and demand curves is at a higher point on both the price and quantity axes, an increase in demand, other things (supply) being equal, will have a *price-increasing effect* and a *quantity-increasing effect*. (The value of graphical analysis is now apparent; we need not fumble with columns of figures in determining the effect on price and quantity but only compare the new with the old point of intersection on the graph.)

A decrease in demand, shown in Figure 4-6b, reveals both *price-decreasing* and *quantity-decreasing effects*. Price falls, and quantity also declines. *In brief, we*

find a direct relationship between a change in demand and resulting changes in both equilibrium price and quantity.

Changing Supply Let's now analyze the effect of a change in supply on price, assuming that demand is constant. If supply increases, as in Figure 4-6c, the new intersection of supply and demand is located at a lower equilibrium price. Equilibrium quantity, however, increases. If supply decreases, product price will rise. Figure 4-6d illustrates this situation. Here, price increases but quantity declines.

In short, an increase in supply has a *price-decreasing* and a *quantity-increasing effect*. A decrease in supply has a *price-increasing* and a *quantity-decreasing effect*. *There is an inverse relationship between a change in supply and the resulting change in equilibrium price, but the relationship between a change in supply and the resulting change in equilibrium quantity is direct.*

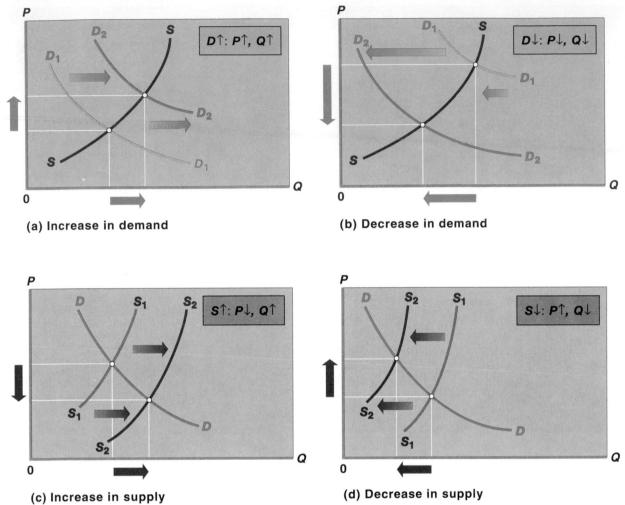

(a) Increase in demand   **(b) Decrease in demand**

(c) Increase in supply   **(d) Decrease in supply**

FIGURE 4-6   Changes in demand and supply and the effects on price and quantity

The increase in demand of (a) and the decrease in demand of (b) indicate a direct relationship between a change in demand and the resulting changes in equilibrium price and quantity. The increase in supply of (c) and the decrease in supply of (d) show an inverse relationship between a change in supply and the resulting change in equilibrium price, but a direct relationship between a change in supply and the accompanying change in equilibrium quantity.

Complex Cases A host of more complex cases might arise, involving changes in both supply and demand.

1 Supply Increase; Demand Decrease Assume first that supply increases and demand decreases. What effect does this have on equilibrium price? This example couples two price-decreasing effects, and the net result will be a price fall greater than what would result from either change alone. How about equilib-

rium quantity? Here the effects of the changes in supply and demand are opposed: The increase in supply increases equilibrium quantity, but the decrease in demand reduces the equilibrium quantity. The direction of the change in quantity depends on the relative sizes of the changes in supply and demand.

2 Supply Decrease; Demand Increase Another possibility is for supply to decrease and demand to increase. Two price-increasing effects are involved here.

We can predict an increase in equilibrium price greater than that caused by either change separately. The effect on equilibrium quantity is again indeterminate, depending on the relative size of the changes in supply and demand. If the decrease in supply is relatively larger than the increase in demand, the equilibrium quantity will be less than initially. But if the decrease in supply is relatively smaller than the increase in demand, the equilibrium quantity will increase as a result of these changes. You should trace through these two cases graphically to verify these conclusions.

3 Supply Increase; Demand Increase What if supply and demand both increase? What is the effect on equilibrium price? It depends. Here we must compare two conflicting effects on price—the price-decreasing effect of the increase in supply and the price-increasing effect of the increase in demand. If the increase in supply is greater than the increase in demand, the equilibrium price will decrease. If the opposite holds, equilibrium price will increase.

The effect on equilibrium quantity is certain: Increases in supply and in demand both have quantity-increasing effects. This means that equilibrium quantity will increase by an amount greater than either change alone.

4 Supply Decrease; Demand Decrease A decrease in both supply and demand can be similarly analyzed. If the decrease in supply is greater than the decrease in demand, equilibrium price will rise. If the reverse holds true, equilibrium price will fall. Because decreases in supply and demand both have quantity-decreasing effects, it can be predicted with certainty that equilibrium quantity will be less than that which prevailed initially.

Special cases might arise where a decrease in demand and a decrease in supply, on the one hand, and an increase in demand and an increase in supply, on the other, exactly cancel out. In both these cases, the net effect on equilibrium price will be zero; price will not change. You should also work out these more complex cases in terms of supply and demand curves to verify all these results.

The Resource Market

As in the product market, resource supply curves are typically upsloping, and resource demand curves are downsloping.

Resource supply curves reflect a *direct* relationship between resource price and quantity supplied, because it is in the interest of resource owners to supply more of a particular resource at a high price than at a low price. High income payments in a particular occupation or industry encourage households to supply more human and property resources. Low-income payments discourage resource owners from supplying resources in this particular occupation or industry and encourage them to supply their resources elsewhere. There is strong evidence, incidentally, that most college students choose their major (their occupation) on the basis of prospective financial rewards.

On the demand side, businesses buy less of a given resource as its price rises, and they substitute other relatively low-priced resources for it. Entrepreneurs will find it profitable to substitute low- for high-priced resources as they try to minimize costs. More of a particular resource will be demanded at a low price than at a high price. The result? A downsloping demand curve for the various resources.

Just as supply decisions of businesses and the demand decisions of consumers determine prices in the product market, so the supply decisions of households and demand decisions of businesses set prices in the resource market.

"Other Things Equal" Revisited

Recall from Chapter 1 that as a substitute for their inability to conduct controlled experiments, economists invoke the "other things being equal" assumption in their analyses. We have seen in the present chapter that a number of forces bear on both supply and demand. Hence, in locating specific supply and demand curves, such as D_1 and S in Figure 4-6a, economists isolate the impact of what they judge to be the most important influence on the amounts supplied and demanded—the price of the specific product under consideration. In thus representing the laws of demand and supply by downsloping and upsloping curves respectively, the economist assumes that the determinants of demand (incomes, tastes, and so forth) and supply (resource prices, technology, and other factors) are constant or unchanging. That is, price and quantity demanded are inversely related, *other things being equal*. And price and quantity supplied are directly related, *other things being equal*.

If you forget the "other things equal" assumption, you can encounter situations which *seem* to be in conflict with the laws of demand and supply. For example, suppose Ford sells 200,000 Escorts in 1990 at $8000; 300,000 at $8500 in 1991; and 400,000 in 1992 at $9000. Price and the number purchased vary *directly,* and these real-world data seem to be at odds with the law of demand. But there is really not a conflict here; these data do *not* refute the law of demand. The catch is that the law of demand's "other things equal" assumption has been violated over the three years in the example. Specifically, because of, for example, growing incomes, population growth, and relatively high gasoline prices which increase the attractiveness of compact cars, the demand curve for Escorts has increased over the years—shifted to the right as from D_1 to D_2 in Figure 4-6a—causing price to rise and, simultaneously, a larger quantity to be purchased.

Conversely, consider Figure 4-6d. Comparing the original S_1D and the new S_2D equilibrium positions, *less* of the product is being sold or supplied at a higher price; that is, price and quantity supplied seem to be *inversely* related, rather than *directly* related as the law of supply indicates. The catch again is that the "other things equal" assumption underlying the upsloping supply curve has been violated. Perhaps production costs have gone up or a specific tax has been levied on this product, shifting the supply curve from S_1 to S_2. These examples also emphasize the importance of our earlier distinction between a "change in quantity demanded (or supplied)" and a "change in demand (supply)."

QUICK REVIEW 4-3

▸ *In competitive markets price adjusts to the equilibrium level at which quantity demanded equals quantity supplied.*

▸ *A change in demand alters both equilibrium price and equilibrium quantity in the same direction as the change in demand.*

▸ *A change in supply causes equilibrium price to change in the opposite direction, but equilibrium quantity to change in the same direction, as the change in supply.*

▸ *Over time equilibrium price and quantity may change in directions which seem at odds with the laws of demand and supply because the "other things equal" assumption is violated.*

APPLICATION: THE FOREIGN EXCHANGE MARKET[6]

We close this chapter by applying our understanding of demand and supply to the **foreign exchange market,** the market where various national currencies are exchanged for one another. At the outset two points merit emphasis.

1 Real-world foreign exchange markets conform closely to the kinds of markets studied in this chapter. These are competitive markets characterized by large numbers of buyers and sellers dealing in a standardized "product" such as the American dollar, the German mark, the British pound, or the Japanese yen.

2 The price or exchange value of a nation's currency is an unusual price in that it links *all* domestic (United States) prices with *all* foreign (say, Japanese or German) prices. Exchange rates enable consumers in one country to translate prices of foreign goods into units of their own currency by multiplying the foreign product price by the exchange rate. For example, if the dollar-yen exchange rate is 1 cent per yen, a Sony cassette player priced at 20,000 yen will cost an American $200 (=20,000 × 1¢). But if the exchange rate is 2 cents per yen, the Sony will cost an American $400 (=20,000 × 2¢). Similarly, all other Japanese products will double in price to American buyers. As we shall see, a change in exchange rates has important implications for a nation's levels of domestic production and employment.

The Dollar–Yen Market

Skirting technical details, we now examine how the foreign exchange market for dollars and yen might work. When nations trade they need to exchange their currencies. American exporters who sell to Japan want to be paid in dollars, not yen; but Japanese importers of American goods possess yen, not dollars. This problem is resolved by Japanese offering or supplying yen in exchange for dollars. Conversely, American importers need to pay Japanese exporters with yen, not dollars. To do so they go to the foreign exchange market as demanders of yen. We can think of Japanese importers as suppliers of yen and American importers as demanders of yen. The interaction of the demand for yen and the supply of yen will establish the dollar price of yen. Suppose the equilibrium dollar price of yen—the dollar–yen exchange rate—is $1 = ¥100. That is, a

---

[6]Some instructors may choose to skip this section.

LAST WORD

THE HIGH PRICE OF MARIJUANA

In late 1990 and early 1991 the Drug Enforcement Agency reported that the price of marijuana reached historic highs.

At the start of this decade the price of a "lid" (an ounce) of marijuana ranged from $200 to $400 in the United States. In comparison an ounce of gold was selling for $370.

Simple supply and demand explains this "reefer madness." On the demand side marijuana is by far the nation's most commonly used illegal drug. It is estimated that about one-third of all American adults— some 66 million people—have used pot at least once during their lives. However, the demand for marijuana is declining. In 1979 over 35 percent of all young adults (aged 18–25) used pot at least once a month. By 1990 this figure had declined to less than 13 percent. Stated differently, over 22 million people smoked marijuana in 1979 compared to slightly over 10 million in 1990. Other things the same, a declining demand should mean lower, not higher, pot prices.

But other things have not been the same. For a variety of reasons substantial reductions in marijuana supply have occurred. First, law enforcement in Mexico—a major exporter of pot to the United States— has improved. Second, many pot producers have shifted their resources to alternative drugs. In particu-

lar, Colombia's incredibly profitable cocaine industry has expanded and attracted resources from marijuana. It is also cheaper and easier to smuggle small quantities of cocaine compared to bulky truck- and planeloads of marijuana. Third, the interdiction of pot smugglers has improved; less marijuana is coming over our borders. Finally, within the United States efforts to apprehend marijuana growers and destroy their crops have been increasingly effective.

How to explain the high price of pot? Quite simply: Supply has fallen much more dramatically than has demand.

---

dollar will buy 100 yen (the "dollar price" of 1 yen is 1 cent) and therefore 100 yen worth of Japanese goods. Conversely, 100 yen will buy $1 worth of American goods.

Changing Rates: Depreciation and Appreciation

What might cause this exchange rate to change? The determinants of the demand for and the supply of yen are similar to those we have already discussed. From the vantage point of the United States, several things might take place to increase the demand for —and therefore the dollar price of—yen. Incomes might rise in the United States, causing Americans to buy not only more domestic goods, but also more Sony televisions, Nikon cameras, and Nissan automobiles from Japan. To do this Americans need more yen, so

the demand for yen increases. Or there may be a change in American tastes which enhances our preferences for Japanese goods. For instance, when gasoline prices soared in the 1970s, many American auto buyers shifted their demands from large, gas-guzzling domestic cars to gas-efficient Japanese compact cars. In so doing the demand for yen increased.

The point is that an increase in the American demand for Japanese goods will increase the demand for yen and raise the dollar price of yen. Let's suppose the dollar price of yen rises from $1 = ¥100 (or 1¢ = ¥1) to $2 = ¥100 (or 2¢ = ¥1). When the dollar price of yen *increases,* a **depreciation** of the dollar relative to the yen has occurred. Dollar depreciation means that it takes more dollars (pennies in this case) to buy a single unit of a foreign currency (the yen). A dollar is worth less because it will buy fewer yen and therefore fewer Japanese goods.

If events opposite to those we have presumed had occurred—that is, if incomes rose in Japan and Japanese preferences for American goods strengthened—then the *supply* of yen in foreign exchange markets would increase. This increase in the supply of yen relative to demand would *decrease* the equilibrium dollar price of yen. For example, supply might increase to the extent that the dollar price of yen declines from the original $1 = ¥100, or 1¢ = ¥1, to $.50 = ¥100 or ½¢ = ¥1.

This *decrease* in the dollar price of yen means there has been an **appreciation** of the dollar relative to the yen. Appreciation means it takes fewer dollars (pennies) to buy a single yen than previously. The dollar is worth more because it can purchase more yen and therefore more Japanese goods.

Economic Consequences

The profound consequences of changes in exchange rates are easily perceived. Suppose America is operating at a point inside its production possibilities curve and the dollar depreciates, that is, the dollar price of yen rises from 1¢ = ¥1 to 2¢ = ¥1. This means that the yen and therefore *all* Japanese goods are now more expensive to Americans. Therefore, American consumers shift their expenditures from Japanese to American goods. The Chevy Corsica is now relatively more attractive than the Honda Accord to American consumers. American industries are stimulated by this shift in expenditures and their production and employment both rise. Conversely, Japanese export industries find the sales of their products diminishing, so output and employment both tend to decline. The depreciation of the dollar has caused America to become more prosperous and Japan less so.

You are urged to confirm that an appreciation of the dollar's value relative to the yen will tend to depress the American economy and stimulate the Japanese economy.

With the economic stakes so high, it is easy to understand why governments often interfere with otherwise "free" foreign exchange markets. Thus, the United States government might attempt to depreciate the dollar when our economy is at less than full employment. The problem, however, is that the consequent shift in American expenditures from foreign goods to domestic goods will lower Japanese exports and tend to depress *their* economy. The Japanese government may well be interested in offsetting the depreciation of the dollar which the Americans desire. Both the economic and political implications of exchange rates are great, and they will be considered in later chapters.

CHAPTER SUMMARY

1 A market is any institution or arrangement which brings buyers and sellers of some product or service together.

2 Demand refers to a schedule which summarizes the willingness of buyers to purchase a given product during a specific time period at each of the various prices at which it might be sold. According to the law of demand, consumers will ordinarily buy more of a product at a low price than they will at a high price. Therefore, other things being equal, the relationship between price and quantity demanded is negative or inverse and demand graphs as a downsloping curve.

3 Changes in one or more of the basic determinants of demand—consumer tastes, the number of buyers in the market, the money incomes of consumers, the prices of related goods, and consumer expectations—will cause the market demand curve to shift. A shift to the right is an increase in demand; a shift to the left, a decrease in demand. A "change in demand" is distinguished from a "change in the quantity demanded," the latter involving movement from one point to another point on a fixed demand curve because of a change in the price of the product under consideration.

4 Supply is a schedule showing the amounts of a product which producers would be willing to offer in the market during a given period at each possible price. The law of supply says that, other things equal, producers will offer more of a product at a high price than they will at a low price. As a result, the relationship between price and quantity supplied is a direct one, and the supply curve is upsloping.

5 A change in resource prices, production techniques, taxes or subsidies, the prices of other goods, price expectations, or the number of sellers in the market will cause the supply curve of a product to shift. A shift to the right is an increase in supply; a shift to the left, a decrease in supply. In contrast, a change in the price of the product under consideration will result in a change in the quantity supplied, that is, a movement from one point to another on a given supply curve.

6 Under competition, the interaction of market demand and market supply will adjust price to that point where quantity demanded and quantity supplied are equal. This is the equilibrium price. The corresponding quantity is the equilibrium quantity.

7 The ability of market forces to synchronize selling and buying decisions to eliminate potential surpluses or shortages is termed the "rationing function" of prices.

8 A change in either demand or supply will cause equilibrium price and quantity to change. There is a positive or direct relationship between a change in demand and the resulting changes in equilibrium price and quantity. Though the relationship between a change in supply and resulting change in equilibrium price is inverse, the relationship between a change in supply and equilibrium quantity is direct.

9 The concepts of supply and demand also apply to the resource market.

10 The foreign exchange market is an important application of demand and supply analysis. Foreign importers are suppliers of their currencies and American importers are demanders of foreign currencies. The resulting equilibrium exchange rates link the price levels of all nations.

11 Depreciation of the dollar reduces our imports and stimulates our domestic economy; dollar appreciation increases our imports and depresses our domestic economy.

TERMS AND CONCEPTS

market	normal (superior) good	supply	rationing function of
demand	inferior good	supply schedule	prices
demand schedule	substitute goods	(curve)	foreign exchange
(curve)	complementary goods	law of supply	market
law of demand	change in demand	surplus	depreciation and
diminishing marginal	(supply) versus	shortage	appreciation of the
utility	change in the	equilibrium price and	dollar
income and	quantity demanded	quantity	
substitution effects	(supplied)		

QUESTIONS AND STUDY SUGGESTIONS

1 Explain the law of demand. Why does a demand curve slope downward? What are the determinants of demand? What happens to the demand curve when each of these determinants changes? Distinguish between a change in demand and a change in the quantity demanded, noting the cause(s) of each.

2 Critically evaluate: "In comparing the two equilibrium positions in Figure 4-6a, I note that a larger amount is actually purchased at a higher price. This refutes the law of demand."

3 Explain the law of supply. Why does the supply curve slope upward? What are the determinants of supply? What happens to the supply curve when each of these determinants changes? Distinguish between a change in supply and a change in the quantity supplied, noting the cause(s) of each.

4 Explain the following news dispatch from Hull, England: "The fish market here slumped today to what local commentators called 'a disastrous level'—all because of a shortage of potatoes. The potatoes are one of the main ingredients in a dish that figures on almost every café-menu—fish and chips."

5 Suppose the total demand for wheat and the total supply of wheat per month in the Kansas City grain market are as follows:

Thousands of bushels demanded	Price per bushel	Thousands of bushels supplied	Surplus (+) or shortage (−)
85	$3.40	72	_____
80	3.70	73	_____
75	4.00	75	_____
70	4.30	77	_____
65	4.60	79	_____
60	4.90	81	_____

a What will be the market or equilibrium price? What is the equilibrium quantity? Using the surplus-shortage column, explain why your answers are correct.

b Using the above data, graph the demand for wheat and the supply of wheat. Be sure to label the axes of your graph correctly. Label equilibrium price *"P"* and equilibrium quantity *"Q."*

c Why will $3.40 not be the equilibrium price in this market? Why not $4.90? "Surpluses drive prices up; shortages drive them down." Do you agree?

d Now suppose that the government establishes a ceiling price of, say, $3.70 for wheat. Explain carefully the effects of this ceiling price. Demonstrate your answer graphically. What might prompt government to establish a ceiling price?

e Assume now that the government establishes a price floor of, say, $4.60 for wheat. Explain carefully the effects of this supported price. Demonstrate your answer graphically. What might prompt the government to establish this price support?

f "Legally fixed prices strip the price mechanism of its rationing function." Explain this statement in terms of your answers to 5d and 5e.

6 Given supply, what effect will each of the following have on the demand for, and the equilibrium price and quantity of, product B?

a Product B becomes more fashionable.

b The price of product C, a good substitute for B, goes down.

c Consumers anticipate declining prices and falling incomes.

d There is a rapid upsurge in population growth.

7 Given demand, what effect will each of the following have on the supply and equilibrium price and quantity of product B?

a A technological advance in the methods of producing B.

b A decline in the number of firms in industry B.

c An increase in the prices of resources required in the production of B.

d The expectation that the equilibrium price of B will be lower in the future than it is currently.

e A decline in the price of product A, a good whose production requires substantially the same techniques and resources as does the production of B.

f The levying of a specific sales tax on B.

g The granting of a 50-cent per unit subsidy for each unit of B produced.

8 Explain and illustrate graphically the effect of:

a An increase in income on the demand curve of an inferior good.

b A drop in the price of product S on the demand for substitute product T.

c A decline in income on the demand curve of a normal good.

d An increase in the price of product J on the demand for complementary good K.

9 "In the corn market, demand often exceeds supply and supply sometimes exceeds demand." "The price of corn rises and falls in response to changes in supply and demand." In which of these two statements are the terms "supply" and "demand" used correctly? Explain.

10 How will each of the following changes in demand and/or supply affect equilibrium price and equilibrium quantity in a competitive market; that is, do price and quantity *rise, fall, remain unchanged,* or are the answers *indeterminate,* depending on the magnitudes of the shifts in supply and demand? You should rely on a supply and demand diagram to verify answers.

a Supply decreases and demand remains constant.

b Demand decreases and supply remains constant.

c Supply increases and demand is constant.

d Demand increases and supply increases.

e Demand increases and supply is constant.

f Supply increases and demand decreases.

g Demand increases and supply decreases.

h Demand decreases and supply decreases.

11 "Prices are the automatic regulator that tends to keep production and consumption in line with each other." Explain.

12 Explain: "Even though parking meters may yield little or no net revenue, they should nevertheless be retained because of the rationing function they perform."

13 Use two market diagrams to explain how an increase in state subsidies to public colleges might affect tuition and enrollments in both public and private colleges.

14 What effects would United States import quotas on Japanese automobiles have on the American price of Japanese cars *and* on the demand for, and price of, American-made cars?

15 Many states have had usury laws stipulating the maximum interest rate which lenders (commercial banks, savings and loan associations, etc.) can charge borrowers. Indicate in some detail what would happen in the loan market during periods when the equilibrium interest rate exceeds the stipulated maximum. On the basis of your analysis, do you favor usury laws?

16 Explain why labor unions—whose members are paid wage rates far above the legal minimum—strongly and actively support increases in the minimum wage.

17 "Our imports create a demand for foreign monies; foreign imports of our goods generate supplies of foreign monies." Do you agree? Other things being equal, would a decline in American incomes or a weakening of American preferences for foreign products cause the dollar to depreciate or appreciate? What would be the effects of that depreciation or appreciation on production and employment domestically and abroad?

18 **Advanced analysis:** Assume that demand for a commodity is represented by the equation $P = 10 - .2Q_d$ and supply by the equation $P = 2 + .2Q_s$, where Q_d and Q_s are quantity demanded and quantity supplied, respectively, and P is price. Using the equilibrium condition $Q_s = Q_d$, solve the equations to determine equilibrium price. Now determine equilibrium quantity. Graph the two equations to substantiate your answers.

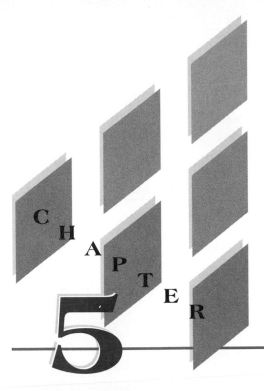

C H A P T E R 5

The Private Sectors and the Market System

Chapters 5 and 6 will put meat on the bare-bones model of capitalism developed thus far. In this chapter we consider the private sectors—households, businesses, and the foreign sector. Chapter 6 is devoted to the public or governmental sector.

Our main goals in this chapter are twofold:

1 Households and businesses are the primary *decision makers* in our economy and we need to know more about them. We flesh out our discussion of a market economy by exploring the characteristics of the household, business, and foreign components of the private economy.

2 A system of markets and prices is the basic *coordinating mechanism* of a capitalistic system. We will examine how the market system synchronizes the innumerable decisions of the consumers, businesses, and resource suppliers which comprise the private sector.

HOUSEHOLDS AS INCOME RECEIVERS

The household sector of American capitalism is currently composed of some 94 million households. These households are the ultimate suppliers of all economic resources and simultaneously the major spending group in the economy. We will consider households first as income receivers and second as spenders.

There are two related approaches to studying the facts of income distribution.

1 The **functional distribution** of income indicates how society's money income is divided among wages, rents, interest, and profits. Here total income is distributed according to the function performed by the income receiver. Wages are paid to labor, rents and interest compensate property resources, and profits flow to the owners of corporations and unincorporated businesses.

2 The **personal distribution** of income shows the way total money income of society is apportioned among individual households.

The Functional Distribution of Income

The functional distribution of the nation's total earned income for 1991 is shown in Figure 5-1. Clearly the largest source of income for households is the wages and salaries paid to workers by the businesses and governmental units hiring them. In our capitalist system the bulk of total income goes to labor and not to

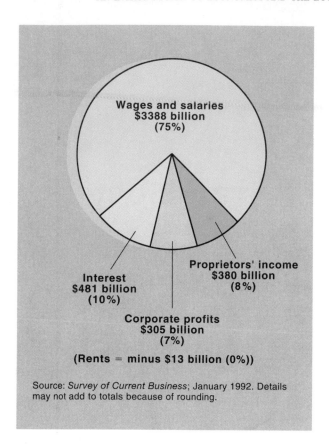

Wages and salaries
$3388 billion
(75%)

Interest
$481 billion
(10%)

Corporate profits
$305 billion
(7%)

Proprietors' income
$380 billion
(8%)

(Rents = minus $13 billion (0%))

Source: *Survey of Current Business*; January 1992. Details may not add to totals because of rounding.

	Billions of dollars	Percent of total
Wages and salaries	$3388	75
Proprietors' income	380	8
Corporate profits	305	7
Interest	481	10
Rents	−13	0
Total earnings	$4541	100

FIGURE 5-1   The functional distribution of income, 1991

Almost three-fourths of national income is received as wages and salaries. Capitalist income—corporate profits, interest, and rents—only account for less than one-fifth of total income. (The "rents" figure is negative because depreciation exceeded rental income.)

"capital." Proprietors' income—that is, the incomes of doctors, lawyers, small business owners, farmers, and other unincorporated enterprises—is in fact a combination of wage, profit, rent, and interest incomes. The other three sources of earnings are virtually self-defining. Some households own corporate stock and receive dividend income on their holdings. Many households also own bonds and savings accounts which yield interest income. Rental income results from households providing buildings, land, and other natural resources to businesses.

Personal Distribution of Income

Figure 5-2 is an overall view of how total income is distributed among households. Here we divide families into five numerically equal groups or *quintiles* and show the percentage of total income received by each group. In 1990 the poorest 20 percent of all families received less than 5 percent of total personal income in contrast to the 20 percent they would have received if income were equally distributed. In comparison the richest 20 percent of all families received over 44 per-

cent of personal income. Thus the richest fifth of the population received almost ten times as much income as the poorest fifth. Given these data, most economists agree there is considerable inequality in the distribution of income.

HOUSEHOLDS AS SPENDERS

How do households dispose of the income they earn? Part flows to government in the form of personal taxes, and the rest is divided between personal consumption expenditures and personal saving. Specifically, households disposed of their total personal income in 1991 as shown in Figure 5-3.[1]

Personal Taxes

Personal taxes, of which the Federal personal income tax is the major component, have risen sharply in both

[1] The income concepts used in Figures 5-1 and 5-3 are different, accounting for the quantitative discrepancy between "total income" in the two figures.

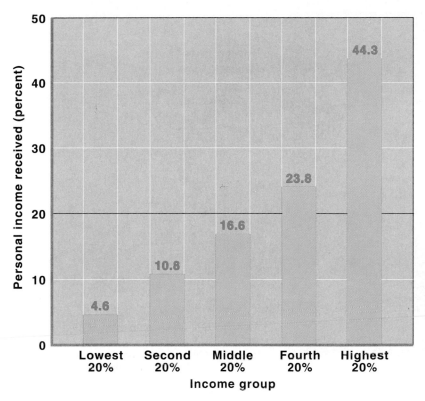

FIGURE 5-2 The distribution of income among families, 1990

Personal income is quite unequally distributed in the United States. An equal distribution would mean that all vertical bars would be equal to the horizontal line drawn at 20 percent; each 20 percent of the families would get 20 percent of total personal income. In fact, the richest fifth of the families gets almost ten times as much income as does the poorest fifth.

absolute and relative terms since World War II. In 1941, households paid $3.3 billion, or about 3 percent of their $95.3 billion total income, in personal taxes, compared to $616 billion, or about 13 percent of that year's $4724 billion total income in 1991.

Personal Saving

Economists define saving as "that part of after-tax income which is *not* consumed"; hence, households have just two choices with their incomes after taxes— to consume or to save.

Saving is defined as that portion of current (this year's) income not paid out in taxes or in the purchase of consumer goods, but which flows into bank accounts, insurance policies, bonds and stocks, and other financial assets.

Reasons for saving are many and diverse, but they center around *security* and *speculation*. Households save to provide a nest egg for unforeseen contingencies—sickness, accident, unemployment—for retirement from the work force, to finance the education of children, or simply for the overall financial security of one's family. On the other hand, saving might well occur for speculation. One might channel part of one's

income to the purchase of securities, speculating as to increases in their monetary values.

The desire or willingness to save, however, is not enough. This willingness must be accompanied by the *ability* to save, which depends basically on the size of one's income. If income is very low, households may *dissave;* that is, they may consume in excess of their after-tax incomes. They do this by borrowing and by digging into savings they may have accumulated in years when their incomes were higher. However, both saving and consumption vary directly with income; as households get more income, they divide it between saving and consumption. In fact, the top 10 percent of income receivers account for most of the personal saving in our society.

Personal Consumption Expenditures

Figure 5-3 shows that the bulk of total income flows from income receivers back into the business sector of the economy as personal consumption expenditures.

The size and composition of the economy's total output depend to a great extent on the size and composition of the flow of consumer spending. It is thus imperative that we examine how households divide their

AN INTRODUCTION TO ECONOMICS AND THE ECONOMY

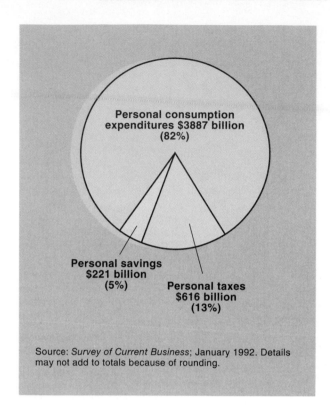

	Billions of dollars	Percent of total
Personal taxes	$ 616	13
Personal saving	221	5
Personal consumption expenditures	3887	82
Total income	$4724	100

Source: *Survey of Current Business*; January 1992. Details may not add to totals because of rounding.

FIGURE 5-3   The disposition of household income, 1991

Household income is apportioned between taxes, saving, and consumption, with consumption being the dominant use of income.

expenditures among the various goods and services competing for their dollars. The U.S. Department of Commerce classifies consumer spending as (1) expenditures on durables, (2) expenditures on nondurables, and (3) expenditures on services. If a product generally has an expected life of one year or more, it is called a **durable good;** if its life is less than one year, it is labeled **nondurable.** Automobiles, video recorders, washing machines, personal computers, and most furniture are good examples of consumer durables. Most food and clothing items are representative of nondurables. **Services** refer to the services which lawyers, barbers, doctors, mechanics, and others provide to consumers. Note in Table 5-1 that *ours is a service-oriented economy in that over one-half of consumer outlays are for services.*

This threefold breakdown, detailed in Table 5-1, implies that many consumer outlays are discretionary or postponable. During prosperity, durable, or "hard," goods are typically traded in or scrapped before they become utterly useless. This is ordinarily the case with automobiles and most major household appliances. But if a recession materializes, consumers tend to forgo expenditures on durables, having little choice but to put up with an old model car and outdated house-

hold appliances. The desire to conserve dollars for the nondurable necessities of food and clothing may cause a radical shrinkage of expenditures on durables. Much the same is true of many services. True, one cannot postpone an operation for acute appendicitis. But education, dental work, and a wide variety of less pressing services can be deferred or, if necessary, forgone entirely. In brief, the durable goods and services segments of personal consumption expenditures are subject to much more variation over time than are expenditures on nondurables.

QUICK REVIEW 5-1

♦   *The functional distribution of income indicates how income is divided among wages, rents, interest, and profits; the personal distribution of income shows how income is apportioned among households.*

♦   *Wages and salaries are the major component of the functional distribution of income. The personal distribution reveals considerable inequality.*

♦   *Over 80 percent of household income is consumed, the remainder being saved or paid in taxes.*

♦   *Over half of consumer spending is for services.*

TABLE 5-1 **The composition of personal consumption expenditures, 1991***

Types of consumption	Amount (billions of dollars)	Percent of total
Durable goods	$ 445	11
Motor vehicles and parts	$184	5
Furniture and household equipment	172	4
All others	90	2
Nondurable goods	1251	32
Food	619	16
Clothing and shoes	211	5
Gasoline and oil	103	3
Fuel oil and coal	12	1
All others	307	8
Services	2191	56
Housing	575	15
Household operations	225	6
Medical care	577	15
Transportation	156	4
Personal services, recreation, and others	658	17
Personal consumption expenditures	$3887	100

*Excludes interest paid to businesses.

Sources: Survey of Current Business, January 1992. Details may not add to totals because of rounding.

THE BUSINESS POPULATION

Businesses constitute the second major aggregate of the private sector. To avoid confusion, we preface our discussion with some comments on terminology. In particular, we must distinguish among a plant, a firm, and an industry.

1 A **plant** is a physical establishment in the form of a factory, farm, mine, retail or wholesale store, or warehouse which performs one or more specific functions in the fabrication and distribution of goods and services.

2 A business **firm,** on the other hand, is the business organization which owns and operates these plants. Although most firms operate only one plant, many own and operate a number of plants. Multiplant firms may be "horizontal," "vertical," or "conglomerate" combinations. For example, without exception all the large steel firms of our economy—USX Corporation (United States Steel), Bethlehem Steel, Republic Steel, and the others—are **vertical combinations** of plants; that is, each company owns plants at various

stages of the production process. Each steelmaker owns ore and coal mines, limestone quarries, coke ovens, blast furnaces, rolling mills, forge shops, foundries, and, in some cases, fabricating shops.

The large chain stores in the retail field— A&P, Kroger, Safeway, J.C. Penney—are **horizontal combinations** in that each plant is at the same stage of production. Other firms are **conglomerates;** they comprise plants which operate across many different markets and industries. For example, International Telephone and Telegraph, apart from operations implied by its name, is involved through affiliated plants on a large-scale basis in such diverse fields as hotels, baking products, educational materials, and insurance.

3 An **industry** is a group of firms producing the same, or at least similar, products. Though an apparently uncomplicated concept, industries are usually difficult to identify in practice. For example, how do we identify the automobile industry? The simplest answer is, "All firms producing automobiles." But automobiles are heterogeneous products. While Cadillacs and Buicks are similar products, and Buicks and Fords are similar, and Fords and Geos are similar, it is clear that Geos and Cadillacs are very dissimilar. At least most buyers think so. And what about trucks? Certainly, small pickup trucks are similar in some respects to station wagons. Is it better to speak of the "motor vehicle industry" rather than of the "automobile industry"?

This matter of delineating an industry becomes even more complex because most enterprises are multiproduct firms. American automobile manufacturers are also responsible for such diverse products as diesel locomotives, buses, refrigerators, guided missiles, and air conditioners. As you can see, industry classifications are usually somewhat arbitrary.

LEGAL FORMS OF BUSINESS ENTERPRISES

The business population is extremely diverse, ranging from giant corporations like General Motors with 1990 sales of $126 billion and 761,000 employees to neighborhood speciality shops and "mom and pop" groceries with one or two employees and sales of only $100 or $150 per day. This diversity makes it necessary to classify business firms by some criterion such as legal structure, industry or product, or size. Figure 5-4 shows how the business population is distributed among the three major legal forms: (1) the sole proprietorship, (2) the partnership, and (3) the corporation.

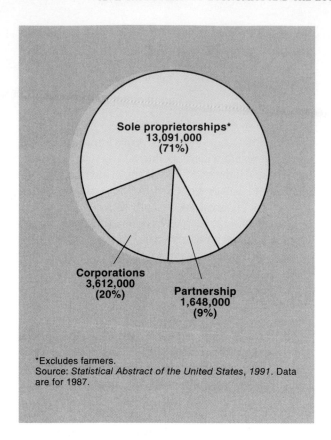

Sole proprietorships*
13,091,000
(71%)

Corporations
3,612,000
(20%)

Partnership
1,648,000
(9%)

*Excludes farmers.
Source: *Statistical Abstract of the United States, 1991.* Data are for 1987.

The business population by form of legal organization and volume of sales

Form	Number of firms	Percent of total	Volume of sales (billions)	Percent of total
Sole pro- prietorships*	13,091,000	71	$ 611	6
Partnerships	1,648,000	9	411	4
Corporations	3,612,000	20	9,185	90
Total	18,351,000	100	$10,207	100

*Excludes farmers.

FIGURE 5-4   The business population by form of legal organization
Although sole proprietorships dominate the business population numerically, corporations account for 90 percent of total sales.

Sole Proprietorship

A **sole proprietorship** is literally an individual in business for himself or herself. The proprietor owns or obtains the materials and capital equipment needed by the business and personally supervises its operation.

Advantages   This simple type of business organization has certain distinct advantages:
1   A sole proprietorship is very easy to organize—there is virtually no legal red tape or expense.
2   The proprietor is his or her own boss and has substantial freedom of action. Since the proprietor's profit income depends on the enterprise's success, there is a strong and immediate incentive to manage the affairs of the business efficiently.

Disadvantages   But the disadvantages of this form of business organization are great. They include financial restrictions on firm growth, the inability to specialize in management, and the fact that all of a proprietor's assets are potentially available to creditors.

1   With rare exceptions, the financial resources of a sole proprietorship are insufficient to permit the firm to grow into a large-scale enterprise. Finances are usually limited to what the proprietor has in his or her bank account and to what he or she can borrow. Since proprietorships often fail, commercial banks are not eager to extend much credit to them.
2   Being in complete control of an enterprise forces the proprietor to carry out all basic management functions. A proprietor must make all basic decisions concerning buying, selling, and the hiring and training of personnel, not to mention the technical aspects involved in producing, advertising, and distributing the product. In short, the potential benefits of specialization in business management are usually inaccessible to the typical small-scale proprietorship.
3   Most important of all, the proprietor is subject to *unlimited liability.* Individuals in business for themselves risk not only the assets of the firm but also their personal assets. If assets of an unsuccessful proprietorship are insufficient to satisfy the claims of creditors, those creditors can file claims against the proprietor's personal property.

Partnership

The **partnership** form of business organization is more or less a natural outgrowth of the sole proprietorship. Partnerships were developed to overcome some of the major shortcomings of proprietorships. In a partnership, two or more individuals agree to own and operate a business. Usually they pool their financial resources and business skills. Similarly, they share the risks and the profits or losses.

Advantages   What are the advantages of a partnership arrangement?
1   Like the sole proprietorship, it is easy to organize. Although a written agreement is almost invariably involved, legal red tape is not great.
2   Greater specialization in management is possible because there are more participants.
3   Again, because there are several participants, the odds are that the financial resources of a partnership will be greater than those of a sole proprietorship. Partners can pool their money capital and are usually somewhat better risks in the eyes of lending institutions.

Disadvantages   The partnership often does less to overcome the shortcomings of the proprietorship than first appears, and raises some new potential problems which the sole proprietorship does not have.
1   Whenever several people participate in management, this division of authority can lead to inconsistent, divided policies or to inaction when action is required. Worse yet, partners may flatly disagree on basic policy. For all these reasons, management in a partnership may be unwieldy and cumbersome.
2   The finances of partnerships are still limited, although generally superior to those of a sole proprietorship. But the financial resources of three or four partners may still not be enough for the growth of a successful enterprise.
3   The continuity of a partnership is very precarious. The withdrawal or death of a partner generally means dissolution and complete reorganization of the firm, disrupting its operations.
4   Finally, unlimited liability plagues a partnership, just as it does a proprietorship. In fact, each partner is liable for all business debts incurred, not only as a result of each partner's own management decisions, but also as a consequence of the actions of any other partner. A wealthy partner risks money on the prudence of less affluent partners.

Corporation

Corporations are legal entities, distinct and separate from the individuals who own them. As such, these governmentally designated "legal persons" can acquire resources, own assets, produce and sell products, incur debts, extend credit, sue and be sued, and carry on all those functions which any other type of enterprise performs.

Advantages   The advantages of the corporate form of business enterprise have catapulted it into a dominant position in modern American capitalism. Although corporations are relatively small in number (Table 5-2), they are frequently large in size and scale of operations. Although only 20 percent of all businesses are corporations, they account for roughly 90 percent of all business sales.
1   The corporation is by far the most effective form of business organization for raising money capital. As this chapter's Last Word reveals, the corporation features unique methods of finance—the selling of stocks and bonds—which allow the firm to tap the savings of untold thousands of households. Through the securities market, corporations can pool the financial resources of extremely large numbers of people.

Financing by the sale of securities also has advantages from the viewpoint of the purchasers of these securities. First, households can now participate in enterprise and share the expected monetary reward therefrom without assuming an active part in management. In addition, an individual can spread any risks by buying the securities of several corporations. Finally, it is usually easy for the holder of corporate securities to dispose of these holdings. Organized stock exchanges facilitate transfer of securities among buyers and sellers, which increases the willingness of savers to buy corporate securities.

Corporations have easier access to bank credit than other types of business organizations. Corporations are better risks and are more likely to provide banks with profitable accounts.
2   Corporations have the distinct advantage of **limited liability.** The owners (stockholders) of a corporation risk *only* what they paid for the stock purchased. Their personal assets are not at stake if the corporation founders on the rocks of bankruptcy. Creditors can sue the corporation as a legal person, but not the owners of the corporation as individuals. Limited liability clearly eases the corporation's task in acquiring money capital.

3 Because of their advantage in attracting money capital, successful corporations find it easier to expand the size and scope of their operations and to realize associated advantages. In particular, corporations can take advantage of mass-production technologies. Similarly, size permits greater specialization in the use of human resources. While the manager of a sole proprietorship may be forced to share her time between production, accounting, and marketing functions, a corporation can hire specialized personnel in these areas and achieve greater efficiency.

4 As a legal entity, the corporation has a life independent of its owners and, for that matter, of its individual officers. Proprietorships are subject to sudden and unpredictable demise, but, legally at least, corporations are immortal. The transfer of corporate ownership through the sale of stock will not disrupt the continuity of the corporation. Corporations have a certain permanence, lacking in other forms of business organization, which is conducive to long-range planning and growth.

Disadvantages The corporation's advantages are of tremendous significance and typically override any accompanying disadvantages. Yet the following drawbacks of the corporate form of organization merit mentioning:

1 There are some red tape and legal expense in obtaining a corporate charter.

2 From the social point of view, the corporate form of enterprise lends itself to certain abuses. Because the corporation is a legal entity, unscrupulous business owners sometimes can avoid personal responsibility for questionable business activities by adopting the corporate form of enterprise. And, despite legislation to the contrary, the corporate form of organization has been a cornerstone for the issue and sale of worthless securities. Note, however, that these are potential abuses of the corporate form, not inherent defects.

3 A further disadvantage of corporations is the **double taxation** of corporate income. That part of corporate income paid out as dividends to stockholders is taxed twice—once as part of corporate profits and again as part of stockholders' personal incomes.

4 In the sole proprietorship and partnership forms, those owning the real and financial assets of the firm also directly manage or control those assets. But, in larger corporations where ownership of common stock is widely diffused over tens or hundreds of thousands of stockholders, a fundamental **separation of ownership and control** will arise. The roots of this cleavage lie in the lethargy of the typical stockholder. Most stockholders do not exercise their voting rights, or, if they do, merely sign these rights over by proxy to the corporation's present officers. And why not? Average stockholders know little or nothing about the efficiency with which "their" corporation is being managed. Because the typical stockholder may own only 1000 of 15,000,000 shares of common stock outstanding, one vote "really doesn't make a bit of difference." Not voting, or the automatic signing over of one's proxy to current corporate officials, makes those officials self-perpetuating.

The separation of ownership and control is of no fundamental consequence so long as the actions of the control (management) group and the wishes of the ownership (stockholder) group are in accord. In fact, the interests of the two groups are not always identical. Management, seeking the power and prestige which accompany control over a *large* enterprise, may favor unprofitable expansion of the firm's operations. Or a conflict of interest can develop on current dividend policies. What portion of corporate earnings after taxes should be paid out as dividends, and what amount should be retained by the firm as undistributed profits? And corporation officials may vote themselves large salaries, pensions, bonuses, and so forth, out of corporate earnings which might otherwise be used for increased dividend payments. In short, the separation of ownership and control raises important and intriguing questions about the distribution of power and authority, the accountability of corporate managers, and the possibility of intramural conflicts between managers and shareholders.

Incorporate or Not?

The need for money capital is a critical determinant of whether or not a firm incorporates. The money capital required to establish and operate a barbershop, a shoeshine stand, or a small gift shop is modest, making incorporation unnecessary. In contrast, modern technology and a much larger dollar volume of business make incorporation imperative in many lines of production. In most branches of manufacturing—automobiles, steel, fabricated metal products, electrical equipment, and household appliances—substantial money requirements for investment in fixed assets and for working capital are involved. Given these circumstances, there is no choice but to incorporate.

INDUSTRIAL DISTRIBUTION AND BIGNESS

What do the 18.4 million firms which compose the business sector of our economy produce?

Types of Industries

Table 5-2 measures the significance of the various industry classifications in several different ways. Column 2 indicates the numerical and percentage distribution of the business population among various industries. Column 3 shows in both absolute and relative terms the portion of the domestic output originating in various industries. Column 4 indicates the absolute and relative amounts of employment provided by each industry. Several points in Table 5-2 are noteworthy:

1 Many firms are engaged in agriculture, but agriculture is relatively insignificant as a provider of incomes and jobs. This implies that agriculture comprises a large number of small, competitive producers.
2 The wholesale and retail industries and the service industries (hotels, motels, and personal services) are heavily populated with firms and are simultaneously important sources of employment and incomes in the economy.

3 Table 5-2 reminds us that not all the economy's income and employment originate in private domestic enterprises. Government and foreign enterprises account for about 13 percent of the economy's domestic output and employ about 16 percent of the labor force.
4 The relatively small number of firms in manufacturing account for almost one-fifth of domestic output and total employment. These figures correctly suggest that our economy is highly industrialized, characterized by gigantic business corporations in its manufacturing industries. This point merits brief elaboration.

Big Business

To what degree does big business prevail in our economy? Casual evidence suggests that many of our major industries are dominated by corporate giants which enjoy assets and annual sales revenues of billions of dollars, employ hundreds of thousands of workers, have a hundred thousand or more stockholders, and earn annual profits after taxes running into hundreds of millions of dollars. We have already cited the vital statistics of General Motors, America's largest corporation, for 1990: sales, about $126 *billion;* assets, about $180 *billion;* employees, about 761,000. Remarkably, there are only 20 or so nations in the world whose

TABLE 5-2 **Industry classes: number of firms, domestic output originating, and employment provided***

(1) Industry	(2) Number of private businesses		(3) Contribution to domestic output		(4) Workers employed	
	Thousands	Percent	Billions	Percent	Thousands	Percent
Agriculture, forestry, and fisheries	2,088	11	$ 114	2	2,863	3
Mining	258	1	80	2	735	1
Construction	2,067	11	248	5	5,204	5
Manufacturing	686	4	966	18	19,063	17
Wholesale and retail trade	3,521	18	826	16	26,150	23
Finance, insurance, and real estate	2,571	13	897	17	6,832	6
Transportation, communications, and public utilities	824	4	461	9	5,839	5
Services	7,384	38	971	19	28,208	25
Government			619	12	18,291	16
Rest of world			38	1		
Total	19,399	100	$5,220	100	113,185	100

*Column 2 is for 1987; 3 for 1989; and 4 for 1990. Includes farms.
Source: Statistical Abstract of the United States, 1991, p. 526; and Survey of Current Business. Details may not add to totals because of rounding.

ingness to buy X will depend on one's preference for X compared to available close substitutes for X and their relative prices. Thus, product prices play a key role in determining spending patterns of consumers.

There is nothing particularly ethical about the market system as a mechanism for distributing output. Households which accumulate large amounts of property resources by inheritance, through hard work and frugality, through business acumen, or by crook will receive large incomes and thus command large shares of the economy's total output. Others, offering unskilled and relatively unproductive labor resources which elicit low wages, will receive meager money incomes and small portions of total output.

Accommodating Change

Industrial societies are dynamic: Consumer preferences, technology, and resource supplies all change. This means that the particular allocation of resources which is *now* the most efficient for a *given* pattern of consumer tastes, for a *given* range of technological alternatives, and for *given* supplies of resources will become obsolete and inefficient as consumer preferences change, new techniques of production are discovered, and resource supplies alter over time. Can the market economy negotiate adjustments to these changes so that resources are still used efficiently?

Guiding Function of Prices Suppose consumer tastes change. Specifically, assume that, because of greater health consciousness, consumers decide they want more exercise bikes and fewer cigarettes than the economy currently provides. This change in consumers' taste will be communicated to producers through an increase in demand for bikes and a decline in demand for cigarettes. Bike prices will rise and cigarette prices will fall. Now, assuming firms in both industries were enjoying precisely normal profits before these changes in consumer demand, higher exercise bike prices mean economic profits for the bike industry, and lower cigarette prices mean losses for the cigarette industry. Self-interest induces new competitors to enter the prosperous bike industry. Losses will in time force firms to leave the depressed cigarette industry.

But these adjustments are both self-limiting. The expansion of the bike industry will continue only until the resulting increase in the market supply of bikes brings bike prices back down to a level where normal profits again prevail. Similarly, contraction in the cigarette industry will persist until the accompanying decline in the market supply of cigarettes brings cigarette

prices up to a level where remaining firms can receive a normal profit. Or, in the extreme, the cigarette industry may cease to exist.

The point is that these adjustments in the business sector are completely appropriate to changes in consumer tastes. Society—meaning consumers—wants more exercise bikes and fewer cigarettes, and that is precisely what it is getting as the bike industry expands and the cigarette industry contracts. These adjustments, incidentally, portray the concept of consumer sovereignty at work.

This analysis assumes that resource suppliers are agreeable to these adjustments. Will the market system prompt resource suppliers to reallocate their human and property resources from the cigarette to the bike industry, thereby permitting the output of bikes to expand at the expense of cigarette production? The answer is "Yes."

The economic profits which initially follow the increase in demand for bikes will not only provide that industry with the inducement to expand but will also give it the revenue needed to obtain the resources essential to its growth. Higher bike prices will permit firms in that industry to pay higher prices for resources, thereby drawing resources from what are now less urgent alternative employments. Willingness and ability to employ more resources in the exercise bike industry will be communicated back into the resource market through an increase in the demand for resources.

The reverse occurs in the adversely affected cigarette industry. The losses which the decline in consumer demand initially entails will cause a decline in the demand for resources in that industry. Workers and other resources released from the contracting cigarette industry can now find employment in the expanding bike industry. Furthermore, the increased demand for resources in the bike industry will mean higher resource prices in that industry than those being paid in the cigarette industry, where declines in resource demand have lowered resource prices. The resulting differential in resource prices will provide the incentive for resource owners to further their self-interests by reallocating their resources from the cigarette to the bike industry. And this is the precise shift needed to permit the bike industry to expand and the cigarette industry to contract.

The ability of the market system to communicate changes in such basic data as consumer tastes and to elicit appropriate responses from both businesses and resource suppliers is called the **directing** or **guiding function of prices.** By affecting product prices and profits, changes in consumer tastes direct the expansion of some industries and the contraction of others. These adjustments carry through to the resource market as expanding industries demand more resources and contracting industries demand fewer. The resulting changes in resource prices guide resources from the contracting to the expanding industries. Without a market system, some administrative agency, presumably a governmental planning board, would have to direct business institutions and resources into specific lines of production.

Similar analysis would indicate that the market system would adjust to similar fundamental changes—for example, to changes in technology and in the relative supplies of various resources.

Initiating Progress Adjusting to changes is one thing; initiating changes, particularly desirable changes, is something else again. Is the competitive market system congenial to technological improvements and capital accumulation—the interrelated changes which lead to greater productivity and a higher level of material well-being for society? This question is not easy to answer. Our answer at this point will not consider qualifications and modifications.

Technological Advance The competitive market system contains the incentive for technological advance. New cost-cutting techniques give the innovating firm a temporary advantage over its rivals. Lower production costs mean economic profits for the pioneering firm. By passing part of its cost reduction to the consumer through a lower product price, the firm can increase sales and obtain economic profits at the expense of rival firms. Furthermore, the competitive market system provides an environment favorable to the rapid spread of a technological advance. Rivals *must* follow the lead of the most progressive firm or suffer immediate losses and eventual bankruptcy.

The lower product price which technological advance permits will cause the innovating industry to expand. This expansion may be the result of existing firms' expanding their rates of output or of new firms entering the industry lured by the economic profits initially created by technological advance. This expansion, that is, the diversion of resources from less progressive to more progressive industries, is as it should be. Sustained efficiency in the use of scarce resources demands that resources be continually reallocated from industries whose productive techniques are relatively less efficient to those whose techniques are relatively more efficient.

Capital Accumulation But technological advance typically requires increased amounts of capital goods. The entrepreneur as an innovator can command through the market system the resources necessary to produce the machinery and equipment upon which technological advance depends.

If society registers dollar votes for capital goods, the product market and the resource market will adjust to these votes by producing capital goods. The market system acknowledges dollar voting for both consumer and capital goods.

But who, specifically, will register votes for capital goods? First, the entrepreneur as a receiver of profit income can be expected to apportion part of that income to accumulation of capital goods. By doing so, an even greater profit income can be achieved in the future if innovation is successful. Furthermore, by paying interest, entrepreneurs can borrow portions of the incomes of households and use these borrowed funds in casting dollar votes for the production of more capital goods.

Competition and Control: The "Invisible Hand"

Though the market system is the organizing mechanism of pure capitalism, competition is the mechanism of control. The market mechanism of supply and demand communicates the wants of consumers (society) to businesses and through businesses to resource suppliers. It is competition, however, which forces businesses and resource suppliers to make appropriate responses.

To illustrate: We have seen that an increase in consumer demand for some product will raise that good's price above the wage, rent, interest, and normal profit costs of production. The resulting economic profits are a signal to producers that society wants more of the product. It is competition—new firms entering the industry—that simultaneously brings an expansion of output and a lowering of price back to a level just consistent with production costs. However, if the industry was dominated by, say, one huge firm (a monopolist) which was able to prohibit entry of potential competitors, that firm could continue to enjoy economic profits by preventing expansion of the industry.

But competition does more than guarantee responses appropriate to the wishes of society. It also forces firms to adopt the most efficient productive techniques. In a competitive market, the failure of some

LAST WORD

THE FINANCING OF CORPORATE ACTIVITY

One of the main advantages of corporations is their ability to finance their operations through the sale of stocks and bonds. It is informative to examine the nature of corporate finance in more detail.

Generally speaking, corporations finance their activities in three different ways. First, a very large portion of a corporation's activity is financed internally out of undistributed corporate profits. Second, like individuals or unincorporated businesses, corporations may borrow from financial institutions. For example, a small corporation which wants to build a new plant or warehouse may obtain the funds from a commercial bank, a savings and loan association, or an insurance company. Third, unique to corporations, common stocks and bonds can be issued.

A common stock is an ownership share. The purchaser of a stock certificate has the right to vote in the selection of corporate officers and to share in any declared dividends. If you own 1000 of the 100,000 shares issued by Specific Motors, Inc. (hereafter SM), then you own 1 percent of the company, are entitled to 1 percent of any dividends declared by the board of directors, and control 1 percent of the votes in the annual election of corporate officials. In contrast, a bond is not an ownership share. A bond purchaser is simply lending money to a corporation. A bond is merely an IOU, in acknowledgment of a loan, whereby the corporation promises to pay the holder a fixed amount at some specified future date and other fixed amounts (interest payments) every year up to the bond's maturity date. For example, one might purchase a ten-year SM bond with a face value of $1000 with a 10 percent stated rate of interest. This means that in exchange for your $1000 SM guarantees you a $100 interest payment for each of the next ten years and then to repay your $1000 principal at the end of that period.

There are clearly important differences between stocks and bonds. First, as noted, the bondholder is not an owner of the company, but is only a lender. Second, bonds are considered to be less risky than stocks for two reasons. On the one hand, bondholders have a "legally prior claim" upon a corporation's earnings. Dividends cannot be paid to stockholders until all interest payments due to bondholders have been paid. On the other hand, holders of SM stock do not know how much their dividends will be or how much they might obtain for their stock if they decide to sell. If Specific Motors falls on hard times, stockholders may receive no dividends at all and the value of their stock

---

firms to use the least costly production technique means their eventual elimination by more efficient firms. Finally, we have seen that competition provides an environment conducive to technological advance.

The operation and adjustments of a competitive market system create a curious and important identity —the identity of private and social interests. Firms and resource suppliers, seeking to further their own self-interest and operating within the framework of a highly competitive market system, will simultaneously, as though guided by an **"invisible hand,"**[2] promote the public or social interest. For example, we have seen

that given a competitive environment, business firms use the least costly combination of resources in producing a given output because it is in their private self-interest to do so. To act otherwise would be to forgo profits or even to risk bankruptcy. But, at the same time, it is clearly also in the social interest to use scarce resources in the least costly, that is, most efficient, manner. Not to do so would be to produce a given output at a greater cost or sacrifice of alternative goods than is necessary.

In our more-bikes–fewer-cigarettes illustration, it is self-interest, awakened and guided by the competitive market system, which induces responses appropriate to the assumed change in society's wants. Businesses seeking to make higher profits and to avoid

[2]Adam Smith, *The Wealth of Nations* (New York: Modern Library, Inc., originally published in 1776), p. 423.

may plummet. Provided the corporation does not go bankrupt, the holder of an SM bond is guaranteed a $100 interest payment each year and the return of his or her $1000 at the end of ten years.

But this is not to imply that the purchase of corporate bonds is riskless. The market value of your SM bond may vary over time in accordance with the financial health of the corporation. If SM encounters economic misfortunes which raise questions about its financial integrity, the market value of your bond may fall. Should you sell the bond prior to maturity you may receive only $600 or $700 for it (rather than $1000) and thereby incur a capital loss.

Changes in interest rates also affect the market prices of bonds. Specifically, increases in interest rates cause bond prices to fall and vice versa. Assume you purchase a $1000 ten-year SM bond this year (1993) when the going interest rate is 10 percent. This obviously means that your bond provides a $100 fixed interest payment each year. But now suppose that by next year the interest rate has jumped to 15 percent and SM must now guarantee a $150 fixed annual payment on its new 1994 $1000 ten-year bonds. Clearly, no sensible person will pay you $1000 for your bond which pays only $100 of interest income per year when new bonds can be purchased for $1000 which pay the holder $150 per year. Hence, if you sell your 1993 bond before maturity, you will suffer a capital loss.

Bondholders face another element of risk due to inflation. If substantial inflation occurs over the ten-year period you hold a SM bond, the $1000 principal repaid to you at the end of that period will represent substantially less purchasing power than the $1000 you loaned to SM ten years earlier. You will have lent "dear" dollars, but will be repaid in "cheap" dollars.

losses, on the one hand, and resource suppliers pursuing greater monetary rewards, on the other, negotiate the changes in the allocation of resources and therefore the composition of output which society demands. The force of competition controls or guides the self-interest motive in such a way that it automatically, and quite unintentionally, furthers the best interests of society. The "invisible hand" tells us that when firms maximize their profits, society's domestic output is also maximized.

The Case for the Market System

The virtues of the market system are implicit in our discussion of its operation. Two merit emphasis.

Allocative Efficiency The basic economic argument for the market system is that it promotes an efficient allocation of resources. The competitive market system guides resources into production of those goods and services most wanted by society. It forces use of the most efficient techniques in organizing resources for production, and is conducive to the development and adoption of new and more efficient production techniques. The "invisible hand" will in effect harness self-interest so as to provide society with the greatest output of wanted goods from its available resources. This, then, suggests the maximum economic efficiency. This presumption of allocative efficiency makes most economists hesitant to advocate governmental interference with, or regulation of, free markets unless reasons for such interference are clear and compelling.

Freedom The major noneconomic argument for the market system is its great emphasis on personal freedom. One of the fundamental problems of social organization is how to coordinate the economic activities of large numbers of individuals and businesses. We recall from Chapter 2 that there are two contrasting ways of providing this coordination: one is central direction and the use of coercion; the other is voluntary cooperation through the market system. Only the market system can coordinate economic activity without coercion. The market system permits—indeed, it thrives on—freedom of enterprise and choice. Entrepreneurs and workers are not herded from industry to industry by government directives to meet production targets established by some omnipotent governmental agency. On the contrary, they are free to further their own self-interests, subject, of course, to the rewards and penalties imposed by the market system itself.

QUICK REVIEW 5-3

✦ **The output mix of the competitive market system is determined by profits. Profits cause industries to expand; losses cause them to contract.**

✦ **Competition forces firms to use the least costly (most efficient) production methods.**

✦ **The distribution of output in a market economy is determined by consumer incomes and product prices.**

✦ **Competitive markets reallocate resources in response to changes in consumer tastes, technological progress, and changes in resource supplies.**

CHAPTER SUMMARY

1 The functional distribution of income shows how society's total income is divided among wages, rents, interest, and profits; the personal distribution of income shows how total income is divided among individual households.

2 Households divide their total incomes among personal taxes, saving, and consumer goods. Consumer expenditures on durables and some services are discretionary and therefore postponable.

3 Sole proprietorships, partnerships, and corporations are the major legal forms of business enterprises. Corporations dominate the business sector because they **a** have limited liability, and **b** are in a superior position to acquire money capital for expansion.

4 Ours is a "big business" economy in that many industries are dominated by a small number of large corporations.

5 United States world trade has grown both absolutely and as a proportion of domestic output. The other industrially advanced nations are our major trading partners.

6 International trade yields significant economic benefits in the form of **a** more efficient use of world resources, and **b** enhanced competition. A potential disadvantage is that a nation's international economic interrelationships may create new sources of macroeconomic instability which complicate policy making.

7 Every economy is confronted with Five Fundamental Questions: **a** At what level should available resources be employed? **b** What goods and services are to be produced? **c** How is that output to be produced? **d** To whom should the output be distributed? **e** Can the system adapt to changes in consumer tastes, resource supplies, and technology?

8 Those products whose production and sale yield total revenue sufficient to cover all costs, including a normal profit, will be produced. Those whose production will not yield a normal profit will not be produced.

9 Economic profits designate an industry as prosperous and signal its expansion. Losses mean an industry is unprosperous and result in contraction of that industry.

10 Consumer sovereignty means that both businesses and resource suppliers channel their efforts in accordance with the wants of consumers.

11 Competition forces firms to use the least costly, and therefore the most economically efficient, productive techniques.

12 The prices commanded by the quantities and types of resources supplied by each household will determine the number of dollar claims against the economy's output which each household receives. Within the limits of each household's money income, consumer preferences and the relative prices of products determine the distribution of total output.

13 The competitive market system can communicate changes in consumer tastes to resource suppliers and entrepreneurs, thereby prompting appropriate adjustments in the allocation of the economy's resources. The competitive market system also provides an environment conducive to technological advance and capital accumulation.

14 Competition, the primary mechanism of control in the market economy, will foster an identity of private and social interests; as though directed by an "invisible hand," competition harnesses the self-interest motives of businesses and resource suppliers to simultaneously further the social interest in using scarce resources efficiently.

TERMS AND CONCEPTS

functional and personal distribution of income	firm	separation of ownership and control	expanding industry versus declining industry
durable and nondurable goods	conglomerates	Five Fundamental Questions	consumer sovereignty
services	industry	normal versus economic profits	derived demand
plant	sole proprietorship	dollar votes	directing (guiding) function of prices
horizontal and vertical combinations	partnership		"invisible hand"
	corporation		
	limited liability		
	double taxation		
	economic costs		

QUESTIONS AND STUDY SUGGESTIONS

1 Distinguish between functional and personal distributions of income. What effects do you think a change in the personal distribution of income from that shown in Figure 5-2 to one of complete equality would have on the composition of output and the allocation of resources?

2 What is the demand for consumer durable goods less stable than that for nondurables?

3 Distinguish clearly between a plant, a firm, and an industry. Why is an "industry" often difficult to define in practice?

4 What are the major legal forms of business organization? Briefly state the advantages and disadvantages of each. How do you account for the dominant role of corporations in our economy? Explain and evaluate the separation of ownership and control which characterizes the corporate form of business enterprise.

5 What are the major industries in American capitalism in terms of **a** the number of firms in operation, and **b** the amount of income and employment provided?

6 Explain and evaluate the following statements:

  a "It is the consumer, and the consumer alone, who casts the vote that determines how big any company should be."

  b "The very nature of modern industrial society requires labor, government, and businesses to be 'big' and their bigness renders impossible the functioning of the older, small-scale, simpler, and more flexible capitalist system."

  c "The legal form which an enterprise assumes is dictated primarily by the financial requirements of its particular line of production."

  d "If we want capitalism, we must also accept inequality of income distribution."

7 What is the quantitative importance of world trade to the United States? Explain: "Nations engage in international trade because it allows them to realize the benefits of specialization."

8 How have persistent United States trade deficits been financed? "Trade deficits mean we get more merchandise from the rest of the world than we provide in return. Therefore, trade deficits are economically desirable." Do you agree?

9 Suppose excessive aggregate expenditures in the United States are causing inflation. Explain the effect of **a** appreciation, and **b** depreciation of the dollar on domestic inflation.

10 Describe in detail how the market system answers the Fundamental Questions. Why must economic choices be made? Explain: "The capitalistic system is a profit and loss economy."

11 Evaluate and explain the following statements:

  a "The most important feature of capitalism is the absence of a central economic plan."

  b "Competition is the indispensable disciplinarian of the market economy."

  c "Production methods which are inferior in the engineering sense may be the most efficient methods in the economic sense."

12 Explain fully the meaning and implications of the following quotation.

The beautiful consequence of the market is that it is its own guardian. If output prices or certain kinds of remuneration stray away from their socially ordained levels, forces are set into motion to bring them back to the fold. It is a curious paradox which thus ensues: the market, which is the acme of individual economic freedom, is the strictest taskmaster of all. One may appeal the ruling of a planning board or win the dispensation of a minister; but there is no appeal, no dispensation, from the anonymous pressures of the market mechanism. Economic freedom is thus more illusory than at first appears. One can do as one pleases in the market. But if one pleases to do what the market disapproves, the price of individual freedom is economic ruination.[3]

13 Assume that a business firm finds that its profits will be at maximum when it produces $40 worth of product A. Suppose also that each of the three techniques shown in the following table will produce the desired output.

Resource	Price per unit of resource	Technique no. 1	Technique no. 2	Technique no. 3
Labor	$3	5	2	3
Land	4	2	4	2
Capital	2	2	4	5
Entrepreneurial ability	2	4	2	4

  a Given the resource prices shown, which technique will the firm choose? Why? Will production entail profits or losses? Will the industry expand or contract? When is a new equilibrium output achieved?

  b Assume now that a new technique, technique No. 4, is developed. It entails the use of 2 units of labor, 2 of land, 6 of capital, and 3 of entrepreneurial ability. Given the resource prices in the table, will the firm adopt the new technique? Explain your answer.

  c Suppose now that an increase in labor supply causes the price of labor to fall to $1.50 per unit, all other resource prices being unchanged. Which technique will the producer now choose? Explain.

  d "The market system causes the economy to conserve most in the use of those resources which are particularly scarce in supply. Resources which are scarcest relative to the demand for them have the highest prices. As a result, producers use these resources as sparingly as is possible." Evaluate this statement. Does your answer to question 13c bear out this contention? Explain.

14 Foreigners frequently point out that, comparatively speaking, Americans are very wasteful of food and material goods and very conscious, and overly economical, in their use of time. Can you provide an explanation for this observation?

[3]Robert L. Heilbroner, *The Worldly Philosophers,* 3d ed. (New York: Simon & Schuster, Inc., 1967), p. 42.

CHAPTER 6

The Public Sector

The economic activities of government affect your well-being every day of your life. If you attend a public college or university, taxpayers heavily subsidize your education. When you receive a check from your part-time or summer job, you see significant deductions for income and social security taxes. The ground beef in your Big Mac has been examined by government inspectors to prevent contamination and to ensure quality. Laws requiring seat belts and motorcycle helmets—not to mention the sprinkler system government mandates in your dormitory—are all intended to enhance your safety. If you are a woman or a member of a minority group, an array of legislation is designed to enhance your education, housing, and employment opportunities.

All real-life economies are "mixed"; government and the market system share the responsibility of responding to the Five Fundamental Questions. Our economy is predominantly a market economy, yet the economic activities of government are of great significance. In this chapter we will (1) state and illustrate the major economic functions of the public sector; (2) add government to the circular flow model; and (3) examine the major expenditures and sources of tax revenue for Federal, state, and local governments.

ECONOMIC FUNCTIONS OF GOVERNMENT

The economic functions of government are many and varied. The economic role of government is so broad that it is virtually impossible to establish an all-inclusive list of its economic functions. The following breakdown of government's economic activities will serve as a pattern for our discussion, although some overlapping is unavoidable.

First, some economic functions of government strengthen and facilitate the operation of the market system. The two major activities of government in this area are:

1 Providing the legal foundation and a social environment conducive to the effective operation of the market system.
2 Maintaining competition.

Through a second group of functions, government supplements and modifies the operation of the market system. The three major functions of government here involve:

3 Redistributing income and wealth.
4 Adjusting the allocation of resources to alter the composition of the domestic output.
5 Stabilizing the economy, that is, controlling unemployment and inflation caused by business fluctuations, and promoting economic growth.

In reality most government activities and policies have *some* impact in all these areas. For example, a program to redistribute income to the poor affects the allocation of resources in that the poor buy somewhat different goods and services than the wealthy. A decline in, say, government military spending to lessen inflationary pressures also reallocates resources from public to private uses.

LEGAL AND SOCIAL FRAMEWORK

Government provides the legal framework and certain basic services prerequisite to the effective operation of a market economy. The necessary legal framework includes providing for the legal status of business enterprises, defining the rights of private ownership, and providing for enforcement of contracts. Government also establishes legal "rules of the game" governing the relationships of businesses, resource suppliers, and consumers with one another. Through legislation, government can referee economic relationships, detect foul play, and exercise authority in imposing appropriate penalties.

Basic services provided by government include police powers to maintain internal order, a system of standards for measuring the weight and quality of products, and a monetary system to facilitate exchange of goods and services.

The Pure Food and Drug Act of 1906 and its various amendments are an excellent example of how government has strengthened the operation of the market system. This act sets rules of conduct governing producers in their relationships with consumers. It prohibits the sale of adulterated and misbranded foods and drugs, requires net weights and ingredients of products to be specified on their containers, establishes quality standards which must be stated on labels of canned foods, and prohibits deceptive claims on patent-medicine labels. All these measures are designed to prevent fraudulent activities on the part of producers and, simultaneously, to increase the public's confidence in the integrity of the market system. Similar legislation pertains to labor-management relations and relations of business firms to one another.

The presumption is that this type of government activity will improve resource allocation. Supplying a medium of exchange, ensuring product quality, defining ownership rights, and enforcing contracts tend to increase the volume of exchange. This widens markets and permits greater specialization in the use of both property and human resources. Such specialization means a more efficient allocation of resources. However, some argue that government has overregulated interactions of businesses, consumers, and workers, stifling economic incentives and impairing productive efficiency.

MAINTAINING COMPETITION

Competition is the basic regulatory mechanism in a capitalistic economy. It is the force which subjects producers and resource suppliers to the dictates of consumer sovereignty. With competition, the supply and demand decisions of *many* sellers and buyers determine market prices. Individual producers and resource suppliers can only adjust to the wishes of buyers as tabulated and communicated by the market system. Profits and survival await the competitive producers who obey the market system; losses and eventual bankruptcy are the lot of those who deviate from it. With competition, buyers are the boss, the market is their agent, and businesses are their servants.

The growth of **monopoly** drastically alters this situation. *Monopoly exists when the number of sellers becomes small enough for each seller to influence total supply and therefore the price of the commodity being sold.*

When monopoly supplants competition, sellers can influence, or "rig," the market in their own self-interests, to the detriment of society as a whole. Through their ability to influence total supply, monopolists can artificially restrict the output of products and enjoy higher prices and, frequently, persistent economic profits. These above-competitive prices and profits directly conflict with the interests of consumers. Monopolists are not regulated by the will of society as are competitive sellers. Producer sovereignty supplants consumer sovereignty to the degree that monopoly supplants competition. Resources are then allocated in terms of the profit-seeking interests of monopolistic sellers rather than in terms of the wants of society as a whole. Monopoly causes a misallocation of economic resources.

In the United States, government has attempted to control monopoly primarily in two ways.
1 In the case of "natural monopolies"—industries in

which technological and economic realities rule out competitive markets—government has created public commissions regulating prices and service standards. Transportation, communications, and electric and other utilities are industries which are regulated in varying degrees. At local levels of government, public ownership of electric and water utilities is common.

2   In the vast majority of markets, efficient production can be attained with a high degree of competition. The Federal government has therefore enacted a series of antimonopoly or antitrust laws, beginning with the Sherman Act of 1890, to maintain and strengthen competition as an effective regulator of business behavior.

Even if the legal foundation of capitalistic institutions is assured and competition is maintained, there is still a need for certain additional economic functions on the part of government. *The market economy has certain biases and shortcomings which compel government to supplement and modify its operation.*

REDISTRIBUTION OF INCOME

The market system is an impersonal mechanism, and the distribution of income to which it gives rise may entail more inequality than society desires. The market system yields very large incomes to those whose labor, by virtue of inherent ability and acquired education and skills, commands high wages. Similarly, those who possess—through hard work or easy inheritance—valuable capital and land receive large property incomes.

But others in our society have less ability and have received modest amounts of education and training. These same people typically have accumulated or inherited no property resources. Hence, their incomes are very low. Furthermore, many of the aged, the physically and mentally handicapped, and husbandless women with dependent children earn only very small incomes or, like the unemployed, no incomes at all through the market system. In short, the market system involves considerable inequality in the distribution of money income (recall Figure 5-2) and therefore in the distribution of total output among individual households. Poverty amidst overall plenty in our economy persists as a major economic and political issue.

Government responsibility for ameliorating income inequality is reflected in a variety of policies and programs.

1   *Transfer payments* provide relief to the destitute, aid to the dependent and handicapped, and unemployment compensation to the unemployed. Similarly, our social security and Medicare programs provide financial support for the retired and aged sick. All these programs transfer income from government to households which would otherwise have little or none.

2   Government also alters the distribution of income by *market intervention,* that is, by modifying the prices established by market forces. Price supports for farmers and minimum-wage legislation are illustrations of government price fixing designed to raise incomes of specific groups.

3   Finally, the personal income tax has been used historically to take a larger proportion of the incomes of the rich than the poor. However, recent revisions of the personal income tax have significantly reduced its redistributive impact.

REALLOCATION OF RESOURCES

Economists recognize two major cases of *market failure,* that is, situations in which the competitive market system would either (1) produce the "wrong" amounts of certain goods and services, or (2) fail to allocate any resources whatsoever to the production of certain goods and services whose output is economically justified. The first case involves "spillovers" or "externalities" and the second "public" or "social" goods.

Spillovers or Externalities

One of the virtues of a competitive market system is that it would result in an efficient allocation of resources. The "right" or optimal amount of resources would be allocated to each of the various goods and services produced. Hence, the equilibrium output in a competitive market is also identified as the optimal output.

But the conclusion that competitive markets automatically bring about allocative efficiency rests on the hidden assumption that *all* the benefits and costs of production and consumption of each product are fully reflected in the market demand and supply curves respectively. It is assumed that there are no *spillovers* or *externalities* associated with the production or consumption of any good or service.

A *spillover*[1] occurs when some of the benefits or costs of production or consumption of a good "spill over" onto third parties, that is, to parties other than the

[1]Spillovers may go by other names—for example, external economies and diseconomies, neighborhood effects, and social benefits and costs.

immediate buyer or seller. Spillovers are also termed *externalities* because they are benefits and costs accruing to some individual or group external to the market transaction.

Spillover Costs When production or consumption of a commodity inflicts costs on a third party without compensation, there exists a **spillover cost.** Obvious examples of spillover costs involve environmental pollution. When a chemical manufacturer or meat-packing plant dumps its wastes into a lake or river, swimmers, fishermen, and boaters—not to mention communities' water supplies—suffer spillover costs. When a petroleum refinery pollutes the air with smoke or a paint factory creates distressing odors, the community bears spillover costs for which it is not compensated.

Figure 6-1a illustrates how spillover or external costs affect the allocation of resources. When spillover costs occur—when producers shift some of their costs onto the community—their production costs are lower than otherwise. The supply curve does not include or "capture" all the costs which can be legitimately associated with production of the good. Hence, the producer's supply curve, S, understates total costs of production and therefore lies to the right of the supply curve which would include all costs, S_t. By polluting, that is, by creating spillover costs, the firm enjoys lower production costs and the supply curve S. The result,

shown in Figure 6-1a, is that equilibrium output Q_e is larger than optimal output Q_o. This means resources are *overallocated* to the production of this commodity.

Correcting for Spillover Costs Government can take several actions to correct the overallocation of resources associated with spillover costs and "internalize" the external costs. Two basic types of corrective action are common: legislative action and specific taxes.

1 Legislation In our examples of air and water pollution, we find that the most direct action is to pass *legislation* prohibiting or limiting pollution. Such legislation forces potential polluters to bear costs of properly disposing of industrial wastes. Firms must buy and install smoke-abatement equipment or facilities to purify water contaminated by manufacturing processes. Such action forces potential offenders, under the threat of legal action, to bear *all* costs associated with their production. In short, legislation can shift the supply curve S toward S_t in Figure 6-1b, bringing equilibrium and optimal outputs into equality.

2 Specific Taxes A second, less direct action is based upon the fact that taxes are a cost and therefore a determinant of a firm's supply curve (Chapter 4). Government might levy a *specific tax* which equals or ap-

FIGURE 6-1   Spillover costs and the overallocation of resources

With spillover costs in (a) we find that the lower costs borne by businesses, as reflected in *S*, fail to reflect all costs, as embodied in *S$_t$*. Consequently, the equilibrium output *Q$_e$* is greater than the efficient or optimal output *Q$_o$*. This overallocation of resources can be corrected by legislation or, as shown in (b), by imposing a specific tax, *T*, which raises the firm's costs and shifts its supply curve from *S* to *S$_t$*.

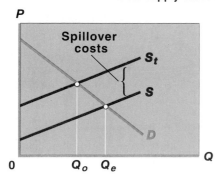
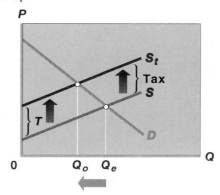

proximates the spillover costs per unit of output. Through this tax, government attempts to shove back onto the offending firm those external or spillover costs which private industry would otherwise avoid. A specific tax equal to T per unit in Figure 6-1b will increase the firm's costs, shifting the supply curve from S to S_t. The result is that the equilibrium output Q_e will decline so that it corresponds with the optimal output Q_o and the overallocation of resources will be eliminated.

Spillover Benefits But spillovers may also take the form of benefits. Production or consumption of certain goods and services may confer spillover or external benefits on third parties or the community at large for which payment or compensation is not required. For example, measles and polio immunization shots result in direct benefits to the immediate consumer. But immunization against these contagious diseases yields widespread and substantial spillover benefits to the entire community.

Education is another example of **spillover benefits.** Education benefits individual consumers: "More educated" people generally achieve higher incomes than "less educated" people. But education also confers sizable benefits upon society. The economy as a whole benefits from a more versatile and more productive labor force, on the one hand, and smaller outlays in crime prevention, law enforcement, and welfare programs, on the other. Significant, too, is the fact that political participation correlates positively with the level of education in that the percentage of persons who vote increases with educational attainment.

Figure 6-2a shows the impact of spillover benefits on resource allocation. The existence of spillover benefits means that the market demand curve, which reflects only private benefits, understates total benefits. The market demand curve fails to capture all the benefits associated with the provision and consumption of goods and services which entail spillover benefits. Thus D in Figure 6-2a indicates the benefits which private individuals derive from education; D_t is drawn to include these private benefits *plus* the additional spillover benefits accruing to society at large. While market demand D and supply S_t would yield an equilibrium output of Q_e, this output would be less than the optimal output Q_o. The market system would not produce enough education; resources would be *underallocated* to education.

Correcting for Spillover Benefits How might the underallocation of resources associated with the presence of spillover benefits be corrected?

1 Increase Demand One approach is to increase demand by providing consumers with purchasing power which can be used *only* to obtain the particular good or service producing spillover benefits. Example: Our food stamp program is designed to improve the diets of low-income families. The food stamps which government provides to such families can be spent

FIGURE 6-2 **Spillover benefits and the underallocation of resources**

Spillover benefits in (a) cause society's total benefits from a product, as shown by D_t, to be understated by the market demand curve, D. As a result, the equilibrium output Q_e is less than the optimal output Q_o. This can be corrected by a subsidy to consumers, as shown in (b), which increases market demand from D to D_t. Alternatively, the underallocation can be eliminated by providing producers with a subsidy of U, which increases their supply curve from S_t to S_t'.

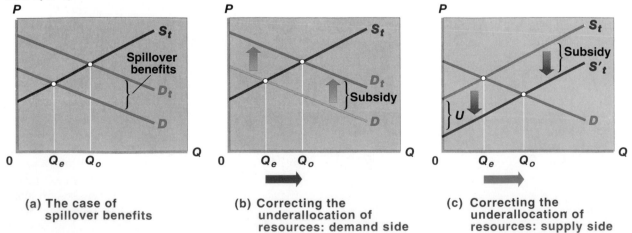

(a) **The case of spillover benefits**

(b) **Correcting the underallocation of resources: demand side**

(c) **Correcting the underallocation of resources: supply side**

only on food. Stores accepting food stamps are reimbursed with money by the government. Part of the rationale for this program is that improved nutrition will help disadvantaged children perform better in school and disadvantaged adults to be better employees. In brief, the program is designed to help disadvantaged people become productive participants in the economy, an outcome benefiting society as a whole. In terms of Figure 6-2b the program increases the demand for food from from D to D_t, thereby alleviating or eliminating the underallocation of resources.

2 Increase Supply An alternative approach works through the supply side of the market. Instead of subsidizing consumers of a particular good, government may find it more convenient and administratively simpler to subsidize producers. A *subsidy* is a specific tax in reverse; taxes impose an extra cost on producers, whereas subsidies reduce their costs. In Figure 6-2c a subsidy of U per unit to producers will reduce costs and shift the supply curve downward from S_t to S_t', and output will increase from Q_e to the optimal level Q_o. Hence, the underallocation of resources will be corrected. Public subsidization of higher education, mass immunization programs, and public hospitals and health clinics are cases in point.

3 Government Provision A third policy option arises if spillover benefits are extremely large: Government may simply choose to finance or, in the extreme, to own and operate such industries. This option leads us into a discussion of public goods and services.

Public Goods and Services

Private goods, which are produced through the market system, are *divisible* in that they come in units small enough to be afforded by individual buyers. Furthermore, private goods are subject to the **exclusion principle,** the idea that those willing and able to pay the equilibrium price get the product, but those unable or unwilling to pay are excluded from the benefits provided by that product.

Certain goods and services—**public** or **social goods**—would not be produced at all by the market system because their characteristics are essentially opposite those of private goods. Public goods are *indivisible,* involving such large units that they cannot be sold to individual buyers. Individuals can buy hamburgers, computers, and automobiles through the market, but not Patriot missiles, highways, and air-traffic control.

More importantly, the exclusion principle does *not* apply; there is no effective way of excluding individuals from the benefits of public goods once those goods come into existence. Obtaining the benefits of private goods is predicated upon *purchase;* benefits from public goods accrue to society from the *production* of such goods.

Illustrations The classic public goods example is a lighthouse on a treacherous coast or harbor. The construction of a lighthouse would be economically justified if benefits (fewer shipwrecks) exceeded production costs. But the benefit accruing to each individual user would not justify the purchase of such a large and indivisible product. In any event, once in operation, its warning light is a guide to *all* ships. There is no practical way to exclude certain ships from its benefits. Therefore, why should any ship owner voluntarily pay for the benefits received from the light? The light is there for all to see, and a ship captain cannot be excluded from seeing it if the ship owner chooses not to pay. Economists call this the **free-rider problem;** *people can receive benefits from a good without contributing to its costs.*

Given the inapplicability of the exclusion principle, there is no economic incentive for private enterprises to supply lighthouses. If the services of the lighthouse cannot be priced and sold, it will be unprofitable for private firms to devote resources to lighthouses. Here is a service which yields substantial benefits but for which the market would allocate no resources. National defense, flood-control, public health, and insect-abatement programs are other public goods. If society is to enjoy such goods and services, they must be provided by the public sector and financed by compulsory charges in the form of taxes.

Large Spillover Benefits While the inapplicability of the exclusion principle sets off public from private goods, many other goods and services are provided by government even though the exclusion principle *could* be applied. Such goods and services as education, streets and highways, police and fire protection, libraries and museums, preventive medicine, and sewage disposal could be subject to the exclusion principle, that is, they could be priced and provided by private producers through the market system. But, as noted earlier, these are all services with substantial spillover benefits and would be underproduced by the market system. Therefore, government undertakes or sponsors their provision to avoid the underallocation of resources which would otherwise occur. Such goods and services are sometimes called *quasi-public goods*. One can understand the long-standing controversies surrounding the status of medical care and housing. Are these private goods to be provided through the market system, or are they quasi-public goods to be provided by government?

Allocating Resources to Public Goods

Given that the price system would fail to allocate resources for public goods and would underallocate resources for quasi-public goods, what is the mechanism by which such goods get produced?

Public goods are purchased through the government on the basis of group, or collective, choices, in contrast to private goods, which are purchased from private enterprises on the basis of individual choices. The types and quantities of the various public goods produced are determined in a democracy by political means, that is, by voting. The quantities of the various public goods consumed are a matter of public policy.[2] These group decisions, made in the political arena, supplement the choices of households and businesses in answering the Five Fundamental Questions.

Given these group decisions, precisely how are resources reallocated from production of private goods to production of public goods? In a full-employment economy, government must free resources from private employment to make them available for production of public goods. The apparent means of releasing resources from private uses is to reduce private demand for them. This is accomplished by levying taxes on businesses and households, diverting some of their incomes—some of their potential purchasing power—out of the income-expenditure streams. With lower incomes, businesses and households must curtail their investment and consumption spending. *Taxes diminish private demand for goods and services, and this decrease in turn prompts a drop in the private demand for resources.* By diverting purchasing power from private spenders to government, taxes free resources from private uses.

Government expenditure of the tax proceeds can then reabsorb these resources in the provision of public goods and services. Corporation and personal income taxes

release resources from production of investment goods—printing presses, boxcars, warehouses—and consumer goods—food, clothing, and television sets. Government expenditures can reabsorb these resources in production of guided missiles, military aircraft, and new schools and highways. Government purposely reallocates resources to bring about significant changes in the composition of the economy's total output.

Stabilization

Historically, the most recent function of government is that of stabilizing the economy—assisting the private economy to achieve both the full employment of resources and a stable price level. At this point we will only outline (rather than fully explain) the stabilization function of government.

The level of output depends directly on total or aggregate expenditures. A high level of total spending means it will be profitable for industries to produce large outputs. This condition, in turn, will necessitate that both property and human resources be employed at high levels. But aggregate spending may either fall short of, or exceed, that particular level which will provide for full employment and price stability. Two possibilities, unemployment or inflation, may then occur.

1 Unemployment The level of total spending in the private sector may be too low for full employment. Thus, the government may choose to augment private spending so that total spending—private *and* public—will be sufficient to generate full employment. Government can do this by using the same techniques—government spending and taxes—as it uses to reallocate resources to production of public goods. Specifically, government might increase its own spending on public goods and services on the one hand, and reduce taxes to stimulate private spending on the other.[3]

2 Inflation The second possibility is that the economy may attempt to spend in excess of its productive capacity. If aggregate spending exceeds the full-employment output, the excess spending will pull up the price level. Excessive aggregate spending is inflationary. Government's obligation here is to eliminate the excess spending. It can do this primarily by cutting its own expenditures and by raising taxes to curtail private spending.

---

[2]There are differences between *dollar voting,* which dictates ouput in the private sector of the economy, and *political voting,* which determines ouput in the public sector. The rich person has many more votes to cast in the private sector than does the poor person. In the public sector, each—at least in theory—has an equal say. Furthermore, the children who cast their votes for bubble gum and comic books in the private sector are banned by virtue of their age from the registering of social choices.

[3]In macroeconomics we learn that government can also use monetary policy—changes in the nation's money supply and interest rates—to help achieve economic stability.

THE CIRCULAR FLOW REVISITED

Government is thoroughly integrated into the real and monetary flows which comprise our economy. It is informative to reexamine the redistributional, allocative, and stabilization functions of government in terms of Chapter 3's circular flow model. In Figure 6-3 flows (1) through (4) restate Figure 3-2. Flows (1) and (2) show business expenditures for the resources provided by households. These expenditures are costs to businesses, but represent wage, rent, interest, and profit income to households. Flows (3) and (4) portray households making consumer expenditures for the goods and services produced by businesses.

Now consider the numerous modifications which stem from the addition of government. Flows (5)

FIGURE 6-3   The circular flow and the public sector
Government expenditures, taxes, and transfer payments affect the distribution of income, the allocation of resources, and the level of economic activity.

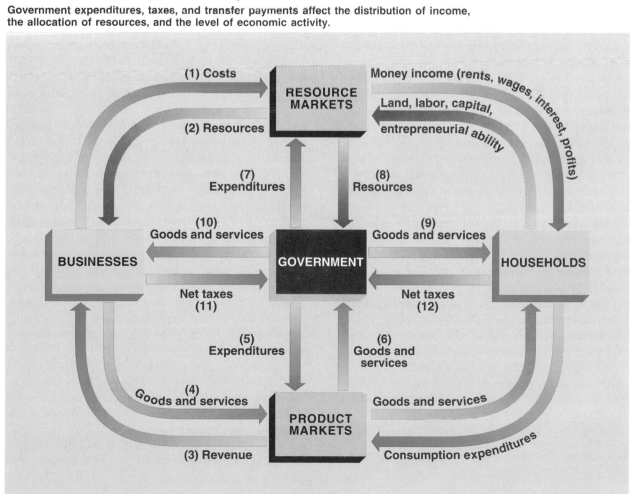

through (8) tell us that government makes purchases in both product and resource markets. Specifically, flows (5) and (6) represent government purchasing such things as paper clips, computers, and military hardware from private businesses. Flows (7) and (8) reflect government purchases of resources. The Federal government employs and pays salaries to members of Congress, the armed forces, Justice Department lawyers, various bureaucrats, and so on. State and local governments hire teachers, bus drivers, police, and firefighters. The Federal government might lease or purchase land to expand a military base; a city may buy land to build a new elementary school.

Government then provides public goods and services to both households and businesses as shown by flows (9) and (10). The financing of public goods and services requires tax payments by businesses and households as reflected in flows (11) and (12). We have labeled these flows as *net* taxes to acknowledge that they also include "taxes in reverse" in the form of transfer payments to households and subsidies to businesses. Thus, flow (11) entails not merely corporate income, sales, and excise taxes flowing from businesses to government, but also various subsidies to farmers, shipbuilders, and some airlines.[4] Similarly, government also collects taxes (personal income taxes, payroll taxes) directly from households and makes available transfer payments, for example, welfare payments and social security benefits as shown by flow (12).

Our expanded circular flow model clearly shows us how government can alter the distribution of income, reallocate resources, and change the level of economic activity. The structure of taxes and transfer payments can have a significant impact on income distribution. In flow (12) a tax structure which draws tax revenues primarily from well-to-do households combined with a system of transfer payments to low-income households will result in greater equality in the distribution of income.

Flows (6) and (8) imply an allocation of resources which differs from that of a purely private economy. Government buys goods and labor services which differ from those purchased by households.

Finally, all governmental flows suggest means by which government might attempt to stabilize the economy. If the economy was experiencing unemployment, an increase in government spending with taxes and

transfers held constant would increase aggregate spending, output, and employment. Similarly, given the level of government expenditures, a decline in taxes or an increase in transfer payments would increase spendable incomes and boost private spending. Conversely, with inflation the opposite government policies would be in order: reduced government spending, increased taxes, and reduced transfers.

GOVERNMENT FINANCE

How large is the public sector? What are the main economic programs of Federal, state, and local governments? How are these programs financed?

Government Growth: Purchases and Transfers

We can get a general impression of the size and growth of government's economic role by examining government purchases of goods and services and government transfer payments. The distinction between these two kinds of outlays is significant.

1 Government purchases are "exhaustive" in that they directly absorb or employ resources and the resulting production is part of the domestic output. For example, the purchase of a missile absorbs the labor of physicists and engineers along with steel, explosives, and a host of other inputs.

2 Transfer payments are "nonexhaustive" in that they do not directly absorb resources or account for production. Social security benefits, welfare payments, veterans' benefits, and unemployment compensation are examples of transfer payments. Their key characteristic is that recipients make no current contribution to output in return for these payments.

Figure 6-4 compares *government purchases* of goods and services with the domestic output, that is, with the total amount of goods and services produced in the economy for the 1929–1991 period. Total government purchases rose significantly relative to domestic output over the 1929–1940 period, but then skyrocketed during World War II. However, since the early 1950s government spending for goods and services has hovered around 20 percent of the domestic output. Of course, the domestic output has expanded dramatically over the 1929–1991 period so that the *absolute* volume of government spending has increased greatly. Government expenditures on goods and services to-

---

[4]Most business subsidies are "concealed" in the form of low-interest loans, loan guarantees, tax concessions, or the public provision of facilities at prices less than costs.

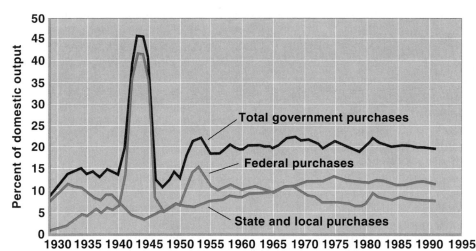

FIGURE 6-4   Government purchases as a percent of domestic output, 1929–1991

Government purchases rose relative to domestic output over the 1929–1940 period, only to increase dramatically during World War II. Since the early 1950s total government purchases have been approximately 20 percent of the domestic output.

taled $1087 billion in 1991 as compared to only $9 billion in 1929!

When transfer payments are added, our impression of government's role and its growth change considerably. Transfers have grown rapidly since the 1960s, rising from $29 billion or 5 percent of the domestic output in 1960, to $759 billion or 13 percent of the domestic output in 1991. The net result is that tax revenues required to finance both government purchases *and* transfers are equal to approximately one-third of the domestic output. In 1990 an average tax bill of about $13,000 was imposed on every family in the United States. In 1991 the average taxpayer spent about 2 hours and 49 minutes of each 8-hour workday to pay taxes. However, the size of our public sector is small compared to other industrialized countries. Taxes in Sweden, Norway, France, Great Britain, and West Germany are 51, 46, 45, 39, and 37 percent of domestic output respectively, compared to about 30 percent in the United States.

Some Causes

Let's now consider some specific factors which account for the historical growth and present size of government spending and taxes.

1 War and Defense   Hot and cold wars have tended to sustain Federal expenditures at high levels for the past four decades. War, national defense, and military-space research are among the major causes of the growth of government spending and taxation which has occurred since 1940.

2 Population Growth   There are over twice as many Americans today as there were a scant sixty years ago. This means there are more people for whom public goods and services must be provided. Even with a constant level of government spending per person, total government spending would have increased dramatically in recent decades.

3 Urbanization and the Demand for Public Goods The increasing urbanization of our economy has necessitated massive expenditures on streets, public transportation facilities, police and fire protection, and sewers. Also, the public has demanded more and better public goods and services to "match" the rising standard of living provided by the private sector of the economy. We want bigger and better highways to accommodate more and better automobiles. We seek more and better educational facilities to upgrade the labor force for the more demanding jobs of private industry.

4 Environmental Quality Population growth and urbanization have contributed to serious and well-publicized problems of environmental quality. Society has become highly aware that the production and consumption of vast quantities of goods can lead to serious external or spillover costs in air, water, and land pollution. Government has inherited a central role in coping with these environmental problems.

5 Egalitarianism Since the mid-1960s there has occurred a sharp expansion of programs designed to alleviate poverty and reduce income inequality. Social security, unemployment compensation, welfare, Medicare, food stamps, and public housing are examples. These programs accounted for about 3 percent of domestic output twenty years ago. They now require approximately 13 percent of domestic output.

FEDERAL FINANCE

Now we will disaggregate the public sector into Federal, state, and local units of government to compare their expenditures and taxes. Table 6-1 tells the story for the Federal government.

Federal Expenditures

Although Table 6-1 reveals a wide variety of Federal expenditures, three important areas of spending stand out: (1) income security, (2) national defense, and (3) interest on the public debt. The *income security* category reflects the myriad income-maintenance programs for the aged, the disabled, the unemployed, the handicapped, the medically indigent, and families with

no breadwinner. *National defense* constitutes about one-fourth of the Federal budget and underscores the high costs of military preparedness. *Interest on the public debt* has grown dramatically in recent years because the public debt itself has grown. The remaining categories of expenditures listed in Table 6-1 are largely self-explanatory.

Federal Receipts

The receipts side of Table 6-1 clearly shows that the personal income tax, payroll taxes, and the corporate income tax are the basic revenue getters, accounting for 45, 37, and 9 cents of each dollar collected.

Personal Income Tax The **personal income tax** is the kingpin of our national tax system and merits special comment. This tax is levied on *taxable income,* that is, on the incomes of households and unincorporated businesses after certain exemptions ($2,150 for each household member) and deductions (business expenses, charitable contributions, home mortgage interest payments, certain state and local taxes) are taken into account.

The Federal personal income tax is a *progressive tax,* that is, people with higher incomes pay a larger percentage of their income as taxes than do persons with lower incomes. The progressivity is achieved through a system of higher tax rates which apply to successive layers or brackets of income.

Columns 1 and 2 of Table 6-2 portray the mechanics of the income tax for a married couple filing a joint return. Note that the 15 percent rate applies to all taxable income up to $34,000, at which point any *additional* income up to $82,150 is taxable at the 28 percent rate.

TABLE 6-1 **The Federal budget, 1990**

Tax receipts	Billions of dollars	Percent of total	Expenditures	Billions of dollars	Percent of total
Personal income tax	$ 467	45	Income security	$ 494	39
Payroll taxes	380	37	National defense	299	24
Corporate income taxes	94	9	Interest on public debt	184	15
Excise taxes	35	3	Commerce, housing, and transportation	97	8
Customs duties	17	2	Education, training, and health	96	8
Estate and gift taxes	12	1	Agriculture, natural resources, and environment	46	4
All other	26	3	All other (net)	36	3
Total receipts	$1031	100	Total expenditures	$1252	100

Source: Economic Report of the President. Because of rounding, figures may not add up to totals.

TABLE 6-2   **Federal personal income tax rates, 1991***

(1) Total taxable income	(2) Marginal tax rate (4) ÷ (3)	(3) Change in income Δ(1)	(4) Change in taxes Δ(5)	(5) Total tax	(6) Average Tax rate (5) ÷ (1)
$ 0	0%	—	—	—	—
34,000	15	$34,000	$ 5,100	$ 5,100	15%
82,150	28	48,150	13,482	18,582	22.6
Over 82,150	31	—	—	—	—

*Data are for a married couple filing a joint return.

Any additional taxable income above $82,150 is taxed at 31 percent.

The tax rates shown in column 2 of Table 6-2 are marginal tax rates. A **marginal tax rate** is the tax paid on additional or incremental income. By definition, it is the *increase* in taxes paid (column 4) divided by the *increase* in income (column 3). Thus, if our couple's taxable income increased from $0 to $34,000 the increase in taxes paid would be $5,100 (=.15 × $34,000) as shown in column 4. If the couple's taxable income rose by an additional $48,150 (column 3)—that is, from $34,000 to $82,150—a higher marginal tax rate of 28 percent would apply so that an additional tax of $13,482 (=.28 × $48,150) would have to be paid (column 4).

The marginal tax rates of column 2 overstate the personal income tax bite because the rising rates apply only to income falling within each successive tax bracket. To get a better picture of the tax burden one must consider average tax rates. The **average tax rate** is the total tax paid divided by total taxable income. In column 6 of Table 6-2 for the $0 to $34,000 tax bracket the average tax rate is $5,100 (column 4) divided by $34,000 (column 1) or 15 percent, the same as the marginal tax rate. But the couple earning $82,150 does *not* pay 28 percent of its income as taxes as the marginal tax rate would suggest. Rather, its average tax rate is only about 22.6 percent (=$18,582 ÷ $82,150). The reason is that the first $34,000 of income it taxed at 15 percent and only the next $48,150 is subject to the 28 percent rate. You should calculate the average tax rate for a couple earning $182,500. What we observe here is that, if the marginal tax rate is higher than the average tax rate, the average tax rate will rise.[5]

By definition, a tax whose average tax rate rises as income increases is called a *progressive tax.* Such a tax claims both a larger absolute amount and a larger proportion of income as income rises. Thus we can say

that our current personal income tax is mildly progressive.

Payroll Taxes   Social security contributions, or **payroll taxes,** are the premiums paid on the compulsory insurance plans—old age insurance and Medicare—provided for by existing social security legislation. These taxes are paid by both employers and employees. Improvements in, and extensions of, our social security programs, plus growth of the labor force, have resulted in very significant increases in payroll taxes in recent years. In 1992 employees and employers each paid a tax of 7.65 percent on the first $55,500 of an employee's annual earnings.

Corporate Income Tax   The Federal government also taxes corporate income. This **corporate income tax** is levied on a corporation's profits—the difference between its total revenue and its total expenses. The basic rate is 34 percent, which applies to annual profits over $335,000. A firm with profits of $1,335,000 would pay corporate income taxes of $340,000. Firms making annual profits less than $335,000 are taxed at lower rates.

Excise Taxes   Commodity or consumption taxes may take the form of **sales taxes** or **excise taxes.** The difference between the two is basically one of coverage. Sales taxes fall on a wide range of products, whereas excises are taxes on a small, select list of commodities. As Table 6-1 suggests, the Federal government collects excise taxes on such commodities as alcoholic beverages, tobacco, and gasoline. Beginning in 1991 a new excise tax applies to certain luxury goods. A 10 percent tax is now levied on that portion of the price above $30,000 for cars, $100,000 for boats, $250,000 for aircraft, and $10,000 for furs and jewelry. If your rich uncle were to buy you a $60,000 Mercedes for graduation, he would have to pay a tax of $3,000. The Federal government does *not* levy a general sales tax; sales taxes are the bread and butter of most state governments.

[5]The arithmetic is the same as what you may have encountered in school. You must get a score on an additional or "marginal" examination higher than your existing average grade to pull your average up!

QUICK REVIEW 6-2

◆ *Government purchases are about 20 percent of the domestic output; the addition of transfers increases government spending to almost one-third of domestic output.*

◆ *Income security and national defense are the main Federal expenditures; personal income, payroll, and corporate income taxes are the primary sources of revenue.*

◆ *States rely primarily on sales and excise taxes for revenue; their spending is largely for education, welfare, and health.*

◆ *Education is the dominant expenditure for local governments and most of their revenue is derived from property taxes.*

Fiscal Federalism

Historically, the tax collections of both state and local governments have fallen substantially short of their expenditures. These revenue shortfalls are largely filled by Federal transfers or grants. It is not uncommon for 15 to 20 percent of all revenue received by state and local governments to come from the Federal government. In addition to Federal grants to state and local governments, the states also make grants to local governmental units. This system of intergovernmental transfers is called **fiscal federalism.** Concern over large and persistent Federal budget deficits has precipitated declines in Federal grants in recent years, causing state and local governments to increase tax rates, impose new taxes, and restrain expenditures.

CHAPTER SUMMARY

1 Government enhances the operation of the market system by **a** providing an appropriate legal and social framework, and **b** acting to maintain competition.

2 Government alters the distribution of income by direct market intervention and through the tax-transfer system.

3 Spillovers or externalities cause the equilibrium output of certain goods to vary from the optimal output. Spillover costs result in an overallocation of resources which can be corrected by legislation or specific taxes. Spillover benefits are accompanied by an underallocation of resources which can be corrected by subsidies to either consumers or producers.

4 Government must provide public goods because such goods are indivisible and entail benefits from which nonpaying consumers cannot be excluded.

5 The manipulation of taxes and its expenditures is one basic means by which government can reduce unemployment and inflation.

6 The circular flow model helps us envision how government performs its redistributional, allocative, and stabilizing functions.

7 Although the absolute level of total government purchases of goods and services has increased greatly, such purchases have been about 20 percent of the domestic output in the entire post-World War II period.

8 Government purchases are exhaustive or resource-absorbing; transfer payments are not. Government purchases and transfers combined amount to about one-third of the domestic output.

9 Wars and national defense, population growth, urbanization, environmental problems, and egalitarianism have been among the more important causes of the historical growth of the public sector.

10 The main categories of Federal spending are for income security, national defense, and interest on the public debt; revenues come primarily from personal income, payroll, and corporate income taxes.

11 The primary sources of revenue for the states are sales and excise taxes; public welfare, education, highways, and health and hospitals are the major state expenditures.

12 At the local level, most revenue comes from the property tax, and education is the most important expenditure.

13 Under our system of fiscal federalism, state and local tax revenues are supplemented by sizable revenue grants from the Federal government.

TERMS AND CONCEPTS

monopoly	public or social goods	personal income tax	corporate income tax
spillover costs and	free-rider problem	marginal and average	sales and excise taxes
spillover benefits	government purchases	tax rates	property taxes
exclusion principle	transfer payments	payroll taxes	fiscal federalism

QUESTIONS AND STUDY SUGGESTIONS

1 Carefully evaluate this statement: "The public, as a general rule . . . gets less production in return for a dollar spent by government than from a dollar spent by private enterprise."

2 Enumerate and briefly discuss the main economic functions of government.

3 Explain why, in the absence of spillovers, equilibrium and optimal outputs are identical in competitive markets. What divergences arise between equilibrium and optimal output when **a** spillover costs and **b** spillover benefits are present? How might government correct for these discrepancies? "The presence of spillover costs suggests underallocation of resources to that product and the need for governmental subsidies." Do you agree? Explain how zoning and seat belt laws might be used to deal with a problem of spillover costs.

4 UCLA researchers have concluded that injuries caused by firearms cost about $429 million a year in hospital expenses alone. Because the majority of those shot are poor and without insurance, almost 86 percent of hospital costs must be borne by taxpayers. Use your understanding of externalities to recommend appropriate policies.

5 What are the basic characteristics of public goods? Explain the significance of the exclusion principle. By what means does government provide public goods?

6 Use your understanding of the characteristics of private and public goods to determine whether the following should be produced through the market system or provided by government: **a** bread; **b** street lighting; **c** bridges; **d** parks; **e** swimming pools; **f** medical care; **g** mail delivery; **h** housing; **i** air traffic control; **j** libraries.

7 Explain how government might manipulate its expenditures and tax revenues to reduce **a** unemployment and **b** the rate of inflation.

8 "Most governmental actions simultaneously affect the distribution of income, the allocation of resources, and the levels of unemployment and prices." Use the circular flow model to confirm this assertion for each of the following: **a** the construction of a new high school in Blackhawk County; **b** a 2 percent reduction in the corporate income tax; **c** an expansion of preschool programs for disadvantaged children; **d** a $50 billion increase in spending for space research; **e** the levying of a tax on air polluters; and **f** a $1 increase in the minimum wage.

9 Draw a production possibilities curve with public goods on the vertical axis and private goods on the horizontal axis. Assuming the economy is initially operating on the curve, indicate the means by which the production of public goods might be increased. How might the output of public goods be increased if the economy is initially functioning at a point inside the curve?

10 Describe and account for the historical growth of the public sector of the economy. In your response carefully distinguish between government purchases and transfer payments.

11 What is the most important source of revenue and the major type of expenditure at the Federal level? At the state level? At the local level?

12 Briefly describe the mechanics of the Federal personal income tax. Use the concepts of marginal and average tax rates to explain why it is a progressive tax.

13 Assume that the structure of a personal income tax is such that you would pay a tax of $2000 if your taxable income was $16,000 and a tax of $3000 if your taxable income was $20,000. What is the average tax rate at the $16,000 and $20,000 levels of taxable income? What marginal tax rate applies to taxable income which falls between $16,000 and $20,000? Is this tax progressive? Explain.

14 Calculate the average and marginal tax rates for the following table. Is this tax progressive? How do you know? What generalization can you offer concerning the relationship between marginal and average tax rates?

Income	Tax	Average tax rate	Marginal tax rate
$ 0	$ 0	_____	
100	10	_____	_____
200	30	_____	_____
300	60	_____	_____
400	100	_____	_____
500	150	_____	_____

15 The Federal government recently increased its excise taxes on gasoline, alcoholic beverages, and tobacco. What effect might these increases have on the revenues which states receive from their excises on these same products?

16 What is "fiscal federalism"? Why does it exist?

National Income, Employment, and Fiscal Policy

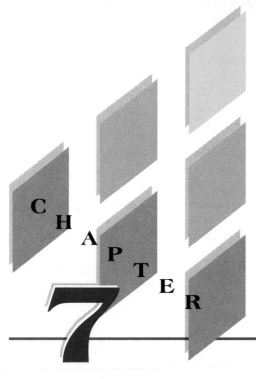

Measuring Domestic Output, National Income, and the Price Level

"**P**ersonal Consumption Expenditures Surge" "Private Domestic Investment Stagnates" "Gross Domestic Product Up 3.4 Percent" "Personal Income Continues To Fall" "Price Level Rises 0.8 Percent for Month"

These are typical headlines in the business and economics sections of the news. Many readers skip these articles, concluding that they are too technical, and therefore of limited interest.

The goal of this chapter is to ensure that you are not one of those readers. The potential payoff from this chapter is large. Upon completing it, you will have learned the basics of how government statisticians and accountants measure and record the levels of domestic output, national income, and prices for the entire United States. Moreover, you will acquire an understanding of important terms such as gross domestic product, net domestic product, national income, personal income, disposable income, and the price level. Finally, this chapter will extend your vocabulary in a way that will aid your comprehension of the macroeconomics in subsequent chapters.

Our specific approach is as follows: First, we explain why it is important to be able to measure the performance of the economy. Second, the key measure of domestic output—gross domestic product or GDP—is defined. We show that GDP can be measured either from the vantage point of expenditures on output or by the income generated from the production of that output. Third, several other important measures of output and income are derived from GDP and their meanings explained. Fourth, we show how the overall level of prices—the price level—is measured. Fifth, we demonstrate how GDP can be adjusted for changes in the price level—that is, for inflation or deflation—so changes in the physical amount of the nation's production are more accurately reflected. Finally, some limitations of our measures of domestic output and national income are surveyed.

THE IMPORTANCE OF MACROECONOMIC MEASUREMENT

Our present aim is to define and understand a group of so-called social or national income accounting concepts which measure the overall production performance of the economy. We do so because national income accounting does for the economy as a whole what private accounting does for the individual business enterprise or, for that matter, for the household. The business executive is vitally interested in knowing how well his or her firm is doing, but the answer is not always immediately discernible.

Measurement of a firm's flows of income and expenditures is needed to assess its operations for the current year. With this information, the executive can gauge the firm's economic health. If things are going well, the accounting data can be used to explain this success. Costs might be down or sales and product prices up, resulting in large profits. If things are going badly, accounting measures can be employed to discover immediate causes. And by examining the accounts over a period of time, the executive can detect growth or decline of profits for the firm and indications of the immediate causes. All this information helps the executive make intelligent business decisions.

A system of **national income accounting** operates in much the same way for the economy as a whole:

1 It allows us to keep a finger on the economic pulse of the nation. The various measures which make up our national income accounting system permit us to measure the level of production in the economy at some point in time and explain the immediate causes of that level of performance.

2 By comparing national income accounts over a period of time, we can plot the long-run course which the economy has been following; the growth or stagnation of the economy will show up in the national income accounts.

3 Finally, information supplied by national income accounts provides a basis for the formulation and application of public policies to improve the performance of the economy; without national income accounts, economic policy would be based on guesswork. *National income accounting allows us to keep tabs on the economic health of society and formulate policies which will improve that health.*

What are these accounting measures?

GROSS DOMESTIC PRODUCT

There are many conceivable measures of the economic well-being of society. But the best available indicator of an economy's health is its annual total output of goods and services or, as it is sometimes called, the economy's aggregate output. There are two closely related basic national income accounting measures of the total output of goods and services: gross national product and gross domestic product. Both measure *the total market value of all final goods and services produced in the economy in one year.* The difference is in how the "economy" is defined.

Gross national product (GNP) consists of the total output produced by land, labor, capital, and entrepreneurial talent supplied by Americans, whether these resources are located in the United States or abroad. Thus, for example, the share of output (income) produced by an American working in France is included in our GNP. Conversely, the share of output (income) produced in the United States by foreign-owned resources is excluded from our GNP.

On the other hand, **gross domestic product** (GDP) comprises the value of the total goods and services produced within the boundaries of the United States, whether by American or foreign-supplied resources. For instance, the full value of the autos produced at a Japanese-owned Nissan factory in the United States, including profits, is a part of American GDP. Conversely, profits earned by an American-owned IBM plant in France are excluded from our GDP.

Most nations use GDP as the chief measure of their output. In 1992 the United States switched from GNP accounting to GDP accounting. Thus, our focus will be on GDP.

In discussing GDP, we will see that all goods *produced* in a particular year may not be *sold;* some may be added to inventories. Any increase in inventories must therefore be included in determining GDP, since GDP measures all current production, whether or not it is sold. Our definition of GDP is very explicit and merits considerable comment.

A Monetary Measure

Note, first, that GDP measures the market value of annual output; it is a monetary measure. Indeed, it must be if we are to compare the heterogeneous collections of goods and services produced in different years and get a meaningful idea of their relative worth. If the

TABLE 7-1   Comparing heterogeneous outputs by using money prices (hypothetical data)

Year	Annual outputs	Market values
1	3 oranges and 2 apples	3 at 20 cents + 2 at 30 cents = $1.20
2	2 oranges and 3 apples	2 at 20 cents + 3 at 30 cents = $1.30

economy produces three oranges and two apples in year 1 and two oranges and three apples in year 2, in which year is output greater? We cannot answer this question until price tags are attached to the various products as indicators of society's evaluation of their relative worth.

The problem is resolved in Table 7-1, where the money price of oranges is 20 cents and the price of apples is 30 cents. Year 2's output is greater than year 1's, because society values year 2's output more highly; society is willing to pay more for the collection of goods produced in year 2 than for goods produced in year 1.

Avoiding Double Counting

To measure total output accurately, all goods and services produced in any given year must be counted once, but not more than once. Most products go through a series of production stages before reaching a market. As a result, parts or components of most products are bought and sold many times. To avoid counting several times the parts of products that are sold and resold, GDP includes only the market value of final goods and ignores transactions involving intermediate goods.

By **final goods** we mean goods and services being purchased for final use and not for resale or further processing or manufacturing. Transactions involving

intermediate goods refer to purchases of goods and services for further processing and manufacturing or for resale. The sale of final goods is *included* and the sale of intermediate goods is *excluded* from GDP. Why? Because the value of final goods already includes all intermediate transactions involved in their production. To count intermediate transactions separately would be **double counting** and an exaggerated estimate of GDP.

To clarify this point, suppose there are five stages of production in getting a wool suit manufactured and to the consumer, who, of course, is the ultimate or final user. As Table 7-2 indicates, firm A, a sheep ranch, provides $60 worth of wool to firm B, a wool processor. Firm A pays out the $60 it receives in wages, rents, interest, and profits. Firm B processes the wool and sells it to firm C, a suit manufacturer, for $100. What does firm B do with this $100? As noted, $60 goes to firm A, and the remaining $40 is used by B to pay wages, rents, interest, and profits for the resources needed in processing the wool. The manufacturer sells the suit to firm D, a clothing wholesaler, who in turn sells it to firm E, a retailer, and then, at last, it is bought for $250 by a consumer, the final user. At each stage, the difference between what a firm has paid for the product and what it receives for its sale is paid out as wages, rent, interest, and profits for the resources used by that firm in helping to produce and distribute the suit.

TABLE 7-2   Value added in a five-stage production process *(hypothetical data)*

(1) Stage of production	(2) Sales value of materials or product	(3) Value added
	0	
Firm A, sheep ranch	$ 60	$60(= $ 60 − $ 0)
Firm B, wool processor	100	40(= 100 − 60)
Firm C, suit manufacturer	125	25(= 125 − 100)
Firm D, clothing wholesaler	175	50(= 175 − 125)
Firm E, retail clothier	250	75(= 250 − 175)
Total sales values	$710	
Value added (total income)		$250

How much should we include in GDP in accounting for the production of this suit? Just $250, the value of the final product. This figure includes all the intermediate transactions leading up to the product's final sale. It would be a gross exaggeration to sum all the intermediate sales figures and the final sales value of the product in column 2 and add the entire amount, $710, to GDP. This would be a serious case of double counting, that is, counting the final product *and* the sale and resale of its various parts in the multistage productive process. The production and sale of the suit has generated $250, not $710, worth of output and income.

To avoid double counting, national income accountants are careful to calculate only the *value added* by each firm. **Value added** is the market value of a firm's output *less* the value of the inputs which it has purchased from others. Thus, in column 3 of Table 7-2 the value added of firm B is $40, the difference between the $100 value of its output and the $60 it paid for the inputs provided by firm A. By adding together the values added by the five firms in Table 7-2 the total value of the suit can be accurately determined. Similarly, by calculating and summing the values added by all firms in the economy, we can determine the GDP, that is, the market value of total output.

GDP Excludes Nonproduction Transactions

GDP measures the annual production of the economy. In doing so, the many nonproduction transactions which occur each year must be carefully excluded. *Nonproduction transactions* are of two major types: (1) purely financial transactions, and (2) secondhand sales.

Financial Transactions Purely financial transactions are of three general types: public transfer payments, private transfer payments, and the buying and selling of securities.

1 We have already mentioned *public transfer payments* (Chapter 5). These are the social security payments, welfare payments, and veterans' payments which government makes to particular households. The basic characteristic of public transfer payments is that recipients make no contribution to *current* production in return for them. Thus, to include them in GDP would be to overstate this year's production.

2 *Private transfer payments*—for example, a university student's monthly subsidy from home or an occasional gift from a wealthy relative—do not entail production but simply the transfer of funds from one private individual to another.

3 *Security transactions*—buying and selling stocks and bonds—are also excluded from GDP. Stock market transactions merely involve swapping paper assets. The amount spent on these assets does not directly involve current production. Only the services provided by the security broker are included in GDP. Note, however, that sales of *new* issues of stocks and bonds transfer money from savers to businesses which often spend the proceeds on capital goods. Thus, these transactions may indirectly contribute to spending, which does account for output.

Secondhand Sales The reason for excluding secondhand sales from GDP is that such sales either reflect no *current* production, or they involve double counting. If you sell your 1982 Ford to a friend, this transaction would be excluded in determining GDP because no current production is involved. Including the sales of goods produced some years ago in this year's GDP would be an exaggeration of this year's output. Similarly, if you purchased a brand new Ford and resold it a week later to your neighbor, we would still exclude the resale transaction from the current GDP. When you originally bought the new car, its value was included in GDP then. To include its resale value would be to count it twice.

Two Sides to GDP: Spending and Income

We now must consider how the market value of total output—or for that matter, any single unit of output—is measured. Returning to Table 7-2, how can we measure, for example, the market value of a suit?

First, we can determine how much a consumer, the final user, spends in obtaining it. Second, we can add up all the wage, rental, interest, and profit incomes created in its production. This second approach is the value-added technique discussed in Table 7-2.

The final-product and value-added approaches are two ways of looking at the same thing. *What is spent on a product is received as income by those who contributed to its production.* Indeed, Chapter 3's circular flow model demonstrated this concept. If $250 is spent on the suit, that is necessarily the total amount of income derived from its production. You can verify this by noting the incomes generated by firms A, B, C, D, and E in Table 7-2 are $60, $40, $25, $50, and $75 respectively, and total $250.

TABLE 7-3 **The output and income approaches to GDP**

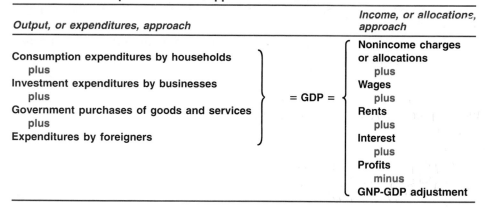

This equality of the expenditure for a product and the income derived from its production is guaranteed, because profit income serves as a balancing item. Profit—or loss—is the income remaining after wage, rent, and interest incomes have been paid by the producer. If the wage, rent, and interest incomes which the firm must pay in getting the suit produced are less than the $250 expenditure for the suit, the difference will be the firm's profits.[1] Conversely, if wage, rent, and interest incomes exceed $250, profits will be negative, that is, losses will be realized, to balance the expenditure on the product and the income derived from its production.

This reasoning is also valid for the output of the economy as a whole. There are two different ways of looking at GDP: One is to see GDP as the sum of all the expenditures involved in taking that total output off the market. This is called the *output,* or **expenditures, approach.** The other views it in terms of the income derived or created from the production of the GDP. This is called the *earnings,* or *allocations,* or **income, approach** to the determination of GDP.

GDP can be determined either by adding up all that is spent to buy this year's total output or by summing up all the incomes derived from the production of this year's output. Putting this in the form of a simple equation, we can say that

Amount spent to purchase this year's total output $\Big\}$ = $\begin{cases} \text{money income} \\ \text{derived from} \\ \text{production of} \\ \text{this year's output} \end{cases}$

This is more than an equation: It is an identity. Buying (spending money) and selling (receiving money income) are two aspects of the same transaction. *What is spent on a product is income to those who have contributed their human and property resources in getting that product produced and to market.*

For the economy as a whole, we can expand the above identity to read as in Table 7-3. This summary statement shows that all final goods produced in the American economy are purchased either by the three domestic sectors—households, businesses, and government—or by foreign consumers. It also demonstrates that, aside from a few complicating factors, discussed later, the total receipts which businesses acquire from the sale of total output are allocated among resource suppliers as wage, rent, interest, and profit income. Using this summary as a point of reference, we next examine in detail the meaning and significance of the types of expenditures and the incomes derived from them.

THE EXPENDITURES APPROACH TO GDP

To determine GDP through the expenditures approach, we must add up all types of spending on finished or final goods and services. But our national income accountants have more precise terms for the different types of spending than those in Table 7-3. We examine these precise terms and their meanings next.

Personal Consumption Expenditures (C)

What we have called "consumption expenditures by households" is **personal consumption expenditures** to national income accountants. It includes ex-

---

[1] The term "profits" is used here in the accounting sense to include both normal profits and economic profits as defined in Chapter 5.

penditures by households on *durable consumer goods* (automobiles, refrigerators, video recorders), *nondurable consumer goods* (bread, milk, beer, cigarettes, shirts, toothpaste), and *consumer expenditures for services* (of lawyers, doctors, mechanics, barbers). We will use the letter C to designate the total of these expenditures.

Gross Private Domestic Investment (I_g)

This term refers to all investment spending by American business firms. Investment spending includes three things:

1   All final purchases of machinery, equipment, and tools by business enterprises
2   All construction
3   Changes in inventories

This is more than we have ascribed to the term "investment" thus far. Hence, we must explain why each of these three items is included under the general heading of gross private domestic investment.

The reason for including the first group of items is apparent. This simply restates our original definition of investment spending as the purchase of tools, machinery, and equipment.

The second item—all construction—merits explanation. Clearly, building a new factory, warehouse, or grain elevator is a form of investment. But why include residential construction as investment rather than consumption? Because apartment buildings are investment goods which, like factories and grain elevators, are income-earning assets. Other residential units which are rented are for the same reason investment goods. Furthermore, owner-occupied houses are classified as investment goods because they could be rented out to yield a money income return, even though the owner may not do so. For these reasons all residential construction is considered as investment.

Finally, changes in inventories are counted as investment because an increase in inventories is, in effect, "unconsumed output," and that precisely is what investment is!

Inventory Changes as Investment   Because GDP is designed to measure total current output, we must include in GDP any products which are produced *but not sold* this year. If GDP is to be an accurate measure of total production, it must include the market value of any additions to inventories which accrue during the year. If we excluded an increase in inventories, GDP

would understate the current year's total production. If businesses have more goods on their shelves and in warehouses at year's end than they had at the start, the economy has produced more than it has purchased during this year. This increase in inventories must be added to GDP as a measure of *current* production.

What about a decline in inventories? This must be subtracted in figuring GDP, because in this situation the economy sells a total output which exceeds current production, the difference being reflected in inventory reduction. Some of the GDP taken off the market this year reflects not current production but, rather, a drawing down of inventories on hand at the beginning of this year. And inventories on hand at the start of any year's production represent the production of previous years. Consequently, a decline in inventories in any given year means that the economy has purchased more than it has produced during the year. Rephrased, society has purchased all of this year's output plus some of the inventories inherited from previous years' production. Because GDP is a measure of the *current* year's output, we must omit any purchases of past production, that is, any drawing down of inventories, in determining GDP.[2]

Noninvestment Transactions   We have discussed what investment is; it is equally important to emphasize what it is not. Specifically, investment does *not* refer to the transfer of paper assets or secondhand tangible assets. The buying of stocks and bonds is excluded from the economist's definition of investment, because such purchases merely transfer the ownership of existing assets. The same holds true of the resale of existing assets.

Investment is the construction or manufacture of *new* capital assets. The creation of these earning assets gives rise to jobs and income, not the exchange of claims to existing capital goods.

Gross versus Net Investment   We have broadened our concepts of investment and investment goods to include purchases of machinery and equipment, all construction, and changes in inventories. Now let's focus our attention on the three modifiers, "gross," "private," and "domestic," which national income ac-

---

[2]Both *planned* and *unplanned* changes in inventories are included as part of investment. In the former, firms may intentionally increase their inventories because aggregate sales are growing. In the latter, an unexpected drop in sales may leave firms with more unsold goods (larger inventories) than intended.

countants use in describing investment. The second and third terms tell us, respectively, that we are talking about spending by private business enterprises as opposed to governmental (public) agencies, and that the investment is in America—as opposed to abroad.

The term "gross," however, cannot be disposed of so easily. **Gross private domestic investment** includes production of *all* investment goods—those which replace machinery, equipment, and buildings used up in the current year's production *plus* any net additions to the economy's stock of capital. In short, gross investment includes both replacement and added investment. On the other hand, the term **net private domestic investment** refers only to the added investment in the current year.

A simple example will make the distinction clear. In 1991 our economy produced about $725 billion worth of capital goods. However, in the process of producing the GDP in 1991, the economy used up some $623 billion worth of machinery and equipment. Thus, our economy added $102 (or $725 minus $623) billion to its stock of capital in 1991. Gross investment was $725 billion in 1991, but net investment was only $102 billion. The difference between the two is the value of the capital used up or depreciated in the production of 1991's GDP.

Net Investment and Economic Growth The relationship between gross investment and *depreciation*—the amount of the nation's capital worn out or used up in a particular year—is a good indicator of whether our economy is expanding, static, or declining. Figure 7-1 illustrates these cases.

1 Expanding Economy When gross investment exceeds depreciation (Figure 7-1a), the economy is expanding in that its productive capacity—measured by its stock of capital goods—is growing. More simply, net investment is a positive figure in an expanding economy. For example, as noted above, in 1991 gross investment was $725 billion, and $623 billion worth of capital goods was consumed in producing that year's GDP. Our economy ended 1991 with $102 billion more capital goods than it had on hand at the start of the year. Bluntly stated, we made a $102 billion addition to our "national factory" in 1991. Increasing the supply of capital goods is a basic means of expanding the productive capacity of the economy (Chapter 2).

2 Static Economy A stationary or static economy is

one in which gross investment and depreciation are equal (Figure 7-1b). The economy is standing pat; it produces just enough capital to replace what is consumed in producing the year's output—no more, no less. Example: During World War II, the Federal government purposely restricted private investment to free resources to produce war goods. In 1942 gross private investment and depreciation (replacement investment) were each about $10 billion and thus net investment was about zero. At the end of 1942 our stock of capital was about the same as at the start of that year. Our economy was stationary; its production facilities failed to expand.

3 Declining Economy A declining economy arises whenever gross investment is less than depreciation, that is, when the economy uses up more capital in a year than it produces (Figure 7-1c). Under these circumstances net investment will be a negative figure—the economy will be *disinvesting*. Depressions foster such circumstances. During bad times, when production and employment are at a low ebb, the nation has a greater productive capacity than it is currently using. There is little or no incentive to replace depreciated capital equipment, much less add to the existing stock. Depreciation is likely to exceed gross investment, with the result that the nation's stock of capital is less at the end of the year than it was at the start.

This was the case during the heart of the Great Depression. In 1933 gross investment was only $1.6 billion, while the capital consumed during that year was $7.6 billion. Net disinvestment was therefore $6 billion. That is, net investment was a minus $6 billion, indicating that the size of our "national factory" shrunk during that year.

We will use the symbol I for domestic investment spending and attach the subscript g when referring to gross and n when referring to net investment.

Government Purchases (G)

This classification of expenditures *includes* all governmental spending, Federal, state, and local, on the finished products of businesses and all direct purchases of resources—labor, in particular—by government. However, it *excludes* all government transfer payments, because such outlays, as previously noted, do not reflect any current production but merely transfer governmental receipts to certain specific households. The letter G will indicate **government purchases.**

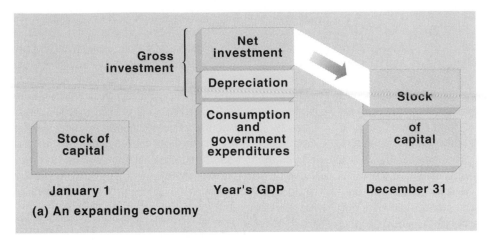

(a) An expanding economy

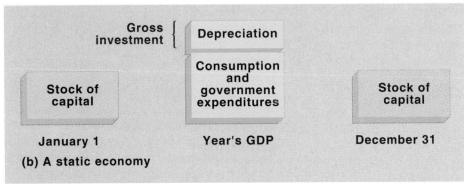

(b) A static economy

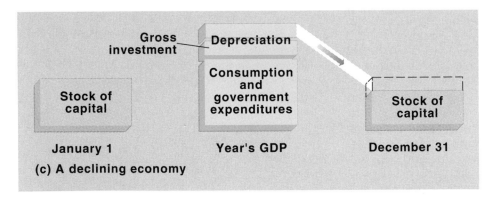

(c) A declining economy

FIGURE 7-1 Expanding, static, and declining economies

In an expanding economy (a), gross investment exceeds depreciation, which means that the economy is making a net addition to its stock of capital facilities. In a static economy (b), gross investment precisely replaces the capital facilities depreciated in producing the year's output, leaving the stock of capital goods unchanged. In a declining economy (c), gross investment is insufficient to replace the capital goods depreciated by the year's production. As a result, the economy's stock of capital declines.

Net Exports (X_n)

How do American international trade transactions enter into national income accounting? We can best explain it in this way: On the one hand, we are trying to add up all spending in American markets which accounts for or induces the production of goods and services in the American economy.

Spending by foreigners on American goods will account for American output just as will spending by Americans. Thus, we must add in what foreigners spend on American goods and services—that is, we must add in the value of American exports—in determining GDP by the expenditures approach.

On the other hand, we must recognize that a portion of consumption, investment, and government purchases is for goods which have been imported, that is, produced abroad, and therefore does *not* reflect production activity in the United States. The value of imports is subtracted to avoid overstating total production in the United States.

TABLE 7-4 **The income statement for the economy, 1991** *(in billions of dollars)*

Receipts: expenditures approach		Allocations: income approach	
Personal consumption expenditures *(C)*	$3887	Consumption of fixed capital	$623
Gross private domestic investment *(I$_g$)*	725	Indirect business taxes...........................	521
Government purchases *(G)*	1087	Compensation of employees	3388
Net exports *(X$_n$)*	−27	Rents	−13
		Interest	481
		Proprietors' income	380
		Corporate income taxes	120
		Dividends	138
		Undistributed corporate profits	47
		Gross national product.........................	$5684
		Less: Net American income earned abroad........	12
Gross domestic product	$5672	Gross domestic product........................	$5672

Source: U.S. Department of Commerce data. Because of rounding, details may not add up to totals.

Rather than treat these two items—American exports and imports—separately, our national income accountants merely take the difference between the two. Thus, net exports of goods and services or, more simply, **net exports,** *is the amount by which foreign spending on American goods and services exceeds American spending on foreign goods and services.*

If foreigners buy $45 billion worth of American exports and Americans buy $35 billion worth of foreign imports in a given year, net exports would be *plus* $10 billion. We must emphasize that our definition of net exports might result in a negative figure. If foreigners spend $30 billion on American exports and Americans spend $40 billion on foreign imports, our "excess" of foreign spending over American spending is *minus* $10 billion. Note in Table 7-4 that in 1991 Americans in fact spent $27 billion more on foreign goods and services than foreigners spent on American goods and services, a matter which will receive our attention in later chapters.

The letter X_n will designate net exports.

$C + I_g + G + X_n$ = GDP

These four categories of expenditures—personal consumption expenditures *(C)*, gross private domestic investment *(I$_g$)*, government purchases *(G)*, and net exports *(X$_n$)*—are comprehensive. They include all possible types of spending. Added together, they measure the market value of the year's output or, in other words, the GDP. That is,

$$C + I_g + G + X_n = \text{GDP}$$

For 1991 (Table 7-4):
$$\$3887 + \$725 + \$1087 - \$27 = \$5672$$

THE INCOME APPROACH TO GDP[3]

How was this $5672 billion of expenditure allocated or distributed as income? It would be simple if we could say that total expenditures on the economy's annual output flow to households as wage, rent, interest, and profit incomes. However, the picture is complicated by two *nonincome charges* against the value of total output (GDP). These are (1) consumption of fixed capital, and (2) indirect business taxes. Also, a complication arises because some of the recorded wage, rent, interest, and profit income comes from resources supplied by Americans abroad.

Depreciation: Consumption of Fixed Capital

The useful life of most capital equipment extends far beyond the year of purchase. Actual expenditures for capital goods and their productive life are not synchronized in the same accounting period. To avoid gross understatement of profit and therefore of total income in the year of purchase and overstatement of profit and total income in succeeding years, individual businesses

[3]Some instructors may choose to omit this section because the expenditures approach is more relevant for the analysis of Chapters 9–12.

estimate the useful life of their capital goods and allocate the total cost of such goods more or less evenly over the life of the machinery. The annual charge which estimates the amount of capital equipment used up in each year's production is called "depreciation." Depreciation is a bookkeeping entry designed to yield a more accurate statement of profit income and hence total income of a firm in each year.

If profits and total income for the economy as a whole are to be stated accurately, a gigantic depreciation charge must be made against the total receipts of the business sector. This depreciation charge is called **consumption of fixed capital.** This is exactly what it is—an allowance for capital goods which have been "consumed" in producing this year's GDP. This huge depreciation charge constitutes the previously noted difference between gross and net investment (I_g and I_n).

For present purposes, the significance of this charge is that part of the business sector's receipts is *not* available for income payments to resource suppliers. Part of the receipts—that is, part of the value of production—is a cost of production which reduces business profits. But, unlike other costs of production, depreciation does not add to anyone's income. In real terms, meaning in terms of physical goods and services, the consumption of fixed capital tells us that a portion of this year's GDP must be set aside to replace the machinery and equipment used up in its production. Not all of GDP can be consumed as income by society without impairing the economy's stock of production facilities.

Indirect Business Taxes

The second complicating nonincome charge arises because government levies certain taxes, called **indirect business taxes,** which business firms treat as costs of production and therefore add to the prices of the products they sell. Such taxes include general sales taxes, excises, business property taxes, license fees, and customs duties. Assume a firm produces a product designed to sell at $1. As we have seen, production of this item creates an equal amount of wages, rental, interest, and profit income. But now government imposes a 5 percent sales tax on all products sold at retail. The retailer adds this 5 percent to the price of the product, raising its price from $1 to $1.05 and thereby shifting the burden of the sales tax to consumers.

This $.05 of tax must be paid to government before the remaining $1 can be paid to households as wage, rent, interest, and profit incomes. Furthermore, this flow of indirect business taxes to government is not earned income, because government contributes nothing directly to the production of the good in return for these tax receipts. For this reason we must exclude indirect business taxes when figuring the total income earned by the factors of production. Part of the value of the annual output reflects the indirect business taxes passed along to consumers as higher product prices. This part of the value of the nation's output is *not* available as either wages, rents, interest, or profits.

Consumption of fixed capital and indirect business taxes account for the nonincome allocations listed in Table 7-3. What remains are wages, rents, interest, profits, and a GNP–GDP adjustment. But national income statisticians need a more detailed breakdown of wages and profits than we have discussed thus far.

Compensation of Employees

This largest income category comprises primarily the wages and salaries paid by businesses and government to suppliers of labor. It also includes an array of wage and salary supplements, in particular, payments by employers into social insurance and into a variety of private pension, health, and welfare funds for workers. These wage and salary supplements are part of the employer's cost of obtaining labor and are treated as a component of the firm's total wage payments.

Rents

Rents consist of income payments received by households which supply property resources. Rents were negative in 1991 because depreciation exceeded rental revenue.

Interest

Interest refers to money income payments flowing from private businesses to the suppliers of money capital. For reasons noted later, interest payments made by government are excluded from interest income.

Proprietors' Income

What we have loosely termed "profits" is also broken into two basic accounts: *proprietors' income* or income of unincorporated businesses, and *corporate profits.* Proprietors' income refers to the net income of sole proprietorships, partnerships, and cooperatives. Corporate profits cannot be dismissed so easily, because corporate earnings may be distributed in several ways.

Corporate Profits

Generally, three things happen with corporate profits:
1 A part will be claimed by, and therefore flow to, government as *corporate income taxes.*
2 A part of the remaining corporate profits will be paid out to stockholders as *dividends.* Such payments flow to households, which are the ultimate owners of all corporations.
3 What remains of corporate profits after both corporate income taxes and dividends have been paid is called *undistributed corporate profits.* These retained corporate earnings, along with consumption of fixed capital, are invested currently or in the future in new plants and equipment, increasing the real assets of the investing businesses.

Net American Income Earned Abroad

When we add employee compensation, rents, interest, proprietors' income, and corporate profits we get the national income earned by American-supplied resources, whether here or abroad. Adding the two nonincome charges to this total yields gross national product (GNP), not GDP. Therefore, to get gross *domestic* product we have to subtract from GNP the *net* income which Americans earned abroad. This net income earned abroad—or net output produced by Americans there—is determined by subtracting total income payments to the rest of the world from total income receipts from the rest of the world. Thus, *net* income from abroad can be either positive or negative. In 1991 it was a positive $12 billion, meaning that American-supplied resources produced and earned more abroad than foreign-owned resources produced and earned in the United States. Subtracting this positive amount from GNP, in 1991 we get:

	Billions
Gross national product	$5672
Net American income earned abroad	−12
Gross domestic product	$5684

Table 7-4 summarizes our discussions of both the expenditure and income approaches to GDP. You will

note that this is a gigantic income statement for the economy as a whole. The left-hand side tells us what the economy produced in 1991 and the total revenue derived from that production. The right-hand side indicates how the income derived from the production of 1991's GDP was allocated.

QUICK REVIEW 7-1

✦ **Gross domestic product (GDP) measures the total market value of all final goods and services produced within the economy in a specific year.**
✦ **The expenditures approach to GDP sums the total spending on final goods and services: $C + I_g + G + X_n$.**
✦ **When net investment is positive, the economy's production capacity expands; when net investment is negative, the economy's production capacity erodes.**
✦ **The income approach to GDP sums the total income earned by American resource suppliers, adds two nonincome charges (depreciation and indirect business taxes), and subtracts net American income earned abroad.**

OTHER SOCIAL ACCOUNTS

Our discussion has centered on GDP as a measure of the economy's annual output. However, there are related social accounting concepts of equal importance which can be derived from GDP. Our plan of attack in identifying these concepts will be to start with GDP and make a series of adjustments—subtractions and additions—necessary to the derivation of the related social accounts. We have already mentioned the first two of these adjustments.

Net Domestic Product (NDP)

GDP as a measure of total output has an important defect: It gives us a somewhat exaggerated picture of this year's production. *It fails to make allowance for that part of this year's output needed to replace the capital goods used up in the year's production.*
Example: Using hypothetical figures, suppose that on January 1, 1993, the economy had $100 billion worth of capital goods on hand. Assume also that during 1993, $40 billion worth of this equipment and machinery is used up in producing a GDP of $800 billion. Thus,

Computing a GDP Price Index

Table 7-6 gives an example of how a GDP price index or deflator can be computed in a particular year for a hypothetical economy. Observe from column 1 that in 1993 this economy produces only four goods: pizzas (a consumption good); industrial robots (a capital good); paper clips (a good purchased by government); and computer disks (an export good). Suppose that in 1993 the outputs of the four goods are 2, 1, 1, and 1 units, respectively, as shown in column 2. Furthermore, assume that the per unit prices of these four products in 1993 are those shown in column 3. The total price (cost) of the 1993 output therefore is $64, an amount found by summing the expenditures on each of the four goods (column 4).

Now, let's arbitrarily select 1987 as our reference or base year to establish a price index for 1993. The 1987 prices of the components of the 1993 output are listed in column 5 of Table 7-6. From columns 5 and 3, we observe that the prices of pizza and paper clips were lower in 1987 than in 1993, the price of robots was higher, and the price of computer disks did not change. Most importantly, the total price (cost) of the 1993 output—shown at the bottom of column 6—was $50 in 1987 rather than $64 as in 1993. This tells us that the 1993 output would have cost $50 if 1987 prices had persisted. To determine the 1993 price index, we divide the 1993 price of the market basket ($64) by the 1987 price of that same collection of goods ($50). The quotient is then multiplied by 100 to express the price index in its conventional form.

$$\text{GDP price index}_{1993} = \frac{\text{price of market basket}_{1993}}{\text{price of 1993 market basket in the base year}_{1987}} \times 100$$

More concretely,

$$\text{GDP price index}_{1993} = \frac{\$64}{\$50} \times 100 = 128$$

The price index for 1993 is 128. This index value may be thought of as the price level for 1993.

These steps can be used to calculate the price level for all years in a series of years. For example, the price index in the 1987 base year is found by discovering the price of the particular collection of goods and services produced in 1987 and comparing this price to the price of that same market basket in the base year. However, in this special case, the "given year" and the "reference year" are the same. That is,

$$\text{GDP price index}_{1987} = \frac{\text{price of market basket}_{1987}}{\text{price of market basket}_{1987}} \times 100$$

The GDP price index for the 1987 base year therefore is 100. In effect, we automatically set the price index at 100 in the base year.

Likewise, if we wanted to know the GDP price index for 1950, we would determine 1950 output and then estimate what that same or a similar collection of goods and services would have cost in the 1987 base year. If prices on the 1950 output had quadrupled between 1950 and 1987, the price ratio of the market basket would be $\frac{1}{4}$ (=.25) and the 1950 GDP price index would be 25 (=.25 × 100).

Once a GDP price index has been constructed for each year in a series of years, comparisons of price levels between years is possible. First example: If the price indexes for 1993 and 1987 are 128 and 100, respectively, we can calculate that the price level increased by 28 percent [=(128 − 100)/100] between

TABLE 7-6 **Computing a GDP price index for 1993** *(hypothetical data)*

(1) Product	(2) Quantities in market basket in 1993	(3) Prices of 1993 market basket in 1993	(4) Expenditures on 1993 market basket in 1993 (3) × (2)	(5) Prices of 1993 market basket in 1987 (base year)	(6) Expenditures on 1993 market basket in 1987 (5) × (2)
Pizzas	2	$12	$24	$ 5	$10
Robots	1	18	18	20	20
Paper clips	1	8	8	6	6
Computer disks	1	14	14	14	14
Total price (cost)			$64		$50
GDP price index 1993			$128\left(=\dfrac{\$64}{\$50} \times 100\right)$		

the two years. Second example: If, as suggested by our previous illustration, the price index for 1950 is 25, we can say that the price level rose by 412 percent [(128 − 25)/25] between 1950 and 1993. Third example: if the price index fell from 100 in 1987 to 98 in 1988, we would know that the price level declined by 2 percent [= (98 − 100)/100].

Conclusions: The GDP price index compares the price of each year's output to the price of that same output in the base year or reference year. A series of price indexes for various years enables us to compare price levels between years. An increase in the GDP price index from one year to the next constitutes *inflation;* a decrease in the price index constitutes *deflation.*

NOMINAL AND REAL GDP

Inflation or deflation complicates gross domestic product because GDP is a price-times-quantity figure. The raw data from which the national income accountants estimate GDP are the total sales figures of business firms; however, these figures include changes in *both* the quantity of output *and* the level of prices. This means that a change in either the quantity of total physical output or the price level will affect the size of GDP. However, it is the quantity of goods produced and distributed to households which affects their standard of living, not the size of the price tags on these goods. The hamburger of 1970 which sold for 65 cents yielded the same satisfaction as will an identical hamburger selling for $2.00 in 1993.

The situation facing our social accountants is this: In gathering statistics from financial reports of businesses and deriving GDP in various years, government accountants come up with nominal GDP figures. They do *not* know directly to what extent changes in price, on the one hand, and changes in quantity of output, on the other, have accounted for the given increases in nominal GDP. For example, they would not know directly if a 4 percent increase in nominal GDP resulted from a 4 percent rise in output and zero inflation, a zero percent change in output and 4 percent inflation, or some other combination of changes in output and the price level, say, a 2 percent increase in output and 2 percent inflation. The problem is one of adjusting a price-times-quantity figure so it will accurately reflect changes in physical output or quantity, not changes in prices.

Fortunately, national income accountants have resolved this difficulty: They *deflate* GDP for rising prices and *inflate* it when prices are falling. These adjustments give us a picture of GDP for various years *as if* prices and the value of the dollar were constant. A GDP figure which reflects current prices, that is, which is *not* adjusted for changes in the price level, is alternatively called *unadjusted, current dollar, money,* or *nominal GDP.* Similarly, GDP figures which are inflated or deflated for price level changes measure *adjusted, constant dollar,* or **real GDP.**

The Adjustment Process

The process for adjusting current dollar or nominal GDP for inflation or deflation is straightforward. The GDP deflator for a specific year tells us the ratio of that year's prices to the prices of the same goods in the base year. The GDP deflator or GDP price index therefore can be used to inflate or deflate nominal GDP figures. The outcome of this adjustment is that GDP for each year gets expressed in real terms: in other words, *as if* base year prices prevailed. *The simplest and most direct method of deflating or inflating a year's nominal GDP is to express that year's index number in decimal form, and divide it into the nominal GDP.* This yields the same result as the more complex procedure of dividing nominal GDP by the corresponding index number and multiplying the quotient by 100. In equation form:

$$\frac{\text{Nominal GDP}}{\text{price index (in hundredths)}} = \text{real GDP}$$

To illustrate in terms of Table 7-6, in 1993 nominal GDP is $64 and the price index for that year is 128 (= 1.28 in hundredths). Real GDP in 1993, therefore, is:

$$\frac{\$64}{1.28} = \$50$$

In summary, the real GDP figures measure the value of total output in the various years *as if* the prices of the products had been constant from the reference or base year throughout all the years being considered. Real GDP thus shows the market value of each year's output measured in terms of constant dollars, that is, dollars which have the same value, or purchasing power, as the base year. Real GDP is clearly superior to nominal GDP as an indicator of the economy's production performance.

Inflating and Deflating

Table 7-7 is a "real-world" illustration of the **inflating** and **deflating** process. Here we are taking actual nomi-

TABLE 7-7 Adjusting GDP for changes in the price level *(selected years, in billions of dollars)*

(1) Year	(2) Nominal, or unadjusted, GDP	(3) Price level index,* percent (1987 = 100)	(4) Real, or adjusted, GDP, 1987 dollars
1960	$ 513.4	26.0	$1974.6 (= 513.4 ÷ 0.260)
1965	702.7	28.4	_____
1970	1010.7	35.1	$2879.5 (= 1010.7 ÷ 0.351)
1975	1585.9	49.2	_____
1980	2708.0	71.7	$3776.8 (= 2708.0 ÷ 0.717)
1983	3405.0	87.2	$3904.8 (= 3405.0 ÷ 0.872)
1985	4038.7	94.4	_____
1986	4268.6	96.9	$4405.2 (= 4268.6 ÷ 0.969)
1987	4539.9	100.0	$4539.9 (= 4539.9 ÷ 1.000)
1988	4900.4	103.9	_____
1989	5244.0	108.4	$4837.6 (= 5244.0 ÷ 1.084)
1990	5513.8	112.9	$4883.1 (= 5513.8 ÷ 1.129)
1991	5671.8	117.0	$4847.7 (= 5671.8 ÷ 1.170)

*U.S. Department of Commerce implicit price deflators.

Source: U.S. Department of Commerce data.

nal GDP figures for selected years and adjusting them with an index of the general price level for these years to obtain real GDP. Note that the base year is 1987.

Because the long-run trend has been for the price level to rise, the problem is one of increasing, or *inflating,* the pre-1987 figures. This upward revision of nominal GDP acknowledges that prices were lower in years prior to 1987 and, as a result, nominal GDP figures understated the real output of those years. Column 4 indicates what GDP would have been in all these selected years if the 1987 price level had prevailed.

The rising price level has caused the nominal GDP figures for the post-1987 years to overstate real output; hence, these figures must be reduced, or *deflated,* as in column 4, to gauge what GDP would have been in 1988, 1990, and so on, if 1987 prices had actually prevailed. In short, while the *nominal* GDP figures reflect both output and price changes, the *real* GDP figures allow us to estimate changes in real output, because the real GDP figures, in effect, hold the price level constant.

Example: For 1991 nominal GDP was $5671.8 billion and the price index was 117.0 or 17.0 percent higher than 1987. To compare 1991's GDP with 1987's we express the 1991 index in hundredths (1.170) and divide it into the nominal GDP of $5671.8 as shown in column 4. The resulting real GDP of $4847.7 is directly comparable to the 1987 base year's GDP because both reflect only changes in output and *not* price level changes. You should trace through the computations involved in deriving the real GDP figures given in Table 7-7 and also determine real GDP for years 1965, 1975, 1985, 1988, for which the figures have been purposely omitted.

QUICK REVIEW 7-3

◆ *A price index compares the combined price of a specific market basket of goods and services in a particular year to the combined price of the same basket in a base year.*

◆ *Nominal GDP is output valued at current prices; real GDP is output valued at constant prices (base year prices).*

◆ *A year's nominal GDP can be adjusted to real GDP by dividing nominal GDP by the GDP price index (expressed in hundredths).*

GDP AND SOCIAL WELFARE

GDP is a reasonably accurate and extremely useful measure of domestic economic performance. It is not, and was never intended to be, an index of social welfare. GDP is merely a measure of the annual volume of market-oriented activity.

> . . . any number of things could make the Nation better off without raising its real [GDP] as measured today: we might start the list with peace, equality of opportunity, the elimination of injustice and violence, greater brotherhood among Americans of different racial and ethnic backgrounds, better understanding between parents and children and between husbands and wives, and we could go on endlessly.[6]

Nevertheless, it is widely held that there should be a strong positive correlation between real GDP and social welfare, that is, greater production should move society toward "the good life." Thus, we must understand some of the shortcomings of GDP—some reasons why it might understate or overstate real output and why more output will not necessarily make society better off.

Nonmarket Transactions

Certain production transactions do not appear in the market. Hence, GDP as a measure of the market value of output fails to include them. Standard examples include the production services of a homemaker, the efforts of the carpenter who repairs his or her own home, or the work of the erudite professor who writes a scholarly but nonremunerative article. Such transactions are *not* reflected in the profit and loss statements of business firms and therefore escape the national income accountants, causing GDP to be understated. However, some quantitatively large nonmarket transactions, such as that portion of farmers' output which farmers consume themselves, are estimated by national income accountants.

Leisure

Over many years, leisure has increased very significantly. The workweek declined from about 53 hours at the turn of the century to approximately 40 hours by the end of World War II. Since then the workweek has declined more slowly and is currently about 35 hours. In addition, the expanded availability of paid vacations, holidays, and leave time has reduced the work year. This increased leisure has had a positive effect upon our well-being. Our system of social accounting under-

states our well-being by not directly recognizing this. Nor do the accounts reflect the satisfaction—the "psychic income"—which people derive from their work.

Improved Product Quality

GDP is a quantitative rather than a qualitative measure. It does not accurately reflect improvements in product quality. This is a shortcoming: quality improvement clearly affects economic well-being as much as does the quantity of goods. To the extent that product quality has improved over time, GDP understates improvement in our material well-being.

Composition and Distribution of Output

Changes in the composition and the allocation of total output among specific households may influence economic welfare. GDP, however, reflects only the size of output and does not tell us anything about whether this collection of goods is "right" for society. A switchblade knife and a Beethoven compact disc, both selling for $14.95, are weighted equally in the GDP. And some economists feel that a more equal distribution of total output would increase national economic well-being. *If* these economists are correct, a future trend toward a less unequal distribution of GDP would enhance the economic welfare of society. A more unequal future distribution would have the reverse effect.

Conclusion: GDP measures the size of the total output but does not reflect changes in the composition and distribution of output which might also affect the economic well-being of society.

Per Capita Output

For many purposes the most meaningful measure of economic well-being is per capita output. Because GDP measures the size of total output, it may conceal or misrepresent changes in the standard of living of individual households in the economy. For example, GDP may rise significantly, but if population is also growing rapidly, the per capita standard of living may be relatively constant or may even be declining.

This is the plight of many of the less developed countries. India's domestic output grew at about 4.3 percent per year over the 1965–1989 period. But annual population growth exceeded 2 percent, resulting in a meager annual increase in per capita output of only 1.8 percent.

---

[6]Arthur M. Okun, "Social Welfare Has No Price Tag," *The Economic Accounts of the United States: Retrospect and Prospect* (U.S. Department of Commerce, July 1971), p. 129.

L A S T   W O R D

THE CONSUMER PRICE INDEX

The consumer price index is the most widely reported measure of inflation; therefore, it is important to have some knowledge of its characteristics and limitations.

The consumer price index (CPI) measures changes in the prices of a "market basket" of some 300 goods and services purchased by urban consumers. The composition of this market basket was determined on the basis of a survey of the spending patterns of urban consumers over the 1982–1984 period. The index is a "fixed-weight" index in that the composition of the market basket is the same in each year as in the base period (1982–1984).

The "fixed-weight" approach used to construct the CPI differs from the technique used to construct the GDP deflator discussed in this chapter. We previously indicated that the GDP deflator is found by establishing the market basket on the basis of the composition of output in *each* particular year and then determining what the price of that same composition of goods would have been in the base year (Table 7-6). Hence, the composition of the market basket used to construct the GDP index changes from year to year. But in the case of the CPI, the composition of the market basket is fixed in the base period and is assumed not to change from one period to another. The reason for this assumption is that the purpose of the CPI is to measure changes in the costliness of a constant standard of living. There are two well-known problems associated with the CPI which lead critics to conclude that this price index overstates increases in the cost of living.

Consumers in fact do change their spending patterns—the composition of the market basket changes—particularly in response to changes in relative prices. If the price of beef rises, consumers will substitute away from beef and buy fish, veal, or mutton instead. This means that over time consumers are buying a market basket which contains more of the relatively low-priced and less of the relatively high-priced goods and services. The fixed-weight CPI assumes these substitutions have not occurred and it therefore overstates the actual cost of living.

The CPI does not take qualitative improvements into account. To the extent that goods and services have improved since 1982–1984, their prices should be higher. Thus we ought to pay more for medical care today than in the early 1980s because it is generally of higher quality. The same can be said for computers, automobile tires, stereos, and many other items. The CPI, however, assumes all of the increase in the money or nominal value of the market basket is due solely to inflation rather than quality improvements. Again, the CPI tends to overstate the rate of inflation.

In general, economists feel that the CPI overstates the rate of inflation, perhaps by a significant margin. So

GDP and the Environment

There are undesirable and much publicized "gross domestic by-products" accompanying the production and growth of the GDP such as dirty air and water, automobile junkyards, congestion, noise, and other forms of environmental pollution. Clearly, the costs of pollution affect our economic well-being adversely.

These spillover costs associated with the production of the GDP are not now deducted from total output and, hence, GDP overstates our national economic welfare. Ironically, as GDP increases, so does pollution and the extent of this overstatement. As put by one economist, "The ultimate physical product of economic life is garbage."[7] A rising GDP means more garbage—more environmental pollution. In fact, under existing ac-

what? The major consequence is that this overstatement may contribute to ongoing inflation because the incomes of large numbers of people are tied directly or indirectly to changes in the CPI. For example, some 40 million social security recipients have their monthly check tied or "indexed" to the CPI. And an estimated 6 million workers have cost-of-living adjustments (COLAs) in their collective bargaining agreements. When prices rise, their money wages automatically increase to further fuel inflation. Furthermore, the wage expectations and demands of virtually all workers—union or nonunion, blue- or white-collar—are linked to the cost of living as measured by the CPI. Thus the CPI is not merely a vehicle for measuring the problem of inflation; it may be part of the problem!

Another consequence of an overstated CPI stems from the "indexing" of personal income tax brackets. This indexing—or adjusting tax brackets upward to account for the rate of inflation—was begun in 1985 to resolve an inequity in the personal income tax. Specifically, the intent of indexing is to prevent inflation from pushing households into higher tax brackets even though their real incomes have not increased. For example, a 10 percent increase in your *nominal* income might put you in a higher marginal tax bracket and increase the proportion of your income paid in taxes. But if product prices are also rising by 10 percent, your *real* or inflation-adjusted income has remained constant. The result would be an unintended redistribution of real income from taxpayers to the Federal government. The purpose of indexing tax brackets was to prevent this redistribution. However, to the extent that the CPI *overstates* inflation, indexing will reduce government's tax share. The Federal government will be deprived of substantial amounts of tax revenue and real income will be redistributed from government to taxpayers.

counting procedures, when a manufacturer pollutes a river and government spends to clean it up, the cleanup expense is added to the GDP while the pollution is not subtracted!

[7]See the delightful and perceptive essay "Fun and Games with the Gross National Product" by Kenneth E. Boulding, in Harold W. Helfrich, Jr. (ed.), *The Environmental Crisis* (New Haven: Yale University Press, 1970), p. 162.

The Underground Economy

Economists agree that there is a relatively large and perhaps expanding underground or subterranean sector in our economy. Some participants in this sector engage in illegal activities such as gambling, loan-sharking, prostitution, and the narcotics trade. These may well be "growth industries." Obviously, persons receiving income from such illegal businesses choose to conceal their incomes.

Most participants in the underground economy are in legal activities, but do not fully report their incomes to the Internal Revenue Service (IRS). A waiter or waitress may underreport tips from customers. A businessperson may record only a portion of sales receipts for the tax collector. A worker who wants to retain unemployment compensation or welfare benefits may obtain an "off the books" or "cash only" job so there is no record of his or her work activities. As inflation and high tax burdens squeeze real disposable incomes, the incentive to receive income in forms (for example, cash and barter) which cannot be readily discovered by the IRS is strengthened.

Although there is no consensus on the size of the underground economy, most estimates suggest that it is between 5 to 15 percent of the recorded GDP. In 1991, that meant official GDP was understated by between $284 and $851 billion. If this additional income had been taxed at a 20 percent average tax rate, the Federal budget deficit for 1991 would have declined from $269 billion to between a $212 billion and a $99 billion deficit.

There is also some evidence to suggest that the underground economy has been growing relative to the legal economy. If so, then national income accounts will increasingly understate our economy's performance and growth through time.

Finally, to the extent that a proportion of the population is involved in illegal activities or in legal activities where income is concealed, our official unemployment statistics will be overstated. This may pose a problem for policy makers. If the existence of the underground economy distorts such basic economic indicators as GDP and the unemployment rate, policies based on these indicators may be inappropriate and harmful. Thus an understated GDP and an overstated unemployment rate might prompt policy makers to stimulate the economy. But, as we will find in Chapter 12, the stimulus may cause unwanted inflation rather than increases in real output and employment.

CHAPTER SUMMARY

1 Gross domestic product (GDP), a basic measure of society's economic performance, is the market value of all final goods and services produced within the United States in a year. Intermediate goods, nonproduction transactions, and secondhand sales are purposely excluded in calculating GDP.

2 GDP may be calculated by summing total expenditures on all final output or by summing the income derived from the production of that output.

3 By the expenditures approach GDP is determined by adding consumer purchases of goods and services, gross investment spending by businesses, government purchases, and net exports; $GDP = C + I_g + G + X_n$.

4 Gross investment can be divided into **a** replacement investment (required to maintain the nation's stock of capital at its existing level), and **b** net investment (the net increase in the stock of capital). Positive net investment is associated with a growing economy; negative net investment with a declining economy.

5 By the income or allocations approach GDP is calculated as the sum of compensation to employees, rents, interest, proprietors' income, corporate income taxes, dividends, undistributed corporate profits, *plus* the two nonincome charges (capital consumption allowance and indirect business taxes) and *minus* net American income earned abroad.

6 Other important national income accounting measures are derived from GDP. Net domestic product (NDP) is GDP less the consumption of fixed capital. National income (NI)

is total income earned by American resource suppliers; it is found by adding net American income earned abroad and subtracting indirect business taxes from NDP. Personal income (PI) is the total income paid to households prior to any allowance for personal taxes. Disposable income (DI) is personal income after personal taxes have been paid. DI measures the amount of income households have available to consume or save.

7 Price indexes are computed by comparing the price of a specific collection or "market basket" of output in a given period to the price (cost) of the same market basket in a base period and multiplying the outcome (quotient) by 100. The GDP deflator is the price index associated with adjusting nominal GDP to account for inflation or deflation and thereby obtaining real GDP.

8 Nominal (current dollar) GDP measures each year's output valued in terms of the prices prevailing in that year. Real (constant dollar) GDP measures each year's output in terms of the prices which prevailed in a selected base year. Because it is adjusted for price level changes, real GDP measures the level of production activity.

9 The various national income accounting measures exclude nonmarket and illegal transactions, changes in leisure and product quality, the composition and distribution of output, and the environmental effects of production. Nevertheless, these measures are reasonably accurate and very useful indicators of the nation's economic performance.

TERMS AND CONCEPTS

national income accounting	**value added**	**government purchases**	**personal income**
gross national product	**expenditures and income approaches**	**net exports**	**disposable income**
gross domestic product	**personal consumption expenditures**	**consumption of fixed capital**	**price index**
final and intermediate goods	**gross and net private domestic investment**	**indirect business taxes**	**GDP deflator**
double counting		**net domestic product**	**nominal GDP**
		national income	**real GDP**
			inflating and deflating

QUESTIONS AND STUDY SUGGESTIONS

1 "National income statistics are a powerful tool of economic understanding and analysis." Explain this statement. "An economy's output is its income." Do you agree?

2 Why do national income accountants include only final goods in measuring total output? How do GDP and NDP differ?

3 What is the difference between gross private domestic investment and net private domestic investment? If you

were to determine net domestic product through the expenditures approach, which of these two measures of investment spending would be appropriate? Explain.

4 Why are changes in inventories included as part of investment spending? Suppose inventories declined by $1 billion during 1993. How would this affect the size of gross private domestic investment and gross domestic product in 1993? Explain.

5 The following is a list of domestic output and national income figures for a given year. All figures are in billions. The ensuing questions ask you to determine the major national income measures by both the expenditure and income methods. Answers derived by each approach should be the same.

Personal consumption expenditures	$245
Net American income earned abroad	4
Transfer payments	12
Rents	14
Consumption of fixed capital (depreciation)	27
Social security contributions	20
Interest	13
Proprietors' income	33
Net exports	3
Dividends	16
Compensation of employees	223
Indirect business taxes	18
Undistributed corporate profits	21
Personal taxes	26
Corporate income taxes	19
Corporate profits	56
Government purchases	72
Net private domestic investment	33
Personal saving	16

a Using the above data, determine GDP and NDP by both the expenditure and income methods.

b Now determine NI (1) by making the required additions and subtractions from GDP, and (2) by adding up the types of income which comprise NI.

c Make those adjustments of NI required in deriving PI.

d Make the required adjustments from PI (as determined in 5c) to obtain DI.

6 Use the concepts of gross and net investment to distinguish between an expanding, a static, and a declining economy. "In 1933 net private domestic investment was minus $6 billion. This means in that particular year the economy produced no capital goods at all." Do you agree? Explain: "Though net investment can be positive, negative, or zero, it is quite impossible for gross investment to be less than zero."

7 Define net exports. Explain how the United States' exports and imports each affect domestic production. Suppose foreigners spend $7 billion on American exports in a given year and Americans spend $5 billion on imports from abroad in the same year. What is the amount of America's net exports? Explain how net exports might be a negative amount.

8 Given the following national income accounting data, compute **a** GDP, **b** NDP, and **c** NI. All figures are in billions.

Compensation of employees	$194.2
U.S. exports of goods and services	13.4
Consumption of fixed capital	11.8
Government purchases	59.4
Indirect business taxes	14.4
Net private domestic investment	52.1
Transfer payments	13.9
U.S. imports of goods and services	16.5
Personal taxes	40.5
Net American income earned abroad	2.2
Personal consumption expenditures	219.1

9 Why do national income accountants compare the market value of the total outputs in various years rather than actual physical volumes of production? Explain. What problem is posed by any comparison over time of the market values of various total outputs? How is this problem resolved?

10 Suppose that in 1974 the total output of a hypothetical economy consisted of three goods—X, Y, and Z—produced in the following quantities: X = 4, Y = 1, Z = 3. Also suppose that in 1974 the prices of X, Y, and Z were as follows: X = $3, Y = $12, and Z = $5. Finally, assume that in 1987 the prices of these goods were X = $5, Y = $10, and Z = $10. Determine the GDP price index for 1974, using 1987 as the base year. By what percent did the price level rise between 1974 and 1987?

11 The following table shows nominal GDP and an appropriate price index for a group of selected years. Compute real GDP. Indicate in each calculation whether you are inflating or deflating the nominal GDP data.

Year	Nominal GDP, billions	Price level index, percent (1987 = 100)	Real GDP, billions
1959	$ 494.2	25.6	$_____
1964	648.0	27.7	$_____
1967	814.3	30.3	$_____
1973	1349.6	41.3	$_____
1978	2232.7	60.3	$_____
1988	4900.4	103.9	$_____

12 Which of the following are included in deriving this year's GDP? Explain your answer in each case.

a Interest on an AT&T bond

b Social security payments received by a retired factory worker

c The services of a painter in painting the family home

d   The income of a dentist

e   The money received by Smith when he sells a 1983 Chevrolet to Jones

f   The monthly allowance which a college student receives from home

g   Rent received on a two-bedroom apartment

h   The money received by Mac when he resells this year's model Plymouth to Ed

i   Interest received on government bonds

j   A 2-hour decline in the length of the workweek

k   The purchase of an AT&T bond

l   A $2 billion increase in business inventories

m   The purchase of 100 shares of GM common stock

n   The purchase of an insurance policy

o   Wages paid to a domestic servant

p   The market value of a homemaker's services

q   The purchase of a Renaissance painting by a public art museum

13 What would be the most likely effect on real GDP of each of the following: a a law mandating an increase in the workweek from 40 hours to 50 hours for every able-bodied adult;   b legalization of all activities currently undertaken in the underground economy; and   c a $1 million increase in the production of burglar alarms offset by a $1 million decline in the provision of prenatal health care services?

Would society's well-being in each of these situations change in the same direction as the change in real GDP? Explain.

Macroeconomic Instability: Unemployment and Inflation

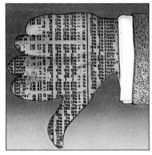

In an ideal economy, real GDP would expand over time at a brisk, steady pace. Additionally, the price level, as measured by the GDP deflator or the consumer price index, would remain constant or only rise slowly. The result would be neither significant unemployment nor inflation. Several periods of U.S. history fit this pattern. But experience shows that steady economic growth, full employment, and a stable price level cannot be taken for granted. Recent cases in point: (1) The inflation rate skyrocketed to 13.5 percent in 1980. (2) During a sixteen-month period in the early 1980s, real output fell by 3.5 percent. (3) Three million more people were unemployed in 1982 than in 1980. (4) The annual inflation rate rose from 1.9 percent in 1986 to 4.8 percent in 1989. (5) In mid-1990, output in the U.S. economy turned downward for the eighth time since 1950.

In this and the next several chapters we explore the problem of achieving macroeconomic stability, or more specifically, steady economic growth, full employment, and price stability. The present chapter proceeds as follows: First, we establish an overview of the business cycle—the periodic fluctuations in output, employment, and price level which characterize our economy. Then we look in more detail at unemployment. What are the various types of unemployment? How is unemployment measured? Why is unemployment an economic problem? Finally, we examine inflation—a serious problem which plagued us throughout the 1970s and into the early 1980s. What are inflation's causes and consequences?

OVERVIEW OF THE BUSINESS CYCLE

Our society seeks economic growth *and* full employment *and* price level stability along with other less quantifiable goals (Chapter 1). The broad spectrum of American economic history reflects remarkable economic growth. Technological progress, rapid increases in productive capacity, and a standard of living which is among the highest in the world are strategic facets of the dynamic character in our economy.

The Historical Record

But our long-run economic growth has not been steady; it has been interrupted by periods of economic

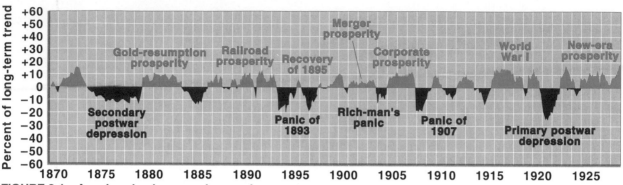

FIGURE 8-1   American business-cycle experience

As indicated by this chart which shows deviations from the long-run trend line of economic activity, the American economy has encountered periods of prosperity and depression. (AmeriTrust Company, Cleveland.)

instability as Figure 8-1 reveals. Periods of rapid economic expansion have sometimes been marred by inflation. At other times, expansion has given way to recession and depression, that is, falling levels of employment and output. On a few occasions—most notably in the 1970s and early 1980s— we have experienced a rising price level and abnormally high unemployment simultaneously. In short, the long-term trend of economic growth has been interrupted and complicated by both unemployment and inflation.

Phases of the Cycle

The term **business cycle** refers to the recurrent ups and downs in the level of economic activity which extend over several years. Individual business cycles vary substantially in duration and intensity. Yet all display common phases which are variously labeled by different economists. Figure 8-2 shows the several phases of a stylized business cycle.

1 Peak   We begin our explanation with a cyclical **peak** at which business activity has reached a temporary maximum such as the middle peak in Figure 8-2. Here the economy is at full employment and the domestic output is also at or very close to capacity. The price level is likely to rise during this cyclical phase.

2 Recession   The peak is followed by a **recession,** which is a period of decline in total output, income, employment, and trade, lasting six months or longer. This downturn is marked by widespread contractions of business in many sectors of the economy. But, be-

cause many prices in our economy are downwardly inflexible, the price level is likely to fall only if the recession is severe and prolonged—that is, if a depression occurs. An old one-liner is: "When your neighbor loses his job, it's a recession; when you lose your job it's a depression."

3 Trough   The **trough** of the recession or depression is where output and employment "bottom out" at their lowest levels. The trough phase of the cycle may be short-lived or quite long.

FIGURE 8-2   The business cycle

Economists distinguish between four phases of the business cycle and recognize that the duration and strength of each phase is highly variable. A recession, for example, need not always entail serious and prolonged unemployment. Nor need a cyclical peak always entail full employment.

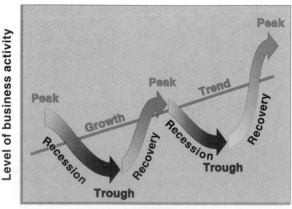

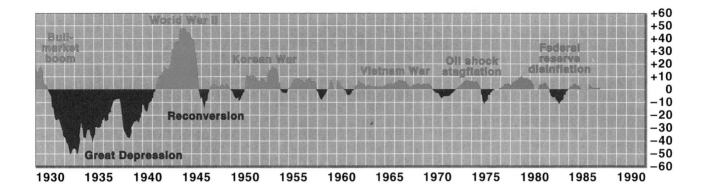

4 Recovery Finally, in the **recovery** phase the economy's levels of output and employment expand toward full employment. As recovery intensifies, the price level may begin to rise before the realization of full employment and full capacity production.

Despite common phases, specific business cycles vary greatly in duration and intensity. Indeed, some economists prefer to talk of business *fluctuations,* rather than *cycles,* because cycles imply regularity while fluctuations do not. The Great Depression of the 1930s resulted in a 40 percent decline in real GDP over a three-year period and seriously undermined business activity for an entire decade. By comparison, our more recent recessions—detailed in Table 8-1—have been minor in both intensity and duration.

Causation: A First Glance

Historically, economists have suggested many theories to explain fluctuations in business activity. Some center on innovation, contending that major innova-tions such as the railroad, the automobile, or synthetic fibers have great impact on investment and consumption spending and therefore on output, employment, and the price level. But these major innovations occur irregularly and thus contribute to the variability of economic activity.

Other economists have explained the business cycle in terms of political and random events, as suggested by some of the labeling in Figure 8-1. Wars, for example, can be economically very disruptive. A virtually insatiable demand for war goods during hostilities can generate a period of overfull employment and sharp inflation, frequently followed by an economic slump when peace returns and military spending plummets. Still other economists view the cycle as a purely monetary phenomenon. When government creates too much money, an inflationary boom is generated; a relative paucity of money will precipitate a declining output and unemployment.

Despite these diverse opinions, most economists believe that the immediate determinant of the levels of domestic output and employment is the level of total or aggregate expenditures. In a largely market-directed economy, businesses produce goods and services only if they can be sold profitably. If total spending is low, most businesses will not find it profitable to produce a large volume of goods and services. Hence, output, employment, and the level of incomes will all be low. A higher level of total spending will mean that more production will be profitable; thus, output, employment, and incomes will all be higher also. Once the economy reaches full employment, real output becomes fixed and added spending will simply pull up the price level. Later in this chapter we will find that the relationship between aggregate spending and the price level is more complex and that, in fact, inflation may arise from causes other than a change in total spending.

TABLE 8-1   United States recessions since 1950

Period	Duration in months	Depth (decline in real output)
1953–54	10	−3.0%
1957–58	8	−3.5
1960–61	10	−1.0
1969–70	11	−1.1
1973–75	16	−4.3
1980	6	−3.4
1981–82	16	−2.6
1990–?		

Source: NBER and Federal Reserve Bank of Boston.

Noncyclical Fluctuations

Not all changes in business activity result from the business cycle. There can be **seasonal variations** in business activity. For example, pre-Christmas and pre-Easter buying rushes cause considerable fluctuations each year in the tempo of business activity, particularly in the retail industry. Agriculture, the automobile industry, construction—all are subject to some degree of seasonality.

Business activity is also subject to a **secular trend**—its expansion or contraction over a long period of years, for example, 25, 50, or 100 years. We note here that the long-run secular trend for American capitalism has been one of rather remarkable expansion (Chapter 19). For present purposes, the importance of this long-run expansion is that the business cycle involves fluctuations in business activity around a long-run growth trend. Note that in Figure 8-1 cyclical fluctuations are measured as deviations from the secular growth trend and that the stylized cycle of Figure 8-2 is drawn against a trend of growth.

Cyclical Impact: Durables and Nondurables

The business cycle is pervasive; it is felt in virtually every nook and cranny of the economy. The interrelatedness of the elements of the economy allows few, if any, to escape the cold hand of depression or the fever of inflation. However, various individuals and various segments of the economy are affected in different ways and degrees by the business cycle.

Insofar as production and employment are concerned, service industries and industries producing nondurable consumer goods are somewhat insulated from the most severe effects of recession. And, of course, recession actually helps some firms such as pawnbrokers and law firms specializing in bankruptcies! Who is hit hardest by recession? Those firms and industries producing capital goods and consumer durables. The construction industry is particularly vulnerable. Industries and workers producing housing and commercial buildings, heavy capital goods, farm implements, automobiles, refrigerators, gas ranges, and similar products bear the brunt of bad times. Conversely, these "hard goods" industries are stimulated most by expansion. Two facts help explain the vulnerability of these industries to the business cycle.

1 Postponability Within limits, purchase of hard goods is postponable. As the economy slips into bad times, producers frequently put off the acquisition of more modern production facilities and construction of new plants. The business outlook simply does not warrant increases in the stock of capital goods. The firm's present capital facilities and buildings will likely still be usable and in excess supply. In good times, capital goods are usually replaced before they completely depreciate. When recession strikes, however, business firms patch up their outmoded equipment and make it do. As a result, investment in capital goods will decline sharply. Some firms, having excess plant capacity, may not even bother to replace all the capital which they are currently consuming. Net investment for them may be a negative figure.

Much the same holds true for consumer durables. When recession occurs and the family must trim its budget, plans for the purchases of durables such as major appliances and automobiles often first feel the ax. People will repair their old appliances and cars rather than buy new models. Food and clothing—consumer nondurables—are a different story. A family must eat and clothe itself. These purchases are much less postponable. True, to some extent the quantity and certainly the quality of these purchases will decline, but not so much as with durables.

2 Monopoly Power Most industries producing capital goods and consumer durables are industries of high concentration, where a small number of large firms dominate the market. As a result, these firms have sufficient monopoly power to temporarily resist lowering prices by restricting output in the face of a declining demand. Consequently, the impact of a fall in demand centers primarily on production and employment. The reverse is true in nondurable, or soft, goods industries, which are for the most part highly competitive and characterized by low concentration. Price declines cannot be resisted in such industries, and the impact of a declining demand falls to a greater extent on prices than on the levels of production.

Figure 8-3 provides historical evidence on this point. It shows the percentage declines in price and quantity which occurred in ten selected industries as the economy fell from peak prosperity in 1929 to the depth of depression in 1933. Generally, high-concentration industries make up the top half of the table and low-concentration industries the bottom half. Note the drastic production declines and relatively modest price declines of the high-concentration industries on the one hand, and the large price declines and relatively small output declines which took place in the low-concentration industries on the other.

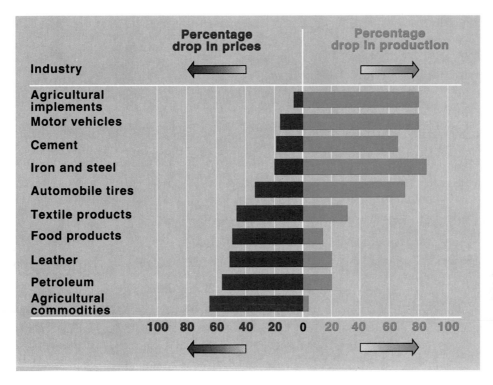

FIGURE 8-3 Relative price and production declines in ten industries, 1929–1933

The high-concentration industries shown in the top half were characterized by relatively small price declines and large declines in output during the early years of the Great Depression. In the low-concentration industries of the bottom half, price declines were relatively large, and production fell by relatively small amounts. [Gardiner C. Means, *Industrial Prices and Their Relative Flexibility* (Washington, 1953), p. 8.]

QUICK REVIEW 8-1

✦   *The long-term secular trend of real domestic output has been upward in the United States.*

✦   *The typical business cycle has four phases: peak, recession, trough, and recovery.*

✦   *Industries producing capital goods and consumer durables normally suffer greater output and employment declines during recession than do service and nondurable consumer goods industries.*

Armed with this thumbnail sketch of the business cycle, let's now examine unemployment and inflation in more detail.

UNEMPLOYMENT

"Full employment" is hard to define. A person might initially interpret it to mean that everyone who is in the labor market—100 percent of the labor force—is employed. But such is not the case; some unemployment is normal or warranted.

Types of Unemployment

In defining full employment, we first distinguish among several different types of unemployment.

Frictional Unemployment Given freedom to choose occupations and jobs, at any time some workers will be "between jobs." Some will be in the process of voluntarily switching jobs. Others will have been fired and are seeking reemployment. Still others will be temporarily laid off from their jobs because of seasonality (for example, bad weather in the construction industry) or model changeovers (as in the automobile industry). And there will be some workers, particularly young people, searching for their first jobs. As these people find jobs or are called back from temporary layoffs, other job seekers and temporarily laid-off workers will replace them in the "unemployment pool." Therefore, even though the specific individuals who are unemployed for these reasons change from month to month, this type of unemployment persists.

Economists use the term **frictional unemployment**—which consists of *search unemployment* and *wait unemployment*—for the group of workers who are either searching for jobs or waiting to take jobs in the near future. The adjective "frictional" correctly implies that the labor market does not operate perfectly and instantaneously—that is, without friction—in matching workers and jobs.

Frictional unemployment is regarded as inevitable and, at least in part, desirable. This is so because many workers who are voluntarily "between jobs" are moving from low-paying, low-productivity jobs to higher-paying, higher-productivity positions. This means more income for workers and a better allocation of labor resources—and therefore a larger real output—for the economy as a whole.

Structural Unemployment Frictional unemployment shades into a second category, called **structural unemployment.** Here, economists use the term "structural" in the sense of "compositional." Important changes occur over time in the "structure" of consumer demand and in technology, which in turn alter the "structure" of the total demand for labor. Because of such changes, some skills will be in less demand or may even become obsolete. Demand for other skills will expand, including new skills which previously did not exist. Unemployment results because the composition of the labor force does not respond quickly or completely to the new structure of job opportunities. As a result, some workers find they have no readily marketable talents; their skills and experience have been rendered obsolete and unwanted by changes in technology and consumer demand. Similarly, the geographic distribution of jobs constantly changes. Witness the migration of industry and employment opportunities from the Snow Belt to the Sun Belt over the past two decades.

Examples: (1) Years ago, highly skilled glass-blowers were thrown out of work by the invention of bottle-making machines. (2) More recently, unskilled and inadequately educated blacks have been dislodged from agriculture in the south as a result of the mechanization of agriculture. Many of these workers have migrated to northern cities and have suffered prolonged unemployment because of insufficient skills. (3) An American shoe worker, unemployed because of import competition, cannot become, say, a computer programmer without considerable retraining and perhaps also geographic relocation. (4) Finally, many oil-field workers in the "oil-patch" states of the United States found themselves structurally unemployed when the world price of oil declined dramatically in the 1980s. Less drilling and other oil-related activity took place, and widespread layoffs resulted.

The distinction between frictional and structural unemployment is hazy. The key difference is that frictionally unemployed workers have salable skills, whereas structurally unemployed workers are not readily reemployable without retraining, additional education, and possibly geographic relocation. Frictional unemployment is more short-term, while structural unemployment is more long-term, and therefore regarded as more serious.

Cyclical Unemployment Cyclical unemployment is unemployment caused by the recession phase of the business cycle, that is, by a deficiency of aggregate or total spending. As the overall demand for goods and services decreases, employment falls, and unemployment rises. For this reason, cyclical unemployment is sometimes called *deficient-demand unemployment.* During the recession year 1982, for example, the unemployment rate rose to 9.7 percent. This compares to a 6.7 percent unemployment rate in the recession year 1991. Cyclical unemployment at the depth of the Great Depression in 1933 was about 25 percent of the labor force.

Defining "Full Employment"

Full employment does *not* mean zero unemployment. Economists regard frictional and structural unemployment as essentially unavoidable; hence, "full employment" is defined as something less than employment of 100 percent of the labor force. Specifically, the **full-employment unemployment rate** is equal to the total of frictional and structural unemployment. Stated differently, the full-employment unemployment rate is achieved when cyclical unemployment is zero. The full-employment rate of unemployment is alternatively referred to as the **natural rate of unemployment.** The real level of domestic output associated with the natural rate of unemployment is called the economy's **potential output.** That is, the economy's potential output is the real output forthcoming when the economy is "fully employed."

From a slightly different vantage point the full or natural rate of unemployment results when labor markets are in balance in the sense that the number of job seekers equals the number of job vacancies. The natural rate of unemployment is some positive amount because it takes time for frictionally unemployed job seekers to find appropriate job openings. And, regarding the structurally unemployed, it also takes time to achieve the skills and geographic relocation needed for reemployment. If the number of job seekers exceeds available vacancies, labor markets are not in balance; there is a deficiency of aggregate demand and cyclical unemployment is present. On the other hand, if aggregate demand is excessive a "shortage" of labor will arise; the number of job vacancies will exceed the number of workers seeking employment. In this situation the actual rate of unemployment is below the natural rate. Unusually "tight" labor markets such as this are associated with inflation.

The concept of the natural rate of unemployment merits elaboration in two respects.

1 The term does *not* mean that the economy will always operate at the natural rate and thereby realize its potential output. We have already suggested in our brief discussion of the business cycle that the economy frequently operates at an unemployment rate in excess of the natural rate. On the other hand, the economy may on rare occasions achieve an unemployment rate lower than the natural rate. For example, during World War II, when the natural rate was 3 or 4 percent, the pressure of wartime production resulted in an almost unlimited demand for labor. Overtime work was common as was "moonlighting" (holding more than one job). The government also froze some people working in "essential" industries in their jobs, reducing frictional unemployment. The actual rate of unemployment was below 2 percent in the entire 1943–1945 period and actually dropped to 1.2 percent in 1944. The economy was producing beyond its potential output, but incurred considerable inflationary pressure in the process.

2 The natural rate of unemployment itself is *not* immutable, but rather is subject to revision because of the shifting demographics of the labor force or institutional changes (changes in society's laws and customs). For example, in the 1960s it was believed that this unavoidable minimum of frictional and structural unemployment was about 4 percent of the labor force. In other words, full employment was said to exist when 96 percent of the labor force was employed. But today, economists generally agree that the natural rate of unemployment is about 5 to 6 percent.

Why is the natural rate of unemployment higher today than in the 1960s? First, the demographic makeup of the labor force has changed. Young workers—who traditionally have high unemployment rates—have become relatively more important in the labor force. Second, institutional changes have occurred. For example, our unemployment compensation program has been expanded both in terms of numbers of workers covered and size of benefits. This is important because, by cushioning the economic impact of unemployment, unemployment compensation permits unemployed workers to engage in a more leisurely job search, thereby increasing frictional unemployment and the overall unemployment rate.

Measuring Unemployment

The controversy over the full employment rate of unemployment is complicated by problems encountered in the actual measurement of the rate of unemployment. Figure 8-4 is a helpful starting point. The total

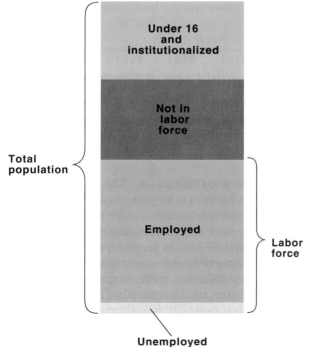

FIGURE 8-4   The labor force, employment, and unemployment, 1991

The labor force consists of persons sixteen years of age or older who are not in institutions and who are employed or unemployed.

Total population	252,666,000
Less: Under 16 and institutionalized . . .	− 62,901,000
Not in labor force	− 64,462,000
Equals: Labor force	125,303,000
Employed	116,877,000
Unemployed	8,426,000

rates of inflation in the 1970s and early 1980s, the prices of video recorders, digital watches, and personal computers actually declined. Indeed, as we will see, one of the troublesome aspects of inflation is that prices rise very unevenly. Some streak upward; others ascend at a more leisurely pace; others do not rise at all.

Measuring Inflation

Inflation is measured by price index numbers such as those introduced in Chapter 7. Recall that a price index measures the general level of prices in reference to a base period.

To illustrate, the consumer price index uses 1982–1984 as the base period in which that period's price level is set equal to 100. In 1991 the price index was approximately 136. This means that prices were 36 percent higher in 1991 than in 1982–1984, or that a given collection of goods which cost $100 in 1982–1984 cost $136 in 1991.

The *rate* of inflation can be calculated for any given year by subtracting last year's (1990) price index from this year's (1991) index, dividing that difference by last year's (1990) index, and multiplying by 100 to express it as a percentage. For example, the consumer price index was 130.7 in 1990 and 136.2 in 1991. The rate of inflation for 1991 is derived as follows:

$$\text{Rate of inflation} = \frac{136.2 - 130.7}{130.7} \times 100 = 4.2\%$$

The so-called **rule of 70** provides a different perspective for gaining a quantitative appreciation of inflation. It permits quick calculation of the number of years it takes the price level to double. We divide the number 70 by the annual rate of inflation:

$$\text{Approximate number of years required to double} = \frac{70}{\text{percentage annual rate of increase}}$$

For example, a 3 percent annual rate of inflation will double the price level in about 23 ($=70 \div 3$) years. Inflation of 8 percent per year will double the price level in about 9 ($=70 \div 8$) years. Inflation at 12 percent will double the price level in only about 6 years. Note that the rule of 70 is generally applicable in that it will allow you, for example, to estimate how long it will take for real GDP *or* your savings account to double.

With these facts in mind, we next examine the historical record of inflation in the United States and

compare annual inflation rates internationally for a recent period. Then we will survey the causes of inflation and its consequences.

The Facts of Inflation

Figure 8-7 surveys inflation in the United States since 1920. The figures shown are annual increases in the consumer price index, which is constructed using a base period of 1982–1984. That is, the CPI for the 1982–1984 period is arbitrarily set at 100. Although most of you have grown up in an "age of inflation," observe that our economy has not always been inflation-prone. The price level was remarkably stable in the prosperous 1920s and declined—that is, *deflation* occurred—during the early years of the Great Depression of the 1930s. Prices then rose sharply in the immediate post–World War II period (1945–1948). However, overall price stability characterized the 1951–1965 period in which the average annual increase in the price level was less than 1½ percent. But the inflation which took hold in the late 1960s and surged ahead in the 1970s introduced Americans to double-digit inflation. In 1979 and 1980 the price level rose at 12 to 13 percent annual rates. By the end of the 1980s, the inflation rate had settled into a 4–5 percent annual range. Specific annual rates of inflation can be found on the inside covers of this textbook.

Inflation is not a distinctly American institution. Virtually all industrial nations have experienced this problem. Figure 8-8 traces the post-1980 annual inflation rates of the United States, the United Kingdom, Japan, France, and Germany. Observe that inflation in the United States has been neither unusually high nor low relative to inflation in these other industrial countries.

Some nations have had double-digit, triple-digit, or still higher annual rates of inflation in recent years. In 1990, for example, the annual inflation rate in Greece was 20 percent; in Poland, 586 percent; and in Yugoslavia, 583 percent. Several Latin American nations experienced astronomical rates of inflation in 1990: Brazil, 2938 percent; Argentina, 2314 percent; and Peru, 7482 percent! The Peruvian inti, worth 7 cents when introduced in 1986, was worth less than two-thousandths of a penny in 1990.

Causes: Theories of Inflation

Economists distinguish between two types of inflation.

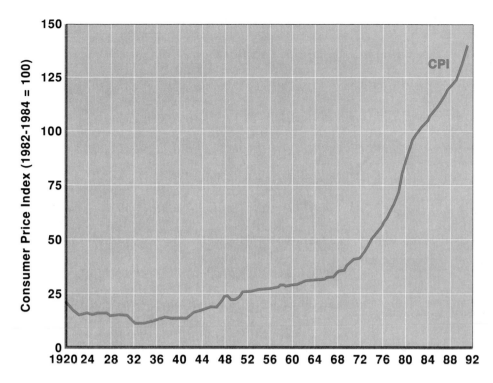

FIGURE 8-7 Price level behavior in the United States since 1920

The price stability of the 1920s and the deflation of the 1930s gave way to sharp inflation in the immediate post-World War II period. The 1951–1965 period was characterized by a reasonably stable price level, but the period since 1965 has clearly been an "age of inflation." (Bureau of Labor Statistics.)

1 Demand-Pull Inflation Traditionally, changes in the price level have been attributed to an excess of total demand. The economy may attempt to spend beyond its capacity to produce; it may seek some point beyond its production possibilities curve. The business sector cannot respond to this excess demand by expanding real output because all available resources are already fully employed. This excess demand will bid up the prices of the fixed real output, causing **demand-pull inflation.** The essence of demand-pull inflation is often expressed as "too much money chasing too few goods."

But the relationship between total demand, on the one hand, and output, employment, and the price level, on the other, is more complex than these comments suggest. Figure 8-9 will help unravel these complications.

Range 1 In *range 1* total spending—the sum of consumption, investment, government, and net export spending—is so low that domestic output is far short of its maximum full-employment level. In other words, a substantial GDP gap exists. Unemployment rates are high and businesses have much idle production capacity. Now assume that total demand increases. Real domestic output will rise and the unemployment rate will fall, but there will be little or no increase in the price level. Large amounts of idle human and property re-

FIGURE 8-8 Inflation rates in five industrial nations, 1980–1991

Inflation rates in the United States over the past eleven years have neither been extraordinarily high nor low relative to rates in other industrial nations. (*Economic Report of the President.*)

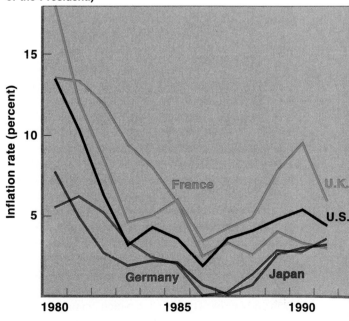

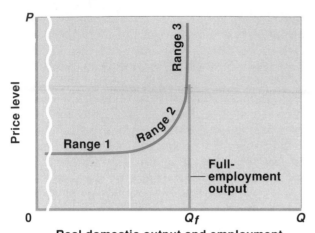

FIGURE 8-9 The price level and the level of employment

As aggregate expenditures increase, the price level generally begins to rise before full employment is reached. At full employment, additional spending tends to be purely inflationary.

sources can be put back to work at their *existing* prices. An unemployed worker does not ask for a wage increase during a job interview!

In terms of Chapter 4's demand and supply analysis, the usual price-raising effects of the assumed increases in demand do not occur because supply is a horizontal line. The increases in the amount of labor and other resources supplied are possible because idle resources are available and the additional production is profitable. The net result is large output-increasing effects and no price-increasing effects.

Range 2   As demand continues to rise, the economy enters *range 2* where it approaches full employment and is closer to fully using its available resources. But note that, before full employment is achieved, the price level may begin to rise. As production expands, supplies of idle resources do not vanish simultaneously in all sectors and industries of the economy. Bottlenecks develop in some industries even though most have excess production capacity. Some industries are using fully their production capacity before others and cannot respond to further increases in demand for their products by increasing output. So their prices rise. As labor markets tighten, some types of labor become fully employed and their money wages rise. This increases production costs and prompts businesses to increase their prices. Finally, as full employment is approached, firms will be forced to employ less efficient (less productive) workers and this contributes to rising costs and prices. The inflation which occurs in range 2

is sometimes called *premature inflation* because it occurs before the economy reaches full employment.

Range 3   As total spending increases into *range 3,* full employment occurs in all sectors of the economy. Industries in the aggregate can no longer respond to increases in demand with increases in output. Real domestic output is at a maximum and further increases in demand will cause demand-pull inflation. Total demand in excess of society's capacity to produce pulls the price level upward.

Reprise: Chapter 7's distinction between nominal and real GDP is helpful at this point. So long as the price level is constant (range 1), increases in nominal and real GDP are identical. But with premature inflation (range 2), nominal GDP is rising faster than real GDP, so nominal GDP must be "deflated" to measure changes in physical output. With pure inflation (range 3), nominal GDP is rising—perhaps rapidly— but real GDP is constant.

2 Cost-Push or Supply-Side Inflation   Inflation may also arise on the supply or cost side of the market. During several periods in our recent economic history the price level has risen despite rather widespread evidence that aggregate demand was not excessive. We have experienced periods when output and employment were both *declining* (evidence of a deficiency of total demand), while at the same time the general price level was *increasing*.

The theory of **cost-push inflation** explains rising prices in terms of factors which raise **per unit production cost.** Per unit production cost is the average cost of a particular level of output. This average cost is found by dividing the total cost of resource inputs by the amount of output produced. That is,

$$\text{Per unit production cost} = \frac{\text{total input cost}}{\text{units of output}}$$

Rising per unit production costs in the economy squeeze profits and reduce the amount of output firms are willing to supply at the existing price level. As a result, the economywide supply of goods and services declines. This decline in supply drives up the price level. Hence, under this scenario, costs are *pushing* the price level upward, rather than demand *pulling* it upward, as with demand-pull inflation.

Two sources of cost-push inflation are increases in nominal wages and increases in the prices of nonwage inputs such as raw materials and energy.

Wage-Push Variant   The wage-push variant of cost-push inflation theorizes that, under some circumstances, unions may be a source of inflation. That is, unions exert some control over nominal wage rates through collective bargaining. Suppose major unions demand and receive large increases in wages. Let's also assume that these wage gains set the standard for wage increases paid to many nonunion workers. If the economywide wage gains are excessive relative to any offsetting factors such as rises in output per hour, then employers will experience rising per unit production costs. Producers will respond by reducing the amount of goods and services offered for sale. Assuming no change in demand, this decline in supply will result in an increase in the price level. Because the culprit is an excessive increase in nominal wages, this type of inflation is called the *wage-push variant* of cost-push inflation.

Supply-Shock Variant   A second major variant of cost-push inflation, labeled *supply shock,* traces rising production costs—and therefore product prices—to abrupt, unanticipated increases in the costs of raw materials or energy inputs. The dramatic run-ups of imported oil prices in 1973–1974 and again in 1979–1980 are good illustrations. As energy prices rose during these periods, the costs of producing and transporting virtually every product in the economy increased. Rapid cost-push inflation ensued.

Complexities

The real world is much more complex than our simple distinction between demand-pull and cost-push inflation suggests. In practice it is difficult to distinguish between the two types of inflation. For example, suppose a boost in health care spending occurs which increases total spending, causing demand-pull inflation. As the demand-pull stimulus works its way through product and resource markets, individual firms find their wage costs, material costs, and fuel prices rising. From their perspective they must raise their prices because production costs have risen. Although inflation in this case is clearly demand-pull, it appears to be cost-push to many business firms. It is not easy to label inflation as demand-side or supply-side without knowing the ultimate source—the original cause—of price and wage increases.

Cost-push and demand-pull inflation differ in another important respect. Demand-pull inflation will continue so long as there is excess total spending. On the other hand, cost-push inflation automatically is self-limiting; it will die out or cure itself. Reduced supply will decrease real domestic output and employment and these declines will constrain further cost increases. Cost-push inflation generates a recession and the recession inhibits additional cost increases. This process will be addressed in more detail in Chapter 17.

QUICK REVIEW 8-3

♪   *Inflation is a rising general level of prices, measured as a percentage change in a price index.*

♪   *The United States' inflation rate has been within the middle range of rates of other advanced industrial nations, and far below the rates experienced by some nations.*

♪   *Demand-pull inflation occurs when total spending exceeds the economy's ability to provide goods and services at the existing price level; total spending pulls the price level upward.*

♪   *Cost-push inflation occurs when factors such as excessive wage increases and rapid increases in raw material prices drive up per unit production costs; higher costs push the price level upward.*

REDISTRIBUTIVE EFFECTS OF INFLATION

Our attention now shifts from causes to effects. We first consider how inflation capriciously redistributes income; second, we examine possible effects on the domestic output.

As we will see, the relationship between the price level and the domestic output is ambiguous. Historically, real output and the price level have risen and fallen together. In the past two decades or so, however, on several occasions real output has fallen while prices have continued to rise. We will dodge this issue for a moment by assuming that real output is constant and at the full-employment level. By holding real output and income constant we can better isolate the effects of inflation on the distribution of that income. Assuming that the size of the national income pie is fixed, how does inflation affect the size of the slices going to different income receivers?

To answer this question we must understand the difference between money or nominal income and real income.[2] *Money* or **nominal income** is the number of

---

[2]Chapter 7's distinction between nominal and real GDP is pertinent and you may want to review the "inflating" and "deflating" process involved in converting nominal GDP to real GDP (Table 7-7).

dollars one receives as wages, rent, interest, or profits. **Real income** measures the amount of goods and services nominal income can buy.

Clearly, if your nominal income increases faster than the price level, your real income will rise. Conversely, if the price level increases faster than your nominal income, your real income will decline. The change in one's real income can be approximated through this formula:

$$\begin{array}{ccc} \text{Percentage} & \text{percentage} & \text{percentage} \\ \text{change in} = & \text{change in} & - \text{change in} \\ \text{real income} & \text{nominal income} & \text{price level} \end{array}$$

Thus, if your nominal income rises by 10 percent in a given year and the price level rises by 5 percent in the same period, your real income will *increase* by about 5 percent. Conversely, a 5 percent increase in nominal income accompanied by 10 percent inflation will *decrease* your real income by approximately 5 percent.[3]

The point is this: While inflation reduces the purchasing power of the dollar—the amount of goods and services a dollar will buy—it does not necessarily follow that a person's real income will fall. The purchasing power of the dollar declines whenever inflation occurs; a decline in your real income or standard of living occurs only when your nominal income fails to keep pace with inflation.

Finally, note that the redistribution effects of inflation are quite different, depending on whether or not it is expected. With **anticipated inflation,** an income receiver *may* be able to take steps to avoid or lessen the adverse effects which inflation would otherwise have on real income. The generalizations which immediately follow assume the presence of **unanticipated inflation.** We will then modify our generalizations by taking the anticipation of inflation into account.

---

[3]A more precise calculation follows Chapter 7's process for changing nominal GDP to real GDP. Hence,

$$\text{Real income} = \frac{\text{nominal income}}{\text{price index (in hundredths)}}$$

Thus, in our first illustration, if nominal income rises by 10 percent from $100 to $110 and the price level (index) increases by 5 percent from 100 to 105, then real income has increased as follows:

$$\frac{\$110}{1.05} = \$104.76$$

The 5 percent increase in real income shown by the simple formula in the text is a good approximation of the 4.76 percent yielded by our more complex formula.

Fixed-Nominal-Income Receivers

Our distinction between nominal and real incomes shows that *inflation penalizes people who receive relatively fixed nominal incomes.* Restated, inflation redistributes income away from fixed income receivers toward others in the economy. The classic case is the elderly couple living on a private pension or annuity which provides a fixed amount of nominal income each month. The pensioner who retired in 1978 on what appeared to be an adequate pension finds by 1991 that the purchasing power of that pension had been cut by one-half.

Similarly, landlords who receive lease payments of fixed dollar amounts will be hurt by inflation as they receive dollars of declining value over time. To a lesser extent some white-collar workers, some public sector employees whose income is dictated by fixed pay scales, and families living on fixed levels of welfare and other transfer income will be victims of inflation. Note, however, that Congress has *indexed* social security benefits; social security payments are tied to the consumer price index to prevent erosion from inflation.

Some people living on flexible incomes *may* benefit from inflation. The nominal incomes of such households may spurt ahead of the price level, or cost of living, with the result that their real incomes are enhanced. Workers in expanding industries and represented by vigorous unions may keep their nominal wages apace with, or ahead of, the rate of inflation.

On the other hand, some wage earners are hurt by inflation. Those in declining industries or without strong, aggressive unions may find that the price level skips ahead of their money incomes.

Business executives and other profit receivers *might* benefit from inflation. *If* product prices rise faster than resource prices, business receipts will grow at a faster rate than costs. Thus some profit incomes will outdistance the rising tide of inflation.

Savers

Inflation also hurts savers. *As prices rise, the real value, or purchasing power, of a nest egg of savings will deteriorate.* Savings accounts, insurance policies, annuities, and other fixed-value paper assets once adequate to meet rainy-day contingencies or provide for a comfortable retirement decline in real value during inflation. The simplest case is the individual who hoards money as a cash balance. For example, a $1000 cash balance would have lost one-half its real value between 1967 and 1977. Of course, most forms of savings earn interest. But the value of savings will still decline if the rate of inflation exceeds the rate of interst.

Example: A household may save $1000 in a certificate of deposit (CD) in a commercial bank or savings and loan association or buy a $1000 bond at 6 percent interest. But if inflation is 13 percent (as in 1980), the real value or purchasing power of that $1000 will be cut to about $938 at the end of the year. That is, the saver will receive $1060 (equal to $1000 plus $60 of interest), but deflating that $1060 for 13 percent inflation means that the real value of $1060 is only about $938 (equal to $1060 divided by 1.13.)

Debtors and Creditors

Inflation also redistributes income by altering the relationship between debtors and creditors. *Unanticipated inflation benefits debtors (borrowers) at the expense of creditors (lenders).* Suppose you borrow $1000 from a bank, to be repaid in two years. If in that time the general level of prices were to double, the $1000 which you repay will have only half the purchasing power of the $1000 originally borrowed. True, if we ignore interest charges, the same number of dollars is repaid as was borrowed. But because of inflation, each of these dollars will now buy only half as much as it did when the loan was negotiated. As prices go up, the value of the dollar comes down. Thus, because of inflation, the borrower is given "dear" dollars but pays back "cheap" dollars. The inflation of the past few decades has been a windfall to those who purchased homes in, say, the mid-1960s with fixed-interest-rate mortgages. On the one hand, inflation has greatly reduced the real burden of their mortgage indebtedness. On the other hand, the nominal value of housing has increased more rapidly than the overall price level.

The Federal government, which has amassed $3600 billion of public debt over the decades, has also been a major beneficiary of inflation. Historically, the Federal government has regularly paid off its loans by taking out new ones. Inflation has permitted the Treasury to pay off its loans with dollars which have less purchasing power than the dollars it originally borrowed. Nominal national income and therefore tax collections rise with inflation; the amount of public debt owed does not. Thus, inflation reduces the real burden of the public debt to the Federal government. Given

that inflation benefits the Federal government in this way, some economists have wondered out loud whether society can really expect government to be particularly zealous in its efforts to halt inflation.

In fact, some nations such as Brazil once used inflation so extensively to reduce the real value of their debts that lenders now force them to borrow money in U.S. dollars or in some other relatively stable currency instead of their own currency. This prevents them from using domestic inflation as a means of subtly "defaulting" on their debt. Any inflation which they generate will reduce the value of their own currencies, but not the value of the dollar-denominated debt they must pay back.

Anticipated Inflation

The redistributive effects of inflation will be less severe or even eliminated if transactors (1) anticipate inflation and (2) have the capacity to adjust their nominal incomes to reflect expected price level changes. For example, the prolonged inflation which began in the late 1960s prompted many unions in the 1970s to insist on labor contracts with **cost-of-living adjustment (COLA)** clauses to automatically adjust workers incomes for inflation.

Similarly, the redistribution of income from lender to borrower which we just observed might be altered *if* inflation is anticipated. Suppose a lender (perhaps a commercial bank or savings and loan) and a borrower (a household) both agree that 5 percent is a fair rate of interest on a one-year loan, *provided* the price level is stable. But assume inflation has been occurring and both lender and borrower agree it is reasonable to anticipate a 6 percent increase in the price level over the next year. If the bank lends the household $100 at 5 percent, the bank will be paid back $105 at the end of the year. But if 6 percent inflation does occur during the year, the purchasing power of that $105 will have been reduced to about $99. The *lender* will in effect have paid the *borrower* $1 to use the lender's money for a year.

The lender can avoid this curious subsidy by charging an *inflation premium,* which means increasing the interest rate by the amount of the anticipated inflation. By charging 11 percent the lender will receive back $111 at the end of the year which, adjusted for the 6 percent inflation, has the real value or purchasing power of about $105. Here there is a mutually agreeable transfer of purchasing power from borrower to lender of $5, or 5 percent, for the use of $100 for one year. Note that savings and loan institutions have developed variable-interest-rate mortgages to protect themselves from the adverse effects of inflation. Incidentally, these examples imply that, rather than being a cause of inflation, high nominal interest rates may be a consequence of inflation.

Our illustration shows the difference between the real rate of interest, on the one hand, and the money or nominal rate of interest, on the other. The **real interest rate** *is the percentage increase in purchasing power that the lender receives from the borrower.* In our example the real interest rate is 5 percent. The **nominal interest rate** *is the percentage increase in money that the lender receives.* The nominal rate of interest is 11 percent in our example. The difference in these two concepts is that the real interest rate is adjusted or "deflated" for the rate of inflation while the nominal interest rate is not. Stated differently, the nominal interest rate is the sum of the real interest rate plus the premium paid to offset the expected rate of inflation.

Addenda

Three final points must be mentioned.

1 Not surprisingly, the effects of deflation are substantially the reverse of those of inflation. *Assuming no change in total output,* those with fixed money incomes will find their real incomes enhanced. Creditors will benefit at the expense of debtors. And savers will discover the purchasing power of their savings has grown because of falling prices.

2 The fact that any given family may be an income earner, a holder of financial assets, and an owner of real assets simultaneously will likely cushion the redistributive impact of inflation. If the family owns fixed-value monetary assets (savings accounts, bonds, and insurance policies), inflation will lessen their real value. But that same inflation may increase the real value of any property assets (a house, land) which the family owns. In short, many families are simultaneously hurt and benefited by inflation. All these effects must be considered before we can conclude that the family's net position is better or worse because of inflation.

3 The final point is that the redistributive effects of inflation are *arbitrary;* they occur regardless of society's goals and values. Inflation lacks a social conscience and takes from some and gives to others, whether they be rich, poor, young, old, healthy, or infirm.

> ### QUICK REVIEW 8-4
>
> ♪ *Inflation arbitrarily "taxes" those who receive relatively fixed nominal incomes and "subsidizes" some people who receive flexible nominal incomes.*
>
> ♪ *Unanticipated inflation arbitrarily penalizes savers and benefits debtors at the expense of creditors.*
>
> ♪ *The nominal interest rate exceeds the real interest rate by the expected rate of inflation.*

OUTPUT EFFECTS OF INFLATION

We have assumed thus far that the economy's real output is fixed at the full-employment level. As a result, the redistributive effects of inflation and deflation have been in terms of some groups gaining absolutely at the expense of others. *If* the size of the pie is fixed and inflation causes some groups to get larger slices, other groups must necessarily get smaller slices. But, in fact, the level of domestic output may vary as the price level changes. The size of the pie itself may vary.

There is much uncertainty and disagreement as to whether inflation will be accompanied by a rising or a falling real domestic output. We will consider three scenarios, the first associating inflation with an expanding output and the remaining two with a declining output.

Stimulus of Demand-Pull Inflation

Some economists argue that full employment can only be achieved if some modest amount of inflation is tolerated. They base their reasoning on Figure 8-9. We know that the levels of real domestic output and employment depend on aggregate spending. If spending is low, the economy will operate in range 1. In this range there is price level stability, but real domestic output is substantially below its potential and the unemployment rate is high. If aggregate spending now increases so that the economy moves into range 2, we find society must accept a higher price level—some amount of inflation—to achieve these higher levels of real domestic output and the accompanying lower unemployment rates. If further increases in aggregate spending pull the economy into range 3, that spending will be purely inflationary because the full-employment or capacity level of real domestic output will have been reached.

The critical point is that in range 2 there appears to be a tradeoff between output (including employment) and inflation. Some moderate amount of inflation must be accepted if we are to realize high levels of output and employment. The high levels of spending which give us higher levels of output and low unemployment rates also cause some inflation. Stated differently, an inverse relationship may exist between the inflation rate and the unemployment rate.

This scenario has been criticized in recent years. Many economists feel that any tradeoff between the inflation rate and the unemployment rate is a transitory or short-run phenomenon at best and there is no such tradeoff in the long run. This controversy will be explored in detail in Chapter 17.

Cost-Push Inflation and Unemployment

There is an equally plausible set of circumstances in which inflation might cause output and employment both to *decline.* Suppose the level of total spending is initially such that the economy is enjoying full employment *and* price level stability. If cost-push inflation now occurs, the amount of real output which the existing level of total demand will buy will be reduced. That is, a given level of total spending will only be capable of taking a smaller real output off the market when cost-push pressures boost the price level. Hence, real output will fall and unemployment will rise.

Economic events of the 1970s support this scenario. In late 1973 the Organization of Petroleum Exporting Countries (OPEC) became effective and exerted its market power to quadruple the price of oil. The cost-push inflationary effects generated rapid price level increases in the 1973–1975 period. At the same time the unemployment rate rose from slightly less than 5 percent in 1973 to 8.5 percent in 1975. Similar outcomes occurred in 1979–1980 in response to a second OPEC oil price shock.

Hyperinflation and Breakdown

Some economists express anxiety over our first scenario. They are fearful that the mild, "creeping" inflation which might initially accompany economic recovery may snowball into a more severe **hyperinflation.** This term is reserved for extremely rapid inflation whose ultimate impact on domestic output and employment can be devastating. The contention is that, as prices persist in creeping upward, households and businesses will expect them to rise further. So, rather than let their idle savings and current incomes depreci-

ate, people are induced to "spend now" to beat anticipated price rises. Businesses do the same in buying capital goods. Action based on this "inflationary psychosis" intensifies pressure on prices, and inflation feeds on itself.

Furthermore, as the cost of living rises, labor demands and gets higher nominal wages. Indeed, unions may seek wage increases sufficient not only to cover last year's price level increase but also to compensate for inflation anticipated during the future life of their new collective bargaining agreement. Prosperity is not a good time for business firms to risk strikes by resisting such demands. Business managers recoup their rising labor costs by boosting the prices they charge consumers. And for good measure, businesses may jack prices up an extra notch or two to be sure that profit receivers keep abreast or ahead of the inflationary parade. As the cost of living moves upward as a result of these price increases, labor once again has an excellent excuse to demand another round of substantial wage increases. But this triggers another round of price increases. The net effect is a cumulative *wage-price inflationary spiral.* Nominal-wage and price rises feed on each other, and this creeping inflation bursts into galloping inflation.

Aside from disruptive redistributive effects, hyperinflation can precipitate economic collapse. Severe inflation encourages a diversion of effort toward speculative, and away from productive, activity. Businesses may find it increasingly profitable to hoard both materials and finished products in anticipation of further price increases. But, by restricting the availability of materials and products relative to the demand for them, such actions will intensify inflationary pressures. Rather than invest in capital equipment, businesses and individual savers may purchase nonproductive wealth—jewels, gold and other precious metals, real estate, and so forth—as hedges against inflation.

In the extreme, as prices shoot up sharply and unevenly, normal economic relationships are disrupted. Business owners do not know what to charge for their products. Consumers do not know what to pay. Resource suppliers will want to be paid with actual output, rather than with rapidly depreciating money. Creditors will avoid debtors to escape the repayment of debts with cheap money. Money becomes virtually worthless and ceases to do its job as a measure of value and medium of exchange. The economy may literally be thrown into a state of barter. Production and exchange grind toward a halt, and the net result is eco-

ters—examined the functioning of capitalistic economies against the backdrop of the Great Depression of the 1930s when unemployment in the United States was as high as 25 percent. In this lamentable economic condition there was ample room to expand production without fear of higher production costs or higher prices. Conversely, Keynes held that declines in real domestic output and employment would *not* be cushioned by price and wage reductions.

Classical (Vertical) Range   At the other extreme, we find that the economy reaches full employment or a natural rate of unemployment at a real domestic output of Q_f. The economy is at a point *on* Chapter 2's production possibilities curve and in the short term no further increase in real output is attainable. Any further increase in the price level will fail to elicit additional real output because the economy is already operating at capacity. At full employment individual firms may try to expand production by bidding resources away from other firms. But the resources and additional production one firm gains will be lost by some other firm. Resource prices (costs) and ultimately product prices will rise because of this process, but real domestic output will remain unchanged.

Two diverse points must be made concerning the vertical range of the aggregate supply curve.

1   This range is associated with classical economics —also to be discussed in the next chapter—which concludes there are forces inherent in a market economy which cause full employment to be the norm. Hence, the vertical range is also known as the **classical range** of the aggregate supply curve.

2   "Full employment" and "full-employment real output" are slippery concepts. This is true not merely because the "full employment or natural unemployment rate" is difficult to quantify (Chapter 8), but also because hours of work and the size of the labor force can sometimes be expanded beyond what is normal. Recall from Figure 8-5 that periodically actual GDP exceeds potential GDP. Thus, in a highly prosperous economy daily working hours and the workweek can be extended. Workers can also engage in "moonlighting," the practice of holding more than one job.

Example: During World War II a 10-hour workday and a six-day workweek were common. Many workers, after their normal workday at a regular job, would work a partial or full night shift in a defense plant. Women and young persons, who would not ordinarily have worked, joined the labor force in response to patriotic appeals and high wages. But for our purposes we assume there is some specific level of real output which corresponds to full employment.

Intermediate (Upsloping) Range   Finally, in the **intermediate range** between Q and Q_f an expansion of real output is accompanied by a rising price level. One reason is that the aggregate economy is in fact comprised of innumerable product and resource markets *and* full employment is not reached evenly or simultaneously in various sectors or industries. As the economy expands in the QQ_f real output range, the high-tech computer industry, for example, may encounter shortages of skilled workers while the automobile or steel industries are still faced with substantial unemployment. Similarly, in certain industries raw-material shortages or similar production bottlenecks may begin to appear. Expansion also means some firms will be forced to use older and less efficient machinery as they approach capacity production. Also, less capable workers may be hired as output expands. For all of these reasons, per unit production costs rise and firms must receive higher product prices for production to be profitable. Thus, in the intermediate range a rising real output is accompanied by a higher price level.

As we have noted, the shape of the aggregate supply curve is a matter of controversy. We will find in later chapters that some economists—called *classical* or *new classical economists*—contend the curve is vertical throughout, implying that a change in aggregate demand will be relatively harmless because it only affects the price level while leaving output and employment unchanged. Other economists—known as *Keynesians* —argue that the aggregate supply curve is either horizontal or upsloping and therefore that decreases in aggregate demand have adverse and very costly effects on output and employment.

Determinants of Aggregate Supply

Our discussion of the shape of the aggregate supply curve revealed that real domestic output increases as the economy moves from left to right through the Keynesian and intermediate ranges of aggregate supply. These changes in output result from *movements along* the aggregate supply curve and must be distinguished from *shifts* in the aggregate supply curve itself. An existing aggregate supply curve identifies the relationship between the price level and real domestic output, *other things being equal*. But when one or more of these "other things" change, the aggregate supply curve itself shifts.

The shift of the curve from AS₁ to AS₂ in Figure 9-4 shows an *increase* in aggregate supply. Over the intermediate and classical range of the aggregate supply curves, this shift is rightward, indicating that businesses collectively will produce more real output at each price level than previously. Over the Keynesian range of the aggregate supply curves, an increase in aggregate supply can best be thought of as a decline in the price level at each level of domestic output (a downward shift of aggregate supply). For convenience we will refer to an increase in aggregate supply as a "rightward" shift of the curve rather than a "rightward or a downward" shift. Conversely, the shift of the curve from AS₁ to AS₃ will be referred to as a "leftward shift," indicating a *decrease* in aggregate supply. That is, businesses now will produce less real output at each price level than before (or charge higher prices at each level of output).

Table 9-2 summarizes the "other things" which shift the aggregate supply curve when they change. These factors are called the **determinants of aggregate supply** because they collectively "determine" or establish the location of the aggregate supply curve. These determinants have one thing in common: When

TABLE 9-2 Determinants of aggregate supply: factors that shift the aggregate supply curve

1 **Change in input prices**
   a **Domestic resource availability**
      a_1 land
      a_2 labor
      a_3 capital
      a_4 entrepreneurial ability
   b **Prices of imported resources**
   c **Market power**
2 **Change in productivity**
3 **Change in legal-institutional environment**
   a **Business taxes and subsidies**
   b **Government regulation**

they change, per unit production costs also change. We established in earlier chapters that the supply decisions of businesses are made on the basis of production costs and revenues. Businesses are profit seekers and profits arise from the difference between product prices and per unit production costs. Producers respond to higher prices for their products—that is, to higher price levels—by increasing their real output. And, production bottlenecks mean that per unit production costs rise as output expands toward full employment. For this reason the aggregate supply curve slopes upward in its intermediate range.

The point is that there are factors *other than changes in real domestic output* which alter per unit production costs (see Table 9-2). When one or more change, per unit production costs change at each price level and the aggregate supply curve shifts positions. Specifically, decreases in per unit production costs of this type shift the aggregate supply curve rightward. Conversely, increases in per unit production costs shift the aggregate supply curve leftward. *When per unit production costs change for reasons other than a change in domestic output, firms collectively alter the amount of domestic output they produce at each price level.*

We now examine how changes in the aggregate supply shifters listed in Table 9-2 affect per unit production costs and thereby shift the aggregate supply curve.

Input Prices Input or resource prices—to be distinguished from the output prices comprising the price level—are an important determinant of aggregate supply. All else being equal, higher input prices increase per unit production costs and therefore reduce aggregate supply. Lower input prices produce just the opposite result. The following factors influence input prices:

FIGURE 9-4 Changes in aggregate supply

A change in one or more of the determinants of aggregate supply listed in Table 9-2 will cause a change in aggregate supply. An increase in aggregate supply is shown as a rightward shift of the AS curve from AS₁ to AS₂; a decrease in aggregate supply, as a leftward shift from AS₁ to AS₃.

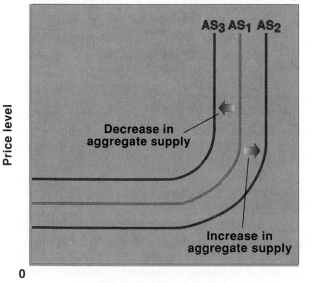

domestic resource availability, the prices of imported resources, and market power.

Domestic Resource Availability We noted in Chapter 2 that a society's production possibilities curve shifts outward when the resources available to it increase. Rightward shifts in the production possibilities curve translate into rightward shifts of our aggregate supply curve. Increases in the supply of domestic resources lower input prices and, as a result, per unit production costs fall. Thus, at any given price level, firms collectively will produce and offer for sale more real domestic output than before. Conversely, declines in resource supplies increase input prices and shift the economy's aggregate supply curve to the left.

How might changes in the availability of land, labor, capital, and entrepreneurial resources work to shift the aggregate supply curve? Several examples will help answer this question.

Land Land resources might become more available through discoveries of mineral deposits, irrigation of land, or new technical innovations which permit us to transform what were previously "nonresources" into valuable factors of production. An increase in the supply of land resources lowers the price of land inputs and thus lowers per unit production costs. For example, the recent discovery that widely available materials at low temperatures can act as superconductors of electricity is expected eventually to reduce per unit production costs by reducing electricity loss during transmission. This lower price of electricity will increase aggregate supply.

Two examples of reductions in land resources availability may also be cited: (1) the widespread depletion of the nation's underground water through irrigation, and (2) the nation's loss of topsoil through intensive farming. Eventually, each of these problems may increase input prices and shift the aggregate supply curve leftward.

Labor About 75 percent of all business costs are wages or salaries. All else being equal, changes in wages thus have a significant impact on per unit production costs and on the location of the aggregate supply curve. An increase in the availability of labor resources reduces the price of labor; a decrease raises labor's price. Examples: The influx of women into the labor force during the past two decades placed a downward pressure on wages and expanded American aggregate supply. Emigration of employable workers

from abroad also has historically increased the availability of labor in the United States.

Conversely, the great loss of life during World War II greatly diminished the postwar availability of labor in the United States, tending to raise per unit production costs. Currently, the AIDS epidemic threatens to reduce the supply of labor and thus diminish the nation's aggregate supply of real output.

Capital Aggregate supply tends to increase when society adds to its stock of capital. Such an addition would happen if society saved more of its income and directed the savings toward purchase of capital goods. In much the same way, an improvement in the quality of capital reduces production costs and increases aggregate supply. For example, businesses over the years have replaced poor quality equipment with new, superior equipment.

Conversely, aggregate supply will decline when the quantity and quality of the nation's stock of capital diminish. Example: In the depths of the Great Depression of the 1930s, our capital stock deteriorated because new purchases of capital were insufficient to offset the normal wearing out and obsolescence of plant and equipment.

Entrepreneurial Ability Finally, the amount of entrepreneurial ability available to the economy can change from one period to the next and shift the aggregate supply curve. Recent media focus on individuals who have amassed fortunes through entrepreneurial efforts might conceivably increase the number of people who have entrepreneurial aspirations, tending to shift the aggregate supply curve rightward.

Prices of Imported Resources Just as foreign demand for American goods contributes to our aggregate demand, the importation of resources from abroad adds to our aggregate supply. Resources add to our productive capacity whether they be domestic or imported. Imported resources reduce input prices and therefore decrease the per unit cost of producing American real domestic output. Generally, a decrease in the prices of imported resources expands our aggregate supply; an increase in the prices of these resources reduces our aggregate supply.

Exchange rate fluctuations are a factor which periodically alter the price of imported resources. Suppose that the dollar price of foreign currency falls—that is, the dollar appreciates—enabling American firms to obtain more foreign currency with each American dollar. This means that American producers face a lower dollar price of imported resources. Under these conditions, American firms would expand their imports of foreign resources and realize reductions in per unit production costs at each level of output. Falling per unit production costs of this type shift the American aggregate supply curve to the right.

Conversely, an increase in the dollar price of foreign currency—dollar depreciation—raises the prices of imported resources. As a result, our imports of these resources fall, our per unit production costs jump upward, and our aggregate supply curve moves leftward.

Market Power   A change in the degree of market power or monopoly power held by sellers of resources can also affect input prices and aggregate supply. *Market power* is the ability to set a price above that which would occur in a competitive situation. The rise and fall of OPEC's market power during the past two decades is a good illustration. The tenfold increase in the price of oil that OPEC achieved during the 1970s permeated our economy, drove up per unit production costs, and jolted the American aggregate supply curve leftward. Conversely, a substantial reduction in OPEC's market power during the mid-1980s reduced the cost of manufacturing and transporting products, and as a direct result, increased American aggregate supply.

A change in union market power also can be expected to affect the location of the aggregate supply curve. Some observers believe that unions experienced growing market power in the 1970s, resulting in union wage increases which widened the gap between union and nonunion workers. This higher pay may well have increased per unit production costs and produced leftward shifts of aggregate supply. Alternatively, union market power greatly waned during the 1980s. Consequently, in many industries the price of union labor fell, resulting in lower per unit production costs. The result was an increase in aggregate supply.

Productivity   Productivity relates a nation's level of real output to the quantity of input used to produce that output. In other words, **productivity** is a measure of average output, or of real output per unit of input:

$$\text{Productivity} = \frac{\text{real output}}{\text{input}}$$

An increase in productivity means that more real domestic output can be obtained from the amount of resources—or inputs—currently available.

How does an increase in productivity affect the aggregate supply curve? We first need to discover how a change in productivity alters per unit production costs. Suppose real domestic output in a hypothetical economy is 10 units, the input quantity needed to produce that quantity is 5, and the price of each input unit is $2. Productivity—output per input—is 2 (=10/5). The per unit cost of output would be found through the following formula:

$$\text{Per unit production cost} = \frac{\text{total input cost}}{\text{units of output}}$$

In this case, per unit cost is $1, found by dividing $10 of input cost (=$2 × 5 units of input) by 10 units of output.

Now suppose that real domestic output doubles to 20 units, while the input price and quantity remain constant at $2 and 5 units. That is, suppose productivity rises from 2 (=10/5) to 4 (=20/5). Because the total cost of the inputs stays at $10 (=$2 × 5 units of input), the per unit cost of the output falls from $1 to $.50 (=$10 of input cost/20 units of output).

By reducing per unit production costs, an increase in productivity will shift the aggregate supply curve rightward; conversely, a decline in productivity will increase per unit production costs and shift the aggregate supply curve leftward.

We will discover in Chapter 19 that productivity growth is a major factor explaining the secular expansion of aggregate supply in the United States and the corresponding growth of real domestic output. The use of more machinery and equipment per worker, improved production technology, a better-educated and trained labor force, and improved forms of business enterprises have interacted to raise productivity, all else being equal, and increase aggregate supply.

Legal-Institutional Environment   Changes in the legal-institutional setting in which businesses collectively operate may alter per units costs of output and shift the aggregate supply curve. Two categories of changes of this type are (1) changes in taxes and subsidies, and (2) changes in the extent of regulation.

Business Taxes and Subsidies   Higher business taxes, such as sales, excise, and social security taxes, increase per unit costs and reduce aggregate supply in much the same way as a wage increase. Example: An increase in the social security taxes paid by businesses will increase production costs and reduce aggregate supply. Similarly, a business subsidy—a payment or tax break by government to firms—reduces production costs and increases aggregate supply. Example: During the 1970s, the government subsidized producers of energy from alternative sources such as wind, oil shale, and solar power. The purpose was to reduce production costs and encourage development of energy sources which might substitute for oil and natural gas. To the extent that these subsidies were successful, the aggregate supply curve moved rightward.

Government Regulation   It is usually costly for businesses to comply with government regulations. Hence, regulation increases per unit production costs and shifts the aggregate supply curve leftward. "Supply-side" proponents of deregulation of the economy have argued forcefully that, by increasing efficiency and reducing paperwork associated with complex regulations, deregulation will reduce per unit costs. In this way, the aggregate supply curve purportedly will shift rightward. Conversely, increases in regulation raise production costs and reduce aggregate supply.

EQUILIBRIUM: REAL OUTPUT AND THE PRICE LEVEL

We found in Chapter 4 that the intersection of the demand for and supply of a particular product will determine the equilibrium price and output of that good. Similarly, as we see in Figure 9-5a and b (Key Graph) the intersection of the aggregate demand and aggregate supply curves determines the **equilibrium price level** and **equilibrium real domestic output.**

In Figure 9-5a note where aggregate demand crosses aggregate supply in its intermediate range. We find that the equilibrium price level and level of real domestic output are P_e and Q_e, respectively. To illustrate why P_e is the equilibrium price and Q_e is the equilibrium level of real domestic output, suppose that the price level were P_1 rather than P_e. We observe from the aggregate supply curve that price level P_1 would entice businesses to produce at most real output level Q_1. How much real output would domestic consumers, businesses, government, and foreign buyers wish to purchase at P_1? We see from the aggregate demand curve that the answer is Q_2. Competition among buyers to purchase the available real output of Q_1 will drive up the price level to P_e. As arrows in Figure 9-5a indicate, the rise in the price level from P_1 to P_e encourages *producers* to increase their real output from Q_1 to Q_e and simultaneously causes *buyers* to scale back their desired level of purchases from Q_2 to Q_e. When equality occurs between the amount of real domestic output produced and the amount purchased, as it does at P_e, the economy has achieved equilibrium.

In Figure 9-5b aggregate demand intersects aggregate supply in the Keynesian range where aggregate supply is perfectly horizontal. In this particular case the price level does *not* play a role in bringing about the equilibrium level of real domestic output. To understand why, first observe that the equilibrium price and real output levels in Figure 9-5b are P_e and Q_e. If the business sector had produced a larger domestic output, such as Q_2, it could not dispose of that output. Aggregate demand would be insufficient to take the domestic output off the market. Faced with unwanted inventories of goods, businesses would reduce their production to the equilibrium level of Q_e—shown by the leftward pointing arrow—and the market would clear. Conversely, if firms had only produced domestic output of Q_1, businesses would find that their inventories of goods would quickly diminish because sales of output would exceed production. Businesses would react by increasing production and domestic output would rise to equilibrium as shown by the rightward pointing arrow.

CHANGES IN EQUILIBRIUM

Now we will shift the aggregate demand and aggregate supply curves and observe the effects on real domestic output (and therefore on employment) and the price level.

KEY GRAPH

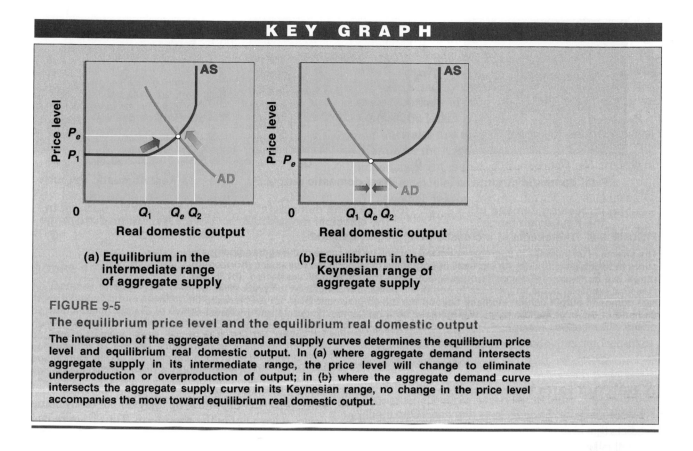

(a) Equilibrium in the intermediate range of aggregate supply

(b) Equilibrium in the Keynesian range of aggregate supply

FIGURE 9-5

The equilibrium price level and the equilibrium real domestic output

The intersection of the aggregate demand and supply curves determines the equilibrium price level and equilibrium real domestic output. In (a) where aggregate demand intersects aggregate supply in its intermediate range, the price level will change to eliminate underproduction or overproduction of output; in (b) where the aggregate demand curve intersects the aggregate supply curve in its Keynesian range, no change in the price level accompanies the move toward equilibrium real domestic output.

Shifting Aggregate Demand

Suppose households and businesses decide to increase their spending, thereby shifting the aggregate demand curve to the right. Our list of determinants of aggregate demand (Table 9-1) provides several possible reasons for this decision. Perhaps consumers become more optimistic in their expectations about future economic conditions. These favorable expectations might stem from new American technological advances which promise to increase the competitiveness of our products in both domestic and world markets and therefore to increase future real income. As a result, consumers would consume more (save less) of their current incomes. Similarly, firms anticipate that future business conditions will enhance profits from current investments in new capital. They increase their investment spending to enlarge their productive capacities. As shown in Figure 9-6, the precise effects of an *increase* in aggregate demand depend on whether the economy is currently in the Keynesian,

intermediate, or classical range of the aggregate supply curve.

In the Keynesian range of Figure 9-6a, where there is high unemployment and much unused production capacity, the effect of an increase in aggregate demand (AD_1 to AD_2) brings about a large increase in real domestic output (Q_1 to Q_2) and employment with no increase in the price level (P_1). In the classical range of Figure 9-6b, where labor and capital are fully employed, an increase in aggregate demand (AD_5 to AD_6) would affect the price level only, increasing it from P_5 to P_6. Real domestic output will remain at the full-employment level Q_f. In the intermediate range of Figure 9-6c an increase in aggregate demand (AD_3 to AD_4) will raise both real domestic output (Q_3 to Q_4) and price level (P_3 to P_4).

The price level increases associated gate demand increases in both the c termediate ranges of the aggregate stitute **demand-pull inflation** aggregate demand are pulling

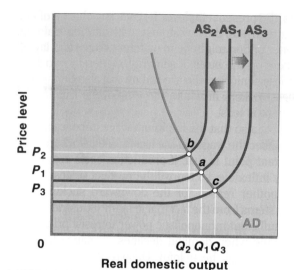

FIGURE 9-8 The effects of changes in aggregate supply

A leftward shift in aggregate supply from AS_1 to AS_2 will cause cost-push inflation in that the price level increases from P_1 to P_2. Real domestic output will fall from Q_1 to Q_2. A rightward shift of aggregate supply from AS_1 to AS_3 will increase the real domestic output from Q_1 to Q_3 and reduce the price level from P_1 to P_3.

Observe that the shift in the aggregate supply curve involves a change in the full-employment level of real domestic output; in particular, a rightward shift of the curve signifies economic growth and indicates that the economy's potential output has increased. In terms of Chapter 2, the economy's production possibilities curve has moved to the right, reflected in the rightward shift of the aggregate supply curve in Figure 9-8.

shown by the movement from AS_1 to AS_2 in Figure 9-8. The price level increase occurring here is clearly **cost-push inflation** (Chapter 8).

Note that, given aggregate demand, the effects of a leftward shift in aggregate supply are doubly bad. When aggregate supply shifts from AS_1 to AS_2, real domestic output will decline from Q_1 to Q_2 *and* the price level will rise from P_1 to P_2. That is, the economy will move from *a* to *b*. Falling employment and inflation will occur.

Alternatively, suppose that one of the factors in Table 9-2 changes so that aggregate supply increases. Specifically, suppose the economy experiences a sharp increase in productivity which is not matched by increases in higher paychecks for workers. Or, perhaps a liberalization of immigration laws increases the supply of labor and pulls wage rates down. Or, finally, maybe lower business tax rates reduce per unit costs (a tax is a cost as viewed by a business), shifting the aggregate supply curve rightward. In Figure 9-8 the shift in the aggregate supply from AS_1 to AS_3 indicates an increase ⌐real output from Q_1 to Q_3 and assuming downward ⌐nd wage flexibility, a simultaneous decline in the ⌐l from P_1 to P_3. In brief, the economy moves

UNANSWERED QUESTIONS: LOOKING AHEAD

Our aggregate demand and aggregate supply model is a useful framework for developing a more detailed and comprehensive understanding of macroeconomics. However, this model raises many questions. Are there features of the economy which ensure that the aggregate demand curve always intersects the aggregate supply curve in the classical range? That is, are there automatic mechanisms which ensure full employment of the nation's resources (Chapter 10)? What economic principles underlie the less-than-full-employment equilibrium implied by an intersection of aggregate demand and aggregate supply in the Keynesian and intermediate ranges of aggregate supply (Chapters 10 and 11)? What, if anything, can the government do to keep aggregate demand from periodically declining and producing widespread unemployment (Chapter 12)?

Still other questions are: What role do money, the banking system, and the Federal Reserve play in determining the location of the aggregate demand curve and the macroeconomic health of the economy (Chapters 13 through 15)? Have government policies to manage aggregate demand contributed to macro-

LAST WORD

JOHN MAYNARD KEYNES (1883–1946)

The English economist John Maynard Keynes is regarded as the originator of modern macroeconomics.

In 1935 George Bernard Shaw received a letter from John Maynard Keynes in which Keynes asserted, "I believe myself to be writing a book on economic theory which will largely revolutionize . . . the way the world thinks about economic problems." And, in fact, Keynes' *The General Theory of Employment, Interest, and Money* (1936) did revolutionize economic analysis and established Keynes as one of the most brilliant and influential economists of all time.

The son of an eminent English economist, Keynes was educated at Eton and Cambridge. While his early interests were in mathematics and probability theory, Keynes ultimately turned to economics.

Keynes was far more than an economist: He was an incredibly active, many-sided man who also played such diverse roles as principal representative of the Treasury at the World War I Paris Peace Conference, deputy for the Chancellor of the Exchequer, a director of the Bank of England, trustee of the National Gallery, chairman of the Council for the Encouragement of Music and the Arts, bursar of King's College, Cambridge, editor of the *Economic Journal*, chairman of the *Nation* and later the *New Statesman* magazines, and chairman of the National Mutual Life Assurance Society. He also ran an investment company, organized the Camargo Ballet (his wife, Lydia Lopokova, was a renowned star of the Russian Imperial Ballet), and built (profitably) the Arts Theatre at Cambridge.*

In addition, Keynes found time to amass a $2 million personal fortune by speculating in stocks, international currencies, and commodities. He was also a

*E. Ray Canterbery, *The Making of Economics*, 3d ed. (Belmont, Calif.: Wadsworth Publishing Company, 1987), p. 126.

leading figure in the "Bloomsbury group," an *avant-garde* group of intellectual luminaries who greatly influenced the artistic and literary standards of England.

Most importantly, Keynes was a prolific scholar. His books encompassed such widely ranging topics as probability theory, monetary economics, and the economic consequences of the World War I peace treaty. His *magnum opus,* however, was the *General Theory,* which has been described by John Kenneth Galbraith as "a work of profound obscurity, badly written and prematurely published." Yet the *General Theory* attacked the classical economists' contention that recession will automatically cure itself. Keynes' analysis suggested that recession could easily spiral downward into a depression. Keynes claimed that modern capitalism contained no automatic mechanism which would propel the economy back toward full employment. The economy might languish for many years in depression. Indeed, the massive unemployment of the worldwide depression of the 1930s seemed to provide sufficient evidence that Keynes was right. His basic policy recommendation—a startling one in view of the balanced-budget sentiment at the time—was for government in these circumstances to increase its spending to induce more production and put the unemployed back to work.

economic stability, or, conversely, have they produced the very instability they are designed to counter (Chapter 16)? What set of aggregate demand and supply circumstances explains periods of "stagflation"—simultaneous rising inflation and recession (Chapter 17)? Where do Federal budget deficits and the national debt fit into this overall framework (Chapter 18)? And,

finally, what are the facts and issues of economic growth—rises of real domestic output and income—and what policies might generate faster growth (Chapter 19)?

Our answers to these and a host of related questions will form the heart of our ensuing study of macroeconomics.

CHAPTER SUMMARY

1 For purposes of analysis we consolidate—or aggregate—the outcomes from the enormous number of individual product markets into a composite market in which key variables are the price level and the level of real domestic output. This is accomplished through an aggregate demand–aggregate supply model of the economy.

2 The aggregate demand curve shows the level of real domestic output which the economy will purchase at each possible price level.

3 The rationale for the downsloping aggregate demand curve is based on the wealth or real balances effect, the interest-rate effect, and the foreign purchases effect. The wealth or real balances effect indicates that inflation will reduce the real value or purchasing power of fixed-value financial assets held by households, causing them to retrench on their consumer spending. The interest-rate effect indicates that, given the supply of money, a higher price level will increase the demand for money, thereby increasing the interest rate and reducing consumption and investment purchases which are interest-rate sensitive. The foreign purchases effect suggests that a change in the United States' price level relative to other countries will change the net exports component of American aggregate demand in the opposite direction.

4 The determinants of aggregate demand are spending by domestic consumers, businesses, government, and foreign buyers. Changes in the factors listed in Table 9-1 cause changes in spending by these groups and shift the aggregate demand curve.

5 The aggregate supply curve shows the levels of real domestic output which will be produced at various possible price levels.

6 The shape of the aggregate supply curve depends on what happens to per unit production costs—and therefore to the prices which businesses must receive to cover costs and make a profit—as real domestic output expands. The Keynesian range of the curve is horizontal because, with substantial unemployment, production can be increased without per unit cost or price increases. In the intermediate range, per unit costs increase as production bottlenecks appear and less efficient equipment and workers are employed. Prices must therefore rise as real domestic output is expanded. The classical range coincides with full employment; real domestic output is at a maximum and cannot be increased, but the price level will rise in response to an increase in aggregate demand.

7 As indicated in Table 9-2, the determinants of aggregate supply are input prices, productivity, and the legal-institutional environment. All else being equal, a change in one of these factors will change per unit production costs at each level of output and therefore alter the location of the aggregate supply curve.

8 The intersection of the aggregate demand and aggregate supply curves determines the equilibrium price level and real domestic output.

9 Given aggregate supply, increases in aggregate demand will **a** increase real domestic output and employment but not alter the price level in the Keynesian range; **b** increase both real domestic output and the price level in the intermediate range; and **c** increase the price level but not change real domestic output in the classical range.

10 The ratchet effect is at work when prices are flexible upward, but relatively inflexible downward. An increase in aggregate demand will raise the price level, but in the short term, prices cannot be expected to fall when demand decreases.

TERMS AND CONCEPTS

aggregation	foreign purchases effect	Keynesian, classical,	equilibrium price level
aggregates	determinants of	and intermediate	equilibrium real
aggregate demand	aggregate demand	ranges of the	domestic output
wealth or real balances	aggregate supply	aggregate supply	demand-pull inflation
effect	determinants of	curve	ratchet effect
interest-rate effect	aggregate supply	productivity	cost-push inflation

QUESTIONS AND STUDY SUGGESTIONS

 1 Why is the aggregate demand curve downsloping? Specify how your explanation differs from the rationale behind the downsloping demand curve for a single product.

 2 Explain the shape of the aggregate supply curve, accounting for the differences between the Keynesian, intermediate, and classical ranges of the curve.

3 Suppose that the aggregate demand and supply schedules for a hypothetical economy are as shown below:

Amount of real domestic output demanded, billions	Price level (price index)	Amount of real domestic output supplied, billions
$100	300	$400
200	250	400
300	200	300
400	150	200
500	150	100

a Use these sets of data to graph the aggregate demand and supply curves. What will be the equilibrium price level and level of real domestic output in this hypothetical economy? Is the equilibrium level of real domestic output also the full-employment level of real domestic output? Explain.

b Why will a price level of 150 *not* be an equilibrium price level in this economy? Why *not* 250?

c Suppose that buyers desire to purchase $200 billion of extra real domestic output at each price level. What factors might cause this change in aggregate demand? What is the new equilibrium price level and level of real domestic output? Over what range of the aggregate supply curve—Keynesian, intermediate, or classical—has equilibrium changed?

4 Suppose that the hypothetical economy in question 3 had the following relationship between its real domestic output and the input quantities necessary for producing that level of output:

Input quantity	Real domestic output
150.0	400
112.5	300
75.0	200

a What is the level of productivity in this economy?

b What is the per unit cost of production if the price of each input is $2?

c Assume that the input price increases from $2 to $3 with no accompanying change in productivity. What is the new per unit cost of production? In what direction would the $1 increase in input price push the aggregate supply curve? What effect would this shift in aggregate supply have on the price level and the level of real domestic output?

d Suppose that the increase in input price had *not* occurred but instead that productivity had increased by 100 percent. What would be the new per unit cost of production? What effect would this change in per unit production cost have on the aggregate supply curve? What effect would this shift in aggregate supply have on the price level and the level of real domestic output?

5 Will an increase in the American price level relative to price levels in other nations shift our aggregate demand curve? If so, in what direction? Explain. Will a decline in the dollar price of foreign currencies shift the American aggregate supply curve rightward or simply move the economy along an existing aggregate supply curve? Explain.

6 What effects might each of the following have on aggregate demand or aggregate supply? In each case use a diagram to show the expected effects on the equilibrium price level and level of real domestic output. Assume that all other things remain constant.

a A widespread fear of depression on the part of consumers

b A large purchase of wheat by Russia

c A 5-cent increase in the excise tax on gasoline

d A reduction in interest rates at each price level

e A cut in Federal spending for higher education

f The expectation of a rapid rise in the price level

g The complete disintegration of OPEC, causing oil prices to fall by one-half

h A 10 percent reduction in personal income tax rates

i An increase in labor productivity

j A 12 percent increase in nominal wages

k Depreciation in the international value of the dollar

l A sharp decline in the national incomes of our western European trading partners

m A decline in the percentage of the American labor force which is unionized

7 What is the relationship between the production possibilities curve discussed in Chapter 2 and the aggregate supply curve discussed in this chapter?

8 Other things being equal, what effect will each of the following have on the equilibrium price level and level of real domestic output:

a An increase in aggregate demand in the classical range of aggregate supply

b An increase in aggregate supply (assume prices and wages are flexible)

c An equal increase in both aggregate demand and aggregate supply

d A reduction in aggregate demand in the Keynesian range of aggregate supply

e An increase in aggregate demand and a decrease in aggregate supply

f A decrease in aggregate demand in the intermediate range of aggregate supply (assume prices and wages are inflexible downward)

9 In the accompanying diagram assume that the aggregate demand curve shifts from AD_1 in year 1 to AD_2 in year 2, only to fall back to AD_1 in year 3. Locate the new year 3 equilibrium position on the assumption that prices and wages are **a** completely flexible and **b** completely rigid downward. Which of the two equilibrium positions is more desirable? Which is more realistic? Explain why the price level might be ratcheted upward when aggregate demand increases.

10 "Unemployment can be caused by a leftward shift of aggregate demand or a leftward shift of aggregate supply." Do you agree? Explain. In each case, specify price level effects.

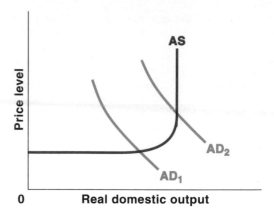

CHAPTER 10

Classical and Keynesian Theories of Employment

In preceding chapters we gained some familiarity with macroeconomic theory and problems through the concepts of aggregate demand and supply. In this and the next chapter we will expand our understanding of macroeconomic principles.

First, we will contrast the extreme forms of classical and Keynesian employment theories and thus clarify Chapter 9's designations of the classical (vertical) and Keynesian (horizontal) ranges of the aggregate supply curve. The comparison is a vivid one. Classical economics suggests that full employment is the norm of a market economy and that a laissez faire policy is best. Keynesian economics holds that unemployment is characteristic of laissez faire capitalism, and activist government policies are required to avoid the wastes of idle resources. We have seen that the market system can provide for an efficient allocation of resources (Chapter 5). The question now is: Can it also achieve and maintain full employment of available resources?

After contrasting these two widely divergent views, our second objective will be to examine the tools of Keynesian employment theory in greater detail. The Keynesian view has dominated macroeconomics since the Great Depression and, with many modifications and embellishments, is the core of modern mainstream macroeconomics. In Chapter 11 we use the tools developed in this chapter to demonstrate how the equilibrium levels of real domestic output and employment are determined in the Keynesian model. This model also explains a curious phenomenon: An initial change in spending ultimately produces a multiple change in national income and domestic output. At the end of Chapter 11, we link the Keynesian analysis directly back to the aggregate demand and aggregate supply model introduced in Chapter 9. Therefore, in subsequent chapters we can bring each of these related perspectives to bear in examining government stabilization policies.

SIMPLIFICATIONS

Four simplifying assumptions will help us achieve our objectives:

1 Although our analysis eventually will involve an "open economy" in which there are international trade transactions, initially we assume a "closed economy." Our discussion in this chapter will deal with the domestic economy, deferring complications arising from exports and imports until midway through Chapter 11.

2 Government will be ignored until Chapter 12, thereby permitting us in Chapters 10 and 11 to determine whether or not laissez faire capitalism can achieve and maintain full employment.

3 Although saving actually occurs in both the business and household sectors of the economy, we will for convenience speak as if all saving were personal saving.

4 For simplicity we will assume that depreciation and *net* American income earned abroad are zero.

Two implications of these assumptions are noteworthy: First, we found in Chapter 7 that there are four components of aggregate spending: consumption, investment, government purchases, and net exports. Our assumptions 1 and 2 mean that, for the moment, we are concerned only with consumption and investment.

Second, assumptions 2 through 4 permit us to treat gross domestic product (GDP), national income (NI), personal income (PI), and disposable income (DI) as being equal. All the items which in practice distinguish them from one another are due to depreciation, net American income earned abroad, government (taxes and transfer payments), and business saving (see Table 7-5). This means if $500 billion worth of goods and services is produced as GDP, exactly $500 billion worth of DI is received by households to split between consumption and saving.

THE CLASSICAL THEORY OF EMPLOYMENT

Until the Great Depression of the 1930s, many prominent economists of the nineteenth and early twentieth centuries—now called classical economists[1]—felt that the market system would ensure full employment of the economy's resources. It was acknowledged that now and then abnormal circumstances such as wars, political upheavals, droughts, speculative crises, and gold rushes would arise to push the economy from the path of full employment (see Figure 8-1). But when these deviations occurred, automatic adjustments within the market system would soon restore the economy to the full-employment level of output.

Classical employment theory is not simply an artifact of economic thought. A few modern economists have reformulated, revitalized, and extended the work of these nineteenth- and twentieth-century economists to generate a "new" classical economics. Indeed, Chapter 16's discussions of monetarism and rational expectations theory explain currently held views of macroeconomics which have strong intellectual roots in classical theory.

The **classical theory of employment** was grounded on two basic concepts:

1 Underspending—that is, a level of spending insufficient to purchase a full-employment output—was most unlikely to occur.

2 Even if a deficiency of total spending were to occur, price-wage (including interest-rate) adjustments would result quickly and ensure that the decline in total spending would *not* entail declines in real output, employment, and real incomes.

Say's Law

Classical theory's denial of the possibility of underspending was based in part on Say's law. **Say's law** is the disarming notion that the very act of producing goods generates an amount of income exactly equal to the value of the goods produced. The production of any output would automatically provide the income needed to take that output off the market. *Supply creates its own demand.*[2]

The essence of Say's law can be understood most easily in terms of a barter economy. A shoemaker, for example, produces or *supplies* shoes as a means of buying or *demanding* the shirts and stockings produced by other craftsmen. The shoemaker's supply of shoes *is* his demand for other goods. And so it allegedly is for other producers and for the entire economy: Demand must be the same as supply! In fact, the circular flow model of the economy and national income accounting both suggest something of this sort. Income generated from the production of any level of total output would, *when spent,* be just sufficient to provide a matching total demand. Assuming that the composition of output is in

---

[1] Most notable among this group of classical economists are David Ricardo, John Stuart Mill, F. Y. Edgeworth, Alfred Marshall, and A. C. Pigou.

[2] Attributed to the nineteenth-century French economist J. B. Say.

accord with consumer preferences, all markets would be cleared of their outputs. It would seem that all business owners need do to sell a full-employment output is to produce that output; Say's law guarantees there will be sufficient consumption spending for its successful disposal.

Saving: A Complicating Factor   However, there is one obvious omission in this simple application of Say's law. Although it is an accepted truism that output gives rise to an identical amount of nominal income (Chapter 7), there is no guarantee that the recipients of this income will spend it all. Some income might be saved (not spent) and therefore not reflected in product demand. Saving would constitute a break, or "leakage," in the income-expenditure flows and would undermine the effective operation of Say's law. Saving is a withdrawal of funds from the income stream which will cause consumption expenditures to fall short of total output. If households saved part of their incomes, supply would not create its own demand. Saving would cause a deficiency of consumption. The consequence would be unsold goods, cutbacks in production, unemployment, and falling incomes.

Saving, Investment, and the Interest Rate   But the classical economists argued that saving would not really result in a deficiency of total demand, because every dollar saved would be invested by businesses. Investment would occur to compensate for any deficiency of consumer spending; investment would fill any consumption "gap" caused by saving. Business firms, after all, do not plan to sell their entire output to consumers, but rather produce much of total output in the form of capital goods for sale to one another. Investment spending by businesses is a supplement or an addition to the income-expenditure stream which may fill any consumption gap arising from saving. Thus, if businesses as a group intend to invest as much as households want to save, Say's law will hold and the levels of domestic output and employment will remain constant. Whether or not the economy could achieve and sustain a level of spending sufficient to provide a full-employment level of output and income therefore would depend on whether businesses were willing to invest enough to offset the amount households want to save.

Classical economists argued that capitalism contained a very special market—the *money market*—which would guarantee an equality of saving and investment plans and therefore full employment. That is,

the money market—and, more specifically, the *interest rate* (the price paid for the use of money)—would ensure that dollars which leaked from the income-expenditure stream as saving would automatically reappear as dollars spent on investment goods.

The rationale underlying the saving and investment equating adjustments of the interest rate was simple and quite plausible. The classical economists contended that, other things being equal, households normally prefer to consume rather than save. Consumption of goods and services satisfies human wants; idle dollars do not. Hence, it was reasoned that consumers would save only if someone would pay them a rate of interest as a reward for their thriftiness. The greater the interest rate, the more dollars saved; that is, the saving (supply-of-dollars) curve of households would be upsloping, as shown by S in Figure 10-1a.

And who would pay for the use of saving? None other than investors—business owners who seek (demand) money capital to replace and enlarge their plants and stocks of capital equipment. Because the interest rate is a cost to borrowing businesses, they will be more willing to borrow and invest at low than at high interest rates. Thus, the investment (demand-for-dollars) curve of businesses is downsloping, as shown by I in Figure 10-1a.

Classical economists concluded that the money market, in which savers supply dollars and investors demand dollars, would establish an equilibrium price for the use of money—an equilibrium interest rate—at which the quantity of dollars saved (supplied) would equal the number of dollars invested (demanded).

In terms of Figure 10-1a, the interest rate would be r and the amounts of saving and investment both would be q. Saving, said the classicists, does not really constitute a break in the income-expenditure stream or a fatal flaw in Say's law, because the interest rate will cause every dollar saved to get into the hands of investors and be spent on capital equipment. Therefore, an increase in thriftiness is no cause for social concern; it simply shifts the supply-of-saving curve to the right, from S to S' in Figure 10-1b. Although saving will momentarily exceed investment and perhaps cause some temporary unemployment, the surplus of saving will drive the interest rate down to a new and lower equilibrium level, r'. And this lower interest rate will expand the volume of investment spending until it again equals the amount of saving at q', thereby preserving full employment.

In short, changes in the interest rate would guarantee the operation of Say's law even in an economy in which substantial saving occurs. As the classical econ-

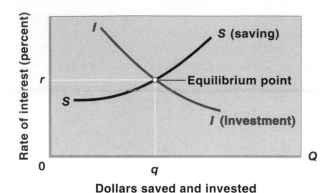

(a) Equilibrium interest rate and dollars saved and invested

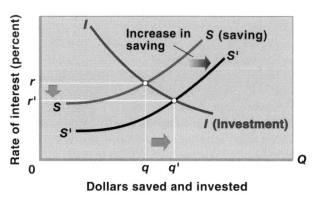

(b) New equilibrium interest rate and dollars saved and invested

FIGURE 10-1   Classical view of the money market

The classical economists believed that the saving plans of households would be reflected in a supply-of-dollars curve S and the investment plans of businesses in a demand-for-dollars curve I in the money market. In (a) the equilibrium interest rate r, the price paid for the use of money, would equate the amounts households and businesses planned to save and invest, thereby guaranteeing a full-employment level of spending. In (b) an increase in desired saving at each interest rate results in a rightward shift of the supply-of-dollars curve to S'. The equilibrium interest rate therefore falls to r' and the new equilibrium amounts of dollars saved and invested increases to q'. At q' the amounts of saving and investment are again equal and the full-employment level of spending is again assured.

omists saw it, the economy was like a gigantic bathtub in which the volume of water measured the levels of output and employment. Any leakage down the drain of saving would be returned to the tub through the spigot of investment. This had to be the case, because the interest rate connected the drainpipe and the spigot!

Price-Wage Flexibility

The classical economists bolstered their conclusion that full employment is the norm of capitalism with the argument that the level of output which businesses can sell depends not only on the level of total spending but also on the level of product prices. Even if the interest rate should somehow temporarily fail to equate the amounts which households wanted to save with the investment intentions of businesses, any resulting decline in total spending would be offset by proportionate declines in the price level. That is, $40 will buy four shirts at $10, but $20 will buy the same number of shirts provided their price falls to $5. Hence, if households temporarily saved more than businesses were willing to invest, the resulting decline in total spending would not result in a prolonged decline in real output, real income, and the level of employment *if* product prices declined in proportion to the decline in expenditures.

And, according to classical economists, this is precisely what would happen. Competition among sellers would ensure price flexibility. As declines in product demand became general, competing producers would lower their prices to dispose of accumulating surpluses. The result of "excess" saving would be to lower prices; and lower prices, by increasing the real value or purchasing power of the dollar, would permit nonsavers to obtain more goods and services with their current money incomes. Saving would therefore lower prices, but not output and employment.

"But," skeptics have asked, "doesn't this ignore the resource market? Although businesses can sustain sales in the face of declining demand by accepting lower product prices, won't they find it unprofitable to do so? As product prices decline, won't resource prices—particularly wage rates—have to decline significantly so businesses can produce *profitably* at the now lower prices?" Classical economists replied that wage rates must and would decline. General declines in product demand would be mirrored in declines in the demand for labor and other resources. The immediate result would be a surplus of labor, that is, unemployment, at the wage rate prevailing prior to these declines in the demand for labor. However, though not willing to employ all workers at the original wage rates, producers would find it profitable to employ these workers at lower wage rates. The demand for labor, in other words, is downsloping; those workers unable to locate employment at the old higher wage rates could find jobs at the new lower wage rates.

Would workers be willing to accept lower wage rates? Competition among unemployed workers, according to the classical economists, would force them to do so. In competing for scarce jobs, idle workers would bid down wage rates until these rates (wage costs to employers) were so low that employers would once again find it profitable to hire all available workers. This would happen at the new lower equilibrium wage rate. The classical economists therefore concluded that *involuntary unemployment* was impossible. Anyone who was willing to work at the market-determined wage rate could readily find employment. Competition in the labor market ruled out involuntary idleness.

Classical Theory and Laissez Faire

In the classical view these market system adjustments —fluctuations in the interest rate on the one hand, and **price-wage flexibility** on the other—were fully capable of maintaining full employment in a capitalistic economy. Working together, the classical economists felt, the two adjustment mechanisms made full employment a foregone conclusion. They came to embrace capitalism as a self-regulating economy in which full employment was the norm. Capitalism was capable of "running itself." Government assistance in operating the economy was unnecessary—nay, harmful. In an economy capable of achieving both full production and full employment, governmental interference could only be a detriment to its efficient operation. The logic of the classical theory led to the conclusion that a laissez faire economic policy was desirable.

KEYNESIAN ECONOMICS

One embarrassing fact persistently denied the validity of the classical theory of employment—recurring periods of prolonged unemployment and inflation. While one might explain a minor recession, such as the brief downswings of 1924 and 1927, in terms of wars and similar external considerations, serious and prolonged downswings, such as the Great Depression of the 1930s, were not easily rationalized. There is a remarkable inconsistency between a theory which concludes that unemployment is virtually impossible and the actual occurrence of a ten-year siege of very substantial unemployment. And so various economists came to criticize both the rationale and the underlying assumptions of classical employment theory. They tried to find a better, more realistic explanation of those forces which determine the level of employment.

Finally, in 1936 the renowned English economist John Maynard Keynes, whom you met in Chapter 9's Last Word, set forth a new explanation of the level of employment in capitalistic economies. In his *General Theory of Employment, Interest, and Money,*[3] Keynes attacked the foundations of classical theory and, in doing so, touched off a major revolution in economic thinking on macroeconomic questions. Although Keynes fathered modern employment theory, many others have since refined and extended his work. In this and following chapters, we explore Keynesian employment theory, or **Keynesian economics,** as it stands today.

Keynesian employment theory contrasts sharply with the classical position. Its blunt conclusion in its extreme form is that capitalism does *not* contain any mechanisms capable of guaranteeing full employment. The economy might come to rest—that is, reach an aggregate output equilibrium—with either considerable unemployment or substantial inflation. Full employment is more of an accident than a norm. Capitalism is *not* a self-regulating system capable of perpetual prosperity; it cannot be depended on to "run itself."

Furthermore, economic fluctuations should not be associated exclusively with external forces such as wars, droughts, and similar abnormalities. Rather, the causes of unemployment and inflation lie mainly in the failure of certain fundamental economic decisions—in particular, saving and investment decisions—to be completely synchronized in a capitalistic system. In addition, product prices and wages tend to be downwardly inflexible; extended and costly periods of recession will prevail before significant declines in prices and wages occur. Internal, in addition to external, forces contribute to economic instability.

Keynesians back these sweeping contentions by rejecting the very mechanisms on which the classical position is grounded—the interest rate and price-wage adjustments.

The Unlinking of Saving and Investment Plans

Keynesian theory rejects Say's law by seriously questioning the ability of the interest rate to match the saving and investment plans of households and businesses. The fact that modern capitalism is amply

---

[3]New York: Harcourt, Brace & World, Inc., 1936.

endowed with an elaborate money market and a wide variety of financial institutions does not diminish this skepticism about the interest rate as a mechanism capable of connecting the saving drain and the investment spigot. Keynesians find untenable the classical contention that business firms would invest more when households increased their rates of saving. After all, does not more saving mean less consumption? Can we really expect business planners to expand their capital facilities as the markets for their products shrink? More generally, the Keynesian view holds that savers and investors formulate their saving and investment plans for different reasons which, in the case of saving, are largely unrelated to the rate of interest.

Savers and Investors are Differently Motivated

Saving decisions are motivated by diverse considerations. Some save to make large purchases which exceed any single paycheck; households save for down payments on houses and to buy automobiles or television sets. Some saving is solely for the convenience of having liquid funds readily available to take advantage of any extraordinarily good buys which may occur. Or saving may provide for future needs of individuals and their families: Households save for the future retirement of the family breadwinner or to provide a college education for their children. Saving may be a precautionary, rainy-day measure—a means of protection against such unpredictable events as prolonged illness and unemployment. Or saving may be merely a deeply ingrained habit practiced on an almost automatic basis with no specific purposes in mind. Much saving is highly institutionalized or contractual: for example, payments for life insurance and annuities or participation in a "bond-a-month" program.

The basic point is that none of these diverse motives for saving is particularly sensitive to the interest rate. In fact, Keynesians argue that one can readily pose a situation in which, contrary to the classical conception (Figure 10-1), saving is *inversely* related to the interest rate. For example, if a family seeks to provide an annual retirement income of $12,000 from saving, it will need to save $200,000 if the interest rate is 6 percent, but only $100,000 if the interest rate is 12 percent.

In the Keynesian view, the primary determinant of both saving and consumption is the level of national income.

Why do businesses purchase capital goods? The motivation for investment spending, as we will see, is complex. The interest rate—the cost of obtaining money capital to invest—*is* a consideration in formulating investment plans, but it is *not* the only factor. The rate of profit which business firms expect to realize on the investment is also a crucial determinant of the amounts they desire to invest. Furthermore, during a major recession or depression, profit expectations may be so bleak that investment will be low and possibly declining despite substantial reductions in the interest rate. Interest rate reductions may not stimulate investment spending when it is most needed.

Money Balances and Banks

Keynesian employment theory sees the classical concept of the money market (Figure 10-1) as oversimplified and therefore incorrect in another sense. Specifically, the classical money market assumes that current saving is the only source of funds for the financing of investment. Keynesian economics holds that there are two other sources of funds which can be made available in the money market: (1) the accumulated money balances—cash and checking account money—held by households, and (2) lending institutions which can add to the money supply.

Keynesian theory stipulates that the public holds money balances not merely to negotiate day-to-day transactions, but also as a form of accumulated wealth not held in savings accounts in banks. The important point here is that, by drawing down or decumulating a portion of these money balances and offering these dollars to investors, a supply of funds in excess of current saving can be made available in the money market. Similarly, as we will find in Chapter 14, when lending institutions make loans, they add to the money supply. Lending by banks and other financial institutions, therefore, is also a means of augmenting current saving as a source of funds for investment.

The consequence is that a reduction in the money balances held by households *and* bank lending can lead to an amount of investment which is in excess of current saving. This implies that Say's law is invalid and that output, employment, and the price level can fluctuate. More specifically, we will see that an excess of investment over saving results in an increase in total spending which has an expansionary effect on the economy. If the economy is initially in recession, output and employment will increase; if the economy is already at full employment, the added spending will cause demand-pull inflation.

Conversely, classical theory is incorrect in assuming that all current saving will appear in the money market. If (1) households add some of their current saving to their money balances rather than channel it into the money market, or (2) some current saving is used to retire outstanding bank loans and these funds are not loaned to someone else, then the amount of funds made available in the money market will be less than that shown by the classical saving curve in Figure 10-1. This suggests that the amount of current saving will exceed the amount invested. Again, Say's law does not hold and macroeconomic instability will result. In this case the excess of saving over investment will mean a decline in total demand which is contractionary; output and employment will tend to fall.

To summarize: *The Keynesian position is that saving and investment plans can be at odds and thereby can result in fluctuations in total output, total income, employment, and the price level.* It is largely a matter of chance that households and businesses will desire to save and invest identical amounts. Keynesian economists feel they are better plumbers than their classical predecessors by recognizing that the saving drain and the investment spigot are *not* connected.

The Discrediting of Price-Wage Flexibility

But what of the second aspect of the classical position—the contention that downward price-wage adjustments will eliminate the unemployment effects of a decline in total spending?

Existence Modern Keynesians recognize that some prices and wages are flexible downward. In the early 1980s some prices fell and large numbers of workers were forced to accept wage freezes, wage cuts, and reduced fringe benefits. Causal factors included (1) back-to-back recessions, one of which was so severe as to bring about the highest unemployment rates since the 1930s; (2) enhanced foreign competition; and (3) deregulation of the airlines and trucking industries. But Keynesians argue that wage-price flexibility does not exist to the overall degree necessary for ensuring the restoration of full employment in the face of a decline in aggregate demand. The market system of capitalism has never been perfectly competitive; it is riddled by market imperfections and circumscribed by practical and political obstacles working against downward price-wage flexibility. In terms of Chapter 9's discussion of the ratchet effect, Keynesians argue that monopolistic producers have both the ability and desire to resist falling product prices as demand declines. And in resource markets, strong labor unions are equally persistent in holding the line against wage cuts.

Union collective bargaining agreements shield wages from downward adjustment for the two- or three-year duration of these contracts. In nonunion labor markets wages usually are adjusted only once a year. Furthermore, employers are often wary of wage cuts, recognizing adverse effects on worker morale and productivity. In short, as a practical matter, downward price-wage flexibility cannot be expected to offset the unemployment effects of a decline in aggregate demand.

Usefulness Even if price-wage declines accompanied a contraction of total spending, these declines might not reduce unemployment. The volume of total money demand cannot remain constant as prices and wages decline. Lower prices and wages necessarily mean lower nominal incomes, and lower nominal incomes in turn entail further reductions in total spending. The net result is likely to be little or no change in the depressed levels of output and employment.

Keynesians point out that the classicists were tripped up in their reasoning by the fallacy of composition. Because any particular group of workers typically buys only a small amount of what it produces, the product and therefore labor demand curves of a single firm can be regarded as independent of any wage (income) changes accorded its own workers. In other words, a decline in its wage rate will move a *single firm* down its stable labor demand curve and result in more employment. But this reasoning, argue Keynesian economists, does not apply to the economy as a whole, to general wage cuts. Wages are the major source of income in the economy. Widespread wage declines will therefore result in declines in incomes and also declines in the demand for both products and the labor used in producing them. The result is that employers will hire little or no additional labor after the general wage cuts. What holds true for a single firm—a wage cut for its employees will not adversely affect labor demand—is not true for the economy as a whole—general wage cuts *will* lower money incomes, causing the demand for products and labor to decline generally.

CLASSICS AND KEYNES: AD-AS RESTATEMENT

These two views of the macroeconomic world—classical and Keynesian—can be meaningfully restated and compared in their crude or extreme forms in terms of Chapter 9's aggregate demand and aggregate supply curves.

Classical View

The classical view is that the aggregate supply curve is vertical and therefore exclusively determines the level of real domestic output. On the other hand, the down-sloping aggregate demand curve is stable and solely establishes the price level.

Vertical Aggregate Supply Curve The classical position sees the aggregate supply curve as a vertical line as shown in Figure 10-2a. This is why we referred to the vertical portion of our aggregate supply curve in Chapter 9 as the "classical range." The vertical aggregate supply curve, remember, is located where the natural or full-employment rate of unemployment is being realized. According to the classical economists, the economy will operate at its full-employment level of output, Q_f, for the reasons previously discussed: Say's law, flexible interest rates, and responsive prices and wages. We stress that classical economists believe that Q_f does *not* change in response to changes in the price level. Observe, for example, that as the price level falls in Figure 10-2a from P_1 to P_2, real domestic output remains firmly anchored at Q_f.

But, you might argue, this stability of output seems at odds with Chapter 4's upsloping supply curves for individual products. There we found that lower prices would make production less profitable and cause producers to offer *less* output and presumably employ *fewer* workers. The classical response to your argument is that input costs would fall along with product prices to leave *real* profits unchanged and therefore output unchanged.

Consider a simplified illustration. Suppose we have a one-firm economy in which the firm's owner must receive a *real* profit of $20 to be induced to produce the full-employment output of, say, 100 units. Recall from Chapter 8 that what ultimately counts is the *real* reward one receives and not the level of prices. Suppose the owner's only input (aside from personal entrepreneurial talent) is 10 units of labor hired at $8 per worker for a total wage cost of $80 (=10 × $8). Also suppose the 100 units of output sell for $1 per unit so that total revenue is $100 (=100 × $1). This firm's *nominal* profit is $20 (=$100 − $80) and, using the $1 price to designate the base price index of 100 percent, its *real* profit is also $20 (=$20 ÷ 1.00). Well and good; full employment is achieved. But suppose that the price level declines by one-half. Would our producer still realize the $20 of real profits needed to induce the production of a 100-unit full-employment output?

The classical answer is Yes. Now that product price is only $.50, total revenue will only be $50 (=100 × $.50). But the cost of 10 units of labor will be

FIGURE 10-2 Classical and Keynesian views of the macroeconomy

According to classical theory (a), aggregate supply will determine the full-employment level of real domestic output while aggregate demand will establish the price level. Aggregate demand normally is stable, but if it should decline, say, as shown from AD₁ to AD₂, the price level will quickly fall from P_1 to P_2 to eliminate the temporary excess supply of *ab* and to restore full employment at *c*. The Keynesian view (b) is that aggregate demand is unstable and that price and wages are downwardly inflexible. An AD₁ to AD₂ decline in aggregate demand has no effect on the price level. Rather, real output falls from Q_f to Q_u and can remain at this equilibrium indefinitely.

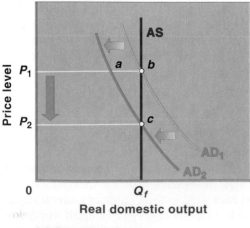

(a) Classical theory

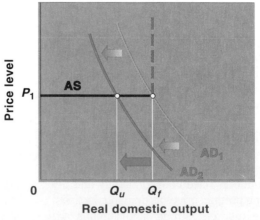

(b) Keynesian theory

reduced to $40 (=10 × $4) because the wage rate will be halved. Although *nominal* profits fall to $10 (=$50 − $40), *real* profits remain at $20. In other words, by dividing money profits of $10 by the new price index (expressed as a decimal) we obtain *real* profits of $20 (=$10 ÷ .50).

Generalization: With perfectly flexible wages there would be no change in the real rewards and therefore the production or output behavior of businesses. Under conditions of perfect wage flexibility, a change in the price level will not cause the economy to stray from its full-employment position.

Stable Aggregate Demand The classical economists theorized that money underlies aggregate demand. Specifically, the amount of real domestic output which can be purchased depends on (1) the quantity of money households and businesses possess and (2) the purchasing power or real value of that money as determined by the price level. Recall that the purchasing power of the dollar simply refers to the real quantity of goods and services a dollar will buy. Thus as we move down the vertical axis of Figure 10-2a the price level is falling. This means that the purchasing power of each dollar increases and therefore the given quantity of money can purchase a larger quantity of real output. If the price level declined by one-half, a given quantity of money would now purchase a real domestic output which is twice as large. Given a fixed money supply, the price level and real domestic output are inversely related.

And what of the *location* of the aggregate demand curve? According to the classical economists, aggregate demand will be reasonably stable if the nation's monetary authorities maintain a constant supply of money. Given aggregate supply, increases in the supply of money will shift the aggregate demand curve rightward and spark demand-pull inflation; reductions in the supply of money will shift the curve leftward and trigger deflation. The key to price-level stability then, according to the classical economists, is to control the nation's money supply to prevent unwarranted shifts in aggregate demand.

A final observation: Even if there are declines in the money supply and therefore in aggregate demand, the economy depicted in Figure 10-2a will *not* experience unemployment. Admittedly, the immediate effect of a decline in aggregate demand from AD_1 to AD_2 is an excess supply of output in that the aggregate output of goods and services exceeds aggregate spending by the amount *ab*. But, given the presumed downward flexibility of product and resource prices, this excess supply will reduce product prices along with workers' wages and the prices of other inputs. As a result, the price level will quickly decline from P_1 to P_2 until the amounts of output demanded and supplied are brought once again into equilibrium, this time at *c*. While the price level has fallen from P_1 to P_2, the level of real domestic output remains at the full-employment level.

Keynesian View

As noted earlier, the core of the Keynesian theory is that, at least in the short run, product prices and wages are downwardly inflexible, resulting in what is graphically represented as a horizontal aggregate supply curve. Additionally, aggregate demand is subject to periodic changes caused by changes in one or more of the determinants of aggregate demand (Table 9-1). Let's explore these two points in terms of Figure 10-2b.

1 Horizontal Aggregate Supply Curve (to Full-Employment Output) The downward inflexibility of prices and wages discussed first in Chapter 9 translates to a horizontal aggregate supply curve as shown in Figure 10-2b. Here, a decline in real domestic output from Q_f to Q_u will have no impact on the price level. Conversely, an increase in domestic output from Q_u to Q_f will also leave the price level unchanged. A "Keynesian range" of the aggregate supply curve therefore extends from zero real domestic output rightward to the full-employment or potential output Q_f. Once full employment is reached, according to Keynesians, the aggregate supply curve becomes vertical. This view is shown by the vertical line extending upward from the horizontal aggregate supply curve at Q_f.

2 Unstable Aggregate Demand Keynesian economists view aggregate demand as being unstable from one period to the next, even if there are no changes in the supply of money. In particular, the investment component of aggregate demand fluctuates, thereby altering the location of the aggregate demand curve. Suppose, for example, that aggregate demand in Figure 10-2b declines from AD_1 to AD_2. The sole impact of this change in aggregate demand will be on output and employment in that real domestic output falls from Q_f to Q_u while the price level remains constant at P_1. Moreover, Keynesians believe that unless there is a fortuitous offsetting increase in aggregate demand, real domestic output may remain at Q_u, which is below the full-employment level Q_f. Active macroeconomic policies of aggregate demand management by government are essential to avoid the wastes of recession and depression.

TOOLS OF KEYNESIAN EMPLOYMENT THEORY

According to Keynesian economics, how are the levels of output and employment determined in modern capitalism? *The amount of goods and services produced and therefore the level of employment depend directly on the level of total or aggregate expenditures.* Subject to the economy's productive potential as determined by the scarce resources available to it, businesses will produce the level of output they can profitably sell. Both workers and machinery are idled when there are no markets for the goods and services they can produce. Aggregate expenditures and total output and employment vary directly with each other.

Aggregate expenditures can best be understood in terms of the four components of GDP discussed in Chapter 7: consumption, investment, government purchases, and net exports. Our plan of attack is to analyze

the consumption and investment components of aggregate expenditures in the rest of this chapter. In Chapter 11 we derive the Keynesian private sector model of equilibrium GDP and employment, with net exports included. Chapter 12 adds government expenditures (along with taxes) to the model.

We preface our discussion with two other comments.

1 Unless specified otherwise we assume that the economy is operating within the horizontal Keynesian range of the aggregate supply curve. That is, the economy is presumed to have a substantial amount of excess productive capacity and unemployed labor so that an increase in aggregate demand will increase real output and employment, but *not* the price level.

2 In the Keynesian model we develop the notion of *aggregate expenditures,* which shows the relationship between real domestic output and national income, on the one hand, and the economy's total spending, on the other. This contrasts with the macro model we have used thus far in which *aggregate demand* portrays the relationship between real domestic output and the price level. In Chapter 11 we reconcile Chapter 9's aggregate demand–aggregate supply model and the Keynesian expenditures-output model which we now begin to construct.

CONSUMPTION AND SAVING

In terms of absolute size, consumption is the main component of aggregate expenditures (Chapter 7). It is therefore important to understand the major determinants of consumption spending. Recall that economists define personal saving as "not spending" or "that part of disposable income (DI) which is not consumed." In other words, disposable income equals consumption plus saving. Hence, in examining the determinants of consumption we are also simultaneously exploring the determinants of saving.

Income-Consumption and Income-Saving Relationships

Many considerations influence the level of consumer spending. But common sense and available statistical data both suggest that the most important determinant of consumer spending is income—in particular, disposable income. And, of course, since saving is that part of disposable income not consumed, DI is also the basic determinant of personal saving.

Consider some recent historical data. In Figure 10-3 each dot indicates the consumption–disposable income relationship for each year since 1960 and the green line is fitted to these points. Consumption is directly related to disposable income and, indeed, households clearly spend most of their income.

But we can say more. The gray 45-degree line is added to the diagram as a point of reference. Because this line bisects the 90-degree angle formed by the vertical and horizontal axes of the graph, each point on the 45-degree line must be equidistant from the two axes. We can therefore regard the vertical distance from any point on the horizontal axis to the 45-degree line as either consumption *or* disposable income. If we regard it as disposable income, then the amount (the vertical distance) by which the actual amount consumed in any given year falls short of the 45-degree guideline indicates the amount of saving in any particular year. For example, in 1991 consumption was $3887 billion, and disposable income was $4218 billion; hence, saving in 1991 was $331 billion. Disposable income less consumption equals saving. By observing these vertical distances as we move to the right in Figure 10-3, we note that saving also varies directly with the level of disposable income. Not shown in Figure 10-3 is the fact that in years of very low income, for example, some of

the worst years of the Great Depression, consumption exceeded disposable income. The dots for these depression years would be located *above* the 45-degree line. Households actually consumed in excess of their current incomes by *dissaving,* that is, by going into debt and liquidating previously accumulated wealth.

In summary, Figure 10-3 suggests that (1) households consume most of their disposable income and (2) both consumption and saving are directly related to the income level.

The Consumption Schedule

Figure 10-3 displays historical data; it shows us how much households *actually did consume* (and save) at various levels of DI over a period of years. For analytical purposes we need to show an income-consumption relationship—a consumption schedule—which indicates the various amounts households *plan* to consume at various possible levels of disposable income which might prevail at some specific *point in time.* A hypothetical **consumption schedule** of the type we require for analysis is shown in columns 1 and 2 of Table 10-1 and is plotted in Figure 10-4a (Key Graph). This consumption schedule reflects the consumption–disposable income relationship suggested by the em-

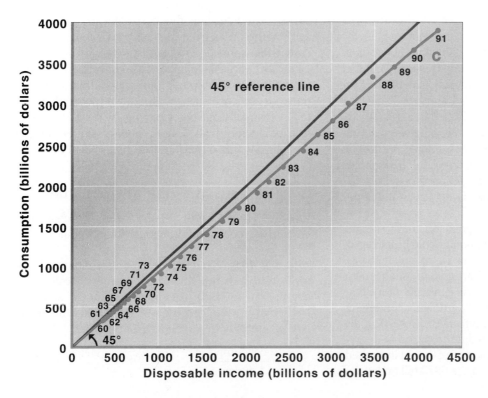

FIGURE 10-3
Consumption and disposable income, 1960–1991

Each dot in this figure shows consumption and disposable income in a given year. The *C* line generalizes on the relationship between consumption and disposable income. It indicates a direct relationship and that households consume the bulk of their incomes.

TABLE 10-1 Consumption and saving schedules *(hypothetical data; columns 1 through 3 in billions)*

(1) Level of output and income (GDP = DI)	(2) Consump- tion, C	(3) Saving, S (1) − (2)	(4) Average propensity to consume (APC) (2)/(1)	(5) Average propensity to save (APS) (3)/(1)	(6) Marginal propensity to consume (MPC) $\Delta(2)/\Delta(1)$*	(7) Marginal propensity to save (MPS) $\Delta(3)/\Delta(1)$*
(1) $370	$375	$−5	1.01	−.01		
					.75	.25
(2) 390	390	0	1.00	.00		
					.75	.25
(3) 410	405	5	.99	.01		
					.75	.25
(4) 430	420	10	.98	.02		
					.75	.25
(5) 450	435	15	.97	.03		
					.75	.25
(6) 470	450	20	.96	.04		
					.75	.25
(7) 490	465	25	.95	.05		
					.75	.25
(8) 510	480	30	.94	.06		
					.75	.25
(9) 530	495	35	.93	.07		
					.75	.25
(10) 550	510	40	.93	.07		

*The Greek letter Δ, delta, means "a change in."

pirical data of Figure 10-3, and is consistent with many empirical family budget studies. The relationship is direct—as common sense would suggest—and we note that households will spend a *larger proportion* of a small disposable income than of a large disposable income.

The Saving Schedule

It is a simple task to derive a **saving schedule.** Because disposable income equals consumption plus saving (DI = C + S), we need only subtract consumption (column 2) from disposable income (column 1) to find the amount saved (column 3) at each level of DI. That is, DI − C = S. Hence, columns 1 and 3 of Table 10-1 constitute the saving schedule, plotted in Figure 10-4b. Note that there is a direct relationship between saving and DI but that saving constitutes a smaller proportion (fraction) of a small DI than of a large DI. If households consume a smaller and smaller proportion of DI as DI goes up (column 4), they must save a larger and larger proportion (column 5).

Remembering that each point on the 45-degree line indicates a point where DI equals consumption, we see that dissaving would occur at the relatively low DI of, say, $370 billion (row 1), where consumption is actually $375 billion. Households will consume more than their current incomes by drawing down accumulated savings or by borrowing. Graphically, the vertical distance of the consumption schedule *above* the 45-degree line is equal to the vertical distance of the saving schedule *below* the horizontal axis at the $370 billion level of

output and income (see Figure 10-4a and b). In this instance, each of these two vertical distances measures the $5 billion of *dissaving* which occurs at the $370 billion income level.

The **break-even income** is at the $390 billion income level (row 2). This is the level at which households consume their entire incomes. Graphically, the consumption schedule cuts the 45-degree line, and the saving schedule cuts the horizontal axis (saving is zero) at the break-even income level. At all higher incomes, households will plan to save part of their income. The vertical distance of the consumption schedule *below* the 45-degree line measures this saving, as does the vertical distance of the saving schedule *above* the horizontal axis. For example, at the $410 billion level of income (row 3), both these distances indicate $5 billion worth of saving (see Figure 10-4a and b).

Average and Marginal Propensities

Columns 4 to 7 of Table 10-1 show additional characteristics of the consumption and saving schedules.

APC and APS   That fraction, or percentage, of any given total income which is consumed is called the **average propensity to consume** (APC), and that fraction of any total income which is saved is the **average propensity to save** (APS). That is,

$$APC = \frac{consumption}{income}$$

KEY GRAPH

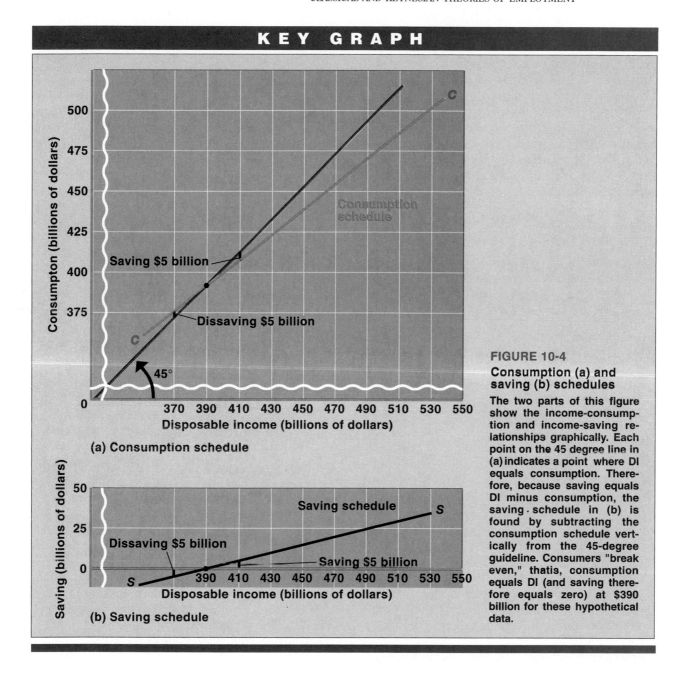

FIGURE 10-4

Consumption (a) and saving (b) schedules

The two parts of this figure show the income-consumption and income-saving relationships graphically. Each point on the 45 degree line in (a) indicates a point where DI equals consumption. Therefore, because saving equals DI minus consumption, the saving schedule in (b) is found by subtracting the consumption schedule vertically from the 45-degree guideline. Consumers "break even," that is, consumption equals DI (and saving therefore equals zero) at $390 billion for these hypothetical data.

and

$$\text{APS} = \frac{\text{saving}}{\text{income}}$$

For example, at the $470 billion level of income (row 6) in Table 10-1, the APC is $\frac{450}{470} = \frac{45}{47}$, or about 96 percent, while the APS is $\frac{20}{470} = \frac{2}{47}$, or about 4 percent. By calculating the APC and APS at each of the ten levels of DI shown in Table 10-1, we find that the APC falls and the APS rises as DI increases. This quantifies a point just

made: The fraction of total DI which is consumed declines as DI rises, a change that makes it necessary for the fraction of DI which is saved to rise as DI rises.

Because disposable income is either consumed or saved, the sum of the fraction of any level of DI which is consumed plus the fraction which is saved (not consumed) must exhaust that level of income. In short, APC + APS = 1. Columns 4 and 5 of Table 10-1 illustrate this point.

MPC and MPS The fact that households consume a certain portion of some given total income—for example, $\frac{45}{47}$ of a $470 billion disposable income—does not guarantee they will consume the same proportion of any *change* in income which they might receive. The proportion, or fraction, of any change in income which is consumed is called the **marginal propensity to consume** (MPC), marginal meaning "extra" or "a change in." Or, alternatively stated, the MPC is the ratio of a *change* in consumption to the *change* in income which brought the consumption change about:

$$MPC = \frac{\text{change in consumption}}{\text{change in income}}$$

Similarly, the fraction of any change in income which is saved is the **marginal propensity to save** (MPS). The MPS is the ratio of a *change* in saving to the *change* in income which brought it about:

$$MPS = \frac{\text{change in saving}}{\text{change in income}}$$

Thus, if disposable income is currently $470 billion (row 6) and household incomes rise by $20 billion to $490 billion (row 7), we find that they will consume $\frac{15}{20}$, or $\frac{3}{4}$, and save $\frac{5}{20}$, or $\frac{1}{4}$, of that increase in income (see columns 6 and 7 of Table 10-1). In other words, the MPC is $\frac{3}{4}$, or .75, and the MPS is $\frac{1}{4}$, or .25. *The sum of the MPC and the MPS for any given change in disposable income must always be 1.* Consuming and saving out of extra income is an either-or proposition; that fraction of any change in income which is not consumed is, by definition, saved. Therefore the fraction consumed (MPC) plus the fraction saved (MPS) must exhaust the whole increase in income:

$$MPC + MPS = 1$$

In our example .75 plus .25 equals 1.

MPC and MPS as Slopes The MPC is the numerical value of the slope of the consumption schedule and the MPS is the numerical value of the slope of the saving schedule. We know from the appendix to Chapter 1 that the slope of any line can be measured by the ratio of the vertical change to horizontal change involved in moving from one point to another on that line.

In Figure 10-5 we highlight the slopes of the consumption and saving lines derived from Table 10-1 by enlarging relevant portions of Figures 10-4a and 10-4b. Observe that consumption changes by $15 billion (vertical change) for each $20 billion change in disposable income (horizontal change); the slope of the consump-

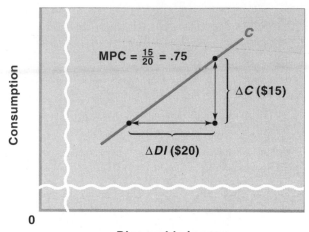

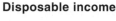

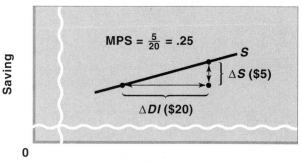

FIGURE 10-5 The marginal propensity to consume and the marginal propensity to save
The MPC is the slope of the consumption schedule and the MPS is the slope of the saving schedule.

tion line is .75 (=$15/$20)—the value of the MPC. Saving changes by $5 billion (vertical change) for every $20 billion change in disposable income (horizontal change). The slope of the saving line therefore is .25 (=$5/$20), which is the value of the MPS.

Nonincome Determinants of Consumption and Saving

The level of disposable income is the basic determinant of the amounts households will consume and save, just as price is the basic determinant of the quantity demanded of a single product. Recall that changes in determinants other than price, such as consumer tastes, incomes, and so forth (Chapter 4), will shift the demand curve for a given product. Similarly, certain determinants might cause households to consume more or less at each possible level of DI and thereby change the locations of the consumption and saving schedules. These factors are familiar to us because they were mentioned in a slightly different context in our discussion of aggregate demand in Chapter 9. There we focused on the downward slope of the aggregate demand curve and the factors which shift that curve. Here we see how these factors alter the consumption–disposable income and savings–disposable income relationships shown in Figure 10-4.

1 Wealth Generally, the greater the amount of wealth households have accumulated, the larger will be the amount of consumption and the smaller the amount of saving out of any level of current income. By *wealth* we mean both real assets (a house, automobiles, television sets, and other durables) and financial assets (cash, savings accounts, stocks, bonds, insurance policies, pensions) which households own. Households save—refrain from consumption—to accumulate wealth. Other things being equal, the more wealth households have accumulated, the weaker the incentive to save to accumulate additional wealth. An increase in wealth shifts the saving schedule downward and the consumption schedule upward.

Example: The dramatic stock market crash of 1929 significantly decreased the financial wealth of many families almost overnight and was undoubtedly a factor in explaining the low levels of consumption in the depressed 1930s. More recent example: The general decline in real estate values during 1989 and 1990 eroded household wealth and contributed to a retrenchment of consumer spending.

For the most part, however, the amount of wealth held by households only changes modestly from year to year and therefore does not typically account for large shifts in the consumption and saving schedules.

2 Price Level An increase in the price level shifts the consumption schedule downward; a decrease in the price level shifts it upward. This generalization is closely related to our discussion of wealth as a determinant of consumption because changes in the price level change the *real value* or *purchasing power* of certain types of wealth. Specifically, the real value of financial assets whose values are fixed in money terms will vary inversely with changes in the price level. This, of course, is the *wealth* or *real balances effect* which you encountered in Chapter 9.

Example: Suppose you own a $10,000 government bond. If the price level increases by, say, 10 percent, the real value of your $10,000 financial asset will decrease by approximately 10 percent. Because your real

financial *wealth* has been reduced, you will be less inclined to consume out of current *income*. Conversely, a decrease in the price level will increase your real financial wealth and induce you to consume more of your current income.

Note that, whenever we draw (locate) a particular consumption or saving schedule as in Figure 10-4, we are implicitly assuming a constant price level. This means that the horizontal axis of that figure measures *real* disposable income, as opposed to nominal or money, disposable income.

3 Expectations Household expectations concerning future prices, money incomes, and the availability of goods may have a significant impact on current spending and saving. Expectations of rising prices and product shortages trigger more spending and less saving currently. This shifts the consumption schedule upward and the saving schedule downward. It is natural for consumers to seek to avoid paying higher prices or having to "do without." Expected inflation and expected shortages induce people to "buy now" to escape higher future prices and bare shelves. The expectation of rising money incomes in the future also tends to make consumers freer in their current spending. Conversely, expected price declines, anticipations of shrinking incomes, and the feeling that goods will be abundantly available may induce consumers to retrench on consumption and build up savings.

4 Consumer Indebtedness The level of consumer debt can also affect the willingness of households to consume and save out of current income. If households are in debt to the degree that, say, 20 or 25 percent of their current incomes are committed to installment payments on previous purchases, consumers may well retrench on current consumption to reduce indebtedness. Conversely, if consumer indebtedness is relatively low, households may consume at an unusually high rate by increasing this indebtedness.

5 Taxation In Chapter 12, where consumption will be plotted against before-tax income, we will find that changes in taxes will shift the consumption and saving schedules. Specifically, we will discover that taxes are paid partly at the expense of consumption *and* partly at the expense of saving. Therefore, an *increase* in taxes will shift *both* the consumption and saving schedules *downward*. Conversely, a tax reduction will be partly consumed and partly saved by households. Thus a tax *decrease* will shift *both* the consumption and saving schedules *upward*.

Shifts and Stability

Three final, related points are relevant to our discussion of the consumption and saving schedules.

1 Terminology The movement from one point to another on a given stable consumption schedule (for example, *a* to *b* on C_0 in Figure 10-6a) is called a *change in the amount consumed*. The sole cause of this change is a change in the level of disposable income. On the other hand, a *change in the consumption schedule* refers to an upward or downward shift of the entire schedule— for example, a shift from C_0 to C_1 or to C_2 in Figure 10-6a. A relocation of the consumption schedule is

FIGURE 10-6 Shifts in the consumption (a) and saving (b) schedules

A change in any one or more of the nonincome determinants will cause the consumption and saving schedules to shift. If households consume more at each level of DI, they are necessarily saving less. Graphically this means that an upshift in the consumption schedule (C_0 to C_1) entails a downshift in the saving schedule (S_0 to S_1). Conversely, if households consume less at each level of DI, they are saving more. A downshift in the consumption schedule (C_0 to C_2) is reflected in an upshift of the saving schedule (S_0 to S_2).

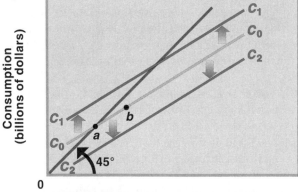

Disposable income (billions of dollars)

(a) Consumption schedule

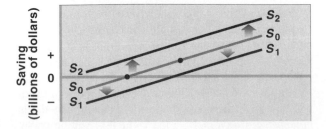

Disposable income (billions of dollars)

(b) Saving schedule

caused by changes in any one or more of the nonincome determinants just discussed. A similar distinction in terminology applies to the saving schedule in Figure 10-6b.

2 Schedule Shifts Insofar as the first four nonincome determinants of consumption are concerned, the consumption and saving schedules will shift in opposite directions. If households decide to consume *more* at each possible level of disposable income, they want to save *less,* and vice versa. Graphically, if the consumption schedule shifts upward from C_0 to C_1 in Figure 10-6, the saving schedule will shift downward from S_0 to S_1. Similarly, a downshift in the consumption schedule from C_0 to C_2 means an upshift in the saving schedule from S_0 to S_2. As just noted, the exception to this involves the fifth nonincome determinant—taxation. Households will consume less *and* save less to pay higher taxes. Thus, a tax increase will lower *both* consumption and saving schedules, whereas a tax cut will shift *both* schedules upward.

3 Stability Economists generally agree that, aside from deliberate governmental actions designed to shift them, the consumption and saving schedules are generally stable. This may be because consumption-saving decisions are strongly influenced by habit or because the nonincome determinants are diverse and changes in them frequently work in opposite directions and therefore tend to be self-canceling.

QUICK REVIEW 10-2

♦ *Consumption spending and saving both rise when disposable income increases; they fall when disposable income decreases.*

♦ *The average propensity to consume (APC) is the fraction of any given level of disposable income which is consumed; the average propensity to save (APS) is the fraction of any given level of disposable income which is saved.*

♦ *The marginal propensity to consume (MPC) is the fraction of any change in disposable income which is spent for consumer goods and is the slope of the consumption schedule; the marginal propensity to save (MPS) is the fraction of any change in disposable income which is saved and is the slope of the saving schedule.*

♦ *Changes in consumer wealth, the price level, consumer expectations, consumer indebtedness, and taxes shift the consumption and saving schedules.*

INVESTMENT

We now turn to investment, the second component of private spending. Recall that investment refers to expenditures on new plants, capital equipment, machinery, and so forth. There are two basic determinants of the level of net investment spending: (1) the expected rate of net profits businesses hope to realize from investment spending, and (2) the interest rate.

Expected Rate of Net Profit

Investment spending is guided by the profit motive; the business sector buys capital goods only when it expects such purchases to be profitable. Suppose the owner of a small cabinetmaking shop is considering investing in a new sanding machine which costs $1000 and has a useful life of only one year. The new machine will presumably increase the firm's output and sales revenue. Specifically, suppose that the *net* expected revenue (that is, net of such operating costs as power, lumber, labor, certain taxes, and so forth) from the machine is $1100. In other words, after operating costs have been accounted for, the remaining expected net revenue is sufficient to cover the $1000 cost of the machine and leave a return of $100. Comparing this $100 return or profit with the $1000 cost of the machine, we find that the expected *rate* of net profit on the machine is 10 percent (=$100/$1000).

The Real Interest Rate

There is one important cost associated with investing which our example has ignored. That, of course, is the interest rate—the financial cost the firm must pay to borrow the *money* capital required to purchase the *real* capital (the sanding machine).

Our generalization is this: If the expected rate of net profits (10 percent) exceeds the interest rate (say, 7 percent), it will be profitable to invest. But if the interest rate (say, 12 percent) exceeds the expected rate of net profits (10 percent), it will be unprofitable to invest.

But what if the firm does *not* borrow, but rather finances the investment internally out of funds saved from past profits? The role of the interest rate as a cost in investing in real capital remains valid. By using this money to invest in the sander, the firm incurs an opportunity cost (Chapter 2) in the sense that it forgoes the interest income it could have realized by lending the funds to someone else.

Note that the *real* rate of interest, rather than the nominal rate, is crucial in making investment deci-

sions. Recall from Chapter 8 that the nominal interest rate is expressed in terms of dollars of current value, while the real interest rate is stated in terms of dollars of constant or inflation-adjusted value. In other words, the real interest rate is the nominal rate less the rate of inflation. In our sanding machine illustration we implicitly assumed a constant price level so that all our data, including the interest rate, were in real terms.

But what if inflation is occurring? Suppose a $1000 investment is estimated to yield a real (inflation-adjusted) expected rate of net profits of 10 percent and the nominal interest rate is 15 percent. At first, one would say the investment is unprofitable and should not be made. But assume now there is ongoing inflation of 10 percent per year. This means that the investor will be paying back dollars with approximately 10 percent less in purchasing power. While the nominal interest rate is 15 percent, the real rate is only 5 percent (=15 percent − 10 percent). Comparing this 5 percent real interest rate with the 10 percent expected real rate of net profits, we find that the investment *is* profitable and should be undertaken.

Investment-Demand Curve

We now move from a single firm's investment decision to an understanding of the total demand for investment goods by the entire business sector. Assume every firm in the economy has estimated the expected rate of net profits from all relevant investment projects and these data have been collected. These estimates can now be *cumulated*—that is, successively summed—by asking: How many dollars' worth of investment projects entail an expected rate of net profit of, say, 16 percent or more? Of 14 percent or more? Of 12 percent or more? And so on.

Suppose there are no prospective investments which will yield an expected net profit of 16 percent or more. But there are $5 billion of investment opportunities with an expected rate of net profits between 14 and 16 percent; an *additional* $5 billion yielding between 12 and 14 percent; still an *additional* $5 billion yielding between 10 and 12 percent; and an *additional* $5 billion in each successive 2 percent range of yield down to and including the 0 to 2 percent range.

By *cumulating* these figures we obtain the data of Table 10-2, which are shown graphically by the **investment-demand curve** in Figure 10-7. Note in Table 10-2 that the number opposite 12 percent, for example, tells us there are $10 billion worth of investment opportunities which will yield an expected net profit of 12 percent *or more;* the $10 billion, in other words, in-

NATIONAL INCOME, EMPLOYMENT, AND FISCAL POLICY

TABLE 10-2 **Profit expectations and investment (hypothetical data)**

Expected rate of net profit (in percent)	Amount of investment (billions of dollars per year)
16%	$ 0
14	5
12	10
10	15
8	20
6	25
4	30
2	35
0	40

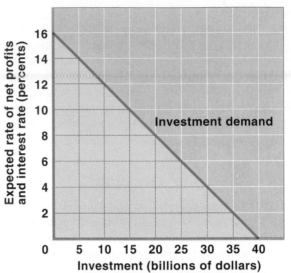

FIGURE 10-7   **The investment-demand curve**

The investment-demand curve for the economy is derived by arraying all relevant investment projects in descending order of their expected rate of net profitability and applying the rule that investment should be undertaken up to the point at which the interest rate is equal to the expected rate of net profits. The investment-demand curve is downsloping, reflecting an inverse relationship between the interest rate (the financial price of investing) and the aggregate quantity of capital goods demanded.

cludes the $5 billion of investment which will yield an expected return of 14 percent or more *plus* the $5 billion which is expected to yield between 12 and 14 percent.

Given this cumulated information on expected net profit rates of all possible investment projects, we again introduce the real interest rate or financial cost of investing. We know from our sanding machine example that an investment project will be undertaken provided its expected net profit rate exceeds the real interest rate. Let's apply this reasoning to Figure 10-7. If we assume that rate of interest is 12 percent, we find that $10 billion of investment spending will be profitable, that is, $10 billion worth of investment projects entail an expected net profit rate of 12 percent or more. Stated differently, at a financial "price" of 12 percent, $10 billion worth of investment goods will be demanded. Similarly, if the interest rate were lower at, say, 10 percent, then an additional $5 billion of investment projects would become profitable and the total amount of investment goods demanded would be $15 billion (=$10 + $5). At an interest rate of 8 percent, a further $5 billion of investment would become profitable and the total demand for investment goods would be $20 billion. At 6 percent, investment would be $25 billion. And so forth.

By applying the rule that all investment projects should be undertaken up to the point at which the expected rate of net profit equals the interest rate, we discover that the curve of Figure 10-7 is the investment-demand curve. Various possible financial prices of investing (various real interest rates) are shown on the vertical axis and the corresponding quantities of investment goods demanded are revealed on the horizontal axis. By definition, any line or curve embodying such data is the investment-demand curve. Consistent with our product and resource demand curves of Chapter 4, observe the *inverse* relationship between the interest rate (price) and the amount of spending on investment goods (quantity demanded).

This conception of the investment decision allows us to anticipate an important aspect of macroeconomic policy. We will find in our discussion of monetary policy in Chapter 15 that by changing the supply of money, government can alter the interest rate. This is done primarily to change the level of investment spending. At any point in time, business firms in the aggregate have a wide variety of investment projects under consideration. If interest rates are high, only those projects with the highest expected rate of net profit will be undertaken. Hence, the level of investment will be small. As the interest rate is lowered, projects whose expected rate of net profit is less will also become commercially feasible and the level of investment will rise.

A final point: Assuming a fixed supply of money, a change in the price level will influence the amount of investment through the *interest-rate effect* described in Chapter 9. A rise in the price level will increase the amount of money that consumers and businesses desire to have available for purchasing the higher-priced output. That is, if prices rise by, say 10 percent, then people will want to have 10 percent more money in their billfolds and checking accounts. With a fixed supply of money, this increase in the demand for money balances elevates the price of money—the interest rate—which, in turn, reduces investment. Likewise, lower price levels reduce the demand for money balances, decrease the interest rate, and bolster investment.

Shifts in Investment Demand

In discussing the consumption schedule, we noted that, although disposable income is the key determinant of the amount consumed, there are other factors which affect consumption. These "nonincome determinants," you will recall, cause shifts in the consumption schedule. So it also is with the investment-demand schedule. Given the expected rates of net profit of various possible investments, Figure 10-7 portrays the interest rate as the main determinant of investment.

But other factors or variables determine the location of the investment-demand curve. We will examine several of the more important "noninterest determinants" of investment demand, noting how changes in these determinants might shift the investment-demand curve. Note that any factor which increases the expected net profitability of investment will shift the investment-demand curve to the right. Conversely, anything which decreases the expected net profitability of investment will shift the investment-demand curve to the left.

1 Acquisition, Maintenance, and Operating Costs
As our sanding machine example revealed, the initial costs of capital goods, along with the estimated costs of operating and maintaining those goods, are important considerations in gauging the expected rate of net profitability of any particular investment. To the extent that these costs rise, the expected rate of *net* profit from prospective investment projects will fall, shifting the investment-demand curve to the left. Conversely, if these costs decline, expected net profit rates will rise, shifting the investment-demand curve to the right. Note that the wage policies of unions may affect the investment-demand curve because wage rates are a major operating cost for most firms.

2 Business Taxes
Business owners look to expected profits *after taxes* in making their investment decisions. Hence, an increase in business taxes will lower profitability and shift the investment-demand curve to the left; a tax reduction will shift it to the right.

3 Technological Change
Technological progress—the development of new products, improvements in existing products, the creation of new machinery and production processes—is a basic stimulus to investment. The development of a more efficient machine, for example, will lower production costs or improve product quality, increasing the expected rate of net profit from investing in the machine. Profitable new products—mountain bikes, digital tape players, high-resolution television, legal drugs, and so on—induce a flurry of investment as firms tool up for expanded production. In short, a rapid rate of technological progress shifts the investment-demand curve to the right, and vice versa.

4 The Stock of Capital Goods on Hand
Just as the stock of consumer goods on hand affects household consumption-saving decisions, so the stock of capital goods on hand influences the expected profit rate from additional investment in a given industry. To the extent that a given industry is well stocked with productive facilities and inventories of finished goods, investment will be retarded in that industry. Obviously, such an industry will be amply equipped to fulfill present and future market demand at prices which yield mediocre profits. If an industry has enough, or even excessive, productive capacity, the expected rate of profit from further investment in the industry will be low, and therefore little or no investment will occur. Excess productive capacity shifts the investment-demand curve to the left; a relative scarcity of capital goods shifts it to the right.

5 Expectations
We noted earlier that business investment is based on *expected* profits. Capital goods are durable—they may have a life expectancy of ten or twenty years—and thus the profitability of any capital investment will depend on business planners' expectations of the *future* sales and *future* profitability of the product which the capital helps produce. Business expectations may be based on elaborate forecasts of future business conditions which incorporate a number of "business indicators." Nevertheless, such elusive and difficult-to-predict factors as changes in the domestic political climate, the thrust of foreign affairs, population growth, and stock market conditions must be taken into account on a subjective or intuitive basis. For

present purposes we note that, if business executives are optimistic about future business conditions, the investment-demand curve will shift to the right; a pessimistic outlook will shift it to the left.

QUICK REVIEW 10-3

◆ *A specific investment will be undertaken if the expected rate of net profits exceeds the real interest rate.*

◆ *The investment demand curve shows the expected rates of net profits for various levels of total investment.*

◆ *Total investment is established where the real interest rate and the expected rate of net profits on investment are equal.*

◆ *The investment demand curve shifts when changes occur in the costs of capital goods, business taxes, technology, the stock of capital goods on hand, and business expectations.*

Investment and Income

To add the investment decisions of businesses to the consumption plans of households (Chapter 11), we must express investment plans in terms of the level of disposable income (DI), or GDP. That is, we will construct an **investment schedule** showing the amounts which business firms as a group plan or intend to invest at each possible level of income or output. Such a schedule will mirror the investment plans or intentions of business owners and managers in the same way the consumption and saving schedules reflect the consumption and saving plans of households.

TABLE 10-3   The investment schedule (hypothetical data; in billions)

(1) Level of output and income	(2) Investment, I_g	(3) Investment, I'_g
$370	$20	$10
390	20	12
410	20	14
430	20	16
450	20	18
470	20	20
490	20	22
510	20	24
530	20	26
550	20	28

We assume that business investment is geared to long-term profit expectations as influenced by technological progress, population growth, and so forth, and therefore is *autonomous* or independent of the level of current disposable income or domestic output. Specifically, suppose that the investment-demand curve is as shown in Figure 10-7 *and* that the current rate of interest is 8 percent. This means that the business sector will find it profitable to spend $20 billion on investment goods. In Table 10-3, columns 1 and 2, we are assuming that this level of investment will be forthcoming at every level of income. The I_g line in Figure 10-8 shows this graphically.

This assumed independence of investment and income is admittedly a simplification. A higher level of business activity may *induce* additional spending on

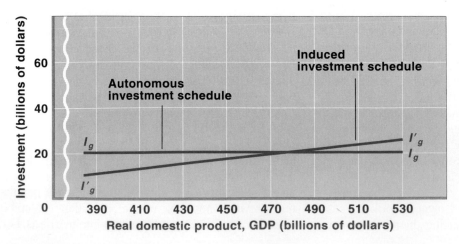

FIGURE 10-8   The investment schedule: two possibilities

Our discussion will be facilitated by employing the investment schedule I_g, which assumes that the investment plans of businesses are independent or autonomous of the current level of income. Actually, the investment schedule may be slightly upsloping, as suggested by I'_g.

capital facilities, as suggested by columns 1 and 3 of Table 10-3 and I'_g in Figure 10-8. There are at least two reasons why investment might vary directly with income. First, investment is related to profits; much investment is financed internally out of business profits. Therefore, it is very plausible that as disposable income and GDP rise, so will business profits and therefore the level of investment. Second, at low levels of income and output, the business sector will have excess production capacity; many industries will have idle machinery and equipment and therefore little incentive to purchase additional capital goods. But, as the level of income rises, this excess capacity disappears and firms are inclined to add to their stock of capital goods. Our simplification, however, is not too unrealistic and will greatly facilitate later analysis.

Instability of Investment

In contrast to the consumption schedule, the investment schedule is unstable. Proportionately, investment is the most volatile component of total spending. Figure 10-9 shows the volatility of investment and also makes clear that this variability is substantially greater than that of GDP. These data also suggest that our simplified treatment of investment as being independent of domestic output (Figure 10-8) is essentially realistic; investment spending does not closely follow GDP.

Some of the more important factors explaining the variability of investment follow:

1 Durability Because of their durability, capital goods have a rather indefinite useful life. Within limits, purchases of capital goods are discretionary and therefore postponable. Older equipment or buildings can be scrapped and entirely replaced, on the one hand, or patched up and used for a few more years, on the other. Optimism about the future may prompt business planners to replace their older facilities, that is, to modernize their plants, and this will call for a high level of investment. A less optimistic view, however, may lead to very small amounts of investment as older facilities are repaired and kept in use.

2 Irregularity of Innovation We have indicated that technological progress is a major determinant of investment. New products and processes provide a major stimulus to investment. However, history suggests that major innovations—railroads, electricity, automobiles, computers, and so forth—occur quite ir-

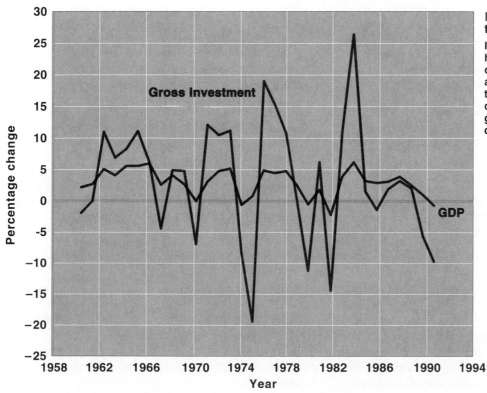

FIGURE 10-9 The volatility of investment

Investment spending is highly volatile. In comparing changes in real investment and real GDP, we observe that the annual percentage changes in investment are greater than the percentage changes in GDP.

LAST WORD

THE SHARE ECONOMY: MAKING WAGES FLEXIBLE

*Can greater downward wage flexibility be achieved to soften the impact of a decline in aggregate demand on employment? MIT's Martin Weitzman has offered a proposal to achieve this goal.**

Our comparisons of the classical and the Keynesian conceptions of the macroeconomy suggest that, if wages are stable, employment will tend to be unstable and vice versa. Most modern economists recognize that long-term union contracts, among other considerations, make wages downwardly inflexible at least in the short run. Hence, the declines in labor demand which accompany recession have their primary effect on employment. Professor Weitzman's proposal seeks to increase the downward flexibility of wage rates so that the functioning of labor markets corresponds more closely with the classical model and thereby results in greater employment stability.

In essence Weitzman's proposal is that some portion of wages should be tied directly to the firm's profitability; some part of worker compensation should be in the form of profit sharing. For example, instead of paying workers a guaranteed wage rate of $10 per hour, Weitzman suggests that workers be guaranteed $5 per hour (the base wage) and additional compensation equal to some predetermined percentage of the firm's profits (the share wage). Total compensation (base wage + share wage) may exceed or fall short of $10 per hour, depending on the firm's economic fortunes.

How would employment be affected by such a plan? Assume initially that workers are receiving $10 per hour—$5 in the form of a guaranteed wage and another $5 as profit-sharing compensation. Now suppose a recession occurs and the employer's sales and

*Martin L. Weitzman, *The Share Economy* (Cambridge, Mass.: Harvard University Press, 1984).

profits both decline. As a result, the $5 of profit-sharing income will fall and might decline to zero so that actual wages paid by the firm fall from $10 to $5. Given the new depressed demand for labor, the firm would clearly choose to hire more workers under Weitzman's proposal where wages have now fallen to $5, than if they were fixed at $10.

There are a number of criticisms of the profit-sharing wage plan. For example, it has been argued that the plan might jeopardize the historical wage gains of labor and result in exploitative wages. A further criticism is that with lower guaranteed wages employers will be inclined to adopt production techniques which involve the use of relatively more labor and relatively less capital. Because the amount of capital equipment per worker is critical to labor productivity and economic growth, the long-run expansion of real GDP might be impaired. At a more pragmatic level there is the fundamental question as to whether workers will accept the prospect of more jobs and greater employment stability in exchange for a reduced wage guarantee. It should be noted, however, that a growing number of union and nonunion labor contracts *do* contain profit-sharing arrangements. Hence, although a full-blown share economy seems improbable, profit-sharing appears to be an idea which is spreading.

---

regularly, and when they do occur, these innovations induce a vast upsurge or "wave" of investment spending which in time recedes. A classic illustration is the widespread acceptance of the automobile in the 1920s. This event not only brought about substantial increases in investment in the automobile industry itself, but also induced tremendous amounts of investment in

such related industries as steel, petroleum, glass, and rubber, not to mention public investment in streets and highways. But when investment in these related industries was ultimately "completed"—that is, when enough capital facilities had been created to meet the needs of the automobile industry—total investment leveled off.

3 Variability of Profits We know that business owners and managers invest only when they feel it will be profitable to do so and that, to a significant degree, the expectation of future profitability is influenced by the size of current profits. Current profits, however, are themselves highly variable (line 13 of the table on the inside covers provides information on undistributed corporate profits). Thus, the variability of profits contributes to the volatile nature of the incentive to invest. Furthermore, the instability of profits may also cause investment fluctuations, because profits are a major source of funds for business investment. American businesses tend to prefer this internal source of financing to increases in external debt or stock issue. In short, expanding profits give business planners both greater incentives and greater means to invest; declining profits have the reverse effects. The fact that actual profits are variable adds to the instability of investment.

4 Variability of Expectations We have already discussed how the durability of capital equipment results in the making of investment decisions on the basis of *expected* net profit. Now, while there is a tendency for business firms to project current business conditions into the future, it is equally true that expectations are sometimes subject to radical revision when some event or combination of events suggests a significant change in future business conditions. What kinds of events make business confidence so capricious? Changes in the domestic political climate, changes in energy developments, changes in population growth and therefore in anticipated market demand, court decisions in key labor or antitrust cases, legislative actions, strikes, changes in governmental economic policies, and a host of similar considerations may give rise to substantial shifts in business optimism or pessimism.

The stock market merits specific comment in this regard. Business planners frequently look to the stock market as an index or barometer of the overall confidence of society in future business conditions; a rising "bull" market signifies public confidence in the business future, whereas a falling "bear" market implies a lack of confidence. The stock market, however, is a highly speculative market, and initially modest changes in stock prices can be seriously intensified by participants who jump on the bandwagon by buying when prices begin to rise and by selling when stock prices start to fall. Furthermore, by affecting the amount of proceeds gained through offerings of new stock, upsurges and slumps in stock values also affect the level of investment—that is, the amount of capital goods purchased.

For these and similar reasons, we can correctly associate most fluctuations in output and employment with changes in investment. In terms of Figure 10-8, we can think of this volatility as being reflected in frequent and substantial upward and downward shifts in the investment schedule.

CHAPTER SUMMARY

1 Classical employment theory envisioned laissez faire capitalism as being capable of providing virtually continuous full employment. This analysis was based on Say's law and the ability of the money market to equate saving and investment.

2 Classical economists argued that because supply creates its own demand, general overproduction was improbable. This conclusion was held to be valid even when saving occurred, because the money market, or more specifically, the interest rate, would automatically synchronize the saving plans of households and the investment plans of businesses.

3 Classical employment theory also held that even if temporary declines in total spending occurred, these declines would be compensated for by downward price-wage adjustments in such a way that real output, employment, and real income would not decline.

4 Keynesian employment theory rejects the notion that the interest rate would equate saving and investment by pointing out that savers and investors make their saving and investment decisions for different reasons—reasons which, for savers, are largely unrelated to the interest rate. Furthermore, because of changes in **a** the public's holdings of money balances, and **b** loans made by banks and other financial institutions, the supply of funds may exceed or fall short of current saving, and saving and investment will not be equal.

5 Keynesian economists discredit price-wage flexibility on both practical and theoretical grounds. They argue that **a** union and business monopolies, minimum-wage legislation, and a host of related factors have virtually eliminated the possibility of substantial price-wage reductions, and **b** price-wage cuts will lower total income and therefore the demand for labor.

6 Classical economist see **a** a vertical aggregate supply curve which establishes the level of output, and **b** a stable aggregate demand curve which establishes the price level; Keynesians see **a** a horizontal aggregate supply curve at less-than-full-employment levels of output, and **b** an inherently unstable aggregate demand curve.

7 The basic tools of Keynesian employment theory are the consumption, saving, and investment schedules, which show the various amounts that households intend to consume and save and that businesses plan to invest at the various possible income-output levels, given a particular price level.

8 The locations of the consumption and saving schedules are determined by such factors as **a** the amount of wealth owned by households; **b** the price level; **c** expectations of future income, future prices, and product availability; **d** the relative size of consumer indebtedness; and **e** taxation. The consumption and saving schedules are relatively stable.

9 The *average* propensities to consume and save show the proportion or fraction of any level of *total* income consumed and saved. The *marginal* propensities to consume and save show the proportion or fraction of any *change* in total income consumed or saved.

10 The immediate determinants of investment are **a** the expected rate of net profit and **b** the real rate of interest.

The economy's investment-demand curve can be determined by cumulating investment projects and arraying them in descending order according to their expected net profitability and applying the rule that investment will be profitable up to the point at which the real interest rate equals the expected rate of net profit. The investment-demand curve reveals an inverse relationship between the interest rate and the level of aggregate investment.

11 Shifts in the investment-demand curve can occur as the result of changes in **a** the acquisition, maintenance, and operating costs of capital goods; **b** business taxes; **c** technology; **d** the stocks of capital goods on hand; and **e** expectations.

12 We make the simplifying assumption that the level of investment determined by the current interest rate and the investment-demand curve does not vary with the level of GDP.

13 The durability of capital goods, the irregular occurrence of major innovations, profit volatility, and the variability of expectations all contribute to the instability of investment spending.

TERMS AND CONCEPTS

classical theory of employment	Keynesian economics consumption and saving schedules	average propensities to consume and save	marginal propensities to consume and save
Say's law		investment-demand	
price-wage flexibility	break-even income	curve	investment schedule

---

QUESTIONS AND STUDY SUGGESTIONS

1 Explain the classical economists' conclusion that Say's law would prevail even in an economy where substantial saving occurred. What arguments have Keynesian economists used in attacking the classical view that Say's law would result in sustained full employment?

2 "Unemployment can be avoided so long as businesses are willing to accept lower product prices, and workers to accept lower wage rates." Critically evaluate.

3 Use the aggregate demand–aggregate supply model to compare classical and Keynesian interpretations of **a** the aggregate supply curve, and **b** the aggregate demand curve. Which model do you think is more realistic?

4 Precisely how are the APC and the MPC different? Why must the sum of the MPC and the MPS equal 1? What are the basic determinants of the consumption and saving schedules? Of your own level of consumption?

5 Explain precisely what relationships are shown by **a** the consumption schedule, **b** the saving schedule,

c the investment-demand curve, and **d** the investment schedule.

6 Explain how each of the following will affect the consumption and saving schedules or the investment schedule:

    a A decline in the amount of government bonds which consumers are holding

    b The threat of limited, nonnuclear war, leading the public to expect future shortages of consumer durables

    c A decline in the real interest rate

    d A sharp decline in stock prices

    e An increase in the rate of population growth

    f The development of a cheaper method of manufacturing pig iron from ore

    g The announcement that the social security program is to be restricted in size of benefits

    h The expectation that mild inflation will persist in the next decade

    i An 8 percent reduction in the price level

7 Explain why an upshift in the consumption schedule typically involves an equal downshift in the saving schedule. What is the exception?

8 Complete the accompanying table.

Level of output and income (GDP = DI)	Consumption	Saving	APC	APS	MPC	MPS
$240	$_____	$−4	___	___	___	___
260	_____	0	___	___	___	___
280	_____	4	___	___	___	___
300	_____	8	___	___	___	___
320	_____	12	___	___	___	___
340	_____	16	___	___	___	___
360	_____	20	___	___	___	___
380	_____	24	___	___	___	___
400	_____	28	___	___	___	___

a Show the consumption and saving schedules graphically.

b Locate the break-even level of income. How is it possible for households to dissave at very low income levels?

c If the proportion of total income consumed decreases and the proportion saved increases as income rises, explain both verbally and graphically how the MPC and MPS can be constant at various levels of income.

9 What are the basic determinants of investment? Explain the relationship between the real interest rate and the level of investment. Why is the investment schedule less stable than the consumption and saving schedules?

10 Assume there are no investment projects in the economy which yield an expected rate of net profit of 25 percent or more. But suppose there are $10 billion of investment projects yielding expected net profit of between 20 and 25 percent; another $10 billion yielding between 15 and 20 percent; another $10 billion between 10 and 15 percent; and so

forth. Cumulate these data and present them graphically, putting the expected rate of net profit on the vertical axis and the amount of investment on the horizontal axis. What will be the equilibrium level of aggregate investment if the real interest rate is **a** 15 percent, **b** 10 percent, and **c** 5 percent? Explain why this curve is the investment-demand curve.

11 **Advanced analysis:** Linear equations (see appendix to Chapter 1) for the consumption and saving schedules take the general form $C = a + bY$ and $S = −a + (1 − b)Y$, where C, S, and Y are consumption, saving, and national income, respectively. The constant a represents the vertical intercept, and b is the slope of the consumption schedule.

a Use the following data to substitute specific numerical values into the consumption and saving equations.

National income (Y)	Consumption (C)
$ 0	$ 80
100	140
200	200
300	260
400	320

b What is the economic meaning of b? Of $(1 − b)$?

c Suppose the amount of saving which occurs at each level of national income falls by $20, but that the values for b and $(1 − b)$ remain unchanged. Restate the saving and consumption equations for the new numerical values and cite a factor which might have caused the change.

12 **Advanced analysis:** Suppose that the linear equation for consumption in a hypothetical economy is $C = 40 + .8Y$. Also suppose that income (Y) is $400. Determine **a** the marginal propensity to consume, **b** the marginal propensity to save, **c** the level of consumption, **d** the average propensity to consume, **e** the level of saving, and **f** the average propensity to save.

Equilibrium Domestic Output in the Keynesian Model

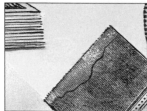

There is a chance that sometime during your lifetime you or a member of your family will experience a layoff because of a decline in total spending. A greater likelihood is that you will live through a period in which total spending suddenly surges, sharply increasing domestic output, national income, and total employment.

In this chapter we continue our development of the Keynesian aggregate expenditures model—a model which helps us understand cyclical changes in total spending, output, income, and employment. We first use the consumption, saving, and investment schedules developed in Chapter 10 to explain the equilibrium levels of output, income, and employment. Next, we will analyze *changes* in the equilibrium levels of output, income, and employment brought about by changes in investment spending. Then, the foreign sector is added to the model to show how exports and imports affect the macroeconomy. The final section reconciles our newly developed aggregate expenditures model with Chapter 9's aggregate demand and supply model.

Until government is included in our discussion in Chapter 12, we continue to assume no depreciation, no *net* American income earned abroad, no government, and no business saving. Recall that these assumptions permit us to equate GDP and DI. In addition, unless explicitly indicated to the contrary, we assume that the price level is constant. In other words, the economy is presumed to be operating within the Keynesian (horizontal) range of the aggregate supply curve. Hence, our analysis will be in terms of *real* domestic output as opposed to *nominal* domestic output.

Note that in this and the next chapter we deal with a *model* of the economy designed to clarify the basic determinants of the levels of output and employment. The specific numbers employed are only illustrative; they are not intended to measure the real world.

EXPENDITURES-OUTPUT APPROACH

In determining and explaining the equilibrium level of output, we employ two closely interrelated approaches: the **aggregate expenditures–domestic output** (or $C + I_g = $ GDP) **approach** and the **leakages-injections** (or the $S = I_g$) **approach.** Let's first discuss the aggregate expenditures–domestic output approach, using both simple arithmetic data and graphical analysis.

Tabular Analysis

Table 11-1 combines the income-consumption and income-saving data of Table 10-1 and the simplified income-investment data of columns 1 and 2 in Table 10-3.

Domestic Output Column 2 of Table 11-1 is the total or domestic output schedule for the economy. It indicates the various possible levels of total output—that is, the various possible real GDPs—which the business sector of the economy might produce. *Producers are willing to offer each of these ten levels of output in the expectation that they will receive an identical amount of receipts of income from its sale.* For example, the business sector will produce $370 billion worth of output, thereby incurring $370 billion worth of costs (wages, rents, interest, and profit), only if businesses expect that this output can be sold for $370 billion worth of receipts. Some $390 billion worth of output will be of-

fered if businesses feel this output can be sold for $390 billion. And so it is for all the other possible levels of output.

Aggregate Expenditures The total, or aggregate, expenditures schedule is shown in column 6 of Table 11-1. It shows the total amount which will be spent at each possible output-income level. In the closed private sector of the economy, the aggregate expenditures schedule shows the amount of consumption and planned gross investment spending $(C + I_g)$ forthcoming at each output-income level. Our initial focus is on *planned* or intended investment as shown in column 5 of Table 11-1. Later analysis will reveal that imbalances in aggregate expenditures and real domestic output will result in unplanned or unintended investment in the form of inventory changes (Column 7).

Equilibrium GDP Of the ten possible levels of GDP in Table 11-1, which one will be the equilibrium level? Which level of total output will the economy be capable of sustaining?

The equilibrium level of output is that output whose production will create total spending just sufficient to purchase that output. In other words, the equilibrium level of GDP is where the total quantity of goods produced (GDP) is equal to the total quantity of goods purchased $(C + I_g)$. Examination of the domestic output schedule of column 2 and the aggregate expenditures schedule of column 6 indicates that this equality exists only at

TABLE 11-1 Determination of the equilibrium levels of employment, output, and income: the closed private sector (*hypothetical data*)

(1) Possible levels of employment, millions	(2) Real domestic output (and income) (GDP = DI),* billions	(3) Consumption, C, billions	(4) Saving, S, billions	(5) Investment, I_g, billions	(6) Aggregate expenditures $(C + I_g)$, billions	(7) Unintended investment (+) or disinvestment (−) in inventories	(8) Tendency of employment, output, and incomes
(1) 40	$370	$375	$−5	$20	$395	$−25	Increase
(2) 45	390	390	0	20	410	−20	Increase
(3) 50	410	405	5	20	425	−15	Increase
(4) 55	430	420	10	20	440	−10	Increase
(5) 60	450	435	15	20	455	−5	Increase
(6) 65	470	450	20	20	470	0	Equilibrium
(7) 70	490	465	25	20	485	+5	Decrease
(8) 75	510	480	30	20	500	+10	Decrease
(9) 80	530	495	35	20	515	+15	Decrease
(10) 85	550	510	40	20	530	+20	Decrease

*If depreciation and net American income earned abroad are zero, government is ignored, and it is assumed that all saving occurs in the household sector of the economy, GDP as a measure of domestic output is equal to NI, PI, and DI. This means that households receive a DI equal to the value of total output.

the $470 billion level of GDP (row 6). This is the only level of output at which the economy is willing to spend precisely the amount necessary to take that output off the market. Here the annual rates of production and spending are in balance. There is no overproduction, which results in a piling up of unsold goods and therefore cutbacks in the production rate. Nor is there an excess of total spending, which draws down inventories and prompts increases in the rate of production. In short, there is no reason for businesses to alter this rate of production; $470 billion is therefore the **equilibrium GDP.**

Disequilibrium To enhance our understanding of the meaning of the equilibrium level of GDP, let's examine other possible levels of GDP to see why they cannot be sustained.

At the $410 billion level of GDP (row 3), businesses would find that if they produced this output, the income created would give rise to $405 billion in consumer spending. Supplemented by $20 billion of planned investment, total expenditures ($C + I_g$) would be $425 billion, as shown in column 6. The economy provides an annual rate of spending more than sufficient to purchase the current $410 billion rate of production. Because businesses are producing at a lower rate than buyers are taking goods off the shelves, an unintended decline in business inventories of $15 billion would occur (column 7) if this situation were sustained. But businesses will adjust to this imbalance between aggregate expenditures and domestic output by stepping up production. A higher rate of output will mean more jobs and a higher level of total income. In short, if aggregate expenditures exceed the domestic output, the latter will be pulled upward.

By making the same comparisons of GDP (column 2) and $C + I_g$ (column 6) at all other levels of GDP below the $470 billion equilibrium level, we find that the economy wants to spend in excess of the level at which businesses are willing to produce. The excess of total spending at all these levels of GDP will drive GDP upward to the $470 billion level.

The reverse is true at all levels of GDP above the $470 billion equilibrium level. Businesses will find that the production of these total outputs fails to generate the levels of spending needed to take them off the market. Being unable to recover their costs, businesses will cut back on production.

To illustrate: At the $510 billion level of output (row 8), business managers will find there is insufficient spending to permit the sale of that output. Of the $510 billion worth of income which this output creates, $480 billion is received back by businesses as consumption spending. Though supplemented by $20 billion worth of planned investment spending, total expenditures ($500 billion) fall $10 billion short of the $510 billion quantity produced. If this imbalance persisted, $10 billion of inventories would pile up (column 7). But businesses will react to this unintended accumulation of unsold goods by cutting back on the rate of production. This decline in GDP will mean fewer jobs and a decline in total income. You should verify that deficiencies of total spending exist at all other levels of GDP in excess of the $470 billion level.

The equilibrium level of GDP exists where the total output, measured by GDP, and aggregate expenditures, $C + I_g$, are equal. Any excess of total spending over total output will drive GDP upward. Any deficiency of total spending will pull GDP downward.

Graphical Analysis

The same analysis can be shown in a simple graph. In Figure 11-1 (Key Graph) the **45-degree line** (used in Chapter 10 to delineate graphically how disposable income is divided between consumption and saving) now takes on increased significance. Recall that the special property of the 45-degree line is that at any point on the line, the value of what is being measured on the horizontal axis (in this case GDP) is equal to the value of what is being measured on the vertical axis (here it is aggregate expenditures or $C + I_g$). Having discovered in our tabular analysis that the equilibrium level of domestic output is determined where $C + I_g$ equals GDP, we can say that the 45-degree line in Figure 11-1 is a graphical statement of this equilibrium condition.

Next, we must add the aggregate expenditures schedule to Figure 11-1. To do this we graph the consumption schedule of Figure 10-4a and add to it *vertically* the constant $20 billion amount from Figure 10-8, which, we assume, businesses plan to invest at each possible level of GDP. More directly, we can plot the $C + I_g$ data of column 6 in Table 11-1. Observe that the aggregate expenditures line shows total spending rising with domestic output and national income, but that expenditures do not rise as much as income. This is so because the marginal propensity to consume—the slope of line C—is less than 1. Because the aggregate expenditures line $C + I_g$ is parallel to the consumption line, the slope of the aggregate expenditures line equals the MPC and is also less than 1. A part of any

KEY GRAPH

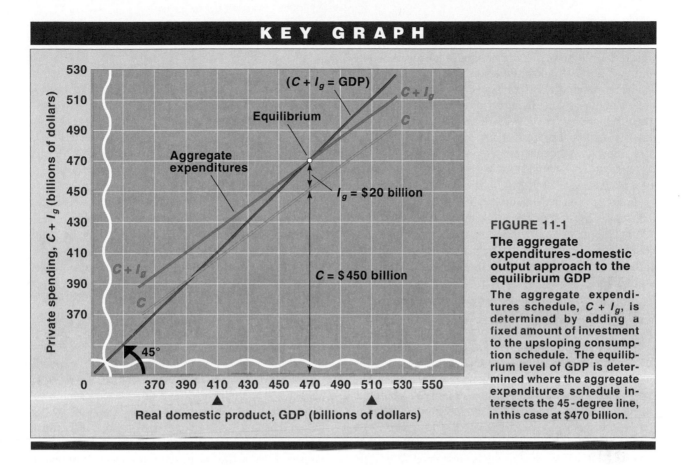

FIGURE 11-1

The aggregate expenditures-domestic output approach to the equilibrium GDP

The aggregate expenditures schedule, $C + I_g$, is determined by adding a fixed amount of investment to the upsloping consumption schedule. The equilibrium level of GDP is determined where the aggregate expenditures schedule intersects the 45-degree line, in this case at $470 billion.

increase in national income will *not* be spent; it will be saved. For our particular data, aggregate expenditures rise by $15 billion for every $20 billion increase in domestic output and national income because $5 billion of each $20 billion income increment is saved.

The equilibrium level of GDP is that GDP which corresponds to the intersection of the aggregate expenditures schedule and the 45-degree line. This intersection locates the only point at which aggregate expenditures (on the vertical axis) are equal to GDP (on the horizontal axis). Because our aggregate expenditures schedule is based on the data of Table 11-1, we once again find that equilibrium output is $470 billion. Observe that consumption at this output is $450 billion and investment is $20 billion.

It is evident from Figure 11-1 that no levels of GDP above the equilibrium level are sustainable, because $C + I_g$ falls short of GDP. Graphically, the aggregate expenditures schedule lies *below* the 45-degree line. For example, at the $510 billion GDP level, $C + I_g$ is only $500 billion. Inventories of unsold goods rise to undesired levels, prompting businesses to readjust

production sights downward in the direction of the $470 billion output level.

Conversely, at all possible levels of GDP less than $470 billion, the economy desires to spend in excess of what businesses are producing. $C + I_g$ exceeds the value of the corresponding output. Graphically, the aggregate expenditures schedule lies *above* the 45-degree line. At the $410 billion GDP, for example, $C + I_g$ totals $425 billion. Inventories decline as the rate of spending exceeds the rate of production, prompting businesses to raise their production sights toward the $470 billion GDP. Unless there is some change in the location of the aggregate expenditures line, the $470 billion level of GDP will be sustained indefinitely.

LEAKAGES-INJECTIONS APPROACH

The expenditures-output approach to determining GDP spotlights total spending as the immediate determinant of the levels of output, employment, and income. Though the leakages-injections approach is less direct, it does have the advantage of underscoring the reason $C + I_g$ and GDP are unequal at all levels of output except the equilibrium level.

The essence of the leakages-injections approach is this: Under our simplifying assumptions we know that the production of any level of domestic output will generate an identical amount of disposable income. But we also know a part of that income may be saved—that is, *not* consumed—by households. Saving therefore represents a *leakage,* withdrawal, or diversion of potential spending from the income-expenditures stream. The consequence of saving is that consumption falls short of total output or GDP; hence, by itself consumption is insufficient to take the domestic output off the market, and this fact would seem to set the stage for a decline in total output.

However, the business sector does not intend to sell its entire output to consumers; some domestic output will consist of capital or investment goods sold within the business sector. Investment can therefore be thought of as an *injection* of spending into the income-expenditures stream which supplements consumption; stated differently, investment is a potential offset to, or replacement for, the leakage of saving.

If the leakage of saving exceeds the injection of investment, then $C + I_g$ will fall short of GDP and this level of GDP will be too high to be sustained. Any GDP where saving exceeds investment will be an above-equilibrium GDP. Conversely, if the injection of investment exceeds the leakage of saving, then $C + I_g$ will be greater than GDP and GDP will be driven upward. Any GDP where investment exceeds saving will be a below-equilibrium GDP. Only where $S = I_g$—where the leakage of saving is exactly offset by the injection of investment—will aggregate expenditures equal the domestic output. And we know that this equality defines the equilibrium GDP.

In the closed private economy assumed here, there are only one leakage (saving) and one injection (investment). In general terms, a *leakage* is any use of income other than its expenditure on domestically produced output. In the more realistic models which follow (the section on international trade in this chapter and Chapter 12), we will need to incorporate the additional leakages of imports and taxes into our analysis.

Similarly, an *injection* is any supplement to consumer spending on domestic production. Again, in later models we must add injections of exports and government purchases to our discussion. But for now we need only compare the single leakage of saving with the sole injection of investment to assess the impact on GDP.

Tabular Analysis

The saving schedule (columns 2 and 4) and the investment schedule (columns 2 and 5) of Table 11-1 are pertinent. Our $C + I_g = $ GDP approach has led us to conclude that all levels of GDP less than $470 billion are unstable because the corresponding $C + I_g$ exceeds these GDPs, driving GDP upward. A comparison of the amounts households and businesses want to save and invest at each of the below-equilibrium GDP levels explains the excesses of total spending. In particular, at each of these relatively low GDP levels, businesses plan to invest more than households want to save.

For example, at the $410 billion level of GDP (row 3), households will save only $5 billion, thereby spending $405 of their $410 billion incomes. Supplemented by $20 billion of business investment, aggregate expenditures $(C + I_g)$ are $425 billion. Aggregate expenditures exceed GDP by $15 billion (=$425 − $410) *because* the amount businesses plan to invest at this level of GDP exceeds the amounts households save by $15 billion. The fact is that a very small leakage of saving at this relatively low income level will be more than compensated for by the relatively large injection of investment spending which causes $C + I_g$ to exceed GDP and induce GDP upward.

Similarly, all levels of GDP above the $470 billion level are also unstable, because here GDP exceeds $C + I_g$. The reason for this insufficiency of aggregate expenditures lies in the fact that at all GDP levels above $470 billion, households will want to save in excess of the amount businesses plan to invest. The saving leakage is not replaced or compensated for by the injection of investment.

For example, households will choose to save at the high rate of $30 billion at the $510 billion GDP (row 8). Businesses, however, will plan to invest only $20 billion at this GDP. This $10 billion excess of saving over planned investment will cause total spending to fall $10 billion short of the value of total output. Specifically, aggregate expenditures are $500 billion and real GDP is $510 billion. This deficiency will reduce GDP.

Again we verify that the equilibrium GDP is $470 billion. Only at this level are the saving desires of households and the investment plans of businesses equal. Only when businesses and households attempt to invest and save at equal rates—where the leakages and injections are equal—will $C + I_g$ = GDP. Only here will the annual rates of production and spending be in balance; only here will unplanned changes in inventories be absent. One can think of it in this way: If saving were zero, consumer spending would always be sufficient to clear the market of any given GDP; consumption would equal GDP. But saving can and does occur, causing consumption to fall short of GDP. Only when businesses are willing to invest at the same rate at which households save will the amount by which consumption falls short of GDP be precisely counterbalanced.

Graphical Analysis

The leakages-injections approach to determining the equilibrium GDP can be demonstrated graphically, as in Figure 11-2. Here we have combined the saving schedule of Figure 10-4b and the investment schedule of Figure 10-8. The numerical data for these schedules are repeated in columns 2, 4, and 5 of Table 11-1. We see the equilibrium level of GDP is at $470 billion, where the saving and investment schedules intersect. Only here do businesses and households invest and save at the same rates; therefore, only here will GDP and $C + I_g$ be equal.

At all higher levels of GDP, households will save at a higher rate than businesses plan to invest. The fact that the saving leakage exceeds the investment injection causes $C + I_g$ to fall short of GDP, driving GDP downward. At the $510 billion GDP, for example, saving of $30 billion will exceed investment of $20 billion by $10 billion, with the result that $C + I_g$ is $500 billion, $10 billion short of GDP.

At all levels of GDP below the $470 billion equilibrium level, businesses will plan to invest more than households save. Here the injection of investment exceeds the leakage of saving so that $C + I_g$ exceeds GDP, driving the latter upward. To illustrate: At the $410 billion level of GDP the $5 billion leakage of saving is more than compensated for by the $20 billion that businesses plan to invest. The result is that $C + I_g$ exceeds GDP by $15 billion, inducing businesses to produce a larger GDP.

PLANNED VERSUS ACTUAL INVESTMENT

We have emphasized that discrepancies in saving and investment can occur and bring about changes in the equilibrium GDP. Now we must recognize that, in another sense, saving and investment must always be equal! This apparent contradiction concerning the equality of saving and investment is resolved when we distinguish between **planned investment** and saving (which need not be equal) and **actual investment** and saving (which by definition must be equal). The catch is that *actual investment consists of both planned and unplanned investment (unplanned changes in inventory*

FIGURE 11-2 The leakages-injections approach to the equilibrium GDP

A second approach is to view the equilibrium GDP as determined by the intersection of the saving (S) and the planned investment (I_g) schedules. Only at the point of equilibrium will households plan to save the amount businesses want to invest. It is the consistency of these plans which equates GDP and $C + I_g$.

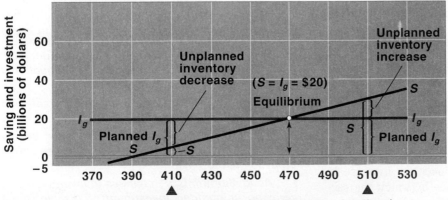

investment), and unplanned investment acts as a balancing item which always equates the actual amounts saved and invested in any period of time.

Disequilibrium and Inventories

Consider, for example, the $490 billion above-equilibrium GDP (row 7 of Table 11-1). What would happen if businesses produced this output, thinking they could sell it? At this level, households save $25 billion of their $490 billion DI, so consumption is only $465 billion. *Planned* investment (column 5) is $20 billion; businesses plan or desire to buy $20 billion worth of capital goods. This means aggregate expenditures $(C + I_g)$ are $485 billion, and sales therefore fall short of production by $5 billion. This extra $5 billion of goods is retained by businesses as an *unintended* or *unplanned* increase in inventories (column 7). It is unintended because it results from the failure of total spending to take total output off the market. Remembering that, by definition, changes in inventories are a part of investment, we note the *actual* investment of $25 billion ($20 planned *plus* $5 unintended or unplanned) equals saving of $25 billion, even though saving exceeds *planned* investment by $5 billion. Businesses, being unwilling to accumulate unwanted inventories at this annual rate, will cut back production.

Now look at the below-equilibrium $450 billion output (row 5 of Table 11-1). Because households save only $15 billion of their $450 billion DI, consumption is $435 billion. Planned investment by businesses is $20 billion, so aggregate expenditures are $455 billion. Sales exceed production by $5 billion. This is so because an unplanned decline in business inventories has occurred. Businesses have unintentionally *dis*invested $5 billion in inventories (column 7). Note once again that *actual* investment is $15 billion ($20 planned *minus* $5 unintended or unplanned) and equal to saving of $15 billion, even though *planned* investment exceeds saving by $5 billion. This unplanned decline in investment in inventories due to the excess of sales over production will induce businesses to increase the GDP by expanding production.

To summarize: At all *above-equilibrium* levels of GDP (where saving exceeds planned investment), actual investment and saving are equal because of unintended increases in inventories which, by definition, are included as a part of actual investment. Graphically (Figure 11-2), the unintended inventory increase is measured by the vertical distance by which the saving schedule lies above the (planned) investment schedule.

At all *below-equilibrium* levels of GDP (where planned investment exceeds saving), actual investment will be equal to saving because of unintended decreases in inventories which must be subtracted from planned investment to determine actual investment. These unintended inventory declines are shown graphically as the vertical distance by which the (planned) investment schedule lies above the saving schedule.

Achieving Equilibrium

These distinctions are important because they correctly suggest that *it is the equality of planned investment and saving which determines the equilibrium level of GDP.* We can think of the process by which equilibrium is achieved as follows:

1 A difference between saving and planned investment causes a difference between the production and spending plans of the economy as a whole.

2 This difference between aggregate production and spending plans results in unintended investment or disinvestment in inventories.

3 As long as unintended investment in inventories persists, businesses will revise their production plans downward and thereby reduce the GDP. Conversely, as long as unintended disinvestment in inventories exists, firms will revise their production plans upward and increase the GDP. Both types of movements in GDP are toward equilibrium because they bring about the equality of planned investment and saving.

4 Only where planned investment and saving are equal will the level of GDP be in equilibrium; that is, only where planned investment equals saving will there be no unintended investment or disinvestment in inventories to drive the GDP downward or upward. Note in column 7 of Table 11-1 that only at the $470 billion equilibrium GDP is there no unintended investment or disinvestment in inventories.

QUICK REVIEW 11-1

♦ *In a closed private economy, equilibrium GDP occurs where aggregate expenditures equal real domestic output (C + I_g = GDP).*

♦ *Alternatively, equilibrium GDP is established where planned investment equals saving (I_g = S).*

♦ *Actual investment consists of planned investment plus unplanned changes in inventories and is always equal to saving.*

♦ *At equilibrium GDP, changes in inventories are zero; no unintended investment or disinvestment occurs.*

CHANGES IN EQUILIBRIUM GDP AND THE MULTIPLIER

Thus far, we have been concerned with explaining the equilibrium levels of total output and income. But we saw in Chapter 8 that the GDP of American capitalism is seldom stable; rather, it is characterized by long-run growth and punctuated by cyclical fluctuations. Let's turn to the questions of *why* and *how* the equilibrium level of real GDP fluctuates.

The equilibrium level of GDP will change in response to changes in the investment schedule or the saving-consumption schedules. Because investment spending generally is less stable than the consumption-saving schedules, we will assume that changes in the investment schedule occur.

The impact of changes in investment can be seen through Figure 11-3a and b. Suppose the expected rate of net profit on investment rises (shifting the investment-demand curve of Figure 10-7 to the right) *or* the

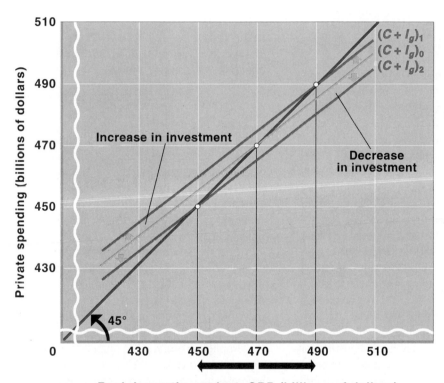

(a) Change in aggregate expenditures schedule

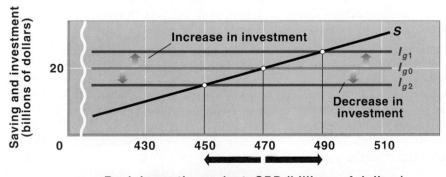

(b) Change in investment schedule

FIGURE 11-3   Changes in the equilibrium GDP caused by shifts in (a) the aggregate expenditures schedule and (b) the investment schedule

An upshift in the aggregate expenditures schedule from, say, $(C + I_g)_0$ to $(C + I_g)_1$ will increase the equilibrium GDP. Conversely, a downshift in the aggregate expenditures schedule from, say, $(C + I_g)_0$ to $(C + I_g)_2$ will lower the equilibrium GDP. In the saving-investment figure an upshift in the investment schedule (I_{g0} to I_{g1}) will raise, and a downshift (I_{g0} to I_{g2}) will lower, the equilibrium GDP.

interest rate falls (moving down the stable curve). As a result, investment spending increases by, say, $5 billion. This is indicated in Figure 11-3a by an upward shift in the aggregate expenditures schedule from $(C + I_g)_0$ to $(C + I_g)_1$, and in Figure 11-3b by an upward shift in the investment schedule from I_{g0} to I_{g1}. In each of these portrayals the consequence is a rise in the equilibrium GDP from $470 to $490 billion.

Conversely, if the expected rate of net profit from investment decreases *or* the interest rate rises, a decline in investment spending of, say, $5 billion will occur. This is shown by the downward shift of the investment schedule from I_{g0} to I_{g2} in Figure 11-3b and the aggregate expenditures schedule from $(C + I_g)_0$ to $(C + I_g)_2$ in Figure 11-3a. In each case, these shifts cause the equilibrium GDP to fall from the original $470 billion level to $450 billion. You should verify these conclusions in terms of Table 11-1 by substituting $25 billion and then $15 billion for the $20 billion planned investment figure in column 5 of the table.

Incidentally—and at the risk of getting ahead of ourselves—the indicated $5 billion changes in investment may be the direct result of economic policy. Looking back at Table 10-2, we find that the initial $20 billion level of investment is associated with an 8 percent interest rate. *If* the economy is in a recession, the monetary authorities may purposely negotiate a reduction in the interest rate to 6 percent (by increasing the money supply), causing a $5 billion increase in investment and thereby in aggregate expenditures to stimulate the economy.

Conversely, *if,* with the initial $20 billion of investment, the economy faces a demand-pull inflation problem, the monetary authorities may increase the interest rate to 10 percent (by reducing the money supply), thereby reducing investment and aggregate expenditures to constrain the inflation. Monetary policy—changing the money supply to alter interest rates and aggregate expenditures—is the subject of Chapter 15.

Changes in the consumption-saving schedules will have similar effects. If households want to consume more (save less) at each level of GDP, the aggregate expenditures schedule will shift upward and the saving schedule downward in Figure 11-3a and b, respectively. In either portrayal these shifts will mean an increase in the equilibrium GDP. If households want to consume less (save more) at each possible GDP, the resulting drop in the consumption schedule and the increase in the saving schedule will reduce the equilibrium GDP.

The Multiplier Effect

You may have noticed a curious feature of these examples: A $5 billion change in investment spending led to a $20 billion change in the output-income level. This surprising result is called the **multiplier effect** or, more simply, the *multiplier.* Specifically, the multiplier is the ratio of a change in equilibrium GDP to the initial change in (investment) spending which caused that change in real GDP. That is:

$$\text{Multiplier} = \frac{\text{change in real GDP}}{\text{initial change in spending}}$$

In this case the multiplier is 4 (change of GDP of 20 ÷ change in investment of 5). Or, by rearranging our equation, we can say that:

$$\text{Change in GDP} = \text{multiplier} \times \frac{\text{initial change in}}{\text{spending}}$$

Three points about the multiplier must be made here.
1 The "initial change in spending" is usually associated with investment spending because investment is the most volatile component of aggregate expenditures (Figure 10-9). But changes in consumption, government purchases, or exports also are subject to the multiplier effect.
2 The "initial change in spending" refers to an upshift or downshift in the aggregate expenditures schedule due to an upshift or downshift in one of its components. In Figure 11-3b we find that real GDP has increased by $20 billion because the investment schedule has shifted upward by $5 billion from I_{g0} to I_{g1}.
3 Implicit in our second point is that the multiplier is a two-edged sword working in both directions. A small increase in spending can give rise to a multiple increase in GDP, or a small decrease in spending can be magnified into a much larger decrease in GDP by the multiplier. Note carefully the effects of the shift in $(C + I_g)_0$ to $(C + I_g)_1$ or to $(C + I_g)_2$ and I_{g0} to I_{g1} or to I_{g2} in Figure 11-3a and b.

Rationale The multiplier is based on two facts.
1 The economy is characterized by repetitive, continuous flows of expenditures and income through which dollars spent by Smith are received as income by Jones.

Any change in income will cause both consumption and saving to vary in the same direction as, and by a fraction of, the change in income.

It follows that an initial change in the rate of spending will cause a spending chain reaction which, although of diminishing importance at each successive step, will cumulate to a multiple change in GDP.

The rationale underlying the multiplier effect is illustrated numerically in Table 11-2. Suppose a $5 billion increase in investment spending occurs. Graphically, this is the upshift of the aggregate expenditures schedule by $5 billion in Figure 11-3a and the upshift of the investment schedule from $20 to $25 billion in Figure 11-3b. We continue to assume that the MPC is .75 and the MPS is .25. Also, we suppose that the economy is initially in equilibrium at $470 billion.

The initial increase in investment generates an equal amount of wage, rent, interest, and profit income because spending and receiving of income are two sides of the same transaction. How much consumption will be induced by this $5 billion increase in the incomes of households? We find the answer by applying the marginal propensity to consume of .75 to this change in income. Thus, the $5 billion increase in income raises consumption by $3.75 (=.75 × $5) billion and saving by $1.25 (=.25 × $5) billion, as shown in columns (2) and (3) of Table 11-2. The $3.75 billion spent is received by other households as income (second round). These households consume .75 of this $3.75 billion or $2.81 billion, and save .25 of it, or $0.94 billion. The $2.81 billion consumed flows to still other households as income (third round). This process continues.

Figure 11-4, which is derived from Table 11-2, shows the cumulative effects of the various rounds of the multiplier process. Observe that each round *adds* the [orange] blocks to national income and GDP. The cumulation of the additional income in each round— the sum of the [orange] blocks—constitutes the total change in income or GDP. Though the spending and respending effects of the initial increase in investment diminish with each successive round of spending, the cumulative increase in the output-income level will be $20 billion if the process is carried through to the last dollar. The $5 billion increase in investment will therefore increase the equilibrium GDP by $20 billion, from $470 to $490 billion. Hence, the multiplier is 4 (=$20 billion ÷ $5 billion).

It is no coincidence that the multiplier effect ends at the point where exactly enough saving has been generated to offset the initial $5 billion increase in investment spending. Only then will the disequilibrium created by the investment increase be corrected. In this case, GDP and total incomes must rise by $20 billion to create $5 billion in additional saving to match the $5 billion increase in investment spending. Income must increase by four times the initial excess of investment over saving, because households save one-fourth of any increase in their incomes (that is, the MPS is .25). As noted, in this example the multiplier—the number of times the ultimate increase in income exceeds the initial increase in investment spending—is 4.

The Multiplier and the Marginal Propensities You may have sensed from Table 11-2 some relationship between the MPS and the size of the multiplier. The fraction of an increase in income saved—that is, the MPS—determines the cumulative respending effects of any initial change in I_g, G, X_n or C, and therefore the multiplier. Specifically, *the size of the MPS and the size of the multiplier are inversely related.* The smaller the fraction of any change in income saved, the greater the respending at each round and, therefore, the greater the multiplier. If the MPS is .25, as in our example, the multiplier is 4. If the MPS were .33, the multiplier

TABLE 11-2 **The multiplier: a tabular illustration** *(hypothetical data; in billions)*

	(1) Change in income	(2) Change in consumption (MPC = .75)	(3) Change in saving (MPS = .25)
Assumed increase in investment	$ 5.00	$ 3.75	$1.25
Second round	3.75	2.81	0.94
Third round	2.81	2.11	0.70
Fourth round	2.11	1.58	0.53
Fifth round	1.58	1.19	0.39
All other rounds	4.75	3.56	1.19
Totals	$20.00	$15.00	$5.00

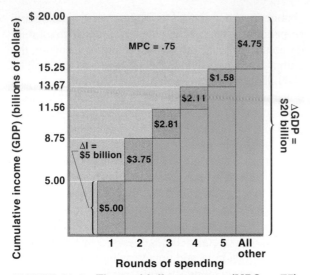

FIGURE 11-4 The multiplier process (MPC = .75)

An initial change in investment spending of $5 billion creates an equal $5 billion of new income in round 1. Households spend $3.75 (=.75 × $5) billion of this new income, creating $3.75 of added income in round 2. Of this $3.75 of new income, households spend $2.81 (=.75 × $3.75) billion and income rises by that amount in round 3. The cumulation of such income increments over the entire process eventually results in a total change of income and GDP of $20 billion. The multiplier therefore is 4 (=$20 billion ÷ $5 billion).

would be 3. If the MPS were .2, the multiplier would be 5.

Look again at Table 11-1 and Figure 11-3b. Initially the economy is in equilibrium at the $470 billion level of GDP. Now businesses increase investment by $5 billion so that planned investment of $25 billion exceeds saving of $20 billion at the $470 billion level. This means $470 billion is no longer the equilibrium GDP. By how much must gross domestic product or national income rise to restore equilibrium? By enough to generate $5 billion of additional saving to offset the $5 billion increase in investment. Because households save $1 out of every $4 of additional income they receive (MPS = .25), GDP must rise by $20 billion—four times the assumed increase in investment—to create the $5 billion of extra saving necessary to restore equilibrium. Hence, the multiplier is 4. If the MPS were .33, GDP would only have to rise by $15 billion (three times the increase in investment) to generate $5 billion of additional saving and restore equilibrium, and the multiplier therefore would be 3. But if the MPS were .20, GDP would have to rise by $25 billion for an extra $5 billion of saving to be forthcoming and equilibrium to be restored, yielding a multiplier of 5.

Furthermore, recall that the MPS measures the slope of the saving schedule. In terms of the leakages-injections $(S = I_g)$ approach, this means that if the MPS is relatively large (say, .5) and the slope of the saving schedule is therefore relatively steep (.5), any given upward shift in investment spending will be subject to a relatively small multiplier. For example, a $5 billion increase in investment will entail a new point of intersection of the S and I_g schedules only $10 billion to the right of the original equilibrium GDP. The multiplier is only 2. But if the MPS is relatively small (say, .10), the slope of the saving schedule will be relatively gentle. Therefore, a $5 billion upward shift in the investment schedule will provide a new intersection point some $50 billion to the right of the original equilibrium GDP. The multiplier is 10 in this case. You should verify these two examples by drawing appropriate saving and investment diagrams.

We can summarize these and all other possibilities by merely saying that *the multiplier is equal to the reciprocal of the MPS*. The reciprocal of any number is the quotient you obtain by dividing 1 by that number. We can say:

$$\text{The multiplier} = \frac{1}{\text{MPS}}$$

This formula provides a shorthand method of determining the multiplier. All you need to know is the MPS to calculate the size of the multiplier. Recall, too, from Chapter 10 that since MPC + MPS = 1, it follows that MPS = 1 − MPC. Therefore, we can also write our multiplier formula as

$$\text{The multiplier} = \frac{1}{1 - \text{MPC}}$$

Significance of the Multiplier The significance of the multiplier is that a relatively small change in the investment plans of businesses or the consumption-saving plans of households can trigger a much larger change in the equilibrium level of GDP. The multiplier magnifies the fluctuations in business activity initiated by changes in spending.

As illustrated in Figure 11-5, the larger the MPC (the smaller the MPS), the greater will be the multiplier. For example, if the MPC is .75 and the multiplier is therefore 4, a $10 billion decline in planned investment will reduce the equilibrium GDP by $40 billion. But if the MPC is only .67 and the multiplier is 3, the same $10 billion drop in investment will cause the equilibrium GDP to fall by only $30 billion. This makes

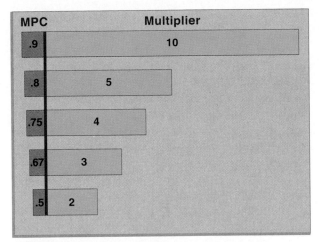

FIGURE 11-5   The MPC and the multiplier

The larger the MPC (the smaller the MPS), the greater is the size of the multiplier.

sense intuitively: A large MPC means the chain of induced consumption shown in Figure 11-4 dampens down slowly and thereby cumulates to a large change in income. Conversely, a small MPC (a large MPS) causes induced consumption to decline quickly so the cumulative change in income is small.

Generalizing the Multiplier   The multiplier concept as presented here is sometimes called the *simple multiplier* because it is based on a simple model of the economy. In terms of the $\frac{1}{\text{MPS}}$ formulation, the simple multiplier reflects only the leakage of saving. But, as noted earlier, in the real world successive rounds of income and spending can also be dampened down by other leakages in the form of imports and taxes. In addition to the leakage into saving, some portion of income at each round would be siphoned off as additional taxes, and

another part would be used to purchase additional goods from abroad. The result of these additional leakages is that the $\frac{1}{\text{MPS}}$ statement of the multiplier can be generalized by changing the denominator to read "fraction of the change in income which is not spent on domestic output" or "fraction of the change in income which leaks, or is diverted, from the income-expenditure stream." The more realistic multiplier which results when all these leakages—saving, taxes, and imports—are taken into account is called the *complex multiplier*. The Council of Economic Advisers, which advises the President on economic matters, has estimated the complex multiplier for the United States to be about 2.

Paradox of Thrift

A curious irony—dubbed the **paradox of thrift**—is suggested by the leakages-injections approach to GDP determination and by our analysis of the multiplier. The paradox is that if society attempts to save more, it may end up actually saving the same amount.

Suppose I_g and S_1 in Figure 11-6 are the current investment and saving schedules which determine a $470 billion equilibrium GDP. Now assume that households, perhaps anticipating a recession, attempt to save $5 billion more at each income level to provide a nest egg against the expected bad times. This attempt to save more is reflected in an upward shift of the saving schedule from S_1 to S_2. But this very upshift creates an excess of saving over planned investment at the current $470 billion equilibrium output. And we know that the multiplier effect will cause this small increase in saving (decline in consumption) to be reflected in a much larger—$20 billion (=$5 × 4) in this case—*decline* in equilibrium GDP.

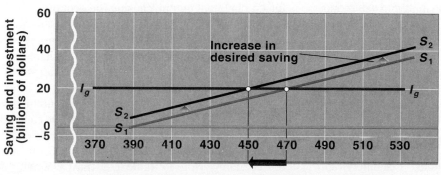

Real domestic product, GDP (billions of dollars)

FIGURE 11-6   The paradox of thrift

Unless offset by an upshift in the planned investment schedule, any attempt by households to save more (S_1 to S_2) will be frustrated by a multiple decline in the equilibrium GDP.

There is a paradox here in several different senses.

1 At the new $450 billion equilibrium GDP, households are saving the same amount they did at the original $470 billion GDP. Society's attempt to save more has been frustrated by the multiple decline in the equilibrium GDP which that attempt itself caused.

2 This analysis suggests that thrift, which has always been held in high esteem in our economy, can be a social vice. From the individual point of view, a penny saved may be a penny earned. But from the social point of view, a penny saved is a penny not spent and therefore causes a decline in someone's income. The act of thrift may be virtuous from the individual's viewpoint but disastrous from the social standpoint because of its potential undesirable effects on total output and employment.

3 It is ironic, if not paradoxical, that households may be most strongly induced to save more (consume less) at the very time when increased saving is most inappropriate and economically undesirable, that is, when the economy seems to be backsliding into recession. Someone fearing the loss of his or her job will hardly be inclined to go on a spending spree. In our scenario more saving has made an anticipated recession a reality.

But the paradox of thrift and its implication that saving is socially undesirable must be altered in two important respects.

1 Assume the economy is initially experiencing rather pronounced demand-pull inflation. That is, the economy is operating, not in the horizontal Keynesian range, but in the vertical classical range of the aggregate supply curve. Here the economy is producing at full employment and an excess of aggregate demand is pulling up the price level. If households saved more (consumed less) in this situation, aggregate demand would shift leftward and the rate of inflation would be reduced. Look back at Figure 9-6b once again. Assume that the aggregate demand curve is initially at AD_6 with the price level at P_6. An increase in saving will reduce aggregate demand to, say, AD_5 and the price level would decline toward P_5. In this case more saving is socially desirable because it restrains inflation.

2 Recall from our discussion of Figure 2-4 that, other things being equal, an economy which saves *and invests* a larger proportion of its domestic output will achieve a higher rate of economic growth. A higher rate of saving frees resources from consumption uses so that they *may* be allocated to the production of more investment goods. This additional machinery and equipment enhances the nation's future productive

capacity. Thus, if we make the classical assumption that the money market effectively links saving and investment decisions (recall Figure 10-1), then the upshift in the saving schedule from S_1 to S_2 in Figure 11-6 would be matched by an equal upshift in the investment schedule so that the equilibrium level of GDP would remain at $470 billion. In this case real output and employment would be unchanged but the composition of output would include more investment goods and fewer consumer goods. The result would be a more rapid rate of future economic growth. If rapid growth is a desired social goal, additional saving in this scenario would clearly be virtuous when matched by an equal increase in investment.

EQUILIBRIUM VERSUS FULL-EMPLOYMENT GDP

We now turn from the task of explaining to that of evaluating the equilibrium GDP.

The $470 billion equilibrium GDP embodied in our analysis (Table 11-1 and Figures 11-1 and 11-2) may or may not entail full employment. The aggregate expenditures schedule might well lie above or below that which would intersect the 45-degree line at the full-employment noninflationary level of output. Indeed, we have assumed thus far that production occurs in the less-than-full-employment Keynesian range of the aggregate supply curve.

Recessionary Gap

Assume in Figure 11-7a that the full-employment noninflationary level of domestic output is $490 billion. Suppose, too, that the aggregate expenditures schedule is at $(C + I_g)_1$, which is the aggregate expenditures schedule developed and employed in this chapter. This schedule intersects the 45-degree line to the left of the full-employment output, causing the economy's aggregate production to fall $20 billion short of its capacity production. In terms of Table 11-1, the economy is failing to employ 5 million of its 70 million available workers and, as a result, is sacrificing $20 billion worth of output.

The amount by which aggregate expenditures fall short of the full-employment level of GDP is called the **recessionary gap** simply because this deficiency of spending has a contractionary or depressing impact on the economy. Note in Table 11-1 that, assuming the full-employment GDP is $490 billion, the correspond-

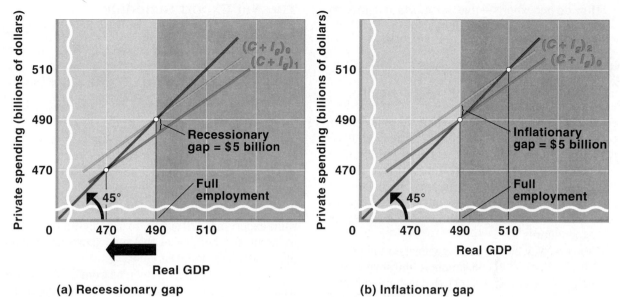

FIGURE 11-7   Recessionary and inflationary gaps

The equilibrium and full-employment GDPs may not coincide. A recessionary gap, shown in (a), is the amount by which aggregate expenditures fall short of the noninflationary full-employment GDP. It will cause a multiple decline in real GDP. The inflationary gap in (b) is the amount by which aggregate expenditures exceed the noninflationary full-employment level of GDP. This gap will cause demand-pull inflation.

ing level of total expenditures is only $485 billion. The recessionary gap is $5 billion, the amount by which the aggregate expenditures schedule would have to shift upward to realize the full-employment noninflationary GDP. Graphically, the recessionary gap is the *vertical* distance by which the aggregate expenditures schedule $(C + I_g)_1$ lies below the full-employment point on the 45-degree line. Because the relevant multiplier is 4, we observe a $20 billion differential (equal to the recessionary gap of $5 billion *times* the multiplier of 4) between the equilibrium GDP and the full-employment GDP. This $20 billion gap is the GDP gap which we encountered in Figure 8-5.

Inflationary Gap

If aggregate expenditures are at $(C + I_g)_2$ in Figure 11-7b, a demand-pull inflationary gap will exist. Specifically, the amount by which aggregate spending exceeds the full-employment level of GDP is called an **inflationary gap.** In this case, a $5 billion inflationary gap exists, as shown by the *vertical* distance between $(C + I_g)_2$ and the full-employment point on the 45-degree line. The inflationary gap is the amount by which the aggregate expenditures schedule would

have to shift downward to realize the full-employment noninflationary GDP.

The effect of this inflationary gap—this excess demand—will be to pull up the prices of the economy's fixed physical volume of production. Businesses as a whole cannot respond to the $5 billion in excess demand by expanding their real outputs, so *demand-pull inflation* will occur; nominal GDP will rise, but real GDP will not.

INTERNATIONAL TRADE AND EQUILIBRIUM OUTPUT

Thus far our aggregate expenditures model has ignored international trade by assuming a closed economy. We now acknowledge the existence of exports and imports and the fact that **net exports** (exports minus imports) may be either positive or negative in a particular period. A glance at line 4 on the inside covers of this book will reveal that net exports in some years have been positive (exports > imports) and in other years negative (imports > exports). Observe that net exports in 1975 were a *positive* $14 billion, for example, while in 1987 they were a *negative* $143 billion.

How do net exports—that is, exports and imports—relate to aggregate expenditures?

Net Exports and Aggregate Expenditures

Recall from Chapters 7 and 9 that—like consumption, investment, and government purchases—exports (X) give rise to domestic production, income, and employment. Even though goods and services produced in response to such spending are sent abroad, foreign spending on American goods increases production and creates jobs and incomes in the United States. Exports must therefore be added as a new component of aggregate expenditures.

Conversely, when an economy is open to international trade, part of its consumption and investment spending will be for imports (M), that is, for goods and services produced abroad rather than in the United States. In order not to overstate the value of domestic production, we must reduce the sum of consumption and investment expenditures for the portions expended on imported goods. Thus, in measuring aggregate expenditures for domestic goods and services, we must subtract expenditures on imports.

In short, for a private nontrading or closed economy, aggregate expenditures are $C + I_g$. But for a trading or open economy, aggregate spending is $C + I_g + (X - M)$. Or, recalling that net exports (X_n) equals $(X - M)$, we can say that aggregate expenditures for a private, open economy are $C + I_g + X_n$.

TABLE 11-3 **Two net export schedules** *(hypothetical data; in billions)*

(1) Level of GDP	(2) Net exports X_{n1} (X > M)	(3) Net exports X_{n2} (X < M)
$370	$+5	$−5
390	+5	−5
410	+5	−5
430	+5	−5
450	+5	−5
470	+5	−5
490	+5	−5
510	+5	−5
530	+5	−5
550	+5	−5

The Net Export Schedule

Table 11-3 shows two potential net export schedules for the hypothetical economy characterized by the data presented in Table 11-1. Similar to consumption and investment schedules, a net export schedule lists the amount of a particular expenditure—in this case net exports—which will occur at each level of GDP. The net export schedule X_{n1} (columns 1 and 2) tells us that exports exceed imports by $5 billion at each level of GDP. Perhaps exports are $15 billion, for example, while imports are $10 billion. The schedule X_{n2} (columns 1 and 3) reveals that imports are $5 billion higher than exports. That is, perhaps imports are $15 billion while exports are $10 billion. To simplify our discussion we assume in both cases that net exports are autonomous or independent of GDP.[1]

The two net export schedules from Table 11-3 are plotted in Figure 11-8b. Schedule X_{n1} reveals that a *positive* $5 billion of net exports are associated with each level of GDP. Conversely, X_{n2} is below the horizontal axis and shows that net exports are a *negative* $5 billion.

Net Exports and Equilibrium GDP

The aggregate expenditures schedule labeled $C + I_g$ in Figure 11-8a is identical to the one found in Table 11-1 and Figure 11-1. That is, $C + I_g$ reflects the combined consumption and gross investment expenditures which will occur at each level of GDP. The equilibrium level of GDP will be $470 billion when there is no foreign sector. Recall that this equilibrium level of output is determined at the intersection of the $C + I_g$ schedule and the 45-degree reference line; only there will aggregate expenditures equal GDP.

But net exports can be either positive or negative. Hence, exports and imports need not be neutral in their effect on the equilibrium level of GDP. How will each of the net export schedules presented in Figure 11-8b affect equilibrium GDP?

---

[1]Although our *exports* depend on *foreign* incomes and are thus independent of American GDP, our *imports* do vary directly with our own *domestic* national income. Just as our domestic consumption varies directly with our GDP, so do our purchases of foreign goods. As our GDP rises, American households buy not only more Pontiacs and more Pepsi but also Porsches and Perrier. However, for now we will ignore the resulting complications of the positive relationship between imports and American GDP.

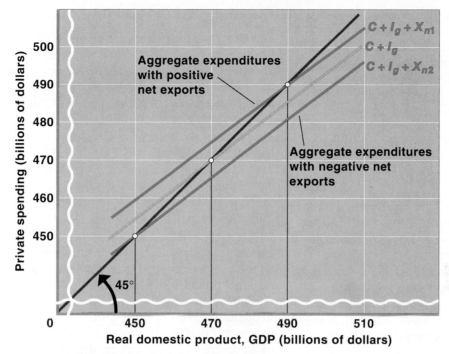

(a) Aggregate expenditures schedule

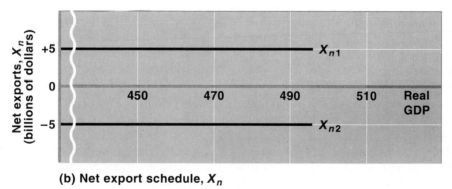

(b) Net export schedule, X_n

FIGURE 11-8 Net exports and the equilibrium GDP

Positive net exports such as shown by the net export schedule X_{n1} in (b) elevate the aggregate expenditures schedule in (a) from the closed-economy level of $C + I_g$ to the open-economy level of $C + I_g + X_{n1}$. Negative net exports such as depicted by the net export schedule X_{n2} in (b) lower the aggregate expenditures schedule in (a) from the closed-economy level of $C + I_g$ to the open-economy level of $C + I_g + X_{n2}$.

Positive Net Exports First, suppose the net export schedule for our hypothetical economy is X_{n1}. The $5 billion of additional net export expenditures by foreigners are accounted for by adding $5 billion to the $C + I_g$ schedule in Figure 11-8a. Restated, aggregate expenditures at each level of GDP are $5 billion higher than indicated by the $C + I_g$ schedule alone. The aggregate expenditures schedule for the open economy thus becomes $C + I_g + X_{n1}$. The presence of international trade has increased equilibrium GDP from $470 billion in the simplified closed economy to $490 billion in the more realistic open economy. You should verify that the new equilibrium GDP is $490 billion by adding $5

billion to each level of aggregate expenditures in Table 11-1 and then determining where $C + I_g + X_n$ equals GDP.

Generalization: *Positive net exports increase aggregate expenditures beyond what they would be in a closed economy and thus have an expansionary effect on domestic GDP.* In this case, adding net exports of $5 billion has increased GDP by $20 billion, implying a multiplier of 4.

Negative Net Exports An extension of our line of reasoning enables us to determine the impact of negative net exports on equilibrium GDP. If net exports are

X_{n2} as shown in Figure 11-8b, rather than X_{n1}, $5 billion of net export spending by foreigners must be subtracted from the aggregate expenditure schedule $C + I_g$ to establish aggregate expenditures for the open economy. The $5 billion of negative net exports mean that our hypothetical economy is importing $5 billion more of goods than it is selling abroad. The aggregate expenditures schedule shown as $C + I_g$ in Figure 11-8a therefore has overstated the expenditures on *domestic* output at each level of GDP. We must reduce the sum of consumption and investment expenditures by the $5 billion net amount expended on imported goods. For example, if imports are $15 billion and exports are $10 billion, we must subtract the $5 billion of *net* imports (= −$5 billion of net exports) from the combined domestic consumption and investment expenditures.

After we subtract $5 billion from the $C + I_g$ schedule in Figure 11-8a, the relevant aggregate expenditures schedule becomes $C + I_g + X_{n2}$ and equilibrium GDP falls from $470 to $450. Again, a change in net exports of $5 billion has resulted in a fourfold change in GDP, telling us that the multiplier is 4. Confirmation of the new equilibrium GDP can be obtained by subtracting $5 billion from aggregate expenditures at each level of GDP in Table 11-1 and ascertaining the new equilibrium GDP.

A corollary to our first generalization emerges: *Negative net exports reduce aggregate expenditures relative to what they would be in the closed economy and hence have a contractionary effect on domestic GDP.* Imports add to the stock of goods available in the economy, but they diminish domestic GDP by reducing expenditures on domestically produced products.

Our generalizations concerning positive and negative net exports and equilibrium GDP allow us to conclude that a decline in net exports—that is, a decrease in exports or an increase in imports—decreases aggregate expenditures and has a contractionary effect on domestic GDP. Conversely, an increase in net exports —the result of either an increase in exports or a decrease in imports—increases aggregate expenditures and has an expansionary effect on domestic GDP. These changes may be in terms of real GDP or the price level, depending on where the economy initially is located relative to its potential output. For example, if the full employment level of GDP in Figure 11-8a is $470 billion, then a rise of net exports from zero to $5 billion will create an inflationary gap of $5 billion, *not* a real GDP increase of $20 billion as implied in our earlier discussion.

International Economic Linkages

Our analysis of net exports and domestic GDP permits us to demonstrate how circumstances or policies abroad can affect our domestic GDP.

Prosperity Abroad A rising level of national income among our trading partners will enable us to sell more of our goods abroad, thus raising our net exports and increasing our domestic GDP. We should be interested in the prosperity of our trading partners because their good fortune enables them to buy more imports. These purchases stimulate our exports and transfer some of their prosperity to us.

Tariffs Suppose our trading partners impose high tariffs on American goods to reduce their imports and stimulate production in their economies. But their imports are our exports. When they restrict their imports to stimulate *their* economies, they are reducing our exports and depressing *our* economy. We may retaliate by imposing trade barriers on their products. If so, their exports will decline and their net exports may be unchanged or even fall. In the Great Depression of the 1930s various nations, including the United States, imposed trade barriers in the hope of reducing domestic unemployment. But rounds of retaliation simply throttled world trade and made the world depression worse.

Exchange Rates Depreciation of the dollar relative to other currencies (Chapters 4 and 9) will permit people abroad to obtain more dollars per unit of their currencies. The price of American goods in terms of these currencies will fall, stimulating purchases of our exports. Conversely, American consumers will find they need more dollars to buy foreign goods and consequently will reduce their spending on imports. The resulting higher American exports and lower imports will increase our net exports and expand our GDP.

Whether depreciation of the dollar raises real GDP or produces inflation depends crucially on the initial location of the economy relative to its full-employment level of output. If the economy initially is operating below its productive capacity, the depreciation of the dollar and the resulting rise in net exports will increase real GDP. Alternatively, if the economy initially is fully employed, the depreciation of the dollar and higher level of net exports will cause domestic inflation.

Finally, while this last example has been cast in terms of a depreciation of the dollar, you should think through the impact that an *appreciation* of the dollar will have on net exports and equilibrium GDP.

QUICK REVIEW 11-2

◢ The multiplier is the principle that initial changes in spending can cause magnified changes in national income and GDP.

◢ The higher the marginal propensity to consume (the lower the marginal propensity to save), the larger is the simple multiplier.

◢ Society may not always be successful in attempts to save more because reduced consumption can cause GDP and national income to fall.

◢ In the Keynesian model, a recessionary gap is the amount by which the aggregate expenditures line must increase for the economy to realize full employment GDP; the inflationary gap is the amount by which the aggregate expenditures line must decrease for the economy to end demand-pull inflation.

◢ Positive net exports increase aggregate expenditures on domestic output and increase equilibrium GDP; negative net exports decrease aggregate expenditures on domestic output and reduce equilibrium GDP.

RECONCILING TWO MACRO MODELS

Our final challenge is to reconcile the Keynesian model of this chapter which shows the relationship between *aggregate expenditures* and real GDP and which assumes a constant price level with Chapter 9's model which portrays the relationship between real GDP and the *price level.* The Keynesian model, developed during the massive unemployment of the 1930s, assumes that an increase in aggregate expenditures will bring about an increase in domestic output at the existing or "going" price level. In contrast, the aggregate demand–aggregate supply model indicates that the price level will rise as aggregate demand increases in the intermediate and classical ranges of the aggregate supply curve. To repeat: The Keynesian expenditures-output analysis is a *constant* price level model; the aggregate demand–aggregate supply analysis is a *variable* price level model.

Deriving the AD Curve

By using familiar concepts and ideas we can forge an important link between our two models by showing how shifts in the aggregate expenditures schedule caused by price level changes permit us to trace out or locate a given downsloping aggregate demand curve.

Wealth Effect We know from Chapter 10 that there is an inverse relationship between the location of the consumption schedule and the price level. An increase in the price level causes the consumption schedule—and therefore the aggregate expenditures schedule—to shift downward and vice versa. A primary reason is the *real balances* or *wealth effect* introduced in Chapter 9. An increase in the price level reduces the real value or purchasing power of people's wealth. To restore the value of their wealth, people must save more and therefore consume less. At the higher price level the consumption schedule and therefore the aggregate expenditures schedule will shift downward and real GDP will fall.

Conversely, a decline in the price level increases the real value of people's wealth. When individuals are wealthier they are more inclined to consume and less inclined to save out of current real income. At the lower price level the consumption and aggregate expenditures curves shift upward and real GDP rises.

Interest-Rate Effect We also know from Chapter 10 that there is an inverse relationship between the location of the investment schedule (Table 10-3 and Figure 10-8) and the price level. An increase in the price level, all else being equal, will increase the interest rate, which in turn will shift the investment and aggregate expenditures schedules downward. This *interest-rate effect,* remember, works as follows: More money will be needed for purchases at the higher price level and, given a fixed supply of money, the increase in money demand will boost the interest rate and reduce investment expenditures. Conversely, a decline in the price level will reduce the demand for money, lower the interest rate, and elevate the investment and aggregate expenditures schedules. Lower price levels will be associated with greater aggregate expenditures and higher equilibrium levels of real GDP.

Foreign Purchases Effect Finally, there is an inverse relationship between the price level and the net export schedule. An increase in the price level will shift the net export schedule downward and thus reduce

KEY GRAPH

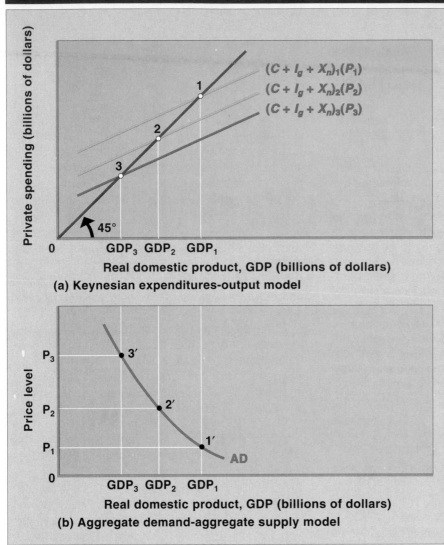

(a) Keynesian expenditures-output model

(b) Aggregate demand–aggregate supply model

FIGURE 11-9

Deriving the aggregate demand curve from the expenditures-output model

Through the wealth, interest-rate, and foreign purchases effects, the consumption, investment, and net exports schedules and therefore the aggregate expenditures schedule will rise when the price level declines and fall when the price level increases. If the aggregate expenditure schedule is at $(C + I_g + X_n)_2$ when the price level is P_2, we can combine that price level and the equilibrium output, GDP_2, to determine one point ($2'$) on the aggregate demand curve. A lower price level such as P_1 shifts aggregate expenditures to $(C + I_g + X_n)_1$, providing us with point $1'$ on the aggregate demand curve. Similarly, a higher price level at P_3 shifts aggregate expenditures down to $(C + I_g + X_n)_3$ so P_3 and GDP_3 yield another point on the aggregate demand curve at $3'$.

aggregate expenditures and equilibrium GDP. Other things being equal, higher prices for American goods will reduce U.S. export sales abroad and increase our imports of relatively cheaper foreign products. American net exports, aggregate expenditures on American goods, and American GDP will all fall due to this *foreign purchases effect*. A lower American price level, on the other hand, will produce the opposite effects.

Combined Models The aggregate demand curve of the variable price-level model merely relates the various possible price levels to the corresponding equilibrium GDPs. Note in Figure 11-9 (Key Graph) that we

can "stack" our Keynesian model of Figure 11-9a and the aggregate demand–aggregate supply model of Figure 11-9b vertically because real domestic output is being measured on the horizontal axis of both models. Now we can start in the top diagram with the aggregate expenditures schedule $(C + I_g + X_n)_2$. The price level relevant to this aggregate expenditures schedule is P_2 as shown in parentheses to remind us of that fact. From this information we can plot the equilibrium real domestic output, GDP_2, and the corresponding price level of P_2. This gives us one point—namely $2'$—on Figure 11-9b's aggregate demand curve.

We can now go through the same procedure but

assume that the price level is lower at P_1. We know that, other things being equal, a lower price level will: (1) increase the value of wealth, boosting consumption expenditures; (2) reduce the interest rate, promoting investment expenditures; and (3) reduce imports and increase exports, increasing net export expenditures. Consequently, the aggregate expenditures schedule will rise from $(C + I_g + X_n)_2$ to, say, $(C + I_g + X_n)_1$, giving us equilibrium at GDP_1. In Figure 11-9b we locate this new price level–real domestic output combination, P_1 and GDP_1, at point 1′.

Similarly, now suppose the price level increases from the original P_2 level to P_3. The real value of wealth falls, the interest rate rises, exports fall, and imports rise. Consequently, the consumption, investment, and net export schedules fall, shifting the aggregate expenditures schedule downward from $(C + I_g + X_n)_2$ to $(C + I_g + X_n)_3$ where real output is GDP_3. This lets us locate a third point on Figure 11-9b's aggregate demand curve, namely point 3′ where the price level is P_3 and real output is GDP_3.

In summary, a decrease in the price level shifts the aggregate expenditures schedule upward and increases real GDP. An increase in the price level shifts the aggregate expenditures schedule downward, reducing real GDP. The resulting price level–real GDP combinations yield various points such as 1′, 2′, and 3′, which locate a given downsloping aggregate demand curve.

Shifting the AD Curve

We know from Chapter 10 that the price level (and its impact on the real value of wealth, the interest rate, and net exports) is only one of many factors which might shift the aggregate expenditures schedule. For example, the consumption component of aggregate expenditures might be affected by expectations, consumer debt, or tax changes. And the investment component might be altered by changes in profit expectations, technological change, business taxes, and so forth. Likewise, the net export component of aggregate expenditures might be influenced by changes in exchange rates, tariff policies, and changes in levels of GDP and income in foreign nations.

What happens if we *hold the price level constant* and consider shifts in aggregate expenditures caused by these determinants of consumption, investment, and net exports? The answer is that the entire aggregate demand curve will shift rightward or leftward. (These aggregate demand shifters were discussed in Chapter 9 and summarized in Table 9-1.)

In Figure 11-10 we begin with the aggregate expenditures schedule at $(C + I_g + X_n)_1$ in the top diagram, yielding a real domestic output of GDP_1. Assume now that more optimistic business expectations cause investment to increase so that the aggregate expenditures schedule rises from $(C + I_g + X_n)_1$ to $(C + I_g + X_n)_2$. (The parenthetical P_1's remind us that in this case the price level is assumed to be constant.) The result will be a multiplied increase in real GDP from GDP_1 to GDP_2. In the lower graph this is reflected in an

FIGURE 11-10   Shifts in the aggregate expenditures schedule and in the aggregate demand curve

In (a) we assume that some determinant of consumption, investment, or net exports other than the price level shifts the aggregate expenditures schedule from $(C + I_g + X_n)_1$ to $(C + I_g + X_n)_2$, thereby increasing real domestic output from GDP_1 to GDP_2. In (b) we find that the aggregate demand counterpart of this is a rightward shift of the aggregate demand curve from AD_1 to AD_2 which is just sufficient to show the same increase in real output as in the expenditures-output model. We previously summarized the "aggregate demand shifters" in Table 9-1.

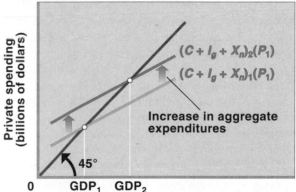

(a) Keynesian expenditures-output model

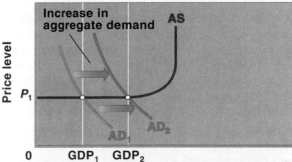

(b) Aggregate demand-aggregate supply model

increase in aggregate demand from AD_1 to AD_2 which shows the same multiplied increase in real GDP from GDP_1 to GDP_2. *The initial increase in investment shown as the upward shift of the aggregate expenditures curve in the top graph has shifted the AD curve in the lower graph by a horizontal distance equal to the change in investment times the multiplier.* Notice that this change in real GDP is associated with the constant price level P_1 because we are in the horizontal Keynesian range of the aggregate supply curve.

Multiplier with Price Level Changes

Thus far our two macro models seem compatible. The aggregate demand curve can be derived from the Keynesian model (Figure 11-9) and the multiplied effect of an initial change in some component of aggregate spending can be seen in both models (Figure 11-10). The two models part company, however, when changes in aggregate expenditures and aggregate demand cause price level changes.

In Figure 11-11, which restates and extends Figure 11-10b, we see that the previously discussed shift in aggregate demand from AD_1 to AD_2 occurs in the horizontal Keynesian range of aggregate supply. In other words, the economy is assumed to be in recession with ample excess productive capacity and a high unemployment rate. Therefore, businesses are willing to produce more output *at existing prices.* Any change in aggregate demand over this range is translated fully into a change in real GDP and employment while the price level remains constant. In the Keynesian range of aggregate supply a "full-strength" multiplier is at work.

If the economy is in the intermediate or classical range of the aggregate supply curve, part or all of any initial increase in aggregate demand will be dissipated in inflation and therefore *not* reflected in increased real output and employment. In Figure 11-11 the shift of aggregate demand from AD_2 to AD_3 is of the same magnitude as the AD_1 to AD_2 shift, but look what happens. Because we are now in the intermediate range of the aggregate supply curve, a portion of the increase in aggregate demand is dissipated in inflation as the price level rises from P_1 to P_2. Thus real GDP rises to only GDP'. If the aggregate supply curve had been horizontal, the AD_2 to AD_3 shift would have increased real domestic output to GDP_3. But inflation has weakened the multiplier so that the actual increase is to GDP' which is only about half as much.

Our conclusions are twofold. First, *for any given initial increase in aggregate demand, the resulting increase in real GDP will be smaller the larger the increase*

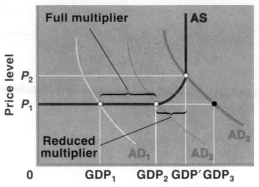

FIGURE 11-11 Inflation and the multiplier
The aggregate demand–aggregate supply model allows us to envision how inflation reduces the size of the multiplier. For the AD_1 to AD_2 increase in aggregate demand the price level is constant and the multiplier is at full strength. Although the increase in aggregate demand from AD_2 to AD_3 is of equal magnitude, it is partly dissipated in inflation (P_1 to P_2) and real output therefore only increases from GDP_2 to GDP'.

in the price level. Price level increases weaken the multiplier. You should sketch an increase in demand equal to the AD_2 to AD_3 shift in the vertical classical range to confirm that this increase in spending would be entirely dissipated in inflation. There would be no multiplier because real GDP would be unchanged. Our second, more general conclusion is that *the aggregate expenditures–output model is not sufficient to explain situations where changes in aggregate expenditures (and hence in aggregate demand) cause the price level to change.*

QUICK REVIEW 11-3

♪   *A change in the price level alters the location of the aggregate expenditures schedule through the wealth, interest rate, and foreign purchases effects.*

♪   *The aggregate demand curve is derived from the aggregate expenditures model by allowing the price level to change and observing the effect on the aggregate expenditures schedule and thus on equilibrium GDP.*

♪   *Holding the price level constant, increases in consumption, investment, and net export expenditures shift the aggregate expenditures schedule upward and the aggregate demand curve to the right.*

♪   *Price level increases occurring in the upsloping intermediate range of aggregate supply weaken the multiplier.*

LAST WORD

SQUARING THE ECONOMIC CIRCLE

Humorist Art Buchwald examines the multiplier.

WASHINGTON—The recession hit so fast that nobody knows exactly how it happened. One day we were the land of milk and honey and the next day we were the land of sour cream and food stamps.

This is one explanation.

Hofberger, the Chevy salesman in Tomcat, Va., a suburb of Washington, called up Littleton, of Littleton Menswear & Haberdashery, and said, "Good news, the new Novas have just come in and I've put one aside for you and your wife."

Littleton said, "I can't, Hofberger, my wife and I are getting a divorce."

"I'm sorry," Littleton said, "but I can't afford a new car this year. After I settle with my wife, I'll be lucky to buy a bicycle."

Hofberger hung up. His phone rang a few minutes later.

"This is Bedcheck the painter," the voice on the other end said. "When do you want us to start painting your house?"

"I changed my mind," said Hofberger. "I'm not going to paint the house."

"But I ordered the paint," Bedcheck said. "Why did you change your mind?"

"Because Littleton is getting a divorce and he can't afford a new car."

That evening when Bedcheck came home his wife said, "The new color television set arrived from Gladstone's TV Shop."

"Take it back," Bedcheck told his wife.

"Why?" she demanded.

"Because Hofberger isn't going to have his house painted now that the Littletons are getting a divorce."

The next day Mrs. Bedcheck dragged the TV set in its carton back to Gladstone. "We don't want it."

Gladstone's face dropped. He immediately called his travel agent, Sandstorm. "You know that trip you had scheduled for me to the Virgin Islands?"

"Right, the tickets are all written up."

"Cancel it. I can't go. Bedcheck just sent back the color TV set because Hofberger didn't sell a car to Lit-

tleton because they're going to get a divorce and she wants all his money."

Sandstorm tore up the airline tickets and went over to see his banker, Gripsholm. "I can't pay back the loan this month because Gladstone isn't going to the Virgin Islands."

Gripsholm was furious. When Rudemaker came in to borrow money for a new kitchen he needed for his restaurant, Gripsholm turned him down cold. "How can I loan you money when Sandstorm hasn't repaid the money he borrowed?"

Rudemaker called up the contractor, Eagleton, and said he couldn't put in a new kitchen. Eagleton laid off eight men.

Meanwhile, General Motors announced it was giving a rebate on its new models. Hofberger called up Littleton immediately. "Good news." he said, "even if you are getting a divorce, you can afford a new car."

"I'm not getting a divorce," Littleton said. "It was all a misunderstanding and we've made up."

"That's great," Hofberger said. "Now you can buy the Nova."

"No way," said Littleton. "My business has been so lousy I don't know why I keep the doors open."

"I didn't realize that," Hofberger said.

"Do you realize I haven't seen Bedcheck, Gladstone, Sandstorm, Gripsholm, Rudemaker or Eagleton for more than a month? How can I stay in business if they don't patronize my store?"

Source: Art Buchwald, "Squaring the Economic Circle," *Cleveland Plain Dealer,* February 22, 1975. Reprinted by permission.

Looking Ahead

What's next? In Chapter 12 we will embellish our expenditures-output and aggregate demand and supply models by moving from a private sector economy to a mixed economy in which government expenditures and taxes are considered. Our main mission will be to explain how government might alter its expenditures and tax collections to alleviate either unemployment or inflation.

CHAPTER SUMMARY

1 For a closed private economy the equilibrium level of GDP is where aggregate expenditures and domestic output are equal or, graphically, where the $C + I_g$ line intersects the 45-degree line. At any GDP greater than equilibrium GDP, domestic output will exceed aggregate spending, resulting in unintended investment in inventories, depressed profits, and eventual declines in output, employment, and income. At any below-equilibrium GDP, aggregate expenditures will exceed domestic output, resulting in unintended disinvestment in inventories, substantial profits, and eventual increases in GDP.

2 A complementary leakages-injections approach determines equilibrium GDP at the point where the amount households save and the amount businesses plan to invest are equal. This is at the point where the saving and planned investment schedules intersect. Any excess of saving over planned investment will cause a shortage of total spending, forcing GDP to fall. Any excess of planned investment over saving will cause an excess of total spending, inducing GDP to rise. These changes in GDP will in both cases correct the indicated discrepancies in saving and planned investment.

3 Shifts in the saving-consumption schedules or in the investment schedule will cause the equilibrium output-income level to change by several times the amount of the initial change in spending. This multiplier effect accompanies both increases and decreases in spending. The simple multiplier is equal to the reciprocal of the marginal propensity to save.

4 The paradox of thrift is the notion that the attempt of society to save more, as reflected in an upshift of the saving schedule, may be frustrated by the multiple decline in the equilibrium GDP which will ensue. If demand-pull inflation exists, however, more saving will reduce the price level. Furthermore, if the additional saving is invested, the equilib-

rium GDP will be unchanged and the economy will realize a more rapid rate of growth.

5 The equilibrium level of GDP and the full-employment noninflationary GDP need not coincide. The amount by which aggregate expenditures fall short of the full-employment GDP is called the recessionary gap; this gap prompts a multiple decline in real GDP. The amount by which aggregate expenditures exceed the full-employment GDP is the inflationary gap; it causes demand-pull inflation.

6 Positive net exports increase aggregate expenditures and thus increase American GDP; negative net exports decrease aggregate expenditures and therefore reduce American GDP. Increases in exports or decreases in imports have an expansionary effect on GDP while decreases in exports or increases in imports have a contractionary effect on GDP.

7 The downsloping aggregate demand curve can be derived from the expenditures-output model by varying the price level and determining how the consequent changes in aggregate expenditures alter the equilibrium level of real domestic output. Shifts in the aggregate demand curve are associated with shifts in the aggregate expenditures curve caused by non-price-level factors that alter consumption, investment, or net export spending.

8 Assuming a constant price level, the aggregate demand–aggregate supply model would show the same multiplied change in real GDP as portrayed in the expenditures-output model.

9 In the intermediate and classical ranges of the aggregate supply curve the aggregate demand–aggregate supply model tells us that the multiplier will be weakened because a portion of any increase in aggregate demand will be dissipated in inflation.

TERMS AND CONCEPTS

aggregate expenditures–
    domestic output
    approach
equilibrium GDP
	leakages-injections
	    approach
	45-degree line
	multiplier effect
		planned and actual
		    investment
		paradox of thrift
			recessionary and
			    inflationary gaps
			net exports

QUESTIONS AND STUDY SUGGESTIONS

1 Explain graphically the determination of the equilibrium GDP by **a** the aggregate expenditures–domestic output approach and **b** the leakages-injections approach for the private sector of a closed economy. Why must these two approaches

always yield the same equilibrium GDP? Explain why the intersection of the aggregate expenditures schedule and the 45-degree line determines the equilibrium GDP.

2 Assuming the level of investment is $16 billion and independent of the level of total output, complete the following table and determine the equilibrium level of output and income which the private sector of this closed economy would provide.

Possible levels of employment, millions	Real domestic output (GDP = DI), billions	Consumption, billions	Saving, billions
40	$240	$244	$___
45	260	260	___
50	280	276	___
55	300	292	___
60	320	308	___
65	340	324	___
70	360	340	___
75	380	356	___
80	400	372	___

a If this economy has a labor force of 70 million, will there exist an inflationary or a recessionary gap? Explain the consequences of this gap.

b Will an inflationary or a recessionary gap exist if the available labor force is only 55 million? Trace the consequences.

c What are the sizes of the MPC and the MPS?

d Use the multiplier concept to explain the increase in the equilibrium GDP which will occur as the result of an increase in planned investment spending from $16 to $20 billion.

3 Using the consumption and saving data given in question 2 and assuming the level of investment is $16 billion, what are the levels of saving and planned investment at the $380 billion level of domestic output? What are the levels of saving and actual investment? What are saving and planned investment at the $300 billion level of domestic output? What are the levels of saving and actual investment? Use the concept of unintended investment to explain adjust-

ments toward equilibrium from both the $380 and $300 billion levels of domestic output.

4 "Planned investment is equal to saving at all levels of GDP; actual investment equals saving only at the equilibrium GDP." Do you agree? Explain. Critically evaluate: "The fact that households may save more than businesses want to invest is of no consequence, because events will in time force households and businesses to save and invest at the same rates."

5 What effect will each of the changes designated in question 6 at the end of Chapter 10 have on the equilibrium level of GDP? Explain your answers.

6 What is the simple multiplier effect? What relationship does the MPC bear to the size of the multiplier? The MPS? What will the multiplier be when the MPS is 0, .4, .6, and 1? When the MPC is 1, .90, .67, .50, and 0? How much of a change in GDP will result if businesses increase their level of investment by $8 billion and the MPC in the economy is .80? If the MPC is .67? Explain the difference between the simple and the complex multiplier.

7 Explain the paradox of thrift. What is its significance? "One's view of the social desirability of saving depends on whether one assumes a Keynesian or classical view of the macroeconomy." Do you agree?

8 The data in columns 1 and 2 of the table below are for a closed economy.

a Use columns 1 and 2 to determine the equilibrium GDP for the closed economy.

b Now open this economy for international trade by including the export and import figures of columns 3 and 4. Calculate net exports and determine the equilibrium GDP for the open economy. Explain why equilibrium GDP differs from the closed economy.

c Given the original $20 billion level of exports, what would be the equilibrium GDP if imports were $10 billion larger at each level of GDP? Or $10 billion smaller at each level of GDP? What generalization concerning the level of imports and the equilibrium GDP is illustrated by these examples?

d What is the size of the multiplier in these examples?

(1) Real domestic output (GDP = DI), billions	(2) Aggregate expenditures, closed economy, billions	(3) Exports, billions	(4) Imports, billions	(5) Net exports, billions	(6) Aggregate expenditures, open economy, billions
$200	$240	$20	$30	$___	$___
250	280	20	30	___	___
300	320	20	30	___	___
350	360	20	30	___	___
400	400	20	30	___	___
450	440	20	30	___	___
500	480	20	30	___	___
550	520	20	30	___	___

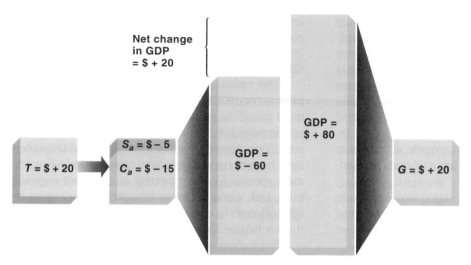

FIGURE 12-3   The balanced-budget multiplier

The balanced-budget multiplier is 1. An equal increase in taxes and government expenditures will increase GDP by an amount equal to the increase in the amount of government expenditures and taxes. Given an MPC of .75, a tax increase of $20 billion will reduce disposable income by $20 billion and lower consumption expenditures by $15 billion. Because the multiplier is 4, GDP will therefore decline by $60 billion. The $20 billion increase in government expenditures, however, will produce a more than offsetting increase in GDP of $80 billion. The net increase in GDP will be $20 billion, which equals the amount of the increase in government expenditures and taxes.

or inflation. When recession exists, an **expansionary fiscal policy** is in order. This entails (1) increased government spending, *or* (2) lower taxes, *or* (3) a combination of the two. In other words, if the budget is balanced at the outset, fiscal policy should move toward a government budget *deficit* during recession or depression.

Conversely, when demand-pull inflation is present, a restrictive or **contractionary fiscal policy** is appropriate. A contractionary policy is composed of (1) decreased government spending, *or* (2) higher taxes, *or* (3) a combination of these two policies. Fiscal policy should move toward a *surplus* in the government's budget when the economy is faced with the problem of controlling inflation.

Keep in mind, however, that not only does the difference between government spending and taxes (the size of a deficit or surplus) affect the GDP, but so does the absolute size of the budget. In our illustration of the balanced-budget multiplier, increases in *G* and *T* of $20 billion increased GDP by $20 billion. If *G* and *T* had both increased by only $10 billion, equilibrium GDP would only have risen by $10 billion.

Financing Deficits and Disposing of Surpluses

Given the size of a deficit, its expansionary effect on the economy will depend upon the method by which it is financed. Similarly, given the size of a surplus, its deflationary impact will depend on its disposition.

Borrowing versus New Money   There are two different ways by which the Federal government can finance a deficit: by borrowing from (selling interest-bearing bonds to) the public, or by issuing new money to its creditors. The impact on aggregate expenditures will be different in each case.

1 Borrowing If the government goes into the money market and borrows, it will be competing with private business borrowers for funds. This added demand for funds will drive the equilibrium interest rate upward. We know from Chapter 10 that investment spending is inversely related to the interest rate. Government borrowing therefore will increase the interest rate and "crowd out" some private investment spending and interest-sensitive consumer spending.

2 Money Creation If deficit spending is financed by issuing new money, crowding-out of private expenditures can be avoided. Federal spending can increase without any adverse effect on investment or consumption. Thus, we can conclude that *the creation of new money is a more expansionary way of financing deficit spending than is borrowing.*

Debt Retirement versus Idle Surplus Demand-pull inflation calls for fiscal action by government which will result in a budget surplus. However, the anti-inflationary effect of this surplus depends on what government does with it.

1 Debt Reduction Since the Federal government has an outstanding debt of some $3.6 trillion, it is logical that government should use a surplus to retire outstanding debt. The anti-inflationary impact of a surplus, however, may be reduced somewhat by paying off debt. In retiring debt held by the general public, the government transfers its surplus tax revenues back into the money market, causing the interest rate to fall and thereby stimulating investment and consumption.

2 Impounding On the other hand, government can realize a greater anti-inflationary impact from its budgetary surplus by impounding the surplus funds, that is, by allowing them to stand idle. An impounded surplus means that the government is extracting and withholding purchasing power from the income-expenditure stream. If surplus tax revenues are not reinjected into the economy, there is no possibility of some portion of the surplus being spent. There is no chance that the funds will create inflationary pressure to offset the deflationary impact of the surplus itself. We conclude that *the impounding of a budgetary surplus is more contractionary than the use of the surplus to retire public debt.*

Policy Options: *G* or *T*?

Is it preferable to use government spending or taxes to eliminate recessionary and inflationary gaps? The answer depends to a considerable extent upon one's view as to whether the public sector is too large or too small. "Liberal" economists, who think the public sector needs to be enlarged to meet various failures of the market system (Chapter 6), can recommend that aggregate expenditures should be expanded during recessions by increasing government purchases *and* that aggregate expenditures should be constrained during inflationary periods by increasing taxes.

Conversely, "conservative" economists, who contend that the public sector is overly large and inefficient, can advocate that aggregate expenditures be increased during recessions by cutting taxes *and* that aggregate expenditures be reduced during inflation by cutting government spending. An active fiscal policy designed to stabilize the economy can be associated with either an expanding or a contracting public sector.

QUICK REVIEW 12-1

✦ **The Employment Act of 1946 commits the Federal government to take positive actions to promote "maximum employment, production, and purchasing power."**

✦ **Government purchases shift the aggregate expenditures schedule upward and raise equilibrium GDP.**

✦ **Taxation reduces disposable income, lowers consumption spending and saving, shifts the aggregate expenditures schedule downward, and reduces equilibrium GDP.**

✦ **The balanced-budget multiplier is 1.**

✦ **Expansionary fiscal policy involves increases in government spending, reductions in taxes, or some combination of the two; contractionary fiscal policy entails the opposite actions.**

NONDISCRETIONARY FISCAL POLICY: BUILT-IN STABILIZERS

To some degree appropriate changes in relative levels of government expenditures and taxes occur automatically. This so-called automatic or *built-in stability* is not included in our discussion of discretionary fiscal policy because we assumed a simple lump-sum tax whereby the same amount of tax revenue was collected at each level of GDP. Built-in stability arises because in reality our net tax system (net taxes equal taxes minus transfers and subsidies) is such that *net tax revenues[1] vary directly with GDP.*

Virtually all taxes will yield more tax revenue as GDP rises. In particular, personal income taxes have progressive rates and result in more than proportionate increases in tax collections as GDP expands. Furthermore, as GDP increases and more goods and services are purchased, revenues from corporate income taxes and sales and excise taxes will increase. And, similarly, payroll tax payments increase as economic

[1]From now on, we will use the term "taxes" in referring to net taxes.

expansion creates more jobs. Conversely, when GDP declines, tax receipts from all these sources will decline. Transfer payments (or "negative taxes") behave in precisely the opposite way. Unemployment compensation payments, welfare payments, and subsidies to farmers all *decrease* during economic expansion and *increase* during a contraction.

Automatic or Built-In Stabilizers

Figure 12-4 helps us understand how the tax system gives rise to built-in stability. Government expenditures G are given and assumed to be independent of the level of GDP; expenditures are decided on at some fixed level by Congress. But Congress does *not* determine the *level* of tax revenues; rather, it establishes tax *rates*. Tax revenues then vary directly with the level of GDP which the economy actually realizes. The direct relationship between tax revenues and GDP is shown in the upsloping T line.

The economic importance of this direct relationship between tax receipts and GDP comes into focus when we remember two things.

1   Taxes are a leakage or withdrawal of potential purchasing power from the economy.

2   It is desirable from the standpoint of stability to increase leakages or withdrawals of purchasing power when the economy is moving toward inflation and to diminish these withdrawals when the economy is tending to slump.

In other words, the kind of tax system portrayed in Figure 12-4 builds some stability into the economy by automatically bringing about changes in tax revenues and therefore in the public budget which tend to counter both inflation and unemployment. Generally speaking, a **built-in stabilizer** is *anything which increases the government's deficit (or reduces its surplus) during a recession and increases its surplus (or reduces its deficit) during inflation without requiring explicit action by policy makers.* As Figure 12-4 clearly reveals, this is precisely what our tax system does.

As GDP rises during prosperity, tax revenues *automatically* increase and, because they are a leakage, restrain the economic expansion. In other words, as the economy moves toward a higher GDP, tax revenues automatically rise and move the budget from a deficit toward a surplus.

Conversely, as GDP falls during recession, tax revenues *automatically* decline and this reduction in leakages cushions the economic contraction. With a falling GDP, tax receipts decline and move the public budget from a surplus toward a deficit. In terms of Figure 12-4, the low level of income GDP_3 will automatically give rise to an expansionary budget deficit; the high and perhaps inflationary income level GDP_2 will automatically generate a contractionary budget surplus.

It is clear from Figure 12-4 that the size of the automatic budget deficits or surpluses and therefore built-in stability depends on the responsiveness of changes in taxes to changes in GDP. If tax revenues change sharply as GDP changes, the slope of line T in the figure will be steep and the vertical distances between T and G—the deficits or surpluses—will be large. Alternatively, if tax revenues change very little when GDP changes, the slope will be gentle and built-in stability will be low.

Said differently, the steepness of T in Figure 12-4 depends on the type of tax system in place. If the tax system is **progressive,** meaning the average tax rate (=tax revenue/GDP) rises with GDP, the T line will be steeper than if the tax system is **proportional** or **regressive.** A proportional tax system is one in which the average tax rate remains constant as GDP rises; in a regressive tax system the average tax rate falls as GDP rises. Tax revenues will rise with GDP under progressive and proportional tax systems and may either rise, fall, or remain the same when GDP increases under a regressive system. But the relevant generalization is this: *The more progressive the tax system, the greater is the economy's built-in stability.*

Changes in public policies or laws which alter the progressivity of the net tax system (taxes minus transfers and subsidies) therefore affect the degree of built-in stability. The tax system became less progressive be-

FIGURE 12-4   Built-in stability

If tax revenues vary directly with GDP the deficits which will occur automatically during recession will help alleviate that recession. Conversely, the surpluses which occur automatically during expansion will assist in offsetting possible inflation.

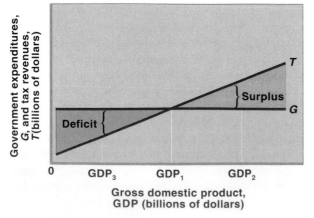

tween 1977 and 1985. Built-in stability fell because social security taxes, which are regressive, rose substantially. Also, in the early 1980s the Federal government "indexed" the personal income tax. Indexing means that income tax brackets are widened each year to adjust for inflation. Before indexing, inflation would push taxpayers into higher marginal tax brackets and thus increase government's tax revenues.

The tax system has become more progressive since 1986. The Tax Reform Act of 1986 greatly reduced the highest marginal tax rates, but also removed tax breaks used by the wealthy. Subsequent tax changes have increased the share of total taxes paid by the wealthy. The Council of Economic Advisers concludes that tax progressivity and therefore the degree of built-in stability is similar to that in the mid-1970s.

The built-in stability provided by our tax system has reduced the severity of business fluctuations. But built-in stabilizers can only diminish, *not* correct, major changes in equilibrium GNP. Discretionary fiscal policy—changes in tax rates and expenditures—therefore may be needed to correct inflation or recession of any appreciable magnitude.

Full-Employment Budget

Built-in stability—the fact that tax revenues vary directly with GDP—makes it hazardous to use the **actual budget** surplus or deficit in any given year as an index of the government's fiscal stance. Suppose the economy is at full employment at GDP_1 in Figure 12-4 and the budget is in balance. Now, assume that C_a or I_g or X_n declines, causing a recession at GDP_3. The government, let's assume, takes no discretionary fiscal action; therefore, the G and T lines remain in the positions shown in the diagram. As the economy moves to GDP_3, tax revenues fall and, with government expenditures unaltered, a deficit occurs. But this **cyclical deficit** is clearly *not* the result of positive countercyclical fiscal actions by the government; rather it is the by-product of fiscal inaction as the economy slides into a recession.

We cannot gain a meaningful picture of the government's fiscal posture—whether Congress was appropriately manipulating taxes and expenditures—by viewing the historical record of budgetary deficits or surpluses. The actual budget surplus or deficit reflects not only possible discretionary decisions about spending and taxes (as shown in the locations of the G and T lines in Figure 12-4), but also the level of equilibrium GDP (where the economy is operating on the horizontal axis of Figure 12-4). Given that tax revenues vary

with GDP, the problem of comparing deficits or surpluses in year 1 and year 2 is that the level of GDP may be vastly different in each of the two years.

Economists have resolved this problem through the concept of a full-employment budget. The **full-employment budget** *measures what the Federal budgetary surplus or deficit would be if the economy were to operate at full employment throughout the year.* Figure 12-5 compares the full-employment budget and the actual budget as percentages of domestic output since 1955. Two features stand out.

1 In many years the sizes of the actual budget deficits or surpluses greatly differed from the sizes of the deficits or surpluses of the full-employment budget. Consider 1961 and 1962, years of above-normal unemployment and sluggish economic growth. A look at the actual budget deficits in these years implies that government was appropriately engaged in an expansionary fiscal policy. But the full-employment budget data tell us that this was *not* the case. The full-employment budget data indicate that, *if* the economy had been at full employment, there would have been a budgetary surplus. Our fiscal policy in 1961 and 1962 was in fact contractionary, and this was partially responsible for the less-than-full-employment levels of domestic output, the consequent poor tax harvests, and the deficits which occurred in the actual budgets for 1961 and 1962.

Also, consider 1969, a year when tax revenues were flowing into the Federal government at a rapid pace because inflation was occurring and the unemployment rate was *less* than the full-employment unemployment rate. Note that even though the actual budget was in surplus, the full-employment budget was in deficit. How could this be? If the unemployment rate were at the higher full-employment level, tax revenues would have been much lower, and given the level of government spending the budget would have been in deficit. Fiscal policy was mildly stimulative in 1969 even though the actual budget was in surplus.

2 Both the actual and full-employment budgets have been in deficit over the past few decades. The last surplus in the actual budget occurred in 1969; the last surplus in the full-employment budget occurred in 1962. In the mid- and late 1980s there were large actual and full-employment budget deficits. These latter budget deficits were also called **structural deficits.** A large portion of the actual deficits during this period did not result from automatic deficiencies in tax revenues brought forth by below-full-employment domestic output and income; they were not mainly cyclical deficits. Rather, they resulted from structural imbalances

Money, Banking, and Monetary Policy

most gas stations will verify, checks are somewhat less generally accepted than currency. But, for practically all major purchases, sellers willingly accept checks as a means of payment. Furthermore, such deposits can be immediately converted into paper money and coins on demand; checks drawn on these deposits are for all practical purposes the equivalent of currency.

To summarize:

Money, $M1$ = currency + checkable deposits

Institutions Offering Checkable Deposits Table 13-1 shows that **checkable deposits** are clearly the largest component of the $M1$ money supply. By glancing ahead at Figure 13-4 we find that many financial institutions offer checkable deposits in the United States.

1 Commercial banks are the mainstays of the system. They accept the deposits of households and businesses and use these financial resources to extend a wide variety of loans. Commercial bank loans provide short-term working capital to businesses and farmers, finance consumer purchases of automobiles and other durable goods, and so on.

2 The commercial banks are supplemented by a variety of other financial institutions—savings and loan associations (S&Ls), mutual savings banks, and credit unions—which are collectively designated as **thrift** or **savings institutions** or, more simply, "thrifts." **Savings and loan associations** and **mutual savings banks** marshal the savings of households and businesses which are then used, among other things, to finance housing mortgages. **Credit unions** accept the deposits of "members"—usually a group of individuals who work for the same company—and lend these funds to finance installment purchases.

The checkable deposits of banks and thrifts go by various exotic names—demand deposits, NOW (negotiable order of withdrawal) accounts, ATS (automatic transfer service) accounts, and share draft accounts. Nevertheless, they are all similar in that depositors can write checks on them whenever, and in whatever amount, they choose.

Qualification A technical qualification of our definition of money must be added: Currency and checkable deposits owned by government (the Treasury) and by the Federal Reserve Banks, commercial banks, or other financial institutions are excluded. A paper dollar in the hands of John Doe obviously constitutes just $1 of the money supply. But, if we counted dollars held by banks as part of the money supply, the same $1 would count for $2 when deposited in a bank. It would count for a $1 demand deposit owned by Doe and also for $1 worth of currency resting in the bank's vault. This problem of double counting can be avoided by excluding currency resting in banks (and currency redeposited in the Federal Reserve Banks or other commercial banks) in determining the total money supply.

The exclusion of currency held by, and demand deposits owned by, government is somewhat more arbitrary. The major reason for this exclusion is that it permits us better to gauge the money supply and rate of spending in the private sector of the economy apart from spending initiated by government policy.

Near-Monies: *M2* and *M3*

Near-monies are certain highly liquid financial assets such as noncheckable savings accounts, time deposits, and short-term government securities which, although they do not directly function as a medium of exchange, can be readily and without risk of financial loss converted into currency or checkable deposits. Thus, on demand you may withdraw currency from a **noncheckable savings account** at a commercial bank or thrift institution. Or, alternatively, you may request that funds be transferred from a noncheckable savings account to a checkable account.

As the term implies, **time deposits** only become available to a depositor at maturity. For example, a 90-day or 6-month time deposit is only available without penalty when the designated period expires. Although time deposits are somewhat less liquid than noncheckable savings accounts, they can be taken as currency or shifted into checkable accounts when they mature.

Alternatively, you can withdraw funds quickly from a **money market deposit account (MMDA).** These are interest-bearing accounts offered by banks and thrifts, which pool individual deposits to buy a variety of short-term securities. MMDAs have minimum balance requirements and limit how often money can be withdrawn. Or, through a telephone call, you can redeem shares in a **money market mutual fund (MMMF)** offered through a financial investment company. These companies use the combined funds of individual shareholders to buy short-term credit instruments such as certificates of deposit and U.S. government securities.

M2 Thus our monetary authorities offer a second and broader definition of money:

$$\text{Money, } M2 = \begin{array}{l} M1 + \text{noncheckable savings} \\ \text{deposits} + \text{small (less than} \\ \$100,000) \text{ time deposits} \\ + \text{MMDAs} + \text{MMMFs} \end{array}$$

In other words, **M2** includes (1) the medium of exchange items (currency and checkable deposits) which compose *M*1 plus (2) other items such as noncheckable savings deposits, small time deposits, money market deposit accounts, and individual money market mutual fund balances. These latter deposits can be quickly and without loss converted into currency and checkable deposits. Table 13-1 shows that the addition of noncheckable savings deposits, small time deposits, MMDAs, and MMMFs yields an *M*2 money supply of $3391 billion as compared to an *M*1 figure of $866 billion.

M3 A third "official" definition, **M3,** recognizes that large ($100,000 or more) time deposits—usually owned by businesses as certificates of deposit—are also easily convertible into checkable deposits. There is a going market for these certificates and they can therefore be sold (liquidated) at any time, although perhaps at the risk of a loss. The addition of these large time deposits to *M*2 yields a still broader definition of money:

$$\text{Money, } M3 = \begin{array}{l} M2 + \text{large (\$100,000 or} \\ \text{more) time deposits} \end{array}$$

Consulting Table 13-1 again, we find that the *M*3 money supply rises to $4143 billion.

Finally, there are still other slightly less liquid assets such as certain government securities (for example, Treasury bills and U.S. savings bonds) which can be easily converted into *M*1 money. There exists a whole spectrum of assets which vary slightly from one another in terms of their liquidity or "moneyness."

Which definition of money shall we adopt? The simple *M*1 definition has a notable virtue: It includes only items *directly* and *immediately* usable as a medium of exchange. For this reason it is the most-cited statistic in discussions of the money supply. However, for some purposes economists prefer the broader *M*2 definition. For example, *M*2 is used as one of the eleven trend variables in the index of leading indicators (Last Word, Chapter 12). And what of *M*3 and still broader definitions of money? These definitions are so inclusive that many economists question their usefulness.

We will adopt the narrow M*1 definition of money in our discussion and analysis, unless stated otherwise.* Bear

in mind that the important principles which apply to *M*1 are also applicable to *M*2 and *M*3 in that *M*1 is a component in these broader measures.

Near-Monies: Implications

Aside from complicating our definition of money, the existence of near-monies is important for several related reasons.

1 Spending Habits The highly liquid assets affect people's consuming-saving habits. Usually, the greater the amount of financial wealth people hold as near-monies, the greater is their willingness to spend out of their money incomes.

2 Stability Conversion of near-monies into money or vice versa can affect the economy's stability. For example, during the prosperity-inflationary phase of the business cycle, a significant conversion of noncheckable deposits into checkable deposits or currency adds to the money supply and, if not offset, could enhance inflationary pressures. Such conversions can complicate the task of the monetary authorities in controlling the money supply and the level of economic activity.

3 Policy The specific definition of money adopted is important for purposes of monetary policy. For example, the money supply as measured by *M*1 might be constant, while money defined as *M*2 might be increasing. Now, if the monetary authorities feel it is appropriate to have an expanding supply of money, acceptance of our narrow *M*1 definition would call for specific actions to increase currency and checkable deposits. But acceptance of the broader *M*2 definition would suggest that the desired expansion of the money supply is already taking place and that no specific policy action is required.

Credit Cards

You may wonder why credit cards—Visa, MasterCard, American Express, Discover, and so forth—have been ignored in our discussion of how money is defined. After all, credit cards are a convenient means of making purchases. The answer is that credit cards are *not* really money, but rather a means of obtaining a short-term loan from the commercial bank or other financial institution which has issued the card.

When you purchase a box of cassettes with a credit card, the issuing bank will reimburse the store. Then later you reimburse the bank. You pay an annual fee for the services provided and, if you repay the bank in installments, you pay a sizable interest charge. Credit cards, in short, are a means of deferring or postponing payment for a short period of time. Your purchase of cassettes is not actually complete until you have paid your credit-card bill.

It is worth noting, however, that credit cards—and, indeed, all other forms of credit—allow individuals and businesses to "economize" in the use of money. Credit cards permit you to have less currency and checkable deposits on hand for transactions. Stated differently, credit cards facilitate the synchronization of your expenditures and your receipt of income, thereby reducing the cash and checkable deposits you must hold.

QUICK REVIEW 13-1

◗ *Money serves as a medium of exchange, a measure of value, and a store of value.*

◗ *The narrow M1 definition of money includes currency and checkable deposits.*

◗ *Thrift institutions as well as commercial banks now offer accounts on which checks can be written.*

◗ *The M2 definition of money includes M1 plus noncheckable savings deposits, small (less than $100,000) time deposits, money market deposit accounts, and money market mutual fund balances; M3 consists of M2 plus large time deposits (more than $100,000).*

WHAT "BACKS" THE MONEY SUPPLY?

This is a slippery question; any reasonably complete answer is likely to be at odds with the preconceptions many of us hold about money.

Money as Debt

The major components of the money supply—paper money and checkable deposits—are debts, or promises to pay. *Paper money is the circulating debt of the Federal Reserve Banks. Checkable deposits are the debts of commercial banks and thrift institutions.*

Furthermore, paper currency and checkable deposits have no intrinsic value. A $5 bill is just a piece of paper, and a checkable deposit is merely a bookkeeping entry. And coins, we know, have an intrinsic value less than their face value. Nor will government redeem the paper money you hold for anything tangible, such as gold. In effect, we have chosen to "manage" our money supply to provide the amount of money needed for that particular volume of business activity which will foster full employment, price level stability, and a healthy rate of economic growth.

Most economists feel that management of the money supply is more sensible than linking it to gold or any other commodity whose supply might arbitrarily and capriciously change. A large increase in the nation's gold stock as the result of new gold discovery or a breakthrough in the extraction of gold from ore might increase the money supply far beyond the amount needed to transact a full-employment level of business activity, and therefore cause inflation. Conversely, the historical decline in domestic gold production could reduce the domestic money supply to the point where economic activity was choked off and unemployment and a retarded growth rate resulted.

The point is that paper money cannot be converted into a fixed amount of gold or some other precious metal but is exchangeable only for other pieces of paper money. The government will swap one paper $5 bill for another bearing a different serial number. That is all you can get if you ask the government to redeem some of your paper money. Similarly, check money cannot be exchanged for gold but only for paper money, which, as we have just seen, will not be redeemed by the government for anything tangible.

Value of Money

If currency and checkable deposits have no intrinsic characteristics which give them value *and* if they are not backed by gold or other precious metals, then why are they money? What gives a $20 bill or a $100 checking account entry its value? A reasonably complete answer to these questions involves three points.

1 Acceptability Currency and checkable deposits are money simply because they are accepted as money. By virtue of long-standing business practice, currency and checkable deposits perform the basic function of money; they are acceptable as a medium of exchange. Suppose you swap a $20 bill for a shirt or blouse at a clothing store. Why does the merchant accept this piece of paper in exchange for that product? The merchant accepts paper money because he or she is confident that others will also be willing to accept it in exchange for goods and services. The merchant knows that paper money can purchase the services of clerks, acquire products from wholesalers, and pay the rent on the store. We accept paper money in exchange because we are confident it will be exchangeable for real goods and services when we choose to spend it.

2 Legal Tender Our confidence in the acceptability of paper money is partly a matter of law; currency has been designated as **legal tender** by government. This means that paper currency must be accepted in the payment of a debt or the creditor forfeits both the privilege of charging interest and the right to sue the debtor for nonpayment. Put more bluntly, the acceptability of paper dollars is bolstered by the fact that government says these dollars are money. The paper money in our economy is basically **fiat money;** it is money because the government says it is, not because of redeemability in terms of some precious metal. The general acceptability of currency is also bolstered by the willingness of government to accept it in the payment of taxes and other obligations due the government.

Lest we be overimpressed by the power of government, it should be noted that the fact that paper currency is generally accepted in exchange is decidedly more important than government's legal tender decree in making these pieces of paper function as money. Indeed, the government has *not* decreed checks (which are also fiat money) to be legal tender, but they nevertheless successfully perform the vast bulk of the economy's exchanges of goods, services, and resources. The fact that a governmental agency—the Federal Deposit Insurance Corporation (FDIC)—insures the deposits of commercial banks and S&Ls undoubtedly contributes to the willingness of individuals and businesses to use checkable deposits as a medium of exchange.

3 Relative Scarcity Basically, the value of money, like the economic value of anything else, is a supply and demand phenomenon. That is, money derives its value from its scarcity relative to its usefulness. The usefulness of money lies in its unique capacity to be exchanged for goods and services, either now or in the future. The economy's demand for money thus depends on its total dollar volume of transactions in any given time period plus the amount of money individuals and businesses want to hold for possible future

transactions. Given a reasonably constant demand for money, the value or "purchasing power" of the monetary unit will be determined by the supply of money.

Money and Prices

The real value or purchasing power of money is the amount of goods and services a unit of money will buy. When money rapidly loses its purchasing power, it rapidly loses its role as money.

Value of the Dollar The amount a dollar will buy varies inversely with the price level; *a reciprocal relationship exists between the general price level and the value of the dollar.* Figure 13-1 shows this inverse relationship. When the consumer price index or "cost-of-living" index goes up, the purchasing power of the dollar necessarily goes down, and vice versa. Higher prices lower the value of the dollar because more dollars will be needed to buy a given amount of goods and services. Conversely, lower prices increase the purchasing power of the dollar because you will need fewer dollars to obtain a given quantity of goods and services. If the price level doubles, the value of the dollar will decline by one-half, or 50 percent. If the price level falls by one-half, or 50 percent, the purchasing power of the dollar will double.

The arithmetic of the relationship between the price level and the value of the dollar is as follows. If we let P equal the price level expressed as an index number (in hundredths) and D equal the value of the dollar, then our reciprocal relationship is

$$D = \frac{1}{P}$$

If the price level P equals 1.00, then the value of the dollar D is 1.00. But, if P rises from 1.00 to 1.20, D will be 0.833, meaning a 20 percent increase in the price level will reduce the value of the dollar by 16.67 percent. Check your understanding of this reciprocal relationship by determining the value of D and its percentage rise when P falls by 20 percent to 0.80.

Inflation and Acceptability We noted in Chapter 8 several situations in which a nation's currency became worthless and unacceptable in exchange. With few exceptions these were circumstances where government issued so many pieces of paper currency that the value of each of these units of money was almost totally undermined. The infamous post-World War I inflation in Germany is a notable example. In December of 1919

KEY GRAPH

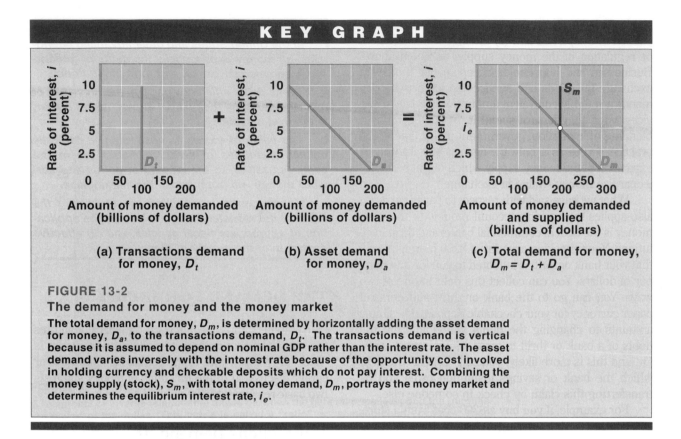

(a) Transactions demand for money, D_t

(b) Asset demand for money, D_a

(c) Total demand for money, $D_m = D_t + D_a$

FIGURE 13-2

The demand for money and the money market

The total demand for money, D_m, is determined by horizontally adding the asset demand for money, D_a, to the transactions demand, D_t. The transactions demand is vertical because it is assumed to depend on nominal GDP rather than the interest rate. The asset demand varies inversely with the interest rate because of the opportunity cost involved in holding currency and checkable deposits which do not pay interest. Combining the money supply (stock), S_m, with total money demand, D_m, portrays the money market and determines the equilibrium interest rate, i_e.

and is independent of the interest rate, we show the transactions demand as a vertical line. For simplicity we assume the amount of money demanded for transactions is unrelated to changes in the interest rate. That is, higher interest rates will not reduce the amount of money demanded for transactions.[4]

We have located the transactions demand at $100 billion arbitrarily, but a rationale can be provided. For example, if each dollar held for transactions purposes is spent on the average three times per year *and* nominal GDP is assumed to be $300 billion, then the public would need $100 billion of money to purchase that GDP.

Asset Demand, D_a

The second reason for holding money is rooted in money's function as a store of value. People may hold

their financial assets in many forms—for example, as corporate stocks, private or government bonds, or as *M*1 money. Hence, there is an **asset demand** for money.

What determines the asset demand for money? First, we must recognize that each of the various forms in which our financial assets may be held has advantages and disadvantages. To simplify, let's compare holding bonds with holding money as an asset. The advantages of holding money are its liquidity and lack of risk. Money is the most liquid of all assets in that it is immediately usable in making purchases. Money is an especially attractive asset to be holding when the prices of goods, services, and other financial assets are expected to decline. When the price of a bond falls, the bondholder will suffer a loss if the bond must be sold before maturity. There is no such risk with holding money.

The disadvantage of holding money as an asset is that, compared to holding bonds, one does *not* earn interest income or, in the case of an interest-bearing checking account, earn as much interest income as on bonds or noncheckable deposits. And idle currency earns no interest at all. Some banks and thrifts require

---

[4]This is a simplification. We would also expect the amount of money held by businesses and households to negotiate transactions to vary inversely with the interest rate. When interest rates are high, consumers and businesses will try to reduce the amount of money held for transactions purposes to have more funds to put into interest-earning assets.

minimum-sized checkable deposits for the depositor to be paid interest; hence, many depositors do not achieve these minimum deposit balances and therefore earn no interest. The interest paid on checkable deposits which exceed the required minimums is less than that paid on bonds and the various noncheckable deposits.

Knowing this, the problem is deciding how much of your financial assets to hold as, say, bonds and how much as money. The solution depends primarily upon the rate of interest. By holding money a household or business incurs an opportunity cost (Chapter 2); interest income is forgone or sacrificed. If a bond pays 10 percent interest, then it costs $10 per year of forgone income to hold $100 as cash or in a noninterest checkable account. It is no surprise that *the asset demand for money varies inversely with the rate of interest.* When the interest rate or opportunity cost of holding money as an asset is low, the public will choose to hold a large amount of money as assets. Conversely, when the interest rate is high, it is costly to "be liquid" and the amount of assets held in the form of money will be small. Stated differently, when it is expensive to hold money as an asset, people will hold less of it; when money can be held cheaply, people will hold more of it. This inverse relationship between the interest rate and the amount of money people will want to hold as an asset is shown by D_a in Figure 13-2b.

Total Money Demand, D_m

As shown in Figure 13-2c, the **total demand** for money, D_m, can be found by adding the asset demand horizontally to the transactions demand. (The vertical blue line in Figure 13-2a represents the transactions demand to which Figure 13-2b's asset demand has been added.) The resulting downsloping line represents the total amount of money the public will want to hold for transactions and as an asset at each possible interest rate. Also note that a change in the nominal GDP—working through the transactions demand for money—will shift the total money demand curve. Specifically, an increase in nominal GDP will mean that the public will want to hold a larger amount of money for transactions purposes and this will shift the total money demand curve to the right. For example, if nominal GDP increases from $300 to $450 billion and we continue to suppose that the average dollar held for transactions is spent three times per year, then the transactions demand line will shift from $100 to $150 billion. Thus the total money demand curve will lie $50 billion further to the right at each possible interest rate

than formerly. Conversely, a decline in nominal GDP will shift the total money demand curve to the left.

THE MONEY MARKET

We can combine the demand for money with the supply of money to portray the **money market** and determine the equilibrium rate of interest. In Figure 13-2c we have drawn a vertical line, S_m, to represent the money supply. The money supply is shown as a vertical line because we assume our monetary authorities and financial institutions have provided the economy with some particular *stock* of money, such as the $M1$ total shown in Table 13-1. Just as in a product or resource market (Chapter 4), the intersection of money demand and money supply determines equilibrium price. The "price" in this case is the equilibrium interest rate, that is, the price paid for the use of money.

If disequilibrium existed in the money market, how would the money market achieve equilibrium? Consider Figure 13-3, which replicates Figure 13-2c and adds two alternative supply-of-money curves.

FIGURE 13-3 Restoring equilibrium in the money market

A decrease in the supply of money creates a temporary shortage of money in the money market. People and institutions attempt to gain more money by selling bonds. The supply of bonds therefore increases, which reduces bond prices and raises interest rates. At higher interest rates, people reduce the amount of money they wish to hold. Hence, the amount of money supplied and demanded once again is equal at the higher interest rate. An increase in the supply of money creates a temporary surplus of money, resulting in an increase in the demand for bonds and higher bond prices. Interest rates fall and equilibrium is reestablished in the money market.

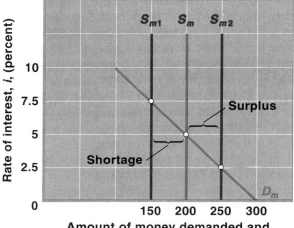

own demand-deposit liabilities increase. And, as we will see, it is on the basis of extra reserves that banks can lend and thereby earn interest income.

Actually, of course, the bank would not deposit *all* its cash in the Federal Reserve Bank. However, because (1) banks as a rule hold vault cash only in the amount of $1\frac{1}{2}$ or 2 percent of their total assets, and (2) vault cash can be counted as reserves, we assume that all the bank's cash is deposited in the Federal Reserve Bank and therefore constitutes the commercial bank's total reserves. The cumbersome process of adding two assets—"cash" and "deposits in the Federal Reserve Bank"—to determine "reserves" is thereby avoided.

At the completion of this transaction, the balance sheet of the Merchants and Farmers Bank will appear as follows:

BALANCE SHEET 4: WAHOO BANK			
Assets		**Liabilities and net worth**	
Cash	$ 0	Demand	
Reserves	110,000	deposits	$100,000
Property	240,000	Capital stock	250,000

Several points relevant to this transaction merit comment:

1 Excess Reserves A note on terminology: The amount by which the bank's **actual reserves** exceed its **required reserves** is the bank's **excess reserves.**

That is,

$$\frac{\text{Excess}}{\text{reserves}} = \frac{\text{actual}}{\text{reserves}} - \frac{\text{required}}{\text{reserves}}$$

In this case,

Actual reserves	$110,000
Required reserves	−20,000
Excess reserves	$90,000

The only reliable way of computing excess reserves is to multiply the bank's demand-deposit liabilities by the reserve ratio to obtain required reserves ($100,000 times 20 percent equals $20,000), then to subtract this figure from the actual reserves listed on the asset side of the bank's balance sheet.

To understand this process, you should compute excess reserves for the bank's balance sheet as it stands at the end of transaction 4, assuming that the reserve ratio is (1) 10 percent, (2) $33\frac{1}{3}$ percent, and (3) 50 percent.

Because the ability of a commercial bank to make loans depends on the existence of excess reserves, this concept is crucial in grasping the money-creating ability of the banking system.

2 Control What is the rationale underlying the requirement that member banks deposit a reserve in the Federal Reserve Bank of their district? One might think that the basic purpose of reserves is to enhance the liquidity of a bank and protect commercial bank depositors from losses. In other words, reserves would constitute a ready source of funds from which commercial banks can meet large and unexpected withdrawals of cash by depositors.

But this reasoning breaks down under close scrutiny. Although historically reserves were seen as a source of liquidity and therefore protection for depositors, *legal,* or required, reserves cannot be used to meet unexpected cash withdrawals. If the banker's nightmare should materialize—everyone with demand deposits in the bank appearing at once to demand these deposits in cash—the banker could not draw upon required reserves to meet this "bank panic" without violating the legal reserve ratio and incurring the wrath and penalties of the Federal Reserve authorities. In practice, legal reserves are *not* an available pool of liquid funds on which commercial banks can rely in times of emergency.[1] In fact, even if legal reserves were accessible to commercial banks, they would not be sufficient to meet a serious "run" on a bank. As already noted, reserves are *fractional;* that is, demand deposits may be 10 or 20 times as large as a bank's required reserves.

Commercial bank depositors must be protected by other means. As noted in Chapter 13, periodic bank

---

[1]This amendment must be added: As depositors withdraw cash from a commercial bank, the bank's demand-deposit liabilities will decline. This lowers the absolute amount of required reserves which the bank must keep, freeing some of the bank's actual reserves for use in meeting cash withdrawals by depositors. To illustrate: Suppose a commercial bank has reserves of $20 and demand-deposit liabilities of $100. If the legal reserve ratio is 20 percent, all the bank's reserves are required. Now, if depositors withdraw, say, $50 worth of their deposits as cash, the bank will only need $10 as required reserves to support the remaining $50 of demand-deposit liabilities. Thus $10 of the bank's actual reserves of $20 are no longer required. The bank can draw on this $10 in helping to meet the cash withdrawals of its depositors. And, of course, if a bank goes out of business, all its reserves will be available to pay depositors and other claimants.

examinations are an important device for promoting prudent commercial banking practices. And banking laws restrict banks as to the kinds of assets they may acquire; for example, banks are generally prohibited from buying common stocks. Furthermore, insurance funds administered by the Federal Deposit Insurance Corporation (FDIC) exist to insure individual deposits in banks and thrifts up to $100,000.

If the purpose of reserves is not to provide for commercial bank liquidity, what is their function? *Control* is the basic answer. Legal reserves permit the Board of Governors to influence the lending ability of commercial banks. Chapter 15 will examine how the Board of Governors can invoke certain policies which either increase or decrease commercial bank reserves and affect the ability of banks to grant credit. The objective is to prevent banks from *over*extending or *under*extending bank credit. To the degree that these policies are successful in influencing the volume of commercial bank credit, the Board of Governors can help the economy avoid the business fluctuations which lead to bank runs, bank failures, and collapse of the monetary system. In this indirect way—controlling commercial bank credit and thereby stabilizing the economy—reserves function to protect depositors, not as a source of liquidity. Another function of reserves is to facilitate the collection or "clearing" of checks.

3 Asset and Liability   Note there is an apparent accounting matter which transaction 4 entails. Specifically, *the reserve created in transaction 4 is an asset to the depositing commercial bank but a liability to the Federal Reserve Bank receiving it.* To the Wahoo bank the reserve is an asset; it is a claim which this commercial bank has against assets of another institution—the Federal Reserve Bank. To the Federal Reserve Bank this reserve is a liability, a claim which another institution—the Wahoo bank—has against it. Just as the demand deposit you get by depositing money in a commercial bank is an asset to you and a liability to your commercial bank, so the deposit or reserve which a commercial bank establishes by depositing money in a bankers' bank is an asset to the commercial bank and a liability to the Federal Reserve Bank. An understanding of this relationship is necessary in pursuing transaction 5.

Transaction 5: A Check Is Drawn Against the Bank
This is a significant and somewhat more complicated transaction. Suppose Clem Bradshaw, a Wahoo farmer who deposited a substantial portion of the $100,000 in

demand deposits which the Wahoo bank received in transaction 3, buys $50,000 worth of farm machinery from the Ajax Farm Implement Company of Beaver Crossing, Nebraska. Bradshaw very sensibly pays for this machinery by writing a $50,000 check, against his deposit in the Wahoo bank, to the Ajax company. We need to know (1) how this check is collected or cleared, and (2) the effect the collection of the check has on the balance sheets of the banks involved in the transaction.

To do this, we must consider the Wahoo bank (Bradshaw's bank), the Beaver Crossing bank (the Ajax Company's bank), and the Federal Reserve Bank of Kansas City.[2] For simplicity's sake, we deal only with changes which occur in those specific accounts affected by this transaction.

We trace this transaction in three related steps, keying the steps by letters to Figure 14-1.

a Bradshaw gives his $50,000 check, drawn against the Wahoo bank, to the Ajax company. Ajax deposits the check in its account with the Beaver Crossing bank. The Beaver Crossing bank increases Ajax's demand deposit by $50,000 when it deposits the check. Ajax is now paid off. Bradshaw is pleased with his new machinery, for which he has now paid.

b Now the Beaver Crossing bank has Bradshaw's check in its possession. This check is simply a claim against the assets of the Wahoo bank. The Beaver Crossing bank will collect this claim by sending this check—along with checks drawn on other banks—to the Federal Reserve Bank of Kansas City. Here a clerk will clear, or collect, this check for the Beaver Crossing bank by *increasing* its reserve in the Federal Reserve Bank by $50,000 and by *decreasing* the Wahoo bank's reserve by a like amount. The check is collected merely by making bookkeeping notations that the Wahoo bank's claim against the Federal Reserve Bank has been reduced by $50,000 and the Beaver Crossing bank's claim increased accordingly. Note these changes on the balance sheets in Figure 14-1.

c Finally, the Federal Reserve Bank sends the cleared check back to the Wahoo bank, and for the first time the Wahoo bank discovers that one of its depositors has drawn a check for $50,000 against his demand deposit. Accordingly, the Wahoo bank reduces Bradshaw's demand deposit by $50,000 and recognizes that the collection of this check has entailed a $50,000 de-

---

[2]Actually, the Omaha branch of the Federal Reserve Bank of Kansas City would handle the process of collecting this check.

For example, if the full-employment GDP is $490 billion, an increase in the money supply from $150 to $175 billion will reduce the interest rate from 8 to 6 percent, as indicated in Figure 15-2a, and increase investment from $20 to $25 billion, as shown in Figure 15-2b. This $5 billion upshift of the investment schedule from I_{g1} to I_{g2} in Figure 15-2c, subject to the relevant income multiplier of 4, will increase equilibrium GDP from $470 billion to the desired $490 billion full-employment level.

Effects of a Tight Money Policy

Conversely, if the original $470 billion GDP generates demand-pull inflation, the Federal Reserve will institute a *tight money policy.*

The Federal Reserve Board will direct Federal Reserve Banks to undertake some combination of the following actions: (1) sell government securities to depository instutitions and the public in the open market, (2) increase the legal reserve ratio, or (3) increase the discount rate. Banks then will discover that their reserves are too low to meet the legal reserve ratio. How can depository institutions meet the reserve ratio when their demand deposits are too high relative to their reserves? The answer is they will need to reduce their demand deposits by refraining from issuing new loans as old loans are paid back. This will shrink money supply and increase the interest rate. The higher interest

rate will reduce investment, decreasing aggregate expenditures and restraining demand-pull inflation.

To illustrate: If the full-employment, noninflationary GDP is $450 billion, an inflationary gap of $5 billion will exist. At the $470 billion level of GDP, planned investment exceeds saving—and therefore aggregate expenditures exceed domestic output—by $5 billion. A decline in the money supply from $150 to $125 billion will increase the interest rate from 8 to 10 percent in Figure 15-2a and reduce investment from $20 to $15 billion in Figure 15-2b. The consequent $5 billion downshift in Figure 15-2c's investment schedule from I_{g1} to I_{g3} will equate planned investment and saving—and therefore aggregate expenditures and domestic output—at the $450 billion GDP, thereby eliminating the initial $5 billion inflationary gap.

Table 15-3 summarizes the traditional or Keynesian interpretation of how monetary policy works. We recommend that you study this table carefully.

Refinements and Feedbacks

The components of Figure 15-2 allow us to (1) appreciate some of the factors which determine the effectiveness of monetary policy and (2) note the existence of a "feedback" or "circularity" problem which complicates monetary policy.

Policy Effectiveness Figure 15-2 indicates the magnitudes by which an easy or tight money policy will change the interest rate, investment, and the equilibrium GDP. These magnitudes are determined by the particular shapes of the demand for money and investment-demand curves. You might pencil in alternative curves to convince yourself that *the steeper the D_m curve, the larger will be the effect of any given change in the money supply on the equilibrium rate of interest. Furthermore, any given change in the interest rate will have a larger impact on investment—and hence on equilibrium GDP—the flatter the investment-demand curve.* In other words, a given change in quantity of money will be most effective when the demand for money curve is relatively steep and the investment-demand curve is relatively flat.

Conversely, a given change in the quantity of money will be relatively ineffective when the money-demand curve is flat and the investment-demand curve is steep. As we will find in Chapter 16, there is controversy as to the precise shapes of these curves and therefore the effectiveness of monetary policy.

TABLE 15-3 Monetary policy: Keynesian interpretation

(1) Easy money policy	(2) Tight money policy
Problem: unemployment and recession	**Problem: inflation**
Federal Reserve buys bonds, lowers reserve ratio, or lowers the discount rate	Federal reserve sells bonds, increases reserve ratio, or increases the discount rate
↓	↓
Money supply rises	Money supply falls
↓	↓
Interest rate falls	Interest rate rises
↓	↓
Investment spending increases	Investment spending decreases
↓	↓
Real GDP rises by a multiple of the increase in investment	Inflation declines

Feedback Effects   You may have sensed in Figure 15-2 a feedback or circularity problem which complicates monetary policy. The nature of this problem is as follows: By reading Figure 15-2 from left to right we discover that the interest rate, working through the investment-demand curve, is an important determinant of the equilibrium GDP. Now we must recognize that causation also runs the other way. The level of GDP is a determinant of the equilibrium interest rate. This link comes about because the transactions component of the money-demand curve depends directly on the level of nominal GDP.

How does this feedback from Figure 15-2c to 15-2a affect monetary policy? It means that the increase in the GDP which an easy money policy brings about will *increase* the demand for money, partially offsetting the interest-reducing effect of the easy money policy. Conversely, a tight money policy will reduce the nominal GDP. But this will *decrease* the demand for money and dampen the initial interest-increasing effect of the tight money policy. This feedback is also at the core of a policy dilemma, as we will see later.

Monetary Policy: AD-AS Framework

We can further refine our understanding of monetary policy by our aggregate demand–aggregate supply model. As with fiscal policy (Chapter 12), monetary policy is subject to constraints implicit in the aggregate supply curve. The cause-effect chain presented in Figure 15-2 and Table 15-3 indicates that monetary policy primarily affects investment spending and, therefore, real output and the price level. The AD-AS model, and the aggregate supply curve in particular, explains how the change in investment may be divided between changes in real output and changes in the price level.

Consider Figure 15-3. You may recall from Chapter 9 that in locating a given aggregate demand curve we assume that the money supply is fixed. An increase in the money supply lowers the interest rate and increases investment spending, which along with consumption, net exports, and government spending is one of the determinants of aggregate demand. The AD curve shifts rightward by a horizontal distance equal to the change in investment times the income multiplier. An increase in the money supply will permit consumers, firms, and government to purchase a larger real output at any given price level.

Conversely, by increasing the interest rate and reducing investment, a reduction in the money supply

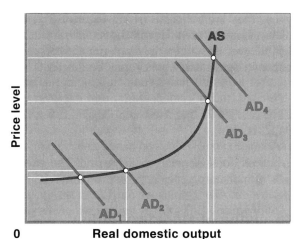

FIGURE 15-3   Monetary policy and the AD-AS model

An easy money policy in the near-horizontal Keynesian range of the aggregate supply curve has its primary effect on real output and employment rather than the price level. In the near-vertical classical range easy money would be inappropriate because it would cause inflation and bring about little or no increase in real output and employment. The effect of tight money on the economy is complicated by the downward stickiness of prices and wages.

shifts the AD curve leftward. The participants in the economy will not wish to buy as much real GDP at any given price level.

We thus note in Figure 15-3 that, if the economy is in the near-horizontal Keynesian or recession range of the aggregate supply curve, an easy money policy will shift the aggregate demand curve rightward as from AD_1 to AD_2 and have a large impact on real domestic output and employment and little or no effect on the price level.

But if the economy was already at or near to full employment, an increase in aggregate demand would have little or no effect on real output and employment. It would, however, cause a substantial increase in the price level. This is shown in Figure 15-3 by the shift of aggregate demand from AD_3 to AD_4 in the near-vertical range of the aggregate supply curve. Needless to say, an easy money policy would be inappropriate when the economy was at or near full employment. Figure 15-3 underscores the reason why: It would be highly inflationary.

You should analyze (1) an easy money policy in the intermediate range of aggregate supply and (2) a tight money policy in all three ranges. In analyzing tight money you also should distinguish between the case where prices are assumed to be flexible downward and

Alternative Views: Monetarism and Rational Expectations

The Keynesian conception of employment theory and stabilization policy, summarized in the discussion represented by Figure 15-4, has dominated the thinking of most economists in all market-oriented industrial economies since World War II. In the United States, Democratic and Republican administrations alike have basically accepted these precepts, if not the Keynesian label.

In the past two decades, however, this theory has been challenged by alternative conceptions of macroeconomics, particularly monetarism and rational expectations theory (RET). Each of these schools of macroeconomic thinking is led by its own set of distinguished scholars. Five Nobel Prize winners—Paul Samuelson, Franco Modigliani, and Robert Solow of MIT; James Tobin of Yale; and Lawrence Klein of Pennsylvania—are members of the older generation of Keynesian spokesmen. Younger economists whose scholarship fits within the Keynesian tradition include Alan Blinder of Princeton, Stanley Fisher of MIT, and Robert Gordon of Northwestern.

The University of Chicago's Milton Friedman is the intellectual leader of the *monetarist school*. Winner of the 1976 Nobel Prize in economics, Friedman's pioneering empirical and theoretical research asserts that the role of money in determining the level of economic activity and the price level is much greater than suggested by early Keynesian theory.

The leading contributors to the *rational expectations theory* (RET)—a facet of the so-called *new classical economics*—are Chicago's Robert Lucas, Stanford's Thomas Sargent, and Harvard's Robert Barro.

The primary purpose of this chapter is to present monetarism and RET and compare them with Keynesianism. In Chapter 17, we will continue the debate over stabilization policy along with analysis of the problem of simultaneous inflation and unemployment. In Chapter 18, issues surrounding the troublesome budget deficits and the public debt are explored. Part 4 concludes with Chapter 19, which examines the important problem of maintaining economic growth.

BASIC DIFFERENCES

We begin by contrasting Keynesian economics and monetarism. For comparison, it first will be useful to characterize Keynesianism and monetarism in their polar forms. In reality, we will discover the lines between many contemporary Keynesians and monetarists are not so clearly drawn. But at the extreme, Keynesians and monetarists have different views on the inherent stability of capitalistic economies. They also have important ideological differences, particularly on the role of government.

Keynesians: Instability and Intervention

Keynesians believe that capitalism and, more particularly, the free-market system suffer from inherent shortcomings. Most important for our discussion is the Keynesian contention that the private sector contains no mechanism to ensure macroeconomic stability. Imbalances of planned investment and saving *do* occur and the result is business fluctuations—periodic episodes of inflation or unemployment.

In particular, many markets are noncompetitive so that prices and wages are inflexible downward. Fluctuations in aggregate expenditures therefore affect primarily output and employment rather than prices. According to Keynesians, government can and should play a positive, activist role in stabilizing the economy; discretionary fiscal and monetary policies are needed to alleviate the economic ups and downs which would otherwise characterize the economy's course.

Monetarists: Stability and Laissez Faire

The **monetarist** view is that markets are highly competitive and that a competitive market system provides the economy with a high degree of macroeconomic stability. Monetarism has its intellectual roots in Chapter 10's classical economics which argues that the price and wage flexibility which competitive markets provide would cause fluctuations in aggregate expenditures to alter product and resource prices rather than output and employment. Thus the market system would provide substantial macroeconomic stability *were it not for governmental interference with the functioning of the economy.*

The problem, as the monetarists see it, is that government has fostered and promoted downward wage-price inflexibility through the minimum-wage law, pro-union legislation, farm price supports, pro-business monopoly legislation, and so forth. The free-market system could provide substantial macroeconomic stability, but, despite good intentions, government interference has undermined this capability. Furthermore, monetarists argue that government has contributed to the instability of the system—to the business cycle—through its clumsy and mistaken attempts to achieve greater stability through *discretionary* fiscal and monetary policies.

Given the above comments, it is no surprise that monetarists have a strong *laissez faire* or free-market orientation. Governmental decision making is held to be bureaucratic, inefficient, harmful to individual incentives, and frequently characterized by policy mistakes which destabilize the economy. Furthermore, centralized decision making by government inevitably erodes individual freedoms.[1] The public sector should be kept to the smallest possible size.

Keynesians and monetarists therefore are opposed in their conceptions of the private and public sectors. To the Keynesian, the instability of private investment causes the economy to be unstable. Government plays a positive role by applying appropriate stabilization medicine. To the monetarist, government has harmful effects on the economy. Government creates rigidities which weaken the capacity of the market system to provide substantial stability and it embarks on monetary and fiscal measures which, although well intentioned, aggravate the very instability they are designed to cure.

THE BASIC EQUATIONS

Keynesian economics and monetarism each build their analysis upon specific equations.

The Aggregate Expenditures Equation

As indicated in previous chapters, Keynesian economics focuses on aggregate spending and its components. Recall that the basic Keynesian equation is:

$$C_a + I_g + X_n + G = \text{GDP} \tag{1}$$

---

[1]Friedman's philosophy is effectively expounded in two of his books: *Capitalism and Freedom* (Chicago: The University of Chicago Press, 1962); and with Rose Friedman, *Free to Choose* (New York: Harcourt Brace Jovanovich, 1980).

This theory says that the aggregate amount of after-tax consumption, gross investment, net exports, and government spending determines the total value of the goods and services sold. In equilibrium, $C_a + I_g + X_n + G$ (aggregate expenditures) is equal to GDP (domestic output).

Equation of Exchange

Monetarism, as the label suggests, focuses on money. The fundamental equation of monetarism is the **equation of exchange:**

$$MV = PQ \tag{2}$$

where M is the supply of money; V is the income **velocity of money,** that is, the number of times per year the average dollar is spent on final goods and services; P is the price level or, more specifically, the average price at which each unit of physical output is sold; and Q is the physical volume of goods and services produced.

The label "equation of exchange" is easily understood. The left side, MV, represents the total amount *spent* by purchasers of output, while the right side, PQ, represents the total amount *received* by sellers of that output.

> The difference between the two approaches can be compared with two ways of looking at the flow of water through a sewer pipe—say, at the rate of 6000 gallons per hour. A neo-Keynesian investigator might say that the flow of 6000 gallons an hour consisted of 3000 gallons an hour from a paper mill, 2000 gallons an hour from an auto plant, and 1000 gallons an hour from a shopping center. A monetarist investigator might say that the sewer flow of 6000 gallons an hour consisted of an average of 200 gallons in the sewer at any one time with a complete turnover of the water 30 times every hour.[2]

Both the Keynesian and monetarist approaches are useful and insightful in understanding macroeconomics. In fact, the Keynesian equation can be readily "translated" into monetarist terms. According to the monetarist approach, total spending is the supply of money multiplied by its velocity. In short, MV is the monetarist counterpart of equilibrium $C_a + I_g + X_n + G$. Because MV is the total amount spent on final goods in one year, it is necessarily equal to nominal GDP. Furthermore, nominal GDP is the sum of the physical outputs of various goods and services *(Q)* multiplied

by their respective prices *(P)*. That is, GDP = PQ. Thus, we can restate the Keynesian $C_a + I_g + X_n + G$ = GDP equation in nominal terms as the monetarist equation of exchange, $MV = PQ$.[3] The two approaches are two ways of looking at much the same thing. But the critical question remains: Which theory more accurately portrays macroeconomics and therefore is the better basis for economic policy?

Spotlight on Money

The Keynesian equation puts money in a secondary role. Indeed, the Keynesian conception of monetary policy entails a rather lengthy transmission mechanism (Chapter 15). This mechanism is shown in Figure 16-1a. A change in monetary policy alters the nation's supply of money. The change in the money supply affects the interest rate, which affects the level of investment. When the economy initially is operating at less than capacity, changes in investment affect nominal GDP (= PQ) by changing real output *(Q)* through the income multiplier effect. Alternatively, when the economy is achieving full employment, changes in investment affect nominal GDP by altering the price level *(P)*.

Keynesians contend there are many loose links in this cause-effect chain with the result that monetary policy is an uncertain and relatively weak stabilization tool compared with fiscal policy. Some of the weaknesses of monetary policy were cited in Chapter 15. For example, recall from Figure 15-2 that monetary policy will be relatively ineffective if the demand for money curve is flat and the investment-demand curve is steep. Also, the investment-demand curve may shift adversely so that the impact of a change in the interest rate on investment spending is muted or offset. Nor will an easy money policy be very effective if banks and other depository institutions are not anxious to lend or the public eager to borrow.

Monetarists believe that money and monetary policy are much more important in determining the level of economic activity than do the Keynesians. *Monetarists hold that changes in the money supply are the single most important factor in determining the levels of output, employment, and prices.* They see a different cause-effect chain between the supply of money and the level

[2]Werner Sichel and Peter Eckstein, *Basic Economic Concepts* (Chicago: Rand McNally College Publishing Company, 1974), p. 344.

[3]Technical footnote: There is an important conceptual difference between the Keynesian $C_a + I_g + X_n + G$ and the MV component of the equation of exchange. Specifically, the former indicates planned or *intended* expenditures, which equal actual expenditures only in equilibrium. MV, on the other hand, reflects *actual* spending.

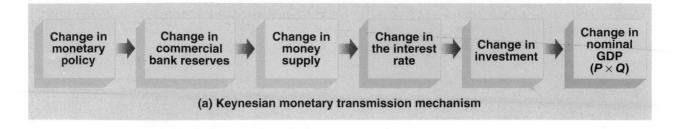

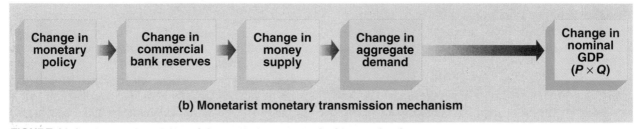

FIGURE 16-1 Alternative views of the monetary transmission mechanism

Keynesians (a) emphasize the roles of interest rates and investment spending in explaining how changes in the money supply affect nominal GDP. On the other hand, monetarists (b) contend that changes in the money supply cause direct changes in aggregate demand and thereby changes in nominal GDP.

of economic activity than the Keynesian model suggests. Rather than limiting the effect of an increase in money to bond purchases and consequent declines in the interest rate, monetarists theorize that an increase in the money supply drives up the demand for all assets—real or financial—as well as for current output. Under conditions of full employment, the prices of all these items will rise. Monetarists also contend that the velocity of money is stable—meaning that it does not fluctuate wildly and does not change in response to a change in the money supply itself. Thus, changes in the money supply will have a predictable effect on the level of nominal GDP ($= PQ$). More precisely, an increase in M will increase P or Q, or some combination of both P and Q; a decrease in M will produce the opposite effects.

Monetarists believe that, although a change in M may cause short-run changes in real output and employment as market adjustments occur, the long-run impact of a change in M will be on the price level. Monetarists think the private economy is inherently stable and tends to operate at the full-employment level of output. The exact level of that full-employment output depends on such "real" factors as the quantity and quality of labor, capital, and land and upon technology (Chapter 19). For present purposes the point is that, if Q is constant at the economy's capacity output, then changes in M will lead to changes in P.

Monetarism implies a more direct transmission mechanism than does the Keynesian model. Observe in Figure 16-1b that monetarists view changes in the money supply as producing direct changes in aggregate demand which alter nominal GDP. We know from previous discussion that monetarists contend that changes in the money supply affect all components of aggregate demand, not just investment. Furthermore, changes in aggregate demand allegedly affect nominal GDP in the long run primarily through changes in the price level, not through changes in real output.

VELOCITY: STABLE OR UNSTABLE?

A critical theoretical issue in the Keynesian–monetarist debate centers on the question of whether the velocity of money, V, is stable. Note that, as used here, the word "stable" is *not* synonymous with the word "constant." Monetarists are well aware that velocity is higher today than in 1945. Shorter pay periods, greater use of credit cards, and faster means of making payments have increased velocity since 1945. These factors have enabled people over the years to reduce their cash and checkbook holdings relative to the size of the nominal GDP.

What monetarists mean when they say that velocity is stable is that the factors which alter velocity change gradually and predictably. Changes in velocity from one year to the next thus can be easily anticipated. Moreover, velocity does *not* change in response to changes in the supply of money itself.

If velocity is stable, the equation of exchange tells us that monetarists are indeed correct in claiming that a direct predictable relationship exists between the money supply and nominal GDP $(= PQ)$.

Suppose M is 100, V is 1, and nominal GDP is 100. Also assume velocity increases annually at a stable rate of 2 percent. Using the equation of exchange, we can predict that a 5 percent annual growth rate of the money supply will result in about a 7 percent increase in nominal GDP. M will increase from 100 to 105, V will rise from 1 to 1.02, and nominal GDP will increase from 100 to about 107 $(= 105 \times 1.02)$.

But if V is not stable, the Keynesian contention that money plays only a secondary role in macroeconomics is valid. If V is variable and unpredictable from one period to another, the link between M and PQ will be loose and uncertain. In particular, a steady growth of M will not necessarily translate into a steady growth of nominal GDP.

Monetarists: *V* Is Stable

What rationale do monetarists offer for their contention that V is stable? Basically, they argue that people have a stable desire to hold money relative to holding other financial and real assets and buying current output. The factors which determine the amount of money people and businesses wish to hold at any given time are independent of the supply of money. Most importantly, the amount of money the public will want to hold will depend on the level of nominal GDP.

Consider a simple example. Suppose that, when the level of nominal GDP is $400 billion, the amount of money the public wants or *desires* to hold to negotiate the purchase of this output is $100 billion. (This implies that V is 4.) If we further assume that the *actual* supply of money is $100 billion, we can say that the economy is in equilibrium with respect to money; the *actual* amount of money supplied equals the amount the public *desires* to hold.

In the monetarist view an increase in the money supply of, say, $10 billion will upset this equilibrium in that the public will now be holding more money or liquidity than it wants to hold; the actual amount of money being held exceeds the desired amount. The

natural reaction of the public (households and businesses) is to restore its desired balance of money relative to other items such as stocks and bonds, factories and equipment, houses and automobiles, and clothing and toys. The public has more money than it wants; the way to get rid of money is to buy things. But one person's spending of money leaves more cash in someone else's checkable deposit or billfold. That person, too, tries to "spend down" excess cash balances.

The collective attempt to reduce cash balances will increase aggregate demand, which will boost the nominal GDP. Because velocity is 4—the typical dollar is spent four times per year—nominal GDP must rise by $40 billion. When nominal GDP reaches $440 billion, the *actual* money supply of $110 billion again will be the amount which the public *desires* to hold, and by definition equilibrium will be reestablished. Spending on goods and services will increase until nominal GDP has increased sufficiently to restore the original equilibrium relationship between nominal GDP and the money supply. In fact, the relationship GDP/M defines V. A stable relationship between GDP and M means a stable V.

Keynesians: *V* Is Unstable

In the Keynesian view the velocity of money is variable and unpredictable. This position can best be understood in reference to the Keynesian conception of the demand for money (Chapter 13). The Keynesian view is that money is demanded, not only to use in negotiating transactions, but also to hold as an asset. Money demanded for *transactions* purposes will be "active" money, which is changing hands and circulating through the income-expenditures stream. In other words, transactions dollars have some positive velocity; the average transactions dollar may be spent, say, six times per year and thereby negotiate $6 worth of transactions. In this case V is 6 for each transactions dollar.

But money demanded and held as an *asset* is "idle" money; these dollars do *not* flow through the income-expenditures stream and therefore their velocity is zero. It follows that the overall velocity of the entire money supply will depend on how it is divided between transactions and asset balances. The greater the relative importance of "active" transactions balances, the larger will be V. Conversely, the greater the relative significance of "idle" asset balances, the smaller will be V.

Given this framework, Keynesians discredit the monetarist transmission mechanism—the allegedly

alleviate output reductions resulting from cost-push inflation. These shifts in short-run aggregate supply frustrate attainment of full employment and increase the price level.

Alternatively, suppose that government recognizes this policy trap and decides *not* to increase aggregate demand from AD to AD'. Instead, government implicitly decides to allow a cost-push induced recession to run its course. Widespread layoffs, plant shutdowns, and business failures eventually will occur. At some point there will be sufficient slack in labor markets to reduce nominal wages and thus undo the initial leftward shift of short-run aggregate supply. Restated, a severe recession will in time shift the short-run aggregate supply from AS_2 back to AS_1. The price level will therefore return to P_1 at a and the potential level of output will be restored along long-run aggregate supply AS_{LR}.

Two generalizations emerge from our analysis:

1 *If government attempts to maintain full employment under conditions of cost-push inflation, an inflationary spiral is likely to occur.*

2 *If government takes a hands-off approach to cost-push inflation, a recession will probably occur.* Although the recession can be expected eventually to undo the initial rise in production costs, the economy in the meanwhile will experience high unemployment and a loss of real output.

QUICK REVIEW 17-2

◆ *The short-run aggregate supply curve has a positive slope because nominal wages are assumed to be fixed as the price level changes.*

◆ *The long-run aggregate supply curve is vertical because input prices eventually respond fully to changes in the price level.*

◆ *In the short run, demand-pull inflation will increase both the price level and domestic output; in the long run, only the price level will rise.*

◆ *Cost-push inflation creates a policy dilemma for government: If it engages in an expansionary stabilization policy to increase output, an inflationary spiral may ensue; if it does nothing, a recession may occur.*

Other Options   Given our experiences with cost-push inflation and the difficulties in using demand-management policies to deal with it (Figure 17-7b), government has sought out additional policy options.

In terms of Figure 17-7b these policies are designed to prevent the aggregate supply curve from shifting leftward as from AS_1 to AS_2. Or, alternatively, if the economy already is experiencing stagflation at the intersection of AD and AS_2, the goal would be to shift the aggregate supply curve rightward toward AS_1. Similarly, in terms of the Phillips Curve (whether conceived of as a downsloping curve or a vertical line) the policy goal is to shift the curve leftward to provide a better inflation rate–unemployment rate tradeoff for society. In particular, economists who interpreted the data points for the 1970s and 1980s in Figure 17-3 as reflecting rightward shifts of the Phillips Curve sought means of shifting the curve back to the more desirable position which seemed relevant for the 1960s.

Generally speaking, three categories of policies have been proposed: (1) market policies; (2) wage-price, or incomes, policies; and (3) the set of policies prescriptions known as "supply-side economics."

MARKET POLICIES

Two kinds of **market policies** can be distinguished. *Employment and training policy* is intended to reduce or eliminate imbalances and bottlenecks in labor markets. A *procompetition policy* attempts to reduce the market power of unions and large corporations. Recall that labor market imbalances and market power constitute the traditional logic underlying the Phillips Curve.

Employment and Training Policy

The goal of employment and training policy is to improve the efficiency of labor markets so that any given level of aggregate demand will be associated with a lower level of unemployment. In other words, the purpose of employment and training policy is to achieve a better matching of workers to jobs, thereby reducing labor market imbalances or bottlenecks. Several different kinds of programs will provide a better matching of workers to jobs. Three of these are vocational training, job information, and antidiscrimination programs.

1 Vocational Training   Programs of vocationally oriented education and training will permit marginal and displaced workers to be more quickly reemployed. Various government programs provide for both institutional and on-the-job training for the unemployed, for disadvantaged youth, and for older workers whose skills are meager or obsolete.

2 Job Information   A second type of employment and training policy is concerned with improving the flow of job information between unemployed workers and potential employers and with enhancing the geographic mobility of workers. For example, a number of attempts have been made recently to modernize the United States Employment Service to increase its effectiveness in bringing job seekers and employers together.

3 Nondiscrimination   Another facet of employment and training policy is concerned with reducing or eliminating artificial obstacles to employment. Discrimination has been an important roadblock in matching workers and jobs; it is a basic factor in explaining why unemployment rates for blacks are roughly twice as high as for whites. The Civil Rights Act of 1964 attempts to improve the use of labor resources by removing discrimination because of race, religion, gender, or ethnic background as an obstacle to employment or union membership.

Procompetition Policy

A second avenue for improving the tradeoff between the unemployment rate and rate of inflation is to reduce the monopoly or market power of unions and businesses. This policy aims at reducing the monopoly power of unions so that they will be less able to push up wage rates ahead of average productivity increases. Similarly, more competition in the product market will reduce the power of large corporations to raise prices.

How can the economy be made more competitive? One recommendation is to apply existing antitrust (antimonopoly) laws much more vigorously to large corporations. Another is to remove remaining legal restrictions on entry to certain regulated industries such as communications, transportation, and power generation and distribution. Similarly, elimination of tariffs and other restrictions on foreign imports will increase competitiveness of American markets.

On the labor front, it is periodically argued that the antimonopoly laws should be applied to unions or that collective bargaining should be less centralized. Also recall that Chapter 10's Last Word outlined a proposal to link a portion of wages to profits in order to make wages more flexible downward. The purpose is to shift the burden of a decline in demand from unemployment to wages.

WAGE-PRICE (INCOMES) POLICIES

A second approach accepts the existence of monopoly power and labor market imbalances as more-or-less inevitable facts of economic life, and seeks to alter the behavior of labor and product-market monopolists to make their wage and price decisions more compatible with the twin goals of full employment and price level stability. Although they differ primarily in degree, it is meaningful to distinguish between **wage-price guideposts** and **wage-price controls.** Guideposts and controls differ in that guideposts rely on the voluntary cooperation of labor and business, whereas controls have the force of law.

Wage-price guideposts and wage-price controls are sometimes called **incomes policies.** The reason for this label is that a person's real income—the amount of goods and services obtained with one's nominal income—depends on the size of that nominal income and the prices of the goods and services bought. Guideposts and controls are designed to constrain both nominal incomes and prices paid, and thus affect real incomes.

There have been five periods in recent history when incomes policies have been applied:

1   Comprehensive controls during World War II
2   Selective controls during the Korean war in the early 1950s
3   Guideposts during the early 1960s under the Kennedy–Johnson administrations
4   The Nixon administration's wage-price controls of 1971–1974
5   The Carter administration's guideposts of 1978

Our discussion will center on the guideposts of the early 1960s and the 1971–1974 controls. These episodes of incomes policies are of more than historical interest; they highlight the basic principles of incomes policies. Governments in several foreign countries experiencing rapid inflation have implemented similar policies within the past decade. Also, invariably there are calls for incomes policies in the United States when inflation begins to approach double-digit levels.

Kennedy–Johnson Guideposts

In the period from 1962 to 1966, the Kennedy and Johnson administrations set forth "guideposts for noninflationary wage and price behavior." These were a set of wage and price rules which, if followed by labor and management, would provide some assurance that the government's plan to stimulate the economy would be translated into increases in real domestic output and employment, rather than dissipated in price increases.

1 Wage Guidepost *The basic wage guidepost was that nominal wage rates in all industries should rise in accordance with the rate of increase in labor productivity for the nation as a whole.* Referring back to equation (1) in our earlier discussion of the productivity decline, we know that nominal wage rate increases equaling the rate of productivity growth will be noninflationary. That is, unit labor costs will be unchanged and there will be no reason for producers to raise prices.

Of course, the productivity increases of some industries will exceed, while those of others will fall short of, the overall or average increase in national productivity. For an industry whose productivity rises by less than national productivity, unit labor costs will rise. For example, if national productivity rose by 3 percent while productivity rose by only 1 percent in industry X, then, with nominal wage rates increasing by 3 percent, that industry would experience approximately a 2 percent *increase* in its unit labor costs. Conversely, if productivity rose by 5 percent in industry Y, then the 3 percent increase in nominal wages would *decrease* its unit labor costs by about 2 percent.

2 Price Guidepost *The basic price guidepost was that prices should change to compensate for changes in unit labor costs.* In industries whose rate of productivity was equal to the national average, prices would be constant because unit labor costs would be unchanged. For industries whose productivity rose by less than the national average, prices could be increased enough to cover the resulting increase in unit labor costs. Industry X, cited earlier, could increase its prices by 2 percent. For industries where productivity increases exceeded the national average, prices would be expected to fall in accordance with the resulting decline in unit labor costs. Industry Y should lower its prices by 2 percent. These price increases and decreases would cancel out and leave the overall price level unchanged.

Nixon Wage-Price Controls

In 1971 controls were put into effect by President Nixon. Faced with stagflation, taxes were cut by some $7 to $8 billion to stimulate aggregate demand and, it was hoped, boost output and employment. The prob-

lem, however, was to prevent this expansionary fiscal policy from being translated into additional inflation rather than into increases in employment and real output. The Nixon response was to order a freeze on wages, prices, and rents. The President's executive order made it illegal to (1) increase wages or salaries, (2) charge more for a product than the highest price charged in the 30-day period prior to the freeze, and (3) raise the rents landlords charged tenants. The Nixon freeze was followed by formal wage and price controls which set maximum legal limits on wage and price hikes. These controls were phased out in 1974, which was in time to reinforce the stagflation already being generated by OPEC, agricultural shortfalls, and depreciation of the dollar.

The Wage-Price Policy Debate

There has been heated and prolonged debate in the United States on the desirability and efficacy of incomes policies. The debate centers on two points.

1 Workability and Compliance Critics argue that the voluntary *guideposts* approach will fail because it asks business and labor leaders to abandon their primary functions and forgo the goals of maximum profits and higher wages. A union leader will not gain favor with the rank and file by reducing wage demands; nor does a corporate official become endeared to stockholders by bypassing potentially profitable price increases. For these reasons little voluntary cooperation can be expected from labor and management.

Wage and price *controls* have the force of law and, therefore, labor and management can be forced to obey. Nevertheless, problems of enforcement and compliance can be severe, particularly if wage and price controls are quite comprehensive and maintained for an extended time. *Black markets*—illegal markets in which prices exceed their legal maximums— become commonplace under these circumstances. Furthermore, firms can circumvent price controls by lowering the quality or size of their product. If the price of a candy bar is frozen at 40 cents, its price can be effectively doubled by reducing its size by one-half!

Proponents of incomes policies point out that inflation is frequently fueled by *inflationary expectations.* Workers demand unusually large nominal wage increases because they expect future inflation to diminish their real incomes. Employers acquiesce in these demands because they, too, anticipate an inflationary environment in which higher costs can be easily passed along to consumers. A strong wage-price control program can quell inflationary expectations by convincing labor and management that the government does not intend to allow inflation to continue. Therefore, workers do not need anticipatory wage increases. And firms are put on notice that they may not be able to shift higher costs to consumers via price increases. Expectations of inflation can generate inflation; wage-price controls can undermine those expectations.

2 Allocative Efficiency and Rationing Opponents of incomes policies contend that effective guideposts or controls interfere with the allocative function of the market system. Specifically, effective price controls prohibit the market system from making necessary price adjustments. If an increase in the demand for some product should occur, its price could *not* rise to signal society's wish for more output and therefore more resources in this area of production.

Also, controls strip the market mechanism of its rationing function, that is, of its ability to equate quantity demanded and quantity supplied, and product shortages will result. Which buyers are to obtain the product and which are to do without? The product can be rationed on a first-come-first-served basis or by favoritism. But this is highly arbitrary and inequitable; those first in line or those able to cultivate a friendship with the seller get as much of the product as they want while others get none at all. Government may therefore have to impartially ration the product to all consumers by issuing ration coupons to buyers on an equitable basis. But governmental rationing contributes to the problem of compliance noted earlier.

Defenders of incomes policies respond as follows: If effective guideposts or controls are imposed on a competitive economy, then in time the resulting rigidities will impair allocative efficiency. But it is *not* correct to assume that resource allocation will be efficient in the absence of a wage-price policy. Cost-push inflation allegedly arises *because* big labor and big businesses possess monopoly power and consequently have the capacity to distort the allocation of resources.

Effectiveness

How effective have incomes policies been? The evidence, in a word, is "mixed." The use of direct wage-price controls during World War II did contain—or at least defer—the serious inflation which would other-

wise have occurred. On the other hand, the 1962 wage and price guideposts did little to arrest the growing demand-pull inflation of the mid-1960s. Additionally, the wage and price controls of 1971–1974 not only failed to achieve their purposes, but worsened stagflation by causing inefficiencies in the allocation of resources.

SUPPLY-SIDE ECONOMICS

In the past decade or so, some economists have stressed low growth of productivity and real output as basic causes of stagflation and the overall poor performance of our economy. These **supply-side economists** assert that mainstream economics does not come to grips with stagflation because its focal point is aggregate demand.

Supply-side economists contend that changes in aggregate supply—shifts in the long-run aggregate supply curve—must be recognized as an "active" force in determining both the levels of inflation *and* unemployment. Economic disturbances can be generated on the supply side, as well as on the demand side. Most importantly for present purposes, by emphasizing the demand side, mainstream economists have neglected certain supply-side policies which might alleviate stagflation.

Tax-Transfer Disincentives

Supply-side economists contend that the spectacular growth of our tax-transfer system allegedly has negatively affected incentives to work, invest, innovate, and assume entrepreneurial risks. In short, the tax-transfer system has eroded the economy's productivity and the decline in efficiency has meant higher production costs and stagflation. The argument is that higher taxes will reduce the after-tax rewards of workers and producers, making work, innovations, investing, and risk bearing less financially attractive. Supply-side economists stress the importance of *marginal tax rates* because these rates are most relevant to decisions to undertake *additional* work and *additional* saving and investing.

Incentives to Work Supply-siders argue that how long and how hard individuals work depends on how much additional *after-tax* earnings they derive from this extra work. To induce more work—to increase aggregate inputs of labor—marginal tax rates on earned incomes should be reduced. Lower marginal tax rates increase the attractiveness of work and simultaneously increase the opportunity cost of leisure. Thus, individuals will choose to substitute work for leisure. This increase in productive effort can occur in many ways: by increasing the number of hours worked per day or week; by encouraging workers to postpone retirement; by inducing more people to enter the labor force; by making people willing to work harder; and by discouraging long periods of unemployment.

Transfer Disincentives Supply-side economists also contend that the existence of a wide variety of public transfer programs has eroded incentives to work. Unemployment compensation and welfare programs have made the loss of one's job less of an economic crisis than formerly. The fear of being unemployed and therefore the need to be a disciplined, productive worker is simply less acute than previously. Indeed, most transfer programs are structured to discourage work. Our social security and aid to families with dependent children programs are such that transfers are reduced sharply if recipients earn income. These programs encourage recipients *not* to be productive by imposing a "tax" in the form of a loss of transfer benefits on those who work.

Incentives to Save and Invest The rewards to saving and investing have also been reduced by high marginal tax rates. Assume you save $1000 at 10 percent, so that you earn $100 interest per year. If your marginal tax rate is 40 percent, your after-tax interest earnings will fall to $60 and the after-tax interest rate you receive is only 6 percent. While you might be willing to save (forgo current consumption) for a 10 percent return on your saving, you might prefer to consume when the return is only 6 percent.

Saving, remember, is the prerequisite of investment. Thus supply-side economists recommend lower marginal tax rates on saving. They also call for lower taxes on investment income to ensure there are ready investment outlets for the economy's enhanced pool of saving. We saw in Chapter 10 that one of the determinants of investment spending is the *after-tax* net profitability of that spending.

To summarize, lower marginal tax rates encourage saving and investing to the end that workers will find themselves equipped with more and technologically superior machinery and equipment. Therefore, labor productivity will rise, and as equation (1) reminds us, this will hold down increases in unit labor costs and the price level.

Laffer Curve

According to supply-side economics, reductions of marginal tax rates will shift Figure 17-4's aggregate supply curve from AS_2 toward AS_1, alleviating inflation, increasing real output, and reducing the unemployment rate. Moreover, according to supply-side economists such as Arthur Laffer, lower tax *rates* are compatible with constant or even enlarged tax *revenues*. Supply-side tax cuts need not cause Federal budget deficits.

This position is based on the **Laffer Curve**, which, as shown in Figure 17-8, depicts the relationship between tax rates and tax revenues. The idea is that, as tax rates increase from zero to 100 percent, tax revenue will increase from zero to some maximum level (at m) and then decline to zero. Tax revenues decline beyond some point because higher tax rates presumably discourage economic activity and therefore the tax base (domestic output and national income) diminishes. This is easiest to envision at the extreme where tax rates are 100 percent. Tax revenues here are reduced to zero because the 100 percent confiscatory tax rate has brought production to a halt. A 100 percent tax rate applied to a tax base of zero yields no revenue.

In the early 1980s Professor Laffer contended we were at some point such as n where tax rates were so high that production had been so discouraged that tax revenues were below the maximum at m. If the economy is at n, then lower tax *rates* are quite compatible

FIGURE 17-8 The Laffer Curve

The Laffer Curve suggests that up to point m higher tax rates will result in larger tax revenues. But still higher rates will adversely affect incentives to produce, reducing the size of the national income tax base to the extent that tax revenues decline. It follows that, if tax rates are above $0m$, tax reductions will result in increases in tax revenues. The controversial empirical question is to determine at what actual tax rates will tax revenues begin to fall.

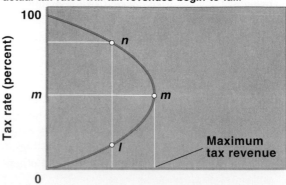

with constant tax *revenues*. In Figure 17-8 we simply lower tax rates, moving from point *n* to point *l*, and government will collect an unaltered amount of tax revenue. Laffer's reasoning is that lower tax rates will stimulate incentives to work, save and invest, innovate, and accept business risks, thus triggering an expansion of domestic output and national income. This enlarged tax base will sustain tax revenues even though tax rates are lower.

According to supply-side economists, a budget deficit can be avoided in two additional ways.

1 Less Tax Evasion   Tax avoidance and evasion will decline. High marginal tax rates prompt taxpayers to avoid taxes through various tax shelters (for example, buying municipal bonds on which interest is tax free) or to conceal income from the Internal Revenue Service. Lower tax rates will reduce the inclination to engage in such activities.

2 Reduced Transfers   The stimulus to production and employment which a tax cut provides will reduce government transfer payments. For example, more job opportunities will reduce unemployment compensation payments and thereby reduce a budget deficit.

Criticisms of the Laffer Curve

The Laffer Curve and its supply-side policy implications have been subject to much criticism.

1 Taxes: Incentives and Time   A fundamental criticism has to do with the sensitivity of economic incentives to changes in tax rates. Skeptics point out that there is ample empirical evidence that the impact of a tax reduction on incentives will be small, of uncertain direction, and relatively slow to emerge. For example, with respect to work incentives, studies indicate that decreases in tax rates lead some people to work more, but others to work less. Those who work more are enticed by the higher after-tax pay; they substitute work for leisure because the opportunity cost of leisure has increased. Those who work less do so because the higher after-tax pay increases their ability to "buy leisure." They can meet their after-tax income goals while working fewer hours.

Furthermore, any positive effects which tax cuts have on real output and therefore tax revenues will be slow to appear:

> In the long run, most tax changes that increase total capital formation and thereby raise the rate of economic growth will eventually raise (tax) revenues. However, the long run is likely to be very long in-

deed since a major proportionate increase in savings and investment will cause only a tiny proportionate increase in the capital stock every year, and it is the latter which is important to economic growth. Consequently, the long run must be measured in terms of decades rather than years.[1]

2 Reinforcing Inflation   Most economists contend that demand-side effects of a tax cut exceed supply-side effects. Hence, tax cuts undertaken when the economy is expanding or at its full-employment output will generate large increases in aggregate demand which will overwhelm any increase in aggregate supply. Large budget deficits and inflation will result.

3 Position on Curve   Skeptics note that the Laffer Curve is merely a logical proposition asserting there must be some level of tax rates between zero and 100 percent at which tax revenues will be maximized. Economists of all persuasions can agree with this statement. But the issue of where a particular economy is located on the Laffer Curve is an empirical question. If we assume—as Laffer did in the early 1980s—that we are at *n* in Figure 17-8, then tax rate cuts will increase tax revenues. But critics contend that the economy's location on the Laffer Curve is undocumented and unknown. If the economy is actually at any point southwest of *m*, then tax reductions will reduce tax revenues and create budget deficits.

Other Supply-Side Tenets

Although removing tax-transfer disincentives is the centerpiece of supply-side economics, there are two additional tenets worth noting.

1 The Tax "Wedge"   Supply-side economists note that the historical growth of the public sector has increased the nation's tax bill both absolutely and as a percentage of the national income. In the Keynesian view, higher taxes represent a withdrawal of purchasing power from the economy and therefore have a contractionary or anti-inflationary effect (Chapter 12). Supply-siders argue to the contrary: They contend that sooner or later most taxes are incorporated into business costs and shifted forward to consumers in the form of higher prices. Taxes, in short, entail a cost-push effect.

Supply-side economists point out that in the 1970s

---

[1]Testimony of R. G. Penner in Senate Budget Committee, *Leading Economists' Views of Kemp–Roth* (Washington, 1978), p. 139.

and 1980s state and local governments negotiated substantial increases in sales and excise taxes and that the Federal government has boosted dramatically payroll (social security) taxes. These are precisely the kinds of taxes incorporated in business costs and reflected in higher prices. Such taxes constitute a "wedge" between the costs of resources and the price of a product. As government has grown, this **tax wedge** has increased, shifting the aggregate supply curve leftward.

2 Overregulation Supply-siders also claim that government involvement in the economy in the form of regulation has also had adverse effects on productivity and costs. Two points should be noted in this regard.
1   It is held that "industrial" regulation—government regulation of specific industries such as transportation or communications—frequently has the effect of providing firms in the regulated industry with a kind of legal monopoly or cartel. Governmental regulation protects such firms from competition with the result that these firms are less efficient and incur higher costs of production than they would otherwise.
2   The "social" regulation of industry has increased substantially in the past two decades. New government regulations have been imposed on industry in response to the problems of pollution, product safety, worker health and safety, and equal access to job opportunities. Supply-side economists point out that social regulation has greatly increased costs of doing business. The overall impact of both varieties of regulation is that costs and prices are higher and there is a tendency toward stagflation.

Reaganomics: The Program

The elements of supply-side economics just outlined provided the intellectual underpinnings for the economic policies of the Reagan administration (1981–1988). Specifically, **Reaganomics** consisted of the following four policies:
1   The growth of the Federal government was restrained by freezes and cuts in spending on social and welfare programs. Defense spending, however, was increased significantly.
2   Substantial reductions in government regulation of private businesses occurred.
3   The administration encouraged the Federal Reserve System to hold the growth rate of the money supply to a rate considered to be noninflationary, yet sufficiently expansive to allow for economic growth.
4   Personal and corporate income tax rates were reduced sharply beginning in 1981. The tax system was

reformed in 1986 so that the marginal tax rate on income of wealthy taxpayers fell from 50 percent to 28 percent.

Reaganomics: Did It Work?

The real world is an imperfect laboratory for judging the success of a vast socioeconomic experiment such as Reaganomics. Also, Congress did not accept all the expenditure reductions which the Reagan administration requested in its program. Finally, the Reagan years witnessed significant declines in inflation and interest rates, a record-long peacetime economic expansion, and attainment of full employment. Having acknowledged these points, it is nevertheless fair to say that, *as such,* supply-side economics largely failed to accomplish its goals.

The facts are these:
1   Any immediate output effects of the Reagan tax cuts were overwhelmed by the tight money policy being undertaken by the Federal Reserve to reduce the then-existing rapid inflation. The economy fell into severe back-to-back recessions in 1980–1982.
2   The inflation rate fell sharply from annual rates of 13.5 percent in 1980 to 3.2 percent in 1983. Since 1983 the inflation rate has remained relatively low. But most economists attribute the decline in inflation to the 1980–1982 recessions, caused by the Federal Reserve's tight money policy, and to declines in oil prices. Rightward shifts in aggregate supply predicted by supply-side economists were *not* a major factor in reducing inflation.
3   The Reagan tax cuts contributed to burgeoning Federal budget deficits (Chapter 18). The prediction of the Laffer Curve that tax cuts would enhance tax revenues beyond those associated with normal economic expansions simply did not bear fruit. These large deficits may have increased interest rates, crowding out some unknown amount of private investment and depressing both export-dependent and import-competing industries (Figures 12-6b and 12-6d). A record high U.S. balance of payments deficit resulted. In 1990, the Bush administration and Congress were forced to enact a tax-spending package designed to reduce the deficit by $500 billion over a five-year period.
4   There is little evidence that Reaganomics has had any significant positive impacts on saving and investment rates or incentives to work. The savings rate trended downward throughout the 1980s. Productivity growth surged in 1983 and 1984, as is usual during recovery, but has been disappointingly low since then.
5   Most economists attribute the post-1982 economic

An example focusing on a recession will clarify the new classical thinking. Suppose that productivity—output per worker—declines because an increase in the world price of oil makes it prohibitively expensive to operate certain types of machinery. This decline in productivity implies a reduction in the economy's ability to produce real output and therefore a leftward shift of its long-run (vertical) aggregate supply curve. As domestic output falls in response to the decline in aggregate supply, less money is needed to exchange the reduced volume of goods and services. That is, the decline in output reduces the demand for money. Moreover, the slowdown in business activity lessens business borrowing from banks, causing a drop in the supply of money. In this scenario, changes in the supply of money respond passively to changes in the demand for money. The decline in the money supply in turn reduces aggregate demand (shifts the AD curve leftward) to the same extent as the initial decline in aggregate supply. The result is that real equilibrium output is lower, while the price level remains unchanged. Like the Keynesian model, then, the real business cycle theory allows for a decline in real output in the presence of a constant price level. (You are urged to

test your comprehension of the r... ory by using the AD-AS model t...

The policy implications of t... theory are as unusual and cont... itself. First, demand-managem... propriate and doomed to fail. I... tion policy in this situation will... put; instead, it will cause inflati... of aggregate supply from its l... should not be the source of soc... to real business cycle theorists,... ness booms roughly match the... from "real" downturns. The *ne*... ness cycles therefore are alleg... emphasis of public policy sho... long-term economic growth ratl... bilize the economy.

Conventional economists v... business cycle theory because... the facts of past business cycl... the theory makes it evident tha... ing, evolving field of study and... roeconomic theory is not the... town.

---

supply curve rightward. The long-run aggregate supply curve therefore is vertical at the potential level of output.

6 In the short run, demand-pull inflation increases the price level *and* real output. Once nominal wages have increased, however, the temporary increase in real output dissipates.

7 In the short run, cost-push inflation increases the price level and reduces real output. Unless government expands aggregate demand, nominal wages eventually will decline under conditions of recession and the short-run aggregate supply curve will shift back to its initial location. Prices and real output will eventually return to their original levels.

8 Market policies, wage-price (incomes) policies, and supply-side policies have been proposed to prevent or alleviate stagflation.

9 Market policies consist of employment and training programs designed to reduce labor market imbalances and

procompetition policies which re... unions and corporations.

10 Incomes policies take the ... posts or controls. Economists del... policies in terms of their worka... resource allocation.

11 Supply-side economists trac... of the public sector and, more ... effects of the tax-transfer systen... tors cited are the growing tax "v... costs and product prices and go... businesses. Based on the Laffe... ents advocated sizable tax cuts s... the Reagan administration as a... dence has cast considerable d... supply-side view.

TERMS AND CONCEPTS

Phillips Curve
stagflation
aggregate supply shocks
inflationary expectations
theory of adaptive expectations

natural rate hypothesis
rational expectations theory
short-run aggregate supply curve
long-run aggregate supply curve

disinflation
new classical economics
price-level surprises
demand-pull inflation
cost-push inflation
market policies

---

recovery to the demand-side expansionary effects of the Reagan tax cuts and not to the use of tax cuts as an antistagflation, supply-side measure.

In summary, the evidence to date casts considerable doubt on the central supply-side proposition that tax cuts can significantly shift the nation's production possibilities curve and aggregate supply curve rightward more rapidly than their historical pace.

QUICK REVIEW 17-3

♦ *Policy options for stagflation include: market policies (employment and training policies, antitrust); incomes policies (wage-price guideposts and controls); and supply-side economics (tax cuts, deregulation).*

♦ *The Laffer Curve contends that, when tax rates are higher than optimal, tax reductions can stimulate real output and simultaneously increase tax revenue.*

♦ *The supply-side policies (tax cuts, deregulation) of Reaganomics did not increase aggregate supply more rapidly than otherwise would have been expected.*

RECAP: ALTERNATIVE MACROECONOMIC PERSPECTIVES

We have seen here and in Chapter 16 that a number of theories purport to explain how the national economy operates. In particular, the central ideas and policy implications of Keynesianism, monetarism, rational expectations theory, and supply-side economics have been presented.

Table 17-1 summarizes major aspects of these theories and policy perspectives. In reviewing the table, note there is no direct reference to the terminology

TABLE 17-1 Alternative macroeconomic theories and policies

| Issue | Keynesianism | Natural rate hypothesis | | Supply-side economics |
		Monetarism	Rational expectations	
View of the private economy	Inherently unstable	Stable in long run at natural rate of unemployment	Stable in long run at natural rate of unemployment	May stagnate without proper work, saving, and investment incentives
Cause of the observed instability of the private economy	Investment plans unequal to saving plans (changes in AD); AS shocks	Inappropriate monetary policy	Unanticipated AD and AS shocks in the short run	Changes in AS
Appropriate macro policies	Active fiscal and monetary policy; occasional use of incomes policies	Monetary rule	Monetary rule	Policies to increase AS
How changes in the money supply affect the economy	By changing the interest rate, which changes investments, and real GDP	By directly changing AD which changes GDP.	No effect on output because price-level changes are anticipated	By influencing investment and thus AS
View of the velocity of money	Unstable	Stable	No consensus	No consensus
How fiscal policy affects the economy	Changes AD and GDP via the multiplier process	No effect unless money supply changes	No effect on output because price-level changes are anticipated	Affects GDP and price level via changes in AS
View of cost-push inflation	Possible (wage-push, AS shock)	Impossible in the long run in the absence of excessive money supply growth	Impossible in the long run in the absence of excessive money supply growth	Possible (productivity decline, higher costs due to regulation, etc.)

LAST WORD

"REAL" BUSINESS CYCLE THEORY

A handful of prominent new classical economists stand traditional economic theory on its head by arguing that business cycles are caused by real factors affecting aggregate supply rather than by fluctuations in aggregate demand.

Keynesians and monetarists hold that business cycles result mainly from changes in aggregate demand. But new classical economists tend to rule out demand changes as causes of permanent changes in real output. They contend that flexible nominal wages and changes in other input prices return real output to its potential level through rapid adjustments in short-run aggregate supply (Figures 17-6b and 17-7a). Yet, historical evidence clearly shows that long-lasting business recessions and booms *do* occur. If changes in aggregate demand are not the reason for these observed fluctuations, what are the reasons?

A small, but influential, group of new classical economists has hypothesized that business cycles are caused by factors which disturb the long-run growth

trend of aggregate supply. Accor[...]
recessions begin on the supply[...]
not on the demand side as tra[...]
other words, "real" factors—[...]
availability, and productivity—[...]
supply are the alleged causes[...]
contrast, traditional theory env[...]
tors affecting aggregate demand[...]
cyclical instability.

"new classical economics." This viewpoint is simply that associated in a general way with the natural rate hypothesis which asserts that the economy tends automatically to achieve equilibrium at its full potential level

of output—that is, at its natural[...]
The natural rate hypothesis i[...]
mists of the monetarist and ra[...]
suasions.

CHAPTER SUMMARY

1 Using the AD-AS model to compare the impacts of small and large increases in aggregate demand on the price level and real domestic output yields the generalization that high rates of inflation should be associated with low rates of unemployment and vice versa. This inverse relationship is known as the Phillips Curve and empirical data for the 1960s were generally consistent with it. Labor market imbalances and monopoly power are used to explain the Phillips Curve tradeoff.

2 In the 1970s the Phillips Curve apparently shifted rightward, a shift consistent with stagflation. A series of supply shocks in the form of higher energy and food prices, a depreciated dollar, and the demise of the Nixon wage-price freeze were involved in the 1973–1975 stagflation. More subtle factors such as inflationary expectations and a decline in the rate of productivity growth also contributed to stagflationary tendencies. Following the recession of 1981–1982, the Phillips Curve shifted inward toward its original position. By 1989 stagflation had largely subsided.

3 The adaptive expectations [...]
hypothesis argues that in the long [...]
Curve tradeoff does not exist [...]
management policies will shift th[...]
upward, resulting in increasing i[...]
decline in unemployment.

4 The rational expectations [...]
hypothesis contends that the in[...]
sionary policies will be anticipate[...]
wage demands. As a result, the [...]
crease in employment and thus r[...]

5 In the short run—where no [...]
increase in the price level increa[...]
Conversely, a decrease in the pri[...]
real output. Thus, the short-run [...]
upward-sloping. In the long run–[...]
variable—price level increases [...]
shift the short-run aggregate s[...]
versely, price level declines sh[...]

QUESTIONS AND STUDY SUGGESTIONS

1 Employ the aggregate demand–aggregate supply model to derive the Phillips Curve. What events occurred in the 1970s to cast doubt on the stability and existence of the Phillips Curve?

2 Use an appropriate diagram to explain the adaptive expectations rationale for concluding that in the long run the Phillips Curve is a vertical line.

3 Explain rational expectations theory and its relevance to analysis of the Phillips Curve.

4 Assume the following information is relevant for an industrially advanced economy in the 1993–1995 period:

Year	Price level index	Rate of increase in labor productivity	Index of industrial production	Unemployment rate	Average hourly wage rates
1993	167	4%	212	4.5%	$6.00
1994	174	3	208	5.2	6.50
1995	181	2.5	205	5.8	7.10

Describe in detail the macroeconomic situation faced by this society. Is cost-push inflation evident? What policy proposals would you recommend?

5 Evaluate or explain the following statements:

a "Taken together, the adaptive expectations and rational expectations theories imply that demand-management policies cannot influence the real level of economic activity in the long run."

b "The essential difference between the adaptive expectations theory and rational expectations theory is that inflation is unanticipated in the former and anticipated in the latter."

6 Use graphical analysis to show (1) demand-pull inflation in the short run and long run, and (2) cost-push inflation in the short run and long run. Assume in the second case that government does *not* increase aggregate demand to offset the real output effect of the cost-push inflation.

7 Suppose the potential level of real domestic output *(Q)* for a hypothetical economy is $250 and the price level *(P)* initially is 100. Use the short-run aggregate supply schedules below to answer the questions which follow.

AS(P₁₀₀)		AS(P₁₂₅)		AS(P₇₅)	
P	Q	P	Q	P	Q
125	280	125	250	125	310
100	250	100	220	100	280
75	220	75	190	75	250

a What will be the level of real domestic output in the *short run* if the price level unexpectedly rises from 100 to 125 because of an increase in aggregate demand? Falls unexpectedly from 100 to 75 because of a decrease in aggregate demand? Explain each situation.

b What will be the level of real domestic output in the *long run* when the price level rises from 100 to 125? Falls from 100 to 75? Explain each situation.

c Show the circumstances described in a and b on graph paper and derive the long-run aggregate supply curve.

8 Explain the Kennedy–Johnson wage-price guideposts, indicating in detail the relationship between nominal wages, productivity, and unit labor costs. What specific problems are associated with the use of wage-price guideposts and controls? Evaluate these problems and note the arguments in favor of guideposts and controls. Would you favor a special tax on firms which grant wage increases in excess of productivity increases?

9 "Controlling prices to halt inflation is like breaking a thermometer to control the heat. In both instances you are treating symptoms rather than causes." Do you agree? Does the correctness of the statement vary when applied to demand-pull and to cost-push inflation? Explain.

10 What reasons do supply-side economists give to explain leftward shifts of the AS curve? Using the Laffer Curve, explain why they recommend tax cuts to remedy stagflation.

11 Review Table 17-1 and explain to your satisfaction each of the elements contained therein. If an item makes little sense to you, search this and previous chapters to find explicit or implicit explanations of the particular point made in the table.

Budget Deficits and the Public Debt

Federal deficits and our rapidly expanding public debt have received much publicity in the past few years. Headlines proclaiming "Exploding Federal Debt" "National Debt Threatens You" and "Runaway Deficits Possible" can hardly escape our attention. Nor can we escape the reality that it took over 200 years for the Federal debt to reach $1 trillion. But, then it required only eight years—1982 to 1990—to pass the $3 trillion mark.

In this chapter we will carefully examine the issues of persistent Federal deficits and the mounting public debt which these deficits have produced. After presenting relevant definitions, we first gain perspective by comparing several different budget philosophies. Next, the quantitative dimensions of the public debt are explored. How large is the debt? How can it be most meaningfully measured? We then consider the problems associated with the public debt and will find that some are essentially false or bogus problems, while others are of substance. Next, we want to assess the great upsurge in the size of deficits and in the public debt occurring in the past decade. We seek to understand why many economists see these deficits as having adverse effects on our domestic investment and international trade. Finally, recent laws and proposals designed to reduce or eliminate budget deficits are examined.

DEFICITS AND DEBT: DEFINITIONS

It is important to understand what we mean by deficits and the public debt. Recall from Chapter 12 that a **budget deficit** is the amount by which government's expenditures exceed its revenues during a particular year. For example, during 1991 the Federal government spent $1323 billion and its receipts were only $1054 billion, giving rise to a $269 billion deficit. The national or **public debt** is the total accumulation of the Federal government's total deficits and surpluses which have occurred through time. At the end of 1991 the public debt was about $3600 billion.

The term "public debt" as ordinarily used does *not* include the entire public sector; in particular, state and local finance is omitted. In fact, while the Federal government has been incurring large deficits, state and local governments in the aggregate have been realizing surpluses. For example, in 1991 all state and local governments combined had a budgetary surplus in excess of $26 billion.[1]

BUDGET PHILOSOPHIES

Is it desirable to incur deficits and realize a growing public debt? Or should the budget be balanced annually, if necessary by legislation or constitutional amendment? Indeed, we saw in Chapter 12 that the essence of countercyclical fiscal policy is that the Federal budget should move toward a deficit during recession and toward a surplus during inflation. This correctly suggests that an activist fiscal policy is unlikely to result in a balanced budget in any particular year. Is this a matter of concern? Let's approach this question by examining the economic implications of several contrasting budget philosophies.

Annually Balanced Budget

Until the Great Depression of the 1930s, the **annually balanced budget** was generally accepted without question as a desirable goal of public finance. Upon examination, however, it becomes evident that an annually balanced budget largely rules out government fiscal activity as a countercyclical, stabilizing force. Worse yet, an annually balanced budget actually intensifies the business cycle. To illustrate: Suppose that the economy encounters a siege of unemployment and falling incomes. As Figure 12-4 indicates, in such circumstances tax receipts will automatically decline. To balance its budget, government must either (1) increase tax rates, (2) reduce government expenditures, or (3) employ a combination of these two. The problem is that all these policies are contractionary; each one further dampens, rather than stimulates, aggregate demand.

Similarly, an annually balanced budget will intensify inflation. Again, Figure 12-4 tells us that, as money incomes rise during the course of inflation, tax collections will automatically increase. To avoid the impending surplus, government must either (1) cut tax rates, (2) increase government expenditures, or (3) adopt a combination of both. All three of these policies will add to inflationary pressures. *An annually balanced budget is not economically neutral; the pursuit of such a policy is procyclical, not countercyclical.* Despite this and other

---

[1]This figure includes the states' pension funds. If these funds are excluded, the states collectively suffered a budgetary deficit in 1991.

problems, there is considerable support for a constitutional amendment requiring an annually balanced budget.

More recently, several prominent economists have advocated an annually balanced budget, not so much because of a fear of deficits and a mounting public debt per se, but rather because they feel an annually balanced budget is essential in constraining an undesirable and uneconomic expansion of the public sector. Budget deficits, they argue, are a manifestation of political irresponsibility. Deficits allow politicians to give the public the benefits of government programs while currently avoiding the associated cost of paying higher taxes.

In other words, these economists believe government has a tendency to grow larger than it should because there is less popular opposition to this growth when it is financed by deficits rather than taxes. Wasteful governmental expenditures are more likely to creep into the Federal budget when deficit financing is readily available. Conservative economists and politicians want legislation or a constitutional amendment to force a balanced budget to slow government growth. They view deficits as a symptom of a more fundamental problem—government encroachment on the private sector.

Cyclically Balanced Budget

The idea of a **cyclically balanced budget** is that government exerts a countercyclical influence and at the same time balances its budget. In this case, however, the budget would not be balanced annually—after all, there is nothing sacred about twelve months as an accounting period—but rather, over the course of the business cycle.

The rationale of this budget philosophy is simple, plausible, and appealing. To offset recession, government should lower taxes and increase spending, thereby purposely incurring a deficit. During the ensuing inflationary upswing, taxes would be raised and government spending slashed. The resulting surplus could then be used to retire the Federal debt incurred in financing the recession. In this way government fiscal operations would exert a positive countercyclical force, and the government could still balance its budget—not annually, but over a period of years.

The problem with this budget philosophy is that the upswings and downswings of the business cycle may not be of equal magnitude and duration (Figure 8-1), and hence the goal of stabilization conflicts with balancing the budget over the cycle. A long and severe slump, followed by a modest and short period of prosperity, would mean a large deficit during the slump, little or no surplus during prosperity, and therefore a cyclical deficit in the budget.

Functional Finance

According to **functional finance,** a balanced budget—either annually or cyclically—is secondary. The primary purpose of Federal finance is to provide for noninflationary full employment, that is, to balance the economy, not the budget. If attainment of this objective means either persistent surpluses or a large and growing public debt, so be it. According to this philosophy, the problems involved in government deficits or surpluses are relatively minor compared with the highly undesirable alternatives of prolonged recession or persistent inflation. The Federal budget is first and foremost an instrument for achieving and maintaining macroeconomic stability. Government should not hesitate to incur any deficits and surpluses required to achieve this goal.

In response to those who express concern about the large Federal debt which the pursuit of functional finance might entail, proponents of this budget philosophy offer three arguments.

1   Our tax system is such that tax revenues automatically increase as the economy expands. Hence, given government expenditures, a deficit which is successful in stimulating equilibrium GDP will be partially self-liquidating (Figure 12-4).

2   Given its taxing powers and the ability to create money, the government's capacity to finance deficits is virtually unlimited.

3   Finally, it is contended that the problems of a large Federal debt are less burdensome than most people think.

THE PUBLIC DEBT: FACTS AND FIGURES

Because modern fiscal policy endorses unbalanced budgets for the purpose of stabilizing the economy, its application will possibly lead to a growing public debt. Let's briefly consider the public debt—its causes, characteristics, and size; and the burdens and benefits associated with it.

Growth of the public debt, as Table 18-1 shows, has been substantial since 1929. As noted, the public debt is the accumulation of all past deficits, minus surpluses, of the Federal budget.

Causes

Why has our public debt increased historically? Or, stated differently, what has caused us to incur large and persistent deficits? The answer is threefold: wars, recessions, and tax cuts.

Wars   A considerable portion of the public debt has arisen from the deficit financing of wars. The public debt grew more than fivefold during World War II and it also increased substantially during World War I.

Consider the World War II situation and the options it posed. The task was to reallocate a substantial portion of the economy's resources from civilian to war goods production. Accordingly, government expenditures for armaments and military personnel soared. Financing options were threefold: Increase taxes, print the needed money, or practice deficit financing. Government feared that tax financing would require tax rates so high they would diminish incentives to work. The national interest required attracting more people into the labor force and encouraging those already participating to work longer hours. Very high tax rates were felt to interfere with these goals. Printing and spending additional money was correctly seen as highly inflationary. Thus, much of World War II was financed by selling bonds to the public, thereby draining off spendable income and freeing resources from civilian production so they would be available for defense industries.

Recessions   A second source of the public debt is recessions and, more specifically, the built-in stability which characterizes our fiscal system. In periods when the national income declines or fails to grow, tax collections automatically decline and tend to cause deficits. Thus the public debt rose during the Great Depression of the 1930s and, more recently, during the recessions of 1974–1975, 1980–1982, and 1990–1991.

Tax Cuts   A third consideration has accounted for much of the large deficits since 1981. The Economic Recovery Tax Act of 1981 provided for substantial cuts in both individual and corporate income taxes. The Reagan administration and Congress did *not* make offsetting reductions in government outlays, thereby building a *structural deficit* into the Federal budget in the sense that the budget would not balance even if the

TABLE 18-1 Quantitative significance of the public debt: the public debt and interest payments in relation to GDP, selected years, 1929–1991*

(1) Year	(2) Public debt, billions	(3) Gross domestic product, billions	(4) Interest payments, billions	(5) Public debt as percentage of GDP, (2) ÷ (3)	(6) Interest payments as percentage of GDP, (4) ÷ (3)	(7) Per capita public debt
1929	$ 16.9	$ 103.2	$ 0.7	16%	0.7%	$ 134
1940	50.7	100.1	1.1	51	1.1	384
1946	271.0	211.6	4.2	128	2.0	1917
1950	256.9	286.7	4.5	90	1.6	1667
1955	274.4	403.3	5.1	68	1.3	1654
1960	290.5	513.4	6.8	57	1.3	1610
1965	322.3	702.7	8.4	46	1.2	1659
1970	380.9	1010.7	14.1	38	1.4	1858
1975	541.9	1585.9	23.0	34	1.5	2507
1980	908.5	2708.0	53.3	34	2.0	3989
1982	1136.8	3149.6	84.6	36	2.7	4889
1984	1564.1	3777.2	115.6	41	3.1	6600
1986	2120.1	4268.6	135.4	50	3.2	8775
1988	2600.8	4900.4	146.0	56	3.0	10611
1990	3206.3	5513.8	177.5	58	3.2	12826
1991	3599.0	5671.8	188.4	63	3.3	14244

*In current dollars.

Source: *Economic Report of the President, 1992;* U.S. Department of Commerce.

economy were operating at the full-employment level. Unfortunately, the economy was not at full employment during most of the early 1980s. In particular, the 1981 tax cuts combined with the severe 1980–1982 recessions to generate rapidly rising annual deficits which were $128 billion in 1982, accelerating to $221 billion by 1986. Although annual budget deficits declined between 1986 and 1990, they remained historically high even though the economy reached full employment. Due partly to the earlier tax rate cuts, tax revenues simply were not sufficiently high to cover rising Federal spending. Annual deficits, and thus the public debt, rose again in 1991 and 1992 as the economy experienced recession and the Federal government began to incur massive expenses in bailing out failed savings and loan associations.

Without being too cynical one might also assert that deficits and a growing public debt are the result of lack of political will and determination. Spending tends to gain votes; tax increases precipitate political disfavor. While opposition to deficits is widely expressed by both politicians and their constituencies, *specific* pro-

posals to raise taxes or cut either domestic or defense programs typically encounter more opposition than support. For example, college students may favor smaller deficits so long as funds for student loans are not eliminated in the process.

In summary, much of the public debt has been caused by wartime finance, recessions, and, more recently, by tax cuts.

Quantitative Aspects

The public debt is estimated to be $3600 billion—that's $3.6 trillion—in 1991. That amount is more than twice what it was a mere seven years ago! How much is $3.6 trillion? Three trillion 600 million $1 bills placed end-to-end would stretch 340 million miles or, in other words, from the earth to the sun and back nearly two times. Or, a stack of $1000 bills 4 inches high would make you a millionaire; it would take a stack 241 miles high to represent our $3.6 trillion public debt.[2]

[2]These illustrations are from *U.S. News & World Report,* September 6, 1985, p. 33. Updated.

But we must not fear large or virtually incomprehensible numbers per se. The reason will become clear when we put the size of the public debt into better perspective.

Debt and GDP A bald statement of the absolute size of the debt glosses over the fact that the wealth and productive ability of our economy have also increased tremendously over the years. A wealthy nation can more easily incur and carry a large public debt than a poor nation. In other words, it is more realistic to measure changes in the public debt *in relation to* changes in the economy's GDP. Column 5 in Table 18-1 presents such data. Note that instead of the thirteenfold increase in the debt between 1955 and 1991 shown in column 2, we find that the relative size of the debt was less in 1991 than in 1955. However, our data also show that the relative size of the debt has doubled since the early 1980s. Column 7 indicates that on a per capita basis the nominal debt has increased more or less steadily through time.

International Comparisons Other industrial nations have relative public debts similar to, or greater than, those in the United States. We will see in this chapter's Last Word that, as a percent of GDP, public debt in 1991 was greater in Italy, Canada, and Japan than in the United States.

Interest Charges Many economists feel that the primary burden of the debt is the annual interest charge that accrues as a result of the debt. The absolute size of these interest payments is shown in column 4 of Table 18-1. Note that interest payments have increased dramatically beginning in the 1970s. This reflects not only increases in the debt, but, more importantly, periods of very high interest rates. Interest on the debt is now the third largest item of expenditures in the Federal budget (Table 6-1). Interest charges as a percentage of the GDP are shown in column 6 of Table 18-1. We find that interest payments as a proportion of GDP have increased significantly in recent years. This ratio reflects the level of taxation (the average tax rate) which is required to service the public debt. In 1991 government had to collect taxes equal to 3.3 percent of the gross domestic product simply to pay interest on its debt.

Ownership Approximately one-third of the total public debt is held by governmental agencies and our central banks, the remaining two-thirds by state and local governments, private individuals, commercial banks, and insurance companies. Only about 12 percent of the total debt is held by foreigners. This statistic is significant because, as we will see shortly, the implications of internally and externally held debt are quite different.

Accounting and Inflation While the data on budget deficits and public debt appear to be straightforward and unassailable, this is not the case. Robert Eisner, past president of the American Economic Association, argues that governmental accounting procedures do not reflect government's actual financial position. He points out that private firms have a separate capital budget because, in contrast to current expenses on labor and raw materials, expenditures for capital equipment represent tangible money-making assets. The Federal government treats expenditures for highways, harbors, and public buildings the same as it does welfare payments, while in fact the former outlays are investments in physical assets. According to Eisner, Federal budget deficits of recent years would be greatly reduced if the Federal government employed a capital budget which included depreciation costs.

Eisner also reminds us that inflation works to benefit debtors. A rising price level reduces the real value or purchasing power of the dollars paid back by borrowers. Taking this "inflationary tax" into account further reduces the sizes of budget deficits and public debt.

All of this is quite controversial. But the important point is that there are different ways of measuring the public debt and government's overall financial position. Some of these alternative views differ significantly from the data presented in Table 18-1.

QUICK REVIEW 18-1

✦ *A budget deficit is an excess of government expenditures above tax revenues in a particular year; the public debt is the total accumulation of budget deficits and surpluses through time.*

✦ *The three major budget philosophies are: a an annually balanced budget; b a budget balanced over the business cycle; and c functional finance, which makes balancing the budget secondary to using it to promote macroeconomic goals.*

✦ *The $3.6 trillion public debt has resulted mainly from wartime financing, recessions, and tax cuts.*

✦ *United States public debt as a percentage of GDP is less than what it was in 1955 and lies in the midrange of such debt among major industrial nations.*

ECONOMIC IMPLICATIONS: FALSE ISSUES

How does the public debt and its growth affect the operation of the economy? Can a mounting public debt bankrupt the nation at some point? Does the debt place an unwarranted economic burden on our children and grandchildren?

These are essentially false or bogus issues. The debt is not about to bankrupt the government or the nation. Nor, except under certain specific circumstances, does the debt place a burden on future generations.

Going Bankrupt?

Can a large public debt bankrupt the government, making it unable to meet its financial obligations? The answer to this question is "No" because of the following three points.

1 Refinancing The first point is that there is no reason why the public debt need be reduced, much less eliminated. In practice, as portions of the debt fall due each month, government does not typically cut expenditures or raise taxes to provide funds to *retire* the maturing bonds. (We know that with depressed economic conditions, this would be unwise fiscal policy.) Rather, the government simply *refinances* the debt; it sells new bonds and uses the proceeds to pay off holders of the maturing bonds.

2 Taxation Government has the constitutional authority to levy and collect taxes. If acceptable to voters, a tax increase is a government option for gaining sufficient revenue to pay interest and principal on the public debt. Financially distressed private households and corporations *cannot* raise revenue via taxes; government *can*. Private households and corporations *can* go bankrupt; the Federal government *cannot*.

3 Creating Money A final, important consideration that makes bankruptcy difficult to imagine is that the Federal government has the power to print money to pay both principal and interest on the debt. A government bond simply obligates the government to redeem that bond for some specific amount of money on its maturity date. Government can use the proceeds from the sale of other bonds *or* it can create the needed money to retire the maturing bonds. The creation of new money to pay interest on debt or to retire debt

may be inflationary. But it is difficult to conceive of governmental bankruptcy when government has the power to create new money by running the printing presses.

Shifting Burdens

Does the public debt impose a burden on future generations? Recall that per capita debt in 1991 was $14,244. Does each newborn child in 1991 enter the world to be handed a $14,244 bill from Uncle Sam? Not really!

We first must ask to whom we owe the public debt. The answer is that, for the most part, we owe it to ourselves. About 88 percent of our government bonds are owned and held by citizens and institutions—banks, businesses, insurance companies, governmental agencies, and trust funds—within the United States. Thus *the public debt is also a public credit.* While the public debt is a liability to the American people (as taxpayers), most of the same debt is simultaneously an asset to the American people (as bondholders).

Retirement of the public debt would therefore call for a gigantic transfer payment whereby Americans would pay higher taxes and government would pay out most of those tax revenues to those same taxpaying individuals and institutions in the aggregate in redeeming the bonds they hold. Although a redistribution of income would result from this gigantic financial transfer, it need not entail any immediate decline in the economy's aggregate wealth or standard of living. Repayment of an internally held public debt entails no leakage of purchasing power from the economy of the country as a whole. New babies who on the average inherit the $14,244 per person public debt obligation will also be bequeathed that same amount of government bonds.

We noted earlier that the public debt increased sharply during World War II. Was some of the economic burden of World War II shifted to future generations by the decision to finance military purchases through the sale of government bonds? Again, the answer is "No." Recalling the production possibilities curve, we realize that the economic cost of World War II was the civilian goods society had to forgo in shifting scarce resources to war goods production. Regardless of whether financing of this reallocation was achieved through higher taxes or borrowing, the real economic burden of the war would have been essentially the same. In short, the burden of the war was borne almost entirely by those who lived during the war; they were the ones who did without a multitude of consumer goods to permit the United States to arm itself and its allies.

Also, wartime production may slow the growth of a nation's stock of capital as resources are shifted from production of capital goods to production of war goods. As a result, future generations inherit a smaller stock of capital goods than they otherwise would. This occurred in the United States during World War II (see table on inside covers, line 2). But, again, this shifting of costs is independent of how a war is financed.

ECONOMIC IMPLICATIONS: SUBSTANTIVE ISSUES

We must be careful not to leave the impression that the public debt is of no concern among economists. The large debt *does* pose some real and potential problems, although economists vary in the importance they attach to these problems.

Income Distribution

The distribution of government bond ownership is undoubtedly uneven. Some people own more than their $14,244 per capita share; others less; others none at all. Although our knowledge of the ownership of the public debt by income class is limited, it is presumed that ownership is concentrated among wealthier groups in society. Because the tax system is at best mildly progressive, payment of interest on the public debt probably increases income inequality. If greater income equality is one of our social goals, then this redistributive effect is clearly undesirable.

Incentives

Table 18-1 indicates that the present public debt necessitates annual interest payments well over $185 billion. With no increase in the size of the debt, this annual interest charge must be paid out of tax revenues. These added taxes may dampen incentives to bear risk, to

innovate, to invest, and to work. In this indirect way, the existence of a large public debt can impair economic growth. As noted earlier, the ratio of interest payments to GDP indicates the level of taxation needed to pay interest on the debt. Thus, some economists are concerned that this ratio has increased quite sharply in recent years (column 6 of Table 18-1).

External Debt

External debt—our U.S. debt held by citizens and institutions of foreign countries—is a burden. This part of the public debt is *not* "owed to ourselves," and in real terms the payment of interest and principal requires transferring a portion of our real output to other nations. It is worth noting that foreign ownership of the public debt has increased in recent years. In 1960 only about 5 percent of the debt was foreign-owned; currently foreign ownership is about 12 percent. The assertion that "we owe the debt to ourselves" and the implication that the debt should be of little concern is less accurate than it was three decades ago.

Crowding Out and the Stock of Capital

This brings us to a potentially more serious problem. As an exception to our earlier comments, there is one important way the public debt can transfer a real economic burden to future generations. That way is by causing future generations to inherit a smaller stock of capital goods—a smaller "national factory." This possibility involves Chapter 12's **crowding-out effect,** the notion that deficit financing will increase interest rates and reduce investment spending. If this should happen, future generations would inherit an economy with a smaller productive capacity and, other things being equal, the standard of living would be lower than otherwise.

How might this come to pass? Suppose the economy is operating at its full-employment or potential level of output and that the Federal budget is initially in balance. Now for some reason government increases its level of spending. We know from earlier discussion of the economic burden of World War II that the impact of an increase in government spending will fall on those living when it occurs. Think of Chapter 2's production possibilities curve with "government goods" on one axis and "private goods" on the other. In a full-employment economy an increase in government spending will move the economy *along* the curve toward the government-goods axis, meaning that fewer private goods will be available.

But private goods may be either consumer or investment goods. If the increased government goods are provided at the expense of consumer goods, then the present generation bears the entire burden in the form of a lower current standard of living. The current investment level is not affected and therefore neither is the size of the national factory inherited by future generations. But if the increase in government goods means a reduction in production of capital goods, then the present generation's level of consumption (standard of living) will be unimpaired. However, in the future our children and grandchildren will inherit a smaller stock of capital goods and will realize lower income levels than otherwise.

Two Scenarios Let's sketch the two scenarios which yield the two results described.

First Scenario Suppose the presumed increase in government spending is financed by an increase in taxation, say, personal income taxes. We know that most income is consumed and that, therefore, consumer spending will fall by almost as much as the increase in taxes. In this case the burden of the increase in government spending falls primarily on today's generation in the form of fewer consumer goods.

Second Scenario Assume that the increase in government spending is financed by increasing the public debt. In this case the government goes into the money market and competes with private borrowers for funds. Given the supply of money, this increase in money demand will increase the interest rate—the "price" paid for the use of money.

In Figure 18-1 the curve I_{d1} reproduces the investment-demand curve of Figure 10-7. (Ignore curve I_{d2} for now.) The investment-demand curve is downsloping, indicating that investment spending varies inversely with the interest rate. In this instance government deficit financing drives up the interest rate, causing private investment to fall. For example, if government borrowing increases the interest rate from 6 to 10 percent, investment spending would fall from $25 to $15 billion. That is, $10 billion of private investment would be crowded out.

Our conclusion is that the assumed increase in public goods production is much more likely to come at the expense of private investment goods when financed by deficits. In comparison with tax financing the future generation inherits a smaller national factory

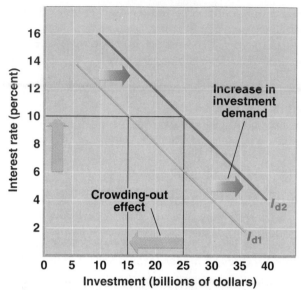

FIGURE 18-1   The investment-demand curve and the crowding-out effect

The crowding-out effect suggests that, given the location of the investment-demand curve (I_{d1}), an increase in the interest rate caused by a government deficit will reduce private investment spending and decrease the size of the "national factory" inherited by future generations. In this case an increase in the interest rate from 6 to 10 percent crowds out $10 billion of private investment. However, if the economy is initially in a recession, the government deficit may improve profit expectations of businesses and shift the investment-demand curve rightward as from I_{d1} to I_{d2}. This shift may offset the crowding-out effect wholly or in part.

and therefore realizes a lower standard of living with deficit financing.

Two Qualifications But there are two important loose ends to our discussion which might mitigate or even eliminate the size of the economic burden shifted to future generations in our second scenario.

1 Public Investment Our discussion has glossed over the character of the increase in government spending. Just as private goods may involve consumption or investment, so it is with public goods. If the increase in government spending is essentially consumption-type outlays—subsidies for school lunches or provision of limousines for government officials—then our second scenario's conclusion that the debt increase has shifted a burden to future generations is correct. But what if the government spending is primarily investment-type outlays, for example, for construction of highways, harbors, and flood-control projects? Similarly, what if they are "human capital" investments in education and health?

Like private expenditures on machinery and equipment, **public investments** increase the economy's future productive capacity. Thus, the capital stock of future generations need not be diminished, but rather its composition is changed so there is more public capital and less private capital.

2 Unemployment The other qualification relates to our assumption that the initial increase in government expenditures occurs when the economy is operating at full employment. Again the production possibilities curve reminds us that, *if* the economy is at less than full employment or, graphically, operating at a point inside the production possibilities frontier, then an increase in government expenditures can move the economy *to* the curve without any sacrifice of either current consumption or capital accumulation. If unemployment exists initially, deficit spending by government need *not* mean a burden for future generations in the form of a smaller national factory.

Consider Figure 18-1 once again. We know that, if deficit financing increases the interest rate from 6 to 10 percent, a crowding-out effect of $10 billion will occur. But now we are saying that the increase in government spending will stimulate a recession economy via the multiplier effect, thereby improving business profit expectations and causing a rightward shift of investment demand to I_{d2}. As a result, in the case shown, investment spending remains at $25 billion despite the higher 10 percent interest rate. Of course, the increase in investment demand might be smaller or larger than that shown in Figure 18-1. In the former case the crowding-out effect would not be fully offset; in the latter case it would be more than offset. The point is that an increase in investment demand counters the crowding-out effect.

RECENT FEDERAL DEFICITS

Federal deficits and the growing public debt have been in the economic spotlight in the last decade. This in part is because of the unusually large size of recent deficits. It also reflects an intertwined group of economic problems which are associated with the deficits.

Growing Concerns

Growing concern over deficits and the public debt spring from several sources.

TABLE 18-2 Recent annual Federal deficits *(selected fiscal years, in billions of dollars)**

Year	Deficit	Year	Deficit
1970	$ 3	1984	$185
1973	15	1985	212
1977	54	1986	221
1979	40	1987	149
1980	74	1988	155
1981	79	1989	154
1982	128	1990	221
1983	208	1991	269

*Fiscal years are twelve-month periods ending September 30 of each year, rather than December 31 as for calendar years. Source: *Economic Report of the President,* 1992.

Enormous Size First, there is the matter of size. As Table 18-2 makes clear, the absolute size of annual Federal deficits increased enormously in the past decade, as did the public debt. The average annual deficit for the 1970s was approximately $35 billion. In the 1980s annual deficits averaged five times that amount. As a consequence, the public debt tripled during the 1980s (Table 18-1).

The Federal deficit increased to $269 billion in 1991, mainly because of the 1990–1991 recession which reduced tax revenues. Government's expensive bailout of failed S&Ls also contributed to this large deficit. The 1992 deficit is expected to exceed the 1991 deficit, perhaps reaching $350 billion.

Understatement? The most recent annual budget deficits shown in Table 18-2 may be severely understated. Over the past few years government has raised more money from social security taxes than it has paid out as benefits to current retirees. The purpose of this surplus is to prepare for the future time when numerous "baby boomers" retire. Some economists argue that these revenues should be excluded when calculating present deficits because they represent future government obligations on a dollar-for-dollar basis. That is, the social security surplus should not be considered as an offset to *current* government spending. When we exclude the social security surplus from the deficit figures, the 1991 budget deficit is $339 billion, not the $269 billion shown in Table 18-2.

Rising Interest Costs Reference to column 4 of Table 18-1 indicates that interest payments on the public debt have increased more than tenfold since 1970. Interest payments were $188 billion in 1991, an amount greater than the entire deficit in many previous years! Because interest payments are part of government expenditures, the debt feeds on itself through interest charges. Interest payments on the debt are the only component of government spending which Congress cannot cut. The spiraling of such payments therefore complicates the problem of controlling government spending and the size of future deficits.

Inappropriate Policy   Another concern is that many of our recent large annual deficits occurred in an economy operating close to full employment. Historically, deficits—particularly sizable ones—have been associated with wartime finance and recessions. While the 1980–1982 and 1990–1991 recessions contributed to large deficits, it is clear that the large size of continuing deficits reflects the 1981 tax cuts and rising government spending. In terms of Figure 12-4, the 1981 tax cuts have shifted the tax line downward. Meanwhile, the government spending line in the figure has shifted upward. Thus, even at a full-employment level of output (GDP_1) sizable structural deficits can be expected.

Large deficits during times of economic prosperity raise the concern of fueling demand-pull inflation. To counteract potentially rising prices, the Federal Reserve is forced to employ a tighter monetary policy than would otherwise be ideal. Along with the strong demand for money in the private sector, the tight money policy raises real interest rates and reduces investment spending. The point is that the greatest potential for budget deficits to produce a crowding-out effect occurs when the economy is near or at full employment.

Balance of Trade Problems   Finally, large budget deficits make it difficult for the nation to achieve a balance in its international trade. As we will see, large annual budget deficits promote imports and stifle exports. Furthermore, budget deficits are thought to be a main cause of two related phenomena much in the news: (1) our recently attained status as the "world's leading debtor nation" and (2) the so-called "selling of America" to foreign investors.

BUDGET DEFICITS AND TRADE DEFICITS

Many, but not all, economists see a direct cause-effect chain between Federal budget deficits and balance of trade deficits. Figure 18-2 is a helpful guide to understanding their thinking.

FIGURE 18-2   Budget deficits and trade deficits

Many economists contend that large deficits have the effects shown below. Deficits increase domestic interest rates, resulting in both crowding out of private investment and an increase in the demand for American securities. The latter increases our externally held debt and the demand for dollars. The strong demand for dollars raises the international value of the dollar, making our exports more expensive to foreigners and imports cheaper to Americans. As our exports fall and our imports rise, a contractionary trade deficit arises.

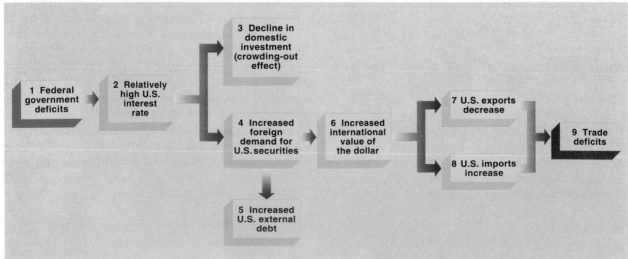

Higher Interest Rates

Beginning with boxes 1 and 2, we note once again that in financing its deficits government must enter the money market to compete with the private sector for funds. We know this drives up interest rates. High interest rates in turn have two important effects. First, as shown in box 3, they discourage private investment spending; this is the crowding-out effect discussed earlier. When the economy is reasonably close to full employment, the crowding-out effect is likely to be large. Therefore, although willing to admit that the short-run impact of deficits is expansionary, some economists express concern that the long-run effect will retard the economy's growth rate. They envision deficits being used to finance defense spending and consumption-type government goods at the expense of investment in modernized factories and equipment. Deficits, it is contended, are forcing the economy onto a slower long-run growth path.

Dollar Appreciation

The second effect, shown by box 4, is that high interest rates on both American government and private securities make financial investment in the United States more attractive for foreigners. While the resulting inflow of foreign funds helps finance both the deficit and private investment, box 5 reminds us that this inflow represents an increase in our external debt. Recall that paying interest on and retiring debts to foreigners means a reduction in future real output available to our domestic economy.

Box 6 indicates that, to purchase high-yielding American securities, foreigners must first buy American dollars with their own currencies. This increases the worldwide demand for dollars and increases the international price or exchange value of the dollar. To illustrate: Suppose that prior to our incurring large deficits, the dollar ($) and the French franc (F) exchanged in the market at a rate of $1 = F10. But now the financing of our large deficits increases interest rates in the United States, increasing the demand for dollars with which to buy American securities. Suppose this raises the price of the dollar to, say, $1 = F11.

Trade Deficits

This appreciation of the dollar will eventually depress our exports (box 7) and increase our imports (box 8), leading to an "unfavorable" balance of trade. Let's see

how this comes about. We know that exchange rates link the price levels of the world's nations. When the value of the dollar increases—when dollars become more expensive to foreigners—all American goods become more expensive to foreign buyers.

In our example the increase in the value of the dollar from $1 = F10 to $1 = F11 increases prices of all American goods by 10 percent to the French. The American product that formerly cost 10 francs now costs 11 francs. The French will react to this by buying fewer American goods; American exports will fall. Conversely, at the higher exchange rate Americans now get 11 rather than 10 francs for a dollar, so French goods are cheaper to Americans. We therefore buy more French goods; our imports rise. Or, to bring these two developments together, American net exports (exports *minus* imports) fall and a trade deficit emerges (box 9).

Net exports are a component of aggregate demand. A trade deficit implies negative net exports and has a contractionary effect on the economy. As our exports fall, unemployment will rise in American exporting industries such as agriculture and computers. American import-competing industries such as automobiles and basic steel will also be adversely affected. The increase in the value of the dollar makes Japanese and German imports of these products cheaper and American auto and steel industries find themselves with excess productive capacity and redundant labor.

Note that the foregoing comments reiterate our earlier analysis (Chapter 12) that an expansionary fiscal policy may be less stimulating to the economy than simple analysis suggests. The expansionary impact of a deficit might be softened by both the *crowding-out effect* (box 3) and the negative *net export effect* (box 9) to which it might give rise.

Related Effects

There are three loose ends to this story.
1 The inflow of foreign funds does augment domestic funds and helps keep American interest rates lower than they otherwise would be. Stated differently, the inflow of foreign funds to the United States diminishes the size of the crowding-out effect. From the standpoint of foreign nations transferring funds to the United States, their domestic investment and long-term economic growth will be smaller than otherwise.
2 Deficit-caused high interest rates in America impose an increased burden on heavily indebted underdeveloped countries such as Mexico and Brazil. Their

dollar-denominated debts to American banks and the banks of other industrially advanced nations become more costly to service when American interest rates rise.

Similarly, if declining American net exports lead to protectionism, these nations will have more difficulty selling their products in the United States. This means they will have greater difficulty in earning dollars to pay interest and principal on their debts.

In short, our large budget deficits—particularly through the upward pressure they exert on domestic interest rates—pose something of a threat to the international credit system and to American banks.

3 A trade deficit means we are not exporting enough goods to pay for our imports. The difference can be paid for in two ways. First, we can borrow from people and institutions in foreign lands. In the late 1980s when the American trade deficit was severe, the United States became the world's leading debtor nation. Second, U.S. assets such as factories, shopping centers, and farms can be sold to foreign investors. This, too, happened in the late 1980s and early 1990s. To pay our debts and repurchase these assets, we must in the future export more than we import. In other words, in the future we will need to consume and invest less than we produce.

Contrary View: Ricardian Equivalence Theorem

A few prominent economists disagree with the mainstream analysis we have outlined. They adhere to the **Ricardian equivalence theorem** (Chapter 12) which holds that financing a deficit by borrowing has the same effect on GDP as financing it through a present tax increase. People are allegedly aware that deficits today will require higher future taxes to pay the added interest expense resulting from the increase in the public debt. Households therefore spend less today—saving more—in anticipation of having less future after-tax income available for consumption. Because the increase in private saving perfectly offsets the increase in government borrowing, the interest rate does not change. Thus neither a crowing-out effect nor a trade deficit necessarily emerges from a budget deficit. In Figure 18-2 the Ricardian equivalence theorem breaks the chain between box 1 and box 2, negating all the effects purportedly following (boxes 3 through 9).

But most economists reject this novel perspective. They claim instead that the 1980s and early 1990s pro-

vide ample evidence of negative foreign-sector effects of large budget deficits. A glance at line 4 on the inside back cover of this text shows that high trade deficits (negative net exports) accompanied the large budget deficits of the late 1980s and early 1990s (Table 18-2).

QUICK REVIEW 18-3

✦ *The borrowing and interest payments associated with the public debt may **a** increase income inequality, **b** require higher taxes which dampen incentives, and **c** impede the growth of the nation's capital stock if public borrowing significantly crowds out private investment.*

✦ *Recent Federal deficits are of concern because of **a** their enormous size, **b** the fact that they may be understated, **c** rising total interest costs, and **d** their inappropriateness when the economy is near, or at, full-employment output.*

✦ *Budget deficits can be linked to trade deficits as follows: Budget deficits increase domestic interest rates; the dollar appreciates; American exports fall, and American imports rise.*

Policy Responses

Concern with large budget deficits and an expanding public debt has spawned several policy responses.

Constitutional Amendment   The most extreme proposal is that a constitutional amendment should be passed which mandates that Congress balance the budget each year. This proposed **balanced budget amendment** is based on the assumption that Congress will continue to act "irresponsibly" because government spending enhances and tax increases diminish a politician's popular support. Political rhetoric notwithstanding, Federal deficits allegedly will continue until a constitutional amendment forces a balanced budget. Critics of this proposal remind us that an annually balanced budget has a procyclical or destabilizing effect on the economy.

Gramm-Rudman-Hollings Act   In December of 1985 Congress passed the **Gramm-Rudman-Hollings Act** (GRH) which was designed to achieve annual reductions in the Federal deficit to ensure that the budget be balanced by 1991. Congress revised the act in 1987 to allow a more gradual reduction in the budget deficits and a balanced budget by 1993.

The idea of GRH was to encourage the President and Congress to agree on an annual budget which achieved the targeted reduction in the deficit. If they could not agree on sufficient spending cuts or tax hikes to achieve the required deficit goals, a series of automatic spending cuts would occur until the deficit goals were realized.

The automatic provisions of GRH were never invoked, and the act probably restrained government spending. But one major problem with the law was that its compliance required only annual submission of a *planned* budget which met the deficit reduction goals. *Actual* budget deficits exceeding those planned did not trigger automatic spending cuts. Also, GRH contained an escape clause exempting the administration from the deficit provisions if the economy experienced recession. Faced with the recession of 1990–1991 and the massive S&L bailout, Congress in effect abandoned the GRH targets as unrealistic.

Budget Legislation of 1990 In November 1990 Congress directly attacked the deficit problem by passing the **Budget Reconciliation Act of 1990,** a package of tax increases and spending cuts designed to reduce budget deficits by $500 billion between 1991 and 1996.

This act sought to enhance tax revenue through (1) an increase in the marginal tax rate for wealthy Americans from 28 to 31 percent; (2) lower allowable deductions and personal exemptions for wealthy individuals; (3) higher payroll taxes for medical care; (4) increased excise taxes on gasoline, tobacco, alcoholic beverages, and airline tickets; and (5) a new luxury tax on expensive jewelry, furs, cars, boats, and personal aircraft. This law also lopped $260 billion from government spending between 1991 and 1996, the brunt of cuts being borne by national defense, farm programs, and Federal pensions.

Tax increases and expenditure cuts in the midst of recession are counter to conventional fiscal policy. But Congress and the Bush administration reasoned that deficit reduction was essential to lower interest rates and increase investment—that is, to achieve a reverse crowding-out effect. They also recognized that without these actions deficits would skyrocket to unprecedented, politically costly heights.

The **Budget Enforcement Act of 1990** accompanied the Budget Reconciliation Act and established a "pay-as-you-go" test for new spending or tax decreases. Between 1991 and 1996 new legislation that increases government spending must be offset by a corresponding decrease in existing spending or an increase in taxes. Likewise, new tax reductions must be accompanied by offsetting tax increases or spending cuts. Also, this law placed legally binding caps (with exceptions for emergencies) on Federal spending for each of these five years.

The budget legislation of 1990 will keep budget deficits from rising as fast as otherwise, but these laws will *not* reduce budget deficits to zero any time soon. Unless Congress takes further direct action, most observers believe that the "reduced" deficits will remain historically high.

Other Proposals Concern with balancing the budget has prompted a variety of other deficit-reduction proposals. Two significant proposals are the call for greater "privatization" of the economy and for reform which would enable the President to veto spending measures on a line-item basis.

1 Privatization **Privatization** refers to government divesting itself of certain assets and programs through their sale to private firms. This is in keeping with the conservative belief that most economic activities can be performed more efficiently in the private sector than in the public sector. More important for present purposes, the sale of government programs and assets would provide revenue to help reduce budget deficits and public debt. It has been proposed that the Navy's petroleum reserves in California and Wyoming, Amtrak, Washington's Dulles and International airports, the Federal Housing Administration, and the Bonneville Power Administration, among other entities, be sold to private firms. While privatization is very controversial, there are precedents. Margaret Thatcher's conservative government in Great Britain sold more than $25 billion of state-owned enterprises in the 1980s.

2 Line-Item Veto The **line-item veto** would permit the President to veto individual spending items in appropriation bills. A typical appropriations bill merges hundreds of programs and projects into a single piece of legislation. Governors of forty-three states currently possess line-item veto authority for their state budgets, but the President does not have that kind of veto power for the Federal budget. Proponents of this reform argue that it would allow the President to cull from appropriation bills projects for which local or regional benefits are less than the costs to the nation's taxpayers. The line-item veto would tend to reduce government spending and help the Federal government balance its budget. Opponents argue that the line-item

LAST WORD

PUBLIC DEBT: INTERNATIONAL COMPARISONS

Although the United States has the world's largest public debt, several other industrial nations have larger debts as a percentage of their GDPs.

Public debt is not exclusively an American phenomenon. All industrial nations have public debts, and, as shown in the accompanying figure, several have larger relative debts than the United States. Note that in 1991 public debt as a percentage of gross domestic product was larger in Italy, Japan, and Canada than in the United States and that the relative debts of France and Germany were only slightly lower than in the United States.

Whatever the particular combinations of forces giving rise to public debts in various nations, the existence of public debts is universal. More importantly, there is no discernible relationship between a nation's public debt as a percentage of its GDP and the overall health of its economy. Japan, with a high relative debt,

has had an enviable growth record during the past several decades; the United Kingdom, with a small relative debt, has generally struggled. Meanwhile, Germany has had strong economic growth, and its relative debt is below that of Italy, Japan, Canada, the United States, and France.

---

veto would give far too much power to the President—power, they say, which might easily be abused for political purposes.

Positive Role of Debt

Having completed this survey of imagined and real problems associated with deficits and the public debt, we conclude our discussion on a more positive note. Debt—both public and private—plays a positive role in a prosperous and growing economy. As income expands, so does saving. Employment theory and fiscal policy tell us that if aggregate expenditures are to be

sustained at the full-employment level, this expanding volume of saving or its equivalent must be obtained and spent by consumers, businesses, or government. The process by which saving is transferred to spenders is *debt creation.* Now, in fact, consumers and businesses *do* borrow and spend a great amount of saving. But if households and businesses are not willing to borrow and thereby increase private debt sufficiently fast to absorb the growing volume of saving, an increase in public debt must absorb the remainder or the economy will falter from full employment and fail to realize its growth potential.

CHAPTER SUMMARY

1 A budget deficit is the excess of government expenditures over its receipts; the public debt is the total accumulation of its deficits and surpluses over time.

2 Budget philosophies include the annually balanced budget, the cyclically balanced budget, and functional finance. The basic problem with an annually balanced budget is that it is procyclical rather than countercyclical. Similarly, it may be difficult to balance the budget over the course of the business cycle if upswings and downswings are not of

roughly comparable magnitude. Functional finance is the view that the primary purpose of Federal finance is to stabilize the economy, and problems associated with consequent deficits or surpluses are of secondary importance.

3 Historically, growth of the public debt has been caused by the deficit financing of wars and by recessions. The large deficits in recent years are primarily the result of earlier tax reductions, accompanied by expenditure increases.

4 The public debt was $3.6 trillion in 1991. Since the

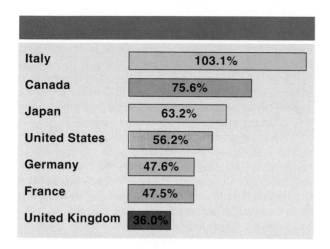

Italy	103.1%
Canada	75.6%
Japan	63.2%
United States	56.2%
Germany	47.6%
France	47.5%
United Kingdom	36.0%

For most economists, the main message from these international comparisons is that Americans need not be overly concerned with the public debt. But other economists warn that the figure demonstrates only that the United States is not alone in making inappropriate fiscal decisions.

1970s the debt and associated interest charges have trended upward as a percentage of the GDP. The debt has also been rising on a per capita basis.

5 The argument that a large public debt may bankrupt the government is false because **a** the debt need only be refinanced rather than refunded and **b** the Federal government has the power to levy taxes and create money.

6 The crowding-out effect aside, the public debt is not a vehicle for shifting economic burdens to future generations.

7 More substantive problems associated with the public debt include the following: **a** Payment of interest on the debt probably increases income inequality. **b** Interest payments on the debt require higher taxes which may impair incentives. **c** Paying interest or principal on the portion of the debt held by foreigners entails a transfer of real output abroad. **d** Government borrowing to refinance or pay interest on the debt may increase interest rates and crowd out private investment spending.

8 Federal budget deficits have been much larger recently than earlier. Many economists think these large deficits have increased interest rates in the United States which in turn have **a** crowded out private investment and **b** increased foreign demand for American securities. Increased demand for American securities has increased the international value of the dollar, causing American exports to fall and American imports to rise. The resulting trade deficits exert a contractionary effect on our domestic economy.

9 Proposed or enacted remedies for deficits and public debt increases include **a** a proposed constitutional amendment mandating an annually balanced budget; **b** the Gramm-Rudman-Hollings Act which required annual deficit reductions; **c** budget legislation of 1990 which raised taxes, cut expenditures, and forced Congress to offset new spending or tax cuts with reductions in existing spending or tax increases; **d** greater privatization of the economy by selling public assets and programs to the private sector; and **e** giving the President line-item veto authority.

TERMS AND CONCEPTS

budget deficit
public debt
annually balanced
   budget
cyclically balanced
   budget

functional finance
external debt
crowding-out effect
Ricardian equivalence
   theorem
public investments

balanced budget
   amendment
Gramm-Rudman-
   Hollings Act
Budget Reconciliation
   Act of 1990

Budget Enforcement
   Act of 1990
privatization
line-item veto

QUESTIONS AND STUDY SUGGESTIONS

1 Assess the potential for using fiscal policy as a stabilization device under **a** an annually balanced budget, **b** a cyclically balanced budget, and **c** functional finance.

2 What have been the major sources of the public debt historically? Why were deficits so large in the 1980s? Why was the deficit so large in 1991?

3 Discuss the various ways of measuring the size of the public debt. How does an internally held public debt differ from an externally held public debt? What would be the effects of retiring an internally held public debt? An externally held public debt? Distinguish between refinancing and retiring the debt.

4 Explain or evaluate each of the following statements:

a "A national debt is like a debt of the left hand to the right hand."

b "The least likely problem arising from a large public debt is that the Federal government will go bankrupt."

c "The basic cause of our growing public debt is a lack of political courage."

d "The social security reserves are not being reserved. They are being spent, masking the real deficit."

5 Is the crowding-out effect likely to be larger during recession or when the economy is near full employment? Use the aggregate demand–aggregate supply model to substantiate your answer.

6 Some economists argue that the quantitative importance of the public debt can best be measured by interest payments on the debt as a percentage of the GDP. Can you explain why?

7 Explain the essence of the 1990 Budget Reconciliation and Budget Enforcement Acts. Would you favor a constitutional amendment requiring the Federal budget to be balanced annually? Do you favor "privatization," either as a means of reducing budget deficits or as a vehicle for reducing the size of the public sector? Do you favor giving the President the authority to veto line-items of appropriation bills?

8 Is our $3.6 trillion public debt a burden to future generations? If so, in what sense? Why might deficit financing be more likely to reduce the future size of our "national factory" than tax financing of government expenditures?

9 Trace the cause-and-effect chain through which large deficits might affect domestic interest rates, domestic investment, the international value of the dollar, and our international trade. Comment: "There is too little recognition that the deterioration of America's position in world trade is more the result of our own policies than the harm wrought by foreigners." Provide a critique of this position, using the idea of Ricardian equivalence.

10 Explain how a significant decline in the nation's budget deficit would be expected to affect a the size of our trade deficit, b the total debt Americans owe to foreigners, and c foreign purchases of U.S. assets such as factories and farms.

Economic
Growth

Although punctuated by periods of cyclical instability, economic growth in the United States has been impressive during this century. Real output has increased twelvefold and population has tripled, yielding approximately a quadrupling of the goods and services available to the average American. *What explains this expansion of real GDP and real GDP per capita?*

During the 1980s and early 1990s saving as a percentage of GDP in the United States fell to less than half its historical average. Also, according to a recent major study, America's technological edge has ended in a full one-third of ninety-four critical technologies in which we had a lead just a decade ago. *What are the implications of these developments for economic growth in the United States?*

In the 1970s and to a lesser degree in the 1980s and early 1990s productivity growth—increases in output per worker-hour—slowed in the United States relative to earlier periods. *How does productivity growth relate to economic growth? What caused this slowdown?*

The foregoing questions preview part of the subject matter of this chapter. Specifically, our discussion of economic growth is organized as follows. First, we examine how growth is defined and why it is important. Our second goal is to gain analytical perspective on economic growth. Third, we present and assess the long-term growth record of the United States. Fourth, the quantitative importance of various factors contributing to growth are explored. Fifth, we explain the slowdown in the productivity growth of American labor which began in the 1970s. Finally, we briefly examine the controversy surrounding growth and take a fleeting look at policies to promote growth.

GROWTH ECONOMICS

Employment theory and stabilization policy are of a static or short-run character. They assume the economy has fixed amounts of resources or inputs available and therefore is capable of producing some capacity or full-employment level of domestic output. The concern of employment theory is what must be done to use fully the nation's *existing* productive capacity. In contrast, growth economics is concerned with how to *increase* the economy's productive capacity or full-employment GDP.

Two Definitions

Economic growth is defined and measured in two related ways. Specifically, it may be defined as:

1 The increase in real GDP which occurs over a period of time

2 The increase in real GDP *per capita* which occurs over time

Both definitions are useful. For example, in measuring military potential or political preeminence, the first definition is more relevant. But per capita output is clearly superior to compare living standards among nations or regions. While India's GDP is $235 billion as compared to Switzerland's $175 billion, per capita GDP is $29,880 in Switzerland and only $340 in India. In this chapter we deal primarily with the growth of real output and income per capita.

Economic growth by either definition is usually calculated in terms of annual percentage *rates* of growth. For example, if real GDP was $200 billion last year and $210 billion this year, we can calculate the rate of growth by subtracting last year's real GDP from this year's real GDP and comparing the difference to last year's real GDP. Specifically, the growth rate in this case is ($210 − $200)/$200, or 5 percent.

Importance of Growth

Growth is a widely held economic goal. The growth of total output relative to population means a higher standard of living. An expanding real output means greater material abundance and implies a more satisfactory answer to the economizing problem. *A growing economy is in a superior position to meet new needs and resolve socioeconomic problems both domestically and internationally.* A growing economy, by definition, enjoys an increment in its annual real output which it can use to satisfy existing needs more effectively or to undertake new programs.

An expanding real wage or salary income makes new opportunities available to a family—a trip to Europe, a new stereo, a college education for each child—without sacrificing other opportunities and enjoyments. Similarly, a growing economy can undertake new programs to alleviate poverty and clean up the environment *without* impairing existing levels of consumption, investment, and public goods production. *Growth lessens the burden of scarcity.* A growing econ-

omy, unlike a static one, can consume more while simultaneously increasing its capacity to produce more in the future. By easing the burden of scarcity—by relaxing society's production constraints—economic growth allows a nation to attain existing economic goals more fully and to undertake new output-absorbing endeavors.

Arithmetic of Growth

People sometimes wonder why economists get excited about seemingly minuscule changes in the rate of growth. But it really *does* matter whether our economy grows at 4 percent or 3 percent. For the United States, with a current real GDP of about $4848 billion, the difference between a 3 and a 4 percent growth rate is about $48 billion of output per year. For a very poor country, a .5 percent change in the growth rate may mean the difference between starvation and mere hunger.

Furthermore, when viewed over a period of years, an apparently small difference in the rate of growth becomes exceedingly important because of the "miracle" of compound interest. Example: Suppose Alphania and Betania have identical GDPs. But Alphania begins to grow at a 4 percent annual rate, while Betania grows at only 2 percent. Recalling our "rule of 70" of Chapter 8, Alphania would find that its GDP would double in about eighteen years (=70 ÷ 4); Betania would take thirty-five years (=70 ÷ 2) to accomplish the same feat. The importance of the growth rate is undeniable.

One can also argue that the realization of growth is more important than achieving economic stability. The elimination of a recessionary gap might increase the national income by, say, 6 percent on a one-time basis. But a 3 percent annual growth rate will increase the national income by 6 percent in two years and will provide that 6 percent biannual increment indefinitely.

CAUSES: INGREDIENTS OF GROWTH

Basically, there are six strategic ingredients in the growth of any economy.

Supply Factors

Four growth factors relate to the physical ability of an economy to grow. They are (1) the quantity and quality of its natural resources, (2) the quantity and quality of its human resources, (3) the supply or stock of capital goods, and (4) technology. These four items are the **supply factors** in economic growth. These are the physical agents of greater production. The availability of more and better resources, including the stock of technological knowledge, is what permits an economy to produce a greater real output.

Demand and Allocative Factors

But the ability to grow and the actual realization of growth may be quite different things. Specifically, two additional considerations contribute to growth. First, there is a **demand factor** in growth. To realize its growing productive potential, a nation must provide for full employment of its expanding supplies of resources. This requires a growing level of aggregate demand.

Second, there is the **allocative factor** in growth. To achieve its productive potential, a nation must provide not only for full employment of its resources, but also for full production from them. The ability to expand production is not sufficient for the expansion of total output; also required are the actual employment of expanded resource supplies *and* the efficient allocation of those resources to get the maximum amount of useful goods produced.

It is notable that the supply and demand factors in growth are related. Unemployment can retard the rate of capital accumulation and slow expenditures for research. And, conversely, a low rate of innovation and investment can cause unemployment.

ECONOMIC GROWTH: GRAPHICAL ANALYSIS

The factors underlying economic growth can be placed in proper perspective through Chapter 2's production possibilities curves and Chapter 17's aggregate demand and aggregate supply analysis.

Growth and Production Possibilities

Recall that a curve such as *AB* in Figure 19-1 is a best-performance curve. It indicates the various *maximum* combinations of products the economy can produce, given the quantity and quality of its natural, human, and capital resources, and its stock of technological knowledge. An improvement in any of the supply factors will push the production possibilities curve to the

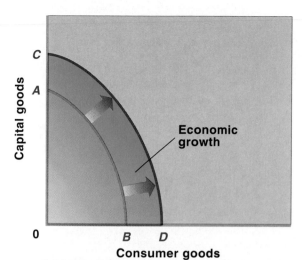

FIGURE 19-1   Economic growth and the production possibilities curve

Economic growth is indicated by an outward shift of the production possibilities curve, as from *AB* to *CD*. Increases in the quantity and quality of resources and technological advance permit this shift; full employment and allocative efficiency are essential to its realization.

right, as shown by the shift from *AB* to *CD* in Figure 19-1. Increases in the quantity or quality of resources and technological progress push the curve to the right. But the demand and allocative factors remind us that the economy need not attain its maximum productive potential; the curve may shift to the right and leave the economy behind at some level of operation *inside* the curve. In particular, the economy's enhanced productive *potential* will not be *realized* unless (1) aggregate demand increases sufficiently to sustain full employment, and (2) the additional resources are employed efficiently so they make the maximum possible contribution to the domestic output.

Example: The net increase in the labor force of the United States is roughly 2 million workers per year. As such, this increment raises the productive capacity, or potential, of the economy. But obtaining the extra output these additional workers are capable of producing presumes they can find jobs and that these jobs are in firms and industries where their talents are fully used. Society doesn't want new labor-force entrants to be unemployed; nor does it want pediatricians working as plumbers.

Although demand and allocative considerations are important, discussions of growth focus primarily on the supply side. Figure 19-2 provides a commonly used framework for discussing the supply factors in growth.

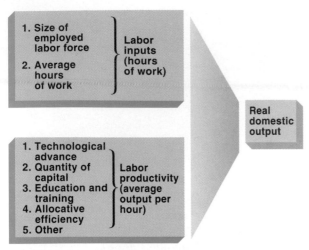

FIGURE 19-2 The determinants of real output
Real GDP can be usefully viewed as the product of the quantity of labor inputs multiplied by labor productivity.

It indicates there are two fundamental ways any society can increase its real output and income: (1) by increasing its inputs of resources, and (2) by increasing the productivity of those inputs. Let's focus on inputs of labor. By so doing we can say that *our real GDP in any year depends on the input of labor (measured in worker-hours) multiplied by* **labor productivity** *(measured as real output per worker per hour)*. That is

Total output = worker-hours × labor productivity

Hypothetical illustration: Assume an economy with 10 workers, each of whom works 2000 hours per year (50 weeks at 40 hours per week) so that total input of worker-hours is 20,000 hours. If productivity—average real output per worker-hour—is $5, then total output or real GDP will be $100,000 (=20,000 × $5).

What determines the number of hours worked each year? And, more importantly, what determines labor productivity? Figure 19-2 provides a framework for answering these questions. The hours of labor input depend on the size of the employed labor force and the length of the average workweek. Labor force size in turn depends on the size of the working age population and the labor force participation rate, that is, the percentage of the working age population actually in the labor force. The average workweek is governed by legal and institutional considerations and by collective bargaining.

Productivity is determined by technological progress, the quantity of capital goods with which workers are equipped, the quality of labor itself, and the efficiency with which inputs are allocated, combined, and managed. Stated differently, productivity increases

when the health, training, education, and motivation of workers are improved; when workers have more and better machinery and natural resources with which to work; when production is better organized and managed; and when labor is reallocated from less efficient industries to more efficient industries.

Note that Figure 19-2 complements Figure 15-4. The latter figure outlines the determinants of the *demand* for domestic output. Figure 19-2 summarizes those factors which determine a nation's capacity to *supply* or produce aggregate output. By locating Figure 19-2 to the left of Figure 15-4, we obtain a more complete model of the economy which sketches the determinants of both the demand for, and the supply of, domestic output.

Aggregate Demand–Aggregate Supply Framework

We can also view economic growth in terms of the long-run aggregate supply and aggregate demand analysis developed in Figures 17-6 and 17-7. Initially, suppose that aggregate demand is AD_1 and long-run and short-run aggregate supply curves are AS_1 and AS_1' as shown in Figure 19-3. Thus, the initial equilibrium price level is P_1 while the level of real output is Q_1.

Recall that the upward slope of short-run aggregate supply curve AS_1' shows that, other things equal, a change in the price level will alter the level of real output. In the long run, however, wages and other input prices will fully adjust to the price level, making the aggregate supply curve vertical at the economy's natural or potential level of real output. As is true of the location of the production possibilities curve, real supply factors—the quantity and quality of resources and technology—determine the long-run level of potential domestic output. Price level changes do not alter the location of the production possibilities curve; neither do price level changes alter the location of the long-run aggregate supply curve.

Aggregate Supply Shifts Now assume that changes in the supply factors listed in Figure 19-2 shift the long-run aggregate supply curve rightward from AS_1 to AS_2. That is, the production possibilities curve in Figure 19-1 has been pushed outward and the long-run aggregate supply curve in Figure 19-3 has shifted to the right. Also, we will soon see that the new relevant short-run aggregate supply curve is AS_2'.

Aggregate Demand Shifts If aggregate demand remains at AD_1, the increase in long-run aggregate

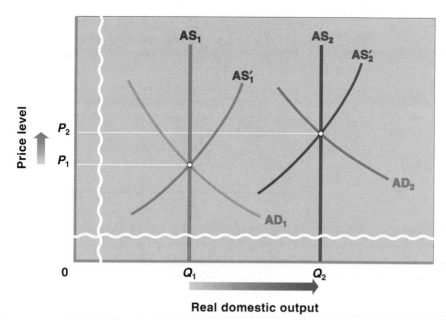

FIGURE 19-3 Economic growth and aggregate demand–aggregate supply analysis

Long-run and short-run aggregate supply curves have shifted rightward over time, as from AS_1 and AS_1' to AS_2 and AS_2'. Meanwhile, aggregate demand has shifted rightward even more rapidly. The outcome of these combined shifts has been economic growth, shown as the increase in real domestic output from Q_1 to Q_2, accompanied by inflation, shown as the rise in the price level from P_1 to P_2.

supply from AS_1 to AS_2 eventually will overcome any downward price and wage rigidity and reduce the price level. But in recent decades a rising, not a falling, price level has accompanied economic growth. This suggests that aggregate demand has increased more rapidly than long-run aggregate supply. We show this reality in Figure 19-3 by shifting aggregate demand from AD_1 to AD_2, which results from changes in one or more of the determinants of aggregate demand (Table 9-1).

The combined increases in aggregate supply and aggregate demand shown in Figure 19-3 have produced economic growth of Q_1Q_2 and a rise in the price level from P_1 to P_2. At price level P_2, the economy confronts a new short-run aggregate supply curve AS_2'. Also, observe that nominal GDP ($=P \times Q$) has increased more rapidly than real GDP ($=Q$) because of inflation. This diagram describes the secular trend of nominal GDP, real GDP, and the price level in the United States, a fact that you can quickly confirm by examining rows 5, 18, and 21 on the inside covers of this book.

GROWTH RECORD OF THE UNITED STATES

Table 19-1 gives us a rough idea of economic growth in the United States over past decades as viewed through our two definitions of growth. Column 2 summarizes

the economy's growth as measured by increases in real GDP. Although not steady, the growth of real GDP has been remarkable. *Real GDP has increased over fivefold since 1940.* But our population has also grown significantly. Thus, using our second definition of growth, we find in column 4 that *real per capita GDP was almost three times larger in 1991 than in 1940.*

TABLE 19-1   Real GDP and per capita GDP, 1929–1991

(1) Year	(2) GDP, billions of 1987 dollars	(3) Population, millions	(4) Per capita GDP, 1987 dollars (2) ÷ (3)
1929	$ 841	122	$ 6,893
1933	592	126	4,698
1940	919	132	6,962
1945	1615	140	11,536
1950	1428	152	9,395
1955	1773	166	10,681
1960	1973	181	10,902
1965	2474	194	12,753
1970	2876	205	14,029
1975	3222	214	15,056
1980	3776	228	16,561
1985	4280	239	17,908
1988	4719	245	19,261
1991	4848	253	19,162

Source: U.S. Department of Commerce.

What about our *rate* of growth? Data presented in Table 19-2 suggest that the post-1948 growth rate of the United States' real GDP has been more than 3 percent per year, while real GDP per capita has grown at almost 2 percent per year.

These bare numbers must be modified in several respects.

1 Improved products The figures of Tables 19-1 and 19-2 do *not* fully take into account improvements in product quality, and thus may understate the growth of economic well-being. Purely quantitative data do not provide an accurate comparison between an era of ice-boxes and one of refrigerators.

2 Added leisure The increases in real GDP and per capita GDP shown in Table 19-1 were accomplished despite sizable increases in leisure. The seventy-hour workweek is a thing of the distant past. The standard workweek is now less than forty hours. The result again is an understatement of economic well-being.

3 Environmental effects On the other hand, these measures of growth do *not* take into account adverse effects which growth may have on the environment and the quality of life itself. To the extent that growth debases the physical environment and creates a stressful work environment our data will overstate the benefits of growth.

4 International comparisons Also, the United States growth record is less impressive than those of several other industrially advanced nations. For example, the growth record of Japan has averaged more than twice that of the United States over the past four decades and there is genuine concern that Japan will overtake America as the world's leading industrial power.

QUICK REVIEW 19-1

◆ Economic growth can be viewed as either the increase in real GDP or real GDP per capita that occurs over time.

◆ Graphically, growth is shown as outward shifts of the production possibilities curve or as combined rightward shifts of aggregate supply and aggregate demand curves.

◆ Annual growth of real GDP in the United States has averaged more than 3 percent since World War II.

ACCOUNTING FOR GROWTH

Edward F. Denison of The Brookings Institution spent most of his professional career trying to quantify the relative importance of the various factors contributing to economic growth. His conceptual framework corresponds closely to the factors in Figure 19-2 and is therefore highly relevant to our discussion. Denison's most recent estimates are shown in Table 19-3. Over the 1929–1982 period he calculates that real national income grew by 2.9 percent per year. He then estimates what percentage of this annual growth was accounted for by each factor shown in the table. We will use Denison's table as a focal point for a series of brief comments on the ingredients in American economic growth.

Inputs versus Productivity

The most evident conclusion from Denison's data is that *productivity growth has been the most important force underlying the growth of our real domestic output*

TABLE 19-2 Growth of real GDP and real GDP per capita in selected countries

	Growth rates of real GDP		Growth rates of real GDP per capita	
	1870–1969	1948–1988	1870–1969	1948–1988
United States	3.7%	3.3%	2.0%	1.9%
Japan	4.2	7.1	—	5.9
Germany	3.0	5.0	1.9	4.2
United Kingdom	1.9	2.6	1.3	2.2
France	2.0	4.1	1.7	3.3
Italy	2.2	4.4	1.5	3.9
Canada	3.6	4.5	1.8	2.7

Source: U.S. Department of Commerce, *Historical Statistics of the United States: Colonial Times to 1970* (Washington, 1975), p. 225; and *Economic Report of the President, 1989*, p. 27.

TABLE 19-3 **The sources of growth in U.S. real national income, 1929–1982**

Sources of growth		Percent of total growth
(1) Increase in quantity of labor		32
(2) Increase in labor productivity		68
(3) Technological advance	28	
(4) Quantity of capital	19	
(5) Education and training	14	
(6) Economies of scale	9	
(7) Improved resource allocation	8	
(8) Legal-human environment and other	−9	
		100

Source: Edward F. Denison, *Trends in American Economic Growth, 1929–1982* (Washington: The Brookings Institution, 1985), p. 30. Details may not add to totals because of rounding.

and national income. Increases in the quantity of labor (item 1) account for only about one-third of the increase in real national income over this period; the remaining two-thirds is attributable to rising labor productivity (item 2).

Quantity of Labor

Our population and labor force have both expanded significantly through time. Over the 1929–1982 period considered by Denison, total population grew from 122 to 232 million and the labor force increased from 49 to 110 million workers. Historical reductions in the length of the average workweek have reduced labor inputs, but the workweek has declined very modestly since World War II. Declining birthrates in the past twenty years or so have slowed the rate of population growth. However, largely because of increased participation by women in labor markets, our labor force continues to grow by about 2 million workers per year.

Technological Advance

We note in Table 19-3 that technological advance (item 3) is an important engine of growth, accounting for 28 percent of the increase in real national income realized over the 1929–1982 period. Technological advance is broadly defined to include, not merely new production techniques, but also new managerial techniques and new forms of business organization. More generally, technological advance is linked with the discovery of new knowledge, which permits combining a given amount of resources in new ways to result in a larger output.

In practice, technological advance and capital formation (investment) are closely related processes; technological advance often entails investment in new machinery and equipment. The idea that there is a more efficient way to catch a rabbit than by running it down led to investment in the bow and arrow. And it is clearly necessary to construct new nuclear power plants to apply nuclear power technology. However, modern crop-rotation practices and contour plowing are ideas which contribute greatly to output, although they do not necessarily use new kinds or increased amounts of capital equipment.

Casual observation suggests that, historically, technological advance has been both rapid and profound. Gas and diesel engines, conveyor belts, and assembly lines come to mind as highly significant developments of the past. More recently, the lamp of technology has freed the automation jinni and with it the potential wonders of the push-button factory. Supersonic jets, the transistor and integrated circuitry, computers, xerography, containerized shipping, and nuclear power—not to mention recent breakthroughs in biotechnology and superconductivity—are technological achievements which were in the realm of fantasy only a generation ago. Table 19-3 merely confirms the importance of such developments in the economic growth process.

Quantity of Capital

Some 19 percent—almost one-fifth—of the annual growth of real national income over the indicated period was attributable to increases in the quantity of capital (item 4). It is no surprise that a worker will be more productive when equipped with a larger amount of capital goods. And how does a nation acquire more capital? Capital accumulation results from saving and the investment in plant and equipment which these savings make possible.

The critical consideration in labor productivity is the amount of capital goods *per worker.* The aggregate stock of capital might expand during a specific period, but if the labor force increases more rapidly, then labor productivity will fall because *each worker* will be less well equipped. Something of this sort happened in the 1970s and contributed to a slowing of productivity growth.

To what extent has real capital per worker increased? One long-run estimate concludes that in the

1889 to 1969 period the stock of capital goods increased sixfold and, over this same period, labor-hours doubled. Hence, the quantity of capital goods per labor-hour was roughly three times as large in 1969 than in 1889.[1] While the capital stock is not easy to calculate, data suggest that the amount of capital equipment (machinery and buildings) per worker is currently about $40,000.

Two addenda are in order.

1 We will see shortly that the United States has been saving and investing a smaller percentage of its GDP in recent years than have most other industrially advanced nations. This helps explain our relatively less impressive growth performance (Table 19-2).

2 Investment is not only private, but also public. Our **infrastructure**—our highways and bridges, port facilities, public transit systems, wastewater treatment facilities, municipal water systems, airports, and so on—is encountering growing problems of deterioration, technological obsolescence, and insufficient capacity to serve future growth. Moreover, public capital—the infrastructure—and private capital may be complementary. Investments in new highways promote private investment in new factories and retail establishments along their routes. Some economists view the deterioration of our infrastructure as a significant source of reduced private investment.

Education and Training

Ben Franklin once said, "He that hath a trade hath an estate." This is an archaic way of saying that education and training improve a worker's productivity and result in higher earnings. Like investment in real capital, investment in human capital is an important means of increasing labor productivity. Denison's estimates in Table 19-3 indicate that 14 percent of the growth in our real national income is attributable to such improvements in the quality of labor (item 5).

Perhaps the simplest measure of labor force quality is the level of educational attainment. Figure 19-4 reflects the gains realized in the past several decades. Currently 86 percent of the labor force has received at least a high school education. Of this group more than 26 percent acquired a college education or more. Less than 6 percent of the labor force has received no more than an elementary school education. It is clear that education has become accessible to more and more people.

But there are persistent concerns about the quality of American education. Scores on Scholastic Aptitude Tests (SATs) have declined relative to scores of a few decades ago. Furthermore, the performance of American students in science and mathematics compares unfavorably to that of students in many other industrialized countries.

Scale Economies and Resource Allocation

Table 19-3 also tells us that labor productivity has increased because of economies of scale (item 6) and improved resource allocation (item 7). Let's consider the latter factor first.

Improved Resource Allocation   Improved resource allocation means that workers over time have reallocated themselves from relatively low-productivity employment to relatively high-productivity employment. For example, historically, much labor has been reallocated from agriculture—where labor productivity is relatively low—to manufacturing—where labor productivity is relatively high. As a result, the average productivity of American workers in the aggregate has increased.

Also, labor market discrimination has denied many women and minorities access to those jobs in which they would be most productive. The decline of such discrimination over time has increased labor productivity.

We will find in Chapter 37 that tariffs, import quotas, and other barriers to international trade are conducive to the allocation of labor to relatively unproductive employments. The long-run movement toward freer international trade has therefore improved the allocation of labor and enhanced productivity.

Economies of Scale   Economies of scale are production advantages which are derived from market and firm size. A large corporation might be able to select a more efficient production technique than could a small-scale firm. A large manufacturer of automobiles can use elaborate assembly lines, with computerization and robotics, while smaller producers must settle for more primitive technologies. The contribution of economies of scale shown in Table 19-3 means that markets have increased in scope and firms have increased in size so that more efficient production methods are being used. Accordingly, labor productivity has increased.

[1] Solomon Fabricant, *A Primer on Productivity* (New York: Random House, Inc., 1969), chap. 5.

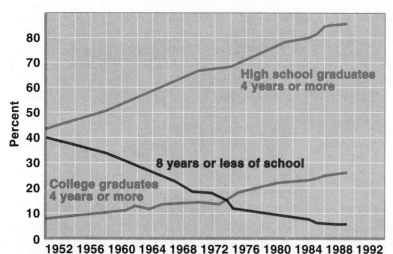

FIGURE 19-4 Recent changes in the educational attainment of the labor force

The percentage of the labor force completing high school and college has been rising steadily in recent years, while the percentage who did not go to high school or complete elementary school has been falling. (*Statistical Abstract of the United States.*)

Detriments to Growth

Unfortunately, some developments detract from labor productivity and growth of real national income. The legal and human environment entry in Table 19-3 (item 8) aggregates these detriments to productivity growth. Over the 1929–1982 period considerable changes were made in the regulation of industry, environmental pollution, and worker health and safety, which have negatively affected growth. The expansion of government regulation of business in such areas as pollution control and worker health and safety diverted investment spending away from productivity-increasing capital goods and toward equipment which provides cleaner air and water and greater worker protection from accident and illness. A firm required to spend $1 million on a new scrubber to meet government standards for air pollution will not have that $1 million to spend on machinery and equipment which would enhance worker productivity. The diversion of resources to deal with dishonesty and crime, the effects of work stoppages because of labor disputes, and the impact of bad weather on agricultural output are also included in item 8.

This point is worth adding. Worker safety, clean air and water, and the overall "quality of life" may come at the expense of productivity. But the reverse is also true. That is, we cannot assume that productivity advances automatically enhance society's welfare. Pro-

ductivity growth may entail opportunity costs of other things (a clean environment) which we value more highly. Productivity measures output per hour of work, not overall "well-being" per hour of work.

Other Factors

There are other difficult-to-quantify considerations which play significant roles in determining an economy's growth rate. For example, the generous and varied supplies of natural resources with which the United States has been blessed have been an important contributor to our economic growth.[2] We enjoy an abundance of fertile soil, desirable climatic and weather conditions, ample quantities of most mineral resources, and generous sources of power. With the possible exception of the former Soviet Union, the United States has a larger variety and greater quantity of natural resources than any other nation.

While an abundant natural resource base is often very helpful to the growth process, a meager resource base does not doom a nation to slow growth. Although Japan's natural resources are severely constrained, its post-World War II growth has been remarkable

[2]Denison omits land (natural resources) from Table 19-3 on the grounds that, unlike inputs of labor and capital, there have been no changes in land inputs to contribute to the growth of real national income. That is, the quantity of land does not change and any qualitative changes are minuscule.

(Table 19-2). On the other hand, some of the less developed countries of Africa and South America have substantial amounts of natural resources.

There are additional unmeasurable factors which affect a nation's growth rate. In particular, the overall social-cultural-political environment of the United States generally has been conducive to economic growth. Several interrelated factors contribute to this favorable environment.

1 As opposed to many other nations, there are virtually no social or moral taboos on production and material progress. Indeed, American social philosophy has embraced material advance as an attainable and desirable economic goal. The inventor, the innovator, and the business executive are generally accorded high degrees of prestige and respect in American society.

2 Americans have traditionally possessed healthy attitudes toward work and risk taking; our society has benefited from a willing labor force and an ample supply of entrepreneurs.

3 Our market system is replete with personal and corporate incentives which encourage growth; our economy rewards actions which increase output.

4 Our economy is founded on a stable political system characterized by internal order, the right of property ownership, the legal status of enterprise, and the enforcement of contracts.

Though not subject to quantification, these characteristics have undoubtedly provided an excellent foundation for American economic growth.

Aggregate Demand, Instability, and Growth

As seen in Table 19-3, Denison's analysis is designed to explain the growth of *actual,* as opposed to *potential* or full-employment, real national income. The 2.9 percent annual growth rate which the table attempts to explain embodies changes in real national income caused by fluctuations in aggregate demand. Denison recognizes that our growth rate would have been higher—3.2 percent per year—if the economy's potential output had been realized year after year. Deviations from full employment due to a deficiency of aggregate demand cause the actual rate of growth to fall short of the potential rate. A glance back at Figure 8-5 reminds us of the extent to which the actual performance of our economy frequently falls short of its potential output. The Great Depression of the 1930s in particular was a serious

blow to the United States' long-run growth record. Between 1929 and 1933 our real GDP (measured in 1987 prices) actually *declined* from $841 to $592 billion. In 1939 the real GDP was approximately at the same level as in 1929 (see line 18 on table inside front cover). More recently it is estimated that the severe 1980–1982 recessions cost the United States more than $600 billion in lost output and income.

But this is only part of the picture. Cyclical unemployment can have certain harmful "carry-over" effects on the growth rate in subsequent years of full employment through the adverse effects it may have on other growth factors. For example, unemployment depresses investment and capital accumulation. Furthermore, the expansion of research budgets may be slowed by recession so that technological progress diminishes; union resistance to technological change may stiffen; and so forth. Though it is difficult to quantify the impact of these considerations on the growth rate, they undoubtedly can be of considerable importance.

QUICK REVIEW 19-2

◆ *Increases in labor productivity account for about two-thirds of increases in real output; the use of more labor inputs accounts for the remaining one-third.*

◆ *Improved technology, more capital, more education and training, economies of scale, and improved resource allocation are the main contributors to growth.*

◆ *Growth rates in the United States have been erratic, particularly because of fluctuations in aggregate demand.*

THE PRODUCTIVITY SLOWDOWN

In the 1970s—and to a lesser degree in the 1980s and early 1990s—the United States experienced a much-publicized productivity slowdown. Table 19-4 portrays the course of United States labor productivity in the post-World War II period. Observe in column 2 that for about two decades following World War II (1948–1966) labor productivity increased at a vigorous average annual rate of 3.2 percent, only to decline rather precipitously in the 1966–1973 period. This was followed by a dismal productivity performance in the 1973–1981 period, and a modest resurgence of productivity growth

TABLE 19-4 **Growth of labor productivity and real per capita GDP, 1948–1990**

(1) Period	(2) Productivity growth rate	(3) Real per capita GDP, growth rate
1948–1966	3.2	2.2%
1966–1973	2.0	2.0
1973–1981	0.7	1.1
1981–1990	1.3	1.8

Source: *Economic Report of the President, 1988,* p. 67. End points of calculations are cyclical peaks. Updated.

in the 1980s. Although labor productivity growth has been slowing worldwide, American productivity growth has been less than that of other major industrialized nations. The United States still enjoys the highest absolute level of output per worker, but its productivity advantage is quickly diminishing.

Significance

The significance of our productivity slowdown is manifold.

1 Standard of Living Productivity growth is the basic source of improvements in real wage rates and the standard of living. Real income per worker-hour can only increase at the same rate as real output per worker-hour. More output per hour means more real income to distribute for each hour worked. The simplest case is the classic one of Robinson Crusoe on his deserted island. The number of fish he can catch or coconuts he can pick per hour *is* his real income or wage per hour.

We observe in column 3 of Table 19-4 that the broadest measure of living standards—the growth of real per capita GDP—followed the path of labor productivity. Living levels thus measured grew by only 1.1 percent per year during the severe 1973–1981 productivity stagnation compared to 2.2 percent in the 1948–1966 postwar decades.

2 Inflation We saw in Chapter 17 that productivity increases offset increases in nominal-wage rates and thereby partly or fully lessen cost-push inflationary pressures. Other things being equal, a decline in the rate of productivity growth contributes to rapidly rising unit labor costs and a higher rate of inflation. Many

economists believe that productivity stagnation contributed to the unusually high inflation rates of the 1970s.

3 World Markets Other things being equal, our slow rate of productivity growth compared to our major international trading partners increases relative prices of American goods in world markets. The result is a decline in our competitiveness and a loss of international markets for American producers.

Causes of the Slowdown

There is no consensus among experts as to why American productivity growth has slowed and fallen behind the rates of Japan and western Europe. Indeed, because so many factors affect productivity, there may be no simple explanation for the slowdown. However, let's survey some of the possible causes.

Labor Quality One possibility is that slower improvements in labor quality may have dampened productivity growth. Three factors may have been at work.

1 Decline in Experience Level The experience level of the labor force may have declined. The large number of baby-boom workers who entered the labor force had little experience and training and were therefore less productive. Similarly, the labor force participation of women increased significantly over the past two decades. Many were married women with little or no prior labor force experience and therefore had low productivity.

2 Less Able Workers The declining test scores of students on standardized examinations during the past few decades perhaps indicates a decline in worker capabilities. If so, this decline may have contributed to the productivity slowdown.

3 Slowing of Increased Educational Attainment The average level of educational attainment of the labor force has been increasing more slowly in recent years. The median number of years of school completed by the adult population was 12.3 in 1960 and increased to only 12.7 by 1989.

Technological Progress Technological advance—usually reflected in improvements in the quality of capital goods and the efficiency with which inputs are combined—may also have faltered. Technological progress is fueled by expenditures for formal research and development (R&D) programs. In the United States, R&D spending declined as a percentage of GDP from a peak of 3 percent in the mid-1960s to about 1 percent by the late 1970s, before rising again in the 1980s.

However, some economists discount the R&D decline in explaining the productivity slowdown. They say R&D *spending* alone tells us little about R&D *accomplishments*. There is evidence of continuing technological advance during the past two decades.

Investment   There is a high positive correlation between the percentage of a nation's GDP devoted to investment goods and the productivity increases it achieves. A worker using a bulldozer can move more earth per hour than the same worker equipped with a hand shovel. An engineer using a computer can complete a design task more rapidly than with pencil and paper.

As Figure 19-5 shows, the United States has recently been investing a smaller percentage of its GDP than in earlier periods. Note the decline in the 1970s and the even greater decline in the 1980s. Several factors may have contributed to the weak growth of investment.

1 Low Saving Rate   The United States has had a relatively low saving rate which, coupled with strong private and public demands for credit, has resulted in high real interest rates relative to historical standards. High interest rates discourage investment spending.

2 Import Competition   Growing import competition may have made some American producers reluctant to invest in new capital equipment. Alternatively, they may have shifted more investment overseas toward nations with low-wage workers.

3 Regulation   As noted earlier, the expansion of government regulations in the areas of pollution control and worker health and safety diverted some investment spending away from output-increasing capital goods. This investment spending may have increased total utility to society, but did not directly increase output itself. That is, the composition of investment may have shifted toward uses which do not increase productivity.

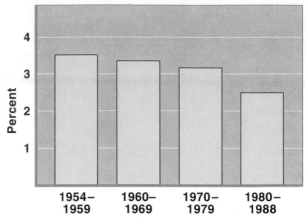

FIGURE 19-5   Investment as a percentage of GDP, selected period averages

Real nonresidental net investment in the United States declined for several reasons in the 1970s and diminished even more significantly in the 1980s. These declines may have been a contributing factor to the slow growth of labor productivity.

4 Reduced Infrastructure Spending   Reduced spending on the economy's infrastructure—its highways, bridges, airports, harbors, power plants, and similar installations—may have slowed productivity growth. These public goods are complementary to private capital goods. For example, public investments in new highways and airports increase the productivity of business travelers and the efficiency with which inputs and finished products are transported. Also, public spending on power plants lowers energy costs and therefore the costs of running private manufacturing plants. Data show that in the 1950–1970 period the public capital stock of infrastructure grew at a 4.1 percent annual rate, and labor productivity growth was 2.0 percent per year. In the 1971–1985 era, however, the yearly increase in the infrastructure fell to only 1.6 percent and the annual productivity increase plummeted to 0.8 percent. A slowing of spending on public investment goods may have contributed to diminishing private investments and to declines in productivity growth.

Energy Prices   Perhaps the prime suspect in the productivity slowdown was the large increases in oil prices which occurred in 1973–1975 and in 1978–1980. Productivity growth fell off sharply after the quadrupling of oil prices in 1973–1975. Also, the impact of skyrocketing energy prices was worldwide, as was the productivity slowdown.

The direct impact of higher oil prices was to increase the cost of operating capital equipment, in effect raising the "price" of capital relative to labor. Producers were therefore more inclined to use less productive labor-intensive techniques.

The indirect macroeconomic effects of dramatically higher energy prices may have been even more important in reducing productivity growth. The two episodes of soaring energy prices precipitated stagflation—inflationary recessions. Government's use of restrictive macroeconomic policies to control inflation undoubtedly worsened and prolonged the periods of recession and slow economic growth. Recessions diminish productivity—output per worker—in that output tends to decline more rapidly than employment. The prolonged periods of underuse of productive capacity in many industries undoubtedly contributed to the productivity slowdown.

Industrial Relations   A different view of the productivity slowdown stresses that forces of an institutional nature—the way work is organized, the attitudes and behavior of workers and managers, communication between labor and management, and the division of authority among managers and workers—account for much of our poor productivity performance compared to Japan and western Europe. The argument is that American industrial relations are characterized by an adversarial relationship between managers and their employees. Feeling alienated from their employers, workers do not participate in the decisions which govern their daily work lives; they do not identify with the objectives of their firms, and therefore are not motivated to work hard and productively. Managers are judged, rewarded, and motivated by short-term profit performance and thus, it is argued, give little attention to long-term plans and strategies critical to attaining high rates of productivity growth.

Japanese industries, in contrast, provide lifetime employment security for a sizable portion of their work force, allow for worker participation in decision making, and use profit-sharing or bonuses to provide a direct link between the economic success of a firm and worker incomes. Furthermore, the direct interest workers have in the competitiveness and profitability of their enterprise reduces the need for supervisory personnel. The result is a commonality of interest and cooperation between management and labor, greater flexibility in job assignment, and enhanced willingness of workers to accept technological change. Lifetime employment is also conducive to heavy investment by employers in training and retraining their workers.

The implication is that an overhaul of our industrial relations system is a key to restoring our productivity growth.

A Resurgence?

The 1981–1990 data in Table 19-4 suggest a modest improvement in productivity growth; the 1.3 percent annual increase for this period compares favorably with the 0.7 percent productivity growth for 1973–1981. Although the recession of 1990–1991 halted this upward trend—productivity growth was only 0.2 percent in 1990—it is evident that some of the factors which may have depressed productivity growth have dissipated or been reversed. Since 1977 R&D spending has generally increased as a percentage of GDP. Important innovations in computerization and robotics may be providing a stimulus to productivity. The inexperienced baby boomers who flooded labor markets in the 1970s are now rapidly becoming mature, experienced, more productive workers.

Also, although American industrial relations remain distinctly different from the cooperative "shared vision" of Japanese managers and workers, the problems imposed by recession and increasing foreign competition are pushing American workers and managers in that direction. Worker involvement and profit-sharing plans are increasingly common in American industry. In fact, employees in the United States collectively now own an estimated $150 billion of stock in the firms for which they work.

Nevertheless, it is unclear at this point whether the recent revival of productivity is transitory or permanent.

IS GROWTH DESIRABLE?

Up to now we have taken for granted that growth is desirable. In fact, growth is an issue of some controversy.

The Case Against Growth

Serious questions have been raised as to the desirability of continued economic growth for already affluent nations. A number of interrelated arguments comprise this antigrowth sentiment.

1 Pollution Concern with environmental deterioration is an important part of the antigrowth position. Industrialization and growth result in serious problems of pollution, industrial noise and stench, ugly cities, traffic jams, and many other disamenities of modern life. These adverse external or spillover costs are held to be the consequence of the hard fact that the production of the GDP changes the form of resources, but does not destroy them. Virtually all inputs in the productive process are eventually returned to the environment in some form of waste.

The more rapid our growth and the higher our standard of living, the more waste there is for the environment to absorb—or attempt to absorb. In an already wealthy society, further growth may mean satisfying increasingly trivial wants at the cost of mounting threats to our ecological system. Antigrowth economists feel that future growth should be purposely constrained.

2 Problem Resolution? There is little compelling evidence that economic growth has solved socioeconomic problems, as its proponents claim. Antigrowth economists assert, for example, that the domestic problem of poverty—income inequality—is essentially a problem of distribution, not production. The requisites for solving the poverty problem are commitment and political courage, not further increases in output. In general, there is no compelling evidence that growth has been, or will be, a palliative for domestic social problems.

3 Human Obsolescence and Insecurity Growth critics contend that rapid growth—and in particular the changing technology at the core of growth—poses new anxieties and new sources of insecurity for workers. Both high-level and low-level workers face the prospect of having their hard-earned skills and experience rendered obsolete by an onrushing technology.

4 Growth and Human Values Critics of growth also offer a group of related arguments which say, in effect, that while growth may permit us to "make a living," it does not give us "the good life." We may, in fact, be producing more, but enjoying it less. More specifically, it is charged that growth means industrialization, uncreative and unsatisfying mass-production jobs, and alienated workers who have little or no control over the decisions affecting their lives.

In Defense of Growth

However, most economists view growth as a high-priority goal. They make the following arguments.

1 Living Standards The primary defense of economic growth is that it is the path to material abundance and rising standards of living for families and individuals (Table 19-1). *Growth makes the unlimited wants–scarce resources dilemma less acute.*

> In a growing economy public choices are less agonizing and divisive. It is possible to modernize the armed forces; keep the nation's infrastructure in repair; provide for the elderly, the sick, and the needy; improve education and other public services; and still have private incomes that rise after taxes.[3]

2 Growth and the Environment Growth proponents feel that the connection between growth, on the one hand, and the environment, on the other, is overdrawn. To a considerable degree these are separable issues. If society should flatly abandon the goal of growth and produce a constant real output every year, it would still have to make choices about the composition of output which would affect the environment and the quality of life. Society would still have to weigh the relative merits of enjoying the natural beauty of a forest or cutting the timber for productive uses. And, if the timber were cut, society would have to decide whether it would be used for housing or fast-food wrappers.

Pollution is not so much a by-product of growth as it is a shortcoming of the market system. Specifically, much of the environment—streams, lakes, oceans, and the air—are treated as "common property" and no charge is made for their use. Thus, our environmental resources are overused and debased. Recalling Chapter 6's terminology, environmental pollution is a case of spillover or external costs, and correcting this problem involves regulatory legislation or specific taxes ("effluent charges") to remedy the market system's flaw and eliminate misuse of the environment. There are, to be sure, serious pollution problems. But limiting growth is the wrong response.

3 Poverty Reduction Economic growth is the only politically feasible way to reduce poverty in our society.

---

[3]Alice M. Rivlin (ed.), *Economic Choices of 1984* (Washington: The Brookings Institution, 1984), p. 2.

Support for highly progressive taxes and major income transfer programs has waned in the United States. In fact, the distribution of income today is more unequal than it was in 1969. It follows that the primary means for improving the economic position of the poor is to move the entire distribution of income upward through economic growth. Similarly, a no-growth policy among industrial nations would most likely end political support for aid to developing nations, perhaps assigning the world's poor to poverty for longer periods.

4 Nonmaterial Considerations Those who defend growth argue that its retardation or cessation will not automatically foster humanistic goals or promote "the good life." Indeed, we should expect the contrary. The ending of growth will not mean elimination of production-line work; historically, growth has been accompanied by a *decline* in the fraction of the labor force so employed. Nor has growth uniformly made labor more unpleasant or hazardous. New machinery is usually less taxing and less hazardous than the machinery it replaces. Air-conditioned workplaces are more pleasant than the sweatshops of old.

Furthermore, why would retardation or prohibition of growth reduce materialism or alienation? Would we not expect results to be the opposite? The loudest protests against materialism are heard in those nations and from those groups who now enjoy the highest levels of material abundance! More positively, it is the high standards of living which growth provides that make it possible for more people "to take the time for education, reflection, and self-fulfillment."[4]

QUICK REVIEW 19-3

♦ *Productivity has slowed down in the past two decades because of declines in labor quality, slowing of technological progress, decreased investment spending as a percentage of GDP, higher energy prices, and deteriorating industrial relations.*

♦ *Although some critics disparage growth because it allegedly increases pollution and fails to solve socioeconomic problems, there are compelling arguments in favor of growth, namely, that it lessens the scarcity problem and increases the standard of living.*

---

[4]Marc J. Roberts, "On Reforming Economic Growth," in Mancur Olson and Hans H. Landsberg (eds.), *The No-Growth Society* (New York: W. W. Norton & Company, Inc., 1973), p. 133.

GROWTH POLICIES

If we accept the view that on balance economic growth is desirable, then the question as to what public policies might best stimulate growth arises. Several types of policy are either in use or have been suggested.

Demand-Side Policies

Low growth is often the consequence of inadequate aggregate demand and resulting GDP gaps. The purpose of demand-side policies is to eliminate or reduce the severity of recessions through active fiscal and monetary policy. The idea is to use government tools to increase aggregate demand at a rapid, noninflationary pace. Strong aggregate demand not only keeps present resources fully employed, it also creates an incentive for firms to expand their operations. In particular, low real interest rates (easy money policy) are conducive to high levels of investment spending. This spending leads to capital accumulation, which expands the economy's capacity to produce.

Supply-Side Policies

These policies emphasize factors which will directly increase the potential or full-capacity output of the economy over time. The goal is to shift Figure 19-3's long-run and short-run aggregate supply curves rightward. Policies which fit this category include tax policies designed to stimulate saving, investment, and entrepreneurship. For example, by lowering or eliminating the tax paid on income placed in saving accounts, the return on saving will increase and therefore so will the amount of saving. Likewise, by lowering or eliminating the deduction of interest expenses on one's personal income tax, consumption will be discouraged and saving encouraged. Some economists favor the introduction of a national consumption tax as a full or partial replacement for the personal income tax. The idea is to penalize consumption and thereby encourage saving.

On the investment side of the picture, some economists propose eliminating the corporate income tax or, more specifically, allowing generous tax credits for business investment spending. If effective, this proposal would simultaneously increase aggregate demand and aggregate supply.

LAST WORD

THE JAPANESE GROWTH MIRACLE

Since World War II Japan has achieved more rapid growth than any other economy (Table 19-2). What factors account for this remarkable progress?

The Japanese economy is showing signs of replacing the United States as the world's leading industrial power. Symbolic of Japan's success is the fact that it surpassed the United States in automobile production in 1980. Similarly, American dominance in the steel and television industries has been usurped by Japan. Japan is also dominant in the production of watches, cameras, electronics equipment, and industrial robots. These economic accomplishments are all the more remarkable because Japan's population is large relative to its land mass and its natural resource base is very limited. For example, Japan is heavily dependent on imported oil and iron ore. Recall, too, that at the end of World War II (1945) the Japanese economy was in ruins. How, then, can we account for the Japanese growth miracle?

1 Saving and investing Japan has achieved high rates of saving and investment. The cultural thriftiness of the Japanese population has been supplemented by special tax incentives to save. The interest earned on small savings accounts is tax-free. On the investment side of the picture, tax laws embody accelerated depre-

ciation of capital goods for tax purposes when investment involves plant modernization or the introduction of new products and technologies. Japan invests a larger proportion of its GDP than does any other advanced capitalist country and this is reflected in a high rate of productivity growth.

2 Labor-management relations Many experts contend that a sizable portion of Japan's economic progress is attributable to its quasi-paternalistic system of labor relations. About one-third of the Japanese labor force enjoys the security of guaranteed lifetime employment in large industrial concerns.

Industrial and Other Policies

There are other potential growth-stimulating policies which economists of various persuasions recommend. Some advocate an **industrial policy** whereby government would take a direct, active role in shaping the structure and composition of industry to promote growth. Thus government might take steps to hasten expansion of high-productivity industries and speed the movement of resources out of low-productivity industries. Government might also increase its expenditures on basic research and development to stimulate technological progress. Also, increased expenditures on education may help increase the quality and productivity of labor.

While the litany of potential growth-enhancing policies is long and involved, most economists agree that it is no simple matter to increase a nation's growth rate.

CHAPTER SUMMARY

1 Economic growth may be defined either as **a** an expanding real output (income) or **b** an expanding per capita real output (income). Growth lessens the burden of scarcity and provides increases in the domestic output which

can be used to resolve domestic and international socioeconomic problems.

2 The supply factors in economic growth are **a** the quantity and quality of a nation's natural resources, **b** the

Furthermore, these enterprises have assumed many functions of the welfare state in that they provide medical care, subsidized housing, and a variety of other fringe benefits. As a result, the adversary labor-management relations which are common to the United States are largely supplanted in Japan by a cooperative relationship. Workers realize that their economic futures are intimately linked to the viability and competitiveness of their enterprise.

Given employment security and the fact that a substantial portion of wages is in the form of profit-related bonuses, workers have a strong incentive to accept technological change, learn new skills, and cooperate with management in increasing productivity. More generally, the Japanese labor force is disciplined and well-educated.

3 National purpose and planning A somewhat less tangible factor in Japan's growth performance has to do with a clearer perception of its national interest and the willingness of economic actors to subordinate their self-interests to national goals. This ability of government, business, and labor to achieve a consensus or common perspective on national economic objectives may have cultural roots or it may spring from a recognition that Japan's economic success hinges on its remaining highly competitive in world markets. The net result is a close positive relationship between the government, business, and labor in promoting the national interest, that is, in furthering economic growth.

In fact, the Japanese engage in "indicative" (as opposed to "imperative" or coercive) planning whereby industrial development objectives are determined along with other economic and social goals. Primary responsibility for the overall regulation and guidance of Japanese industries toward these goals rests with the Ministry of International Trade and Industry (MITI). Business and labor are expected to subordinate their private interests to the national goals set forth by MITI. The overall result is that government and business are in a more cooperative posture, as compared to the adversary relationship generally existing in the United States.

Japan, in short, has a more coherent industrial policy and a more clearly defined sense of national purpose than do most of its capitalistic competitors. And economic growth ranks high as a national goal in Japan.

4 Other factors The Japanese growth story has other roots. Since World War II the Japanese have diverted few resources—less than 1 percent of the GDP—to military spending. This has freed high-level personnel and capital goods to improve the productivity of industry. Similarly, the Japanese have been very adept at transferring, applying, and improving on the technological advances of other countries.

While Japan's progress has not been achieved without conflicts and problems, its overall growth record is enviable.

---

quantity and quality of its human resources, **c** its stock of capital facilities, and **d** its technology. Two other factors— a sufficient level of aggregate demand and allocative efficiency—are essential if the economy is to realize its growth potential.

3 Economic growth can be shown graphically as a rightward shift of a nation's production possibilities curve or as a rightward shift of its long-run aggregate supply curve.

4 The post-World War II growth rate of real GDP for the United States has been more than 3 percent; real GDP per capita has grown at about 2 percent.

5 Real GDP in the United States has grown, partly because of increased inputs of labor, and primarily because of increases in the productivity of labor. Technological progress, increases in the quantity of capital per worker, improvements in the quality of labor, economies of scale, and improved allocation of labor are among the more important factors which increase labor productivity.

6 The rate of productivity growth declined sharply in the 1970s, causing a slowdown in the rise of our living standards and contributing to inflation. Although productivity has risen in the 1980s and early 1990s, it remains substantially below the levels attained in the two decades following World War II.

7 Critics of economic growth **a** cite adverse environmental effects; **b** argue that domestic and international problems are matters of distribution, not production; **c** contend that growth is a major source of human obsolescence and insecurity; and **d** argue that growth is frequently in conflict with certain human values.

8 Proponents of growth stress that **a** growth means a better solution to the wants-means dilemma; **b** environmental problems are only loosely linked to growth; **c** growth is the only feasible means by which poverty can be reduced; and **d** growth is more consistent with "the good life" than is stagnation.

TERMS AND CONCEPTS

supply, demand, and
allocative factors in
growth

economic growth
labor productivity

infrastructure

industrial policy

QUESTIONS AND STUDY SUGGESTIONS

1 Why is economic growth important? Explain why the difference between a 2.5 percent and a 3.0 percent annual growth rate might be of great importance.

2 What are the major causes of economic growth? "There are both a demand and a supply side to economic growth." Explain. Illustrate the operation of both sets of factors in terms of the production possibilities curve.

3 Suppose an economy's real GDP is $30,000 in year 1 and $31,200 in year 2. What is the growth rate of its GDP? Assume that population was 100 in year 1 and 102 in year 2. What is the growth rate of GDP per capita? Between 1948 and 1991 the nation's price level has risen by over 440 percent while its real output has increased by almost 275 percent. Use the aggregate demand–aggregate supply model to show these outcomes graphically.

4 Briefly describe the growth record of the United States. Compare the rates of growth in real GDP and real GDP per capita, explaining any differences. To what extent might these figures understate or overstate economic well-being?

5 To what extent have increases in our real GDP been the result of more labor inputs? Of increasing labor productivity? Discuss the factors which contribute to productivity growth in order of their quantitative importance.

6 Using examples, explain how changes in the allocation of labor can affect labor productivity.

7 How do you explain the close correlation which exists between changes in the rate of productivity growth and changes in real wage rates? Discuss the relationship between productivity growth and inflation.

8 Account for the recent slowdown in the United States' rate of productivity growth. What are the consequences of this slowdown? "Most of the factors which contributed to poor productivity growth in the 1970s are now behind us and are unlikely to recur in the near future." Do you agree?

9 "If we want economic growth in a free society, we may have to accept a measure of instability." Evaluate. The noted philosopher Alfred North Whitehead once remarked that "the art of progress is to preserve order amid change and to preserve change amid order." What did he mean? Is this contention relevant for economic growth? What implications might this have for public policy? Explain.

10 Comment on the following statements:
  a "Technological advance is destined to play a more important role in economic growth in the future than it has in the past."
  b "Poverty reduction is a matter of redistribution, not of further growth."
  c "The issues of economic growth and environmental pollution are separable and distinct."

11 What specific policies would you recommend to increase the productivity of American workers?

PART

5

Micro-economics of Product and Resource Markets

CHAPTER 20

Demand and Supply: Elasticities and Applications

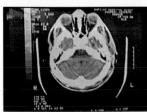

Scarce resources and unlimited wants are the foundation of economic science. The efficient management of scarce resources is a major goal of our economic system. There are two major facets to achieving efficient resource use. The first, examined in Parts 2, 3, and 4, centers on the full employment of available resources.

The second aspect of the economizing problem—the one to which we now turn—deals with the efficient use of employed resources. This is the task we undertake in Part 5.

A major characteristic of capitalistic economies is their heavy reliance on the market system for allocating resources. Major topics of discussion, then, are individual prices and the market system. Specifically, our goal in this and ensuing chapters is to acquire an understanding of the operation and relative efficiency of the *market* or *price system* in allocating resources within the framework of capitalism. In achieving this primary goal, we will analyze *individual* prices under a variety of contrasting market arrangements.

In Chapter 4 we examined demand and supply analysis. If your recollection of that material is hazy, you might reread that chapter or at least examine the chapter summary. In this chapter we will extend our understanding of demand and supply. Specifically, this chapter's tasks are threefold.

1 We will examine the concept of price elasticity as it applies to both demand and supply.

2 We will generalize the elasticity concept by introducing both cross and income elasticity of demand.

3 Finally, as an application of demand and supply analysis, we will examine the potential effects of legally fixed prices on individual markets.

PRICE ELASTICITY OF DEMAND

The law of demand means consumers will respond to a price decline by buying more of a product. But the degree of consumer responsiveness to a price change may vary considerably from product to product. We also will find that consumer responsiveness typically varies substantially between different price ranges for the same product.

The responsiveness, or sensitivity, of consumers to a change in the price of a product is measured by the concept of **price elasticity of demand.** Demand for some products is such that consumers are relatively responsive to price changes; modest price changes lead to very considerable changes in the quantity purchased. The demand for such products is said to be *relatively elastic* or simply *elastic.* For other products, consumers are relatively unresponsive to price changes; substantial price changes result only in modest changes in the amount purchased. In such cases demand is *relatively inelastic* or simply *inelastic.*

The Price Elasticity Formula

Economists measure the degree of elasticity or inelasticity by the coefficient E_d in this price elasticity formula:

$$E_d = \frac{\text{percentage change in quantity demanded of product X}}{\text{percentage change in price of product X}}$$

These *percentage* changes are calculated by dividing the change in price by the original price and the consequent change in quantity demanded by the original quantity demanded. Thus, our formula restated:

$$E_d = \frac{\text{change in quantity demanded of X}}{\text{original quantity demanded of X}} \div \frac{\text{change in price of X}}{\text{original price of X}}$$

Use of Percentages Why use percentages rather than absolute amounts in measuring consumer responsiveness? The answer is twofold.

1 If we use absolute changes, our impression of buyer responsiveness will be arbitrarily affected by the choice of units. To illustrate: If the price of product X falls from $3 to $2 and consumers increase their purchases from 60 to 100 pounds, it appears that consumers are quite sensitive to price changes and therefore that demand is elastic. After all, a price change of "one" has caused a change in the amount demanded of "forty." But by changing the monetary unit from dollars to pennies (why not?), we find a price change of "one hundred" causes a quantity change of "forty," giving the impression of inelasticity. Using percentage changes avoids this problem. The given price decline is 33 percent whether measured in terms of dollars ($1/$3) or pennies (100¢/300¢).

2 The other reason for using percentages is that we can more meaningfully compare consumer responsiveness to changes in the prices of different products. It makes little sense to compare the effects on quantity demanded of a $1 increase in the price of a $10,000 auto with a $1 increase in the price of a $1 can of Coors. Here the price of the auto is rising by .0001 percent while the beer price is up by 100 percent! If we increased the price of both products by 1 percent—$100 for the car and 1¢ for the can—we would obtain a sensible comparison of consumer sensitivity to the price changes.

Ignore Minus Sign We know from the downsloping demand curve that price and quantity demanded are inversely related. This means that the price elasticity coefficient of demand will always yield a *negative* number. For example, if price declines, then quantity demanded will increase. This means that the numerator in our formula will be positive and the denominator negative, yielding a negative coefficient. Conversely, for an increase in price, the numerator will be negative but the denominator positive, again yielding a negative coefficient.

Economists usually ignore the minus sign and simply present the *absolute value* of the elasticity coefficient to avoid an ambiguity which might otherwise arise. It can be confusing to say that an elasticity coefficient of -4 is greater than one of -2; this possible confusion is avoided when we say a coefficient of 4 indicates greater elasticity than one of 2. Hence, in what follows we ignore the minus sign in the coefficient of price elasticity of demand and merely show the absolute value. Incidentally, the noted ambiguity does not arise with supply because price and quantity are positively related.

Interpretations Now let's interpret our formula. Demand is **elastic** if a given percentage change in price results in a *larger* percentage change in quantity demanded. Example: If a 2 percent decline in price results in a 4 percent increase in quantity demanded, demand is elastic. In such cases where demand is elastic, the elasticity coefficient will be greater than 1; in this case it will be 2.

If a given percentage change in price is accompanied by a relatively smaller change in quantity demanded, demand is **inelastic.** Illustration: If a 3 percent decline in price leads to only a 1 percent increase in amount demanded, demand is inelastic. Specifically, the elasticity coefficient is .33 in this instance. It is apparent that the elasticity coefficient will always be less than 1 when demand is inelastic.

The borderline case separating elastic and inelastic demands occurs where a percentage change in price and the accompanying percentage change in quantity demanded are equal. For example, a 1 percent drop in price causes a 1 percent increase in amount sold. This special case is termed **unit elasticity,** because the elasticity coefficient is exactly 1, or unity.

When economists say demand is "inelastic," they do not mean consumers are completely unresponsive to a price change. The term **perfectly inelastic** demand refers to the extreme situation where a price change results in no change whatsoever in the quantity demanded. Approximate examples: an acute diabetic's demand for insulin or an addict's demand for heroin. A demand curve parallel to the vertical axis—such as D_1 in Figure 20-1—shows this graphically. Conversely, when economists say demand is "elastic," they do not mean that consumers are completely responsive to a price change. In the extreme situation, where a small price reduction would cause buyers to increase their purchases from zero to all they could obtain, we say that demand is **perfectly elastic.** A perfectly elastic demand curve is a line parallel to the horizontal axis such as D_2 in Figure 20-1. We will see in Chapter 23 that such a demand curve applies to a firm selling in a purely competitive market.

Refinement: Midpoints Formula

The hypothetical demand data shown in Table 20-1 are useful in explaining an annoying problem which arises in applying the price elasticity formula. In calculating the elasticity coefficient for the $5–$4 price range, should we use the $5–4 units price–quantity combination or the $4–5 units combination as a point of reference in calculating percentage changes in price and quantity which the elasticity formula requires? Our choice will influence the outcome.

Using the $5–4 unit reference point, the percentage decrease in price is 20 percent and the percentage increase in quantity, 25 percent. Substituting in the formula, the elasticity coefficient is 25/20, or 1.25, indicating that demand is somewhat elastic. But, using the $4–5 unit reference point, the percentage increase in price is 25 percent and the percentage decline in quantity 20 percent. The elasticity coefficient is therefore 20/25, or 0.80, meaning demand is slightly inelastic. Which is it? Is demand elastic or inelastic?

A workable solution to this problem is achieved by using *averages* of the two prices and two quantities under consideration for reference points. In the $5–$4 price-range case, the price reference is $4.50 and the quantity reference, 4.5 units. The percentage change in price is now about 22 percent and the percentage change in quantity also about 22 percent, giving us an elasticity coefficient of 1. Instead of gauging elasticity at either one of the extremes of this price–quantity range, this solution estimates elasticity at the midpoint of the $5–$4 price range. We now can refine our earlier statement of the elasticity formula to read:

$$E_d = \frac{\text{change in quantity}}{\text{sum of quantities}/2} \div \frac{\text{change in price}}{\text{sum of prices}/2}$$

Substituting data for the $5–$4 price range, we get

$$E_d = \frac{1}{9/2} \div \frac{1}{9/2} = 1$$

FIGURE 20-1   Perfectly inelastic and elastic demand

A perfectly inelastic demand curve, D_1, graphs as a line parallel to the vertical axis; a perfectly elastic demand curve, D_2, is drawn parallel to the horizontal axis.

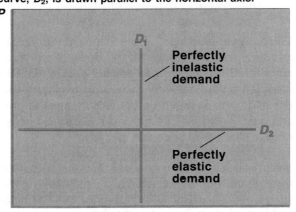

gain in total revenue caused by the higher unit price (area P_7P_8ac) is *less* than the *loss* in revenue associated with the accompanying fall in sales (Q_1cbQ_2). *If demand is elastic, a price change will cause total revenue to change in the opposite direction.*

2 Inelastic Demand If demand is *inelastic,* a price *decrease* will cause total revenue to *decrease.* The modest increase in sales which occurs will not offset the decline in revenue per unit, and the net result is that total revenue declines. This is true for the $2–$1 price range of our demand curve, as shown in Figure 20-2a. Initially, total revenue is OP_2fQ_7 ($14) when price is P_2 ($2) and quantity demanded is Q_7 (7 units). If we reduce price to P_1 ($1), quantity demanded will increase to Q_8 (8 units). Total revenue will change to OP_1hQ_8 ($8), which is clearly less than OP_2fQ_7. It is smaller because the loss in revenue from the lower unit price (area P_1P_2fg) *is larger* than the *gain* in revenue from the accompanying increase in sales (area Q_7ghQ_8). The $1 decline in price applies to 7 units (Q_7) with a consequent revenue loss of $7. The sales increase accompanying this lower price is 1 unit (Q_7 to Q_8) which results in a revenue gain of $1. The overall result is a *net decrease* in total revenue of $6 (=$1 − $7).

Again, our analysis is reversible: If demand is inelastic, a price increase will increase total revenue. *If demand is inelastic, a price change will cause total revenue to change in the same direction.*

3 Unit Elasticity In the special case of *unit elasticity,* an increase or decrease in price will leave total revenue unchanged. Loss in revenue from a lower unit price will be exactly offset by the gain in revenue from the accompanying increase in sales. Conversely, the gain in revenue from a higher unit price will be exactly offset by the revenue loss associated with the accompanying decline in the amount demanded.

In Figure 20-2a we find that at the $5 price 4 units will be sold to yield total revenue of $20. At $4 a total of 5 units will be sold, again resulting in $20 of total revenue. The $1 price reduction causes the loss of $4 in revenue on the 4 units that could have been sold for $5 each. This is exactly offset by a $4 revenue gain which results from the sale of 1 more unit at the lower $4 price.

Graphical Portrayal The relationship between price elasticity of demand and total revenue can be demonstrated graphically by comparing Figures 20-2a and 20-2b. In Figure 20-2b we have graphed the eight total revenue–quantity demanded points from columns 1 and 4 of Table 20-1.

Lowering price over the $8–$5 price range increases total revenue. We know from the elasticity coefficient calculations in Table 20-1 that demand is *elastic* in this range so any given percentage decline in price results in a larger percentage increase in the quantity demanded. The lower price per unit is more than offset by the increase in sales and, consequently, total revenue rises.

The $5–$4 price range is characterized by *unit* elasticity. Here the percentage decline in price causes an equal percentage increase in the quantity demanded. The price cut is exactly offset by increased purchases so total revenue is unchanged.

Finally, our coefficient calculations tell us that in the $4–$1 price range demand is *inelastic,* which means that any given percentage decline in price will be accompanied by a smaller percentage increase in sales, causing total revenue to diminish. Question 2 at the end of this chapter is recommended at this point.

Our logic is reversible. A price *increase* in the elastic $8–$5 price range will reduce total revenue. Similarly, a price *increase* in the inelastic $4–$1 range causes total revenue to increase.

Reprise Table 20-2 provides a convenient summary of the characteristics of price elasticity of demand and merits careful study.

Determinants of Price Elasticity of Demand

There are no ironclad generalizations concerning determinants of the elasticity of demand. The following points, however, are valid and helpful.

1 Substitutability Generally, the larger the number of good substitute products available, the greater the elasticity of demand. We will find later that in a purely competitive market, where by definition there are many perfect substitutes for the product of any given seller, the demand curve to that single seller will be perfectly elastic. If one competitive seller of wheat or corn raises its price, buyers will turn to the readily available perfect substitutes of its many rivals. At the other extreme, the diabetic's demand for insulin or an addict's demand for heroin is highly inelastic.

TABLE 20-2 Price elasticity of demand: a summary

Absolute value of elasticity coefficient	Terminology	Description	Impact on total revenue (expenditures) of a price:	
			Increase	Decrease
Greater than 1 ($E_d > 1$)	"Elastic" or "relatively elastic"	Quantity demanded changes by a larger percentage than does price	Total revenue decreases	Total revenue increases
Equal to 1 ($E_d = 1$)	"Unit" or "unitary elastic"	Quantity demanded changes by the same percentage as does price	Total revenue is unchanged	Total revenue is unchanged
Less than 1 ($E_d < 1$)	"Inelastic" or "relatively inelastic"	Quantity demanded changes by a smaller percentage than does price	Total revenue increases	Total revenue decreases

The elasticity of demand for a product depends on how narrowly the product is defined. Demand for Texaco motor oil is more elastic than is the overall demand for motor oil. Many other brands are readily substitutable for Texaco's oil, but there is no good substitute for motor oil.

2 Proportion of Income Other things being equal, the higher the price of a good relative to one's budget, the greater will be the elasticity of demand for it. A 10 percent increase in the price of pencils or chewing gum will amount to only a few pennies, with little response in the amount demanded. A 10 percent increase in the price of automobiles or housing means price increases of perhaps $1500 and $10,000 respectively. These increases are significant fractions of the annual incomes of many families, and quantities purchased could be expected to diminish significantly.

3 Luxuries versus Necessities The demand for "necessities" tends to be inelastic; for "luxuries," elastic. Bread and electricity are generally regarded as necessities; we can't get along without them. A price increase will not reduce significantly the amount of bread consumed or the amounts of lighting and power used in a household. Note the very low price elasticities of these goods in Table 20-3. A more extreme case: You will not decline an operation for acute appendicitis because the physician's fee has just gone up!

On the other hand, French cognac and emeralds are luxuries which, by definition, can be forgone. If the price of cognac or emeralds rises, you need not buy and will encounter no hardship.

The demand for salt is highly inelastic on several counts. It is a "necessity"; there are few good substitutes available; and, finally, salt is a negligible item in the family budget.

4 Time Generally, product demand is more elastic the longer the time period under consideration because many consumers are creatures of habit. When the price of a product rises, it takes time to find and experiment with other products to see if they are acceptable. Consumers may not immediately reduce their purchases very much when the price of beef rises by 10 percent, but in time they may shift to chicken or fish, for which they have now "developed a taste." Another consideration is product durability. Studies show that "short-run" demand for gasoline is more inelastic at 0.2 than is "long-run" demand at 0.7. In the long run, large, gas-guzzling automobiles wear out and, with rising gasoline prices, are replaced by smaller, higher-mileage cars.

An empirical study of commuter rail transportation in the Philadelphia area estimates that "long-run" elasticity of demand is almost three times as great as "short-run" elasticity. Specifically, short-run commuter responses (defined as those occurring immediately at the time of a fare change) are inelastic at 0.68. In contrast, the long-run response (defined as those occurring over a four-year period) is elastic at 1.84. The greater long-run elasticity occurs because over time

TABLE 20-3 Selected price elasticities of demand

Product or service	Price elasticity of demand	Product or service	Price elasticity of demand
Housing	.01	Milk	.63
Electricity (household)	.13	Household appliances	.63
Bread	.15	Movies	.87
Telephone service	.26	Beer	.90
Medical care	.31	Shoes	.91
Eggs	.32	Motor vehicles	1.14
Legal services	.37	China, glassware, tableware	1.54
Automobile repair	.40	Restaurant meals	2.27
Clothing	.49	Lamb and mutton	2.65

Main sources: H. S. Houthakker and Lester D. Taylor, *Consumer Demand in the United States: Analyses and Projections,* 2d ed. (Cambridge, Mass.: Harvard University Press, 1970); P. S. George and G. A. King, *Consumer Demand for Food Commodities in the United States with Projections for 1980* (Berkeley: University of California Press, 1971); and Ahsan Mansur and John Whalley, "Numerical Specification of Applied General Equilibrium Models: Estimation, Calibration, and Data," in Herbert E. Scarf and John B. Shoven, *Applied General Equilibrium Analysis* (New York: Cambridge University Press, 1984).

potential rail commuters can make choices concerning automobile purchases, car pooling, and the locations of residences and employment. These different elasticities led to the prediction that the commuter system, with about 100,000 riders, could immediately *increase* daily revenues by $8000 by increasing the price of a one-way ticket by $.25 or about 9 percent. Why? Because short-run demand is inelastic. But in the long run the same 9 percent fare increase is estimated to *reduce* total revenue per day by over $19,000 because demand is elastic. This implies that a fare increase which is profitable in the short run may lead to financial difficulties in the long run.[1]

Table 20-3 shows estimated price elasticities of demand for a number of products. You should use the elasticity determinants just discussed to explain or rationalize each of these elasticity coefficients.

QUICK REVIEW 20-2

◢ *A price change will cause total revenue to vary in the opposite direction when demand is elastic and in the same direction when demand is inelastic.*

◢ *Price elasticity of demand is greater a the larger the number of substitutes available; b the*

higher the price of a product relative to one's budget; c the greater the extent to which the product is a luxury; and d the longer the time period involved.

Some Practical Applications

The concept of price elasticity of demand has great practical significance, as seen in the following examples.

1 Wage Bargaining The United Automobile Workers once contended that automobile manufacturers should raise wages and simultaneously cut automobile prices. Arguing that the elasticity of demand for automobiles was about 4, the UAW concluded that a price cut would help check inflation, boost the total revenue of manufacturers, and preserve or even increase the profits of producers. A spokesman for the Ford Motor Company, however, claimed that available studies suggest an elasticity of demand for automobiles in the 0.5–1.5 range. He held that price cuts would therefore shrink profits or result in losses for manufacturers. In this case, elasticity of demand for automobiles was a strategic factor in labor-management relations and wage bargaining.

[1]Richard Voith, "Commuter Rail Ridership: The Long and the Short Haul," *Business Review* (Federal Reserve Bank of Philadelphia), November–December 1987, pp. 13–23.

2 Bumper Crops Studies indicate that demand for most farm products is highly inelastic, perhaps 0.20 or 0.25. As a result, increases in the output of farm products due to a good growing season or to productivity increases depress both the prices of farm products and total revenues (incomes) of farmers. For farmers as a group, the inelastic nature of demand for their products means that a bumper crop may be undesirable. For policy makers it means that higher total farm income depends on the restriction of farm output.

3 Automation The impact of automation, that is, of rapid technological advance, on the level of employment depends in part on the elasticity of demand for the product being manufactured. Suppose a firm installs new laborsaving machinery, resulting in technological unemployment of 500 workers. Suppose too that part of the cost reduction resulting from this technological advance is passed on to consumers in the form of reduced product prices. The effect of this price reduction on the firm's sales and therefore the quantity of labor it requires will depend on the elasticity of product demand. An elastic demand might increase sales to the extent that some of, all, or even more than the 500 displaced workers are reabsorbed by the firm. An inelastic demand will mean that few, if any, displaced workers will be reemployed, because the increase in the volume of the firm's sales and output will be small.

4 Airline Deregulation Deregulating the airlines in the late 1970s initially increased the profits of many carriers. The reason was that deregulation increased competition among the airlines, lowering air fares. Lower fares, coupled with an elastic demand for air travel, increased revenues. Because additional costs associated with flying full, as opposed to partially empty, aircraft are minimal, revenues increased ahead of costs and profits were enhanced. Unfortunately for the airlines, this profitability was not to last, for three reasons: The competitive scramble for new routes competed profits away; rising fuel prices increased operating costs; and persistent "fare wars" cut into profits.

5 Excise Taxes Government pays attention to elasticity of demand when selecting goods and services on which to levy excise taxes. Assume a $1 tax is currently levied on a product and 10,000 units are sold. Tax revenue is $10,000. If the tax is now raised to $1.50, and the consequent higher price reduces sales to 5,000 because of an elastic demand, tax revenue will *decline* to $7,500. A higher tax on a product, the demand for which is elastic, will bring in less tax revenue. Hence, legislatures will seek out products for which demand is inelastic—liquor, gasoline, and cigarettes—when levying excises. It is not by chance that the Federal government increased taxes on these three categories of goods in 1991 in trying to reduce the budget deficit.

6 Cocaine and Street Crime The fact that the demand for crack-cocaine by addicts is highly inelastic poses some awkward tradeoffs in law enforcement. The approach typically used in attempting to reduce cocaine addiction is restricting supply, that is, making the drug less readily available by cracking down on its shipment into the United States. But what will happen if this policy is successful? Given the highly inelastic demand, the street price to addicts will rise sharply while the amount purchased will decrease only slightly. From the drug dealers' viewpoint this means greatly increased revenues and profits. From the addicts' viewpoint it means greater total expenditures on cocaine. Because much of the income which addicts spend on cocaine comes from crime—shoplifting, burglary, prostitution, muggings—these crimes will increase as addicts increase their total expenditures for cocaine. Here, the effort of law-enforcement authorities to control the spread of drug addiction may increase the amount of crime committed by addicts.

In recent years the controversial proposal to legalize drugs has been widely debated. Proponents contend that drugs should be treated like alcohol; they should be made legal for adults and regulated for purity and potency. The current war on drugs, it is argued, has been unsuccessful and the associated costs—including enlarged police forces, the construction of more prisons, an overburdened court system, and untold human costs—have increased markedly. Legalization would allegedly reduce drug trafficking greatly by taking the profit out of it. Crack-cocaine, for example, is cheap to produce and could be sold at a low price in a legal market. Because the demand of addicts is highly inelastic, the amount consumed at the lower price will only increase modestly. Total expenditures for cocaine by addicts will decline and so will the street crime which finances these expenditures.

Opponents of legalization take the position that, in addition to the addict's inelastic demand, there is another segment to the market where demand may be more elastic. This is the segment populated by occasional users or "dabblers." Dabblers will use cocaine when its price is low, but abstain or substitute, say, alcohol when cocaine's price is high. For this group the lower price of cocaine associated with legalization will increase consumption by dabblers and in time turn many of them into addicts. This will increase street crime and enlarge all the social costs associated with drug use.

7 Minimum Wage   The Federal minimum wage prohibits employers from paying covered workers less than $4.25 per hour. Critics contend that an above-equilibrium minimum wage moves employers back up their downsloping labor demand curves and causes unemployment, particularly among teenage workers. On the other hand, workers who remain employed at the minimum wage will receive higher incomes than otherwise. The amount of income lost by the unemployed and the income gained by those who keep their jobs will clearly depend on the elasticity of demand for teenage labor. Research studies suggest that demand for teenage labor is quite inelastic, possibly as low as 0.15 or 0.25. If these estimates are correct, it means that income gains associated with the minimum wage exceed income losses. The case made by critics of the minimum wage would be stronger if the demand for teenage workers were elastic.

More examples could be cited but you can see that elasticity of demand is vitally important to businesses, farmers, labor, and government policy makers.

PRICE ELASTICITY OF SUPPLY

The concept of price elasticity also applies to supply. If producers are responsive to price changes, supply is elastic. If they are relatively insensitive to price changes, supply is inelastic.

The elasticity formula is pertinent in determining the degree of elasticity or inelasticity of supply. The only required alteration is substitution of "percentage change in quantity *supplied*" for "percentage change in quantity *demanded*."

$$E_s = \frac{\text{percentage change in quantity supplied of product X}}{\text{percentage change in price of product X}}$$

For reasons explained earlier, the midpoints of the changes in quantity supplied and price are used in calculations. Suppose price were to increase from $4 to $6, causing quantity supplied to rise from 8 to 12. The percentage change in quantity supplied would be $\frac{2}{10}$, or 20 percent, and the percentage change in price would be $\frac{2}{5}$, or 40 percent. Substituting in our formula, we determine elasticity of supply to be $\frac{20}{40}$ or $+0.50$. Note that, because price and quantity supplied are directly related, the coefficient will always be positive.

The main determinant of the **price elasticity of supply** is the amount of *time* which a producer has to respond to a given change in product price. We can expect a greater output response—and therefore greater elasticity of supply—the longer the amount of time a producer has to adjust to a given price change. A producer's response to an increase in the price of product X depends on its ability to shift resources from the production of other products (whose prices we assume remain constant) to the production of X. And shifting resources takes time: the greater the time, the greater the resource "shiftability." Hence, the greater will be the output response and the elasticity of supply.

In analyzing the impact of time on elasticity of supply, economists distinguish between the immediate market period, the short run, and the long run.

1 The Market Period   The immediate **market period** is so short a time that producers cannot respond to a change in demand and price. Suppose a small truck farmer brings an entire season's output of tomatoes—one truckload—to market. The supply curve will be perfectly inelastic; the farmer will sell the truckload whether the price is high or low. Why? Because he cannot offer more tomatoes than his one truckload if the price of tomatoes should be higher than he had anticipated. Though he might like to offer more, tomatoes cannot be produced overnight. Another full growing season is needed to respond to a higher-than-expected price by producing more than one truckload. Similarly, because the product is perishable, the farmer cannot withhold it from the market. If the price is lower than anticipated, he will still sell the entire truckload. Costs of production, incidentally, will not be important in this decision. Though the price of tomatoes may fall far short of production costs, the farmer will nevertheless sell out to avoid a total loss through spoilage. In a very short time, then, our farmer's supply of tomatoes is fixed; only one truckload can be offered no matter how high the price. The perishability of the product

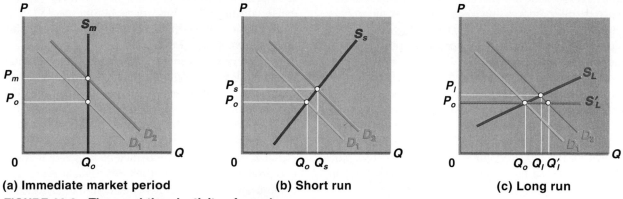

(a) Immediate market period   (b) Short run   (c) Long run

FIGURE 20-3 Time and the elasticity of supply

The greater the amount of time producers have to adjust to a change in demand, the greater will be their output response. In the immediate market period (a) there is insufficient time to change output, and so supply is perfectly inelastic. In the short run (b) plant capacity is fixed, but output can be altered by changing the intensity of its use; supply is therefore more elastic. In the long run (c) all desired adjustments—including changes in plant capacity—can be made, and supply becomes still more elastic.

forces the farmer to sell all, no matter how low the price.

Figure 20-3a illustrates the truck farmer's perfectly inelastic supply curve in the market period. Note that this and other truck farmers cannot respond to an assumed increase in demand; they do not have time to increase the amount supplied. The price increase from P_o to P_m simply rations a fixed supply to buyers, but elicits no increase in output.[2]

2 The Short Run In the **short run,** the plant capacity of individual producers and the industry is presumed fixed. But firms *do* have time to use their plants more or less intensively. Thus, in the short run, our truck farmer's plant—comprised of land and farm machinery—is fixed. But he does have time in the short run to cultivate tomatoes more intensively by applying more labor and more fertilizer and pesticides to the crop. The result is a greater output response to the presumed increase in demand; this greater output response is reflected in a more elastic supply of tomatoes, as shown by S_s in Figure 20-3b. Note that the increase

in demand is met by a larger quantity adjustment (Q_o to Q_s) and a smaller price adjustment (P_o to P_s) than in the market period; price is therefore lower than in the market period.

3 The Long Run The **long run** is a time period sufficiently long so that firms can make all desired resource adjustments; individual firms can expand (or contract) their plant capacities, and new firms can enter (or existing firms can leave) the industry. In the "tomato industry" our truck farmer can acquire additional land and buy more machinery and equipment. Furthermore, more farmers may be attracted to tomato production by increased demand and higher price. These adjustments mean an even greater supply response, that is, an even more elastic supply curve S_L. The result, shown in Figure 20-3c, is a small price effect (P_o to P_l) and a large output effect (Q_o to Q_l) in response to the increase in demand.

The dark supply curve in Figure 20-3c entails a new long-run equilibrium price, P_l, somewhat higher than the original price, P_o, in Figure 20-3a. The presumption is that tomato farming is an **increasing-cost industry,** meaning simply that the industry's expansion causes prices of relevant resources to rise. Increased demand for fertilizer and farm equipment has pushed their prices up somewhat; expanded demand for land has increased its market or rental value. In

---

[2]The supply curve need not be perfectly inelastic (vertical) in the market period. If the product is not perishable, producers may choose, at low current prices, to store some of their product for future sale. This will cause the market supply curve to have some positive slope.

short, it is realistic to expect the expansion of an industry to result in "increasing costs." Hence, while P_o was sufficient for profitable production in Figure 20-3a, a higher price, P_b, is required for profitable production in the enlarged industry.

If the tomato industry hired very small or negligible portions of relevant resources, then its increased demand for these inputs would leave their prices unchanged. In this **constant-cost industry** case the long-run supply curve would be perfectly elastic, as shown by the light red curve S'_L in Figure 20-3c. The new price would be equal to the original price, P_o, in Figure 20-3a.

There is no total-revenue test for elasticity of supply. Supply shows a positive or direct relationship between price and amount supplied; that is, the supply curve is upsloping. Thus, regardless of the degree of elasticity or inelasticity, price and total revenue will always move together.

CROSS AND INCOME ELASTICITY OF DEMAND

In addition to price elasticity, two other elasticity concepts are significant.

Cross Elasticity of Demand

We have seen that *price elasticity of demand* measures the effect of a change in a product's price on the quantity of *that* product demanded. The concept of **cross elasticity of demand** measures how sensitive consumer purchases of *one* product (say X) are to a change in the price of some *other* product (say Y). Our formula for the coefficient of cross elasticity of demand is similar to simple price elasticity except that we are relating the percentage change in the consumption of X to a percentage change in the price of Y:

$$E_{xy} = \frac{\text{percentage change in quantity demanded of X}}{\text{percentage change in price of Y}}$$

This elasticity concept allows us to quantify and more fully understand substitute and complementary goods as introduced in Chapter 4.

If cross elasticity of demand is *positive*—that is, the quantity demanded of X varies directly with a change in the price of Y—then X and Y are *substitute goods*. For

example, an increase in the price of butter (Y) will cause consumers to buy more margarine (X). The larger the positive coefficient, the greater the substitutability between the two products.

When cross elasticity is *negative,* then we know that X and Y "go together" and are *complementary goods.* Thus an increase in the price of cameras will decrease the amount of film purchased. The larger the negative coefficient, the greater the complementarity between the two goods.

A zero or near-zero coefficient suggests that the two products are unrelated or *independent goods.* For example, we would not expect a change in the price of butter to have any significant impact on the purchases of film.

Income Elasticity of Demand

The concept of **income elasticity of demand** measures the percentage change in the quantity of a product demanded which results from some percentage change in consumer incomes:

$$E_i = \frac{\text{percentage change in quantity demanded}}{\text{percentage change in income}}$$

For most goods the income elasticity coefficient will be *positive.* Again recalling Chapter 4, those products of which more is purchased as incomes increase are called *normal* or *superior* goods. But the positive elasticity coefficient varies greatly among products. For example, the income elasticity of demand for automobiles has been estimated to be about $+3.00$, while for most farm products it is only about $+0.20$.

A *negative* income elasticity coefficient designates an *inferior good.* Retreaded tires, cabbage, bus tickets, used clothing, and muscatel wine are likely candidates. Consumers *decrease* their purchases of such products as incomes *increase.*

The practical significance of income elasticity coefficients is that they help us predict which industries are likely to be prosperous, expanding industries and which will probably be unprosperous, declining industries. Specifically, other things being equal, a high positive income elasticity implies that that industry will share more than proportionately in the overall income growth of the economy. A small positive or, worse yet, a negative coefficient implies a declining industry. For example, the indicated high positive income elasticity of demand for automobiles portends a greater likelihood of long-run prosperity for that industry in comparison to agriculture's low coefficient which suggests chronic problems.

APPLICATIONS: LEGAL PRICES

Supply and demand analysis and the elasticity concept will be applied repeatedly in the remainder of this book. Let's strengthen our understanding of these analytical tools and their significance by examining some of the implications of legal prices.

On occasion the general public and government feel that the forces of supply and demand result in prices that are either unfairly high to buyers or unfairly low to sellers. In such instances government may intervene by legally limiting how high or low the price may go.

Price Ceilings and Shortages

A **price ceiling** *is the maximum legal price a seller may charge for a product or service.* The rationale for ceiling prices on specific products is that they purportedly enable consumers to obtain some "essential" good or service they could not afford at the equilibrium price. Rent controls and usury laws (which specify maximum interest rates which may be charged to borrowers) are

FIGURE 20-4   Price ceilings result in persistent shortages

Because a price ceiling such as P_c results in a persistent product shortage, indicated by the distance Q_sQ_d, government must undertake the job of rationing the product to achieve an equitable distribution.

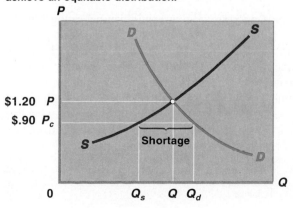

examples. More generally, ceiling prices or general price controls have been used in attempting to restrain the overall rate of inflation in the economy. Price controls were invoked during World War II and to a lesser extent during the Korean conflict. Similarly, President Nixon froze prices, wages, and rents in the early 1970s.

World War II Price Controls   Let's turn back the clock to World War II and analyze the effects of a ceiling price on butter. The booming wartime prosperity of the early 1940s was shifting demand for butter to the right so that, as in Figure 20-4, the equilibrium or market price P was, say, $1.20 per pound. On the one hand, the rapidly rising price of butter was contributing to inflation and, on the other, rationing out of the butter market those families whose money incomes were not keeping up with the soaring cost of living. To help stop inflation and to keep butter on the tables of the poor, government imposed a ceiling price P_c of, say, $0.90 per pound. Note that to be effective a ceiling price must be *below* the equilibrium price. A ceiling price of $1.50 would have no immediate impact on the butter market.

What will be the effects of this ceiling price? The rationing ability of the free market will be rendered ineffective. At the ceiling price there will be a persistent shortage of butter. The quantity of butter demanded at P_c is Q_d and the quantity supplied is only Q_s; a persistent excess demand or shortage in the amount Q_sQ_d occurs. The size of this shortage varies directly with the price elasticities of supply and demand.

The important point is that the legal price P_c prevents the usual market adjustment where competition among buyers would bid up price, thereby inducing more production and rationing some buyers out of the market until the shortage disappears at the equilibrium price and quantity, P and Q.

By preventing these market-clearing adjustments from occurring, the ceiling price poses problems born of the market disequilibrium.

1   How is the available supply Q_s to be apportioned among buyers who want amount Q_d? Should supply be distributed on a first-come, first-served basis, that is, to those willing and able to stand in line the longest? Or should the grocer distribute butter on the basis of favoritism? An unregulated shortage is hardly conducive to the equitable distribution of butter. To avoid catch-as-catch-can distribution, government must establish some formal system of rationing the product to consumers. This was done during World War II by issuing ration coupons to individuals on an equitable basis. An effective rationing system entails the printing of ration coupons equal to Q_s pounds of butter and their equitable distribution among consumers so that the rich family of four and the poor family of four will both get the same number of coupons.

2 But the use of ration coupons does not prevent a second problem from arising. Specifically, the demand curve in Figure 20-4 tells us there are many buyers who are willing to pay more than the ceiling price. And, of course, it is more profitable for grocers to sell above the ceiling price. Thus, despite the sizable enforcement bureaucracy which accompanied World War II price controls, illegal *black markets*—markets where products were bought and sold at prices above the legal limits—flourished for many goods. Counterfeiting of ration coupons was also a problem.

Rent Controls Some 200 American cities—including New York City, Boston, and San Francisco—have rent controls. Such legislation is well-intended. Its goals are to protect low-income families from escalating rents caused by perceived housing shortages and to make housing more affordable to the poor.

What are the actual economic effects? On the demand side, it is true that below-equilibrium rents will mean that more families are willing to consume rental housing; the quantity of rental housing demanded will increase at the lower price. The problem occurs on the supply side. Price controls make it less attractive for landlords to offer housing on the rental market. In the short run they may sell their apartments or convert them to condominiums. In the long run low rents make it unprofitable for owners to maintain or renovate their rental units. Rent controls are one cause of the many abandoned apartment buildings found in larger cities. Also, potential new investors in housing such as insurance companies and pension funds will find it more profitable to invest in office buildings, shopping malls, or motels where rents are not controlled,

In brief, rent controls distort market signals so that resources are misallocated: Too few resources are allocated to rental housing, too many to alternative uses. Ironically, although rent controls are often legislated to mitigate the effects of perceived housing shortages, in fact, controls are a primary cause of such shortages.

Credit Card Interest Ceilings In recent years several bills have been introduced in Congress to impose a nationwide interest rate ceiling on credit card accounts. In fact, several states now have such laws and others have legislation under consideration. The usual rationale for interest rate ceilings is that the banks and retail stores issuing such cards are presumably "gouging" users and, in particular, lower-income users by charging interest rates that average about 18 percent. In late 1991 President Bush sought such ceilings on the grounds that lower interest rates would stimulate consumer spending and help the economy recover from recession.

What might be the responses to the legal imposition of below-equilibrium interest rates on credit cards? According to a study by the Federal Reserve,[3] profits on bank-issued credit cards have been low, while retail store cards have generally entailed losses for their issuers. Hence, lower interest income associated with a legal interest ceiling would require adjustments by issuers to reduce costs or enhance revenues. What forms might these responses take?

1 Card issuers might tighten credit standards to reduce nonpayment losses and collection costs. In particular, low-income people and young people who have not yet established their creditworthiness would find it more difficult to obtain credit cards.

2 The annual fee charged card holders might be increased as might the fee charged merchants for processing credit card sales. Similarly, card users might be charged a fee for every transaction.

3 Card users now have a "grace period" when the credit provided is interest-free. This period might be shortened or eliminated.

4 Finally, retail stores which issue cards might increase their merchandise prices to help offset the decline of interest income. This would mean that customers who pay cash would in effect be subsidizing customers who use credit cards. Empirical studies of states which now have ceilings on credit card interest rates have confirmed our first and final predictions.

Rock Concerts Below-equilibrium pricing should not be associated solely with government policies. Superstars such as Madonna or Michael Jackson frequently price their concert tickets below the market-clearing price. Tickets are usually rationed on a first-come, first-served basis and black market "scalping" is common. Why should rock stars want to subsidize their fans—at least those fortunate enough to obtain tickets—with below-equilibrium prices? Why not set

[3]Glenn B. Canner and James T. Fergus, "The Economic Effects of Proposed Ceilings on Credit Card Interest Rates," *Federal Reserve Bulletin,* January 1987, pp. 1–13.

ticket prices at a higher, market-clearing level and realize more income from a tour?

The answer is that long lines of fans waiting hours or days for bargain-priced tickets catch the attention of the press, as does an occasional attempt by ticketless fans to "crash" a sold-out concert. The millions of dollars worth of free publicity undoubtedly stimulates record and CD sales from which much of any rock group's income is derived. Hence, the "gift" of below-equilibrium ticket prices a rock star gives to fans also benefits the star. The gift also imposes costs upon fans—the opportunity cost of time spent waiting in line to buy tickets.

Price Floors and Surpluses

Price floors—*minimum prices fixed by government which are above equilibrium prices*—have generally been invoked when society has felt that the free functioning of the market system has not provided a sufficient income for certain groups of resource suppliers or producers. Minimum-wage legislation and the support of agricultural prices are the two most widely discussed examples of government price floors. Let's examine price floors as applied to a specific farm commodity.

FIGURE 20-5 Price floors result in persistent surpluses

A price floor such as P_f gives rise to a persistent product surplus, indicated by the distance Q_dQ_s. Government must either purchase these surpluses or take measures to eliminate them by restricting product supply or increasing product demand.

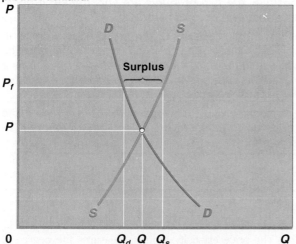

Suppose the going market price for corn is $2 per bushel, and as a result of this price, many farmers realize extremely low incomes. Government decides to lend a helping hand by establishing a legal floor price of $3 per bushel.

What will be the effects? At any price above the equilibrium price, quantity supplied will exceed quantity demanded; that is, there will be a persistent excess supply or surplus of the product. Farmers will be willing to produce and offer for sale more than private buyers are willing to purchase at the price floor. The size of this surplus will vary directly with the elasticity of demand and supply. The greater the elasticity of demand and supply, the greater the resulting surplus. As is the case with a ceiling price, the rationing ability of the free market has been disrupted by imposing a legal price.

Figure 20-5 illustrates the effect of a price floor. Let SS and DD be the supply and demand curves for corn. Equilibrium price and quantity are P and Q, respectively. If government imposes a price floor of P_f, farmers will produce Q_s, but private buyers will only take Q_d off the market at that price. The surplus is measured by the excess of Q_s over Q_d.

Government may cope with the surplus a price floor entails in two basic ways.

1   It might restrict supply (for example, acreage allotments by which farmers agree to take a certain amount of land out of production) or increase demand (for example, researching new uses for agricultural products). In these ways the difference between the equilibrium price and the price floor and thereby the size of the resulting surplus might be reduced.

2   If these efforts are not wholly successful, then government must purchase the surplus output (thereby subsidizing farmers) and store or otherwise dispose of it (Chapter 34).

Recapitulation

Price ceilings and floors rob the free-market forces of supply and demand of their ability to bring the supply decisions of producers and the demand decisions of buyers into accord with one another. Freely determined prices automatically ration products to buyers; legal prices do not. Therefore, government must accept the administrative problem of rationing which stems from price ceilings and the problem of buying or eliminating surpluses which price floors entail. Legal prices entail controversial tradeoffs. Alleged benefits of price ceilings and floors to consumers and producers

LAST WORD

THE TROUBLESOME MARKET FOR HEALTH CARE

Changes in demand and supply help explain why health care costs have risen dramatically.

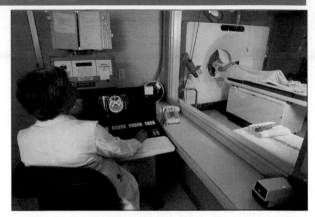

Health care costs in the United States are currently over 12 percent of GDP, up from about 5 percent in 1960. In 1990 we spent about $662 billion on health care, compared to $359 billion and $299 billion on education and national defense, respectively. The Department of Health and Human Services projects that $1.6 trillion—over 16 percent of domestic output— will be spent on health care by the turn of the century. Although it is a complex problem, an analysis of factors at work on the demand and supply sides of the health care market yield important insights as to why medical costs have soared.

Let's first consider the demand side. First, medical care is a normal good so the demand for medical care has increased as per capita incomes have grown. Second, our population is aging and older people encounter more frequent and prolonged spells of illness. Third, social and lifestyle factors such as high rates of violence and drug abuse as compared to most other countries create demands for medical services.

Fourth, the way we pay for health care has greatly increased demand. About three-fourths of all medical costs are paid, not as an out-of-pocket expense by individual users, but by private and public insurance. This has had two demand-increasing effects. On the one hand, Medicare and Medicaid, respectively, finance health care for the aged and the poor, thereby bringing many people into the health care market who might not otherwise have been there. On the other hand, individ-

respectively must be set against costs associated with consequent shortages and surpluses.

Furthermore, our discussions of World War II price controls, rent controls, and interest rate ceilings on credit cards show that governmental interference with the market can have unintended, undesirable side effects. Rent controls may discourage housing construction and repair. Instead of protecting low-income families from high interest charges, interest rate ceilings may simply make credit unavailable to them.

QUICK REVIEW 20-3

◆ Price elasticity of supply is the ratio of the percentage change in quantity supplied to the percentage change in price. The elasticity of supply varies directly with the amount of time producers have to respond to the price change.

◆ Cross elasticity of demand is the percentage change in the quantity demanded of one product divided by the percentage change in the price of another product. If the cross elasticity coefficient is positive, the two products are substitutes; if negative, they are complements.

◆ Income elasticity is the percentage change in quantity demanded divided by the percentage change in income. A positive coefficient indicates a normal or superior good. The coefficient is negative for an inferior good.

◆ Legal prices—ceilings and floors—negate the rationing function of prices and cause unintended side effects.

CHAPTER SUMMARY

1   Price elasticity of demand measures consumer response to price changes. If consumers are relatively sensitive to price changes, demand is elastic. If they are relatively unresponsive to price changes, demand is inelastic.

2   The price elasticity formula measures the degree of elasticity or inelasticity of demand. The formula is

uals pay a fixed insurance fee and then, aside from a modest deductible, medical care is "free" to the individual. In most markets the buyer or demander is confronted with a price that reflects the opportunity cost of that good or service. The price provides a direct economic incentive to restrict the use of that product. But through insurance one's health care is prepaid, creating an incentive to overuse the system. We demand medical services and procedures which we might forgo if directly confronted with their price.

The costs of health care services underlying the supply of health care have greatly increased, tending to reduce or slow the growth of supply. In the first place, new technological advances have made medical care much more costly. For example, increasingly sophisticated body scanners have usurped x-ray machines. A $20 or $40 x-ray has given way to a scan costing as much as $1000 or $2500. Fearful of becoming technologically obsolete, hospitals want to offer the most sophisticated equipment and procedures. Doctors and hospital administrators both realize that to pay for such equipment it must be used extensively. Second, in a litigious society such as ours physicians are prone to recommend more tests and procedures than might be medically warranted to protect themselves from malpractice suits. Third, doctors are paid on a fee-for-

service basis. More surgery is performed in the United States on a fee basis than in foreign countries, where doctors are paid annual salaries unrelated to the number of procedures performed. A recent study concluded that doctors who own x-ray or ultrasound machines did four to four-and-one-half times as many tests as doctors who referred their patients to radiologists. Finally, economists have long argued that the American Medical Association has kept admissions to medical schools and hence the supply of physicians artificially low. All of this increases costs and restricts the supply of health care.

As the demand for medical care has increased relative to supply, prices have soared. The consequences are predictable. Some 35 million Americans—13 percent of the population—lack health insurance. Companies and their workers are increasingly at odds over the sharing of health insurance costs. Politicians are debating the creation of a national health insurance program. Finally, the increasing acuteness of our health care problems is forcing us to face the hard fact that medical care is a scarce service which must be rationed. Can we continue to provide $5000 per-day intensive care to a comatose ninety-year-old who is unlikely to be restored to reasonable health?

$$E_d = \frac{\text{percentage change in quantity demanded of X}}{\text{percentage change in price of X}}$$

The averages of prices and quantities under consideration are used as reference points in determining percentage changes in price and quantity. If E_d is greater than 1, demand is elastic. If E_d is less than 1, demand is inelastic. Unit elasticity is the special case in which E_d equals 1. A perfectly inelastic demand curve is portrayed by a line parallel to the vertical axis; a perfectly elastic demand curve is shown by a line above and parallel to the horizontal axis.

3   Elasticity varies at different price ranges on a demand curve, tending to be elastic in the northwest segment and inelastic in the southeast segment. Elasticity cannot be judged by the steepness or flatness of a demand curve on a graph.

4   If price and total revenue move in opposite directions, demand is elastic. If price and total revenue move in the same direction, demand is inelastic. Where demand is of unit elasticity, a change in price will leave total revenue unchanged.

5   The number of available substitutes, the size of an item in one's budget, whether the product is a luxury or necessity, and time are all determinants of elasticity of demand.

6   The elasticity concept also applies to supply. Elasticity of supply depends on the shiftability of resources between alternative employments. This shiftability in turn varies directly with the time producers have to adjust to a given price change.

7   Cross elasticity gauges how sensitive the purchases of one product are to changes in the price of another product. It is measured by the percentage change in the quantity demanded of product X divided by the percentage change in the price of product Y.

8   Income elasticity indicates the responsiveness of consumer purchases to a change in income. It is measured by the percentage change in the quantity demanded of the product divided by the percentage change in income.

9   Legally fixed prices upset the rationing function of equilibrium prices. Effective price ceilings result in persistent product shortages and, if an equitable distribution of the product is sought, government will have to ration the product to consumers. Price floors lead to product surpluses; government must purchase these surpluses or eliminate them by imposing restrictions on production or by increasing private demand.

TERMS AND CONCEPTS

price elasticity of demand	perfectly elastic demand	increasing- and constant-cost industries	short run and long run income elasticity of demand
elastic versus inelastic demand	total-revenue test price elasticity of supply	cross elasticity of demand	price ceiling price floor
perfectly inelastic demand	market period		

QUESTIONS AND STUDY SUGGESTIONS

1 Answer questions 1, 3, and 10 at the end of Chapter 4.

2 Graph the accompanying demand data and then use both the elasticity coefficient and the total-revenue test to determine price elasticity of demand for each possible price change. What can you conclude about the relationship between the slope of a curve and its elasticity? Explain in a nontechnical way *why* demand is elastic in the northwest segment of the demand curve and inelastic in the southeast segment. Graph the total revenue data below the demand curve and generalize on the relationship between price elasticity and total revenue.

Product price	Quantity demanded
$5	1
4	2
3	3
2	4
1	5

3 In some industries, for example, the petroleum industry, producers justify their reluctance to lower prices by arguing that demand for their products is inelastic. Explain.

4 How will the following changes in price affect total revenue (expenditures)—that is, will total revenue *increase, decline,* or *remain unchanged?*

   a Price falls and demand is inelastic.
   b Price rises and demand is elastic.
   c Price rises and supply is elastic.
   d Price rises and supply is inelastic.
   e Price rises and demand is inelastic.
   f Price falls and demand is elastic.
   g Price falls and demand is of unit elasticity.

5 What are the major determinants of price elasticity of demand? Use these determinants in judging whether demand for each of the following products is elastic or inelastic: **a** oranges; **b** cigarettes; **c** Winston cigarettes; **d** gasoline; **e** butter; **f** salt; **g** automobiles; **h** football games; **i** diamond bracelets; and **j** this textbook.

6 Empirical estimates suggest the following demand elasticities: 0.6 for physicians' services; 4.0 for foreign travel; and 1.2 for radio and television receivers. Use the generalizations for the determinants of elasticity developed in this chapter to explain each of these figures.

7 What effect would a rule stating that university students must live in university dormitories have on the price elasticity of demand for dormitory space? What impact might this in turn have on room rates?

8 You are sponsoring an outdoor rock concert. Your major costs—for the band, land rent, and security—are largely independent of attendance. Use the concept of price elasticity of demand to explain how you might establish ticket prices to maximize profits.

9 "If the demand for farm products is highly price inelastic, a bumper crop may reduce farm incomes." Evaluate and illustrate graphically.

10 You are chairperson of a state tax commission responsible for establishing a program to raise new revenue through excise taxes. Would elasticity of demand be important to you in determining those products on which excises should be levied? Explain.

11 In May 1990 Vincent van Gogh's painting "Portrait of Dr. Gachet" sold at auction for $82.5 million. Portray this sale in a demand and supply diagram and comment on the elasticity of supply.

12 In the 1970s the Organization of Petroleum Exporting Countries (OPEC) became operational as a cartel which reduced the world supply of oil, greatly increasing OPEC's revenues and profits. What can you infer regarding the elasticity of demand for oil? Would you expect countries exporting bananas or pineapples to be able to emulate OPEC? Explain.

13 In 1987 the average price of a home rose from $97,000 in April to $106,800 in May. During the same period home sales fell from 724,000 to 616,000 units. If we assume that mortgage interest rates and all other factors affecting home sales are constant, what do these figures suggest about the elasticity of demand for housing?

14 In the 1950s the local Boy Scout troop in Jackson, Wyoming, decided to gather and sell at auction elk antlers shed by thousands of elk wintering in the area. Buyers were mainly local artisans who used the antlers to make belt buckles, buttons, and tie clasps. Price per pound was 6¢ and the troop took in $500 annually. In the 1970s a fad developed in Asia which involved grinding antlers into powder to sprinkle on food for purported aphrodisiac benefits. In 1979 the price per pound of elk antlers in the Jackson auction was $6 per pound and the Boy Scouts earned $51,000! Show graphically and explain these dramatic increases in price and total revenue. Assuming no shift in the supply curve of elk antlers, use the midpoints formula to calculate the coefficient for the elasticity of supply.

15 Suppose the cross elasticity of demand for products A and B is +3.6 and for products C and D it is −5.4. What can you conclude about how products A and B and products C and D are related?

16 The income elasticities of demand for movies, dental services, and clothing have been estimated to be +3.4, +1.0, and +0.5, respectively. Interpret these coefficients. What does it mean if the income elasticity coefficient is negative?

17 Why is it desirable for ceiling prices to be accompanied by government rationing? And for price floors to be accompanied by surplus-purchasing or output-restricting or demand-increasing programs? Show graphically why price ceilings entail shortages and price floors result in surpluses. What effect, if any, does elasticity of demand and supply have on the size of these shortages and surpluses? Explain.

18 New York City has had rent controls since 1941. What effect do you think they have had on the amount of housing demanded? On the construction of new housing? Explain: "Rent controls are a kind of self-fulfilling prophecy. They are designed to cope with housing shortages, but instead create such shortages." Can you predict the economic consequences of laws which impose ceilings on interest rates? Show diagrammatically the expected effect of the minimum wage upon employment of low-wage workers.

21

Consumer Behavior and Utility Maximization[1]

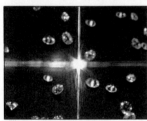

You have probably seen the bumper sticker which asserts: "I'd rather be shopping!" Indeed, we seem to be a nation of shoppers. Fact: Consumers spent about $3.9 trillion on goods and services in 1991. Fact: Americans consume 92 percent of their after-tax incomes. Fact: Consumption per person was $15,383 in the United States in 1991.

One concern of microeconomics is explaining consumer spending. If you were to compare the shopping carts of two consumers leaving a supermarket, you would observe striking differences. Why does Paula have potatoes, parsnips, pomegranates, and Pepsi in her cart, while Sam has sugar, saltines, soap, and 7-Up in his? Why didn't Paula also buy pork and pimentos? Why didn't Sam have soup and spaghetti on his grocery list? In this chapter, we will learn how individual consumers allocate their money incomes among the various goods and services available to them. Why does a consumer buy some specific bundle of goods rather than any one of a number of other collections of goods available? As we examine these issues we will also strengthen our understanding of the law of demand.

TWO EXPLANATIONS OF THE LAW OF DEMAND

The law of demand may be treated as a commonsense notion. A high price discourages consumers from buying; a low price encourages them to buy. We now explore two complementary explanations of the downsloping nature of the demand curve which will back up our everyday observations. (A third explanation, based on indifference curves, is more advanced and is summarized in the appendix to this chapter.)

Income and Substitution Effects

In Chapter 4 the law of demand—the downsloping demand curve—was explained in terms of income and substitution effects. Whenever a product's price decreases, two things happen to cause the amount demanded to increase.

---

[1]Some instructors may choose to omit this chapter. This can be done without impairing the continuity and meaning of ensuing chapters.

1 Income Effect   The **income effect** is the impact of a change in the price of a product on a consumer's real income and consequently on the quantity of that product demanded. If the price of a product—say, steak—declines, the real income or purchasing power of anyone buying that product will increase. This increase in real income will be reflected in increased purchases of many products, including steak. With a constant money income of $20 per week you can buy 10 pounds of steak at $2 per pound. But if the price of steak falls to $1 per pound and you buy 10 pounds, $10 per week is freed to buy more of this and other commodities. A decline in the price of steak increases the consumer's real income, enabling him or her to purchase more steak.[2] This is called the *income effect.*

2 Substitution Effect   The **substitution effect** is the impact a change in a product's price has on its relative expensiveness, and consequently on the quantity demanded. The lower price of a product means it is now cheaper relative to all other products. Consumers will substitute the cheaper product for other products which are now relatively more expensive. In our example, as the price of steak falls—prices of other products being unchanged—steak will become more attractive to the buyer. At $1 per pound it is a "better buy" than at $2. The lower price will induce the consumer to substitute steak for some of the now relatively less attractive items in the budget. Steak may well be substituted for pork, chicken, veal, fish, and other foods. A lower price increases the relative attractiveness of a product and the consumer will buy more of it. This is the *substitution effect.*

The income and substitution effects combine to make a consumer able and willing to buy more of a specific good at a low price than at a high price.

Law of Diminishing Marginal Utility

A second explanation of the downsloping demand curve is that, although consumer wants in general may be insatiable, wants for specific commodities can be fulfilled. In a given span of time, where buyers' tastes are unchanged, consumers can get as much of specific goods and services as they want. The more of a specific product consumers obtain, the less they will want more units of the same product.

This can be most readily seen for durable goods. A consumer's want for an automobile, when he or she has none, may be very strong; the desire for a second car is much less intense; for a third or fourth, very weak. Even the wealthiest families rarely have more than a half-dozen cars, although their incomes would allow them to purchase a whole fleet of them.

Terminology   Economists theorize that specific consumer wants can be fulfilled with succeeding units of a commodity in the **law of diminishing marginal utility.** Recall that a product has utility if it can satisfy a want. **Utility** is want-satisfying power. Two characteristics of this concept must be emphasized.

1   "Utility" and "usefulness" are not synonymous. Paintings by Picasso may be useless in a functional sense and yet be of tremendous utility to art connoisseurs.

2   Implied in the first point is the fact that utility is a subjective notion. The utility of a specific product will vary widely from person to person. A bottle of muscatel wine may yield substantial utility to the Skid Row alcoholic, but zero or negative utility to the local temperance union president. Eyeglasses have great utility to someone who is extremely far- or near-sighted, but no utility to a person having 20-20 vision.

By *marginal* utility we simply mean the extra utility, or satisfaction, a consumer gets from one additional unit of a specific product. In any short time wherein the consumer's tastes do not change, the marginal utility derived from successive units of a given product will decline.[3] A consumer will eventually become relatively saturated, or "filled up," with that particular product. The fact that marginal utility will decline as the consumer acquires additional units of a specific product is known as the law of diminishing marginal utility.

Because it is a subjective concept, utility is not susceptible to precise quantitative measurement. But for purposes of illustration, assume we can measure satisfaction with units we will call "utils." This mythical unit of satisfaction is a convenient pedagogical device allowing us to quantify consumer behavior. Thus, in Table 21-1, we can illustrate the relationship between the quantity obtained of a product—say, fast-food hamburgers—and the accompanying extra utility derived from each successive unit. Here we assume that the law of diminishing marginal utility sets in with the first hamburger consumed. Each successive hamburger

---

[2]We assume here that steak is a *normal* or *superior* good.

[3]For a time the marginal utility of successive units of a product may increase. A third can of beer may yield a larger amount of extra satisfaction than the first or second. But beyond some point, we can expect the marginal utility of added units to decline. With beer, this decline may be abrupt.

TABLE 21-1 The law of diminishing marginal utility as applied to hamburgers (*hypothetical data*)

Unit of hamburgers	Marginal utility, utils	Total utility, utils
First	10	10
Second	6	16
Third	2	18
Fourth	0	18
Fifth	−5	13

yields less and less extra utility than the previous one as the consumer's want for hamburgers comes closer and closer to fulfillment. *Total utility* can be found for any number of hamburgers by cumulating the marginal-utility figures as indicated in Table 21-1. This is so because marginal utility is the change in total utility associated with the consumption of one more unit of a good. Thus, the third hamburger has a marginal utility of 2 utils; 3 hamburgers yield a total utility of 18 utils (=10 + 6 + 2). Notice that marginal utility becomes zero for the fourth hamburger and negative for the fifth.

Relation to Demand and Elasticity How does the law of diminishing marginal utility explain why the demand curve for a specific product is downsloping? If successive units of a good yield smaller and smaller amounts of marginal, or extra, utility, then the consumer will buy additional units of a product only if its price falls. The consumer for whom these utility data are relevant may buy 2 hamburgers at a price of $1. But, owing to diminishing marginal utility from additional hamburgers, a consumer will choose *not* to buy more at this price, because giving up money really means giving up other goods, that is, alternative ways of getting utility. Therefore, additional hamburgers are "not worth it" unless the price (sacrifice of other goods) declines. (When marginal utility becomes negative, McDonald's or Burger King would have to pay *you* to consume another hamburger!) From the seller's viewpoint, diminishing marginal utility forces the producer to lower the price so buyers will take more of the product. This rationale supports the notion of a downsloping demand curve.

The amount by which marginal utility declines as more units of a product are consumed will determine its price elasticity of demand. Other things being equal, if marginal utility falls sharply as successive units are consumed, we would expect demand to be inelastic.

Conversely, modest declines in marginal utility as consumption increases imply an elastic demand.

THEORY OF CONSUMER BEHAVIOR

As well as providing a basis for explaining the law of demand, the idea of diminishing marginal utility is critical in explaining how consumers should allocate their money income among the many goods and services available for purchase.

Consumer Choice and Budget Restraint

The situation of the typical consumer is something like this:

1 Rational Behavior The consumer is a rational person, trying to dispose of his or her money income so as to derive the greatest amount of satisfaction, or utility, from it. Consumers want to get "the most for their money" or, more technically, to maximize total utility.

2 Preferences The consumer has rather clear-cut preferences for various goods and services available in the market. We assume buyers have a good idea of how much marginal utility they will get from successive units of the various products they might purchase.

3 Budget Restraint The consumer's money income is limited. Because a consumer supplies limited amounts of human and property resources to businesses, the money income received will be limited. With few possible exceptions—the Rockefellers, Bob Hope, Michael Jackson, and Saudi Arabia's King Fahd —all consumers are subject to a *budget restraint.*

4 Prices   The goods and services available to consumers have price tags on them. They are scarce in relation to the demand for them, or, stated differently, their production uses scarce and therefore valuable resources. In our examples we will suppose that product prices are not affected by the amounts of specific goods which the individual consumer buys; pure competition exists on the buying or demand side of the market.

If a consumer has limited dollars and the products he or she wants have price tags on them, the consumer can purchase only a limited amount of goods. The consumer cannot buy everything wanted when each purchase exhausts a portion of a limited money income. It is precisely this point which brings the economic fact of scarcity home to the individual consumer.

> In making his choices, our typical consumer is in the same position as the Western prospector . . . who is restocking for his next trip into the back country and who is forced by the nature of the terrain to restrict his luggage to whatever he can carry on the back of one burro. If he takes a great deal of one item, say baked beans, he must necessarily take much less of something else, say bacon. His job is to find that collection of products which, in view of the limitations imposed on the total, will best suit his needs and tastes.[4]

The consumer must compromise; he or she must choose among alternative goods to obtain with limited money income the most satisfying mix of goods and services.

Utility-Maximizing Rule

Of all the collections of goods and services a consumer can obtain within his or her budget, which specific collection will yield the maximum utility or satisfaction? The rule to be followed in maximizing satisfaction is that *the consumer's money income should be allocated so that the last dollar spent on each product purchased yields the same amount of extra (marginal) utility.* We shall call this the **utility-maximizing rule.** When the consumer is "balancing his margins" in accordance with

this rule, there will be no incentive to alter his or her expenditure pattern. The consumer will be in *equilibrium* and, barring a change in tastes, income, or the prices of the various goods, will be worse off—total utility will decline—by any alteration in the collection of goods purchased.

Numerical Example   An illustration will help explain this rule. For simplicity's sake we limit our discussion to just two products, but the analysis can readily be extended to any number of goods. Suppose consumer Brooks is trying to decide which combination of two products—A and B—she should purchase with her limited daily income of $10. Brooks's preferences for these two products and their prices will be basic data determining the combinations of A and B which will maximize her satisfactions. Table 21-2 summarizes Brooks's preferences for products A and B. Column 2a shows the amount of extra or marginal utility she will derive from each successive unit of A. Column 3a reflects her preferences for product B. In each case the relationship between the number of units of the product obtained and the corresponding marginal utility reflects the law of diminishing marginal utility. Diminishing marginal utility is assumed to begin with the first unit of each product purchased.

Marginal Utility per Dollar   Before we apply the utility-maximizing rule to these data, we must put the

---

[4]E. T. Weiler, *The Economic System* (New York: The Macmillan Company, 1952), p. 89.

TABLE 21-2   The utility-maximizing combination of products A and B obtainable with an income of $10* *(hypothetical data)*

(1) Unit of product	(2) Product A: price = $1		(3) Product B: price = $2	
	(a) Marginal utility, utils	(b) Marginal utility per dollar (MU/price)	(a) Marginal utility, utils	(b) Marginal utility per dollar (MU/price)
First	10	10	24	12
Second	8	8	20	10
Third	7	7	18	9
Fourth	6	6	16	8
Fifth	5	5	12	6
Sixth	4	4	6	3
Seventh	3	3	4	2

*It is assumed in this table that the amount of marginal utility received from additional units of each of the two products is independent of the quantity of the other product. For example, the marginal utility schedule for product A is independent of the amount of B obtained by the consumer.

marginal-utility information of two columns 2a and 3a on a per-dollar-spent basis. A consumer's choices will be influenced not only by the extra utility which successive units of product A will yield, but also by how many dollars (and therefore how many units of alternative good B) she must give up to obtain those added units of A.

The rational consumer must compare the extra utility from each product with its cost. Suppose you prefer a pizza whose marginal utility is, say, 36 utils to a movie whose marginal utility is just 24 utils. But if the pizza's price is $12 and the movie only $6, you would choose the movie rather than the pizza! Why? Because the marginal utility per dollar spent would be 4 utils for the movie (4 = 24 ÷ $6) compared to only 3 utils for the pizza (3 = 36 ÷ $12). You could buy two movies for $12 and, assuming the marginal utility of the second movie is, say, 16 utils, total utility would be 40 utils. Forty units of satisfaction from two movies is clearly superior to 36 utils from the same $12 expenditure on one pizza. *To make the amounts of extra utility derived from differently priced goods comparable, marginal utility must be put on a per-dollar-spent basis.* This is done in columns 2b and 3b. These figures are obtained by dividing the marginal-utility data of columns 2a and 3a by the assumed prices of A and B—$1 and $2, respectively.

Decision-Making Process   Now we have Brooks's preferences—on unit and per dollar bases—and the price tags of A and B before us. Brooks stands patiently with $10 to spend on A and B. In what order should she allocate her dollars on units of A and B to achieve the highest degree of utility within the limits imposed by her money income? What specific combination of A and B will she have obtained at the time that she exhausts her $10?

Concentrating on columns 2b and 3b of Table 21-2, we find that Brooks should first spend $2 on the first unit of B, because its marginal utility per dollar of 12 utils is higher than A's of only 10 utils. But now Brooks finds herself indifferent about whether she should buy a second unit of B or the first unit of A, because the marginal utility per dollar of both is 10. So she buys both of them. Brooks now has 1 unit of A and 2 of B. With this combination of goods the last dollar spent on each yields the same amount of extra utility. Does this combination of A and B therefore represent the maximum amount of utility which Brooks can obtain? The answer is "No." This collection of goods only costs $5 [=(1 × $1) + (2 × $2)]; Brooks has $5 remaining,

which she can spend to achieve a still higher level of total utility.

Examining columns 2b and 3b again, we find Brooks should spend the next $2 on a third unit of B because marginal utility per dollar for the third unit of B is 9 compared to 8 for the second unit of A. But now, with 1 unit of A and 3 of B, we find she is again indifferent to a second unit of A and a fourth unit of B. Again assume Brooks purchases one more unit of each. Marginal utility per dollar is now the same at 8 utils for the last dollar spent on each product, *and* Brooks's money income of $10 is exhausted [(2 × $1) + (4 × $2)]. *The utility-maximizing combination of goods attainable by Brooks is 2 units of A and 4 of B.*[5] By summing the marginal utility information of columns 2a and 3a we find that Brooks is realizing 18 (=10 + 8) utils of satisfaction from the 2 units of A and 78 (=24 + 20 + 18 + 16) utils of satisfaction from the 4 units of B. Her $10, optimally spent, yields 96 (=18 + 78) utils of satisfaction. Table 21-3 summarizes this step-by-step process for maximizing consumer utility and merits your careful study.

Inferior Options   There are other combinations of A and B which are obtainable with $10. But none will yield a level of total utility as high as 2 units of A and 4 of B. For example, 4 units of A and 3 of B can be obtained for $10. However, this combination violates the utility-maximizing rule; total utility here is only 93 utils, clearly inferior to the 96 utils yielded by 2 of A and 4 of B. Furthermore, there are other combinations of A and B (such as 4 of A and 5 of B *or* 1 of A and 2 of B) where the marginal utility of the last dollar spent is the same for both A and B. But all such combinations are either unobtainable with Brooks's limited money income (as 4 of A and 5 of B) or fail to exhaust her money income (as 1 of A and 2 of B) and therefore do not yield her the maximum utility attainable.

Problem: Suppose that Brooks's money income was $14 rather than $10. What now would be the utility-maximizing combination of A and B? Are A and B normal or inferior goods?

Algebraic Restatement

Our rule merely says that a consumer will maximize her satisfaction when she allocates her money income

---

[5]To simplify, we assume in this example that Brooks spends her entire income; she neither borrows nor saves. Saving can be regarded as a utility-yielding commodity and incorporated in our analysis. It is treated thus in question 5 at the end of the chapter.

TABLE 21-3 Sequence of purchases in achieving consumer equilibrium

Potential choice	Marginal utility per dollar	Purchase decision	Income remaining
1 { First unit of A	10	First unit of B for $2	$8 = $10 − $2
First unit of B	12		
2 { First unit of A	10	First unit of A for $1	$5 = $8 − $3
Second unit of B	10	and second unit of B for $2	
3 { Second unit of A	8	Third unit of B for $2	$3 = $5 − $2
Third unit of B	9		
4 { Second unit of A	8	Second unit of A for $1	$0 = $3 − $3
Fourth unit of B	8	and fourth unit of B for $2	

so that the last dollar spent on product A, the last on product B, and so forth, yield equal amounts of additional, or marginal, utility. Now the marginal utility per dollar spent on A is indicated by MU of product A/price of A (column 2b of Table 21-2) and the marginal utility per dollar spent on B by MU of product B/price of B (column 3b of Table 21-2). Our utility-maximizing rule merely requires that these ratios be equal. That is,

$$\frac{\text{MU of product A}}{\text{price of A}} = \frac{\text{MU of product B}}{\text{price of B}}$$

and, of course, the consumer must exhaust her available income. Our tabular illustration has shown us that the combination of 2 units of A and 4 of B fulfills these conditions in that

$$\frac{8}{1} = \frac{16}{2}$$

and the consumer's $10 income is spent.

If the equation is not fulfilled, there will be some reallocation of the consumer's expenditures between A and B, from the low to the high marginal-utility-per-dollar product, which will increase the consumer's total utility. For example, if the consumer spent $10 on 4 of A and 3 of B, we would find that

$$\frac{\text{MU of A: 6 utils}}{\text{price of A: \$1}} < \frac{\text{MU of B: 18 utils}}{\text{price of B: \$2}}$$

The last dollar spent on A provides only 6 utils of satisfaction, and the last dollar spent on B provides 9 (=18 ÷ $2). On a per dollar basis, units of B provide more extra satisfaction than units of A. Hence, the consumer will increase total satisfaction by purchasing

more of B and less of A. As dollars are reallocated from A to B, the marginal utility from additional units of B will decline as the result of moving *down* the diminishing marginal-utility schedule for B, and the marginal utility of A will rise as the consumer moves *up* the diminishing marginal-utility schedule for A. At some new combination of A and B—specifically, 2 of A and 4 of B—the equality of the two ratios and therefore consumer equilibrium will be achieved. As we already know, the net gain in utility is 3 utils (=96 − 93).

MARGINAL UTILITY AND THE DEMAND CURVE

It is a simple step from the utility-maximizing rule to the construction of a downsloping demand curve. Recall that the basic determinants of an individual's demand curve for a specific product are (1) preferences or tastes, (2) money income, and (3) prices of other goods. The utility data of Table 21-2 reflect our consumer's preferences. We continue to suppose that her money income is $10. And, concentrating on the construction of a simple demand curve for product B, we assume that the price of A—representing "other goods"—is $1.

Deriving the Demand Curve We can now derive a simple demand schedule for B by considering alternative prices at which B might be sold and determining the quantity our consumer will purchase. We have already determined one such price-quantity combination in explaining the utility-maximizing rule: Given tastes, income, and prices of other goods, the rational consumer will purchase 4 units of B at $2. Now assume the price of B falls to $1. The marginal-utility-per-dollar data of column 3b of Table 21-2 will double, because the price of B has been halved; the new data for column 3b are in fact identical to those in column 3a. The purchase of 2 units of A and 4 of B is no longer an equilibrium combination. By applying the same reasoning used to develop the utility-maximizing rule, we now find Brooks's utility-maximizing position is 4 units of A and 6 of B. We sketch Brooks's demand curve for B as in Table 21-4, confirming a downsloping demand curve.

Income and Substitution Effects Revisited At the beginning of this chapter we indicated that increased purchases of a good whose price had fallen could be understood in terms of the substitution and income effects. Although our analysis does not let us sort out these two effects quantitatively, we can see intuitively how each is involved in the increased purchase of product B.

The *substitution effect* can be understood by referring back to our utility-maximizing rule. Before the price of B declined, Brooks was in equilibrium in that $MU_A(8)/P_A(\$1) = MU_B(16)/P_B(\$2)$, when purchasing 2 units of A and 4 units of B. But after B's price falls from $2 to $1, $MU_A(8)/P_A(\$1) < MU_B(16)/P_B(\$1)$ or, more simply stated, the last dollar spent on B now yields more utility (16 utils) than does the last dollar spent on A (8 utils). This indicates that a switching of expenditures from A to B is needed to restore equilibrium; that is, a *substitution* of now cheaper B for A will occur in the bundle of goods which Brooks purchases.

What about the *income effect?* The assumed decline in the price of B from $2 to $1 increases Brooks's real income. Before the price decline, Brooks was in equilibrium when buying 2 of A and 4 of B. But at the lower $1 price for B, Brooks would have to spend only $6 rather than $10 on this same combination of goods. She has $4 left over to spend on more of A, more of B, or more of both. In short, the price decline of B has caused Brooks's *real* income to increase so that she can now obtain larger amounts of A and B with the same $10 *money* income. The portion of the 2-unit increase in her purchase of B due to this increase in real income is the income effect.

TABLE 21-4   **The demand schedule for product B**

Price per unit of B	Quantity demanded
$2	4
1	6

THE TIME DIMENSION

The theory of consumer behavior has been generalized to take the economic value of *time* into account. Both consumption and production activities have a common characteristic—they take time. Time is a valuable economic resource; by working—by using an hour in productive activity—one may earn $6, $10, $50, or more, depending on one's education and skills. By using that hour for leisure or in consumption activities, one incurs the opportunity cost of forgone income; you sacrifice the $6, $10, or $50 you could have earned by working.

The Value of Time

In the marginal-utility theory of consumer behavior economists traditionally have assumed that consumption is an instantaneous act. However, it is logical to argue that "prices" of consumer goods should include, not merely market price, but also the value of the time required in consumption of the good. In other words, the denominators of our earlier marginal-utility/price ratios are incomplete because they do not reflect the "full price"—market price *plus* the value of consumption time—of the product.

Imagine a consumer who is considering the purchase of a round of golf, on the one hand, and a concert, on the other. The market price of the golf game is $15 and the concert is $20. But the golf game is more time-intensive than the concert. Suppose you will spend four hours on the golf course, but only two hours at the concert. If your time is worth $7 per hour—as evidenced by the $7 wage rate you can obtain by working—then the "full price" of the golf game is $43 (the $15 market price *plus* $28 worth of time). Similarly, the "full price" of the concert is $34 (the $20 market price

LAST WORD

THE WATER–DIAMOND PARADOX

Water is clearly one of the most useful products in the world; our very survival depends on it. Yet water is very cheap. In contrast, diamonds—which are merely decorative and have little practical value—are very expensive. Why do prices apparently fail to measure the usefulness of goods? Our theory of consumer behavior and the distinction between total and marginal utility help resolve this paradox.

The explanation of the water–diamond paradox lies in two related considerations. First, the supplies of the two products are much different. Water is plentiful and, as a consequence, its price is low and we therefore consume large quantities of it. In doing so we extend our use of water to uses wherein the utility from the last unit of water—water's marginal utility—is very low. For example, we water our lawns, make ice cubes, and wash our cars. In contrast, diamonds are rare and costly to mine, cut, and polish. Therefore, their supply is restricted and they are available only at a high price. The marginal utility of diamonds is therefore very large.

The second consideration relates back to the utility-maximizing rule which states that consumers should purchase any good until the ratio of its marginal utility to price is the same as that for all other goods. Although the *marginal* utility of water may be low because it is plentiful and its price is low, the *total* utility derived from its consumption is exceedingly large because of the great quantity consumed. Conversely, the total utility derived from diamonds is low because the very high price which reflects the scarcity of diamonds causes consumers to purchase relatively few of them. In short, the total utility derived from water is relatively great and the total utility derived from diamonds is relatively small, but it is *marginal* utility which is relevant to the price people are willing to pay for a good. Water yields much more total utilty to us than do diamonds, even though the utility of an additional gallon of water is much less than the utility of an additional diamond. Society would gladly give up *all* of the diamonds in the world if that were necessary to obtain *all* of the water in the world. But society would rather have an *additional* diamond than an *additional* gallon of water, given the abundant stock of water available.

---

plus $14 worth of time). We find that, contrary to what market prices alone indicate, the "full price" of the concert is really *less* than the "full price" of the golf game.

If we now assume that the marginal utilities derived from successive golf games and concerts are identical, traditional theory would indicate that one should consume more golf games than concerts because the market price of the former is lower ($15) than the latter ($20). But when time is taken into account, the situation is reversed and golf games are more expensive ($43) than concerts ($34). Hence, it is rational in this case to consume more concerts than golf games.

Some Implications

By taking time into account, we can explain certain observable phenomena which traditional theory does not. It may be rational for the unskilled worker or retiree whose time has little or no market value to ride a bus from Peoria to Pittsburgh. But the corporate executive, whose time is very valuable, will find it cheaper to fly, even though bus fare is only a fraction of plane fare. It is sensible for the retiree, living on a modest social security check and having ample time, to spend many hours shopping for bargains. It is equally intelligent for the highly paid physician, working 55 hours per week, to patronize the hospital cafeteria and to buy a new television set over the phone.

Foreigners feel affluent Americans are "wasteful" of food and other material goods, but "overly economical" in the use of time. Americans who visit less developed countries find that time is used casually or "squandered," while material goods are very highly prized and carefully used. These differences are not a paradox or a case of radically different temperaments. The differences are primarily a rational reflection that the high labor productivity characteristic of an advanced society gives time a high market value, whereas the opposite is true in a less developed country.

A final point: As labor productivity has increased historically with the growth of our economy, time has become more valuable in the labor market. Or, stated differently, time used on pure leisure and various consumer activities has become more expensive. Thus we make a great effort to use nonwork time more "productively." Where possible, we try to increase the pleasure or utility yield per hour by consuming more per unit of time. In some cases this means making consumption more goods-intensive; for example, by buying or renting a motorized golf cart, the time required for a round of golf can be reduced. One watches the news on television because it takes less time than reading the newspaper. In other instances, we consume two or more items simultaneously. After dinner, the consumer "may find himself drinking Brazilian coffee, smoking a Dutch cigar, sipping a French cognac, reading *The New York Times,* listening to a Brandenburg Concerto and entertaining his Swedish wife—all at the same time, with varying degrees of success."[6]

But the yield from certain uses of time—pure idleness, cultural pursuits, and the "cultivation of mind and spirit"—cannot be readily increased. Hence, time tends to be shifted from these uses to areas where the yield is greater. This helps explain why, although economic development may bring affluence in the form of goods, it also increases the relative scarcity of time and creates a more hectic life-style. Economic growth, it is argued, cannot produce abundance in all respects; total affluence—an abundance of *both* goods and time—is a logical fallacy. Advanced economies are goods-rich and time-poor, while less developed countries are time-rich and goods-poor.

[6]Staffan B. Linder, *The Harried Leisure Class* (New York: Columbia University Press, 1970), p. 79.

CHAPTER SUMMARY

1 The law of demand can be explained in terms of the income and substitution effects or the law of diminishing marginal utility.

2 The income effect says that a decline in the price of a product will enable the consumer to buy more of it with a fixed money income. The substitution effect points out that a lower price will make a product relatively more attractive and therefore increase the consumer's willingness to substitute it for other products.

3 The law of diminishing marginal utility states that beyond some point, additional units of a specific good will yield ever-declining amounts of extra satisfaction to a consumer.

4 We may assume that the typical consumer is rational and acts on the basis of well-defined preferences. Because income is limited and goods have prices on them, the consumer cannot purchase all the goods and services he or she might like to have. The consumer should therefore select that attainable combination of goods which will maximize his or her utility or satisfaction.

5 The consumer's utility will be maximized when income is allocated so that the last dollar spent on each product purchased yields the same amount of extra satisfaction. Algebraically, the utility-maximizing rule is fulfilled when

$$\frac{\text{MU of product A}}{\text{price of A}} = \frac{\text{MU of product B}}{\text{price of B}}$$

and the consumer's income is spent.

6 The utility-maximizing rule and the demand curve are logically consistent. Because marginal utility declines, a lower price will be needed to induce the consumer to buy more.

7 The theory of consumer choice has been generalized by taking into account the value of the time required in the consumption of various goods and services.

TERMS AND CONCEPTS

income effect	law of diminishing	utility
substitution effect	marginal utility	utility-maximizing rule

QUESTIONS AND STUDY SUGGESTIONS

1 Explain the law of demand through the income and substitution effects, using a price increase as a point of departure for your discussion. Explain the law of demand in terms of diminishing marginal utility.

2 Mrs. Peterson buys loaves of bread and quarts of milk each week at prices of $1 and 80 cents, respectively. At present she is buying these two products in amounts such that the marginal utilities from the last units purchased of the two products are 80 and 70 utils, respectively. Is she buying the utility-maximizing combination of bread and milk? If not, how should she reallocate her expenditures between the two goods?

3 You are choosing between two goods, X and Y, and your marginal utility from each is as shown below. If your income is $9 and the prices of X and Y are $2 and $1 respectively, what quantities of each will you purchase in maximizing utility? Specify the amount of total utility you will realize. Assume that, other things remaining unchanged, the price of X falls to $1. What quantities of X and Y will you now purchase? Using the two prices and quantities you have derived for X, graph your demand curve for X.

Units of X	MU_x	Units of Y	MU_y
1	10	1	8
2	8	2	7
3	6	3	6
4	4	4	5
5	3	5	4
6	2	6	3

4 "Nothing is more useful than water: but it will purchase scarce any thing; scarce any thing can be had in exchange for it. A diamond, on the contrary, has scarce any value in use; but a very great quantity of other goods may frequently be had in exchange for it."[7] Explain.

[7]Adam Smith, *The Wealth of Nations* (New York: Modern Library, Inc., originally published in 1776), p. 28.

5 Columns 1 through 4 of the table at the bottom of this page show the marginal utility, measured in terms of utils, which Mr. Black would get by purchasing various amounts of products A, B, C, and D. Column 5 shows the marginal utility Black gets from saving. Assume that the prices of A, B, C, and D are $18, $6, $4, and $24, respectively, and that Black has a money income of $106.

  a What quantities of A, B, C, and D will Black purchase in maximizing his satisfactions?

  b How many dollars will Black choose to save?

  c Check your answers by substituting them into the algebraic statement of the utility-maximizing rule.

6 "In the long run it may be irrational to purchase goods on the basis of habit; but in the short run habitual buying may prove to be a very sensible means of allocating income." Do you agree? Explain.

7 How can time be incorporated into the theory of consumer behavior? Foreigners frequently point out that Americans are very wasteful of food and other material goods and very conscious of, and overly economical in, their use of time. Can you explain this observation?

8 Explain:

  a "Before economic growth, there were too few goods; after growth, there is too little time."

  b "It is irrational for an individual to take the time to be completely rational in economic decision making."

9 In the last decade or so there has been a dramatic expansion of small retail convenience stores—such as Kwik Shops, 7-Elevens, Gas 'N Shops—although their prices are generally much higher than those in the large supermarkets. Can you explain their success?

10 **Advanced analysis:** Let $MU_a = z = 10 - x$ and $MU_b = z = 21 - 2y$, where z is marginal utility measured in utils, x is the amount spent on product A, and y is the amount spent on B. Assume the consumer has $10 to spend on A and B; that is, $x + y = 10$. How is this $10 best allocated between A and B? How much utility will the marginal dollar yield?

Column 1		Column 2		Column 3		Column 4		Column 5	
Units of A	MU	Units of B	MU	Units of C	MU	Units of D	MU	No. of dollars saved	MU
1	72	1	24	1	15	1	36	1	5
2	54	2	15	2	12	2	30	2	4
3	45	3	12	3	8	3	24	3	3
4	36	4	9	4	7	4	18	4	2
5	27	5	7	5	5	5	13	5	1
6	18	6	5	6	4	6	7	6	$\frac{1}{2}$
7	15	7	2	7	$3\frac{1}{2}$	7	4	7	$\frac{1}{4}$
8	12	8	1	8	3	8	2	8	$\frac{1}{8}$

Indifference Curve Analysis

A more advanced explanation of consumer behavior and equilibrium is based upon (1) budget lines and (2) indifference curves.

The Budget Line: What Is Attainable

A **budget line** *shows various combinations of two products which can be purchased with a given money income.* If the price of product A is $1.50 and the price of B $1.00, then the consumer could purchase all the combinations of A and B shown in Table 1 with $12 of money income. At one extreme the consumer might spend all of his or her income on 8 units of A and have nothing left to spend on B. Or, by giving up 2 units of A and thereby "freeing" $3, the consumer could have 6 units of A and 3 of B. And so on to the other extreme, at which the consumer could buy 12 units of B at $1.00 each, spending his or her entire money income on B with nothing left to spend on A.

Figure 1 shows the budget line graphically. The slope of the budget line measures the ratio of the price of B to the price of A; more precisely, the absolute value of the slope is $P_B/P_A = \$1.00/\$1.50 = 2/3$. This is the mathematical way of saying that the consumer must forgo 2 units of A (measured on the vertical axis) at $1.50 each to have $3 to spend on 3 units of B (measured on the horizontal axis). In moving down the budget or price line, 2 of A (at $1.50 each) must be given up to obtain 3 of B (at $1.00 each). This yields a slope of $\frac{2}{3}$.

Two other characteristics of the budget line merit comment.

1 Income Changes The location of the budget line varies with money income. An *increase* in money income will shift the budget line to the *right;* a *decrease* in money income will move it to the *left*. To verify these statements, recalculate Table 1 assuming that money income is (*a*) $24 and (*b*) $6 and plot the new budget lines in Figure 1.

2 Price Changes A change in product prices will also shift the budget line. A decline in the prices of both products—the equivalent of a real income increase—will shift the curve to the right. You can verify this by recalculating Table 1 and replotting Figure 1 assuming that $P_A = \$.75$ and $P_B = \$.50$. Conversely, an increase

TABLE 1   **The budget line: combinations of A and B attainable with an income of $12 (*hypothetical data*)**

Units of A (price = $1.50)	Units of B (price = $1.00)	Total expenditures
8	0	$12 (=$12 + $0)
6	3	$12 (=$9 + $3)
4	6	$12 (=$6 + $6)
2	9	$12 (=$3 + $9)
0	12	$12 (=$0 + $12)

FIGURE 1   **A consumer's budget line**

The budget line shows all the various combinations of any two products which can be purchased, given the prices of the products and the consumer's money income.

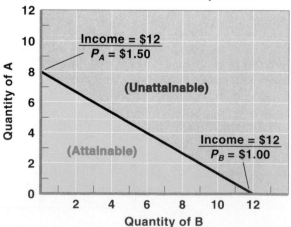

in the prices of A and B will shift the curve to the left. Again, assume $P_A = \$3$ and $P_B = \$2$ and rework Table 1 and Figure 1 to substantiate this statement. Note in particular what happens if we change P_B while holding P_A (and money income) constant. The reader should verify that, if we lower P_B from $\$1.00$ to $\$.50$, the budget line will fan outward to the right. Conversely, by increasing P_B from $\$1.00$ to $\$1.50$, the line will fan inward to the left. In both instances the line remains "anchored" at 8 units on the vertical axis because P_A has not changed.

Indifference Curves: What Is Preferred

Budget lines reflect "objective" market data involving income and prices. The budget line reveals combinations of A and B which are attainable, given money income and prices. Indifference curves, on the other hand, embody "subjective" information about consumer preferences for A and B. An **indifference curve** *shows all combinations of products A and B which will yield the same level of satisfaction or utility to the consumer.* Table 2 and Figure 2 present a hypothetical indifference curve involving products A and B. The consumer's subjective preferences are such that he or she will realize the same total utility from each combination of A and B shown in the table or curve; hence, the consumer will be indifferent as to which combination is actually obtained.

It is essential to understand several characteristics of indifference curves.

1 Downsloping Indifference curves are downsloping because both product A and product B yield utility to the consumer. Hence, in moving from combination *j* to combination *k*, the consumer is obtaining more of B and increasing his or her total utility; therefore, some of A must be taken away to decrease total utility by a precisely offsetting amount. In brief, "more of B" necessitates "less of A" so that the quantities of A and B are inversely related. Any curve which reflects inversely related variables is downsloping.

TABLE 2   An indifference schedule (*hypothetical data*)

Combination	Units of A	Units of B
j	12	2
k	6	4
l	4	6
m	3	8

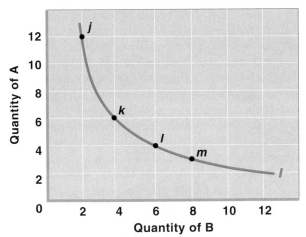

FIGURE 2   A consumer's indifference curve
Every point on an indifference curve represents some combination of products A and B which is equally satisfactory to the consumer; that is, each combination of A and B embodies the same level of total utility.

2 Convex to Origin But, as viewed from the origin, a downsloping curve can be concave (bowed outward) or convex (bowed inward). A concave curve has an increasing (steeper) slope as one moves down the curve, while a convex curve has a diminishing (flatter) slope as one moves down it. (Recall that the production possibilities curve of Figure 2-1 is concave, reflecting the law of increasing opportunity costs.) Note in Figure 2 that *the indifference curve is convex as viewed from the origin.* That is, the slope diminishes or becomes flatter as we move from *j* to *k*, to *l*, to *m*, and so on down the curve. Technically, the slope of the indifference curve measures the **marginal rate of substitution** (MRS) because it shows the rate, at the margin, at which the consumer will substitute one good for the other (B for A) to remain equally satisfied. The diminishing slope of the indifference curve means the willingness to substitute B for A *diminishes* as one moves down the curve.

The rationale for this convexity, that is, for a diminishing MRS, is that a consumer's subjective willingness to substitute B for A (or vice versa) will depend on the amounts of B and A he or she has to begin with. Consider Table 2 and Figure 2 once again, beginning at point *j*. Here, in relative terms, the consumer has a substantial amount of A and very little of B. This means that "at the margin" B is very valuable (that is, its marginal utility is high), while A is less valuable at the margin (its marginal utility is low). The consumer will then be willing to give up a substantial amount of A to get, say, 2 more units of B. In this particular case, the consumer is willing to forgo 6 units of A to get 2 more units of B; the MRS is $\frac{6}{2}$, or 3. But at point k the consumer now has less A and more B. Now A will be somewhat more valuable, and B somewhat less valuable, at the margin. Considering the move from point k to point l, the consumer is only willing to give up 2 units of A to get 2 more units of B so the MRS is now only $\frac{2}{2}$, or 1. Having still less of A and more of B at point l, the consumer is only willing to give up 1 unit of A in return for 2 more of B and and the MRS falls to $\frac{1}{2}$.

In general, as the amount of B *increases,* the marginal utility of additional units of B *decreases.* Similarly, as the quantity of A *decreases,* its marginal utility *increases.* In Figure 2 we see that in moving down the curve the consumer will be willing to give up smaller and smaller amounts of A to offset acquiring each additional unit of B. The result is a curve with a diminishing slope, one which is convex when viewed from the origin. The MRS declines as one moves southeast along the indifference curve.

3 Indifference Map   The single indifference curve of Figure 2 reflects some constant (but unspecified) level of total utility or satisfaction. It is possible—and useful for our analysis—to sketch a whole series of indifference curves or, in other words, an **indifference map** as shown in Figure 3. Each curve reflects a different level of total utility. Specifically, each curve to the *right* of our original curve (labeled I_3 in Figure 3) reflects combinations of A and B which yield *more* utility than I_3. Each curve to the *left* of I_3 reflects *less* total utility than I_3. As we move out from the origin each successive indifference curve entails a higher level of utility. This can be demonstrated by drawing a line in a northeasterly direction from the origin and noting that its points of intersection with each successive curve entail larger amounts of *both* A and B and therefore a higher level of total utility.

Equilibrium at Tangency

Noting that the axes of Figures 1 and 3 are identical, we can now determine the consumer's **equilibrium position** by combining the budget line and the indifference map as shown in Figure 4. By definition, the budget line indicates all combinations of A and B the consumer can attain, given his or her money income and the prices of A and B. Of these attainable combinations, the consumer will most prefer that combination which yields the greatest satisfaction or utility. Specifically,

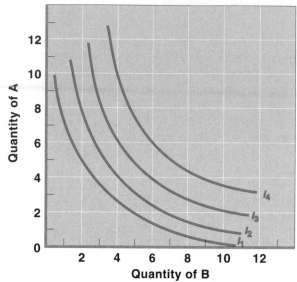

FIGURE 3   An indifference map

An indifference map is comprised of a set of indifference curves. Each successive curve further from the origin indicates a higher level of total utility. That is, any combination of products A and B shown by a point on I_4 is superior to any combination of A and B shown by a point on I_3, I_2, or I_1.

the utility-maximizing combination will be the one lying on the highest attainable indifference curve.

In terms of Figure 4 the consumer's utility-maximizing or equilibrium combination of A and B is at point X where the budget line is *tangent* to I_3. Why not point Y? Because Y is on a lower indifference curve, I_2. By trading "down" the budget line—by shifting dollars from purchases of A to purchases of B—the consumer can get on an indifference curve further from the origin and thereby increase total utility from the same income. Why not Z? Same reason: Point Z is on a lower indifference curve, I_1. By trading "up" the budget line—by reallocating dollars from B to A—the consumer can get on higher indifference curve I_3 and increase total utility.

How about point W on indifference curve I_4? While it is true that W yields a higher level of total utility than does X, point W is beyond (outside) the budget line and hence *not* attainable to the consumer. Point X is the best or optimal *attainable* combination of products A and B. At this point we note that, by definition of tangency, the slope of the highest attainable indifference curve equals the slope of the budget line. Because the slope of the indifference curve reflects the MRS and

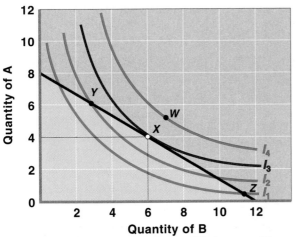

FIGURE 4   The consumer's equilibrium position

The consumer's equilibrium position is at point *X*, where the budget line is tangent to the highest attainable indifference curve, *I₃*. In this case the consumer will buy 4 units of A at $1.50 per unit and 6 of B at $1 per unit with a $12 money income. Points *Z* and *Y* also represent attainable combinations of A and B, but yield less total utility as is evidenced by the fact they are on lower indifference curves. While *W* would entail more utility than *X*, it is outside the budget line and therefore unattainable.

the slope of the budget line is P_B/P_A, the optimal or equilibrium position is where

$$MRS = P_B/P_A$$

Digression: The Measurement of Utility

There is an important difference between the marginal-utility theory and the indifference curve theory of consumer demand. The marginal-utility theory assumes that utility is *numerically* measurable. That is, the consumer is assumed to be able to say *how much* extra utility he or she derives from an extra unit of A or B. Given the prices of A and B, the consumer must be able to measure the marginal utility derived from successive units of A and B to realize the utility-maximizing (equilibrium) position as previously indicated by

$$\frac{\text{Marginal utility of A}}{\text{price of A}} = \frac{\text{marginal utility of B}}{\text{price of B}}$$

The indifference curve approach poses a less stringent requirement for the consumer: He or she need only specify whether a given combination of A and B

yields more, less, or the same amount of utility than some other combination of A and B. The consumer need only say, for example, that 6 of A and 7 of B yield more (or less) satisfaction than 4 of A and 9 of B; indifference curve analysis does *not* require the consumer to specify *how much* more (or less) satisfaction will be realized.

When the equilibrium situations in the two approaches are compared we find that (1) in the indifference curve analysis the MRS equals P_B/P_A; however, (2) in the marginal-utility approach the ratio of marginal utilities equals P_B/P_A. We therefore deduce that the MRS is equivalent in the marginal-utility approach to the ratio of marginal utilities of the two goods.[8]

Deriving the Demand Curve

We noted earlier that, given the price of A, an increase in the price of B will cause the budget line to fan inward to the left. This fact can now be used to derive a demand curve for product B. In Figure 5a we reproduce Figure 4 showing our initial consumer equilibrium at point *X*. The budget line involved in determining this equilibrium position assumes a money income of $12 and that P_A = $1.50 and P_B = $1.00. Let's examine what happens to the equilibrium position if we increase P_B to $1.50, holding money income and the price of A constant.

The result is shown in Figure 5a. The budget line fans to the left, yielding a new equilibrium point of tangency with indifference curve I_2 at point X'. At X' the consumer is buying 3 units of B and 5 of A compared to 4 of A and 6 of B at *X*. Our interest is in B and we note that we have sufficient information to locate the demand curve for product B. We know that at equilibrium point *X* the price of B is $1.00 and 6 units are purchased; at equilibrium point X' the price of B is $1.50 and 3 units are purchased.

These data are shown graphically as a demand curve for B in Figure 5b. Note that the horizontal axes of Figure 5a and b are identical; both measure the quantity demanded of B. Hence, we can drop gray perpendiculars from Figure 5a down to the horizontal axis of Figure 5b. On the vertical axis of Figure 5b we locate the two chosen prices of B. Connecting these prices

[8]Technical footnote: If we begin with the utility-maximizing rule, $MU_A/P_A = MU_B/P_B$, then multiply through by P_B and divide through by MU_A, we obtain $P_B/P_A = MU_B/MU_A$. In indifference curve analysis we know that the optimal or equilibrium position is where $MRS = P_B/P_A$. Hence, MRS also equals MU_B/MU_A.

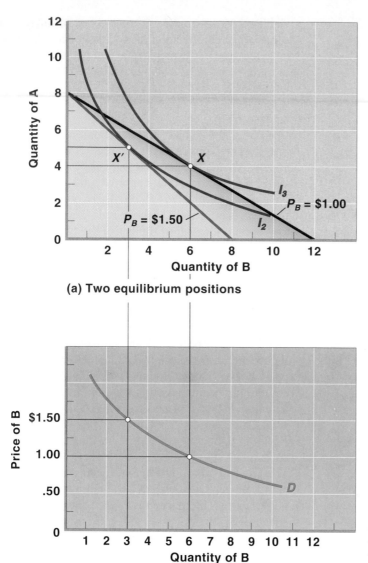

(a) Two equilibrium positions

(b) The demand curve for product B

FIGURE 5   Deriving the demand curve

When the price of B is increased from $1.00 to $1.50 in (a) the equilibrium position moves from *X* to *X′*, decreasing the quantity of B demanded from 6 to 3 units. The demand curve for B is determined in (b) by plotting the $1.00–6 units and the $1.50–3 units price-quantity combinations for B.

with the relevant quantities demanded, we locate two points on the demand curve for B. By simple manipulation of the price of B in an indifference curve–budget line context, a downsloping demand curve for B can be derived. We have derived the law of demand under the correct assumption of "other things being equal" since *only* the price of B has been changed. The price of A as well as the consumer's income and tastes have remained constant when deriving the consumer's demand curve for product B.

APPENDIX SUMMARY

1   The indifference curve approach to consumer behavior is based on the consumer's budget line and indifference curves.

2   The budget line shows all combinations of two products which the consumer can purchase, given money income and product prices.

3 A change in product prices or money income will shift the budget line.
4 An indifference curve shows all combinations of two products which will yield the same level of total utility to the consumer. Indifference curves are downsloping and convex to the origin.
5 An indifference map consists of a number of indifference curves; the further from the origin, the higher the level of utility associated with each curve.

6 The consumer will select that point on the budget line which puts him or her on the highest attainable indifference curve.
7 Changing the price of one product shifts the budget line and determines a new equilibrium position. A downsloping demand curve can be determined by plotting the price-quantity combinations associated with the old and new equilibrium positions.

APPENDIX TERMS AND CONCEPTS

budget line
indifference curve

marginal rate of
substitution

indifference map
equilibrium position

APPENDIX QUESTIONS AND STUDY SUGGESTIONS

1 What information is embodied in a budget line? What shifts will occur in the budget line when money income **a** increases and **b** decreases? What shifts will occur in the budget line as the product price shown on the horizontal axis **a** increases and **b** decreases?
2 What information is contained in an indifference curve? Why are such curves **a** downsloping and **b** convex to the origin? Why does total utility increase as the consumer moves to indifference curves further from the origin? Why can't indifference curves intersect?
3 Using Figure 4, explain why the point of *tangency* of the budget line with an indifference curve is the consumer's equilibrium position. Explain why any point where the budget line *intersects* an indifference curve will *not* be equilibrium. Explain: "The consumer is in equilibrium where $MRS = P_B/P_A$."
4 Assume that the data in the accompanying table indicate an indifference curve for Mr. Chen. Graph this curve,

putting A on the vertical and B on the horizontal axis. Assuming the prices of A and B are $1.50 and $1.00, respectively, and that Chen has $24 to spend, add the resulting budget line to your graph. What combination of A and B will Chen purchase? Does your answer meet the $MRS = P_B/P_A$ rule for equilibrium?

Units of A	Units of B
16	6
12	8
8	12
4	24

5 Explain graphically how indifference analysis can be used to derive a demand curve.
6 **Advanced analysis:** Demonstrate that the equilibrium condition $MRS = P_B/P_A$ is the equivalent of the utility-maximizing rule $MU_A/P_A = MU_B/P_B$.

The Costs of Production

Product prices are determined by the interaction of demand and supply. In preceding chapters we examined factors underlying demand. As observed in Chapter 4, the basic factor underlying the ability and willingness of firms to supply a product in the market is the cost of production. Production of any good requires economic resources which, because of their relative scarcity, bear price tags. The amount of any product a firm is willing to supply depends on the prices (costs) and the productivity of the resources essential to its production, on the one hand, and the price the product will bring in the market, on the other.

This chapter considers the general nature of production costs. Product prices are introduced in the following chapters, and supply decisions of producers are then explained.

ECONOMIC COSTS

Costs exist because resources are scarce and have alternative uses. To use a bundle of resources in producing some particular good means that certain alternative production opportunities have been forgone. *Costs in economics deal with forgoing the opportunity to produce alternative goods and services.* The **economic,** or **opportunity cost** of any resource in producing a good is its value or worth in its best alternative use.

This conception of costs is embodied in the production possibilities curve of Chapter 2. Note that at point *C* in Table 2-1 the opportunity cost of producing 100,000 *more* pizzas is the 3,000 industrial robots which must be forgone. The steel used for armaments is not available for manufacturing automobiles or apartment buildings. And if an assembly-line worker can produce automobiles or washing machines, then the cost to society in employing this worker in an automobile plant is the contribution the worker would otherwise have made in producing washing machines. The cost to you in reading this chapter is the alternative uses of your time—studying for a biology exam or going to a movie—which you must forgo while you read it.

Explicit and Implicit Costs

Let's now consider costs from the firm's viewpoint. Given the notion of opportunity costs, we can say that *economic costs are those payments a firm must make, or incomes it must provide, to resource suppliers to attract these resources away from alternative production oppor-*

tunities. These payments or incomes may be either explicit or implicit.

The monetary payments—the "out-of-pocket" or cash expenditures a firm makes to "outsiders" who supply labor services, materials, fuel, transportation services, and power—are called **explicit costs.** Explicit costs are payments to nonowners of the firm for the resources they supply.

But, in addition, a firm may use certain resources the firm itself owns. Our concept of opportunity costs tells us that, regardless of whether a resource is owned or hired by an enterprise, there is a cost involved in using that resource in a specific employment. The costs of such self-owned, self-employed resources are nonexpenditure or **implicit costs.** To the firm, those implicit costs are the money payments the self-employed resources could have earned in their best alternative employments.

Example: Suppose Holly operates a corner grocery as a sole proprietor. She owns outright her store building and supplies all her own labor and money capital. Though her enterprise has no explicit rental or wage costs, implicit rents and wages are incurred. By using her own building for a grocery, Holly sacrifices the $800 monthly rental income she otherwise could have earned by renting it to someone else. Similarly, by using her money capital and labor in her own enterprise, Holly sacrifices the interest and wage incomes she otherwise could have earned by supplying these resources in their best alternative employments. And, finally, by running her own enterprise, Holly forgoes earnings she could have realized by supplying her managerial efforts to another firm.

Normal Profits as a Cost

The minimum payment required to keep Holly's entrepreneurial talents engaged in this enterprise is called a **normal profit.** As is true of implicit rent or implicit wages, her normal return for performing entrepreneurial functions is an implicit cost. If this minimum, or normal, return is not realized, the entrepreneur will withdraw her efforts from this line of production and reallocate them to a more attractive line of production. Or she may cease being an entrepreneur and become a wage or salary earner.

The economist includes as costs all payments— explicit and implicit, the latter including a normal profit —required to attract and retain resources in a given line of production.

Economic, or Pure, Profits

Economists and accountants use the term "profits" differently. *Accounting profits are the firm's total revenue less its explicit costs.* But economists define profits differently. **Economic profits** *are total revenue less all costs (explicit and implicit, the latter including a normal profit to the entrepreneur).* Therefore, when an economist says a firm is just covering its costs, it means that all explicit and implicit costs are being met and that the entrepreneur is receiving a return just large enough to retain his or her talents in the present line of production.

If a firm's total receipts exceed all its economic costs, any residual accrues to the entrepreneur. This residual is called an *economic,* or *pure, profit.* In short:

$$\begin{array}{c} \text{Economic} \\ \text{profits} \end{array} = \begin{array}{c} \text{total} \\ \text{revenue} \end{array} - \begin{array}{c} \text{opportunity cost} \\ \text{of all inputs} \end{array}$$

An economic profit is *not* a cost, because by definition it is a return in excess of the normal profit required to retain the entrepreneur in this particular line of production.

Figure 22-1 shows the relationships between various cost and profit concepts and merits close examination. You should also consider question 2 at the end of this chapter.

Short Run and Long Run

The costs a firm or industry incurs in producing any given output will depend on the types of adjustments it can make in the amounts of the various resources it

FIGURE 22-1 Economic and accounting profits

Economic profits are equal to total revenue less opportunity costs. Opportunity costs are the sum of explicit and implicit costs and include a normal profit to the entrepreneur. Accounting profits are equal to total revenue less accounting (explicit) costs.

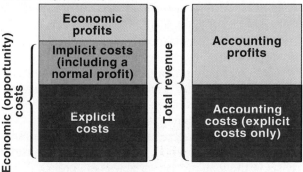

employs. The quantities employed of many resources —most labor, raw materials, fuel, and power—can be varied easily and quickly. Other resources require more time for adjustment. The capacity of a manufacturing plant, that is, the size of the factory building and the amount of machinery and equipment therein, can only be varied over a considerable period of time. In some heavy industries it may take several years to alter plant capacity.

Short Run: Fixed Plant   These differences in the time necessary to vary quantities of various resources used in the productive process make it essential to distinguish between the short run and the long run. The **short run** is a period of time too brief for an enterprise to alter its plant capacity, yet long enough to permit a change in the level at which the fixed plant is used. The firm's plant capacity is fixed in the short run, but output can be varied by applying larger or smaller amounts of labor, materials, and other resources to that plant. Existing plant capacity can be used more or less intensively in the short run.

Long Run: Variable Plant   From the viewpoint of existing firms, the **long run** is a period of time extensive enough for these firms to change the quantities of *all* resources employed, including plant capacity. From the industry's viewpoint, the long run also encompasses enough time for existing firms to dissolve and leave the industry or for new firms to be created and enter the industry. *While the short run is a "fixed-plant" time period, the long run is a "variable-plant" time period.*

Illustrations   If a General Motors plant hired 100 extra workers or added an entire shift of workers, this would be a short-run adjustment. If the same GM plant added a new wing to its building and installed more equipment, this would be a long-run adjustment.

Note that the short run and the long run are *conceptual* rather than specific calendar time periods. In light manufacturing industries, changes in plant capacity may be negotiated almost overnight. A small T-shirt firm can increase its plant capacity in a few days or less by ordering and installing a couple of new cutting tables and several extra sewing machines. But heavy industry is a different story. It may take Exxon several years to construct a new oil refinery.

We will now analyze production costs in the short-run, or fixed-plant, period. Following this we consider costs in the long-run, or variable-plant, period.

PRODUCTION COSTS IN THE SHORT RUN

A firm's costs of producing any output will depend not only on prices of needed resources, but also on technology—the quantity of resources it takes to produce that output. It is the latter, technological aspect of costs which we now consider. In the short run a firm can change its output by adding variable resources to a fixed plant. But how does output change as more and more variable resources are added to the firm's fixed resources?

Law of Diminishing Returns

The answer is provided in general terms by the **law of diminishing returns,** also called the "law of diminishing marginal product" and the "law of variable proportions." This law states that *as successive units of a variable resource (say, labor) are added to a fixed resource (say, capital or land), beyond some point the extra, or marginal, product attributable to each additional unit of the variable resource will decline.* If additional workers are applied to a given amount of capital equipment, as is the case in the short run, eventually output will rise by smaller and smaller amounts as more workers are employed.

Rationale   Suppose a farmer has a fixed amount of land—80 acres—planted in corn. If the farmer does not cultivate the cornfields at all, the yield will be 40 bushels per acre. If the land is cultivated once, output may rise to 50 bushels per acre. A second cultivation may increase output to 57 bushels per acre, a third to 61, and a fourth to 63. Further cultivations will add little or nothing to total output. Successive cultivations add less and less to the land's yield. If this were not so, the world's needs for corn could be fulfilled by extremely intense cultivation of this single 80-acre plot of land.

Indeed, if diminishing returns did not occur, the world could be fed out of a flowerpot.

The law of diminishing returns also holds true in nonagricultural industries. Assume a small planing mill is manufacturing wood furniture frames. It has a given amount of equipment—lathes, planers, saws, sanders. If this firm hired just one or two workers, total output and productivity (output per worker) would be very low. These workers would perform many different jobs, and the advantages of specialization would be lost. Time would also be lost in switching from one job to another, and machines would stand idle much of the time. In short, the plant would be understaffed, and production inefficient because there is too much capital relative to labor.

These difficulties would disappear as more workers were added. Equipment would be more fully used, and workers could now specialize on a single job. Time would no longer be lost from job switching. Thus, as more workers are added to the initially understaffed plant, the extra or marginal product of each will tend to rise due to more efficient production.

But this cannot go on indefinitely. As still more workers are added, problems of overcrowding will arise. Workers must wait in line to use the machinery, so now *workers* are under-used. Total output increases at a diminishing rate because, given the fixed plant size, each worker will have less capital equipment to work with as more and more labor is hired. The extra, or marginal, product of additional workers declines because the plant is more intensively staffed. There now is more labor in proportion to the fixed amount of capital goods. In the extreme case, the continuous addition of labor to the plant would use up all standing room, and production would be brought to a standstill.

Note that the law of diminishing returns assumes that all units of variable inputs—workers in this case—are of equal quality. Each successive worker is presumed to have the same innate ability, motor coordination, education, training, and work experience. Marginal product ultimately diminishes, not because successive workers are qualitatively inferior, but because more workers are being used relative to the amount of capital goods available.

Numerical Example Table 22-1 presents a numerical illustration of the law of diminishing returns. Column 2 indicates the **total product** resulting from combining each level of labor input in column 1 with a fixed amount of capital goods.

Column 3, **marginal product,** shows the *change* in total output associated with each additional input of labor. Note that with no labor inputs, total product is zero; an empty plant will yield no output. The first two workers reflect increasing returns, their marginal products being 10 and 15 units of output respectively. But then, beginning with the third worker, marginal product—the increase in total product—diminishes continuously and actually becomes zero with the eighth worker and negative with the ninth.

Average product or output per worker (also called "labor productivity") is shown in column 4. It is calculated by dividing total product (column 2) by the corresponding number of workers (column 1).

TABLE 22-1 **The law of diminishing returns** *(hypothetical data)*

(1) Inputs of the variable resource (labor)	(2) Total product	(3) Marginal product $\Delta 2/\Delta 1$		(4) Average product (2)/(1)
0	0			—
1	10	10 ⎱ Increasing	marginal returns	10
2	25	15 ⎰		$12\frac{1}{2}$
3	37	12		$12\frac{1}{3}$
4	47	10	Diminishing	$11\frac{3}{4}$
5	55	8	marginal returns	11
6	60	5		10
7	63	3		9
8	63	0	Negative marginal	$7\frac{7}{8}$
9	62	−1	returns	$6\frac{8}{9}$

Shifting the Cost Curves

Changes in either resource prices or technology will cause cost curves to shift. If fixed costs had been higher—say, $200 rather than the $100 we assumed in Table 22-2—then the AFC curve in Figure 22-5 would be shifted upward. The ATC curve would also be at a higher position because AFC is a component of ATC. But the positions of the AVC and MC curves would be unaltered because their locations are based on the prices of variable rather than fixed resources. Thus, if the price (wage) of labor or some other variable input rose, the AVC, ATC, and MC curves would all shift upward, but the position of AFC would remain unchanged. Reductions in the prices of fixed or variable resources will entail cost curve shifts exactly opposite to those just described.

If a more efficient technology were discovered, then the productivity of all inputs would increase. The cost figures in Table 22-2 would all be lower. To illustrate, if labor is the only variable input and wages are $10 per hour and average product is 10 units, then AVC would be $1. But if a technological improvement increases the average product of labor to 20 units, then AVC will decline to $.50. More generally, an upward shift in the productivity curves shown in the top portion of Figure 22-6 will mean a downward shift in the cost curves portrayed in the bottom portion of that diagram.

QUICK REVIEW 22-2

♦ **The law of diminishing returns indicates that, beyond some point, output will increase by diminishing amounts as a variable resource (labor) is added to a fixed resource (capital).**

♦ **In the short run the total cost of any level of output is the sum of fixed and variable costs (TC = TFC + TVC).**

♦ **Average fixed, average variable, and average total costs are fixed, variable and total cost per unit of output; marginal cost is the cost of producing one more unit of output.**

♦ **Average fixed cost declines continuously as output increases; average variable cost and average total cost are U-shaped, reflecting increasing and then diminishing returns; marginal cost falls but then rises, intersecting both average variable and average total cost at their minimum points.**

PRODUCTION COSTS IN THE LONG RUN

In the long run an industry and the individual firms it comprises can undertake all desired resource adjustments. The firm can alter its plant capacity; it can build a larger plant or revert to a smaller plant than assumed in Table 22-2. The industry can also change its plant size; the long run allows sufficient time for new firms to enter or existing firms to leave an industry. The impact of the entry and exodus of firms into and from an industry will be discussed in the next chapter; here we are concerned only with changes in plant capacity made by a single firm. We will couch our analysis in terms of ATC, making no distinction between fixed and variable costs because all resources, and therefore all costs, are variable in the long run.

Firm Size and Costs

Suppose a single-plant manufacturing enterprise begins on a small scale and then, as the result of successful operations, expands to successively larger plant sizes. What happens to average total costs as this occurs? For a time successively larger plants will bring lower average total costs. However, eventually the building of a still larger plant may cause ATC to rise.

Figure 22-7 illustrates this situation for five possible plant sizes. ATC-1 is the average-total-cost curve for the smallest of the five plants, and ATC-5 for the largest. The relationship of the five plant sizes to one another is clearly that stated above. Constructing a larger plant will entail lower minimum per unit costs through plant size 3. But beyond this point a larger plant will mean a higher level of minimum average total costs.

The Long-Run Cost Curve

The vertical lines perpendicular to the output axis in Figure 22-7 are crucial. They indicate those outputs at which the firm should change plant size to realize the lowest attainable per unit costs of production. In Figure 22-7 we see that for all outputs up to 20 units, the lowest per unit costs are attainable with plant size 1. However, if the firm's volume of sales expands to some level greater than 20 but less than 30 units, it can achieve lower per unit costs by constructing a larger plant—plant size 2. Although *total* cost will be higher at the greater levels of production, the cost *per unit* of output

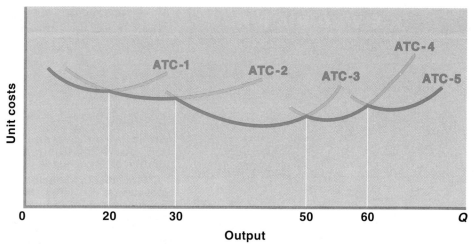

FIGURE 22-7   The long-run average-cost curve: five possible plant sizes

The long-run average-cost curve is made up of segments of the short-run cost curves (ATC-1, ATC-2, etc.) of the various-sized plants from which the firm might choose. Each point on the bumpy planning curve shows the least unit cost attainable for any output when the firm has had time to make all desired changes in its plant size.

will be less than before. For any output between 30 and 50 units, plant size 3 will yield the lowest per unit costs. For the 50- to 60-unit range of output, plant size 4 must be built to achieve the lowest unit costs. Lowest per unit costs for any output over 60 units demand construction of the still larger plant size 5.

Tracing these adjustments, we can conclude that the long-run ATC curve for the enterprise will comprise segments of the short-run ATC curves for the various plant sizes which can be constructed. *The long-run ATC curve shows the least per unit cost at which any output can be produced after the firm has had time to make all appropriate adjustments in its plant size.* In Figure 22-7 the heavy, bumpy curve is the firm's long-run ATC curve or, as it is often called, the firm's planning curve.

In most lines of production the choice of plant sizes is much wider than that in our illustration. In fact, in many industries the number of possible plant sizes is virtually unlimited, and in time quite small changes in the volume of output (sales) will lead to changes in plant size. Graphically, this implies an unlimited number of short-run ATC curves, as suggested by Figure 22-8 (Key Graph). The minimum ATC of producing each possible level of output is shown by the long-run ATC curve. Rather than being comprised of *segments* of short-run ATC curves as in Figure 22-7, the long-run

ATC curve is made up of all the *points of tangency* of the theoretically unlimited number of short-run ATC curves from which the long-run ATC curve is derived. Hence, the planning curve is smooth rather than bumpy.

Economies and Diseconomies of Scale

We have accepted the contention that for a time larger and larger plant size will entail lower unit costs but that beyond some point successively larger plants will mean higher average total costs. Exactly why is the long-run ATC curve U-shaped? Note, first, that the law of diminishing returns does *not* apply here, because it presumes one resource is fixed in supply while the long run assumes all resources are variable. Also, our discussion assumes resource prices are constant. We can explain the U-shaped long-run average-cost curve in terms of economies and diseconomies of large-scale production.

Economies of Scale   **Economies of scale** or, more commonly, economies of mass production, explain the downsloping part of the long-run ATC curve, as indicated in Figure 22-9a. As plant size increases, a number

producer able to expand its scale of operations. From a slightly different perspective, an increase in *all* resources of, say, 10 percent will cause a more-than-proportionate increase in output of, say, 20 percent. The necessary result will be a decline in ATC.

It is of interest that the notion of economies of scale has been invoked in debate over the national defense budget. When the Pentagon was proposing a fleet of 132 B-2 Stealth bombers, the estimated cost per plane was $580 million. But a proposed cut to 75 bombers by the Secretary of Defense caused the cost per plane to surge to over $800 million. The per plane cost increase was allegedly due to the loss of scale economies associated with the smaller order.

Diseconomies of Scale   But in time the expansion of a firm *may* lead to diseconomies and therefore higher per unit costs.

The main factor causing **diseconomies of scale** lies with managerial problems in efficiently controlling and coordinating a firm's operations as it becomes a large-sclae producer. In a small plant a single key executive may make all the basic decisions for the plant's operation. Because of the firm's smallness, the executive is close to the production line and can readily comprehend the firm's operations, easily digest information gained from subordinates, and make clear and efficient decisions.

This neat picture changes, however, as a firm grows. There are many management levels between the executive suite and the assembly line; top management is far removed from the actual production operations of the plant. One person cannot assemble, understand, and digest all the information essential to rational decision making in a large-scale enterprise. Authority must be delegated to innumerable vice-presidents, second vice-presidents, and so forth. This expansion in depth and width of the management hierarchy leads to problems of communication, coordination, and bureaucratic red tape, and the possibility that decisions of various subordinates will fail to mesh. The result is impaired efficiency and rising average costs.

Also, in massive production facilities workers may feel alienated from their jobs and have little commitment to productive efficiency. Opportunities to shirk—to avoid work in favor of on-the-job leisure—may be greater in large plants than in small ones. Large plants susceptible to worker alienation and shirking may require additional worker supervision, which increases costs.

Again, thought of differently, an increase in *all* resources of 10 percent will cause a less-than-proportionate increase in output of, say, 5 percent. As a consequence, ATC will increase. Diseconomies of scale are illustrated by the rising portion of the long-run cost curve in Figure 22-9a.

Constant Returns to Scale   In some instances there may exist a rather wide range of output between the output level at which economies of scale are exhausted and the point at which diseconomies of scale are encountered. That is, there will be a range of **constant returns to scale** over which long-run average cost is constant. The q_1q_2 output range of Figure 22-9a is relevant. Here a given percentage increase in *all* inputs of 10 percent will cause a proportionate 10 percent increase in output. Thus, ATC does not change.

Relevance   In many American manufacturing industries economies of scale have been of great significance. Firms which have expanded their scale of operations to realize economies of mass production have survived and flourished. Those unable to achieve this expansion are in the unenviable position of being high-cost producers, doomed to a marginal existence or ultimate insolvency.

There is some difference of opinion among economists as to the relevance of diseconomies of scale. Some feel that the existence and continued growth of such gigantic corporations as General Motors, AT&T, Exxon, and Prudential Life Insurance cast doubt on the concept. In practice, computerized information and communication systems have often been developed and applied to overcome or forestall the decision-making problems embodied in the notion of diseconomies of scale. Where these efforts are successful, the long-run average-cost curve would fall and then become more or less constant as economies of scale are exhausted.

But there is case study and anecdotal evidence to suggest that diseconomies of scale are a fact of industrial life and, when encountered, can be significant. Large firms often design their organizational structures in the hope of avoiding diseconomies of scale. Among its many subdivisions, General Motors has established five automobile-producing divisions (Chevrolet, Buick, Oldsmobile, Pontiac, and Cadillac), each of which is largely autonomous and competing. GM's recent Saturn automobile project entailed the creation of a separate company. In short, a degree of decentralization has been sought which will allow full attainment of economies of scale yet help avoid diseconomies of scale.

Some economists contend that small companies have fueled much of the technological innovation and job creation of the last fifteen or twenty years. They also point out that huge American corporations in such industries as steel, automobiles, and consumer electronics have failed to meet cost and quality competition of foreign firms, some of which are smaller. It is also relevant that some of the more successful big companies such as Johnson & Johnson (pharmaceuticals) and Hewlett-Packard (computers) have organized themselves into groups of smaller, essentially independent firms.

Former executives of large corporations attest to the reality of diseconomies of scale. A former General Motors president commented thus on GM's Chevrolet division:

> Chevrolet is such a big monster that you twist its tail and nothing happens at the other end for months and months. It is so gigantic that there isn't any way to really run it. You just sort of try to keep track of it.

Similarly, a former GM vice-president provided this insider's view of Chevrolet:

> One of the biggest . . . problems was in the manufacturing staff. It was overburdened with layer upon layer of management. . . . A plant manager reported to a city manager who reported to a regional manager who reported to a manager of plants who reported to me, the general manager. Consequently, the manager of the Chevrolet Gear and Axle plant on Detroit's near east side who was only a few miles away from my office, was almost light years away in terms of management reporting channels.

Adams and Brock[1] recently examined the steel and automobile industries, concluding that the hierarchical, bureaucratic managements which accompany the large size of firms in those industries tend to inhibit efficiency. They also note that in recent years many large and highly diversified corporations have divested themselves of various divisions and subsidiaries to enhance managerial efficiency.

[1] Walter Adams and James W. Brock, *The Bigness Complex* (New York: Pantheon Books, 1986), chap. 3. The above two quotations are cited in Adams and Brock.

MES and Industry Structure

Economies and diseconomies of scale are an important determinant of an industry's structure. Here it is helpful to introduce the concept of **minimum efficient scale** (MES) which is the smallest level of output at which a firm can minimize long-run average costs. In Figure 22-9a this occurs at Oq_1 units of output. Because of the extended range of constant returns to scale, firms producing substantially larger outputs could also realize the minimum attainable average costs. Specifically, firms would be equally efficient within the q_1q_2 range. We would therefore not be surprised to find an industry with such cost conditions to be populated by firms of quite different sizes. The meatpacking, furniture, wood products, and small appliance industries provide approximate examples. With an extended range of constant returns to scale, relatively large and relatively small firms could coexist in an industry and be equally viable.

Compare this with Figure 22-9b where economies of scale are extensive and diseconomies are remote. Here the long-run average-cost curve will decline over a long range of output, the case in the automobile, aluminum, steel, and other heavy industries. Given consumer demand, efficient production will be achieved only with a small number of industrial giants. Small firms cannot realize the minimum efficient scale and will not be viable. In the extreme, economies of scale might extend beyond the market's size, resulting in what is termed a natural monopoly (Chapter 24). A **natural monopoly** is a market situation where unit costs are minimized by having one firm produce the particular good or service.

Where economies of scale are few and diseconomies quickly encountered, minimum efficient size occurs at a small level of output as shown in Figure 22-9c. In such industries a given level of consumer demand will support a large number of relatively small producers. Many retail trades and some types of farming fall into this category. So do certain types of light manufacturing, such as the baking, clothing, and shoe industries. Fairly small firms are as efficient as, or more efficient than, large-scale producers in such industries.

The point is that the shape of the long-run average-cost curve, as determined by economies and diseconomies of scale, can be significant in determining the structure and competitiveness of an industry. Whether

LAST WORD

ECONOMIES OF SCALE AND INDUSTRIAL CONCENTRATION

Is market concentration explainable in terms of economies of scale?

It is sometimes argued that industrial concentration—the dominance of a market by a small number of firms—is justified on the basis of economies of scale. If a firm's long-run average-cost curve declines over an extended range of output, total consumption of the product may only support a few efficient (minimum unit cost) producers (Figure 22-9b).

Research studies suggest that industrial concentration is generally *not* warranted on the basis of economies of scale. The minimum efficient scale (MES)—the smallest plant size at which minimum unit cost would be attained—has been determined for a number of industries, twelve of which are listed in the accompanying table. Column 2 compares the MES output with domestic consumption of each product to determine the percentage of total consumption which a single MES plant could produce. We find, for example, that a cigarette manufacturer of minimum efficient scale could produce about 6.6 percent of the domestic consumption of cigarettes.

By dividing the percentage of domestic consumption which an MES plant could produce into 100 percent (total domestic consumption), one can calculate the number of efficient plants which consumption will support. Thus we observe in column 3 that 15 MES plants (=100 percent ÷ 6.6 percent) are compatible with domestic cigarette consumption.

In a few industries—small diesel engines, turbogenerators, electric motors, and refrigerators—some

level of concentration is required to realize scale economies. But for most of the industries shown, the minimum efficient plant sizes are small compared to the domestic market for each product. This suggests that economies of scale do *not* provide a rationale or justification for a high degree of concentration in most of the studied industries. The fact that the four largest firms in the beer industry actually provide 77 percent of

an industry is "competitive"—populated by a relatively large number of small firms—or "concentrated"—dominated by a few large producers—is sometimes a reflection of an industry's technology and the resulting shape of its long-run average-cost curve.

But we must be cautious in making this statement because industry structure does not depend on cost conditions alone. Government policies, geographic size of a market, managerial ability, and other factors must be considered in explaining the structure of a given industry. Indeed, this chapter's Last Word presents empirical evidence suggesting that many industries are much more concentrated than can be justified on the basis of economies of scale.

QUICK REVIEW 22-3

♦ *Most firms have U-shaped long-run average-cost curves, reflecting economies and then diseconomies of scale.*

♦ *Economies of scale are the consequence of greater specialization of labor and management, more efficient capital equipment, and the use of by-products.*

♦ *Diseconomies of scale are caused by problems of coordination and communication which arise in large firms.*

♦ *Minimum efficient scale is the lowest level of output at which a firm's long-run average costs are at a minimum.*

Minimum efficient plant sizes as a percentage of domestic consumption

(1) Industry	(2) Minimum efficient scale as a percentage of domestic consumption	(3) Number of efficient plants compatible with domestic consumption
Diesel engines (small)	25.5%	4
Turbogenerators	23.0	4
Electric motors	15.0	7
Refrigerators	14.1	7
Cellulosic synthetic fiber	11.1	9
Passenger automobile production	11.0	9
Commercial aircraft	10.0	10
Cigarettes	6.6	15
Printing paper	4.4	23
Beer brewing	3.4	29
Bicycles	2.1	48
Petroleum refining	1.9	53

Source: F. M. Scherer, *Industrial Market Structure and Economic Performance*, 2d ed. (Boston: Houghton Mifflin Company, 1980), pp. 96–97.

domestic beer output and the four largest cigarette manufacturers control 90 percent of the domestic cigarette market (Table 26-1) is not explainable solely in terms of economies of scale.

There are some qualifications which must be appended. The data cited in the table refer only to *production* economies. Multiplant firms—and therefore higher levels of industrial concentration than those suggested by column 3 of the table—may be justified on the basis of other nonproduction advantages. For example, a large multiplant firm may be able to economize on management services by drawing on a common pool of accountants, lawyers, and financial planners to serve all of its plants. Similarly, a multiplant firm may realize economies in advertising, raising money capital, or in product distribution. On the other hand, it is conceivable that diseconomies could be associated with some aspects of multiplant operation. In any event, even when adjustments are made for such factors, the general conclusion remains that economic concentration in many industries cannot be justified on the basis of economies of scale.

CHAPTER SUMMARY

1 Economic costs include all payments which must be received by resource owners to ensure continued supply of these resources in a particular line of production. This definition includes explicit costs, which flow to resource suppliers separate from a given enterprise, and also implicit costs, the remuneration of self-owned and self-employed resources. One of the implicit cost payments is a normal profit to the entrepreneur for functions performed.

2 In the short run a firm's plant capacity is fixed. The firm can use its plant more or less intensively by adding or subtracting units of variable resources, but the firm does not have sufficient time to alter plant size.

3 The law of diminishing returns describes what happens to output as a fixed plant is used more intensively. The law states that as successive units of a variable resource such as labor are added to a fixed plant, beyond some point the resulting marginal product associated with each additional worker will decline.

4 Because some resources are variable and others fixed, costs can be classified as variable or fixed in the short run. Fixed costs are independent of the level of output; variable costs vary with output. The total cost of any output is the sum of fixed and variable costs at that output.

5 Average fixed, average variable, and average total costs are fixed, variable, and total costs per unit of output. Average fixed costs decline continuously as output increases, because a fixed sum is being spread over a larger and larger number of units of production. Average variable costs are

U-shaped, reflecting the law of diminishing returns. Average total cost is the sum of average fixed and average variable costs; it too is U-shaped.

6 Marginal cost is the extra, or additional, cost of producing one more unit of output. Graphically, the marginal cost curve intersects the ATC and AVC curves at their minimum points.

7 Lower resource prices shift cost curves downward as does technological progress. Higher input prices shift cost curves upward.

8 The long run is a period of time sufficiently long for a firm to vary the amounts of all resources used, including plant size. In the long run all costs are variable. The long-run ATC, or planning, curve is composed of segments of the short-run ATC curves, representing the various plant sizes a firm can construct in the long run.

9 The long-run ATC curve is generally U-shaped. Economies of scale are first encountered as a small firm expands. A number of considerations—particularly greater specialization in the use of labor and management, ability to use the most efficient equipment, and more complete utilization of by-products—contribute to these economies of scale. Diseconomies of scale stem from the managerial complexities which accompany large-scale production. The relative importance of economies and diseconomies of scale in an industry is often an important determinant of the structure of that industry.

TERMS AND CONCEPTS

economic (opportunity) cost	law of diminishing returns	average fixed cost	constant returns to scale
explicit and implicit costs	total, marginal, and average product	average variable cost	minimum efficient scale
normal and economic profits	fixed costs	average total cost	natural monopoly
short run and long run	variable costs	marginal cost	
	total costs	economies and diseconomies of scale	

QUESTIONS AND STUDY SUGGESTIONS

1 Distinguish between explicit and implicit costs, giving examples of each. What are the explicit and implicit costs of going to college? Why does the economist classify normal profits as a cost? Are economic profits regarded as a cost of production?

2 Gomez runs a small firm which makes pottery. He hires one helper at $12,000 per year, pays annual rent of $5,000 for his shop, and materials cost $20,000 per year. Gomez has $40,000 of his own funds invested in equipment (pottery wheels, kilns, and so forth) which could earn him $4,000 per year if alternatively invested. Gomez has been offered $15,000 per year to work as a potter for a competitor. He estimates his entrepreneurial talents are worth $3,000 per year. Total annual revenue from pottery sales is $72,000. Calculate accounting profits and economic profits for Gomez's pottery.

3 Which of the following are short-run and which are long-run adjustments? **a** Wendy's builds a new restaurant; **b** Acme Steel Corporation hires 200 more workers; **c** A farmer increases the amount of fertilizer used on his corn crop; and **d** An Alcoa plant adds a third shift of workers.

4 Why can the distinction between fixed and variable costs be made in the short run? Classify the following as fixed or variable costs: advertising expenditures, fuel, interest on company-issued bonds, shipping charges, payments for raw materials, real estate taxes, executive salaries, insurance premiums, wage payments, depreciation and obsolescence charges, sales taxes, and rental payments on leased office machinery. "There are no fixed costs in the long run; all costs are variable." Explain.

5 List the fixed and variable costs associated with owning and operating an automobile. Suppose you are considering whether to drive your car or fly 1000 miles to Florida for spring break. Which costs—fixed, variable, or both—would you take into account in making your decision? Would any implicit costs be relevant? Explain.

6 Use the following data to calculate marginal product and average product. Plot total, marginal, and average product and explain in detail the relationship between each pair of curves. Explain why marginal product first rises, then declines, and ultimately becomes negative. What bearing does the law of diminishing returns have on short-run costs? Be specific. "When marginal product is rising, marginal cost is falling. And when marginal product is diminishing, marginal cost is rising." Illustrate and explain graphically and through a numerical example.

Inputs of labor	Total product	Marginal product	Average product
1	15	———	———
2	34	———	———
3	51	———	———
4	65	———	———
5	74	———	———
6	80	———	———
7	83	———	———
8	82	———	———

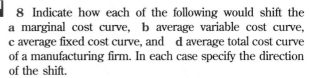

7 A firm has fixed costs of $60 and variable costs as indicated in the table below. Complete the table. When finished, check your calculations by referring to question 4 at the end of Chapter 23.

   a Graph fixed cost, variable cost, and total cost. Explain how the law of diminishing returns influences the shapes of the variable-cost and total-cost curves.
   b Graph AFC, AVC, ATC, and MC. Explain the derivation and shape of each of these four curves and the relationships they bear to one another. Specifically, explain in nontechnical terms why the MC curve intersects both the AVC and ATC curves at their minimum points.
   c Explain how the locations of each of the four curves graphed in question 7b would be altered if (1) total fixed cost had been $100 rather than $60, and (2) total variable cost had been $10 less at each level of output.

8 Indicate how each of the following would shift the **a** marginal cost curve, **b** average variable cost curve, **c** average fixed cost curve, and **d** average total cost curve of a manufacturing firm. In each case specify the direction of the shift.

   a A reduction in business property taxes
   b An increase in the nominal wages of production workers
   c A decrease in the price of electricity
   d An increase in insurance rates on plant and equipment
   e An increase in transportation costs

9 Suppose a firm has only three possible plant size options as shown in the accompanying figure. What plant size will the firm choose in producing **a** 50, **b** 130, **c** 160, and **d** 250 units of output? Draw the firm's long-run average-cost curve on the diagram and define this curve.

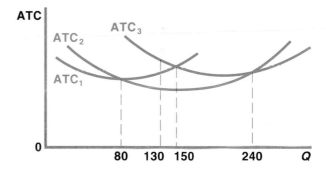

Total product	Total fixed cost	Total variable cost	Total cost	Average fixed cost	Average variable cost	Average total cost	Marginal cost
0	$———	$ 0	$———	$———	$———	$———	
1	———	45	———	———	———	———	$———
2	———	85	———	———	———	———	———
3	———	120	———	———	———	———	———
4	———	150	———	———	———	———	———
5	———	185	———	———	———	———	———
6	———	225	———	———	———	———	———
7	———	270	———	———	———	———	———
8	———	325	———	———	———	———	———
9	———	390	———	———	———	———	———
10	———	465	———	———	———	———	———

 10 Use the concepts of economies and diseconomies of scale to explain the shape of a firm's long-run ATC curve. What is the concept of minimum efficient scale? What bearing may the exact shape of the long-run ATC curve have on the structure of an industry?

CHAPTER 23

Price and Output Determination: Pure Competition

Chapters 20 to 22 have given us the basic tools of analysis for understanding how product price and output are determined. But a firm's decisions concerning price and production will vary depending on the character of the industry in which it is operating. There is no such thing as an "average" or "typical" industry. Detailed examination of the business sector of our economy reveals an almost infinite number of different market situations; no two industries are alike. At one extreme we find a single producer dominating a market; at the other thousands of firms, each supplying a minute fraction of market output. Between these extremes lies an unlimited variety of market structures.

PRELUDE: FOUR MARKET MODELS

Any attempt to examine each specific industry would be an impossible task. We seek a more realistic objective—to define and discuss several basic market structures, or models. In so doing, we will acquaint ourselves with the *general* way in which price and output are determined in most of the market types characterizing our economy.

Economists envision four relatively distinct market situations: (1) pure competition, (2) pure monopoly, (3) monopolistic competition, and (4) oligopoly. They will be considered in this order here and in the next three chapters. These four market models differ in the number of firms in the industry, whether the product is standardized or differentiated, and how easy or difficult it is for new firms to enter the industry.

The main characteristics of these four models are outlined below and in Table 23-1 with more detailed definitions to follow.

1 In **pure competition** there are a very large number of firms producing a standardized product (for example, wheat or peanuts). New firms can enter the industry very easily.

2 At the other extreme, **pure monopoly** (Chapter 24) is a market in which one firm is the sole seller of a product or service (a local electric company). Entry of additional firms is blocked so that the firm *is* the industry. Because there is only one product, there is no product differentiation.

3 **Monopolistic competition** (Chapter 25) is characterized by a relatively large number of sellers producing differentiated products (women's clothing, furniture, books). Differentiation is the basis for product promotion and development. Entry to a monopolistically competitive industry is quite easy.

438

4 Finally, in **oligopoly** (Chapter 26) there are a few sellers; this "fewness" means that pricing and output decisions are interdependent. Each firm is affected by the decisions of rivals and must take these decisions into account in determining its own price-output behavior. Products may be standardized (steel or aluminum) or differentiated (automobiles and computers). Generally, entry to oligopolistic industries is very difficult.

These definitions and the characteristics outlined in Table 23-1 will come into sharper focus as we examine each model in detail.

We will find it convenient occasionally to distinguish between the characteristics of a purely competitive market and those of all other basic market structures—pure monopoly, monopolistic competition, and oligopoly. To facilitate such comparisons we will employ **imperfect competition** as a generic term to designate all those market structures deviating from the purely competitive market model.

PURE COMPETITION: CONCEPT AND OCCURRENCE

Let's focus our attention on pure competition, beginning with an elaboration of our definition.

1 Very Large Numbers A basic feature of a purely competitive market is the presence of a large number of independently acting sellers, usually offering their products in a highly organized market. Markets for farm commodities, the stock market, and the foreign exchange market are illustrative.

2 Standardized Product Competitive firms produce a standardized or homogeneous product. Given price, the consumer is indifferent as to the seller from which the product is purchased. In a competitive market the products of firms, B, C, D, and E, are viewed by the buyer as perfect substitutes for that of firm A. Because of product standardization, there is no reason for *nonprice competition,* that is, competition based on differences in product quality, advertising, or sales promotion.

3 "Price Taker" In a purely competitive market *individual firms* exert no significant control over product price. This characteristic follows from the preceding two. Under pure competition each firm produces such a small fraction of total output that increasing or decreasing its output will not perceptibly influence total supply or, therefore, product price. Assume there are 10,000 competing firms, each currently producing 100

TABLE 23-1 **Characteristics of the four basic market models**

| Characteristic | Market Model | | | |
	Pure competition	Monopolistic competition	Oligopoly	Pure monopoly
Number of firms	A very large number	Many	Few	One
Type of product	Standardized	Differentiated	Standardized or differentiated	Unique; no close substitutes
Control over price	None	Some, but within rather narrow limits	Circumscribed by mutual interdependence; considerable with collusion	Considerable
Conditions of entry	Very easy, no obstacles	Relatively easy	Significant obstacles present	Blocked
Nonprice competition	None	Considerable emphasis on advertising, brand names trademarks, etc.	Typically a great deal, particularly with product differentiation	Mostly public relations advertising
Examples	Agriculture	Retail trade, dresses, shoes	Steel, automobiles, farm implements, many household appliances	Local utilities

units of output. Total supply is therefore 1,000,000. Now suppose one of these firms cuts its output to 50 units. This will not affect price, because this restriction of output by a single firm has almost no impact on total supply. Specifically, the total quantity supplied declines from 1,000,000 to 999,950. This is not enough of a change in total supply to affect product price noticeably. In short, the individual competitive producer is a **price taker;** the competitive firm cannot adjust market price, but can only adjust to it.

Stated differently, the individual competitive producer is at the mercy of the market; product price is a given datum over which the producer exerts no influence. The firm gets the same price per unit for a large output as it does for a small output. To ask a price higher than the going market price would be futile. Consumers will not buy from firm A at $2.05 when its 9999 competitors are selling an identical, and therefore perfect substitute, product at $2 per unit. Conversely, because firm A can sell as much as it chooses at $2 per unit, there is no reason for it to charge a lower price, say, $1.95, for to do so would shrink its profits.

4 Free Entry and Exit   New firms can freely enter and existing firms can freely leave purely competitive industries. No significant obstacles—legal, technological, financial, or other—exist to prohibit new firms from forming and selling their outputs in competitive markets.

Relevance   Pure competition is quite rare in practice. This does not mean, however, that an analysis of how competitive markets work is irrelevant:
1   A few industries more closely approximate the competitive model than any other market structure. For example, much can be learned about American agriculture by understanding the operation of competitive markets.
2   Pure competition provides the simplest context in which to apply the revenue and cost concepts developed in previous chapters. Pure competition is a clear and meaningful starting point for any discussion of price and output determination.
3   In the concluding section of this chapter we will discover that the operation of a purely competitive economy gives us a standard, or norm, against which the efficiency of the real-world economy can be compared and evaluated.

In short, pure competition is a market model of considerable analytical and some practical importance.

Our analysis of pure competition has four major objectives. First, we will examine demand from the competitive seller's viewpoint. Second, we consider how a competitive producer adjusts to market price in the short run. Next, the nature of long-run adjustments in a competitive industry is explored. Finally, we evaluate the efficiency of competitive industries from the standpoint of society.

DEMAND TO A COMPETITIVE SELLER

Because each competitive firm offers a negligible fraction of total supply, the individual firm cannot perceptibly influence the market price which the forces of total demand and supply have established. The competitive firm does *not* have a price policy, that is, the ability to adjust price. Rather, the firm can merely *adjust to* the market price, which it must regard as a given datum determined by the market. As noted, the competitive seller is a *price taker,* rather than a *price maker.*

Perfectly Elastic Demand

Stated technically, the demand curve of the individual competitive firm is *perfectly elastic.* Columns 1 and 2 of Table 23-2 show a perfectly elastic demand curve

TABLE 23-2   **The demand and revenue schedules for an individual purely competitive firm (hypothetical data)**

Firm's demand or average-revenue schedule		Revenue data	
(1) Product price (average revenue)	(2) Quantity demanded (sold)	(3) Total revenue	(4) Marginal revenue
$131	0	$ 0	
131	1	131	$131
131	2	262	131
131	3	393	131
131	4	524	131
131	5	655	131
131	6	786	131
131	7	917	131
131	8	1048	131
131	9	1179	131
131	10	1310	131

where market price is assumed to be $131. Note that the firm cannot obtain a higher price by restricting output; nor need it lower price to increase its sales volume.

We are *not* saying that the *market* demand curve is perfectly elastic in a competitive market. Instead, it is typically a downsloping curve as a glance ahead at Figure 23-7b reveals. In fact, the total-demand curves for most agricultural products are quite *in*elastic, even though agriculture is the most competitive industry in our economy. However, the demand schedule faced by the *individual firm* in a purely competitive industry is perfectly elastic.

The distinction comes about in this way. For the industry—for all firms producing a particular product—a larger sales volume can be realized only by accepting a lower product price. All firms, acting independently but simultaneously, can and do affect total supply and therefore market price. But not so for the individual firm. If a *single* producer increases or decreases output, the outputs of all other competing firms being constant, the effect on total supply and market price is negligible. The single firm's demand or sales schedule is therefore perfectly elastic, as shown in Figures 23-1 and 23-7a. This is an instance in which the fallacy of composition is worth remembering. What is true for the industry or group of firms (a downsloping, less than perfectly elastic, demand curve) is *not* true for the individual, purely competitive firm (a perfectly elastic demand curve).

Average, Total, and Marginal Revenue

The firm's demand schedule is simultaneously a revenue schedule. What appears in column 1 of Table 23-2 as price per unit to the purchaser is revenue per unit, or **average revenue,** to the seller. To say that a buyer must pay $131 per unit is to say that the revenue per unit, or average revenue, received by the seller is $131. Price and average revenue are the same thing seen from different points of view.

Total revenue for each sales level can be determined by multiplying price by the corresponding quantity the firm can sell. Multiply column 1 by column 2, and the result is column 3. In this case, total revenue increases by a constant amount, $131, for each additional unit of sales. Each unit sold adds exactly its price to total revenue.

When a firm is pondering a change in its output, it will consider how its revenue will *change* as a result of that shift in output. What will be the additional revenue from selling another unit of output? **Marginal revenue** is the change in total revenue, that is, the extra revenue, which results from selling one more unit of output. In column 3 of Table 23-2 total revenue is obviously zero when zero units are being sold. The first unit of output sold increases total revenue from zero to $131. Marginal revenue—the increase in total revenue from the sale of the first unit of output—is therefore

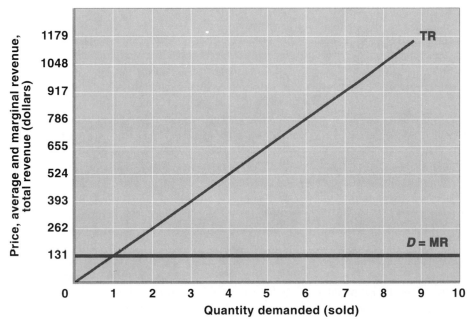

FIGURE 23-1 Demand, marginal revenue, and total revenue of a purely competitive firm

Because it can sell additional units of output at a constant price, the marginal-revenue curve (MR) of a purely competitive firm coincides with its perfectly elastic demand curve (*D*). The firm's total-revenue curve (TR) is a straight upsloping line.

$131. The second unit sold increases total revenue from $131 to $262, so marginal revenue is again $131. Note in column 4 that marginal revenue is a constant figure of $131, because total revenue increases by a constant amount with every extra unit sold.

Under purely competitive conditions, product price is constant to the individual firm; added units therefore can be sold without lowering product price. Each additional unit of sales adds exactly its price—$131 in this case—to total revenue, and marginal revenue *is* this increase in total revenue. Marginal revenue is constant under pure competition because additional units can be sold at a constant price.

Graphical Portrayal

The competitive firm's demand curve and total- and marginal-revenue curves are shown graphically in Figure 23-1. The demand or average-revenue curve is perfectly elastic. The marginal-revenue curve coincides with the demand curve because product price is constant to the competitive firm. Each extra unit of sales increases total revenue by $131. Total revenue is a straight line up to the right. Its slope is constant—it is a straight line—because marginal revenue is constant.

QUICK REVIEW 23-1

♦ *In a purely competitive industry there are a large number of firms producing a homogeneous product and no significant entry barriers.*

♦ *The competitive firm's demand curve is perfectly elastic at the market price.*

♦ *Marginal and average revenue coincide with the firm's demand curve; total revenue rises by the amount of product price for each additional unit sold.*

PROFIT MAXIMIZATION IN THE SHORT RUN: TWO APPROACHES

In the short run the competitive firm has a fixed plant and maximizes its profits or minimizes its losses by adjusting its output through changes in the amounts of variable resources (materials, labor, and so forth) it employs. The economic profits it seeks are defined as the difference between total revenue and total costs. Indeed, this is the direction of our analysis. The revenue data of the previous section and the cost data of Chapter 22 must be brought together so the profit-maximizing output for the firm can be determined.

There are two complementary approaches to determining the level of output at which a competitive firm will realize maximum profits or minimum losses. The first compares total revenue and total costs; the second compares marginal revenue and marginal costs. Both approaches apply not only to a purely competitive firm but also to firms operating in any of the other three basic market structures. To understand output determination under pure competition, we will use both approaches, emphasizing the marginal approach. Also, hypothetical data in both tabular and graphical form will be employed to clarify the two approaches.

Total-Revenue–Total-Cost Approach

Given the market price of its product, the competitive producer is faced with three related questions: (1) Should we produce? (2) If so, what amount? (3) What profit (or loss) will be realized?

At first, the answer to question 1 seems obvious: "You should produce if it is profitable to do so." But the situation is more complex than this. In the short run part of the firm's total costs is variable costs, and the remainder is fixed costs. The latter have to be paid "out of pocket" even when the firm is closed down. In the short run a firm takes a loss equal to its fixed costs when it produces zero units of output. This means that, although there may be no level of output at which the firm can realize a profit, the firm might still produce if it can realize a loss less than the fixed-cost loss it will face in closing down. Thus, the correct answer to the "Should we produce?" question is: *The firm should produce in the short run if it can realize either (1) a profit or (2) a loss less than its fixed costs.*

Assuming the firm *will* produce, the second question becomes relevant: "How much should be produced?" The answer here is evident: *In the short run the firm should produce that output at which it maximizes profits or minimizes losses.*

We now examine three cases demonstrating the validity of these two generalizations and answer our third query by indicating how profits and losses can be calculated. In the first case the firm will maximize its profits by producing. In the second case it will minimize its losses by producing. In the third case the firm will minimize its losses by closing down. We will assume the same short-run cost data for all three cases and explore the firm's production decisions when faced with three different product prices.

Profit-Maximizing Case In all three cases we employ cost data with which we are already familiar. Columns 3 through 5 of Table 23-3 repeat the fixed-, variable-, and total-cost data developed in Table 22-2. Assuming that market price is $131, we derive total revenue for each output level by multiplying output by price, as we did in Table 23-2. These data are presented in column 2. Then in column 6 the profit or loss encountered at each output is found by subtracting total cost (column 5) from total revenue (column 2). Now we have all the data needed to answer the three questions.

Should the firm produce? Yes, because it can realize a profit by doing so. How much? Nine units, because column 6 tells us this is the output at which total economic profits will be at a maximum. The size of that profit in this **profit-maximizing case?** $299.

Figure 23-2a compares total revenue and total cost graphically. Total revenue is a straight line, because under pure competition each additional unit adds the same amount—its price—to total revenue (Table 23-2).

Total costs increase with output; more production requires more resources. But the rate of increase in total costs varies with the relative efficiency of the firm. Specifically, the cost data reflect Chapter 22's law of diminishing returns. For a time the rate of increase in total cost is less and less as the firm uses its fixed resources more efficiently. Then, after a time, total cost begins to rise by ever-increasing amounts because of the inefficiencies accompanying more intensive use of the firm's plant.

Comparing total cost with total revenue in Figure 23-2a, note that a **break-even point** occurs at about 2 units of output. If our data were extended beyond 10 units of output, another such point would be incurred where total cost would catch up with total revenue, as shown in Figure 23-2a. Any output outside these points will entail losses. Any output within these break-even points will produce an economic profit. Maximum profit is achieved where the vertical difference between total revenue and total cost is greatest. For our particular data this is at 9 units of output and the resulting maximum profit is $299.

Loss-Minimizing Case Assuming no change in costs, the firm may not realize economic profits if the market yields a price considerably below $131. Suppose the market price is only $81. As column 6 of Table 23-4 indicates, at this price all levels of output will lead to losses. But the firm will *not* close down because, by producing, it realizes a loss considerably less than the

TABLE 23-3 The profit-maximizing output for a purely competitive firm: total-revenue–total-cost approach (price = $131) (hypothetical data)

(1) Total product	(2) Total revenue	(3) Total fixed cost	(4) Total variable cost	(5) Total cost	(6) Total economic profit (+) or loss (−), = (2) − (5)
0	$ 0	$100	$ 0	$ 100	$−100
1	131	100	90	190	− 59
2	262	100	170	270	− 8
3	393	100	240	340	+ 53
4	524	100	300	400	+124
5	655	100	370	470	+185
6	786	100	450	550	+236
7	917	100	540	640	+277
8	1048	100	650	750	+298
9	1179	100	780	880	+299
10	1310	100	930	1030	+280

$100 fixed-cost loss it would incur by closing down, that is, producing zero units of output. Specifically, in this **loss-minimizing case,** the firm will minimize its losses by producing 6 units of output. The resulting $64 loss is clearly preferable to the $100 loss which closing down would involve. By producing 6 units the firm earns a total revenue of $486, sufficient to pay all the firm's variable costs ($450) and also a substantial portion—$36 worth—of the firm's $100 of fixed costs.

In general terms, whenever total revenue exceeds total *variable* costs, the firm will produce because all variable costs as well as some portion of total fixed costs can be paid out of revenue. If the firm closed down, all of its total fixed costs would have to be paid out of the entrepreneur's pocket. By producing some output, the firm's loss will be less than its total fixed cost. Note that there are several other outputs which entail a loss less than the firm's $100 fixed costs; but at 6 units of output the loss is minimized.

Close-Down Case Assume finally that the market price is a mere $71. Given short-run costs, column 9 of Table 23-4 indicates that at all levels of output, losses will exceed the $100 fixed-cost loss the firm will incur by closing down. Thus, in this **close-down case,** the firm will minimize its losses by halting production, that is, by producing zero units of output.

Figure 23-2b demonstrates the loss-minimizing and close-down cases graphically. In the loss-minimiz-

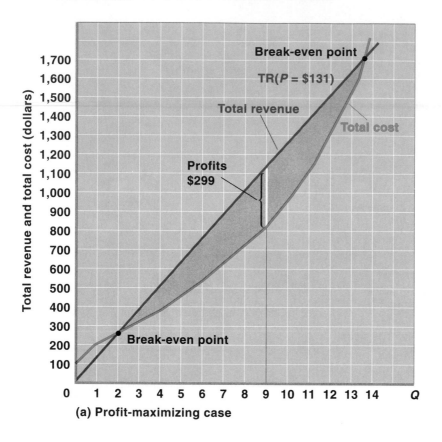

(a) Profit-maximizing case

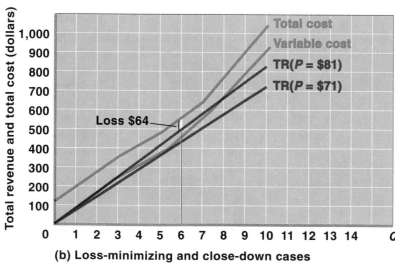

(b) Loss-minimizing and close-down cases

FIGURE 23-2 The profit-maximizing (a), loss-minimizing, and close-down cases (b), as shown by the total-revenue–total-cost approach

A firm's profits are maximized in (a) at that output at which total revenue exceeds total cost by the maximum amount. A firm will minimize its losses in (b) by producing at that output at which total cost exceeds total revenue by the smallest amount. However, if there is no output at which total revenue exceeds variable costs, the firm will minimize losses in the short run by closing down.

ing case, the total revenue line TR (P = 81) exceeds total variable cost by the maximum amount at 6 units of output. Here total revenue is $486, and the firm recovers all its $450 of variable costs and also $36 worth of its fixed costs. The firm's minimum loss is $64, superior to the $100 fixed-cost loss involved in closing down. In the

close-down case, the total-revenue line TR (P = 71) lies below the total-variable-cost curve at all points; there is no output at which variable costs can be recovered. By producing the firm would incur losses exceeding its fixed costs. The firm's best choice is to close down and pay its $100 fixed-cost loss out of pocket.

TABLE 23-4 The loss-minimizing outputs for a purely competitive firm: total-revenue–total-cost approach (prices = $81 and $71) (hypothetical data)

Product price = $81						Product price = $71		
(1) Total product	(2) Total revenue	(3) Total fixed cost	(4) Total variable cost	(5) Total cost	(6) Total economic profit (+) or loss (−), = (2) − (5)	(7) Total revenue	(8) Total cost	(9) Total economic profit (+) or loss (−), = (7) − (8)
0	$ 0	$100	$ 0	$ 100	$−100	$ 0	$ 100	$−100
1	81	100	90	190	−109	71	190	−119
2	162	100	170	270	−108	142	270	−128
3	243	100	240	340	− 97	213	340	−127
4	324	100	300	400	− 76	284	400	−116
5	405	100	370	470	− 65	355	470	−115
6	486	100	450	550	− 64	426	550	−124
7	567	100	540	640	− 73	497	640	−143
8	648	100	650	750	−102	568	750	−182
9	729	100	780	880	−151	639	880	−241
10	810	100	930	1030	−220	710	1030	−320

QUICK REVIEW 23-2

◗ *In the short run a firm should produce if it can achieve a profit or attain a loss which is smaller than its total fixed costs.*

◗ *Profits are maximized where the excess of total revenue over total cost is greatest.*

◗ *Losses are minimized where the excess of total cost over total revenue is smallest and is some amount less than total fixed costs.*

◗ *If losses at all levels of output exceed total fixed costs, the firm should close down in the short run.*

Marginal-Revenue–Marginal Cost Approach

An alternative means for determining the amounts a competitive firm would offer in the market at each possible price is for the firm to determine and compare the amounts that each *additional* unit of output will add to total revenue, on the one hand, and to total cost, on the other. The firm should compare the *marginal revenue* (MR) and the *marginal cost* (MC) of each successive unit of output. Any unit of output whose marginal revenue exceeds its marginal cost should be produced, because on each such unit the firm gains more in revenue from its sale that it adds to costs in producing that unit.

Hence, the unit of output is adding to total profits or, as the case may be, subtracting from losses. Similarly, if the marginal cost of a unit of output exceeds its marginal revenue, the firm should avoid producing that unit. It will add more to costs than to revenue; such a unit will not "pay its way."

MR = MC Rule In the initial stages of production, where output is relatively low, marginal revenue will usually (but not always) exceed marginal cost. It is therefore profitable to produce through this range of output. But at later stages of production, where output is relatively high, rising marginal costs will cause the reverse to be true. Marginal cost will exceed marginal revenue. Obviously, to maximize profits, producing units of output in this range is to be avoided.

Separating these two production ranges will be a unique point at which marginal revenue equals marginal cost. This point is the key to the output-determining rule: *The firm will maximize profits or minimize losses by producing at that point where marginal revenue equals marginal cost.* For convenience we call this profit-maximizing guide the **MR = MC rule.** For most sets of MR and MC data, there will be no nonfractional level of output at which MR and MC are precisely equal. In such instances the firm should produce the last complete unit of output whose MR exceeds its MC.

TABLE 23-5 The profit-maximizing output for a purely competitive firm: marginal-revenue-equals-marginal-cost approach (price = $131) *(hypothetical data)*

(1) Total product	(2) Average fixed cost	(3) Average variable cost	(4) Average total cost	(5) Marginal cost	(6) Price = marginal revenue	(7) Total economic profit (+) or loss (−)
0						$−100
1	$100.00	$90.00	$190.00	$ 90	$131	− 59
2	50.00	85.00	135.00	80	131	− 8
3	33.33	80.00	113.33	70	131	+ 53
4	25.00	75.00	100.00	60	131	+124
5	20.00	74.00	94.00	70	131	+185
6	16.67	75.00	91.67	80	131	+236
7	14.29	77.14	91.43	90	131	+277
8	12.50	81.25	93.75	110	131	+298
9	11.11	86.67	97.78	130	131	+299
10	10.00	93.00	103.00	150	131	+280

Three Characteristics Three features of this MR = MC rule merit comment.

1 The rule assumes that the firm will choose to produce rather than close down. Shortly, we will note that marginal revenue must be equal to, or must exceed, average variable cost, or the firm will find it preferable to close down rather than produce the MR = MC output.

2 The MR = MC rule is an accurate guide to profit maximization for all firms, be they purely competitive, monopolistic, monopolistically competitive, or oligopolistic. The rule's application is *not* limited to the special case of pure competition.

3 The MR = MC rule can be conveniently restated in a slightly different form when being applied to a purely competitive firm. Product price is determined by the market forces of supply and demand, and although the competitive firm can sell as much or as little as it chooses at that price, the firm cannot manipulate the price itself. In technical terms the demand, or sales, schedule faced by a competitive seller is perfectly elastic at the going market price. The result is that product price and marginal revenue are equal; that is, each extra unit sold adds precisely its price to total revenue as shown in Table 23-2 and Figure 23-1. Thus, under pure competition—and *only* under pure competition—we may substitute price for marginal revenue in the rule, so that it reads as follows: *To maximize profits or minimize losses the competitive firm should produce at that point where price equals marginal cost* (P = MC). This *P* = **MC rule** is simply a special case of the MR = MC rule.

Now let's apply the MR = MC or, because we are considering pure competition, the *P* = MC rule, using the same three prices as in our total-revenue–total-cost approach to profit maximization.

Profit-Maximizing Case Table 23-5 reproduces the unit- and marginal-cost data derived in Table 22-2. It is, of course, the marginal-cost data of column 5 in Table 23-5 which we will compare with price (equal to marginal revenue) for each unit of output. Suppose first that market price, and therefore marginal revenue, is $131, as shown in column 6.

What is the profit-maximizing output? We see that every unit of output up to and including the ninth adds more to total revenue than to cost. Price, or marginal revenue, exceeds marginal cost on all the first 9 units of output. Each unit therefore adds to the firm's profits and should be produced. The tenth unit, however, will not be produced, because it would add more to costs ($150) than to revenue ($131).

Profit Calculations The level of economic profits realized by the firm can be calculated from the unit-cost data. Multiplying price ($131) times output (9), we find total revenue to be $1179. Total cost of $880 is found by multiplying average total cost ($97.78) by output (9).[1]

---

[1]In most instances the unit-cost data are rounded figures. Therefore, economic profits calculated from them will typically vary by a few cents from the profits determined in the total-revenue–total-cost approach. We here ignore the few-cents differentials and make our answers consistent with the results of the total-revenue–total-cost approach.

KEY GRAPH

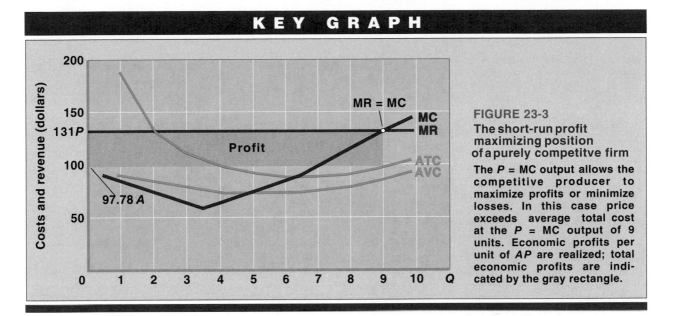

FIGURE 23-3

The short-run profit maximizing position of a purely competitve firm

The *P* = MC output allows the competitive producer to maximize profits or minimize losses. In this case price exceeds average total cost at the *P* = MC output of 9 units. Economic profits per unit of *AP* are realized; total economic profits are indicated by the gray rectangle.

The difference of $299 (=$1179 − $880) is economic profits.

Another means of calculating economic profits is to determine profit *per unit* by subtracting average total cost ($97.78) from product price ($131) and multiplying the difference (per unit profits of $33.22) by the level of output (9). By verifying the figures in column 7 of Table 23-5 you will find that any output other than that indicated to be most profitable by the MR (=*P*) = MC rule will mean either losses or profits less than $299.

Graphical Portrayal   Figure 23-3 (Key Graph) compares price and marginal cost graphically. Here per unit economic profit is indicated by the distance *AP*. When multiplied by the profit-maximizing output, the resulting total economic profit is shown by the gray rectangular area.

Note that the firm is seeking to maximize its *total* profits, not its *per unit* profits. Per unit profits are largest at 7 units of output, where price exceeds average total cost by $39.57 (= $131 − $91.43). But by producing only 7 units, the firm would be forgoing the production of two additional units of output which would clearly contribute to total profits. The firm is happy to accept lower per unit profits if the additional profits associated with the extra units of sales more than compensate for the lower per unit profits.

Loss-Minimizing Case   Now let's assume that market price is $81 rather than $131. Should the firm produce? If so, how much? And what will the resulting profits or losses be? The answers, respectively, are "Yes," "Six units," and "A loss of $64."

Column 6 of Table 23-6 shows the new price (equal to marginal revenue) beside the same unit- and marginal-cost data presented in Table 23-5. Comparing columns 5 and 6, we find that the first unit of output adds $90 to total cost but only $81 to total revenue. One might conclude: "Don't produce—close down!" But this would be hasty. Remember that in the very early stages of production, marginal product is low, making marginal cost unusually high. The price–marginal-cost relationship improves with increased production. On the next 5 units—2 through 6—price exceeds marginal cost. Each of these 5 units adds more to revenue than to cost, more than compensating for the "loss" taken on the first unit. Beyond 6 units, however, MC exceeds MR (=*P*). The firm should therefore produce at 6 units. In general, the profit-seeking producer should always compare marginal revenue (or price under pure competition) with the *rising* portion of the marginal-cost schedule or curve.

Loss Determination   Will production be profitable? No, because at 6 units of output average total costs of $91.67 exceed price of $81 by $10.67 per unit. Multiply by the 6 units of ouput, and we find the firm's total loss is $64. Then why produce? Because this loss is less than the firm's $100 of fixed costs—the $100 loss the firm would incur in the short run by closing down. The firm receives enough revenue per unit ($81) to cover

TABLE 23-6 The loss-minimizing outputs for a purely competitive firm: marginal-revenue-equals-marginal-cost approach (prices = $81 and $71) *(hypothetical data)*

(1) Total product	(2) Average fixed cost	(3) Average variable cost	(4) Average total cost	(5) Marginal cost	(6) $81 price = marginal revenue	(7) Profit (+) or loss (−), $81 price	(8) $71 price = marginal revenue	(9) Profit (+) or loss (−), $71 price
0						$−100		$−100
1	$100.00	$90.00	$190.00	$90	$81	−109	$71	−119
2	50.00	85.00	135.00	80	81	−108	71	−128
3	33.33	80.00	113.33	70	81	− 97	71	−127
4	25.00	75.00	100.00	60	81	− 76	71	−116
5	20.00	74.00	94.00	70	81	− 65	71	−115
6	16.67	75.00	91.67	80	81	− 64	71	−124
7	14.29	77.14	91.43	90	81	− 73	71	−143
8	12.50	81.25	93.75	110	81	−102	71	−182
9	11.11	86.67	97.78	130	81	−151	71	−241
10	10.00	93.00	103.00	150	81	−220	71	−320

its average variable costs of $75 and also provide $6 per unit, or a total of $36, to apply against fixed costs. Therefore, the firm's loss is only $64 (=$100 − $36), rather than $100.

Graphical Portrayal This case is shown graphically in Figure 23-4. Whenever price exceeds the minimum average variable cost but falls short of average total cost, the firm can pay part of, but not all, its fixed costs by producing. In this instance total variable costs are shown by the area *OVGF*. Total revenue, however, is *OPEF,* greater than total variable costs by *VPEG*. This excess of revenue over variable costs can be applied

against total fixed costs, represented by area *VACG*. If it produces 6 units the firm's loss is only area *PACE;* if it closes down, its loss would be its fixed costs shown by the larger area *VACG*.

Close-Down Case Suppose now that the market yields a price of only $71. It will now pay the firm to close down, to produce nothing, because there is no output at which the firm can cover its average variable costs, much less its average total cost. In other words, the smallest loss it can realize by producing is greater than the $100 worth of fixed costs it will lose by closing down. The best action is to close down.

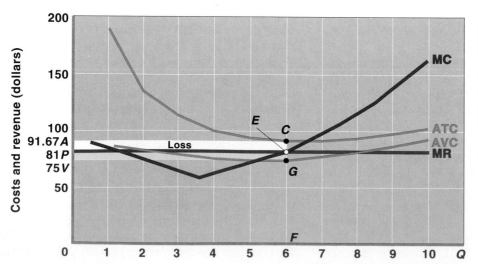

FIGURE 23-4 The short-run loss-minimizing position of a purely competitive firm

If price exceeds the minimum AVC but is less than ATC, the *P* = MC output of 6 units will permit the firm to minimize its losses. In this instance losses are *AP* per unit; total losses are shown by the area *PACE*.

This can be verified by comparing columns 3 and 8 of Table 23-6 and can be seen in Figure 23-5. Price comes closest to covering average variable costs at the MR $(=P)$ = MC output of 5 units. But even here, price or revenue per unit would fall short of average variable cost by $3 $(=\$74 - \$71)$. By producing at the MR $(=P)$ = MC output, the firm would lose its $100 worth of fixed costs *plus* $15 ($3 on each of the 5 units) worth of variable costs, for a total loss of $115. This clearly compares unfavorably with the $100 fixed-cost loss the firm would incur by closing down and thereby producing no output. In short, it will pay the firm to close down rather than operate at a $71 price or, for that matter, at any price less than the minimum average variable cost of $74.

The close-down case obligates us to modify our MR $(=P)$ = MC rule for profit maximization or loss minimization. *A competitive firm will maximize profits or minimize losses in the short run by producing at that output at which* MR $(=P)$ = MC, *provided that price exceeds minimum average variable cost.*

Marginal Cost and the Short-Run Supply Curve

You will recognize that we have simply selected three different prices and asked how much the profit-seeking competitive firm, faced with certain costs, would choose to offer or supply in the market at each of these prices. This information—product price and corresponding quantity supplied—constitutes the supply schedule for the competitive firm.

Table 23-7 summarizes the supply schedule data for the three prices chosen—$131, $81, and $71. You

TABLE 23-7 The supply schedule of a competitive firm confronted with the cost data of Table 23-5 (hypothetical data)

Price	Quantity supplied	Maximum profit (+) or minimum loss (−)
$151	10	$_____
131	9	+299
111	8	_____
91	7	_____
81	6	− 64
71	0	−100
61	0	_____

are urged to apply the MR $(=P)$ = MC rule (modified by the close-down case) to verify the quantity-supplied data for the $151, $111, $91, and $61 prices and calculate the corresponding profits or losses. We confirm that the supply schedule is upsloping. Here price must be $74 (equal to minimum average variable cost) or greater before any output is supplied. And because the marginal cost of successive units of output is increasing, the firm must get successively higher prices for it to be profitable to produce these additional units of output.

Figure 23-6 (Key Graph) generalizes on our application of the MR $(=P)$ = MC rule. We have drawn the appropriate cost curves and from the vertical axis have extended a series of marginal-revenue lines from some possible prices the market might set for the firm. The crucial prices are P_2 and P_4. Our close-down case reminds us that at any price *below* P_2—that price equal to

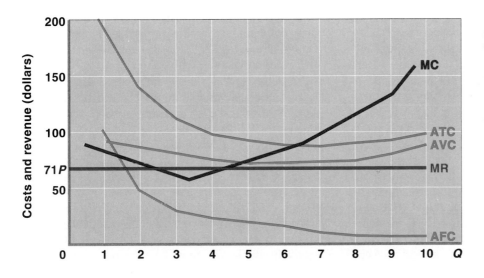

FIGURE 23-5 The short-run close-down position of a purely competitive firm

If price falls short of minimum AVC, the competitive firm will minimize its losses in the short run by closing down. There is no level of output at which the firm can produce and realize a loss smaller than its fixed costs.

KEY GRAPH

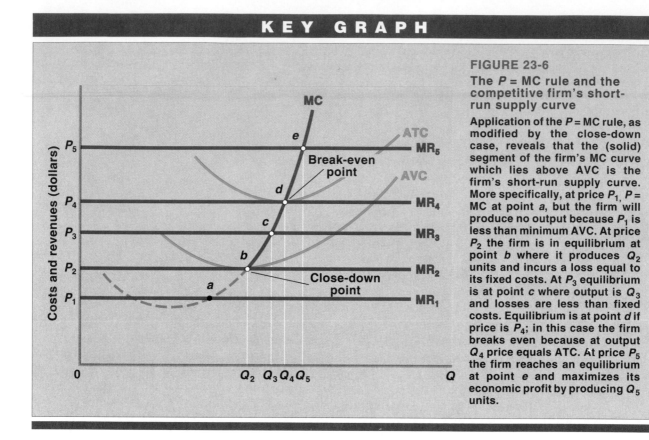

FIGURE 23-6

The *P* = MC rule and the competitive firm's short-run supply curve

Application of the *P* = MC rule, as modified by the close-down case, reveals that the (solid) segment of the firm's MC curve which lies above AVC is the firm's short-run supply curve. More specifically, at price P_1, *P* = MC at point *a*, but the firm will produce no output because P_1 is less than minimum AVC. At price P_2 the firm is in equilibrium at point *b* where it produces Q_2 units and incurs a loss equal to its fixed costs. At P_3 equilibrium is at point *c* where output is Q_3 and losses are less than fixed costs. Equilibrium is at point *d* if price is P_4; in this case the firm breaks even because at output Q_4 price equals ATC. At price P_5 the firm reaches an equilibrium at point *e* and maximizes its economic profit by producing Q_5 units.

the minimum average variable cost—the firm should close down and supply nothing. Actually, by producing Q_2 units of output *at* a price of P_2, the firm will just cover its variable costs, and its loss will be equal to its fixed costs. The firm therefore would be indifferent as to closing down *or* producing Q_2 units of output. But at any price below P_2, such as P_1, the firm will close down and supply zero units of output.

P_4 is strategic because it is the price at which the firm will just break even by producing Q_4 units of output, as indicated by the MR $(=P)$ = MC rule. Here total revenue will just cover total costs (including a normal profit). At P_3 the firm supplies Q_3 units of output and minimizes its losses. At any other price between P_2 and P_4 the firm will minimize its losses by producing to the point where MR $(=P)$ = MC.

At any price above P_4 the firm will maximize its economic profits by producing to the point where MR $(=P)$ = MC. Thus at P_5 the firm will realize the greatest profits by supplying Q_5 units of output. The basic point is that each of the various MR $(=P)$ = MC intersection points shown as *b,c,d,* and *e* in Figure 23-6 indicates a possible product price (on the vertical axis) and

the corresponding quantity which the profit-seeking firm would supply at that price (on the horizontal axis). These points, by definition, locate the supply curve of the competitive firm. Because nothing would be produced at any price below the minimum average variable cost, we can conclude that *the portion of the firm's marginal-cost curve which lies above its average-variable-cost curve is its* **short-run supply curve.** The solid segment of the marginal cost curve is the short-run supply curve in Figure 23-6. This is the link between production costs and supply in the short run.

In Chapter 22 we saw that changes in such factors as the prices of variable inputs or in technology will shift the marginal cost or short-run supply curve to a new location. For example, a wage increase would shift the supply curve upward as viewed from the horizontal axis (leftward as viewed from the vertical axis), constituting a decrease in supply. Similarly, technological progress which increases the productivity of labor would shift the marginal cost or supply curve downward as viewed from the horizontal axis (rightward as viewed from the vertical axis). This represents an increase in supply. You should determine how (1) a specific tax on the product and (2) a per unit subsidy on this product would shift the supply curve.

Recapitulation

Let's pause to summarize the main points made concerning short-run competitive pricing. Table 23-8 is a convenient check sheet on the total-revenue–total-cost and MR = MC approaches to determining the competitive firm's profit-maximizing output. This table warrants careful study.

Firm and Industry: Equilibrium Price

Now, having developed the competitive firm's short-run supply curve by applying the MR $(=P)$ = MC rule, we must determine which of the various price possibilities will actually be the equilibrium price.

From Chapter 4 we know that in a purely competitive market, equilibrium price is determined by *total,* or market, supply and total demand. To derive total supply, the supply schedules or curves of the individual competitive sellers must be summed. Thus in Table 23-9, columns 1 and 3 repeat the individual competitive firm's supply schedule just derived in Table 23-7. We now conveniently assume that there are a total of 1000 competitive firms in this industry, each having the

TABLE 23-9 Firm and market supply and market demand (hypothetical data)

(1) Quantity supplied, single firm	(2) Total quantity supplied, 1000 firms	(3) Product price	(4) Total quantity demanded
10	10,000	$151	4,000
9	9,000	131	6,000
8	8,000	111	8,000
7	7,000	91	9,000
6	6,000	81	11,000
0	0	71	13,000
0	0	61	16,000

same total and unit costs as the single firm we discussed. This lets us calculate the total- or market-supply schedule (columns 2 and 3) by multiplying the quantity-supplied figures of the single firm (column 1) by 1000.

Market Price and Profits To determine equilibrium price and output, this total-supply data must be compared with total-demand data. Let's assume total-demand data are as shown in columns 3 and 4 of Table 23-9. Comparing the total quantity supplied and total quantity demanded at the seven possible prices, we determine that equilibrium price is $111 and equilibrium quantity 8000 units for the industry—8 units for each of the 1000 identical firms.

Will these conditions of market supply and demand make this a prosperous or an unprosperous industry? Multiplying product price ($111) by output (8), we find the total revenue of each firm is $888. Total cost is $750, found by multiplying average total cost of $93.75 by 8, or simply by looking at column 5 of Table 23-3. The $138 difference is the economic profit of each

TABLE 23-8 Summary of competitive output determination in the short run

	Total-revenue–total-cost approach	Marginal-revenue–marginal-cost approach
Should the firm produce?	Yes, if TR exceeds TC or if TC exceeds TR by some amount less than total fixed cost.	Yes, if price is equal to, or greater than, minimum average variable cost.
What quantity should be produced to maximize profits?	Produce where the excess of TR over TC is a maximum or where the excess of TC over TR is a minimum (and less than total fixed costs).	Produce where MR or price equals MC.
Will production result in economic profit?	Yes, if TR exceeds TC. No, if TC exceeds TR.	Yes, if price exceeds average total cost. No, if average total cost exceeds price.

firm. Another way of calculating economic profits is to determine *per unit* profit by subtracting average total cost ($93.75) from product price ($111) and multiplying the difference (per unit profits of $17.25) by the firm's equilibrium level of output (8). For the industry, total economic profit is $138,000. This, then, is a prosperous industry.

Graphical Portrayal Figure 23-7a and b shows this analysis graphically. The individual supply curves of each of the 1000 identical firms—one of which is shown as *s* in Figure 23-7a—are summed horizontally to get the total supply curve *S* of Figure 23-7b. Given total demand *D,* equilibrium price is $111, and equilibrium quantity for the industry is 8000 units. This equilibrium price is given and unalterable to the individual firm; that is, each firm's demand curve is perfectly elastic at the equilibrium price, indicated by *d.* Because price is given and constant to the individual firm, the marginal-revenue curve coincides with the demand curve. This $111 price exceeds average total cost at the firm's equilibrium MR (=*P*) = MC output, resulting in a situation of economic profits similar to that already portrayed in Figure 23-3.

Assuming no changes in cost or market demands, these diagrams reveal a genuine *short-run* equilibrium situation. There are no shortages or surpluses in the market to cause price or total quantity to change. Nor can any of the firms in the industry improve their profits by altering their output. Note, too, that higher unit and marginal costs, on the one hand, or a weaker market demand situation, on the other, could pose a loss situation similar to Figure 23-4. You are urged to sketch, in Figure 23-7a and b, how higher costs and a less favorable demand could cause a short-run equilibrium situation entailing losses.

Firm versus Industry Figure 23-7a and b underscores a point made earlier: Product price is a given datum to the *individual* competitive firm, but at the same time, the supply plans of all competitive producers *as a group* are a basic determinant of product price. If we recall the fallacy of composition, we find there is no inconsistency here. Though each firm, supplying a negligible fraction of total supply, cannot affect price, the sum of the supply curves of all the firms in the industry constitutes the industry supply curve, and this curve does have an important bearing on price. *Under competition, equilibrium price is a given datum to the individual firm and simultaneously is the result of the production (supply) decisions of all firms taken as a group.*

FIGURE 23-7 Short-run competitive equilibrium for a firm (a) and the industry (b)

The horizontal sum of the 1000 firms' supply curves (*s*) determines the industry supply curve (*S*). Given industry demand (*D*), the short-run equilibrium price and output for the industry are $111 and 8000 units. Taking the equilibrium price as given datum, the representative firm establishes its profit-maximizing output at 8 units and, in this case, realizes the economic profit shown by the gray area.

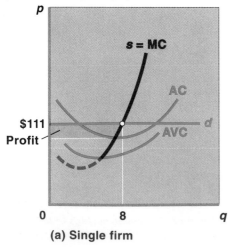

(a) Single firm

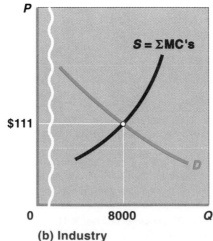

(b) Industry

PROFIT MAXIMIZATION IN THE LONG RUN

The long run permits firms to make certain adjustments which time does not allow in the short run. In the short run there are a given number of firms in an industry, each of which has a fixed, unalterable plant. True, firms may close down in the sense that they produce zero units of output in the short run; but they do not have sufficient time to liquidate their assets and go out of business. By contrast, in the long run firms already in an industry have sufficient time either to expand or contract their plant capacities. More importantly, the number of firms in the industry may either increase or decrease as new firms enter or existing firms leave. We now examine how these long-run adjustments modify our conclusions concerning short-run output and price determination.

Assumptions and Goal

We will make certain simplifying assumptions, none of which will impair the general validity of our conclusions.

1 Entry and Exodus   We will suppose that the only long-run adjustment is the entry and exodus of firms. Furthermore, for simplicity's sake we ignore the short-run adjustments already analyzed, in order to grasp the nature of long-run competitive adjustments.

2 Identical Costs   We also assume that all firms in the industry have identical cost curves. This lets us discuss an "average," or "representative," firm knowing that all other firms in the industry are similarly affected by any long-run adjustments which occur.

3 Constant-Cost Industry   We assume for the moment that the industry under discussion is a constant-cost industry. This means that the entry and exodus of firms will *not* affect resource prices or, therefore, the locations of the unit-cost schedules of individual firms.

We will describe long-run competitive adjustments both verbally and through graphical analysis. The basic conclusion we seek to explain is as follows: *After all long-run adjustments are completed, that is, when long-run equilibrium is achieved, product price will be exactly equal to, and production will occur at, each firm's point of minimum average total cost.*

This conclusion follows from two basic facts: (1) Firms seek profits and shun losses, and (2) under competition, firms are free to enter and leave industries. If price initially exceeds average total costs, the resulting economic profits will attract new firms to the industry. But this industry expansion will increase product supply until price is brought back down into equality with average total cost. Conversely, if price is initially less than average total cost, resulting losses will cause firms to leave the industry. As they leave, total product supply will decline, bringing price back up into equality with average total cost.

Zero-Profit Model

Our conclusion can best be demonstrated and its significance evaluated by assuming that the average or representative firm in a purely competitive industry is initially in long-run equilibrium. This is shown in Figure 23-8a, where price and minimum average total cost are equal at, say, $50. Economic profits here are zero; the industry is in equilibrium or "at rest," because there is no tendency for firms to enter or leave the industry. The going market price is determined by total, or industry, demand and supply, as shown by D_1 and S_1 in Figure 23-8b. (The market supply schedule, incidentally, is a *short-run* schedule; the industry's long-run supply schedule will be developed in our discussion.) By examining the quantity axes of the two graphs, we note that if all firms are identical, there must be 1000 firms in the industry, each producing 100 units, to achieve the industry's equilibrium output of 100,000 units.

Entry of Firms Eliminates Profits

Now our model is set up. Let's upset the long-run equilibrium of Figure 23-8 and trace subsequent adjustments. Suppose a change in consumer tastes increases product demand from D_1 to D_2. This favorable shift in demand will make production profitable; the new price of $60 exceeds average total cost of $50. *These economic profits will lure new firms into the industry.* Some entrants will be newly created firms; others will shift from less prosperous industries.

As firms enter, the market supply of the product will increase, causing product price to gravitate downward from $60 toward the original level. Assuming, as we are, that entry of new firms has no effect on costs, economic profits will persist, and entry will therefore

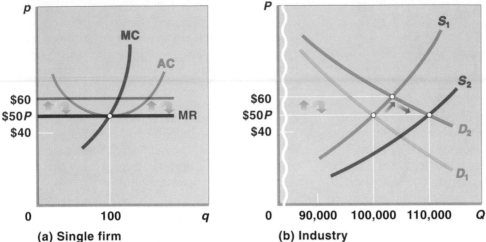

(a) Single firm   **(b) Industry**

FIGURE 23-8   Temporary profits and the reestablishment of long-run equilibrium in a representative firm (a) and the industry (b)

A favorable shift in demand (D_1 to D_2) will upset the original equilibrium and produce economic profits. But profits will cause new firms to enter the industry, increasing supply (S_1 to S_2) and lowering product price until economic profits are once again zero.

continue until short-run market supply has increased to S_2. At this point, price is again equal to minimum average total cost at $50. The economic profits caused by the boost in demand have been competed away to zero, and as a result, the previous incentive for more firms to enter the industry has disappeared. Long-run equilibrium is restored at this point.

Figure 23-8 tells us that upon reestablishment of long-run equilibrium, industry output is 110,000 units and that each firm in the now expanded industry is producing 100 units. We can conclude that the industry is now composed of 1100 firms; that is, 100 new firms have entered the industry.

Exodus of Firms Eliminates Losses

To strengthen our understanding of long-run competitive equilibrium, let's reverse our analysis. In Figure 23-9a and b, the $50 price and curves S_1 and D_1 show the initial long-run equilibrium situation used as a point of departure in our previous analysis of how the entry of firms eliminates economic profits.

Now suppose that consumer demand falls from D_1 to D_3. This forces price down to $40, making production unprofitable. *In time resulting losses will induce firms to leave the industry.* The reason is that owners can realize a normal profit elsewhere as opposed to the below-normal profit (losses) now confronting them. As capital equipment wears out and contractual obligations expire, some firms will simply fold. As this exodus of firms proceeds, however, industry supply will de-

crease, moving from S_1 toward S_3. As this occurs, price will begin to rise from $40 back toward $50. Assuming costs are unchanged by the exodus of firms, losses will force firms to leave the industry until supply has declined to S_3, at which point price is again exactly $50, barely consistent with minimum average total cost. The exodus continues until losses are eliminated and long-run equilibrium is again restored.

Observe in Figure 23-9a and b that total quantity supplied is now 90,000 units and each firm is producing 100 units. The industry is now populated by only 900 firms rather than the original 1000 since losses have forced 100 firms out of business.

You may have noted that we have sidestepped the question of which firms will leave the industry when losses occur by assuming all firms have identical cost curves. In the "real world" entrepreneurial talents differ so that, even if resource prices and technology are the same for all firms, inferior entrepreneurs would incur higher costs and therefore be the first to leave the industry when product demand declined. Similarly, other resources may be heterogeneous and also give rise to cost differences. For example, firms with less productive labor forces will be high-cost producers and likely candidates to quit the industry when product demand decreases.

Our prestated conclusion has now been verified. Competition, reflected in the entry and exodus of firms, forces price into equality with the minimum long-run average total cost of production, and each firm produces at the point of minimum long-run average total

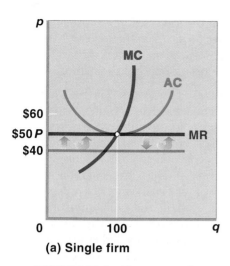

(a) Single firm

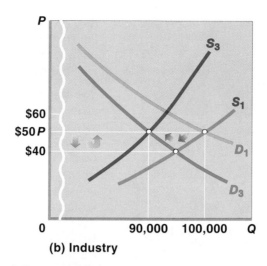

(b) Industry

FIGURE 23-9 Temporary losses and the reestablishment of long-run equilibrium in a representative firm (a) and the industry (b)

An unfavorable shift in demand (D_1 to D_3) will upset the original equilibrium and produce losses. But losses will cause firms to leave the industry, decreasing supply (S_1 to S_3) and increasing product price until all losses have disappeared.

cost. Note, too, that these expanding- and declining-industry cases explain the functioning of consumer sovereignty, a concept we discussed in Chapter 5.

Long-Run Supply for a Constant-Cost Industry

What is the character of the **long-run supply curve** which evolves from this analysis of the expansion or contraction of a competitive industry? Although our discussion deals with the long run, we have noted that the market supply curves of Figures 23-8b and 23-9b are short-run industry supply curves. However, the analysis itself permits us to sketch the nature of the long-run supply curve for this competitive industry. The crucial factor in determining the shape of the industry's long-run supply curve is the effect, if any, which changes in the number of firms in the industry will have on the costs of the individual firms in the industry.

Constant-Cost Industry   In the foregoing analysis of long-run competitive equilibrium we assumed the industry under discussion was a **constant-cost industry.** This means that industry expansion through the entry of new firms will not affect resource prices or, therefore, production costs. Graphically, the entry of new firms does *not* change the position of the long-run average-cost curves of individual firms in the industry. When will this be the case? For the most part, when the industry's demand for resources is small in relation to

the total demand for those resources. This is most likely to occur when the industry employs unspecialized resources which are being demanded by many other industries. In short, when the particular industry's demand for resources is a negligible component of total demand, the industry can expand without significantly affecting resource prices and costs.

Perfectly Elastic Supply   What will the long-run supply curve for a constant-cost industry look like? The answer is contained in our previous discussion of the long-run adjustments toward equilibrium which profits or losses will initiate. Here we assumed that entrance or departure of firms would not affect costs. The result was that entry or exodus of firms would alter industry output but always bring product price back to the original $50 level, where it is just consistent with the unchanging minimum average total cost of production. Specifically, we discovered that the industry would supply 90,000, 100,000, or 110,000 units of output, all at a price of $50 per unit. *The long-run supply curve of a constant-cost industry is perfectly elastic.*

This is demonstrated graphically in Figure 23-10, where the data from Figures 23-8 and 23-9 are retained. Suppose that industry demand is originally D_1, industry output is Q_1 (100,000), and product price is Q_1P_1 ($50). This situation, referring to Figure 23-8, is one of long-run equilibrium. Now assume that demand increases to D_2, upsetting this equilibrium. The resulting economic profits will attract new firms. Because this is a constant-cost industry, entry will continue and indus-

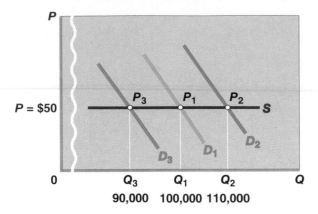

FIGURE 23-10 The long-run supply curve for a constant-cost industry is perfectly elastic

Because the entry or exodus of firms does not affect resource prices or, therefore, unit costs, an increase in demand (D_1 to D_2) will cause an expansion in industry output (Q_1 to Q_2) but no alteration in price ($Q_1P_1 = Q_2P_2$). Similarly, a decrease in demand (D_1 to D_3) will cause a contraction of output (Q_1 to Q_3) but no change in price ($Q_1P_1 = Q_3P_3$). This means that the long-run industry supply curve (S) will be perfectly elastic.

try output will expand until price is driven back down to the unchanged minimum average-total-cost level. This will be at price Q_2P_2 ($50) and output Q_2 (110,000).

This analysis, now referring to Figure 23-9, is reversible. A decline in short-run industry demand from D_1 to D_3 will cause an exodus of firms and ultimately restore equilibrium at price Q_3P_3 ($50) and output Q_3 (90,000). A line connecting all points, such as these three, shows the various price–quantity supplied combinations most profitable when firms have had enough time to make *all* desired adjustments to assumed changes in industry demand. By definition, this line is the industry's long-run supply curve. In a constant-cost industry this line, S in Figure 23-10, is perfectly elastic.

Long-Run Supply for an Increasing-Cost Industry

But constant-cost industries are a special case. Most industries are **increasing-cost industries** in that their average cost curves shift upward as the industry expands and downward as the industry contracts. Usually, the entry of new firms will bid up resource prices and therefore raise unit costs for individual firms in the industry. When an industry is using a significant portion of some resource whose total supply is not readily increased, the entry of new firms will increase resource demand in relation to supply and boost resource prices. This is particularly so in industries using specialized resources whose initial supply is not readily aug-

mented. Higher resource prices will result in higher long-run average costs for firms in the industry. The higher costs take the form of an upward shift in the long-run average-cost curve for the representative firm.

Two-Way Profit Squeeze The net result is that when an increase in product demand causes economic profits and attracts new firms to the industry, a two-way squeeze on profits will occur to eliminate those profits. On the one hand, the entry of new firms will increase market supply and lower product price and, on the other, the entire average-total-cost curve of the representative firm will shift upward. The equilibrium price will now be higher than it was originally. The industry will only produce a larger output at a higher price because industry expansion has increased average total costs, and in the long run product price must cover these costs. Greater output will be forthcoming at a higher price, or, more technically, the industry supply curve for an increasing-cost industry will be upsloping. Instead of getting either 90,000, 100,000, or 110,000 units at the same price of $50, in an increasing-cost industry 90,000 units might be forthcoming at $45; 100,000 at $50; and 110,000 at $55. The higher price is required to induce more production because costs per unit of output increase as the industry expands.

This can be seen graphically in Figure 23-11. Original market demand, industry output, and price are D_1, Q_1 (100,000), and Q_1P_1 ($50) respectively. An increase in demand to D_2 will upset this equilibrium and lead to economic profits. As new firms enter, (1) industry supply will increase, driving product price down to minimum average cost, and (2) resource prices will rise, causing average total costs of production to rise. Because of these average-total-cost increases, the new long-run equilibrium price will be established at some level *above* the original price, such as Q_2P_2 ($55). Conversely, a decline in demand from D_1 to D_3 will make production unprofitable and cause firms to leave the industry. The resulting decline in the demand for resources relative to their supply will lower resource prices and reduce average total costs of production. The new equilibrium price will be established at some level *below* the original price, such as Q_3P_3 ($45). Connecting these three equilibrium positions, we derive an upsloping long-run supply curve shown by S in Figure 23-11.

Long-Run Supply for a Decreasing-Cost Industry

In some industries firms may experience lower costs as the industry expands. Such industries are **de-**

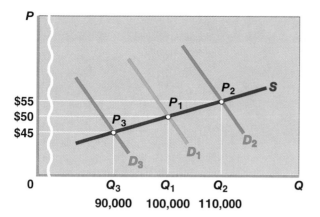

FIGURE 23-11 The long-run supply curve for an increasing-cost industry is upsloping

In an increasing-cost industry the entry of new firms in response to an increase in demand (D_3 to D_1 to D_2) will bid up resource prices and thereby increase unit costs. As a result, an increased industry output (Q_3 to Q_1 to Q_2) will be forthcoming only at higher prices ($Q_2P_2 > Q_1P_1 > Q_3P_3$). The long-run industry supply curve (S) is therefore upsloping.

creasing-cost industries. Classic example: As more mines are established in a given locality, each firm's costs in pumping out water seepage may decline. With more mines pumping, seepage into each is less, and pumping costs are therefore reduced. Furthermore, with only a few mines in an area, industry output might be so small that only relatively primitive and therefore costly transportation facilities are available. But as the number of firms and industry output expand, a railroad might build a spur into the area and thereby significantly reduce transportation costs.

You are urged to replicate the analysis underlying Figure 23-11 to show that the long-run supply curve of a decreasing-cost industry will be *downsloping*.

PURE COMPETITION AND EFFICIENCY

Whether a purely competitive industry is one of constant or increasing costs, the final long-run equilibrium position for each firm will have the same basic characteristics. As shown in Figure 23-12 (Key Graph) price (and marginal revenue) will settle where they are equal to minimum average cost. However, we discovered in Chapter 22 that the marginal-cost curve intersects, and is therefore equal to, average cost at the point of minimum average cost. In the long-run equilibrium position, "everything is equal." MR ($=P$) = minimum AC = MC.

This triple equality tells us that, although a com-

petitive firm may realize economic profits or losses in the short run, it will barely break even by producing in accordance with the MR ($=P$) = MC rule in the long run. Also, this triple equality suggests certain conclusions of great social significance concerning the efficiency of a purely competitive economy.

Economists agree that, subject to certain limitations and exceptions, a purely competitive economy will lead to the most efficient use of society's scarce resources. *A competitive price economy will allocate the limited amounts of resources available to society so as to maximize the satisfactions of consumers.* Actually, efficient use of limited resources requires that two conditions—which we have called allocative efficiency and productive efficiency—are fulfilled.

First, to achieve **allocative efficiency** resources must be apportioned among firms and industries to obtain the particular mix of products which is most wanted by society (consumers). Allocative efficiency is realized when it is impossible to alter the composition of total output to achieve a net gain for society.

Second, **productive efficiency** requires that each good in this optimum product mix be produced in the least costly way. To facilitate our discussion of how these conditions would be achieved under purely competitive conditions, let's examine the second point first.

1 Productive Efficiency: P = Minimum AC We know that, in the long run, competition forces firms to produce at the point of minimum average total cost of production and to charge that price which is just consistent with these costs. This is a most desirable situation from the consumer's point of view. It means that firms must use the best available (least-cost) technology or they will not survive. Stated differently, the minimum amount of resources will be used to produce any given output.

For example, glance back at the final equilibrium position shown in Figure 23-9a. Each firm in the industry is producing 100 units of output by using $5000 (equal to average cost of $50 *times* 100 units) worth of resources. If that same output had been produced at a total cost of, say, $7000, resources would be being used inefficiently. Society would be faced with the net loss of $2000 worth of alternative products. Note, too, that consumers benefit from the lowest product price possible under the cost conditions currently prevailing. Finally, the costs involved in each instance are only those costs essential in producing a product. Because products are standardized in competitive industries, there will be no selling or promotional costs added to production costs in determining product price.

KEY GRAPH

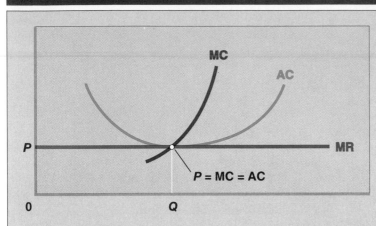

FIGURE 23-12
The long-run equilibrium position of a competitive firm, *P* = minimum AC = MC

The equality of price and minimum average cost indicates that the firm is using the most efficient known technology and is charging the lowest price *P* and producing the greatest output *Q* consistent with its costs. The equality of price and marginal cost indicates that resources are being allocated in accordance with consumer preferences.

2 Allocative Efficiency: *P* = MC   But the competitive production of *any* collection of goods does not necessarily make for an efficient allocation of resources. Production must not only be technologically efficient, but must also be the "right goods," goods consumers want most. The competitive market system functions so that resources are allocated to produce a total output whose composition best fits consumer preferences.

We must first grasp the social meaning of competitive product and resource prices. *The money price of any product—product X—is society's measure, or index, of the relative worth of that product at the margin.* Similarly, recalling the notion of opportunity costs, *the marginal cost of producing X measures the value, or relative worth, of the other goods the resources used in producing an extra unit of X could otherwise have produced.* In short, product price measures the benefit, or satisfaction, which society gets from additional units of X, and the marginal cost of an additional unit of X measures the sacrifice, or cost to society, of other goods in using resources to produce more of X.

Underallocation: *P* > MC   Now, under competition, the production of each product will occur up to that precise point at which price is equal to marginal cost (Figure 23-12). The profit-seeking competitor will realize the maximum possible profit only by equating price and marginal cost. To produce short of the MR (=*P*) = MC point will mean less than maximum profits to the individual firm and an *under*allocation of resources to this product from society's standpoint. The fact that price exceeds marginal cost indicates that society values additional units of X more highly than the alterna-

tive products the appropriate resources could otherwise produce.

To illustrate, if the price of a shirt is $10 and its marginal cost is $8, producing an additional shirt will cause a net increase in total output of $2. Society will gain a shirt valued at $10, while the alternative products sacrificed by allocating more resources to shirts would only be valued at $8. Whenever society can gain something valued at $10 by giving up something valued at $8, the initial allocation of resources must have been inefficient.

Overallocation: *P* < MC   For similar reasons, the production of X should not go beyond the output at which price equals marginal cost. To do so would entail less than maximum profits for producers and an *over*allocation of resources to X from the standpoint of society. To produce X at some point at which marginal cost exceeds price means resources are being used in the production of X by sacrificing alternative goods society values more highly than the added units of X. For example, if the price of a shirt is $10 and its marginal cost $13, then the production of one less shirt would result in a net increase in society's total output of $3. Society would lose a shirt valued at $10, but reallocating the freed resources to their best alternative uses would increase the output of some other good valued at $13. Again, whenever society is able to give up something valued at $10 in return for something valued at $13, the original allocation of resources must have been inefficient.

Efficient Allocation   Our conclusion is that *under pure competition, profit-motivated producers will pro-*

duce each commodity up to that precise point at which price and marginal cost are equal. *This means that resources are efficiently allocated under competition.* Each good is produced to the point at which the value of the last unit is equal to the value of the alternative goods sacrificed by its production. To alter the production of X would necessarily reduce consumer satisfactions. To produce X beyond the $P = MC$ point would sacrifice alternative goods whose value to society exceeds that of the extra units of X. To produce X short of the $P = MC$ point would sacrifice units of X which society values more than the alternative goods resources can produce.

Dynamic Adjustments A further attribute of purely competitive markets is their ability to restore efficiency in the use of resouces when disrupted by dynamic changes in the economy. In a competitive economy, any changes in consumer tastes, resource supplies, or technology will automatically set in motion appropriate realignments of resources. As we have already explained, an increase in consumer demand for product X will increase its price. Disequilibrium will occur in that, at its present output, the price of X will now exceed its marginal cost. This will create economic profits in industry X and stimulate its expansion. Its profitability will permit the industry to bid resources away from now less pressing uses. Expansion in this industry will end only when the price of X again equals its marginal cost, that is, when the value of the last unit produced once again equals the value of the alternative goods society forgoes in producing that last unit of X.

Similarly, changes in supplies of particular resources or in production techniques will upset existing price–marginal-cost equalities by either raising or lowering marginal cost. These inequalities will cause business executives, in either pursuing profits or shunning losses, to reallocate resources until price once again equals marginal cost in each line of production. In so doing, they correct any inefficiencies in the allocation of resources which changing economic data may temporarily impose on the economy.

"Invisible Hand" Revisited A final point: The highly efficient allocation of resources which a purely competitive economy fosters comes about because businesses and resource suppliers freely seek to further their own self-interests. That is, the "invisible hand" (Chapter 5) is at work in a competitive market system. In a competitive economy, businesses employ resources until the extra, or marginal, costs of production equal the product price. This not only maximizes profits for individual

producers but simultaneously results in a pattern of resource allocation which maximizes consumer satisfaction. The competitive market system organizes the private interests of producers along lines which are fully in accord with society's interest in using scarce resources efficiently.

QUICK REVIEW 23-4

♦   *In the long run the entry of firms will compete away profits and the exodus of firms will eliminate losses so that price equals minimum average cost.*

♦   *The long-run supply curves of constant-, increasing-, and decreasing-cost industries are perfectly elastic, upsloping, and downsloping, respectively.*

♦   *In purely competitive markets both productive efficiency (price equals minimum average cost) and allocative efficiency (price equals marginal cost) are achieved in the long run.*

Qualifications

Our conclusion that a purely competitive market system results in both productive and allocative efficiency must be qualified in several important respects.

The Income Distribution Problem The contention that pure competition will allocate resources efficiently is predicated on some given distribution of money income. Money income is distributed among households in some specific way, and this distribution results in a certain structure of demand. The competitive market system then brings about an efficient allocation of resources or, stated differently, an output of goods and services whose composition maximizes fulfillment of these particular consumer demands.

But if the distribution of money income is altered so that the structure of demand changes, would the competitive market system negotiate a new allocation of resources? The answer is "Yes"; the market system would reallocate resources and therefore change the composition of output to maximize the fulfillment of this new pattern of consumer wants. The question, then, is which of these two "efficient" allocations of resources is the "most efficient"? Which allocation of resources yields the greatest level of satisfaction to society?

There is no *scientific* answer to this question because we cannot measure and compare the satisfaction derived by various individuals from goods and services. If all people were alike in their capacities to ob-

LAST WORD

THE THEORY OF CONTESTABLE MARKETS

The concept of contestable markets suggests that the market power of imperfectly competitive producers may be severely constrained by potential industry entrants.

As noted in this chapter, the outcomes of purely competitive markets set standards of efficiency by which imperfectly competitive markets are judged. Both allocative and productive efficiency are realized when an industry is purely competitive. Princeton's William Baumol argues that the *potential* entry of firms to industries which are *not* purely competitive may also bring about the efficient results associated with pure competition.

Baumol has developed the notion of a *contestable market,* which means a market in which firm entry and exit are costless or virtually so. Envision a contestable market which is oligopolistic, that is, comprised of three or four large firms. The contestability of the market means that it is subject to "hit and run" entry by other firms because they can enter and leave virtually without cost. It follows that any economic profits or production inefficiencies on the part of the several firms in the industry will attract new entrants. (Productive inefficiencies imply that profits are being forgone by existing producers and new entrants can realize such profits by producing efficiently.) Hence, in contestable markets the mere presence of potential competition will force existing firms to produce efficiently and to charge prices which yield only a normal profit. Stated differently, incumbent firms are forced to behave as would purely competitive firms to forestall entry of other firms. We thus realize the socially desirable outcomes of purely competitive markets in contestable markets even though the latter are populated by only a few firms. The important factor which promotes these outcomes is not the number of firms in the industry, but costless entry and exit.

The most cited example of a contestable market is the airline industry. Assume there are just two airlines flying the Omaha–Chicago route. If entry and exit were costly, the market would *not* be contestable and the two incumbent airlines might realize substantial economic profits from their protected market position.

But in fact additional airlines can enter and leave this particular segment of the air transportation market with minimal cost. The reason is that the relevant capital equipment—the airplanes themselves—are highly mobile. Hence, if an additional airline were to enter and find the Omaha–Chicago route to be unprofitable, it could simply "pull out" by flying its equipment to some other route. The important point is that the awareness of the possibility of costless entry will compel the two airlines currently flying the Omaha–Chicago route to provide their transportation services efficiently and at prices which yield only a normal profit.

The main policy implication of contestable markets is that the focus of antimonopoly policy should shift from the current structure or competitive conditions within an industry to the conditions of entry. The primary criticism of contestable market theory is that its applicability is extremely limited. Critics contend that there are few, if any, industries—including the aforementioned airline industry—where entry and exit are costless.

tain satisfaction from income, economists could recommend that income be distributed equally and that the allocation of resources appropriate to *that* distribution would be the "best" or "most efficient" of all. But, people differ in their education, experiences, and environment, not to mention their inherited mental and physical characteristics. Such differences can be used to argue for an unequal distribution of income.

The distribution of income associated with the workings of a purely competitive market system is in fact quite unequal (Chapter 35) and therefore may lead to the production of trifles for the rich while denying basic needs of the poor. Many economists believe that the distribution of income which pure competition provides should be modified by public action. They maintain that allocative efficiency is hardly a virtue if it is a response to an income distribution which offends prevailing standards of equity.

Market Failure: Spillovers and Public Goods Under competition each producer will assume only those costs which it *must* pay. This correctly implies that in some lines of production there are significant costs producers can and do avoid, usually by polluting the environment. Recall from Chapter 6 that these avoided costs accrue to society and are aptly called *spillover* or *external costs*. On the other hand, consumption of certain goods and services, such as chest x-rays and measles vaccinations, yields widespread satisfactions, or benefits, to society as a whole. These satisfactions are called *external* or *spillover benefits*.

The profit-seeking activities of producers will bring about an allocation of resources which is efficient from society's point of view only if marginal cost embodies *all* the costs which production entails and product price accurately reflects *all* the benefits which society gets from a good's production. Only in this case will competitive production at the MR $(=P) =$ MC point balance the *total* sacrifices and satisfactions of society and result in an efficient allocation of resources. To the extent that price and marginal cost are not accurate indexes of sacrifices and satisfactions—to the extent that spillover costs and benefits exist—production at the MR $(=P) =$ MC point will *not* signify an efficient allocation of resources (see Figures 6-1 and 6-2).

Remember, too, the point of the lighthouse example in Chapter 6: The market system does not provide for social or public goods, that is, for goods to which the exclusion principle does *not* apply. Despite its other virtues, the competitive price system ignores an important class of goods and services—national defense, flood-control programs, and so forth—which can and do yield satisfaction to consumers but which cannot be priced and sold through the market system.

Productive Techniques Purely competitive markets may not always entail the use of the most efficient productive techniques or encourage development of improved techniques. There are both a static (or "right now") aspect and a dynamic (or "over time") aspect of this criticism.

Natural Monopolies The static aspect involves the *natural monopoly* problem introduced in Chapter 22. In

certain lines of production, existing technology may be such that a firm must be a large-scale producer to realize the lowest unit costs of production. Given consumer demand, this suggests that a relatively small number of large-scale producers is needed if production is to be carried on efficiently. Existing mass-production economies might be lost if such an industry were populated by the large number of small-scale producers pure competition requires.

Technological Progress The dynamic aspect of this criticism concerns the willingness and ability of purely competitive firms to undertake technological advance. The progressiveness of pure competition is debated by economists. Some authorities believe that a purely competitive economy would *not* foster a very rapid rate of technological progress. They argue, first, that the incentive for technological advance may be weak under pure competition because the profit rewards accruing to an innovating firm from a cost-reducing technological improvement will be quickly competed away by rival firms adopting the new technique. Second, the small size of the typical competitive firm and the fact that it tends to "break even" in the long run raise serious questions whether such producers could finance substantial programs of organized research. We will return to this controversy in Chapter 26.

Range of Consumer Choice A purely competitive economy might not provide a sufficient range of consumer choice or foster development of new products. This criticism, like the previous one, has both a static and a dynamic aspect. Pure competition, it is contended, means product standardization, whereas other market structures—for example, monopolistic competition and, frequently, oligopoly—encompass a wide range of types, styles, and quality gradations of any product. This product differentiation widens the consumer's range of free choice and simultaneously allows the buyer's preferences to be more completely fulfilled. Similarly, critics of pure competition point out that, just as pure competition is not likely to be progressive in developing new productive techniques, neither is this market structure conducive to improving existing products or creating completely new ones.

The question of the progressiveness of various market structures in terms of both productive techniques and product development will recur in the following three chapters.[2]

---

[2]Instructors who want to consider agriculture as a case study in pure competition should insert Chapter 34 at this point.

CHAPTER SUMMARY

1 The market models of **a** pure competition, **b** pure monopoly, **c** monopolistic competition, and **d** oligopoly are classifications into which most industries can be fitted with reasonable accuracy.

2 A purely competitive industry comprises a large number of independent firms producing a standardized product. Pure competition assumes that firms and resources are mobile among different industries.

3 No single firm can influence market price in a competitive industry; the firm's demand curve is perfectly elastic and price therefore equals marginal revenue.

4 Short-run profit maximization by a competitive firm can be analyzed by a comparison of total revenue and total cost or through marginal analysis. A firm will maximize profits by producing that output at which total revenue exceeds total cost by the greatest amount. Losses will be minimized by producing where the excess of total cost over total revenue is at a minimum and less than total fixed costs.

5 Provided price exceeds minimum average variable cost, a competitive firm will maximize profits or minimize losses in the short run by producing that output at which price or marginal revenue equals marginal cost. If price is less than average variable cost, the firm will minimize its losses by closing down. If price is greater than average variable cost but less than average total cost, the firm will minimize its losses by producing the $P = MC$ output. If price exceeds average total cost, the $P = MC$ output will provide maximum economic profits for the firm.

6 Applying the MR $(=P) = MC$ rule at various possible market prices leads to the conclusion that the segment of the firm's short-run marginal-cost curve lying above average variable cost is its short-run supply curve.

7 In the long run, competitive price will equal the minimum average cost of production because economic profits will cause firms to enter a competitive industry until those profits have been competed away. Conversely, losses will force the exodus of firms from the industry until product price once again barely covers unit costs.

8 The long-run supply curve is perfectly elastic for a constant-cost industry, upsloping for an increasing-cost industry, and downsloping for a decreasing-cost industry.

9 The long-run equality of price and minimum average cost means that competitive firms will use the most efficient known technology and charge the lowest price consistent with their production costs.

10 The equality of price and marginal cost implies that resources will be allocated in accordance with consumer tastes. The competitive price system will reallocate resources in response to a change in consumer tastes, technology, or resource supplies to maintain allocative efficiency over time.

11 Economist recognize four possible deterrents to allocative efficiency in a competitive economy. **a** There is no reason why the competitive market system will result in an optimal distribution of income. **b** In allocating resources, the competitive model does not allow for spillover costs and benefits or for the production of public goods. **c** A purely competitive industry may preclude the use of the best-known productive techniques and foster a slow rate of technological advance. **d** A competitive system provides neither a wide range of product choice nor an environment conducive to the development of new products.

TERMS AND CONCEPTS

pure competition	price taker	close-down case	constant-cost industry
pure monopoly	average, total, and	MR $(=P) = MC$ rule	decreasing-cost
monopolistic	marginal revenue	short-run supply curve	industry
competition	profit-maximizing case	long-run supply curve	allocative efficiency
oligopoly	break-even point	increasing-cost	productive efficiency
imperfect competition	loss-minimizing case	industry	

QUESTIONS AND STUDY SUGGESTIONS

1 Briefly indicate the basic characteristics of pure competition, pure monopoly, monopolistic competition, and oligopoly. Under which of these market classifications does each of the following most accurately fit? **a** a supermarket in your home town; **b** the steel industry; **c** a Kansas wheat farm; **d** the commercial bank in which you or your family has an account; **e** the automobile industry. In each case justify your classification.

2 Strictly speaking, pure competition never has existed and probably never will. Then why study it?

3 Use the following demand schedule to determine total and marginal revenues for each possible level of sales.

Product price	Quantity demanded	Total revenue	Marginal revenue
$2	0	$____	
2	1	____	$____
2	2	____	____
2	3	____	____
2	4	____	____
2	5	____	____

a What can you conclude about the structure of the industry in which this firm is operating? Explain.

b Graph the demand, total-revenue, and marginal-revenue curves for this firm.

c Why do the demand and marginal-revenue curves coincide?

d "Marginal revenue is the change in total revenue." Do you agree? Explain verbally and graphically, using the data in the table.

4 Assume the following unit-cost data are for a purely competitive producer:

Total product	Average fixed cost	Average variable cost	Average total cost	Marginal cost
0				
1	$60.00	$45.00	$105.00	$45
2	30.00	42.50	72.50	40
3	20.00	40.00	60.00	35
4	15.00	37.50	52.50	30
5	12.00	37.00	49.00	35
6	10.00	37.50	47.50	40
7	8.57	38.57	47.14	45
8	7.50	40.63	48.13	55
9	6.67	43.33	50.00	65
10	6.00	46.50	52.50	75

a At a product price of $32, will this firm produce in the short run? Why, or why not? If it does produce, what will be the profit-maximizing or loss-minimizing output? Explain. Specify the amount of economic profit or loss per unit of output.

b Answer the questions of 4a assuming product price is $41.

c Answer the questions of 4a assuming product price is $56.

d Complete the short-run supply schedule for the firm, and indicate the profit or loss incurred at each output (columns 1 to 3).

(1) Price	(2) Quantity supplied, single firm	(3) Profit (+) or loss (−)	(4) Quantity supplied, 1500 firms
$26	____	$____	____
32	____	____	____
38	____	____	____
41	____	____	____
46	____	____	____
56	____	____	____
66	____	____	____

e Explain: "That segment of a competitive firm's marginal-cost curve which lies above its average-variable-cost curve constitutes the short-run supply curve for the firm." Illustrate graphically.

f Now assume there are 1500 identical firms in this competitive industry; that is, there are 1500 firms, each of which has the same cost data shown here. Calculate the industry supply schedule (column 4).

g Suppose the market demand data for the product are as follows:

Price	Total quantity demanded
$26	17,000
32	15,000
38	13,500
41	12,000
46	10,500
56	9,500
66	8,000

What will equilibrium price be? What will equilibrium output be for the industry? For each firm? What will profit or loss be per unit? Per firm? Will this industry expand or contract in the long run?

5 Why is the equality of marginal revenue and marginal cost essential for profit maximization in all market structures? Explain why price can be substituted for marginal revenue in the MR = MC rule when an industry is purely competitive.

6 Explain: "A competitive producer must look to average variable cost in determining whether or not to produce in the short run, to marginal cost in deciding on the best volume of production, and to average total cost to calculate profits or losses." Why might a firm produce at a loss in the short run rather than close down?

7 Using diagrams for both the industry and a representative firm, illustrate competitive long-run equilibrium. Employing these diagrams, show how **a** an increase, and **b** a decrease, in market demand will upset this long-run equilibrium. Trace graphically and describe verbally the adjustment processes by which long-run equilibrium is restored. Assume the industry is one of constant costs.

8 Distinguish carefully between constant-cost, increasing cost, and decreasing-cost industries. Answer question 7 assuming that the industry is one of increaasing costs. Compare the long-run supply curves of constant-cost, increasing-cost and decreasing-cost industries.

9 Suppose a decrease in demand occurs in a competitive increasing-cost industry. Contrast the product price and industry output existing after all long-run adjustments are completed with those which originally prevailed.

10 In long-run equilibrium, $P = AC = MC$. Of what significance for economic efficiency is the equality of P and AC? The equality of P and MC? Distinguish between productive efficiency and allocative efficiency in your answer.

11 Explain why some economists believe that an unequal distribution of income might impair the allocative efficiency of a competitive market system. What other criticisms can be made of a purely competitive economy?

Price and Output Determination: Pure Monopoly

You deal with monopolies—sole sellers of products and services—daily. When you mail a letter, you are using the services of the United States Postal Service, a governmentally sponsored monopoly. Similarly, when you use your telephone, turn on your lights, or subscribe to cable TV, you are patronizing monopolies.

We now jump from pure competition to the opposite end of the industry spectrum (Table 23-1) and examine the characteristics, bases, price-output behavior, and social desirability of monopoly. How is a pure monopoly defined? What conditions underlie its existence? How does a monopolist's price-output behavior compare with that of a purely competitive industry? Do monopolists achieve the allocative and productive efficiency associated with pure competition? If not, can government policies improve the price-output behavior of a pure monopolist?

PURE MONOPOLY: AN INTRODUCTION

Absolute or **pure monopoly** exists when *a single firm is the sole producer of a product for which there are no close substitutes*. Let's first examine the characteristics of pure monopoly and then provide examples.

Characteristics

1 Single Seller A pure, or absolute, monopolist is a one-firm industry. A single firm is the only producer of a specific product or the sole supplier of a service; the firm and the industry are synonymous.

2 No Close Substitutes Thus, the monopolist's product is unique in that there are no good, or close, substitutes. From the buyer's viewpoint, there are no reasonable alternatives. The buyer must buy the product from the monopolist or do without it.

3 "Price Maker" We saw that the individual firm operating under pure competition exercises no influence over product price; it is a "price taker." This is so because it contributes only a negligible portion of total supply. In contrast, the pure monopolist is a *price maker;* the firm exercises considerable control over price because it is responsible for, and therefore controls, the total quantity supplied. Given a downsloping demand curve for its product, the monopolist can change product price by manipulating the quantity of the product supplied. If it is advantageous, the monopolist will use this power.

4 Blocked Entry A pure monopolist has no immediate competitors because there are barriers to entry. Economic, technological, legal, or other obstacles must exist to keep new competitors from coming into the industry if monopoly is to persist. Entry under conditions of pure monopoly is totally blocked.

5 Advertising The fact there are no close substitutes for the monopolized product has interesting implications for advertising. Depending on the type of product or service offered, a monopolist may or may not engage in extensive advertising and sales promotion. For example, a pure monopolist selling a luxury good such as diamonds might advertise heavily to increase demand for the product. The result might be that more people will buy diamonds rather than take vacations. Local public utilities, on the other hand, normally see no point in large expenditures for advertising: People wanting water, gas, electric power, and local telephone service already know from whom they must buy these necessities.

Examples

In most cities governmentally owned or regulated public utilities—gas and electric companies, the water company, the cable TV company, and the telephone company—are all monopolies or virtually so. There are no close substitutes for services provided by these public utilities. Of course, there is almost always *some* competition. Candles or kerosene lights are very imperfect substitutes for electricity; telegrams, letters, and courier services can be substituted for the telephone. But such substitutes are either costly, inconvenient, or unappealing.

The classic example of a private, unregulated monopoly is the De Beers diamond syndicate which effectively controls 80 to 90 percent of the world's diamond supply. But in the United States major manufacturing monopolies are rare and frequently transient in that in time new competitors emerge to erode their single-producer status.

> . . . monopoly in the sense of a single seller is virtually nonexistent in nationwide U.S. manufacturing industries of appreciable size. The rate at which near-monopolies have faded appears to have exceeded the rate of new appearance by a substantial margin. In 1962 Gillette made 70 percent of domes-

tic razor blade sales, but its position was eroded, first by the appearance of Wilkinson's stainless steel blades and then by Bic's aggressive marketing of disposable razors. Eastman Kodak's 90 percent share of amateur film sales and 65 percent share of all film sales, including instant photo packs, was sharply challenged in the 1980s by import competition from Fuji. General Motors' share of diesel locomotive sales probably remains near 75 percent. For decades Western Electric supplied roughly 85 percent of U.S. telephone equipment, but its position faded rapidly owing to technological changes of the 1970s and the antitrust-induced divestiture in 1984 of affiliated Bell Telephone local operating companies, ending a captive market situation. IBM's 72 to 82 percent share of the digital computer market during the 1960s fell as new rivals captured mini- and microcomputer applications. Xerox's 75 to 80 percent share of electrostatic copier revenues declined with the erosion of its patent position during the 1970s. . . . During much of the 1960s and 1970s, Boeing controlled roughly two-thirds of noncommunist world jet airliner placements. With the rise of Europe's Airbus Consortium, Boeing's share declined to 50 percent in the late 1980s.[1]

Professional sports leagues embody monopoly power by granting member clubs franchises to be the sole suppliers of their services in designated geographic areas. Aside from Chicago, New York, and one or two other extremely large metropolitan areas, larger American cities are served by a single professional baseball, football, hockey, or basketball team. If you want to see a live major-league professional basketball game in Phoenix or Seattle, you must patronize the Suns and the Sonics respectively.

Monopoly may also be geographic. A small town may have only one airline or railroad. The local bank, movie, or bookstore may approximate a monopoly in a small, isolated community.

Importance

Analysis of pure monopoly is important for at least two reasons.

1 A not insignificant amount of economic activity—perhaps 5 or 6 percent of domestic output—is carried out under conditions approaching pure monopoly.

2 A study of pure monopoly yields valuable insights concerning the more common market structures of

[1]F. M. Scherer and David Ross, *Industrial Market Structure and Economic Performance,* 3d ed. (Chicago: Rand McNally College Publishing Company, 1990), p. 82.

monopolistic competition and oligopoly, discussed in Chapters 25 and 26. These two market situations combine in differing degrees characteristics of pure competition and pure monopoly.

BARRIERS TO ENTRY

The absence of competitors characterizing pure monopoly is largely explainable in terms of factors which prohibit additional firms from entering an industry. These **barriers to entry** are also pertinent in explaining the existence of oligopoly and monopolistic competition between the market extremes of pure competition and pure monopoly.

In pure monopoly, entry barriers effectively block all potential competition. Somewhat less formidable barriers permit the existence of oligopoly, a market dominated by a few firms. Still weaker barriers result in the fairly large number of firms which characterizes monopolistic competition. The virtual absence of entry barriers helps explain the very large number of competing firms which is the basis of pure competition. The point is that barriers to entry are pertinent not only to the extreme case of pure monopoly but also to the "partial monopolies" so characteristic of our economy.

Economies of Scale

Modern technology in some industries is such that efficient, low-cost production can be achieved only if producers are extremely large both absolutely and in relation to the market. Where economies of scale are very significant, a firm's long-run average-cost schedule will decline over a wide range of output (Figure 22-9b). Given market demand, the achieving of low unit costs and therefore low unit prices for consumers depends on the existence of a small number of firms or, in the extreme case, only one firm.

The automobile, aluminum, and basic steel industries are a few of many heavy industries which reflect such conditions. If three firms currently enjoy all available economies of scale and each has roughly one-third of a market, it is easy to see why new competitors may find it extremely difficult to enter this industry. New firms entering the market as small-scale producers will have little or no chance to survive and expand. As small-scale entrants they cannot realize the cost economies enjoyed by the existing "Big Three" and therefore will be unable to realize the profits necessary for survival and growth. New competitors in the basic steel and automobile industries will not come from the suc-

cessful operation and expansion of small "backyard" producers. They simply will not be efficient enough to survive.

The other option is to start out big, that is, to enter the industry as a large-scale producer. In practice, this is extremely difficult. It is very difficult for a new and untried enterprise to secure the money capital needed to obtain capital facilities comparable to those of the Big Three in the automobile industry. The financial obstacles in the way of starting big are so great in many cases as to be prohibitive.

Public Utilities: Natural Monopolies

In a few industries, economies of scale are particularly pronounced; they extend throughout the range of market demand. This can be envisioned graphically by looking ahead to Figure 24-6. At the same time competition is impractical, inconvenient, or simply unworkable. Such industries are called *natural monopolies,* and most of the so-called public utilities—electric and gas companies, bus firms, cable television, and water and communication facilities—fit into this category. These industries are generally given exclusive franchises by government. But in return for this sole right to supply electricity, water, or bus service to a given geographic area, government reserves the right to regulate the operations of such monopolies to prevent abuses of the monopoly power it has granted.

As an illustration, it would be exceedingly wasteful if a community had several firms supplying water or electricity. Technology is such in these industries that large-scale and extensive capital expenditures on generators, pumping and purification equipment, water mains, and transmission lines are required. This problem is aggravated because capital equipment must be sufficient to meet peak demands which occur on hot summer days when lawns are being watered and air conditioners operated. The point is that unit costs of production decline with the number of cubic feet of water or kilowatt hours of electricity supplied by each firm, that is, as the firm expands its size. The presence of several water and electricity suppliers would divide the total market and reduce the sales of each competitor. Each firm would be pushed back up its declining long-run average-cost curve. Firms would be too small to achieve minimum long-run average costs and therefore electricity and water rates would be unnecessarily high.

In addition, competition could be extremely inconvenient. The presence of a half-dozen telephone companies in an area could mean having six telephones and six telephone books—not to mention six telephone bills—to ensure communication with all other residents in the same area.

Because natural monopolies can lower their average costs by expanding output, they try to increase sales by price cutting. As a result, cutthroat price competition breaks out when several firms exist in these public utilities industries. The result will be losses, bankruptcy of weaker rivals, and eventual merger of survivors. The evolving pure monopoly will be anxious to recoup past losses and to profit fully from its new position of market dominance by charging monopoly prices for its goods or services.

To spare society such disadvantageous results, government will usually grant an exclusive franchise to a single firm to supply water, natural gas, electricity, telephone service, or bus transportation. In return, government reserves the right to designate the monopolist's geographic area of operation, to regulate the quality of its services, and to control the prices it charges. The result is a regulated or government-sponsored monopoly—monopoly designed to achieve low unit costs but regulated so that consumers will benefit from these cost economies. Some of the problems associated with regulation are considered later in this chapter and in Chapter 33.

Legal Barriers: Patents and Licenses

We have already noted that government frequently gives exclusive franchises to natural monopolies. Government also creates legal entry barriers in awarding patents and licenses.

Patents   By granting an inventor the exclusive right to produce or license a product for seventeen years, American patent laws aim to protect the inventor from having the product or process usurped by rival enterprises which have not shared in the time, effort, and money outlays which have gone into its development. By the same token patents provide the inventor with a monopoly position for the life of the patent.

Patent control figured prominently in the growth of many modern-day industrial giants such as National Cash Register, General Motors, Xerox, Polaroid, General Electric, and du Pont. The United Shoe Machinery Company is a notable example of patent control being abused to achieve monopoly power. In this case United Shoe became the exclusive supplier of certain essential shoemaking machines through patent control. It extended its monopoly power to other types of shoemak-

ing machinery by requiring all lessees of its patented machines to sign a "tying agreement" in which shoe manufacturers agreed also to lease all other shoemaking machinery from United Shoe. This allowed United Shoe to monopolize the market until partially effective antitrust action was taken by the government in 1955.

Research underlies the development of patentable products. Firms which gain a measure of monopoly power by their own research or by purchasing the patents of others are in a strategic position to consolidate and strengthen their market position. The profits from one important patent can finance the research required to develop new patentable products. The pharmaceutical industry is a case in point. Patents on prescription drugs have produced large monopoly profits which have helped finance the discovery of new patentable medicines. Monopoly power achieved through patents may well be cumulative.

Licenses   Entry into an industry or occupation may be limited by government through the issuing of licenses. At the national level the Federal Communications Commission licenses radio and television stations. In many large cities one needs a municipal license to drive a taxicab. The consequent restriction of the supply of cabs creates monopolistic earnings for cab owners and drivers. In a few instances government might license itself to provide some product and thereby create a public monopoly. For example, the sale of liquor in some states is exclusively through state-owned retail outlets. Similarly, many states have in effect "licensed" themselves to run lotteries (Chapter 6). This chapter's Last Word discusses how generous contracts granted to national park concessionaires have resulted in monopoly power and monopoly profits.

Ownership of Essential Resources

The institution of private property can be used by a monopoly as an effective obstacle to potential rivals. A firm owning or controlling a resource essential to the production process can prohibit the creation of rival firms. The Aluminum Company of America retained its monopoly position in the aluminum industry for many years by virtue of its control of all basic sources of bauxite, the major ore used in aluminum fabrication. At one time the International Nickel Company of Canada (now called Inco) controlled approximately 90 percent of the world's known nickel reserves. As noted earlier, most of the world's known diamond mines are owned or effectively controlled by the De Beers Company of South Africa. Similarly, it is very difficult for new professional sports leagues to evolve when existing leagues have contracts with the best players and leases on the major stadiums and arenas.

Two Implications

Our discussion of barriers to entry suggests two noteworthy points about monopoly.

1 Relatively Rare Barriers to entry are rarely complete. This is merely another way of stating our earlier point that pure monopoly is relatively rare. Although research and technological advance may strengthen the market position of a firm, technology may also undermine existing monopoly power. Existing patent advantages may be circumvented by the development of new and distinct, yet substitutable, products. New sources of strategic resources may be found. It is probably only a modest overstatement to say that monopoly in the sense of a one-firm industry persists over time only with the sanction or aid of government, as with the postal service's monopoly on the delivery of first-class mail.

2 Desirability We have implied that monopolies may be desirable or undesirable from the standpoint of economic efficiency. The public utilities and economies-of-scale arguments suggest that market demand and technology may be such that efficient low-cost production presupposes the existence of monopoly. On the other hand, our comments on resource ownership, patents, and licensing as sources of monopoly imply more undesirable connotations of business monopoly.

MONOPOLY DEMAND

Let's begin our analysis of the price-output behavior of a pure monopolist by making three assumptions.

1 Our monopolist's status is secured by patents, economies of scale, or resource ownership.

2 The firm is *not* governmentally regulated.

3 The firm is a single-price monopolist; it charges the same price for all units of output.

The crucial difference between a pure monopolist and a purely competitive seller lies on the demand side of the market. Recall from Chapter 23 that the purely competitive seller faces a perfectly elastic demand schedule at the market price determined by industry supply and demand. The competitive firm is a "price taker" which can sell as much or as little as it wants at the going market price. It follows that each additional unit sold will add a constant amount—its price—to the firm's total revenue. In other words, marginal revenue for the competitive seller is constant and equal to product price. This means that total revenue increases by a constant amount, that is, by the constant price of each unit sold. (Refer back to Table 23-2 and Figure 23-1 for price, marginal-revenue, and total-revenue relationships for the purely competitive firm.)

The monopolist's demand curve—indeed, the demand curve of *any* imperfectly competitive seller—is much different. Because the pure monopolist *is* the industry, its demand, or sales, curve is the industry demand curve.[2] And the industry demand curve is not perfectly elastic, but rather is downsloping, as illustrated by columns 1 and 2 of Table 24-1.

There are three implications of a downsloping demand curve which must be understood.

Price Exceeds Marginal Revenue

A downsloping demand curve means that a pure monopoly can increase its sales only by charging a lower unit price for its product. *Because the monopolist must lower price to boost sales, marginal revenue is less than price (average revenue) for every level of output except the first.* The reason? Price cuts will apply not only to the extra output sold but also to *all* other units of output which otherwise could have been sold at a higher price. Each additional unit sold will add to total revenue its price *less* the sum of the price cuts which must be taken on all prior units of output.

In Figure 24-1 we have extracted two price–quantity combinations—$142-3 and $132-4—from the monopolist's demand curve. By lowering price from $142 to $132, the monopolist can sell one more unit and thus gain as revenue the fourth unit's price of $132. This gain is designated as the gray rectangle. But to sell this fourth unit for $132, the monopolist must lower price on the first three units from $142 to $132. This $10 reduction on 3 units results in a $30 revenue loss indicated by the light red rectangle in Figure 24-1. The *net* change in total revenue, or marginal revenue, from selling the fourth unit is $102, the $132 gain minus the $30 loss.

---

[2]Recall in Chapter 23 that we presented separate diagrams for the purely competitive industry *and* for a single firm in that industry. Because with pure monopoly the firm and the industry are one and the same, we need only a single diagram.

TABLE 24-1 Revenue and cost data of a pure monopolist (hypothetical data)

Revenue data				Cost data			
(1) Quantity of output	(2) Price (average revenue)	(3) Total revenue	(4) Marginal revenue	(5) Average total cost	(6) Total cost	(7) Marginal cost	(8) Profit (+) or loss (−)
0	$172	$ 0			$ 100		$−100
			$162			$ 90	
1	162	162		$190.00	190		− 28
			142			80	
2	152	304		135.00	270		+ 34
			122			70	
3	142	426		113.33	340		+ 86
			102			60	
4	132	528		100.00	400		+128
			82			70	
5	122	610		94.00	470		+140
			62			80	
6	112	672		91.67	550		+122
			42			90	
7	102	714		91.43	640		+ 74
			22			110	
8	92	736		93.73	750		− 14
			2			130	
9	82	738		97.78	880		−142
			−18			150	
10	72	720		103.00	1030		−310

This same point is evident in Table 24-1, where we observe that the marginal revenue of the second unit of output is $142 rather than its $152 price, because a $10 price cut must be taken on the first unit to increase sales from 1 to 2 units. Similarly, to sell 3 units the firm must lower price from $152 to $142. The resulting marginal revenue will be just $122—the $142 addition to total revenue which the third unit of sales provides less $10 price cuts on the first 2 units of output. It is this rationale which explains why the marginal-revenue data of column 4 of Table 24-1 fall short of product price in column 2 for all levels of output except the first. Because marginal revenue is, by definition, the increase in total revenue associated with each additional unit of output, the declining marginal-revenue figures mean that total revenue will increase at a diminishing rate as shown in column 3 of Table 24-1.

The relationships between the demand, marginal-revenue, and total-revenue curves, which were introduced in Chapter 20, are portrayed graphically in Figure 24-2a and b. In drawing this diagram we have extended the demand and revenue data of columns 1 through 4 of Table 24-1 by continuing to assume that successive $10 price cuts will each elicit one additional unit of sales. That is, 11 units can be sold at $62, 12 at $52, and so forth.

In addition to the fact that the marginal-revenue curve lies *below* the demand curve, note the special relationship between total revenue and marginal revenue. Because marginal revenue is, by definition, the change in total revenue, we observe that so long as total revenue is increasing, marginal revenue is positive. When total revenue reaches its maximum, marginal revenue is zero. When total revenue is diminishing, marginal revenue is negative.

FIGURE 24-1 Price and marginal revenue under pure monopoly

A pure monopolist—or, in fact, any imperfect competitor with a downsloping demand curve—must reduce price to sell more output. As a consequence, marginal revenue will be less than price. In our example, by reducing price from $142 to $132 the monopolist gains $132 from the sale of the fourth unit. But from this gain must be subtracted $30 which reflects the $10 price cut which has been made on each of the first three units. Hence, the fourth unit's marginal revenue is $102 (=$132 − $30), considerably less than its $132 price.

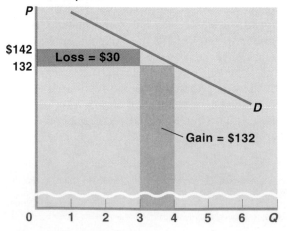

Price Maker

In all imperfectly competitive markets in which down-sloping demand curves are relevant—that is, purely monopolistic, oligopolistic, and monopolistically competitive markets—firms have a price policy. By virtue of their ability to influence total supply, the output decisions of these firms necessarily affect product price.

This is most evident in pure monopoly, where one firm controls total output. Faced with a downsloping demand curve, in which each output is associated with some unique price, the monopolist unavoidably determines price in deciding what volume of output to produce. The monopolist simultaneously chooses both price and output. In columns 1 and 2 of Table 24-1 we find that the monopolist can sell only an output of 1 unit at a price of $162, only an output of 2 units at a price of $152 per unit, and so forth.

This does not mean that the monopolist is "free" of market forces in establishing price and output or that the consumer is completely at the monopolist's mercy. In particular, the monopolist's downsloping demand curve means that it cannot raise price without losing sales, or gain sales without charging a lower price.

Price Elasticity

The total-revenue test for price elasticity of demand is the basis for our third conclusion. Recall from Chapter 20 that the total-revenue test tells us that, when demand is elastic, a decline in price will increase total revenue. Similarly, when demand is inelastic, a decline in price will reduce total revenue. Beginning at the top of the demand curve in Figure 24-2, observe that for all price reductions from $172 down to approximately $82, total revenue increases (and marginal revenue therefore is positive). This means that demand is elastic in this price range. Conversely, for price reductions below $82, total revenue decreases (marginal revenue is negative), which indicates that demand is inelastic.

Our generalization is that a monopolist will never choose a price-quantity combination where price declines cause total revenue to decrease (marginal revenue to be negative). *The profit-maximizing monopolist will always want to avoid the inelastic segment of its demand curve in favor of some price-quantity combination in the elastic segment.* By lowering price into the inelastic range, total revenue will decline. But the lower price is associated with a larger output and therefore increased total costs. Lower revenue and higher costs mean diminished profits.

QUICK REVIEW 24-1

♦ *A pure monopolist is the sole supplier of a product or service for which there are no close substitutes.*

♦ *Monopolies exist because of entry barriers such as economies of scale, patents and licenses, and the ownership of essential resources.*

♦ *The monopolist's demand curve is downsloping, causing the marginal revenue curve to lie below it.*

♦ *Price declines in the elastic range of the monopolist's demand curve will increase total revenues, and marginal revenue will be positive; in the inelastic portion of the demand curve price declines will decrease total revenue, and marginal revenue will be negative.*

OUTPUT AND PRICE DETERMINATION

What specific price-quantity combination on its demand curve will a profit-maximizing monopolist choose? To answer this we must add production costs to our understanding of monopoly demand.

Cost Data

On the cost side, we will assume that, although the firm is a monopolist in the product market, it hires resources competitively and employs the same technology as our competitive firm in the preceding chapter. This lets us use the cost data developed in Chapter 22 and applied in Chapter 23 to compare the price-output decisions of a pure monopoly with those of a pure competitor. Columns 5 through 7 of Table 24-1 restate the pertinent cost concepts of Table 22-2.

MR = MC Rule

A profit-seeking monopolist will employ the same rationale as a profit-seeking firm in a competitive industry. It will produce each successive unit of output so long as it adds more to total revenue than it does to total cost. The firm will produce up to that output at which marginal revenue equals marginal cost (MR = MC).

A comparison of columns 4 and 7 in Table 24-1 indicates that the profit-maximizing output is 5 units;

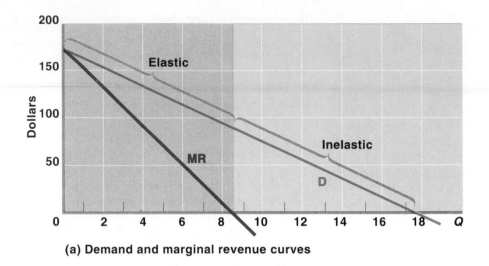

(a) Demand and marginal revenue curves

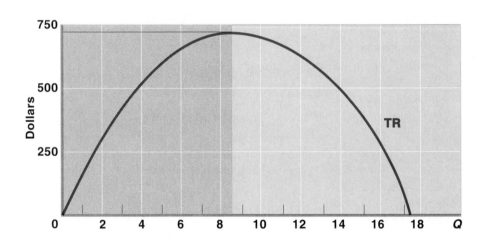

(b) Total revenue curve

FIGURE 24-2 Demand, marginal revenue, and total revenue of an imperfectly competitive firm

Because it must lower price to increase its sales, an imperfectly competitive firm's marginal-revenue curve (MR) lies below its downsloping demand curve (*D*). Total revenue (TR) increases at a decreasing rate, reaches a maximum, and then declines. Note that, because MR is the change in TR, a unique relationship exists between MR and TR. In moving down the elastic segment of the demand curve, TR is increasing and, hence, MR is positive. When TR reaches its maximum, MR is zero. And in moving down the inelastic segment of the demand curve, TR is declining, so MR is negative. A monopolist or other imperfectly competitive seller will never choose to lower price into the inelastic segment of its demand curve because by doing so it will simultaneously reduce total revenue and increase production costs, thereby lowering profits.

the fifth unit is the last unit of output whose marginal revenue exceeds its marginal cost. What price will the monopolist charge? The downsloping demand curve of columns 1 and 2 in Table 24-1 indicates that there is only one price at which 5 units can be sold: $122.

This analysis is presented graphically in Figure 24-3 (Key Graph), where the demand, marginal-revenue, average-total-cost, and marginal-cost data of Table 24-1 have been drawn. Comparing marginal revenue and marginal cost confirms that the profit-maximizing

KEY GRAPH

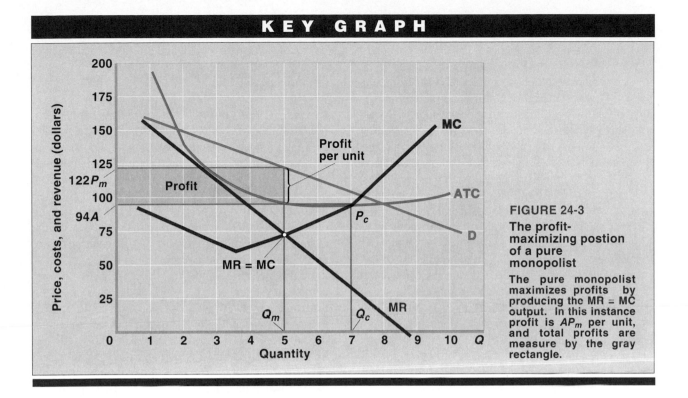

FIGURE 24-3

The profit-maximizing postion of a pure monopolist

The pure monopolist maximizes profits by producing the MR = MC output. In this instance profit is AP_m per unit, and total profits are measure by the gray rectangle.

output is 5 units or, more generally, Q_m. The unique price at which Q_m can be sold is found by extending a perpendicular line up from the profit-maximizing point on the output axis and then at right angles from the point at which it hits the demand curve to the vertical axis. The indicated price is P_m. To charge a price higher than P_m, the monopolist must move up the demand curve, meaning that sales will fall short of the profit-maximizing level Q_m. Specifically, the firm will fail to produce units of output whose marginal revenue exceeds their marginal cost. If the monopolist charges less than P_m, it would involve a sales volume in excess of the profit-maximizing output.

Columns 2 and 5 of Table 24-1 indicate that, at 5 units of output, product price of $122 exceeds average total cost of $94. Economic profits are therefore $28 per unit; total economic profits are then $140 ($= 5 \times \$28$). In Figure 24-3, per unit profit is indicated by the distance AP_m, and total economic profits—the gray area—are found by multiplying this unit profit by the profit-maximizing output Q_m.

The same profit-maximizing combination of output and price can also be determined by comparing the total revenue and total costs incurred at each possible level of production. You should employ columns 3 and 6 of Table 24-1 to verify the conclusions reached through our marginal-revenue–marginal-cost analysis. Similarly, an accurate graphing of total revenue and total cost against output will also show the greatest differential (the maximum profit) at 5 units of output.

No Monopoly Supply Curve

Recall that the supply curve of a purely competitive firm is that portion of its marginal-cost curve lying above average variable costs (Figure 23-6). The supply curve is determined by applying the $P = MC$ profit-maximization rule. At any given market-determined price the purely competitive seller will maximize profits by equating that price (which is equal to marginal revenue) with marginal cost. When market price increases or decreases, the competitive firm will move up or down its marginal-cost curve because it is profitable to produce more or less output. We find each price to be uniquely associated with a specific output, thus defining the supply curve.

At first glance we would suspect that the pure monopolist's marginal-cost curve would also be its supply curve. But this is *not* the case. *The pure monopolist has no supply curve.* The reason is that there is no unique relationship between price and quantity supplied. The price and amount supplied depend on the location of the demand (and therefore marginal-revenue) curves. Like the competitive firm, the monopolist equates marginal revenue and marginal cost, but for the monopolist marginal revenue is less than price. Because the monopolist does *not* equate marginal cost to price, it is possible for different demand conditions to bring about different profit-maximizing prices for the same output. To convince yourself of this, go back to Figure 24-3 and pencil in a steeper (less elastic) demand curve, drawing its corresponding marginal-revenue curve so that it intersects marginal cost at the same point as does the present marginal-revenue curve. With the steeper demand curve, this new MR = MC output will yield a higher price. Conclusion: There is no single, unique price associated with output level Q_m, and therefore no supply curve for the pure monopolist.

Misconceptions Concerning Monopoly Pricing

Our analysis explodes some popular fallacies concerning monopoly behavior.

1 Not Highest Price Because a monopolist can manipulate output and price, it is often alleged that it "will charge the highest price it can get." This is a misguided assertion. There are many prices above P_m in Figure 24-3, but the monopolist shuns them because they entail a smaller-than-maximum profit. *Total* profits are the difference between *total* revenue and *total* costs, and each of these two determinants of profits depends on quantity sold as much as on price and unit cost.

2 Total, Not Unit, Profits The monopolist seeks maximum *total* profits, not maximum *unit* profits. In Figure 24-3 a careful comparison of the vertical distance between average cost and price at various possible outputs indicates that per unit profits are greater at a point slightly to the left of the profit-maximizing output Q_m. This is seen in Table 24-1, where unit profits are $32 at 4 units of output compared with $28 at the profit-maximizing output of 5 units. Here the monopolist accepts a lower-than-maximum per unit profit be-

cause additional sales more than compensate for lower unit profits. A profit-seeking monopolist would rather sell 5 units at a profit of $28 per unit (for a total profit of $140) than 4 units at a profit of $32 per unit (for a total profit of only $128).

3 Losses Pure monopoly does *not* guarantee economic profits. True, the likelihood of economic profits is greater for a pure monopolist than for a purely competitive producer. In the long run the latter is doomed by the free and easy entry of new firms to a normal profit; barriers to entry permit the monopolist to perpetuate economic profits in the long run.[3] Unlike the competitive situation, entry barriers keep out potential entrants who would increase supply, drive price down, and eliminate economic profits.

Like the pure competitor, the monopolist will not persistently operate at a loss. Faced with losses, the firm's owners will move their resources to alternative industries offering higher returns. Thus we can expect the monopolist to realize a normal profit or better in the long run. However, if the demand and cost situation faced by the monopolist is sufficiently less favorable than shown in Figure 24-3, short-run losses will be realized. Despite its dominance in the market, the monopolist shown in Figure 24-4 realizes a loss of an amount shown by the light red area by virtue of weak demand and relatively high costs. Yet it continues to operate for the time being because its total loss is less than its fixed costs. More precisely, observe that at Q_m the monopolist's price P_m exceeds its average variable cost. Although the government's rail corporation AMTRAK has a virtual monopoly in long-distance passenger train service, it frequently operates at a loss.

ECONOMIC EFFECTS OF MONOPOLY

Let's now evaluate pure monopoly from the standpoint of society as a whole. We will examine (1) price, output, and resource allocation; (2) income distribution; (3) some uncertainties caused by difficulties in making

---

[3]A related point is that the distinction between the short run and the long run is less important under monopoly than it is under pure competition. With pure competition the entry or exit of firms guarantees that economic profits will be zero in the long run. But with pure monopoly barriers to entry prevent the competing away of economic profits by new firms.

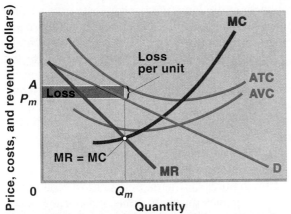

FIGURE 24-4 The loss-minimizing position of a pure monopolist

If demand *D* is weak and costs are high, the pure monopolist may be unable to make a profit. Because P_m exceeds AVC at Q_m, it will minimize losses in the short run by producing at that output where MR = MC. Loss per unit is AP_m, and total losses are indicated by the light red rectangle.

cost comparisons between competitive and monopolistic firms; and (4) technological progress.

Price, Output, and Resource Allocation

In Chapter 23 we concluded that pure competition would result in both "productive efficiency" and "allocative efficiency." Productive efficiency is realized because free entry and exodus of firms would force firms to operate at the optimal rate of output where unit costs of production would be at a minimum. Product price would be at the lowest level consistent with average total costs. In Figure 24-3 the competitive firm would sell Q_c units of output at a price of Q_cP_c.

Allocative efficiency is reflected in the fact that production under competition would occur up to that point at which price (the measure of a product's value to society) would equal marginal cost (the measure of the alternative products forgone by society in producing any given commodity).

Figure 24-3 indicates that, *given the same costs,* a purely monopolistic firm will produce much less desirable results. The pure monopolist will maximize profits by producing an output of Q_m and charging a price of P_m. *The monopolist will find it profitable to sell a smaller output and to charge a higher price than would a compet-*

itive producer.[4] Output Q_m is short of the Q_c point where average total costs are minimized (the intersection of MC and ATC). In column 5 of Table 24-1, ATC at the monopolist's 5 units of output is $94.00 compared to the $91.43 which would result under pure competition. Also, at Q_m units of output, product price is considerably greater than marginal cost. This means that society values additional units of this monopolized product more highly than it does the alternative products resources could otherwise produce. The monopolist's profit-maximizing output results in an underallocation of resources; the monopolist finds it profitable to restrict output and therefore employ fewer resources than are justified from society's standpoint.

[4]In Figure 24-3 the price-quantity comparison of monopoly and pure competition is from the vantage point of the single purely competitive *firm* of Figure 23-7a. An equally illuminating approach is to start with the purely competitive *industry* of Figure 23-7b, reproduced below. Recall that the competitive industry's supply curve *S* is the horizontal sum of the marginal-cost curves of all the firms in the industry. Comparing this with industry demand *D*, we get the purely competitive price and output of P_c and Q_c. Now suppose that this industry becomes a pure monopoly as a result of a wholesale merger or one firm's somehow buying out all its competitors. Assume, too, that no changes in costs or market demand result from this dramatic change in the industry's structure. What were formerly, say, 100 competing firms are now a pure monopolist consisting of 100 branch plants.

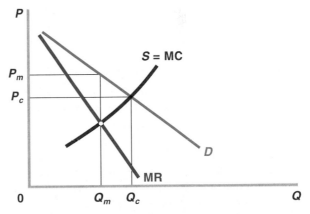

The industry supply curve is now the marginal-cost curve of the monopolist, the summation of the MC curves of its many branch plants. The important change, however, is on the market demand side. From the viewpoint of each individual competitive firm, demand was perfectly elastic, and marginal revenue was therefore equal to price. Each firm equated MC to MR (and therefore to *P*) in maximizing profits (Chapter 23). But industry demand and individual demand are the same to the pure monopolist; the firm *is* the industry, and thus the monopolist correctly envisions a downsloping demand curve *D*. This means that marginal revenue MR will be less than price; graphically the MR curve lies below the demand curve. In choosing the profit-maximizing MC = MR position, the monopolist selects an output Q_m which is smaller, and a price P_m which is greater, than if the industry were organized competitively.

Income Distribution

Business monopoly probably contributes to inequality in income distribution. By virtue of their market power, monopolists charge a higher price than would a purely competitive firm with the same costs; monopolists in effect can levy a "private tax" on consumers and thereby realize substantial economic profits. These monopolistic profits, it should be noted, are not widely distributed because corporate stock ownership is largely concentrated in the hands of upper income groups. The owners of monopolistic enterprises tend to be enriched at the expense of the rest of society.

Cost Complications

Our evaluation of pure monopoly has led us to conclude that, *given identical costs,* a purely monopolistic firm will find it profitable to charge a higher price, produce a smaller output, and foster an allocation of economic resources inferior to that of a purely competitive industry. These contrasting results are rooted in the entry barriers characterizing monopoly.

Now we must recognize that costs may *not* be the same for purely competitive and monopolistic producers. Unit costs incurred by a monopolist may be either larger or smaller than those facing a purely competitive firm. Several potentially conflicting considerations are involved: (1) economies of scale, (2) the notion of "X-inefficiency," (3) monopoly-preserving expenditures, and (4) the "very long-run" perspective which allows for technological progress. We examine the first three issues in this section and technological progress in the ensuing section.

Economies of Scale Revisited   The assumption that unit costs available to the purely competitive and the purely monopolistic firm are the same may not hold in practice. Given production techniques and therefore production costs, consumer demand may not be sufficient to support a large number of competing firms producing at an output which permits each one to realize all *existing* economies of scale. In such instances a firm must be large in relation to the market—it must be monopolistic—to produce efficiently (at low unit cost).

This is shown diagrammatically in Figure 24-5. The argument is that with pure competition or its approximation each firm would have only a small share of the market such as Q_c. This small share forces each

firm back up the long-run average-cost curve so that unit costs are high (AC_c). Economies of scale are *not* being realized and average costs are therefore high.

But with monopoly (or oligopoly) the single (or each of the few) firm(s) can achieve existing scale economies and lower unit costs. In other words, a monopolist or oligopolist may realize output Q_m with the consequent lower average cost of AC_m. Presumably these lower costs—even after allowing for an economic profit—translate into a lower product price than competitive firms could charge.

How important is this exception? Most economists feel that it applies mostly to public utilities and is not significant enough to undermine our general conclusions concerning the restrictive nature of monopoly. Evidence suggests that the large corporations in many manufacturing industries now have more monopoly power than can be justified on the grounds that they are merely availing themselves of existing economies of scale. Again, Chapter 22's Last Word provides relevant evidence suggesting that most industries could be quite competitive at smaller firm sizes without sacrificing economies of scale.

X-Inefficiency   While economies of scale *might* argue for monopoly in a few cases, the notion of X-inefficiency suggests that monopoly costs might be *higher* than those associated with more competitive industries. What is X-inefficiency? Why might it plague monopolists more than competitors?

All the average-cost curves used in this and other chapters are based on the assumption that the firm chooses from *existing* technologies the most efficient one or, in other words, that technology which permits the firm to achieve the minimum average cost for each level of output. **X-inefficiency** occurs when a firm's actual costs of producing any output are greater than the minimum possible costs. In Figure 24-5 X-inefficiency is represented by unit costs of AC_x (as opposed to AC_c) for output Q_c and average costs of AC'_x (rather than AC_m) for output Q_m. Any point above the average-cost curve in Figure 24-5 is attainable but reflects internal inefficiency or "bad management" on the part of the firm.

Why does X-inefficiency occur when it reduces profits? The answer is that managers may often have goals—firm growth, an easier work life, avoidance of business risk, providing jobs for incompetent friends and relatives—which conflict with cost minimization. Or X-inefficiency may arise because a firm's workers

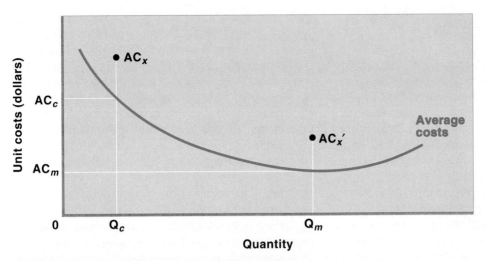

FIGURE 24-5 Economies of scale and X-inefficiency

This diagram serves to demonstrate two unrelated points. First, given the existence of extensive economies of scale, we note that a monopolist can achieve low unit costs of AC_m at Q_m units of output. In contrast, if the market were divided among a number of competing firms so that each produced only Q_c, then scale economies would be unrealized and unit costs of AC_c would be high. The second point is that X-inefficiency—the inefficient internal operation of a firm—results in higher-than-necessary costs. For example, unit costs might be AC_x rather than AC_c for Q_c units of output and AC_x' rather than AC_m for the Q_m level of output.

are poorly motivated. Or a firm may simply become lethargic and relatively inert, relying on rules-of-thumb in decision making as opposed to relevant calculations of costs and revenues.

For our purposes the relevant question is whether monopolistic firms are more susceptible to X-inefficiency than are competitive producers. Presumably this is the case. Theoretically, firms in competitive industries are continually under pressures from rivals which force them to be internally efficient to survive. But monopolists and oligopolists are sheltered from competitive forces by entry barriers and such an environment leads to X-inefficiency. Empirical evidence on X-inefficiency is largely anecdotal and sketchy, but it does suggest that X-inefficiency is greater the smaller the amount of competition. A reasonable estimate is that X-inefficiency may be 5 percent or more of costs for monopolists, but only 3 percent for an "average" oligopolistic industry in which the four largest firms produce 60 percent of total output.[5] In the words of one authority: "The evidence is fragmentary, but it points in the same direction. X-inefficiency exists, and it is more

apt to be reduced when competitive pressures are strong than when firms enjoy insulated market positions."[6]

Rent-Seeking Expenditures Economists use the term **rent-seeking behavior** in referring to activities designed to transfer income or wealth to a particular firm or resource supplier at someone else's or society's expense. We have seen that a monopolist can earn economic profits even in the long run. Therefore, it is no surprise a firm may go to considerable expense to acquire or maintain monopoly privileges granted by government. A monopolist's barrier to entry may depend on legislation or an exclusive license provided by government as in radio and television broadcasting. To sustain or enhance the consequent economic profits, the monopolist may spend large amounts on legal fees, lobbying, and public relations advertising to persuade government to grant or sustain its privileged position. These expenditures add nothing to the firm's output, but clearly increase its costs. Rent-seeking expenditures mean that monopoly might entail higher costs and a greater efficiency loss than suggested by Figure 24-3.

[5]William G. Shepherd, *The Economics of Industrial Organization,* 3d ed. (Englewood Cliffs, N.J.: Prentice-Hall, Inc., 1990), p. 129. For a rather extensive review of case study evidence of X-inefficiency, see Scherer and Ross, pp. 668–672.

[6]Scherer and Ross, p. 672.

Technological Progress: Dynamic Efficiency

We have noted that our condemnation of monopoly must be qualified where *existing* mass-production economies might be lost if an industry comprises a large number of small, competing firms. Now we must consider the issue of **dynamic efficiency,** or whether monopolists are more likely to develop more efficient production techniques over time than competitive firms. Are monopolists more likely to improve productive technology, thereby lowering (shifting downward) their average-cost curves, than are competitive producers? Although we will concentrate on changes in productive techniques, the same question applies to product improvement. Do monopolists have greater means and incentives to improve their products and thus enhance consumer satisfaction? This is fertile ground for honest differences of opinion.

The Competitive Model   Competitive firms certainly have the incentive—indeed, a market mandate—to employ the most efficient *known* productive techniques. Their very survival depends on being efficient. But competition deprives firms of economic profit—an important means and a major incentive to develop *new* and improved productive techniques or *new* products. The profits of technological advance may be short-lived to the innovating competitor. An innovating firm in a competitive industry will find that its rivals will soon duplicate or imitate any technological advance it may achieve; rivals will share the rewards but not the costs of successful technological research.

The Monopoly Model   In contrast—thanks to entry barriers—a monopolist may persistently realize substantial economic profits. Hence, the pure monopolist will have greater financial resources for technological advance than competitive firms. But what about the monopolist's incentives for technological advance? Here the picture is clouded.

There is one imposing argument suggesting that the monopolist's incentives to develop new techniques or products will be weak: The absence of competitors means there is no automatic stimulus to technological advance in a monopolized market. Because of its sheltered market position, the pure monopolist can afford to be inefficient and lethargic. The keen rivalry of a competitive market penalizes the inefficient; an inefficient monopolist does not face this penalty simply because it has no rivals. The monopolist has every reason to be satisfied with the status quo, to become complacent. It might well pay the monopolist to withhold or "file" technological improvements in both productive techniques and products to exploit existing capital equipment fully. New and improved techniques and products may be suppressed by monopolists to avoid losses caused by the sudden obsolescence of existing machinery and equipment. And, even when improved techniques are belatedly introduced by monopolists, the accompanying cost reductions will accrue to the monopolist as increases in profits and only partially, if at all, to consumers in the form of lower prices and increased output.

Proponents of this view point out that in a number of industries which approximate monopoly—for example, steel and aluminum—interest in research has been minimal. Such advances as have occurred have come largely from outside the industry or from smaller firms which make up the "competitive fringe" of the industry.

Basically, there are at least two counterarguments:
1   Technological advance lowers unit costs and thereby expands profits. As our analysis of Figure 24-3 implies, lower costs will give rise to a profit-maximizing position which involves a larger output and a lower price than previously. Any expansion of profits will not be of a transitory nature; barriers to entry protect the monopolist from profit encroachment by rivals. In short, technological progress is profitable to the monopolist and therefore will be undertaken.
2   Research and technological advance may be one of the monopolist's barriers to entry; hence, the monopolist must persist and succeed in technological advance or fall prey to new competitors, including those located abroad. Technological progress, it is argued, is essential to the maintenance of monopoly.

A Mixed Picture   What can be offered by way of a summarizing generalization on the economic efficiency of pure monopoly? In a static economy, where economies of scale are equally accessible to purely competitive and monopolist firms, pure competition will be superior to pure monopoly in that pure competition forces use of the best-known technology and allocates resources according to the wants of society. However, when economies of scale available to the monopolist are not attainable by small competitive producers, or in a dynamic context in which changes in the rate of technological advance must be considered, the inefficiencies of pure monopoly are somewhat less evident.

◆ *The monopolist maximizes profits (or minimizes losses) at the output where MR = MC and charges the price on its demand curve which corresponds to this output.*

◆ *Given identical costs, a monopolist will be less efficient than a purely competitive firm because the monopolist produces less output and charges a higher price.*

◆ *The inefficiencies of monopoly may be offset or lessened by economies of scale and technological progress, but intensified by the presence of X-inefficiency and rent-seeking expenditures.*

PRICE DISCRIMINATION

Up to now we have assumed that the monopolist charges a uniform price to all buyers. Under certain conditions the monopolist can exploit its market position more fully and thus increase profits by charging different prices to different buyers. In so doing the seller is engaging in price discrimination. **Price discrimination** *occurs when a given product is sold at more than one price and these price differences are not justified by cost differences.*

Conditions

The opportunity to engage in price discrimination is not readily available to all sellers. In general, price discrimination is workable when three conditions are realized.

1 Monopoly Power The seller must be a monopolist or, at least, possess some degree of monopoly power, that is, some ability to control output and price.

2 Market Segregation The seller must be able to segregate buyers into separate classes where each group has a different willingness or ability to pay for the product. This separation of buyers is usually based on different elasticities of demand as later illustrations will make clear.

3 No Resale The original purchaser cannot resell the product or service. If buyers in the low-price segment of the market can easily resell in the high-price segment, the monopolist's price discrimination strategy creates competitive sellers with the monopolist in the high-price segment of the market. This competition will reduce price in the high-price segment and undermine the monopolist's price discrimination policy. This correctly suggests that service industries such as the transportation industry or legal and medical services, where resale is impossible, are especially susceptible to price discrimination.

Illustrations

Price discrimination is widely practiced in our economy. The sales representative who must communicate important information to corporate headquarters has a highly inelastic demand for long-distance telephone service and pays the high daytime rate. The college student making a periodic "reporting in" call to the folks at home has an elastic demand and defers the call to take advantage of lower evening or weekend rates. Electric utilities frequently segment their markets by end uses, such as lighting and heating. The absence of reasonable substitutes means that the demand for electricity for illumination is inelastic and the price per kilowatt hour for this use is high. But the availability of natural gas and petroleum as alternatives to electrical heating makes the demand for electricity less inelastic for this purpose and the price charged is lower. Similarly, industrial users of electricity are typically charged lower rates than residential users because the former may have the alternative of constructing their own generating equipment while the individual household does not.

Movie theaters and golf courses vary their charges on the basis of time (higher rates in the evening and on weekends when demand is strong) and age (ability to pay). Railroads vary the rate charged per ton mile of freight according to the market value of the product being shipped. The shipper of 10 tons of television sets or costume jewelry will be charged more than the shipper of 10 tons of gravel or coal. Airlines charge high fares to traveling executives, whose demand for travel is inelastic, and offer a variety of lower fares in the guise of "family rates" and "standby fares" to attract vacationers and others whose demands are more elastic. Hotels, restaurants, theaters, and pharmacies frequently give discounts to retired people. In international trade, price discrimination is called "dumping." A South Korean electronics manufacturer, for example, might sell TV sets for $100 less in the United States than it charges domestically.

MICROECONOMICS OF PRODUCT AND RESOURCE MARKETS

Consequences

The economic consequences of price discrimination are twofold.

1 It is not surprising that a monopolist will be able to increase its profits by practicing price discrimination.

2 Other things being equal, a discriminating monopolist will produce a larger output than a nondiscrimination monopolist.

1 More Profits The simplest way to understand why price discrimination can yield additional profits is to look again at our monopolist's downsloping demand curve in Figure 24-3. Although the profit-maximizing uniform price is $122, the segment of the demand curve lying above the profit area in Figure 24-3 tells us there are buyers willing to pay *more than* P_m ($122) rather than forgo the product.

If the monopolist can identify and segregate each of these buyers and charge the maximum price each would pay, the sale of any given level of output will be more profitable. In columns 1 and 2 of Table 24-1 we note that buyers of the first 4 units of output would be willing to pay more than the equilibrium price of $122. If the seller could practice perfect price discrimination by extracting the maximum price each buyer would pay, total revenue would increase from $610 (=$122 × 5) to $710 (=$122 + $132 + $142 + $152 + $162) and profits would increase from $140 (=$610 − $470) to $240 (=$710 − $470).

2 More Production Other things being the same, the discriminating monopolist will choose to produce a larger output than the nondiscriminating monopolist. Recall that when the nondiscriminating monopolist lowers price to sell additional output, the lower price will apply not only to the additional sales but also to *all* prior units of output. As a result, marginal revenue is less than price and, graphically, the marginal-revenue curve lies below the demand curve. The fact that marginal revenue is less than price is a disincentive to increased production.

But when a perfectly discriminating monopolist lowers price, the reduced price applies *only* to the additional unit sold and *not* to prior units. Hence, price and marginal revenue are equal for any unit of output. Graphically, the perfectly discriminating monopolist's marginal-revenue curve will coincide with its demand curve and the disincentive to increased production is removed. As indicated in Table 24-1, because marginal revenue now equals price, the monopolist will find that it is profitable to produce 7, rather than 5, units of out-

put. The additional revenue from the sixth and seventh units is $214 (=$112 + $102). Thus total revenue for 7 units is $924 (=$710 + $214). Total costs for 7 units are $640, so profits are $284.

Ironically, although price discrimination increases the monopolist's profit compared to a nondiscriminating monopolist, it also results in greater output and thus less allocative inefficiency. In our example, the output level of 7 units matches that which would occur in pure competition. That is, allocative efficiency (P = MC) is achieved.

Questions 5 and 6 at the end of this chapter may be helpful in comparing the price and output decisions of a nondiscriminating and a discriminating monopolist.

REGULATED MONOPOLY

Most purely monopolistic industries are natural monopolies and subject to regulation. In particular, the prices or rates public utilities—telephone companies, natural gas and electricity suppliers—can charge are determined by a Federal, state, or local regulatory commission or board.

Figure 24-6 shows the demand and long-run cost conditions of a natural monopoly. Because of the advantages of larger firm size, demand cuts the average-cost curve at a point where long-run average cost is still falling. It would be inefficient to have many firms in

FIGURE 24-6 Regulated monopoly

Price regulation can improve the social consequences of a natural monopoly. The socially optimal price P_r will result in an efficient allocation of resources but is likely to entail losses and therefore call for permanent public subsidies. The "fair-return" price P_f will allow the monopolist to break even, but will not fully correct the underallocation of resources.

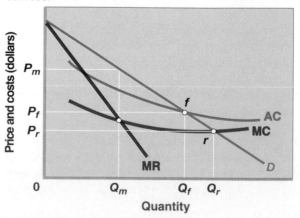

such an industry because, by dividing the market, each firm would move further to the left on its average-cost curve so unit costs would be substantially higher. The relationship between market demand and costs is such that the attainment of low unit costs presumes only one producer.

We know by application of the MR = MC rule that P_m and Q_m are the profit-maximizing price and output which the unregulated monopolist would choose. Because price exceeds average total cost at Q_m, the monopolist enjoys a substantial economic profit. Furthermore, price exceeds marginal cost, indicating an underallocation of resources to this product or service. Can government regulation bring about better results from society's point of view?

Socially Optimal Price: *P* = MC

If the objective of our regulatory commission is to achieve allocative efficiency, it should attempt to establish a legal (ceiling) price for the monopolist equal to *marginal cost*. Remembering that each point on the market demand curve designates a price-quantity combination, and noting that marginal cost cuts the demand curve only at point r, it is clear that P_r is the only price equal to marginal cost. The imposition of this maximum or ceiling price causes the monopolist's effective demand curve to become $P_r r D$; the demand curve becomes perfectly elastic, and therefore P_r = MR, out to point r, where the regulated price ceases to be effective.

The important point is that, given the legal price P_r, the monopolist will maximize profits or minimize losses by producing Q_r units of output, because it is at this output that MR ($= P_r$) = MC. By making it illegal to charge more than P_r per unit, the regulatory agency has eliminated the monopolist's incentive to restrict output to benefit from a higher price.

In short, by imposing the legal price P_r and letting the monopolist choose its profit-maximizing or loss-minimizing output, the allocative results of pure competition can be simulated. Production takes place where P_r = MC, and this equality indicates an efficient allocation of resources to this product or service.[7] This price which achieves allocative efficiency is called the **socially optimal price.**

[7]While "allocative efficiency" is achieved, "productive efficiency" would only be achieved by chance. In Figure 24-6 we note that production takes place at Q_r which is less than the output at which average costs are minimized. Can you redraw Figure 24-6 to show those special conditions where both allocative and productive efficiency are realized?

"Fair-Return" Price: *P* = AC

But the socially optimal price P_r may pose a problem of losses for the regulated firm. The price which equals marginal cost may be so low that average total costs are not covered, as is shown in Figure 24-6. The inevitable result is losses. The reason for this lies in the basic character of public utilities. Because they are required to meet "peak" demands (both daily and seasonally) for their product or service, they have substantial excess productive capacity when demand is relatively "normal." This high level of investment in capital facilities means that unit costs of production are likely to decline over a wide range of output. In technical terms, the market demand curve in Figure 24-6 cuts marginal cost at a point to the left of the marginal-cost–average-total-cost intersection, so the socially optimal price is necessarily below AC. Therefore, to enforce a socially optimal price on the regulated monopolist would mean short-run losses, and in the long run, bankruptcy for the utility.

What to do? One option would be a public subsidy to cover the loss which marginal-cost pricing would entail. Another possibility is condoning price discrimination and hoping that the additional revenue gained will permit the firm to cover costs.

In practice, regulatory commissions have pursued a third option; they tend to back away somewhat from the objective of allocative efficiency and marginal-cost pricing. Most regulatory agencies in the United States are concerned with establishing a **"fair-return" price.** This is so because, as the courts have seen it, a socially optimal price would lead to losses and eventual bankruptcy and thereby deprive the monopoly's owners of their private property without "due process of law." Indeed, the Supreme Court has held that regulatory agencies must permit a "fair return" to owners.

Remembering that total costs include a normal or "fair" profit, we see that the "fair" or "fair-return" price in Figure 24-6 would be P_f, where price equals *average* cost. Because the demand curve cuts average cost only at point f, clearly P_f is the only price which permits a fair return. The corresponding output at regulated price P_f will be Q_f. Total revenue of $0P_f f Q_f$ will equal total costs of the same amount and the firm will realize a normal profit.

Dilemma of Regulation

Comparing results of the socially optimal price (P = MC) and the fair-return price (P = AC) suggests a policy dilemma, sometimes termed the **dilemma of regu-**

LAST WORD

MONOPOLIES IN THE NATIONAL PARKS

Few people recognize that the facilities found in our national parks are operated by government-sponsored monopolies.

In the early years of the National Park Service (NPS), officials felt that it was necessary to provide services— modern campgrounds, restaurants, motels and lodges, shops and stores, and ski lifts—to attract visitors. To achieve this, the NPS negotiated long-term contracts on highly favorable terms to private concessionaires. For example, in 1963 the Curry Company, a subsidiary of entertainment giant Music Corporation of America, was granted virtually exclusive rights to do business in Yosemite National Park for a fee of 0.75 percent of gross revenues. In 1988 the NPS collected only $590,000 on the basis of gross sales by Curry of almost $79 million. Critics estimate Curry's 1988 profits were from $10 to $20 million. Across the nation NPS fees averaged only about 2.5 percent of gross revenues. At the Grand Canyon the government received $1.2 million on the basis of concessionaire revenues of almost $49 million. In 1990 the 75 largest concessionaires paid the government just $12.3 million or 2.5 percent on sales of $486 million.

Critics contend, first, that this is an outrageous, wholly unjustified granting of monopoly power by the NPS. Second, environmentalists argue that concessionaires are opposed to policies designed to protect the parks from deterioration through overuse. For example, they say the Curry Company has been successful in stalling a plan to restrict greatly automobile traffic

and to remove some motel rooms and employee housing from Yosemite because of potentially adverse effects on sales revenues.

The concessionaires defend current arrangements, contending that they have resulted in a high level of visitor services under adverse conditions of short visitor seasons and high construction and operating costs. Furthermore, the private concessionaires assert they are able to maintain and modify facilities without the inevitable delays associated with governmental bureaucracies. In short, concessionaires hold that the present system has worked in the public interest.

Many concessionaire agreements are soon coming up for renewal and the NPS is seeking to shorten the duration of contracts and to raise its fees to 22 percent of gross revenues.

---

lation. When price is set to achieve the most efficient allocation of resources ($P = MC$), the regulated utility is likely to suffer losses. Survival of the firm would presumably depend on permanent public subsidies out of tax revenues. On the other hand, although a fair-return price ($P = AC$) allows the monopolist to cover costs, it only partially resolves the underallocation of resources which the unregulated monopoly would foster. That is, the fair-return price would only increase output from Q_m to Q_f, while the socially optimal output is Q_r. Despite this problem, regulation can improve on the results of monopoly from the social point of view. Price regulation can simultaneously reduce price, increase output, and reduce the economic profits of monopolies.

QUICK REVIEW 24-3

♦ *Price discrimination occurs when a seller charges different prices which are not based on cost differentials.*

♦ *The conditions necessary for price discrimination are: **a** monopoly power; **b** the segregation of buyers on the basis of different demand elasticities; and **c** the inability of buyers to resell the product.*

♦ *Monopoly price can be reduced and output increased through government regulation.*

♦ *The socially optimal price (P = MC) achieves allocative efficiency but may result in losses; the fair-return price (P = AC) yields a normal profit but falls short of allocative efficiency.*

CHAPTER SUMMARY

1 A pure monopolist is the sole producer of a commodity for which there are no close substitutes.

2 Barriers to entry, in the form of **a** economies of scale, **b** natural monopolies, **c** patent ownership and research, and **d** ownership or control of essential resources, help explain the existence of pure monopoly and other imperfectly competitive market structures. Barriers to entry which are formidable in the short run may prove to be surmountable in the long run.

3 The pure monopolist's market situation differs from a competitive firm's in that the monopolist's demand curve is downsloping, causing the marginal-revenue curve to lie below the demand curve. Like the competitive seller, the pure monopolist will maximize profits by equating marginal revenue and marginal cost. Barriers to entry may permit a monopolist to acquire economic profits even in the long run. Note, however, that **a** the monopolist does not charge "the highest price it can get"; **b** the maximum total profit sought by the monopolist rarely coincides with maximum unit profits; **c** high costs and a weak demand may prevent the monopolist from realizing any profit at all; and **d** the monopolist will want to avoid the inelastic range of its demand curve.

4 Given the same costs, the pure monopolist will find it profitable to restrict output and charge a higher price than would a competitive seller. This restriction of output causes resources to be misallocated, as is evidenced by the fact that price exceeds marginal cost in monopolized markets.

5 Monopoly also tends to increase income inequality.

6 The costs of monopolists and competitive producers may not be the same. On the one hand, economies of scale may make lower unit costs accessible to monopolists but not to competitors. On the other hand, X-inefficiency—the failure to produce with the least-costly combination of inputs—is more common to monopolists than to competitive firms and monopolists may make sizable expenditures to maintain monopoly privileges conferred by government.

7 Economists disagree as to how conducive pure monopoly is to technological advance. Some feel pure monopoly is more progressive than pure competition because its ability to realize economic profits helps finance technological research. Others, however, argue that absence of rival firms and the monopolist's desire to exploit fully its existing capital facilities weaken the monopolist's incentive to innovate.

8 A monopolist can increase its profits by practicing price discrimination, provided it can segregate buyers on the basis of different elasticities of demand and the product or service cannot be readily transferred between the segregated markets. Other things being equal, the discriminating monopolist will produce a larger output than will the nondiscriminating monopolist.

9 Price regulation can be invoked to eliminate wholly or partially the tendency of monopolists to underallocate resources and to earn economic profits. The "socially optimal" price is determined where the demand and marginal-cost curves intersect; the "fair-return" price is determined where the demand and average-cost curves intersect.

TERMS AND CONCEPTS

pure monopoly	rent-seeking behavior	socially optimal price	the dilemma of
barriers to entry	dynamic efficiency	fair-return price	regulation
X-inefficiency	price discrimination		

QUESTIONS AND STUDY SUGGESTIONS

1 "No firm is completely sheltered from rivals; all firms compete for consumer dollars. Pure monopoly, therefore, does not exist." Do you agree? Explain.

2 Discuss the major barriers to entry. Explain how each barrier can foster monopoly or oligopoly. Which barriers, if any, do you feel give rise to monopoly that is socially justifiable?

3 How does the demand curve faced by a purely monopolistic seller differ from that confronting a purely competitive firm? Why does it differ? Of what significance is the difference? Why is the pure monopolist's demand curve not perfectly inelastic?

4 Use the demand schedule below to calculate total revenue and marginal revenue. Plot the demand, total-revenue, and marginal-revenue curves and carefully explain the relationships between them. Explain why the marginal revenue of the fourth unit of output is $3.50, even though its price is $5.00. Use Chapter 20's total-revenue test for price elasticity to designate the elastic and inelastic segments of your graphed demand curve. What generalization can you make regarding the relationship between marginal revenue and elasticity of demand? Suppose that somehow the marginal cost of successive units of output were zero. What output would the profit-seeking firm produce? Finally, use your analysis to explain why a monopolist would never produce in that range of its demand curve which is inelastic.

Price	Quantity demanded	Price	Quantity demanded
$7.00	0	$4.50	5
6.50	1	4.00	6
6.00	2	3.50	7
5.50	3	3.00	8
5.00	4	2.50	9

5 Suppose a pure monopolist is faced with the demand schedule shown below and the same cost data as the competitive producer discussed in question 4 at the end of Chapter 23. Calculate total and marginal revenue and determine the profit-maximizing price and output for this monopolist. What is the level of profits? Verify your answer graphically and by comparing total revenue and total cost. If this firm could engage in perfect price discrimination, what would be the level of output? Of profits?

Price	Quantity demanded	Total revenue	Marginal revenue
$115	0	$_____	
100	1	_____	$_____
83	2	_____	_____
71	3	_____	_____
63	4	_____	_____
55	5	_____	_____
48	6	_____	_____
42	7	_____	_____
37	8	_____	_____
33	9	_____	_____
29	10	_____	

6 Draw a diagram showing the relevant demand, marginal-revenue, average-cost, and marginal-cost curves and the equilibrium price and output for a nondiscriminating monopolist. Use the same diagram to show the equilibrium position of a monopolist able to practice perfect price discrimination. Compare equilibrium outputs, total revenues, and economic profits in the two cases. Comment on the economic desirability of price discrimination.

7 Assume a pure monopolist and a purely competitive firm have the same unit costs. Contrast the two with respect to **a** price, **b** output, **c** profits, **d** allocation of resources, and **e** impact upon the distribution of income. Since both monopolists and competitive firms follow the MC = MR rule in maximizing profits, how do you account for the different results? Why might the costs of a purely competitive firm and a monopolist *not* be the same? What are the implications of such cost differences?

8 Carefully evaluate the following widely held viewpoint. Can you offer any arguments to the contrary?

A monopoly is usually not under pressure to *invent* new products or methods. Nor does it have strong incentives to *innovate:* to apply those new inventions in practice and bring new products to the market. *The monopoly may choose to invent and innovate, but it will do so only at its own pace.* Because the new product cuts the value of the existing products, the monopoly will tend to hold back on innovation. Typically it innovates only when a smaller competitor forces its hand. Even if its capital is outdated or its products mediocre, a monopolist may prefer to protect and continue them rather than to replace them with better ones.[8]

9 Critically evaluate and explain:
    a "Because they can control product price, monopolists are always assured of profitable production by simply charging the highest price consumers will pay."
    b "The pure monopolist seeks that output which will yield the greatest per unit profit."
    c "An excess of price over marginal cost is the market's way of signaling the need for more production of a good."
    d "The more profitable a firm, the greater its monopoly power."
    e "The monopolist has a price policy; the competitive producer does not."
    f "With respect to resource allocation, the interests of the seller and of society coincide in a purely competitive market but conflict in a monopolized market."
    g "In a sense the monopolist makes a profit for not producing; the monopolist produces profits more than it does goods."

10 Assume a monopolistic publisher has agreed to pay an author 15 percent of the total revenue from the sales of a text. Will the author and the publisher want to charge the same price for the text? Explain.

11 Suppose a firm's demand curve lies below its average-total-cost curve at all levels of output. Can you conceive of any circumstance in which production might be profitable?

12 Are colleges and universities engaging in price discrimination when they charge full tuition to some students and provide financial aid to others? What are the advantages and disadvantages of this practice?

13 Explain verbally and graphically how price (rate) regulation may improve the performance of monopolies. In your answer distinguish between **a** socially optimal (marginal-cost) pricing and **b** fair-return (average-cost) pricing. What is the "dilemma of regulation"?

14 It has been proposed that natural monopolists should be allowed to determine their profit-maximizing outputs and prices and then government should tax their profits away and distribute them to consumers in proportion to their purchases from the monopoly. Is this proposal as socially desirable as requiring monopolists to equate price with marginal cost or average cost?

[8]William G. Shepherd, *Public Policies Toward Business,* 8th ed. (Homewood, Ill.: Richard D. Irwin, Inc., 1991), p. 36.

Price and Output Determination: Monopolistic Competition

If you live in a town or city of any reasonable size, you have a wide array of choices in buying many products. Suppose you want to purchase a sweater. You might patronize a discount store whose newspaper flier advertises an imported acrylic for $12. Or you might select a fleece pullover with your college's logo and colors advertised in your campus newspaper for $20 on sale at your bookstore. Alternatively, you might buy a cotton knit for $45 from any one of a number of mail-order catalogs. Or you could shop at an "upscale" clothier and pay $80 or $90 or more for a wool sweater. These product choices reflect the world of monopolistic competition where competition is not only based on price, but also on product quality, services, and advertising.

Pure competition and pure monopoly are the exception, not the rule, in our economy. Most market structures fall somewhere between these two extremes. In Chapter 26 we will discuss oligopoly, a market structure close to pure monopoly. In this chapter we examine monopolistic competition. Monopolistic competition correctly suggests a blending of monopoly and competition; more specifically, monopolistic competition involves a very considerable amount of competition mixed with a small dose of monopoly power.

Our objectives are to (1) define and discuss the nature and prevalence of monopolistic competition, (2) analyze and evaluate the price-output behavior of monopolistically competitive firms, and (3) explain and assess the role of nonprice competition, that is, competition based on product quality and advertising, in monopolistically competitive industries.

MONOPOLISTIC COMPETITION: CONCEPT AND OCCURRENCE

Let's recall and expand on our definition of monopolistic competition.

Relatively Large Numbers

Monopolistic competition refers to that market situation in which a relatively large number of small producers or sellers offer similar but not identical products. The contrasts between this and pure competition are important. Monopolistic competition does not require the presence of hundreds or thousands of firms but only a fairly large number—say 25, 35, 60, or 70.

Several important characteristics of monopolistic competition follow from the presence of relatively large numbers.

1 Small Market Share Each firm has a comparatively small percentage of the total market, so each has a very limited amount of control over market price.

2 No Collusion The presence of a relatively large number of firms also ensures that collusion—concerted action by firms to restrict output and rig price—is all but impossible.

3 Independent Actions Finally, with numerous firms in the industry, there is no feeling of mutual interdependence among them; each firm determines its policies without considering possible reactions of rival firms. This is a very reasonable way to act in a market in which one's rivals are numerous. After all, the 10 or 15 percent increase in sales which firm X may realize by cutting price will be spread so thinly over its 20, 40, or 60 rivals that, for all practical purposes, the impact on their sales will be imperceptible. Rivals' reactions can be ignored because the impact of one firm's actions on each of its many rivals is so small that these rivals will have no reason to react.

Product Differentiation

Also in contrast to pure competition, monopolistic competition has the fundamental feature of **product differentiation.** Purely competitive firms produce a standardized or homogeneous product; monopolistically competitive producers turn out variations of a given product. In fact, product differentiation may take a number of different forms.

1 Product Quality Product differentiation may take the form of physical or qualitative differences in products themselves. "Real" differences in functional features, materials, design, and workmanship are vitally important aspects of product differentiation. Personal computers, for example, differ in terms of hardware capacity, software, graphics, and how "user-friendly" they are. There are scores of competing principles of economics texts which differ in content, organization, presentation and readability, pedagogical aids, and

graphics and design. Any good-sized city will have a variety of retail stores selling men's and women's clothing varying greatly in styling, materials, and quality of workmanship. Similarly, one fast-food hamburger chain may feature lean beef, while a competitor stresses the juiciness of its hamburgers.

2 Services Services and conditions surrounding the sale of a product are important aspects of product differentiation. One grocery store may stress the helpfulness of its clerks who bag your groceries and carry them to your car. A "warehouse" competitor may leave bagging and carrying to its customers, but feature lower prices. "One-day" clothes cleaning may be preferred to cleaning of equal quality which takes three days. The "snob appeal" of a store, the courteousness and helpfulness of clerks, the firm's reputation for servicing or exchanging its products, and credit availability are all service aspects of product differentiation.

3 Location Products may also be differentiated as to location and accessibility. Small minigroceries or convenience stores successfully compete with large supermarkets, even though they have a more limited range of products and charge higher prices. They compete on the basis of location—being close to customers and on busy streets—and by staying open 24 hours a day. Similarly, a gas station's proximity to the interstate highway gives it a locational advantage which may allow it to sell gasoline at a higher price than could a gas station in a city 2 or 3 miles from the interstate.

4 Promotion and Packaging Product differentiation may also arise from perceived differences created through advertising, packaging, and the use of brand names and trademarks. A celebrity's name associated with jeans or perfume may enhance those products in the minds of buyers. Many consumers regard toothpaste packaged in a "pump" container as preferable to the same toothpaste in a conventional tube. While there are many aspirin-type products, product promotion and advertising may convince many consumers that Bayer or Anacin is superior and worth a higher price than a generic substitute.

One important implication of product differentiation is that, despite the presence of a relatively large number of firms, monopolistically competitive producers do have limited control over the prices of their products. Consumers prefer the products of specific sellers and *within limits* will pay more to satisfy those preferences. Sellers and buyers are no longer linked at random, as in a purely competitive market.

Nonprice Competition

Under monopolistic competition economic rivalry centers not only on price, but also on such nonprice factors as product quality, advertising, and conditions associated with the sale of a product. Because products are differentiated, they can be varied over time and the differentiating features of each firm's product will be susceptible to advertising and other forms of sales promotion. Great emphasis is placed on trademarks and brand names to convince consumers that a firm's product is better than its rivals.

Easy Entry

Entry into monopolistically competitive industries tends to be relatively easy. The fact that monopolistically competitive producers are typically small-sized firms, both absolutely and relatively, suggests that economies of scale and capital requirements are few. On the other hand, compared with pure competition, added financial barriers may result from the need to develop a product different from one's rivals and the obligation to advertise it. Existing firms may hold pat-

ents on their products and copyrights on their brand names and trademarks, enhancing the difficulty and cost of successfully imitating them.

Illustrations

Table 25-1 lists a group of manufacturing industries which approximate monopolistic competition. In addition, retail stores in metropolitan areas are generally monopolistically competitive; grocery stores, gasoline stations, barber shops, dry cleaners, clothing stores, and so forth, operate under conditions similar to those we have described.

PRICE AND OUTPUT DETERMINATION

We now analyze the price-output behavior of a monopolistically competitive firm. We assume initially that the firms in the industry are producing *given* products and engaging in a *given* amount of promotional activity. Later we note how product variation and advertising modify our discussion.

The Firm's Demand Curve

Our explanation is couched in terms of Figure 25-1 (Key Graph). The basic feature of this diagram, which sets it off from our analyses of pure competition and pure monopoly, is the elasticity of the firm's individual demand, or sales, curve. *The demand curve faced by a monopolistically competitive seller is highly, but not perfectly, elastic.* It is much more elastic than the demand curve of the pure monopolist, because the monopolistically competitive seller is faced with many rivals producing close-substitute goods. The pure monopolist, of course, has no rivals at all. Yet, for two reasons, the monopolistically competitive seller's sales curve is not perfectly elastic as is the purely competitive producer's: First, the monopolistically competitive firm has fewer rivals, and, second, the products of these rivals are close but not perfect substitutes.

Generally speaking, the precise degree of elasticity embodied in the monopolistically competitive firm's demand curve will depend on the exact number of rivals and the degree of product differentiation. The larger the number of rivals and the weaker the product differentiation, the greater will be the elasticity of each seller's demand curve, that is, the closer the situation will be to pure competition.

TABLE 25-1 **Percentage of output* produced by firms in selected low-concentration manufacturing industries**

Industry	Four largest firms	Eight largest firms	Twenty largest firms
Men's and boys' suits and coats	25%	37%	57%
Mattresses and bedsprings	23	31	43
Prefab metal buildings	21	31	50
Women's and misses' suits and coats	19	28	40
Book publishing	17	30	56
Upholstered furniture	17	25	39
Wood furniture	16	23	37
Metal house furniture	16	26	44
Paperboard boxes	15	26	43
Bolts, nuts, and rivets	13	23	38
Fur goods	12	19	33
Metal doors	11	17	30
Women's and misses' dresses	6	10	17

*As measured by value of industry shipments. Data are for 1982.
Source: Bureau of the Census, *1982 Census of Manufacturers.*

KEY GRAPHS

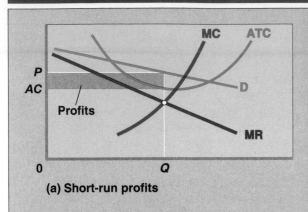

(a) Short-run profits

FIGURE 25-1
Monopolistically competitive firms tend to realize a normal profit in the long run

The economic profits shown in (a) will induce new firms to enter, causing the profits to be competed away. The losses indicated in (b) will cause an exodus of firms until normal profits are restored. Thus in (c), where price just covers unit costs at the MR = MC output, the firm's long-run equilibrium position is portrayed.

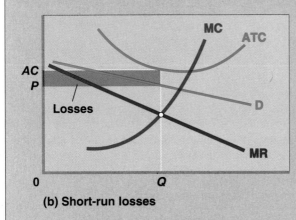

(b) Short-run losses

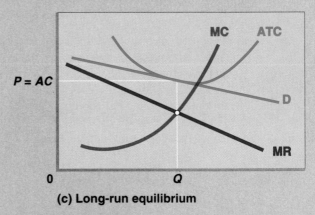

(c) Long-run equilibrium

The Short Run: Profits or Losses

The firm will maximize its profits or minimize its losses in the short run by producing that output designated by the equality of marginal cost and marginal revenue, for reasons with which we are now familiar. Our firm of Figure 25-1a produces an output Q, charges a price P, and realizes a total profit of the size indicated in gray. But a less favorable cost and demand situation may exist, putting the monopolistically competitive firm in the position of realizing losses in the short run. This is illustrated by the light red area in Figure 25-1b. In the short run the monopolistically competitive firm may either realize an economic profit or be faced with losses.

The Long Run: Break Even

In the long run, however, the *tendency* is for monopolistically competitive firms to earn a normal profit or, in other words, to break even.

Profits: Firms Enter   In the short-run profits case, Figure 25-1a, economic profits will attract new rivals, because entry is relatively easy. As new firms enter, the demand curve faced by the typical firms will fall (shift to the left) and become more elastic. Why? Because each firm has a smaller share of the total demand and now faces a larger number of close-substitute products. This in turn tends to cause the economic profits to disappear. When the demand curve is tangent to the average-cost curve at the profit-maximizing output, as shown in Figure 25-1c, the firm is just breaking even. Output Q is the equilibrium output for the firm; as Figure 25-1c clearly indicates, any deviation from that output will entail average costs which exceed product price and, therefore, losses for the firm. Furthermore, economic profits have been competed away, and there is no incentive for more firms to enter.

Losses: Firms Leave   In the short-run losses case, Figure 25-1b, an exodus of firms would occur in the long run. Faced with fewer substitute products and blessed with an expanded share of total demand, surviving firms will find that their losses disappear and gradually give way to approximately normal profits. (For simplicity's sake we have assumed constant costs; shifts in the cost curves as firms enter or leave would complicate our discussion slightly, but would not alter the conclusions.)

Complications We have been careful to say that the representative firm in a monopolistically competitive market *tends* to break even, or earn a normal profit, in the long run. Certain complicating factors prevent us from being more definite than this.

1 Some firms may achieve a measure of product differentiation which cannot be duplicated by rivals even over a long span of time. A given gasoline station may have the only available location at the busiest intersection in town. Or a firm may hold a patent giving it a slight and more-or-less permanent advantage over imitators. Such firms may realize a sliver of economic profits even in the long run.

2 Remember that entry is not completely unrestricted. Because of product differentiation, there are likely to be greater financial barriers to entry than otherwise would be the case. This again suggests that some economic profits may persist even in the long run.

3 A final consideration may work in the opposite direction, causing losses—below-normal profits—to persist in the long run. The proprietors of a corner delicatessen persistently accept a return less than they could earn elsewhere because their business is a "way of life" to them. The suburban barber ekes out a meager existence, because cutting hair is "all he wants to do." With all things considered, however, the long-run normal profit equilibrium of Figure 25-1c is a reasonable portrayal of reality.

WASTES OF MONOPOLISTIC COMPETITION

Recalling our evaluation of competitive pricing in Chapter 23, we know that economic efficiency requires the triple equality of price, marginal cost, and average cost. The equality of price and marginal cost is necessary for the realization of *allocative efficiency,* that is, the allocation of the right amount of resources to the product. The equality of price with minimum average total cost suggests the achievement of *productive efficiency* or the use of the most efficient (least-cost) technology; this equality means consumers will enjoy the largest volume of the product and the lowest price which least-cost conditions allow.

Excess Capacity

In monopolistically competitive markets neither allocative nor productive efficiency is realized. An examination of Figure 25-2, which enlarges the relevant portion of Figure 25-1c and adds detail, suggests that the monopolistic element in monopolistic competition causes a modest underallocation of resources to goods produced under this market structure. Price (*a*) exceeds marginal cost (*b*) in long-run equilibrium, indicating that society values additional units of this commodity more than the alternative products the needed resources can otherwise produce.

Furthermore, in contrast to purely competitive firms, we observe in Figure 25-2 that monopolistically competitive firms produce somewhat short of the most efficient (least unit cost) output. Production entails higher unit costs (*a*) than the minimum attainable (*c*). This means a somewhat higher price (*a*) than would result under competition (*c*). Consumers do *not* benefit from the largest output and lowest price which cost conditions permit. Indeed, monopolistically competitive firms must charge a higher than competitive price in the long run to achieve a normal profit. Viewed differently, if each firm could produce at the most efficient output, fewer firms could produce the same total output, and the product could be sold at a lower price. Monopolistically competitive industries tend to be overcrowded with firms, each of which is underutilized, that is, operating short of optimal capacity. This is typified by many kinds of retail establishments, for example, the thirty or forty gasoline stations, all operating with excess capacity, that populate a medium-sized city. These are the so-called **wastes of monopolistic competition,** the underutilized plants and consumers penalized through higher than competitive prices for this underutilization.

Redeeming Features?

In many monopolistically competitive industries, however, the price and output results are not drastically different from those of pure competition. The highly elastic nature of each firm's demand curve guarantees that results are nearly competitive.

Furthermore, the product differentiation characterizing monopolistic competition means buyers can select from many variations of the same general product, better satisfying the diverse tastes of consumers.

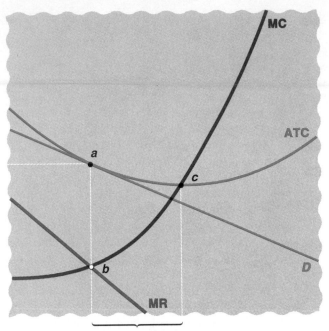

Excess capacity

FIGURE 25-2   The inefficiency aspects of monopolistic competition

In long-run equilibrium a monopolistically competitive firm achieves neither allocative nor productive efficiency. An underallocation of resources is reflected in the fact that the product price of *a* exceeds marginal cost of *b*. Productive efficiency is not realized because production occurs where unit costs of *a* exceed the minimum attainable unit cost of *c*.

In fact, there is a tradeoff between product differentiation and the production of a given product at the minimum average cost. The stronger the product differentiation (the less elastic the demand curve), the further to the left of the minimum average costs will production take place. But the greater the product differentiation, the more likely diverse tastes will be fully satisfied. The greater the excess capacity problem, the wider the range of consumer choice.

QUICK REVIEW 25-1

♦   *Monopolistic competition refers to industries which comprise a relatively large number of firms, operating noncollusively, in the production of differentiated products.*

♦   *In the short run a monopolistically competitive firm will maximize profits or minimize losses by producing that output at which marginal revenue equals marginal cost.*

♦   *In the long run easy entry and exodus of firms generates a strong tendency for firms to break even.*

♦   *A monopolistically competitive firm's equilibrium output is such that price exceeds marginal cost (indicating that resources are underallocated to the product) and price exceeds minimum average total cost (implying that consumers do not get the product at the lowest unit cost and price attainable).*

NONPRICE COMPETITION

For reasons cited above, we can conclude that the situation portrayed in Figure 25-1c and Figure 25-2 may not be the most beneficial to society. It is also not very satisfying to the monopolistically competitive producer which barely captures a normal profit for its efforts. We can therefore expect monopolistically competitive producers to try to improve on the long-run equilibrium position.

How can this be accomplished? The answer lies in product differentiation. Each firm has a product distinguishable in some more-or-less tangible way from those of its rivals. The product is presumably subject to further variation, that is, to product development. The emphasis on real product differences and the creation of perceived differences also may be achieved through advertising and related sales promotion. In short, the profit-realizing firm of Figure 25-1a will not stand by and watch new competitors encroach on its profits by duplicating or imitating its product, copying its advertising, and matching its services to consumers. Rather, the firm will attempt to sustain these profits and stay ahead of competitors through further product development and by enhancing the quantity and quality of advertising. In this way it might prevent the long-run tendency of Figure 25-1c from becoming a reality. True, product development and advertising will add to the firm's costs, but they can also increase the demand for its product. If demand increases by more than enough to compensate for development and promotional costs, the firm will have improved its profit position. As Figure 25-1c suggests, the firm may have little or no prospect of increasing profits by price cutting. So why not practice **nonprice competition?**

Product Differentiation and Product Development

The likelihood that easy entry will promote product variety and product improvement is possibly a redeeming feature of monopolistic competition which may offset, wholly or in part, the "wastes" associated with this market structure. There are two considerations here: (1) product differentiation at a point in time, and (2) product improvement over a period of time.

1 Differentiation Product differentiation means that at any point in time the consumer will be offered a wide range of types, styles, brands, and quality gradations of any given product. Compared with the situation of pure competition, this suggests possible advantages to the consumer. The range of choice is widened, and variations and shadings of consumer tastes are more fully met by producers.

But skeptics warn that product differentiation is a mixed blessing. Product proliferation may reach the point where the consumer becomes confused and rational choice becomes time-consuming and difficult. Variety may add spice to the consumer's life, but only up to a point. A woman shopping for lipstick may be bewildered by the vast array of products available. Revlon alone offers 157 shades of lipstick, of which 41 are "pink"! Worse yet, some observers fear that the consumer, faced with a myriad of similar products, may judge product quality by price; the consumer may irrationally assume that price is necessarily an index of product quality.

2 Development Product competition is vital to technological innovation and product betterment over a period of time. Such product development may be cumulative in two different ways. First, a successful product improvement by one firm obligates rivals to imitate or, if they can, improve on this firm's temporary market advantage or suffer the penalty of losses. Second, profits realized from a successful product improvement can finance further improvements.

Again, however, there are criticisms of the product development which may occur under monopolistic competition. Critics point out that many product alterations are more apparent than real, consisting of frivolous and superficial changes which do *not* improve the product's durability, efficiency, or usefulness. A more exotic container, bright packaging, or "shuffling the chrome" is frequently the focus for product development. It is argued, too, that particularly with durable and semidurable consumer goods, development may follow a pattern of "planned obsolescence," where firms improve their product only by that amount necessary to make the average consumer dissatisfied with last year's model.

Do the advantages of product differentiation, properly discounted, outweigh the "wastes" of monopolistic competition? It is difficult to say, short of examining specific cases; and even then, concrete conclusions are difficult to come by.

THE ECONOMICS OF ADVERTISING

A monopolistically competitive producer may gain at least a temporary edge on rivals by altering its product. It may also seek the same result by attempting to influence consumer preferences through advertising and sales promotion. Advertising *may* be a mechanism through which a firm can increase its share of the market and enhance consumer loyalty to its particular product.

Controversy and Scope

In fact, there is considerable disagreement as to the economic and social desirability of advertising. Since advertising and promotional expenditures in the United States were estimated to be almost $129 billion in 1990, the issues involved are significant. This amount exceeded by a wide margin the amount all state and local governments spent on public welfare. Hence, if advertising is generally wasteful, any potential virtues of monopolistically competitive markets are thereby dimmed, and the need for corrective public policies is indicated.

Two Views

The controversy over advertising has generated two diametrically opposed views of advertising.[1] In outlin-

[1]The ensuing discussion draws upon Robert B. Eklund, Jr., and David S. Saurman, *Advertising and the Market Process* (San Francisco: Pacific Research Institute for Public Policy, 1988).

ing these two positions, bear in mind that advertising is not confined to monopolistic competition. Product differentiation and heavy advertising are also characteristic of many oligopolistic industries (Chapter 26). Hence, our comments are equally germane to these industries.

The **traditional view** envisions advertising as a redundant and economically wasteful expenditure which generates economic concentration and monopoly power. The **new perspective** on advertising sees it as an efficient means for both providing information to consumers and enhancing competition. Let's contrast these two views in three critical areas.

1 Persuasion or Information? The traditional view holds that the main purpose of advertising is to manipulate or persuade consumers, that is, to alter their preferences in favor of the advertiser's product. A television beer commercial or a newspaper cigarette ad conveys little or no useful information to consumers. Advertising is often based on misleading and extravagant claims which confuse and frequently insult the intelligence of consumers, not enlighten them. Indeed, advertising may well persuade consumers in some cases to pay high prices for much-acclaimed but inferior products, forgoing better but unadvertised products selling at lower prices.

The new perspective contends that consumers need extensive information about product characteristics and prices to make rational (efficient) decisions. Advertising is alleged to be a low-cost means of providing that information. Suppose you are in the market for a CD player and there was no newspaper or magazine advertising of this product. To make a rational choice you might have to spend several days visiting electronics stores to determine the prices and features of various brands. This entails both direct costs (gasoline, parking fees) and indirect costs (the value of your time). Advertising, it is argued, reduces your "search time" and minimizes these costs.

2 Concentration or Competition? Does advertising generate monopoly or stimulate competition? The traditional view envisions some firms as being more successful than others in establishing "brand loyalty" through advertising, that is, in persuading consumers to buy their products. As a consequence, such firms are able to increase their sales, expand their market share, and enjoy enlarged profits. Enhanced profits permit still more advertising and further enlargement of the firm's market share and profits. In short, successful advertising leads to the expansion of some firms at the expense of others and therefore to increased industrial concentration. Consumers in time lose the advantages of competitive markets and face the disadvantages of monopolized markets. Furthermore, potential new entrants to the industry will be faced with the need to incur large advertising expenditures to establish their product in the marketplace; hence, advertising expenditures may be a formidable barrier to entry.

The traditional view is portrayed graphically in Figure 25-3a. By successfully generating brand loyalty through advertising, the firm's demand curve shifts rightward from D_1 to D_2, implying a larger market share. The fact that curve D_2 is less elastic than D_1 indicates a lessening of competition; successful advertising has convinced consumers that there exist fewer good substitutes for this firm's product. The less elastic demand curve also means that the producer can charge higher prices with less loss of sales.

The new perspective sees advertising as a force which enhances competition. By providing information about the wide variety of substitute products available to buyers, advertising diminishes monopoly power. In fact, advertising is frequently associated with the introduction of new products designed to compete with existing brands. Could the Hyundai and Isuzu automobiles have gained a foothold in the American market without advertising? How about Act II microwave popcorn and Softsoap?

In terms of Figure 25-3b, advertising, in a world of costly and imperfect knowledge, makes consumers more aware of the range of substitutable products available to them and provides them with valuable information on the prices and characteristics of these goods. Before advertising, consumers may have only been aware that products B and C were good substitutes for A. But advertising provides them with the knowledge that D, E, and F are also substitutable for A. As a consequence of the advertising of all firms in the industry, the demand curve of firm A shifts leftward, as from D_3 to D_4 in Figure 25-3b, and becomes more elastic. Both of these changes reflect enhanced competition.

3 Wasteful or Efficient? The traditional view contends that advertising is economically wasteful. First, it makes markets less competitive and therefore obstructs the realization of either allocative or productive efficiency. Second, advertising allegedly diverts human and property resources from higher-valued uses. For example, timber, which is sorely needed in the produc-

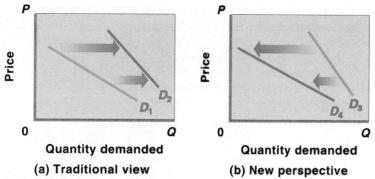

FIGURE 25-3   Advertising and a firm's demand curve: two views

The traditional view of advertising sees advertising as a device which increases the successful advertiser's market share and enhances brand loyalty. The result is greater market concentration as the demand curve of the successful advertiser shifts rightward and becomes more inelastic as shown by the D_1 to D_2 movement in panel (a). The new perspective regards advertising as a means of increasing consumer awareness of substitute products, thereby enhancing competition. Consequently, advertising in an industry will cause a firm's demand curve to shift leftward and become more elastic as portrayed by the movement from D_3 to D_4 in panel (b).

tion of housing, is squandered on unsightly billboards and on producing the paper used for the ubiquitous advertising supplements in local newspapers. Advertising allegedly constitutes an inefficient use of scarce resources. Finally, advertising expenditures contribute to higher costs which are ultimately reflected in higher prices to consumers.

The new perspective, as we have seen, views advertising as an efficiency-enhancing activity. It is an inexpensive means of providing useful information to consumers and thus lowers search costs. By enhancing competition advertising is conducive to both greater allocative and productive efficiency. Finally, by facilitating the successful introduction of new products advertising is conducive to technological progress.

Empirical Evidence

There are important empirical studies which lend credence to both of these views. For example, Comanor and Wilson have examined the role of advertising in forty-one industries manufacturing consumer goods. They concluded that advertising is generally anticompetitive. Specifically, they report that "the heavy volume of advertising expenditures in some industries serves as an important barrier to new competition in the markets served by these industries."[2] Prices of

heavily advertised goods exceed their marginal costs, reflecting a misallocation of resources. Furthermore, for many of the studied industries expenditures for advertising were found to be "excessive" and wasteful of scarce resources.

In contrast, Eckard has concluded that advertising is a procompetitive force. He reasons that, if advertising promotes monopoly power, then industries which advertise most heavily should be the ones which increase their prices the most and their outputs the least over time (recall Figure 24-3). Examining price and output changes of some 150 major industries over the 1963–1977 period, Eckard found that generally those industries with higher-than-average levels of advertising had *lower*-than-average rates of price increases and had *higher*-than-average rates of output increase. Conclusion: Rather than contributing to monopoly power, advertising generally enhances competition.[3]

There are also other industry studies which suggest that advertising enhances competition and has economically desirable results. For example, a study of the eyeglasses industry compared prices in states where professional codes of ethics permitted optometrists to advertise with those where codes prohibited or restricted advertising. The conclusion was that prices of eyeglasses were 25 to 40 percent higher in states

[2]William S. Comanor and Thomas A. Wilson, *Advertising and Market Power* (Cambridge, Mass.: Harvard University Press, 1974), p. 239.

[3]E. Woodrow Eckard, Jr., "Advertising, Concentration, and Consumer Welfare," *Review of Economics and Statistics,* May 1988, pp. 340–343.

LAST WORD

THE MARKET FOR PRINCIPLES OF ECONOMICS TEXTBOOKS*

The market for principles texts embraces a number of the characteristics of monopolistic competition.

Currently there are fifty or more economics texts which could be used in the principles course. If you undertook the arduous task of comparing a number of them, you would find considerable differences. While there is some variation in subject matter, most leading texts cover the same core topics. Books do vary considerably as to the rigor and detail with which material is presented. They also vary as to reading level. Some books have a one-color format, others a multicolor presentation. Books vary greatly in the use of such pedagogical devices as photos, "boxed features," cartoons, learning objectives, intrachapter summaries, and glossaries. Publishers seek the mix of these features which will be most appealing to instructors and students.

Texts are also differentiated by their accompanying "packages" of ancillary materials. These include study guides, videos, and computer tutorial and simulation programs to aid student understanding. Instructor manuals, test banks, and overhead transparencies are designed to save instructor time and enhance teacher

*Based on Timothy Tregarthen, "The Market for Principles of Economics Texts," *The Margin,* March 1987, pp. 14–15; and Joseph E. Stiglitz, "On the Market for Principles of Economics Textbooks: Innovation and Product Differentiation," *Journal of Economic Education,* Spring 1988, pp. 171–177.

productivity. Were you to trace the introduction and development of these various pedagogical aids and instructional materials, you would find that when any one of them was introduced and proved attractive to adopters, that feature would be quickly incorporated into future editions of most other old and new books.

Product differentiation is accompanied by considerable nonprice competition. Texts are advertised by direct mail and in widely read economics journals. Publishers provide potential adopters with free copies and use "trade fair" booths at economics conventions to publicize their wares. Sales representatives of the various publishers—who receive bonuses for exceeding sales quotas—prowl the halls of academia to make

---

where advertising was restricted.[4] A similar study of retail drug prices, comparing states where advertising was permitted with those in which it was not, found that prescription drug prices were about 5 percent lower in states which permitted advertising.[5] Finally, a study of the toy industry yielded the conclusion that television advertising had the effect of bringing about substantial price reductions:

[4]Lee and Alexandra Benham, "Regulating the Professions: A Perspective on Information Control," *Journal of Law and Economics,* October 1975, pp. 421–447.

[5]John F. Cady, *Restricted Advertising and Competition: The Case of Retail Drugs* (Washington, D.C.: American Enterprise Institute, 1976).

Advertising cuts distribution margins on advertised brands for two reasons: *first,* advertising causes goods to turn over rapidly so they can be sold profitably with smaller markups; and *second,* advertising creates product identity—which, in differentiated products, permits the public to compare prices between stores, thus setting a limit on the retailer's freedom to mark up. Products which are both heavily advertised and are fast sellers will be pulled through the distribution channels with the lowest markups of all.[6]

[6]Robert L. Steiner, "Does Advertising Lower Consumer Prices?" *Journal of Marketing,* October 1973, p. 21.

professors aware of the distinguishing features and alleged advantages of their particular text. Over 1 million students take principles courses each year so the battle for market shares is vigorous.

Price competition probably plays a secondary role in the textbook market. First, unlike most markets, the product is chosen for the consumer by a second party. Your instructor—who gets a free text from the publisher and may not even be aware of its retail price—decides the text you must read for the course. Second, instructors usually put textbook quality above price. It would prove very costly to students to use an inaccurate, poorly written text which might impair the teaching-learning process. The significant exception is that over the years more and more instructors have opted for lower-priced paperbacks which split micro and macro components of the course. Thus, a student taking only one semester of economics can avoid the higher cost of a two-semester hardback.

While there are no artificial barriers to entering the market, the widespread use of multicolor formats and the obligation to provide an array of student-instructor ancillary items poses a significant financial barrier. It may take an investment of $1 million or more for a publisher to enter the market with a text and ancillaries comparable to those already on the market. Even so, it is not uncommon to find two or three new entries in the market every year.

In summary, the economics textbook market is characterized by product differentiation and nonprice competition. Price competition is muted and the only entry barrier is financial.

Evidence on the economic effects of advertising is mixed because studies are usually plagued by data problems and difficulties in determining cause and effect. Suppose it is found that firms which do a great deal of advertising seem to have considerable monopoly power and large profits. Does this mean that advertising creates barriers to entry which in turn generate monopoly power and profits? Or do entry barriers associated with factors remote from advertising cause monopoly profits which in turn allow firms to spend lavishly in advertising their products? In any event, at this

time there is simply no consensus on the economic implications of advertising.

QUICK REVIEW 25-2

♪ *Monopolistically competitive firms may seek economic profits through product differentiation, product development, and advertising.*

♪ *The traditional view of advertising alleges that it is a persuasive rather than informative activity; it promotes economic concentration and monopoly power; and it is a source of economic waste and inefficiency.*

♪ *According to the new perspective, advertising is a low-cost source of information for consumers; a means of increasing competition by making consumers aware of substitutable products; and a source of greater efficiency in the use of resources.*

Monopolistic Competition and Economic Analysis

Our discussion of nonprice competition correctly implies that the equilibrium situation of a monopolistically competitive firm is actually more complex than the previous graphical analysis indicates. Figure 25-1a, b, and c *assumes* a given product and a given level of advertising expenditures. But we now know these are not given in practice. The monopolistically competitive firm must actually juggle three variable factors—price, product, and promotion—in seeking maximum profits. What specific variety of product, selling at what price, and supplemented by what level of promotional activity, will result in the greatest level of profits attainable? This complex situation is not easily expressed in a simple, meaningful economic model. At best we can note that each possible combination of price, product, and promotion poses a different demand and cost (production plus promotion) situation for the firm, some one of which will allow it maximum profits. In practice, this optimal combination cannot be readily forecast but must be sought by trial and error. Even here, certain limitations may be imposed by the actions of rivals. A firm may not eliminate its advertising expenditures for fear its share of the market will decline sharply, benefiting its rivals who do advertise. Similarly, patents held by rivals will rule out certain desirable product variations.

CHAPTER SUMMARY

1 The distinguishing features of monopolistic competition are: **a** There are enough firms so that each has little control over price, mutual interdependence is absent, and collusion is virtually impossible; **b** products are characterized by real and perceived differences and by varying conditions surrounding their sale; **c** economic rivalry entails both price and nonprice competition; and **d** entry to the industry is relatively easy. Many aspects of retailing, and some industries where economies of scale are few, approximate monopolistic competition.

2 Monopolistically competitive firms may earn economic profits or incur losses in the short run. The easy entry and exodus of firms give rise to a tendency for them to earn a normal profit in the long run.

3 The long-run equilibrium position of the monopolistically competitive producer is less socially desirable than that of a purely competitive firm. Under monopolistic competition, price exceeds marginal cost, suggesting an underallocation of resources to the product, and price exceeds minimum average total cost, indicating that consumers do not get the product at the lowest price which cost conditions would allow. However, because the firm's demand curve is highly elastic, these "wastes" of monopolistic competition should not be overemphasized.

4 Product differentiation provides a means by which monopolistically competitive firms can offset the long-run tendency for economic profits to approximate zero. Through product development and advertising outlays, a firm may strive to increase the demand for its product more than nonprice competition increases its costs.

5 Although subject to certain dangers and problems, product differentiation affords the consumer a greater variety of products at any point in time and improved products over time. Whether these features fully compensate for the "wastes" of monopolistic competition is a complex and unresolved question.

6 The traditional and new perspective views of advertising differ as to whether advertising **a** is persuasive or informative, **b** promotes monopoly or competition, and **c** impairs or improves efficiency in resource use. Empirical evidence reveals no consensus as to whether advertising is an anti- or procompetitive force.

7 In practice the monopolistic competitor seeks that specific combination of price, product, and promotion which will maximize its profits.

TERMS AND CONCEPTS

monopolistic competition

product differentiation

traditional and new perspective views of advertising

wastes of monopolistic competition

nonprice competition

QUESTIONS AND STUDY SUGGESTIONS

1 How does monopolistic competition differ from pure competition? From pure monopoly? Explain fully what product differentiation entails.

2 Compare the elasticity of the monopolistically competitive producer's demand curve with that of **a** a pure competitor, and **b** a pure monopolist. Assuming identical long-run costs, compare graphically the prices and outputs which would result under pure competition and monopolistic competition. Contrast the two market structures in terms of allocative and productive efficiency. Explain: "Monopolistically competitive industries are characterized by too many firms, each of which produces too little."

3 "Monopolistic competition is monopoly up to the point at which consumers become willing to buy close-substitute products and competitive beyond that point." Explain.

4 "Competition in quality and in service may be quite as effective in giving the buyer more for her money as is price competition." Do you agree? Explain why monopolistically competitive firms frequently prefer nonprice to price competition.

5 Critically evaluate and explain:

  a "In monopolistically competitive industries economic profits are competed away in the long run; hence, there is no valid reason to criticize the performance and efficiency of such industries."

  b "In the long run monopolistic competition leads to a monopolistic price but not to monopolistic profits."

6 Compare the traditional and new perspective view of advertising. Which do you feel is more accurate?

7 Do you agree with the following statements?

a   "The amount of advertising which a firm does is likely to vary inversely with the real differences in its product."

b   "If each firm's advertising expenditures merely tend to cancel the effects of its rivals' advertising, it is clearly irrational for these firms to maintain large advertising budgets."

8   Carefully evaluate the two views expressed in the following statements:

a   "It happens every day. Advertising builds mass demand. Production goes up—costs come down. More people can buy—more jobs are created. These are the ingredients of economic growth. Each stimulates the next in a cycle of productivity and plenty which constantly creates a better life for you."

b   "Advertising constitutes 'inverted education'—a costly effort to induce people to buy without sufficient thought and deliberation and therefore to buy things they don't need. Furthermore, advertising outlays vary directly with the level of consumer spending."

Which view do you feel is the more accurate? Justify your position.

The answer is evident: The firms will all be motivated to collude—to "get together and talk it over"—and agree to charge the same price *PQ*. In addition to reducing the omnipresent possibility of price warring, each firm will obtain the maximum profit. And for society, the result is the same as if the industry were a pure monopoly composed of three identical plants (see Chapter 24).

Overt Collusion: the OPEC Cartel Collusion may assume a variety of forms. The most comprehensive form of collusion is the **cartel** which typically involves a formal written agreement with respect to both price and production. Output must be controlled—that is, the market must be shared—to maintain the agreed-upon price.

The most spectacularly successful international cartel of recent decades has been OPEC (the Organization of Petroleum Exporting Countries). Comprising thirteen nations, OPEC was extremely effective in the 1970s in restricting oil supply and raising prices. The cartel was able to raise world oil prices from $2.50 to $11.00 per barrel within a six-month period in 1973–1974. By early 1980 price hikes had brought the per barrel price into the $32 to $34 range. The result was enormous profits for cartel members, a substantial stimulus to worldwide inflation, and serious international trade deficits for oil importers.

OPEC was highly effective in the 1970s for several reasons. First, it dominated the world market for oil. If a nation imported oil, it was almost obligated to do business with OPEC. Second, world demand for oil was strong and expanding in the 1970s. Finally, the "short-run" demand for oil was highly inelastic because the economies of oil-importing nations such as the United States were locked into gas-guzzling automobiles and energy-intensive housing and capital equipment. This inelasticity meant that a small restriction of output by OPEC would result in a relatively large price increase. Thus, as shown in Figure 26-4, in 1973–1974 and again in 1979–1980 OPEC was able to achieve dramatic increases in oil prices and only incur a very modest decline in sales. Given this inelastic demand, higher prices meant greatly increased total revenues to OPEC members. The accompanying smaller output meant lower total costs. The combination of more total revenue and lower total costs resulted in greatly expanded profits. (We discuss the serious weakening of the OPEC cartel in the 1980s later in this chapter.)

Covert Collusion: The Electrical Equipment Conspiracy Cartels are illegal in the United States and hence collusion has been covert or secret. In 1960 an extensive price-fixing and market-sharing scheme involving heavy electrical equipment such as transformers, turbines, circuit breakers, and switchgear was uncovered. Elaborate covert schemes were developed by such participants as General Electric, Westinghouse, and Allis-Chalmers to rig prices and divide the market.

> The manner in which prices were fixed, bids controlled, and markets allocated may be illustrated by *power switch gear assemblies* . . . five companies and twelve individuals were involved. It was charged that at least twenty-five meetings were held between the middle of November 1958 and October 1959 in various parts of the country. . . .
>
> At these periodic meetings, a scheme or formula for quoting nearly identical prices to electric utility companies, private industrial corporations and contractors was used by defendant corporations, designated by their representatives as a "phase of the moon" or "light of the moon" formula. Through cyclic rotating positioning inherent in the formula one defendant corporation would quote the low price, others would quote intermediate prices and another would quote the high price; these positions would be periodically rotated among the defendant corporations. . . . This formula was designed to permit each

FIGURE 26-4   The OPEC cartel and the world oil market

Because of the inelasticity of the demand for oil, in 1973–1974 and again in 1979–1980 the OPEC cartel was able to obtain a dramatic increase in the price of oil (P_1 to P_2) accompanied by only a very modest decline in production and sales (Q_1 to Q_2). Total revenue thus rose.

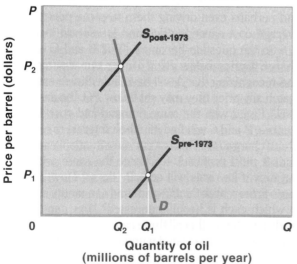

Quantity of oil
(millions of barrels per year)

defendant corporation to know the exact price it and every other defendant corporation would quote on each prospective sale.

At these periodic meetings, a cumulative list of sealed bid business secured by all of the defendant corporations was also circulated and the representatives present would compare the relative standing of each corporation according to its agreed upon percentage of the total sales pursuant to sealed bids. The representatives present would then discuss particular future bid invitations and designate which defendant corporation should submit the lowest bid therefore, the amount of such bid, and the amount of the bid to be submitted by others.[1]

Twenty-nine manufacturers and forty-six company officials were indicted in this "great electrical conspiracy" which violated our antitrust laws. Substantial fines, jail penalties, and lawsuits by victimized buyers were the final outcome.

In innumerable other instances collusion is even more subtle. **Gentlemen's agreements** frequently are struck at cocktail parties, on the golf course, or at trade association meetings where competing firms reach a verbal agreement on product price, leaving market shares to the ingenuity of each seller as reflected in nonprice competition. Although they too collide with the antitrust laws, the elusive character of gentlemen's agreements makes them more difficult to detect and prosecute successfully.

Obstacles to Collusion   In practice cartels and similar collusive arrangements are difficult to establish and maintain. Let's briefly consider several important barriers to collusion.

1 Demand and Cost Differences   When oligopolists' costs and product demands differ, it is more difficult to agree on price. Where products are differentiated and changing frequently over time, this would be the case. Indeed, even with highly standardized products, we would expect that firms might have somewhat different market shares and would operate with differing degrees of productive efficiency. Thus it is likely that even homogeneous oligopolists would have different demand and cost curves.

In either event, differences in costs and demand will mean that the profit-maximizing price for each firm will differ, there will be no single price readily accept-

able to all. Price collusion therefore depends on the ability to achieve compromises and concessions—to arrive at a degree of "understanding" which in practice is often difficult to attain. For example, the MR = MC positions of firms A, B, and C may call for them to charge $12, $11, and $10 respectively, but this price cluster or range may be unsatisfactory to one or more of the firms. Firm A may feel that differences in product quality justify only a $1.50, rather than a $2, price differential between its product and that of firm C. In short, cost and demand differences make it difficult for oligopolists to agree on a single price or a "proper" cluster of prices; these differentials are therefore an obstacle to collusion.

2 Number of Firms   Other things being equal, the larger the number of firms, the more difficult it is to achieve a cartel or other form of price collusion. Agreement on price by three or four producers that control an entire market is much more readily accomplished than it is when ten firms each have roughly 10 percent of the market, or where the Big Three have, say, 70 percent of the market, while a "competitive fringe" of eight or ten smaller firms battles for the remainder.

3 Cheating   As our game theory model made clear, there is a more-or-less persistent temptation for collusive oligopolists to engage in clandestine price cutting, that is, to make secret price concessions to get additional business.

The difficulty with cheating is that buyers paying a high price may get wind of the lower-priced sales and demand similar treatment. Or buyers receiving price concessions from one oligopolist may use this concession as a wedge to get even larger price concessions from the firm's rivals. The attempt of buyers to play sellers against one another may precipitate price warring among the firms. In short, although it is potentially profitable, secret price concessions threaten the maintenance of collusive oligopoly over time. Collusion is more likely to persist when cheating is deterred because it is easy to detect and punish.

4 Recession   Recession is usually an enemy of collusion because slumping markets increase average costs. In technical terms, as the oligopolists' demand and marginal-revenue curves shift to the left (Figure 26-3), each firm moves back to a higher point on its average-cost curve. Firms find they have substantial excess productive capacity, sales are down, unit costs are up, and profits are being squeezed. Under these

---

[1]Jules Backman, *The Economics of the Electrical Machinery Industry* (New York: New York University Press, 1962), pp. 135–138, abridged. Reprinted by permission.

conditions, businesses may feel they can better avoid serious profit reductions by price cutting in the hope of gaining sales at the expense of rivals.

5 Potential Entry The enhanced prices and profits which result from collusion may attract new entrants, including foreign firms. Such entry would increase market supply and reduce prices and profits. Therefore, successful collusion requires that colluding oligopolists can block entry of new producers.

6 Legal Obstacles: Antitrust Our antitrust laws (Chapter 33) prohibit cartels and the kind of price-fixing collusion we have been discussing. Therefore, less obvious means of price rigging—such as price leadership—have evolved in the United States.

OPEC in Disarray The highly successful OPEC oil cartel of the 1970s fell into disarray in the 1980s. The reasons for OPEC's decline relate closely to the obstacles to collusion we have just enumerated.

First, the dramatic runup of oil prices in the 1970s stimulated the search for new oil reserves, and soon non-OPEC nations, which OPEC could not block from entering world markets, became part of the world oil industry. Great Britain, Norway, Mexico, and the former Soviet Union have all become major world oil suppliers. As a result, OPEC's share of world oil production fell sharply.

Second, on the demand side, oil conservation, worldwide recession in the early 1980s, and expanded use of alternative energy sources (such as coal, natural gas, and nuclear power) all reduced the demand for oil. The combination of greater production by non-OPEC nations and a decline in world demand generated an "oil glut" and seriously impaired OPEC's ability to control world oil prices.

Third, OPEC has had a serious cheating problem stemming from the relatively large number of members (thirteen) and the diversity of their economic circumstances. Saudi Arabia is the dominant cartel member; it has the largest oil reserves and is probably the lowest-cost producer. Saudi Arabia has favored a "moderate" pricing policy because it has feared that very high oil prices would hasten development of alternative energy sources (such as solar power and synthetic fuels) and increase the attractiveness of existing substitutes such as coal and natural gas. These developments would greatly reduce the value of its vast oil reserves. Saudi Arabia also has a small population and a very high per capita domestic output. But other members—for example, Nigeria and Venezuela—are very poor, have large populations, and are burdened with large external debts. Still others—Iran, Iraq, and Libya—have had large military commitments. All of these members have had immediate needs for cash. Hence, there has been substantial cheating whereby some members have exceeded assigned production quotas and have sold oil at prices below those agreed to by the cartel. Thus, although OPEC's official oil price reached $34 per barrel in 1979, it is currently about $17 per barrel.

Price Leadership

Price leadership is a type of gentlemen's agreement by which oligopolists can coordinate their price behavior without engaging in outright collusion. Formal agreements and clandestine meetings are *not* involved. Rather, a practice evolves whereby the "dominant" firm—usually the largest or the most efficient in the industry—initiates price changes, and all other firms more-or-less automatically follow that price change. The importance of price leadership is evidenced in the fact that such industries as farm machinery, anthracite coal, cement, copper, gasoline, newsprint, tin cans, lead, sulfur, rayon, fertilizer, glass containers, steel, automobiles, and nonferrous metals are practicing, or have in the recent past practiced, price leadership.

Cigarette Pricing Consider the cigarette industry, a classic example of tight price leadership. In this instance the Big Three, producing from 68 to 90 percent of total output, evolved a highly profitable practice of price leadership which resulted in virtually identical prices over the entire 1923 to 1941 period.

> In 1918 American Tobacco tried to lead a price rise, but Reynolds (the largest seller) refused to follow. In 1921, American cut its price and Reynolds retaliated with a further cut, which American and the other sellers matched. This experience apparently had a profound educational impact on American and the other major brand sellers, none of whom challenged Reynolds' leadership again for a decade. Between 1923 and 1941, virtual price identity prevailed continuously among the Big Three's standard brands, although certain other cigarettes of similar size and quality sold in smaller quantities at premium prices, and premium-priced Philip Morris grew through heavy advertising to a 6 percent market share. During this period there were eight standard brand list price changes. Reynolds led six of them, five upward and one downward, and was followed each time, in

most cases within twenty-four hours of its announcement. The other two changes were downward revisions during 1933 led by American and followed by the other standard brand vendors. American also attempted to lead a price increase in 1941, but Reynolds again refused to follow and the change was rescinded. Throughout this period, the return on invested capital realized by Reynolds, American, and Ligget & Myers averaged 18 percent after taxes—roughly double the rate earned by American manufacturing industry as a whole.[2]

Since 1946 cigarette pricing has been somewhat less rigid, reflecting both successful antitrust action and the development of increasingly heterogeneous product lines. But overall there has been little evidence of enhanced price rivalry.

Leadership Tactics   The examination of price leadership in a variety of industries suggests that the price leader is likely to observe the following tactics.
1   Because price changes always carry some risk that rivals will not follow, price adjustments will be made infrequently. The price leader will *not* respond pricewise to minuscule day-to-day changes in cost and demand conditions. Price will be changed only when cost and demand conditions have been altered significantly and on an industry-wide basis by, for example, industrywide wage increases, an increase in taxes, or an increase in the price of some basic input such as energy. In the automobile industry price adjustments traditionally have been made when new models are introduced each fall.
2   Impending price adjustments are often communicated by the price leader to the industry through speeches by major executives, trade publication interviews, and so forth. By publicizing "the need to raise prices" the price leader can elicit a consensus among its competitors for the actual increase.
3   The price leader does not necessarily choose the price which maximizes short-run profits for the industry. The reason for this is that the industry may want to discourage new firms from entering. If barriers to entry are based on cost advantages (economies of scale) of existing firms, these cost barriers may be surmounted by new entrants *if* product price is set high enough. New firms which are relatively inefficient because of their small size may survive and grow if the industry's price is very high. To discourage new competitors and

maintain the current oligopolistic structure of the industry, price may be established below the short-run profit-maximizing level.

Cost-Plus Pricing

A final view of oligopolistic price behavior centers on what is variously known as *markup, rule-of-thumb,* or **cost-plus pricing.** In this case the oligopolist uses a formula or procedure to estimate cost per unit of output and a markup is applied to cost to determine price. Unit costs, however, vary with output and therefore the firm must assume some typical or target level of output. For example, the firm's average-cost figure may be that which is realized when the firm is operating at, say, 75 or 80 percent of capacity. A markup, usually in the form of a percentage, is applied to average cost in determining price. An appliance manufacturer may estimate unit costs of dishwashers to be $250, to which a 50 percent markup is applied. This yields a $375 price to retailers.

The markup is 50 percent rather than 25 or 100 percent because the firm is seeking some target profit or rate of return on its investment. To illustrate, consider the pricing technique used by General Motors for over four decades prior to the advent of aggressive foreign competition in the mid-1970s.

> GM started with the goal of earning, on the average over the years, a return of approximately 15 percent after taxes on total invested capital. Not knowing how many autos would be sold and hence unit costs (including prorated fixed costs), it calculated costs on the assumption of operation at 80 percent of conservatively rated capacity. A standard price was calculated by adding to unit cost a sufficient profit margin to yield the desired 15 percent after-tax return. The rule would be adjusted across the product line to take account of actual and potential competition, business conditions, long-run strategic goals and other factors. Actual profit then depended on the number of vehicles sold. Between 1960 and 1979, GM's actual return on stockholders' equity fell below 15 percent in only four years, all marked by recession and/or OPEC-induced gasoline price shocks. The average return was 17.6 percent. After 1979, however, recession and intensifying import competition caused GM frequently to fall short of its target.[3]

Two final points. First, this method of pricing is consistent with collusion or price leadership. If producers in an industry have roughly similar costs, adherence to a common pricing formula will result in highly

---

[2]F. M. Scherer and David Ross, *Industrial Market Structure and Economic Performance,* 3d ed. (Boston: Houghton Mifflin Company, 1990), p. 250.

[3]Ibid., p. 262.

similar prices and price changes. As we will find in the case study which concludes this chapter, General Motors used cost-plus pricing *and* was until recently the price leader in the automobile industry.

Second, cost-plus pricing has special advantages for multiproduct firms which would otherwise be faced with the difficult and costly process of estimating demand and cost conditions for perhaps hundreds of different products. In practice, it is virtually impossible to allocate correctly certain common overhead costs such as power, lighting, insurance, and taxes to specific products.

ROLE OF NONPRICE COMPETITION

We have noted that, for several reasons, oligopolists have an aversion to price competition. This aversion may lead to some more-or-less informal type of collusion on price. In the United States, however, price collusion is usually accompanied by nonprice competition. It is typically through nonprice competition that each firm's share of the total market is determined. This emphasis on nonprice competition has its roots in two basic facts.

1 Less Easily Duplicated Price cuts can be quickly and easily met by a firm's rivals. Because of this the possibility of significantly increasing one's share of the market through price competition is small; rivals will promptly cancel any potential gain in sales by matching price cuts. And, of course, the risk is always present that price competition will precipitate disastrous price warring. Nonprice competition is less likely to get out of hand. Oligopolists seem to feel that more permanent advantages can be gained over rivals through nonprice competition because product variations, improvements in productive techniques, and successful advertising gimmicks cannot be duplicated so quickly and completely as price reductions.

2 Greater Financial Resources There is a more evident reason for the tremendous emphasis which oligopolists put on nonprice competition: Manufacturing oligopolists are typically blessed with substantial financial resources with which to support advertising and product development. Thus, although nonprice competition is a basic characteristic of both monopolistically competitive and oligopolistic industries, the latter are typically in a financial position to indulge in nonprice competition more fully.

OLIGOPOLY AND ECONOMIC EFFICIENCY

Is oligopoly an "efficient" market structure from society's standpoint? How does the price–output behavior of the oligopolist compare with that of a purely competitive firm? Because there are a variety of oligopoly models—kinked demand, collusion, price leadership, and cost-plus pricing—it is difficult to make such a comparison.

Allocative and Productive Efficiency

Many economists believe that the outcome of oligopolistic markets is approximately that shown in Figure 26-3. Note that, as compared to the benchmark of pure competition (Figure 23-12), production occurs where price exceeds marginal cost and short of that output where average total cost is minimized. In terms of the terminology of Chapters 23 and 24, neither allocative efficiency ($P = $ MC) nor productive efficiency ($P = $ minimum ATC) is likely to occur under oligopoly.

One may even argue that oligopoly is actually less desirable than pure monopoly simply because pure monopoly in the United States is frequently subject to government regulation to mitigate abuses of market power. Informal collusion among oligopolists may yield price and output results similar to pure monopoly, yet at the same time maintain the outward appearance of several independent and "competing" firms.

Two qualifications are relevant. First, in recent years foreign competition has generated more rivalry in a number of oligopolistic markets—autos and steel come immediately to mind—and has tended to undermine such cozy arrangements as price leadership and cost-plus pricing and stimulate more competitive pricing. Second, recall that oligopolistic firms may purposely keep prices below the short-run, profit-maximizing level to deter entry where entry barriers are less formidable.

Dynamic Efficiency

What about the "very long run" perspective where we allow for innovation in terms of improvements in product quality and more efficient production methods?

Competitive View One view is that competition provides a compelling incentive to be technologically progressive. If a given competitive firm does not seize the initiative, one or more rivals will introduce an improved product or a cost-reducing production technique which may drive it from the market. In short, as a matter of short-term profits and long-term survival, competitive firms are under persistent pressure to improve products and lower costs through innovation.

Some adherents of this **competitive view** allege that oligopolists may often have a strong incentive to impede innovation and restrain technological progress. The larger corporation wants to maximize profits by exploiting fully all its capital assets. Why rush to develop and introduce a new product (for example, fluorescent lights) when that product's success will render obsolete all equipment designed to produce an existing product (incandescent bulbs)? Furthermore, it is not difficult to cite oligopolistic industries in which interest in research and development has been modest at best: The steel, cigarette, and aluminum industries are cases in point.

Schumpeter–Galbraith View In contrast, the **Schumpeter–Galbraith view** holds that large oligopolistic firms with market power are necessary for rapid technological progress.

High R&D Costs It is argued, first, that modern research to develop new products and new productive techniques is incredibly expensive. Therefore, only large oligopolistic firms can finance extensive research and development (R&D) activities.

Barriers and Profits Second, the existence of barriers to entry gives the oligopolist some assurance that it will realize any profit rewards from successful R&D endeavors. In Galbraith's words:

> The modern industry of a few large firms [is] an excellent instrument for inducing technical change. It is admirably equipped for financing technical development. Its organization provides strong incentives for undertaking development and for putting it into use. . . . In the modern industry shared by a few large firms, size and the rewards accruing to market power combine to insure that resources for research and technical development will be available. The power that enables the firm to have some influence on prices insures that the resulting gains will not be passed on to the public by imitators (who have stood none of the costs of development) before the outlay for development can be recouped. In this way market power protects the incentive to technical development.[4]

Bluntly put, small competitive firms have neither the *means* nor the *incentives* to be technologically progressive; large oligopolists do.

If the Schumpeter–Galbraith view is correct, it suggests that over time oligopolistic industries will foster rapid product improvement, lower unit production costs, lower prices, and perhaps a greater output and more employment than would the same industry organized competitively. There is anecdotal and case-study evidence suggesting that many oligopolistic manufacturing industries—television and other electronics products, home appliances, automobile tires—have been characterized by substantial improvements in product quality, falling relative prices, and expanding levels of output and employment.

Technological Progress: The Evidence

Which view is more nearly correct? Empirical studies have yielded ambiguous results. The consensus, however, seems to be that giant oligopolies are probably *not* a fountainhead of technological progress. A pioneering study[5] of sixty-one important inventions made from 1880 to 1965 indicates that over half were the work of independent inventors disassociated from corporate industrial research laboratories. Such substantial advances as air conditioning, power steering, the ballpoint pen, cellophane, the jet engine, insulin, xerography, the helicopter, and the catalytic cracking of petroleum have this individualistic heritage. Other equally important advances have come from small- and medium-sized firms.

According to this study, about two-thirds—forty out of sixty-one—of the basic inventions of this century have been initiated by independent inventors or the research activities of relatively small firms. This is not to deny that in a number of oligopolistic industries— for example, the aircraft, chemical, petroleum, and electronics industries—research activity has been pursued vigorously and fruitfully. But even here the picture is clouded by the fact that a very substantial portion of the research carried on in the aircraft-missile, electronics, and communications industries is heavily subsidized with public funds.

Some leading researchers in this field have tentatively concluded that technological progress in an industry may be determined more by the industry's sci-

[4]John Kenneth Galbraith, *American Capitalism,* rev. ed. (Boston: Houghton Mifflin Company, 1956), pp. 86–88. Also see Joseph Schumpeter, *Capitalism, Socialism, and Democracy* (New York: Harper & Row Publishers, Inc., 1942).

[5]John Jewkes, David Sawers, and Richard Stillerman, *The Sources of Invention,* rev. ed. (New York: St. Martin's Press, Inc., 1968).

entific character and "technological opportunities" than by its market structure. There may simply be more ways to progress in the electronics and computer industries than in the brickmaking and cigarette industries, regardless of whether they are organized competitively or oligopolistically.

AUTOMOBILES: A CASE STUDY[6]

The automobile industry provides an informative case study of oligopoly, illustrating many of the points made in this chapter. It also indicates that market structure is not permanent and, in particular, that foreign competition can upset the oligopolists' "quiet life."

Market Structure Although there were over eighty auto manufacturers in the early 1920s, several mergers (most notably the combining of Chevrolet, Pontiac, Oldsmobile, Buick, and Cadillac into General Motors), many failures during the Great Depression of the 1930s, and the increasing importance of entry barriers —all reduced numbers in the industry. Currently, three large firms—General Motors (GM), Ford, and Chrysler—dominate the market for domestically produced automobiles.

These firms are gigantic: According to *Fortune* magazine, GM, Ford, and Chrysler were the first, third, and eleventh largest manufacturing companies in the United States in 1990 as measured by sales. All three are leading truck manufacturers, produce household appliances, are involved in defense contracting and finance and banking, and have extensive overseas interests. GM has a virtual monopoly in producing buses and diesel locomotives in the United States.

Entry Barriers Entry barriers are substantial, as evidenced by the fact that it has been about six decades since an American firm successfully entered the automobile industry. The primary barrier is economies of scale. It is estimated that the minimum efficient scale for a producer is about 300,000 units of output per year. However, given the uncertainties of consumer tastes, experts feel a truly viable firm must produce at least two different models. Hence, to have a reasonable prospect of success a new firm would have to produce about 600,000 autos per year.

The estimated cost of an integrated plant (involving the production of engines, transmissions, other components, and product assembly) might be as much as $1.2 to $1.4 billion. Other entry barriers include the need for extensive advertising and far-flung dealer networks (GM has over 15,500 dealers and Chrysler has 10,500) which provide spare parts and repair service. A newcomer also would face the expensive task of overcoming existing brand loyalties. Given that the domestic automobile industry spent $2.6 billion on advertising in 1990, this is no small matter.

Price Leadership and Profits The indicated industry structure—a few firms with high entry barriers— has been fertile ground for collusive or coordinated pricing. GM traditionally was the price leader. Each fall, with the introduction of new models, GM would establish prices for its basic models and Ford and Chrysler would set the prices of their comparable models accordingly. (Details of how GM established its prices were outlined in the earlier section on cost-plus pricing.)

In the past several decades automobile prices have moved up steadily and at a rate in excess of the overall rate of inflation. And despite large periodic declines in demand and sales, automobile prices have displayed considerable downward rigidity, although import competition and recession have caused rebates and financing subsidies to become common in recent years.

---

[6]This section draws heavily on Walter Adams and James W. Brock, "The Automobile Industry," in Walter Adams (ed.), *The Structure of American Industry,* 8th ed. (New York: The Macmillan Company, 1990), pp. 101–127.

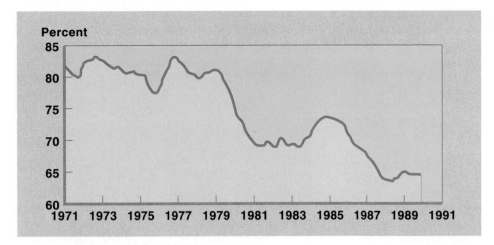

FIGURE 26-5 Big Three sales as a share of the United States automobile market

Although GM, Ford, and Chrysler commanded about 80 percent of domestic car sales in the 1970s, that share fell sharply in the late 1970s and early 1980s and is now less than 65 percent.

Over the years price leadership has proved to be very profitable. Over the 1947–1977 period the Big Three earned an average profit rate significantly greater than that of all United States manufacturing corporations taken as a whole.

Styling and Technology   In addition to advertising, nonprice competition has centered on styling and technological advance. In practice the former has been stressed over the latter. As early as the 1920s GM recognized that the replacement market was becoming increasingly important compared to the market for first-time purchasers. Therefore, its strategy—later adopted by other manufacturers—became one of annual styling changes accompanied by model proliferation. The purpose is to achieve higher sales and profits by encouraging consumers to replace their autos with greater frequency and to encourage buyers to shift their purchase from basic to "upscale" models.

As summarized by Adams and Brock, technological progress represents a mixed picture over time:

First, the rate, breadth, and depth of product innovation were greatest in the era prior to World War II, when the field was populated by many independent producers. Competition was intense, and new people with new ideas could put their ideas (the bad along with the good) into commercial practice. . . .

Second, with the demise of a vigorous independent sector, and with the consolidation of the industry into a tight oligopoly, the pace of genuine product innovation slackened. Innovations like front-wheel drive, disc brakes, fuel injection, utilitarian minivans and fuel-efficient subcompacts, and four-wheel steering languished in the hands of the Big Three. . . .

Third, while the domestic oligopoly luxuriated in complacency and the cosmetic style game, foreign producers took the lead in aggressively exploiting the frontiers of automobile technology. . . . This lead persists to the present day, with foreign producers commercializing such recent product innovations as four-wheel steering, electronically controlled active suspensions, multivalve engines, and ceramic engine componentry.

Fourth, with regard to *process* innovation, the domestic oligopoly's performance is hardly more enviable. Here, too, foreign firms—especially the Japanese—have exhibited far more entrepreneurship in seeking out and implementing improved manufacturing techniques. . . . In their devotion to production, and in their relentless willingness to experiment, the Japaneses seem to have been far more astute students of Henry Ford than the chieftains of the U.S industry, who succumbed to satisfaction with the status quo.

In the 1980s the Big Three have struggled to advance, both in product innovation as well as in production technology. They have progressed on both fronts—examples are the successful Ford Taurus program, GM's "Saturn" project, billions of dollars in cost reductions, and productivity gains on the factory floor.[7]

Foreign Competition   In the last two decades the automobile market in the United States has become more competitive than the tight oligopolistic structure of the domestic industry would suggest. GM, Ford, and Chrysler have been challenged by foreign (particularly Japanese) producers. As Figure 26-5 shows, the Big Three's share of the United States market has declined

[7]Ibid., pp. 117–119.

LAST WORD

THE BEER INDUSTRY: OLIGOPOLY BREWING?

The beer industry was once populated by hundreds of firms and an even larger number of brands. But this industry has increasingly become concentrated and is now an oligopoly.

The brewing industry has undergone profound changes since World War II which have increased the degree of concentration in the industry. In 1947 slightly over 400 independent brewing companies existed in the United States. By 1967 the number had declined to 124 and by 1980 only 33 survived. While the five largest brewers sold only 19 percent of the nation's beer in 1947, the Big Five brewers currently sell 93 percent of the nation's domestically produced beer as shown in the accompanying table. The Big Two—Anheuser-Busch and Miller—produce 68 percent. Why the change?

Market share for domestically produced beer, 1990

Firm	Market share
Anheuser-Busch	45%
Miller	23
Coors	10
Stroh	8
Heileman	7
All others	7
	100%

Changes on the demand side of the market have contributed to the "shake-out" of small brewers from the industry. First, there is evidence that in the 1970s consumer tastes shifted from the stronger-flavored beers of the small brewers to the light, dry products of the larger brewers. Second, there has been a relative shift from the consumption of beer in taverns to consumption in the home. The significance of this change is that taverns were usually supplied with kegs from local brewers to avoid the relatively high cost of shipping kegs. But the acceptance of metal containers for home consumption made it possible for large, distant brewers to compete with the local brewers because the former could now ship their products by truck or rail without breakage.

from 80 percent as recently as 1979 to less than 65 percent currently.

The reasons for growth of foreign competition are manifold.

1 Rising Gas Prices The OPEC-inspired increases in gasoline prices in the 1970s prompted a shift in consumer demand toward smaller, fuel-efficient imports from Japan and Germany. Many analysts contend that domestic producers seriously misjudged the scope and apparent permanence of this shift.

2 Quality In addition, many consumers perceive that imports have quality advantages. A 1990 consumer survey with respect to perceived automobile quality found seven Japanese models, two German models,

and only one American-made car in the top ten. The American car ranked fifth.

3 Costs Finally, lower overseas wages and higher labor productivity have given the Japanese and Koreans a substantial cost advantage on compact cars.

The response of the domestic automobile industry to enhanced foreign competition has been essentially threefold.

1 Protection The industry—with the support of organized labor—successfully lobbied government for protection. The result, beginning in 1981, was "voluntary" import quotas on Japanese cars which effectively restrained competition. Reduced foreign competition allowed domestic manufacturers to boost their prices

Developments on the supply side of the market have been even more profound. In particular, technological advances have speeded up the bottling or closing lines so that, for example, the number of cans of beer which could be filled and closed per minute increased from 900 to 1500 between 1965 and the late 1970s. Currently the most modern canning lines can close 2000 cans per minute. Large plants are also able to reduce labor costs through the automating of brewing and warehousing. Furthermore, plant construction costs per barrel are about one-third less for a 4.5-million-barrel plant than for a 1.5-million-barrel plant. As a consequence of these and other economies, it is estimated that unit production costs decline sharply up to the point at which a plant produces 1.25 million barrels per year. Average costs continue to decline, but less significantly, up to the 4.5-million-barrel capacity at which all scale economies seem to be exhausted. Evidence of the importance of scale economies is reflected in statistics which show that over time there has been a steady decline in breweries producing less than 2 million barrels per year. Because the construction of a modern 4-million-barrel capacity brewery costs about $250 million, economies of scale may now constitute a significant barrier to entry.

Although mergers have occurred, they have not been a fundamental cause of increased concentration in the brewing industry. Rather, mergers have been largely the result of failing small breweries selling out.

On the other hand, the ascendancy of the Miller Brewing Company from the seventh to the second largest producer in the 1970s was due in large measure to advertising and product differentiation. When Miller was acquired by the Philip Morris Company in 1970, the new management made two salient changes. First, Miller High Life beer was "repositioned" into that segment of the market where potential sales were the greatest. Sold previously as the "champagne of beers," High Life had appealed heavily to upper-income consumers and women who only drank beer occasionally. Miller's new television ads featured young blue-collar workers who were inclined to be greater beer consumers. Second, Miller then developed its low-calorie Lite beer which was extensively promoted with the infusion of Philip Morris advertising dollars. Lite proved to be the most popular new product in the history of the beer industry and contributed significantly to Miller's dramatic rise in the industry.

Currently, the beer industry does not appear to have engaged in economically undesirable behavior. There has been no evidence of collusion and current excess productive capacity prompts the large brewers to compete for market shares. The fact that historically there has been considerable turnover in the ranking of the largest firms is further evidence of competition. Miller, ranked eighth in 1968, rose to number two in 1977 and has maintained that position. In comparison, Schlitz and Pabst were the second and third largest brewers in the mid-1970s, but now are only "also rans."

Source: This synopsis is based on Kenneth G. Elzinga, "The Beer Industry," in Walter Adams (ed.), *The Structure of American Industry,* 8th ed. (New York: Macmillan Publishing Co., Inc. 1990), pp. 128–160. Updated.

---

to consumers. For example, one authoritative estimate suggests that the import quotas strengthened the domestic oligopoly to the extent that on the average domestic producers earned an additional $400 in profits on each car sold in 1983. Given that the output of domestic producers was 7 million cars in 1983, the aggregate increase in profits of domestic manufacturers was $2.8 billion.[8] These estimates clearly indicate that American consumers have a great stake in free international trade and the competition it generates (Chapter 37).

But the Japanese in turn have responded to import quotas and the uncertainties inherent in the changing dollar–yen exchange rate by building automobile plants in the United States. These so-called "transplants" now produce about 10 percent of the cars sold in the United States. The success of Japanese production in America is reflected in the fact that they built eight new factories in the United States in the 1980s, precisely the number closed by the Big Three in the 1987–1989 period. It is significant that the Japanese have not sacrificed their production cost advantage by producing in the United States. The transplants embody state-of-the-art equipment, Japanese industrial relations techniques, and in some cases nonunion workers. The result is an automobile built for $500 to $800 less than in most of the Big Three's plants.

---

[8]"Carving Up the Car Buyer," *Newsweek,* March 5, 1984, pp. 72–73. The estimates are those of Robert Crandall of The Brookings Institution. The import quotas further hurt American consumers by restricting the supply and increasing the prices of Japanese cars.

2 Joint Ventures The second response of domestic producers has been to co-opt and mitigate foreign competition by initiating an elaborate network of joint ownership arrangements and joint ventures with foreign producers. Chrysler owns about one-fourth of Mitsubishi and imports both compact cars and parts from the latter. Mitsubishi in turn is a part owner of Korea's Hyundai Motor Company. General Motors has a joint production arrangement with Toyota in California and has significant ownership shares in other lesser-known Japanese auto manufacturers. Ford owns about one-fourth of Mazda. These arrangements cast a cloud of doubt on the contention that foreign competition has had an important "disciplining" effect on American auto manufacturers.

Adams and Brock, two astute observers of the industry, point out that ". . . a decade of joint ventures in the automotive industry has secured an interlocking system of mutually acceptable accords, and may well have forged the groundwork for cartelizing the world automobile industry."[9]

[9]Walter Adams and James W. Brock, "Joint Ventures, Antitrust, and Transnational Cartelization," *Northwestern Journal of International Law & Business,* Winter 1991, p. 465.

3 Altered Pricing Another effect of Japanese competition has been to alter the GM price leadership pattern which characterized the industry for many decades. In 1977–1978 the dollar significantly declined in value relative to the yen, meaning that each dollar earned by the Japanese on auto sales in the United States translated into a smaller amount of yen profits. Led by Toyota, the Japanese raised their prices in four steps during the 1978 model year. American producers generally followed these increases. Again in 1985–1988 a depreciating dollar further increased Japanese car prices but, perhaps alarmed by declining market shares, the Big Three only boosted prices by about one-third of the Japanese increases. In short, the price leadership role of GM has been clouded by a new group of foreign rivals.

We have now finished our analysis of the four basic product market models—pure competition, pure monopoly, monopolistic competition, and oligopoly. You should reexamine Table 23-1 to ensure that you clearly understand the main characteristics of each of these models.

CHAPTER SUMMARY

1 Oligopolistic industries are characterized by the presence of a few firms, each of which has a significant fraction of the market. Firms thus situated are mutually interdependent; the behavior of any one firm directly affects, and is affected by, the actions of rivals. Products may be virtually uniform or significantly differentiated. Underlying reasons for the evolution of oligopoly are economies of scale, other entry barriers, and the advantages of merger.

2 Concentration ratios can be used as a measure of oligopoly and market power. By giving more weight to larger firms, the Herfindahl index is designed to measure market dominance in an industry.

3 Game theory **a** shows the mutual interdependence of oligopolists' price policies; **b** reveals the tendency to act collusively; and **c** explains the temptation to cheat on collusive agreements.

4 Important models of oligopoly include: **a** the kinked-demand model, **b** collusive oligopoly, **c** price leadership, and **d** cost-plus pricing.

5 Noncollusive oligopolists may face a kinked demand curve. This curve and the accompanying marginal-revenue curve help explain the price rigidity which characterizes such markets; they do not, however, explain the level of price.

6 The uncertainties inherent in noncollusive pricing are conducive to collusion. There is a tendency for collusive oligopolists to maximize joint profits—that is, to behave somewhat like pure monopolists. Demand and cost differences, the presence of a "large" number of firms, "cheating" through secret price concessions, recessions, and the antitrust laws are all obstacles to collusive oligopoly.

7 Price leadership is a less formal means of collusion where the largest or most efficient firm in the industry initiates price changes and the other firms follow.

8 With cost-plus or markup pricing, oligopolists estimate their unit costs at some target level of output and add a percentage "markup" to determine price.

9 Market shares in oligopolistic industries are usually determined on the basis of nonprice competition. Oligopolists emphasize nonprice competition because **a** advertising and product variations are less easy for rivals to match, and **b** oligopolists frequently have ample resources to finance nonprice competition.

10 It is unlikely that either allocative or productive efficiency is realized in oligopolistic markets. The competitive view envisions oligopoly as being inferior to more competitive market structures in promoting product improvement and cost-decreasing innovations. The Schumpeter–Galbraith view is that oligopolists have both the incentive and financial resources to be technologically progressive.

TERMS AND CONCEPTS

oligopoly	import competition	collusion	cartel
homogeneous and	Herfindahl index	kinked demand curve	price leadership
differentiated	game theory model	price war	cost-plus pricing
oligopoly	duopoly	collusive oligopoly	competitive and
concentration ratios	mutual	gentlemen's	Schumpeter–
interindustry	interdependence	agreements	Galbraith views
competition			

QUESTIONS AND STUDY SUGGESTIONS

1 Why do oligopolies exist? List five or six oligopolists whose products you own or regularly purchase. What distinguishes oligopoly from monopolistic competition?

2 "Fewness of rivals means mutual interdependence, and mutual interdependence means uncertainty as to how those few rivals will react to a price change by any one firm." Explain. Of what significance is this for determining demand and marginal revenue? Other things being equal, would you expect mutual interdependence to vary directly or inversely with the degree of product differentiation? With the number of firms? Explain.

3 What is the meaning of a four-firm concentration ratio of 60 percent? 90 percent? What are the shortcomings of concentration ratios as measures of market power?

4 Suppose that in industry A five firms have annual sales of 30, 30, 20, 10, and 10 percent of total industry sales. For the five firms in industry B the figures are 60, 25, 5, 5, and 5 percent. Calculate the Herfindahl index for each industry and compare their likely competitiveness.

5 Explain the general character of the data in the following profits-payoff matrix for oligopolists C and D. All profit figures are in thousands.

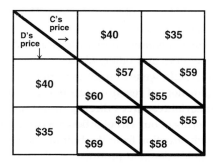

a Use the table to explain the mutual interdependence which characterizes oligopolistic industries.
b Assuming no collusion, what is the likely outcome of this game?
c Given your answer to question **b,** explain why price collusion is mutually profitable. Why might there be a temptation to cheat on the collusive agreement?

6 What assumptions concerning a rival's responses to price changes underlie the kinked demand curve? Why is there a gap in the marginal-revenue curve? How does the kinked demand curve help explain oligopolistic price rigidity? What are the shortcomings of the kinked-demand model?

7 Why might price collusion occur in oligopolistic industries? Assess the economic desirability of collusive pricing. Explain: "If each firm knows that the price of each of its few rivals depends on its own price, how can the prices be determined?" What are the main obstacles to collusion? Apply these obstacles to the weakening of OPEC in the 1980s.

8 Assume the demand curve shown in question 4 in Chapter 24 applies to a pure monopolist which has a constant marginal cost of $4. What price and output will be most profitable for the monopolist? Now assume the demand curve applies to a two-firm industry (a "duopoly") and that each firm has a constant marginal cost of $4. If the firms collude, what price and quantity will maximize their joint profits? Demonstrate why it might be profitable for one of the firms to cheat. If the other firm becomes aware of this cheating, what will happen?

9 Explain how price leadership might evolve and function in an oligopolistic industry. Is cost-plus pricing compatible with collusion?

10 "Oligopolistic industries have both the means and the inclination for technological progress." Do you agree? Explain.

11 "If oligopolists really want to compete, they should do so by cutting their prices rather than by squandering millions of dollars on advertising and other forms of sales promotion." Do you agree? Why don't oligopolists usually compete by cutting prices?

12 Using Figure 26-3, explain how a collusive oligopolist might increase its profits by offering secret price concessions to buyers. On the diagram, indicate the amount of additional profits which the firm may realize. What are the risks involved in such a policy?

13 Review the case study of the automobile industry and identify aspects of industry structure and behavior which are oligopolistic. What responses have domestic producers made to increasing foreign competition?

sume an acre of land, a John Deere tractor, or the labor services of a farmer, but households do want to consume the various food and fiber products these resources help produce.

Marginal Revenue Product (MRP)

The derived nature of resource demand implies that the strength of the demand for any resource will depend on (1) the productivity of the resource in helping to create a good, and (2) the market value or price of the good it is producing. A resource which is highly productive in turning out a commodity highly valued by society will be in great demand. On the other hand, demand will be very weak for a relatively unproductive resource which is only capable of producing some good not in great demand by households. There will be no demand for a resource which is phenomenally efficient in producing something no one wants to purchase!

Productivity　The roles of productivity and product price in determining resource demand can be clearly seen in Table 27-1. Here we assume a firm adds one variable resource—labor—to its fixed plant. Columns 1 through 3 remind us that the law of diminishing returns will apply in this situation, causing the **marginal product** (MP) of labor to fall beyond some point. (It might be helpful to review the section, "Law of Diminishing Returns," in Chapter 22 at this point.) For simplicity, we assume that diminishing marginal productivity sets in with the first worker hired.

Product Price　But the derived demand for a resource also depends on the price of the commodity it

produces. Column 4 adds this price information. Note that product price is constant, in this case at $2, because we are supposing a competitive product market.

Multiplying column 2 by column 4, we get the total-revenue data of column 5. From these total-revenue data we can compute **marginal revenue product** (MRP)—*the increase in total revenue resulting from the use of each additional variable input (labor, in this case)*. This is indicated in column 6.

Rule for Employing Resources: MRP = MRC

The MRP schedule—columns 1 and 6—is the firm's demand schedule for labor. To explain this, we must first discuss the rule which guides a profit-seeking firm in hiring any resource. *To maximize profits, a firm should hire additional units of any given resource so long as each successive unit adds more to the firm's total revenue than it does to its total costs.*

Economists have special terms designating what each additional unit of labor or other variable resource adds to total cost and what it adds to total revenue. We noted that, by definition, MRP measures how much each successive worker adds to total revenue. The amount which each additional unit of a resource adds to the firm's total (resource) cost is called **marginal resource cost** (MRC). Thus we can restate our rule for hiring resources as follows: *It will be profitable for a firm to hire additional units of a resource up to the point at which that resource's MRP is equal to its MRC.* If the number of workers a firm is currently hiring is such that the MRP of the last worker exceeds his or her MRC, the firm can clearly profit by hiring more workers. But if the number being hired is such that the

TABLE 27-1　**The demand for a resource: pure competition in the sale of the product** *(hypothetical data)*

(1) Units of resource	(2) Total product	(3) Marginal product (MP), or Δ(2)	(4) Product price	(5) Total revenue, or (2) × (4)	(6) Marginal revenue product (MRP), or Δ(5)
0	0		$2	$ 0	
		7			$14
1	7		2	14	
		6			12
2	13		2	26	
		5			10
3	18		2	36	
		4			8
4	22		2	44	
		3			6
5	25		2	50	
		2			4
6	27		2	54	
		1			2
7	28		2	56	

MRC of the last worker exceeds the MRP, the firm is hiring workers who are not "paying their way," and it can thereby increase its profits by laying off some workers. You may have recognized that this **MRP = MRC rule** is very similar to the MR = MC profit-maximizing rule employed throughout our discussion of price and output determination. The rationale of the two rules is the same, but the point of reference is now *inputs* of resources, rather than *outputs* of product.

MRP Is a Demand Schedule

Just as product price and marginal revenue are equal in a purely competitive product market, so *resource price and marginal resource cost are equal when a firm is hiring a resource competitively.* In a purely competitive labor market the wage rate is set by the total, or market, supply of, and the market demand for, labor. Because it hires such a small fraction of the total supply of labor, a single firm cannot influence this wage rate. This means that total resource cost increases by exactly the amount of the going wage rate for each additional worker hired; the wage rate and MRC are equal. It follows that so long as it is hiring labor competitively, *the firm will hire workers to the point at which their wage rate (or MRC) is equal to their MRP.*[1]

In terms of the data in column 6 of Table 27-1, if the wage rate is $13.95, the firm will hire only one worker. This is so because the first worker adds $14 to total revenue and slightly less—$13.95—to total costs. For each successive worker, however, MRC exceeds MRP, indicating that it will not be profitable to hire any of those workers. If the wage rate is $11.95, by the same reasoning we discover that it will pay the firm to hire both the first and second workers. Similarly, if the wage rate is $9.95, three will be hired. If $7.95, four. If $5.95, then five. And so forth. It is evident that *the MRP schedule constitutes the firm's demand for labor, because each point on this schedule (curve) indicates the number of workers which the firm would hire at each possible wage rate which might exist.* This is shown graphically in Figure 27-1.

The rationale employed here is familiar to us. Recall in Chapter 23 that we applied the price-equals-marginal-cost or *P* = MC rule for the profit-maximizing *output* to discover that the portion of the competitive firm's short-run marginal-cost curve lying above average variable cost is the short-run *product supply* curve (Figure 23-6). Presently we are applying the

[1]The logic here is the same as that which allowed us to change the MR = MC profit-maximization rule to *P* = MC for the purely competitive seller of Chapter 23.

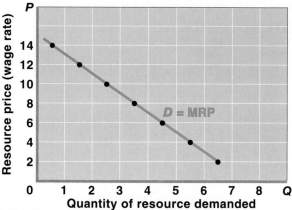

FIGURE 27-1   The purely competitive seller's demand for a resource

The MRP curve is the resource demand curve. The location of the curve depends on the marginal productivity of the resource and the price of the product. Under pure competition product price is constant; therefore, diminishing marginal productivity is the sole reason why the resource demand curve is downsloping.

MRP = MRC rule for the profit-maximizing *input* to the firm's MRP curve and determining that this curve is the input or *resource demand* curve.

Resource Demand under Imperfect Competition

Our analysis of labor demand becomes more complex when we assume that the firm is selling its product in an imperfectly competitive market. Pure monopoly, oligopoly, and monopolistic competition in the product market all mean that the firm's product demand curve is downsloping; the firm must accept a lower price to increase its sales.

Table 27-2 takes this into account. The productivity data of Table 27-1 are retained in columns 1–3, but we now assume in column 4 that product price must be lowered to sell the marginal product of each successive worker. The MRP of the purely competitive seller falls for one reason: Marginal product diminishes. But the MRP of the imperfectly competitive seller falls for two reasons: Marginal product diminishes *and* product price falls as output increases.

It must be emphasized that the lower price accompanying every increase in output applies in each case not only to the marginal product of each successive worker but also to all prior units which otherwise could have sold at a higher price. To illustrate: The second worker's marginal product is 6 units. These 6 units can be sold for $2.40 each or, as a group, for $14.40. But this is *not* the MRP of the second worker. To sell these 6

TABLE 27-2 The demand for a resource: imperfect competition in the sale of the product (hypothetical data)

(1) Units of resource	(2) Total product	(3) Marginal product (MP), or Δ(2)	(4) Product price	(5) Total revenue, or (2) × (4)	(6) Marginal revenue product (MRP), or Δ(5)
0	0		$2.80	$ 0	
		7			$18.20
1	7		2.60	18.20	
		6			13.00
2	13		2.40	31.20	
		5			8.40
3	18		2.20	39.60	
		4			4.40
4	22		2.00	44.00	
		3			2.25
5	25		1.85	46.25	
		2			1.00
6	27		1.75	47.25	
		1			−1.05
7	28		1.65	46.20	

units, the firm must take a 20-cent price cut on the 7 units produced by the first worker—units which could have been sold for $2.60 each. Thus, the MRP of the second worker is only $13.00 [= $14.40 − (7 × 20 cents)]. Similarly, the third worker's MRP is $8.40. Although the 5 units this worker produces are worth $2.20 each in the market, the third worker does not add $11.00 to the firm's total revenue when account is taken of the 20-cent price cut which must be taken on the 13 units produced by the first two workers. In this case the third worker's MRP is only $8.40 [= $11.00 − (13 × 20 cents)]. The other figures in column 6 are similarly explained.

The net result is that the MRP curve—the resource demand curve—of the imperfectly competitive producer tends to be less elastic than that of a purely competitive producer. At a wage rate or MRC of $11.95, both the purely competitive and the imperfectly competitive seller will hire two workers. But at $9.95, the competitive firm will hire three and the imperfectly competitive firm only two. And at $7.95, the purely competitive firm will take on four employees and the imperfect competitor only three. This difference in elasticity can be readily seen by graphing the MRP data of Table 27-2 as in Figure 27-2 and comparing them with Figure 27-1.[2]

It is not surprising that the imperfectly competitive producer is less responsive to wage cuts in terms of workers employed than is the purely competitive producer. The imperfect competitor's relative reluctance to employ more resources and thereby produce more output when resource prices fall is merely the resource market reflection of the imperfect competitor's tendency to restrict output in the product market. Other things being equal, the imperfectly competitive seller will produce less of a product than would a purely com-

FIGURE 27-2 The imperfectly competitive seller's demand for a resource

An imperfectly competitive seller's resource demand curve slopes downward because marginal product diminishes and product price falls as output increases.

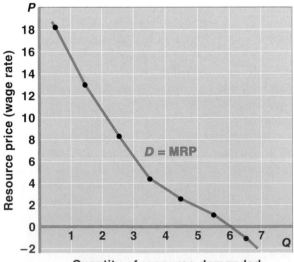

Quantity of resource demanded

[2]Note that the points in Figures 27-1 and 27-2 are plotted halfway between each number of workers because MRP is associated with the *addition* of one more worker. Thus, in Figure 27-2, for example, the MRP of the second worker ($13.00) is plotted not at 1 or 2, but rather at 1½. This "smoothing" technique also allows us to present a continuously downsloping curve rather than one which moves downward in discrete steps as each worker is hired.

petitive seller. In producing this smaller output, it will demand fewer resources.

But one important qualification exists. We noted in Chapters 24 and 26 that the market structures of pure monopoly and oligopoly *might* lead to technological progress and a higher level of production, more employment, and lower prices in the long run than would a purely competitive market. The resource demand curve in these cases would not be restricted.

Market Demand for a Resource

We can now derive the market demand curve for a resource. You will recall that the total, or market, demand curve for a product is developed by summing horizontally the demand curves of all individual buyers in the market. Similarly, the market demand curve for a particular resource can be derived in essentially the same fashion, that is, by summing the individual demand or MRP curves for all firms hiring that resource.

QUICK REVIEW 27-1

♪ *A resource will be employed in the profit-maximizing amount where its marginal revenue product equals its marginal resource cost (MRP = MRC).*

♪ *Application of the MRP = MRC rule to a firm's MRP curve demonstrates that the MRP curve is the firm's resource demand curve.*

♪ *The resource demand curve of a purely competitive seller is downsloping solely because the marginal product of the resource diminishes; the resource demand curve of an imperfectly competitive seller is downsloping because marginal product diminishes and product price falls as output is increased.*

DETERMINANTS OF RESOURCE DEMAND

What will alter the demand for a resource, that is, shift the demand curve? What are the determinants of labor demand? The very derivation of resource demand immediately suggests two related factors—the resource's productivity and the market price of the product it is producing. And our previous analysis of changes in product demand (Chapter 4) suggests another factor—changes in the prices of other resources.

Changes in Product Demand

Because resource demand is a derived demand, any change in the demand for the product will affect product price and therefore the MRP of the resource. Other things being equal, *a change in the demand for the product that a particular type of labor is producing will shift labor demand in the same direction.*

In Table 27-1, assume an increase in product demand which boosts product price from $2 to $3. If you calculate the new labor demand curve and plot it in Figure 27-1, you will find it lies to the right of the old curve. Similarly, a drop in product demand and price will shift the labor demand curve to the left.

Real-world examples: The 1987 stock market crash resulted in a decline in the volume of stocks traded daily and a consequent decline in the demand for stockbrokers, causing widespread layoffs on Wall Street. Similarly, the increases in the prices of oil, natural gas, and electricity which have occurred since the mid-1970s increased the demand for woodburning stoves. An interesting labor market impact was an increase in the demand for chimney sweeps. Finally, in late 1987 McDonald's used television commercials to attract housewives and retirees to work in its 1600 company-owned restaurants. Why did this recruitment campaign begin in 1987 rather than a decade or two earlier? A major reason was that more and more women were working outside the house and thus had less time for meal preparation. The result was an increase in the demand for restaurant meals and an increase in the demand for fast-food workers which could not be entirely filled by teenagers, the traditional source of labor for fast-food restaurants.

Productivity Changes

Other things being unchanged, *a change in the productivity of labor will shift the labor demand curve in the same direction.* If we were to double the MP data of column 3 in Table 27-1 we would find that the MRP data would also double, indicating an increase in labor demand.

The productivity of any resource can be altered in several ways.

1 The marginal productivity data for, say, labor will depend on the quantities of other resources with which it is combined. The greater the amount of capital and land resources with which labor is combined, the greater will be the marginal productivity and the demand for labor.

2 Technological improvements will have the same effect. The better the quality of the capital, the greater the productivity of labor. Steelworkers employed with a given amount of real capital in the form of modern oxygen furnaces are more productive than when employed with the same amount of real capital embodied in old open-hearth furnaces.

3 Improvements in the quality of the variable resource itself—labor—will increase marginal productivity and therefore the demand for labor. In effect, we have a new demand curve for a different, more skilled, kind of labor.

All these considerations, incidentally, are important in explaining why the average level of (real) wages is higher in the United States than in many other nations. American workers are generally healthier and better trained than those of these other nations, and in most industries they work with a larger and more efficient stock of capital goods and more abundant natural resources. This spells a strong demand for labor. On the supply side of the market, labor is *relatively* scarce compared with some other nations. A strong demand and a relatively scarce supply result in high wage rates. This will be discussed further in Chapter 28.

Prices of Other Resources

Just as changes in the prices of other products will change the demand for a specific commodity, so changes in the prices of other resources can be expected to alter the demand for a particular resource. Just as the effect of a change in the price of product X on the demand for product Y depends on whether X and Y are substitute or complementary goods (Chapter 4), so the effect of a change in the price of resource A on the demand for resource B will depend on their substitutability or their degree of complementarity.

Substitute Resources Suppose in a certain production process that technology is such that labor and capital are substitutable for one another. In other words, a firm can produce some given output with a relatively small amount of labor and a relatively large amount of capital or vice versa. Now assume a decline in the price of machinery occurs. The resulting impact on the demand for labor will be the net result of two opposed effects: the substitution effect and the output effect.

1 Substitution Effect The decline in the price of machinery will prompt the firm to substitute machinery for labor. This is the obvious adjustment to make if the firm seeks to produce any given output in the least costly fashion. At given wage rates, smaller quantities of labor will now be employed. In short, this **substitution effect** will decrease the demand for labor.

2 Output Effect Because the price of machinery has fallen, the costs of producing various outputs will also have declined. With lower costs, the firm will find it profitable to produce and sell a larger output. This greater output will increase the demand for all resources, including labor. For a reduction in the price of machinery, this **output effect** will increase the demand for labor.

The substitution and output effects clearly work in opposite directions. For a decline in the price of machinery, the substitution effect decreases and the output effect increases the demand for labor. The net impact on labor demand will depend on the relative sizes of the two opposed effects. If the substitution effect outweighs the output effect, the reduction in the price of capital reduces the demand for labor. If the reverse holds true, the demand for labor will increase. *If the substitution effect outweighs the output effect, a change in the price of a substitute resource will change the demand for labor in the same direction. If the output effect exceeds the substitution effect, a change in the price of a substitute resource will change the demand for labor in the opposite direction.*

Complementary Resources Recall from Chapter 4 that certain products, such as cameras and film or computers and software, are complementary goods in that they "go together" and are jointly demanded. Resources may also be complementary; an increase in the quantity of one of them used in the production process will require an increase in the amount used of the other as well, and vice versa. For example, suppose a small manufacturer of metal products uses punch presses as its basic piece of capital equipment. Each press is designed to be operated by one worker; the machine is not automated—it won't run itself—and a second worker would be wholly redundant.

Assume that a significant technological advance in the production of these presses substantially reduces their costs. Now there can be no negative substitution effect because labor and capital must be used in fixed proportions, one person for one machine. Capital cannot be substituted for labor. But there is a positive output effect for labor. Other things being equal, the reduction in the price of capital goods means lower production costs. It will therefore be profitable to produce a larger output. In doing so the firm will use both more capital and more labor. When labor and capital are complementary, a decline in the price of machinery will increase the demand for labor through the output effect. Conversely, in the case of an increase in the price of capital, the output effect will reduce the demand for labor. *A change in the price of a complementary resource will cause the demand for labor to change in the opposite direction.*

Recapitulation: The demand curve for labor will *increase* (shift rightward) when:

1 The demand for (and therefore the price of) the product produced by that labor increases
2 The productivity (MP) of labor increases
3 The price of a substitute input decreases, provided the output effect is greater than the substitution effect
4 The price of a substitute input increases, provided the substitution effect exceeds the output effect
5 The price of a complementary input decreases

ELASTICITY OF RESOURCE DEMAND

The factors just discussed are responsible for shifts in the location of resource demand curves. Such changes in demand must be distinguished from a change in the quantity of a resource demanded. The latter does not entail a shift in the resource demand curve but rather a movement from one point to another on a stable resource demand curve, because of a change in the price of the specific resource under consideration. In Table 27-1 and Figure 27-1 we note that an increase in the wage rate from $5.95 to $7.95 will reduce the quantity of labor demanded from five to four workers.

What determines the sensitivity of producers to changes in resource prices? Or, more technically, what determines the elasticity of resource demand? Several generalizations provide important insights in answering this question.

1 *Rate of MP Decline* A purely technical consideration—the rate at which the marginal product of the variable resource declines—is crucial. *If the marginal product of labor declines slowly as it is added to a fixed amount of capital, the MRP, or demand curve for labor, will decline slowly and tend to be highly elastic.* A small decline in the price of such a resource will yield a relatively large increase in the amount demanded. Conversely, if the marginal productivity of labor declines sharply, the MRP, or labor demand curve, will decline rapidly. This means that a relatively large decline in the wage rate will be accompanied by a very modest increase in the amount of labor hired; resource demand will be inelastic.

2 *Ease of Resource Substitutability* The degree to which resources are substitutable is also a determinant of elasticity. *The larger the number of good substitute resources available, the greater will be the elasticity of demand for a particular resource.* If a furniture manufacturer finds that five or six different types of wood are equally satisfactory in making coffee tables, a rise in the price of any one type of wood may cause a very sharp drop in the amount demanded as the producer substitutes other woods. At the other extreme, it may be impossible to substitute; bauxite is absolutely essential in the production of aluminum ingots. Thus, the demand for it by aluminum producers is inelastic.

Note that *time* can play an important role in the input substitution process. For example, a firm's truck drivers may obtain a substantial wage increase with little or no immediate decline in employment. But over time, as the firm's trucks wear out and are replaced, the company may purchase larger trucks and thereby be able to deliver the same total output with fewer drivers. Alternatively, as the firm's trucks depreciate, it might turn to entirely different means of transportation. As a second example, recently developed commercial aircraft have been specifically designed to require only two pilots rather than the customary three.

3 *Elasticity of Product Demand* The elasticity of demand for any resource will depend on the elasticity of demand for the product it helps produce. *The greater the elasticity of product demand, the greater the elasticity of resource demand.* The derived nature of resource demand would lead us to expect this relationship. A small rise in the price of a product with great elasticity of demand will sharply reduce output and therefore bring about a relatively large decline in the amounts of various resources demanded. This correctly implies that the demand for the resource is elastic. Remember that the resource demand curve of Figure 27-1 is more elastic than the resource demand curve shown in Figure 27-2. The difference arises because in Figure 27-1 we assume a perfectly elastic product demand curve, while Figure 27-2 is based on a downsloping or less than perfectly elastic product demand curve.

4 Labor Cost–Total Cost Ratio *The larger the proportion of total production costs accounted for by a resource, the greater will be the elasticity of demand for that resource.* In the extreme, if labor costs were the only production cost, then a 20 percent increase in wage rates would shift the firm's cost curves upward by 20 percent. Given the elasticity of product demand, this substantial increase in costs would cause a relatively large decline in sales and a sharp decline in the amount of labor demanded. Labor demand would be elastic. But if labor costs were only 50 percent of production costs, then a 20 percent increase in wage rates would only increase costs by 10 percent. Given the same elasticity of product demand, a relatively small decline in sales and therefore in the amount of labor would result. The demand for labor would be inelastic.

QUICK REVIEW 27-2

◆   *A resource demand curve will shift because of changes in product demand, changes in the productivity of the resource, and changes in the prices of other inputs.*

◆   *If resources A and B are substitutable, a decline in the price of A will decrease the demand for B provided the substitution effect exceeds the output effect. But if the output effect exceeds the substitution effect, the demand for B will increase.*

◆   *If resources C and D are complements, a decline in the price of C will increase the demand for D.*

◆   *The elasticity of demand for a resource will be less the more rapid the decline in marginal product; the smaller the number of substitutes; the smaller the elasticity of product demand; and the smaller the proportion of total cost accounted for by the resource.*

OPTIMAL COMBINATION OF RESOURCES

So far we have centered our discussion on one variable input, namely, labor. But in the long run firms can vary the amounts of *all* the resources they use. It is therefore important to consider what combination of resources a firm will choose when all are variable. While our analysis will be based on two resources, it can be extended to any number one chooses to consider.

We will consider two interrelated questions:

1   What is the least-cost combination of resources to use in producing *any* given level of output?

2   What combination of resources will maximize a firm's profits?

The Least-Cost Rule

A firm is producing *any* given output with the **least-cost combination of resources** when the last dollar spent on each resource entails the same marginal product. That is, *the cost of any output is minimized when the marginal product per dollar's worth of each resource used is the same.* With just two resources, labor and capital, the cost-minimizing position occurs where

$$\frac{\text{MP of labor}}{\text{price of labor}} = \frac{\text{MP of capital}}{\text{price of capital}} \qquad (1)$$

You can see why fulfilling this condition means least-cost production. Suppose that the prices of capital and labor are both $1 per unit, but that capital and labor are currently employed in such amounts that the marginal product of labor is 10 and the marginal product of capital is 5. Our equation immediately tells us this is *not* the least costly combination of resources: MP_L/P_L is 10/1 and MP_C/P_C is 5/1.

If the firm spends a dollar less on capital and shifts that dollar to labor, it will lose the 5 units of output produced by the marginal dollar's worth of capital, but will gain the 10 units of output from the extra dollar's worth of labor. *Net* output will increase by 5 (= 10 − 5) units for the same total cost. This shifting of dollars from capital to labor will push the firm down its MP curve for labor and back up its MP curve for capital, moving the firm toward a position of equilibrium where equation (1) is fulfilled. At that point the MP of both labor and capital might be, for example, 7.

Whenever the same total cost results in a greater total output, the cost per unit—and therefore the total cost of any given level of output—is being reduced. To be able to produce a *larger* output with a *given* total-cost outlay is the same thing as being able to produce a *given* output with a *smaller* total-cost outlay. From a slightly different perspective, if the firm buys $1 less of capital, its output will fall by 5 units. By spending only $.50 on labor the firm will increase its output by a compensating 5 units (= $\frac{1}{2}$ of the marginal product of a dollar's worth of labor). Thus, the firm will realize the same total output at a $.50 lower total cost.

The cost of producing any given output can be reduced so long as $MP_L/P_L \neq MP_C/P_C$. But when dollars have been shifted among capital and labor to the point where equation (1) holds, there are no further changes in the amounts of capital and labor employed which will further reduce costs. The least-cost combination of capital and labor is being realized for that output.

All long run[3] cost curves developed in Chapter 22 and applied in the ensuing product market chapters implicitly assume that each possible level of output is being produced with the least costly combination of inputs. If this were not so, then presumably there would exist lower attainable positions for the cost curves, and consequently there would be some other (larger) output and lower price at equilibrium. In terms of Chapter 24 a firm which combines resources in violation of the least-cost rule would incur X-inefficiency.

The producer's least-cost rule is analogous to the consumer's utility-maximizing rule of Chapter 21. In achieving the utility-maximizing collection of goods, the consumer considers both his or her preferences as reflected in diminishing marginal-utility data *and* prices of the various products. Similarly, a producer wants to minimize costs, just as the consumer seeks to maximize utility. In pursuing this combination of resources, the producer must consider both the productivity of the resource as reflected in diminishing marginal productivity data *and* prices (costs) of the various resources. A firm may well find it profitable to employ very small amounts of an extremely productive resource if its price is particularly high. Conversely, a firm might hire large amounts of a relatively unproductive resource if its price is sufficiently low.

The Profit-Maximizing Rule

Minimizing cost is not sufficient for maximizing profit. There are many different levels of output which a firm can produce in the least costly way, but there is only one unique output which will maximize profits. Recalling our earlier analysis of product markets, this profit-maximizing *output* is where marginal revenue equals marginal cost (MR = MC). We now derive a comparable rule from the standpoint of resource *inputs*.

In deriving the demand schedule for labor early in this chapter we determined that the profit-maximizing quantity of labor to employ is that quantity at which the wage rate, or price of labor (P_L), equals the marginal *revenue* product of labor (MRP_L) or, more simply, $P_L = MRP_L$.

The same rationale applies to any other resource —for example, capital. Capital will also be employed in the profit-maximizing amount when its price equals its marginal revenue product, or $P_C = MRP_C$. Thus, in

general, we can say that when hiring resources *in competitive markets,* a firm will realize the **profit-maximizing combination of resources** when each input is employed up to the point at which its price equals its marginal revenue product:

$$P_L = MRP_L$$

$$P_C = MRP_C$$

Dividing both sides of each equation by their respective prices, we have

$$\frac{MRP_L}{P_L} = \frac{MRP_C}{P_C} = 1 \qquad (2)$$

Note in equation (2) that it is not sufficient that the MRPs of the two resources be *proportionate to* their prices; the MRPs must be *equal to* their prices and the ratios therefore equal to 1. For example, if $MRP_L = \$15, P_L = \$5, MRP_C = \$9$, and $P_C = \$3$, the firm would be underemploying both capital and labor even though the ratios of MRP to resource price were identical for both resources. The firm could expand its profits by hiring additional amounts of both capital and labor until it had moved down their downsloping MRP curves to the points at which MRP_L was equal to \$5 and MRP_C was \$3. The ratios would now be 5/5 and 3/3 and equal to 1.[4]

---

[3]We specify long run because application of the least-cost rule assumes that quantities of both labor and capital are variable.

[4]It is not difficult to demonstrate that equation (2) is consistent with (indeed, the equivalent of) the $P = MC$ rule for determining the profit-maximizing output of Chapter 23. We begin by taking the reciprocal of equation (2):

$$\frac{P_L}{MRP_L} = \frac{P_C}{MRP_C} = 1$$

Recall that, assuming pure competition in the product market, marginal revenue product, MRP, is found by multiplying marginal product, MP, by product price, P_x. Thus we can write:

$$\frac{P_L}{MP_L \cdot P_x} = \frac{P_C}{MP_C \cdot P_x} = 1$$

Multiplying through by product price, P_x, we get:

$$\frac{P_L}{MP_L} = \frac{P_C}{MP_C} = P_x$$

The two ratios measure marginal cost. That is, if we divide the cost of an additional input of labor or capital by the associated marginal product we have the addition to total cost, that is, the *marginal cost,* of each additional unit of output. For example, if the price of an extra worker (P_L) is \$10 and that worker's marginal product (MP_L) is 5 units, then the marginal cost of each of those 5 units is \$2. The same reasoning applies to capital. We thus obtain:

$$MC_x = P_x$$

Our conclusion is that equation (2) in the text, showing the profit-maximizing combination of *inputs,* is the equivalent of our earlier $P = MC$ rule which identified the profit-maximizing *output.*

Although we have separated the two for discussion purposes, the profit-maximizing position of equation (2) subsumes the least-cost position of equation (1). (Note that if we divide the MRP numerators in equation [2] by product price we obtain equation [1].) A firm which is maximizing its profits *must* be producing the profit-maximizing output with the least costly combination of resources. If it is *not* using the least costly combination of labor and capital, then it could produce the same output at a smaller total cost and realize a larger profit. Thus, a necessary condition for profit maximization is the fulfillment of equation (1). But equation (1) is not a sufficient condition for profit maximization. It is quite possible for a firm to produce the "wrong" output, that is, an output which does not maximize profits, but to produce that output with the least costly combination of resources.

Numerical Illustration

A numerical illustration may help us in grasping the least-cost and profit-maximizing rules. In columns 2, 3, 2′, and 3′ of Table 27-3 we show the total products and marginal products for various amounts of labor and capital which are assumed to be the only inputs needed in producing product X. Both inputs are subject to the law of diminishing returns.

We also assume that labor and capital are supplied in competitive resource markets at $8 and $12 respectively and that product X is sold competitively at $2 per unit. For both labor and capital we can determine the total revenue associated with each input level by multiplying total product by the $2 product price. These data

are shown in columns 4 and 4′. This allows us to calculate the marginal revenue product of each successive input of labor and capital as shown in columns 5 and 5′.

Producing at Least Cost What is the least-cost combination of labor and capital to use in producing, say, 50 units of output? Answer: 3 units of labor and 2 units of capital. Note from columns 3 and 3′ that in hiring 3 units of labor $MP_L/P_L = 6/8 = 3/4$ and for 2 units of capital $MP_C/P_C = 9/12 = 3/4$, so equation (1) is fulfilled. And columns 2 and 2′ indicate that this combination of labor and capital does, indeed, result in the specified 50 (= 28 + 22) units of output. How can we verify that costs are actually minimized? First, note that the total cost of employing 3 units of labor and 2 of capital is $48 [= (3 × $8) + (2 × $12)] or, alternatively stated, cost per unit of output is $.96 (= $48/50).

Observe that there are other combinations of labor and capital which will yield 50 units of output. For example, 5 units of labor and 1 unit of capital will produce 50 (= 37 + 13) units, but we find that total cost is now higher at $52 [= (5 × $8) + (1 × $12)], meaning that average unit cost has risen to $1.04 (= $52/50). By employing 5 units of labor and 1 of capital the least-cost rule would be violated in that $MP_L/P_L = 4/8$ is less than $MP_C/P_C = 13/12$, indicating that more capital and less labor should be employed to produce this output.

Similarly, 50 units of output also could be produced with 2 units of labor and 3 of capital. The total cost of the 50 units of output would again be $52 [= (2 × $8) + (3 × $12)], or $1.04 per unit. Here equation (1) is not fulfilled in that $MP_L/P_L = 10/8$

TABLE 27-3 **The least-cost and profit-maximizing combination of labor and capital** *(hypothetical data)**

Labor (price = $8)					Capital (price = $12)				
(1) Quantity	(2) Total product	(3) Marginal product	(4) Total revenue	(5) Marginal revenue product	(1′) Quantity	(2′) Total product	(3′) Marginal product	(4′) Total revenue	(5′) Marginal revenue product
0	0	0	$ 0	$ 0	0	0	0	$ 0	$ 0
1	12	12	24	24	1	13	13	26	26
2	22	10	44	20	2	22	9	44	18
3	28	6	56	12	3	28	6	56	12
4	33	5	66	10	4	32	4	64	8
5	37	4	74	8	5	35	3	70	6
6	40	3	80	6	6	37	2	74	4
7	42	2	84	4	7	38	1	76	2

*To simplify, it is assumed in this table that the productivity of each resource is independent of the quantity of the other. For example, the total and marginal product of labor is assumed not to vary with the quantity of capital employed.

which exceeds $MP_C/P_C = 6/12$. This inequality suggests that the firm should use more labor and less capital.

To recapitulate: While there may be several combinations of labor and capital capable of producing any given output—in this case 50 units—only that combination which fulfills equation (1) will minimize costs.

Maximizing Profits   Will 50 units of output maximize the firm's profits? Answer: No, because the profit-maximizing rule stated in equation (2) is *not* fulfilled when employing 3 units of labor and 2 of capital. We know that to maximize profits any given input should be employed until its price equals its marginal revenue product ($P_L = MRP_L$ and $P_C = MRP_C$). But for 3 units of labor we find in column 5 that labor's MRP is $12 while its price is only $8. This means it is profitable to hire more labor. Similarly, for 2 units of capital we observe in column 5' that MRP is $18 and capital's price is only $12, indicating that more capital should be employed. When hiring 3 units of labor and 2 of capital to produce 50 units of output, the firm is underemploying both inputs. Labor and capital are both being used in less than profit-maximizing amounts.

The marginal revenue products of labor and capital are equal to their prices and equation (2) is fulfilled when the firm is employing 5 units of labor and 3 units of capital. This is therefore the profit-maximizing combination of outputs.[5] The firm's total cost will be $76, which is made up of $40 (= 5 × $8) worth of labor and $36 (= 3 × $12) worth of capital. Total revenue of $130 is determined by multiplying total output of 65 (= 37 + 28) by the $2 product price or, alternatively, by simply summing the total revenue attributable to labor ($74) and to capital ($56). The difference between total revenue and total cost is, of course, the firm's economic profit which in this instance is $54 (= $130 − $76). Equation (2) is fulfilled when 5 units of labor and 3 of capital are employed: $MRP_L/P_L = 8/8 = MRP_C/P_C = 12/12 = 1$. You should experiment with other combinations of labor and capital to demonstrate that they will yield an economic profit less than $54.

Our example also verifies our earlier assertion that a firm using the profit-maximizing combination of inputs is also necessarily producing the resulting output

with the least cost. In fulfilling equation (2) the firm is automatically fulfilling equation (1). In this case for 5 units of labor and 3 of capital we observe that $MP_L/P_L = 4/8 = MP_C/P_C = 6/12$. Questions 5 and 7 at the end of this chapter are also recommended to further your understanding of the least-cost and profit-maximizing combination of inputs.[6]

MARGINAL PRODUCTIVITY THEORY OF INCOME DISTRIBUTION

Our discussion of resource pricing is the cornerstone of the controversial view that economic justice is one of the outcomes of a competitive capitalist economy. Table 27-1 tells us, in effect, that labor receives an income payment equal to the marginal contribution it makes to the firm's revenue. Bluntly stated, labor is paid what it is economically worth. Therefore, if one is willing to accept the ethical proposition "To each according to what one creates," the marginal productivity theory seems to provide a fair and equitable distribution of income. Because the marginal productivity theory equally applies to capital and land, the distribution of all incomes can be held as equitable.

At first glance an income distribution whereby workers and owners of property resources are paid in accordance with their contribution to output sounds eminently fair. But there are serious criticisms of the **marginal productivity theory of income distribution.**

1 Inequality   Critics argue that the distribution of income resulting from payment according to marginal productivity may be highly unequal because productive resources are very unequally distributed in the first place. Aside from differences in genetic endowments, individuals encounter substantially different opportunities to enhance their productivity through education and training. Some may not be able to participate in production at all because of mental or physical handicaps and would obtain no income under a system of distribution based solely on marginal productivity.

---

[5]Given that we are dealing with discrete (nonfractional) increases in the two outputs, you should also be aware that in fact the employment of 4 units of labor and 2 of capital is equally profitable. The fifth unit of labor's MRP and its price are equal (at $8), so that the fifth unit neither adds to, nor subtracts from, the firm's profits. The same reasoning applies to the third unit of capital.

[6]Footnote 1 in Chapter 28 modifies our least-cost and profit-maximizing rules for the situation in which a firm is hiring resources under imperfectly competitive conditions. Where there is imperfect competition in the resource market, the marginal resource cost (MRC)—the cost of an extra input—exceeds the resource price (P). Hence, we must substitute MRC for P in the denominators of equations (1) and (2).

LAST WORD

INPUT SUBSTITUTION: THE CASE OF CABOOSES

Substituting among inputs—particularly when jobs are at stake—can be quite controversial.

We have found that a firm will achieve the least-cost combination of inputs when the last dollar spent on each makes the same contribution to total output. This rule also implies that a firm is unimpeded in changing its input mix in response to technological changes or changes in input prices. Unfortunately, in the real world the substitution of new capital for old capital and the substitution of capital for labor may be controversial and difficult to achieve.

Consider the case of railroad cabooses. The railroads claim that technological advance has made the caboose obsolete. In particular, railroads want to substitute a "trainlink" which can be attached to the coupler of the last car of a train. This small black box contains a revolving strobe light and instruments which monitor train speed, airbrake pressure, and other relevant data which it transmits to the locomotive engineer. The trainlink costs only $4000 in comparison to $80,000 for a new caboose. And, of course, the trainlink replaces one member of the train crew.

The railroads cite substantial cost economies— perhaps as much as $400 million per year—from this rearrangement of capital and labor inputs. But the United Transportation Union (UTU) which represents railroad conductors and brakemen fears that the recent trend toward the demise of the caboose portends a decline in the demand for its members. The union therefore has made a concerted, but largely unsuccessful, effort to halt the elimination of cabooses on trains. The UTU argues that the elimination of cabooses will reduce railroad safety.

The union contends that, unlike humans, trainlink cannot detect broken wheels or axles nor overheated bearings. From the vantage point of the railroads this looks like featherbedding, that is, the protection of unnecessary jobs. The railroads contend that available data show no safety differences between trains using and those not using cabooses. Indeed, safety may be enhanced without cabooses because many injuries are incurred by crew who are riding in cabooses.

While cabooses are virtually extinct in Europe, they are the rule in Canada. In the United States the railway unions have lobbied successfully for legislation in four states which makes cabooses mandatory. In all other states the use of cabooses remains a matter of collective bargaining negotiations. In any event, the case of cabooses indicates clearly that input substitution is not as simple as economic analysis would suggest.

Ownership of property resources is also highly unequal. Many landlords and capitalists obtain their property by inheritance rather than through their own productive effort. Hence, income from inherited property resources conflicts with the "To each according to what one creates" proposition. This reasoning can lead one to advocate government policies to modify the income distribution resulting from payments made strictly according to marginal productivity.

2 Monopsony and Monopoly   The marginal productivity theory rests on the assumption of competitive markets. We will find in Chapter 28 that labor markets,

for example, are riddled with imperfections. Some employers exert monopsony power in hiring workers. And some workers, through labor unions and professional associations, brandish monopoly power in selling their services. Indeed, the process of collective bargaining over wages suggests a power struggle over the division of income. In this struggle market forces— and income shares based on marginal productivity— are pushed into the background. In short, we will find that, because of real-world market imperfections, wage rates and other resource prices frequently do *not* measure contributions to domestic output.

CHAPTER SUMMARY

1 Resource prices are a major determinant of money incomes, and simultaneously perform the function of rationing resources to various industries and firms.

2 The fact that the demand for any resource is derived from the product it helps produce means that the demand for a resource will depend on its productivity and the market value (price) of the good it is producing.

3 The marginal revenue product schedule of any resource is the demand schedule for that resource. This follows from an application of the rule that a firm hiring under competitive conditions will find it most profitable to hire a resource up to the point where the price of the resource equals its marginal revenue product.

4 The demand curve for a resource is downsloping because the marginal product of additional inputs of any resource declines in accordance with the law of diminishing returns. When a firm is selling in an imperfectly competitive market, the resource demand curve will fall for a second reason: Product price must be reduced to permit the firm to sell a larger output. The market demand for a resource can be derived by summing horizontally the demand curves of all firms hiring that resource.

5 The demand for a resource will shift as the result of **a** a change in the demand for, and therefore the price of, the product the resource is producing; **b** changes in the productivity of the resource; and **c** changes in prices of other resources.

6 If resources A and B are substitutable, a decline in the price of A will decrease the demand for B provided the substitution effect is greater than the output effect. But if the output effect exceeds the substitution effect, a decline in the price of A will increase the demand for B.

7 If resources C and D are complementary or jointly demanded, there is only an output effect and a change in the price of C will change the demand for D in the opposite direction.

8 The elasticity of resource demand will be greater **a** the slower the rate at which the marginal product of the resource declines, **b** the larger the number of good substitute resources available, **c** the greater the elasticity of demand for the product, and **d** the larger the proportion of total production costs attributable to the resource.

9 Any level of output will be produced with the least costly combination of resources when the marginal product per dollar's worth of each input is the same, that is, when

$$\frac{\text{MP of labor}}{\text{price of labor}} = \frac{\text{MP of capital}}{\text{price of capital}}$$

10 A firm will employ the profit-maximizing combination of resources when the price of each resource is equal to its marginal *revenue* product or, algebraically, when

$$\frac{\text{MRP of labor}}{\text{price of labor}} = \frac{\text{MRP of capital}}{\text{price of capital}} = 1$$

TERMS AND CONCEPTS

derived demand	MRP = MRC rule	profit-maximizing	marginal productivity
marginal product	substitution and output	combination of	theory of income
marginal revenue	effects	resources	distribution
product	least-cost combination		
marginal resource cost	of resources		

QUESTIONS AND STUDY SUGGESTIONS

1 What is the significance of resource pricing? Explain in detail how the factors determining resource demand differ from those underlying product demand. Explain the meaning and significance of the notion that the demand for a resource is a *derived* demand. Why do resource demand curves slope downward?

 2 Complete the following labor demand table (page 532) for a firm which is hiring labor competitively and selling its product in a competitive market.

    a How many workers will the firm hire if the going wage rate is $27.95? $19.95? Explain why the firm will not

hire a larger or smaller number of workers at each of these wage rates.

b Show in schedule form and graphically the labor demand curve of this firm.

c Now redetermine the firm's demand curve for labor, assuming that it is selling in an imperfectly competitive market and that, although it can sell 17 units at $2.20 per unit, it must lower product price by 5 cents to sell the marginal product of each successive worker. Compare this demand curve with that derived in question 2b. Which curve is more elastic? Explain.

Units of labor	Total product	Marginal product	Product price	Total revenue	Marginal revenue product
1	17		$2	$_____	
2	31	_____	2	_____	$_____
3	43	_____	2	_____	$_____
4	53	_____	2	_____	$_____
5	60	_____	2	_____	$_____
6	65	_____	2	_____	$_____

3 Distinguish between a change in resource demand and a change in the quantity of a resource demanded. What specific factors might lead to a change in resource demand? A change in the quantity of a resource demanded?

4 What factors determine the elasticity of resource demand? What effect will each of the following have on the elasticity *or* the location of the demand for resource C, which is being used in the production of commodity X? Where there is any uncertainty as to the outcome, specify the causes of that uncertainty.

  a An increase in the demand for product X.
  b An increase in the price of substitute resource D.
  c An increase in the number of resources substitutable for C in producing X.
  d A technological improvement in the capital equipment with which resource C is combined.
  e A decline in the price of complementary resource E.
  f A decline in the elasticity of demand for product X due to a decline in the competitiveness of the product market.

5 Suppose the productivity of labor and capital are as shown below. The output of these resources sells in a purely competitive market for $1 per unit. Both labor and capital are hired under purely competitive conditions at $1 and $3 respectively.

Units of capital	MP of capital	Units of labor	MP of labor
1	24	1	11
2	21	2	9
3	18	3	8
4	15	4	7
5	9	5	6
6	6	6	4
7	3	7	1
8	1	8	$\frac{1}{2}$

  a What is the least-cost combination of labor and capital to employ in producing 80 units of output? Explain.
  b What is the profit-maximizing combination of labor and capital for the firm to employ? Explain. What is the resulting level of output? What is the economic profit?
  c When the firm employs the profit-maximizing combination of labor and capital determined in 5b, is this combination also the least costly way of producing the profit-maximizing output? Explain.

6 Using the substitution and output effects, explain how a decline in the price of resource A *might* cause an increase in the demand for substitute resource B. If resources C and D are complementary and used in fixed proportions, what will be the impact of an increase in the price of C on the demand for D?

7 In each of the following four cases MRP_L and MRP_C refer to the marginal revenue products of labor and capital, respectively, and P_L and P_C refer to their prices. Indicate in each case whether the conditions are consistent with maximum profits for the firm. If not, state which resource(s) should be used in larger amounts and which resource(s) should be used in smaller amounts.

  a $MRP_L = \$8$; $P_L = \$4$; $MRP_C = \$8$; $P_C = \$4$.
  b $MRP_L = \$10$; $P_L = \$12$; $MRP_C = \$14$; $P_C = \$9$.
  c $MRP_L = \$6$; $P_L = \$6$; $MRP_C = \$12$; $P_C = \$12$.
  d $MRP_L = \$22$; $P_L = \$26$; $MRP_C = \$16$; $P_C = \$19$.

8 **Advanced analysis:** Demonstrate algebraically that the condition for the profit-maximizing level of output is the equivalent of the condition for the profit-maximizing combination of inputs.

9 If each input is paid in accordance with its marginal revenue product, will the resulting distribution of income be ethically just?

The Pricing and Employment of Resources: Wage Determination

The most important price you will encounter in your lifetime will most likely be your wage rate. It will be critical in determining your economic well-being. The following facts and questions may be of more than casual interest.

Fact: Real wages and therefore living standards have increased historically in the United States. Question: What forces account for these increases?

Fact: Union workers generally receive higher wages than nonunion workers in the same occupation. Question: How are unions able to accomplish this wage advantage?

Fact: The average salary for major league baseball players in 1991 was $890,844 compared to about $33,000 for teachers. Question: What causes differences in wages and incomes?

Fact: Most people are paid a certain hourly wage rate. But some workers are paid by the number of units produced or receive commissions and royalties. Question: What is the rationale for various compensation schemes?

Having explored the strategic factors underlying resource demand, we now introduce supply as it characterizes the markets for labor, land, capital, and entrepreneurial ability, to understand how wages, rents, interest, and profits are determined. We discuss wages before other resource prices because to the vast majority of households the wage rate is the most important price in the economy; it is the sole or basic source of income. About three-fourths of the national income is in the form of wages and salaries.

Our basic objectives in discussing wage determination are to (1) understand the forces underlying the general level of wage rates in the United states; (2) see how wage rates are determined in particular labor markets by presenting several representative labor market models; (3) analyze the impact of unions on the structure and level of wages; (4) discuss the economic effects of the minimum wage; (5) explain wage differentials; and (6) survey a number of compensation schemes which link pay to worker performance.

Throughout this chapter we will rely on the marginal productivity theory of Chapter 27 as an explanation of labor demand.

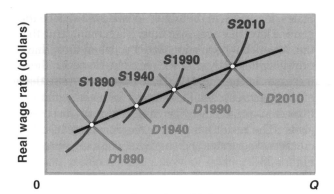

FIGURE 28-2   The secular trend of real wages in the United States

The productivity of American labor has increased substantially in the long run, causing the demand for labor to increase in relation to the supply. The result has been increases in real wages.

Market Demand   Suppose there are many—say, 200—firms demanding a particular type of semiskilled or skilled labor. These firms need not be in the same industry; industries are defined in terms of the products they produce and not of the resources they employ. Thus, firms producing wood-frame furniture, window and door frames, and cabinets will all demand carpenters. The total, or market, demand for the labor in question can be determined by summing horizontally the labor demand curves (the MRP curves) of the individual firms, as suggested in Figure 28-3a and b (Key Graph).

Market Supply   On the supply side of the picture, we assume there is no union; workers compete individually for available jobs. The supply curve for a particular type of labor will be upsloping, reflecting the fact that, in the absence of unemployment, hiring firms as a group will be forced to pay higher wage rates to obtain more workers. This is so because firms must bid these workers away from other industries, occupations, and localities. Within limits, workers have alternative job opportunities; that is, they may work in other industries in the same locality, or they may work in their present occupations in different cities or states. In a full-employment economy the group of firms in this particular labor market must pay higher and higher wage rates to attract this type of labor away from these alternative job opportunities. Similarly, higher wages are necessary to induce individuals not currently in the labor force to seek employment.

More technically, the market supply curve rises because it is an *opportunity cost* curve. To attract workers to this particular employment the wage rate paid must cover the opportunity costs of alternative uses of time spent, either in other labor markets, in household activities, or in leisure. Higher wages attract more people to this employment—people who were not attracted by lower wages because their opportunity costs were too high.

Market Equilibrium   The equilibrium wage rate and the equilibrium level of employment for this type of labor are determined at the intersection of the labor demand and labor supply curves. In Figure 28-3b the equilibrium wage rate is W_c ($6), and the number of workers hired is Q_c (1000). To the individual firm the wage rate W_c is given. Each of the many hiring firms employs such a small fraction of the total available supply of this type of labor that none can influence the wage rate. The supply of labor is perfectly elastic to the individual firm, as shown by S in Figure 28-3a.

Each individual firm will find it profitable to hire workers up to the point at which the going wage rate is equal to labor's MRP. This is merely an application of the MRP = MRC rule developed in Chapter 27. (Indeed, the demand curve in Figure 28-3a is based on Table 27-1.)

As Table 28-1 indicates, *because resource price is given to the individual competitive firm, the marginal cost of that resource* (MRC) *will be constant and equal to resource price (the wage rate).* In this case the wage rate and hence the marginal cost of labor are constant to the individual firm. Each additional worker hired adds precisely his or her wage rate ($6 in this case) to the firm's

TABLE 28-1   The supply of labor: pure competition in the hire of labor (hypothetical data)

(1) Units of labor	(2) Wage rate	(3) Total labor cost (wage bill)	(4) Marginal resource (labor) cost
0	$6	$ 0	
			$6
1	6	6	
			6
2	6	12	
			6
3	5	18	
			6
4	6	24	
			6
5	6	30	
			6
6	6	36	

KEY GRAPH

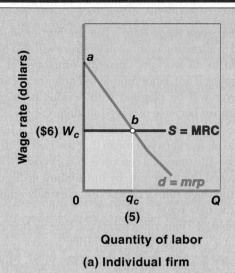

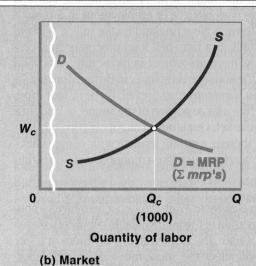

(a) Individual firm

(b) Market

FIGURE 28-3

The supply of, and the demand for, labor in a single competitive firm (a) and in a competitive market (b)

In a competitive labor market the equilibrium wage rate W_c and number of workers employed Q_c are determined by supply SS and demand DD, as shown in (b). Because this wage rate is given to the individual firm hiring in the market, its labor supply curve, $S = MRC$, is perfectly elastic, as in (a). The firm finds it most profitable to hire workers up to the MRP = MRC point. The area $0abq_c$ represents the firm's total revenue of which the green area $0W_cbq_c$ is its total wage cost; the remaining orange area W_cab is available for paying nonlabor resources.

total resource cost. The firm then will maximize its profits by hiring workers to the point at which their wage rate, and therefore marginal resource cost, equals their marginal revenue product. In Figure 28-3a the "typical" firm will hire q_c (5) workers.

Note that the firm's total revenue from hiring q_c workers can be found by summing their MRPs. In this case the total revenue from the five workers is indicated by the area $0abq_c$ in Figure 28-3a. Of this total revenue, the green area $0W_cbq_c$ is the firm's total wage cost and the orange triangular area W_cab represents additional revenue available to reward other inputs such as capital, land, and entrepreneurship.

Monopsony Model

In a purely competitive labor market each employer hires too small an amount of labor to influence the wage rate. Each firm is a "wage taker"; it can hire as

little or as much labor as it needs at the market wage, as reflected in its perfectly elastic labor supply curve.

Characteristics Let's now consider the case of **monopsony**, which describes an employer with monopolistic buying (hiring) power. Monopsony has the following characteristics:

1 The given firm's employment is a large portion of the total employment of a particular kind of labor.
2 This type of labor is relatively immobile, either geographically or in the sense that, if workers sought alternative employment, they would have to acquire new skills.
3 The firm is a "wage maker" in that the wage rate it must pay varies directly with the number of workers it employs.

In some instances the monopsonistic power of employers is virtually complete because there is only one major employer in a labor market. For example,

their salaries and MRPs into close accord as our competitive model suggests.

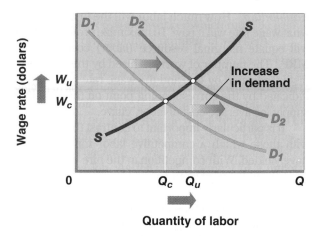

FIGURE 28-5   Unions and the demand for labor
When unions can increase the demand for labor (D_1D_1 to D_2D_2), higher wage rates (W_c to W_u) and more jobs (Q_c to Q_u) can be realized.

Some Union Models

Thus far, we have assumed that workers actively compete in the sale of their labor services. In some markets workers "sell" their labor services collectively through unions. To view the economic impact of unions in the simplest context, let's first suppose a union is formed in an otherwise competitive labor market. That is, a union is now bargaining with a relatively large number of employers.

Unions seek many goals. The basic economic objective, however, is to raise wage rates. The union can pursue this objective in several different ways.

Increasing the Demand for Labor   From the union's viewpoint, the most desirable technique for raising wage rates is to increase the demand for labor. As shown in Figure 28-5, an increase in the demand for labor will result in *both* higher wage rates and more jobs. The relative sizes of these increases will depend on the elasticity of labor supply.

A union might increase labor demand by altering one or more of the determinants of labor demand (Chapter 27). Specifically, a union can attempt to (1) increase the demand for the product or service it is producing, (2) enhance labor productivity, or (3) alter the prices of other inputs.

1 Increase Product Demand   Unions may attempt to increase the demand for the products they help produce—and hence increase the derived demand for

their own labor services—by advertising, political lobbying, or "featherbedding."

Union television ads urging consumers to "buy the union label" are relevant. Historically, The International Ladies Garment Workers Union (ILGWU) has joined with its employers to finance advertising campaigns to bolster demand for their products. Also, the Communications Workers of America (CWA) helped finance a $2 million "Call or Buy Union" campaign to convince telephone users to choose the long-distance services and equipment of AT&T and Western Union Corporation, which together provided almost 100,000 CWA jobs.

On the political front we see construction unions lobbying for new highway or urban renewal projects. Similarly, teachers' unions and associations push for increased public spending on education. Unions connected with the aerospace industry lobby to increase military spending. And it is no accident that some unions have vigorously supported their employers in seeking protective tariffs or import quotas designed to exclude competing foreign products. The steelworkers and automobile workers both have sought such forms of protection. Thus, a decline in the supply of imported cars through tariffs or negotiated agreements between nations will increase import prices, increasing the demand for highly substitutable American-made autos and boosting the derived demand for American auto workers.

Some unions have sought to expand the demand for labor by forcing make-work, or "featherbedding," rules on employers. Prior to recent court rulings, the Railway Brotherhoods forced railroads to hire train crews of a certain minimum size; diesel engines had to have a fireman even though there was no fire.

2 Increase Productivity While many decisions affecting labor productivity—for example, decisions concerning quantity and quality of real capital—are made unilaterally by management, there is a growing interest in establishing joint labor-management committees designed to increase labor productivity.

3 Increase Prices of Substitutes Unions might enhance the demand for their own labor by increasing the prices of substitute resources. A good example is that unions—whose workers are generally paid significantly more than the minimum wage—strongly support increases in the minimum wage. An alleged reason for this position is that unions want to increase the price of potentially substitutable low-wage, nonunion labor. A higher minimum wage for nonunion workers will deter employers from substituting them for union workers, thereby bolstering the demand for union workers.

Similarly, unions can also increase the demand for their labor by supporting public actions which *reduce* the price of a complementary resource. Unions in industries using large amounts of energy might actively oppose rate increases proposed by electric or natural gas utilities. Where labor and energy are complemen-

tary, energy price increase might reduce the demand for labor through Chapter 27's output effect.

Unions recognize that their capacity to influence the demand for labor is tenuous and uncertain. As many of our illustrations imply, unions are frequently trying to forestall *declines* in labor demand rather than actually increasing it. In view of these considerations, it is not surprising that union efforts to increase wage rates have concentrated on the supply side of the market.

Exclusive or Craft Unionism Unions may boost wage rates by reducing the supply of labor. Historically, organized labor has favored policies designed to restrict the supply of labor to the economy as a whole to bolster the general level of wages. Labor unions have supported legislation which has (1) restricted immigration, (2) reduced child labor, (3) encouraged compulsory retirement, and (4) enforced a shorter workweek.

More relevant for present purposes, specific types of workers have adopted, through unions, techniques designed to restrict their numbers. This is especially true of *craft unions*—unions which comprise workers of a given skill, such as carpenters, bricklayers, and plumbers. These unions have frequently forced employers to agree to hire only union workers, giving the union virtually complete control of the supply of labor. Then, by following restrictive membership policies—long apprenticeships, exorbitant initiation fees, the limitation or flat prohibition of new members—the union causes an artificial restriction of the labor supply. As indicated in Figure 28-6, this results in higher wage rates. This approach to achieving wage increases is called **exclusive unionism.** Higher wages result from excluding workers from the union and therefore from the supply of labor.

Occupational licensing is another widely used means of restricting the supplies of specific kinds of labor. Here a group of workers in an occupation will pressure state or municipal governments to pass a law which provides that, say, barbers (physicians, plumbers, beauticians, egg graders, pest controllers) can practice their trade only if they meet certain specified requirements. These requirements might specify the level of education, amount of work experience, the passing of an examination, and personal characteristics ("the practitioner must be of good moral character"). The licensing board administering the law is typically dominated by members of the licensed occupation. The result is self-regulation, conducive to polices that

FIGURE 28-6 Exclusive or craft unionism

By reducing the supply of labor (S_1S_1 to S_2S_2) through the use of restrictive membership policies, exclusive unions achieve higher wage rates (W_c to W_u). However, the restriction of labor supply also reduces the number of workers employed (Q_c to Q_u).

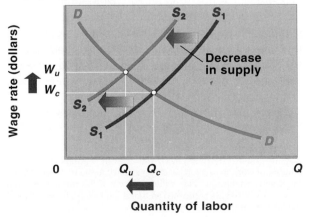

reflect self-interest. In short, imposing arbitrary and irrelevant entrance requirements or constructing an unnecessarily stringent examination can restrict entrants to the occupation. Ostensibly, the purpose of licensing is to protect consumers from incompetent practitioners. But in fact licensing laws are frequently abused in that the number of qualified workers is artificially restricted, resulting in above-competitive wages and earnings for those in the occupation (Figure 28-6). Furthermore, licensing requirements often specify a residency requirement which tends to inhibit the interstate movement of qualified workers. It is estimated that some 600 occupations are now licensed in the United States.

Many economists feel that the very high earnings of physicians are attributable in part to the American Medical Association's ability to control licensing of doctors. Practicing physicians must be licensed and licenses are awarded only to graduates of medical schools approved by the AMA. By restricting the number of approved schools and by indirectly influencing the number of medical school acceptances, the AMA has allegedly restricted the supply of physicians relative to demand and thereby increased the incomes of licensed doctors.

Inclusive or Industrial Unionism Most unions, however, do not attempt to limit their membership. On the contrary, they seek to organize all available or potential workers. This is characteristic of the so-called *industrial unions*—unions, such as the automobile workers and steelworkers, which seek all unskilled, semiskilled, and skilled workers in an industry as members. A union can afford to be exclusive when its members are skilled craftsmen for whom substitute workers are not readily available in quantity. But a union that comprises largely unskilled and semiskilled workers will undermine its own existence by limiting its membership, causing numerous highly substitutable nonunion workers to be available for employment.

If an industrial union includes virtually all workers in its membership, firms will be under great pressure to agree to the wage rate demanded by the union. By going on strike the union can deprive the firm of its entire labor supply.

Inclusive unionism is illustrated in Figure 28-7. Initially, the competitive equilibrium wage rate is W_c, and the level of employment is Q_c. Now suppose an industrial union is formed, and it imposes a higher, above-equilibrium wage rate of, say, W_u. This wage rate changes the supply curve of labor to the firm from

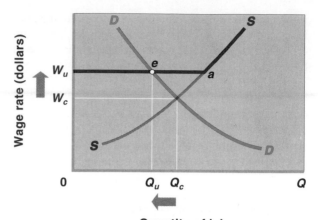

FIGURE 28-7   Inclusive or industrial unionism

By organizing virtually all available workers and thereby controlling the supply of labor, inclusive industrial unions may impose a wage rate, such as W_u, which is above the competitive wage rate W_c. The effect is to change the labor supply curve from *SS* to $W_u aS$. At the W_u wage rate, employers will cut employment from Q_c to Q_u.

the preunion *SS* curve to the postunion $W_u aS$ curve shown by the dark red line.[4] No workers will be forthcoming at a wage rate less than that demanded by the union. If employers decide it is better to pay this higher wage rate than to suffer a strike, they will cut back on employment from Q_c to Q_u.

By agreeing to the union's W_u wage demand, individual employers become "wage takers" at this wage and therefore face a perfectly elastic labor supply curve over the $W_u a$ range. Because labor supply is perfectly elastic, MRC is equal to the W_u wage over this range. The Q_u level of employment results from employers equating MRC ($=W_u$) with MRP as embodied in the labor demand curve.

Note that at W_u there is an excess supply or surplus of labor in the amount *ea*. Without the union—that is, in a purely competitive labor market—these unemployed workers might accept lower wages and the wage rate would thereby fall to the W_c competitive equilibrium level. But this doesn't happen because workers are acting collectively through their union.

---

[4]Technically, the wage rate W_u makes the labor supply curve perfectly elastic over the $W_u a$ range in Figure 28-7. If employers hire any number of workers in this range, the union-imposed wage rate is effective and must be paid, or the union will supply no labor at all—the employers will be faced with a strike. If employers want a number of workers over $W_u a$, they will have to bid up wages above the union's minimum. This will only occur if the market demand curve for labor shifts rightward so that it intersects the aS range of the labor supply curve.

Workers cannot individually offer to work for less than W_u; nor can employers contractually pay less.

Wage Increases and Unemployment

Have unions been successful in raising the wages of their members? The best evidence suggests that union members on the average achieve a 10 to 15 percent wage advantage over nonunion workers.

As Figures 28-6 and 28-7 suggest, the wage-raising actions of both exclusive and inclusive unionism cause employment to decline. A union's success in achieving above-equilibrium wage rates is tempered by the consequent decline in the number of workers employed. This unemployment effect can act as a restraining influence on union wage demands. A union cannot expect to maintain solidarity within its ranks if it seeks a wage rate so high that joblessness will result for, say, 20 or 30 percent of its members.

The unemployment impact of wage increases might be mitigated from the union's standpoint in two ways.

1 Growth The normal growth of the economy increases the demand for most kinds of labor through time. Thus a rightward shift of the labor demand curves in Figures 28-6 and 28-7 could offset, or more than offset, any unemployment effects which would otherwise be associated with the indicated wage increases. There would still be an employment restricting aspect to the union wage increases but it would take the form of a decline in the rate of growth of job opportunities, not of an absolute decline in the number of jobs.

2 Elasticity The size of the unemployment effect will depend on the elasticity of demand for labor. The more inelastic the demand, the smaller will be the amount of unemployment accompanying a given wage-rate increase. If unions have sufficient bargaining strength, they *may* obtain provisions in their collective bargaining agreements which reduce the substitutability of other inputs for labor and thereby reduce the elasticity of demand for union labor. For example, a union may force employer acceptance of rules blocking the introduction of new machinery and equipment. Or the union may bargain successfully for severance or layoff pay, which increases the cost to the firm of substituting capital for labor when wage rates are increased. Similarly, the union might gain a contract provision prohibiting the firm from subcontracting

production to nonunion (lower-wage) firms, effectively restricting the substitution of cheaper labor for union workers.

For these and other reasons the unemployment restraint on union wage demands may be less pressing than our exclusive and inclusive union models suggest.

Bilateral Monopoly Model

Suppose now that a strong industrial union is formed in a labor market which is monopsonistic rather than competitive. In other words, we combine the monopsony model with the inclusive unionism model. The result is **bilateral monopoly.** The union is a monopolistic "seller" of labor in that it controls labor supply and can influence wage rates; it faces a monopsonistic employer (or combination of oligopsonistic employers) of labor who can also affect wages by altering its employment. This is not an extreme or special case. In such important industries as steel, automobiles, meatpacking, and farm machinery, "big labor"—one huge industrial union—bargains with "big business"—a few huge industrial giants.

Indeterminate Outcome This situation is shown in Figure 28-8, which merely superimposes Figure 28-7 on 28-4. The monopsonistic employer will seek the below-competitive-equilibrium wage rate W_m and the union presumably will press for some above-competitive-equilibrium wage rate such as W_u. Which of these

FIGURE 28-8 Bilateral monopoly in the labor market

When a monopsonistic employer seeks the wage rate W_m and the inclusive union it faces seeks an above-equilibrium wage rate such as W_u, the actual outcome is logically indeterminate.

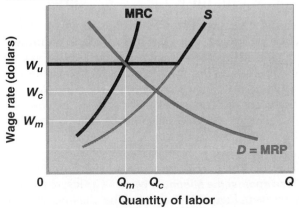

two possibilities will result? We cannot say with certainty. The outcome is logically indeterminate since economic theory does not explain what the resulting wage rate will be. We should expect the resulting wage to lie somewhere between W_m and W_u. Beyond that, about all we can say is that the party with the most bargaining power and the most effective bargaining strategy will be able to get its opponent to agree to a wage close to the one it seeks.

Desirability These comments suggest another important feature of the bilateral monopoly model. It is possible that the wage and employment outcomes might be more socially desirable than the term bilateral monopoly would imply. Monopoly on one side of the market *might* in effect cancel out the monopoly on the other side of the market, yielding competitive or near-competitive results. If either the union or management prevailed in this market—that is, if the actual wage rate were determined at either W_u or W_m—employment would be restricted to Q_m (where MRP = MRC), which is below the competitive level. But now suppose the monopoly power of the union roughly offsets the monopsony power of management, and a bargained wage rate of about W_c, which is the competitive wage, is agreed upon. Once management agrees to this wage rate, its incentive to restrict employment disappears; no longer can the employer depress wage rates by restricting employment. Thus management equates the bargained wage rate W_c (= MRC) with MRP and finds it most profitable to hire Q_c workers. In short, with monopoly on both sides of the labor market, it may be possible that the resulting wage rate and level of employment will be closer to competitive levels than if monopoly existed on only one side of the market.

The Minimum-Wage Controversy

Since the passage of the Fair Labor Standards Act in 1938, the United States has had a Federal **minimum wage.** The minimum wage has ranged from about 40 to 50 percent of the average wage paid to manufacturing workers and is currently $4.25 per hour. Roughly 90 percent of all nonsupervisory workers are covered. Our analysis of the effects of union wage-fixing raises the much-debated question of how effective minimum-wage legislation is as an antipoverty device.

Case against the Minimum Wage Critics, reasoning in terms of Figure 28-7, contend that the imposition of

effective (above-equilibrium) minimum wages will simply push employers back up their MRP or labor demand curves as it is now profitable to hire fewer workers. The higher wage costs may even force some firms out of business. The result is that some of the poor, low-wage workers whom the minimum wage was designed to help will now find themselves out of work. Critics say a worker who is unemployed at a minimum wage of $4.25 per hour is clearly worse off than if he or she were employed at the market wage rate of, say, $3.50 per hour.

A second major criticism is that the minimum wage is poorly targeted as an antipoverty device. It is designed to provide a "living wage" which will allow less-skilled workers to earn enough so that they and their families can escape poverty. However, critics argue that the primary impact of the minimum wage is on teenage workers, many of whom belong to relatively affluent families.

Case for the Minimum Wage Advocates allege that critics have analyzed the impact of the minimum wage in an unrealistic context. Figure 28-7, advocates claim, assumes a competitive and static market. The imposition of a minimum wage in a monopsonistic labor market (Figure 28-8) suggests that the minimum wage can increase wage rates without causing unemployment; indeed, higher minimum wages may even result in more jobs by eliminating the monopsonistic employer's motive to restrict employment.

Furthermore, the imposition of an effective minimum wage may increase labor productivity, shifting the labor demand curve to the right and offsetting any unemployment effects which the minimum wage might otherwise induce.

But how might a minimum wage increase productivity? First, a minimum wage may have a *shock effect* on employers. Firms using low-wage workers may be inefficient in the use of labor; the higher wage rates imposed by the minimum wage will presumably shock these firms into using labor more efficiently, and so the productivity of labor rises. Second, it is argued that higher wages will increase the real incomes and therefore the health, vigor, and motivation of workers, making them more productive.

Evidence Which view is correct? The consensus of the many research studies of the minimum wage is that it does cause some unemployment, particularly among teenage (16 to 19 years) workers. It is estimated that a 10 percent increase in the minimum wage will reduce teenage employment by 1 to 3 percent. Young adults (age 20 to 24) are also adversely affected; a 10 percent increase in the minimum wage would reduce employment for this group by 1 percent or less. Blacks and women, who are disproportionately represented in low-wage occupations, tend to suffer larger declines in employment than do white males. The other side of the coin, of course, is that those who remain employed receive higher incomes and tend to escape poverty. The overall antipoverty effect of the minimum wage may thus be a mixed, ambivalent one. Those who lose their jobs are plunged deeper into poverty; those who remain employed tend to escape poverty.

WAGE DIFFERENTIALS

We have discussed the general level of wages and the role of supply and demand in a series of specific labor market situations. We now consider the wage differences which persist between different occupations and different individuals in the same occupations. Why does a corporate executive or professional athlete receive $300,000, $500,000, or even $1,000,000 or more per year while laundry workers and retail clerks get a paltry $13,000 or $14,000 per year? Why is the average annual salary almost $891,000 for major-league baseball players compared to $27,000 for acute-care nurses and $33,000 for teachers? What rationale lies behind Chrysler Corporation paying its chairman, Lee Iacocca, total compensation of over $23 million in 1987? Table 28-3 indicates the substantial **wage differentials** which exist among certain common occupational groups. Our objective is to gain some insight as to why these differentials exist.

Once again the forces of supply and demand provide a general answer. If the supply of a particular type of labor is very great in relation to the demand for it, the resulting wage rate will be low. But if demand is great and the supply relatively small, wages will be very high. Though it is a good starting point, this supply and demand explanation is not particularly revealing. To discover *why* supply and demand conditions differ in various labor markets, we must probe those factors underlying the supply and demand of particular types of labor.

If (1) all workers were homogeneous, (2) all jobs were equally attractive to workers, and (3) labor markets were perfectly competitive, all workers would receive precisely the same wage rate. As such, this is not a particularly startling statement. It suggests that in an

TABLE 28-3 Average hourly and weekly earnings in selected industries, September 1991

Industry	Average hourly gross earnings	Average weekly gross earnings
Bituminous coal	$17.30	$787
Motor vehicles	15.66	689
Chemicals	14.22	616
Construction	14.14	551
Printing and publishing	11.67	446
Fabricated metals	11.32	475
Food products	9.87	409
Hotels and motels	7.23	225
Laundries and dry cleaning	7.11	241
Retail trade	7.07	204
Apparel and finished textiles	6.86	258

Source: U.S. Department of Labor, *Employment and Earnings*, November 1991.

economy having one type of labor and in effect one type of job, competition would result in a single wage rate for all workers. The statement is important in that it suggests reasons why wage rates do differ in practice. (1) Workers are not homogeneous. They differ in innate abilities and in education and training and, as a result, fall into noncompeting occupational groups. (2) Jobs vary in attractiveness; the nonmonetary aspects of various jobs are not the same. (3) Labor markets are typically characterized by imperfections.

Noncompeting Groups

Workers are not homogeneous; they differ significantly in their mental and physical capacities *and* in their education and training. At any point in time the labor force can be thought of as falling into many **noncompeting groups,** each of which may be composed of one or several occupations for which the members of this group qualify.

Ability Relatively few workers have the inherent abilities to be brain surgeons, concert violinists, research chemists, or professional athletes. The result is that supplies of these particular types of labor are very small in relation to the demand for them and consequently wages and salaries are high. These and similar groups do not compete with one another nor with other skilled or semiskilled workers. The violinist does not compete with the surgeon, nor does the garbage collector or retail clerk compete with either the violinist or the surgeon.

The concept of noncompeting groups is a flexible one; it can be applied to various subgroups and even to specific individuals in a given group. Some especially skilled surgeons can command higher fees than their run-of-the-mill colleagues performing the same operations. Michael Jordan, Larry Bird, Isiah Thomas, Patrick Ewing, and a few others demand and get salaries many times that of the average professional basketball player. In each instance their less-talented colleagues are only imperfect substitutes.

Investing in Human Capital: Education Noncompeting groups—and therefore wage differentials—also exist because of differing amounts of investment in human capital. A **human capital investment** refers to expenditures on education and training which improve the skills or, in other words, the productivity, of workers. Like business purchases of machinery and equipment, expenditures which increase one's productivity can be regarded as investments because *current* expenditures or costs are incurred with the intention that these costs will be more than compensated for by an enhanced *future* flow of earnings.

Figure 28-9 indicates, first, that individuals with larger investments in education do achieve higher incomes during their work careers than those who have made smaller education investments. A second point is that the earnings of more-educated workers rise more rapidly than those of less-educated workers. The primary reason for this is that more-educated workers usually get more on-the-job training.

Although education yields higher incomes, it also entails costs. For example, a college education entails not only direct costs (tuition, fees, books) but also indirect or opportunity costs (forgone earnings). Question: Does the higher pay received by more-educated workers compensate for these costs? The answer is "Yes." Rates of return have recently been estimated to be 10 to 13 percent for investing in a secondary education and 8 to 10 percent for higher education. Also, in recent years the pay gap between college graduates and high school graduates has been widening.

Equalizing Differences

If a group of workers in a particular noncompeting group is equally capable of performing several different jobs, one might expect that the wage rate would be identical for each of these jobs. But this is not the case. A group of high school graduates may be equally capable of becoming bank clerks or unskilled construction workers. But these jobs pay different wages. In virtually all localities, construction laborers receive higher wages than do bank clerks.

These differences can be explained on the basis of the *nonmonetary aspects* of the two jobs. The construction job involves dirty hands, a sore back, the hazard of accidents, and irregular employment, both seasonally and cyclically. The banking job means a white shirt, pleasant air-conditioned surroundings, and little fear of injury or layoff. Other things being equal, it is easy to see why workers would rather pick up a deposit slip than a shovel. The result is that contractors must pay higher wages than banks pay to compensate for the unattractive nonmonetary aspects of construction jobs. These wage differentials are called **equalizing differences** because they must be paid to compensate for nonmonetary differences in various jobs.

Market Imperfections

The notion of noncompeting groups helps explain wage differentials between various jobs for which limited numbers of workers are qualified. Equalizing differences aid in understanding wage differentials on certain jobs for which workers in the same noncompeting group are equally qualified. Market imperfections in the form of various immobilities help explain wage differences paid on identical jobs.

1 Geographic Immobilities Workers take root geographically. They are reluctant to leave friends, relatives, and associates, to force their children to change schools, to sell their houses, and to incur the costs and inconveniences of adjusting to a new job and a new community. Geographic mobility is likely to be particularly low for older workers with seniority rights and substantial claims to pension payments upon retirement. Similarly, an optometrist or dental hygienist qualified to practice in one state may not meet licensing requirements of other states, and therefore his or her ability to move geographically is impeded. Also, workers who may be willing to move may simply be ignorant of job opportunities and wage rates in other areas. As Adam Smith noted over two centuries ago, "A man is of all sorts of luggage the most difficult to be trans-

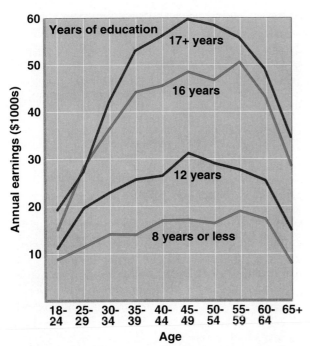

FIGURE 28-9   Education levels and individual income

Investment in education yields a return in the form of an income differential enjoyed throughout one's work-life. (*U.S. Bureau of the Census.* Data are for males in 1990.)

ported." The reluctance or inability of workers to move causes geographic wage differentials for the same occupation to persist.

2 Institutional Immobilities   Geographic immobilities may be reinforced by artificial restrictions on mobility imposed by institutions. We have noted that craft unions find it to their advantage to restrict membership. After all, if carpenters and bricklayers become plentiful, the wages they can command will decline. Thus the low-paid nonunion carpenter of Brush, Colorado, may be willing to move to Chicago in the pursuit of higher wages. But his chances of successfully doing so are slim. He may be unable to get a union card; and no card, no job. The professions impose similar artificial restraints. For example, at most universities individuals lacking advanced degrees are automatically not considered for employment as teachers. Apart from one's competence as a teacher and command of the subject matter, a "union card"—an M.A. or preferably a Ph.D.—is the first requisite for employment.

3 Sociological Immobilities   Finally, we must acknowledge sociological immobilities. Despite legislation to the contrary, women workers frequently receive less pay than men on the same job. The consequence of racial and ethnic discrimination is that blacks, Hispanics, and other minorities historically have been forced to accept lower wages on given jobs than fellow workers receive.

A final point: It is typical that all three of these considerations—noncompeting groups, equalizing differences, and market imperfections—will play a role in the explanation of actual wage differentials. For example, the differential between the wages of a physician and a construction worker is largely explainable on the basis of noncompeting groups. Physicians fall into a noncompeting group where, because of mental and financial requisites to entry, the supply of labor is small in relation to demand, and wages are therefore high. In construction work, where mental and financial prerequisites are much less significant, the supply of labor is great in relation to demand and wages are low when compared with those of physicians. However, were it not for the unpleasantness of the construction worker's job and the fact that his craft union pursues restrictive membership policies, the differential would probably be even greater than it is.

QUICK REVIEW 28-2

◆   *Unions may achieve above-equilibrium wage rates by increasing labor demand, restricting supply (exclusive unionism) or by bargaining (inclusive unionism).*

◆   *Bilateral monopoly occurs where a monopsonist bargains with an inclusive union. Wages and employment are indeterminant in this situation.*

◆   *Proponents of the minimum wage argue that it is an effective means of assisting the working poor; critics contend that it is poorly targeted and causes unemployment.*

◆   *Wage differentials are attributable in part to differences in worker abilities and education, nonmonetary differences in jobs, and market imperfections.*

PAY AND PERFORMANCE

The models of wage determination presented in this chapter presume that worker compensation is always

LAST WORD

PAY AND PERFORMANCE IN PROFESSIONAL BASEBALL

Professional baseball has provided an interesting "laboratory" in which the predictions of wage theory have been empirically tested.

Until 1976 professional baseball players were bound to a single team through the so-called "reserve clause" which prevented players from selling their talents on the open (competitive) market. Stated differently, the reserve clause conferred monopsony power on the team which originally drafted a player. As we have seen in the present chapter, labor market theory would lead us to predict that this monopsony power would permit teams to pay wages less than a player's marginal revenue product (MRP). However, since 1976 major league players have been able to become "free agents" at the end of their sixth season of play and at that time can sell their services to any team. Orthodox theory suggests that free agents should be able to increase their salaries and bring them more closely into accord with their MRPs. Research confirms both of the indicated predictions.

Scully* found that before baseball players could become free agents their salaries were substantially below their MRPs. Scully estimated a player's MRP as follows. First, he determined the relationship between a team's winning percentage and its revenue. Then he estimated the relationship between various possible measures of player productivity and a team's winning percentage. He found the ratio of strikeouts to walks for pitchers and the slugging averages for hitters (all nonpitchers) to be the best indicators of a player's contribution to the winning percentage. These two estimates were combined to calculate the contribution of a player to a team's total revenue.

*Gerald W. Scully, "Pay and Performance in Major League Baseball," *American Economic Review*, December 1974, pp. 915–930.

As noted, Scully calculated that prior to free agency the estimated MRPs of both pitchers and hitters were substantially greater than player salaries. Table 1 shows the relevant data for pitchers. Column 1 indicates pitcher performance as measured by lifetime strikeout-to-walk ratio. A higher ratio indicates a better pitcher. Column 2 indicates MRP after player training costs are taken into account and column 3 shows actual average salary for pitchers in each quality class. As expected, salaries were far less than MRPs. Even the lowest quality pitchers (those with a 1.60 strikeout-to-walk ratio) received on the average salaries amounting to only about 54 percent of their MRPs. Observe, too, that the gap between MRP and average salary widens

in the form of a standard hourly wage rate, for example, $5, $10, or $25 per hour. In fact, pay schemes are often more complex in composition and purpose. For example, many workers receive annual salaries rather than hourly pay. Also, pay plans are frequently designed by employers to elicit some desired level of performance by workers.

The Principal–Agent Problem

Firms hire workers because workers help produce goods or services which firms can sell for a profit. Workers may be thought of as the firm's *agents,* that is, parties who are hired to advance the interests of the firm. Similarly, firms may be regarded as *principals* or parties who hire others (agents) to help them achieve

TABLE 1 Marginal revenue products and salaries of professional baseball pitchers, 1968–1969

(1) Performance*	(2) Marginal revenue product	(3) Salary
1.60	$ 57,600	$31,100
1.80	80,900	34,200
2.00	104,100	37,200
2.20	127,400	40,200
2.40	150,600	43,100
2.60	173,900	46,000
2.80	197,100	48,800
3.00	220,300	51,600
3.20	243,600	54,400
3.40	266,800	57,100
3.60	290,100	59,800

*Strikeout-to-walk ratio.

Source: Scully, op. cit., p. 923.

TABLE 2 Estimated marginal revenue products and player costs, 1977

(1) Pitcher	(2) Marginal revenue product	(3) Annual contract cost*
Garland	$282,091	$230,000
Gullett	340,846	349,333
Fingers	303,511	332,000
Campbell	205,639	210,000
Alexander	166,203	166,667

*Includes annual salary, bonuses, the value of insurance policies and deferred payments, etc.

Source: Sommers and Quinton, op. cit., p. 432.

as player quality improves. "Star" players were exploited more than other players. The best pitchers received salaries which were only about 21 percent of their MRPs, according to Scully. The same general results apply to hitters. For example, the least productive hitters on the average received a salary equal to about 37 percent of their MRPs.

Sommers and Quinton[†] have assessed the economic fortunes of fourteen players who constituted the "first family" of free agents. In accordance with the predictions of labor market theory, their research indicates that the competitive bidding of free agency has brought the salaries of free agents more closely into accord with their estimated MRPs. The data for the five free-agent pitchers are shown in Table 2 where we find

[†]Paul M. Sommers and Noel Quinton, "Pay and Performance in Major League Baseball: The Case of the First Family of Free Agents," *Journal of Human Resources,* Summer 1982, pp. 426–435.

a surprisingly close correspondence between estimated MRPs and salaries. Although MRP and salary differences are larger for hitters, Sommers and Quinton conclude that the overturn of the monopsonistic reserve clause "has forced owners into a situation where there is a greater tendency to pay players in relation to their contribution to team revenues."

How have baseball team owners reacted to the escalating salaries under free agency? In early 1986 the players' union filed a grievance charging that the twenty-six professional baseball clubs had acted in concert against signing any of the players who became free agents in 1985. In fact, of the sixty-two players who became free agents in 1985, only two had signed contracts with a different team before the season began. In effect, the players charged that owners had attempted to restore some of the monopsony power which they previously had possessed. Such collusive action is illegal because it violates the basic collective bargaining agreement which exists between players and owners. In the fall of 1987 an arbitrator ruled that baseball owners had conspired to "destroy" the free-agent market and in 1990 the courts ordered club owners to pay $102.5 million in lost salaries to players.

their goals. Principals and their agents have a common interest. The principal's (firm's) objective is profits, and agents (workers) are willing to help firms earn profits in return for payments of wage income.

But the interests of firms and workers are not identical and when these interests diverge a so-called **principal–agent problem** arises. Agents might increase their utility by **shirking** on the job, that is, by providing

less than agreed-upon worker effort or by taking unauthorized work breaks. Workers may improve their well-being by increasing their leisure—through reduced work effort and work time—without forfeiting income. The night watchman in a warehouse may leave work early or spend time reading a novel as opposed to making the assigned rounds. A salaried manager may spend much time out of the office, visiting about personal interests with friends, rather than attending to urgent company business.

Firms (principals) have a profit incentive to reduce or eliminate shirking. One option is to monitor workers; but monitoring is often difficult and costly. Hiring another worker to monitor our night watchman might double the costs of having a secure warehouse. Another way of resolving a principal–agent problem is through some sort of **incentive pay plan** which ties worker compensation more closely to worker output or performance. Such incentive pay schemes include piece rates, commissions and royalties, bonuses and profit sharing, seniority pay, and efficiency wages.

Piece Rates   *Piece rates* are compensation paid in proportion to the number of units a worker produces. By paying fruit pickers by the bushel and typists by the page, the principal need not be concerned with shirking or monitoring costs.

Commissions and Royalties   Unlike piece rates, which link pay to units of output, commissions and royalties tie pay to the *value* of sales. Realtors, insurance agents, stockbrokers and retail salespersons commonly receive *commissions* based on the monetary value of their sales. *Royalties* are paid to recording artists and authors based on a certain percentage of sales revenue.

Bonuses and Profit Sharing   *Bonuses* are payments beyond one's annual salary based on some factor such as performance of the individual or the firm. A professional baseball player may receive bonuses for a high batting average, the number of home runs, or the number of runs batted in. A manager may receive bonuses based on the profit performance of his or her unit. *Profit sharing* allocates a specified percentage of a firm's profits to its employees.

Seniority Pay   Wages and earnings generally increase with job tenure. One recent explanation of this is that it is advantageous to both workers and employers to pay junior workers less than their MRPs and senior workers more than their MRPs. *Seniority pay* may be an inexpensive way of reducing shirking when monitoring costs are high. If shirkers are found out and dismissed, they will forgo the high seniority pay accruing in later years of employment. From the firm's standpoint, turnover is reduced because workers who quit will forfeit the high seniority pay. Less turnover means a more experienced and therefore more productive work force. The increased productivity of workers is the source of extra sales revenue from which the firm and the workers, respectively, enhance their profits and lifetime pay. Young workers accept wages which are initially less than their MRPs for the opportunity to participate in a labor market where in time the reverse will be true. The increased work effort and higher average productivity are appealing to workers because they are the source of higher lifetime earnings.

Efficiency Wages   The notion of *efficiency wages* suggests that employers might get greater effort from their workers by paying them relatively high, above-equilibrium wage rates. Glance back at Figure 28-3 for a competitive labor market where the equilibrium wage rate is $6. What if an employer decided to pay an above-equilibrium wage of $7 per hour? Rather than put the firm at a cost disadvantage compared to rival firms paying only $6, the higher wage *might* improve worker effort and productivity so that unit labor costs actually fall. For example, if each worker produces 10 units of output per hour at the $7 wage rate compared to only 6 units at the $6 wage rate, unit labor costs will be only $.70 (= $7 ÷ 10) for the high-wage firm as opposed to $1.00 (= $6 ÷ 6) for firms paying the equilibrium wage.

An above-equilibrium wage might enhance worker efficiency in several ways. The higher wage permits the firm to attract higher-quality workers. Worker morale should be higher. Turnover will be reduced, resulting in a more experienced work force, greater worker productivity, and also lower recruitment and training costs. Because the opportunity cost of losing a high-wage job is greater, workers are likely to put forth their best efforts with less supervision and monitoring.

Equilibrium Revisited

Labor market equilibrium is often more complex than the simple determination of wage rates and employment (Figures 28-3 through 28-8). When principal–agent problems involving shirking and monitoring costs arise, decisions must also be made with respect to the most effective compensation scheme. When we recognize that work effort and productivity are related to the form of worker compensation, the choice of pay plan is not a matter of indifference to either employer or employee.

CHAPTER SUMMARY

1 Wages are the price paid per unit of time for the services of labor.

2 The general level of wages in the United States is higher than in most foreign nations because the demand for labor is great in relation to the supply. The strong demand for American labor is based on its high productivity. Over time various productivity-increasing factors have caused the demand for labor to increase in relation to the supply, accounting for the long-run rise of real wages in the United States.

3 The determination of specific wage rates depends on the structure of the particular labor market. In a competitive market the equilibrium wage rate and level of employment are determined at the intersection of labor supply and demand.

4 Under monopsony, however, the marginal resource cost curve will lie above the resource supply curve, because the monopsonist must bid up wage rates in hiring extra workers and pay that higher wage to *all* workers. The monopsonist will hire fewer workers than under competitive conditions to achieve less-than-competitive wage rates (costs) and thereby greater profits.

5 A union may raise competitive wage rates by **a** increasing the derived demand for labor **b** restricting the supply of labor through exclusive unionism, and

c directly enforcing an above-equilibrium wage rate through inclusive unionism.

6 In many important industries the labor market takes the form of bilateral monopoly, in which a strong union "sells" labor to a monopsonistic employer. The wage rate outcome of this labor market model is logically indeterminate.

7 On the average, unionized workers realize wage rates 10 to 15 percent higher than comparable nonunion workers.

8 Economists disagree about the desirability of the minimum wage as an antipoverty mechanism. While it causes unemployment for some low-income workers, it raises the incomes of others who retain their jobs.

9 Wage differentials are largely explainable in terms of **a** noncompeting groups arising from differences in the capacities and education of different groups of workers, **b** equalizing differences, that is, wage differences which must be paid to offset nonmonetary differences in jobs; and **c** market imperfections in the form of geographic, artificial, and sociological immobilities.

10 The principal–agent problem arises when workers shirk, that is, provide less-than-expected work effort. Firms may combat this problem by monitoring workers or by creating incentive pay schemes which link worker compensation to work effort.

TERMS AND CONCEPTS

nominal and real wages	**monopsony**	**noncompeting groups**	**principal–agent**
competitive labor	**occupational licensing**	**human capital**	**problem**
market	**bilateral monopoly**	**investment**	**shirking**
exclusive and inclusive	**the minimum wage**	**equalizing differences**	**incentive pay plan**
unionism	**wage differentials**		

QUESTIONS AND STUDY SUGGESTIONS

1 Explain why the general level of wages is higher in the United States than in most foreign nations. What is the most important single factor underlying the long-run increase in average real wage rates in the United States?

2 Describe wage determination in a labor market in which workers are unorganized and many firms actively compete for the services of labor. Show this situation graphically, using W_1 to indicate the equilibrium wage rate and Q_1 to show the number of workers hired by the firms as a group. Compare the labor supply curve of the individual firm with that of the total market and explain any differences. In the firm's diagram identify total revenue, total

wage cost, and revenue available for the payment of nonlabor resources.

    a Suppose now that the formerly competing firms form an employers' association which hires labor as a monopsonist would. Describe verbally the impact upon wage rates and employment. Adjust the market graph you have just drawn, showing the monopsonistic wage rate and employment level as W_2 and Q_2, respectively.

    b Using the monopsony model, explain why hospital administrators frequently complain about a "shortage" of nurses. Do you have suggestions for correcting this shortage?

3 Describe the techniques which unions might employ to raise wages. Evaluate the desirability of each from the viewpoint of **a** the union, and **b** society as a whole. Explain: "Craft unionism directly restricts the supply of labor; industrial unionism relies upon the market to restrict the number of jobs."

4 Assume a monopsonistic employer is paying a wage rate of W_m and hiring Q_m workers, as indicated in Figure 28-8. Now suppose that an industrial union is formed and that it forces the employer to accept a wage rate of W_c. Explain verbally and graphically why in this instance the higher wage rate will be accompanied by an *increase* in the number of workers hired.

5 Complete the accompanying labor supply table for a firm hiring labor competitively.

Units of labor	Wage rate	Total labor cost (wage bill)	Marginal resource (labor) cost
0	$14	$_____	$ _____
1	14	_____	_____
2	14	_____	_____
3	14	_____	_____
4	14	_____	_____
5	14	_____	_____
6	14	_____	

a Show graphically the labor supply and marginal resource (labor) cost curves for this firm. Explain the relationships of these curves to one another.
b Compare these data with the labor demand data of question 2 in Chapter 27. What will the equilibrium wage rate and level of employment be? Explain.
c Now redetermine this firm's supply schedule for labor, assuming that it is a monopsonist and that, although it can hire the first worker for $6, it must increase the wage rate by $3 to attract each successive worker. Show the new labor supply and marginal labor

cost curves graphically and explain their relationships to one another. Compare these new data with those of question 2 for Chapter 27. What will be the equilibrium wage rate and the level of employment? Why do these differ from your answer to question 5b?

6 A critic of the minimum wage has contended, "The effects of minimum wage legislation are precisely the opposite of those predicted by those who support them. Government can legislate a minimum wage, but cannot force employers to hire unprofitable workers. In fact, minimum wages cause unemployment among low-wage workers who can least afford to give up their small incomes." Do you agree? What bearing does the elasticity of labor demand have on this assessment? What factors might possibly offset the potential unemployment effects of a minimum wage?

7 On the average do union workers receive higher wages than comparable nonunion workers?

8 What are the basic considerations which help explain wage differentials? What long-run effect would a substantial increase in safety for underground coal miners have on their wage rates in comparison to other workers?

9 "Many of the lowest-paid people in society—for example, short-order cooks—also have relatively poor working conditions. Hence, the notion of equalizing wage differentials is disproved." Do you agree? Explain.

10 What is meant by investment in human capital? Use this concept to explain **a** wage differentials, and **b** the long-run rise of real wage rates in the United States.

11 What is meant by the principal–agent problem? Have you ever worked in a setting where this problem has arisen? If so, do you think increased monitoring would have eliminated the problem? Why don't firms simply hire more supervisors to eliminate shirking?

12 The notion of efficiency wages suggests that an above-equilibrium wage rate will elicit a more-than-offsetting increase in worker productivity. By what specific means might the higher wage cause worker productivity to rise? Why might young workers accept a seniority pay plan under which they are initially paid less than their MRPs?

The Pricing and Employment of Resources: Rent, Interest, and Profits

7.75%
1-Year Introductory Rate

Emphasis in the previous two chapters was on labor markets because wages and salaries account for about three-fourths of our national income. In this chapter we focus on three other sources of income—rent, interest, and profits—which compose the remaining one-fourth of national income.

You undoubtedly are aware of these income sources. We read stories of incredibly high land rents in urban areas such as Tokyo, where an acre of land may sell for more than $85 million. An acre of desert may cost $650,000 along the Las Vegas casino strip; meanwhile, an acre of land in the middle of the Nevada desert can be bought for about $60. *How do land prices and rents get established?*

If you put money in a three-month certificate of deposit in early 1991, you probably received an interest rate of about 7 percent. One year later that CD paid only about 3.7 percent. *What factors determine interest rates and explain why they change?*

The news media continually document the profit and loss performance of various firms and industries. The maker of Nintendo video games has reaped large profits. And the firm which produces AZT, a drug which prolongs the life of AIDS patients, doubled its profits over a three-year period. Meanwhile, some automakers and airlines have recently suffered record losses. *What are the sources of profits and losses? What functions do they serve?*

ECONOMIC RENT

To most people the term "rent" means the amount one must pay for a two-bedroom apartment or a dormitory room. To the business executive, "rent" is a payment made for use of a factory building, machinery, or warehouse facilities. Closer examination finds these commonsense definitions of rent to be confusing and ambiguous. Dormitory room rent, for example, includes interest on the money capital the univeristy has borrowed to finance the dormitory's construction, wages for custodial service, utility payments, and so forth.

Economists therefore use the term "rent" in a narrower, less ambiguous sense: **Economic rent** *is the price paid for use of land and other natural resources which are completely fixed in total supply.* The unique

553

supply conditions of land and other natural resources—their fixed supply—make rental payments distinguishable from wage, interest, and profit payments.

Let's examine this feature and some of its implications through supply and demand analysis. To avoid complications, assume, first, that all land is the same grade or quality—in other words, each available acre of land is equally productive. Suppose, too, that all land has just one use, being capable of producing just one product—say, corn. And assume that land is being rented in a competitive market—that many corn farmers are demanding and many landowners offering land in the market.

In Figure 29-1, SS indicates the supply of arable farmland available in the economy as a whole and D_2 the demand of farmers for use of that land. As with all economic resources, demand is a derived demand. It is downsloping because of the law of diminishing returns and the fact that, for farmers as a group, product price must be reduced to sell additional units of output.

Perfectly Inelastic Supply

The unique feature of our analysis is on the supply side: For all practical purposes the supply of land is perfectly inelastic, as reflected in SS. Land has no production cost; it is a "free and nonreproducible gift of nature." The economy has so much land, and that's that. It is true, of course, that within limits existing land can be made more usable by clearing, drainage, and irrigation. But these programs are capital improvements and not changes in the amount of land as such. Furthermore, such variations in the usability of land are a very small fraction of the total amount of land in existence and do not undermine the basic argument that land and other natural resources are in virtually fixed supply.

Changes in Demand

The fixed nature of the supply of land means that demand is the only active determinant of land rent; supply is passive. And what determines the demand for land? Those factors discussed in Chapter 27—the price of the product grown on the land, the productivity of land (which depends in part on the quantity and quality of the resources with which land is combined), and the prices of those other resources which are combined with land. If in Figure 29-1, the demand for land should increase from D_2 to D_1 or decline from D_2 to D_3, land rent would change from R_2 to R_1 or R_3, but the amount of land supplied would remain unchanged at $0S$. Changes in economic rent will have no impact on the amount of land available; the supply of land is simply not augmentable. In technical terms, there is a large price effect and no quantity effect when the demand for land changes. If demand for land is only D_4, land rent will be zero; land will be a "free good" because it is not scarce enough in relation to demand for it to command a price. This situation was approximated in the free-land era of American history.

Land Rent Is a Surplus

The perfect inelasticity of the supply of land must be contrasted with the relative elasticity of such property resources as apartment buildings, machinery, and warehouses. These resources are *not* fixed in total supply. A higher price will give entrepreneurs the incentive to construct and offer larger quantities of these property resources. Conversely, a decline in their prices will induce suppliers to allow existing facilities to depreciate and not be replaced. The same general reasoning applies to the total supply of labor. Within limits, a higher average level of wages will induce more workers to enter the labor force, and lower wages will cause them to drop out of the labor force. The supplies of nonland resources are upsloping or, stated differently, the prices paid to such resources perform an **incentive**

FIGURE 29-1   The determination of land rent

Because the supply of land and other natural resources is perfectly inelastic (SS), demand is the sole active determinant of land rent. An increase (D_2 to D_1) or decrease (D_2 to D_3) in demand will cause considerable changes in rent (R_2 to R_1 and R_2 to R_3). If demand is very small (D_4) relative to supply, land will be a "free good."

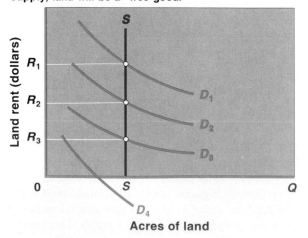

Acres of land

function. A high price provides an incentive to offer more; a low price, to offer less.

Not so with land. Rent serves no incentive function, because the total supply of land is fixed. If rent is $10,000, $500, $1, or $0 per acre, the same amount of land will be available to society to make a contribution to production. Rent, in other words, could be eliminated without affecting the productive potential of the economy. For this reason economists consider rent to be a *surplus,* that is, a payment which is not necessary to ensure that land will be available to the economy as a whole.[1]

A Single Tax on Land

If land is a free gift of nature, costs nothing to produce, and would be available even in the absence of rental payments, why should rent be paid to those who by historical accident, by inheritance, or by crook happen to be landowners? Socialists have long argued that all land rents are unearned incomes. Therefore, they argue, land should be nationalized—owned by the state—so that any payments for its use can be used by the state to further the well-being of the entire population rather than being used by a landowning minority.

Henry George's Proposal   In the United States, criticism of rental payments has taken the form of a **single-tax movement** which gained much support in the late nineteenth century. Spearheaded by Henry George's provocative book *Progress and Poverty* (1879), this reform movement maintained that economic rent could be taxed away completely without impairing the available supply of land or, therefore, the productive potential of the economy as a whole.

George observed that as population grew and the geographic frontier closed, landowners enjoyed larger and larger rents from their landholdings. These increments in rent were the result of a growing demand for a resource whose supply was perfectly inelastic; some landlords were receiving fabulously high incomes, not

through rendering any productive effort, but solely from holding advantageously located land. Henry George stated that these increases in land rent belonged to the economy as a whole; he held that land rents should be taxed away and spent for public uses.

Indeed, George held that there was no reason to tax away only 50 percent of the landowner's unearned rental income. Why not take 70 or 90 or 99 percent? In seeking popular support for his ideas on land taxation, Henry George proposed that taxes on rental income be the *only* tax levied by government.

George's case for taxing land was based not only on equity or fairness, but also on efficiency grounds. In particular, unlike virtually every other tax, a tax on land does *not* alter or distort the allocation of resources. For example, a tax on wages will reduce after-tax wages and might weaken incentives to work. An individual who decides to participate in the labor force at a $6 before-tax wage rate may decide to drop from the labor force and go on welfare when an income tax reduces the after-tax wage rate to $4.50. Similarly, a property tax on buildings lowers returns to investors in such property, causing them in time to reallocate their money capital toward other investments. But no such reallocations of resources occur when land is taxed. The most profitable use for land before it is taxed remains the most profitable use after the tax is imposed. Of course, a landlord could withdraw land from production when a tax is imposed, but this would mean no rental income at all.

Criticisms   Critics of the single tax on land make these points:

1   Current levels of government spending are such that a land tax alone would clearly not bring in enough revenue; it cannot be considered realistically as a *single* tax.

2   As noted earlier, in practice most income payments combine elements of interest, rent, wages, and profits. Land is typically improved in some manner by productive effort, and economic rent cannot be readily disentangled from payments for capital improvements. As a practical matter, it would be difficult to determine how much of any given income payment is actually rent.

3   The question of unearned income goes beyond land and land ownership. One can argue that many individuals and groups other than landowners benefit from receipt of "unearned" income associated with the overall advance of the economy. For example, consider the capital gains income received by someone who,

---

[1] A portion—in some instances a major portion—of wage and salary incomes may be a surplus in that these incomes exceed the minimum amount necessary to keep an individual in his or her current line of work. For example, in 1991 the *average* salary paid to major league baseball players was about $891,000 per year. In the next best occupational option as, say, a college coach, a player might earn only $40,000 or $50,000 per year. Most of his current income is therefore a surplus. Observe that in the twilight of their careers, professional athletes sometimes accept sizable salary reductions rather than seek employment in alternative occupations.

some twenty or twenty-five years ago, chanced to purchase (or inherit) stock in a firm which has experienced rapid growth (say, IBM or Xerox). How is this income different from the rental income of the landowner?

4   Finally, historically a piece of land is likely to have changed ownership many times. *Former* owners may have been the beneficiaries of past increases in land rent. It is hardly fair to tax *current* owners who paid the competitive market price for land.

Productivity Differences

Thus far we have assumed that all units of land are of the same grade. In practice, this is plainly not so. Different acres vary greatly in productivity. These productivity differences stem primarily from differences in soil fertility and such climatic factors as rainfall and temperature. These factors explain why Iowa soil is excellently suited to corn production, the plains of eastern Colorado are much less so, and desert wasteland of New Mexico is incapable of corn production. These productivity differences will be reflected in resource demand. Competitive bidding by farmers will establish a high rent for the very productive Iowa land. Less productive Colorado land will command a much lower rent, and New Mexico land no rent at all.

Location may be equally important in explaining differences in land rent. Other things being equal, renters will pay more for a unit of land which is strategically located with respect to materials, labor, and customers than for a unit of land whose location is remote from these markets. Witness the extremely high land rents in large metropolitan areas.

The rent differentials to which quality differences in land would give rise can be seen by viewing Figure 29-1 from a slightly different point of view. Suppose, as before, that only one agricultural product, say corn, can be produced on four grades of land, *each* of which is available in the fixed amount $0S$. When combined with identical amounts of capital, labor, and other cooperating resources, the productivity—or, more specifically, the marginal revenue productivity—of each grade of land is reflected in demand curves D_1, D_2, D_3, and D_4. Grade 1 land is the most productive, as reflected in D_1, whereas grade 4 is the least productive, as is shown by D_4. The resulting economic rents for grades 1, 2, and 3 land will be R_1, R_2, and R_3 respectively, the rent differentials mirroring differences in productivity of the three grades of land. Grade 4 land is so poor in quality

that it would not pay farmers to bring it fully into production; it would be a "free" and only partially used resource.

Alternative Uses and Costs

We have also supposed, thus far, that land has only one use. Actually, we know that land normally has a number of alternative uses. An acre of Iowa farm land may be useful in raising not only corn, but also wheat, oats, milo, and cattle; or it may be useful as a house or factory site.

What is the importance of this obvious point? It indicates that, although land is a free gift of nature and has no production cost from the viewpoint of society as a whole, the rental payments of individual producers are *costs*. The total supply of land will be available to society even if no rent at all is paid for its use. But, from the standpoint of individual firms and industries, land has alternative uses, and therefore payments must be made by specific firms and industries to attract that land from those other uses. Such payments by definition are costs. Again, the fallacy of composition (Chapter 1) has entered our discussion. From the standpoint of society, there is no alternative but for land to be used by society. Therefore, to society, rents are a surplus, not a cost. But because land has alternative uses, the rental payments of corn farmers or any other individual user are a cost; such payments are required to attract land from alternative uses.

QUICK REVIEW 29-1

∮   *Economic rent is the price paid for resources such as land, the supply of which is perfectly inelastic.*

∮   *Land rent is a surplus in that land would be available to society even if rent were not paid.*

∮   *The surplus nature of land rent was the basis for Henry George's single-tax movement.*

∮   *Differential rents allocate land among alternative uses.*

INTEREST

The interest rate is the price paid for the use of money. It is the amount of money one must pay for the use of one dollar for a year. Two aspects of this income payment are notable.

1 Stated as Percentage   Because it is paid in kind, interest is typically stated as a percentage of the amount of money being borrowed rather than as an absolute amount. It is less clumsy to say one is paying 12 percent interest than to proclaim that interest is "$120 per year per $1000." Furthermore, stating interest as a percentage facilitates comparison of interest paid on loans of much different absolute amounts. By expressing interest as a percentage, we can immediately compare an interest payment of, say, $432 per year per $2880 and one of $1800 per year per $12,000. In this case both interest payments are 15 percent—a fact not obvious from the absolute figures.

The **Truth in Lending Act** was passed in 1968 and requires lenders to state the costs and terms of consumer credit in concise and uniform language. In particular, the act requires that interest must be stated as an annual rate. Nevertheless, as this chapter's Last Word explains, it is not always simple to determine how much interest is being charged.

2 Money Not a Resource   Money is *not* an economic resource. As such, money is not productive; it cannot produce goods and services. However, businesses "buy" the use of money, because money can be used to acquire capital goods—factory buildings, machinery, warehouses, and so forth. These facilities clearly do contribute to production. Thus, in hiring the use of money capital, business executives are ultimately buying the use of real capital goods.

Determining the Interest Rate

The theory of interest rate determination and its relationship to aggregate investment have been presented in Part 3 and need only be summarized here.[2] Glancing back at Figure 15-2, we recall in Figure 15-2a that the total demand for money comprises **transactions** and **asset demands.** The former is directly related to the level of nominal GDP, while the latter is inversely related to the interest rate. Graphed against the interest rate, the total demand for money curve is downsloping.

The money supply is a vertical line on the assumption that the monetary authorities determine some stock of money (money supply) independent of the rate of interest. The intersection of the demand for

money curve and the money supply curve determines the equilibrium rate of interest.

The Investment Decision   Now consider Figure 15-2b which shows how the interest rate relates to the purchase of real capital. The investment-demand curve is constructed by aggregating all possible investment projects and ranking them from highest to lowest in terms of their expected rates of net profits. By projecting the equilibrium interest rate of Figure 15-2a off the investment-demand curve of Figure 15-2b, we determine the amount of investment the business sector will find profitable to undertake. All investment projects whose expected rate of net profits exceeds the equilibrium interest rate will be undertaken.

Nominal and Real Interest Rates   This discussion of the role of the interest rate in the investment decision assumes there is no inflation. If inflation occurs, we must distinguish between money or nominal interest rates and real interest rates. The **nominal interest rate** is the rate of interest expressed in terms of dollars of current value. The **real interest rate** is the rate of interest expressed in terms of dollars of constant or inflation-adjusted value. The real interest rate is the nominal rate less the rate of inflation.

An example will clarify this distinction. Suppose that the nominal interest rate and the rate of inflation are both 10 percent. If you borrow $100, you must pay back $110 a year from now. However, because of 10 percent inflation each of these 110 dollars will be worth 10 percent less. Hence, the real value or purchasing power of your $110 repayment at the end of the year is only $100. In terms of inflation-adjusted dollars you are borrowing $100 and at year's end paying back $100. While the nominal interest rate is 10 percent, the real interest rate is zero. By subtracting the 10 percent inflation rate from the 10 percent nominal interest rate we determine that the real interest rate is zero.

The distinction is relevant to our discussion because it is the real interest rate, not the nominal rate, which is important in making investment decisions. Thus in the late 1970s and early 1980s nominal interest rates were unusually high; 12, 15, and 18 percent rates were common. At first glance one would think these high nominal rates would choke off investment; after all, there are relatively few investment opportunities promising an expected rate of return over 15 or 18 percent. But this didn't occur; investment spending was quite strong during this period. The reason was that,

---

[2]You should review the following sections: "The Demand for Money" in Chapter 13; "Monetary Policy, Equilibrium GDP, and the Price Level," in Chapter 15; and "Investment" in Chapter 10.

than are payments which would be made if outsiders had supplied these resources. Economic profits are a residual—the total revenue remaining after *all* costs are taken into account.

Role of the Entrepreneur

The economist views profits as the return to a very special type of human resource—entrepreneurial ability. The functions of the entrepreneur were summarized in Chapter 2. They entail (1) taking the initiative to combine other resources in producing a good or service; (2) making basic, nonroutine policy decisions for the firm; (3) introducing innovations in the form of new products or production processes; and (4) bearing the economic risks associated with all these functions.

Part of the entrepreneur's return is called a **normal profit.** This is the minimum return or payment necessary to retain the entrepreneur in some specific line of production. This normal profit payment is a cost (Chapter 22). However, we know that a firm's total revenue may exceed its total costs (explicit, implicit, the latter inclusive of a normal profit). This extra or excess revenue above all costs is an economic, or pure, profit. This residual—which is *not* a cost because it is in excess of the normal profit required to retain the entrepreneur in the industry—accrues to the entrepreneur. The entrepreneur is the residual claimant.

Economists offer several theories to explain why this residual of economic profit might occur. These explanations relate to:

1 The *risks* which the entrepreneur bears by functioning in a dynamic and therefore uncertain environment or by undertaking innovational activity.
2 The possibility of attaining *monopoly power.*

Sources of Economic Profit

Our understanding of economic profits and the entrepreneur's functions can be enhanced by describing an artificial economic environment within which pure profits would be zero. Then, by noting real-world deviations from this environment, we can lay bare the sources of economic profit.

In a purely competitive static economy, pure profits would be zero. By a **static economy** we mean one in which basic data—resource supplies, technological knowledge, and consumer tastes—are constant and unchanging. A static economy is a changeless one in which all determinants of cost and supply data, on the

one hand, and demand and revenue data, on the other, are constant.

Given the static nature of these data, the economic future is perfectly foreseeable; economic uncertainty is nonexistent. The outcome of price and production policies is accurately predictable. Furthermore, the static nature of such a society precludes innovational change. Under pure competition any pure profits (positive or negative) which might have existed initially in various industries will disappear with the entry or exodus of firms in the long run. All costs—explicit and implicit—will therefore be covered in the long run, leaving no residual in the form of pure profits (Figure 23-12).

The notion of zero economic profits in a static, competitive economy enhances our understanding of profits by suggesting that the presence of profits is linked to the dynamic nature of real-world capitalism and its accompanying uncertainty. Furthermore, it indicates that economic profits may arise from a source apart from the directing, innovating, risk-bearing functions of the entrepreneur. And that source is the presence of some degree of monopoly power.

Uncertainty, Risk, and Profits In a dynamic economy the future is always uncertain. This means that the entrepreneur necessarily assumes risks. Profits can be thought of in part as a reward for assuming these risks.

In linking pure profits with uncertainty and risk bearing, we must distinguish between risks which are insurable and those which are not. Some types of risks—fires, floods, theft, and accidents to employees—are measurable in that actuaries can accurately estimate their average occurrence. As a result, these risks are typically insurable. Firms can avoid, or at least provide for, them by incurring a known cost in the form of an insurance premium. It is the bearing of **uninsurable risks,** then, which is a potential source of economic profits.

Basically, such uninsurable risks are uncontrollable and unpredictable changes in demand (revenue) and supply (cost) conditions facing the firm. Some of these uninsurable risks stem from unpredictable changes in the general economic environment or, more specifically, from the business cycle. Prosperity brings substantial windfall profits to most firms, whereas depression means widespread losses. In addition, changes are constantly taking place in the structure of the domestic and world economies. Even in a full-employment, noninflationary economy, changes are always occurring in consumer tastes, technology, and resource supplies. Example: Technological change has been such that vinyl long-playing records have given way to cassettes and the latter in turn have partially lost their market to compact discs. Digital audio tapes may soon challenge compact discs.

Such changes continually alter the revenue and cost data faced by individual firms and industries, leading to changes in the structure of the business population as favorably affected industries expand and adversely affected industries contract. Changes in government policies are pertinent at both levels. Appropriate fiscal and monetary policies of government may reverse a recession, whereas the establishment or elimination of a tariff may alter significantly the demand and revenue data of the affected industry.

The point is that profits and losses can be associated with the bearing of uninsurable risks stemming from cyclical, structural, and policy changes in the economy.

Uncertainty, Innovations, and Profits   The uncertainties just discussed are external to the firm; they are beyond the control of the individual firm or industry. One other extremely important dynamic feature of capitalism—innovation—occurs at the initiative of the entrepreneur. Business firms deliberately introduce new methods of production and distribution to affect their costs favorably and new products to influence their revenue favorably. The entrepreneur purposely undertakes to upset existing cost and revenue data in a way which hopefully will be profitable.

But once again, uncertainty enters the picture. Despite exhaustive market surveys, new products or modifications of existing products may prove to be economic failures. Three-dimensional movies, not to mention Yugo and Fiero automobiles, and disk cameras come readily to mind. Similarly, of the many new novels, textbooks, records, and tapes which appear every year, only a handful garner large profits. Nor is it known with certainty whether a new machine will actually provide the cost economies predicted for it while it is still in the blueprint stage. Innovations purposely undertaken by entrepreneurs entail uncertainty, just as do those changes in the economic environment over which an individual enterprise has no control. In a sense, innovation as a source of profits is merely a special case of risk bearing.

Under competition and in the absence of patent laws, innovational profits will be temporary. Rival firms will imitate successful (profitable) innovations, compet-

ing away all economic profits. Nevertheless, innovational profits may always exist in a progressive economy as new, successful innovations replace older ones whose associated profits have been eroded or competed away.

Monopoly Profits   Thus far, we have emphasized that profits are related to the uncertainties and uninsurable risks surrounding dynamic events which enterprises are exposed to or initiate themselves. The existence of monopoly in some form or other is a final source of economic profits. Because of its ability to restrict output and deter entry, a monopolist may persistently enjoy above-competitive prices and economic profits, provided demand is strong relative to costs (Figure 24-3).

There are both a causal relationship and a notable distinction between uncertainty, on the one hand, and monopoly, on the other, as sources of profits. The causal relationship involves the fact that an entrepreneur can reduce uncertainty, or at least manipulate its effects, by achieving monopoly power. The competitive firm is unalterably exposed to the vagaries of the market; the monopolist, however, can control the market to a degree and offset or minimize potentially adverse effects of uncertainty. Furthermore, innovation is an important source of monopoly power; the short-run uncertainty associated with the introduction of new techniques or new products may be borne for the purpose of achieving a measure of monopoly power.

The notable distinction between profits stemming from uncertainty and from monopoly has to do with the social desirability of the two sources of profits. Bearing the risks inherent in a dynamic and uncertain economic environment and the undertaking of innovations are socially desirable functions. The social desirability of monopoly profits, on the other hand, is very doubtful. Monopoly profits typically are founded on output restriction, above-competitive prices, and a contrived misallocation of resources.

Functions of Profits

Profit is the prime mover, or energizer, of the capitalistic economy. As such, profits influence both the level of resource utilization and the allocation of resources among alternative uses.

Investment and Domestic Ouput   It is profits—or better, the *expectation* of profits—which induce firms to innovate. Innovation stimulates investment, total output, and employment. Innovation is a fundamental aspect of the process of economic growth, and it is the pursuit of profit which underlies most innovation. However, profit expectations are volatile, with the result that investment, employment, and the rate of growth have been unstable. Profits have functioned imperfectly as a spur to innovation and investment.

Profits and Resource Allocation   Perhaps profits perform more effectively the task of allocating resources among alternative lines of production. Entrepreneurs seek profits and shun losses. The occurrence of economic profits is a signal that society wants that particular industry to expand. Profit rewards are more than an inducement for an industry to expand; they also are the financial means by which firms in such industries can add to their productive capacities.

Losses, on the other hand, signal society's desire for the afflicted industries to contract; losses penalize businesses which fail to adjust their productive efforts to those goods and services most preferred by consumers. This is not to say that profits and losses result in an allocation of resources now and forever attuned to consumer preferences. In particular, the presence of monopoly in both product and resource markets impedes the shiftability of firms and resources, as do the various geographic, artificial, and sociological immobilities discussed in Chapter 28.

> **QUICK REVIEW 29-3**
>
> ♪   *Pure or economic profits are determined by subtracting all explicit and implicit costs (including a normal profit) from a firm's total revenue.*
>
> ♪   *Economic profits result from* **a** *the bearing of uninsurable risks,* **b** *innovation, and* **c** *monopoly power.*
>
> ♪   *Profits and profit expectations affect the levels of investment and domestic output and also allocate resources among alternative uses.*

INCOME SHARES

The discussions of Chapters 28 and 29 would be incomplete without a brief empirical summary on the importance of wages, rent, interest, and profits as proportions or relative shares of the national income. Table 29-2 provides an historical look at income shares in terms of the income categories used in our national income accounts. Although these accounting conceptions of income do not neatly fit the economist's definitions of wages, rent, interest, and profits, they do yield some usable insights about the relative size and trends of income shares.

Current Shares

The most recent 1982–1990 figures in the table reveal the dominant role of labor income. Defining labor in-

---

TABLE 29-2   **Relative shares of national income, 1900–1990** *(decade or period averages of shares for individual years)*

| (1)
Decade | (2)
Wages
and
salaries | (3)
Pro-
prietors'
income | Property (capital) income | | | (7)
Total |
			(4) Cor- porate profits	(5) Interest	(6) Rent	
1900–1909	55.0%	23.7%	6.8%	5.5%	9.0%	100%
1910–1919	53.6	23.8	9.1	5.4	8.1	100
1920–1929	60.0	17.5	7.8	6.2	7.7	100
1930–1939	67.5	14.8	4.0	8.7	5.0	100
1939–1948	64.6	17.2	11.9	3.1	3.3	100
1949–1958	67.3	13.9	12.5	2.9	3.4	100
1954–1963	69.9	11.9	11.2	4.0	3.0	100
1963–1970	71.7	9.6	12.1	3.5	3.2	100
1971–1981	75.9	7.1	8.4	6.4	2.2	100
1982–1990	73.6	7.3	8.3	10.0	1.0	100

Source: Irving Kravis, "Income Distribution: Functional Share," *International Encyclopedia of Social Sciences,* vol. 7 (New York: The Macmillan Company and Free Press, 1968), p. 134, updated.

e narrowly as "wages and salaries," labor currently eives almost 75 percent of the national income. But ne economists argue that since proprietors' income argely composed of wages and salaries, it should be ded to the official "wages and salaries" category to etermine labor income. When we use this broad definition, labor's share rises to about 80 percent of national income. Interestingly, although we label our system a "capitalist economy," the capitalist share of national income—the sum of "corporate profits," "interest," and "rent"—is only about 20 percent of the national income.

Historical Trends

What can be deduced from Table 29-2 about historical trends? Let's concentrate on the dominant wage share. Using the narrow definition of labor's share as simply "wages and salaries," we note an increase from about 55 to almost 75 percent in this century.

Structural Changes   Although these are several tentative explanations of these data, one prominent theory stresses the structural changes which have occurred in our economy. Two specific points are made.

1 Corporate Growth   Noting the relative constancy of the capitalist share (the sum of columns 4, 5, and 6)—roughly 20 percent in both the 1900–1909 and the 1982–1990 periods—we find that the expansion of labor's share has come primarily at the expense of the share going to proprietors. This suggests that the evolution of the corporation as the dominant form of business enterprise is an important explanatory factor. Individuals who would have operated their own corner groceries in the 1920s are the hired managers of corporate supermarkets in the 1980s or 1990s.

2 Changing Industry-Mix   The changing output-mix and therefore the industry-mix which have occurred historically have increased labor's share. Over-

all, there has been a long-term change in the composition of output and industry away from land- and capital-intensive production and toward labor-intensive production. Again, crudely stated, there has been an historical reallocation of labor from agriculture (where labor's share is quite low) to manufacturing (where labor's share is rather high) and, finally, to private and public services (where labor's share is very high). These shifts account for much of the growth of labor's share reflected in column 2 of Table 29-2.

Unions?   It is tempting to explain an expanding wage share in terms of the growth of labor unions. But there are difficulties with this approach.

1   The growth of the labor movement in the United States does not fit very well chronologically with the growth of labor's share of the national income. Much of the growth of "wages and salaries" occurred between 1900 and 1939; much of the growth in the labor movement came in the last few years of the 1930s and the war years of the early 1940s.

2   Wage increases for union members may come at the expense of wages of unorganized workers. That is, in obtaining higher wages, unions restrict employment opportunities (Figures 28-6 and 28-7) in organized industries. Unemployed workers and new labor-force entrants therfore seek jobs in nonunion sectors. Resulting increases in labor supply depress wage rates in nonunion jobs. If this scenario is correct, then higher wages for union workers may be achieved, not at the expense of the capitalist share, but rather at the expense of the nonunion wage share. Overall, the total labor share—union plus nonunion—could well be unaffected by unions.

3   If the national income is disaggregated into industry sectors (as in Table 5-5) and the historical trend of the wage share in each sector is examined, we reach a curious conclusion. Generally, labor's share has grown more rapidly in those sectors where unions are weak than in sectors which are highly unionized.

CHAPTER SUMMARY

Economic rent is the price paid for the use of land and r natural resources whose total supplies are fixed.

Rent is a surplus since land would be available to the omy as a whole even without rental payments. The no- f land rent as a surplus gave rise to the single-tax move- of the late 1800s.

3   Differences in land rent are explainable in terms of differences in productivity due to the fertility and climatic features of land and in its location.

4   Land rent is a surplus rather than a cost to the economy as a whole; however, because land has alternative uses from the standpoint of individual firms and industries, rental pay-

DETERMINING THE PRICE OF CREDIT

There are a variety of lending practices which can cause the effective interest rate to be quite different from what it appears to be.

Borrowing and lending—receiving and granting credit—are a way of life. Individuals receive credit when they negotiate a mortgage loan and when they use their credit cards. Conversely, individuals make loans when they open a savings account in a commercial bank or buy a government bond.

Despite the passage of the Truth in Lending Act of 1968, it remains difficult to determine exactly how much interest one pays and receives in borrowing and lending. A few illustrations will be helpful. Let's suppose that you borrow $10,000 which you agree to repay plus $1,000 of interest at the end of the year. In this instance the interest rate is 10 percent. To determine the interest rate (r) one merely compares interest paid with the amount borrowed:

$$r = \frac{\$1,000}{\$10,000} = 10\%$$

But in some cases a lender, say, a bank, will *discount* the interest payment at the time the loan is made. Thus, instead of giving the borrower $10,000, the bank discounts the $1,000 interest payment in advance, giving the borrower only $9,000. This increases the interest rate:

$$r = \frac{\$1,000}{\$9,000} = 11\%$$

While the absolute amount of interest paid is the same, in this second case the borrower has only $9,000 available for the year.

An even more subtle point is that, in order to simplify their calculations, many financial institutions assume a 360-day year (twelve 30-day months). This means the borrower has the use of the lender's funds for five days less than the normal year. This use of a "short year" also increases the interest rate paid by the borrower.

The interest rate paid can change dramatically if a loan is repaid in installments. Suppose a bank lends you $10,000 and charges interest in the amount of $1,000 to be paid at the end of the year. But the loan contract requires you to repay the $10,000 loan in 12 equal monthly installments. The effect of this is that the average amount of the loan outstanding during the year is only $5,000. Hence:

$$r = \frac{\$1,000}{\$5,000} = 20\%$$

Here interest is paid on the total amount of the loan ($10,000) rather than the outstanding balance (which averages $5,000 for the year), making for a much higher interest rate.

Another fact which influences the effective interest rate is whether or not interest is *compounded*. Suppose you deposit $10,000 in a savings account which pays a 10 percent interest rate compounded semiannually. In other words, interest is paid on your [funds] to the bank twice a year. At the end of the first six months, $500 of interest (10% of $10,000 for [half] a year) is added to your account. At the end of [the year] interest is calculated on $10,500 so that the [second] interest payment is $525 (10% of $10,500 for [half] a year). Hence:

$$r = \frac{\$1,025}{\$10,000} = 10.25\%$$

This means that a bank advertising a 10 [percent] interest rate compounded semiannually is [paying] more interest to its customers than a co[mpetitor paying] a simple (noncompounded) interest r[ate of 10 per]cent.

"Let the borrower beware" is a [good rule in the] world of credit.

ments of firms and industries are correctly regarded as costs.

5 Interest is the price paid for the use of money. The theory of interest envisions a total demand for money comprised of transactions and asset demands. The supply of money is primarily the consequence of monetary policy.

6 The equilibrium interest rate influences the level of investment and helps ration financial and physical capital to specific firms and industries. The real interest rate, not the nominal rate, is critical to the investment decision.

7 Economic, or pure, profits are the difference between a firm's total revenue and its total costs, the latter defined to include implicit costs, which include a normal profit. Profits accrue to entrepreneurs for assuming the uninsurable risks

associated with organizing and directing economic resources and innovating. Profits also result from monopoly power.

8 Profit expectations influence innovating and investment activities and therefore the level of employment. The basic function of profits and losses, however, is to induce that allocation of resources which is in general accord with the tastes of consumers.

9 The largest share of the national income goes to labor. Narrowly defined as "wages and salaries," labor's relative share has increased through time. When more broadly defined to include "proprietors' income," labor's share has been about 80 percent and the capitalist share about 20 percent of national income since 1900.

TERMS AND CONCEPTS

economic rent	transactions and asset	pure rate of interest	economic or pure
incentive function	demands for money	explicit and implicit	profit
single-tax movement	nominal versus real	costs	static economy
Truth in Lending Act	interest rate	normal profit	uninsurable risks

QUESTIONS AND STUDY SUGGESTIONS

1 How does the economist's usage of the term "rent" differ from everyday usage? "Though rent need not be paid by society to make land available, rental payments are very useful in guiding land into the most productive uses." Explain.

2 Explain why economic rent is a surplus to the economy as a whole but a cost of production from the standpoint of individual firms and industries. Explain: "Rent performs no 'incentive function' in the economy." What arguments can be made for and against a heavy tax on land?

3 If money capital is not an economic resource, why is interest paid and received for its use? What considerations account for the fact that interest rates differ greatly on various types of loans? Use these considerations to explain the relative size of the interest rates charged on the following:

    a a ten-year $1000 government bond;

    b a $20 pawnshop loan;

    c an FHA thirty-year mortgage loan on a $97,000 house;

    d a 24-month $12,000 commercial bank loan to finance an automobile; and

    e a 60-day $100 loan from a personal finance company.

4 What is the basic determinant of the transactions demand for money? The asset demand for money? Combine these graphically with the supply of money to determine the equilibrium interest rate. Comment: "The interest rate is an administered price."

5 What are the major economic functions of the interest rate? Of economic profits? How might the fact that more and more businesses are financing their investment activities internally affect the efficiency with which the interest rate performs its functions?

6 Distinguish between nominal and real interest rates. Which is more relevant in making investment decisions? If the nominal interest rate is 12 percent and the inflation rate is 8 percent, what is the real rate of interest? At various times during the 1970s savers earned nominal rates of interest on their savings accounts which were less than the rate of inflation so that their savings earned negative real interest. Why, then, did they save?

7 Historically, usury laws which put below-equilibrium ceilings on interest rates have been used by some states on the grounds that such laws will make credit available to poor people who could not otherwise afford to borrow. Critics of such laws contend that it is poor people who are most likely to be hurt by such laws. Which view is correct?

8 How do the concepts of business profits and economic profits differ? Why are economic profits smaller than business profits? What are the three basic sources of economic profits? Classify each of the following in accordance with these sources:

    a a firm's profits from developing and patenting a ball-point pen containing a permanent ink cartridge;

Following through on this disposition-of-output procedure for all five sectors, note that each vertical column must and does show the units of output of each producing sector which are consumed as inputs by the five sectors. For example, we find in column 2 that to produce 200 units of machinery, inputs of 65 units of metal, 25 of machinery, 5 of fuel, 10 of agricultural products, and 200 of labor are required. In this way, the table vividly reveals the highly interdependent character of the various sectors or industries. Any given industry or sector employs the outputs of other sectors—and indeed, some of its own output—as its inputs. And the outputs of that given sector are the inputs of the other sectors. To cite a real-world example: While outputs of steel are inputs in the production of railroad cars, these railroad cars are, in turn, used to transport both finished steel and the various inputs—coke, pig iron, and so forth—which are necessary to steel production.

Interdependence

The interdependence of the economy's sectors or industries can be further demonstrated by tracing the repercussions of an assumed change in the output of a commodity.

Consider the repercussions of a 20-unit (10 percent) increase in machinery production. This means that a 10 percent increase in the production of all the outputs used as inputs in the production of machinery is required.[3] These inputs are listed in column 2 of Table 30-1. Applying the 10 percent figure, we find that 6.5 *additional* units (outputs) of metal, 2.5 units of machinery, 0.5 unit of fuel, 1 unit of agricultural products, and 20 units of labor will be needed to produce another 20 units of machinery.

But further adjustments are also required. Because each sector which supplies inputs to the machinery sector must expand *its* output, these supplying sectors in turn will require more inputs from other sectors. The additional 6.5 units of metal needed as inputs to produce the extra 20 units of machinery will in turn call for an appropriate—6.5 percent, in this case—increase in the production of all the inputs shown in column 1 to be needed in producing metal.

The same reasoning applies to the fuel, agriculture, and labor sectors. That is, the 0.5-unit increase in

fuel production required in producing the extra 20 units of machinery will call for an appropriate (1 percent) increase in the production of all the inputs listed in column 3, and similarly for the agricultural and labor sectors.

Note that the production of 20 more units of machinery output requires as inputs the production of 2.5 units of machinery. This 2.5-unit increase will require "second-round" increases (of 1.25 percent here) in the inputs of all the resources shown in column 2 in the same fashion as did the initial 20-unit increase in machinery output.

The chain reaction is by no means at an end. All the repercussions cited in these examples call for still further adjustments similar to those already described. The crucial point is that, because of the high degree of interrelatedness among the sectors of the economy, a change in the figure in any one "cell" or "box" of the input-output table will precipitate an almost endless series of adjustments in other figures. In our illustration, expansion of production in one sector has nearly innumerable repercussions reaching into virtually every nook and cranny of the economy. This is why economists sometimes remark, not entirely facetiously, that "in economics everything depends on everything else."

QUICK REVIEW 30-1

∮ *Partial equilibrium analysis examines adjustments in one market in isolation; general equilibrium analysis considers how an event which disturbs equilibrium in one market may affect other related markets.*

∮ *Demand and supply analysis can be used to trace interactions between various product markets and between those product markets and relevant resource markets.*

∮ *Input-output analysis systematically analyzes the interrelationships between an industry's output and the inputs needed to produce that output.*

MARKET INTERRELATIONSHIPS: OPEC AND OIL PRICES

Just as a rock dropped into a pond causes widening circles of ripples, any change in the economy precipitates further changes which radiate outward with gradually diminishing force. And just as these ripples some-

---

[3]We invoke here one of the simplifying assumptions underlying the input-output table, namely, that production occurs under conditions of constant returns to scale (Chapter 22).

times reach shore and rebound eventually to affect the initial point of impact, so too are there feedback effects of initial changes occurring in single markets in the economy. This process of reverberation continues throughout the domestic economy—indeed, throughout the world economy—as a new equilibrium is approached in all markets.

To gain further insight as to the interrelatedness of markets, let's consider one of the most dramatic series of price changes of recent history—the run-up of oil prices in the 1970s. In 1973–1974 the OPEC (Organization of Petroleum Exporting Countries) oil cartel—which then accounted for 90 percent of world oil exports—restricted production and increased oil prices by about $8 per barrel. In relative terms the price of a barrel of oil quadrupled within a few months. Then in 1979–1980 OPEC succeeded in imposing a much larger price increase of about $21 per barrel. Thus the barrel of oil which sold for $2.50 in 1972 was priced at $34 in 1980.

According to partial equilibrium analysis, the restriction of output by OPEC would simply reduce the supply of oil, increase its equilibrium price, and reduce its equilibrium output. And that would be the end of the matter. But this narrow perspective would overlook most of the important ramifications of the price increase. What were some of the more salient implications of these oil price increases? Although the two are not neatly separable, we first consider impacts on the domestic economy and then international effects.

The United States Economy

One of the initial effects of much higher oil prices was that users conserved oil and derivative products and sought substitute products. For example, many power producers converted their plants from oil to natural gas or coal. Wood-burning stoves and furnaces became popular in homes once again. High oil prices affected locational decisions as many firms moved from the Snow Belt to the Sun Belt.

The prices of products derived from oil—for example, plastics and commercial fertilizer—rose sharply, causing higher costs and many adjustments for manufacturers and farmers who used these products as inputs. The rise in gasoline prices from about $.30 per gallon in the pre-OPEC era to $.65 per gallon in 1974 had far-reaching effects on both automobile users and producers. The immediate effect of sharply higher gasoline prices was to cause drivers to curtail use of their cars. Carpools suddenly became popular. Resort owners were adversely affected as many drivers canceled or cut short vacation plans.

Demands for goods and services complementary to automobiles—car washes, motor oil, tires, and auto repairs—declined. Demand for substitutes—for example, public transportation—increased. Over time, automobile purchasers redirected their expenditures from large gas-guzzling American-made cars to compact fuel-efficient imports from Japan and Germany. The OPEC-inspired upsurge in oil and gasoline prices was an important contributor to the growing share of imports in the United States automobile market.

Households using oil for heating also took steps to conserve. Demands increased for insulation, weather-stripping, thermopane windows, and storm doors. Impacts on resource markets were predictable and, in some cases, profound. Less labor was needed in the production of domestic automobiles and more was needed in the production and installation of insulation. Less capital was used to build gas stations and more was employed in oil-drilling rigs and offshore platforms. Generally, high energy prices made the plants and equipment of some industries obsolete. In some cases this was the direct result of higher operating costs. Capital goods which were economic and usable when oil was $2 per barrel became uneconomic when oil was $10, $15, or $25 per barrel. In other instances the obsolescence reflected the impact of higher oil prices on the structure of product demand. The plants of American auto producers were heavily committed to producing large fuel-inefficient cars, the demand for which lagged as consumers shifted to more fuel-efficient imports.

Many more subtle ripples emanating from higher oil and gas prices occurred because the demands for oil and gas are inelastic. For example, elasticity of demand for gasoline is estimated to be in the .20 to .40 range, meaning that a 10 percent increase in price will only result in a 2 to 4 percent decrease in consumption. Recalling our total revenue (expenditures) test for elasticity (Chapter 20), this means that after a price increase consumers will spend more of their income on oil and gasoline and therefore will have less to spend on a whole host of other goods and services unrelated to oil and gasoline as either substitutes or complements.

The OPEC oil price increases were the equivalent of a gigantic tax levied on imported oil. American consumers and manufacturers were forced to pay this tax and the OPEC nations served as tax collectors. This "OPEC tax"—which totaled as much as $40 to $50 billion per year—had significant contractionary effects.

Inadequate Information About Buyers

Just as inadequate information about sellers can keep markets from achieving allocative efficiency, so can inadequate information about *buyers*. These buyers can either be consumers buying products or firms buying resources.

Moral Hazard Problem   Private markets may underallocate resources to a particular good or service for which there is a severe **moral hazard problem.** *The moral hazard problem is the tendency of one party to a contract to alter her or his behavior in ways which are costly to the other party.* A contract will not be profitable to a seller, for example, if the seller must incur large costs to identify those buyers most likely to alter their behavior in cost-imposing ways.

To understand this point, suppose a firm offers an insurance policy which pays a set amount of money per month to people who suffer divorces. The attraction of this insurance is that it pools the economic risk of divorce among thousands of people and, in particular, protects nonworking spouses and children from the economic hardship which divorce often brings. Unfortunately, the moral hazard problem reduces the likelihood that insurance companies can profitably provide this type of insurance contract.

After taking out this insurance, some people will alter their behavior in ways which impose heavy costs on the insurer. Specifically, married couples will have less of an incentive to get along and to iron out marital difficulties. At the extreme, some people might be motivated to obtain a divorce, collect the insurance, and then live together. The problem is that the insurance promotes *more* divorces, the very outcome it protects against. The moral hazard difficulty will force the insurer to charge such high premiums for this insurance that few policies will be bought. If the insurer could identify in advance those people most prone to alter their behavior, the firm could exclude them from buying it. But the firm's marginal cost of getting this information is too high compared to the marginal benefit. Thus, this market fails.

Divorce insurance is not available in the marketplace, but society recognizes the benefits of insuring against the hardships of divorce. It has corrected for this underallocation of "hardship insurance" through child-support laws which dictate payments—when the economic circumstances so warrant—to the spouse who retains the children. Alimony laws also play a role.

Finally, government provides "divorce insurance" of sorts through the Aid to Families with Dependent Children (AFDC) program. If a divorce leaves a spouse with children destitute, the family is eligible for AFDC payments. Government intervention does not eliminate the moral hazard problem; instead, it overcomes or offsets it. Unlike private firms, government need not earn a profit to continue the insurance.

The moral hazard concept has numerous applications. We mention them only in passing, to reinforce your understanding of the basic principle.

1   Drivers may be less cautious because they have car insurance.
2   Medical malpractice insurance may increase the amount of malpractice.
3   Guaranteed contracts for professional athletes may reduce their performance.
4   Unemployment compensation insurance may lead some workers to shirk.
5   Government insurance on bank deposits may encourage banks to make risky loans.

Adverse Selection Problem   Another information problem resulting from inadequate information about buyers is the **adverse selection problem.** *The adverse selection problem arises when information known by the first party to a contract is not known by the second, and, as a result, the second party incurs major costs.* Unlike the moral hazard problem, which arises *after* a person signs a contract, the adverse selection problem arises *at the time* a person signs the contract.

In insurance, the adverse selection problem is that people most likely to receive insurance payouts are those who will buy insurance. For example, those in poorest health will seek to buy the most generous health insurance policies. Or, at the extreme, a person planning to hire an arsonist to "torch" his failing business has an incentive to buy fire insurance.

Our example of hypothetical divorce insurance sheds further light on the adverse selection problem. If the insurance firm sets the premiums on the basis of the average rate of divorce, many of the married couples about to get a divorce will buy insurance. An insurance premium based on average probabilities will make for a great insurance buy for those about to get divorced. Meanwhile, those in highly stable marriages will opt against buying it. In summary, the adverse selection problem will eliminate the pooling of risk which is the basis for profitable insurance. The insurance rates needed to cover payouts will be so high that few people will wish or be able to buy this insurance.

Where private firms underprovide insurance because of information problems, government often establishes some type of social insurance. Government can require everyone in a particular group to enter the insurance pool and therefore can overcome the adverse selection problem. Although the social security system in the United States is partly an insurance and partly a welfare program, in its broadest sense it is insurance against poverty in one's senior years. The social security insurance program overcomes the adverse selection problem by requiring nearly universal participation. People who are most likely to need the minimum benefits that social security provides automatically are participants in the program. So, too, are those not likely to need the benefits.

Workplace Safety   The labor market also provides an example of how inadequate information about buyers (employers) can produce market failures.

For several reasons employers have an economic incentive to provide safe workplaces. A safe workplace reduces the amount of disruption of the production process created by job accidents and lowers the costs of recruiting, screening, training, and retaining new workers. It also reduces a firm's worker compensation insurance premiums (legally required insurance against job injuries).

But a safe workplace comes at an expense. Safe equipment, protective gear, and slower paces of work all entail costs. Thus, the firm will compare its marginal cost and marginal benefit of providing a safer workplace in deciding how much safety to provide. Will this amount of job safety achieve allocative efficiency, as well as maximize the firm's profits?

The answer is "Yes" if the labor and product markets are competitive and workers are fully aware of job risks at various places of employment. With full information, workers will avoid employers having unsafe workplaces. Hence, the supply of labor to these establishments will be greatly restricted, forcing them to boost their wages to attract a work force. These higher wages give the employer an incentive to provide socially desirable levels of workplace safety; safer workplaces will reduce wage expenses. Only firms which find it very costly to provide safer workplaces will choose to pay high compensating wage differentials, rather than reduce workplace hazards.

But a serious problem arises when workers *do not know* that particular occupations or workplaces are unsafe. Because information about the buyer is inadequate—that is, about the employer and the workplace

—the firm may *not* need to pay a wage premium to attract its work force. Its incentive to remove safety hazards therefore is diminished and its profit-maximizing level of workplace safety will be less than socially desirable. In brief, the labor market will fail because of inadequate information about buyers (employers).

Government has several options for remedying this information problem.

1   It can directly provide information to workers about the injury experience of various employers, much like it publishes the on-time performance of the various airlines.

2   It can mandate that firms provide information to workers about known workplace hazards.

3   It can establish standards of workplace safety and enforce them through inspection and penalties.

The Federal government has mainly employed the "standards and enforcement" approach to improve workplace safety, but some contend that an "information" strategy might be less costly and more effective.

QUICK REVIEW 31-3

✦   *Inadequate information can cause markets to fail, causing society's scarce resources to be allocated inefficiently.*

✦   *The moral hazard problem is the tendency of some parties to a contract to alter their behavior in ways which are costly to the other party; for example, a person who buys insurance may incur added risk.*

✦   *As it relates to insurance, the adverse selection problem is the tendency of people who are most likely to collect insurance benefits to buy large amounts of insurance.*

Qualification

People have found many ingenious ways to overcome information difficulties short of government intervention. For example, many firms offer product warranties to overcome the lack of information about themselves and their products. Franchising also helps overcome this problem. When you visit McDonald's or Holiday Inn, you know precisely what you are going to get, as opposed to Sam's Hamburger Shop or the Bates Motel.

Also, some private firms and organizations have specialized in providing information to buyers and sellers. *Consumer Reports* and the *Mobil Travel Guide* provide product information, labor unions collect and dis-

20 percent of the population fell slightly from 9.3 to 8.6 percent of their incomes. Meanwhile, the tax burden of the richest 20 percent fell from 27.2 to 26.8 percent over the same period. The burdens of all other income receivers increased only slightly. The slightly enhanced progressivity of the personal income tax, together with the increasing importance of the social security payroll tax, go far to explain the unchanged overall progressivity of the Federal tax system. When the largely regressive tax structures of state and local governments are combined with the Federal data, the overall tax structure is proportional or slightly progressive.

It is significant to note that, while our tax system does *not* substantially alter the distribution of income, our system of transfer payments has a pronounced effect in reducing income inequality. For example, transfers almost quadrupled the incomes of the poorest fifth of the income receivers.

QUICK REVIEW 32-2

∮ *The benefits-received principle holds that government should assess taxes on individuals according to the amount of benefits they receive, regardless of their income; the ability-to-pay tax principle holds that people should be taxed according to their income, regardless of the benefits they receive from government.*

∮ *As income increases, the average tax rate rises when a tax is progressive, remains the same when a tax is proportional, and falls when a tax is regressive.*

∮ *The more inelastic the demand for a product, the more of an excise tax that is borne by consumers; the more inelastic the supply, the larger the portion borne by producers.*

∮ *The efficiency loss of a tax is the loss of output for which marginal benefits exceed marginal costs.*

∮ *Considering the probable incidences of American taxes (Table 32-2), the American tax structure is deemed to be proportional or slightly progressive.*

TAX ISSUES

While the Tax Reform Act of 1986 embodied perhaps the most sweeping changes in the Federal tax code in the past half-century, there is still considerable pressure for further changes in our tax system. These pressures reflect two quite different objectives.

Taxes and Reindustrialization

Some observers recommend that the entire tax system be recast or restructured to encourage the "reindustrialization" of the American economy. The argument essentially is that in the past two decades the productivity of American workers has stagnated relative to workers in Japan, Germany, and a number of other industrialized nations. A major consequence is that a number of our basic industries—for example, automobiles, steel, and electronics—have fallen prey to foreign competition. In aggregative terms the United States has been incurring massive balance of international trade deficits or, simply stated, our imports have greatly exceeded our exports.

Some economists contend that we must "reindustrialize" our economy by making massive new investments in machinery and equipment to offset our relative economic decline. Retooled with large amounts of modern machinery and equipment, the productivity of American workers will once again increase. But you will recall from Chapter 2's production possibilities curve that with reasonably full employment, more investment implies offsetting cuts in consumption. Some feel that a major structural overhaul of our present tax system can bring about the required increases in investment and reductions in consumption.

One proposal is that the corporate income tax should be lowered or eliminated. This allegedly would greatly enhance the expected profitability of investment and stimulate spending on new plants and equipment. But if the economy is at or close to full employment, how can the required resources be released from the production of consumer goods? A widely discussed means for achieving this is to levy a **value-added tax (VAT)** on consumer goods. VAT is much like a retail sales tax, except that the tax applies only to the difference between the value of a firm's sales and the value of its purchases from other firms. In essence, VAT would amount to a national sales tax on consumer goods. A number of European countries—for example, Great Britain and Sweden—currently use VAT as a major source of revenue.

For present purposes the point to note is that VAT penalizes consumption. One can avoid paying VAT by saving rather than consuming. And we know that saving (refraining from consumption) will release resources from consumer goods production and thereby make them available for investment goods production. In short, elimination of the corporate income tax and the installation of VAT will allegedly alter the composition of our domestic output away from consumption and toward investment with the result that our productivity growth and "competitive edge" will be restored.

Cutting the Budget Deficit

Others feel that higher tax rates or entirely new taxes are required to contain large and persistent Federal budget deficits. In recent years large Federal deficits have caused the public debt to rise sharply. Because many Federal expenditure programs are regarded to be "politically untouchable," any resolution of the deficit problem will undoubtedly entail tax increases. One option is to introduce VAT. Another option is to increase the progressivity of the personal income tax.

In 1990 Congress passed tax and spending legislation designed to reduce the Federal budget deficit by $500 billion over a five-year period. Part of this reduction is to come through reduced government spending; part, through enhanced tax revenues. These higher tax revenues will derive from modifications in various provisions of the personal income tax and higher user fees charged to those benefiting from government services. Additionally, Congress increased excise taxes on alcohol, gasoline, and cigarettes and placed an excise tax on certain luxuries such as expensive cars, yachts, and private aircraft. Nevertheless, this tax-spending package will *not* be sufficient to eliminate Federal budget deficits any time soon.

THE ISSUE OF FREEDOM

Finally, we end our discussion of government decision making by considering an important, but elusive, question: What is the nature of the relationship between the role and size of the public sector, on the one hand, and freedom, on the other? Although no attempt is made here to explore this issue in depth, we will outline two divergent views on this question.

The Conservative Position

Many conservative economists feel that, in addition to the economic costs in any expansion of the public sector, there is also a cost in the form of diminished individual freedom. Several related points constitute this position.

First, there is the "power corrupts" argument.[3] "Freedom is a rare and delicate plant . . . history confirms that the great threat to freedom is the concentration of power . . . by concentrating power in political hands, [government] is . . . a threat to freedom."

Second, one can be selective in the market system of the private sector, using one's income to buy precisely what one chooses and rejecting unwanted commodities. But, as noted earlier, in the public sector—even assuming a high level of political democracy—conformity and coercion are inherent. If the majority decides in favor of certain governmental actions—to build a reservoir, to establish a system of national health insurance, to provide a guaranteed annual income—the minority must conform. Hence, the "use of political channels, while inevitable, tends to strain the social cohesion essential for a stable society."[4] To the extent that decisions can be rendered selectively by individuals through markets, the need for conformity and coercion is lessened and this "strain" reduced. The scope of government should be strictly limited.

Finally, the power and activities of government should be dispersed and decentralized.

> If government is to exercise power, better in the county than in the state, better in the state than in Washington. If I do not like what my local community does, be it in sewage disposal, or zoning, or schools, I can move to another local community, and though few may take this step, the mere possibility acts as a check. If I do not like what my state does, I can move to another. If I do not like what Washington imposes, I have few alternatives in this world of jealous nations.[5]

The Liberal Stance

But liberal economists are skeptical of the conservative position. They hold that the conservative view is based on the **fallacy of limited decisions.** That is, conservatives implicitly assume that during any particular period there is a limited, or fixed, number of decisions to be made in the operation of the economy. If government makes more of these decisions in performing its stated functions, the private sector of the economy will necessarily have fewer "free" decisions or choices to make. This is held to be fallacious reasoning. By spon-

[3]Milton Friedman, *Capitalism and Freedom* (Chicago: The University of Chicago Press, 1962), p. 2.
[4]Ibid., p. 23.
[5]Ibid., p. 3.

trust of big business came into full bloom in the decades following the Civil War. The widening of local markets into national markets as transportation facilities improved, the ever-increasing mechanization of production, and the increasingly widespread adoption of the corporate form of business enterprise were important forces causing development of "trusts"—that is, monopolies—in the 1870s and 1880s. Trusts developed in the petroleum, meatpacking, railroad, sugar, lead, coal, whiskey, and tobacco industries, among others, during this era.

Not only were questionable tactics employed in monopolizing various industries, but the resulting market power was almost invariably exerted to the detriment of all who did business with these monopolies. Farmers and small businesses, being particularly vulnerable to the growth and tactics of giant corporate monopolies, were among the first to censure their development. Consumers and labor unions were not far behind in voicing their disapproval of monopoly power.

Because of development of industries in which market forces no longer provided adequate control to ensure socially tolerable behavior, two techniques of control have been adopted as substitutes for, or supplements to, the market.

1 In those few markets where economic realities preclude the effective working of the market—that is, where there is "natural monopoly"—we have established public *regulatory agencies* to control economic behavior.

2 In most other markets in which economic and technological conditions have not made monopoly essential, social control has taken the form of antimonopoly or *antitrust legislation* designed to inhibit or prevent the growth of monopoly.

First, we will consider the major pieces of antitrust legislation which, as refined and extended by various amendments, constitute the basic law of the land with respect to corporate size and concentration.

Sherman Act of 1890

Acute public resentment of the trusts which developed in the 1870s and 1880s culminated in passage of the **Sherman Act** in 1890. This cornerstone of antitrust legislation is surprisingly brief and, at first glance, directly to the point. The core of the act is embodied in two major provisions:

In Section 1:

> Every contract, combination in the form of a trust or otherwise, or conspiracy, in restraint of trade or

commerce among the several states, or with foreign nations is hereby declared to be illegal. . . .

In Section 2:

> Every person who shall monopolize, or attempt to monopolize, or combine or conspire with any person or persons, to monopolize any part of the trade or commerce among the several states, or with foreign nations, shall be deemed guilty of a misdemeanor. . . .

This act made monopoly and "restraints of trade"—for example, collusive price fixing or the dividing up of markets among competitors—criminal offenses against the Federal government. Either the Department of Justice or parties injured by monopoly or anticompetitive behavior could file suits under the Sherman Act. Firms found in violation of the act could be ordered dissolved by the courts, or injunctions could be issued to prohibit practices deemed unlawful under the act. Fines and imprisonment were also possible results of successful prosecution. Further, parties injured by illegal combinations and conspiracies could sue for **treble damages**—triple the amount of monetary injury done them. The Sherman Act seemed to provide a sound foundation for positive government action against business monopolies.

However, early court interpretations raised serious questions about the effectiveness of the Sherman Act and it became clear that a more explicit statement of the government's antitrust sentiments was in order. Indeed, the business community itself sought a clearer statement of what was legal and illegal.

Clayton Act of 1914

This needed elaboration of the Sherman Act took the form of the 1914 **Clayton Act.** The following sections of the Clayton Act were designed to strengthen and make explicit the intent of the Sherman Act:

Section 2 *outlaws price discrimination* between purchasers when such discrimination is not justified on the basis of cost differences.

Section 3 *forbids exclusive,* or **"tying," contracts** whereby a producer would sell a product only on condition that the buyer acquire other products from the same seller and not from competitors.

Section 7 *prohibits acquisition of stocks* of competing corporations when the effect is to lessen competition.

Section 8 *prohibits formation of* **interlocking directorates**—the situation where a director of one firm is also a board member of a competing firm—in large corporations where the effect would be to reduce competition.

Actually, there was little in the Clayton Act which had not already been stated by implication in the Sherman Act. The Clayton Act merely attempted to sharpen and clarify the general provisions of the Sherman Act. Furthermore, the Clayton Act sought to outlaw the techniques by which monopoly might develop and, in this sense, was a preventive measure. The Sherman Act, by contrast, was aimed more at punishing existing monopolies.

Federal Trade Commission Act of 1914

This legislation created the five-member Federal Trade Commission (FTC) and charged it with the responsibility of enforcing the antitrust laws and the Clayton Act in particular. The FTC was given the power to investigate unfair competitive practices on its own initiative or at the request of injured firms. The Commission could hold public hearings on such complaints and, if necessary, issue **cease-and-desist orders** where "unfair methods of competition in commerce" were discovered.

The **Wheeler-Lea Act** of 1938 charged the FTC with the additional responsibility of policing "deceptive acts or practices in commerce" and, as a result, the FTC also undertakes the task of protecting the public against false or misleading advertising and the misrepresentation of products.

The importance of the **Federal Trade Commission Act** is twofold: (1) the act broadened the range of illegal business behavior and (2) it established an independent antitrust agency with the authority to investigate and to initiate court cases. Today, the FTC and the U.S. Justice Department have joint responsibility in enforcing the antitrust laws.

Celler-Kefauver Act of 1950

This act amended Section 7 of the Clayton Act, which prohibits a firm from acquiring the *stock* of competitors when the acquisition would reduce competition. Firms could evade Section 7 by acquiring the physical *assets* (plant and equipment) of competing firms, rather than their stocks. The **Celler-Kefauver Act** plugged this loophole by prohibiting one firm from obtaining physical assets of another firm when the effect would be to lessen competition.

ANTITRUST: ISSUES AND IMPACT

The effectiveness of any law depends on the vigor with which the government enforces it and how the law is interpreted by the courts. The Federal government has varied considerably in its willingness to apply the antitrust acts. Administrations having a laissez-faire philosophy about industrial concentration have sometimes emasculated the acts simply by ignoring them or by cutting budget appropriations of enforcement agencies.

Similarly, the courts have run hot and cold in interpreting antitrust laws. At times, they have applied them with vigor, adhering closely to the spirit and objectives of the laws. In other cases, the courts have interpreted the acts in such ways as to render them all but completely innocuous. With this in mind let's examine two major issues which arise in interpreting antitrust laws.

Behavior or Structure?

A comparison of two landmark Court decisions reveals the existence of two distinct approaches in the application of antitrust. In the 1920 **U.S. Steel case** the courts applied the **rule of reason,** saying in effect that not every monopoly is illegal. Only those which "unreasonably" restrain trade—so-called "bad trusts"—are subject to antitrust action. The Court held in this case that mere size was not an offense; although U.S. Steel clearly *possessed* monopoly power, it was innocent because it had not resorted to illegal acts against competitors in obtaining that power, nor had it unreasonably used its monopoly power.

In the **Alcoa case** of 1945 the courts did a turnabout. The Court held that, even though a firm's behavior might be legal, mere possession of monopoly power (Alcoa had 90 percent of the aluminum ingot market) violated the antitrust laws.

These two cases point to a continuing controversy in antitrust policy. Should an industry be judged by its *behavior* (as in the U.S. Steel case) or by its *structure* (as in the Alcoa case)? "Structuralists" contend that an industry which is highly concentrated will behave like a monopolist. Thus, the economic performance of these industries will necessarily be undesirable. Such industries are therefore legitimate targets for antitrust action.

Alternatively, the "behavioralists" argue that the relationship between structure and performance is tenuous and unclear. They feel that a highly concentrated

planes and then fly to their more distant destinations. This system has reduced unit costs by allowing airlines to use smaller planes on the spoke routes and make use of wide-bodied craft between the major hub airports. Wide-body aircraft cost less to operate per seat-mile than smaller aircraft.

Also, the entry of "nonunion" airlines has forced the major carriers to negotiate wage reductions—often as much as 10 to 20 percent—with their unions. Some airlines have established a two-tier wage system whereby new workers are paid less on a given job than current employees. In many instances union work rules have been made more flexible to increase worker productivity and reduce wage costs. In short, some of the major cost reductions *and* adjustment problems associated with deregulation have occurred in relevant labor markets.

Service and Safety Although critics of airline deregulation predicted that airline service—particularly to smaller communities—would be curtailed or abandoned, this fear has turned out to be exaggerated. While some major airlines have withdrawn from a few smaller cities, commuter airlines have often filled the resulting void. Statistics indicate that the hub and spoke system has increased flight frequencies at most airports. It also has reduced the amount of airline switching required of passengers.

On the negative side, more frequent stopovers now required in hub cities have increased average travel time between cities. Also, by increasing the volume of air traffic, deregulation has contributed to greater airport congestion resulting in more frequent and longer flight delays.

Has deregulation reduced the "safety margin" of air transportation as some critics charge? There is mixed evidence on this question. On the one hand, the increased volume of air traffic has resulted in higher reported instances of near-collisions in midair. On the other hand, the accident and fatal accident rates of airlines are lower today than they were before deregulation. Furthermore, because lower air fares have caused people to substitute air travel for more-dangerous automobile travel, deregulation has prevented an estimated 800 deaths annually on the nation's highways.

Industry Structure Airline deregulation initially brought with it entry of numerous new carriers. In the past few years, however, the industry has gone through a "shakeout" in which many firms have failed

and others have merged with stronger competitors. In 1991 eight airlines accounted for 90 percent of domestic air traffic.

Growing concentration in the airline industry is of considerable concern. Some think consolidation of the industry may be detrimental to the very goals of deregulation itself. Single carriers control 75 percent or more of departures at six large "fortress" hubs. The General Accounting Office found that in 1990 fares at fifteen airports dominated by one or two airlines were about 20 percent higher than at twenty-two airports where competition was more brisk. Moreover, two factors make entry of new carriers into lucrative hubs difficult.

1 Lack of Airport Capacity The lack of airport capacity—at least in the short term—means that airline markets are far from being perfectly contestable. A firm wishing to enter a market because existing carriers are earning economic profits cannot do so if long-term leases allow existing carriers to control the airline gates at the profitable airports. It is alleged that some gates, in fact, go unused because dominant carriers refuse to release them to competitors.

2 Airline Practices Several tactics make it difficult for new firms to successfully enter the airline industry. Airline reservation systems developed by the major carriers give their own flights priority listings on the computers used by travel agents. Also, frequent-flyer programs—discounts based on accumulated flight mileage—encourage passengers to use dominant existing carriers rather than new entrants. Finally, price matching by existing carriers makes it exceedingly difficult for new entrants to lure customers through lower ticket prices.

Although it is too soon for a definitive assessment of airline deregulation, most economists view the outcome to date as positive. The Federal government has estimated that airline deregulation produced a $100 billion net benefit to society during the 1980s. The tight oligopoly which seems to be emerging in the industry, however, is a mixed blessing. While it may lead to a handful of financially strong airlines, each having cost-minimizing route structures, it predictably will lead to price leadership and other business practices associated with oligopoly. At a minimum, strict enforcement against anticompetitive mergers and business tactics may be needed to preserve the gains from deregulation. Another procompetitive option would be to repeal laws which bar foreign airlines from flying domestic routes in the United States.

SOCIAL REGULATION

The "old" regulation just discussed has been labeled economic or **industrial regulation.** Here government is concerned with the overall economic performance of a few specific industries, and concern focuses on pricing and service to the public.

Beginning largely in the early 1960s, government regulation of a new type evolved and experienced rapid growth. This **social regulation** is concerned with the conditions under which goods and services are pro-

TABLE 33-2 The main Federal regulatory commissions: social regulation

Commission (year established)	Jurisdiction
Food and Drug Administration (1906)	Safety and effectiveness of food, drugs, and cosmetics
Equal Employment Opportunity Commission (1964)	Hiring, promotion, and discharge of workers
Occupational Safety and Health Administration (1971)	Industrial health and safety
Environmental Protection Agency (1972)	Air, water, and noise pollution
Consumer Product Safety Commission (1972)	Safety of consumer products

duced, the impact of production on society, and the physical characteristics of goods themselves. For example, the Occupational Safety and Health Administration (OSHA) is concerned with protecting workers against occupational injuries and illnesses and the Consumer Products Safety Commission (CPSC) specifies minimum standards for potentially unsafe products.

The main Federal regulatory commissions dealing with social regulation are listed in Table 33-2.

Distinguishing Features

Social regulation differs from economic regulation in several ways.

1 Social regulation is often applied "across the board" to virtually all industries and directly affects far more people. While the Interstate Commerce Commission (ICC) focuses only on specific portions of the transport industry, OSHA's rules and regulations apply to every employer.

2 The nature of social regulation involves government in the very details of the production process. For example, rather than simply specifying safety standards for products, CPSC mandates—often in detail—certain characteristics which products must have.

3 A final distinguishing feature of social regulation is its rapid expansion. Between 1970 and 1979 government created twenty new Federal regulatory agencies.

The names of the better-known regulatory agencies in Table 33-2 suggest the basic reason for their creation and growth: Much of our society had achieved a reasonably affluent level of living by the 1960s and attention shifted to improvements in the quality of life. This improvement called for safer and better products, less pollution, better working conditions, and greater equality of opportunity.

Costs and Criticisms

It is generally agreed that the overall objectives of social regulation are laudable. But there is great controversy as to whether the benefits of these regulatory efforts justify the costs.

Costs The costs of social regulation are of two types: *administrative costs,* such as salaries paid to employees of the commissions, office expenses, and the like; and *compliance costs,* which are the costs incurred by businesses and state and local governments in meeting the requirements of regulatory commissions. In 1991 total

perts conclude that we have been only modestly successful in such endeavors.

2 Domestic and Foreign Demand Government has initiated a variety of programs to augmuent domestic consumption of farm products. For example, the *food-stamp program* is designed to bolster low-income families' demand for food. Similarly, our **Food for Peace program** under Public Law 480 has permitted less developed countries to buy our surplus farm products with their own currencies, rather than with dollars. Furthermore, in international trade bargaining, our negotiators have pressed hard to persuade foreign nations to reduce protective tariffs and other barriers against our farm products.

Although the government's supply-restricting and demand-increasing efforts undoubtedly helped reduce the amount of surplus production, they have not been successful in eliminating surpluses. As noted earlier, farm subsidies in the 1985–1990 period totaled some $80 billion.

CRITICISMS OF FARM POLICY

After more than a half century of experience with government policies designed to stabilize and enhance farm incomes, there is considerable evidence to suggest that these programs are not working well. There is growing feeling among economists and political leaders that the traditional goals and techniques of farm policy must be reexamined and revised. Some of the more important criticisms of agricultural policy follow.

Symptoms and Causes

Our farm programs have failed to get at the causes of the farm problem. Public policy toward agriculture is designed to treat symptoms and not causes. The root *cause* of the farm problem has been a misallocation of resources between agriculture and the rest of the economy. Historically, the problem has been one of too many farmers. The effect or symptom of this misallocation of resources is relatively low farm incomes. *For the most part, public policy in agriculture has been oriented toward supporting farm prices and incomes rather than toward alleviating the resource allocation problem, which is the fundamental cause of relatively low farm incomes.*

Some critics go further and argue that price-income supports have encouraged people to stay in

agriculture when they otherwise would have migrated to some nonfarm occupation. That is, the price-income orientation of the farm program has deterred the very reallocation of resources necessary to resolve the long-run farm problem.

Misguided Subsidies

Price-income support programs have most benefited those farmers who least need government assistance. Assuming the goal of our farm program is bolstering of low farm incomes, it follows that any program of government aid should be aimed at farmers at the bottom of the farm income distribution. But the poor, small-output farmer simply does not produce and sell enough in the market to get much aid from price supports. It is the large corporate farm which reaps the benefits by virtue of its large output.

In 1990, for example, the 5 percent of all farms with sales of $250,000 or more received over 38 percent of all direct government subsidies. The poorest 59 percent of all farmers—those who earned less than $20,000 from farming in 1990—received under 3 percent of all direct subsidy payments.[1] If public policy must be designed to supplement farm incomes, a strong case can certainly be made for making those benefits vary inversely, rather than directly, with one's position in the income distribution. An income-support program should be geared to *people,* not *commodities.* Many economists contend that, on equity grounds, direct income subsidies to poor farmers are highly preferable to indirect price support subsidies which go primarily to large and prosperous farmers.

A related point concerns land values. The price and income benefits which various farm programs provide are eventually capitalized into higher farmland values. By making crops more valuable, price supports have made the land itself more valuable. Sometimes this is helpful to farmers, but often it is not. Farmers rent about 40 percent of their farmland, mostly from relatively well-to-do nonfarm landlords. Thus, price supports become a subsidy to people *not* actively engaged in farming.

Policy Contradictions

The complexity and multiple objectives embedded in farm policy yield a number of conflicts and contradic-

[1]U.S. Department of Agriculture, *Economic Indicators of the Farm Sector: National Financial Summary, 1990,* p. 44.

tions. Subsidized research is aimed at increasing farm productivity and increasing the supply of farm products, while acreage reserve and "set aside" programs pay farmers to take land out of production to reduce supply. Price supports for crops mean increased feed costs for ranchers and high prices for animal products to consumers. Tobacco farmers have been subsidized at a time when serious health problems are associated with tobacco consumption. Our sugar program raises sugar prices for domestic growers by imposing import quotas which conflict with our free trade policies.

Declining Effectiveness

There is also reason to believe that farm policy has simply become less effective in accomplishing its goals, In the 1930s most farms were relatively small, semi-isolated units which employed relatively modest amounts of machinery and equipment and provided most of their own inputs. Now, however, farms are larger, highly capital-intensive, and closely integrated with both domestic and international economies.

Farmers now depend on others for seed, fertilizers, insecticides, and so forth. American agriculture uses more than twice as much physical capital (machinery and buildings) per worker as does the economy as a whole. This means that farmers now need to borrow large amounts of money to finance purchases of capital equipment and land *and* for operating capital. Despite an elaborate farm policy designed to enhance farm incomes, high interest rates can easily precipitate losses or bankruptcy for many farmers. Dependence on export markets can also undermine farm policy. A fall in foreign incomes or an increase in the international value of the dollar (which makes American farm products more expensive to foreigners) can unexpectedly reduce American farm exports and easily wipe out any positive effects of agricultural programs on farm incomes. In short, a much wider range of variables may now alter farm incomes and diminish the effectiveness of farm programs.

THE POLITICS OF FARM POLICY

In view of these criticisms, we may well ask why we have an extensive and costly farm program. Why not abandon price supports and return to free markets? Why do farm programs persist although the farm population—and the farm vote—has declined historically (Table 34-1)?

Public Choice Theory Revisited

We can respond to these questions in terms of Chapter 32's public choice theory. Recall that *rent-seeking behavior* involves a group—a labor union, firms in a particular industry, or farmers producing a particular product—pursuing political means to transfer income or wealth to themselves at the expense of another group or society as a whole. The *special-interest effect* refers to a program or policy from which a small group receives *large* benefits at the expense of a much larger group who *individually* suffer *small* losses.

Suppose a specific group of farmers—peanut or sugar growers or dairy farmers—organize themselves and establish a well-financed political action committee (PAC). The PAC's job is to promote the establishment and perpetuation of government programs which will transfer income to the group (rent-seeking behavior). Thus the PAC vigorously lobbies senators and representatives to enact or perpetuate price supports and establish import quotas for peanuts, sugar, or milk. They do this by making political contributions to potentially sympathetic legislators. Thus, although peanut production is heavily concentrated in a few states such as Georgia, Alabama, and Texas, the PAC will make contributions to nonpeanut state legislators to gain support.

However, if an interest group—peanut or sugar growers—is small, how can it successfully line its own pockets at the expense of society as a whole? The answer: Although the aggregate costs of the group's program might be considerable, the cost imposed on *each individual* taxpayer is small (the special-interest effect). Indeed, citizen-taxpayers are likely uninformed about and indifferent to issues like these because they have little at stake. Unless you grow sugar beets or peanuts, you have probably no idea how much those programs cost you as an individual taxpayer and consumer, and you do not raise cain, so to speak, if your legislator votes for a sugar program. Civil rights, educational reform, and peace in the Middle East may seem to be much more urgent political issues to you than a program for a handful of peanut or sugar farmers.

There is also political *logrolling* (Chapter 32), the trading of votes on policies and programs to change a negative outcome into a positive outcome. Senator Foghorn votes for a program which benefits Senator Moribund's constituents and Moribund returns the favor. For example: Many members of Congress who represent low-income urban areas vote in favor of farm subsidies. In return, representatives of agricultural areas support such programs as food stamps which provide subsidized food for the poor. Thus we have a rural-urban coalition through which representatives from both areas provide benefits for their constituents and enhance their reelection chances. Such coalitions help explain why farm subsidies persist and why the food stamp program has been greatly expanded over the years.

Public choice theory also tells us that politicians are more likely to favor programs having hidden costs. As we have seen, this is often true of farm programs. In discussing Figure 34-5 we found that price supports involve, not simply an explicit transfer from taxpayer to farmer, but also the costs hidden in higher food prices, storage costs for surplus output, bureaucratic costs of administering farm programs, and costs associated with both domestic and international misallocations of resources. While the explicit or direct cost of the peanut program to taxpayers is only about $4 million a year, the price increase provided by the program carries a hidden subsidy (cost) of $190 million per year. Because the cost of the peanut program is largely indirect and hidden, the program is much more acceptable to politicians and the public than if all costs were explicit.

New Directions?

There is reason to predict that farm subsidies may decline in the future.

1 Declining Farm Population   As farm population has declined, its political clout has also diminished. The farm population was about 25 percent of the total in the 1930s when many of our farm programs were established. That population now is less than 2 percent of the total. Urban lawmakers have a 9-to-1 advantage over their rural colleagues. More and more legislators are critically examining farm programs from the vantage point of their effect on consumers' grocery bills rather than farm incomes.

2 Budget Deficits   Continued pressures to balance the Federal budget have brought farm subsidies under increased political scrutiny.

3 Program Excesses   Program excesses have been increasingly publicized, perhaps weakening the special-interest effect. Examples: In one year in the late 1980s a large California cotton grower received $12 million is subsidy payments; the crown prince of Liechtenstein received a subsidy in excess of $2 million as a partner in a Texas rice farm; and 112 dairy farmers received $1 million each under a program designed to reduce the size of dairy herds. Also, the nonfarm population has become increasingly aware and critical of farm programs. Programs created in the 1930s to help smaller farms are being reevaluated now that agriculture is dominated by large farms increasingly like any other business.

4 Policy Conflicts   It is increasingly apparent that domestic farm programs are seriously at odds with the objective of free world trade. This conflict merits more detailed consideration.

WORLD TRADE AND FARM POLICY

A more critical attitude toward farm subsidies is reflected in American negotiations designed to reduce world trade barriers to agricultural products.

Policy Impacts

Consider the impacts of current farm programs on world trade. Virtually every industrialized country— the United States, Canada, Japan, among others— intervenes in agriculture by subsidizing and providing protective trade barriers. For example, the European Community (EC)—made up of twelve western European nations—has established high prices for its domestic agricultural products. These price supports have a number of consequences.

1   To maintain high domestic prices the EC must restrict imports (supplies) of foreign farm products. It does this by imposing import tariffs and quotas, the former being excise taxes and the latter specific quantitative limits on foreign goods.

2   Although the EC was once an importer of food, high price supports have induced European farmers to produce much more output than European consumers want to purchase.

3   To rid itself of these agricultural surpluses the EC has heavily subsidized their export into world markets.

The effects on the United States are that: (1) our farmers have great difficulty in selling to EC nations because of their trade barriers; and (2) subsidized exports from the EC depress world prices for agricultural products, making these markets less attractive to our farmers.

Perhaps most importantly, from an international perspective farm programs such as those of the EC and the United States distort world agricultural trade and thereby the international allocation of agricultural resources. Encouraged by artificially high prices, farmers in industrially advanced nations produce more agricultural output than they would otherwise. The resulting surpluses flow into world markets where they depress prices. This means that farmers in countries with no farm programs—often less developed countries—face artificially low prices for their exports, which signals them to produce less. In this way farm price distortions alter production away from that based on productive efficiency or comparative advantage (Chapter 3). For example, price supports cause American agricultural resources to be allocated to sugar production, although sugar can be produced at perhaps half the cost in the Caribbean and Australia.

One estimate suggests that the benefits of free, undistorted agricultural trade to the industrially advanced economies alone would be about $35 billion per year, with the United States, the EC, and Japan as the major beneficiaries. Corollary benefits are (1) increased American farm exports, which would reduce our international balance of payments deficit; and (2) reduced expenditures on our domestic farm programs, which would help reduce the Federal budget deficit. Thus the United States has compelling economic reasons to favor the liberalization of international agricultural trade.

QUICK REVIEW 34-2

‣ *The parity ratio, which is the basis for price supports, shows the ratio of prices received to prices paid by farmers.*

‣ *Price supports cause surplus production which government must buy and store; raise both farmer incomes and food prices to consumers; and generate an overallocation of resources to agriculture.*

‣ *Farm policy has been criticized for: delaying the exodus of resources from farming; allocating most subsidies to wealthier farmers; conflicting with other policies such as freer world trade; not effectively resolving farm problems; and being very costly.*

‣ *The persistence of farm programs is explainable in terms of rent-seeking behavior, the special-interest effect, and other aspects of public choice theory.*

‣ *The farm programs of the United States, the European Community, and other industrialized nations have contributed to a misallocation of the world's agricultural resources.*

GATT Negotiations

The United States—along with a number of food-exporting nations known as the Cairns Group (including Australia, New Zealand, Canada, and Argentina)—has been a leading advocate for elimination of trade barriers on agricultural products and, by implication, an advocate for the dismantling of price-support programs. Under the aegis of the General Agreement on Tariffs and Trade (GATT)—an international association of over 100 nations dedicated to the promotion of free world trade—the United States has proposed: (1) a ten-year phaseout of all agricultural tariffs; (2) elimination of agricultural export subsidies over a five-year period; and (3) a phaseout of all domestic farm supports which distort world agricultural trade. Unfortunately, under pressure from their politically powerful farm groups, the EC and Japan have rejected these proposals and negotiations have stalled.

Farm Act of 1990

Despite the failure of the GATT negotiations, recent farm legislation reflects efforts to (1) cut the cost of farm subsidies and (2) increase the role of market (as opposed to supported) prices in agricultural decision making. Specifically, the **Farm Act of 1990** reduces by 15 percent the acreage covered by price guarantees, thereby reducing the cost of subsidy programs. The potential blow to farmers is softened by allowing them to plant the affected acres in alternative crops. Farmers' decisions on these alternative crops will be based on market price signals. For example, many corn and wheat farmers may put the 15 percent reduction in price-supported land into soybeans or sunflowers, based on growing conditions and anticipated prices. In short, the new farm act simultaneously reduces farm subsidies and increases the role of market forces.

Market-Oriented Income Stabilization

From a long-term perspective it seems increasingly likely that farm policy will shift from the goal of enhancing to that of stabilizing farm incomes. The goal of *stabilization* is to reduce the sharp year-to-year fluctuations in farm incomes and prices, but to accept the long-run average of farm prices and incomes which free markets would provide. This contrasts with income *enhancement,* which seeks to provide farmers with commodity prices and incomes above those which free markets would yield. Government might moderate the boom and bust character of agricultural markets by

LAST WORD

THE SUGAR PROGRAM: A SWEET DEAL

The sugar program is a sweet deal for domestic sugar producers, but it imposes heavy costs on domestic consumers and foreign producers.

The United States' program of price supports for sugar has entailed significant costs both domestically and internationally. Recent price supports for some 12,000 American producers have maintained domestic sugar prices at almost double the world price. The estimated aggregate cost to domestic consumers is $3 billion per year.

As a consequence of our high domestic price supports, foreign sugar producers have a very strong incentive to sell their outputs in the United States. But an influx of much cheaper foreign sugar into our domestic market would undermine domestic price supports. Hence, our government has imposed import quotas on foreign sugar. As the difference between United States-supported prices and world prices has increased, import quotas have become more restrictive, with the result that imported sugar has become a declining proportion of our consumption of sweeteners. About 30 percent of our sugar was imported in 1975; currently

supporting prices and accumulating surplus stocks when prices fall significantly below the long-run trend of prices. Conversely, government would augment supply by selling from these stocks when prices rise significantly above the long-run trend.

Proponents feel that the **market-oriented income stabilization policy** has a number of advantages. First, government involvement in agriculture would be diminished in that programs of supply management through acreage reduction would be abandoned. Second, prices would reflect long-run equilibrium levels and therefore lead to an efficient allocation of resources between agriculture and the rest of the economy. By providing farmers with incomes consistent with market-clearing prices, the market system would provide the needed signals to accelerate movement of farmers to nonfarm jobs. Third, taxpayer costs would be significantly reduced. And, finally, the lower average level of farm prices would help to stimulate agricultural exports.

GLOBAL VIEW: FEAST OR FAMINE?

The American farm problem—supply outrunning demand and farm policies which foster surplus production—is not common to most other nations. Many less developed nations, not to mention the former Soviet Union, must presistently import foodstuffs. We frequently read of malnutrition, chronic food shortages, and famine in Africa and elsewhere. In the future—say, four or five decades from now—will the world be unable to feed itself?

While there is no simple response to this question, it is of interest to summarize some of the pros and cons pertinent to the issue. Pessimists, envisioning impending famine as demand increases ahead of supply, make these arguments:

1   The quantity of arable land is finite and its quality is being seriously impaired by wind and water erosion.

2   Urban sprawl and industrial expansion continue to

only 3 or 4 percent is imported. Note that our agricultural policy in the domestic sugar industry largely dictates our international trade policy with respect to that product.

The loss of the American market has had a number of very harmful effects on many of the less developed sugar-exporting countries such as the Philippines, Brazil, and a number of Central American countries. First, exclusion from the American market has significantly reduced their export earnings and national incomes. The decline in export revenues is particularly important because many of the sugar-producing countries are highly dependent on such revenues to pay interest and principal on massive external debts owed to the United States and other industrially advanced nations.

Second, barred by quotas from sale in the United States market, the sugar produced by the less developed countries has been added to world markets, where the increased supply has depressed the world price of sugar.

Third, under the impetus of domestic price supports, American sugar production has increased to the extent that the United States may soon change from a sugar-importing to a sugar-exporting nation. That is, our sugar program may soon be a source of new competition for the sugar producers of the less developed

countries. Sugar price supports in the European Community have already turned that group of nations into sugar exporters.

Finally, from both a domestic and a global perspective, the sugar price support programs of the United States and other industrially advanced economies have distorted the worldwide allocation of agricultural resources. Price supports have signaled an overallocation of resources to sugar production by relatively less efficient American producers. American import quotas and consequent low world sugar prices have signaled more efficient foreign producers to restrict their production. In short, high-cost producers are producing more and low-cost producers are producing less sugar with the result being an inefficient allocation of the world's agricultural resources.

Aside from higher sugar prices to consumers, the sugar program has cost jobs in the United States. In the past decade an estimated 7000 jobs have been lost because of refinery closings due to the decline of sugar imports. The Brach Candy Company recently announced that it would probably move some 3500 jobs from Chicago to Canada where sugar prices are lower.

Based primarily on *Economic Report of the President, 1987* (Washington, D.C.: 1987), pp. 165–169. Updated.

convert prime land from agriculture to nonagricultural uses.
3 Our underground water system upon which farmers depend for irrigation is being mined at such a rapid rate that farmlands in some areas will have to be abandoned.
4 World population continues to grow; every day there are thousands of new mouths to feed.
5 Some environmentalists suggest that unfavorable long-run climatic changes will undermine future agricultural production.

Optimists offer the following counterarguments.
1 The number of acres planted to crops has been increasing and the world is far from bringing all its arable land into production.
2 Agricultural productivity continues to rise and the possibility of dramatic productivity breakthroughs lies ahead as we enter the age of genetic engineering.

There is also room for substantial productivity increases in the agricultural sectors of less developed countries. For example, improved economic incentives for farm workers in China helped expand agricultural output by about one-third between 1980 and 1985.
3 The rate of growth of world population has in fact been diminishing.
4 We must reckon with the adjustment processes elicited by the market system. If food shortages were to develop, food prices would rise. Higher prices would simultaneously induce more production, constrain the amount demanded and head off the shortages.

Admittedly, the "feast or famine" debate is highly speculative; a clear picture of the world's future production capabilities and consumption needs is not easily discerned. Perhaps the main point is that American agricultural policies should take global considerations into account.

CHAPTER SUMMARY

1 In the short run, the highly inelastic nature of agricultural demand translates small changes in output and small shifts in domestic or foreign demand into large fluctuations in prices and incomes.

2 Rapid technological advance, coupled with a highly inelastic and relatively constant demand for agricultural output, has caused agriculture to be a declining industry.

3 Historically, agricultural policy has been price-centered and based on the parity concept which suggests that the relationship between prices received and paid by farmers should remain constant.

4 The use of price floors or supports has a number of economic effects: **a** surplus production occurs; **b** the incomes of farmers are increased; **c** consumers pay higher prices for farm products; **d** society at large pays higher taxes to purchase and store surplus output, and also bears the cost of an overallocation of resources to agriculture; and **e** other nations bear the costs associated with import barriers and depressed world farm commodity prices.

5 Government has pursued with limited success a variety of programs to reduce the supply of, and increase the demand for, agricultural products to reduce the surpluses associated with price supports.

6 Farm policy has been criticized for **a** confusing symptoms (low farm incomes) with causes (excess capacity); **b** providing the largest subsidies to high-income farmers; **c** contradictions among specific farm programs; and **d** declining effectiveness.

7 The persistence of agricultural subsidies can be explained in terms of public choice theory and, in particular, in terms of rent-seeking behavior, the special-interest effect, and political logrolling.

8 The United States has unsuccessfully sought through GATT to reduce barriers to international agricultural trade.

9 The Farm Act of 1990 reduces the amount of land to which price supports apply and enhances the use of market prices in agricultural decision making.

10 The United States may be moving toward a policy of stabilizing, but not enhancing, farm incomes.

TERMS AND CONCEPTS

short-run farm problem	**price supports**	**Food for Peace**	**market-oriented**
long-run farm problem	**acreage allotment**	**program**	**income stabilization**
parity concept	**programs**	**Farm Act of 1990**	**policy**
parity ratio			

QUESTIONS AND STUDY SUGGESTIONS

1 Explain how each of the following contributes to the farm problem: **a** the inelasticity of demand for farm products, **b** rapid technological progress in farming, **c** the modest long-run growth in demand for farm commodities, **d** the competitiveness of agriculture, and **e** the relative fixity or immobility of agricultural resources. Do exports increase or reduce the instability of demand for farm products?

2 What relationship, if any, can you detect between the fact that the farmer's fixed costs of production are large and the fact that the supply of most agricultural products is generally inelastic? Be specific in your answer.

3 "The supply and demand for agricultural products are such that small changes in agricultural supply will result in drastic changes in prices. However, large changes in farm prices have modest effects on agricultural output." Carefully evaluate. *Hint:* A brief review of the distinction between *supply* and *quantity supplied* may be of assistance.

4 The key to efficient resource allocation is the shifting of resources from low-productivity to high-productivity uses. Given the high and expanding physical productivity of agricultural resources, explain why many economists want to divert resources from farming in the interest of greater allocative efficiency.

5 "Industry complains of the higher taxes it must pay to finance subsidies to agriculture. Yet the fact that the trend of agricultural prices has been downward while industrial prices have been moving upward suggests that on balance agriculture is actually subsidizing industry." Explain and evaluate.

6 "Because consumers as a whole must ultimately pay the total incomes received by farmers, it makes no real difference whether this income is paid through free farm markets or through supported prices supplemented by subsidies financed out of tax revenues." Do you agree?

7 Suppose you are president of a local chapter of one of the major farm organizations. You are directed by the chapter's membership to formulate policy statements for the chapter covering the following topics: **a** antitrust policy, **b** monetary policy, **c** fiscal policy, and **d** tariff policy. Briefly outline the policy statements which will best serve the interests of farmers. What is the rationale underlying each statement? Do you see any conflicts or inconsistencies in your policy statements?

8 Carefully demonstrate the economic effects of price supports. On what grounds do economists contend that price supports cause a misallocation of resources?

9 If in a given year the indexes of prices received and paid by farmers were 120 and 165 respectively, what would the parity ratio be? Explain the meaning of this ratio.

10 Reconcile these two statements: "The farm problem is one of overproduction." "Despite the tremendous productive capacity of American agriculture, plenty of Americans are going hungry." What assumptions about the market system are implied in your answer?

11 Use public choice theory to explain the size and persistence of subsidies to agriculture.

12 What are the effects of farm programs such as those of the United States and the European Community on **a** domestic agricultural prices; **b** world agricultural prices; **c** the international allocation of agricultural resources. Use your responses to explain the United States' proposals in the recent GATT negotiations.

13 What are the major criticisms of farm policy? Do you feel that government should attempt to enhance farm incomes, stabilize farm incomes, or allow farm incomes to be determined by free markets? Justify your position.

CHAPTER 35

Income
Inequality
and Poverty

It is not difficult to muster casual evidence which suggests substantial economic disparity in the United States.

Boxer Mike Tyson was estimated to have made over $28 million in 1990; actor Jack Nicholson will reportedly earn $50 million or more for his role in the *Batman* movie.

A recent study concludes that 5.5 million American children—one in eight—go hungry and that another 6 million are nutritionally "at risk." In certain rural counties of the Deep South infant mortality rates exceed those of some less developed countries of Asia and Latin America.

The Census Bureau reports that almost 34 million Americans—over 13 percent of the population—live in poverty. Estimates indicate that 500,000 to 600,000 Americans are homeless.

The average salary in major league baseball is about $900,000 per year. Boston Red Sox pitcher Roger Clemens earns almost $5.4 million per year, which has been estimated to be $1536 per pitch.

Government data indicate that income disparity is increasing in the United States; at present the richest fifth of the population receive almost 45 percent of total income while the poorest fifth receive less than five percent.

The question of how income should be distributed has a long and controversial history in both economics and philosophy. Should our national income and wealth be more or less equally distributed than is now the case? Or, in terms of Chapter 5, is society making the proper response to the "For whom" question?

We begin by surveying some basic facts concerning the distribution of income in the United States. Next, the major causes of income inequality are considered. Third, we examine the debate over income inequality and the tradeoff between equality and efficiency implied by this debate. Fourth, we will look at the poverty problem. Finally, we consider public policy; existing income-security programs are outlined and alternative approaches to welfare reform are discussed.

INCOME INEQUALITY: THE FACTS

How equally—or unequally—is income distributed in the United States? How wide is the gulf between rich and poor? Has the degree of income inequality increased or lessened over time?

Personal Income Distribution

Average income in the United States is among the highest in the world. The average income for all families was $35,353 in 1990. But now we must examine how income is distributed around the average. In Table 35-1 we see that at the low end of the scale 9 percent of all families receive only 1 percent of total personal income. Only 3 percent of the total income went to the 17 percent of families receiving under $15,000 per year in 1990. At the top of the income pyramid 6 percent of families received incomes of $100,000 or more per year; this group received about 18 percent of total personal income. These figures suggest *there is considerable* **income inequality** *in the United States.*

Trends in Income Inequality

Over a period of years economic growth has raised incomes: *Absolutely,* the entire distribution of income has been moving upward over time. Has this changed the *relative* distribution of income? Incomes can move up absolutely, and the degree of inequality may or may not be affected. Table 35-2 is instructive on the relative distribution of income. We divide the total number of income receivers into five numerically equal groups, or *quintiles,* and show the percentage of total personal (before-tax) income received by each in selected years. It is useful to examine the data in Table 35-2 over three periods: 1929–1947, 1947–1969, and 1969–1990.

1929–1947 Period   Comparison of the income distribution data for 1929 and 1947 suggests that a significant reduction in income inequality occurred between these years. Note in Table 35-2 the declining percentage of personal income going to the top quintile and the increasing percentage received by the other four quintiles. Many of the forces at work during World War II undoubtedly contributed to this decline in inequality. Warborn prosperity eliminated the many low incomes caused by the severe unemployment of the 1930s, brought a reduction of wage and salary differentials, boosted depressed farm incomes through sharp increases in farm prices, temporarily diminished discrimination in employment, and was accompanied by a decline in property incomes as a share of the national income.

1947–1969 Period   Many of the forces making for greater equality during World War II became less effective after the war. During the period between 1947 and 1969, the quintile distribution continued its previous trend toward less inequality, but at a far slower pace. The income share of the lowest income group rose by

TABLE 35-1   **The distribution of personal income by families, 1990**

(1) Personal income class	(2) Percentage of all families in this class	(3) Percentage of total personal income received by families in this class	(4) Percentage of all families in this class and all lower classes	(5) Percentage of income received by this class and all lower classes
Under $10,000	9	1	9	1
$10,000–$14,999	8	2	17	3
$15,000–$24,999	16	8	33	11
$25,000–$34,999	16	11	49	22
$35,000–$49,999	20	19	69	41
$50,000–$74,999	18	27	87	68
$75,000–$99,999	7	14	94	82
$100,000 and over	6	18	100	100
	100	100		

Source: Bureau of the Census, *Money Income of Households, Families, and Persons in the United States: 1990,* Current Population Reports, Series P–60, No. 174, 1991.

TABLE 35-2 Percentage of total before-tax income received by each one-fifth, and by the top 5 percent, of families, selected years

Quintile	1929	1935–1936	1947	1955	1969	1979	1990
Lowest 20 percent	12.5	4.1	5.0	4.8	5.6	5.3	4.6
Second 20 percent		9.2	11.8	12.2	12.4	11.6	10.8
Third 20 percent	13.8	14.1	17.0	17.7	17.7	17.5	16.6
Fourth 20 percent	19.3	20.9	23.1	23.7	23.7	24.1	23.8
Highest 20 percent	54.4	51.7	43.0	41.6	40.6	41.6	44.3
Total	100.0	100.0	100.0	100.0	100.0	100.0	100.0
Top 5 percent	30.0	26.5	17.2	16.8	15.6	15.7	17.9

.6 of a percentage point between 1947 and 1969, while that of the wealthiest quintile fell by 2.4 percentage points.

1969–1990 Period The distribution of income by quintiles has become more unequal since 1969. In 1990 the lowest 20 percent of families received only 4.6 percent of total before-tax income, compared to 5.6 percent in 1969. Meanwhile, the income share received by the highest 20 percent rose from 40.6 percent to 44.3 percent. The reasons for this latest trend in income inequality are in dispute. This chapter's Last Word considers a number of possible causes.

In summary, income inequality fell significantly between 1929 and 1947 but declined more slowly in the 1947–1969 period. More recently, income inequality has increased. But, as a direct comparison of the data for 1947 and 1990 in Table 35-2 reveals, the relative distribution in 1990 was similar to what it was over four decades ago.

The Lorenz Curve

The degree of income inequality can be seen through a **Lorenz curve** as shown in Figure 35-1. Here we *cumulate* the "percentage of families" on the horizontal axis and the "percentage of income" on the vertical axis. The theoretical possibility of a completely equal distribution of income is represented by the diagonal line brown because such a line indicates that any given percentage of families receives that same percentage of income. That is, if 20 percent of all families receive 20 percent of total income, 40 percent receive 40 percent, 60 percent receive 60 percent, and so on, all these points will fall on the diagonal line.

By plotting the 1990 data from Table 35-2 we locate the Lorenz curve to visualize the actual distribution of income. Observe that the bottom 20 percent of all families received about 4.6 percent of the income as shown by point *a*; the bottom 40 percent received 15.4 percent (=4.6 + 10.8) as shown by point *b*; and so forth. The orange area, determined by the extent to which the resulting Lorenz curve sags away from the line of perfect equality, indicates the degree of income inequality. The larger this area or gap, the greater the degree of income inequality. If the actual income distribution were perfectly equal, the Lorenz curve and the diagonal would coincide and the gap would disappear.

At the opposite extreme is the situation of complete inequality where 1 percent of families have 100 percent of the income and the rest have none. In this

FIGURE 35-1 The Lorenz curve

The Lorenz curve is a convenient means of visualizing the degree of income inequality. Specifically, the orange area between the line of perfect equality and the Lorenz curve reflects the degree of income inequality.

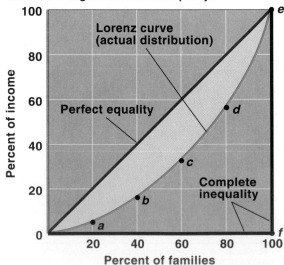

case the Lorenz curve would coincide with the horizontal and right vertical axes of the graph, forming a right angle at point f as indicated by the heavy black lines. This extreme degree of inequality would be indicated by the entire area southeast of the diagonal.

The Lorenz curve can be used to contrast the distribution of income at different points in time, among different groups (for example, blacks and whites), before and after taxes and transfer payments are taken into account, or among different countries. As previously observed, the data in Table 35-2 tell us that the Lorenz curve shifted slightly toward the diagonal between 1947 and 1969 and then back away from the diagonal between 1969 and 1990. Comparisons with other nations suggest that the distribution of income in the United States is quite similar to those in most other industrially advanced countries.

ALTERNATIVE INTERPRETATIONS

There has been controversy in recent years as to whether the Bureau of Census data of Tables 35-1 and 35-2 provide an accurate portrayal of the degree of income inequality. Some scholars feel that the yearly census figures are inadequate. To understand the nature of these alleged deficiencies, we must first review these data. The census figures of Tables 35-1 and 35-2 show the distribution of *nominal* income and include not only wages, salaries, dividends, and interest, but also all *cash transfer payments* such as social security and unemployment compensation benefits. The data are *before taxes* and therefore do not account for the effects of personal income and payroll (social security) taxes which are levied directly on income receivers.

Two major criticisms of the census data are, first, that the income concept employed is too narrow, and second, that the income accounting period of one year is too short.

Broadened Income Concept

Edgar K. Browning[1] has made several adjustments in the Census Bureau data, resulting in a quite different picture of income distribution. Among other adjustments, Browning estimates the market value and distribution of *in-kind transfers,* that is, transfers of goods and services under such programs as Medicare, Medicaid, housing subsidies, and food stamps. Similarly, he takes into account the value and distribution of governmentally provided education. Next, he adds capital gains such as increases in the value of stocks, bonds, and real estate. Finally, he subtracts the amounts families pay as Federal personal income and payroll taxes. The picture which emerges from these adjustments not only is a much more equal distribution of income in each year, but it also indicates a trend toward greater equality over time. The movement toward greater equality is primarily a reflection of the rapid growth of in-kind transfers in the past twenty years or so.

It should be noted that Browning has been criticized for overadjusting the census data and thereby concluding that there is greater income equality than actually exists. Indeed, our point is that income distribution data are subject to many interpretations. In this regard, a recent study by the Census Bureau has confirmed that a broader definition of income translates into reduced inequality in the distribution of income. The Census Bureau has found, however, that its broader income concept tightens the "official" income distribution by only 4 percent.[2]

Lifetime Income

Another objection to the census data is that they portray the distribution of income in a single year and thereby conceal the possibility that the *lifetime earnings* of families might be more equal. If Ben earns $1000 in year 1 and $100,000 in year 2, while Holly earns $100,000 in year 1 and only $1000 in year 2, do we have income inequality? The answer depends on the period of measurement. Annual data would reveal great income inequality; but for the two-year period we have complete equality.

This is important because there is evidence to suggest that there is considerable "churning around" in the distribution of income over time. In fact, most income receivers follow an age-earnings profile where their income starts at relatively low levels, reaches a peak during middle age, and then declines. A glance back at Figure 28-9 reveals this general pattern. It follows that, even if people received the same stream of income over their lifetimes, considerable income inequality would still exist in any given year because of

[1]Edgar K. Browning, "The Trend Toward Equality in the Distribution of Net Income," *Southern Economic Journal,* July 1976, pp. 912–923; and Browning, "How Much More Equality Can We Afford?" *The Public Interest,* Spring 1976, pp. 90–110.

[2]Bureau of the Census, *Measuring the Effect of Benefits and Taxes on Income and Poverty: 1990,* Current Population Report, Series P–60, No. 176, 1991, p. 11.

age differences. In any year the young and old would receive low incomes while the middle-aged received high incomes. This would occur despite complete equality of lifetime incomes.

Morton Paglin[3] has adjusted the quintile data of Table 35-2 for age differences. He found that (1) there is greater income equality when the time factor is taken into account and (2) there was a trend toward greater income equality during the period studied: 1947–1972. The latter conclusion is attributed to the expansion of postsecondary education.

GOVERNMENT AND REDISTRIBUTION

One of the basic functions of government is to redistribute income. As Figure 35-2 and the accompanying table reveal, the distribution of household income *before* taxes and transfers are taken into account is substantially less equal than the distribution *after* taxes and transfers are included.[4] *Government's tax system and transfer programs do reduce significantly the degree of inequality in the distribution of income.* Most of the reduction in income inequality—roughly 80 percent of it—is attributable to transfer payments. Recall from Chapter 32 that our tax system (Federal, state, and local taxes combined) is not highly progressive and, hence, the before-tax and after-tax distributions of income do not differ greatly. But transfers are vital in contributing to greater income equality. More specifically, government transfer payments account for over 75 percent of the income of the lowest quintile and have clearly been the most important means of alleviating poverty in the United States.

INCOME INEQUALITY: CAUSES

Why does the United States have the degree of income inequality evidenced in Tables 35-1 and 35-2? In general, we note that the market system is an impersonal mechanism. It has no conscience, and does not cater to

ethical standards concerning what is an "equitable," or "just," distribution of income. In fact, the basically individualistic environment of the capitalist economy is very permissive of a high degree of income inequality. Factors contributing to income inequality include:

1 Ability Differences People have different mental, physical, and esthetic talents. Some have inherited the exceptional mental qualities essential to entering the high-paying fields of medicine, dentistry, and law. Others, rated as "dull normals" or "mentally retarded," are assigned to the most menial and low-paying occupations or are incapable of earning income at all. Some are blessed with the physical capacity and coordination to become highly paid professional athletes. A few have the talent to become great artists or musicians. In brief, native talents enable some individuals to make contributions to total output which command very high incomes. Others are in much less fortunate circumstances.

2 Education and Training Individuals differ significantly in the amounts of education and training they have obtained and, hence, in their capacities to earn income. In part, these differences are a matter of voluntary choice. Smith chooses to enter the labor force upon high school graduation, while Jones decides to attend college. On the other hand, such differences may be involuntary: Smith's family may simply be unable to finance a college education.

3 Tastes and Risks Incomes differ because of differences in "job tastes." Those willing to take arduous, unpleasant jobs—for example, underground mining and garbage collecting—and to work long hours with great intensity will tend to earn more. Some people boost their incomes by "moonlighting," that is, by holding two jobs. Individuals also differ in their willingness to assume risk. We refer here not only to the steeplejack and prize fighter but to the entrepreneur who assumes risk. Though most fail, the fortunate few who gamble successfully on the introduction of a new product or service may realize very substantial incomes.

4 Discrimination Simple supply and demand analysis suggests how discrimination—in this case labor market discrimination—generates income inequality. Suppose that gender discrimination restricts women to such occupations as secretaries, nurses, and teachers—once considered strictly "female" jobs. This means that the supplies of female workers will be great relative to demand in these few occupations so that

[3]Morton Paglin, "The Measurement and Trend of Inequality: A Basic Revision," *American Economic Review,* September 1975, pp. 598–609.

[4]The "before" data in this table differ from the data of Table 35-2 because the latter includes cash transfers. Also, the data in Table 35-2 are for families (a group of two persons or more related by birth, marriage, or adoption and residing together), whereas the data in Figure 35-2 are for all households (one or more persons occupying a housing unit). Finally, the data in Figure 35-2 are based on a broader concept of income than the data in Table 35-2.

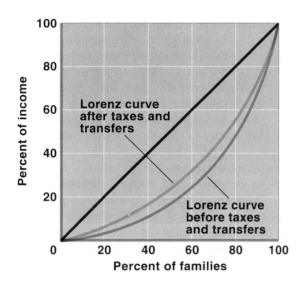

Percent of income received, 1990

Quintile	Before taxes and transfers	After taxes and transfers
Lowest 20 percent	1.1	5.1
Second 20 percent	7.9	11.1
Third 20 percent	15.5	16.5
Fourth 20 percent	24.7	23.8
Highest 20 percent	50.7	43.5

Source: Bureau of the Census, *Measuring the Effect of Benefits and Taxes on Income and Poverty: 1990*, Current Population Report, Series P-60, No. 176-RD, 1991, p. 5. The data include all money income from private sources, including realized capital gains and employer-provided health insurance. The "after taxes and transfers" data include the value of noncash transfers as well as cash transfers.

FIGURE 35-2 The impact of government taxes and transfers on income inequality

The distribution of personal income is significantly more equal after taxes and transfer payments are taken into account. Transfers account for most of the lessening of inequality and provide most of the income received by the lowest quintile of families.

wages and incomes will be low. Conversely, discrimination means males do not have to compete with women in "male" occupations (carpenters, pilots, accountants). This means supply is artificially limited relative to demand in these occupations, with the result that wages and incomes are high.

5 Property Ownership Ownership of property resources and receipt of property incomes are very unequal. The vast majority of households own little or no property resources, while the remaining few supply very great quantities of machinery, real estate, farmland, and so forth. A government study shows that in 1983 the top 10 percent of income receivers in the United States (those with annual incomes of $50,000 or more) owned 72 percent of all stocks, 86 percent of all tax-free bonds, 70 percent of all taxable bonds, and 50 percent of all real estate. The top 2 percent of American income receivers (with annual incomes of $100,000 or more) owned 50 percent of all stocks, 71 percent of all tax-free bonds, 39 percent of all taxable bonds, and 20 percent of all real estate.[5] Similarly, an IRS study for

1986 indicates that nearly 28.5 percent of the nation's personal wealth is held by the richest 1.6 percent of its adults. Asset holdings are much more highly concentrated than are family incomes. Basically, property incomes account for the position of those households at the very pinnacle of the income pyramid. The right of inheritance and the fact that "wealth begets wealth" reinforce the role played by unequal ownership of property resources in determining income inequality.

6 Market Power Ability to "rig the market" on one's own behalf is undoubtedly a major factor in accounting for income inequality. Certain unions and professional groups have adopted policies limiting the supplies of their productive services, thereby boosting the incomes of those "on the inside." Legislation which provides for occupational licensing for barbers, beauticians, taxi drivers, and so forth, can also exert market power favoring the licensed group. The same holds true in the product market; profit receivers in particular stand to benefit when their firm develops some degree of monopoly power.

7 Luck, Connections, and Misfortune There are other important forces which play a part in explaining income inequality. Luck, chance, and "being in the right place at the right time" have all caused individuals

[5]"Survey of Consumer Finances, 1983," *Federal Reserve Bulletin,* September 1984, pp. 679–692. Also see "Financial Characteristics of High-Income Families," *Federal Reserve Bulletin,* March 1986, pp. 163–177.

of income so as to minimize the adverse effects on economic efficiency. Consider this *leaky-bucket analogy*. Assume society agrees to shift income from the rich to the poor. But the money must be transferred from affluent to indigent in a leaky bucket. The leak represents an efficiency loss—the loss of output and income—due to the harmful effects of the tax-transfer process on incentives to work, to save and invest, and to accept entrepreneurial risk. It also reflects the fact that resources must be diverted to the bureaucracies which administer the tax-transfer system.

How much leakage will society accept and continue to endorse the redistribution? If cutting the income pie in more equal slices tends to shrink the pie, what amount of shrinkage will society tolerate? Is a loss of one cent on each redistributed dollar acceptable? Five cents? Twenty-five cents? Fifty cents? This is clearly a basic question which will permeate future political debates over extensions and contractions of our income-maintenance programs.

Fueling this debate over the equality–efficiency tradeoff are studies which suggest that the loss from the redistribution bucket may be quite high.

> Edgar Browning and William Johnson . . . concluded that the upper-income groups bearing the costs of the taxes would sacrifice $350 for every $100 that the poor gained—a net efficiency loss of $250. In Arthur Okun's terms, the leaks in the redistribution bucket are enormous—starting out with a bucket of $350 raised from the nonpoor, $250 is lost on the way to delivering it to the poor. For several reasons, critics of this study have found the estimate to be substantially too high. However, even if cut in half, this loss would be troublesome. Would our society be willing to accept a loss of economic efficiency of $125—or even $100—in order to equalize the distribution of income by transferring $100 to the poor? The answer is by no means clear.[8]

THE DISMAL ECONOMICS OF POVERTY

Many people are less concerned with the larger question of income distribution than they are with the more specific issue of income inadequacy. Therefore, armed with some background information on income inequality, we now turn to the poverty problem. How extensive is poverty in the United States? What are the characteristics of the poor? And what is the best strategy to take to lessen poverty?

Defining Poverty

Poverty does not lend itself to precise definition. But, in general, we might say that a family lives in poverty when its basic needs exceed its available means of satisfying them. A family's needs have many determinants: its size, its health, the ages of its members, and so forth. Its means include currently earned income, transfer payments, past savings, property owned, and so on.

The definitions of poverty developed by concerned government agencies are based on family size. In 1990 an unattached individual receiving less than $6,652 per year was living in poverty. For a family of four the poverty line was $13,359. For a family of six, it was $17,839. Applying these definitions to income data for the United States, it is found that *about 13.5 percent of the nation—some 33.6 million people—lives in poverty.*

Who Are the Poor?

Unfortunately for purposes of public policy, the poor are heterogeneous; they can be found in all geographic regions, they are whites and nonwhites, they include large numbers of both rural and urban people, they are both old and young. Yet, as Table 35-3 clearly indicates, poverty is far from randomly distributed. While the total **poverty rate** —the percentage of the population living in poverty—was 13.5 percent for the entire population, blacks and Hispanics bore a disproportionate share compared to whites. On the other hand, thanks to a generous social security system, the incidence of poverty among the elderly is less than that for the population as a whole.

TABLE 35-3 The distribution of poverty, 1990

Population group	Percent in poverty
Total population	13.5
Whites	10.7
Blacks	31.9
Hispanics	28.1
Families headed by women	33.4
Children under 18	20.6
Elderly (65 or older)	10.9

Source: Bureau of the Census, Money Income and Poverty Status in the United States: 1990, Current Population Reports, series P–60, no. 175, 1991.

[8]Robert H. Haveman, "New Policy for the New Poverty," *Challenge,* September-October 1988, p. 32.

The incidence of poverty is extremely high among female-headed families and a full one-fifth of all children under 18 years of age live in poverty. The poverty rate among black children was 45 percent in 1990.

The high poverty rates for children are especially disturbing because in a very real sense poverty breeds poverty. Poor children are at greater risk for a range of long-term problems, including poor health and inadequate education, crime, drugs, and teenage pregnancy. Many of today's impoverished children will reach adulthood unhealthy, illiterate, and unemployable. The increased concentration of poverty among children bodes poorly for reducing poverty in the near future. It also implies problems for increasing the future productivity of the labor force because poor children receive less and generally inferior education.

Recalling our previous comments on movement or "churning" within the income distribution, we know that there is considerable movement in and out of poverty. Just over half of those who are in poverty one year will remain below the poverty line the next year. On the other hand, poverty is much more persistent for some groups, in particular black families and families headed by women.

Poverty Trends

Not revealed in Table 35-3 is the fact that the percentage of the population living in poverty was higher in 1990 than it was a decade or so ago. This disturbing reality is revealed in Figure 35-4, which traces out the percentage of people in poverty—or the poverty rate—for each year since 1960. Observe that the poverty rate fell significantly between 1960 and 1968, remained relatively unchanged from 1969–1978, and then increased sharply during the early 1980s. This recent increase in the poverty rate resulted from sluggish economic growth, high unemployment rates, and lower real levels of transfer payments. Beginning in 1984, the poverty rate gradually declined as the economy vigorously expanded toward full employment. As has been observed, the poverty rate in 1990 was 13.5 percent.

We need to add a qualification: Although the income levels used to compute the poverty rates shown in Figure 35-4 include cash transfer payments, they do *not* include the monetary value of such noncash transfers as medical care, housing assistance, and food stamps the poor receive. These noncash transfers are similar to income in that they enable the poor to purchase needed goods and services. Recently, the Census Bureau began estimating an alternative poverty

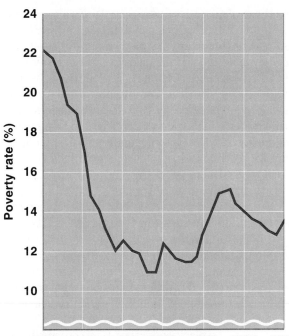

FIGURE 35-4 The U.S. poverty rate, 1960–1990

The percentage of the population living in poverty fell dramatically between 1960 and 1968, remained relatively constant for the next decade, and then climbed between 1978 and 1983. Beginning in 1984, the poverty rate once again began to decline but remained higher in 1990 than it was in the 1970s. Poverty rates for blacks have persistently exceeded those for whites.

rate which includes the value of noncash transfers. The poverty rate for 1990 was 9.8 percent using this expanded definition of income. But, irrespective of definitions of income, the basic point remains: poverty continues to be a persistent and difficult problem.

A "Black Underclass"?

Some observers contend that the city ghettos are spawning a "black underclass" which is trapped in a permanent cycle of poverty, broken homes, welfare, and, frequently, drugs and crime. Relevant statistics are alarming: 1 out of 2 black youths lives in poverty; 1 out of 2 black youths grows up without a father; nearly 40 percent of black teenagers are unemployed; 1 out of 4 births is to a teenager; more than 80 percent of children born to black teenagers are illegitimate; and 1 of every 21 young black men is a homicide victim.

It is argued that in the social and economic isolation of the urban ghetto a new culture—a culture of poverty and dependency—has evolved where attitudes, values, and morality are substantially different from those of mainstream America. Welfare programs —Aid to Families with Dependent Children (AFDC), food stamps, housing subsidies, and the rest—have allegedly undermined incentives to work and have created welfare-dependent families. Furthermore, the historical exodus from the central city of middle-class blacks has left drug dealers, prostitutes, hustlers, and small-time criminals as role models for youngsters. Low-quality schools grossly underprepare minority youth for the job market, while a lenient and overburdened legal system increases the attractiveness of crime as an alternative to work.

At the level of policy, the black underclass view asserts that, although there has been a significant diminution in discrimination over the past several decades and although hundreds of billions have been expended on antipoverty programs, the poverty problem persists. The implication is that the responsibility for poverty rests largely on the poor themselves and that self-help is essential to the alleviation of poverty.

Critics of the black underclass view contend that it is a simplistic and callous position which incorrectly implies that the blame for poverty rests with its victims and not with larger social and economic considerations. Critics of the underclass view also contend that central-city poverty is heterogeneous and has a multitude of causes. What is needed is a far-reaching effort to eliminate racial segregation in housing and schooling, compensatory training and education, more accessible job opportunities, and an income maintenance program which does not discourage work.

The "Invisible" Poor

These facts and figures on the extent and character of poverty may be difficult to accept. After all, ours is an affluent society. How does one square the depressing statistics on poverty with everyday observations of abundance? The answer lies mainly in the fact that much American poverty is hidden; it is largely invisible.

There are three major reasons for this invisibility. First, a sizable proportion of the people in the poverty pool change from year to year. Research has shown that as many as one-half of those in poverty are poor for only one or two years before successfully climbing out of poverty.[9] Hence, many of these people are not visible to us as being permanently downtrodden and needy. Second, the "permanently poor" are increasingly iso-

lated. Poverty persists in the slums and ghettos of large cities and is not readily visible from the freeway or commuter train. Similarly, rural poverty and the chronically depressed areas of Appalachia, the South, and the Southwest are also off the beaten path. Third, and perhaps most important,

> The poor are politically invisible. . . . [They] do not, by far and large, belong to unions, to fraternal organizations, or to political parties. They are without lobbies of their own; they put forward no legislative program. As a group they are atomized. They have no face; they have no voice.[10]

Indeed, the American poor have been labeled "the world's least revolutionary proletariat."

THE INCOME MAINTENANCE SYSTEM

The existence of a wide variety of income-maintenance programs (Table 35-4) is evidence that alleviation of poverty has been accepted as a legitimate goal of public policy. Despite cutbacks in many programs in recent years, income-maintenance programs involve substantial monetary outlays and large numbers of beneficiaries. Total spending for income maintenance has expanded from about 4 percent of domestic production in 1940 to about 13 percent currently.

Our income-maintenance system consists of two kinds of programs: (1) social insurance programs and (2) public assistance or "welfare" programs.

Social Insurance Programs

Social insurance programs partially replace earnings lost due to retirement and temporary unemployment. "Social security" (technically Old Age, Survivors, and Disability Health Insurance or OASDHI), unemployment compensation, and Medicare are the main social insurance programs. Benefits are viewed as earned rights and do not carry the stigma of public charity. These programs are financed primarily out of Federal payroll taxes.

OASDHI and Medicare OASDHI is a gigantic social insurance program financed by compulsory payroll taxes levied upon both employers and employees. Ge-

[9]Greg J. Duncan, *Years of Poverty, Years of Plenty* (Ann Arbor, Mich.: University of Michigan Press, 1984).

[10]Michael Harrington, *The Other America: Poverty in the United States,* rev. ed. (New York: The Macmillan Company, 1970), p. 14.

TABLE 35-4 Characteristics of major income-maintenance programs

| Program | Basis of eligibility | Source of funds | Form of aid | Fiscal 1990 | |
				Expenditures* (billions of dollars)	Beneficiaries (millions)
Social Insurance Programs					
Old Age, Survivors, and Disability Health Insurance (OASDHI)	Age, disability, or death of parent or spouse; individual earnings	Federal payroll taxes on employers and employees	Cash	$248	40
Medicare	Age or disability	Federal payroll tax on employers and employees	Subsidized health insurance	98	34
Unemployment compensation	Unemployment	State and Federal payroll taxes on employers	Cash	7	14
Public Assistance Programs					
Supplemental Security Income (SSI)	Age or disability; income	Federal revenues	Cash	6	5
Aid to Families with Dependent Children (AFDC)	Certain families with children; income	Federal-state-local revenues	Cash and services	18	12
Food stamps	Income	Federal revenues	Vouchers	14	20
Medicaid	Persons eligible for AFDC or SSI and medically indigent	Federal-state-local revenues	Subsidized medical services	55	24

*Expenditures by Federal, state, and local governments; excludes administrative expenses.

Source: Social Security Bulletin, September 1991, and Statistical Abstract of the United States, 1991.

nerically known as "social security," the program replaces earnings lost because of a worker's retirement, disability, or death. A payroll tax of 7.65 percent is levied on both worker and employer and applies to the first $55,500 of wage income. Workers may retire at 65 with full benefits or at 62 with reduced benefits. When the worker dies, benefits accrue to the survivors. Special provisions provide benefits for disabled workers. Currently, social insurance covers over 90 percent of all employed persons in the United States. In 1989 some 40 million people received OASDHI checks averaging about $600 per month.

Medicare was appended to OASDHI in 1965. The hospital insurance it provides for the elderly and disabled is financed out of the payroll tax. Medicare also makes available a low-cost voluntary insurance program which helps pay doctor fees.

Unemployment Compensation All fifty states sponsor unemployment insurance programs. **Unemploy-**ment **compensation** is financed by a modest payroll tax which varies by state and according to each firm's employment history. Any insured worker who becomes unemployed can, after a short waiting period (usually a week), become eligible for benefit payments. Almost 90 percent of all civilian workers are covered by the program. Size of payments and the number of weeks they may be received vary considerably from state to state. Generally speaking, benefits approximate one-half of a worker's after-tax wages up to a certain maximum payment. Benefits averaged $152 weekly in 1990. The number of beneficiaries and the level of total disbursements vary greatly over the business cycle.

Public Assistance Programs

Public assistance, or *welfare, programs* provide benefits for those who are unable to earn income because of permanent handicaps or dependent children. These programs are financed out of general tax revenues and are regarded as public charity. Individuals and families must demonstrate low incomes in order to qualify for aid. The Federal government finances about two-thirds of the welfare program expenditures.

Many needy persons who do not qualify for social insurance programs are assisted through other programs. Beginning in 1972 Federal grants to states for public assistance to the aged, the blind, and the disabled were terminated and a new Federally financed and administered **Supplemental Security Income (SSI) program** was created. The purpose of SSI is to establish a uniform, nationwide minimum income for these three categories of people who are unable to work. Over half the states provide additional income supplements to the aged, blind, and disabled.

The **Aid to Families with Dependent Children (AFDC) program** is state-administered, but partly financed with Federal grants. The program provides aid to families in which dependent children do not have the financial support of a parent, usually the father, because of death, disability, divorce, or desertion.

The **food stamp program** is designed to provide all low-income Americans with a "nutritionally adequate diet." Under the program eligible households receive monthly allotments of coupons which are redeemable for food. The amount of food stamps received varies inversely with a family's earned income.

Medicaid helps finance medical expenses of individuals participating in both the SSI and the AFDC programs.

QUICK REVIEW 35-2

◆ *The fundamental argument for income equality is that it maximizes consumer utility; the basic argument for income inequality is that it is necessary to stimulate economic incentives.*

◆ *By government standards almost 34 million people or 13.5 percent of the population live in poverty.*

◆ *Our income maintenance system comprises both social insurance programs and public assistance ("welfare") programs.*

"The Welfare Mess"

There is no doubt that the income maintenance system—not to mention local relief, housing subsidies, minimum-wage legislation, veterans' benefits, private transfers through charities, pensions, and supplementary unemployment benefits—provides important means of alleviating poverty. On the other hand, the system has been subject to many criticisms in recent years.

1 Administrative Inefficiencies Critics charge that the willy-nilly growth of our welfare programs has created a clumsy and inefficient system, characterized by red tape and dependent on a huge bureaucracy for its administration. Administrative costs account for relatively large portions of the total budget of many programs.

> The amount necessary to lift every man, woman, and child in America above the poverty line has been calculated, and it is *one-third* of what is in fact spent on poverty programs. Clearly, much of the transfer ends up in the pockets of highly paid administrators, consultants, and staff as well as higher income recipients of benefits from programs advertised as antipoverty efforts.[11]

2 Inequities Serious inequities arise in welfare programs in that people with similar needs may be treated very differently.

> Benefit levels vary widely among States and among different demographic and family groups. Geographic differentials arise primarily because benefits under the two major public assistance programs—AFDC and Medicaid—are essentially controlled by the States. As a result, sharp disparities in benefit levels exist between the poorer, rural States and the wealthier, more urban areas. . . .[12]

A family in New York City might receive welfare benefits two times as great as the same family in Mississippi. Furthermore, control of the system is fragmented and some low-income families "fall between the cracks" while other families collect benefits to which they are not entitled.

3 Work Incentives A major criticism is that most of our income-maintenance programs impair incentives to work. This is because all welfare programs are constructed so that a dollar's worth of earned income yields less than a dollar of net income. As earned income increases, program benefits are reduced. An in-

---

[11]Thomas Sowell, *Markets and Minorities* (New York: Basic Books, Inc., Publishers, 1981), p. 122.

[12]*Economic Report of the President, 1978,* pp. 225–226.

dividual or family participating in several welfare programs may find that, when the loss of program benefits and the effect of payroll taxes on earnings are taken into account, the individual or family is absolutely worse off by working. In effect, the marginal tax rate on earned income exceeds 100 percent!

There are other criticisms. Noncash transfers interfere with freedom of consumer choice. Public assistance programs sap initiative and encourage dependency. AFDC regulations in some states promote family breakup by encouraging unemployed fathers to abandon their families so the spouse and children can qualify for benefits. AFDC benefits subsidize birth outside of marriage; nearly one-half of the mothers in the AFDC program have illegitimate children. Various welfare programs foster social divisiveness between workers and welfare recipients. For example, working mothers with small children may wonder out loud why poor mothers receiving AFDC should not also work for their money.

REFORM PROPOSALS

These criticisms have led to calls to reform the public assistance system. Although reform proposals have taken numerous forms, two broad approaches have dominated: negative income tax schemes and "workfare" plans.

Negative Income Tax

One contention is that the entire patchwork of existing welfare programs should be replaced by a **negative income tax** (NIT). The term NIT suggests that, just as the present (positive) income tax calls for families to "subsidize" the government through taxes when their incomes rise *above* a certain level, the government should subsidize households with NIT payments when household incomes fall *below* a certain level.

Comparing Plans Let's examine the two critical elements of any NIT plan. First, a NIT plan specifies a **guaranteed annual income** below which family incomes would not be allowed to fall. Second, the plan embodies a **benefit-loss rate** which indicates the rate at which subsidy benefits are reduced or "lost" as a consequence of earned income. Consider Plan One of the three plans shown in Table 35-5. In Plan One guaranteed annual income is assumed to be $8000 and the benefit-loss rate is 50 percent. If the family earns no income, it will receive a NIT subsidy of $8000. If it earns $4000, it will lose $2000 ($4000 of earnings *times* the 50 percent benefit-loss rate) of subsidy benefits and total income will be $10,000 (=$4000 of earnings *plus* $6000 of subsidy). If $8000 is earned, the subsidy will fall to $4000, and so on. Note that at $16,000 the NIT subsidy becomes zero. The level of earned income at which the subsidy disappears and at which normal (positive) income taxes apply to further increases in earned income is called the **break-even income.**

One might criticize Plan One on the grounds that a 50 percent benefit-loss rate is too high and therefore does not provide sufficient incentives to work. Hence, in Plan Two the $8000 guaranteed income is retained, but the benefit-loss rate is reduced to 25 percent. However, note that the break-even level of income increases to $32,000 and many more families would now qualify for NIT subsidies. Furthermore, a family with any given earned income will now receive a larger NIT sub-

TABLE 35-5 **The negative income tax: three plans** *(hypothetical data for a family of four)*

Plan One ($8000 guaranteed income and 50% benefit-loss rate)			Plan Two ($8000 guaranteed income and 25% benefit-loss rate)			Plan Three ($12,000 guaranteed income and 50% benefit-loss rate)		
Earned income	NIT subsidy	Total income	Earned income	NIT subsidy	Total income	Earned income	NIT subsidy	Total income
$ 0	$8,000	$ 8,000	$ 0	$8,000	$ 8,000	$ 0	$12,000	$12,000
4,000	6,000	10,000	8,000	6,000	14,000	8,000	8,000	16,000
8,000	4,000	12,000	16,000	4,000	20,000	16,000	4,000	20,000
12,000	2,000	14,000	24,000	2,000	26,000	24,000*	0	24,000
16,000*	0	16,000	32,000*	0	32,000			

*Indicates break-even income. Determined by dividing the guaranteed income by the benefit-loss rate.

CHAPTER SUMMARY

1 The distribution of personal income in the United States reflects considerable inequality. The Lorenz curve shows the degree of income inequality graphically.

2 Income inequality lessened significantly between 1929 and the end of World War II, but inequality has increased since 1969.

3 Critics contend that **a** the use of a broadened concept of income and **b** recognition that the positions of individual families in the distribution of income change over time would reveal less income inequality than do Census data.

4 Government taxes and transfers—particularly the latter—lessen the degree of income inequality significantly.

5 Causes of income inequality include discrimination and differences in abilities, education and training, job tastes, property ownership, and market power.

6 The basic argument for income equality is that it maxi-

mizes consumer satisfaction from a given income. The main argument against income equality is that equality undermines incentives to work, invest, and assume risks, thereby reducing the amount of income available for distribution.

7 Current statistics suggest that 13.5 percent of the nation lives in poverty. Poverty is concentrated among blacks, Hispanics, female-headed families, and young children.

8 Our present income-maintenance system is composed of social insurance programs (OASDHI, Medicare, and unemployment compensation) and public assistance programs (SSI, AFDC, food stamps, and Medicaid).

9 Present welfare programs have been criticized as being administratively inefficient, fraught with inequities, and detrimental to work incentives. Reform proposals have been of two basic types: negative income tax proposals and "workfare" plans.

TERMS AND CONCEPTS

income inequality	Medicare	Aid to Families with	guaranteed annual
Lorenz curve	unemployment	Dependent Children	income
tradeoff between	compensation	(AFDC)	break-even income
equality and	Supplemental Security	Medicaid	workfare proposals
efficiency	Income (SSI)	negative income tax	Family Support Act of
poverty rate	food stamp program	benefit-loss rate	1988
OASDHI			

QUESTIONS AND STUDY SUGGESTIONS

1 What criticisms have been made of Census Bureau data on income inequality? How and to what extent does government contribute to income equality?

2 Assume Al, Beth, Carol, David, and Ed receive incomes of $500, $250, $125, $75, and $50 respectively. Construct and interpret a Lorenz curve for this five-person economy.

3 Briefly discuss the major causes of income inequality. With respect to income inequality, is there any difference between inheriting property and inheriting a high IQ? Explain.

4 Use the "leaky-bucket analogy" to discuss the equality–efficiency tradeoff. Compared to our present income-maintenance system, do you feel that a negative income tax would reduce the leak?

5 Should a nation's income be distributed to its members according to their contributions to the production of that total income or to the members' needs? Should society attempt to equalize income *or* economic opportunities? Are the issues of "equity" and "equality" in the distribution of

income synonymous? To what degree, if any, is income inequality equitable?

6 Analyze in detail: "There need be no tradeoff between equality and efficiency. An 'efficient' economy which yields an income distribution which many regard as unfair may cause those with meager income rewards to become discouraged and stop trying. Hence, efficiency is undermined. A fairer distribution of rewards may generate a higher average productive effort on the part of the population, thereby enhancing efficiency. If people think they are playing a fair economic game and this belief causes them to try harder, an economy with an equitable income distribution may be efficient as well."[14]

7 Comment on or explain:

a "To endow everyone with equal income will cer-

[14]Paraphrased from Andrew Schotter, *Free Market Economics* (New York: St. Martin's Press, 1985), pp. 30–31.

tainly make for very unequal enjoyment and satisfaction."

b   "Equality is a 'superior good'; the richer we become, the more of it we can afford."

c   "The mob goes in search of bread, and the means it employs is generally to wreck the bakeries."

d   "Under our welfare system we have foolishly clung to the notion that employment and receipt of assistance must be mutually exclusive."

e   "Some freedoms may be more important in the long run than freedom from want on the part of every individual."

f   "Capitalism and democracy are really a most improbable mixture. Maybe that is why they need each other—to put some rationality into equality and some humanity into efficiency."

8   What are the essential differences between social insurance and public assistance programs? What are the major criticisms of our present income-maintenance system?

9   The table shown below contains three illustrative negative income tax (NIT) plans.

    a   Determine the basic benefit, the benefit-loss rate, and the break-even income for each plan.

    b   Which plan is the most costly? The least costly? Which plan is most effective in reducing poverty? The least effective? Which plan embodies the strongest disincentive to work? The weakest disincentive to work?

    c   Use your answers in part **b** to explain the following statement: "The dilemma of the negative income tax is that you cannot bring families up to the poverty level on the one hand, and simultaneously preserve work incentives and minimize program costs on the other."

10   "The father of a child has a responsibility to help support that child, irrespective of whether or not he is married to the mother. In addition, the able-bodied single mother has a responsibility to help support her child by working." Do you agree? How might these "principles" be incorporated into a welfare program? What problems might arise in implementing this program in the real world?

Plan One			Plan Two			Plan Three		
Earned income	NIT subsidy	Total income	Earned income	NIT subsidy	Total income	Earned income	NIT subsidy	Total income
$ 0	$4,000	$4,000	$ 0	$4,000	$ 4,000	$ 0	$8,000	$ 8,000
2,000	3,000	5,000	4,000	3,000	7,000	4,000	6,000	10,000
4,000	2,000	6,000	8,000	2,000	10,000	8,000	4,000	12,000
6,000	1,000	7,000	12,000	1,000	13,000	12,000	2,000	14,000

CHAPTER 36

Labor-Market Issues: Unionism, Discrimination, and Immigration*

In this chapter we examine three important labor market issues: unionism, discrimination, and immigration. Although largely unrelated to each other, each issue is significant in its own right.

    1   Much of the chapter consists of a detailed look at organized labor, collective bargaining, and the economic effects of unionism. What are the reasons for the historical growth and the recent decline of unionism? What impact do unions have on wages, efficiency and productivity, the distribution of earnings, and inflation?

    2   We next discuss discrimination, its dimensions, and its costs.

    3   Finally, we consider the much publicized issue of immigration of foreign labor to the United States. How many people enter the United States legally and illegally each year? What are the economic ramifications of this inflow of people?

BRIEF HISTORY OF AMERICAN UNIONISM

Some 17 million workers—16 percent of the employed labor force—now belong to labor unions. Bare statistics, however, may understate the importance of unions. The wage rates, hours, and working conditions of nonunionized firms and industries are influenced by those determined in organized industries. Unions are clearly important economic institutions of American capitalism.

    As we consider how the labor movement evolved in the United States, we must examine government policy toward organized labor because labor legislation and union growth are intimately related. In terms of national labor policy, the American labor movement

has gone through three phases: repression (1790 to 1930), encouragement (1930 to 1947), and intervention (1947 to date). Though the dates are somewhat arbitrary, these three phases serve as an excellent guide for our discussion.

Repression Phase: 1790 to 1930

Labor unions have existed in the United States for 200 years. Shoemakers, carpenters, printers, and other skilled craftsmen formed unions of some permanence in the early 1790s. As Figure 36-1 indicates, despite this early start, union growth was relatively slow and spo-

*Instructors may choose to treat the three topics in this chapter selectively.

672

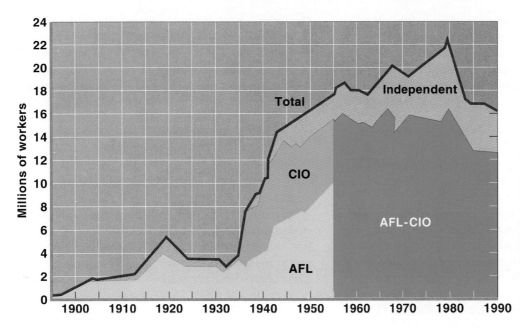

FIGURE 36-1 The growth and decline of union membership

Most of the absolute growth in organized labor has occurred since 1935. However, organized labor has been declining as a percentage of the labor force for some time and, in recent years, the absolute number of union members has also diminished. (U.S. Bureau of the Census and Bureau of Labor Statistics.)

radic until the 1930s. Two factors may account for this meager progress: (1) the hostility of the courts toward labor unions, and (2) the reluctance of American businesses to recognize and bargain with unions.

Unions and the Courts Not until the 1930s did legislation spell out the Federal government's policy toward labor unions. Lacking a national labor policy, it was up to the courts to decide on specific union-management conflicts. And, much to the dismay of organized labor, the courts were generally hostile toward unions. Their hostility had two sources. First, most judges had propertied-class backgrounds. Second, the courts are inherently conservative institutions charged with the responsibility of protecting *established* property rights. Unions, throughout the 1800s and the early decades of the 1900s, were in the unenviable position of seeking rights for labor at the expense of the *existing* rights of management.

The hostility of the courts was first given vent in the **criminal conspiracy doctrine.** This doctrine, "imported" by American courts from English common law at the turn of the nineteenth century, concluded that organizations of workers to raise wages were criminal conspiracies and hence illegal. Although unions as such were later recognized by the courts as legal organizations, the techniques employed by unions to press their demands—strikes, picketing, and boycotting— were generally held to be illegal. And, in the latter part

of the 1800s, the courts employed both antitrust laws and injunctions to impede the labor movement significantly.

Although Congress passed the Sherman Act of 1890 (Chapter 33) for the expressed purpose of thwarting the growth of business monopolies, the courts interpreted the loose wording of the act to include labor unions as conspiracies in restraint of trade and frequently so applied the act.

A simpler and equally effective antiunion device was the **injunction.** An injunction, or restraining order, is a court order directing that some act not be carried out, on the ground that irreparable damage will be done to those affected by the action. The attitude of the courts toward unions was such that it was easy for employers to obtain injunctions from the courts, prohibiting unions from enforcing their demands by striking, picketing, and boycotting. Stripped of these weapons, unions were relatively powerless to obtain the status and rights they sought.

Antiunion Techniques of Management The business community, hostile to unions from their inception, developed a group of techniques to undermine unions. A simple antiunion technique was ferreting out and firing prounion workers. Too, many employers felt it their duty to inform fellow employers that the discharged workers were "troublemakers" and "labor agitators" not fit to be hired. This combination of **discriminatory**

discharge and **blacklisting** made it extremely risky for workers to seek to organize a union. One's present and future employment opportunities were at stake.

Another potent weapon in management's struggle to keep unions down was the **lockout,** management's counterpart of the strike. By closing up shop for a few weeks, employers were frequently able to bring their employees to terms and destroy any notions they might have about organizing a union. Workers of the late 1800s and early 1900s were not blessed with savings accounts or multimillion-dollar strike funds to draw upon in such emergencies.

Where workers were determined to organize, pitched battles often ensued. Rocks, clubs, shotguns, and an occasional stick of dynamite were the shadowy ancestors of collective bargaining. Some of the darkest pages of American labor history concern the violent clashes between workers and company-hired *strikebreakers*. The Homestead strike of 1892, the Pullman strike of 1894, and the Ludlow Massacre of 1914 are cases in point. Less dramatic skirmishes erupt down to the present time.

But management tactics were often more subtle than a cracked skull. The **yellow-dog contract** was one of the more ingenious antiunion devices fostered by management. In such contracts workers agreed to remain nonunion as a condition of employment. They often had little choice but to sign such contracts—no contract, no job. Violation of a yellow-dog contract exposed a worker to a lawsuit by his employer, the result of which might be a court-imposed fine or even imprisonment.

As a last resort, an employer might shower his work force with such amenities as group insurance, pension programs, and stock ownership and profit-sharing schemes to convince them that employers would look after workers' interests as effectively as unions established by "outsiders." The next step beyond company *paternalism* was employee-representation schemes or **company unions,** that is, employer-dominated "dummy" unions which, it was hoped, would discourage the establishment of genuine unions. Paternalism and company unions were decidedly effective in retarding union growth as late as the 1920s.[1]

Evolution of Business Unionism   The labor movement growth which occurred in the 1800s not only was modest, but it also embraced a variety of union philosophies. The mid-1800s were in effect a laboratory in which American labor experimented with alternative forms of unionism—Marxism, utopianism, reformism, and other isms. But such unions usually floundered in the span of a few short years because of the internal conflict between the workers' interest in short-run practical goals (higher wages and shorter hours) and the long-run utopian goals (producer cooperatives, creation of a labor party) of the union leaders.

Then, in 1886, a new labor organization—the **American Federation of Labor (AFL)**—which was to dominate the labor movement for the next fifty years was formed. Under the leadership of Samuel Gompers, labor charted a conservative course which has been very influential down to the present.[2] Appropriately honored as "the father of the American labor movement," Gompers preached three fundamental ideas: (1) practical business unionism, (2) political neutrality for labor, and (3) the autonomy of each trade or craft.

1 Business Unionism   Gompers was firmly convinced that "safe and sane" **business unionism** was the only course for American labor to follow. Gompers rejected long-run idealistic schemes aimed at overthrow of the capitalistic system. He spurned intellectuals and theorizers and emphasized that unions should be concerned with practical short-run economic objectives—higher pay, shorter hours, and improved working conditions. In the words of one scholar, Gompers felt that "you must offer the American working man bread and butter in the here and now instead of pie in the sky in the sweet by and by."[3]

2 Political Neutrality   Gompers was convinced that government should keep its nose out of labor-management relations and collective bargaining. Although he recognized that governmental interference on behalf of labor might be a boon to union growth, Gompers was equally certain that antiunion government policies could stifle the progress of the entire labor movement.

---

[1]During a prolonged strike in the bituminous coal industry in 1902, a spokesman for the mine operators, George F. Baer, issued the classic statement of business paternalism: "The rights and interests of the laboring man will be protected and cared for—not by the labor agitators, but by the Christian men to whom God in His infinite wisdom has given the control of the property interests of this country."

[2]This is not to say that all unions have followed conservative paths since Gompers first espoused the virtues of business unionism. The Industrial Workers of the World, founded in 1905, advocated a decidedly revolutionary brand of left-wing unionism. In 1949 and 1950, the CIO expelled eleven affiliated unions whose leadership had come to be dominated by Communists.

[3]Charles C. Killingsworth, "Organized Labor in a Free Enterprise Economy," in Walter Adams (ed.), *The Structure of American Industry,* 3d ed. (New York: The Macmillan Company, 1961), p. 570.

Gompers cautioned organized labor not to align itself with any political party. Preoccupation with long-run political goals, he argued, causes labor to lose sight of the short-run economic objectives it should seek. Gompers admonished organized labor to reward labor's friends and punish its enemies at the polls regardless of political affiliation.

3 Trade Autonomy Finally, Gompers was firmly convinced that "autonomy of the trade," that is, unions organized on the basis of specific crafts, was the only permanent foundation for the labor movement. Unions composed of many different crafts lack the cohesiveness essential to strong, hard-hitting, business unionism. These craft unions should then be affiliated in a national federation. "One union to each trade, affiliated for one labor movement."

This philosophy—conservative business unionism, political "neutrality," and the craft principle of union organization—was destined to dominate the AFL and the entire labor movement for the next half-century. Indeed, the AFL, operating under Gompers' leadership, met with considerable success—at least for a time. AFL membership hit a high-water mark of about 4 million members by the end of World War I. Then a combination of circumstances in the 1920s forced the AFL into an eclipse (see Figure 36-1). One factor was a strong antiunion drive by employers. Also, many firms introduced employee representation plans, company unions, and a host of paternalistic schemes to convince workers that employers were better prepared to look out for their employees' interests than were labor leaders. Finally, the AFL clung tenaciously to the craft principle of union organization, ignoring the ever-increasing number of unskilled workers employed by the rapidly expanding mass-production industries—the automobile and steel industries in particular.

Encouragement Phase: 1930 to 1947

Two significant events occurred in the 1930s which revived the labor movement and inaugurated a period of rapid growth.
1   The attitude of the Federal government toward unions changed from one of indifference, not to say hostility, to one of encouragement.
2   A major structural change in the labor movement accompanied the founding of the Committee (later the Congress) of Industrial Organizations in 1936. Both events, coupled with the wartime prosperity of the 1940s, greatly swelled the ranks of organized labor.

Prolabor Legislation of the 1930s   Against the background of the depressed thirties, the Federal government enacted two decidedly prolabor acts. In part, the passage of these acts reflected the strong opposition of organized labor to the previously described weapons employed by the courts and by management to suppress unions. In part, they reflected a Democratic administration replacing a Republican administration. In part, they echoed the widely held opinion that strong unions, by achieving higher wages through collective bargaining, would increase aggregate demand—or at least prevent it from falling—and help alleviate the Great Depression.

Norris–La Guardia Act of 1932   The **Norris–La Guardia Act of 1932** did much to clear the path for union growth by outlawing two of the more effective antiunion weapons. Specifically, the act
1   Made it decidedly more difficult for employers to obtain injunctions against unions
2   Declared that yellow-dog contracts were unenforceable

Wagner Act of 1935   Three years later, in 1935, the Federal government took more positive steps to encourage union growth. The **Wagner Act of 1935** (officially the National Labor Relations Act) guaranteed the "twin rights" of labor: the right of self-organization and the right to bargain collectively with employers.

The act specified a number of "unfair labor practices" on the part of management. Specifically it
1   Forbade employers from interfering with the right of workers to form unions
2   Outlawed company unions
3   Prohibited antiunion discrimination by employers in hiring, firing, and promoting
4   Outlawed discrimination against any worker who files charges or gives testimony under the act
5   Obligated employers to bargain in good faith with a union duly established by their employees
The Wagner Act was clearly "labor's Magna Charta."

A **National Labor Relations Board (NLRB)** was established by the act and charged with the authority to investigate unfair labor practices occurring under the act, to issue cease-and-desist orders in the event of violations, and to conduct worker elections in deciding which specific union, if any, workers might want to represent them.

The Wagner Act was tailored to accelerate union growth and was extremely successful in achieving this goal. The protective umbrella provided to unions by this act along with the Norris–La Guardia Act played a major role in increasing the ranks of organized labor from about 4 million in 1935 to 15 million in 1947.

Industrial Unionism: the CIO

Industrial Unionism: the CIO Recall that one of the causes of stagnation in the AFL during the 1920s was its unwillingness to organize the growing masses of unskilled assembly-line workers. Though the majority of AFL leaders chose to ignore unskilled workers, a vocal minority under the leadership of John L. Lewis contended that craft unionism would be ineffective as a means of organizing the hundreds of thousands of workers in the growing mass-production industries. According to Lewis and his followers, the basis for organization should be shifted from **craft unionism** to **industrial unionism,** that is, away from unions which only encompass a specific type of skilled workers (carpenters, bricklayers) to unions including all workers—both skilled and unskilled—in a given industry or group of related industries (steelworkers, autoworkers).[4] This conflict came to a head, and in 1936 Lewis and his sympathizers withdrew their unions (and were simultaneously expelled) from the AFL.

The withdrawing unions established themselves as the **Congress of Industrial Organizations (CIO).** The CIO met with startling success in organizing the automobile and steel industries. So great was this success that the AFL also moved in the direction of organizing on an industrial basis. By 1940, total union membership approximated 9 million workers.

Intervention Phase: 1947 to Date

The prolabor legislation of the 1930s, the birth of industrial unionism, and the booming prosperity of the war years brought rapid union growth (see Figure 36-1). As unions gathered strength—both numerical and financial—it became increasingly evident that they could no longer be regarded as the weak sister or underdog in negotiations with management. Just as the growing power of business monopolies brought a clamor for public control in the 1870s and 1880s, the upsurge of union power in the 1930s and 1940s brought a similar outcry for regulation. This pressure for union control came to a head in the years immediately following World War II and culminated in the passage of the **Taft-Hartley Act of 1947.**

---

[4]Figures 28-6 and 28-7 compare the techniques employed by craft and industrial unions in attempting to raise wages.

Taft-Hartley Act of 1947 Officially called the Labor-Management Relations Act, the provisions of this detailed piece of legislation generally fall under four headings: (1) provisions which designate and outlaw certain "unfair union practices," (2) provisions which regulate the internal administration of unions, (3) provisions which specify collective bargaining procedures and regulate the actual contents of bargaining agreements, and (4) provisions for handling of strikes imperiling the health and safety of the nation.

1 Unfair Union Practices The Wagner Act outlined a number of "unfair labor practices" on the part of management. A new and crucial feature of the Taft-Hartley Act was that it listed a number of "unfair labor practices" on the part of unions. These unfair practices, which constitute some of the most controversial sections of the act, are as follows: *(a)* Unions are prohibited from coercing employees to become union members. *(b)* **Jurisdictional strikes** (disputes between unions over the question of which has the authority to perform a specific job) are forbidden, as are **secondary boycotts** (refusing to buy or handle products produced by another union or group of workers) and certain **sympathy strikes** (strikes designed to assist some other union in gaining employer recognition or some other objective). *(c)* Unions are prohibited from charging excessive or discriminatory initiation fees or dues. *(d)* **Featherbedding,** a mild form of extortion where the union or its members receive payment for work not actually performed, is outlawed. *(e)* Unions cannot refuse to bargain in good faith with management.

2 Union Administration Taft-Hartley also imposed controls on the internal processes of labor unions: *(a)* Unions must make detailed financial reports to the National Labor Relations Board and make such information available to its members. *(b)* Welfare and pension funds must be kept separate from other union funds and jointly administered by the union and management. *(c)* Unions are prohibited from making political contributions in elections, primaries, or conventions which involve Federal offices. *(d)* Originally, union officials were required to sign non-Communist affidavits.

3 Contract Contents Other Taft-Hartley provisions are designed to control the actual collective bargaining process and the contents of the resulting work agreement: *(a)* The **closed shop** (which requires that a firm hire only workers who are already union members) is specifically outlawed for workers engaged in interstate commerce; that is, a closed-shop arrangement cannot be written into a collective bargaining agreement. *(b)* Bargaining agreements must contain termination or *reopening clauses* in which both labor and management must give the other party 60 days' notice of intent to modify or terminate the existing work agreement.

4 "Health and Safety" Strikes Finally, the Taft-Hartley Act outlines a procedure for avoiding major strikes which might disrupt the entire economy and imperil the health or safety of the nation, for example, a nationwide strike of port workers. According to this procedure, the President may obtain an injunction to delay such strikes for an 80-day "cooling off" period. Within this period striking workers are polled by the NLRB on the acceptability of the last offer of the employer. If the last offer is rejected, the union can then strike. The government's only recourse—one of questionable legality—is seizure of the industry.

Landrum-Griffin Act of 1959 Government regulation of the internal processes of labor unions was extended by passage of the **Landrum-Griffin Act** (officially the Labor-Management Reporting and Disclosure Act) in 1959. The act regulates union elections by requiring regularly scheduled elections of officers and the use of secret ballots; restrictions are placed on ex-convicts and Communists in holding union offices. Furthermore, union officials are now held strictly accountable for union funds and property. Officers handling union funds must be bonded; the embezzlement of union funds is made a Federal offense; and close restrictions are placed on a union's loans to its officers and members. The act is also aimed at preventing autocratic union leaders from infringing on the individual worker's rights to attend and participate in union meetings, to vote in union proceedings, and to nominate officers. The act permits a worker to sue his union if it denies him these rights.

UNIONISM'S DECLINE

In 1955 unity was formally reestablished in the American labor movement with the merger of the AFL and CIO. Two factors were especially important in closing the breach which had existed for almost two decades.
1 The political and legislative setbacks which labor had encountered since the prolabor era of the 1930s convinced labor leaders that unity in the labor movement was a necessary first step toward bolstering the political influence of organized labor.
2 Failure to achieve the desired rate of growth in the ranks of organized labor in the post-World War II years made it evident to organized labor that a concerted, unified effort was needed to organize currently nonunion firms and industries.

In fact, however, the period since the AFL-CIO merger has *not* been characterized by a resurgence of organized labor. The growth of union membership has failed to keep pace with the growth of the labor force. While 25 percent of the labor force was organized in the mid-1950s, currently less than 15 percent are members. Indeed, in recent years the absolute number of union members has declined significantly. Over 22 million workers were unionized in 1980; that figure had fallen to only about 17 million in 1990.

Let's consider two possible explanations as to why this has happened.

1 Structural Changes One view, the **structural-change hypothesis,** is that many structural changes unfavorable to the expansion of union membership have occurred both in our economy and in the labor force.
1 Consumer demand and therefore employment patterns have shifted away from traditional union strongholds. Generally, the industry-mix of domestic output has been shifting away from manufactured goods (where unions have been strong) to services (where unions have been weak). This change in industry-mix may be reinforced by increased competition from imports in highly unionized sectors such as automobiles and steel. Growing import competition in these industries has curtailed domestic employment and therefore union membership.
2 An unusually large proportion of the increase in employment in recent years has been concentrated among women, youths, and part-time workers, groups allegedly difficult to organize because of their less firm attachment to the labor force.
3 Spurred by high energy costs, the long-run trend for industry to shift from the Northeast and Midwest where unionism is "a way of life" to "hard to organize" areas of the South and Southwest may have impeded expansion of union membership.
4 An ironic possibility is that the relative decline of unionism may in part reflect the success unions have

had in gaining a sizable wage advantage over nonunion workers in the United States and abroad. Confronted with high union wages, we would expect union employers to substitute machinery for workers, subcontract more work to nonunion suppliers, open nonunion plants in less industrialized areas, or have components produced in low-wage nations. These actions reduce the growth of employment opportunities in the union sector compared to the nonunion sector. Perhaps more important, we would also expect output and employment in low-cost nonunion firms and industries to increase at the expense of output and employment in higher-cost union firms and industries. In short, union success in raising wages may have changed the composition of industry to the disadvantage of union employment and membership.

2 Managerial-Opposition Hypothesis   Another view is that intensified **managerial opposition** to unions has been a major deterrent to union growth. It is argued that in the past decade or so unions have increased the union wage advantage which they enjoy compared to nonunion workers and, as a result, union firms have become less profitable than nonunion firms. As a reaction, managerial opposition to unions has crystallized and become more aggressive. One managerial strategy has been to employ labor-management consultants who specialize in mounting aggressive antiunion drives to dissuade workers from unionizing or, alternatively, to persuade union workers to decertify their union.

It is also alleged that there has been a dramatic increase in the use of illegal antiunion tactics. In particular, it has become increasingly common to identify and dismiss leading prounion workers even though this is prohibited by the Wagner Act. Coupling these antiunion strategies with evidence that unions are devoting fewer resources to organizing the unorganized and that NLRB rulings have become increasingly antilabor, the labor movement has gone into relative and absolute eclipse.

COLLECTIVE BARGAINING

Despite the decline of unionism, collective bargaining remains an important feature of labor-management relations. Nearly 2000 major collective bargaining agreements—those involving 1000 or more workers—cover 8.5 million workers in the United States. Many million other workers are covered under collective bargaining agreements in smaller firms.

The Bargaining Process

To the outsider, collective bargaining is a dramatic clash every two or three years between labor and management. It is easy to get the impression from the newspapers that labor and management settle their differences only with strikes, picketing, and occasional acts of violence.

These impressions are largely inaccurate. Collective bargaining is a somewhat less colorful process than most people believe. In negotiating important contracts, the union is represented by top local and national officials, duly supplemented with lawyers and research economists. Management representatives include top policy-making executives, plant managers, personnel and labor relations specialists, lawyers, and staff economists.

The union usually assumes the initiative, outlining its demands. These take the form of specific adjustments in the current work agreement. The merits and demerits of these demands are then debated. Typically, a compromise solution is reached and written into a new work agreement. Strikes, picketing, and violence are clearly the exception and not the rule. About 95 percent of all bargaining contracts are negotiated without resort to work stoppages. Generally, in recent years less than one-fifth of 1 percent of all working time has been lost each year from work stoppages resulting from labor-management disputes. *Labor and management display a marked capacity for compromise and agreement.* Strikes and labor-management violence are newsworthy, whereas peaceful renewal of a work agreement hardly rates a page-5 column.

The Work Agreement

Collective bargaining agreements assume many forms. Some agreements are brief, covering two or three typewritten pages; others are highly detailed, involving 200 or 300 pages of fine print. Some agreements involve only a local union and a single plant; others set wages, hours, and working conditions for entire industries. There is no such thing as an "average" or "typical" collective bargaining agreement.

At the risk of oversimplification, collective bargaining agreements usually cover four basic areas: (1) the degree of recognition and status accorded the union and the prerogatives of management, (2) wages and hours, (3) seniority and job opportunities, and (4) a procedure for settling grievances.

Union Status and Managerial Prerogatives   Unions enjoy differing degrees of recognition from management. Listed in order of the union's preference are (1) the closed shop, (2) the union shop, and (3) the open shop.

Prior to being outlawed by the Taft-Hartley Act, the closed shop afforded the greatest security to a union. Under a closed shop a worker must be a member of the union before being hired. A **union shop,** on the other hand, permits the employer to hire nonunion workers but provides that these workers must join the union in a specified period—say, thirty days—or relinquish their jobs. Some twenty states now have so-called **right-to-work laws** which make compulsory union membership, and therefore the union shop, illegal.

Under the **open shop,** management may hire union or nonunion workers. Those who are nonunion are not obligated to join the union; they may continue on their jobs indefinitely as nonunion workers. Finally, there is the **nonunion shop.** Here no union exists, and the employer makes a conscious effort to hire those workers who are least inclined to form or join a union.

The other side of the union-status coin is the issue of *managerial prerogatives.* Most work agreements contain clauses outlining certain decisions which are to be made solely by management. These managerial prerogatives usually cover such matters as size and location of plants, products to be manufactured, types of equipment and materials used in production, and production scheduling. Frequently the hiring, transfer, discipline, discharge, and promotion of workers are decisions made solely by management but are subject to the general principle of seniority and to challenge by the union through the grievance procedure.

Wages and Hours   The focal point of any bargaining agreement is wages and hours. Both labor and management tend to be highly pragmatic and opportunistic in wage bargaining. The criteria, or "talking points," most frequently invoked by labor in demanding (and by management in resisting) wage boosts are (1) "what others are getting," (2) ability to pay, (3) cost of living, and (4) productivity. If a given firm's basic rates are below those of comparable firms, the union is likely to stress that wages should be increased to bring them into line with what workers in other firms are getting. Similarly, if the firm has had a very profitable year, the union is likely to demand high wages on the ground that the company has ample ability to grant such increments. Unions have often achieved considerable success in tying wages to the cost of living. About 40 percent of all union workers are covered by some kind of *cost-of-living adjustment* (COLA). Finally, unions bargain for their "fair share" of the additional revenues associated with increases in productivity.

The four wage criteria are clearly two-edged propositions. For example, the cost-of-living criterion is invoked by the union only when prices are hurrying upward; unions conveniently ignore this criterion when prices are stable or declining. Similarly, the union considers the ability-to-pay argument to be important only when profits are large. Management is equally opportunistic in the evaluation it places on the various wage-bargaining standards.

Hours of work, overtime pay, holiday and vacations provisions, and **fringe benefits**—health plans and pension benefits—are other important "economic" issues which must be addressed in the bargaining process.

Seniority and the Control of Job Opportunities   The uncertainty of employment in a market economy, coupled with the fear of antiunion discrimination on the part of employers, have made workers and their unions decidedly "job-conscious." The explicit and detailed provisions covering job opportunities which most work agreements contain reflect this concern. Unions stress **seniority** as the basis for worker promotion and for layoff and recall. The worker with the longest continuous service has first chance at relevant promotions, is last to be laid off, and first to be recalled from a layoff.

Grievance Procedure   Even the most detailed and comprehensive work agreement cannot anticipate all the issues and problems which might occur during its life. What if workers show up for work on a Monday morning to find that for some reason—say, a mechanical failure—the plant is closed down? Should they be given "show-up" pay amounting to, say, two or four hours' pay? Or management and the union may disagree as to whether the worker with the most seniority has the ability to perform the job to which he or she wants to be promoted. Such events and disagreements cannot be anticipated by even the most detailed collective bargaining contracts and therefore must be ironed out through a *grievance procedure.* Virtually all bargaining agreements contain an explicit grievance procedure to handle disputes which arise during the life of an agreement.

QUICK REVIEW 36-1

◆ *Union growth was slowed during the repression phase (1790–1930) by a use of the criminal conspiracy doctrine and injunctions by the courts, and b employer hostility.*

◆ *In the encouragement phase (1930–1947) union growth was stimulated by prounion legislation (the Norris–La Guardia and Wagner acts) and the evolution of industrial unionism.*

◆ *The Taft-Hartley and Landrum-Griffin acts inaugurated the intervention phase (1947 to the present) by regulating union tactics and their internal operations.*

◆ *The decline of unionism in recent decades has been attributed to a changes in the structures of the economy and the labor force, and b growing managerial opposition to unions.*

◆ *Collective bargaining agreements determine a union status and managerial prerogatives, b wages and hours, c control of job opportunities, and d the resolution of grievances.*

Given the historical and legislative background of the labor movement and some understanding of collective bargaining, let's now consider the economic implications of unions.

THE ECONOMIC EFFECTS OF UNIONS

Are the economic effects of labor unions positive or negative? We will respond to this important issue by examining several questions: Do unions raise wages? Do they increase or diminish economic efficiency? Do they make the distribution of earnings more or less equal? Do unions contribute to inflation? The reader should be forewarned that there is considerable uncertainty and debate on the answers to these questions.

The Union Wage Advantage

The three union models of Chapter 28 (see Figures 28-5, 28-6, and 28-7 and the accompanying discussions) all imply that unions have the capacity to raise wages. Has unionization in fact caused wage rates to be higher than otherwise?

Empirical research overwhelmingly does suggest that *unions do raise the wages of their members relative to comparable nonunion workers,* although the size of the union wage advantage varies according to occupation, industry, race, and sex. There is also evidence to suggest that the union wage advantage increased in the 1970s. Hence, early research suggests that over the 1923–1958 period the average union–nonunion pay difference was on the order of 10 to 15 percent.

More recent studies indicate that the difference widened to 20 to 30 percent in the 1970s. Note that these are average differentials and that there is considerable variation among industries and occupations. Furthermore, the wage freezes and pay cuts ("wage give-backs") suffered by organized labor in the early and mid-1980s most likely have significantly diminished the 20 to 30 percent union wage advantage. Labor economists have speculated that the union wage advantage may have returned to the 10 to 15 percent range by the early 1990s.

These estimates of the union wage advantage tend to be under stated because union workers enjoy substantially la ger *fringe benefits* than nonunion workers. Union workers are more likely to have private pensions, medical and dental insurance, and paid vacations and sick leaves than nonunion workers. Where such benefits are available to both union and nonunion workers, their magnitude is greater for union workers. Thus the total compensation (wage rates plus fringe benefits) advantage of union workers is greater than the previously indicated 10 to 15 percent.

Economists also generally agree that *unions have probably had little or no impact on the average level of real wages received by labor—both organized and unorganized—taken as a whole.* At first, these two conclusions—that unions gain a wage advantage but do not affect the average level of real wages—may seem inconsistent. But they need not be if the wage gains of organized workers are at the expense of unorganized workers. As we will see (Figure 36-2), higher wages in unionized labor markets may cause employers to move back up their labor demand curves and hire fewer workers. These unemployed workers may seek employment in nonunion labor markets. The resulting increase in the supply of labor will depress wage rates in these nonunion markets. The net result may well be no change in the average level of wages.

Indeed, the tight relationship between productivity and the average level of real wages shown in Figure 28-1 correctly suggests that unions have little power to raise real wage rates for labor as a whole. But Figure 28-1 is an average relationship and therefore compatible with certain groups of (union) workers getting higher relative wages if other (nonunion) workers are simultaneously getting lower real wages.

Efficiency and Productivity

Are unions a positive or negative force insofar as economic efficiency and productivity are concerned? How do unions affect the allocation of resources? While there is much disagreement as to the efficiency aspects of unionism, it is instructive to consider some of the ways unions might affect efficiency both negatively and positively. We will consider the negative view first.

Negative View There are essentially three basic means by which unions might exert a negative impact on efficiency.

1 Featherbedding and Work Rules Some unions have undoubtedly diminished productivity growth by engaging in "make-work" or "featherbedding" practices and resisting the introduction of output-increasing machinery and equipment. These productivity-reducing practices often arise against a backdrop of technological change. Labor and management may agree to a crew size which is reasonable and appropriate at the time the agreement is concluded. But labor-saving technology may then emerge which renders the crew too large. The union is likely to resist the potential loss of jobs. For many years the Brotherhood of Locomotive Firemen and Engineers retained a fireman on train crews, even though his function was eliminated by the shift from steam to diesel engines.

Similarly, union painters sometimes eschewed the use of spray guns and in some instances limited the width of paint brushes. In more recent years, typographer unions resisted the introduction of computers in setting type. Historically, the musicians' union insisted on oversized orchestras for musical shows and required that a union standby orchestra be paid by employers using nonunion orchestras.

More generally, one can argue that unions are responsible for the establishment of work rules and practices which impede efficient production. For example, under seniority rules workers may be promoted in accordance with their employment tenure, rather than in terms of who can perform the available job with the greatest efficiency. Also, unions may impose jurisdictional restrictions on the kinds of jobs workers may perform. Sheet-metal workers or bricklayers may be prohibited from performing the simple carpentry work often associated with their jobs. Observance of such rules means, in this instance, that unneeded and underutilized carpenters must be available. Finally, it is often contended that unions constrain managerial prerogatives to establish work schedules, determine production targets, and to make freely the decisions contributing to productive efficiency.

2 Strikes A second way unions may adversely affect efficiency is through strikes. If union and management reach an impasse in their negotiations, a strike will result and the firm's production will cease for the strike's duration. The firm will forgo sales and profits and workers will sacrifice income.

Simple statistics on strike activity suggest that strikes are relatively rare and the associated aggregate economic losses are relatively minimal. In 1990, 687 major collective bargaining agreements—those covering 1000 or more workers—were negotiated. Strikes occurred in only 43 of these instances. Furthermore, many strikes last only a few days. As indicated earlier, the average amount of work-time lost each year because of strikes is only about one-fifth of 1 percent of total work-time. This loss is the equivalent of 4 hours per worker per year, which is less than 5 minutes per worker per week!

Note that economic costs associated with strikes may be greater or less than suggested by the amount of work-time lost. Costs may be greater if production of nonstruck firms is disrupted. An extended strike in the steel or rail transportation industries could have serious adverse repercussions for production and employment in many other industries and sectors of the economy.

On the other hand, costs may be less than implied by workdays lost by strikers as nonstruck firms increase their output to offset the loss of production by struck firms. While the output of General Motors will fall when its workers strike, car buyers may shift their demand to Ford and Chrysler which respond by increasing their employment and outputs. While GM and its employees are hurt by a strike, society as a whole may experience little or no decline in employment, real output, and income.

3 Labor Misallocation A third and more subtle avenue through which unions might adversely affect efficiency is the union wage advantage itself. In Figure 36-2 we have drawn (for simplicity's sake) identical labor demand curves for the unionized and nonunion sectors of the labor market for some particular kind of labor.[5] If there were no union present initially, then the wage rate which would result from the competitive hire

[5]Technical note: Our discussion assumes pure competition in both product and resource markets.

GOVERNMENT AND CURRENT ECONOMIC PROBLEMS

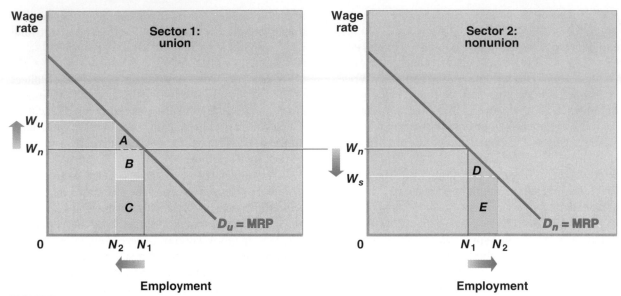

FIGURE 36-2 **The effect of the union wage advantage on the allocation of labor**

The higher wage W_u which the union achieves in sector I causes the displacement of N_1N_2 workers. The reemployment of these workers in nonunion sector 2 reduces the wage rate there from W_n to W_s. The associated loss of output in the union sector is area $A + B + C$, while the gain in the nonunion sector is only area $D + E$. Hence, the net loss of output is equal to area B. This suggests that the union wage advantage has resulted in the misallocation of labor and a decline in economic efficiency.

of labor would be, say, W_n. We now assume a union comes into being in sector 1 and succeeds in increasing the wage rate from W_n to W_u. As a consequence, N_1N_2 workers lose their jobs in the union sector. Assume they all move to nonunion sector 2 where they secure employment. This increase in labor supply in the nonunion sector depresses the wage rate from W_n to W_s.

Recall that the labor demand curves reflect the marginal revenue products (MRPs) of workers or, in other words, the contributions which workers make to the domestic output. This means that the shaded areas $A + B + C$ in the union sector represents the *decrease* in domestic output caused by the N_1N_2 employment decline in that sector. This $A + B + C$ area is the sum of the MRPs—the total contribution to domestic output—of the workers displaced by the W_n to W_u wage increase achieved by the union. The reemployment of these workers in nonunion sector 2 results in an *increase* in domestic output indicated by the shaded areas $D + E$. Because area $A + B + C$ exceeds area $D + E$, there is a net loss of domestic output. More precisely, because $A = D$ and $C = E$, the *net* loss attributable to the union wage advantage is equal to area B. Since the same amount of employed labor is now

producing a smaller output, labor is clearly being misallocated and inefficiently used.

Viewed from a slightly different perspective, *after* the shift of N_1N_2 workers from the union to the nonunion sector has occurred, workers will be paid a wage rate equal to their MRPs in both sectors. But the MRPs of the union workers will be higher than the MRPs of the nonunion workers. The economy will always benefit from a larger domestic output when any given type of labor is reallocated from a relatively low MRP use to a relatively high MRP use. But, given the union's presence and its ability to maintain the W_u wage rate in its sector, this reallocation from sector 2 to 1 will *not* occur.

Attempts to estimate the output loss due to the allocative inefficiency associated with union wage gains suggest that the loss is relatively small. One pioneering study assumed a 15 percent union wage advantage and estimated that approximately 0.14 percent—only about one-seventh of 1 percent—of the domestic output was lost! Similarly, a more recent estimate indicates that union wage gains cost the economy 0.2 to 0.4 percent of domestic product. In 1991 this cost would amount to about $11 to $23 billion or $45.00 to $90.00 per person.

Positive View Other economists take the position that on balance unions make a positive contribution to productivity and efficiency.

1 Managerial Performance: The Shock Effect The *shock effect* is the idea that a wage increase, imposed by a union in this instance, may induce affected firms to adopt improved production and personnel methods and become more efficient. One may carry Figure 36-2's analysis of labor misallocation one step further and argue that the union wage advantage will prompt union firms to *accelerate* the substitution of capital for labor (Chapter 27) and *hasten* the search for cost-reducing (productivity-increasing) technologies. When faced with higher production costs due to the union wage advantage, employers will be pushed to reduce costs by using more machinery and by seeking improved production techniques using less of both labor and capital per unit of output. In fact, if the product market is reasonably competitive, a unionized firm with labor costs 10 to 15 percent higher than nonunion competitors will simply not survive unless productivity can be raised. In short, union wage pressure may generate managerial actions which increase national productivity.

2 Reduced Worker Turnover Unions may also contribute to rising productivity within firms through their effects on worker turnover and worker security. Unions function as a **collective voice** for members in resolving disputes and improving working conditions. That is, if a group of workers is dissatisfied with its conditions of employment, it has two potential means of response. These are the "exit mechanism" and the "voice mechanism."

The **exit mechanism** simply refers to the use of the labor market—leave or exit your present job in search of a better one—as a means of reacting to "bad" employers and "bad" working conditions.

In contrast, the **voice mechanism** involves communication by workers with the employer to improve working conditions and resolve worker grievances. It might be risky for *individual* workers to express their dissatisfaction to employers because employers may retaliate by firing them as "troublemakers." But unions can provide workers with a *collective* voice to communicate problems and grievances to management and to press for their satisfactory resolution.

More specifically, unions may help reduce worker turnover in two ways.

1 Unions provide the voice mechanism as a substitute for the exit mechanism. Unions are effective in correcting job dissatisfactions which would otherwise be "resolved" by workers through the exit mechanism of changing jobs.

2 The union wage advantage is a deterrent to job changes. Higher wages make unionized firms more attractive places to work. Several studies suggest that the decline in quit rates attributable to unionism is substantial, ranging from 31 to 65 percent.

A lower quit rate increases efficiency in several ways. First, lower turnover means a more experienced and, hence, more productive labor force. Second, fewer quits reduce the firm's recruitment, screening, and hiring costs. Finally, reduced turnover makes employers more willing to invest in the training (and therefore the productivity) of their workers. If a worker quits or "exits" at the end of, say, a year's training, the employer will get no return from the higher worker productivity attributable to that training. Lower turnover increases the likelihood that employers will receive a return on any training they provide, thereby making them more willing to upgrade their labor forces.

3 Seniority and Informal Training Much productivity-increasing training is transmitted informally. More-skilled workers may explain their functions to less-skilled workers on the job, during lunch, or during a coffee break. However, a more-skilled senior worker may want to conceal his or her knowledge from less-skilled junior workers *if* the latter can become competitive for the former's job. Because of union insistence on the primacy of seniority in such matters as promotion and layoff, worker security is enhanced. Given this security, senior workers will be more willing to pass on their job knowledge and skills to new or subordinate workers. This informal training enhances the quality and productivity of the firm's work force.

Mixed Research Findings A relatively large number of studies have measured the impact of unionization on productivity. These studies attempt to control for differences in labor quality, the amount of capital equipment used per worker, and other factors aside from unionization which might contribute to productivity differences. Unfortunately, evidence from these studies is inconclusive. For every study which finds a positive union effect on productivity, another study using different methodology or data concludes that there is a negative effect. Hence, at present there is no generally accepted conclusion regarding the overall impact of unions on labor productivity.

Distribution of Earnings

Labor unions envision themselves as institutions which enhance economic equality. Do unions in fact reduce the inequality with which earnings are distributed? The most convincing evidence suggests that unions do reduce earnings inequality.

Increasing Inequality Some economists employ Figure 36-2's analysis of labor misallocation to conclude that unions increase earnings inequality. They contend that, in the absence of the union, competition would bring wages into equality at W_n in these two sectors or submarkets. But the higher union wage realized in sector 1 displaces workers who seek reemployment in the nonunion sector. In so doing they depress nonunion wages. Instead of wage equality at W_n, we have higher wage rates of W_u for union workers and lower wages of W_s for nonunion workers. The impact of the union is clearly to increase earnings inequality. Furthermore, the fact that unionization is more extensive among the more highly skilled, higher-paid blue-collar workers than among less skilled, lower-paid blue-collar workers also suggests that the obtaining of a wage advantage by unions increases dispersion of earnings.

Promoting Equality There are other aspects of union wage policies which suggest that unionism promotes greater, not less, equality in the distribution of earnings.

1 Uniform Wages within Firms In the absence of unions employers are apt to pay different wages to individual workers on the same job. These wage differences are based on perceived differences in job performance, length of job tenure, and, perhaps, favoritism. Unions traditionally seek uniform wage rates for all workers performing a particular job. In short, while nonunion firms tend to assign wage rates to *individual workers,* unions—in the interest of worker allegiance and solidarity—seek to assign wage rate to *jobs.* To the extent that unions are successful, wage and earnings differentials based on supervisory judgments of individual worker performance are eliminated. An important side effect of this standard-wage policy is that wage discrimination against blacks, other minorities, and women is likely to be less when a union is present.

2 Uniform Wages among Firms In addition to seeking standard wage rates for given occupational classes *within* firms, unions also seek standard wage rates among firms. The rationale is that the existence of substantial wage differences among competing firms may undermine the ability of unions to sustain and enhance wage advantages. For example, if one firm in a four-firm oligopoly is allowed to pay significantly lower wages to its union workers, the union is likely to find it difficult to maintain the union wage advantage in the other three firms. In particular, during a recession high-wage firms are likely to put great pressure on the union to lower wages to the level of the low-wage firm. To avoid this kind of problem unions seek to "take wages out of competition" by standardizing wage rates among firms, thereby reducing the degree of wage dispersion.

What is the *net* effect of unionism on the distribution of earnings? Although the issue remains controversial, one authoritative study concludes that the wage effects indicated in Figure 36-2 *increase* earnings inequality by about 1 percent, but the standardization of wage rates within and among firms *decreases* inequality by about 4 percent. The net result is a 3 percent decline in earnings inequality due to unionism. Because only a small proportion of the labor force is unionized, this 3 percent reduction in inequality is substantial.

Unions and Inflation[6]

We now examine the complicated and controversial question of whether unions can increase the average level of money wages and generate cost-push or, more specifically, wage-push inflation.

Two Models We have explored two general models of inflation, namely, the demand-pull and the cost-push models (Figures 9-6b and c and Figure 9-8). The demand-pull model suggests that, given aggregate supply, an increase in aggregate demand will result in a higher price level. Whether due to, say, an increase in the money supply or an increase in investment, the cause or impetus for inflation arises on the demand side of product markets which then increases the derived demands for labor and pulls up nominal wages. The important point is that in the demand-pull theory of

---

[6]This section presupposes that the reader has taken a course in macroeconomic principles.

inflation wage increases are an *effect* or symptom of inflation, not a *cause*. Wage increases do *not* cause inflation but are rather the *result* of excess aggregate demand. Wage increases simply transmit inflation, but do not initiate it.

In comparison, cost-push models allow union wage determination to play a causal role in inflation. Specifically, we know from equation (1) in Chapter 17 that if nominal-wage increases exceed increases in labor productivity, then unit labor costs will rise. Given that labor costs comprise about three-fourths of total production costs, product prices will rise roughly in accord with the increase in unit labor costs. In terms of Figure 9-8 a decrease in aggregate supply from AS_1 to AS_2 results in a higher price level. Some economists contend that union-inspired nominal-wage increases in excess of productivity increases can be an important cause of the indicated leftward shift of the aggregate supply curve.

Tentative Conclusions Which view is correct? While there is no universally accepted conclusion, most experts downgrade union wage-setting as a causal force in inflation. We know from our experience in the early 1960s that union wage determination can be compatible with price level stability. And one can argue with considerable credibility that the major episodes of rapid inflation in the United States were started either by expansions of aggregate demand or major supply shocks which had little or nothing to do with wage increases. Hence, the "great inflation" of the 1970s was rooted in increases in government military spending in the late 1960s, on the one hand, and supply shocks associated with the OPEC oil cartel and crop shortages, on the other.

More important perhaps is the fact that the cost-push model indicates that the decrease in aggregate supply which accompanies a union-induced increase in unit labor costs causes declines in output and increases in unemployment which act to restrain union wage demands (Figure 9-8). This suggests that rising unit labor costs could not generate continuing inflation unless accommodating monetary and fiscal policies gave rise to increases in aggregate demand to offset the falling output and rising unemployment which wage inflation would create (Figure 17-7b). Hence, the most reasonable judgment is that unions do *not* appear to be an initiating cause of inflation. Stated differently, unions do *not* seem to cause initial bursts of inflation or major increases in the rate of existing inflation independently of other causes.

QUICK REVIEW 36-2

♦   *Union workers receive wage rates 10 to 15 percent higher than comparable nonunion workers.*

♦   *Union work rules, strikes, and the misallocation of labor associated with the union wage advantage are ways unions may reduce efficiency.*

♦   *Unions may enhance productivity through the shock effect, by reducing worker turnover, and by providing the worker security prerequisite to informal on-the-job training.*

♦   *On balance, unions probably reduce wage inequality by achieving wage uniformity within and among firms.*

♦   *Most economists do not regard unions as an independent cause of inflation.*

With this survey of unionism and collective bargaining complete, we now consider two additional factors affecting American labor markets—the problem of discrimination, and the controversial immigration issue.

DISCRIMINATION

In Chapter 35 we noted that blacks, Hispanics, and women bear a disproportionately large burden of poverty. The low incomes received by these groups are a consequence of the operation of the labor market. Thus, it is important that we consider the labor market aspects of discrimination.

Economic discrimination occurs when female or minority workers, who have the same abilities, education, training, and experience as white male workers, are accorded inferior treatment with respect to hiring, occupational access, promotion, or wage rate. Discrimination also occurs when females or minorities are denied access to education and training. Table 36-1 provides casual evidence which suggests the presence of racial discrimination. Similar data imply discrimination on the basis of gender. For example, the weekly earnings of full-time female workers is only about 70 percent that of males.

Dimensions of Discrimination

As Table 36-1 and our definition both suggest, discrimination may take several forms. Our discussion is in terms of racial and gender discrimination, but these

TABLE 36-1 Selected measures of discrimination and inequality of opportunity, 1990

Selected measure	Whites	Blacks
Income		
Median income of families	$36,915	$21,423
Percent of households in poverty	10.7	31.9
Percent of families with incomes of $75,000 or more	13.7	4.8
Unemployment rate (percent of civilian labor force)		
All males	4.8	11.8
All females	4.6	10.8
Teenage† males	14.2	32.1
Teenage† females	12.6	30.0
Education		
Percent of population 25 years and over completing 4 years of high school or more	78.4	64.6
Percent of population 25 years and over completing 4 years of college or more	21.8	11.8
Occupational distribution (percent of total civilian employment)		
Managerial and professional occupations	27.1	16.0
Service occupations	12.0	22.9

†Males and females, 16–19 years old.

Sources: Statistical Abstract of the United States, 1991; Economic Report of the President, 1991; and *Employment and Earnings,* February 1991.

remarks also generally apply to discrimination based on age or ethnic background.

1 Wage discrimination occurs when black and other minority workers are paid less than whites for doing the same work. This kind of discrimination is of declining importance because of its explicitness and the fact that it clearly violates Federal law. But, as this chapter's Last Word demonstrates, wage discrimination can sometimes be very subtle and difficult to detect.

2 Employment discrimination means that unemployment is concentrated among minorities. Blacks are frequently the last hired and the first fired. Hence, the unemployment rate for blacks has been roughly double that for whites (Table 36-1).

3 Human-capital discrimination occurs when investments in education and training are lower for blacks than for whites. The smaller amount (Table 36-1) and inferior quality of the education received by blacks have cost them the opportunity to increase their productivity and qualify for better jobs. Unfortunately, a vicious circle seems to exist here. Many blacks are poor because they have acquired little human capital. Being poor, blacks have less financial ability to invest in education and training. They also have less economic motivation to invest in human capital. Facing the very

real possibility of wage, employment, and occupational discrimination, blacks tend to receive a lower rate of return on their investments in education and training.

4 Occupational discrimination means that minority workers have been arbitrarily restricted or prohibited from entering the more desirable, higher-paying occupations. Black executives and salespeople, not to mention electricians, bricklayers, and plumbers, are relatively few and far between. Historically, many craft unions effectively barred blacks from membership and hence from employment.

Occupational Segregation: The Crowding Model

This latter form of discrimination—**occupational segregation**—is particularly apparent in our economy. Women are disproportionately concentrated in a limited number of occupations such as nursing, public school teaching, secretarial and clerical jobs, and retail clerks. Blacks are crowed into a limited number of low-paying jobs such as laundry workers, cleaners and servants, hospital orderlies, and other manual jobs.

Assumptions The character and income consequences of occupational discrimination can be revealed

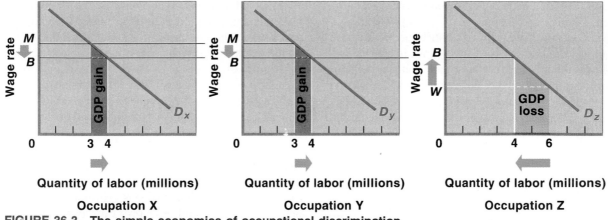

FIGURE 36-3   The simple economics of occupational discrimination

By crowding women into one occupation, men enjoy high wage rates of *OM* in occupations X and Y while women receive low wages of *OW* in occupation Z. The abandonment of discrimination will equalize wage rates at *OB and* result in a net increase in domestic output.

through a simple supply and demand model similar to that used to analyze the efficiency consequences of unions. We make the following simplifying assumptions.

1   The labor force is equally divided between male and female (or white and black) workers. Let's say there are 6 million male and 6 million female workers.
2   The economy is comprised of three occupations, each having identical labor demand curves, as shown in Figure 36-3.
3   Men and women (whites and blacks) have identical labor force characteristics; each of the three occupations could be filled equally well by men or women.

Effects of Crowding   Suppose now that, as a consequence of irrational discrimination, the 6 million women are excluded from occupations X and Y and crowded into occupation Z. Men distribute themselves equally among occupations X and Y so there are 3 million male workers in each occupation and the resulting common wage rate for men is *OM.* (Assuming no barriers to mobility, any initially different distribution of males between X and Y would result in a wage differential which would prompt labor shifts from low- to high-wage occupation until wage equality was realized.) Note that women, on the other hand, are crowded into occupation Z and, because of this occupational segregation, receive a much lower wage rate *OW.* Given the reality of discrimination, this is an "equilibrium" situation. Women *cannot,* because of discrimination, reallocate themselves to occupations X and Y in the pursuit of higher wage rates.

Eliminating Discrimination   But now assume that through legislation or sweeping changes in social attitudes, discrimination disappears. Women, attracted by higher wage rates, will shift from Z to X and Y. Specifically, 1 million women will shift into X and another 1 million into Y, leaving 4 million workers in Z. At this point 4 million workers will be in each occupation and wage rates will be equal to *OB* in all three occupations. Wage equality eliminates the incentive for further reallocations of labor.

This new, nondiscriminatory equilibrium is clearly to the advantage of women, who now receive higher wages, and to the disadvantage of men, who now receive lower wages. Women were initially harmed through discrimination to the benefit of men; the termination of discrimination corrects that situation.

There is also a net gain to society. Recall that the labor demand curve reflects labor's marginal revenue product (Chapter 27) or, in other words, labor's contribution to the domestic output.[7] Hence, the gray areas for occupations X and Y show the *increases* in domestic output—the market value of the marginal or extra output—realized by adding 1 million women workers in each of those two occupations. Similarly, the orange area for occupation Z shows the *decline* in domestic output caused by the shifting of the 2 million women workers from occupation Z. We note that the sum of the two additions to domestic output exceeds the sub-

[7]Technical note: This assumes pure competition in product and resource markets.

traction from domestic output when discrimination is ended. Women workers are reallocating themselves from occupation Z, where their contribution to domestic output (their MRP) is relatively low, to alternative employments in X and Y, where their contributions to domestic output (their MRPs) are relatively high. Conclusion: *Society gains from a more efficient allocation of resources when discrimination is abandoned.* Discrimination influences the distribution of a *diminished* domestic output. That is, discrimination places the nation on a point inside of its production possibilities curve.

Costs of Discrimination

Given the diverse types of discrimination, the economic costs of discrimination are difficult to estimate. However, one estimate is that if economic and social policies were successful in lowering the black unemployment rate to the level of the white rate, and if education and training opportunities were made available to the black labor force so that the average productivity of black labor became equal to that of white workers, the total output of the economy would rise by about 4 percent. For example, in 1991 the economic cost of racial discrimination alone would be about $227 billion.

Addenda

We must consider two important additions to our discussion of discrimination.

Comparable Worth Doctrine   The first involves public policy. The reality of pervasive occupational segregation has given rise to the issue of comparable worth. Legislation such as the Equal Pay Act of 1963 which forced employers to pay equal wages to men and women performing the same jobs was of no help to many women because occupational segregation limited their access to jobs held by men. The essence of the **comparable worth doctrine** is that female secretaries, nurses, and clerks should receive the same salaries as male truck drivers or construction workers if the levels of skill, effort, and responsibility in these disparate jobs are comparable. The basic advantage of comparable worth is that it is a means of quickly correcting perceived pay inequities.

While the concept of comparable worth has considerable appeal, there are a number of important objections. For example, any comparison of the relative worth of various jobs is necessarily subjective and therefore arbitrary, opening the door to endless controversies and lawsuits. Second, wage setting by administrative or bureaucratic judgment, rather than supply and demand, does not bode well for long-run efficiency. To the extent that the calculated worth of specific jobs varies from their market or equilibrium value, worker shortages or surpluses will develop. Furthermore, increasing the wages of women could attract even more females to traditionally "women jobs" and prolong occupational segregation.

Nondiscriminatory Factors   Not all the average income differentials found between blacks and whites *and* males and females are necessarily due to discrimination. Most researchers agree, for example, that some part of the male-female earnings differential is attributable to factors other than discrimination. For example, the work-life cycle of married women who have children historically has involved a continuous period of work until birth of the first child. Then there is a five- to ten-year period of nonparticipation or partial participation in the labor force related to childbearing and child care, followed by a more continuous period of work experience when the mother is in her late thirties or early forties. The net result is that, on the average, married women have accumulated much less labor force experience than men in the same age group. Hence, on the average females are less productive workers and are therefore paid a lower average wage rate.

Furthermore, family ties apparently provide married women with less geographical mobility in job choice than males. In fact, married women may give up good positions to move with husbands who accept jobs elsewhere. And some married women may put convenience of job location and flexibility of working hours ahead of occupational choice. Again, women may have purposely crowded into such occupations as nursing and elementary school teaching because such occupations have the greatest carryover value for productive activity within the home. Finally, in the past decades more women have entered the labor force than have men. This large increase in the supply of female workers has acted as a drag on women's wages and earnings.

All this implies that some portion of the male-female earnings differential is due to considerations other than discrimination by gender. It also suggests that the male-female wage gap will narrow in the future, now that more women are attending college, working through their childbearing years, and pursuing higher-paying professional jobs.

QUICK REVIEW 36-3

● *Discrimination may mean **a** paying different wages to equally qualified workers, **b** higher unemployment rates for minorities, **c** less education and training for women and minorities, and **d** the concentration of minorities and women in a limited number of occupations.*

● *The crowding model demonstrates how **a** men can increase their wages at the expense of women, and **b** occupational segregation diminishes the domestic output.*

● *Comparable worth means that females in one occupation should receive the same wages as males in another occupation if the levels of skill, effort, responsibility and working conditions are comparable.*

IMMIGRATION

The immigration issue has long been clouded in controversy and misunderstanding. Should more or fewer people be allowed to migrate to the United States? How should the much-publicized problem of illegal entrants be handled? We will illuminate this problem by (1) briefly summarizing United States' immigration history and policy, (2) presenting a bare-bones model of the economic effects of immigration, and (3) embellishing this simple model by considering some of the more subtle costs and benefits associated with the international movement of labor.

History and Policy

During the first 140 years of our history as an independent nation, immigration to the United States was virtually unimpeded. There is little question that the great infusion of foreign labor into our labor-scarce country was a major contributing factor to our nation's economic growth. But the great flood of immigrants which came to the United States in the quarter-century prior to World War I was sharply curtailed by the war itself and by a series of restrictive immigration laws enacted in the 1920s. However, after World War II, immigration policy was liberalized and the annual inflows of **legal immigrants** were roughly 250,000 in the 1950s, 320,000 in the 1960s, and 500,000 or more during most of the 1970s and early 1980s.

These data are very imperfect, however, because they do not include **illegal immigrants.** Estimates suggest that, in recent years, as many as 500,000 illegal aliens may enter the United States each year, most coming from Mexico, the Caribbean, and Latin America. Despite this large annual influx of illegals, the total number of illegal aliens in the United States may only be about $3\frac{1}{2}$ to 5 million (estimates vary from 2 to 12 million). Many illegal aliens come to the United States for a year or so to earn a "grubstake" and then return to their native countries.

Current legislation increases the number of legal immigrants to 700,000 per year. The legislation stresses family reunification by allowing United States citizens to bring in immediate relatives—spouses, children, and parents. But there has also been a substantial increase in the number of visas made available to highly skilled professionals such as researchers, engineers, and scientists. In addition, some 10,000 visas have been earmarked for wealthy immigrants who are willing to invest at least $1 million in the United States. Emphasis is clearly on the kinds of immigrants who are likely to make significant contributions to American economic growth.

Immigration and immigration policy have been highly controversial, focusing largely on illegal immigrants. Public concern over illegal immigration gave rise to the Immigration Reform and Control Act of 1986, popularly known as the **Simpson-Rodino Act.** It has three major provisions.

1 Amnesty The law provides amnesty and grants legal status to undocumented individuals who have lived in the United States since 1982. Qualified workers receive work authorization cards and after five years of continuous residence become eligible to apply for citizenship.

2 Employer Sanctions Employers who knowingly hire illegal immigrants are subject to fines and possible imprisonment for repeated offenses.

3 Temporary Farm Labor The law allows temporary migrants or "guest workers" to enter the country to harvest perishable crops.

Economics of Immigration

We can gain some insight into the economic effects of immigration by employing a variation of the crowding model of discrimination (Figure 36-3). In Figure 36-4 we portray the demand for labor in the United States as D_u in the left diagram and the demand for labor in Mexico as D_m in the right diagram. The demand for

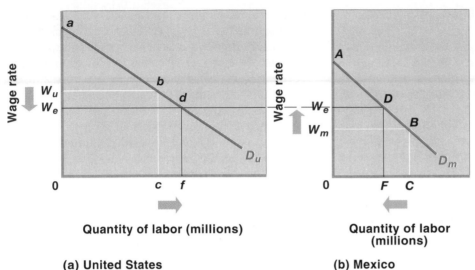

FIGURE 36-4   The simple economics of immigration

The migration of labor to high-income United States (a) from low-income Mexico (b) will increase the domestic output, reduce the average level of wages, and increase business incomes in the United States, while having the opposite effects in Mexico. The United States' domestic output gain of *cbdf* exceeds Mexico's domestic output loss of *FDBC*; hence, there is a net increase in world output.

labor is greater in the United States, presumably because of the presence of more capital equipment and more advanced technologies which enhance the productivity of labor. (Recall from Chapter 27 that the labor demand curve is based on the marginal revenue product of labor.) Conversely, we assume that machinery and equipment are scarce in Mexico and that technology is less sophisticated; hence, labor demand is weak. We also assume that the premigration labor forces of the United States and Mexico are Oc and OC respectively, *and* that full employment exists in both countries.

Wage Rates and World Output   If we further assume that (1) migration is costless; (2) it occurs solely in response to wage differentials; and (3) is unimpeded by legislation in either country, workers will migrate from Mexico to the United States until wage rates in the two countries are equal at W_e. In this case some FC (= fc) million workers will have migrated from Mexico to the United States before equilibrium is achieved. Although the average level of wage rates falls from W_u to W_e in the United States, the domestic output (the sum of the marginal revenue products of the labor force) increases from $Oabc$ to $Oadf$. In Mexico, average wage rates rise from W_m to W_e, but domestic output declines

from $OABC$ to $OADF$.[8] Observing that the domestic output gain of *cbdf* in the United States exceeds the *FDBC* loss in Mexico, we conclude that the world's real output has increased.

Just as elimination of the barrier of sex or racial discrimination enhances economic efficiency within a country, so the elimination of legislative barriers to the international flow of labor increases worldwide economic efficiency. The world gains because freedom to migrate moves people to countries where they can make a larger contribution to world production. To repeat: Migration involves an efficiency gain. It enables the world to produce a larger real output with a given amount of resources.

Income Shares   Our model also suggests that this flow of immigrants will enhance business or capitalist incomes in the United States and reduce them in Mexico. We have just noted that the before-immigration

---

[8]What happens to the wage bill (wage rate multiplied by the number of workers) in each of the two countries depends on the elasticity of labor demand. If the demand for labor is elastic in the W_uW_e wage range in the United States, the absolute size of the wage bill will increase. Conversely, if labor demand is inelastic in the W_uW_e wage range, the absolute size of the wage bill will decline. A similar application of the total revenue (earnings) test for elasticity applies to Mexico.

domestic output in the United States is *Oabc*. The total wage bill is *OW*$_u$*bc*, that is, the wage rate multiplied by the number of workers. The remaining triangular area *W*$_u$*ab* is "business" or capitalist income. The same reasoning applies to Mexico.

Unimpeded immigration will increase business income from *W*$_u$*ab* to *W*$_e$*ad* in the United States and reduce it from *W*$_m$*AB* to *W*$_e$*AD* in Mexico. Business benefits from immigration in the United States; Mexican businesses are hurt by emigration. This is what we would expect intuitively; America is receiving "cheap" labor, Mexico is losing "cheap" labor. This conclusion is consistent with the historical fact that American employers have often actively recruited immigrants.

Complications and Modifications

Our model includes a number of simplifying assumptions and also omits several relevant considerations. Let's therefore release some of the more critical assumptions and introduce omitted factors, observing how our conclusions are affected.

1 Cost of Migration   The international movement of workers is not costless. Costs are not only the explicit or out-of-pocket costs of geographically moving oneself and one's possessions, but also the implicit or opportunity cost of lost income during the period of movement and reestablishing oneself in the host country. Still more subtle costs are involved in adapting to a new culture, language, climate, and so forth. All such *costs* must be estimated by the potential immigrant and weighed against the expected *benefits* of higher wages in the host country. If benefits are estimated to exceed costs, it is rational to migrate. If costs exceed benefits, one should not migrate.

In Figure 36-4 the existence of migration costs means that the flow of labor from Mexico to the United States will *not* occur to the extent that wages are equalized. Wages will remain higher in the United States than in Mexico. Furthermore, the world gain from migration will be reduced.

2 Remittances and Backflows   Many migrants view their moves as temporary. Their plan is to move to a wealthier country, accumulate some desired level of wealth through hard work and frugality, and return home to establish their own enterprises. During their period in the host country, migrants frequently make sizable **remittances** to their families at home. This causes a redistribution of the net gain from migration

between the countries involved. In Figure 36-4 remittances by Mexican workers in the United States to their relatives would cause the *gain* in United States' domestic output to be less than that shown and the *loss* of Mexican domestic output to also be less than that shown.

Actual **backflows**—the return of migrants to their home countries—might also alter gains and losses through time. For example, if some of the Mexican workers who migrated to the United States acquired substantial labor-market or managerial skills and then returned home, their enhanced human capital might then make a substantial contribution to economic development in Mexico. Evidence suggests, however, that migrant workers who acquire skills in the receiving country tend *not* to return home. In fact, at various times the United States has been a beneficiary of "brain drains" as professional and other highly skilled workers have left western Europe and other nations for higher wages and better job opportunities in the United States.

3 Full Employment versus Unemployment   Our model assumes full employment in both the sending and receiving country. Mexican workers presumably leave low-paying jobs to more-or-less immediately take higher-paying jobs in the United States. However, in many cases the factor that "pushes" immigrants from their homelands is not low wages, but chronic unemployment and underemployment. Many less developed countries are characterized by overpopulation and surplus labor; workers are either unemployed or so grossly underemployed that their marginal revenue product is zero.

Again, allowance for this possibility affects our discussion of gains and losses. Specifically, Mexico would *gain* (not lose!) by having such workers emigrate. These unemployed workers are making no contribution to Mexico's domestic output and must be sustained by transfers from the rest of the labor force. The remaining Mexican labor force will be better off by the amount of the transfers after the unemployed workers have migrated to the United States. Conversely, if the Mexican immigrant workers are unable to find jobs in the United States and are sustained through transfers from employed American workers, then the after-tax income of native American workers will decline.

4 Fiscal Aspects   What impacts do immigrants have on tax revenues and government spending in the receiving country? Although evidence is scanty and

impact as a tariff with one big difference: While tariffs generate revenue for the United States government, a quota transfers that revenue to foreign producers.

Suppose in Figure 37-3 that, instead of imposing a tariff of P_wP_t per unit, the United States prohibits any Japanese imports of recorders in excess of bc units. In other words, an import quota of bc recorders is imposed on Japan. Note that we have deliberately chosen the size of this quota to be the same amount as imports would be under a P_wP_t tariff, so we are comparing "equivalent" situations. As a consequence of the quota, the supply of recorders is $S_d + Q$ in the United States. This is comprised of the domestic supply plus the constant amount bc ($=Q$) which importers will provide at each domestic price.[3]

Most of the economic results are the same as with a tariff. Recorder prices are higher (P_t instead of P_w) because imports have been reduced from ad to bc. Domestic consumption of recorders is down from Od to Oc. American producers enjoy both a higher price (P_t rather than P_w) and increased sales (Ob rather than Oa).

The critical difference is that the price increase of P_wP_t paid by American consumers on imports of bc— that is, the orange area—no longer goes to the United States Treasury as tariff (tax) revenue, but rather flows to those Japanese firms which have acquired the rights to sell recorders in the United States. For Americans, a tariff produces a better economic outcome than a quota, other things being the same. A tariff generates government revenue which can be used to cut other taxes or to finance public goods and services which benefit Americans. In contrast, the higher price created by quotas results in additional revenue for foreign producers.

It is relevant that in the early 1980s the American automobile industry with the support of its workers successfully lobbied for an import quota on Japanese autos. The Japanese government in turn apportioned this quota among its various auto producers. The restricted supply of Japanese cars in the American market allowed Japanese manufacturers to increase their prices and, hence, their profits. The American import quotas in effect provided Japanese auto manufacturers with a cartel-like arrangement which enhanced their profits. It is significant that when American import quotas were dropped in the mid-1980s, the Japanese government replaced them with its own system of export quotas for Japanese automakers.

THE CASE FOR PROTECTION: A CRITICAL REVIEW

Although free-trade advocates prevail in the classroom, protectionists sometimes dominate the halls of Congress. What arguments do protectionists make to justify trade barriers? How valid are these arguments?

Military Self-Sufficiency Argument

The argument here is not economic but of a political-military nature: Protective tariffs are needed to preserve or strengthen industries producing strategic goods and materials essential for defense or war. It plausibly contends that in an uncertain world, political-military objectives (self-sufficiency) must take precedence over economic goals (efficiency in the allocation of world resources).

Unfortunately, there is no objective criterion for weighing the relative worth of the increase in national security on the one hand, and the decrease in productive efficiency on the other, which accompany reallocation of resources toward strategic industries when such tariffs are imposed. The economist can only point out that certain economic costs are involved when tariffs are levied to enhance military self-sufficiency.

Although we might all agree that it is probably not a good idea to import our missile guidance systems from China, the self-sufficiency argument is nevertheless open to serious abuse. Virtually every industry can directly or indirectly claim a contribution to national security. Can you name an industry which did *not* contribute in some small way to World War II? Aside from abuses, are there not better ways than tariffs to provide for needed strength in strategic industries? When achieved through tariffs, self-sufficiency creates costs in the form of higher domestic prices on the output of the shielded industry. The cost of enhanced military security is apportioned arbitrarily among those consumers who buy the industry's product. A direct subsidy to strategic industries, financed out of general tax revenues, would more equitably distribute these costs.

Increase Domestic Employment

This "save American jobs" argument for tariffs becomes increasingly fashionable as an economy en-

---

[3]The $S_d + Q$ supply curve does not exist below price P_w because Japanese producers would not export recorders to the United States at any price *below* P_w when they can sell them to other countries *at* the world market prices of P_w.

counters a recession. It is rooted in macro analysis. Aggregate expenditures in an open economy are comprised of consumption expenditures (C) plus investment expenditures (I_g) plus government expenditures (G) plus net export expenditures (X_n). Net export expenditures consist of exports (X) minus imports (M). By reducing imports, M, aggregate expenditures will rise, stimulating the domestic economy by boosting income and employment. But there are important shortcomings associated with this policy.

1 Job Creation from Imports While imports may eliminate some American jobs, they create others. Imports may have eliminated jobs of American steel and textile workers in recent years, but others have gained jobs selling Hondas and imported electronics equipment. While import restrictions alter the composition of employment, they may actually have little or no effect on the volume of employment.

2 Fallacy of Composition All nations cannot simultaneously succeed in import restriction; what is true for *one* nation is not true for *all* nations. The exports of one nation must be the imports of another. To the extent that one country is able to stimulate its economy through an excess of exports over imports, another economy's unemployment problem is worsened by the resulting excess of imports over exports. It is no wonder that tariff and import quotas to achieve domestic full employment are termed "beggar my neighbor" policies. They achieve short-run domestic goals by making trading partners poorer.

3 Retaliation Nations adversely affected by tariffs and quotas are likely to retaliate, causing a competitive raising of trade barriers which will choke off trade to the end that all nations are worse off. The **Smoot-Hawley Tariff Act of 1930,** which imposed the highest tariffs ever enacted in the United States, backfired miserably. Rather than stimulate the American economy, this tariff act only induced a series of retaliatory restrictions by adversely affected nations. This caused a further contraction of international trade and lowered the income and employment levels of all nations.

4 Long-Run Feedbacks In the long run an excess of exports over imports is doomed to failure as a device for stimulating domestic employment. It is through American imports that foreign nations earn dollars with which to purchase American exports. In the long run a nation must import in order to export. The long-run impact of tariffs is not to increase domestic employ-

ment but at best to reallocate workers away from export industries and toward protected domestic industries. This shift implies a less efficient allocation of resources.

In summary, the argument that tariffs increase net exports and therefore create jobs is misleading:

> Overall employment in an economy is determined by internal conditions and macroeconomic policies, not by the existence of trade barriers and the level of trade flows. The United States created [more than 18] million payroll jobs over the course of the [1982–1990] economic expansion, a period of U.S. trade deficits and relatively open U.S. markets. During the same period the European Community (EC) created virtually no net new jobs, even though they experienced trade surpluses. The same level of employment can be obtained in the total absence of free trade as when trade is completely free. But without foreign trade a nation will be worse off economically because, in effect, it will throw away part of its productive capability—the ability to convert surplus goods into other goods through foreign trade.[4]

Diversification for Stability

Closely related to the increase-domestic-employment argument for tariff protection is the diversification-for-stability argument. The point here is that highly specialized economies—for example, Saudi Arabia's oil economy or Cuba's sugar economy—are highly dependent on international markets for their incomes. Wars, cyclical fluctuations, and adverse changes in the structure of industry will force large and frequently painful readjustments on such economies. Tariff and quota protection is therefore allegedly needed to promote greater industrial diversification and consequently less dependence on world markets for just one or two products. This will help insulate the domestic economy from international political developments, depressions abroad, and from random fluctuations in world supply and demand for one or two particular commodities, thereby providing greater domestic stability.

There is some truth in this argument. There are also serious qualifications and shortcomings.
1 The argument has little or no relevance to the United States and other advanced economies.
2 The economic costs of diversification may be great; for example, one-crop economies may be highly inefficient in manufacturing.

[4]*Economic Report of the President, 1988,* p. 131. Updated

QUICK REVIEW 37-2

◆ *Trade barriers include tariffs, import quotas, nontariff barriers, and voluntary export restrictions.*

◆ *A tariff on a specific product increases price, reduces consumption, increases domestic production, reduces imports, and generates tariff revenue for government; an import quota does the same, except that a quota generates revenue for foreign producers rather than the government imposing the quota.*

◆ *Most arguments for trade protection are special-interest pleas which, if followed, would create gains for protected industries and their workers at the expense of much greater losses for the economy.*

INTERNATIONAL TRADE POLICIES

As Figure 37-4 makes clear, tariffs in the United States have had their ups and downs.[6] Generally, the United States was a high-tariff nation over much of its history. Note that the Smoot-Hawley Tariff Act of 1930 enacted some of the highest tariff rates ever imposed by the United States.

In view of the strong case for free trade, this high-tariff heritage may be a bit surprising. If tariffs are economically undesirable, why has Congress been willing to employ them? As suggested earlier in this chapter, the answer lies in the political realities of tariff making and, more specifically, in the special-interest effect. A small group of domestic producers who will receive large economic gains from tariffs and quotas will press vigorously for protection through well-financed and well-informed political lobbyists. The large number of consumers who individually will have small losses imposed on them will be generally uninformed and indifferent.

Indeed, the public may be won over, not only by the vigor, but also by the apparent plausibility ("Cut imports and prevent domestic unemployment") and the patriotic ring ("Buy American!") of the protectionists. Alleged tariff benefits are immediate and clear-cut to the public. The adverse effects cited by economists are obscure and widely dispersed over the economy. Then, too, the public is likely to stumble on the fallacy

[6]Technical footnote: Average tariff-rate figures understate the importance of tariffs by not accounting for the fact that some goods are *excluded* from American markets because of existing tariffs. Then, too, average figures conceal the high tariffs on particular items: watches, china, hats, textiles, scissors, wine, jewelry, glassware, wood products, and so forth.

of composition: "If a quota on Japanese automobiles will preserve profits and employment in the American automobile industry, how can it be detrimental to the economy as a whole?" When political logrolling (Chapter 32) is added in —"You back tariffs for the apparel industry in my state and I'll do the same for the auto industry in your state"—the sum can be protective tariffs and import quotas.

Reciprocal Trade Act and GATT

The downward trend of tariffs since Smoot-Hawley was inaugurated with the **Reciprocal Trade Agreements Act of 1934.** Specifically aimed at tariff reduction, the act had two main features:

1 Negotiating Authority It authorized the President to negotiate agreements with foreign nations which would reduce American tariffs up to 50 percent of the existing rates. Tariff reductions were to hinge on the willingness of other nations to reciprocate by lowering tariffs on American exports.

2 Generalized Reductions By incorporating **most-favored-nation clauses** in these agreements, the resulting tariff reductions not only would apply to the specific nation negotiating with the United States, but they would be *generalized* so as to apply to all nations.

But the Reciprocal Trade Act gave rise to only bilateral (two-nation) negotiations. This approach was broadened in 1947 when twenty-three nations, including the United States, signed a **General Agreement on Tariffs and Trade (GATT).** GATT is based on three cardinal principles: (1) equal, nondiscriminatory treatment for all member nations; (2) the reduction of tariffs by *multilateral* negotiations; and (3) the elimination of import quotas. Basically, GATT is a forum for the negotiation of reductions in trade barriers on a multilateral basis. One hundred nations currently belong to GATT, and there is little doubt that it has been an important force in the trend toward liberalized trade. Under its sponsorship, seven "rounds" of negotiations to reduce trade barriers have been completed in the post-World War II period.

In 1986, the eighth "round" of GATT negotiations began in Uruguay. Proposals discussed at the "Uruguay Round" included (1) eliminating trade barriers and domestic subsidies in agriculture, (2) removing barriers to trade in services (which now account for 20 percent of international trade), (3) ending restrictions on foreign economic investments, and (4) establishing and enforcing patent, copyright, and trademark rights

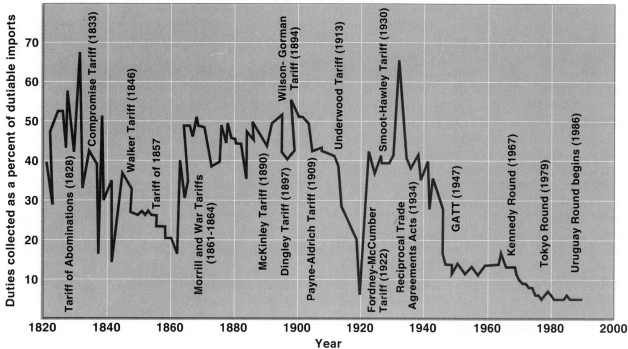

FIGURE 37-4   United States' tariff rates, 1820–1991
American tariff rates have fluctuated historically. But beginning with the Reciprocal Trade Agreements Act of 1934, the trend has been downward. (U.S. Department of Commerce data.)

—so-called *intellectual property rights*—on an international basis.

Reaching agreement on the ambitious Uruguay Round proposals has been difficult. In 1990 the negotiations temporarily collapsed, the main dispute being over European opposition to phasing out export subsidies on agricultural goods and domestic farm subsidies. **Export subsidies** are government payments which reduce the price of a good to buyers abroad; domestic farm subsidies are direct payments to farmers which boost domestic food output. Both types of subsidies artificially reduce export prices and provide unfair advantages to exporting nations. In 1991 the Uruguay Round negotiations were reconvened to try to resolve the remaining trade disagreements.

Economic Integration

Another crucial development in trade liberalization has taken the form of **economic integration**—the joining of the markets of two or more nations into a free-trade zone. Three illustrations of economic integration are the European Economic Community (EC), the U.S.–Canadian Free-Trade Agreement, and the proposed North American free-trade zone.

The Common Market   The most dramatic example of economic integration is the **European Economic Community** (EC), or the **Common Market,** as it is popularly known. Begun in 1958, the EC now comprises twelve western European nations (France, Germany, Italy, Belgium, the Netherlands, Luxemborg, Denmark, Ireland, United Kingdom, Greece, Spain, and Portugal).

Goals   The Common Market called for (1) gradual abolition of tariffs and import quotas on all products traded among the twelve participating nations; (2) establishment of a common system of tariffs applicable to all goods received from nations outside the Common Market; (3) free movement of capital and labor within the Market; and (4) creation of common policies with respect to other economic matters of joint concern, such as agriculture, transportation, and restrictive business practices. By 1992 most of these goals had been achieved.

Results   Motives for creating the Common Market were both political and economic. The primary economic motive was to gain the advantages of freer trade for members. While it is difficult to determine the extent to which EC prosperity and growth has been due to economic integration, it is clear that integration creates the mass markets essential to Common Market industries if economies of large-scale production are to be realized. More efficient production for a large-scale market permits European industries to achieve the lower costs which small, localized markets have historically denied them.

Effects on nonmember nations, such as the United States, are less certain. On the one hand, a peaceful and increasingly prosperous Common Market makes member nations better potential customers for American exports. On the other hand, American firms encounter tariffs which make it difficult to compete in EC markets. For example, *before* the establishment of the Common Market, American, German, and French automobile manufacturers all faced the same tariff in selling their products to, say, Belgium. However, with the establishment of internal free trade among EC members, Belgian tariffs on German Volkswagens and French Renaults fell to zero, but an external tariff still applies to American Chevrolets and Fords. This clearly puts American firms and those of other nonmember nations at a serious competitive disadvantage.

The elimination of this disadvantage has been one of the United States' motivations for promoting freer trade through GATT. And, in fact, the so-called "Kennedy Round" of negotiations completed in 1967 and the "Tokyo Round" which ended in 1979 were quite successful in reducing tariffs.

U.S.–Canadian Free-Trade Agreement A second example of economic integration is the **U.S.–Canadian Free-Trade Agreement** enacted in 1989. Although three-fourths of the trade between the United States and Canada was already duty-free in 1988, the U.S.–Canadian accord is highly significant: It will create the largest free-trade area in the world. Under terms of the agreement, all trade restrictions such as tariffs, quotas, and nontariff barriers will be eliminated within a ten-year period. Canadian producers will gain increased access to a market ten times the size of Canada, while U.S. consumers will gain the advantage of lower-priced Canadian goods. In return, Canada will cut its tariffs by more than the United States because Canadian tariffs are higher than those in the United States. These reduced Canadian tariffs will help American producers and Canadian consumers.

We know from Table 5-3 that Canada is the United States' most significant trade partner quantitatively. Similarly, the United States is the main buyer of Canadian exports. Thus, the potential gain to each country from the U.S.–Canadian accord is large. It has been estimated that the free-trade agreement will generate $1 billion to $3 billion of annual gains for each nation when it is fully implemented.

The U.S.–Canadian accord has global significance. In particular, it is expected to prod multilateral tariff reductions through GATT negotiations, since nations which are not party to the free-trade agreement do not wish to be disadvantaged in a relative sense in selling their goods in the United States and Canada.

Proposed North American Free-Trade Zone The U.S.–Canadian Free-Trade Agreement has stimulated the United States, Canada, and Mexico to begin discussion of a North American free-trade zone constituting the three nations. This zone would have a combined output similar to the European Economic Community.

Free trade with Mexico is more controversial in the United States than is free trade with Canada. Critics fear a loss of American jobs as firms move to Mexico to take advantage of lower wages and less stringent regulations on pollution and workplace safety. Critics also are concerned that Japan and South Korea will build plants in Mexico to ship goods tariff-free to the United States, further hurting U.S. firms and workers.

Proponents of free trade with Mexico cite the standard free-trade argument: Specialization according to comparative advantage will enable the United States to obtain more total output from its scarce resources. Proponents also note this zone would encourage worldwide investment in Mexico, which would enhance Mexican productivity and national income. Some of this increased income will be used to buy United States' exports. Also, a higher standard of living in Mexico would help stem the flow of illegal immigrants to the United States. Finally, advocates point out that any loss of specific American jobs will occur in any event to other low-wage countries such as South Korea, Taiwan, and Hong Kong. The free-trade zone will enable and encourage American firms to be more efficient, enhancing their competitiveness with firms in Japan and the Common Market countries.

Both critics and defenders of the North American free-trade zone agree on one point: It would constitute a powerful trade bloc to counter the European Common Market. Access to the vast North American market is as important to Common Market nations as is access to the European market by the United States, Canada, and Mexico. Observers believe negotiations between the North American trade bloc and the Common Market would surely follow, eventually resulting in a free-trade agreement between the two blocs. Japan, not wishing to be left out of the world's wealthiest trade markets, would be forced to reduce its tariff and non-tariff trade barriers, as well.

QUICK REVIEW 37-3

◆ *The various "rounds" of the General Agreement on Tariffs and Trade (GATT) have established multinational reductions in tariffs and import quotas among the 100 signatory nations.*

◆ *The European Economic Community (EC) and the U.S.–Canadian Free-Trade Agreement of 1989 have reduced trade barriers by establishing large free-trade zones.*

◆ *Proponents of the proposed North American free-trade zone (United States, Canada, and Mexico) contend it will enable all three nations to increase their standards of living; critics suggest that it will result in large losses of American jobs as firms move to Mexico to take advantage of less costly Mexican labor.*

Protectionism Reborn

Despite marked progress in reducing and eliminating tariffs, much remains to be done. The previously mentioned "Uruguay Round" agenda is a case in point. In the past, GATT negotiations have focused on manufactured goods, with other aspects of international trade and finance receiving little attention. These neglected areas include agriculture, services (for example, transportation, insurance, and banking), international investment, and patents and copyrights. There is also the problem of integrating the many nonmember less developed countries into the GATT framework.

More ominously, there has recently occurred a vigorous resurgence of protectionist pressures. Nontariff barriers continue to be a serious problem; import quotas and voluntary export restrictions have been on the rise.

Causes A number of factors explain the new pressures for protection.

1 Backlash They are in part a backlash to past reductions in trade barriers. Industries and workers whose profits and jobs have been adversely affected by freer trade have sought restoration of protection.

2 Internationalized Economy A closely related point is that the American economy is much more "internationalized" than it was a decade or so ago (Table 37-2); there are simply more firms and workers potenti-

ally adversely affected by increased foreign competition.

3 Increased Competition Other nations have in fact become increasingly competitive with American producers. In the late 1970s and 1980s rates of labor productivity growth in Japan and much of western Europe exceeded those of the United States. The result was lower unit labor costs and lower relative prices for imported goods. Competition from a number of the so-called "newly industrialized countries" such as Korea, Taiwan, Hong Kong, and Singapore is also asserting itself.

4 Trade Deficits In the past several years American imports have greatly exceeded American exports. Rising imports have a negative short-run impact on production and employment in those domestic industries which directly compete with imported products. The industries and workers hurt seek government help in the form of trade barriers. Our persistent trade deficit has provided a convenient rationale for the enactment of protectionist measures to help injured industries. Furthermore, the trade deficit has rallied public support for proposals to retaliate against trading partners which restrict the sale of our products in their countries.

Examples While the United States is formally committed to work for reduction of trade barriers through GATT, we have in fact invoked a number of trade-restricting measures during the last decade.

In 1981 a "voluntary" agreement was reached with Japan to limit the number of Japanese automobiles imported to the United States. This agreement expired in 1985 but continues informally today. In 1982 import quotas were imposed on sugar, causing potentially severe problems for Central American and Caribbean nations which are heavily dependent upon sugar exports to the United States. Also in 1982, the United States negotiated a "voluntary" agreement with the Common Market nations which imposed a quota on their steel exports to the United States. Finally, the industrially advanced nations have revised the international textile agreement to tighten restrictions on textile imports from the less developed countries.

Protectionist sentiment is also evidenced in recent trade proposals and laws. The Comprehensive Trade Act of 1988 contains provisions which ease procedures for initiating unfair-trade investigations of countries with consistent patterns of unfair-trade practices (tariffs, quotas, nontariff barriers, dumping).

LAST WORD

PETITION OF THE CANDLEMAKERS, 1845

The French economist Frédéric Bastiat (1801–1850) devastated the proponents of protectionism by satirically extending their reasoning to its logical and absurd conclusions.

Petition of the Manufacturers of Candles, Waxlights, Lamps, Candlesticks, Street Lamps, Snuffers, Extinguishers, and of the Producers of Oil Tallow, Rosin, Alcohol, and, Generally, of Everything Connected with Lighting.

TO MESSIEURS THE MEMBERS
OF THE CHAMBER
OF DEPUTIES.

Gentlemen—You are on the right road. You reject abstract theories, and have little consideration for cheapness and plenty. Your chief care is the interest of the producer. You desire to emancipate him from external competition, and reserve the *national market* for *national industry.*

We are about to offer you an admirable opportunity of applying your—what shall we call it? your theory? No; nothing is more deceptive than theory; your doctrine? your system? your principle? but you dislike doctrines, you abhor systems, and as for principles, you deny that there are any in social economy: we shall say, then, your practice, your practice without theory and without principle.

We are suffering from the intolerable competition

of a foreign rival, placed, it would seem, in a condition so far superior to ours for the production of light, that he absolutely *inundates* our *national market* with it at a price fabulously reduced. The moment he shows himself, our trade leaves us—all consumers apply to him; and a branch of native industry, having countless ramifications, is all at once rendered completely stagnant. This rival . . . is no other than the Sun.

In 1990 both houses of Congress passed protective legislation for the textile industry. The President vetoed this legislation, which would have limited the growth of textile imports to 1 percent a year. Ironically, the U.S. textile industry imports one-half of its machinery.

We should also note that, although overall American tariffs are low, the United States does have very high tariffs on some goods and imposes quantitative restrictions (quotas) on a small but important list of products. Dairy and meat products, tobacco, fruit juices, motorcycles, and cookware are all subject to significant restrictions. In addition, the footwear, ma-

chine tool, copper, shipbuilding, wine, costume jewelry, and shrimp and tuna industries, among others, have all sought additional protection during the past decade.

Costs How costly is existing U.S. trade protection to American consumers? The consumer cost of trade restrictions can be calculated by determining the effect they have on prices of protected goods. Specifically, protection will raise the price of a product in three ways.

1 The price of the imported product goes up (Figure 37-3).

What we pray for is, that it may please you to pass a law ordering the shutting up of all windows, sky-lights, dormer windows, outside and inside shutters, curtains, blinds, bull's-eyes; in a word, of all openings, holes, chinks, clefts, and fissures, by or through which the light of the sun has been in use to enter houses, to the prejudice of the meritorious manufactures with which we flatter ourselves we have accommodated our country,—a country which, in gratitude, ought not to abandon us now to a strife so unequal.

If you shut up as much as possible all access to natural light, and create a demand for artificial light, which of our French manufactures will not be encouraged by it?

If more tallow is consumed, then there must be more oxen and sheep; and, consequently, we shall behold the multiplication of artificial meadows, meat, wool, hides, and, above all, manure, which is the basis and foundation of all agricultural wealth.

The same remark applies to navigation. Thousands of vessels will proceed to the whale fishery; and, in a short time, we shall possess a navy capable of maintaining the honor of France, and gratifying the patriotic aspirations of your petitioners, the undersigned candlemakers and others.

Only have the goodness to reflect, Gentlemen, and you will be convinced that there is, perhaps, no Frenchman, from the wealthy coalmaster to the humblest vender of lucifer matches, whose lot will not be ameliorated by the success of this our petition.

Source: Frédéric Bastiat, *Economic Sophisms* (Edinburgh: Oliver and Boyd, Tweeddale Court, 1873), pp. 49–53, abridged.

2 The higher price of imports will cause some consumers to shift their purchases to higher-priced domestically produced goods.

3 The prices of domestically produced goods may rise because import competition has declined.

Several research studies indicate the costs to consumers of protected products is strikingly high. One study examined thirty-one classes of protected products and found that total annual consumer losses from protection on these goods was about $82.6 billion.[7]

Annual consumer losses from trade restrictions were particularly large for clothing ($27 billion), petroleum products ($6.9 billion), carbon steel ($6.8 billion), automobiles ($5.8 billion), and dairy products ($5.5 billion). These large costs indicate that trade barriers are an expensive means of saving jobs. Specifically, the estimated cost of trade restrictions per job saved is $750,000 in the carbon steel industry; $550,000 in the bolt, nuts, and large screws industry; $220,000 in the dairy industry; $240,000 in the orange juice industry; and $200,000 in the glassware industry. Because wages per job in these industries are only a fraction of these amounts, protectionism can hardly be called a bargain.

Other studies show that import restrictions affect low-income families proportionately more than high-income families.[8] Given that tariffs and quotas are much like sales taxes, it is no surprise that these trade restrictions are highly regressive. For example, the cost of protection was found to be seven times as large for the lowest-income group (incomes under $10,000 per year) as for the highest-income group (incomes over $60,000 per year).

But might not the gains to American producers together with the tariff revenues received by the U.S. government outweigh the high consumer costs of trade protection? The answer is a definite "No." Research studies indicate that gains from trade restrictions are substantially less than costs imposed on consumers.[9] Furthermore, net losses from trade barriers are greater than the losses estimated by the statistical studies. Tariffs and quotas produce myriad costly, difficult-to-quantify secondary effects. For example, import restraints on foreign steel drive up the price of steel to all American buyers of steel—such as American automakers. Therefore American automakers have higher costs and are less competitive in world markets.

Also, industries employ large amounts of economic resources for the purpose of influencing Congress to pass and retain protectionist laws. To the extent that these rent-seeking efforts divert resources away from more socially desirable purposes, society bears an added cost of trade restrictions.

To repeat: *The gains which trade barriers create for protected industries come at the expense of much greater losses for the economy as a whole.*

[7]Cletus C. Coughlin et al., "Protectionist Trade Policies: A Survey of Theory, Evidence and Rationale," *Review* (Federal Reserve Bank of St. Louis), January/February 1988), pp. 17–18.

[8]"The Consumer Cost of U.S. Trade Restraints," *Quarterly Review* (Federal Reserve Bank of New York), Summer 1985, pp. 1–12.
[9]Coughlin et al., op. cit., p. 19.

CHAPTER SUMMARY

1 International trade is important, quantitatively and otherwise, to most nations. World trade is vital to the United States in several respects. **a** The absolute volumes of American imports and exports exceed those of any other single nation. **b** The United States is completely dependent on trade for certain commodities and materials which cannot be obtained domestically. **c** Changes in the volume of net exports can have magnified effects on domestic levels of output and income.

2 International and domestic trade differ in that **a** resources are less mobile internationally than domestically: **b** each nation uses a different currency; and **c** international trade is subject to more political controls.

3 World trade is based on two considerations: the uneven distribution of economic resources among nations, and the fact that efficient production of various goods requires particular techniques or combinations of resources.

4 Mutually advantageous specialization and trade are possible between any two nations so long as the domestic cost ratios for any two products differ. By specializing according to comparative advantage, nations can realize larger real incomes with fixed amounts of resources. The terms of trade determine how this increase in world output is shared by the trading nations. Increasing costs impose limits on gains from specialization and trade.

5 Trade barriers take the form of protective tariffs, quotas, nontariff barriers, and "voluntary" export restrictions. Supply and demand analysis reveals that protective tariffs and quotas increase the prices and reduce the quantities demanded of affected goods. Foreign exporters find their sales diminish. Domestic producers, however, enjoy higher prices and enlarged sales. Tariffs and quotas promote a less efficient allocation of domestic and world resources.

6 When applicable, the strongest arguments for protection are the infant-industry and military self-sufficiency arguments. Most of the other arguments for protection are half-truths, emotional appeals, or fallacies which typically emphasize the immediate effects of trade barriers while ignoring long-run consequences. Numerous historical examples suggest that free trade promotes economic growth and protectionism does not.

7 The Reciprocal Trade Agreements Act of 1934 was the beginning of a trend toward lower American tariffs. In 1947 the General Agreement on Tariffs and Trade (GATT) was formed **a** to encourage nondiscriminatory treatment for all trading nations, **b** to achieve tariff reduction, and **c** to eliminate import quotas.

8 Economic integration is an important means of liberalizing trade. The outstanding illustration is the European Common Market in which internal trade barriers are abolished, a common system of tariffs is applied to nonmembers, and free internal movement of labor and capital occurs. The 1989 U.S.–Canadian Free-Trade Agreement is another example of economic integration, as is the proposed United States–Canadian–Mexican free-trade zone.

9 In recent years there has been a resurgence of protectionist pressures, but empirical evidence indicates that costs of protectionist policies outweigh benefits.

TERMS AND CONCEPTS

labor- (land-, capital-) intensive commodity	gains from trade	strategic trade policy	General Agreement on Tariffs and Trade (GATT)
cost ratio	revenue and protective tariffs	dumping	European Economic Community (Common Market)
principle of comparative advantage	import quotas	Reciprocal Trade Agreements Act of 1934	U.S.–Canadian Free-Trade Agreement
terms of trade	nontariff barriers	most-favored-nation clauses	
trading possibilities line	voluntary export restrictions	export subsidies	
	Smoot-Hawley Tariff Act of 1930	economic integration	

QUESTIONS AND STUDY SUGGESTIONS

1 In what ways are domestic and foreign trade similar? In what ways do they differ?

2 Assume that by using all its resources to produce X, nation A can produce 80 units of X; by devoting all its resources to Y, it can produce 40 Y. Comparable figures for nation B are 60 X and 60 Y. Assuming constant costs, in which product should each nation specialize? Why? Indicate the limits of the terms of trade.

3 "The United States can produce product X more efficiently than can Great Britain. Yet we import X from Great Britain." Explain.

4 State the economist's case for free trade. Given this case, how do you explain the existence of artificial barriers to international trade?

5 Draw a domestic supply and demand diagram for a product in which the United States does not have a comparative advantage. Indicate the impact of foreign imports on domestic price and quantity. Now show a protective tariff which eliminates approximately one-half the assumed imports. Indicate the price-quantity effects of this tariff to **a** domestic consumers, **b** domestic producers, and **c** foreign exporters. How would the effects of a quota which gave rise to the same amount of imports differ?

6 "The most valid arguments for tariff protection are also the most easily abused." What are these arguments? Why are they susceptible to abuse? Carefully evaluate the use of artificial trade barriers, such as tariffs and import quotas, as a means of achieving and maintaining full employment.

7 The following are production possibilities tables for Japan and Hawaii. Assume that prior to specialization and trade, the optimal product-mix for Japan is alternative B and for Hawaii alternative D.

Product	Japan's production alternatives					
	A	B	C	D	E	F
Radios (in thousands)	30	24	18	12	6	0
Pineapples (in tons)	0	6	12	18	24	30

Product	Hawaii's production alternatives					
	A	B	C	D	E	F
Radios (in thousands)	10	8	6	4	2	0
Pineapples (in tons)	0	4	8	12	16	20

a Are comparative-cost conditions such that the two areas should specialize? If so, what product should each produce?

b What is the total gain in radio and pineapple output which results from this specialization?

c What are the limits of the terms of trade? Suppose actual terms of trade are 1 unit of radios for $1\frac{1}{2}$ units of pineapples and that 4 units of radios are exchanged for 6 units of pineapples. What are the gains from specialization and trade for each area?

d Can you conclude from this illustration that specialization according to comparative advantage results in more efficient use of world resources? Explain.

8 Carefully evaluate the following statements:

a "Protective tariffs limit both the imports and the exports of the nation levying tariffs."

b "The extensive application of protective tariffs destroys the ability of the international market system to allocate resources efficiently."

c "Apparent unemployment can often be reduced through tariff protection, but by the same token disguised unemployment typically increases."

d "Foreign firms which 'dump' their products onto the American market are in effect presenting the American people with gifts."

e "Given the rapidity with which technological advance is dispersed around the world, free trade will inevitably yield structural maladjustments, unemployment, and balance of payments problems for industrially advanced nations."

f "Free trade can improve the composition and efficiency of domestic output. Only the Volkswagen forced Detroit to make a compact car, and only foreign success with the oxygen process forced American steel firms to modernize."

g "In the long run foreign trade is neutral with respect to total employment."

9 In the 1981–1985 period the Japanese agreed to a voluntary export restriction which reduced American imports of Japanese automobiles by about 10 percent. What would you expect the short-run effects to have been on the American and Japanese automobile industries? If this restriction were permanent, what would be its long-run effects on **a** the allocation of resources, **b** the volume of employment, **c** the price level, and **d** the standard of living in the two nations?

10 Use "economies of scale" analysis to explain why the Common Market has enabled many European industries to compete more effectively in international markets. Explain: "Economic integration leads a double life: It can promote free trade among members, but pose serious trade obstacles for nonmembers."

11 What are the benefits and the costs of protectionist policies? Compare the two.

12 Explain the following findings from a study on the effects of the 1984 imports restraints which limited the level of steel imports to the United States: increased employment in the steel industry, 14,000; increased employment in the industries producing inputs for steel, 2,800; job losses by American steel-using firms, 52,400.[10]

[10]Arthur T. Denzau, "How Import Restraints Reduce Employment" (Washington University Center for the Study of American Business, Formal Publication #80, June 1987), as reported in Coughlin, op. cit., p. 6.

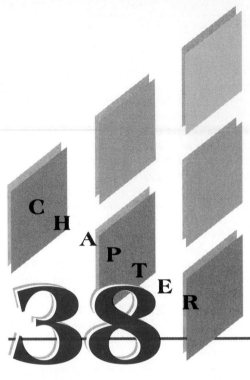

Exchange Rates, the Balance of Payments, and Trade Deficits

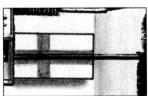

If you take an American dollar to the bank and ask to exchange it for United States currency, you will get a puzzled look. If you persist, you may get in exchange another dollar. One American dollar can buy exactly one American dollar. But, as of January 24, 1992, one United States dollar could buy 5340 Turkish lira, 1.34 Australian dollars, .56 British pounds, 1.16 Canadian dollars, 5.48 French francs, 1.61 German marks, 123.93 Japanese yen, or 5.84 Swedish krona. What explains this seemingly haphazard array of exchange rates?

In Chapter 37 we examined comparative advantage as the underlying economic basis of world trade and discussed the effects of barriers to free trade. In this chapter we first introduce the monetary or financial aspects of international trade. How are currencies of different nations exchanged when import and export transactions occur? Second, we analyze and interpret a nation's international balance of payments. What is meant by a "favorable" or "unfavorable" balance of trade? Third, the kinds of exchange rate systems which trading nations have used are explained and evaluated. In this discussion we examine the polar extremes of freely flexible and fixed exchange rates and then survey actual systems which have existed historically. Finally, we explore the balance of trade deficits the United States has encountered over the past decade.

FINANCING INTERNATIONAL TRADE

A basic feature distinguishing international from domestic payments is that two different national currencies are exchanged. When American firms export goods to British firms, the American exporter wants to be paid in dollars. But British importers have pounds sterling. The problem, then, is to exchange pounds for dollars to permit the American export transaction to occur.

This problem is resolved in *foreign exchange markets* where dollars can be used to purchase British pounds, Japanese yen, German marks, Italian lira, and so forth, and vice versa. Sponsored by major banks in New York, London, Zurich, Tokyo, and elsewhere, foreign exchange markets facilitate American exports and imports.

American Export Transaction

Suppose an American exporter agrees to sell $30,000 worth of computers to a British firm. Assume that the *rate of exchange*—the rate or price at which pounds can be exchanged for, or converted into, dollars, and vice versa—is $2 for £1. This means that the British importer must pay £15,000 to the American exporter. Let's summarize what occurs in terms of simple bank balance sheets (Figure 38-1).

a To pay for the American computers, the British buyer draws a check on its demand deposit in a London bank for £15,000. This is shown by the −£15,000 demand deposit entry in the righthand side of the balance sheet of the London bank.

b The British firm then sends this £15,000 check to the American exporter. But the American exporting firm must pay its employees and materials suppliers, as well as its taxes, in dollars, not pounds. So the exporter sells the £15,000 check or draft on the London bank to a large American bank, probably in New York City, which is a dealer in foreign exchange. The American firm is given a $30,000 demand deposit in the New York bank in exchange for the £15,000 check. Note the new demand deposit entry of +$30,000 in the New York bank.

c What does the New York bank do with the £15,000? It deposits it in a correspondent London bank for future sale. Thus, +£15,000 of demand deposits appear in the liabilities column of the balance sheet of the London bank. This +£15,000 ($30,000) is an asset as viewed by the New York bank. To simplify, we assume that the correspondent bank in London is the same bank from which the British importer obtained the £15,000 draft.

Note these salient points.

1 *American exports create a foreign demand for dollars, and the satisfaction of this demand generates a supply of foreign monies—pounds, in this case—held by American banks and available to American buyers.*

2 The financing of an American export (British import) reduces the supply of money (demand deposits) in Britain and increases the supply of money in the United States by the amount of the purchase.

American Import Transaction

But why would the New York bank be willing to give up dollars for pounds sterling? As just indicated, the New York bank is a dealer in foreign exchange; it is in the business of buying—for a fee—and, conversely, in selling—also for a fee—pounds for dollars.

Having just explained that the New York bank would buy pounds with dollars in connection with an American export transaction, we will now examine how it would sell pounds for dollars in financing an American import (British export) transaction. Suppose that an American retail concern wants to import £15,000 worth of woolens from a British mill. Again, simple commercial bank balance sheets summarize our discussion (Figure 38-2).

a Because the British exporting firm must pay its obligations in pounds rather than dollars, the American importer must exchange dollars for pounds. It does this by going to the New York bank and purchasing £15,000 for $30,000—perhaps the American importer

FIGURE 38-1 **Financing a U.S. export transaction**
American export transactions create a foreign demand for dollars. The satisfaction of this demand increases the supplies of foreign monies held by American banks.

LONDON BANK	
Assets	Liabilities and net worth
	Demand deposit of British importer −£15,000(*a*)
	Deposit of New York bank +£15,000(*c*)

NEW YORK BANK	
Assets	Liabilities and net worth
Deposit in London bank +£15,000(*c*) ($30,000)	Demand deposit of American exporter +$30,000(*b*)

LONDON BANK	
Assets	**Liabilities and net worth**
	Demand deposit of British exporter +£15,000(*b*)
	Deposit of New York bank −£15,000(*a*)

NEW YORK BANK	
Assets	**Liabilities and net worth**
Deposit in London bank −£15,000(*a*) ($30,000)	Demand deposit of American importer −$30,000(*a*)

FIGURE 38-2 Financing a U.S. import transaction
American import transactions create an American demand for foreign monies. The satisfaction of that demand reduces the supplies of foreign monies held by American banks.

purchases the same £15,000 which the New York bank acquired in the previous American export transaction. In Figure 38-2, this purchase reduces the American importer's demand deposit in the New York bank by $30,000 and the New York bank gives up its £15,000 deposit in the London bank.

b The American importer sends its newly purchased check for £15,000 to the British firm, which deposits it in the London bank. Note the +£15,000 deposit in the liabilities and net worth column of Figure 38-2.

We find that:

1 *American imports create a domestic demand for foreign monies (pounds sterling, in this case) and that fulfillment of this demand reduces the supplies of foreign monies held by American banks.*

2 An American import transaction increases the money supply in Britain and reduces the money supply in the United States.

By combining these two transactions, a further point comes into focus. American exports (computers) make available, or "earn," a supply of foreign monies for American banks, and American imports (British woolens) create a demand for these monies. In a broad sense, *any nation's exports finance or "pay for" its imports.* Exports provide the foreign currencies needed to pay for imports. From Britain's point of view, its exports of woolens earn a supply of dollars, which are then used to meet the demand for dollars associated with Britain's imports of computers.

Postscript: Although our examples are confined to the exporting and importing of goods, we will find that demands for and supplies of pounds also arise from transactions involving services and the payment of in-

terest and dividends on foreign investments. Thus Americans demand pounds not only to finance imports, but also to purchase insurance and transportation services from the British, to vacation in London, to pay dividends and interest on British investments in the United States, and to make new financial and real investments in Britain.

THE INTERNATIONAL BALANCE OF PAYMENTS

We now explore the wide variety of international transactions which create a demand for and generate a supply of a given currency. This spectrum of international trade and financial transactions is reflected in the United States' international **balance of payments.** A nation's balance of payments statement records *all* transactions which take place between its residents (including individuals, businesses, and governmental units) and the residents of all foreign nations. These transactions include merchandise exports and imports, tourist expenditures, purchases and sales of shipping and insurance services, interest and dividends received or paid abroad, purchases and sales of financial or real assets abroad, and so forth. The United States' balance of payments shows the balance between all the payments the United States receives from foreign countries and all the payments which we make to them. A simplified balance of payments for the United States in 1990 is shown in Table 38-1. Let's analyze this accounting statement to see what it reveals about our international trade and finance.

TABLE 38-1 The United States' balance of payments, 1990 (in billions)

Current account		
(1) U.S. merchandise exports	$+390	
(2) U.S. merchandise imports	−498	
(3) Balance of trade		$−108
(4) U.S. exports of services..	+133	
(5) U.S. imports of services..	−107	
(6) Balance on goods and services		−82
(7) Net investment income...	+12	
(8) Net transfers	−22	
(9) Balance on current account		−92
Capital account		
(10) Capital inflows to the U.S.	+117*	
(11) Capital outflows from the U.S.................................	−59	
(12) Balance on capital account.................................		+58
(13) Current and capital account balance........................		−34
(14) Official reserves		+34
		$ 0

*Includes a $64 billion statistical discrepancy which is believed to be comprised primarily of unaccounted capital inflows.

Source: Survey of Current Business, December 1991.

Current Account

The top portion of Table 38-1 summarizes the United States' trade in currently produced goods and services and is called the **current account.** Items 1 and 2 show American exports and imports of merchandise (goods) respectively in 1990. We have designated American exports with a *plus* sign and our imports with a *minus* sign because American merchandise exports (and other export-type transactions) are **credits** in that they create or earn supplies of foreign exchange. As we saw in our discussion of how international trade is financed, any export-type transaction obligating foreigners to make "inpayments" to the United States generates supplies of foreign monies in American banks.

Conversely, American imports (and other import-type transactions) are **debits;** they use up foreign exchange. Again, our earlier discussion of trade financing indicated that American imports obligate Americans to make "outpayments" to the rest of the world which draw down available supplies of foreign currencies held by American banks.

Trade balance Items 1 and 2 in Table 38-1 tell us that in 1990 our merchandise exports of $390 billion did *not* earn enough foreign monies to finance our merchandise imports of $498 billion. Specifically, the merchan-

dise balance of trade or, more simply, the **trade balance** refers to the difference between a country's merchandise exports and merchandise imports. If exports exceed imports, then a *trade surplus* or "favorable balance of trade" is being realized. If imports exceed exports, then a *trade deficit* or "unfavorable balance of trade" is occurring. We note in item 3 that in 1990 the United States incurred a trade deficit of $108 billion.

Balance on Goods and Services Item 4 reveals that the United States not only exports autos and computers, but also sells transportation services, insurance, and tourist and brokerage services to residents of foreign countries. These service sales or "exports" totaled $133 billion in 1990. Item 5 indicates that Americans buy or "import" similar services from foreigners. These service imports were $107 billion in 1990.

The **balance on goods and services,** shown in Table 38-1 as item 6, is the difference between our exports of goods and services (items 1 and 4) and our imports of goods and services (items 2 and 5). In 1990 our exports of goods and services fell short of our imports of goods and services by $82 billion.

Balance on Current Account Item 7 reflects that historically the United States has been a net international lender. Over time we have invested more abroad than foreigners have invested in the United States. Thus net investment income represents the excess of interest and dividend payments which foreigners have paid us for the services of our exported capital over what we paid in 1990 in interest and dividends for their capital invested in the United States. Table 38-1 shows that, on balance, our net investment income earned us $12 billion worth of foreign currencies for "exporting" the services of American money capital invested abroad.

Item 8 reflects net transfers, both public and private, from the United States to the rest of the world. Included here is American foreign aid, pensions paid to Americans living abroad, and remittances of immigrants to relatives abroad. These $22 billion of transfers are "outpayments" and exhaust available supplies of foreign exchange. As it has been facetiously put, net transfers entail the importing of "goodwill" or "thank-you notes."

By taking all transactions in the current account into consideration we obtain the **balance on current account** shown by item 9 in Table 38-1. In 1990 the United States realized a current account deficit of $92 billion. This means that our current account import transactions (items 2, 5, and 8) created a demand for a larger dollar amount of foreign currencies than our export transactions (items 1, 4, and 7) supplied.

Capital Account

The **capital account** reflects capital flows in the purchase or sale of real and financial assets which occurred in 1990. For example, Honda or Nissan might acquire an automobile assembly plant in the United States. Or, alternatively, the investments may be of a financial nature, for example, an Arabian oil sheik might purchase GM stock or Treasury bonds. In either event such transactions generate supplies of foreign currencies for the United States. They are therefore credit or inpayment items, designated with a plus sign. The United States is exporting stocks and bonds and thereby earning foreign exchange. Item 10 in Table 38-1 shows that such transactions amounted to $117 billion in 1990.

Conversely, Americans invest abroad. General Electric might purchase a plant in Hong Kong or Singapore to assemble pocket radios or telephones. Or an American might buy stock in an Italian shoe factory. Or an American bank might finance construction of a meat processing plant in Argentina. These transactions have a common feature; they all use up or exhaust supplies

of foreign currencies. We therefore attach a minus sign to remind us that these are debit or outpayment transactions. The United States is importing stocks, bonds, and IOUs from abroad. Item 11 in Table 38-1 reveals that $59 billion of these transactions occurred in 1990. When items 10 and 11 are combined, the **balance on the capital account** was a *plus* $58 billion—the United States enjoyed a capital account surplus of $58 billion in 1990.

Interrelationships

The current and capital accounts are interrelated; they are essentially reflections of one another. The current account *deficit* means that American exports of goods and services were not sufficient to pay for our imports of goods and services.[1] How did we finance the difference? The answer is that the United States must either borrow from abroad or give up ownership of some of its assets to foreigners as reflected in the capital account.

A simple analogy is useful here. Suppose in a given year your expenditures exceed your earnings. How will you finance your "deficit"? You might sell some of your assets or borrow. You might sell some real assets (your car or stereo) or perhaps some financial assets (stocks or bonds) which you own. Or you might obtain a loan from your family or a bank.

Similarly, when a nation incurs a deficit in its current account, its expenditures for foreign goods and services (its imports) exceed the income received from the international sales of its own goods and services (its exports). It must somehow finance that current account deficit by selling assets and by borrowing, that is, by going into debt. And that is what is reflected in the capital account surplus. Our capital account surplus of $58 billion (item 12) indicates that in 1990 the United States "sold off" real assets (buildings, farmland) and received loans from the rest of the world in that amount to help finance our current account deficit of $92 billion.

Recap: A nation's current account deficit will be financed essentially by a net capital inflow in its capital account. Conversely, a nation's current account *surplus* would be accompanied by a net capital *outflow* in its capital account. The excess earnings from its current account surplus will be used to purchase real assets of, and make loans to, other nations.

---

[1]We ignore transfer payments (item 8) in making this statement.

Official Reserves

The central banks of nations hold quantities of foreign currencies called **official reserves** which are added to or drawn on to settle any *net* differences in current and capital account balances. In 1990 the surplus in our capital account was considerably less than the deficit in our current account so we had a $34 billion net deficit on the combined accounts (item 13). That is, the United States earned less foreign monies in all international trade and financial transactions than it used. This deficiency of earnings of foreign currencies was subtracted from the existing balances of foreign monies held by our central banks. The *plus* $34 billion of official reserves shown by item 14 in Table 38-1 represents this reduction of our stocks of foreign currencies. The plus sign indicates this is a credit or "export-type" transaction which represents a supply of foreign exchange.

Frequently the relationship between the current and capital account is just the opposite of that shown in Table 38-1. That is, the current account deficit is less than the capital account surplus. Hence, our central banks would experience an increase in their holdings of foreign currencies. This would show as a *minus* item in the balance of payments; it is a debit or "import-type" transaction because it represents a use of foreign exchange.

The important point here is that the three components of the balance of payments statement—the current account, the capital account, and the official reserves account—must sum to zero. Every unit of foreign exchange used (as reflected in our "minus" outpayment or debit transactions) in our international transactions must have a source (our "plus" inpayment or credit transactions).

Payments Deficits and Surpluses

Although the balance of payments must always sum to zero, economists and political officials frequently speak of **balance of payments deficits and surpluses.** In doing so they are referring to the "current and capital account balance" shown as item 13 in Table 38-1. If this is a negative item, a balance of payments deficit is being realized as was the case for the United States in 1990. In 1990 the United States earned less foreign monies from all its trade and financial transactions than it used. The United States did not "pay its way" in world trade and finance and therefore depleted its official reserves

of foreign monies. If the current and capital account balance were positive, then the United States would be faced with a balance of payments surplus. The United States would have earned sufficient foreign exchange from its export-type transactions to pay for its import-type transactions. As we have just seen, it would add to its stocks of foreign monies—that is, increase its official reserve holdings.

A decrease in official reserves (shown by a positive official reserves item in Table 38-1) measures a nation's balance of payments deficit; an increase in official reserves (shown by a negative official reserves item) measures its balance of payments surplus.

Deficits and Surpluses: Bad or Good?

Having defined a variety of deficits and surpluses, we must now inquire as to their desirability. Are deficits bad, as the term implies? Is a surplus desirable, as that word suggests? The answer to both questions is "not necessarily." A large merchandise trade deficit such as the United States has been incurring in recent years is regarded by many as "unfavorable" or "adverse," as it suggests American producers are losing their competitiveness in world markets. Our industries seem to be having trouble selling their goods abroad and are simultaneously facing strong competition from imported goods. On the other hand, a trade deficit is *favorable* from the vantage point of American consumers who are currently receiving more goods as imports than they are forgoing as exports.

Similarly, the desirability of a balance of payments deficit or surplus depends on (1) the events causing them and (2) their persistence through time. For example, the large payments deficits imposed on the United States and other oil-importing nations by OPEC's dramatic runup of oil prices in 1973–1974 and 1979–1980 were very disruptive in that they forced the United States to invoke policies to curtail oil imports.

Also, any nation's official reserves are limited. Persistent or long-term payments deficits, which must be financed by drawing down those reserves, would ultimately deplete reserves. In this case that nation would have to undertake policies to correct its balance of payments. These policies might require painful macroeconomic adjustments, trade barriers and similar restrictions, or changing the international value of its currency.

low-priced British goods, increasing the demand for pounds. Conversely, the British will purchase fewer American goods, reducing the supply of pounds. This combination of an increase in the demand for, and a reduction in the supply of, pounds will cause the dollar to depreciate.

In fact, differences in relative price levels among nations—which reflect changes in price levels over time—help explain persistent differences in exchange rates. In 1992 an American dollar could buy .56 British pounds, 124 Japanese yen, or 5340 Turkish lira. One reason for these differences is that the prices of British goods and services in pounds were far lower than the prices of Japanese goods and services in yen and the prices of Turkish goods and services in lira. For example, the same market basket of products costing $500 in the United States might cost 250 pounds in England, 67,500 yen in Japan, and 2,500,000 lira in Turkey. *Generally, the higher the prices of a nation's goods and services in terms of its own currency, the greater the amount of that currency which can be obtained with an American dollar.*

Taken to its extreme, this **purchasing power parity theory** holds that differences in exchange rates *equate* the purchasing power of various currencies. That is, the exchange rates among national currencies perfectly adjust in such a way as to equal the ratios of the nations' price levels. For example, if a market basket of goods costs $100 in the United States and £50 in Great Britain, the exchange rate should be $2 = £1. Thus, a dollar spent on goods sold in Britain, Japan, Turkey, and other nations supposedly will have equal purchasing power. In practice, however, exchange rates depart significantly from purchasing power parity, even over long periods. Nevertheless, relative price levels are clearly a major determinant of exchange rates.

Relative Real Interest Rates Suppose the United States restricts the growth of its money supply (tight money policy), as it did in the late 1970s and early 1980s, to control inflation. As a result, *real* interest rates—nominal interest rates adjusted for the rate of inflation—were high in the United States compared to most other nations. Consequently, British individuals and firms found the United States an attractive place to make financial investments. This increase in the demand for American financial assets meant an increase in the supply of British pounds and the dollar therefore appreciated in value.

Speculation Suppose it is widely anticipated that the American economy will *(a)* grow faster than the Brit-

ish economy, *(b)* experience more rapid inflation than the British economy, and *(c)* have lower future real interest rates than Britain. All these expectations would lead one to believe that in the future the dollar will depreciate and, conversely, the pound will appreciate. Holders of dollars will thus attempt to convert them into pounds, increasing the demand for pounds. This conversion causes the dollar to depreciate and the pound to appreciate. A self-fulfilling prophecy arises: The dollar depreciates and the pound appreciates because speculators act on the supposition that these changes in currency values will in fact happen.

Flexible Rates and the Balance of Payments Proponents of flexible exchange rates argue that such rates have a compelling virtue: *They automatically adjust so as eventually to eliminate balance of payments deficits or surpluses.* We can explain this by looking at S and D in Figure 38-5 which restate the demand for, and supply of, pounds curves from Figure 38-3. The equilibrium exchange rate of $2 = £1 correctly suggests there is no balance of payments deficit or surplus. At the $2 = £1 exchange rate the quantity of pounds demanded by Americans to import British goods, buy

FIGURE 38-5 Adjustments under flexible exchange rates, fixed exchange rates, and the gold standard

Under flexible rates an American trade deficit at the $2-for-£1 rate would be corrected by an increase in the rate to $3 for £1. Under fixed rates the *ab* shortage of pounds would be met out of international monetary reserves. Under the gold standard the deficit would cause changes in domestic price and income levels which would shift the demand for pounds (*D′*) to the left and the supply (*S*) to the right, sustaining equilibrium at the $2-for-£1 rate.

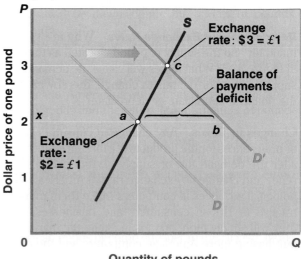

British transportation and insurance services, and pay interest and dividends on British investments in the United States equals the amount of pounds supplied by the British in buying American exports, purchasing services from Americans, and making interest and dividend payments on American investments in Britain. In brief, there would be no change in official reserves in Table 38-1.

Now suppose tastes change and Americans decide to buy more British automobiles. Or assume that the American price level has increased relative to Britain, or that interest rates have fallen in the United States compared to Britain. Any or all of these changes will cause the American demand for British pounds to increase from D to, say, D' in Figure 38-5.

We observe that *at the initial $2 = £1 exchange rate* an American balance of payments deficit has been created in the amount *ab*. That is, at the $2 = £1 rate there is a shortage of pounds in the amount *ab* to Americans. American export-type transactions will earn *xa* pounds, but Americans will want *xb* pounds to finance import-type transactions. Because this is a free competitive market, the shortage will change the exchange rate (the dollar price of pounds) from $2 = £1 to, say, $3 = £1; that is, the dollar has *depreciated*.

At this point it must be emphasized that *the exchange rate is a very special price which links all domestic (United States') prices with all foreign (British) prices.* Specifically, the dollar price of a foreign good is found by multiplying the foreign product price by the exchange rate in dollars per unit of the foreign currency. At an exchange rate of $2 = £1, a British Triumph automobile priced at 9000 will cost an American $18,000 (= 9000 × $2).

A change in the exchange rate therefore alters the prices of all British goods to Americans and all American goods to potential British buyers. Specifically, the change in the exchange rate from $2 = £1 to $3 = £1 will alter the relative attractiveness of American imports and exports in such a way as to restore equilibrium in the balance of payments of the United States. From the American point of view, as the dollar price of pounds changes from $2 to $3, the Triumph priced at £9000, which formerly cost an American $18,000, now costs $27,000 (= 9000 × $3). Other British goods will also cost more to Americans, and American imports of British goods and services will decline. Graphically, this is shown as a move from point *b* toward point *c* in Figure 38-5.

Conversely, from Britain's standpoint the exchange rate, that is, the pound price of dollars, has fallen (from £$\frac{1}{2}$ to £$\frac{1}{3}$ for $1). The international value of the pound has *appreciated*. The British previously got only $2 for £1; now they get $3 for £1. American goods are therefore cheaper to the British, and American exports to Great Britain will rise. In Figure 38-5 this is shown by the move from point *a* toward point *c*.

The two adjustments described—a decrease in American imports from Great Britain and an increase in American exports to Great Britain—are precisely those needed to correct the American balance of payments deficit. (You should reason through the operation of freely fluctuating exchange rates in correcting an initial American balance of payments *surplus* in its trade with Great Britain.)

In summary, the free fluctuation of exchange rates in response to shifts in the supply of, and demand for, foreign monies automatically corrects balance of payments deficits and surpluses.

Disadvantages Even though freely fluctuating exchange rates automatically work eventually to eliminate payments imbalances, they may involve several significant problems:

1 Uncertainty and Diminished Trade The risks and uncertainties associated with flexible exchange rates may discourage the flow of trade. Suppose an American automobile dealer contracts to purchase ten Triumph cars for £90,000. At the current exchange rate of, say $2 for £1, the American importer expects to pay $180,000 for these automobiles. But if in the three-month delivery period the rate of exchange shifts to $3 for £1, the £90,000 payment contracted by the American importer will now be $270,000.

This unheralded increase in the dollar price of pounds may easily turn the potential American importer's anticipated profits into substantial losses. Aware of the possibility of an adverse change in the exchange rate, the American importer may not be willing to assume the risks involved. The American firm therefore may confine its operations to domestic automobiles, with the result that international trade does not occur in this item.

The same rationale applies to investment. Assume that, when the exchange rate is $3 to £1, an American firm invests $30,000 (or £10,000) in a British enterprise. It estimates a return of 10 percent, that is, it anticipates earnings of $3000 or £1000. Suppose these expectations prove correct in that the British firm earns £1000 the first year on the £10,000 investment. But suppose that during the year, the value of the dollar *appreciates* to $2 = £1. The absolute return is now only $2000 (rather than $3000) and the rate of return falls from the anticipated 10 percent to only 6⅔ percent (= $2000/ $30,000). Investment is inherently risky. The added risk posed by adverse changes in exchange rates may persuade the potential American investor to avoid overseas ventures.[2]

2 Terms of Trade A nation's terms of trade will be worsened by a decline in the international value of its currency. For example, an increase in the dollar price of pounds will mean that the United States must export more goods and services to finance a given level of imports from Britain.

3 Instability Freely fluctuating exchange rates may also have destabilizing effects on the domestic economy as wide fluctuations stimulate and then depress those industries producing internationally traded goods. If the American economy is operating at full employment and the international value of its currency depreciates as in our illustration, the results will be inflationary for two reasons. Foreign demand for American goods will increase, that is, the net exports component of aggregate expenditures will increase and cause demand-pull inflation. Also, prices of all American imports will increase. Conversely, appreciation of the dollar would lower exports and increase imports, causing unemployment.

From the vantage point of policy, acceptance of floating exchange rates may complicate the use of domestic fiscal and monetary policies in seeking full employment and price stability. This is especially so for nations whose exports and imports are large relative to their GDPs (Table 37-1).

Fixed Exchange Rates

At the other extreme nations have often fixed or "pegged" their exchange rates to circumvent the disadvantages associated with floating rates. To analyze the implications and problems associated with fixed rates,

assume that the United States and Britain agree to maintain a $2 = £1 exchange rate.

The basic problem is that a governmental proclamation that a dollar will be worth so many pounds does *not* mandate stability of the demand for, and supply of, pounds. As demand and supply shift over time, government must intervene directly or indirectly in the foreign exchange market if the exchange rate is to be stabilized.

In Figure 38-5 suppose the American demand for pounds increases from D to D' and an American payments deficit of *ab* arises. This means that the American government is committed to an exchange rate ($2 = £1) which is below the equilibrium rate ($3 = £1). How can the United States prevent the shortage of pounds—reflecting an American balance of payments deficit—from driving the exchange rate up to the equilibrium level? The answer is to alter market demand or supply or both so that they continue to intersect at the $2 = £1 rate of exchange. There are several means for achieving this.

1 Use of Reserves The most desirable means of pegging an exchange rate is to manipulate the market through the use of official reserves. International monetary *reserves* are stocks of foreign monies owned by a particular government. How do reserves originate? Let's assume that in the past the opposite market condition prevailed in which there was a surplus, rather than a shortage, of pounds, and the United States government had acquired that surplus. That is, at some earlier time the United States government spent dollars to buy surplus pounds which were threatening to reduce the $2 = £1 exchange rate to, say, $1 = £1. By now selling part of its reserve of pounds, the United States government could shift the supply of pounds curve to the right so that it intersects D' at *b* in Figure 38-5, thereby maintaining the exchange rate at $2 = £1.

Historically nations have used gold as "international money" or, in other words, as reserves. Thus, in our example the United States government might sell some of the gold it owns to Britain for pounds. The pounds thus acquired could be used to augment the supply earned through American trade and financial transactions to shift the supply of pounds to the right to maintain the $2 = £1 exchange rate.

It is critical that the amount of reserves be enough to accomplish the required increase in the supply of pounds. This is *not* a problem if deficits and surpluses occur more or less randomly and are of approximately

---

[2]At some cost and inconvenience a *trader* can circumvent part of the risk of unfavorable exchange rate fluctuations by "hedging" in the "futures market" for foreign exchange. For example, our American auto importer can purchase the needed pounds at the current $2 for £1 exchange rates to be made available three months in the future when the British cars are delivered. Unfortunately, this does not eliminate entirely exchange rate risks. Suppose the dollar price of pounds *falls* (the dollar appreciates) in the three-month delivery period and a competing importing firm did not hedge its foreign exchange purchase. This means the competitor will obtain its shipment of Triumphs at a lower price and will be able to undersell our original importer.

equivalent size. That is, last year's balance of payments surplus with Britain will increase the United States' reserve of pounds and this reserve can be used to "finance" this year's deficit. But if the United States encounters persistent and sizable deficits for an extended period, the reserves problem can become critical and force the abandonment of a system of fixed exchange rates. Or, at least, a nation whose reserves are inadequate must resort to less appealing options to maintain exchange rate stability. Let's consider these other options.

2 Trade Policies

One set of policy options includes measures designed to control the flows of trade and finance directly. The United States might try to maintain the $2 = £1 exchange rate in the face of a shortage of pounds by discouraging imports (thereby reducing the demand for pounds) and by encouraging exports (thereby increasing the supply of pounds). Imports can be reduced by imposing tariffs or import quotas. Similarly, special taxes may be levied on the interest and dividends Americans receive for foreign investments. Also, the United States government might subsidize certain American exports and thus increase the supply of pounds.

The fundamental problem with these policies is that they reduce the volume of world trade and distort its composition or pattern away from that which is economically desirable. Tariffs, quotas, and the like can be imposed only at the sacrifice of some portion of the economic gains or benefits attainable from a free flow of world trade based on comparative advantage. These effects should not be underestimated; the imposition of trade barriers can elicit retaliatory responses from other nations which are adversely affected.

3 Exchange Controls: Rationing

Another option is exchange controls or rationing. Under exchange controls the United States government would handle the problem of a pound shortage by requiring that all pounds obtained by American exporters be sold to it. Then, in turn, the government allocates or rations this short supply of pounds (*xa* in Figure 38-5) among various American importers who demand the quantity *xb*. In this way the American government would restrict American imports to the amount of foreign exchange earned by American exports. American demand for British pounds in the amount *ab* would be unfulfilled. Government eliminates a balance of payments deficit by restricting imports to the value of exports.

There are many objections to exchange controls.

1 Like trade controls—tariffs, quotas, and export subsidies—exchange controls distort the pattern of international trade away from that based on comparative advantage.

2 The process of rationing scarce foreign exchange necessarily involves discrimination among importers. Serious problems of equity and favoritism are implicit in the rationing process.

3 Controls impinge on freedom of consumer choice. Americans who prefer Mazdas may be forced to buy Mercuries. The business opportunities of some American importers will necessarily be impaired because imports are being constrained by government.

4 There are likely to be enforcement problems. The market forces of demand and supply indicate there are American importers who want foreign exchange badly enough to pay *more* than the $2 = £1 official rate; this sets the stage for extralegal or "black market" foreign exchange dealings.

4 Domestic Macro Adjustments

A final means of maintaining a stable exchange rate is to use domestic fiscal and monetary policies to eliminate the shortage of pounds. In particular, restrictive fiscal and monetary measures will reduce the United States' national income relative to Britain's. Because American imports vary directly with our national income, our demand for British goods, and therefore for pounds, will be restrained.

To the extent that these contractionary policies reduce our price level relative to Britain's, American buyers of consumption and investment goods will divert their demands from British to American goods, also restricting the demand for pounds. Finally, a restrictive (tight) money policy will increase United States' interest rates compared to Britain and reduce American demand for pounds to make financial investments in Britain.

From Britain's standpoint lower prices on American goods and higher American interest rates will increase British imports of American goods and stimulate British financial investment in the United States. Both developments will increase the supply of pounds. The combination of a decrease in the demand for and an increase in the supply of pounds will eliminate the initial American payments deficit. In Figure 38-5 the new supply and demand curves will intersect at some new equilibrium point on the *ab* line where the exchange rate persists at $2 = £1.

This means of maintaining pegged exchange rates is hardly appealing. The "price" of exchange rate stability for the United States is falling output, employment, and price levels—in other words, a recession. Achieving a balance of payments equilibrium and realizing domestic stability are both important national economic objectives; but to sacrifice the latter for the former is to let the tail wag the dog.

QUICK REVIEW 38-2

◆ *In a system where exchange rates are free to float, they are determined by the demand for, and supply of, individual national currencies.*

◆ *Determinants of freely floating exchange rates—factors which shift currency supply and demand curves—include changes in tastes, changes in relative national incomes, relative price level changes, relative real interest rate changes, and speculation.*

◆ *Under a system of fixed exchange rates, nations set their exchange rates and then maintain them by buying or selling reserves of foreign currencies, incurring inflation or recession, establishing trade barriers, or employing exchange controls.*

INTERNATIONAL EXCHANGE RATE SYSTEMS

There have been three different exchange rate systems which nations have employed in recent history.

The Gold Standard: Fixed Exchange Rates

Over the 1879–1934 period—except for the World War I years—an international monetary system known as the gold standard prevailed. The **gold standard** provided for fixed exchange rates. A look at its operation and ultimate downfall is instructive as to the functioning and some of the advantages and problems associated with fixed-rate systems. Currently a number of economists advocate fixed exchange rates and a few even call for a return to the international gold standard.

Conditions A nation is on the gold standard when it fulfills three conditions:
1 It must define its monetary unit in terms of a certain quantity of gold.
2 It must maintain a fixed relationship between its stock of gold and its domestic money supply.
3 It must allow gold to be freely exported and imported.

If each nation defines its monetary unit in terms of gold, the various national currencies will have a fixed relationship to one another. For example, suppose the United States defines a dollar as being worth 25 grains of gold and Britain defines its pound sterling as being worth 50 grains of gold. This means that a British pound is worth 50⁄25 dollars or, simply, £1 equals $2.

Gold flows Now, ignoring costs of packing, insuring, and shipping gold between countries, under the gold standard the rate of exchange would not vary from this $2-for-£1 rate. No one in the United States would pay more than $2 for £1, because you could always buy 50 grains of gold for $2 in the United States, ship it to Britain, and sell it for £1. Nor would the English pay more than £1 for $2. Why should they, when they could buy 50 grains of gold in England for £1, send it to the United States, and sell it for $2?

In practice the costs of packing, insuring, and shipping gold must be taken into account. But these costs would only amount to a few cents per 50 grains of gold. If these costs were 3 cents for 50 grains of gold, Americans wanting pounds would pay up to $2.03 for a pound rather than buy and export 50 grains of gold to get the pound. Why? Because it would cost them $2 for the 50 grains of gold plus 3 cents to send it to England to be exchanged for £1. This $2.03 exchange rate, above which gold would begin to flow out of the United States, is called the **gold export point.**

Conversely, the exchange rate would fall to $1.97 before gold would flow into the United States. The English, wanting dollars, would accept as little as $1.97 in exchange for £1, because from the $2 which they could get by buying 50 grains of gold in England and reselling it in the United States, 3 cents must be subtracted to pay shipping and related costs. This $1.97 exchange rate, below which gold would flow into the United States, is called the **gold import point.**

Our conclusion is that *under the gold standard the flow of gold between nations would result in exchange rates which for all practical purposes are fixed.*

Domestic Macro Adjustments Figure 38-5 helps explain the kinds of adjustments the gold standard would entail. Here, initially the demand for and the supply of pounds are D and S respectively and the resulting intersection point at a coincides with the fixed exchange rate of $2 = £1 which results from the "in gold" definitions of the pound and the dollar. Now suppose for some reason American preferences for British goods increase, shifting the demand for pounds curve to D'. In Figure 38-5 there is now a shortage of pounds equal to *ab,* implying an American balance of payments deficit.

What will happen? Remember that the rules of the gold standard prohibit the exchange rate from moving from the fixed $2 = £1 relationship; the rate can *not* move up to a new equilibrium of $3 = £1 at point *c* as it would under freely floating rates. Instead, the exchange rate would rise by a few cents to the American gold export point at which gold would flow from the United States to Britain.

Recall that the gold standard requires participants to maintain a fixed relationship between their domestic money supplies and their quantities of gold. Therefore, the flow of gold from the United States to Britain would bring about a contraction of the money supply in America and an expansion of the money supply in Britain. Other things being equal, this will reduce aggregate demand and, therefore, lower real domestic output, employment, and the price level in the United States. Also, the reduced money supply will boost American interest rates.

The opposite occurs in Britain. The inflow of gold increases the money supply, causing aggregate demand, national income, employment, and the price level to all increase. The increased money supply will also lower interest rates in Britain.

In Figure 38-5 declining American incomes and prices will reduce our demand for British goods and services and therefore reduce the American demand for pounds. Lower relative interest rates in Britain will make it less attractive for Americans to invest there, also reducing the demand for pounds. For all these reasons the D' curve will shift to the left.

Similarly, higher incomes and prices in Britain will increase British demand for American goods and services and higher American interest rates will encourage the British to invest more in the United States. These developments all increase the supply of pounds available to Americans, shifting the S curve of Figure 38-5 to the right.

In short, domestic macroeconomic adjustments in America and Britain, triggered by the international flow of gold, will produce new demand and supply for pound curves which intersect at some point on the horizontal line between points *a* and *b*.

Note the critical difference in the adjustment mechanisms associated with freely floating exchange rates and the fixed rates of the gold standard. With floating rates the burden of the adjustment is on the exchange rate itself. In contrast, the gold standard in-

volves changes in the domestic money supplies of participating nations which in turn precipitate changes in price levels, real domestic output and employment, and interest rates.

Although the gold standard boasts the advantages of stable exchange rates and the automatic correction of balance of payments deficits and surpluses, its basic drawback is that nations must accept domestic adjustments in such distasteful forms as unemployment and falling incomes, on the one hand, or inflation, on the other. In using the gold standard nations must be willing to submit their domestic economies to painful macroeconomic adjustments. Under this system a nation's monetary policy would be determined largely by changes in the demand for and supply of foreign exchange. If the United States, for example, was already moving toward recession, the loss of gold under the gold standard would reduce its money supply and intensify the problem. Under the international gold standard nations would have to forgo independent monetary policies.

Demise The worldwide Great Depression of the 1930s signaled the end of the gold standard. As domestic outputs and employment plummeted worldwide, the restoration of prosperity became the primary goal of afflicted nations. Protectionist measures such as the United States' Smoot-Hawley Tariff were enacted as nations sought to increase net exports and stimulate their domestic economies. And each nation was fearful that its economic recovery would be aborted by a balance of payments deficit which would lead to an outflow of gold and consequent contractionary effects. Indeed, nations attempted to devalue their currencies in term of gold to make their exports more attractive and imports less attractive. These devaluations undermined a basic condition of the gold standard and the system broke down.

The Bretton Woods System

Not only did the Great Depression of the 1930s lead to the downfall of the gold standard, it also prompted erection of trade barriers which greatly impaired international trade. World War II was similarly disruptive to world trade and finance. Thus, as World War II drew to a close the world trading and monetary systems were in shambles.

To lay the groundwork for a new international monetary system, an international conference of Allied nations was held at Bretton Woods, New Hampshire, in

1944. Out of this conference evolved a commitment to an *adjustable-peg system* of exchange rates, sometimes called the **Bretton Woods system.** The new system sought to capture the advantages of the old gold standard (fixed exchange rates), while avoiding its disadvantages (painful domestic macroeconomic adjustments).

Furthermore, the conference created the **International Monetary Fund** (IMF) to make the new exchange rate system feasible and workable. This international monetary system, emphasizing relatively fixed exchange rates and managed through the IMF, prevailed with modifications until 1971. The IMF continues to play a basic role in international finance and in recent years has performed a major role in ameliorating debt problems of the less developed countries.

IMF and Pegged Exchange Rates   Why did the Bretton Woods adjustable-peg system evolve? We have noted that during the depressed 1930s, various countries resorted to the practice of **devaluation**—devaluing[3] their currencies to try to stimulate domestic employment. For example, if the United States was faced with growing unemployment, it might devalue the dollar by *increasing* the dollar price of pounds from $2.50 for £1 to, say, $3 for £1. This action would make American goods cheaper to the British and British goods dearer to Americans, increasing American exports and reducing American imports. The resulting increase in net exports, abetted by the multiplier effect, would stimulate output and employment in the United States.

But the problem is that every nation can play the devaluation game, and most gave it a whirl. The resulting rounds of competitive devaluations benefited no one; on the contrary, they actually contributed to further demoralization of world trade. Nations at Bretton Woods therefore agreed that the postwar monetary system must provide for overall exchange rate stability whereby disruptive currency devaluations could be avoided.

What was the adjustable-peg system of exchange rates like? First, as with the gold standard, each IMF member was obligated to define its monetary unit in terms of gold (or dollars), thereby establishing par

rates of exchange between its currency and the currencies of all other members. Each nation was further obligated to keep its exchange rate stable vis-à-vis any other currency.

But how was this obligation to be fulfilled? The answer, as we saw in our discussion of fixed exchange rates, is that governments must use international monetary reserves to intervene in foreign exchange markets. Assume, for example, that under the Bretton Woods system the dollar was "pegged" to the British pound at $2 = £1. Now suppose in Figure 38-5 that the American demand for pounds temporarily increases from D to D' so that a shortage of pounds of *ab* arises at the pegged rate. How can the United States keep its pledge to maintain a $2 = £1 rate when the new market or equilibrium rate would be at $3 = £1? The United States could supply additional pounds in the exchange market, shifting the supply of pounds curve to the right so that it intersects D' at b and thereby maintains the $2 = £1 rate of exchange.

Where would the United States obtain the needed pounds? Under the Bretton Woods system there were three main sources.

1 Reserves   The United States might currently possess pounds in a "stabilization fund" as the result of the opposite exchange market condition existing in the past. That is, at some earlier time the United States government may have spent dollars to purchase surplus pounds which were threatening to reduce the $2 = £1 exchange rate to, say, $1 = £1.

2 Gold Sales   The United States government might sell some of the gold it holds to Britain for pounds. The proceeds would then be offered in the exchange market to augment the supply of pounds.

3 IMF Borrowing   The needed pounds might be borrowed from the IMF. Nations participating in the Bretton Woods system were required to make contributions to the IMF on the basis of the size of their national income, population, and volume of trade. Thus, if necessary, the United States could borrow pounds on a short-term basis from the IMF by supplying its own currency as collateral.

Fundamental Imbalances: Adjusting the Peg   A fixed-rate system such as Bretton Woods functions well so long as a nation's payments deficits and surpluses occur more or less randomly and are approximately equal in size. If a nation's payments surplus last year

---

[3]A note on terminology is in order. We noted earlier in this chapter that the dollar has *appreciated (depreciated)* when its international value has increased (decreased) as the result of changes in the demand for, or supply of, dollars in foreign exchange markets. The terms *revalue* and *devalue* are used to describe an increase or decrease, respectively, in the international value of a currency which occurs as the result of governmental action.

allows it to add a sufficient amount to its international monetary reserves to finance this year's payments deficit, no problems will arise. But what if the United States, for example, encountered a "fundamental imbalance" in its international trade and finance and was confronted with persistent and sizable payments deficits? In this case it is evident that the United States would eventually run out of reserves and be unable to maintain its fixed exchange rate.

Under the Bretton Woods system, a fundamental payments deficit was corrected by devaluation, that is, by an "orderly" reduction in the nation's pegged exchange rate. Also, the IMF allowed each member nation to alter the value of its currency by 10 percent without explicit permission from the Fund to correct a deeply rooted or "fundamental" balance of payments deficit. Larger exchange rate changes required the sanction of the Fund's board of directors. By requiring approval of significant rate changes, the Fund guarded against arbitrary and competitive currency devaluation prompted by nations seeking a temporary stimulus to their domestic economies. In our illustration, devaluing the dollar would increase American exports and lower American imports, correcting its persistent payments deficits.

The objective of the adjustable-peg system was to realize a world monetary system which embraced the best features of both a fixed exchange rate system (such as the old international gold standard) and a system of freely fluctuating exchange rates. By reducing risk and uncertainty, short-term exchange rate stability—pegged exchange rates—would presumably stimulate trade and lead to the efficient use of world resources. Periodic exchange rate adjustments—adjustments of the pegs—made in an orderly fashion through the IMF, and on the basis of permanent or long-run changes in a country's payments position, provided a mechanism by which persistent international payments imbalances could be resolved by means other than painful changes in domestic levels of output and prices.

Demise of the Bretton Woods System   Under the Bretton Woods system gold and the dollar came to be accepted as international reserves. The acceptability of gold as an international medium of exchange was derived from its role under the international gold standard of an earlier era. The dollar became acceptable as international money for two reasons.

1   The United States emerged from World War II as the free world's strongest economy.

2   The United States had accumulated large quantities of gold and between 1934 and 1971 maintained a policy of buying gold from, and selling gold to, foreign monetary authorities at a fixed price of $35 per ounce. Thus the dollar was convertible into gold on demand; the dollar came to be regarded as a substitute for gold and therefore "as good as gold."

But the role of the dollar as a component of international monetary reserves contained the seeds of a dilemma. Consider the situation as it developed in the 1950s and 1960s. The problem with gold as international money was a quantitative one. The growth of the world's money stock depends on the amount of newly mined gold, less any amounts hoarded for speculative purposes or used for industrial and artistic purposes. Unfortunately, the growth of the gold stock lagged behind the rapidly expanding volume of international trade and finance. Thus the dollar came to occupy an increasingly important role as an international monetary reserve.

Economies of the world acquire dollars as reserves as the result of United States' balance of payments deficits. With the exception of some three or four years, the United States incurred persistent payments deficits throughout the 1950s and 1960s. These deficits were financed in part by drawing down American gold reserves. But for the most part United States' deficits were financed by growing foreign holdings of American dollars which were "as good as gold" until 1971.

As the amount of dollars held by foreigners soared and as our gold reserves dwindled, other nations inevitably began to question whether the dollar was really "as good as gold." The ability of the United States to maintain the convertibility of the dollar into gold became increasingly doubtful, and, therefore, so did the role of the dollar as generally accepted international monetary reserves. Hence, the dilemma: ". . . to preserve the status of the dollar as a reserve medium, the payments deficit of the United States had to be eliminated; but elimination of the deficit would mean a drying up of the source of additional dollar reserves for the system."[4] The United States had to reduce or eliminate its payments deficits to preserve the dollar's status as an international medium of exchange. But success in this endeavor would limit the expansion of international reserves or liquidity and restrict the growth of international trade and finance.

[4]Delbert A. Snider, *Introduction to International Economics,* 7th ed. (Homewood, Ill.: Richard D. Irwin, Inc., 1979), p. 352.

This problem came to a head in the early 1970s. Faced with persistent and growing United States' payments deficits, President Nixon suspended the dollar's convertibility into gold on August 15, 1971. This suspension abrogated the policy to exchange gold for dollars at $35 per ounce, which had existed for thirty-seven years. This new policy severed the link between gold and the international value of the dollar, thereby "floating" the dollar and allowing its value to be determined by market forces. The floating of the dollar withdrew American support from the old Bretton Woods system of fixed exchange rates and sounded the death knell for that system.

The Managed Float

The system of exchange rates which has since evolved is not easily described; it can probably best be labeled a system of **managed floating exchange rates.** It is recognized that changing economic conditions among nations require continuing changes in exchange rates to avoid persistent payments deficits or surpluses; exchange rates must be allowed to float. But short-term changes in exchange rates—perhaps accentuated by purchases and sales by speculators—disrupt and discourage the flow of trade and finance. Thus, it is generally agreed that the central banks of the various nations should buy and sell foreign exchange to smooth out such fluctuations in rates. That is, central banks should "manage" or stabilize short-term speculative variations in their exchange rates.

These characteristics were formalized by a leading group of IMF nations in 1976. Thus, ideally, the managed floating system will have not only the needed long-term exchange rate flexibility to correct fundamental payments imbalances, but also sufficient short-term stability of rates to sustain and encourage international trade and finance.

Actually, the current exchange rate system is more complicated than the previous paragraphs suggest. While the major currencies—German marks, American and Canadian dollars, Japanese yen, and the British pound—fluctuate or float in response to changing demand and supply conditions, most of the European Common Market nations are attempting to peg their currencies to one another. Furthermore, many less developed nations peg their currencies to the dollar and allow their currencies to fluctuate with it. Finally, some nations peg the value of their currencies to a "basket" or group of other currencies.

How well has the managed floating system worked? It has both proponents and critics.

Pros Proponents argue that the system has functioned well—far better than anticipated—during its relatively brief existence.

1 Trade Growth In the first place, fluctuating exchange rates did not lead to the diminution of world trade and finance that skeptics had predicted. In real terms world trade has grown at approximately the same rate under the managed float as it did during the decade of the 1960s under the fixed exchange rates of the Bretton Woods system.

2 Managing Turbulence Proponents argue that the managed float has weathered severe economic turbulence which might well have caused a fixed exchange regime to have broken down. Such dramatic events as worldwide agricultural shortfalls in 1972–1974, extraordinary oil-price increases in 1973–1974 and again in 1979–1980, worldwide stagflation in 1974–1976 and 1981–1983, and large U.S. budget deficits in the 1980s, all generated substantial international trade and financial imbalances. Flexible rates facilitated international adjustments to these developments, whereas the same events would have put unbearable pressures on a fixed-rate system.

Cons But there is still considerable sentiment in favor of a system characterized by greater exchange rate stability. Those favoring stable rates see problems with the current system.

1 Volatility and Adjustment Critics argue that exchange rates have been excessively volatile under the managed float. This volatility, it is argued, has occurred even when underlying economic and financial conditions of particular nations have been stable. Perhaps more importantly, the managed float has not readily resolved balance of payments imbalances as flexible rates are presumably capable of doing. Thus the United States has run persistent trade deficits in recent years, while Germany and Japan have had persistent surpluses. Changes in the international values of the dollar, mark, and yen have not yet corrected these imbalances.

2 A "Nonsystem"? Skeptics feel that the managed float is basically a "nonsystem"; the rules and guidelines circumscribing the behavior of each nation as to its exchange rate are not sufficiently clear or constraining to make the system viable in the long run. Nations will inevitably be tempted to intervene in foreign exchange markets, not merely to smooth out short-term or speculative fluctuations in the value of their currencies, but to prop up their currency if it is chronically weak or to manipulate the value of their currency to achieve domestic stabilization goals. In brief, there is fear that in time there may be more "managing" and less "floating" of exchange rates, and this may be fatal to the present loosely defined system.

An example of more "managing" and less "floating" of exchange rates occurred in February 1987 when the "Group of Seven" industrial nations **(G-7 nations)**—the United States, West Germany, Japan, Britain, France, Italy, and Canada—agreed to take actions to stabilize the value of the dollar. In the previous two years the dollar had declined rapidly because of a sizable U.S. trade deficit. Although the U.S. trade deficit remained large, it was felt that a further depreciation of the dollar might be disruptive to economic growth in several G-7 economies. The G-7 nations thus bought large quantities of dollars to prop up the dollar's value. Since 1987 the G-7 nations have periodically intervened in foreign exchange markets to help stabilize the value of the dollar. Do these actions represent an admission by the industrial economies that the system of flexible exchange rates is seriously flawed?

The jury is still out on the managed float and no clear assessment has been reached: "Flexible rates have neither attained their proponents' wildest hopes nor confirmed their opponents' worst fears. But they have seen the major industrial economies through [two decades] mined with major disturbances to the international economy."[5]

QUICK REVIEW 38-3

✶ Under the gold standard (1789–1934), nations fixed exchange rates by valuing their currencies in terms of gold, by tying their stocks of money to gold, and by allowing gold to flow between nations when balance of payment deficits and surpluses occurred.

✶ The Bretton Woods, or adjustable-peg, system of exchange rates (1944–1971) fixed or pegged short-run exchange rates, but permitted orderly long-run adjustments of the pegs.

✶ The managed floating system of exchange rate (1971–present) relies on foreign exchange markets to establish equilibrium exchange rates, but permits central banks to buy and sell foreign currencies to manage or stabilize short-term speculative changes in exchange rates.

---

[5]Richard E. Caves and Ronald W. Jones, *World Trade and Payments,* 3d ed. (Boston: Little, Brown and Company, 1981), p. 471.

RECENT UNITED STATES' TRADE DEFICITS

As shown in Figure 38-6, the United States had large trade deficits in the 1980s and early 1990s. Specifically, our merchandise trade deficit jumped from $25 billion in 1980 to $160 billion in 1987, then fell to $74 billion in 1991. In 1980 the United States had a current account surplus of $2 billion; by 1987 this had changed to a $160 billion deficit. By 1991 the current account deficit had narrowed to $92 billion.

What caused these large trade deficits? What were their effects? Why have they recently diminished?

Causes of the Trade Deficits

It is generally agreed that three major factors contributed to the large trade deficits of the 1980s and early 1990s.

The Rise of the Dollar As Figure 38-7 indicates, there was a pronounced rise in the international value of the dollar between 1980 and 1985. Here the value of the dollar is compared to ten other major currencies (weighted by the amount of trade we carry on with each country). By the end of 1984 the dollar was about 65 percent above its 1980 average value and at the highest level since floating exchange rates were adopted in the early 1970s. A strong or appreciated dollar means that foreign monies are cheaper to Americans and, conversely, dollars are more expensive to foreigners. As a result, foreign goods are cheap to Americans and our imports rise. Conversely, American goods are expensive to foreigners and our exports fall.

But why did the value of the dollar surge between 1980 and 1985? The basic answer is that real interest rates in the United States—nominal interest rates less the rate of inflation—rose in the United States compared to foreign countries. High real interest rates made the United States a very attractive place for foreigners to invest. As a result, the demand for dollars to make such investments increased, causing the dollar to appreciate in value.

Real interest rates were relatively high in America for two reasons.

1 The large Federal budget deficits of the 1980s are cited by many economists as a basic cause of high interest rates. Simply put, government borrowing to finance its deficits increased the domestic demand for money and boosted interest rates.

2 In 1979 the United States shifted to a tighter money policy in its efforts to control inflation. This

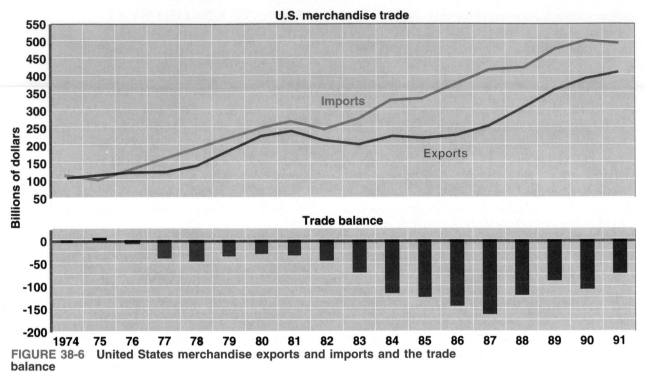

FIGURE 38-6 United States merchandise exports and imports and the trade balance

In recent years American trade deficits have been persistently large.

action increased interest rates directly by reducing the supply of money relative to its demand. Indirectly the lower rate of inflation kept the demand of foreign investors for dollars high because lower inflation means a higher *real* rate of return on investments in the United States.

By 1985 the value of the dollar had reached record heights relative to other currencies. Two factors then began to interact to reduce the dollar's value sharply over the next two years.

1 Five industrial nations—the United States, West Germany, Great Britain, France, and Japan—collectively decided to nudge the dollar downward to help correct the massive U.S. trade deficit and the trade surpluses in Japan and other nations. These five nations agreed to increase the supply of dollars in foreign exchange markets to reduce the dollar's value.

2 The demand for foreign currency in the United States rose sharply because more foreign money was needed to pay for the expanding volume of imports. This increase in the demand for yen, francs, and other foreign currencies increased the value of these currencies relative to the dollar. As shown in Figure 38-7, the value of the dollar declined sharply relative to other currencies over the 1985–1987 period.

Despite the sharp decline in the dollar between 1985 and 1987, the American trade imbalance stubbornly persisted. The major reason was that Japanese and other foreign importers did not immediately increase their dollar prices of products by as much as the decline in the international value of the dollar. Instead of increasing their prices, major importers accepted lower per unit profits on their goods. Therefore, imports to the United States for a time continued to rise, offsetting increases in American exports. Also, recall that in 1987 the G-7 nations agreed to halt the decline in the value of the dollar. Only in the second half of 1988 did the American trade deficit finally begin to shrink.

Rapid American Growth A second cause of the large trade deficits of the 1980s and 1990s is that the United States experienced a more rapid recovery from the 1980–1982 world recession than did its major trading partners. For example, American growth was about double that of Europe in 1983 and nearly triple the European rate in 1984. Although the gap in growth rates narrowed, the American growth rate continued to outpace the European rate between 1985 and 1990. This is significant because, like domestic consumption, a nation's purchases of foreign goods (its imports) vary di-

Index, March 1973 = 1.0

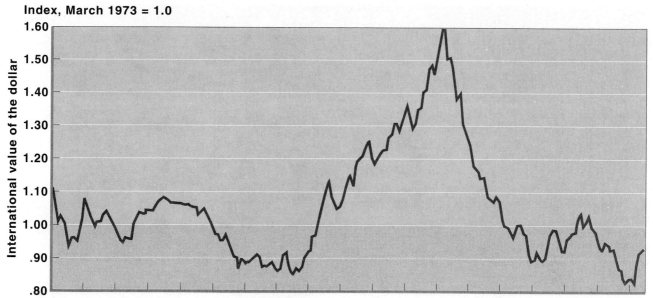

FIGURE 38-7   The international value of the dollar

Between 1980 and 1985 the value of the dollar increased greatly relative to other major currencies, tending to increase our imports and decrease our exports. The dollar fell sharply from 1985 through 1987 but trade deficits continued into the 1990s.

rectly with the level of domestic income. Because our national income expanded relatively rapidly, our imports also expanded rapidly. The slower growth of foreign national incomes meant their imports (our exports) grew slowly.

Exports to Less Developed Countries   A third factor contributing to the large trade deficits was a falloff in our exports to the less developed countries (LDCs). An important source of the LDCs' external debt problem was their need to finance large international trade deficits by borrowing from the industrially advanced nations. As part of rescheduling and restructuring their debts in the 1980s, the less developed countries agreed to lessen their trade deficits. Thus they reduced their imports by using more restrictive monetary and fiscal policies to restrain the growth of their national incomes. In so doing their demands for imported goods declined. Part of those import reductions involved American goods, that is, United States exports. Many LDCs also *devalued* their currencies or, in other words, lowered the exchange rate value of their currencies by governmental decree. Devaluation restricted their imports and stimulated their exports. Thus the LDCs bought less from, and sold more to, the United States.

Effects of U.S. Trade Deficits

What have been the effects or consequences of our foreign trade deficits?

Dampened Aggregate Demand   A trade deficit—more specifically, negative net exports—reduces aggregate demand and therefore, unless offset by other spending, diminishes the levels of real domestic output and employment via the multiplier effect. While this was a factor in keeping our level of employment below the full-employment rate for much of the 1980s, it also helped restrain inflation. A strong, appreciated dollar lowers the prices of all imported goods. Furthermore, a surging volume of imports exerts downward pressure on the prices of domestic goods that compete with those imports.

The constraining effect of a trade deficit is concentrated on industries which are highly dependent on export markets or are most competitive with imports. Some of the problems faced by American farmers, automobile manufacturers, and steel producers in the 1980s, for example, were related to the strong dollar and the associated trade deficits. These difficulties contributed greatly to the upsurge in political pressure for protectionist policies discussed in Chapter 37. They

LAST WORD

BUY AMERICAN: THE GLOBAL REFRIGERATOR

Humorist Art Buchwald pokes fun at those who suggest we could end our trade deficits by buying American consumer products.

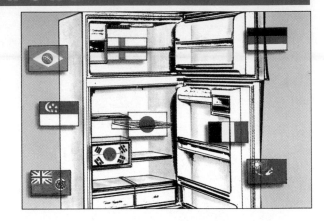

"There is only one way the country is going to get on its feet," said Baleful.

"How's that?" I asked, as we drank coffee in his office at the Baleful Refrigerator Company.

"The consumer has to start buying American," he said, slamming his fist down on the desk. "Every time an American buys a foreign refrigerator it costs one of my people his job. And every time one of my people is out of work it means he or she can't buy refrigerators."

"It's a vicious circle," I said.

Baleful's secretary came in. "Mr. Thompson, the steel broker is on the phone."

My friend grabbed the receiver. "Thompson, where is that steel shipment from Japan that was supposed to be in last weekend? . . . I don't care about weather. We're almost out of steel, and I'll have to close down the refrigerator assembly line next week. If you can't deliver when you promise, I'll find myself another broker."

"You get your steel from Japan?" I asked Baleful.

"Even with shipping costs, their price is still lower than steel made in Europe. We used to get all our sheets from Belgium, but the Japanese are now giving them a run for their money."

The buzzer on the phone alerted Baleful. He listened for a few moments and then said, "Excuse me, I have a call from Taiwan. Mark Four? Look, R&D designed a new push-button door handle and we're going to send the specs to you. Tell Mr. Chow if his people send us a sample of one and can make it for us at the same price as the old handle, we'll give his company the order."

A man came in with a plastic container and said, "Mr. Baleful, you said you wanted to see one of these before we ordered them. They are the containers for the ice maker in the refrigerator."

Baleful inspected it carefully and banged it on the floor a couple of times. "What's the price on it?"

"Hong Kong can deliver it at $2 a tray, and Dong-Fu Plastics in South Korea said they can make it for $1.70."

"It's just a plastic tray. Take the South Korea bid. We'll let Hong Kong supply us with the shelves for the freezer. Any word on the motors?"

"There's a German company in Brazil that just came out with a new motor, and it's passed all our tests, so Johnson has ordered 50,000."

"Call Cleveland Motors and tell them we're sorry, but the price they quoted us was just too high."

"Yes, sir," the man said and departed.

---

also generated interest in industrial policies designed to provide special help for allegedly "key" industries deemed critical to American industrial preeminence.

Increased American Indebtedness A trade deficit is also considered "unfavorable" because it must be financed by increased American indebtedness to foreigners. A trade deficit means we must borrow from the rest of the world to finance that deficit. This failure to "pay our way" in international trade is usually interpreted as a sign of domestic economic weakness and, hence, undesirable. However, economists point out that, at the time a trade or current account deficit is

occurring, it is clearly beneficial to American consumers. After all, a trade deficit means that Americans are currently receiving more goods and services as imports from the rest of the world than we are sending to the rest of the world as exports. Trade deficits augment our domestic living standards during the period in which they occur.

A related consequence of our recent trade deficits is that in 1985 the United States' status changed from that of a net creditor to that of a *net debtor* for the first time since 1914. That is, the United States now owes foreigners more than they owe this country. Recall that current account deficits are financed primarily by net

The secretary came in again and said, "Harry telephoned and wanted to let you know the defroster just arrived from Finland. They're unloading the box cars now."

"Good. Any word on the wooden crates from Singapore?"

"They're at the dock in Hoboken."

"Thank heaven. Cancel the order from Boise Cascade."

"What excuse should I give them?"

"Tell them we made a mistake in our inventory, or we're switching to plastic. I don't care what you tell them."

Baleful turned to me. "Where were we?"

"You were saying that if the consumer doesn't start buying American, this country is going to be in a lot of trouble."

"Right. It's not only his patriotic duty, but his livelihood that's at stake. I'm going to Washington next week to tell the Senate Commerce Committee that if they don't get off the stick, there isn't going to be a domestic refrigerator left in this country. We're not going to stay in business for our health."

"Pour it to them," I urged him.

Baleful said, "Come out with me into the showroom."

I followed him. He went to his latest model, and opened the door. "This is an American refrigerator made by the American worker, for the American consumer. What do you have to say to that?"

"It's beautiful," I said. "It puts foreign imports to shame."

Source: Art Buchwald, "Being Bullish on Buying American." Reprinted by permission. We discovered this article in *Master Curriculum Guide in Economics: Teaching Strategies for International Trade* (New York: Joint Council on Economic Education, 1988).

capital inflows to the United States. When our exports are insufficient to pay for our imports, we finance the difference by borrowing from foreigners or, in other words, by going into debt. The financing of our recent large trade deficits has caused foreigners to accumulate a larger volume of claims against American assets than we have accumulated against foreign assets. The U.S. foreign debt burden climbed to $721 billion in 1990, making us the largest debtor nation in the world.

One implication of net debtor status is that we can no longer look forward to a net inflow of dividend and interest payments (see item 7 in Table 38-1's balance of payments) to help cover deficits in our merchandise

and services trade. A second implication is that more of our corporations are foreign-owned.

The above comments on the economic effects of our trade deficit for the United States economy can be reversed as far as our industrialized trading partners are concerned. The current accounts of Japan and Germany, for example, tended to move toward surplus. These countries experienced an expansionary-inflationary stimulus and unusual growth in their export-dependent industries. They also increased their holdings of American debt.

QUICK REVIEW 38-4

♦ *In the 1980s and early 1990s the United States experienced large trade deficits, caused by a strong dollar, relatively rapid American growth prior to the 1990–1991 recession, and reduced purchases of our exports by less developed nations.*

♦ *These large deficits had a contractionary, anti-inflationary impact, hurt export-dependent industries, and resulted in the United States becoming a debtor nation; they also temporarily enhanced America's standard of living.*

Reducing the Trade Deficit

Two kinds of policies for reducing large trade deficits are most often cited: reduction of the Federal budget deficit and measures to accelerate economic growth abroad.

Reduction of the Budget Deficit Many economists agree that the most critical cause of our continuing trade deficits has been our large annual Federal budget deficits. It is argued that a reduction in the size of our Federal budget deficit will lower the real interest rate in the United States compared to other nations. In other words, a reduction in the government's demand for funds to finance its deficits will lower domestic interest rates and thus make financial investments in the United States less attractive to foreigners. The demand for dollars by foreigners will decline and the dollar will depreciate. Given a depreciated dollar, our exports will increase and imports will fall, correcting our trade deficit. This scenario is exactly opposite to the one shown earlier in Figure 18-2.

Would not a "managed" depreciation of the dollar by the G-7 nations produce a decline in the U.S. trade deficit, even without a reduction in our budget deficit? Perhaps so, but this point may be moot. Our trading partners have not been interested in allowing the dollar to fall appreciably below its 1988 level, unless we reduce our budget deficit. In effect, these nations contend that the United States must "get its fiscal house in order" to achieve a better balance of international trade.

Economic Growth Abroad The American trade deficit can also be reduced if nations abroad speed up their rates of economic growth. Higher levels of foreign national income increase the demand for American exports. The G-7 group of industrial nations has recognized the importance of economic growth in the nations which have trade surpluses as a way to reduce these surpluses and lower the American trade deficit. In the late 1980s, the governments of Japan and Germany established expansionary fiscal and monetary policies to bolster national income and increase the demand for goods produced in America.

Other "Remedies" There are several other possible "remedies" to the persistent United States' trade deficits.

Easy Money Policy Under appropriate circumstances, an easy money policy lowers real interest rates and reduces a trade deficit. The process works as follows. The decline in interest rates reduces the international demand for dollars, which results in a depreciation of the dollar. Dollar depreciation raises our exports and lowers our imports (Table 15-4).

Protective Tariffs Protective tariffs can be used to reduce imports, but this strategy results in the loss of the gains from specialization and international trade. Furthermore, it may not be successful: Tariffs which reduce our *imports* foster retaliatory tariffs abroad which reduce our *exports*. Trade deficits do not disappear in this circumstance; instead, all trading partners suffer declines in their living standards.

Recession Recessions in the United States reduce disposable income and thus spending on all goods, including imports. Because exports are largely unaffected, the decline in imports trims the trade deficit. This is precisely what happened in the United States during the recession of 1990–1991. But recession is an undesirable way to reduce trade deficits; it imposes higher economic costs (lost output) on society than the costs associated with the trade deficit itself. Also, unless the fundamental causes of the deficits have in the meanwhile been remedied, imports and thus trade deficits again rise when the economy begins to recover from recession.

Increased American Competitiveness The American trade deficits can be reduced by lowering the costs of, and improving the quality of, American goods and services relative to foreign goods. Cost-saving production technologies, development of improved products, and more efficient management techniques each can contribute to a decline in the trade deficit by lowering United States demand for imported goods and increasing foreign demand for American goods.

Direct Foreign Investment Ironically, our persistent trade deficit has set off a chain of events which has begun to feed back to reduce the trade deficit itself. The vast accumulation of American dollars in foreign hands has enabled foreign individuals and firms to buy American factories or to build new plants in the United States. Furthermore, the fall in the value of the dollar has provided an incentive for foreign firms to produce in the United States rather than in their own nations.

In short, the trade deficit has given rise to an increase in *direct foreign investment* in the form of plant and equipment. Foreign-owned factories are beginning to turn out increasing volumes of goods that otherwise would have been imported. Hondas and Mazdas, produced in American factories, have replaced Hondas and Mazdas formerly imported from Japan. Other examples abound. The upshot is that the American trade deficit may shrink as imports are replaced with goods produced in foreign-owned factories in the United States.

CHAPTER SUMMARY

1 American exports create a foreign demand for dollars and make a supply of foreign exchange available to Americans. Conversely, American exports simultaneously create a demand for foreign exchange and make a supply of dollars available to foreigners. Generally, a nation's exports earn the foreign currencies needed to pay for its imports.

2 The balance of payments records all international trade and financial transactions taking place between a given nation and the rest of the world. The trade balance compares merchandise exports and imports. The balance on goods and services compares exports and imports of both goods and services. The current account balance considers not only goods and services transactions, but also net investment income and net transfers.

3 A deficit on the current account will be largely offset by a surplus on the capital account. Conversely, a surplus on the current account will be largely offset by a deficit on the capital account. A balance of payments deficit occurs when the sum of the current and capital accounts is in deficit. A payments deficit is financed by drawing down official reserves. A balance of payments surplus occurs when the sum of the current and capital accounts is in surplus. A payments surplus results in an increase in official reserves. The desirability of a balance of payments deficit or surplus depends on its causes and its persistence over time.

4 Flexible or floating exchange rates are determined by the demand for and supply of foreign currencies. Under floating rates a currency will depreciate or appreciate as a result of changes in tastes, relative income changes, relative price changes, relative changes in real interest rates, and speculation.

5 Maintenance of fixed exchange rates requires adequate reserves to accommodate periodic payments deficits. If reserves are inadequate, nations must invoke protectionist trade policies, engage in exchange controls, or endure undesirable domestic macroeconomic adjustments.

6 Historically, the gold standard provided exchange rate stability until its disintegration during the 1930s. Under this system, gold flows between nations precipitated sometimes painful changes in price, income, and employment levels in bringing about international equilibrium.

7 Under the Bretton Woods system exchange rates were pegged to one another and were stable. Participating nations were obligated to maintain these rates by using stabilization funds, gold, or borrowings from the IMF. Persistent or "fundamental" payments deficits could be resolved by IMF-sanctioned currency devaluations.

8 Since 1971 a system of managed floating exchange rates has been in use. Rates are generally set by market forces, although governments intervene with varying frequency to alter their exchange rates.

9 Between 1980 and 1991 the United States experienced large international trade deficits. Causes include **a** a rapidly appreciating dollar between 1980 and 1985; **b** relatively rapid expansion of the American economy prior to the recession of 1990–1991; and **c** curtailed purchases of our exports by the less developed countries.

10 The effects of large trade deficits have been manifold. They have had a contractionary, anti-inflationary effect on our domestic economy. American export-dependent industries have experienced declines in output, employment, and profits, thereby generating political pressures for protection. The United States has become the world's largest debtor nation. However, the trade deficit has meant a current increase in the living standards of American consumers.

11 Two solutions to the trade deficit are **a** reduction of the budget deficit and **b** faster economic growth abroad. Other "remedies" are an easy money policy, protective tariffs, recession, improved U.S. competitiveness, and direct foreign investment.

TERMS AND CONCEPTS

balance of payments
current account
credits
debits
trade balance
balance on goods and services
balance on current account

capital account
balance on the capital account
official reserves
balance of payments deficits and surpluses
fixed exchange rates

flexible or floating exchange rates
depreciation and appreciation
purchasing power parity
gold standard
gold import and export

points
Bretton Woods system
International Monetary Fund
devaluation
managed floating exchange rates
G-7 nations

QUESTIONS AND STUDY SUGGESTIONS

1 Explain how an American automobile importer might finance a shipment of Toyotas from Japan. Demonstrate how an American export of machinery to Italy might be financed. Explain: "American exports earn supplies of foreign monies which Americans can use to finance imports."

2 "A rise in the dollar price of yen necessarily means a fall in the yen price of dollars." Do you agree? Illustrate and elaborate: "The critical thing about exchange rates is that

they provide a direct link between the prices of goods and services produced in all trading nations of the world." Explain the purchasing power parity theory of exchange rates.

3 The Swedish auto company Saab imports car components from Germany and exports autos to the United States. In 1990 the dollar depreciated, and the German mark appreciated, relative to the Swedish krona. Speculate as to how this hurt Saab—twice.

💾 **4** Indicate whether each of the following creates a demand for, or a supply of, French francs in foreign exchange markets:

    a An American importer purchases a shipload of Bordeaux wine

    b A French automobile firm decides to build an assembly plant in Los Angeles

    c An American college student decides to spend a year studying at the Sorbonne

    d A French manufacturer exports machinery to Morocco on an American freighter

    e The United States incurs a balance of payments deficit in its transactions with France

    f A United States government bond held by a French citizen matures

    g It is widely believed that the international value of the franc will fall in the near future

💾 **5** Explain why the American demand for Mexican pesos is downsloping and the supply of pesos to Americans is upsloping. Assuming a system of floating exchange rates between Mexico and the United States, indicate whether each of the following would cause the Mexican peso to appreciate or depreciate:

    a The United States unilaterally reduces tariffs on Mexican products

    b Mexico encounters severe inflation

    c Deteriorating political relations reduce American tourism in Mexico

    d The United States' economy moves into a severe recession

    e The Board of Governors embarks on a tight money policy

    f Mexican products become more fashionable to Americans

    g The Mexican government invites American firms to invest in Mexican oil fields

    h The rate of productivity growth in the United States diminishes sharply

6 Explain whether or not you agree with the following statements:

    a "A country which grows faster than its major trading partners can expect the international value of its currency to depreciate."

    b "A nation whose interest rate is rising more rapidly than in other nations can expect the international value of its currency to appreciate."

    c "A country's currency will appreciate if its inflation rate is less than that of the rest of the world."

7 "Exports pay for imports. Yet in 1990 the rest of the world exported about $108 billion more worth of goods and services to the United States than were imported from the United States." Resolve the apparent inconsistency of these two statements.

8 Answer the following questions on the basis of Scorpio's balance of payments for 1993 as shown below. All figures are in billions of dollars. What is the balance of trade? The balance on goods and services? The balance on current account? The balance on capital account? Does Scorpio have a balance of payments deficit or surplus? Would you surmise that Scorpio is participating in a system of fixed or flexible exchange rates? Are Scorpio's international transactions having a contractionary or expansionary effect on its domestic economy?

Merchandise exports	+$40	Net transfers	+$10
Merchandise imports	− 30	Capital inflows	+ 10
Service exports	+ 15	Capital outflows	− 40
Service imports	− 10	Official reserves	+ 10
Net investment income	− 5		

9 Explain in detail how a balance of payments deficit would be resolved under **a** the gold standard, **b** the Bretton Woods system, and **c** freely floating exchange rates. What are the advantages and shortcomings of each system?

10 Outline the major costs and benefits associated with a large trade or current account deficit. Explain: "A current account deficit means we are receiving more goods and services from abroad than we are sending abroad. How can that be called 'unfavorable'?"

11 Some people assert that the United States is facing a foreign trade crisis. What do you think they mean? What are the major causes of this "crisis"?

12 Cite and explain two reasons for the decline in the international value of the dollar between 1985 and 1987. Why did the U.S. trade deficit remain high, even though the dollar fell in value?

13 Explain how a reduction in the Federal budget deficit could contribute to a decline in the U.S. trade deficit. Why do trade deficits fall during recessions? Is recession a desirable remedy to trade deficits?

Growth and the Less Developed Countries

It is exceedingly difficult for the typical American family, whose 1990 average income was $35,353, to grasp the hard fact that some two-thirds of the world's population persistently lives at, or perilously close to, the subsistence level. In fact, hunger, squalor, and disease are commonplace in many nations of the world. The World Bank estimates that over 1 billion people—approximately 20 percent of the world's population—lives on less than $1 per day!

In this chapter we first identify the poor or less developed nations of the world. Second, we seek to determine why they are poor. What are the obstacles to growth? Third, the potential role of government in the process of economic development is considered. Fourth, international trade, private capital flows, and foreign aid are examined as vehicles of growth. Fifth, the external debt problems faced by many of the poor nations are analyzed. Finally, we present the demands of poor nations to establish a "new international economic order."

THE RICH AND THE POOR

Just as there is considerable income disparity among individual families within a nation (Chapter 35), so there also is great economic inequality among the family of nations. Table 39-1 identifies the following groups of nations.

1 Industrially Advanced Countries The **industrially advanced countries (IACs)** include the United States, Canada, Australia, New Zealand, Japan, and most of the nations of western Europe. These nations have developed market economies based on large stocks of capital goods, advanced production technolo-

gies, and well-educated labor forces. As column 1 of Table 39-1 indicates, the salient feature of these nineteen economies is a high per capita (per person) GNP.

2 Less Developed Countries Most of the remaining nations of the world[1]—located in Africa, Asia, and Latin America—are underdeveloped or **less developed countries (LDCs).** These ninety-seven nations are unindustrialized with their labor forces heavily committed to agriculture. Literacy rates are low, unem-

---

[1]We omit here the former Soviet Union and the eastern European nations which currently do not report their economic data.

are employed fewer hours or days per week than they desire, or work at jobs that do not fully use their skills.

Many economists contend that unemployment is high—perhaps as much as 15 to 20 percent—in the rapidly growing urban areas of the LDCs. Most less developed countries have experienced substantial migration of population from rural to urban areas. This migration is motivated by the *expectation* of finding jobs with higher wage rates than are available in agricultural and other rural employments. But this huge migration makes it unlikely that a migrant will in fact obtain a job. Migration to the cities has greatly exceeded the growth of urban job opportunities, resulting in very high urban unemployment rates. Thus, rapid rural-urban migration has given rise to urban unemployment rates which are two or three times as great as rural rates.

Underemployment is widespread and endemic to most LDCs. In many LDCs rural agricultural labor may be so abundant relative to capital and natural resources that a significant percentage of this labor contributes little or nothing to agricultural output. Similarly, many LDC workers are self-employed as proprietors of small shops, in handicrafts, or as street vendors. A lack of demand means that small shop owners or vendors spend more time in idleness in the shop or on the street. While they are not without jobs, they are underemployed.

Low Labor Productivity   Labor productivity tends to be very low in most LDCs. As we will see, the LDCs have found it difficult to invest in *physical capital*. As a result, their workers are underequipped with machinery and tools and are relatively unproductive.

In addition, most poor countries have not been able to invest sufficiently in their *human capital* (Table 39-2, columns 4 and 5); that is, expenditures on health and education have been meager. Low levels of literacy, malnutrition, absence of proper medical care, and insufficient educational facilities all contribute to populations ill equipped for economic development and industrialization.

Particularly vital is the absence of a vigorous entrepreneurial class willing to bear risks, accumulate capital, and provide the organizational requisites essential to economic growth. Closely related is the dearth of labor prepared to handle the routine supervisory functions basic to any program of development. Ironically, the higher education systems of many LDCs are oriented heavily toward the humanities and offer little work in business, engineering, and the sciences.

An additional irony is that, while migration from the LDCs has modestly offset rapid population growth, it has also deprived some LDCs of highly productive workers. Often the best-trained and most highly motivated workers—physicians, engineers, teachers, and nurses—leave the LDCs to seek their fortunes in the IACs. This so-called **brain drain** contributes to the deterioration in the overall skill level and productivity of the labor force.

Capital Accumulation

An important focal point of economic development is the accumulation of capital goods. There are several reasons for this emphasis on capital formation:

1   All LDCs suffer from a critical shortage of capital goods—factories, machinery and equipment, public utilities, and so forth. Better-equipped labor forces would greatly enhance their productivity and help boost the per capita standard of living. As we found in Chapter 19, there is a close relationship between output per worker (labor productivity) and real income per worker. A nation must produce more goods and services per worker to enjoy more goods and services per worker as income. One basic means of increasing labor productivity is to provide each worker with more tools and equipment. Indeed, empirical studies for the LDCs confirm a significant positive relationship between investment and the growth of GDP. On the average a 1 percentage point increase in the ratio of investment to GDP raises the overall growth rate by about one-tenth of 1 percentage point. Thus an increase in the investment-to-GDP ratio from 10 to 15 percent would increase the growth of real GDP by one-half of 1 percentage point.[3]

2   Increasing the stock of capital goods is crucial because of the very limited possibility of increasing the supply of arable land. If there is little likelihood of increasing agricultural output by increasing the supply of land, an alternative is to use more and better capital equipment with the available agricultural work force.

3   Once initiated, the process of capital accumulation *may* be cumulative. If capital accumulation can increase output ahead of population growth, a margin of saving may arise which permits further capital formation. In a sense, capital accumulation can feed on itself.

Let's first consider the prospects for less developed nations to accumulate capital domestically. Then

[3]International Monetary Fund, *World Economic Outlook* (Washington, D.C., 1988), p. 76.

we will examine the possibility of foreign capital flowing into them.

Domestic Capital Formation   A less developed nation—or any nation for that matter—accumulates capital through the processes of saving and investing. A nation must save or, in other words, refrain from consumption, to release resources from consumer goods production. Investment spending must then occur to absorb these released resources in the production of capital goods. But impediments to saving and investing are much greater in a low-income nation that in an advanced economy.

Savings Potential   Consider first the savings side of the picture. The situation here is mixed and varies greatly between countries. Some of the very poor countries such as Ethiopia, Bangladesh, Uganda, Haiti, and Madagascar save only from 2 to 5 percent of their domestic outputs. They simply are too poor to save a significant portion of their incomes. Interestingly, however, other less developed countries save as large a percentage of their domestic outputs as do advanced industrial countries. In 1989 India and China saved 21 and 36 percent of their domestic outputs, respectively, compared to 33 percent for Japan, 27 percent for West Germany, and 13 percent for the United States. The problem is that the domestic outputs of the LDCs are so low that even when saving rates are comparable to advanced nations, the total absolute volume of saving is not large. As we will see, foreign capital inflows and foreign aid are means of supplementing domestic saving.

Capital Flight   Many of the LDCs have experienced a substantial **capital flight.** Citizens of the LDCs have transferred their savings to, or invested their savings in, the IACs. The primary reason is that citizens of many LDCs regard the risks of investing at home to be high compared to the industrially advanced nations. These risks include loss of savings or real capital due to government expropriation, taxation, higher rates of inflation, or changes in exchange rates. If an LDC's political climate is volatile, savers may shift their funds overseas to a "save haven" in fear that a new government might confiscate their wealth. Likewise, rapid or galloping inflation in an LDC would have similar confiscatory effects (Chapter 8). The transfer of savings overseas may also be a means of evading domestic taxes on interest income or capital gains. Finally, financial capital may flow to the IACs because of higher interest rates or simply because of the greater variety of investment opportunities available in the industrialized countries.

Whatever the motivation, research studies suggest that capital flight from the LDCs is quantitatively significant. One estimate suggested that the five largest Latin American debtors had capital outflows of $101 billion of private assets between 1979 and 1984. At the end of 1987 Mexicans are estimated to have held some $84 billion in assets abroad. Foreign asset holdings for Venezuelans, Argentinians, and Brazilians were $58, $46, and $31 billion respectively. The critical point is that a significant portion of capital lending by the IACs to the LDCs is offset by LDC capital flights to the industrially advanced nations. The World Bank estimates that the inflows of foreign aid and loans to Latin America were essentially negated by corresponding capital flight in the 1980s.

Investment Obstacles   The investment side of the capital formation process abounds with equally serious obstacles. These obstacles undermine the rate of capital formation even when a sufficient volume of saving is available to finance the needed investment. Major obstacles to investment fall into two categories: lack of investors and lack of incentives to invest.

Oddly enough, in some less developed countries the major obstacle to investment is basically the lack of business executives willing to assume the risks associated with investment. This, of course, is a special case of qualitative deficiencies of the labor force previously discussed.

But even if substantial savings and a vigorous entrepeneurial class are present, an essential ingredient in capital formation—the incentive to invest—may be weak. A host of factors may combine in an LDC to cripple investment incentives. Indeed, we have just mentioned such factors as political instability and higher rates of inflation in our discussion of capital flight. Similarly, very low incomes mean a limited domestic market—a lack of demand—for most nonagricultural goods. This factor is especially crucial when one recognizes that the chances of successfully competing with mature industries of advanced nations in international markets are meager. Then, too, the previously cited lack of trained administrative and operating personnel may be a vital factor in retarding investment. Finally, many LDCs simply do not have an adequate **infrastructure,** that is, the public capital goods, which are prerequisite to private investment of a productive nature. Poor roads and bridges, inadequate railways, little gas and electricity production, antiquated communications, unsatisfactory housing, and meager educational and public health facilities scarcely provide an inviting environment for investment spending.

The absence of an adequate infrastructure presents more of a problem than one might first surmise. The dearth of public capital goods means that a great deal of investment spending which does not *directly* result in the production of goods and which may not be capable of bearing profits must take place before, and simultaneously with, productive investment in manufacturing machinery and equipment. Statistics for advanced nations indicate that about 60 percent of gross investment goes for housing, public works, and public utilities, leaving about 40 percent for directly productive investment in manufacturing, agriculture, and commerce.[4] These figures probably understate the percentage of total investment which must be devoted to infrastructure in emerging nations. The volume of investment required to initiate economic development may be much greater than it first appears.

One potential bright spot in this picture is the possibility of accumulating capital through *in-kind* or **nonfinancial investment.** Given leadership and willingness to cooperate, capital can be accumulated by transferring surplus agricultural labor to improvement of agricultural facilities or the infrastructure. If each agricultural village allocated its surplus labor to the construction of irrigation canals, wells, schools, sanitary facilities, and roads, significant amounts of capital might be accumulated at no significant sacrifice of consumer goods production. Nonfinancial investment simply bypasses the problems inherent in the financial aspects of the capital accumulation process. Such investment does not require consumers to save portions of their money income, nor does it presume the presence of an entrepreneurial class anxious to invest. In short, when leadership and cooperative spirit are present, nonfinancial investment is a promising avenue for accumulation of basic capital goods.

Technological Advance

Technological advance and capital formation are frequently part of the same process. Yet, there are advantages in treating technological advance—the discovery and application of new methods of producing—and capital formation, or the accumulating of capital goods, as separate processes.

[4]W. Arthur Lewis, *The Theory of Economic Growth* (Homewood, Ill.: Richard D. Irwin, Inc., 1955), p. 210.

The rudimentary state of technology in the LDCs puts these nations far from the frontiers of technological advance. There already exists an enormous body of technological knowledge accumulated by advanced nations which less developed countries *might* adopt and apply without undertaking expensive research. Adopting modern crop-rotation practices and contour plowing require no additional capital equipment, and may contribute significantly to productivity. By raising grain storage bins a few inches above ground, a large amount of grain spoilage can be avoided. Such changes may sound trivial to people of advanced nations. However, resulting gains in productivity can mean the difference between subsistence and starvation in some poverty-ridden nations.

In most instances application of either existing or new technological knowledge involves use of new and different capital goods. But, within limits, this capital can be obtained without an increase in the rate of capital formation. If the annual flow of replacement investment is rechanneled from technologically inferior to technologically superior capital equipment, productivity can be increased out of a constant level of investment spending. Actually, some technological advances may be **capital-saving** rather than **capital-using.** A new fertilizer, better adapted to a nation's topography and climate, might be cheaper than that currently employed. A seemingly high-priced metal plow which will last ten years may be cheaper in the long run than an inexpensive but technologically inferior wooden plow which requires annual replacement.

To what extent have LDCs transferred and effectively used available IAC technological knowledge? The picture is mixed. There can be no doubt that such technological borrowing has been instrumental in the rapid growth of such Pacific Rim countries as Japan, South Korea, Taiwan, and Singapore. Similarly, the OPEC nations benefited greatly from IAC knowledge of oil exploration, production, and refining. Recently the former Soviet Union and other eastern European nations are seeking western technology to revitalize their faltering economies.

At the same time, we must be realistic about the transferability of advanced technologies to less developed countries. In industrially advanced nations technologies are usually predicated on relatively scarce, highly skilled labor and relatively abundant capital. Such technologies tend to be capital-using or, alternatively stated, labor-saving. In contrast, less developed economies require technologies appropriate to *their* resource endowments or, in other words, to large quantities of abundant, unskilled labor and very limited quantities of capital goods. Labor-using and capital-saving technologies are typically appropriate to LDCs. Much of the highly advanced technology of advanced nations is therefore inappropriate in the less developed countries; they must develop their own technologies. Recall, too, that many less developed nations have "traditional economies" (Chapter 2) and are not highly receptive to change. This is particularly true in peasant agriculture which dominates the economies of most LDCs. A potential technological advance which fails can mean hunger and malnutrition; therefore, there is a strong propensity to retain traditional production techniques.

Sociocultural and Institutional Factors

Purely economic considerations are not sufficient to explain the occurrence or absence of economic growth. Substantial social and institutional readjustments are usually an integral part of the growth process. Economic development means not only changes in a nation's physical environment (new transportation and communications facilities, new schools, new housing, new plants and equipment), but also drastic changes in the ways people think, behave, and associate with one another. Emancipation from custom and tradition is frequently a fundamental prerequisite of economic development. A potentially critical but intangible ingredient in economic development is **the will to develop.** Economic growth may hinge on "what individuals and social groups *want,* and *whether they want it badly enough to change their old ways of doing things* and to work hard at installing the new."[5]

Sociocultural Obstacles Sociocultural impediments to growth are numerous and varied.
1 Some of the least developed countries have failed to achieve the preconditions for a national economic unit. Tribal allegiances take precedence over national identity. Warring tribes confine all economic activity within the tribe, eliminating any possibility for production-increasing specialization and trade.
2 Religious beliefs and observances may seriously restrict the length of the workday and divert resources which might have been used for investment to ceremonial uses. In rural India total ceremonial expenditures

are estimated at about 7 percent of per capita income.[6] Generally, religious and philosophical beliefs may be dominated by the **capricious universe view,** that is, the notion that there is little or no correlation between an individual's activities and endeavors, on the one hand, and the outcomes or experiences which that person encounters, on the other.

> If the universe is deemed capricious, the individual will learn to expect little or no correlation between actions and results. This will result in a fatalistic attitude. . . .
>   These attitudes impinge on all activities including saving, investment, long-range perspective, supply of effort, and family planning. If a higher standard of living and amassing of wealth is treated as the result of providence rather than springing from hard work and saving, there is little rationale for saving, hard work, innovations, and enterprise.[7]

3 The existence of a caste system—formal or informal—causes labor to be allocated to occupations on the basis of caste or tradition rather than on the basis of skill or merit. The result is clearly a misallocation of human resources.

Institutional Obstacles Political corruption and bribery are commonplace in many LDCs. School systems and public service agencies are often ineptly administered and their functioning impaired by petty politics. Tax systems are frequently arbitrary, unjust, cumbersome, and detrimental to incentives to work and invest. Political decisions are often motivated by a desire to enhance the nation's international prestige, rather than to foster development. For example, India's explosion of a nuclear bomb in 1974 created a substantial controversy over societal priorities.

Because of the predominance of farming in LDCs, the problem of achieving that institutional environment in agriculture most conducive to increasing production must be a vital consideration in any growth program. Specifically, the institutional problem of **land reform** demands attention in virtually all LDCs. But needed reform may vary tremendously between specific nations. In some LDCs the problem is excessive concentration of land ownership in the hands of a few wealthy families. This situation is demoralizing for tenants,

[5]Eugene Staley, *The Future of Underdeveloped Countries,* rev. ed. (New York: Frederick A. Praeger, 1961), p. 218.

[6]Inder P. Nijhawan, "Socio-Political Institutions, Cultural Values, and Attitudes: Their Impact on Indian Economic Development," in J. S. Uppal (ed.), *India's Economic Problems* (New Delhi: Tata McGraw-Hill Publishing Company, Ltd., 1975), p. 31.
[7]Ibid., p. 33.

weakening their incentive to produce, and is typically not conducive to capital improvements. At the other extreme is the absurd arrangement whereby each family owns and farms a minute fragment of land far too small for the application of modern agricultural technology. An important complication to the problem of land reform lies in the fact that political considerations sometimes push reform in that direction which is least defensible on economic grounds. For many nations, land reform may well be the most acute institutional problem to be resolved in initiating the process of economic development.

Examples: Land reform in South Korea undermined the political control of the landed aristocracy and made way for the development of strong commercial and industrial middle classes, all to the benefit of the country's economic development. In contrast, the prolonged dominance of the landed aristocracy in the Philippines has helped stifle the development of that economy.[8]

QUICK REVIEW 39-1

♦ **About three-fourths of the world's population lives in the LDCs of Africa, Asia, and Latin America.**

♦ **Natural resource scarcities and inhospitable climates restrict growth in many LDCs.**

♦ **The LDCs are characterized by overpopulation, high unemployment rates, underemployment, and low labor productivity.**

♦ **Low saving rates, capital flight, weak infrastructures, and lack of investors impair capital accumulation.**

♦ **Sociocultural and institutional factors are often serious impediments to growth.**

THE VICIOUS CIRCLE: A SUMMING UP

Many of the characteristics of LDCs just described are simultaneously causes and consequences of their poverty. These countries are caught in a **vicious circle of poverty.** They *stay* poor because they *are* poor! Consider Figure 39-1. The fundamental feature of an LDC is low per capita income. Being poor, a family has little ability or incentive to save. Furthermore, low incomes mean low levels of demand. Thus, there are few avail-

[8]Mrinal Datta-Chaudhuri, "Market Failure and Government Failure," *Journal of Economic Perspectives,* Summer, 1990, p. 36

able resources, on the one hand, and no strong incentives, on the other, for investment in physical or human capital. This means labor productivity is low. And, since output per person is real income per person, it follows that per capita income is low.

Many experts feel that the key to breaking out of this vicious circle is to increase the rate of capital accumulation, to achieve a level of investment of, say, 10 percent of the national income. But Figure 39-1 reminds us that the real villain for many LDCs—rapid population growth—may be waiting in the wings to undo the potentially beneficial effects of this higher rate of capital accumulation. For example, using hypothetical figures, suppose that initially an LDC is realizing no growth in its real GDP. But now it somehow manages to increase its saving and investment to 10 percent of its GDP. As a result, its real GDP begins to grow at, say, 2.5 percent per year. Given a stable population, real GDP per capita will also grow at 2.5 percent per year. If this persists, the standard of living will *double* in about 28 years. But what if population grows at the Latin American rate of 2.5 percent per year? Then real income per person is unchanged and the vicious circle persists.

More optimistically, *if* population can be kept constant or constrained to some growth rate significantly below 2.5 percent, then real income per person will rise. This implies the possibility of still further enlargement in the flows of saving and investment, continued advances in productivity, and the continued growth of per capita real income. In short, if a process of self-sustaining expansion of income, saving, investment, and productivity can be achieved, the self-perpetuating vicious circle of poverty can be transformed into a self-regenerating, beneficent circle of economic progress. The trick is to make effective those policies and strategies which will accomplish this transition.

ROLE OF GOVERNMENT

Economists do not agree on the appropriate role of government in seeking economic growth.

A Positive Role

One view is that, at least during initial stages of development, government should play a major role. The reasons for this stem in large part from the character of the obstacles facing LDCs.

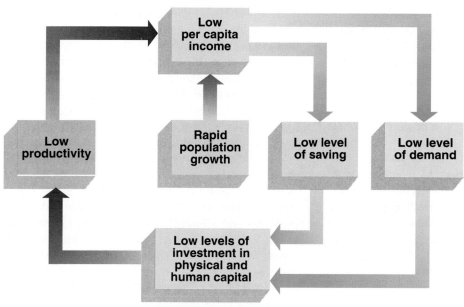

FIGURE 39-1 **The vicious circle of poverty**
Low per capita incomes make it extremely difficult for poor nations to save and invest, a condition that perpetuates low productivity and low incomes. Furthermore, rapid population growth may quickly absorb increases in per capita real income and thereby may negate the possibility of breaking out of the poverty circle.

1 Law and Order   Some of the poorest countries are plagued by widespread banditry and intertribal warfare which divert both attention and resources from the task of development. A strong and stable national government is needed to establish domestic law and order and to achieve peace and unity.

2 Lack of Entrepreneurship   The absence of a sizable and vigorous entrepreneurial class, ready and willing to accumulate capital and initiate production, indicates than in many cases private enterprise is intrinsically not capable of spearheading the growth process.

3 Infrastructure   Many obstacles to economic growth center on deficiencies of public goods and services, or, in other words, an inadequate infrastructure. Sanitation and basic medical programs, education, irrigation and soil conservation projects, and construction of highways and transportation-communication facilities are all essentially nonmarketable goods and services yielding widespread spillover benefits. Government is the sole institution in a position to provide these goods and services in required quantities.

4 Forced Saving and Investment   Government action may also be required to break through the saving-investment dilemma which impedes capital formation in LDCs.

It may well be that only governmental fiscal action can provide a solution by forcing the economy to accumulate capital. There are two alternatives. One is to force the economy to save by increasing taxes. These tax revenues can then be channeled into priority investment projects. The problems of honestly and efficiently administering the tax system and achieving a relatively high degree of compliance with tax laws are frequently very great.

The other alternative is to force the economy to save through inflation. Government can finance capital accumulation by creating and spending new money or by selling bonds to banks and spending the proceeds. The resulting inflation is the equivalent of an arbitrary tax on the economy.

There are serious arguments against the advisability of saving through inflation. In the first place, inflation tends to distort the composition of investment away from productive facilities to such items as luxury housing, precious metals and jewels, or foreign securities, which provide a better hedge against rising prices. Furthermore, significant inflation may reduce voluntary private saving as potential savers become less willing to accumulate depreciating money or securities payable in money of declining value. Internationally, inflation may boost the nation's imports and retard its flow of exports, creating balance of payments difficulties.

5 Social-Institutional Problems Government is in the key position to deal effectively with the social-institutional obstacles to growth. Controlling population growth and land reform are basic problems which call for the broad approach that only government can provide. And government is in a position to stimulate the will to develop, to change a philosophy of "Heaven and faith will determine the course of events" to one of "God helps those who help themselves."

Public Sector Problems

But serious problems and disadvantages may exist with a governmentally directed development program. If entrepreneurial talent is lacking in the private sector, can we expect leaders of quality to be present in the ranks of government? Is there not a real danger that government bureaucracy will impede, not stimulate, much-needed social and economic change? And what of the tendency of centralized economic planning to favor spectacular "showpiece" projects at the expense of less showy but more productive programs? Might not political objectives take precedence over the economic goals of a governmentally directed development program?

Development experts are significantly less enthusiastic about the potential role of government in the growth process than they were twenty-five or thirty years ago. Government maladministration and corruption are commonplace in many LDCs. Government officials often line their own pockets with foreign aid funds. Similarly, political leaders frequently confer monopoly privileges on relatives, friends, and political supporters. A political leader may grant exclusive rights to relatives or friends to produce, import, or export certain products. These monopoly privileges lead to higher domestic prices for the relevant products and diminish the LDC's ability to compete in world markets. Similarly, managers of state-owned enterprises are often appointed on the basis of cronyism rather than competence. In recent years the perception of

government has shifted from that of catalyst and promoter of growth to that of a potential impediment to development.

Once again it is possible to muster casual evidence on both sides of this question. Positive government contributions to development are evident in the cases of Japan, South Korea, and Taiwan. In comparison, Mobutu's Zaire, Marcos' Philippines, and Haiti under the Duvaliers are recognized examples of corrupt and inept governments which functioned as substantial impediments to economic progress. Certainly the revolutionary transformations of the former Soviet Union and other eastern European nations away from communism and toward market-oriented economies makes it clear that central planning is no longer widely recognized as an effective mechanism for development. Most LDCs have come to recognize that competition and individual economic incentives are important ingredients in the development process, and that their citizens need to see direct personal gains from their efforts to motivate them to take actions which will expand production.

ROLE OF THE ADVANCED NATIONS

What are the ways by which industrially advanced nations can help less developed countries in their quest for growth? To what degree have these avenues of assistance been pursued?

Generally, less developed nations can benefit from (1) an expanding volume of trade with advanced nations; (2) foreign aid in the form of grants and loans from governments of advanced nations; and (3) flows of private capital from more affluent nations. Let's consider these possibilities in the order stated.

Expanding Trade

Some authorities maintain that the simplest and most effective means by which the United States and other industrially advanced nations can aid less developed nations is by lowering international trade barriers, enabling LDCs to expand their national incomes through increased trade.

Though there is some truth in this view, lowered trade barriers are not a panacea. It is true that some poor nations need only large foreign markets for their raw materials to achieve growth. But the problem for many is not that of obtaining markets for utilizing existing productive capacity or the sale of relatively abundant raw materials, but the more fundamental one of getting the capital and technical assistance needed to produce something for export.

Furthermore, close trade ties with advanced nations are not without disadvantages. The old quip, "When Uncle Sam gets his feet wet, the rest of the world gets pneumonia," contains considerable truth for many less developed nations. A recession among the IACs can have disastrous consequences for the prices of raw materials and the export earnings of the LDCs. For example, in mid-1974 copper was $1.52 per pound; by the end of 1975 it had fallen to $.53 per pound! Stability and growth in industrially advanced nations are clearly important to progress in less developed countries.

Foreign Aid: Public Loans and Grants

Our vicious circle of poverty emphasizes the importance of capital accumulation in achieving economic growth. Foreign capital—both public and private—can be used to supplement an emerging country's saving and investment efforts and play a crucial role in breaking the circle of poverty.

As noted earlier, most LDCs have inadequate infrastructures. They are sadly lacking in basic public goods—irrigation and public health programs and educational, transportation, and communications systems—prerequisites to attracting either domestic or foreign private capital. Foreign public aid is needed to tear down this major roadblock to the flow of private capital to the LDCs.

Direct Aid The United States and other IACs have assisted LDCs directly through a variety of programs and through participating in international institutions designed to stimulate economic development. Over the 1976–1989 period. American aid to the LDCs—including both loans and grants—averaged $10 billion per year. In 1992 American aid was almost $15 billion. The bulk of this aid is administered by our Agency for International Development (AID). Some, however, takes the form of grants of surplus food under the Food for Peace program. Other advanced nations have also embarked on substantial foreign aid programs. In 1989 foreign aid from all industrially advanced nations was about $47 billion. In addition, the OPEC nations donated almost $2.5 billion.

The aid programs of the IACs merit several additional comments. First, aid is typically distributed on the basis of political and military, rather than economic, considerations. Israel, Turkey, and Greece are major recipients of American aid at the potential expense of Asian, Latin American, and African nations with much lower standards of living. Second, aid from the IACs only amounts to about one-third of 1 percent of the IACs' collective GDPs. Finally, LDCs are increasingly concerned that the shift of the former Soviet Union and eastern Europe toward more democratic, market-oriented systems will make these nations "new players" in the foreign aid field. The LDCs worry that IAC aid which formerly flowed to Latin America, Asia, and Africa may be partially redirected to, say, Poland, Hungary, and Russia.

The World Bank Group The United States is a major participant in the **World Bank,** whose major objective is assisting LDCs in achieving growth. Supported by some 157 member nations, the World Bank not only lends out of its capital funds, but also (1) sells bonds and lends the proceeds, and (2) guarantees and insures private loans.

Several characteristics of the World Bank merit comment.
1   The World Bank is a "last resort" lending agency; its loans are limited to productive projects for which private funds are not readily available.
2   Because many World Bank loans have been for basic development projects—multipurpose dams, irrigation projects, health and sanitation programs, communications and transportation facilities—it has been hoped that the Bank's activities will provide the infrastructure prerequisite to substantial flows of private capital.
3   The Bank has played a significant role in providing technical assistance to the LDCs by helping them discover what avenues of growth seem most appropriate for their economic development.

Two World Bank affiliates function in areas where the World Bank has been weak. The *International Finance Corporation (IFC)* has the primary function of investing in *private* enterprises in the LDCs. The *International Development Association (IDA)* makes "soft loans"—loans which may not be self-liquidating—to the poorest of the LDCs on more liberal terms than does the World Bank.

Private Capital Flows

The LDCs have also received substantial flows of private capital from the IACs. These private investors for the most part are large corporations and commercial

Solutions?

What, if anything, can be done to alleviate or correct the lingering LDC debt crisis? There seem to be two general routes to follow in seeking a solution.

One is to continue the piecemeal, country-by-country approach followed since 1982. The problem with this approach is that it may go on for decades, and, as it does, continue to thwart the possibilities that the highly indebted LDCs will achieve significant growth.

The other option is debt relief. The IACs might simply forgive a significant portion of outstanding LDC debt. There are several problems with this solution. First and most obviously, the forgiving of private debt imposes costs upon the lending commercial banks and their stockholders. The forgiving of public debt imposes costs on American and other IAC taxpayers. Second, any significant "write-down" of the debt will undoubtedly have a highly adverse effect on new private lending to LDCs. It is unrealistic to expect creditors to take large losses and then turn around and extend new loans. On the borrowing side, the problem is that debt forgiveness may be an invitation for LDCs to default on debts incurred in the future. Obviously, no easy solution to the debt issue presents itself.

QUICK REVIEW 39-2

♦ *LDC governments may encourage growth by a providing law and order; b engaging in entrepreneurial activities; c improving the infrastructure; d forcing higher levels of saving and investing; and e resolving social-institutional problems.*

♦ *The IACs can assist the LDCs through expanded trade, foreign aid, and private capital flows.*

♦ *Many LDCs have huge external debts which have become an additional obstacle to growth.*

TOWARD A "NEW INTERNATIONAL ECONOMIC ORDER"?[9]

Despite flows of private investment and foreign aid, the LDCs are far from content with their relationships with industrially advanced nations. As noted earlier, the absolute income gap between IACs and LDCs has widened over time. Furthermore, despite achieving political independence, LDCs feel that an economic-based **neocolonialism** persists. Both private investment and public aid, it is contended, have tended to exploit LDCs and keep them dependent upon, and subservient to, rich nations. In the past decade or so the LDCs have pressed more aggressively for basic changes in the international economic order which would accelerate their growth and redistribute world income to their benefit. In arguing for the creation of a **New International Economic Order (NIEO),** spokesmen for the LDCs make the following arguments and proposals.

1 Rules of the Game   Although they represent the vast majority of the world's population, LDCs have less than one-third of the total votes in the key international institutions which formulate the overall character of the world economy. Indeed, LDCs were simply not involved in the creation of the post-World War II institutions and programs which establish the rules and regulations by which international trade, finance, and investment are conducted. For example, the industrially advanced nations control the International Monetary Fund which provides monetary reserves for the financing of international trade. The LDCs question the equity and legitimacy of these rules and argue that the institutions and programs of the existing economic order are stacked against them.

2 Trade Barriers   Poor nations contend that, rhetoric to the contrary, advanced nations have retarded their development by using a variety of trade barriers—for example, tariffs and import quotas—to deprive them of export markets. The LDCs feel they are in a "Catch-22" situation. If they effectively use the financial and technical aid provided by advanced nations to create efficient low-cost manufacturing industries, the LDCs then become competitive with industries in the advanced nations. The IACs respond to this situation by using trade barriers to protect their domestic industries from the new competition. The LDCs have argued for **preferential tariff treatment**—that is, lower tariffs than those paid by developed countries—to stimulate their industrial growth.

---

[9]This section draws on Edwin P. Reubens, ed., *The Challenge of the New International Economic Order* (Boulder, Colo.: Westview Press, 1981), chap. 1; and Todaro, op. cit., pp. 559–565. For a detailed statement on the NIEO, see Mahbub ul Haq, *The Third World and the International Economic Order* (Washington: Overseas Development Council, 1976). The term "New International Economic Order" arose from a 1974 United Nations declaration on the problem of economic development.

3 Exploitation and Dependence   The LDCs also contend that most of the contracts, leases, and concessions which multinational corporations of advanced countries have negotiated with them have benefited the multinationals at the expense of the host countries. The poor countries argue that the major portion of benefits from the exploitation of their natural resources accrues to others. Furthermore, LDCs seek to achieve greater diversification and therefore greater stability in their economies. Foreign private capital, however, seeks out those industries which are currently the most profitable, that is, the ones now producing for the export market. In brief, while LDCs strive for less dependence on world markets, flows of foreign private capital often enhance that dependence. Exxon, Alcoa, United Fruit, and the rest are after profits and allegedly have no particular interest in either the economic independence, diversification, or overall progress of the LDCs.

4 Terms of Trade   As exporters of raw materials (bauxite, tin, copper, manganese) and basic farm products (cocoa, coffee, cotton, rubber, tea, timber), the LDCs are greatly affected by the extreme price fluctuations which characterize these highly competitive markets. In particular, the high variability of their import earnings makes it very difficult for LDCs to plan and finance development programs. Worse yet, the long-run price trend of LDC commodity exports has been downward. On the other hand, the LDCs import manufactured goods produced by the corporate giants of the advanced nations which have the market power to charge high prices. Thus the LDCs argue that over time the **terms of trade** have shifted against them; the prices of their exports tend to be depressed while the prices of their imports tend to rise. Hence, it takes more of the LDCs' exports to purchase a given quantity of imports.

The poor countries have pushed two proposals designed to relieve this alleged inequality. First, they seek establishment of a **stabilization fund** for some twenty basic food and raw material exports of major importance to them. The fund would be used to buy each of these various products when its world price fell and, conversely, to sell those products when world prices rose. Thus, prices would tend to be stabilized. The second proposal involves *indexing*. That is, LDCs want to tie the prices of their commodity exports to the prices they must pay for their imports from the IACs to maintain the purchasing power of their exports.

5 Debt Relief   The LDCs have also sought debt relief. Their view is that the present debt is so large that it constitutes a severe obstacle to LDC growth. Arguing that the prosperity of the IACs depends on the prosperity of the LDCs, LDCs feel that forgiving some portion of the debt would be mutually beneficial. Thus, in the fall of 1987 some twenty-four LDC governments sought both debt relief and additional loans at the annual joint meeting of the World Bank and the International Monetary Fund.

6 Aid and Redistribution   The LDCs take the position that past foreign aid has been insufficient and ineffective. It has been insufficient in that, as a group, the advanced nations have only made annual aid contributions equal to about one-third of 1 percent of their GDPs. Aid has been relatively ineffective for several reasons. First, much of it is "tied" to the donor country; for example, American aid must be spent on American goods and services. This means that the LDCs cannot "shop around" in world markets for potentially better buys on capital goods and technological assistance. Second, inflation has greatly eroded the real value of aid dollars to recipient nations. Third, as already noted, a large portion of aid must be used to pay interest on the external debts of the LDCs and, hence, is not available for development.

One of the objectives of the NIEO is to have each of the IACs progressively increase its aid to 0.7 percent of its GDP as recommended by the United Nations over a decade ago. This aid should have "no strings attached" and should be provided on a long-term and automatic basis. The influential Brandt Commission[10] has endorsed this 0.7 percent goal. This implies a doubling of the current level of developmental aid.

The NIEO agenda is very controversial. While the poor countries feel the NIEO proposals are egalitarian and just, many advanced nations envision them as a demand for a massive redistribution of world income and wealth which is simply not in the cards. Many industrialized nations feel that there is no "quick fix" for underdevelopment and that the LDCs must undergo the same process of patient hard work and gradual capital formation as did the advanced nations over the past two centuries.

---

[10]*North-South: A Program for Survival* (Cambridge, Mass.: MIT Press, 1980). This commission, which studied a far-ranging agenda of international economic issues, was chaired by Willy Brandt, former Chancellor of West Germany.

LAST WORD

FAMINE IN AFRICA

The roots of Africa's persistent famines include both natural and human causes.

Famine in Africa is not uncommon. The world was shocked during the 1984–1985 Ethiopian famine by pictures of fly-tormented, emaciated children with bloated bellies. Despite an outpouring of aid from the rich nations, that famine caused 1 million deaths. A number of African nations—including Ethiopia, Sudan, Angola, Liberia, Mozambique, and Malawi—are persistently threatened by famine. Various estimates put from 5 to 20 million Africans at risk. This tragic situation is especially ironic because most African countries were self-sufficient in food at the time they became independent nations; they are now heavily dependent on imported foodstuffs for survival.

The immediate and much-publicized cause of this catastrophe is drought. But the ultimate causes of Africa's declining ability to feed itself are more complex and multifaceted, an interplay of natural and human conditions. In addition to a lack of rainfall, these include chronic civil strife, rapid population growth, widespread soil erosion, and counterproductive public policies.

1   Civil Strife   Regional rebellions and prolonged civil wars have devastated some African nations. Both Ethiopia and the Sudan, for example, have been plagued by decades of civil strife. Not only do these conflicts divert precious resources from civilian uses, but they greatly complicate the ability of wealthy nations to provide famine and developmental aid. Ethiopia's government has often denied food aid to areas occupied by antigovernment forces. Donated food is frequently diverted to the army and denied to starving civilians.

2   Population Growth   The hard fact is that in Africa population is growing more rapidly than is food production. Specifically, population is increasing at about 3 percent per year while food output is growing at only 2 percent per year. This grim arithmetic suggests de-

CHAPTER SUMMARY

1   Most of the nations of the world are less developed (low per capita income) nations. While some LDCs have been achieving quite rapid growth rates in recent years, others have realized little or no growth at all.

2   Initial scarcities of natural resources and the limited possibility of augmenting existing supplies may impose a serious limitation on a nation's capacity to develop.

3   The presence of large and rapidly growing populations in most LDCs contributes to low per capita incomes. In particular, increases in per capita incomes frequently induce rapid population growth, to the end that per capita incomes again deteriorate to near subsistence levels.

4   Most LDCs suffer from both unemployment and underemployment. Labor productivity is low because of insufficient investment in physical and human capital.

5   In many LDCs both the saving and investment aspects of capital formation are impeded by formidable obstacles. In some of the poorest LDCs the savings potential is very low. Many LDC savers have chosen to transfer their funds to the IACs rather than invest domestically. The absence of a vig-

clining living standards, hunger, and malnutrition. The World Bank reports that during the 1980s the per capita incomes of the sub-Saharan nations fell to about three-quarters of the level reached by the end of the 1970s.

3 Ecological Degradation But apart from the simple numbers involved, population growth has apparently contributed to the ecological degradation of Africa. Given population pressures and the increasing need for food, marginal land has been deforested and put into crop production. In many cases trees which have served as a barrier to the encroachment of the desert have been cut for fuel, allowing the fragile topsoil to be blown away by desert winds. The ultimate scarcity of wood which has accompanied deforestation has forced the use of animal dung for fuel, thereby denying its traditional use as fertilizer. Furthermore, traditional fallow periods have been shortened, resulting in overplanting and overgrazing and, in simple terms, a wearing out of the soil. Deforestation and land overuse have reduced the capacity of the land to absorb moisture, diminishing its productivity and its ability to resist drought. Some authorities feel that the diminished ability of the land to absorb water reduces the amount of moisture which evaporates into the clouds to return ultimately as rainfall. All of this is complicated by the fact that there are few facilities for crop storage. Thus, even when crops are good, it is difficult to accumulate a surplus for future lean years. A large percentage of domestic farm output in some parts of Africa is lost to rats, insects, and spoilage.

4 Public Policies and Debt Ill-advised public policies have contributed to Africa's famines. In the first place, African governments have generally neglected investment in agriculture in favor of industrial develop-

ment and military strength. It is estimated that African governments on the average spend four times as much on armaments as they do on agriculture. Over 40 percent of Ethiopia's budget is for the support of an oppressive military. Second, many African governments have followed the policy of establishing the prices of agricultural commodities at low levels to provide cheap food for growing urban populations. This low-price policy has diminished the incentives of farmers to increase productivity. While foreign aid has helped to ease the effects of Africa's food-population problems, most experts reject aid as a long-term solution. Indeed, experience suggests that aid in the form of foodstuffs can only provide temporary relief and may undermine the realization of long-run local self-sufficiency. Foreign food aid, it is contended, merely treats symptoms and not causes.

All of this is made more complex by the fact that the sub-Saharan nations are burdened with relatively large and growing external debts. The IMF reports that the aggregate debt of these nations rose from $21 billion in 1976 to $127 billion in 1990. As a condition of further aid, these nations have had to invoke austerity programs which have contributed to declines in their per capita incomes. One tragic consequence is that many of these nations have cut back on social service programs for children. A UNICEF spokesman has indicated that 3 million children died in 1987 worldwide "because they didn't have 50 cents worth of vaccine in them."

To summarize: the famine confronting much of Africa is partly a phenomenon of nature and in part self-inflicted. Drought, overpopulation, ecological deterioration, and errant public policies have all been contributing factors. This complex of causes implies that hunger and malnutrition in Africa may persist long after the rains return.

---

orous entrepreneurial class and the weakness of investment incentives are also serious impediments to capital accumulation.

6   Appropriate social and institutional changes and, in particular, the presence of "the will to develop" are essential ingredients in economic development.

7   The vicious circle of poverty brings together many of the obstacles to growth, saying in effect that "poor countries stay poor because of their poverty." Low incomes inhibit saving and accumulation of physical and human capital, making it difficult to increase productivity and incomes. Rapid population growth can offset otherwise promising attempts to break the vicious circle.

8   The nature of the obstacles to growth—the absence of an entrepreneurial class, the dearth of infrastructure, the saving-investment dilemma, and the presence of social-institutional obstacles to growth—suggests the need for government action in initiating the growth process. However, the corruption and maladministration which are quite common to the public sectors of the LDCs suggest that government may be relatively ineffective as an instigator of growth.

9   Advanced nations can assist in development by reducing trade barriers and by providing both public and private capital.

10   Rising energy prices, declining export prices, depreciation of the dollar, and concern about LDCs' creditworthiness

combined to create an LDC debt crisis in the early 1980s. External debt problems of LDCs remain serious and inhibit their growth.

11 The LDCs are calling for a New International Economic Order (NIEO) which will give them **a** a greater voice in the policies of international financial institutions, **b** preferential tariff treatment, **c** a greater share of the income derived from contracts and leases negotiated with multinational corporations, **d** improved terms of trade, **e** cancellation or rescheduling of their external debts, and **f** a larger and automatic inflow of foreign aid.

TERMS AND CONCEPTS

industrially advanced
    countries (IACs)
less developed
    countries (LDCs)
unemployment and
    underemployment
brain drain
capital flight

infrastructure
nonfinancial
    investment
capital-saving and
    capital-using
    technological
    advance

the will to develop
capricious universe
    view
land reform
vicious circle of poverty
World Bank
neocolonialism

New International
    Economic Order
    (NIEO)
preferential tariff
    treatment
terms of trade
stabilization fund

QUESTIONS AND STUDY SUGGESTIONS

1 What are the major characteristics of an LDC? List the major avenues of economic development available to such a nation. State and explain obstacles which face LDCs in breaking the poverty barrier. Use the "vicious circle of poverty" to outline in detail steps an LDC might take to initiate economic development.

2 Explain how the absolute per capita income gap between rich and poor nations might increase, even though per capita GDP is growing faster in LDCs than it is in IACs.

3 Discuss and evaluate:

    a "The path to economic development has been clearly blazed by American capitalism. It is only for the LDCs to follow this trail."

    b "Economic inequality is conducive to saving, and saving is the prerequisite of investment. Therefore, greater inequality in the income distribution of the LDCs would be a spur to capital accumulation and growth."

    c "The IACs fear the complications which stem from oversaving; the LDCs bear the yoke of undersaving."

    d "The core of the development process involves changing human beings more than it does altering a nation's physical environment."

    e "America's 'foreign aid' program is a sham. In reality it represents neocolonialism—a means by which the LDCs can be nominally free in a political sense but remain totally subservient in an economic sense."

    f "Poverty and freedom cannot persist side by side; one must triumph over the other."

    g "The biggest obstacle facing poor nations in their quest for development is the lack of capital goods."

    h "A high per capita GDP does not necessarily identify an industrially advanced nation."

4 Explain how population growth might be an impediment to economic growth. How would you define the optimal population of a country? Some experts argue that children are "net assets" in poor countries, but "net liabilities" in rich countries. Can you provide a rationale for this assertion? If the statement is true, does it imply that a rising per capita income is the prerequisite for population control?

5 Much of the initial investment in an LDC must be devoted to infrastructure which does not directly or immediately lead to a greater production of goods and services. What bearing might this have on the degree of inflation which results as government finances capital accumulation through the creating and spending of new money?

6 "The nature of the problems faced by the LDCs creates a bias in favor of a governmentally directed as opposed to a decentralized development process." Do you agree? Substantiate your position.

7 What is the LDC debt crisis? How did it come about? What solutions can you offer?

8 What types of products do the LDCs export? Can you use Chapter 37's law of comparative advantage to explain the character of these exports?

9 Outline the main components of the New International Economic Order proposed by the LDCs. Which of these demands do you feel are most justified?

10 What would be the implications of a worldwide policy of unrestricted immigration between nations for economic efficiency and the global distribution of income?

11 Use Figure 39-1 (changing box labels as necessary) to explain rapid economic growth in a country such as Japan or South Korea. What factors other than those contained in the figure might contribute to growth?

C H A P T E R
40

The Soviet Economy in Transition

In 1957 Communist Party Chairman Nikita Khrushchev bluntly asserted that the centrally planned Soviet economy would prove itself superior to the United States economy:

> We declare war upon you—excuse me for using such an expression—in the peaceful field of trade. We declare war. We will win over the United States. The threat to the United States is not the ICBM, but in the field of peaceful production. We are relentless in this and it will prove the superiority of our system.

But in October of 1990 Soviet President Mikhail Gorbachev announced to the world that the Soviet economy was unraveling:

> The position of the economy continues to deteriorate. The volume of production is declining. Economic links are being broken. Separatism is on the increase. The consumer market is in dire straits. The budget deficit and the solvency of the government are now at critical levels. Antisocial behavior and crime are increasing. People are finding life more and more difficult and are losing their interest in work and their belief in the future. The economy is in very great danger. The old administrative system of management has been destroyed but the impetus to work under a market system is lacking. Energetic measures must be taken, with the consent of the public, to stabilize the situation and to accelerate progress towards a market economy.

In the early 1990s there was compelling evidence that the economy of the former Soviet Union was in severe disarray. Consumers were queuing up for hours to buy food and shoddy consumer goods, frequently to find only empty store shelves. One-fifth of 1991's grain production was either unharvested or left to rot because of inadequate storage and transportation. Government rationing of consumer staples was common and black markets were flourishing. Confidence in the monetary unit—the ruble—was rapidly waning and exchange by the use of such "hard" foreign currencies as dollars, yen, and marks and by barter was be-

early years of planning there was substantial surplus labor in agriculture which the plans reallocated to industrial production. Similarly, a larger proportion of the population was induced or coerced into the labor force. Early Soviet growth was achieved through the use of more inputs rather than using given inputs more productively. In the 1930s and again in the early post-World War II era, this strategy produced growth rates greater than the United States and other industrialized nations.

4 Allocation by Directives   Soviet central planners directed the allocation of inputs among industries and firms, thereby determining the composition of output. Planning directives were substituted for the market or price system as an allocational mechanism.

5 Government Price Fixing   In the former Soviet Union prices were set by government direction rather than by the forces of demand and supply. Consumer good prices were changed infrequently and, as a matter of social policy, the prices of "necessities"—for example, housing and many foodstuffs—were established at low levels. Rents on Soviet housing averaged only about 3 percent of income and did not change between 1928 and 1992! Input prices and the price of an enterprise's output were also governmentally determined and were used primarily as accounting devices to gauge a firm's progress in meeting its production target.

6 Self-Sufficiency   The Soviet Union viewed itself as a single socialist nation surrounded by hostile capitalistic countries. Therefore, the central plans stressed economic self-sufficiency. Trade with western nations was greatly restricted because the ruble was not convertible into other currencies. Soviet trade was largely with the other communist bloc nations of eastern Europe.

7 Passive Macroeconomic Policies   The Soviet economy has been a quantity-directed system with money and prices playing only a limited role in resource allocation. Unlike most market economies, monetary and fiscal policies were passive rather than active in the Soviet Union. In the United States and other market systems, monetary and fiscal policies are used to manipulate the aggregate levels of output, employment, and prices. Historically, unemployment in the Soviet Union has been kept very low, perhaps only 1 or 2 percent of the labor force. This is partly the result of ambitious planning targets and various admonitions to work. Low unemployment has also been due to over-staffing (managers cannot fire redundant workers), a disinterest in cost-minimization (gross output being the overriding objective), and a population whose growth rate has been steadily diminishing.

Similarly, government price determination was the primary device used to control the price level. The state banking system, *Gosbank,* issued credit or working capital to enterprises, based on what was needed to fulfill their planned production targets. But it did not use, and did not have the control mechanisms, to manipulate the money supply to achieve macroeconomic stability.

The Coordination Problem

The market system is a powerful organizing force which coordinates millions of individual decisions by consumers, resources suppliers, and businesses, and fosters a reasonably efficient allocation of scarce resources. It is not an easy matter to substitute central planning as a coordinating mechanism.

A simple example illustrates this problem. Suppose a Soviet enterprise in Minsk is producing men's shoes. Planners must establish a realistic production target for that enterprise and then see that all the necessary inputs—labor, electric power, leather, rubber, thread, nails, appropriate machinery, transportation—for production and delivery of that product are made available. When we move from a simple product such as shoes to more complex products such as television sets and farm tractors, planners' allocational problems are greatly compounded.

Because the outputs of many industries are inputs to other industries, the failure of any single industry to fulfill its output target is likely to cause a whole chain of adverse repercussions. If iron mines—for want of machinery or labor or transportation inputs—fail to supply the steel industry with the required inputs of iron ore, the steel industry in turn will be unable to fulfill the input needs of the myriad industries dependent on steel. All these steel-using industries—for example, automobiles, tractors, and transportation—will therefore be unable to fulfill their planned production goals. And so the bottleneck chain reaction goes on to all those firms which use steel parts or components as inputs.

There were some 47,000 industrial enterprises producing goods in the former Soviet Union. The central planners had to see that all the resources needed by these enterprises to fulfill their assigned production targets were somehow allocated to them.

The literally billions of planning decisions that must be made to achieve consistency result in a complex and complete interlocking of macro- and micro- management . . . . The number of planned interconnections increases more rapidly than the size of the economy . . . . Even with the most sophisticated mathematical techniques and electronic computers, the task of interrelating demands and factor inputs for every possible item by every possible subcategory becomes impossible for the central planners alone.[3]

There is much evidence from Soviet sources indicating that bottlenecks occurred with alarming regularity in the 1980s and early 1990s. Moreover, bottlenecks were nothing new to the Soviet economy.

> The Byelorussian Tractor Factory, which has 227 suppliers, had its production line stopped 19 times in 1962 because of the lack of rubber parts, 18 times because of ball bearings, and 8 times because of transmission components. The pattern of breakdowns continued in 1963. During the first quarter of 1963 only about one-half of the plant's ball bearing and rubber needs were satisfied, and only half of the required batteries were available. One supplier shipped 19,000 less wheels than called for in the contract. In total, they were short of 27 different items. . . .
>
> It is not surprising that 90 enterprises out of 100 surveyed in the Chelyabinsk region blamed their underfulfillment of production plans in 1962 on supply deficiencies.[4]

QUICK REVIEW 40-1

＊ *Marxian ideology is based on the labor theory of value and views capitalism as a system for expropriating profits or surplus value from workers.*

＊ *The primary institutional features of the former Soviet economy were state ownership of property resources and central economic planning.*

＊ *Soviet plans were characterized by a an emphasis on rapid industrialization and military power, b resource overcommitment; c growth through the use of more inputs rather than greater efficiency; d resource allocation by government directives rather than markets; e government price determination; f an emphasis on economic self-sufficiency; and g passive monetary and fiscal policies.*

＊ *The basic planning problem is to direct needed resources to each enterprise so that production targets can be achieved.*

THE FAILURE OF SOVIET COMMUNISM

Soviet economic growth in the 1950s and 1960s was impressive. In the 1950s Soviet real domestic output expanded at roughly 6 percent per year compared to about 3 percent for the United States. The Soviet economy continued to grow at about 5 percent per year in the 1960s. But growth fell to an annual rate of about $2\frac{1}{2}$ or 3 percent in the 1970s and further declined to 2 percent by the mid-1980s. More recent data indicate that growth has halted and in the last few years real domestic output has declined. Official Soviet estimates indicate that real domestic output fell by 4 percent in 1990 and 14 percent in 1991.

Further evidence of economic failure is reflected in the quality of goods. In such vital manufacturing sectors as computers and machine tools it is estimated that Soviet technology lags some seven to twelve years behind that of the United States. Overall, the quality of most Soviet manufactured goods is far short of international standards. Consumer goods are of notoriously poor quality and product assortment is greatly limited. Durable goods— automobiles, refrigerators, and consumer electronics products—are primitive by world standards. Furthermore, widespread shortages of basic goods, interminable shopper queues, black markets, and corruption in the distribution of products are all characteristic of the consumer sector.

The major contributing factor to the downfall of Soviet communism has been its inability to efficiently supply the goods and services which consumers want to buy. In the early decades of Soviet communism the government established a "social contract" with its citizenry to the effect that, by enduring the consumer sacrifices associated with the high rates of saving and investment necessary for rapid industrialization and growth, the population would be rewarded with consumer abundance in the future (Figure 2-4). The failure of the system to meet consumer expectations has contributed to frustration and deteriorating morale among consumers and workers. "All future and no present, certainly as in the USSR after six decades, begins to appear after a while more like a long term confidence game than a meaningful program of economic development."[5]

Comparisons with the United States are revealing. While the United States has 565 cars and 789 tele-

[3]Barry M. Richman, *Soviet Management* (Englewood Cliffs, N.J.: Prentice-Hall, Inc., 1965), p. 17.
[4]Ibid., p. 123.

[5]Marshall I. Goldman, *USSR in Crisis: The Failure of an Economic System* (New York: W. W. Norton & Company, 1983), p. 175.

tional markets. In general, over an extended period Soviet enterprises produced the same products with the same techniques, with both goods and techniques becoming increasingly obsolete by world standards.

Nor were individual workers motivated to work hard, because of a lack of material incentives. Because of the low priority assigned to consumer goods in the Five-year Plans, there was only a limited array of relatively low-quality goods and services available to Soviet workers–consumers. (The price of an automobile is far beyond the means of average factory workers, and for those able to buy, the waiting period may be one to five years.) While hard work might result in promotions and bonuses, the increase in *money* income did not translate into a proportionate increase in *real* income. As we will note later, there was a substantial amount of involuntary saving—a "ruble overhang"—in the Soviet Union because of a lack of consumer goods. Why work hard for additional income if there is nothing to buy with the money you earn? As a Soviet worker once lamented to a western journalist: "The government pretends to pay us and we pretend to work."

THE GORBACHEV REFORMS

The deteriorating Soviet economy of the 1970s and early 1980s prompted President Mikhail Gorbachev to introduce in 1986 a reform program described as **perestroika,** a restructuring of the economy. This economic restructuring was accompanied by **glasnost,** a campaign for greater openness and democratization in both political and economic affairs. Under *glasnost,* workers, consumers, enterprise managers, political leaders, and others were provided greater opportunity to voice complaints and make suggestions for improving the functioning of the economy.

Basically, the **Gorbachev reforms** involved six interrelated elements: (1) the modernization of industry; (2) greater decentralization of decision making; (3) provision for a limited private enterprise sector; (4) improved worker discipline and incentives; (5) a more rational price system; (6) an enlarged role in the international economy.

Modernization was sought through reallocation of investment toward research and development and toward high-tech industries. Decentralization of decision making was intended to keep the planning bureaucracy from interfering in the day-to-day internal operations of individual enterprises. In exchange for greater enterprise autonomy, enterprise success indicators were reoriented from output targets to profitability, thus obligating enterprises to be more conscious of the salability (quality) of their products.

Small-scale private production of some consumer goods and services—such as clothing, furniture, rugs, taxi transport, hairdressing, and appliance repair—was also permitted. But those engaged in such activities also had to hold full-time state jobs or be housewives or retirees. The size of these private enterprises was limited by the Marxist prohibition on hiring someone else's labor.

The Gorbachev reforms also attempted to improve the human factors in production. Actions were taken to dismiss incompetent planners and enterprise managers, trim the size of the planning bureaucracies, and improve worker attitudes and behavior. Campaigns against corruption and alcoholism would reduce inefficiency resulting from theft, absenteeism, industrial accidents, and high worker turnover.

Price reforms would reduce over time the number of prices fixed by central planning with such prices ultimately applying only to what was regarded as the most essential consumer and producer goods. Enterprises were to be able to negotiate sales contracts in much the same manner as capitalist firms.

The reforms also hinted at closer economic relationships with the industrialized nations of the west. A related effort was to encourage joint ventures in the Soviet Union with western firms in a wide variety of activities ranging from fast-food restaurants to construction and operation of petrochemical plants. Such ventures were undoubtedly viewed by the Soviets as an inexpensive means of acquiring western technologies and management skills.

While *perestroika* met with some initial success, it did not comprehensively address the systemic economic problems facing the Soviet Union. In retrospect, *perestroika* was more in the nature of traditional Soviet "campaigns" to elicit better performance within the general framework of the planned economy. It was *not* an overall program of institutional change such as those adopted by Poland and Hungary. Thus, in 1986–1987 the Soviet economy was stagnating; some estimates put its growth rate at only 2 percent per year, while others indicated it did not grow at all. Sharply declining world oil prices also were damaging because the Soviet Union is a major oil exporter. In any event, by 1990 *perestroika* had given way to a greater emphasis on sweeping reforms designed to create a western-style market economy.

◢   *The failure of central planning in the former Soviet Union was evidenced by diminished growth rates, low-quality goods, and the failure to provide a rising standard of living.*

◢   *The recent collapse of the Soviet economy is attributable to a a large military burden; b chronic inefficiencies in agriculture; c the need to expand real output by increasing input productivity rather than increasing the quantity of inputs; d the inability of traditional planning techniques to deal with the growing complexity of the Soviet economy; e inadequate success indicators; and f ineffectual incentives to produce, innovate, and work.*

◢   *The Gorbachev reforms of the late 1980s centered on* perestroika *("restructuring") and* glasnost *("openness") but failed to provide major systemic change.*

TRANSITION TO A MARKET SYSTEM

The former Soviet republics—particularly Russia—have committed themselves to making the transition to a market economy. What are the components of such a dramatic reform program?

Privatization

If entrepreneurship is to come into existence, private property rights must be established and protected by law. This means that existing government property—farmland, housing, factories, machinery and equipment, stores—must be transferred to private owners. It also means that new private firms must be allowed to form and develop.

It is not yet clear how this can be effectively and equitably accomplished, but there are a number of options. Small enterprises and retail outlets might be sold directly to private individuals or cooperatives through public auctions. Another possibility is employee stock ownership plans where workers, aided by government loans, buy an enterprise and then retire their debt from future earnings. The privatization of large state enterprises may be more difficult. One proposal is for the government to distribute vouchers, each having a designated monetary value, to all citizens. Owners of these vouchers can then pool them in the purchase of enterprises. An interim option is the "commercialization" of

Soviet enterprises, meaning that the firm is made financially and managerially independent but remains publicly owned. Privatization is made more complex because it is difficult to determine the economic value of an enterprise in the absence of genuine product and resource prices.

Promotion of Competition

The industrial sector of the former Soviet Union consisted of some 47,000 large state-owned enterprises in which average employment exceeded 800 workers. An estimated 30 to 40 percent of total industrial production comprised products for which there was only one producer. When several enterprises produce a given product, their actions were usually coordinated by the planning process to create a cartel. In short, much Commonwealth production took place under monopoly or near-monopoly conditions.

Realization of a reasonably efficient market economy requires the dismantling of these public monopolies and the creation of antitrust laws to sustain competition. Privatization without "demonopolization" will be of limited benefit to the economy. Existing monopolies must be restructured or split apart as separate, competing firms. For example, a tractor manufacturing enterprise with four plants could be separated into four independent and competing firms. The establishment and guarantee of property rights are prerequisite to the creation and entry of new firms into previously monopolized industries. Joint ventures between Commonwealth and foreign companies provide a further avenue for increasing competition, as does opening the economy to international trade. Recent legislation has opened the door for foreign firms to invest directly in the new Commonwealth.

Limited and Reoriented Role for Government

The transition to a market economy will sharply curtail government's economic role. The government must reduce its involvement to those tasks associated with a market economy: providing an appropriate legal framework; maintaining competition; reducing excessive inequality in the distribution of income and wealth; making market adjustments where spillover costs or benefits are large; providing public goods and services; and stabilizing the economy (Chapter 6).

Many of these functions will be new to the governments within the Commonwealth, at least in the environment of a market system. Unemployment and overt inflation were not evident to Soviet citizens under central planning. Historically, ambitious production plans and overstaffing of enterprises have made for very low unemployment rates while government price-setting has been a direct means of controlling the price level. The task will be to develop monetary and fiscal policies—and institutional arrangements appropriate to their implementation—to indirectly provide macroeconomic stability. Restructuring will likely result in substantial short-run unemployment as inefficient public enterprises are closed or fail to be viable under private ownership. Thus, a priority goal will be to establish a social safety net for Soviet citizens. In particular, a program of unemployment insurance must be established, not only on equity grounds but also to reduce worker resistance to the transition. Similarly, antitrust legislation of some sort will be needed to maintain reasonably competitive markets.

Price Reform: Removing Controls

Unlike competitive market prices, the prices established by the government bear no relationship to the economic value of either products or resources. In an effectively functioning competitive market system the price of a product equates, at the margin, the value consumers place on that good and the value of the resources used in its production. When free markets achieve this equality for all goods and services, the economy's scarce resources are being used efficiently to satisfy consumer wants.

But, as noted, in the former Soviet Union both input and output prices were fixed by government and in many instances were not changed for extended periods of time. Because input prices did not measure the relative scarcities of various resources, it was impossible for a firm to minimize real production costs. That is, with fixed prices it is impossible to produce a unit of X in such a way as to minimize sacrifice of alternative goods. Example: Relatively high energy prices have caused firms in market economies to curtail its use. But energy has been underpriced in the former Soviet Union (the world's largest producer of energy) and its industries use two to three times as much energy per unit of output as do leading industrial countries.

A difficult problem arises in making the transition from government- to market-determined prices because historically the prices of many basic consumer goods have been fixed at low levels. The Soviet rationale for this was that low prices would ensure everyone

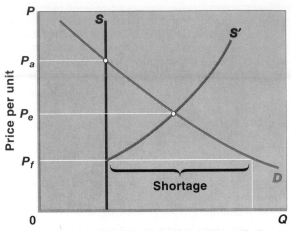

FIGURE 40-1   The effects of government price fixing

Central planners establish below-equilibrium prices such as P_f on many basic consumer goods to make them widely available to everyone. But in fact at such low prices quantity demanded exceeds quantity supplied and this shortage means that many consumers cannot obtain such goods. Assuming no privatization, abandonment of government price fixing would raise price from P_f to P_a. With privatization and an accompanying increase in output as price rises, price would increase from P_f to P_e. In either event, the decontrol of prices can be expected to be inflationary.

ready access to such goods. As Figure 40-1 shows, this pricing policy helps explain the chronic product shortages and long queues which frustrate consumers in the former Soviet Union. The perfectly inelastic supply curve S reflects the fixed output of, say, shoes for which the plan provides. (Disregard supply curve S' for the moment.) The demand curve slopes downward as it would in a market economy. Given S, the equilibrium price would be P_a. But in an effort to make shoes accessible to those with lower incomes, the government fixes the price at P_f.

However, Figure 40-1 makes clear that not everyone who wants shoes at price P_f will be able to obtain them. At P_f quantity demanded is substantially greater than quantity supplied, so there is excess demand or, in other words, a shortage. This explains the long, impatient lines of consumers and the empty shelves we saw in television news clips of Soviet shoppers. It is no surprise that black markets—illegal markets where goods are sold at much higher prices than those fixed by the government—were widespread in the former Soviet Union.

Given that Figure 40-1 was characteristic of most Soviet markets, it is obvious that the transition to free markets poses a serious inflationary problem. Without privatization, shoe prices will rise from P_f to P_a when the market for shoes is decontrolled. Similarly, prices will rise for butter, soap, meat, housing, vodka, and a host of other goods. With privatization, this runup of prices will be dampened somewhat by the extra output induced by the rising prices. As shown by supply curve S' in Figure 40-1, private producers will respond to higher prices by increasing quantity supplied. Nevertheless, prices will rise substantially, as from P_f to P_e. An important need during the transition period will be to control inflationary pressures through appropriate macroeconomic policies. The prospect of rampant inflation is an important reason why many Soviet citizens are apprehensive about the transition to a market economy.

In January of 1992 Boris Yeltsin unilaterally decontrolled prices in the Russian Republic. Prices on many products tripled or quadrupled overnight. His strategy is based on the expectation that higher prices will induce farms to supply in the market foodstuffs they are now hoarding and thereby ease growing food shortages. But if inflation continues, the needed food may be withheld in the anticipation of still higher prices.

Joining the World Economy

The Soviet Union was largely isolated from the world economy for almost three-quarters of a century. A key aspect of transition is to open the economy to international trade and finance.

One basic task is to make the ruble a convertible currency, meaning that it must be exchangeable for other foreign currencies. Convertibility is necessary for the former Soviet Union to achieve an enlarged role in international trade and finance. Firms cannot buy from or sell to the former Soviet Union unless a realistic exchange rate is established for the ruble (Chapter 38). Nor can western firms be expected to invest in the former Soviet Union unless they are certain that rubles can be exchanged for dollars. American and other western firms want their profits in dollars, yen, pounds, and marks, not rubles.

Opening the Soviet economy to world trade will be beneficial because world markets are important sources of competition and a means of acquiring much-needed superior technologies from industrially advanced capitalist nations. Liberalized international trade will put pressure on privatized Soviet firms to produce efficiently products which meet world quality standards. Furthermore, free world trade will allow the former Soviet Union to realize the benefits from production based on comparative advantage—income gains which its isolation has long denied it.

Macroeconomic Stability

Unfortunately, the transition to free markets can be accompanied by high rates of inflation. There are several reasons for this.

1 Decontrolling Prices As just discussed (Figure 40-1), the government has kept consumer prices artificially low for decades. Decontrol of these prices will result in a substantially higher price level. If workers respond by demanding and receiving higher nominal wages, a serious and prolonged price-wage spiral could result.

2 Ruble Overhang In what is called the **ruble overhang,** Soviet households have stored massive amounts of currency and deposits at savings banks during years of waiting for scarce consumer goods to become more abundant. Historically, consumer prices fixed at low levels and restricted supplies of consumer goods gave consumers no other choice but to save. This ruble overhang—estimated to be 250 billion rubles—could generate an inflationary surge when prices are decontrolled and more goods begin to appear in consumer markets.

3 Inflationary Finance The most important potential source of inflation is the recent financing of government deficits by printing additional currency. The Soviet government incurred large deficits in the late 1980s and early 1990s, the result of two considerations. First, the main source of government revenue is the *turnover tax,* which is essentially an excise tax of varying amounts on consumer goods. Because of the stagnation and decline of economic activity, revenues from the turnover tax have declined. Second, given the uncertainty as to the future of the Soviet Union as a political entity, the various republics have withheld their tax collections from the central government.

The consequence is that the central government has incurred substantial deficits which it has financed by the expedient of printing and distributing additional rubles. This is the most inflationary form of government finance and a potential cause of hyperinflation. More money chasing a diminishing amount of goods is a classic inflationary scenario. In fact, in late 1991 Soviet economists estimated that inflation was occurring at almost a 100 percent annual rate and accelerating.

The problem is that an environment of high and volatile inflation greatly complicates achieving other components of transition. The purchase of formerly public enterprises by private buyers, the establishing of a convertible ruble, and the encouragement of both domestic and foreign investment to modernize the economy are all more difficult with the uncertainties posed by a rapidly rising price level.

CAN THE TRANSITION BE IMPLEMENTED?

What are the prospects for transforming the former Soviet economy from central planning to a market system? It is not difficult to list obstacles to such a transformation.

Technical Problems

Our discussion of the components of the transition to a market economy has touched on many of the technical economic problems involved. How can the state efficiently and equitably divest itself of public enterprises? How is an effective degree of competition to be achieved and maintained in an economy which has been dominated by public monopolies for some seven decades? Can government create an effective unemployment insurance program, a workable system of antitrust laws, consumer protection legislation, and the legal framework to protect private property and enterprise? Will it be possible to create the institutions and mechanisms needed to implement monetary and fiscal policies? How can the potential inflationary effects of the ruble overhang be offset?

Public Support: Attitudes and Values

The reforms comprising the transition from central planning to a market system must have wide public support. Consider some of the potential difficulties.

1 Bureaucratic Resistance   The reforms threaten the jobs and status of many former party members and bureaucrats. These individuals continue in many instances to have positions of power and prestige and therefore have a strong interest in maintaining the

status quo. Ironically, there is fear that those most likely to have access to Soviet enterprises and other assets will be those very same bureaucrats who formerly administered the failed system of central planning.

2 Worker Incentives   Under a system of capitalist incentives most workers and managers will be required to be more disciplined and to work harder and more productively. This may be difficult to accept in an economy which historically has served consumers–workers poorly. Money wage increases do not provide incentives without corresponding improvements in the quantity and quality of housing, food, and other consumer goods and services.

Some observers say that many citizens in the former Soviet Union and other communist nations have acquired work habits and personality traits which will only change slowly. These include working at a leisurely pace, avoiding responsibility, resistance to innovation and change, stressing output quantity over quality, and promotion based on connections and party affiliation rather than productive efficiency. It may be wishful thinking to assume that the Soviet populace is imbued with a strong work ethic and a latent entrepreneurial spirit, and that these attributes will emerge when the heavy hand of central planning is removed. The Soviet citizenry has been indoctrinated for some seventy years regarding the evils of private property, profits, and capitalist enterprise. The "mental residue" of communism may not be easily removed.

The Political Problem: National Disintegration

At this time (early 1992), the political status of the former Soviet republics is unclear. The Baltic states have declared themselves independent nations and the Georgian Republic may follow suit. It is uncertain at this point as to the nature of the future political alignment, if any, which may evolve among the remaining republics.

What is vital to the success of the transition process is that the republics *not* become separate and distinct *economic* entities. The worst scenario would be that each republic establish its own currency, its own external tariffs and import quotas, its own banking and tax systems and its own economic laws and policies. By becoming distinct economic units the advantages of specialization based on comparative advantage would be partially sacrificed and each political unit would suffer diminished domestic output.

In fact, diminishing trade between the republics in 1991 contributed to the former Soviet Union's economic and political deterioration. Given impending food shortages, the Ukraine (the main agricultural producer among the republics) stopped food shipments to other republics to conserve stocks for its own citizens. Other republics adopted similar policies. Azerbaijan curtailed its shipments of oil-drilling equipment to the Russian Republic and the latter responded by stopping oil shipments to Azerbaijan. An "every republic for itself" policy could be especially devastating because an estimated 40 percent of Soviet industrial production comes from state monopolies. For example, if for some curious reason Ford should decide not to sell its autos in Illinois, there is no doubt that General Motors and Chrysler, along with foreign producers, would be more than pleased to serve the market. But when Azerbaijan cuts off shipments of oil-drilling equipment to Russia, no alternative domestic source of that equipment is available.

A related point is that the transition process will be greatly facilitated by the influx of foreign investment. This will not occur until the former Soviet Union demonstrates political stability and continuity.

The Simultaneity Problem

A more subtle problem is that the components of reform must be pursued, not piecemeal, but more or less simultaneously. Reform components are interlinked; not to move forward on all fronts is to enhance the prospects for failure. Examples: Private ownership will do little to increase productive efficiency unless prices are reformed to accurately measure relative scarcities. Privatization—the selling off of state enterprises—may be helpful in reducing budget deficits. When market prices for inputs and output are unknown, it is extremely difficult to determine the value of an enterprise when it is being privatized. The creation of a more competitive environment depends significantly on the economy being opened to world trade and foreign investment.

Positive Factors

There are also several positive factors which may facilitate the plan-to-market economy transition.

1 Natural Resource Base   The former Soviet Union has a generous and varied natural resource base. Although differing significantly in composition, the natural resources of the Commonwealth are roughly comparable with those of the United States. The Commonwealth comprises about one-sixth of the earth's land mass and its resources include gold, diamonds, timber, oil, and natural gas. Its population is 288 million, compared to 252 million for the United States.

2 Peace Dividend   The end of the cold war will allow Russia, the Ukraine, and other former Soviet republics to reduce their heavy commitment of resources to the military and to reallocate freed resources to the civilian sector. Westerners estimate that a 50 percent reduction in military spending could save $90 billion per year. Recent arms agreements with the United States and its allies, the withdrawal of Soviet troops from Afghanistan, and reductions in the size of the Red army have been motivated by the desire to revitalize the lagging economy.

3 The "Second Economy"   For years the former Soviet Union has had a thriving underground or "second" economy. Black markets where scarce goods sell at two or three times government-fixed prices were widespread. Peasants "borrowed" government fertilizer to use on their "private" plots of ground. Physicians stole medicines for their unofficial private practices. Plant managers hired "expediters" to illegally obtain needed inputs which the planning system failed to supply. The point is that all of these second economy activities reflected a degree of initiative and entrepreneurship which could be legal and useful in a market economy.

4 Democratization   Democratization and, more specifically, freedom from the ideological baggage of the Communist Party, is a prerequisite for the transition to capitalism. The Communist Party was created to abolish private property, free enterprise, and genuine markets. It would be unrealistic to expect the Party to reverse these accomplishments. The Soviet Union under *glasnost* has made great strides toward democratization in the past several years. The dissolution of the Communist Party in 1991 was as significant economically as it was politically.

ROLE OF ADVANCED CAPITALIST NATIONS

What might the world's industrialized capitalist nations do to facilitate the Soviet plan-to-market economy metamorphosis?

LAST WORD

OBITUARY: THE SOVIET UNION

Contradictions of the world's first communist state killed Marx's vision of a free and prosperous society.

The Soviet Union is dead. It was 74.

Marketed as utopia, run by slogan and fear, it blended genuine achievement with elaborate facade. It created a system whose top priority seemed to be concealing its own failings.

Foreigners, intimidated by its military prowess and obsessive secrecy, frequently overestimated its strength. Its own citizens, bombarded by buoyant propaganda as they went about their harsh existence, sometimes had no idea if their lives were really growing better or worse.

Irony and artifice were everywhere. The Soviet Union led the world in production of steel, oil, tractors and locomotives, all as it moved inexorably to economic ruin.

Construction crews competed to build whole apartment buildings in a month, a week, a day. Yet the Soviet dream of abolishing "communal apartments," where three or four families had to share a tiny kitchen and toilet, was never achieved.

The Soviets were a nuclear super-power that projected military and diplomatic strength around the world. Yet at home, medical care was poor, citizens' diets poorer, and shoddy goods were the norm.

And a nation that claimed to publish more books and newspapers than any other had a ruthless system of censorship, political control and suppression of free ideas.

What went wrong? Why did a nation rich in natural resources—with a literate, educated work force and one-sixth of the world's land mass to stretch out in—fail to build the vibrant, prosperous, free society that was supposed to be a beacon to the world?

Most Soviets blame, first of all, "scientific socialism," the shaky and untested economic model that Lenin's Communists forced on backward Russia.

It was imposed from above and preserved through brute force. There were huge economic advances at first, but accomplished through intimidation as much as economic logic. After World War II, the "planned economy" operated as a continent-wide shell game, with resources wastefully rushed here and there to maintain an illusion of economic progress.

Since the economy essentially did not work, the leaders who depended on it had to find other ways to preserve their strength and build national pride.

They created a genuine center of accomplishment in the Soviet military, which was denied no human or financial resource. The Soviets also excelled in areas of high technology, mathematics and space; brought electricity, communications and industry to backward zones of their nation; and provided an example of quick, forced economic development that many in the Third World admired and attempted to emulate.

For anyone who was unimpressed by these accomplishments, the Soviets also created a system of terror that silenced political dissidents, religious activists, nationalist agitators and anyone else whose cause might be more appealing than communism.

But perhaps most important of all, the leaders built their strength on a suffocating cradle-to-grave so-

Foreign Aid

In 1991 President Gorbachev appealed to the industrialized countries for $20 to $30 billion in aid. The argument for granting this aid was that it would ease the painful transition process when central planning was being dismantled and free enterprise had not yet taken

hold. During this critical period the Soviet economy may further deteriorate. In addition, the abortive August 1991 coup indicates clearly that economic collapse can threaten to reverse the Soviet Union's substantial progress toward political democracy and the apparent demise of the cold war.

cial structure that made citizens totally beholden to the state—and then demanded practically nothing of them.

The state provided food, apartments, medicine, education, jobs and old-age pensions. It ran factories, department stores, farms, film studios and excellent orchestras and ballet companies. It may not have provided the weather, but it certainly controlled the news and sports.

This benevolence, such as it was, was practically free of charge. Citizens were judged mainly by political reliability—or political indifference, which also was acceptable.

During Leonid Brezhnev's reign, the situation steadily worsened and hypocrisy was elevated to the level of state policy. Bluster covered the increasing weakness.

Incompetence, sloppiness and corruption at work were widely overlooked. Citizens quickly learned that an effective way to get along was to do the minimum and challenge nothing—neither politics, nor the efficiency of their workplace.

Under such conditions, many believed the Soviet economy—and the country's whole spirit—was heading for a crash long before Mikhail Gorbachev came to power in 1985. He accelerated the slide by public openness about the country's troubles, a tactic that invigorated a few reformers but threw millions into despair and inactivity when facades came down and they realized how far their country had already crumbled.

Gorbachev's attempts at restructuring the economy were too tentative and too late. They could not make up for seven decades of an economic system that did not work, and the intricate structure established to maintain it at all cost.

That cost included stamping out personal initiative and putting political order ahead of everything else—including the welfare of the Soviet people.

Source: Thomas Kent, "Soviets Mixed Achievement, Facade as Dreams Failed," *The Lincoln Star,* Lincoln, Nebraska, December 26, 1991. Reprinted by permission.

The United States and the other market democracies have a great economic stake in the former Soviet Union's transition to democracy and capitalism. If the transition fails, the peace dividend associated with the end of the cold war will not be realized and the possibility of accelerated economic growth through expanded international trade with a free-market Commonwealth will also be sacrificed. The political benefit is that a democratic Commonwealth will isolate the last strongholds of communism—China, Cuba, North Korea, and Vietnam—and perhaps force their leaders toward political and economic reform.

But there are serious reservations concerning aid to the Soviet Union. One argument is that aid is likely to be ineffectual and wasteful until the transition to market capitalism has been accomplished. Aside from humanitarian aid in the form of foodstuffs and medicine, economic aid is not likely to be of much help under existing institutional arrangements.

A second contention is that the Soviet Union has not yet exploited the opportunity it now has to divert vast amounts of resources from the military to the civilian sector. Cutting military spending in half would release resources three or four times as large as the amount of aid Gorbachev requested.

Third, it is pointed out that the Soviet Union is in fact a gigantic $2 trillion economy. Even granting the $30 billion in aid would only amount to about $100 per year per Soviet citizen.

Finally, there is the hard political fact that foreign aid for a long-time cold war foe may not be popular among the voters of industrialized nations who see their own countries troubled with problems of unemployment, poor education, poverty, and drug abuse.

The United States' position has been that at this time it is appropriate to provide food and other humanitarian aid along with technical and educational assistance to Soviet enterprises and political officials, but to withhold unrestricted aid until substantial reform of the economy has been achieved.

In fact, in the spring of 1992 the United States and its G-7 partners (Germany, Japan, France, Britain, Canada, and Italy) have promised Russia a $24 billion aid package. This includes $11 billion in direct aid; $6 billion to provide a fund for stabilizing the ruble; $4.5 billion of IMF and World Bank loans; and $2.5 billion in debt rescheduling (on an estimated $89 billion debt). The United States' share is approximately $5 billion.

Private Investment

As the former Soviet Union attempts to move toward a capitalistic system, will it be able to attract foreign investment to shore up its economy? Given the vast potential market provided by some 288 million citizens, we would expect the answer to be "Yes." Furthermore, it is undoubtedly true that flows of private investment could be extremely helpful to the Soviet economy, perhaps more so than public aid. The reason is that, in addition to providing real capital, profit-seeking private investors will bring in managerial skills, entrepreneurial behavior, and marketing connections.

But in fact there are serious obstacles to foreign firms in doing business in the former Soviet Union. One is determining who is in charge. As the country moves toward decentralization politically, companies must discover whether they should deal with a Commonwealth trade minister in Minsk, officials at the republic level, or both. To whom does a foreign firm pay taxes, and with whom does one sign contracts? Who issues the necessary permits and licenses?

A second problem is that neither suppliers of inputs nor a dependable infrastructure are available. Enterprises manufacturing inputs are still generally committed to selling most of their supplies to the state. How do new "outsiders" acquire necessary resources? Furthermore, Soviet communication and transportation systems are grossly inadequate by world standards. McDonald's spent fourteen years establishing its Moscow fast-food restaurant and its earnings are in rubles rather than dollars.

A third difficulty is the inconvertibility of the ruble. How does an American firm which establishes a successful company in Kiev or St. Petersburg withdraw its profits? The attractive feature of *joint ventures*—businesses in which American firms and Soviet enterprises cooperate in a productive endeavor—is that the convertibility problem may be circumvented. Firms such as Chevron and Amoco which intend to help the former Soviet Union exploit its vast oil reserves can take their earnings in oil rather than currency.

Membership in International Institutions

Historically the Soviet Union has distanced itself from the major international trade and financial institutions such as the International Monetary Fund (IMF), the World Bank, and the General Agreement on Tariffs and Trade (GATT). There is no doubt that membership in these institutions could benefit the Soviet Union. For example, membership in the IMF and World Bank could provide additional sources of economic aid. Membership in GATT would result in lower tariff barriers for Soviet exports. In the spring of 1992 Russia was

admitted to the IMF and other republics are expected to follow. IMF and World Bank officials have indicated they would provide $45 to $50 billion in aid to the Commonwealth over the next four years.

QUICK REVIEW 40-3

◆ *The former Soviet Union has made the commitment to become a capitalistic system. Ingredients in the transition from planning to markets include: a creating private property and property rights; b promoting competition; c limiting and reformulating government's role; d removing domestic price controls; e opening the economy to international market forces; and f establishing monetary and fiscal policies to stabilize the economy.*

◆ *In addition to the technical economic problems associated with the transition, reforms require widespread public support, the maintenance of economic unity among the republics, and more-or-less simultaneous realization of the reform components.*

◆ *Factors helpful to the transition include a generous natural resource base, the potential release of large amounts of resources from the military sector, the entrepreneurship implicit in the underground economy, and substantial strides toward political democracy.*

◆ *The reform effort in the former Soviet Union may also be assisted by foreign technical and economic aid, private investment by foreign firms, and membership in international trade and lending institutions.*

PROSPECTS

What are the prospects for a successful transition from central planning to markets? At this time there is no definitive answer. The failed August 1991 coup suggests that anarchy and civil war are not beyond imagination. And there is some consensus that the damage done to the Soviet economy by seven decades of communism will not be easily nor quickly undone. The immediate future may bring considerable pain and suffering to citizens in Russia and the other Commonwealth republics. Yet we must keep in mind that the political and economic changes which have occurred in the former Soviet Union in the past several years have been remarkable and justify some measure of optimism.

CHAPTER SUMMARY

1 The labor theory of value is a central principle of Marxian ideology. Capitalists, as property owners, allegedly expropriate most of labor's value as profits or surplus value.

2 Virtually complete state ownership of property resources and central planning historically were the major institutional features of the Soviet economy.

3 Characteristics of Soviet planning included **a** emphasis on industrialization and military strength; **b** overcommitment of resources; **c** economic growth based on additional inputs rather than increased productivity; **d** allocation of resources by bureaucratic rather than market decisions; **e** economic self-sufficiency; and **f** passive macroeconomic policies.

4 The basic problem facing central planners is achieving coordination or internal consistency in their plans to avoid bottlenecks and the chain reaction of production failures which they cause.

5 Diminishing growth rates, shoddy consumer goods, and the inability to provide a promised high standard of living are all evidence of the failure of Soviet central planning.

6 Stagnation of the agricultural sector, a growing labor shortage, and the burden of a large military establishment contributed to the failure of the Soviet economy. However, the primary causes of failure were the inability of central planning to coordinate a more complex economy, the absence of rational success indicators, and the lack of adequate economic incentives.

7 The recent Gorbachev reforms attempted to restructure the economy and introduce greater political "openness," but did not address fundamental systemic deficiencies.

8 To change from central planning to a market economy, the former Soviet Union must move from public to private ownership of property; establish a competitive environment for businesses; restructure government's role to activities appropriate to capitalism; abandon state-determined prices in favor of market-determined prices; bring its economy into nomic policies and institutions to provide employment and price level stability.

9 In addition to resolving the technical economic problems inherent in the transformation of the Soviet economy to a market system, it is also necessary to achieve the support of bureaucrats and workers, preserve economic unity among the republics, and put reforms into effect simultaneously.

10 Reform efforts by the former Soviet republics may be furthered by the Commonwealth's abundant natural resources; the freeing of resources from the military; entrepreneurial talent evident in the underground economy; the democratization of the political system; and the assistance provided by foreign governments, foreign private investment, and international lending and trade institutions.

TERMS AND CONCEPTS

labor theory of value	**central economic**	**Gorbachev reforms**	*glasnost*
surplus value	**planning**	*perestroika*	**ruble overhang**
state ownership			

QUESTIONS AND STUDY SUGGESTIONS

1 Compare the ideology and institutional framework of the former Soviet economy with that of American capitalism. Contrast the manner in which production is motivated in these two systems.

2 Discuss the problem of coordination which faces central planners. Explain how a planning failure can cause a chain reaction of additional failures.

3 How was the number of automobiles to be produced determined in the former Soviet Union? In the United States? How are the decisions implemented in the two different types of economies?

4 What have been the major characteristics and goals of Soviet central planning?

5 What is the evidence of the failure of Soviet planning? Explain why Soviet economic growth diminished after 1970.

6 Explain why the use of quantitative output targets as the major success indicator for Soviet enterprises contributed to economic inefficiency.

7 Use a supply and demand diagram to explain the persistent shortages of many Soviet consumer goods. Why might the transformation to a market economy be accompanied by inflation? Why were black markets so common in the Soviet Union?

8 What specific changes must be made to transform the Soviet economy to a market system? Why is it important that these changes be introduced simultaneously?

9 Citing both specific obstacles and facilitating factors, do you think that the former Soviet Union will be successful in becoming a capitalistic system?

10 "It has become increasingly difficult for thoughtful men to find meaningful alternatives posed in the traditional choices between socialism and capitalism, planning and the free market, regulation and laissez faire, for they find their actual choices neither simple nor so grand."[7] Explain and evaluate.

[7]Robert A. Dahl and Charles E. Lindblom, *Politics, Economics and Welfare* (New York: Harper & Row, Publishers, Inc., 1953), p. 1.

GLOSSARY

Ability-to-pay principle The belief that those who have greater income (or wealth) should be taxed absolutely and relatively more than those who have less.

Abstraction Elimination of irrelevant and noneconomic facts to obtain an economic principle.

Acreage-allotment program The program which determines the total number of acres that are to be used to produce various agricultural products and allocates these acres among individual farmers who are required to limit their plantings to the number of acres allotted to them if they wish to obtain the Support price for their crops.

Actual budget The amount spent by the Federal government (to purchase goods and services and for transfer payments) less the amount of tax revenue collected by it in any (fiscal) year; and which can *not* reliably be used to determine whether it is pursuing an expansionary or contractionary fiscal policy. Compare (*see*) the Full-employment budget.

Actual deficit The size of the Federal government's Budget deficit (*see*) or surplus actually measured or recorded in any given year.

Actual investment The amount which business Firms do invest; equal to Planned investment plus Unplanned investment.

Actual reserves The amount of funds which a Member bank has on deposit at the Federal Reserve Bank of its district (plus its Vault cash).

Adaptive expectations theory The idea that people determine their expectations about future events (for example, inflation) on the basis of past and present events (rates of inflation) and only change their expectations as events unfold.

Adjustable pegs The device used in the Bretton Woods system (*see*) to change Exchange rates in an orderly way to eliminate persistent Payments deficits and surpluses: each nation defined its monetary unit in terms of (pegged it to) gold or the dollar, kept the Rate of exchange for its money stable in the short run, and changed (adjusted) it in the long run when faced with international disequilibrium.

Adverse selection problem A problem which arises when information known to one party to a contract is not known to the other party, causing the latter to incur major costs. Example: Individuals who have the poorest health are more likely to buy health insurance.

AFDC (*See*** Aid to families with dependent children.)**

Aggregate demand A schedule or curve which shows the total quantity of goods and services that will be demanded (purchased) at different price levels.

Aggregate demand–aggregate supply model The macroeconomic model which uses Aggregate demand and Aggregate supply (*see* both) to determine and explain the Price level and the real Domestic output.

Aggregate expenditures The total amount spent for final goods and services in the economy.

Aggregate expenditures–domestic output approach Determination of the Equilibrium gross domestic product (*see*) by finding the real GDP at which Aggregate expenditures are equal to the Domestic output.

Aggregate expenditures schedule A schedule or curve which shows the total amount spent for final goods and services at different levels of real GDP.

Aggregate supply A schedule or curve which shows the total quantity of goods and services that will be supplied (produced) at different price levels.

Aggregation Combining individual units or data into one unit or number. For example, all prices of individual goods and services are combined into a Price level, or all units of output are aggregated into Real gross domestic product.

Agricultural Adjustment Act The Federal act of 1933 which established the Parity concept (*see*) as the cornerstone of American agricultural policy and provided Price supports for farm products, restriction of agricultural production, and the disposal of surplus output.

Aid to families with dependent children (AFDC) A state-administered and partly federally funded program in the United States which provides aid to families in which dependent children do not have the support of a parent because of his or her death, disability, or desertion.

Alcoa case The case decided by the Federal courts in 1945 in which the courts ruled that the possession of monopoly power, no matter how reasonably that power had been used, was a violation of the antitrust laws; and which overturned the Rule of reason (*see*) applied in the U.S. Steel case (*see*).

Allocative efficiency The apportionment of resources among firms and industries to obtain the production of the products most wanted by society (consumers); the output of each product at which its Marginal cost and Price are equal.

Allocative factor The ability of an economy to reallocate resources to achieve the Economic growth which the Supply factors (*see*) make possible.

American Federation of Labor (AFL) The organization of affiliated Craft unions formed in 1886.

Annually balanced budget The equality of government expenditures and tax collections during a year.

Anticipated inflation Inflation (*see*) at a rate which was equal to the rate expected in that period of time.

Applied economics (*See* Policy economics.)

Appreciation of the dollar An increase in the value of the dollar relative to the currency of another nation; a dollar now buys a larger amount of the foreign currency. For example, if the dollar price of a British pound changes from $3 to $2, the dollar has appreciated.

Asset Anything of monetary value owned by a firm or individual.

Asset demand for money The amount of money people want to hold as a Store of value (the amount of their financial assets they wish to have in the form of Money); and which varies inversely with the Rate of interest.

Authoritarian capitalism An economic system (method of organization) in which property resources are privately owned and government extensively directs and controls the economy.

Average fixed costs The total Fixed cost (*see*) of a Firm divided by its output (the quantity of product produced).

Average product The total output produced per unit of a resource employed (total product divided by the quantity of a resource employed).

Average propensity to consume Fraction of Disposable income which households spend for consumer goods and services; consumption divided by Disposable income.

Average propensity to save Fraction of Disposable income which households save; Saving divided by Disposable income.

Average revenue Total revenue from the sale of a product divided by the quantity of the product sold (demanded); equal to the price at which the product is sold so long as all units of the product are sold at the same price.

Average tax rate Total tax paid divided by total (taxable) income; the tax rate on total (taxable) income.

Average (total) cost The Total cost of a Firm divided by its output (the quantity of product produced); equal to Average fixed cost (*see*) plus Average variable cost (*see*).

Average variable cost The total Variable cost (*see*) of a Firm divided by its output (the quantity of product produced).

Backflows The return of workers to the countries from which they originally migrated.

Balanced-budget amendment Proposed constitutional amendment which would require Congress to balance the Federal budget annually.

Balanced budget multiplier The effect of equal increases (decreases) in government spending for goods and services and in taxes is to increase (decrease) the Equilibrium gross domestic product by the amount of the equal increases (decreases).

Balance of payments deficit The sum of the Balance on current account (*see*) and the Balance on the capital account (*see*) is negative.

Balance of payments surplus The sum of the Balance on current account (*see*) and the Balance on the capital account (*see*) is positive.

Balance on current account The exports of goods (merchandise) and services of a nation less its imports of goods (merchandise) and services plus its Net investment income and Net transfers.

Balance on goods and services The exports of goods (merchandise) and services of a nation less its imports of goods (merchandise) and services.

Balance on the capital account The Capital inflows (*see*) of a nation less its Capital outflows (*see*).

Balance sheet A statement of the Assets (*see*), Liabilities (*see*), and Net worth (*see*) of a firm or individual at some given time.

Bank deposits The deposits which banks have at the Federal Reserve Banks (*see*).

Bankers' bank A bank which accepts the deposits of and makes loans to Depository institutions; a Federal Reserve Bank.

Bank reserves Bank reserves held at the Federal Reserve Banks (*see*) plus bank Vault cash (*see*).

Barrier to entry Anything that artificially prevents the entry of Firms into an industry.

Barter The exchange of one good or service for another good or service.

Base year The year with which prices in other years are compared when a Price index (*see*) is constructed.

Benefit-cost analysis Deciding whether to employ resources and the quantity of resources to employ for a project or program (for the production of a good or service) by comparing the marginal benefits with the marginal costs.

Benefit-loss rate   The percentage by which subsidy benefits in a Negative income tax plan (*see*) are reduced as earned income rises.

Benefits-received principle   The belief that those who receive the benefits of goods and services provided by government should pay the taxes required to finance them.

Big business   A business Firm which either produces a large percentage of the total output of an industry, is large (in terms of number of employees or stockholders, sales, assets, or profits) compared with other Firms in the economy, or both.

Bilateral monopoly   A market in which there is a single seller (Monopoly) and a single buyer (Monopsony).

Blacklisting   The passing from one employer to another of the names of workers who favor the formation of labor unions and who ought not to be hired.

Board of Governors   The seven-member group that supervises and controls the money and banking system of the United States; formally, the Board of Governors of the Federal Reserve System; the Federal Reserve Board.

Brain drain   The emigration of highly educated, highly skilled workers from a country.

Break-even income   The level of Disposable income at which Households plan to consume (spend) all of their income (for consumer goods and services) and to save none of it; also denotes that level of earned income at which subsidy payments become zero in an income maintenance program.

Break-even point   Any output which a (competitive) Firm might produce at which its Total cost and Total revenue would be equal; an output at which it has neither an Economic profit nor a loss.

Bretton Woods system   The international monetary system developed after World War II in which Adjustable pegs (*see*) were employed, the International Monetary Fund (*see*) helped to stabilize Foreign exchange rates, and gold and the dollar (*see*) were used as International monetary reserves (*see*).

Budget deficit   The amount by which the expenditures of the Federal government exceed its revenues in any year.

Budget line   A line which shows the different combinations of two products a consumer can purchase with a given money income.

Budget restraint   The limit the size of the consumer's income (and the prices that must be paid for the goods and services) imposes on the ability of an individual consumer to obtain goods and services.

Built-in stability   The effect of Nondiscretionary fiscal policy (*see*) on the economy; when Net taxes vary directly with the Gross domestic product, the fall (rise) in Net taxes during a recession (inflation) helps to eliminate unemployment (inflationary pressures).

Business cycle   Recurrent ups and downs over a period of years in the level of economic activity.

Business unionism   The belief that the labor union should concern itself with such practical and short-run objectives as higher wages, shorter hours, and improved working conditions and should not concern itself with long-run and idealistic changes in the capitalistic system.

Capital   Human-made resources used to produce goods and services; goods which do not directly satisfy human wants; capital goods.

Capital account   The section in a nation's International balance of payments (*see*) in which are recorded the Capital inflows (*see*) and the Capital outflows (*see*) of that nation.

Capital account deficit   A negative Balance on the capital account (*see*).

Capital account surplus   A positive Balance on the capital account (*see*).

Capital flight   The transfer of savings from less developed to industrially advanced countries to avoid government expropriation, taxation, and high rates of inflation or to realize better investment opportunities.

Capital gain   The gain realized when securities or properties are sold for a price greater than the price paid for them.

Capital goods (*See* Capital.)

Capital inflow   The expenditures made by the residents of foreign nations to purchase real and financial capital from the residents of a nation.

Capital-intensive commodity   A product which requires a relatively large amount of Capital to produce.

Capital outflow   The expenditures made by the residents of a nation to purchase real and financial capital from the residents of foreign nations.

Capital-saving technological advance   An improvement in technology that permits a greater quantity of a product to be produced with a given amount of Capital (or the same amount of the product to be produced with a smaller amount of Capital).

Capital-using technological advance   An improvement in technology that requires the use of a greater amount of Capital to produce a given quantity of a product.

Cartel   A formal written or oral agreement among Firms to set the price of the product and the outputs of the individual firms or to divide the market for the product geographically.

Causation A cause-and-effect relationship; one or several events bring about or result in another event.

CEA (*See* Council of Economic Advisers.)

Cease-and-desist order An order from a court or government agency (commission or board) to a corporation or individual to stop engaging in a specified practice.

Ceiling price (*See* Price ceiling.)

Celler-Kefauver Act The Federal act of 1950 which amended the Clayton Act (*see*) by prohibiting the acquisition of the assets of one firm by another firm when the effect would be to lessen competition.

Central bank A bank whose chief function is the control of the nation's money supply.

Central economic planning Government determination of the objectives of the economy and the direction of its resources to the attainment of these objectives.

Ceteris paribus assumption (*See* "Other things being equal" assumption.)

Change in amount consumed Increase or decrease in consumption spending that results from an increase or decrease in Disposable income, the Consumption schedule (curve) remaining unchanged; movement from one row (point) to another on the same Consumption schedule (curve).

Change in amount saved Increase or decrease in Saving that results from an increase or decrease in Disposable income, the Saving schedule (curve) remaining unchanged; movement from one row (point) to another on the same Saving schedule (curve).

Change in the consumption schedule An increase or decrease in consumption at each level of Disposable income caused by changes in the Nonincome determinants of consumption and saving (*see*); an upward or downward movement of the Consumption schedule.

Change in the saving schedule An increase or decrease in Saving at each level of Disposable income caused by changes in the Nonincome determinants of consumption and saving (*see*); an upward or downward movement of the Saving schedule.

Checkable deposit Any deposit in a commercial bank or Thrift institution against which a check may be written; includes Demand deposits and NOW, ATS, and share draft accounts.

Checking account A Checkable deposit (*see*) in a Commercial bank or Thrift institution.

Circuit velocity of money (*See* Velocity of money.)

Circular flow of income The flow of resources from Households to Firms and of products from Firms to Households accompanied in an economy using money by flows of money from Households to Firms and from Firms to Households.

Classical range The vertical segment of the Aggregate supply curve along which the economy is at Full employment.

Classical theory The Classical theory of employment (*see*).

Classical theory of employment The Macroeconomic generalizations accepted by most economists before the 1930s which led to the conclusion that a capitalistic economy would employ its resources fully.

Clayton Act The Federal antitrust act of 1914 which strengthened the Sherman Act (*see*) by making it illegal for business firms to engage in certain specified practices.

Clean Air Act of 1990 Legislation embodying a variety of specific measures to deal with air pollution, urban smog, motor vehicle emissions, ozone depletion, and acid rain.

Closed economy An economy which neither exports nor imports goods and services.

Close-down case The circumstance in which a Firm would experience a loss greater than its total Fixed cost if it were to produce any output greater than zero; alternatively, a situation in which a firm would cease to operate when the price at which it can sell its product is less than its Average variable cost.

Closed shop A place of employment at which only workers who are already members of a labor union may be hired.

Coase theorem The idea that Externality problems may be resolved through private negotiations of the affected parties.

Coincidence of wants The item (good or service) which one trader wishes to obtain is the same item which another trader desires to give up and the item which the second trader wishes to acquire is the same item the first trader desires to surrender.

COLA (*See* Cost-of-living adjustment.)

Collection of checks The process by which funds are transferred from the checking accounts of the writers of checks to the checking accounts of the recipients of the checks; also called the "clearing" of checks.

Collective voice The function a union performs for its members as a group when it communicates their problems and grievances to management and presses management for a satisfactory resolution to them.

Collusion A situation in which Firms act together and in agreement (collude) to set the price of the product and the output each firm will produce or to determine the geographic area in which each firm will sell.

Collusive oligopoly Occurs when the few firms composing an oligopolistic industry reach an explicit or unspoken agreement to fix prices, divide a market, or otherwise restrict competition; may take the form of a Cartel (*see*), Gentleman's agreement (*see*), or Price leadership (*see*).

Command economy An economic system (method of organization) in which property resources are publicly owned and Central economic planning (*see*) is used to direct and coordinate economic activities.

Commercial bank Firm which has a charter from either a state government or the Federal government to engage in the business of banking.

Commercial banking system All Commercial banks and Thrift institutions as a group.

Communism (*See* Command economy.)

Company union An organization of employees which is dominated by the employer (the company) and does not engage in genuine collective bargaining with the employer.

Comparable worth doctrine The belief that women should receive the same salaries (wages) as men when the levels of skill, effort, and responsibility in their different jobs are the same.

Comparative advantage A lower relative or Comparative cost (*see*) than another producer.

Comparative cost The amount the production of one product must be reduced to increase the production of another product; Opportunity cost (*see*).

Compensation to employees Wages and salaries paid by employers to workers plus Wage and salary supplements (*see*).

Competing goods (*See* Substitute goods.)

Competition The presence in a market of a large number of independent buyers and sellers and the freedom of buyers and sellers to enter and leave the market.

Competitive industry's short-run supply curve The horizontal summation of the short-run supply curves of the Firms in a purely competitive industry (*See* Pure competition); a curve which shows the total quantities that will be offered for sale at various prices by the Firms in an industry in the Short run (*see*).

Competitive labor market A market in which a large number of (noncolluding) firms demand a particular type of labor from a large number of nonunionized workers.

Complementary goods Goods or services for which there is an inverse relationship between the price of one and the demand for the other; when the price of one falls (rises) the demand for the other increases (decreases).

Complex multiplier The Multiplier (*see*) when changes in the Gross domestic product change Net taxes and Imports, as well as Saving.

Concentration ratio The percentage of the total sales of an industry made by the four (or some other number) largest sellers (Firms) in the industry.

Conglomerate combination A group of Plants (*see*) owned by a single Firm and engaged at one or more stages in the production of different products (of products which do not compete with each other).

Conglomerate merger The merger of a Firm in one Industry with a Firm in another Industry (with a Firm that is neither supplier, customer, nor competitor).

Congress of Industrial Organizations (CIO) The organization of affiliated Industrial unions formed in 1936.

Constant-cost industry An industry in which the expansion of the Industry by the entry of new Firms has no effect on the prices the Firms in the industry pay for resources and no effect, therefore, on their cost schedules (curves).

Consumer goods Goods and services which satisfy human wants directly.

Consumer sovereignty Determination by consumers of the types and quantities of goods and services that are produced from the scarce resources of the economy.

Consumption of fixed capital Estimate of the amount of Capital worn out or used up (consumed) in producing the Gross domestic product; depreciation.

Consumption schedule Schedule which shows the amounts Households plan to spend for Consumer goods at different levels of Disposable income.

Contractionary fiscal policy A decrease in Aggregate demand brought about by a decrease in Government expenditures for goods and services, an increase in Net taxes, or some combination of the two.

Corporate income tax A tax levied on the net income (profit) of Corporations.

Corporation A legal entity ("person") chartered by a state or the Federal government, and distinct and separate from the individuals who own it.

Correlation Systematic and dependable association between two sets of data (two kinds of events).

Cost-of-living adjustment An increase in the incomes (wages) of workers which is automatically received by them when there is inflation in the economy and guaranteed by a clause in their labor contracts with their employer.

Cost-plus pricing A procedure used by (oligopolistic) Firms to determine the price they will charge for a product and in which a percentage markup is added to the estimated average cost of producing the product.

Cost-push inflation Inflation that results from a decrease in Aggregate supply (from higher wage rates and raw material prices) and which is accompanied by decreases in real output and employment (by increases in the Unemployment rate).

Cost ratio The ratio of the decrease in the production of the product to the increase in the production of another product when resources are shifted from the production of the first to the production of the second product; the amount the production of one product decreases when the production of a second product increases by one unit.

Council of Economic Advisers A group of three persons which advises and assists the President of the United States on economic matters (including the preparation of the economic report of the President to Congress).

Craft union A labor union which limits its membership to workers with a particular skill (craft).

Credit An accounting notation that the value of an asset (such as the foreign money owned by the residents of a nation) has increased.

Credit union An association of persons who have a common tie (such as being employees of the same Firm or members of the same Labor union) which sells shares to (accepts deposits from) its members and makes loans to them.

Criminal-conspiracy doctrine The (now outdated) legal doctrine that combinations of workers (Labor unions) to raise wages were criminal conspiracies and, therefore, illegal.

Cross elasticity of demand The ratio of the percentage change in Quantity demanded of one good to the percentage change in the price of some other good. A negative coefficient indicates the two products are Substitute goods; a positive coefficient indicates Complementary goods.

Crowding model of occupational discrimination A model of labor markets that assumes Occupational discrimination (*see*) against women and blacks has kept them out of many occupations and forced them into a limited number of other occupations in which the large Supply of labor (relative to the Demand) results in lower wages and incomes.

Crowding-out effect The rise in interest rates and the resulting decrease in planned investment spending in the economy caused by increased borrowing in the money market by the Federal government.

Currency Coins and Paper money.

Currency appreciation (*See* Exchange rate appreciation.)

Currency depreciation (*See* Exchange rate depreciation.)

Current account The section in a nation's International balance of payments (*see*) in which are recorded its exports and imports of goods (merchandise) and services, its net investment income, and its net transfers.

Current account deficit A negative Balance on current account (*see*).

Current account surplus A positive Balance on current account (*see*).

Customary economy (*See* Traditional economy.)

Cyclical deficit A Federal Budget deficit which is caused by a recession and the consequent decline in tax revenues.

Cyclical unemployment Unemployment caused by insufficient Aggregate expenditures.

Cyclically balanced budget The equality of Government expenditures and Net tax collections over the course of a Business cycle; deficits incurred during periods of recession are offset by surpluses obtained during periods of prosperity (inflation).

Debit An accounting notation that the value of an asset (such as the foreign money owned by the residents of a nation) has decreased.

Declining economy An economy in which Net private domestic investment (*see*) is less than zero (Gross private domestic investment is less than Depreciation).

Declining industry An industry in which Economic profits are negative (losses are incurred) and which will, therefore, decrease its output as Firms leave the industry.

Decrease in demand A decrease in the Quantity demanded of a good or service at every price; a shift of the Demand curve to the left.

Decrease in supply A decrease in the Quantity supplied of a good or service at every price; a shift of the Supply curve to the left.

Deduction Reasoning from assumptions to conclusions; a method of reasoning that tests a hypothesis (an assumption) by comparing the conclusions to which it leads with economic facts.

Deflating Finding the Real gross domestic product (*see*) by decreasing the dollar value of the Gross domestic product produced in a year in which prices were higher than in the Base year (*see*).

Deflation A fall in the general (average) level of prices in the economy.

Demand A Demand schedule or a Demand curve (*see* both).

Demand curve A curve which shows the amounts of a good or service buyers wish to purchase at various prices during some period of time.

Demand deposit A deposit in a Commercial bank against which checks may be written; a Checking account or checking-account money.

Demand-deposit multiplier (*See* Monetary multiplier.)

Demand factor The increase in the level of Aggregate demand which brings about the Economic growth made possible by an increase in the productive potential of the economy.

Demand management The use of Fiscal policy (*see*) and Monetary policy (*see*) to increase or decrease Aggregate demand.

Demand-pull inflation Inflation which is the result of an increase in Aggregate demand.

Demand schedule A schedule which shows the

amounts of a good or service buyers wish to purchase at various prices during some period of time.

Dependent variable A variable which changes as a consequence of a change in some other (independent) variable; the "effect" or outcome.

Depository institution A Firm that accepts the deposits of Money of the public (businesses and persons); Commercial banks, Savings and loan associations, Mutual savings banks, and Credit unions.

Depository Institutions Deregulation and Monetary Control Act Federal legislation of 1980 which, among other things, allowed Thrift institutions to accept Checkable deposits and to use the check-clearing facilities of the Federal Reserve and to borrow from the Federal Reserve Banks; subjected the Thrifts to the reserve requirements of the Fed; and provided for the gradual elimination of the maximum interest rates that could be paid by Depository institutions on Savings and Time deposits.

Depreciation (*See* Consumption of fixed capital.)

Depreciation of the dollar A decrease in the value of the dollar relative to another currency; a dollar now buys a smaller amount of the foreign currency. For example, if the dollar price of a British pound changes from $2 to $3, the dollar has depreciated.

Derived demand The demand for a good or service which is dependent on or related to the demand for some other good or service; the demand for a resource which depends on the demand for the products it can be used to produce.

Descriptive economics The gathering or collection of relevant economic facts (data).

Determinants of aggregate demand Factors such as consumption, investment, government, and net export spending which, if they change, will shift the aggregate demand curve.

Determinants of aggregate supply Factors such as input prices, productivity, and the legal-institutional environment which, if they change, will shift the aggregate supply curve.

Determinants of demand Factors other than its price which determine the quantities demanded of a good or service.

Determinants of supply Factors other than its price which determine the quantities supplied of a good or service.

Devaluation A decrease in the defined value of a currency.

DI (*See* Disposable income.)

DIDMCA (*See* Depository Institutions Deregulation and Monetary Control Act.)

Differentiated oligopoly An Oligopoly in which the firms produce a Differentiated product (*see*).

Differentiated product A product which differs physically or in some other way from the similar products produced by other Firms; a product which is similar to but not identical with and, therefore, not a perfect substitute for other products; a product such that buyers are not indifferent to the seller from whom they purchase it so long as the price charged by all sellers is the same.

Dilemma of regulation When a Regulatory agency (*see*) must establish the maximum legal price a monopolist may charge, it finds that if it sets the price at the Socially optimal price (*see*) this price is below Average cost (and either bankrupts the Firm or requires that it be subsidized) and if it sets the price at the Fair-return price (*see*) it has failed to eliminate fully the underallocation of resources that is the consequence of unregulated monopoly.

Directing function of prices (*See* Guiding function of prices.)

Directly related Two sets of economic data that change in the same direction; when one variable increases (decreases) the other increases (decreases).

Direct relationship The relationship between two variables which change in the same direction, for example, product price and quantity supplied.

Discount rate The interest rate which the Federal Reserve Banks charge on the loans they make to Depository institutions.

Discouraged workers Workers who have left the Labor force (*see*) because they have not been able to find employment.

Discretionary fiscal policy Deliberate changes in taxes (tax rates) and government spending (spending for goods and services and transfer payment programs) by Congress to achieve a full-employment noninflationary Gross domestic product and economic growth.

Discriminatory discharge The firing of workers who favor formation of labor unions.

Diseconomies of scale Forces which increase the Average cost of producing a product as the Firm expands the size of its Plant (its output) in the Long run (*see*).

Disinflation A reduction in the rate of Inflation (*see*).

Disposable income Personal income (*see*) less personal taxes; income available for Personal consumption expenditures (*see*) and Personal saving (*see*).

Dissaving Spending for consumer goods and services in excess of Disposable income; the amount by which Personal consumption expenditures (*see*) exceed Disposable income.

Division of labor Dividing the work required to produce a product into a number of different tasks which are performed by different workers; Specialization (*see*) of workers.

Dollar votes The "votes" which consumers and entrepreneurs in effect cast for the production of the different kinds of consumer and capital goods, respectively, when they purchase them in the markets of the economy.

Domestic capital formation Adding to a nation's stock of Capital by saving part of its own domestic output.

Domestic economic goal Assumed to be full employment with little or no inflation.

Domestic output Gross (or net) domestic product; the total output of final goods and services produced in the economy.

Double counting Including the value of Intermediate goods (*see*) in the Gross domestic product; counting the same good or service more than once.

Double taxation Taxation of both corporate net income (profits) and the dividends paid from this net income when they become the Personal income of households.

Dumping The sale of products below cost in a foreign country.

Du Pont cellophane case The antitrust case brought against du Pont in which the U.S. Supreme Court ruled (in 1956) that while du Pont (and one licensee) had a monopoly in the narrowly defined market for cellophane it did not monopolize the more broadly defined market for flexible packaging materials, and was not guilty, therefore, of violating the Sherman Act.

Durable good A consumer good with an expected life (use) of one year or more.

Dynamic progress The development over time of more efficient (less costly) techniques of producing existing products and of improved products; technological progress.

Earnings The money income received by a worker; equal to the Wage (rate) multiplied by the quantity of labor supplied (the amount of time worked) by the worker.

Easy money policy Expanding the Money supply.

EC European Economic Community (*See* European Common Market).

Economic analysis Deriving Economic principles (*see*) from relevant economic facts.

Economic concentration A description or measure of the degree to which an industry is monopolistic or competitive. (*See* Concentration ratio.)

Economic cost A payment that must be made to obtain and retain the services of a resource; the income a Firm must provide to a resource supplier to attract the resource away from an alternative use; equal to the quantity of other products that cannot be produced when resources are employed to produce a particular product.

Economic efficiency The relationship between the input of scarce resources and the resulting output of a good or service; production of an output with a given dollar-and-cents value with the smallest total expenditure for resources; obtaining the largest total production of a good or service with resources of a given dollar-and-cents value.

Economic growth (1) An increase in the Production possibilities schedule or curve that results from an increase in resource supplies or an improvement in Technology; (2) an increase either in real output (Gross domestic product) or in real output per capita.

Economic integration Cooperation among and the complete or partial unification of the economies of different nations; the elimination of the barriers to trade among these nations; the bringing together of the markets in each of the separate economies to form one large (a common) market.

Economic law (*See* Economic principle.)

Economic model A simplified picture of reality; an abstract generalization.

Economic perspective A viewpoint which envisions individuals and institutions making rational or purposeful decisions based on a consideration of the benefits and costs associated with their actions.

Economic policy Course of action intended to correct or avoid a problem.

Economic principle Generalization of the economic behavior of individuals and institutions.

Economic profit The Total revenue of a firm less all its Economic costs; also called "pure profit" and "above normal profit."

Economic regulation (*See* Industrial regulation.)

Economic rent The price paid for the use of land and other natural resources, the supply of which is fixed (perfectly inelastic).

Economics Social science concerned with using scarce resources to obtain the maximum satisfaction of the unlimited material wants of society.

Economic theory Deriving economic principles (*see*) from relevant economic facts; an Economic principle (*see*).

Economies of scale The forces which reduce the Average cost of producing a product as the Firm expands the size of its Plant (its output) in the Long run (*see*); the economies of mass production.

Economizing problem Society's material wants are unlimited but the resources available to produce the goods and services that satisfy wants are limited (scarce); the inability of any economy to produce unlimited quantities of goods and services.

Efficiency loss of a tax The loss of net benefits to society because a tax reduces the production and consumption of a taxed good below the allocatively efficient level.

Efficiency wage A wage which minimizes wage costs per unit of output.

Efficient allocation of resources   That allocation of the resources of an economy among the production of different products which leads to the maximum satisfaction of the wants of consumers.

Elastic demand   The Elasticity coefficient (*see*) is greater than one; the percentage change in Quantity demanded is greater than the percentage change in price.

Elasticity coefficient   The number obtained when the percentage change in Quantity demanded (or supplied) is divided by the percentage change in the price of the commodity.

Elasticity formula   The price elasticity of demand (supply) is equal to

$$\frac{\text{percentage change in quantity}}{\text{percentage change in price}}$$
demanded (supplied)

which is equal to

$$\frac{\text{change in quantity demanded (supplied)}}{\text{original quantity demanded (supplied)}}$$

divided by $\dfrac{\text{change in price}}{\text{original price}}$

Elastic supply   The Elasticity coefficient (*see*) is greater than one; the percentage change in Quantity supplied is greater than the percentage change in price.

Emission fees   Special fees that might be levied against those who discharge pollutants into the environment.

Employment Act of 1946   Federal legislation which committed the Federal government to the maintenance of economic stability (Full employment, stable prices, and Economic growth); established the Council of Economic Advisers (*see*); and the Joint Economic Committee (*see*); and provided for the annual economic report of the President to Congress.

Employment discrimination   The employment of whites before blacks (and other minority groups) are employed and the discharge of blacks (and other minority groups) before whites are discharged.

Employment rate   The percentage of the Labor force (*see*) employed at any time.

Entrepreneurial ability   The human resource which combines the other resources to produce a product, makes nonroutine decisions, innovates, and bears risks.

Equality vs. efficiency tradeoff   The decrease in Economic efficiency (*see*) that appears to accompany a decrease in Income inequality (*see*); the presumption that an increase in Income inequality is required to increase Economic efficiency.

Equalizing differences   The differences in the Wages received by workers in different jobs which compensate for nonmonetary differences in the jobs.

Equation of exchange $MV = PQ$; in which M is the Money supply (*see*), V is the Income velocity of money (*see*), P is the Price level, and Q is the physical volume of final goods and services produced.

Equilibrium domestic output   The real Domestic output at which the Aggregate demand curve intersects the Aggregate supply curve.

Equilibrium gross domestic product   The Gross domestic product at which the total quantity of final goods and services produced (the Domestic output) is equal to the total quantity of final goods and services purchased (Aggregate expenditures).

Equilibrium position   The point at which the Budget line (*see*) is tangent to an Indifference curve (*see*) in the indifference curve approach to the theory of consumer behavior.

Equilibrium price   The price in a competitive market at which the Quantity demanded (*see*) and the Quantity supplied (*see*) are equal; at which there is neither a shortage nor a surplus; and at which there is no tendency for price to rise or fall.

Equilibrium price level   The price level at which the Aggregate demand curve intersects the Aggregate supply curve.

Equilibrium quantity   The Quantity demanded (*see*) and Quantity supplied (*see*) at the Equilibrium price (*see*) in a competitive market.

Equilibrium real domestic output   The real domestic output which is determined by the equality (intersection) of Aggregate demand and Aggregate supply.

European Common Market   The association of twelve European nations initiated in 1958 to abolish gradually the Tariffs and Import quotas that exist among them, to establish common Tariffs for goods imported from outside the member nations, to allow the eventual free movement of labor and capital among them, and to create other common economic policies.

European Economic Community (EC)   (*See* European Common Market.)

Excess reserves   The amount by which a member bank's Actual reserves (*see*) exceed its Required reserves (*see*); Actual reserves minus Required reserves.

Exchange control   (*See* Foreign exchange control.)

Exchange rate   The Rate of exchange (*see*).

Exchange rate appreciation   An increase in the value of a nation's money in foreign exchange markets; an increase in the Rates of exchange for foreign monies.

Exchange rate depreciation   A decrease in the value of a nation's money in foreign exchange markets; a decrease in the Rates of exchange for foreign monies.

Exchange rate determinant   Any factor other than the Rate of exchange (*see*) that determines the demand for and the supply of a currency in the Foreign exchange market (*see*).

Excise tax A tax levied on the expenditure for a specific product or on the quantity of the product purchased.

Exclusion principle The exclusion of those who do not pay for a product from the benefits of the product.

Exclusive unionism The policies employed by a Labor union to restrict the supply of labor by excluding potential members in order to increase the Wages received by its members; the Policies typically employed by a Craft union (*see*).

Exhaustive expenditure An expenditure by government that results directly in the employment of economic resources and in the absorption by government of the goods and services these resources produce; a Government purchase (*see*).

Exit mechanism Leaving a job and searching for another one in order to improve the conditions under which a worker is employed.

Expanding economy An economy in which Net private domestic investment (*see*) is greater than zero (Gross private domestic investment is greater than Depreciation).

Expanding industry An industry in which Economic profits are obtained by the firms in the industry and which will, therefore, increase its output as new firms enter the industry.

Expansionary fiscal policy An increase in Aggregate demand brought about by an increase in Government expenditures for goods and services, a decrease in Net taxes, or some combination of the two.

Expectations What consumers, business Firms, and others believe will happen or what conditions will be in the future.

Expected rate of net profits Annual profits which a firm anticipates it will obtain by purchasing Capital (by investing) expressed as a percentage of the price (cost) of the Capital.

Expenditures approach The method which adds all the expenditures made for Final goods and services to measure the Gross domestic product.

Expenditures-output approach (*See* Aggregate expenditures–domestic output approach.)

Explicit cost The monetary payment a Firm must make to an outsider to obtain a resource.

Exports Goods and services produced in a given nation and sold to customers in other nations.

Export subsidies Government payments which reduce the price of a product to foreign buyers.

Export transactions A sale of a good or service which increases the amount of foreign money held by the citizens, firms, and governments of a nation.

External benefit (*See* Spillover benefit.)

External cost (*See* Spillover cost.)

External debt Public debt (*see*) owed to foreign citizens, firms, and institutions.

External economic goal (*See* International economic goal.)

Externality (*See* Spillover.)

Face value The dollar or cents value stamped on a coin.

Factors of production Economic resources: Land, Capital, Labor, and Entrepreneurial ability.

Fair-return price The price of a product which enables its producer to obtain a Normal profit (*see*) and which is equal to the Average cost of producing it.

Fallacy of composition Incorrectly reasoning that what is true for the individual (or part) is therefore necessarily true for the group (or whole).

Fallacy of limited decisions The false notion that there are a limited number of economic decisions to be made so that, if government makes more decisions, there will be fewer private decisions to render.

Farm Act of 1990 Farm legislation which reduces the amount of acreage that is covered by price supports and allows farmers to plant these uncovered acres in alternative crops.

Farm problem The relatively low income of many farmers (compared with incomes in the nonagricultural sectors of the economy) and the tendency for farm income to fluctuate sharply from year to year.

FDIC (*See* Federal Deposit Insurance Corporation.)

Featherbedding Payment by an employer to a worker for work not actually performed.

Federal Advisory Committee The group of twelve commercial bankers which advises the Board of Governors (*see*) on banking policy.

Federal Deposit Insurance Corporation (FDIC) The Federally chartered corporation which insures the deposit liabilities of Commercial banks and Thrift Institutions.

Federal funds rate The interest rate that lending depository institutions charge borrowing institutions for the use of excess reserves.

Federal Open Market Committee (*See* Open Market Committee.)

Federal Reserve Bank Any one of the twelve banks chartered by the United States government to control the Money supply and perform other functions; (*See* Central bank, Quasi-public bank, *and* Banker's bank.)

Federal Reserve Note Paper money issued by the Federal Reserve Banks.

Federal Trade Commission (FTC) The commission of five members established by the Federal Trade Commission Act of 1914 to investigate unfair competitive practices of business Firms, to hold hearings of the complaints of such practices, and to issue Cease-and-desist orders (*see*) when Firms were found to engage in such practices.

Federal Trade Commission Act The Federal act of 1914 which established the Federal Trade Commission (*see*).

Feedback effects The effects which a change in the money supply will have (because it affects the interest rate, planned investment, and the equilibrium GDP) on the demand for money which is itself directly related to the GDP.

Female labor force participation rate The percentage of the female population of working age in the Labor force (*see*).

Fewness A relatively small number of sellers (or buyers) of a good or service.

Fiat money Anything that is Money because government has decreed it to be Money.

Final goods Goods which have been purchased for final use and not for resale or further processing or manufacturing (during the year).

Financial capital (*See* Money capital.)

Financing exports and imports The use of Foreign exchange markets by exporters and importers to receive and make payments for goods and services they sell and buy in foreign nations.

Firm An organization that employs resources to produce a good or service for profit and owns and operates one or more Plants (*see*).

(The) firm's short-run supply curve A curve which shows the quantities of a product a Firm in a purely competitive industry (*see* Pure competition) will offer to sell at various prices in the Short run (*see*); the portion of the Firm's short-run Marginal cost (*see*) curve which lies above its Average variable cost curve.

Fiscal federalism The system of transfers (grants) by which the Federal government shares its revenues with state and local governments.

Fiscal policy Changes in government spending and tax collections for the purpose of achieving a full-employment and noninflationary domestic output.

Five fundamental economic questions The five questions which every economy must answer: what to produce, how to produce, how to divide the total output, how to maintain Full employment, and how to assure economic flexibility.

Fixed cost Any cost which in total does not change when the Firm changes its output; the cost of Fixed resources (*see*).

Fixed exchange rate A Rate of exchange that is prevented from rising or falling.

Fixed resource Any resource employed by a Firm the quantity of which the firm cannot change.

Flexible exchange rate A rate of exchange that is determined by the demand for and supply of the foreign money and is free to rise or fall.

Floating exchange rate (*See* Flexible exchange rate.)

Food for peace program The program established under the provisions of Public Law 480 which permits less developed nations to buy surplus American agricultural products and pay for them with their own monies (instead of dollars).

Food stamp program A program in the United States which permits low-income persons to purchase for less than their retail value, or to obtain without cost, coupons that can be exchanged for food items at retail stores.

Foreign competition (*See* Import competition.)

Foreign exchange control The control a government may exercise over the quantity of foreign money demanded by its citizens and business firms and over the Rates of exchange in order to limit its outpayments to its inpayments (to eliminate a Payments deficit, *see*).

Foreign exchange market A market in which the money (currency) used by one nation is used to purchase (is exchanged for) the money used by another nation.

Foreign exchange rate (*See* Rate of exchange.)

Foreign purchases effect The inverse relationship between the Net exports (*see*) of an economy and its Price level (*see*) relative to foreign Price levels.

45-degree line A line along which the value of the GDP (measured horizontally) is equal to the value of Aggregate expenditures (measured vertically).

Fractional reserve A Reserve ratio (*see*) that is less than 100 percent of the deposit liabilities of a Commercial bank.

Freedom of choice Freedom of owners of property resources and money to employ or dispose of these resources as they see fit, of workers to enter any line of work for which they are qualified, and of consumers to spend their incomes in a manner which they deem to be appropriate (best for them).

Freedom of enterprise Freedom of business Firms to employ economic resources, to use these resources to produce products of the firm's own choosing, and to sell these products in markets of their choice.

Freely floating exchange rates Rates of exchange (*see*) which are not controlled and which may, therefore, rise and fall; and which are determined by the demand for and the supply of foreign monies.

Free-rider problem The inability of those who might

provide the economy with an economically desirable and indivisible good or service to obtain payment from those who benefit from the good or service because the Exclusion principle (*see*) cannot be applied to it.

Free trade   The absence of artificial (government imposed) barriers to trade among individuals and firms in different nations.

Frictional unemployment   Unemployment caused by workers voluntarily changing jobs and by temporary layoffs; unemployed workers between jobs.

Fringe benefits   The rewards other than Wages that employees receive from their employers and which include pensions, medical and dental insurance, paid vacations, and sick leaves.

Full employment   (1) Using all available resources to produce goods and services; (2) when the Unemployment rate is equal to the Full-employment unemployment rate and there is Frictional and Structural but no Cyclical unemployment (and the Real output of the economy is equal to its Potential real output).

Full-employment budget   What government expenditures and revenues and its surplus or deficit would be if the economy were to operate at Full employment throughout the year.

Full-employment unemployment rate   The Unemployment rate (*see*) at which there is no Cyclical unemployment (*see*) of the Labor force (*see*); and because some Frictional and Structural unemployment is unavoidable, equal to about 5 or 6 percent.

Full production   The maximum amount of goods and services that can be produced from the employed resources of an economy; the absence of Underemployment (*see*).

Functional distribution of income   The manner in which the economy's (the national) income is divided among those who perform different functions (provide the economy with different kinds of resources); the division of National income (*see*) into wages and salaries, proprietors' income, corporate profits, interest, and rent.

Functional finance   Use of Fiscal policy to achieve a full-employment noninflationary Gross domestic product without regard to the effect on the Public debt (*see*).

Game theory   A theory which compares the behavior of participants in games of strategy, such as poker and chess, with that of a small group of mutually interdependent firms (an Oligopoly).

GATT   (*See* General Agreement on Tariffs and Trade.)

GDP   (*See* Gross domestic product.)

GDP deflator   The Price index (*see*) for all final goods and services used to adjust the money (or nominal) GDP to measure the real GDP.

GDP gap   Potential Real gross domestic product less actual Real gross domestic product.

General Agreement on Tariffs and Trade   The international agreement reached in 1947 by twenty-three nations (including the United States) in which each nation agreed to give equal and nondiscriminatory treatment to the other nations, to reduce tariff rates by multinational negotiations, and to eliminate Import quotas.

General equilibrium analysis   A study of the Market system as a whole; of the interrelations among equilibrium prices, outputs, and employments in all the different markets of the economy.

Generalization   Statistical or probability statement; statement of the nature of the relation between two or more sets of facts.

Gentleman's agreement   An informal understanding on the price to be charged among the firms in an Oligopoly.

Glasnost   A Soviet campaign of the mid-1980s for greater "openness" and democratization in political and economic activities.

GNP   (*See* Gross national product.)

Gold export point   The rate of exchange for a foreign money above which—when nations participate in the International gold standard (*see*)—the foreign money will not be purchased and gold will be sent (exported) to the foreign country to make payments there.

Gold flow   The movement of gold into or out of a nation.

Gold import point   The Rate of exchange for a foreign money below which—when nations participate in the International gold standard (*see*)—a nation's own money will not be purchased and gold will be sent (imported) into that country by foreigners to make payments there.

Gorbachev's reforms   A mid-1980s series of reforms designed to revitalize the Soviet economy. The reforms stressed the modernization of productive facilities, less centralized control, improved worker discipline and productivity, more emphasis on market prices, and an expansion of private economic activity.

Gosbank   The state-owned and operated bank in the former U.S.S.R.

Government purchases   Disbursements of money by government for which government receives a currently produced good or service in return; the expenditures of all governments in the economy for Final goods (*see*) and services.

Government transfer payment   The disbursement of money (or goods and services) by government for which government receives no currently produced good or service in return.

Gramm-Rudman-Hollings Act   Legislation enacted in 1985 by the Federal government requiring annual reductions in Federal budget deficits and, as amended, a balanced budget by 1993; and mandating an automatic decrease in expenditures when Congress and the President cannot agree on how to meet the targeted reductions in the budget deficit.

Grievance procedure   The methods used by a Labor union and the Firm to settle disputes that arise during the life of the collective bargaining agreement between them.

Gross domestic product (GDP)   The total market value of all Final goods (*see*) and services produced annually within the boundaries of the United States, whether by American or foreign-supplied resources.

Gross national product (GNP)   The total market value of all Final goods (*see*) and services produced annually by land, labor, and capital, and entrepreneurial talent supplied by American residents, whether these resources are located in the United States or abroad.

Gross private domestic investment   Expenditures for newly produced Capital goods (*see*)—machinery, equipment, tools, and buildings—and for additions to inventories.

Guaranteed income   The minimum income a family (or individual) would receive if a Negative income tax (*see*) were to be adopted.

Guiding function of prices   The ability of price changes to bring about changes in the quantities of products and resources demanded and supplied (*See* Incentive function of price.)

Herfindahl index   A measure of the concentration and competitiveness of an industry; calculated as the sum of the squared market shares of the individual firms.

Homogeneous oligopoly   An Oligopoly in which the firms produce a Standardized product (*see*).

Horizontal axis   The "left–right" or "west–east" axis on a graph or grid.

Horizontal combination   A group of Plants (*see*) in the same stage of production which are owned by a single Firm (*see*).

Horizontal merger   The merger of one or more Firms producing the same product into a single Firm.

Household   An economic unit (of one or more persons) which provides the economy with resources and uses the money paid to it for these resources to purchase goods and services that satisfy material wants.

Human-capital discrimination   The denial to blacks (and other minority groups) of the same quality and quantity of education and training received by whites.

Human-capital investment   Any action taken to increase the productivity (by improving the skills and abilities) of workers; expenditures made to improve the education, health, or mobility of workers.

Hyperinflation   A very rapid rise in the price level.

Illegal immigrant   A person who unlawfully enters a country.

IMF   (*See* International Monetary Fund.)

Immobility   The inability or unwillingness of a worker or another resource to move from one geographic area or occupation to another or from a lower-paying to a higher-paying job.

Imperfect competition   All markets except Pure competition (*see*); Monopoly, Monopsony, Monopolistic competition, Oligopoly, and Oligopsony (*see all*).

Implicit cost   The monetary income a Firm sacrifices when it employs a resource it owns to produce a product rather than supplying the resource in the market; equal to what the resource could have earned in the best-paying alternative employment.

Import competition   Competition which domestic firms encounter from the products and services of foreign suppliers.

Import quota   A limit imposed by a nation on the quantity of a good that may be imported during some period of time.

Imports   Spending by individuals, Firms, and governments of an economy for goods and services produced in foreign nations.

Import transaction   The purchase of a good or service which decreases the amount of foreign money held by citizens, firms, and governments of a nation.

Incentive function of price   The inducement which an increase (a decrease) in the price of a commodity offers to sellers of the commodity to make more (less) of it available; and the inducement which an increase (decrease) in price offers to buyers to purchase smaller (larger) quantities; the Guiding function of prices (*see*).

Incentive pay plan   A compensation scheme which ties worker pay directly to performance. Such plans include piece rates, bonuses, commissions, and profit sharing.

Inclusive unionism   A union which attempts to include all workers employed in an industry as members.

Income approach   The method which adds all the incomes generated by the production of Final goods and services to measure the Gross domestic product.

Income effect   The effect which a change in the price of a product has on the Real income (purchasing power) of a consumer and the resulting effect on the quantity of that product the consumer would purchase after the consequences of the Substitution effect (*see*) have been taken into account (eliminated).

Income elasticity of demand   The ratio of the percentage change in the Quantity demanded of a good to the percentage change in income; it measures the responsiveness of consumer purchases to income changes.

Income inequality The unequal distribution of an economy's total income among persons or families in the economy.

Income-maintenance system The programs designed to eliminate poverty and to reduce inequality in the distribution of income.

Incomes policy Government policy that affects the Nominal incomes of individuals (the wages workers receive) and the prices they pay for goods and services and thereby affects their Real incomes; (*see* Wage-price policy).

Income velocity of money (*See* Velocity of money.)

Increase in demand An increase in the Quantity demanded of a good or service at every price; a shift in the Demand curve to the right.

Increase in supply An increase in the Quantity supplied of a good or service at every price; a shift in the Supply curve to the right.

Increasing-cost industry An Industry in which the expansion of the Industry through the entry of new firms increases the prices the Firms in the Industry must pay for resources and, therefore, increases their cost schedules (moves their cost curves upward).

Increasing returns An increase in the Marginal product (*see*) of a resource as successive units of the resource are employed.

Independent goods Goods or services such that there is no relationship between the price of one and the demand for the other; when the price of one rises or falls the demand for the other remains constant.

Independent variable The variable which causes a change in some other (dependent) variable.

Indifference curve A curve which shows the different combinations of two products which give a consumer the same satisfaction or Utility (*see*).

Indifference map A series of Indifference curves (*see*), each of which represents a different level of Utility; and which together show the preferences of the consumer.

Indirect business taxes Such taxes as Sales, Excise, and business Property taxes (*see all*), license fees, and Tariffs (*see*) which Firms treat as costs of producing a product and pass on (in whole or in part) to buyers of the product by charging them higher prices.

Individual demand The Demand schedule (*see*) or Demand curve (*see*) of a single buyer of a good or service.

Individual supply The Supply schedule (*see*) or Supply curve (*see*) of a single seller of a good or service.

Induction A method of reasoning that proceeds from facts to Generalization (*see*).

Industrially advanced countries (IACs) Countries such as the United States, Canada, Japan, and the nations of western Europe which have developed Market economies based on large stocks of technologically advanced capital goods and skilled labor forces.

Industrial policy Any policy in which government takes a direct and active role in shaping the structure and composition of industry to promote economic growth.

Industrial regulation The older and more traditional type of regulation in which government is concerned with the prices charged and the services provided the public in specific industries; in contrast to Social regulation (*see*).

Industrial union A Labor union which accepts as members all workers employed in a particular industry (or by a particular firm) and which contains largely unskilled or semiskilled workers.

Industry The group of (one or more) Firms that produce identical or similar products.

Inelastic demand The Elasticity coefficient (*see*) is less than one; the percentage change in price is greater than the percentage change in Quantity demanded.

Inelastic supply The Elasticity coefficient (*see*) is less than one; the percentage change in price is greater than the percentage change in Quantity supplied.

Inferior good A good or service of which consumers purchase less (more) at every price when their incomes increase (decrease).

Inflating Finding the Real gross domestic product (*see*) by increasing the dollar value of the Gross domestic product produced in a year in which prices are lower than they were in the Base year (*see*).

Inflation A rise in the general (average) level of prices in the economy.

Inflationary expectations The belief of workers, business Firms, and consumers that there will be substantial inflation in the future.

Inflationary gap The amount by which the Aggregate-expenditures schedule (curve) must decrease (shift downward) to decrease the nominal GDP to the full-employment noninflationary level.

Inflationary recession (*See* Stagflation.)

Infrastructure For the economy, the capital goods usually provided by the Public sector for the use of its citizens and Firms (e.g., highways, bridges, transit systems, wastewater treatment facilities, municipal water systems, and airports). For the Firm, the services and facilities which it must have to produce its products, which would be too costly for it to provide for itself, and which are provided by governments or other Firms (e.g., water, electricity, waste treatment, transportation, research, engineering, finance, and banking).

Injection An addition of spending to the income-expenditure stream: Investment, Government purchases, and Exports.

Injunction An order from a court of law that directs a person or organization not to perform a certain act because the act would do irreparable damage to some other person or persons; a restraining order.

In-kind investment Nonfinancial investment (*see*).

In-kind transfer The distribution by government of goods and services to individuals and for which the government receives no currently produced good or service in return; a Government transfer payment (*see*) made in goods or services rather than in money.

Innovation The introduction of a new product, the use of a new method of production, or the employment of a new form of business organization.

Inpayments The receipts of (its own or foreign) money which the individuals, Firms, and governments of one nation obtain from the sale of goods and services, investment income, Remittances, and Capital inflows from abroad.

Input-output analysis Using an Input-output table (*see*) to examine interdependence among different parts (sectors and industries) of the economy and to make economic forecasts and plans.

Input-output table A table which lists (along the left side) the producing sectors and (along the top) the consuming or using sectors of the economy and which shows quantitatively in each of its rows how the output of a producing sector was distributed among consuming sectors and quantitatively in each of its columns the producing sectors from which a consuming sector obtained its inputs during some period of time (a year).

Insurable risk An event, the average occurrence of which can be estimated with considerable accuracy, which would result in a loss that can be avoided by purchasing insurance.

Interest The payment made for the use of money (of borrowed funds).

Interest income Income of those who supply the economy with Capital (*see*).

Interest rate The Rate of interest (*see*).

Interest-rate effect The tendency for increases (decreases) in the Price level to increase (decrease) the demand for money; raise (lower) interest rates; and, as a result, to reduce (expand) total spending in the economy.

Interindustry competition Competition or rivalry between the products produced by Firms in one Industry (*see*) and the products produced by Firms in another industry (or in other industries).

Interlocking directorate A situation in which one or more of the members of the board of directors of one Corpo-

ration are also on the board of directors of another Corporation; and which is illegal when it reduces competition among the Corporations.

Intermediate goods Goods which are purchased for resale or further processing or manufacturing during the year.

Intermediate range The upsloping segment of the Aggregate supply curve that lies between the Keynesian range and the Classical range (*see both*).

Internal economic goal (*See* Domestic economic goal.)

Internal economies The reduction in the cost of producing or marketing a product that results from an increase in output of the Firm [*see* Economies of (large) scale].

Internally held public debt Public debt (*see*) owed to (United States government securities owned by) American citizens, Firms, and institutions.

International balance of payments Summary statement of the transactions which took place between the individuals, Firms, and governments of one nation and those in all other nations during the year.

International balance of payments deficit (*See* Balance of payments deficit.)

International balance of payments surplus (*See* Balance of payments surplus.)

International Bank for Reconstruction and Development (*See* World Bank.)

International economic goal Assumed to be a current-account balance of zero.

International gold standard An international monetary system employed in the nineteenth and early twentieth centuries in which each nation defined its money in terms of a quantity of gold, maintained a fixed relationship between its gold stock and money supply, and allowed the free importation and exportation of gold.

International Monetary Fund The international association of nations which was formed after World War II to make loans of foreign monies to nations with temporary Payments deficits (*see*) and to administer the Adjustable pegs (*see*).

International monetary reserves The foreign monies and such assets as gold a nation may use to settle a Payments deficit (*see*).

International value of the dollar The price that must be paid in foreign currency (money) to obtain one American dollar.

Interstate Commerce Commission The commission established in 1887 to regulate the rates and monitor the services of the railroads in the United States.

Interstate Commerce Commission Act The Federal legislation of 1887 which established the Interstate Commerce Commission (*see*).

Intrinsic value   The market value of the metal in a coin.

Inverse relationship   The relationship between two variables which change in opposite directions, for example, product price and quantity demanded.

Investment   Spending for (the production and accumulation of) Capital goods (*see*) and additions to inventories.

Investment curve   A curve which shows the amounts firms plan to invest (along the vertical axis) at different income (Gross domestic product) levels (along the horizontal axis).

Investment-demand curve   A curve which shows Rates of interest (along the vertical axis) and the amount of Investment (along the horizontal axis) at each Rate of interest.

Investment-demand schedule   Schedule which shows Rates of interest and the amount of Investment at each Rate of interest.

Investment in human capital   (*See* Human-capital investment.)

Investment schedule   A schedule which shows the amounts Firms plan to invest at different income (Gross domestic product) levels.

Invisible hand   The tendency of Firms and resource suppliers seeking to further their self-interests in competitive markets to further the best interest of society as a whole (the maximum satisfaction of wants).

JEC   (*See* Joint Economic Committee.)

Joint Economic Committee   Committee of Senators and members of Congress which investigates economic problems of national interest.

Jurisdictional strike   Withholding from an employer the labor services of its members by a Labor union that is engaged in a dispute with another Labor union over which is to perform a specific kind of work for the employer.

Keynesian economics   The macroeconomic generalizations which are today accepted by most (but not all) economists and which lead to the conclusion that a capitalistic economy does not always employ its resources fully and that Fiscal policy (*see*) and Monetary policy (*see*) can be used to promote Full employment (*see*).

Keynesianism   The philosophical, ideological, and analytical views of the prevailing majority of economists; and their employment theory and stabilization policies.

Keynesian range   The horizontal segment of the Aggregate-supply curve along which the price level is constant as real domestic output changes.

Kinked demand curve   The demand curve which a noncollusive oligopolist sees for its output and which is based on the assumption that rivals will follow a price decrease and will not follow a price increase.

Labor   The physical and mental talents (efforts) of people which can be used to produce goods and services.

Labor force   Persons sixteen years of age and older who are not in institutions and who are employed or are unemployed and seeking work.

Labor-intensive commodity   A product which requires a relatively large amount of Labor to produce.

Labor-Management Relations Act   (*See* Taft-Hartley Act.)

Labor-Management Reporting and Disclosure Act   (*See* Landrum-Griffin Act.)

Labor productivity   Total output divided by the quantity of labor employed to produce the output; the Average product (*see*) of labor or output per worker per hour.

Labor theory of value   The Marxian notion that the economic value of any commodity is determined solely by the amount of labor required to produce it.

Labor union   A group of workers organized to advance the interests of the group (to increase wages, shorten the hours worked, improve working conditions, etc.).

Laffer curve   A curve which shows the relationship between tax rates and the tax revenues of government and on which there is a tax rate (between zero and 100 percent) at which tax revenues are a maximum.

Laissez faire capitalism   (*See* Pure capitalism.)

Land   Natural resources ("free gifts of nature") which can be used to produce goods and services.

Land-intensive commodity   A product which requires a relatively large amount of Land to produce.

Landrum-Griffin Act   The Federal act of 1959 which regulates the elections and finances of Labor unions and guarantees certain rights to their members.

Law of conservation of matter and energy   The notion that matter can be changed to other matter or into energy but cannot disappear; all production inputs are ultimately transformed into an equal amount of finished product, energy, and waste (pollution).

Law of demand   The inverse relationship between the price and the Quantity demanded (*see*) of a good or service during some period of time.

Law of diminishing marginal utility   As a consumer increases the consumption of a good or service, the Marginal utility (*see*) obtained from each additional unit of the good or service decreases.

Law of diminishing returns   When successive equal

increments of a Variable resource (*see*) are added to the Fixed resources (*see*), beyond some level of employment, the Marginal product (*see*) of the Variable resource will decrease.

Law of increasing opportunity cost As the amount of a product produced is increased, the Opportunity cost (*see*)—Marginal cost (*see*)—of producing an additional unit of the product increases.

Law of supply The direct relationship between the price and the Quantity supplied (*see*) of a good or service during some period of time.

Leakage (1) A withdrawal of potential spending from the income-expenditures stream: Saving (*see*), tax payments, and Imports (*see*); (2) a withdrawal which reduces the lending potential of the Commercial banking system.

Leakages-injections approach Determination of the Equilibrium gross domestic product (*see*) by finding the Gross domestic product at which Leakages (*see*) are equal to Injections (*see*).

Least-cost combination rule (of resources) The quantity of each resource a Firm must employ if it is to produce any output at the lowest total cost; the combination on which the ratio of the Marginal product (*see*) of a resource to its Marginal resource cost (*see*) (to its price if the resource is employed in a competitive market) is the same for all resources employed.

Legal cartel theory of regulation The hypothesis that industries want to be regulated so that they may form legal Cartels (*see*) and that government officials (the government) provide the regulation in return for their political and financial support.

Legal immigrant A person who lawfully enters a country.

Legal reserves (deposit) The minimum amount which a Depository institution (*see*) must keep on deposit with the Federal Reserve Bank in its district, or in Vault cash (*see*).

Legal tender Anything that government has decreed must be accepted in payment of a debt.

Lending potential of an individual commercial bank The amount by which a single Commercial bank can safely increase the Money supply by making new loans to (or buying securities from) the public; equal to the Commercial bank's Excess reserves (*see*).

Lending potential of the banking system The amount by which the Commercial banking system (*see*) can increase the Money supply by making new loans to (or buying securities from) the public; equal to the Excess reserves (*see*) of the Commercial banking system multiplied by the Monetary multiplier (*see*).

Less developed countries (LDCs) Most countries of Africa, Asia, and Latin America which are characterized by a lack of capital goods, primitive production technologies, low literacy rates, high unemployment, rapid population growth, and labor forces heavily committed to agriculture.

Liability A debt with a monetary value; an amount owed by a Firm or an individual.

Limited liability Restriction of the maximum that may be lost to a predetermined amount; the maximum amount that may be lost by the owners (stockholders) of a Corporation is the amount they paid for their shares of stock.

Line-item veto A proposal to give the President the power to delete specific expenditure items from spending legislation passed by Congress.

Liquidity Money or things which can be quickly and easily converted into Money with little or no loss of purchasing power.

Loaded terminology Terms which arouse emotions and elicit approval or disapproval.

Loanable funds theory of interest The concept that the supply of and demand for loanable funds determines the equilibrium rate of interest.

Lockout The temporary closing of a place of employment and the halting of production by an employer in order to discourage the formation of a Labor union or to compel a Labor union to modify its demands.

Logrolling The trading of votes by legislators to secure favorable outcomes on decisions to provide public goods and services.

Long run A period of time long enough to enable producers of a product to change the quantities of all the resources they employ; in which all resources and costs are variable and no resources or costs are fixed.

Long-run aggregate supply curve The aggregate supply curve associated with a time period in which input prices (especially nominal wages) are fully responsive to changes in the price level.

Long-run competitive equilibrium The price at which Firms in Pure competition (*see*) neither obtain Economic profit nor suffer losses in the Long run and the total quantity demanded and supplied at that price are equal; a price equal to the minimum long-run average cost of producing the product.

Long-run farm problem The tendency for the incomes of many farmers to decline relative to incomes in the rest of the economy.

Long-run supply A schedule or curve which shows the prices at which a Purely competitive industry will make various quantities of the product available in the Long run.

Lorenz curve A curve which shows the distribution of income in an economy; and when used for this purpose the cumulated percentage of families (income receivers) is measured along the horizontal axis and the cumulated percentage of income is measured along the vertical axis.

Loss-minimizing case The circumstances which result in a loss which is less than its Total fixed cost when a Firm produces the output at which total profit is a maximum (or total loss is a minimum): when the price at which the firm can sell its product is less than Average total cost but greater than Average variable cost.

M1 The narrowly defined Money supply; the Currency and Checkable deposits (*see*) not owned by the Federal government, Federal Reserve Banks, or Depository institutions.

M2 A more broadly defined Money supply; equal to *M1* (*see*) plus Noncheckable savings deposits, small Time deposits (deposits of less than $100,000), Money market deposit accounts, and individual Money market mutual fund balances.

M3 A still more broadly defined Money supply; equal to *M2* (*see*) plus large Time deposits (deposits of $100,000 or more).

Macroeconomics The part of economics concerned with the economy as a whole; with such major aggregates as the household, business, and governmental sectors and with totals for the economy.

Managed floating exchange rate An Exchange rate that is allowed to change (float) to eliminate persistent Payments deficits and surpluses and is controlled (managed) to reduce day-to-day fluctuations.

Managerial-opposition hypothesis The explanation that attributes the relative decline of unionism in the United States to the increased and more aggressive opposition of management to unions.

Managerial prerogatives The decisions, often enumerated in the contract between a Labor union and a business Firm, that the management of the Firm has the sole right to make.

Marginal cost The extra (additional) cost of producing one more unit of output; equal to the change in Total cost divided by the change in output (and in the short run to the change in total Variable cost divided by the change in output).

Marginal labor cost The amount by which the total cost of employing Labor increases when a Firm employs one additional unit of Labor (the quantity of other resources employed remaining constant); equal to the change in the total cost of Labor divided by the change in the quantity of Labor employed.

Marginal product The additional output produced when one additional unit of a resource is employed (the quantity of all other resources employed remaining constant); equal to the change in total product divided by the change in the quantity of a resource employed.

Marginal productivity theory of income distribution The contention that the distribution of income is equitable when each unit of each resource receives a money payment equal to its marginal contribution to the firm's revenue (its Marginal revenue product).

Marginal propensity to consume Fraction of any change in Disposable income which is spent for Consumer goods; equal to the change in consumption divided by the change in Disposable income.

Marginal propensity to save Fraction of any change in Disposable income which households save; equal to change in Saving (*see*) divided by the change in Disposable income.

Marginal rate of substitution The rate (at the margin) at which a consumer is prepared to substitute one good or service for another and remain equally satisfied (have the same total Utility); and equal to the slope of an Indifference curve (*see*).

Marginal resource cost The amount by which the total cost of employing a resource increases when a Firm employs one additional unit of the resource (the quantity of all other resources employed remaining constant); equal to the change in the Total cost of the resource divided by the change in the quantity of the resource employed.

Marginal revenue The change in the Total revenue of the Firm that results from the sale of one additional unit of its product; equal to the change in Total revenue divided by the change in the quantity of the product sold (demanded).

Marginal-revenue–marginal-cost approach The method which finds the total output at which Economic profit (*see*) is a maximum (or losses a minimum) by comparing the Marginal revenue (*see*) and the Marginal cost (*see*) of each additional unit of output.

Marginal revenue product The change in the Total revenue of the Firm when it employs one additional unit of a resource (the quantity of all other resources employed remaining constant); equal to the change in Total revenue divided by the change in the quantity of the resource employed.

Marginal tax rate The fraction of additional (taxable) income that must be paid in taxes.

Marginal utility The extra Utility (*see*) a consumer obtains from the consumption of one additional unit of a good or service; equal to the change in total Utility divided by the change in the quantity consumed.

Market Any institution or mechanism that brings together the buyers (demanders) and sellers (suppliers) of a particular good or service.

Market demand (*See* Total demand.)

Market economy An economy in which only the private decisions of consumers, resource suppliers, and business Firms determine how resources are allocated; the Market system.

Market failure The failure of a market to bring about the allocation of resources that best satisfies the wants of society (that maximizes the satisfaction of wants). In particular, the over- or underallocation of resources to the production of a particular good or service (because of Spillovers or informational problems) and no allocation of resources to the production of Public goods **(see)**.

Market for externality rights A market in which the Perfectly inelastic supply **(see)** of the right to pollute the environment and the demand for the right to pollute would determine the price which a polluter would have to pay for the right.

Market-oriented income stabilization The proposal to shift the goal of farm policy from the enhancement to the stabilization of farm prices and incomes; allow farm prices and incomes to move toward their free-market levels in the long run; and have government stabilize farm prices and incomes from year to year by purchasing farm products when their prices fall below and by selling surplus farm products when their prices rise above their long-run trend of prices.

Market period A period of time in which producers of a product are unable to change the quantity produced in re sponse to a change in its price; in which there is Perfect inelasticity of supply **(see)**; and in which all resources are Fixed resources **(see)**.

Market policies Government policies designed to reduce the market power of labor unions and large business firms and to reduce or eliminate imbalances and bottlenecks in labor markets.

Market socialism An economic system (method of organization) in which property resources are publicly owned and markets and prices are used to direct and coordinate economic activities.

Market system All the product and resource markets of the economy and the relationships among them; a method which allows the prices determined in these markets to allocate the economy's scarce resources and to communicate and coordinate the decisions made by consumers, business firms, and resource suppliers.

Median-voter model The view that under majority rule the median (middle) voter will be in the dominant position to determine the outcome of an election.

Medicaid A Federal program in the United States which helps to finance the medical expenses of individuals covered by the Supplemental security income **(see)** and the Aid to families with dependent children **(see)** programs.

Medicare A Federal program which is financed by Payroll taxes **(see)** and provides for (1) compulsory hospital insurance for senior citizens and (2) low-cost voluntary insurance to help older Americans pay physicians' fees.

Medium of exchange Money **(see)**; a convenient means of exchanging goods and services without engaging in Barter **(see)**; what sellers generally accept and buyers generally use to pay for a good or service.

Microeconomics The part of economics concerned with such individual units within the economy as Industries,

Firms, and Households; and with individual markets, particular prices, and specific goods and services.

Minimum wage The lowest Wage (rate) employers may legally pay for an hour of Labor.

Mixed capitalism An economy in which both government and private decisions determine how resources are allocated.

Monetarism An alternative to Keynesianism **(see)**; the philosophical, ideological, and analytical view of a minority of American economists; and their employment theory and stabilization policy which stress the role of money.

Monetary multiplier The multiple of its Excess reserves **(see)** by which the Commercial banking system **(see)** can expand the Money supply and Demand deposits by making new loans (or buying securities); and equal to one divided by the Required reserve ratio **(see)**.

Monetary policy Changing the Money supply **(see)** to assist the economy to achieve a full-employment, noninflationary level of total output.

Monetary rule The rule suggested by Monetarism **(see)**; the Money supply should be expanded each year at the same annual rate as the potential rate of growth of the Real gross domestic product; the supply of money should be increased steadily at from 3 to 5 percent.

Money Any item which is generally acceptable to sellers in exchange for goods and services.

Money capital Money available to purchase Capital goods **(see)**.

Money income (See Nominal income.)

Money interest rate The Nominal interest rate **(see)**.

Money market The market in which the demand for and the supply of money determine the Interest rate (or the level of interest rates) in the economy.

Money market deposit account (MMDA) Interest-earning accounts at banks and thrift institutions which pool the funds of depositors to buy various short-term securities.

Money market mutual funds (MMMF) Interest-bearing accounts offered by brokers which pool depositors' funds for the purchase of short-term securities; depositors may write checks in minimum amounts or more against their accounts.

Money supply Narrowly defined **(see)** $M1$, more broadly defined **(see)** $M2$ and $M3$.

Money wage The amount of money received by a worker per unit of time (hour, day, etc.); nominal wage.

Money wage rate (See Money wage.)

Monopolistic competition A market in which many Firms sell a Differentiated product **(see)**, into which entry is relatively easy, in which the Firm has some control over the price at which the product it produces is sold, and in which there is considerable Nonprice competition **(see)**.

Monopoly A market in which the number of sellers is so small that each seller is able to influence the total supply and the price of the good or service.

Monopsony A market in which there is only one buyer of the good, service, or resource.

Moral hazard problem The possibility that individuals or institutions will change their behavior in unanticipated ways as the result of a contract or agreement. Example: A bank whose deposits are insured against loss may make riskier loans and investments.

Most-favored-nation clause A clause in a trade agreement between the United States and another nation which provides that the other nation's Imports into the United States will be subjected to the lowest tariff levied then or later on any other nation's Imports into the United States.

MR = MC rule A Firm will maximize its Economic profit (or minimize its losses) by producing the output at which Marginal revenue (*see*) and Marginal cost (*see*) are equal— provided the price at which it can sell its products is equal to or greater than Average variable cost (*see*).

MRP = MRC rule To maximize Economic profit (or minimize losses) a Firm should employ the quantity of a resource at which its Marginal revenue product (*see*) is equal to its Marginal resource cost (*see*).

Multiplier The ratio of the change in the Equilibrium GDP to the change in Investment (*see*), or to the change in any other component of the Aggregate expenditures schedule or to the change in Net taxes; the number by which a change in any component in the Aggregate expenditures schedule or in Net taxes must be multiplied to find the resulting change in the Equilibrium GDP.

Multiplier effect The effect on Equilibrium gross domestic product of a change in the Aggregate expenditures schedule (caused by a change in the Consumption schedule, Investment, Net taxes, Government expenditures for goods and services, or Net exports).

Mutual interdependence Situation in which a change in price (or in some other policy) by one Firm will affect the sales and profits of another Firm (or other Firms) and any Firm which makes such a change can expect the other Firm(s) to react in an unpredictable (uncertain) way.

Mutually exclusive goals Goals which conflict and cannot be achieved simultaneously.

Mutual savings bank A Firm without stockholders which accepts deposits primarily from small individual savers and which lends primarily to individuals to finance the purchases of residences.

National bank A Commercial bank (*see*) chartered by the United States government.

National income Total income earned by resource suppliers for their contributions to the production of the Gross domestic product (*see*); equal to the Gross domestic product minus the Nonincome charges (*see*) plus net American income earned abroad (*see*).

National income accounting The techniques employed to measure (estimate) the overall production of the economy and other related totals for the nation as a whole.

National Labor Relations Act (*See* Wagner Act.)

National Labor Relations Board The board established by the Wagner (National Labor Relations) Act (*see*) of 1935 to investigate unfair labor practices, issue Cease-and-desist orders (*see*), and to conduct elections among employees to determine if they wish to be represented by a Labor union and which union they wish to represent them.

Natural monopoly An industry in which the Economies of scale (*see*) are so great that the product can be produced by one Firm at an average cost which is lower than it would be if it were produced by more than one Firm.

Natural rate hypothesis The idea that the economy is stable in the long run at the natural rate of unemployment; views the long-run Phillips Curve (*see*) as being vertical at the natural rate of unemployment.

Natural rate of unemployment (*See* Full-employment unemployment rate.)

NDP (*See* Net domestic product.)

Near-money Financial assets, the most important of which are Noncheckable savings accounts, Time deposits, and U.S. short-term securities and savings bonds, that are not a medium of exchange but can be readily converted into Money.

Negative income tax The proposal to subsidize families and individuals with money payments when their incomes fall below a Guaranteed income (*see*); the negative tax would decrease as earned income increases. (*See* Benefit-loss rate.)

Negative relationship (*See* Inverse relationship.)

Net American income earned abroad Receipts of resource income from the rest of the world minus payments of resource income to the rest of the world; the difference between GDP (*see*) and GNP (*see*).

Net capital movement The difference between the real and financial investments and loans made by individuals and Firms of one nation in the other nations of the world and the investments and loans made by individuals and Firms from other nations in a nation; Capital inflows less Capital outflows.

Net domestic product Gross domestic product (*see*) less that part of the output needed to replace the Capital goods worn out in producing the output (Consumption of fixed capital, *see*).

Net export effect The notion that the impact of a change in Monetary policy (Fiscal policy) will be strengthened (weakened) by the consequent change in Net exports (*see*). For example, a tight (easy) money policy will increase (decrease) domestic interest rates, thereby increasing (decreasing) the foreign demand for dollars. As a result, the dollar appreciates (depreciates) and causes American net exports to decrease (increase).

Net exports Exports (*see*) minus Imports (*see*).

Net investment income The interest and dividend income received by the residents of a nation from residents of other nations less the interest and dividend payments made by the residents of that nation to the residents of other nations.

Net private domestic investment Gross private domestic investment (*see*) less Consumption of fixed capital (*see*); the addition to the nation's stock of Capital during a year.

Net taxes The taxes collected by government less Government transfer payments (*see*).

Net transfers The personal and government transfer payments made to residents of foreign nations less the personal and government transfer payments received from residents of foreign nations.

Net worth The total Assets (*see*) less the total Liabilities (*see*) of a Firm or an individual; the claims of the owners of a firm against its total Assets.

New classical economics The theory that, although unanticipated price level changes may create macroeconomic instability in the short run, the economy is stable at the full-employment level of domestic output in the long run because of price and wage flexibility.

New International Economic Order A series of proposals made by the Less developed countries (LDCs) (*see*) for basic changes in their relationships with the advanced industrialized nations that would accelerate the growth of and redistribute world income to the LDCs.

New perspective view of advertising Envisions advertising as a low-cost source of consumer information which increases competition by making consumers more aware of substitute products.

NIEO New International Economic Order (*see*).

NIT (*See* Negative income tax.)

NLRB (*See* National Labor Relations Board.)

Nominal gross domestic output (GDP) The GDP (*see*) measured in terms of the price level at the time of measurement (unadjusted for changes on the price level).

Nominal income The number of dollars received by an individual or group during some period of time.

Nominal interest rate The rate of interest expressed in dollars of current value (not adjusted for inflation).

Nominal wage The Money wage (*see*).

Noncheckable savings account A Savings account (*see*) against which a check can not be written.

Noncollusive oligopoly An Oligopoly (*see*) in which the Firms do not act together and in agreement to determine the price of the product and the output each Firm will produce or to determine the geographic area in which each Firm will sell.

Noncompeting groups Groups of workers in the economy that do not compete with each other for employment because the skill and training of the workers in one group are substantially different from those of the workers in other groups.

Nondiscretionary fiscal policy The increases (decreases) in Net taxes (*see*) which occur without Congressional action when the gross domestic product rises (falls) and which tend to stabilize the economy.

Nondurable good A Consumer good (*see*) with an expected life (use) of less than one year.

Nonexhaustive expenditure An expenditure by government that does not result directly in the employment of economic resources or the production of goods and services; *see* Government transfer payment.

Nonfinancial investment An investment which does not require households to save a part of their money incomes; but which uses surplus (unproductive) labor to build Capital goods.

Nonincome charges Consumption of fixed capital (*see*) and Indirect business taxes (*see*).

Nonincome determinants of consumption and saving All influences on consumption spending and saving other than the level of Disposable income.

Noninterest determinants of investment All influences on the level of investment spending other than the rate of interest.

Noninvestment transaction An expenditure for stocks, bonds, or second-hand Capital goods.

Nonmarket transactions The production of goods and services not included in the measurement of the Gross domestic product because the goods and services are not bought and sold.

Nonprice competition The means other than decreasing the prices of their products which Firms employ to attempt to increase the sale of their products; and which includes Product differentiation (*see*), advertising, and sales promotion activities.

Nonproductive transaction The purchase and sale of any item that is not a currently produced good or service.

Nontariff barriers All barriers other than Tariffs (*see*) which nations erect to impede trade among nations: Import quotas (*see*), licensing requirements, unreasonable product-quality standards, unnecessary red tape in customs procedures, etc.

Nonunion shop A place of employment at which none of the employees are members of a Labor union (and at which the employer attempts to hire only workers who are not apt to join a union).

Normal good A good or service of which consumers will purchase more (less) at every price when their incomes increase (decrease).

Normal profit Payment that must be made by a Firm to obtain and retain Entrepreneurial ability (*see*); the minimum payment (income) Entrepreneurial ability must (expect to) receive to induce it to perform the entrepreneurial functions for a Firm; an Implicit cost (*see*).

Normative economics That part of economics which pertains to value judgments about what the economy should be like; concerned with economic goals and policies.

Norris-LaGuardia Act The Federal act of 1932 which made it more difficult for employers to obtain Injunctions (*see*) against Labor unions in Federal courts and which declared that Yellow-dog contracts (*see*) were unenforceable.

NTBs (*See* Nontariff barriers.)

OASDHI (*See* Old age, survivors, and disability health insurance.)

Occupational discrimination The arbitrary restrictions which prevent blacks (and other minority groups) or women from entering the more desirable and higher-paying occupations.

Occupational licensure The laws of state or local governments which require a worker to obtain a license from a licensing board (by satisfying certain specified requirements) before engaging in a particular occupation.

Official reserves The foreign monies (currencies) owned by the central bank of a nation.

Okun's law The generalization that any one percentage point rise in the Unemployment rate above the Full-employment unemployment rate will increase the GDP gap by 2.5 percent of the Potential output (GDP) of the economy.

Old age, survivors, and disability health insurance The social program in the United States which is financed by Federal Payroll taxes (*see*) on employers and employees and which is designed to replace the Earnings lost when workers retire, die, or become unable to work.

Oligopoly A market in which a few Firms sell either a Standardized or Differentiated product, into which entry is difficult, in which the Firm's control over the price at which it sells its product is limited by Mutual interdependence (*see*) (except when there is collusion among firms), and in which there is typically a great deal of Nonprice competition (*see*).

Oligopsony A market in which there are a few buyers.

OPEC An acronym for the Organization of Petroleum Exporting Countries (*see*).

Open economy An economy which both exports and imports goods and services.

Open Market Committee The twelve-member group that determines the purchase-and-sale policies of the Federal Reserve Banks in the market for United States government securities.

Open-market operations The buying and selling of United States government securities by the Federal Reserve Banks.

Open shop A place of employment at which the employer may hire either Labor union members or workers who are not (and need not become) members of the union.

Opportunity cost The amount of other products that must be forgone or sacrificed to produce a unit of a product.

Optimal amount of externality reduction That reduction of pollution or other negative externality where society's marginal benefit and marginal cost of reducing the externality are equal.

Organization of Petroleum Exporting Countries The cartel formed in 1970 by thirteen oil-producing countries to control the price at which they sell crude oil to foreign importers and the quantity of oil exported by its members and which accounts for a large proportion of the world's export of oil.

"Other things being equal" assumption Assuming that factors other than those being considered are constant.

Outpayments The expenditures of (its own or foreign) money which the individuals, Firms, and governments of one nation make to purchase goods and services, for Remittances, as investment income, and Capital outflows abroad.

Output effect The impact which a change in the price of a resource has on the output a Firm finds it most profitable to produce and the resulting effect on the quantity of the resource (and the quantities of other resources) employed by the Firm after the consequences of the Substitution effect (*see*) have been taken into account (eliminated).

Paper money Pieces of paper used as a Medium of exchange (*see*); in the United States, Federal Reserve Notes (*see*).

Paradox of thrift The attempt of society to save more results in the same amount of, or less, Saving.

Paradox of voting A situation where voting by majority rule fails to provide a consistent ranking of society's preferences for public goods or services.

Parity concept The notion that year after year a given

output of a farm product should enable a farmer to acquire a constant amount of nonagricultural goods and services.

Parity price The price at which a given amount of an agricultural product would have to be sold to enable a farmer to obtain year after year money income needed to purchase a constant total quantity of nonagricultural goods and services.

Parity ratio The ratio (index) of the price received by farmers from the sale of an agricultural commodity to the (index of the) prices paid by them; used as a rationale for Price supports (*see*).

Partial equilibrium analysis The study of equilibrium prices and equilibrium outputs or employments in a particular market which assumes prices, outputs, and employments in the other markets of the economy remain unchanged.

Partnership An unincorporated business Firm owned and operated by two or more persons.

Patent laws The Federal laws which grant to inventors and innovators the exclusive right to produce and sell a new product or machine for a period of seventeen years.

Payments deficit (*See* Balance of payments deficit.)

Payments surplus (*See* Balance of payments surplus.)

Payroll tax A tax levied on employers of Labor equal to a percentage of all or part of the wages and salaries paid by them; and on employees equal to a percentage of all or part of the wages and salaries received by them.

Perestroika The essential feature of Mikhail Gorbachev's reform program to "restructure" the Soviet economy; includes modernization, decentralization, some privatization, and improved worker incentives.

Perfect elasticity of demand A change in the Quantity demanded requires no change in the price of the commodity; buyers will purchase as much of a commodity as is available at a constant price.

Perfect elasticity of supply A change in the Quantity supplied requires no change in the price of the commodity; sellers will make available as much of the commodity as buyers will purchase at a constant price.

Perfect inelasticity of demand A change in price results in no change in the Quantity demanded of a commodity; the Quantity demanded is the same at all prices.

Perfect inelasticity of supply A change in price results in no change in the Quantity supplied of a commodity; the Quantity supplied is the same at all prices.

Per se violations Collusive actions, such as attempts to fix prices or divide a market, which are violations of the antitrust laws even though the actions are unsuccessful.

Personal consumption expenditures The expenditures of Households for Durable and Nondurable consumer goods and services.

Personal distribution of income The manner in which the economy's Personal or Disposable income is divided among different income classes or different households.

Personal income The income, part of which is earned and the remainder of which is unearned, available to resource suppliers and others before the payment of Personal taxes (*see*).

Personal income tax A tax levied on the taxable income of individuals (households and unincorporated firms).

Personal saving The Personal income of households less Personal taxes (*see*) and Personal consumption expenditures (*see*); Disposable income not spent for Consumer goods (*see*).

Phillips Curve A curve which shows the relationship between the Unemployment rate (*see*) (on the horizontal axis) and the annual rate of increase in the Price level (on the vertical axis).

Planned economy An economy in which only government determines how resources are allocated.

Planned investment The amount which business firms plan or intend to invest.

Plant A physical establishment (Land and Capital) which performs one or more of the functions in the production (fabrication and distribution) of goods and services.

P = MC rule A firm in Pure competition (*see*) will maximize its Economic profit (*see*) or minimize its losses by producing the output at which the price of the product is equal to Marginal cost (*see*), provided that price is equal to or greater than Average variable cost (*see*) in the short run and equal to or greater than Average (total) cost (*see*) in the long run.

Policy economics The formulation of courses of action to bring about desired results or to prevent undesired occurrences (to control economic events).

Political business cycle The tendency of Congress to destabilize the economy by reducing taxes and increasing government expenditures before elections and to raise taxes and lower expenditures after elections.

Positive economics The analysis of facts or data to establish scientific generalizations about economic behavior; compare Normative economics.

Positive relationship The relationship between two variables which change in the same direction, for example, product price and quantity supplied.

***Post hoc, ergo propter hoc* fallacy** Incorrectly reasoning that when one event precedes another the first event is the cause of the second.

Potential competition The possibility that new competitors will be induced to enter an industry if firms now in that industry are realizing large economic profits.

Potential output   The real output (GDP) an economy is able to produce when it fully employs its available resources.

Poverty   An existence in which the basic needs of an individual or family exceed the means to satisfy them.

Poverty rate   The percentage of the population with incomes below the official poverty income levels established by the Federal government.

Preferential hiring   A practice (often required by the provisions of a contract between a Labor union and an employer) which requires the employer to hire union members so long as they are available and to hire nonunion workers only when union members are not available.

Preferential tariff treatment   Setting Tariffs lower for one nation (or group of nations) than for others.

Premature inflation   Inflation (*see*) which occurs before the economy has reached Full employment (*see*).

Price   The quantity of money (or of other goods and services) paid and received for a unit of a good or service.

Price ceiling   A legally established maximum price for a good or service.

Price-decreasing effect   The effect in a competitive market of a decrease in Demand or an increase in Supply upon the Equilibrium price (*see*).

Price discrimination   The selling of a product (at a given time) to different buyers at different prices when the price differences are not justified by differences in the cost of producing the product for the different buyers; and a practice made illegal by the Clayton Act (*see*) when it reduces competition.

Price elasticity of demand   The ratio of the percentage change in Quantity demanded of a commodity to the percentage change in its price; the responsiveness or sensitivity of the quantity of a commodity buyers demand to a change in the price of a commodity.

Price elasticity of supply   The ratio of the percentage change in Quantity supplied of a commodity to the percentage change in its price; the responsiveness or sensitivity of the quantity of a commodity supplied to a change in the price of a commodity.

Price floor   A legally determined price which is above the Equilibrium price.

Price guidepost   The price charged by an industry for its product should increase by no more than the increase in the Unit labor cost (*see*) of producing the product.

Price increasing effect   The effect in a competitive market of an increase in Demand or a decrease in Supply on the equilibrium price.

Price index   An index number which shows how the average price of a "market basket" of goods changes through time. A price index is used to change nominal output (income) into real output (income).

Price leadership   An informal method which the Firms in an Oligopoly (*see*) may employ to set the price of the product they produce: one firm (the leader) is the first to announce a change in price and the other firms (the followers) quickly announce identical (or similar) changes in price.

Price level   The weighted average of the Prices paid for the final goods and services produced in the economy.

Price level surprises   Unanticipated changes in the price level.

Price maker   A seller (or buyer) of a commodity that is able to affect the price at which the commodity sells by changing the amount it sells (buys).

Price support   The minimum price which government allows sellers to receive for a good or service; a price which is a legally established or maintained minimum price.

Price taker   A seller (or buyer) of a commodity that is unable to affect the price at which a commodity sells by changing the amount it sells (or buys).

Price-wage flexibility   Changes in the prices of products and in the Wages paid to workers; the ability of prices and Wages to rise or to fall.

Price war   Successive and continued decreases in the prices charged by the firms in an oligopolistic industry by which each firm hopes to increase its sales and revenues and from which firms seldom benefit.

Prime interest rate   The interest rate banks charge their most credit-worthy borrowers, for example, large corporations with impeccable financing credentials.

Principal-agent problem   A conflict of interest which occurs when agents (workers) pursue their own objectives to the detriment of the principal's (employer's) goals.

Private good   A good or service to which the Exclusion principle (*see*) is applicable and which is provided by privately owned firms to those who are willing to pay for it.

Private property   The right of private persons and Firms to obtain, own, control, employ, dispose of, and bequeath Land, Capital, and other Assets.

Private sector   The Households and business firms of the economy.

Product differentiation   Physical or other differences between the products produced by different Firms which result in individual buyers preferring (so long as the price charged by all sellers is the same) the product of one Firm to the Products of the other Firms.

Production possibilities curve   A curve which shows the different combinations of two goods or services that can be produced in a Full-employment (*see*), Full-production (*see*) economy in which the available supplies of resources and technology are constant.

Production possibilities table   A table which shows

the different combinations of two goods or services that can be produced in a Full-employment (*see*), Full-production (*see*) economy in which the available supplies of resources and technology are constant.

Productive efficiency   The production of a good in the least costly way; occurs when production takes place at the output where Average total cost is at a minimum and where Marginal product per dollar's worth of each input is the same.

Productivity   A measure of average output or real output per unit of input. For example, the productivity of labor may be determined by dividing hours of work into real output.

Productivity slowdown   The recent decline in the rate at which Labor productivity (*see*) in the United States has increased.

Product market   A market in which Households buy and Firms sell the products they have produced.

Profit   (*See*) Economic profit and Normal profit; without an adjective preceding it, the income of those who supply the economy with Entrepreneurial ability (*see*) or Normal profit.

Profit-maximizing case   The circumstances which result in an Economic profit (*see*) for a Firm when it produces the output at which Economic profit is a maximum; when the price at which the Firm can sell its product is greater than the Average (total) cost of producing it.

Profit-maximizing rule (combination of resources)   The quantity of each resource a Firm must employ if its Economic profit (*see*) is to be a maximum or its losses a minimum; the combination in which the Marginal revenue product (*see*) of each resource is equal to its Marginal resource cost (*see*) (to its price if the resource is employed in a competitive market).

Progressive tax   A tax such that the Average tax rate increases as the taxpayer's income increases and decreases as income decreases.

Property tax   A tax on the value of property (Capital, Land, stocks and bonds, and other Assets) owned by Firms and Households.

Proportional tax   A tax such that the Average tax rate remains constant as the taxpayer's income increases and decreases.

Proprietors' income   The net income of the owners of unincorporated Firms (proprietorships and partnerships).

Prosperous industry   (*See* Expanding industry.)

Protective tariff   A Tariff (*see*) designed to protect domestic producers of a good from the competition of foreign producers.

Public assistance programs   Programs which pay benefits to those who are unable to earn income (because of permanent handicaps or because they are dependent chil-

dren) which are financed by general tax revenues, and which are viewed as public charity (rather than earned rights).

Public choice theory   Generalizations that describe how government (the Public sector) makes decisions for the use of economic resources.

Public debt   The total amount owed by the Federal government (to the owners of government securities) and equal to the sum of its past Budget deficits (less its budget surpluses).

Public finance   The branch of economics which analyzes government revenues and expenditures.

Public good   A good or service to which the Exclusion principle (*see*) is not applicable; and which is provided by government if it yields substantial benefits to society.

Public interest theory of regulation   The presumption that the purpose of the regulation of an Industry is to protect the public (consumers) from the abuse of the power possessed by Natural monopolies (*see*).

Public sector   The part of the economy that contains all its governments; government.

Public-sector failure   The failure of the Public sector (government) to resolve socioeconomic problems because it performs its functions in an economically inefficient fashion.

Public utility   A Firm which produces an essential good or service, has obtained from a government the right to be the sole supplier of the good or service in the area, and is regulated by that government to prevent the abuse of its monopoly power.

Purchasing power parity   The idea that exchange rates between nations equate the purchasing power of various currencies; exchange rates between any two nations adjust to reflect the price level differences between the countries.

Pure capitalism   An economic system (method of organization) in which property resources are privately owned and markets and prices are used to direct and coordinate economic activities.

Pure competition   (1) A market in which a very large number of Firms sells a Standardized product (*see*), into which entry is very easy, in which the individual seller has no control over the price at which the product sells, and in which there is no Nonprice competition (*see*); (2) a market in which there is a very large number of buyers.

Pure monopoly   A market in which one Firm sells a unique product (one for which there are no close substitutes), into which entry is blocked, in which the Firm has considerable control over the price at which the product sells, and in which Nonprice competition (*see*) may or may not be found.

Pure profit (*See* Economic profit.)

Pure rate of interest (*See The* rate of interest.)

Quantity-decreasing effect The effect in a competitive market of a decrease in Demand or a decrease in Supply on the Equilibrium quantity **(*see*)**.

Quantity demanded The amount of a good or service buyers wish (or a buyer wishes) to purchase at a particular price during some period of time.

Quantity-increasing effect The effect in a competitive market of an increase in Demand or an increase in Supply on the Equilibrium quantity **(*see*)**.

Quantity supplied The amount of a good or service sellers offer (or a seller offers) to sell at a particular price during some period of time.

Quasi-public bank A bank which is privately owned but governmentally (publicly) controlled; each of the Federal Reserve Banks.

Quasi-public good A good or service to which the Exclusion principle **(*see*)** could be applied, but which has such a large Spillover benefit **(*see*)** that government sponsors its production to prevent an underallocation of resources.

R&D Research and development; activities undertaken to bring about Technological progress.

Ratchet effect The tendency for the Price level to rise when Aggregate demand increases, but not fall when Aggregate demand declines.

Rate of exchange The price paid in one's own money to acquire one unit of a foreign money; the rate at which the money of one nation is exchanged for the money of another nation.

Rate of interest Price paid for the use of Money or for the use of Capital; interest rate.

Rational An adjective that describes the behavior of any individual who consistently does those things that will enable him or her to achieve the declared objective of the individual; and that describes the behavior of a consumer who uses money income to buy the collection of goods and services that yields the maximum amount of Utility **(*see*)**.

Rational expectations theory The hypothesis that business firms and households expect monetary and fiscal policies to have certain effects on the economy and take, in pursuit of their own self-interests, actions which make these policies ineffective.

Rationing function of price The ability of a price in a competitive market to equalize Quantity demanded and Quantity supplied and to eliminate shortages and surpluses by rising or falling.

Reaganomics The policies of the Reagan administration based on Supply-side economics **(*see*)** and intended to reduce inflation and the Unemployment rate (Stagflation).

Real-balances effect The tendency for increases (decreases) in the price level to lower (raise) the real value (or purchasing power) of financial assets with fixed money values; and, as a result, to reduce (expand) total spending in the economy.

Real capital (*See* Capital.)

Real gross domestic product Gross domestic product **(*see*)** adjusted for changes in the price level; Gross domestic product in a year divided by the GDP deflator **(*see*)** for that year expressed as a decimal.

Real income The amount of goods and services an individual or group can purchase with his, her, or its Nominal income during some period of time. Nominal income adjusted for changes in the Price level.

Real interest rate The rate of interest expressed in dollars of constant value (adjusted for inflation); and equal to the Nominal interest rate **(*see*)** less the rate of inflation.

Real rate of interest The Real interest rate **(*see*)**.

Real wage The amount of goods and services a worker can purchase with his or her Nominal wage **(*see*)**; the purchasing power of the Nominal wage; the Nominal wage adjusted for changes in the Price level.

Real wage rate (*See* Real wage.)

Recessionary gap The amount by which the Aggregate expenditures schedule (curve) must increase (shift upward) to increase the real GDP to the full-employment noninflationary level.

Reciprocal Trade Agreements Act of 1934 The Federal act which gave the President the authority to negotiate agreements with foreign nations and lower American tariff rates by up to 50 percent if the foreign nations would reduce tariff rates on American goods and which incorporated Most-favored-nation clauses **(*see*)** in the agreements reached with these nations.

Refinancing the public debt Paying owners of maturing United States government securities with money obtained by selling new securities or with new securities.

Regressive tax A tax such that the Average tax rate decreases (increases) as the taxpayer's income increases (decreases).

Regulatory agency An agency (commission or board) established by the Federal or a state government to control for the benefit of the public the prices charged and the services offered (output produced) by a Natural monopoly **(*see*)**.

Remittance A gift or grant; a payment for which no good or service is received in return; the funds sent by workers who have legally or illegally entered a foreign nation to their families in the nations from which they have migrated.

Rental income Income received by those who supply the economy with Land (*see*).

Rent-seeking behavior The pursuit through government of a transfer of income or wealth to a resource supplier, business, or consumer at someone else's or society's expense.

Required reserve ratio (*See* Reserve ratio.)

Required reserves (*See* Legal reserves.)

Reserve ratio The specified minimum percentage of its deposit liabilities which a Member bank (*see*) must keep on deposit at the Federal Reserve Bank in its district, or in Vault cash (*see*).

Resolution Trust Corporation (RTC) A Federal institution created in 1989 to oversee the closing and sale of failed savings and loan institutions.

Resource market A market in which Households sell and Firms buy the services of resources.

Retiring the public debt Reducing the size of the Public debt by paying money to owners of maturing United States government securities.

Revaluation An increase in the defined value of a currency.

Revenue tariff A Tariff (*see*) designed to produce income for the (Federal) government.

Ricardian equivalence theorem The idea that an increase in the public debt will have little or no effect on real output and employment because taxpayers will save more in anticipation of future higher taxes to pay the higher interest expense on the debt.

Right-to-work law A law which has been enacted in twenty states that makes it illegal in those states to require a worker to join a Labor union in order to retain his or her job with an employer.

Roundabout production The construction and use of Capital (*see*) to aid in the production of Consumer goods (*see*).

Ruble overhang The large amount of forced savings held by Russian households due to the scarcity of consumer goods; these savings could fuel inflation when Russian prices are decontrolled.

Rule of reason The rule stated and applied in the U.S. Steel case (*see*) that only combinations and contracts that unreasonably restrain trade are subject to actions under the antitrust laws and that size and the possession of monopoly were not themselves illegal.

Rule of 70 A method by which the number of years it will take for the Price level to double can be calculated; divide 70 by the annual rate of inflation.

Sales tax A tax levied on expenditures for a broad group of products.

Saving Disposable income not spent for Consumer goods (*see*); not spending for consumption; equal to Disposal income minus Personal consumption expenditures (*see*).

Savings account A deposit in a Depository institution (*see*) which is interest-earning and which can normally be withdrawn by the depositor at any time.

Savings and loan association A Firm which accepts deposits primarily from small individual savers, and lends primarily to individuals to finance purchases of residences.

Saving schedule Schedule which shows the amounts Households plan to save (plan not to spend for Consumer goods, *see*) at different levels of Disposable income.

Savings institution A Thrift institution (*see*).

Say's law The (discredited) macroeconomic generalization that the production of goods and services (supply) creates an equal Aggregate demand for these goods and services.

Scarce resources The fixed (limited) quantities of Land, Capital, Labor, and Entrepreneurial ability (*see all*) which are never sufficient to satisfy the material wants of humans because their wants are unlimited.

Schumpeter-Galbraith view (of oligopoly) The belief shared by these two economists that large oligopolistic firms are necessary if there is to be a rapid rate of technological progress (because only this kind of firm has both the means and the incentive to introduce technological changes).

Seasonal variation An increase or decrease during a single year in the level of economic activity caused by a change in the season.

Secondary boycott The refusal of a Labor union to buy or to work with the products produced by another union or a group of nonunion workers.

"Second economy" The semilegal and illegal markets and activities which existed side by side with the legal and official markets and activities in the former U.S.S.R.

Secular trend The expansion or contraction in the level of economic activity over a long period of years.

Selective controls The techniques the Federal Reserve Banks employ to change the availability of certain specific types of credit.

Self-interest What each Firm, property owner, worker, and consumer believes is best for itself and seeks to obtain.

Seniority The length of time a worker has been employed by an employer relative to the lengths of time the employer's other workers have been employed; the principle which is used to determine which workers will be laid off when there is insufficient work for them all and who will be rehired when more work becomes available.

Separation of ownership and control Difference between the group that owns the Corporation (the stockholders) and the group that manages it (the directors and officers) and between the interests (goals) of the two groups.

Service That which is intangible (invisible) and for which a consumer, firm, or government is willing to exchange something of value.

Sherman Act The Federal antitrust act of 1890 which made monopoly, restraint of trade, and combinations and conspiracies to monopolize or to restrain trade criminal offenses; and allowed the Federal government or injured parties to take legal action against those committing these offenses.

Shirking Attempts by workers to increase their utility or well-being by neglecting or evading work.

Shortage The amount by which the Quantity demanded of a product exceeds the Quantity supplied at a given (below-equilibrium) price.

Short run A period of time in which producers of a product are able to change the quantity of some but not all of the resources they employ; in which some resources—the Plant (*see*)—are Fixed resources (*see*) and some are Variable resources (*see*); in which some costs are Fixed costs (*see*) and some are Variable costs (*see*); a period of time too brief to allow a Firm to vary its plant capacity but long enough to permit it to change the level at which the plant capacity is used; a period of time not long enough to enable Firms to enter or to leave an Industry (*see*).

Short-run aggregate supply curve The aggregate supply curve relevant to a time period in which input prices (particularly nominal wages) remain constant when the price level changes.

Short-run competitive equilibrium The price at which the total quantity of a product supplied in the Short run (*see*) by a purely competitive industry and the total quantity of the product demanded are equal and which is equal to or greater than the Average variable cost (*see*) of producing the product.

Short-run farm problem The sharp year-to-year changes in the prices of agricultural products and in the incomes of farmers.

Simple multiplier The Multiplier (*see*) in an economy in which government collects no Net taxes (*see*), there are no Imports (*see*), and Investment (*see*) is independent of the level of income (Gross domestic product); equal to one divided by the Marginal propensity to save (*see*).

Simpson-Rodino Act of 1986 Immigration legislation which provides amnesty to qualified illegal aliens; includes penalties for employers who knowingly hire illegal aliens; and allows temporary migrants to harvest perishable crops.

Single-tax movement The attempt of a group which followed the teachings of Henry George to eliminate all taxes except one which would tax all Rental income (*see*) at a rate of 100 percent.

Slope of a line The ratio of the vertical change (the rise or fall) to the horizontal change (the run) in moving between two points on a line. The slope of an upward sloping line is positive, reflecting a direct relationship between two variables; the slope of a downward sloping line is negative, reflecting an inverse relationship between two variables.

Smoot-Hawley Tariff Act Passed in 1930, this legislation established some of the highest tariffs in United States history. Its objective was to reduce imports and stimulate the domestic economy.

Social accounting (*See* National income accounting.)

Socially optimal price The price of a product which results in the most efficient allocation of an economy's resources and which is equal to the Marginal cost (*see*) of the last unit of the product produced.

Social regulation The type of regulation in which government is concerned with the conditions under which goods and services are produced, their physical characteristics, and the impact of their production on society; in contrast to Industrial regulation (*see*).

Social security programs The programs which replace the earnings lost when people retire or are temporarily unemployed, which are financed by Payroll taxes (*see*), and which are viewed as earned rights (rather than charity).

Sole proprietorship An unincorporated business firm owned and operated by a single person.

Special-interest effect Effect on public decision making and the allocation of resources in the economy when government promotes the interests (goals) of small groups to the detriment of society as a whole.

Specialization The use of the resources of an individual, a Firm, a region, or a nation to produce one or a few goods and services.

Spillover A benefit or cost associated with the consumption or production of a good or service which is obtained by or inflicted without compensation on a party other than the buyer or seller of the good or service (*see* Spillover benefit and Spillover cost).

Spillover benefit The benefit obtained neither by producers nor by consumers of a product but without compensation by a third party (society as a whole).

Spillover cost The cost of producing a product borne neither by producers nor by consumers of the product but without compensation by a third party (society as a whole).

SSI (*See* Supplemental security income.)

Stabilization fund A stock of money or of a commodity that is used to prevent the price of the commodity from changing by buying (selling) the commodity when its price decreases (increases).

Stabilization policy dilemma The use of monetary and fiscal policy to decrease the Unemployment rate increases the rate of inflation, and the use of monetary and fiscal policy to decrease the rate of inflation increases the Unemployment rate.

Stagflation Inflation accompanied by stagnation in the rate of growth of output and a high unemployment rate in the economy; simultaneous increases in both the Price level and the Unemployment rate.

Standardized product A product such that buyers are indifferent to the seller from whom they purchase it so long as the price charged by all sellers is the same; a product such that all units of the product are perfect substitutes for each other (are identical).

State bank A Commercial bank chartered to engage in the business of banking by a state government.

State ownership The ownership of property (Land and Capital) by government (the state); in the former U.S.S.R by the central government (the nation).

Static economy (1) An economy in which Net private domestic investment (*see*) is equal to zero—Gross private domestic investment (*see*) is equal to the Consumption of fixed capital (*see*); (2) an economy in which the supplies of resources, technology, and the tastes of consumers do not change and in which, therefore, the economic future is perfectly predictable and there is no uncertainty.

Store of value Any Asset (*see*) or wealth set aside for future use.

Strategic trade policy The use of trade barriers to reduce the risk of product development by domestic firms, particularly products involving advanced technology.

Strike The withholding of their labor services by an organized group of workers (a Labor union).

Strikebreaker A person employed by a Firm when its employees are engaged in a strike against the firm.

Structural-change hypothesis The explanation that attributes the relative decline of unionism in the United States to changes in the structure of the economy and of the labor force.

Structural deficit The difference between Federal tax revenues and expenditures when the economy is at full employment.

Structural unemployment Unemployment caused by changes in the structure of demand for Consumer goods and in technology; workers who are unemployed either because their skills are not demanded by employers or because they lack sufficient skills to obtain employment.

Subsidy A payment of funds (or goods and services) by a government, business firm, or household for which it receives no good or service in return. When made by a government, it is a Government transfer payment (*see*).

Substitute goods Goods or services such that there is a direct relationship between the price of one and the Demand for the other; when the price of one falls (rises) the Demand for the other decreases (increases).

Substitution effect (1) The effect which a change in the price of a Consumer good would have on the relative expensiveness of that good and the resulting effect on the quantity of the good a consumer would purchase if the consumer's Real income (*see*) remained constant; (2) the effect which a change in the price of a resource would have on the quantity of the resource employed by a firm if the firm did not change its output.

Superfund Law of 1980 Legislation which taxes manufacturers of toxic products and uses these revenues to finance the cleanup of toxic-waste sites; assigns liability for improperly dumped waste to the firms producing, transportings, and dumping that waste.

Superior good (*See* Normal good.)

Supplemental security income A program federally financed and administered which provides a uniform nationwide minimum income for the aged, blind, and disabled who do not qualify for benefits under the Old age, survivors, and disability health insurance (*see*) or Unemployment insurance (*see*) programs in the United States.

Supply A Supply schedule or a Supply curve (*see both*).

Supply curve A curve which shows the amounts of a good or service sellers (a seller) will offer to sell at various prices during some period of time.

Supply factor An increase in the available quantity of a resource, an improvement in its quality, or an expansion of technological knowledge which makes it possible for an economy to produce a greater output of goods and services.

Supply schedule A schedule which shows the amounts of a good or service sellers (or seller) will offer at various prices during some period of time.

Supply shock One of several events of the 1970s and early 1980s which increased production costs, decreased Aggregate supply, and generated Stagflation in the United States.

Supply-side economics The part of modern macroeconomics that emphasizes the role of costs and Aggregate supply in its explanation of Inflation, unemployed labor, and Economic growth.

Supply-side view The view of fiscal policy held by the advocates of Supply-side economics which emphasizes increasing Aggregate supply (*see*) as a means of reducing the Unemployment rate and Inflation and encouraging Economic Growth.

Support price   (*See* Price support.)

Surplus   The amount by which the Quantity supplied of a product exceeds the Quantity demanded at a given (above-equilibrium) price.

Surplus value   A Marxian term; the amount by which the value of a worker's daily output exceeds his daily wage; the output of workers appropriated by capitalists as profit.

Sympathy strike   Withholding from an employer the labor services of its members by a Labor union that does not have a disagreement with the employer but wishes to assist another Labor union that does have a disagreement with the employer.

Tacit collusion   Any method used in a Collusive oligopoly (*see*) to set prices and outputs or the market area of each firm that does not involve outright (or overt) collusion (formal agreements or secret meetings); and of which Price leadership (*see*) is a frequent example.

Taft-Hartley Act   The Federal act of 1947 which marked the shift from government sponsorship to government regulation of Labor unions.

Tangent   The point at which a line touches, but does not intersect, a curve.

Target dilemma   A problem which arises because monetary authorities cannot simultaneously stabilize both the money supply and the level of interest rates.

Tariff   A tax imposed (only by the Federal government in the United States) on an imported good.

Tax   A nonvoluntary payment of money (or goods and services) to a government by a Household or Firm for which the Household or Firm receives no good or service directly in return and which is not a fine imposed by a court for an illegal act.

Tax incidence   The income or purchasing power which different persons and groups lose as a result of the imposition of a tax after Tax shifting (*see*) has occurred.

Tax shifting   The transfer to others of all or part of a tax by charging them a higher price or by paying them a lower price for a good or service.

Tax-transfer disincentives   Decreases in the incentives to work, save, invest, innovate, and take risks that allegedly result from high Marginal tax rates and Transfer-payment programs.

Tax "wedge"   Such taxes as Indirect business taxes (*see*) and Payroll taxes (*see*) which are treated as a cost by business firms and reflected in the prices of the products produced by them; equal to the price of the product less the cost of the resources required to produce it.

Technology   The body of knowledge that can be used to produce goods and services from Economic resources.

Terms of trade   The rate at which units of one product can be exchanged for units of another product; the Price (*see*) of a good or service; the amount of one good or service that must be given up to obtain one unit of another good or service.

Theory of human capital   Generalization that Wage differentials (*see*) are the result of differences in the amount of Human-capital investment (*see*); and that the incomes of lower-paid workers are increased by increasing the amount of such investment.

***The* rate of interest**   The Rate of interest (*see*) which is paid solely for the use of Money over an extended period of time and which excludes the charges made for the riskiness of the loan and its administrative costs; and which is approximately equal to the rate of interest paid on the long-term and virtually riskless bonds of the United States government.

Thrift institution   A Savings and loan association, Mutual savings bank, or Credit union (*see all*).

Tight money policy   Contracting, or restricting the growth of, the nation's Money supply (*see*).

Till money   (*See* Vault cash.)

Time deposit   An interest-earning deposit in a Depository institution (*see*) which may be withdrawn by the depositor without a loss of interest on or after a specific date or at the end of a specific period of time.

Token money   Coins which have a Face value (*see*) greater than their Intrinsic value (*see*).

Total cost   The sum of Fixed cost (*see*) and Variable cost (*see*).

Total demand   The Demand schedule (*see*) or the Demand curve (*see*) of all buyers of a good or service.

Total demand for money   The sum of the Transactions demand for money (*see*) and Asset demand for money (*see*); the relationship between the total amount of money demanded, nominal GDP, and the Rate of Interest.

Total product   The total output of a particular good or service produced by a firm (a group of firms or the entire economy).

Total revenue   The total number of dollars received by a Firm (or Firms) from the sale of a product; equal to the total expenditures for the product produced by the Firm (or firms); equal to the quantity sold (demanded) multiplied by the price at which it is sold—by the Average revenue (*see*) from its sale.

Total-revenue test   A test to determine whether Demand is Elastic (*see*), Inelastic (*see*), or of Unitary elasticity (*see*) between any two prices: Demand is elastic (inelastic, unit elastic) if the Total revenue (*see*) of sellers of the commodity increases (decreases, remains constant) when the price of the commodity falls; or Total revenue decreases (increases, remains constant) when its price rises.

Total-revenue–total-cost approach The method which finds the output at which Economic profit (*see*) is a maximum or losses a minimum by comparing the Total revenue and the Total costs of a Firm at different outputs.

Total spending The total amount buyers of goods and services spend or plan to spend.

Total supply The Supply schedule (*see*) or the Supply curve (*see*) of all sellers of a good or service.

Trade balance The export of merchandise (goods) of a nation less its imports of merchandise (goods).

Trade controls Tariffs (*see*), export subsidies, Import quotas (*see*), and other means a nation may employ to reduce Imports (*see*) and expand Exports (*see*).

Trade deficit The amount by which a nation's imports of merchandise (goods) exceed its exports of merchandise (goods).

Trade surplus The amount by which a nation's exports of merchandise (goods) exceed its imports of merchandise (goods).

Trading possibilities line A line which shows the different combinations of two products an economy is able to obtain (consume) when it specializes in the production of one product and trades (exports) this product to obtain the other product.

Traditional economy An economic system (method of organization) in which traditions and customs determine how the economy will use its scarce resources.

Traditional view of advertising The position that advertising is persuasive rather than informative; promotes industrial concentration; and is essentially inefficient and wasteful.

Transactions demand for money The amount of money people want to hold to use as a Medium of exchange (to make payments); and which varies directly with the nominal GDP.

Transfer payment A payment of money (or goods and services) by a government or a Firm to a Household or Firm for which the payer receives no good or service directly in return.

Truth in Lending Act Federal law enacted in 1968 that is designed to protect consumers who borrow; and that requires the lender to state in concise and uniform language the costs and terms of the credit (the finance charges and the annual percentage rate of interest).

Tying agreement A promise made by a buyer when allowed to purchase a product from a seller that it will make all of its purchases of certain other products from the same seller; and a practice forbidden by the Clayton Act (*see*).

Unanticipated inflation Inflation (*see*) at a rate which was greater than the rate expected in that period of time.

Underemployment Failure to produce the maximum amount of goods and services that can be produced from the resources employed; failure to achieve Full production (*see*).

Undistributed corporate profits The after-tax profits of corporations not distributed as dividends to stockholders; corporate or business saving.

Unemployment Failure to use all available Economic resources to produce goods and services; failure of the economy to employ fully its Labor force (*see*).

Unemployment compensation (*See* Unemployment insurance).

Unemployment insurance The insurance program which in the United States is financed by state Payroll taxes (*see*) on employers and makes income available to workers who are unable to find jobs.

Unemployment rate The percentage of the Labor force (*see*) that is unemployed at any time.

Uninsurable risk An event, the occurrence of which is uncontrollable and unpredictable, which would result in a loss that cannot be avoided by purchasing insurance and must be assumed by an entrepreneur (*See* Entrepreneurial ability); sometimes called "uncertainty."

Union shop A place of employment at which the employer may hire either labor union members or workers who are not members of the union but who must become members within a specified period of time or lose their jobs.

Unitary elasticity The Elasticity coefficient (*see*) is equal to one; the percentage change in the quantity (demanded or supplied) is equal to the percentage change in price.

United States–Canadian Free-Trade Agreement An accord signed in 1988 to eliminate all trade barriers between the two nations over a ten-year period.

Unit labor cost Labor costs per unit of output; equal to the Nominal wage rate (*see*) divided by the Average product (*see*) of labor.

Unlimited liability Absence of any limit on the maximum amount that may be lost by an individual and that the individual may become legally required to pay; the amount that may be lost and that a sole proprietor or partner may be required to pay.

Unlimited wants The insatiable desire of consumers (people) for goods and services that will give them pleasure or satisfaction.

Unplanned investment Actual investment less Planned investment; increases or decreases in the inventories of business firms that result from production greater than sales.

Unprosperous industry (*See* Declining industry.)

U.S. Steel case The antitrust action brought by the

Federal government against the U.S. Steel Corporation in which the courts ruled (in 1920) that only unreasonable restraints of trade were illegal and size and the possession of monopoly power were not violations of the antitrust laws.

Utility The want-satisfying power of a good or service; the satisfaction or pleasure a consumer obtains from the consumption of a good or service (or from the consumption of a collection of goods and services).

Utility-maximizing rule To obtain the greatest Utility (*see*) the consumer should allocate Money income so that the last dollar spent on each good or service yields the same Marginal utility (*see*); so that the Marginal utility of each good or service divided by its price is the same for all goods and services.

Value added The value of the product sold by a Firm less the value of the goods (materials) purchased and used by the Firm to produce the product; and equal to the revenue which can be used for Wages, rent, interest, and profits.

Value-added tax A tax imposed on the difference between the value of the goods sold by a firm and the value of the goods purchased by the firm from other firms.

Value judgment Opinion of what is desirable or undesirable; belief regarding what ought or ought not to be (regarding what is right or just and wrong or unjust).

Value of money The quantity of goods and services for which a unit of money (a dollar) can be exchanged; the purchasing power of a unit of money; the reciprocal of the Price level.

Variable cost A cost which in total increases (decreases) when the firm increases (decreases) its output; the cost of Variable resources (*see*).

Variable resource Any resource employed by a firm the quantity of which can be increased or decreased (varied).

VAT Value-added tax (*see*).

Vault cash The Currency (*see*) a bank has in its safe (vault) and cash drawers.

Velocity of money The number of times per year the average dollar in the Money supply (*see*) is spent for Final goods (*see*).

VERs (*See* Voluntary export restrictions.)

Vertical axis The "up–down" or "north–south" axis on a graph or grid.

Vertical combination A group of Plants (*see*) engaged in different stages of the production of a final product and owned by a single Firm (*see*).

Vertical intercept The point at which a line meets the vertical axis of a graph.

Vertical merger The merger of one or more Firms engaged in different stages of the production of a final product into a single Firm.

Vicious circle of poverty A problem common to the less developed countries where their low per capita incomes are an obstacle to realizing the levels of saving and investment requisite to acceptable rates of economic growth.

Voice mechanism Communication by workers through their union to resolve grievances with an employer.

Voluntary export restrictions The limitations by firms of their exports to particular foreign nations to avoid the erection of other trade barriers by the foreign nations.

Wage The price paid for Labor (for the use or services of Labor, *see*) per unit of time (per hour, per day, etc.).

Wage and salary supplements Payments made by employers of Labor into social insurance and private pension, health, and welfare funds for workers; and a part of the employer's cost of obtaining Labor.

Wage differential The difference between the Wage (*see*) received by one worker or group of workers and that received by another worker or group of workers.

Wage discrimination The payments to blacks (or other minority groups) of a wage lower than that paid to whites for doing the same work.

Wage guidepost Wages (*see*) in all industries in the economy should increase at an annual rate equal to the rate of increase in the Average product (*see*) of Labor in the economy.

Wage-price controls A Wage-price policy (*see*) that legally fixes the maximum amounts by which Wages (*see*) and prices may be increased in any period of time.

Wage-price guideposts A Wage-price policy (*see*) that depends on the voluntary cooperation of Labor unions and business firms.

Wage-price inflationary spiral Increases in wage rates which bring about increases in prices which in turn result in further increases in wage rates and in prices.

Wage-price policy Government policy that attempts to alter the behavior of Labor unions and business firms in order to make their Wage and price decisions more nearly compatible with the goals of Full employment and a stable Price level.

Wage rate (*See* Wage.)

Wages The income of those who supply the economy with Labor (*see*).

Wagner Act The Federal act of 1935 which established the National Labor Relations Board (*see*), guaranteed the rights of Labor unions to organize and to bargain collectively with employers, and listed and prohibited a number of unfair labor practices by employers.

Wastes of monopolistic competition The waste of economic resources resulting from producing an output at which price is more than marginal cost and average cost is more than the minimum average cost.

Wealth effect   (*See* Real balances effect.)

Welfare programs   (*See* Public assistance programs.)

Wheeler-Lea Act The Federal act of 1938 which amended the Federal Trade Commission Act (*see*) by prohibiting and giving the commission power to investigate unfair and deceptive acts or practices of commerce (false and misleading advertising and the misrepresentation of products).

(The) "will to develop" Wanting economic growth strongly enough to change from old to new ways of doing things.

Workfare plans Reforms of the welfare system, particularly AFDC, designed to provide education and training for recipients so that they may move from public assistance to gainful employment.

World Bank A bank which lends (and guarantees loans) to less developed nations to assist them to grow; formally, the International Bank for Reconstruction and Development.

X-inefficiency Failure to produce any given output at the lowest average (and total) cost possible.

Yellow-dog contract The (now illegal) contract in which an employee agrees when accepting employment with a Firm that he or she will not become a member of a Labor union while employed by the Firm.

INDEX

National income and related statistics for selected years, 1968–1991*

National income statistics are in billions of current dollars. Details may not add to totals because of rounding.

			1968	1969	1970	1971	1972	1973	1974	1975	1976	1977
THE SUM OF	1	Personal consumption expenditures	559.1	603.7	646.5	700.3	767.8	848.1	927.7	1,024.9	1,143.1	1,271.5
			139.9	155.2	150.3	175.5	205.6	243.1	245.8	226.0	286.4	358.3
	3	Government purchases	191.5	201.8	212.7	224.3	241.5	257.7	288.3	321.4	341.3	368.0
	4	Net exports	–1.3	–1.2	1.2	–3.0	–8.0	0.6	–3.1	13.6	–2.3	–23.7
EQUALS	5	Gross domestic product	889.3	959.5	1,010.7	1,097.2	1,207.0	1,349.6	1,458.6	1,585.9	1,768.4	1,974.1
LESS	6	Consumption of fixed capital	73.9	81.5	88.8	97.6	109.9	120.4	140.2	165.2	182.8	205.2
EQUALS	7	Net domestic product	815.4	878.0	921.9	999.6	1,097.1	1,229.2	1,318.4	1,420.7	1,585.6	1,768.9
PLUS	8	Net American income earned abroad	6.2	6.1	6.4	7.7	8.7	12.7	15.7	13.3	17.1	20.5
LESS	9	Indirect business taxes	80.6	85.5	94.8	107.8	112.9	122.4	135.3	148.7	167.2	180.3
EQUALS	10	National income	741.0	798.6	833.5	899.5	992.9	1,119.5	1,198.8	1,285.3	1,435.5	1,609.1
LESS	11	Social security contributions	50.4	57.9	62.2	68.9	79.0	97.6	110.5	118.5	134.5	149.8
	12	Corporate income taxes	39.4	39.7	34.4	37.7	41.9	49.3	51.8	50.9	64.2	73.0
	13	Undistributed corporate profits	28.5	24.6	19.3	28.8	35.6	39.0	22.3	40.8	47.3	61.9
PLUS	14	Transfer payments	87.2	97.3	113.4	129.4	144.1	165.1	191.5	232.2	256.8	276.9
EQUALS	15	Personal income	709.9	773.7	831.0	893.5	980.5	1,098.7	1,205.7	1,307.3	1,446.3	1,601.3
LESS	16	Personal taxes	92.1	109.9	109.0	108.7	132.0	140.6	159.1	156.4	182.3	210.0
EQUALS	17	Disposable income	617.8	663.8	722.0	784.9	848.5	958.1	1046.5	1,150.9	1,264.0	1,391.3
	18	Real gross domestic product (in 1987 dollars)	2,801.0	2,877.1	2,875.8	2,965.1	3,107.1	3,268.6	3,248.1	3,221.7	3,380.8	3,533.2
	19	Percent change in real GDP	4.1	2.7	0.0	3.1	4.8	5.2	–0.6	–0.8	4.9	4.5
	20	Real disposable income per capita (in 1987 dollars)	9,399.0	9,606.0	9,875.0	10,111.0	10,414.0	11,013.0	10,832.0	10,906.0	11,192.0	11,406.0

RELATED STATISTICS			1968	1969	1970	1971	1972	1973	1974	1975	1976	1977
	21	Consumer price index (1982–84 = 100)	34.8	36.7	38.8	40.5	41.8	44.4	49.3	53.8	56.9	60.6
	22	Rate of inflation (%)	4.2	5.5	5.7	4.4	3.2	6.2	11.0	9.1	5.8	6.5
	23	Index of industrial production (1987 = 100)	60.7	63.5	61.4	62.2	68.3	73.8	72.7	66.3	72.4	78.2
	24	Supply of money, M1 (in billions of dollars)	197.5	204.0	214.5	228.4	249.3	262.9	274.4	287.6	306.4	331.3
	25	Prime interest rate (%)	6.30	7.96	7.91	5.72	5.25	8.03	10.81	7.86	6.84	6.83
	26	Population (in millions)	200.7	202.7	205.1	207.7	209.9	211.9	213.9	216.0	218.0	220.2
	27	Civilian labor force (in millions)	78.7	80.7	82.8	84.4	87.0	89.4	91.9	93.8	96.2	99.0
	28	Unemployment (in millions)	2.8	2.8	4.1	5.0	4.9	4.4	5.2	7.9	7.4	7.0
	29	Unemployment rate as % of civilian labor force	3.6	3.5	4.9	5.9	5.6	4.9	5.6	8.5	7.7	7.1
	30	Index of productivity (1982 = 100)	85.4	85.9	87.0	90.2	92.6	95.0	93.3	95.5	98.3	99.8
	31	Annual change in productivity (%)	3.0	0.5	1.3	3.6	2.7	2.6	–1.8	2.3	3.0	1.6
	32	Trade balance on current account (in billions of dollars)	0.6	0.4	2.3	–1.4	–5.8	7.1	2.0	18.1	4.2	–14.5
	33	Public debt (in billions of dollars)	368.7	365.8	380.9	408.2	435.9	466.3	483.9	541.9	629.0	706.4

*Revised series beginning with 1959. Revised data for GDP and its components for 1929–1958 were not available at the time of publication.
**Preliminary data.